# THE RECOVERY BIBLE

# THE RECOVERY BIBLE

BILL W., EMMET FOX, JAMES ALLEN,
WILLIAM JAMES, HENRY DRUMMOND,
AND MORE

A TarcherPerigee Book

tarcherperigee
An imprint of Penguin Random House LLC
penguinrandomhouse.com

First Jeremy P. Tarcher/Penguin edition 2013

Published simultaneously in Canada



Library of Congress Cataloging-in-Publication Data

W., Bill.
The recovery bible / Bill W., Emmet Fox, James Allen, William James,
Henry Drummond, and more.—First Tarcher/Penguin edition.
p. cm.
ISBN 978-0-399-16505-4
1. Alcoholics—Rehabilitation. 2. Twelve-step programs—History—Sources.
I. W., Bill. Alcoholics Anonymous. II. Drummond, Henry, 1851–1897. Greatest thing in the world.
III. Trine, Ralph Waldo, 1866–1958. In tune with the infinite. IV. Fox, Emmet. Mental equivalent.
V. Allen, James, 1864–1912. As a man thinketh. VI. Shoemaker, Samuel M. (Samuel Moor), 1893–1963.
Religion that works. VII. James, William, 1842–1910. Varieties of religious experience. VIII. Title.
HV5275.W155 2013 2013020722
616.86'103—dc23

Printed in the United States ofAmerica
1 3 5 7 9 10 8 6 4 2

# Contents

23rd and 91st Psalms 1

*Alcoholics Anonymous* by Bill W. (1939 original edition) 7

*The Greatest Thing in the World* by Henry Drummond 231

*In Tune with the Infinite* by Ralph Waldo Trine 251

*The Mental Equivalent* by Emmet Fox 351

*As a Man Thinketh* by James Allen 367

*Religion That Works* by the Rev. Sam Shoemaker 393

*The Varieties of Religious Experience* by William James 465

About the Authors 801

# THE RECOVERY BIBLE

## Psalms 23 and 91

adapted from the American Standard Version translation of 1901

## Psalm 23

The Lord is my shepherd; I shall not want.
He maketh me to lie down in green pastures;
He leadeth me beside still waters.
He restoreth my soul:
He guideth me in the paths of righteousness for his name's sake.
Yea, though I walk through the valley of the shadow of death,
I will fear no evil; for thou art with me;
Thy rod and thy staff, they comfort me.
Thou preparest a table before me in the presence of mine enemies:
Thou hast anointed my head with oil;
My cup runneth over.
Surely goodness and lovingkindness shall follow me all the days of my life;
And I shall dwell in the house of the Lord for ever.

## Psalm 91

He that dwelleth in the secret place of the Most High
Shall abide under the shadow of the Almighty.
I will say of the Lord, He is my refuge and my fortress;
My God, in whom I trust.
For he will deliver thee from the snare of the fowler,
And from the deadly pestilence.
He will cover thee with his pinions,
And under his wings shalt thou take refuge:
His truth is a shield and a buckler.
Thou shalt not be afraid for the terror by night,
Nor for the arrow that flieth by day;
For the pestilence that walketh in darkness,
Nor for the destruction that wasteth at noonday.
A thousand shall fall at thy side,
And ten thousand at thy right hand;
But it shall not come nigh thee.
Only with thine eyes shalt thou behold,
And see the reward of the wicked.
For thou, O Lord, art my refuge!
Thou hast made the Most High thy habitation;
There shall no evil befall thee,
Neither shall any plague come nigh thy tent.
For he will give his angels charge over thee,
To keep thee in all thy ways.
They shall bear thee up in their hands,
Lest thou dash thy foot against a stone.
Thou shalt tread upon the lion and adder:
The young lion and the serpent shalt thou trample under foot.
Because he hath set his love upon me, therefore will I deliver him:
I will set him on high, because he hath known my name.
He shall call upon me, and I will answer him;
I will be with him in trouble:
I will deliver him, and honor him.
With long life will I satisfy him,
And show him my salvation.

# ALCOHOLICS ANONYMOUS

BILL W. (BILL WILSON)

1939

# Contents


Foreword 11

The Doctor's Opinion 13

1. Bill's Story 19
2. There Is a Solution 28
3. More About Alcoholism 35
4. We Agnostics 43
5. How It Works 50
6. Into Action 58
7. Working with Others 67
8. To Wives 75
9. The Family Afterward 84
10. To Employers 92
11. A Vision for You 100

PERSONAL STORIES

The Doctor's Nightmare 111

The Unbeliever 117

The European Drinker 123

A Feminine Victory 129

Our Southern Friend 134

A Business Man's Recovery 142

A Different Slant 147

Traveler, Editor, Scholar 148

The Back-Slider 154

Home Brewmeister 159

The Seven Month Slip 163
My Wife and I 166
A Ward of the Probate Court 171
Riding the Rods 175
The Salesman 182
Fired Again 186
The Fearful One 190
Truth Freed Me! 193
Smile with Me, At Me 195
A Close Shave 200
Educated Agnostic 202
Another Prodigal Story 205
The Car Smasher 209
Hindsight 213
On His Way 216
An Alcoholic's Wife 218
An Artist's Concept 220
The Rolling Stone 223
Lone Endeavor 226

# Foreword

We, of Alcoholics Anonymous, are more than one hundred men and women who have recovered from a seemingly hopeless state of mind and body. To show other alcoholics PRECISELY HOW WE HAVE RECOVERED is the main purpose of this book. For them, we hope these pages will prove so convincing that no further authentication will be necessary. We think this account of our experiences will help everyone to better understand the alcoholic. Many do not comprehend that the alcoholic is a very sick person. And besides, we are sure that our way of living has its advantages for all.

It is important that we remain anonymous because we are too few, at present, to handle the overwhelming number of personal appeals which may result from this publication. Being mostly business or professional folk we could not well carry on our occupations in such an event. We would like it understood that our alcoholic work is an avocation.

When writing or speaking publicly about alcoholism, we urge each of our Fellowship to omit his personal name, designating himself instead as "A Member of Alcoholics Anonymous."

Very earnestly we ask the press also, to observe this request, for otherwise we shall be greatly handicapped.

We are not an organization in the conventional sense of the word. There are no fees nor dues whatsoever. The only requirement for membership is an honest desire to stop drinking. We are not allied with any particular faith, sect or denomination, nor do we oppose anyone. We simply wish to be helpful to those who are afflicted.

We shall be interested to hear from those who are getting results from this book, particularly from those who have commenced work with other alcoholics. We should like to be helpful to such cases.

Inquiry by scientific, medical, and religious societies will be welcomed.

ALCOHOLICS ANONYMOUS.

# The Doctor's Opinion

We of Alcoholics Anonymous believe that the reader will be interested in the medical estimate of the plan of recovery described in this book. Convincing testimony must surely come from medical men who have had experience with the sufferings of our members and have witnessed our return to health. A well-known doctor, chief physician at a nationally prominent hospital specializing in alcoholic and drug addiction, gave Alcoholics Anonymous this letter:

To Whom It May Concern:

I have specialized in the treatment of alcoholism for many years.

About four years ago I attended a patient who, though he had been a competent business man of good earning capacity, was an alcoholic of a type I had come to regard as hopeless.

In the course of his third treatment he acquired certain ideas concerning a possible means of recovery. As part of his rehabilitation he commenced to present his conceptions to other alcoholics, impressing upon them that they must do likewise with still others. This has become the basis of a rapidly growing fellowship of these men and their families. This man and over one hundred others appear to have recovered.

I personally know thirty of these cases who were of the type with whom other methods had failed completely.

These facts appear to be of extreme medical importance; because of the extraordinary possibilities of rapid growth inherent in this group they may mark a new epoch in the annals of alcoholism. These men may well have a remedy for thousands of such situations.

You may rely absolutely on anything they say about themselves.

Very truly yours,
(Signed) ----- M.D.

The physician who, at our request, gave us this letter, has been kind enough to enlarge upon his views in another statement which follows. In this statement he confirms what we who have suffered alcoholic torture must believe—that the body of the alcoholic is quite as abnormal as his mind. It did not satisfy us to be told that we could not control our drinking just because we were maladjusted to life, that we were in full flight from reality, or were outright mental defectives. These things were true to some extent, in fact, to a considerable extent with some of us. But we are sure that our bodies were sickened as well. In our belief, any picture of the alcoholic which leaves out this physical factor is incomplete.

The doctor's theory that we have an allergy to alcohol interests us. As laymen, our opinion as to its soundness may, of course, mean little. But as ex-alcoholics, we can say that his explanation makes good sense. It explains many things for which we cannot otherwise account.

Though we work out our solution on the spiritual as well as an altruistic plane, we favor hospitalization for the alcoholic who is very jittery or befogged. More often than not, it is imperative that a man's brain be cleared before he is approached, as he has then a better chance of understanding and accepting what we have to offer.

The doctor writes:

The subject presented in this book seems to me to be of paramount importance to those afflicted with alcoholic addiction.

I say this after many years' experience as Medical Director of one of the oldest hospitals in the country treating alcoholic and drug addiction.

There was, therefore, a sense of real satisfaction when I was asked to contribute a few words on a subject which is covered in such masterly detail in these pages.

We doctors have realized for a long time that some form of moral psychology was of urgent importance to alcoholics, but its application presented difficulties beyond our conception. What with our ultra-modern standards, our scientific approach to everything, we are perhaps not well equipped to apply the powers of good that lie outside our synthetic knowledge.

About four years ago one of the leading contributors to this book came under our care in this hospital and while here he acquired some ideas which he put into practical application at once.

Later, he requested the privilege of being allowed to tell his story to other patients here and with some misgiving, we consented. The cases we have followed through have been most interesting; in fact, many of them are amazing. The unselfishness of these men as we have come to know them, the entire absence of profit motive, and their community spirit, is indeed inspiring to one who has labored long and wearily in this alcoholic field. They believe in themselves, and still more in the Power which pulls chronic alcoholics back from the gates of death.

Of course an alcoholic ought to be freed from his physical craving for liquor, and this often requires a definite hospital procedure, before psychological measures can be of maximum benefit.

We believe, and so suggested a few years ago, that the action of alcohol on these chronic alcoholics is a manifestations of an allergy; that the phenomenon of craving is limited to this class and never occurs in the average temperate drinker. These allergic types can never safely use alcohol in any form at all; and once having formed the habit and found they cannot break it, once having lost their self-confidence, their reliance upon things human, their problems pile up on them and become astonishingly difficult to solve.

Frothy emotional appeal seldom suffices. The message which can interest and hold these alcoholic people must have depth and weight. In nearly all cases, their ideals must be grounded in a power greater than themselves, if they are to re-create their lives.

If any feel that as psychiatrists directing a hospital for alcoholics we appear somewhat sentimental, let them stand with us a while on the firing line, see the tragedies, the despairing wives, the little children; let the solving of these problems become a part of their daily work, and even of their sleeping moments, and the most cynical will not wonder that we have accepted and encouraged this movement. We feel, after many years of experience, that we have found nothing which has contributed more to the rehabilitation of these men than the altruistic movement now growing up among them.

Men and women drink essentially because they like the effect produced by alcohol. The sensation is so elusive that, while they admit it is injurious, they cannot after a time differentiate the true from the false. To them, their alcoholic life seems the only normal one. They are restless, irritable and discontented, unless they can again experience the sense of ease and comfort which comes at once by taking a few drinks—drinks which they see others taking with impunity. After they have succumbed to the desire again, as so many do, and the phenomenon of craving develops, they pass through the well-known stages of a spree, emerging remorseful, with a firm resolution not to drink again. This is repeated over and over, and unless this person can experience an entire psychic change there is very little hope of his recovery.

On the other hand—and strange as this may seem to those who do not understand—once a psychic change has occurred, the very same person who seemed doomed, who had so many problems he despaired of ever solving them, suddenly finds himself easily able to control his desire for alcohol, the only effort necessary being that required to follow a few simple rules.

Men have cried out to me in sincere and despairing appeal: "Doctor, I cannot go on like this! I have everything to live for! I must stop, but I cannot! You must help me!"

Faced with this problem, if a doctor is honest with himself, he must sometimes feel his own inadequacy. Although he gives all that is in him, it often is not enough. One feels that something more than human power is needed to produce the essential psychic change. Though the aggregate of recoveries resulting from psychiatric effort is considerable, we physicians must admit we have made little impression upon the problem as a whole. Many types do not respond to the ordinary psychological approach.

I do not hold with those who believe that alcoholism is entirely a problem of mental control. I have had many men who had, for example, worked a period of months on some problem or business deal which was to be settled on a certain date, favorably to them. They took a drink a day or so prior to the date, and then the phenomenon of craving at once became paramount to all other interests so that the important appointment was not met. These men were not drinking to escape; they were drinking to overcome a craving beyond their mental control.

There are many situations which arise out of the phenomenon of craving which cause men to make the supreme sacrifice rather than continue to fight.

The classification of alcoholics seems most difficult, and in much detail is outside the scope of this book. There are, of course, the psychopaths who are emotionally unstable. We are all familiar with this type. They are always "going on the wagon for keeps." They are over-remorseful and make many resolutions, but never a decision.

There is the type of man who is unwilling to admit that he cannot take a drink. He plans various ways of drinking. He changes his brand or his environment. There is the type who always believes that after being entirely free from alcohol for a period of time he can take a drink without danger. There is the manic-depressive type, who is, perhaps, the least understood by his friends, and about whom a whole chapter could be written.

Then there are types entirely normal in every respect except in the effect alcohol has upon them. They are often able, intelligent, friendly people.

All these, and many others, have one symptom in common: they cannot start drinking without developing the phenomenon of craving. This phenomenon, as we have suggested, may be the manifestation of an allergy which differentiates these people, and sets them apart as a distinct entity. It has never been, by any treatment with which we are familiar, permanently eradicated. The only relief we have to suggest is entire abstinence.

This immediately precipitates us into a seething caldron of debate. Much has been written pro and con, but among physicians, the general opinion seems to be that most chronic alcoholics are doomed.

What is the solution? Perhaps I can best answer this by relating an experience of two years ago.

About one year prior to this experience a man was brought in to be treated for chronic alcoholism. He had but partially recovered from a gastric hemorrhage and seemed to be a case of pathological mental deterioration. He had lost everything worth while in life and was only living, one might say, to drink. He frankly admitted and believed that for him there was no hope. Following the elimination of alcohol, there was found to be no permanent brain injury. He accepted the plan outlined in this book. One year later he called to see me, and I experienced a very strange sensation. I knew the man by name, and partly recognized his features, but there all resemblance ended. From a trembling, despairing, nervous wreck, had emerged a man brimming over with self-reliance and contentment. I talked with him for some time, but was not able to bring myself to feel that I had known him before. To me he was a stranger, and so he left me. More than three years have now passed with no return to alcohol.

When I need a mental uplift, I often think of another case brought in by a physician prominent in New York City. The patient had made his own diagnosis, and deciding his situation hopeless, had hidden in a deserted barn determined to die. He was rescued by a searching party, and, in desperate condition, brought to me. Following his physical rehabilitation, he had a talk with me in which he frankly stated he thought the treatment a waste of effort, unless I could assure him, which no one ever had, that in the future he would have the "will power" to resist the impulse to drink.

His alcoholic problem was so complex, and his depression so great, that we felt his only hope would be through what we then called "moral psychology," and we doubted if even that would have any effect.

However, he did become "sold" on the ideas contained in this book. He has not had a drink for more than three years. I see him now and then and he is as fine a specimen of manhood as one could wish to meet.

I earnestly advise every alcoholic to read this book through, and though perhaps he came to scoff, he may remain to pray.

CHAPTER 1

# Bill's Story

War fever ran high in the New England town to which we new, young officers from Plattsburg were assigned, and we were flattered when the first citizens took us to their homes, making us feel heroic. Here was love, applause, war; moments sublime with intervals hilarious. I was part of life at last, and in the midst of the excitement I discovered liquor. I forgot the strong warnings and the prejudices of my people concerning drink. In time we sailed for "Over There." I was very lonely and again turned to alcohol.

We landed in England. I visited Winchester Cathedral. Much moved, I wandered outside. My attention was caught by a doggerel on an old tombstone:

*"Here lies a Hampshire Grenadier*
*Who caught his death*
*Drinking cold small beer.*
*A good soldier is ne'er forgot*
*Whether he dieth by musket*
*Or by pot."*

Ominous warning—which I failed to heed.

Twenty-two, and a veteran of foreign wars, I went home at last. I fancied myself a leader, for had not the men of my battery given me a special token of appreciation? My talent for leadership, I imagined, would place me at the head of vast enterprises which I would manage with utmost assurance.

I took a night law course, and obtained employment as investigator for a surety company. The drive for success was on. I'd prove to the world I was important. My work took me about Wall Street and little by little I became interested in the market. Many people lost money—but some became very rich. Why not I? I studied economics and business as well as law. Potential alcoholic that I was, I nearly failed my law course. At one of the finals I was too drunk to think or write. Though my drinking was not yet continuous, it disturbed my wife. We had long talks when I would still her forebodings by telling her that men of genius conceived their best projects when drunk; that the most majestic constructions of philosophic thought were so derived.

By the time I had completed the course, I knew the law was not for me. The inviting maelstrom of Wall Street had me in its grip. Business and financial leaders were my heroes. Out of this alloy of drink and speculation, I commenced to forge the weapon that one day would turn in its flight like a boomerang and all but cut me to ribbons. Living modestly, my wife and I saved $1,000. It went into certain securities then cheap and rather unpopular. I rightly imagined that they would some day have a great rise. I failed to persuade my broker friends to send me out looking over factories and managements, but my wife and I decided to go anyway. I had developed a theory that most people lost money in stocks through ignorance of markets. I discovered many more reasons later on.

We gave up our positions and off we roared on a motorcycle, the sidecar stuffed with tent, blankets, change of clothes, and three huge volumes of a financial reference service. Our friends thought a lunacy commission should be appointed. Perhaps they were right. I had had some success at speculation, so we had a little money, but we once worked on a farm for a month to avoid drawing on our small capital. That was the last honest manual labor on my part for many a day. We covered the whole eastern United States in a year. At the end of it, my reports to Wall Street procured me a position there and the use of a large expense account. The exercise of an option brought in more money, leaving us with a profit of several thousand dollars for that year.

For the next few years fortune threw money and applause my way. I had arrived. My judgment and ideas were followed by many to the tune of paper millions. The great boom of the late twenties was seething and swelling. Drink was taking an important and exhilarating part in my life. There was loud talk in the jazz places uptown. Everyone spent in thousands and chattered in millions. Scoffers could scoff and be damned. I made a host of fair-weather friends.

My drinking assumed more serious proportions, continuing all day and almost every night. The remonstrances of my friends terminated in a row and I became a lone wolf. There were many unhappy scenes in our sumptuous apartment. There had been no real infidelity, for loyalty to my wife, helped at times by extreme drunkenness, kept me out of those scrapes.

In 1929 I contracted golf fever. We went at once to the country, my wife to applaud while I started out to overtake Walter Hagen. Liquor caught up with me much faster than I came up behind Walter. I began to be jittery in the morning. Golf permitted drinking every day and every night. It was fun to carom around the exclusive course which had inspired such awe in me as a lad. I acquired the impeccable coat of tan one sees upon the well-to-do. The local banker watched me whirl fat checks in and out of his till with amused skepticism.

Abruptly in October 1929 hell broke loose on the New York stock exchange. After one of those days of inferno, I wobbled from a hotel bar to a brokerage office. It was eight o'clock—five hours after the market closed. The ticker still clattered. I was staring at an inch of the tape which bore the inscription XYZ-32. It had been 52 that morning. I was finished and so were many friends. The papers reported men jumping to death from the towers of High Finance. That disgusted me. I would not jump. I went back to the bar. My friends had dropped several million since ten o'clock—so what? Tomorrow was another day. As I drank, the old fierce determination to win came back.

Next morning I telephoned a friend in Montreal. He had plenty of money left and thought I had better go to Canada. By the following spring we were living in our accustomed style. I felt like Napoleon returning from Elba. No St. Helena for me! But drinking caught up with me again and my generous friend had to let me go. This time we stayed broke.

We went to live with my wife's parents. I found a job; then lost it as the result of a brawl with a taxi driver. Mercifully, no one could guess that I was to have no real employment for five years, or hardly draw a sober breath. My wife began to work in a department store, coming home exhausted to find me drunk. I became an unwelcome hanger-on at brokerage places.

Liquor ceased to be a luxury; it became a necessity. "Bathtub" gin, two bottles a day, and often three, got to be routine. Sometimes a small deal would net a few hundred dollars, and I would pay my bills at the bars and delicatessens. This went on endlessly, and I began to waken very early in the morning shaking violently. A tumbler full of gin followed by half a dozen bottles of beer would be required if I were to eat any breakfast. Nevertheless, I still thought I could control the situation, and there were periods of sobriety which renewed my wife's hope.

Gradually things got worse. The house was taken over by the mortgage holder, my mother-in-law died, my wife and father-in-law became ill.

Then I got a promising business opportunity. Stocks were at the low point of 1932, and I had somehow formed a group to buy. I was to share generously in the profits. Then I went on a prodigious bender, and that chance vanished.

I woke up. This had to be stopped. I saw I could not take so much as one drink. I was through forever. Before then, I had written lots of sweet promises, but my wife happily observed that this time I meant business. And so I did.

Shortly afterward I came home drunk. There had been no fight. Where had been my high resolve? I simply didn't know. It hadn't even come to mind. Someone had pushed a drink my way, and I had taken it. Was I crazy? I began to wonder, for such an appalling lack of perspective seemed near being just that.

Renewing my resolve, I tried again. Some time passed, and confidence began to be replaced by cocksureness. I could laugh at the gin mills. Now I had what it takes! One day I walked into a cafe to telephone. In no time I was beating on the bar asking myself how it happened. As the whiskey rose to my head I told myself I would manage better next time, but I might as well get good and drunk then. And I did.

The remorse, horror and hopelessness of the next morning are unforgettable. The courage to do battle was not there. My brain raced uncontrollably and there was a terrible sense of impending calamity. I hardly dared cross the street, lest I collapse and be run down by an early morning truck, for it was scarcely daylight. An all night place supplied me with a dozen glasses of ale. My writhing nerves were stilled at last. A morning paper told me the market had gone to hell again. Well, so had I. The market would recover, but I wouldn't. That was a hard thought. Should I kill myself? No—not now. Then a mental fog settled down. Gin would fix that. So two bottles, and—oblivion.

The mind and body are marvelous mechanisms, for mine endured this agony two more years. Sometimes I stole from my wife's slender purse when the morning terror and madness were on me. Again I swayed dizzily before an open window, or the medicine cabinet where there was poison, cursing myself for a weakling. There were flights from city to country and back, as my wife and I sought escape. Then came the night when the physical and mental torture was so hellish I feared I would burst through my window, sash and all. Somehow I managed to drag my mattress to a lower floor, lest I suddenly leap. A doctor came with a heavy sedative. Next day found me drinking both gin and sedative. This combination soon landed me on the rocks. People feared for my sanity. So did I. I could eat little or nothing when drinking, and I was forty pounds under weight.

My brother-in-law is a physician, and through his kindness and that of my mother I was placed in a nationally-known hospital for the mental and physical rehabilitation of alcoholics. Under the so-called belladonna treatment my brain cleared. Hydrotherapy and mild exercise helped much. Best of all, I met a kind doctor who explained that though certainly selfish and foolish, I had been seriously ill, bodily and mentally.

It relieved me somewhat to learn that in alcoholics the will is amazingly weakened when it comes to combating liquor, though it often remains strong in other respects. My incredible behavior in the face of a desperate desire to stop was explained. Understanding myself now, I fared forth in high hope. For three or four months the goose hung high. I went to town regularly and even made a little money. Surely this was the answer—self-knowledge.

But it was not, for the frightful day came when I drank once more. The curve of my declining moral and bodily health fell off like a ski-jump. After a time I returned to the hospital. This was the finish, the curtain, it seemed to me. My weary and despairing wife was informed that it would all end with heart failure during delirium tremens, or I would develop a wet brain, perhaps within a year. She would soon have to give me over to the undertaker or the asylum.

They did not need to tell me. I knew, and almost welcomed the idea. It was a devastating blow to my pride. I, who had thought so well of myself and my abilities, of my capacity to surmount obstacles, was cornered at last. Now I was to plunge into the dark, joining that endless procession of sots who had gone on before. I thought of my poor wife. There had been much happiness after all. What would I not give to make amends. But that was over now.

No words can tell of the loneliness and despair I found in that bitter morass of self-pity. Quicksand stretched around me in all directions. I had met my match. I had been overwhelmed. Alcohol was my master.

Trembling, I stepped from the hospital a broken man. Fear sobered me for a bit. Then came the insidious insanity of that first drink, and on Armistice Day 1934, I was off again. Everyone became resigned to the certainty that I would have to be shut up somewhere, or would stumble along to a miserable end. How dark it is before the dawn! In reality that was the beginning of my last debauch. I was soon to be catapulted into what I like to call the fourth dimension of existence. I was to know happiness, peace, and usefulness, in a way of life that is incredibly more wonderful as time passes.

Near the end of that bleak November, I sat drinking in my kitchen. With a certain satisfaction I reflected there was enough gin concealed about the house to carry me through that night and the next day. My wife was at work. I wondered whether I dared hide a full bottle of gin near the head of our bed. I would need it before daylight.

My musing was interrupted by the telephone. The cheery voice of an old school friend asked if he might come over. *He was sober.* It was years since I could remember his coming to New York in that condition. I was amazed. Rumor had it that he had been committed for alcoholic insanity. I wondered how he had escaped. Of course he would have dinner, and then I could drink openly with him. Unmindful of his welfare, I thought only of recapturing the spirit of other days. There was that time we had chartered an airplane to complete a jag! His coming was an oasis in this dreary desert of futility. The very thing—an oasis! Drinkers are like that.

The door opened and he stood there, fresh-skinned and glowing. There was something about his eyes. He was inexplicably different. What had happened?

I pushed a drink across the table. He refused it. Disappointed but curious, I wondered what had got into the fellow. He wasn't himself.

"Come, what's all this about?" I queried.

He looked straight at me. Simply, but smilingly, he said, "I've got religion."

I was aghast. So that was it—last summer an alcoholic crackpot; now, I suspected, a little cracked about religion. He had that starry-eyed look. Yes, the old boy was on fire all right. But bless his heart, let him rant! Besides, my gin would last longer than his preaching.

But he did no ranting. In a matter of fact way he told how two men had appeared in court, persuading the judge to suspend his commitment. They had told of a simple religious idea and a practical program of action. That was two months ago and the result was self evident. It worked!

He had come to pass his experience along to me—if I cared to have it. I was shocked, but interested. Certainly I was interested. I had to be, for I was hopeless.

He talked for hours. Childhood memories rose before me. I could almost hear the sound of the preacher's voice as I sat, on still Sundays, way over there on the hillside; there was that proffered temperance pledge I never signed; my grandfather's good natured contempt of some church folk and their doings; his insistence that the spheres really had their music; but his denial of the preacher's right to tell him how he must listen; his fearlessness as he spoke of these things just before he died; these recollections welled up from the past. They made me swallow hard.

That war-time day in old Winchester Cathedral came back again.

I had always believed in a power greater than myself. I had often pondered these things. I was not an atheist. Few people really are, for that means blind faith in the strange proposition that this universe originated in a cipher and aimlessly rushes nowhere. My intellectual heroes, the chemists, the astronomers, even the evolutionists, suggested vast laws and forces at work. Despite contrary indications, I had little doubt that a mighty purpose and rhythm underlay all. How could there be so much of precise and immutable law, and no intelligence? I simply had to believe in a Spirit of the Universe, who knew neither time nor limitation. But that was as far as I had gone.

With ministers, and the world's religions, I parted right there. When they talked of a God personal to me, who was love, superhuman strength and direction, I became irritated and my mind snapped shut against such a theory.

To Christ I conceded the certainty of a great man, not too closely followed by those who claimed Him. His moral teaching—most excellent. For myself, I had adopted those parts which seemed convenient and not too difficult; the rest I disregarded.

The wars which had been fought, the burnings and chicanery that religious dispute had facilitated, made me sick. I honestly doubted whether, on balance, the religions of mankind had done any good. Judging from what I had seen in Europe and since, the power of God in human affairs was negligible, the Brotherhood of Man a grim jest. If there was a Devil, he seemed the Boss Universal, and he certainly had me.

But my friend sat before me, and he made the point-blank declaration that God had done for him what he could not do for himself. His human will had failed. Doctors had pronounced him incurable. Society was about to lock him up. Like myself, he had admitted complete defeat. Then he had, in effect, been raised from the dead, suddenly taken from the scrap heap to a level of life better than the best he had ever known!

Had this power originated in him? Obviously it had not. There had been no more power in him than there was in me at that minute; and this was none at all.

That floored me. It began to look as though religious people were right after all. Here was something at work in a human heart which had done the impossible. My ideas about miracles were drastically revised right then. Never mind the musty past; here sat a miracle directly across the kitchen table. He shouted great tidings.

I saw that my friend was much more than inwardly reorganized. He was on a different footing. His roots grasped a new soil.

Despite the living example of my friend there remained in me the vestiges of my old prejudice. The word God still aroused a certain antipathy. When the thought was expressed that there might be a God personal to me this feeling was intensified. I didn't like the idea. I could go for such conceptions as Creative Intelligence, Universal Mind or Spirit of Nature but I resisted the thought of a Czar of the Heavens however loving His sway might be. I have since talked with scores of men who felt the same way.

My friend suggested what then seemed a novel idea. He said, *"Why don't you choose your own conception of God?"*

That statement hit me hard. It melted the icy intellectual mountain in whose shadow I had lived and shivered many years. I stood in the sunlight at last.

*It was only a matter of being willing to believe in a power greater than myself. Nothing more was required of me to make my beginning.* I saw that growth could start from that point. Upon a foundation of complete willingness I might build what I saw in my friend. Would I have it? Of course I would!

Thus was I convinced that God is concerned with us humans when we want Him enough. At long last I saw, I felt, I believed. Scales of pride and prejudice fell from my eyes. A new world came into view.

The real significance of my experience in the Cathedral burst upon me. For a brief moment, I had needed and wanted God. There had been a humble willingness to have Him with me—and He came. But soon the sense of His Presence had been blotted out by worldly clamors, mostly those within myself. And so it had been ever since. How blind I had been.

At the hospital I was separated from alcohol for the last time. Treatment seemed wise, for I showed signs of delirium tremens.

There I humbly offered myself to God, as I then understood Him, to do with me as He would. I placed myself unreservedly under His care and direction. I admitted for the first time that of myself I was nothing; that without Him I was lost. I ruthlessly faced my sins and became willing to have my new-found Friend take them away, root and branch. I have not had a drink since.

My school mate visited me, and I fully acquainted him with my problems and deficiencies. We made a list of people I had hurt or toward whom I felt resentment. I expressed my entire willingness to approach these individuals, admitting my wrong. Never was I to be critical of them. I was to right all such matters to the utmost of my ability.

I was to test my thinking by the new God-consciousness within. Common sense would thus become uncommon sense. I was to sit quietly when in doubt, asking only for direction and strength to meet my problems as He would have me. Never was I to pray for myself, except as my requests bore on my usefulness to others. Then only might I expect to receive. But that would be in great measure.

My friend promised when these things were done I would enter upon a new relationship with my Creator; that I would have the elements of a way of living which answered all my problems. Belief in the power of God, plus enough willingness, honesty and humility to establish and maintain the new order of things, were the essential requirements.

Simple, but not easy; a price had to be paid. It meant destruction of self-centeredness. I must turn in all things to the Father of Lights who presides over us all.

These were revolutionary and drastic proposals, but the moment I fully accepted them, the effect was electric. There was a sense of victory, followed by such a peace and serenity as I had never known. There was utter confidence. I felt lifted up, as though the great clean wind of a mountain top blew through and through. God comes to most men gradually, but His impact on me was sudden and profound.

For a moment I was alarmed, and called my friend, the doctor, to ask if I were still sane. He listened in wonder as I talked.

Finally he shook his head saying, "Something has happened to you I don't understand. But you had better hang on to it. Anything is better than the way you were." The good doctor now sees many men who have such experiences. He knows they are real.

While I lay in the hospital the thought came that there were thousands of hopeless alcoholics who might be glad to have what had been so freely given me. Perhaps I could help some of them. They in turn might work with others.

My friend had emphasized the absolute necessity of demonstrating these principles in all my affairs. Particularly was it imperative to work with others as he had worked with me. Faith without works was dead, he said. And how appallingly true for the alcoholic! For if an alcoholic failed to perfect and enlarge his spiritual life through work and self sacrifice for others, he could not survive the certain trials and low spots ahead. If he did not work, he would surely drink again, and if he drank, he would surely die. Then faith would be dead indeed. With us it is just like that.

My wife and I abandoned ourselves with enthusiasm to the idea of helping other alcoholics to a solution of their problems. It was fortunate, for my old business associates remained skeptical for a year and a half, during which I found little work. I was not too well at the time, and was plagued by waves of self-pity and resentment. This sometimes nearly drove me back to drink. I soon found that when all other measures failed, work with another alcoholic would save the day. Many times I have gone to my old hospital in despair. On talking to a man there, I would be amazingly lifted up and set on my feet. It is a design for living that works in rough going.

We commenced to make many fast friends and a fellowship has grown up among us of which it is a wonderful thing to feel a part. The joy of living we really have, even under pressure and difficulty. I have seen one hundred families set their feet in the path that really goes somewhere; have seen the most impossible domestic situations righted; feuds and bitterness of all sorts wiped out. I have seen men come out of asylums and resume a vital place in the lives of their families and communities. Business and professional men have regained their standing. There is scarcely any form of trouble and misery which has not been overcome among us. In one western city and its environs there are eighty of us and our families. We meet frequently at our different homes, so that newcomers may find the fellowship they seek. At these informal gatherings one may often see from 40 to 80 persons. We are growing in numbers and power.

An alcoholic in his cups is an unlovely creature. Our struggles with them are variously strenuous, comic, and tragic. One poor chap committed suicide in my home. He could not, or would not, see our way of life.

There is, however, a vast amount of fun about it all. I suppose some would be shocked at our seeming worldliness and levity. But just underneath there is deadly earnestness. Faith has to work twenty-four hours a day in and through us, or we perish.

Most of us feel we need look no further for Utopia. We have it with us right here and now. Each day my friend's simple talk in our kitchen multiplies itself in a widening circle of peace on earth and good will to men.

CHAPTER 2

# There Is a Solution

We, of ALCOHOLICS ANONYMOUS, know one hundred men who were once just as hopeless as Bill. All have recovered. They have solved the drink problem.

We are average Americans. All sections of this country and many of its occupations are represented, as well as many political, economic, social, and religious backgrounds. We are people who normally would not mix. But there exists among us a fellowship, a friendliness, and an understanding which is indescribably wonderful. We are like the passengers of a great liner the moment after rescue from shipwreck when camaraderie, joyousness and democracy pervade the vessel from steerage to Captain's table. Unlike the feelings of the ship's passengers, however, our joy in escape from disaster does not subside as we go our individual ways. The feeling of having shared in a common peril is one element in the powerful cement which binds us. But that in itself would never have held us together as we are now joined.

The tremendous fact for every one of us is that we have discovered a common solution. We have a way out on which we can absolutely agree, and upon which we can join in brotherly and harmonious action. This is the great news this book carries to those who suffer alcoholism.

An illness of this sort—and we have come to believe it an illness—involves those about us in a way no other human sickness can. If a person has cancer all are sorry for him and no one is angry or hurt. But not so with the alcoholic illness, for with it there goes annihilation of all the things worth while in life. It engulfs all whose lives touch the sufferer's. It brings misunderstanding, fierce resentment, financial insecurity, disgusted friends and employers, warped lives of blameless children, sad wives and parents—anyone can increase the list.

We hope this volume will inform and comfort those who are, or who may be affected. They are many.

Highly competent psychiatrists who have dealt with us found it sometimes impossible to persuade an alcoholic to discuss his situation without reserve. Strangely enough, wives, parents and intimate friends usually find us even more unapproachable than do the psychiatrist and the doctor.

*But the ex-alcoholic who has found this solution, who is properly armed with facts about himself, can generally win the entire confidence of another alcoholic in a few hours. Until such an understanding is reached, little or nothing can be accomplished.*

That the man who is making the approach has had the same difficulty, that he obviously knows what he is talking about, that his whole deportment shouts at the new prospect that he is a man with a real answer, that he has no attitude of holier than thou, nothing whatever except the sincere desire to be helpful; that there are no fees to pay, no axes to grind, no people to please, no lectures to be endured—these are the conditions we found most effective. After such an approach many take up their beds and walk again.

None of us makes a sole vocation of this work, nor do we think its effectiveness would be increased if we did. We feel that elimination of our drinking is but a beginning. A much more important demonstration of our principles lies before us in our respective homes, occupations, and affairs. All of us spend much of our spare time in the sort of effort which we are going to describe. A few are fortunate enough to be so situated that they can give nearly all of their time to the work.

If we keep on the way we are going there is little doubt that much good will result, but the surface of the problem would hardly be scratched. Those of us who live in large cities are overcome by the reflection that close by hundreds are dropping into oblivion every day. Many could recover if they had the opportunity we have enjoyed. How then shall we present that which has been so freely given us?

We have concluded to publish an anonymous volume setting forth the problem as we see it. We shall bring to the task our combined experience and knowledge. This should suggest a useful program for anyone concerned with a drinking problem.

Of necessity there will have to be discussion of matters medical, psychiatric, social, and religious. We are aware that these matters are, from their very nature, controversial. Nothing would please us so much as to write a book which would contain no basis for contention or argument. We shall do our utmost to achieve that ideal. Most of us sense that real tolerance of other people's shortcomings and viewpoints and a respect for their opinions are attitudes which make us more useful to others. Our very lives, as ex-alcoholics, depend upon our constant thought of others and how we may help meet their needs.

You may already have asked yourself why it is that all of us became so very ill from drinking. Doubtless you are curious to discover how and why, in the face of expert opinion to the contrary, we have recovered from a hopeless condition of mind and body. If you are an alcoholic who wants to get over it, you may already be asking—"What do I have to do?"

It is the purpose of this book to answer such questions specifically. We shall tell you what we have done. Before going into a detailed discussion, it may be well to summarize some points as we see them.

How many times people have said to us: "I can take it or leave it alone. Why can't he?" "Why don't you drink like a gentleman or quit?" "That fellow can't handle his liquor." "Why don't you try beer and wine?" "Lay off the hard stuff." "His will power must be weak." "He could stop if he wanted to." "She's such a sweet girl, I should think he'd stop for her." "The doctor told him that if he ever drank again it would kill him, but there he is all lit up again."

Now these are commonplace observations on drinkers which we hear all the time. Back of them is a world of ignorance and misunderstanding. We see that these expressions refer to people whose reactions are very different from ours.

Moderate drinkers have little trouble in giving up liquor entirely if they have good reason for it. They can take it or leave it alone.

Then we have a certain type of hard drinker. He may have the habit badly enough to gradually impair him physically and mentally. It may cause him to die a few years before his time. If a sufficiently strong reason—ill health, falling in love, change of environment, or the warning of a doctor—becomes operative, this man can also stop or moderate, although he may find it difficult and troublesome and may even need medical attention.

But what about the real alcoholic? He may start off as a moderate drinker; he may or may not become a continuous hard drinker; but at some stage of his drinking career he begins to lose all control of his liquor consumption, once he starts to drink.

Here is the fellow who has been puzzling you, especially in his lack of control. He does absurd, incredible, tragic things while drinking. He is a real Dr. Jekyll and Mr. Hyde. He is seldom mildly intoxicated. He is always more or less insanely drunk. His disposition while drinking resembles his normal nature but little. He may be one of the finest fellows in the world. Yet let him drink for a day, and he frequently becomes disgustingly, and even dangerously anti-social. He has a positive genius for getting tight at exactly the wrong moment, particularly when some important decision must be made or engagement kept. He is often perfectly sensible and well balanced concerning everything except liquor, but in that respect is incredibly dishonest and selfish. He often possesses special abilities, skills, and aptitudes, and has a promising career ahead of him. He uses his gifts to build up a bright outlook for his family and himself, then pulls the structure down on his head by a senseless series of sprees. He is the fellow who goes to bed so intoxicated he ought to sleep the clock around. Yet early next morning he searches madly for the bottle he misplaced the night before. If he can afford it, he may have liquor concealed all over his house to be certain no one gets his entire supply away from him to throw down the waste-pipe. As matters grow worse, he begins to use a combination of high-powered sedative and liquor to quiet his nerves so he can go to work. Then comes the day when he simply cannot make it and gets drunk all over again. Perhaps he goes to a doctor who gives him morphine or some sedative with which to taper off. Then he begins to appear at hospitals and sanitariums.

This is by no means a comprehensive picture of the true alcoholic, as our behavior patterns vary. But this description should identify him roughly.

Why does he behave like this? If hundreds of experiences have shown him that one drink means another debacle with all its attendant suffering and humiliation, why is it he takes that one drink? Why can't he stay on the water wagon? What has become of the common sense and will power that he still sometimes displays with respect to other matters?

Perhaps there never will be a full answer to these questions. Opinions vary considerably as to why the alcoholic reacts differently from normal people. We are not sure why, once a certain point is reached, little can be done for him. We cannot answer the riddle.

We know that while the alcoholic keeps away from drink as he may do for months or years, he reacts much like other men. We are equally positive that once he takes any alcohol whatever into his system, something happens, both in the bodily and mental sense, which makes it virtually impossible for him to stop. The experience of any alcoholic will abundantly confirm that.

These observations would be academic and pointless if our friend never took the first drink thereby setting the terrible cycle in motion. Therefore, the main problem of the alcoholic centers in his mind, rather than in his body. If you ask him why he started on that last bender, the chances are he will offer you any one of a hundred alibis. Sometimes these excuses have a certain plausibility, but none of them really make sense in the light of the havoc an alcoholic's drinking bout creates. They sound like the philosophy of the man who, having a headache, beat himself on the head with a hammer so that he couldn't feel the ache. If you draw this fallacious reasoning to the attention of an alcoholic, he will laugh it off, or become irritated and refuse to talk.

Once in a while he may tell the truth. And the truth, strange to say, is usually that he has no more idea why he took that first drink than you have. Some drinkers have excuses with which they are satisfied part of the time. But in their hearts they really do not know why they do it. Once this malady has a real hold, they are a baffled lot. There is the obsession that somehow, some day, they will beat the game. But they often suspect they are down for the count.

How true this is, few realize. In a vague way their families and friends sense that these drinkers are abnormal, but everybody hopefully waits the day when the sufferer will rouse himself from his lethargy and assert his power of will.

The tragic truth is that if the man be a real alcoholic, the happy day will seldom arrive. He has lost control. At a certain point in the drinking of every alcoholic, he passes into a state where the most powerful desire to stop drinking is of absolutely no avail. This tragic situation has already arrived in practically every case long before it is suspected.

*The fact is that most alcoholics, for reasons yet obscure, have lost the power of choice in drink. Our so-called will power becomes practically non-existent. We are unable at certain times, to bring into our consciousness with sufficient force the memory of the suffering and humiliation of even a week or a month ago. We are without defense against the first drink.*

The almost certain consequences that follow taking even a glass of beer do not crowd into the mind to deter us. If these thoughts occur, they are hazy, and readily supplanted with the old threadbare idea that this time we shall handle ourselves like other people. There is a complete failure of the kind of defense that keeps one from putting his hand on a hot stove.

The alcoholic may say to himself in the most casual way, "It won't burn me this time, so here's how!" Or perhaps he doesn't think at all. How often have some of us begun to drink in this nonchalant way, and after the third or fourth, pounded on the bar and said to ourselves, "For God's sake, how did I ever get started again?" Only to have that thought supplanted by "Well, I'll stop with the sixth drink." Or "What's the use anyhow?"

When this sort of thinking is fully established in an individual with alcoholic tendencies, he has probably placed himself beyond human aid, and unless locked up, may die, or go permanently insane. These stark and ugly facts have been confirmed by legions of alcoholics throughout history. But for the grace of God, there would have been one hundred more convincing demonstrations. So many want to stop, but cannot.

*There is a solution.* Almost none of us liked the self-searching, the leveling of our pride, the confession of shortcomings which the process requires for its successful consummation. But we saw that it really worked in others, and we had come to believe in the hopelessness and futility of life as we had been living it. When, therefore, we were approached by those in whom the problem had been solved, there was nothing left for us but to pick up the simple kit of spiritual tools laid at our feet. We have found much of heaven and we have been rocketed into a fourth dimension of existence, of which we had not even dreamed.

The great fact is just this, and nothing less: that we have had deep and effective spiritual experiences, which have revolutionized our whole attitude toward life, toward our fellows, and toward God's universe. The central fact of our lives today is the absolute certainty that our Creator has entered into our hearts and lives in a way which is indeed miraculous. He has commenced to accomplish those things for us which we could never do by ourselves.

If you are as seriously alcoholic as we were, we believe there is no middle-of-the-road solution. We were in a position where life was becoming impossible, and if we had passed into the region from which there is no return through human aid, we had but two alternatives: one was to go on to the bitter end, blotting out the consciousness of our intolerable situation as best we could; and the other, to accept spiritual help. This we did because we honestly wanted to, and were willing to make the effort.

A certain American business man had ability, good sense, and high character. For years he had floundered from one sanitarium to another. He had consulted the best known American psychiatrists. Then he had gone to Europe, placing himself in the care of a celebrated physician who prescribed for him. Though experience had made him skeptical, he finished his treatment with unusual confidence. His physical and mental condition were unusually good. Above all, he believed he had acquired such a profound knowledge of the inner workings of his mind and its hidden springs, that relapse was unthinkable. Nevertheless, he was drunk in a short time. More baffling still, he could give himself no satisfactory explanation for his fall.

So he returned to this doctor, whom he admired, and asked him point-blank why he could not recover. He wished above all things to regain self-control. He seemed quite rational and well-balanced with respect to other problems. Yet he had no control whatever over alcohol. Why was this?

He begged the doctor to tell him the whole truth, and he got it. In the doctor's judgment he was utterly hopeless; he could never regain his position in society and he would have to place himself under lock and key, or hire a bodyguard if he expected to live long. That was a great physician's opinion.

But this man still lives, and is a free man. He does not need a bodyguard, nor is he confined. He can go anywhere on this earth where other free men may go without disaster, provided he remains willing to maintain a certain simple attitude.

Some of our alcoholic readers may think they can do without spiritual help. Let us tell you the rest of the conversation our friend had with his doctor.

The doctor said: "You have the mind of a chronic alcoholic. I have never seen one single case recover, where that state of mind existed to the extent that it does in you." Our friend felt as though the gates of hell had closed on him with a clang.

He said to the doctor, "Is there no exception?"

"Yes," replied the doctor, "there is. Exceptions to cases such as yours have been occurring since early times. Here and there, once in a while, alcoholics have had what are called vital spiritual experiences. To me these occurrences are phenomena. They appear to be in the nature of huge emotional displacements and rearrangements. Ideas, emotions, and attitudes which were once the guiding forces of the lives of these men are suddenly cast to one side, and a completely new set of conceptions and motives begin to dominate them. In fact, I have been trying to produce some such emotional rearrangement within you. With many individuals the methods which I employed are successful, but I have never been successful with an alcoholic of your description."

Upon hearing this, our friend was somewhat relieved, for he reflected that, after all, he was a good church member. This hope, however, was destroyed by the doctor's telling him that his religious convictions were very good, but that in his case they did not spell the necessary vital spiritual experience.

Here was the terrible dilemma in which our friend found himself when he had the extraordinary experience, which as we have already told you, made him a free man.

We, in our turn, sought the same escape, with all the desperation of drowning men. What seemed at first a flimsy reed, has proved to be the loving and powerful hand of God. A new life has been given us or, if you prefer, "a design for living" that really works.

The distinguished American psychologist, William James, in his book "Varieties of Religious Experience," indicates a multitude of ways in which men have discovered God. We have no desire to convince anyone that there is only one way by which faith can be acquired. If what we have learned, and felt, and seen, means anything at all, it means that all of us, whatever our race, creed, or color, are the children of a living Creator with whom we may form a relationship upon simple and understandable terms as soon as we are willing and honest enough to try. Those having religious affiliations will find here nothing disturbing to their beliefs or ceremonies. There is no friction among us over such matters.

We think it no concern of ours what religious bodies our members identify themselves with as individuals. This should be an entirely personal affair which each one decides for himself in the light of past associations, or his present choice. Not all of us have joined religious bodies, but most of us favor such memberships.

In the following chapter, there appears an explanation of alcoholism as we understand it, then a chapter addressed to the agnostic. Many who once were in this class are now among our members; surprisingly enough, we find such convictions no great obstacle to a spiritual experience.

Further on clear-cut directions are given showing how we recovered. These are followed by more than a score of personal experiences.

Each individual, in the personal stories, describes in his own language, and from his own point of view the way he established his relationship with God. These give a fair cross section of our membership and a clear-cut idea of what has actually happened in their lives.

We hope no one will consider these self-revealing accounts in bad taste. Our hope is that many alcoholic men and women, desperately in need, will see these pages, and we believe that it is only by fully disclosing ourselves and our problems that they will be persuaded to say, "Yes, I am one of them too; I must have this thing."

CHAPTER 3

# More About Alcoholism

Most of us have been unwilling to admit we were real alcoholics. No person likes to think he is bodily and mentally different from his fellows. Therefore, it is not surprising that our drinking careers have been characterized by countless vain attempts to prove we could drink like other people. The idea that somehow, someday he will control and enjoy his liquor drinking is the great obsession of every abnormal drinker. The persistence of this illusion is astonishing. Many pursue it into the gates of insanity or death.

We learned that we had to fully concede to our innermost selves that we were alcoholics. This is the first step in recovery. The delusion that we are like other people, or presently may be, has to be smashed.

We alcoholics are men and women who have lost the ability to control our drinking. We know that no real alcoholic ever recovered control. All of us felt at times that we were regaining control, but such intervals—usually brief—were inevitably followed by still less control, which led in time to pitiful and incomprehensible demoralization. We are convinced to a man that alcoholics of our type are in the grip of a progressive illness. Over any considerable period we get worse, never better.

We are like men who have lost their legs; they never grow new ones. Neither does there appear to be any kind of treatment which will make alcoholics of our kind like other men. We have tried every imaginable remedy. In some instances there has been brief recovery, followed always by still worse relapse. Physicians who are familiar with alcoholism agree there is no such thing as making a normal drinker out of an alcoholic. Science may one day accomplish this, but it evidently hasn't done so yet.

Despite all we can say, many who are real alcoholics are not going to believe they are in that class. By every form of self-deception and experimentation, they will try to prove themselves exceptions to the rule, therefore non-alcoholic. If anyone, who is showing inability to control his drinking, can do the right-about face and drink like a gentleman, our hats are off to him. Heaven knows, we have tried hard enough and long enough to drink like other people!

Here are some of the methods we have tried: drinking beer only, limiting the number of drinks, never drinking alone, never drinking in the morning, drinking only at home, never having it in the house, never drinking during business hours, drinking only at parties, switching from scotch to brandy, drinking only natural wines, agreeing to resign if ever drunk on the job, taking a trip, not taking a trip, swearing off forever (with and without a solemn oath), taking more physical exercise, reading inspirational books, going to health farms and sanitariums, accepting voluntary commitment to asylums—we could increase the list ad infinitum.

We do not like to brand any individual as an alcoholic, but you can quickly diagnose yourself. Step over to the nearest barroom and try some controlled drinking. Try to drink and stop abruptly. Try it more than once. It will not take long for you to decide, if you are honest with yourself about it. It may be worth a bad case of jitters if you get a full knowledge of your condition.

Though there is no way of proving it, we believe that early in our drinking careers most of us could have stopped drinking. But the difficulty is that few alcoholics have enough desire to stop while there is yet time. We have heard of a few instances where people, who showed definite signs of alcoholism, were able to stop for a long period because of an overpowering desire to do so. Here is one.

A man of thirty was doing a great deal of spree drinking. He was very nervous in the morning after these bouts and quieted himself with more liquor. He was ambitious to succeed in business, but saw that he would get nowhere if he drank at all. Once he started, he had no control whatever. He made up his mind that until he had been successful in business and had retired, he would not touch another drop. An exceptional man, he remained bone dry for twenty-five years, and retired at the age of fifty-five, after a successful and happy business career. Then he fell victim to a belief which practically every alcoholic has—that his long period of sobriety and self-discipline had qualified him to drink as other men. Out came his carpet slippers and a bottle. In two months he was in a hospital, puzzled and humiliated. He tried to regulate his drinking for a while, making several trips to the hospital meantime. Then, gathering all his forces, he attempted to stop altogether and found he could not. Every means of solving his problem which money could buy was at his disposal. Every attempt failed. Though a robust man at retirement, he went to pieces quickly, and was dead within four years.

This case contains a powerful lesson. Most of us have believed that if we remained sober for a long stretch, we could thereafter drink normally. But here is a man who at fifty-five years found he was just where he had left off at thirty. We have seen the truth demonstrated again and again: "once an alcoholic, always an alcoholic." Commencing to drink after a period of sobriety, we are in a short time as bad as ever. If we are planning to stop drinking, there must be no reservation of any kind, nor any lurking notion that someday we will be immune to alcohol.

Young people may be encouraged by this man's experience to think that they can stop, as he did, on their own will power. We doubt if many of them can do it, because none will really want to stop, and hardly one of them, because of the peculiar mental twist already acquired, will find he can win out. Several of our crowd, men of thirty-five or less, had been drinking only a few years, but they found themselves as helpless as those who had been drinking twenty years.

To be gravely affected, one does not necessarily have to drink a long time, nor take the quantities some of us have. This is particularly true of women. Potential feminine alcoholics often turn into the real thing and are gone beyond recall in a few years. Certain drinkers, who would be greatly insulted if called alcoholics, are astonished at their inability to stop. We, who are familiar with the symptoms, see large numbers of potential alcoholics among young people everywhere. But try and get them to see it!

As we look back, we feel we had gone on drinking many years beyond the point where we could quit on our will power. If anyone questions whether he has entered this dangerous area, let him try leaving liquor alone for one year. If he is a real alcoholic and very far advanced, there is scant chance of success. In the early days of our drinking we occasionally remained sober for a year or more, becoming serious drinkers again later. Though you may be able to stop for a considerable period, you may yet be a potential alcoholic. We think few, to whom this book will appeal, can stay dry anything like a year. Some will be drunk the day after making their resolutions; most of them within a few weeks.

For those who are unable to drink moderately the question is how to stop altogether. We are assuming, of course, that the reader desires to stop. Whether such a person can quit upon a non-spiritual basis depends upon the extent to which he has already lost the power to choose whether he will drink or not. Many of us felt that we had plenty of character. There was a tremendous urge to cease forever. Yet we found it impossible. This is the baffling feature of alcoholism as we know it—this utter inability to leave it alone, no matter how great the necessity or the wish.

How then shall we help our readers determine, to their own satisfaction, whether they are one of us? The experiment of quitting for a period of time will be helpful, but we think we can render an even greater service to alcoholic sufferers, and perhaps to the medical fraternity. So we shall describe some of the mental states that precede a relapse into drinking, for obviously this is the crux of the problem.

What sort of thinking dominates an alcoholic who repeats time after time the desperate experiment of the first drink? Friends, who have reasoned with him after a spree which has brought him to the point of divorce or bankruptcy, are mystified when he walks directly into a saloon. Why does he? Of what is he thinking?

Our first example is a friend we shall call Jim. This man has a charming wife and family. He inherited a lucrative automobile agency. He had a commendable world war record. He is a good salesman. Everybody likes him. He is an intelligent man, normal so far as we can see, except for a nervous disposition. He did no drinking until he was thirty-five. In a few years he became so violent when intoxicated that he had to be committed. On leaving the asylum, he came into contact with us.

We told him what we knew of alcoholism and the answer we had found. He made a beginning. His family was re-assembled, and he began to work as a salesman for the business he had lost through drinking. All went well for a time, but he failed to enlarge his spiritual life. To his consternation, he found himself drunk half a dozen times in rapid succession. On each of these occasions we worked with him, reviewing carefully what had happened. He agreed he was a real alcoholic and in serious condition. He knew he faced another trip to the asylum if he kept on. Moreover, he would lose his family for whom he had deep affection.

Yet he got drunk again. We asked him to tell us exactly how it happened. This is his story: "I came to work on Tuesday morning. I remember I felt irritated that I had to be a salesman for a concern I once owned. I had a few words with the boss, but nothing serious. Then I decided to drive into the country and see one of my prospects for a car. On the way I felt hungry so I stopped at a roadside place where they have a bar. I had no intention of drinking. I just thought I would get a sandwich. I also had the notion that I might find a customer for a car at this place, which was familiar, for I had been going to it for years. I had eaten there many times during the months I was sober. I sat down at a table and ordered a sandwich and a glass of milk. Still no thought of drinking. I ordered another sandwich and decided to have another glass of milk.

*"Suddenly the thought crossed my mind that if I were to put an ounce of whiskey in my milk, it couldn't hurt me on a full stomach. I ordered a whiskey and poured it into the milk. I vaguely sensed I was not being any too smart, but felt reassured, as I was taking the whiskey on a full stomach.* The experiment went so well that I ordered another whiskey and poured it into more milk. That didn't seem to bother me so I tried another."

Thus started one more journey to the asylum for Jim. Here was the threat of commitment, the loss of family and position, to say nothing of that intense mental and physical suffering which drinking always caused him. *He had much knowledge about himself as an alcoholic. Yet all reasons for not drinking were easily pushed aside in favor of the foolish idea he could take whiskey if only he mixed it with milk!*

Whatever the precise definition of the word may be, we call this plain insanity. How can such a lack of proportion, of the ability to think straight, be called anything else?

You may think this an extreme case. To us it is not far-fetched, for this kind of thinking has been characteristic of every single one of us. We have sometimes reflected more than Jim did upon the consequences. But there was always the curious mental phenomenon, that parallel with our sound reasoning there inevitably ran some insanely trivial excuse for taking the first drink. Our sound reasoning failed to hold us in check. The insane idea won out. Next day we would ask ourselves, in all earnestness and sincerity, how it could have happened.

In some circumstances we have gone out deliberately to get drunk, feeling ourselves justified by nervousness, anger, worry, depression, jealousy or the like. But even in this type of beginning we are obliged to admit that our justification for a spree was insanely insufficient in the light of what always happened. We now see that when we began to drink deliberately, instead of casually, there was little serious or effective thought during the period of premeditation of what the terrific consequences might be.

Our behavior is as absurd and incomprehensible with respect to the first drink as that of an individual with a passion, say, for jay-walking. He gets a thrill out of skipping in front of fast-moving vehicles. He enjoys himself a few years in spite of friendly warnings. Up to this point you would label him as a foolish chap having queer ideas of fun. Luck then deserts him and he is slightly injured several times in succession. You would expect him, if he were normal, to cut it out. Presently he is hit again and this time has a fractured skull. Within a week after leaving the hospital a fastmoving trolley car breaks his arm. He tells you he has decided to stop jay-walking for good, but in a few weeks he breaks both legs.

On through the years this conduct continues, accompanied by his continual promises to be careful or to keep off the streets altogether. Finally, he can no longer work, his wife gets a divorce, he is held up to ridicule. He tries every known means to get the jay-walking idea out of his head. He shuts himself up in an asylum, hoping to mend his ways. But the day he comes out he races in front of a fire engine, which breaks his back. Such a man would be crazy, wouldn't he?

You may think our illustration is too ridiculous. But is it? We, who have been through the wringer, have to admit if we substituted alcoholism for jay-walking, the illustration would fit us exactly. However intelligent we may have been in other respects, where alcohol has been involved, we have been strangely insane. It's strong language—but isn't it true?

Some of you are thinking: "Yes, what you tell us is true, but it doesn't fully apply. We admit we have some of these symptoms, but we have not gone to the extremes you fellows did, nor are we likely to, for we understand ourselves so well after what you have told us that such things cannot happen again. We have not lost everything in life through drinking and we certainly do not intend to. Thanks for the information."

That may be true of certain non-alcoholic people who, though drinking foolishly and heavily at the present time, are able to stop or moderate, because their brains and bodies have not been damaged as ours were. But the actual or potential alcoholic, with hardly an exception, will be *absolutely unable to stop drinking on the basis of self-knowledge.* This is a point we wish to emphasize and re-emphasize, to smash home upon our alcoholic readers as it has been revealed to us out of bitter experience. Let us take another illustration.

Fred is partner in a well-known accounting firm. His income is good, he has a fine home, is happily married and the father of promising children of college age. He is so attractive a personality that he makes friends with everyone. If ever there was a successful business man, it is Fred. To all appearance he is a stable, well balanced individual. Yet, he is alcoholic. We first saw Fred about a year ago in a hospital where he had gone to recover from a bad case of jitters. It was his first experience of this kind, and he was much ashamed of it. Far from admitting he was an alcoholic, he told himself he came to the hospital to rest his nerves. The doctor intimated strongly that he might be worse than he realized. For a few days he was depressed about his condition. He made up his mind to quit drinking altogether. It never occurred to him that perhaps he could not do so, in spite of his character and standing. Fred would not believe himself an alcoholic, much less accept a spiritual remedy for his problem. We told him what we knew about alcoholism. He was interested and conceded that he had some of the symptoms, but he was a long way from admitting that he could do nothing about it himself. He was positive that this humiliating experience, plus the knowledge he had acquired, would keep him sober the rest of his life. Self-knowledge would fix it.

We heard no more of Fred for a while. One day we were told that he was back in the hospital. This time he was quite shaky. He soon indicated he was anxious to see us. The story he told is most instructive for here was a chap absolutely convinced he had to stop drinking, who had no excuse for drinking, who exhibited splendid judgment and determination in all his other concerns, yet was flat on his back nevertheless.

Let him tell you about it: "I was much impressed with what you fellows said about alcoholism, but I frankly did not believe it would be possible for me to drink again. I somewhat appreciated your ideas about the subtle insanity which precedes the first drink, but I was confident it could not happen to me after what I had learned. I reasoned I was not so far advanced as most of you fellows, that I had been usually successful in licking my other personal problems, that I would therefore be successful where you men failed. I felt I had every right to be self-confident, that it would be only a matter of exercising my will power and keeping on guard.

"In this frame of mind, I went about my business and for a time all was well. I had no trouble refusing drinks, and began to wonder if I had not been making too hard work of a simple matter. One day I went to Washington to present some accounting evidence to a government bureau. I had been out of town before during this particular dry spell, so there was nothing new about that. Physically, I felt fine. Neither did I have any pressing problems or worries. My business came off well, I was pleased and knew my partners would be too. It was the end of a perfect day, not a cloud on the horizon.

"I went to my hotel and leisurely dressed for dinner. *As I crossed the threshold of the dining room, the thought came to mind it would be nice to have a couple of cocktails with dinner. That was all. Nothing more.* I ordered a cocktail and my meal. Then I ordered another cocktail. After dinner I decided to take a walk. When I returned to the hotel it struck me a highball would be fine before going to bed, so I stepped into the bar and had one. I remember having several more that night and plenty next morning. I have a shadowy recollection of being in an airplane bound for New York, of finding a friendly taxicab driver at the landing field instead of my wife. The driver escorted me about for several days. I know little of where I went, or what I said and did. Then came the hospital with unbearable mental and physical suffering.

"As soon as I regained my ability to think, I went carefully over that evening in Washington. *Not only had I been off guard, I had made no fight whatever against that first drink. This time I had not thought of the consequences at all.* I had commenced to drink as carelessly as though the cocktails were ginger ale. I now remembered what my alcoholic friends had told me, how they prophesied that if I had an alcoholic mind, the time and place would come—I would drink again. They had said that though I did raise a defense, it would one day give way before some trivial reason for having a drink. Well, just that did happen and more, for what I had learned of alcoholism did not occur to me at all. I knew from that moment that I had an alcoholic mind. I saw that will power and self-knowledge would not help in those strange mental blank spots. I had never been able to understand people who said that a problem had them hopelessly defeated. I knew then. It was a crushing blow.

"Two of the members of Alcoholics Anonymous came to see me. They grinned, which I didn't like so much, and then asked me if I thought myself alcoholic and if I were really licked this time. I had to concede both propositions. They piled on me heaps of evidence to the effect that an alcoholic mentality, such as I had exhibited in Washington, was a hopeless condition. They cited cases out of their own experience by the dozen. This process snuffed out the last flicker of conviction that I could do the job myself.

"Then they outlined the spiritual answer and program of action which a hundred of them had followed successfully. Though I had been only a nominal churchman, their proposals were not, intellectually, hard to swallow. But the program of action, though entirely sensible, was pretty drastic. It meant I would have to throw several lifelong conceptions out of the window. That was not easy. But the moment I made up my mind to go through with the process, I had the curious feeling that my alcoholic condition was relieved, as in fact it proved to be.

"Quite as important was the discovery that spiritual principles would solve all my problems. I have since been brought into a way of living infinitely more satisfying and, I hope, more useful than the life I lived before. My old manner of life was by no means a bad one, but I would not exchange its best moments for the worst I have now. I would not go back to it even if I could."

Fred's story speaks for itself. We hope it strikes home to thousands like him. He had felt only the first nip of the wringer. Most alcoholics have to be pretty badly mangled before they really commence to solve their problems.

Many doctors and psychiatrists agree with our conclusions. One of these men, staff member of a world-renowned hospital, recently made this statement to some of us: "What you say about the general hopelessness of the average alcoholic's plight is, in my opinion, correct. As to two of you men, whose stories I have heard, there is no doubt in my mind that you were 100% hopeless, apart from Divine help. Had you offered yourselves as patients at this hospital, I would not have taken you, if I had been able to avoid it. People like you are too heartbreaking. Though not a religious person, I have profound respect for the spiritual approach in such cases as yours. For most cases, there is virtually no other solution."

Once more: the alcoholic at certain times has no effective mental defense against the first drink. Except in a few rare cases, neither he nor any other human being can provide such a defense. His defense must come from a higher Power.

CHAPTER 4

# We Agnostics

In the preceding chapters, you have learned something of alcoholism. We hope we have made clear the distinction between the alcoholic and the non-alcoholic. If, when you honestly want to, you find you cannot quit entirely, or if, when drinking, you have little control over the amount you take, you are probably alcoholic. If that be the case, you may be suffering from an illness which only a spiritual experience will conquer.

To one who feels he is an atheist or agnostic such an experience seems impossible, but to continue as he is means disaster especially if he is an alcoholic of the hopeless variety. To be doomed to an alcoholic death or to live on a spiritual basis—not always easy alternatives to face.

But it isn't so difficult. About half our fellowship were of exactly that type. At first some of us tried to avoid the issue, hoping against hope we were not true alcoholics. But after a while we had to face the fact that we must find a spiritual basis of life—or else. Perhaps it is going to be that way with you. But cheer up, something like fifty of us thought we were atheists or agnostics. Our experience shows that you need not be disconcerted.

If a mere code of morals, or a better philosophy of life were sufficient to overcome alcoholism, many of us would have recovered long ago. But we found that such codes and philosophies did not save us, no matter how much we tried. We could wish to be moral, we could wish to be philosophically comforted, in fact, we could will these things with all our might, but the needed power wasn't there. Our human resources, as marshalled by the will, were not sufficient; they failed utterly.

Lack of power, that was our dilemma. We had to find a power by which we could live, and it had to be *A Power Greater Than Ourselves.* Obviously. But where and how were we to find this Power?

Well, that's exactly what this book is about. Its main object is to enable you to find a Power greater than yourself, which will solve your problem. That means we have written a book which we believe to be spiritual as well as moral. And it means, of course, that we are going to talk about God. Here difficulty arises with agnostics.

Many times we talk to a new man and watch his hope rise as we discuss his alcoholic problems and explain our fellowship. But his face falls when we speak of spiritual matters, especially when we mention God, for we have re-opened a subject which our man thought he had neatly evaded or entirely ignored.

We know how he feels. We have shared his honest doubt and prejudice. Some of us have been violently anti-religious. To others, the word "God" brought up a particular idea of Him with which someone had tried to impress them during childhood. Perhaps we rejected this particular conception because it seemed inadequate. With that rejection we imagined we had abandoned the God idea entirely. We were bothered with the thought that faith and dependence upon a Power beyond ourselves was somewhat weak, even cowardly. We looked upon this world of warring individuals, warring theological systems, and inexplicable calamity, with deep skepticism. We looked askance at many individuals who claimed to be godly. How could a Supreme Being have anything to do with it all? And who could comprehend a Supreme Being anyhow? Yet, in other moments, we found ourselves thinking, when enchanted by a starlit night, "Who, then, made all this?" There was a feeling of awe and wonder, but it was fleeting and soon lost.

Yes, we of agnostic temperament have had these thoughts and experiences. Let us make haste to reassure you. We found that as soon as we were able to lay aside prejudice and express even a willingness to believe in a Power greater than ourselves, we commenced to get results, even though it was impossible for any of us to fully define or comprehend that Power, which is God.

Much to our relief, we discovered we did not need to consider another's conception of God. Our own conception, however inadequate, was sufficient to make the approach and to effect a contact with Him. As soon as we admitted the possible existence of a Creative Intelligence, a Spirit of the Universe underlying the totality of things, we began to be possessed of a new sense of power and direction, provided we took other simple steps. We found that God does not make too hard terms with those who seek Him. To us, the Realm of Spirit is broad, roomy, all inclusive; never exclusive or forbidding, to those who earnestly seek. It is open, we believe, to all men.

When, therefore, we speak to you of God, we mean your own conception of God. This applies, too, to other spiritual expressions which you find in this book. Do not let any prejudice you may have against spiritual terms deter you from honestly asking yourself what they mean to you. At the start, this is all we needed to commence spiritual growth, to effect our first conscious relation with God as we understood Him. Afterward, we found ourselves accepting many things which then seemed entirely out of reach. That is growth, but if we wished to grow, we had to begin somewhere. So we used our own conception, however limited it was.

We needed to ask ourselves but one short question. "Do I now believe, or am I even willing to believe, that there is a Power greater than myself?" As soon as a man can say that he does believe, or is willing to believe, we emphatically assure him that he is on his way. It has been repeatedly proven among us that upon this simple cornerstone a wonderfully effective spiritual structure can be built.

That was great news to us, for we had assumed we could not make use of spiritual principles unless we accepted many things on faith which seemed difficult to believe. When people presented us with spiritual approaches, how frequently did we all say: "I wish I had what that man has. I'm sure it would work if I could only believe as he believes. But I cannot accept as surely true the many articles of faith which are so plain to him." So it was comforting to learn that we could commence at a simpler level.

Besides a seeming inability to accept much on faith, we often found ourselves handicapped by obstinacy, sensitiveness, and unreasoning prejudice. Many of us have been so touchy that even casual reference to spiritual things made us bristle with antagonism. This sort of thinking had to be abandoned. Though some of us resisted, we found no great difficulty in casting aside such feelings. Faced with alcoholic destruction, we soon became as open minded on spiritual matters as we had tried to be on other questions. In this respect alcohol was a great persuader. It finally beat us into a state of reasonableness. Sometimes this was a tedious process; we hope no one will be prejudiced as long as some of us were.

The reader may still ask why he should believe in a Power greater than himself. We think there are good reasons. Let us have a look at some of them.

The practical individual of today is a stickler for facts and results. Nevertheless, the twentieth century readily accepts theories of all kinds, provided they are firmly grounded in fact. We have numerous theories, for example, about electricity. Everybody believes them without a murmur of doubt. Why this ready acceptance? Simply because it is impossible to explain what we see, feel, direct, and use, without a reasonable assumption as a starting point.

Everybody nowadays, believes in scores of assumptions for which there is good evidence, but no perfect visual proof. And does not science demonstrate that visual proof is the weakest proof? It is being constantly revealed, as mankind studies the material world, that outward appearances are not inward reality at all. To illustrate:

The prosaic steel girder is a mass of electrons whirling around each other at incredible speed. These tiny bodies are governed by precise laws, and these laws hold true throughout the material world. Science tells us so. We have no reason to doubt it. When, however, the perfectly logical assumption is suggested that underneath the material world and life as we see it, there is an All Powerful, Guiding, Creative Intelligence, right there our perverse streak comes to the surface and we laboriously set out to convince ourselves it isn't so. We read wordy books and indulge in windy arguments, thinking we believe this universe needs no God to explain it. Were our contentions true, it would follow that life originated out of nothing, means nothing, and proceeds nowhere.

Instead of regarding ourselves as intelligent agents, spearheads of God's ever advancing Creation, we agnostics and atheists chose to believe that our human intelligence was the last word, the alpha and the omega, the beginning and end of all. Rather vain of us, wasn't it?

We, who have traveled this dubious path, beg you to lay aside prejudice, even against organized religion. We have learned that whatever the human frailties of various faiths may be, those faiths have given purpose and direction to millions. People of faith have a logical idea of what life is all about. Actually, we used to have no reasonable conception whatever. We used to amuse ourselves by cynically dissecting spiritual beliefs and practices when we might have observed that many spiritually-minded persons of all races, colors, and creeds were demonstrating a degree of stability, happiness and usefulness which we should have sought ourselves.

Instead, we looked at the human defects of these people, and sometimes used their shortcomings as a basis of wholesale condemnation. We talked of intolerance, while we were intolerant ourselves. We missed the reality and the beauty of the forest because we were diverted by the ugliness of some of its trees. We never gave the spiritual side of life a fair hearing.

In our personal stories you will find wide variation in the way each teller approaches and conceives of the Power which is greater than himself. Whether we agree with a particular approach or conception seems to make little difference. Experience has taught that these are matters about which, for our purpose, we need not be worried. They are questions for each individual to settle for himself.

On one proposition, however, these men and women are strikingly agreed. Everyone of them has gained access to, and believes in, a Power greater than himself. This Power has in each case accomplished the miraculous, the humanly impossible. As a celebrated American statesman puts it, "Let's look at the record."

Here are one hundred men and women, worldly indeed. They flatly declare that since they have come to believe in a Power greater than themselves, to take a certain attitude toward that Power, and to do certain simple things, there has been a revolutionary change in their way of living and thinking. In the face of collapse and despair, in the face of the total failure of their human resources, they found that a new Power, peace, happiness, and sense of direction flowed into them. This happened soon after they whole-heartedly met a few simple requirements. Once confused and baffled by the seeming futility of existence, they will show the underlying reasons why they were making heavy going of life. Leaving aside the drink question, they tell why living was so unsatisfactory. They will show how the change came over them. When one hundred people, are able to say that the consciousness of The Presence of God is today the most important fact of their lives, they present a powerful reason why one should have faith.

This world of ours has made more material progress in the last century than in all the milleniums which went before. Almost everyone knows the reason. Students of ancient history tell us that the intellect of men in those days was equal to the best of today. Yet in ancient times material progress was painfully slow. The spirit of modern scientific inquiry, research and invention was almost unknown. In the realm of the material, men's minds were fettered by superstition, tradition, and all sorts of fixed ideas. The contemporaries of Columbus thought a round earth preposterous. Others like them came near putting Galileo to death for his astronomical heresies.

We asked ourselves this: are not some of us just as biased and unreasonable about the realm of the spirit as were the ancients about the realm of the material? Even in the present century, American newspapers were afraid to print an account of the Wright Brothers' first successful flight at Kitty Hawk. Had not all efforts at flight failed before? Did not Professor Langley's absurd flying machine go to the bottom of the Potomac river? Was it not true that the best mathematical minds had proved man could never fly? Had not people said God had reserved this privilege to the birds? Only thirty years later the conquest of the air was almost an old story and airplane travel was in full swing.

But in most fields our generation has witnessed complete liberation of our thinking. Show any longshoreman a Sunday supplement describing a proposal to explore the moon by means of a rocket and he will say, "I bet they do it—maybe not so long either." Is not our age characterized by the ease with which we discard old ideas for new, by the complete readiness with which we throw away the theory or gadget which does not work for something new which does?

We had to ask ourselves why we shouldn't apply to our human problems this same readiness to change the point of view. We were having trouble with personal relationships, we couldn't control our emotional natures, we were a prey to misery and depression, we couldn't make a living, we had a feeling of uselessness, we were full of fear, we were unhappy, we couldn't seem to be of real help to other people—was not a basic solution of these bedevilments more important than whether we should see newsreels of lunar flight? Of course it was.

When we saw others solve their problems by simple reliance upon the Spirit of this universe, we had to stop doubting the power of God. Our ideas did not work. But the God idea did.

The Wright Brothers' almost childish faith that they could build a machine which would fly was the mainspring of their accomplishment. Without that, nothing could have happened. We agnostics and atheists were sticking to the idea that self-sufficiency would solve our problems. When others showed us that "God-sufficiency" worked with them, we began to feel like those who had insisted the Wrights would never fly.

Logic is great stuff. We liked it. We still like it. It is not by chance we were given the power to reason, to examine the evidence of our senses, and to draw conclusions. That is one of man's magnificent attributes. We agnostically inclined would not feel satisfied with a proposal which does not lend itself to reasonable approach and interpretation. Hence we are at pains to tell why we think our present faith is reasonable, why we think it more sane and logical to believe than not to believe, why we say our former thinking was soft and mushy when we threw up our hands in doubt and said, "We don't know."

When we became alcoholics, crushed by a self-imposed crisis we could not postpone or evade, we had to fearlessly face the proposition that either God is everything or else He is nothing. God either is, or He isn't. What was our choice to be?

Arrived at this point, we were squarely confronted with the question of faith. We couldn't duck the issue. Some of us had already walked far over the Bridge of Reason toward the desired shore of faith. The outlines and the promise of the New Land had brought lustre to tired eyes and fresh courage to flagging spirits. Friendly hands had stretched out in welcome. We were grateful that Reason had brought us so far. But somehow, we couldn't quite step ashore. Perhaps we had been leaning too heavily on Reason that last mile and we did not like to lose our support.

That was natural, but let us think a little more closely. Without knowing it, had we not been brought to where we stood by a certain kind of faith? For did we not believe in our own reasoning? Did we not have confidence in our ability to think? What was that but a sort of faith? Yes, we had been faithful, abjectly faithful to the God of Reason. So, in one way or another, we discovered that faith had been involved all the time!

We found, too, that we had been worshippers. What a state of mental goose-flesh that used to bring on! Had we not variously worshipped people, sentiment, things, money, and ourselves? And then, with a better motive, had we not worshipfully beheld the sunset, the sea, or a flower? Who of us had not loved something or somebody? How much did these feelings, these loves, these worships, have to do with pure reason? Little or nothing, we saw at last. Were not these things the tissue out of which our lives were constructed? Did not these feelings, after all, determine the course of our existence? It was impossible to say we had no capacity for faith, or love, or worship. In one form or another we had been living by faith and little else.

Imagine life without faith! Were nothing left but pure reason, it wouldn't be life. But we believed in life—of course we did. We could not prove life in the sense that you can prove a straight line is the shortest distance between two points: yet, there it was. Could we still say the whole thing was nothing but a mass of electrons, created out of nothing, meaning nothing, whirling on to a destiny of nothingness? Of course we couldn't. The electrons themselves seemed more intelligent than that. At least, so the chemist said.

Hence, we saw that reason isn't everything. Neither is reason, as most of us use it, entirely dependable though it emanate from our best minds. What about people who proved that man could never fly?

Yet we had been seeing another kind of flight, a spiritual liberation from this world, people who rose above their problems. They said God made these things possible, and we only smiled. We had seen spiritual release, but liked to tell ourselves it wasn't true.

Actually we were fooling ourselves, for deep down in every man, woman, and child, is the fundamental idea of God. It may be obscured by calamity, by pomp, by worship of other things, but in some form or other it is there. For faith in a Power greater than ourselves, and miraculous demonstrations of that power in human lives, are facts as old as man himself.

We finally saw that faith in some kind of God was a part of our make-up, just as much as the feeling we have for a friend. Sometimes we had to search fearlessly, but He was there. He was as much a fact as we were. We found the Great Reality deep down within us. In the last analysis it is only there that He may be found. It was so with us.

We can only clear the ground a bit. If our testimony helps sweep away prejudice, enables you to think honestly, encourages you to search diligently within yourself, then if you wish you can join us on the Broad Highway. With this attitude you cannot fail. The consciousness of your belief is sure to come to you.

In this book you will read the experience of a man who thought he was an atheist. His story is so interesting that some of it should be told now. His change of heart was dramatic, convincing, and moving.

Our friend was a minister's son. He attended church school, where he became rebellious at what he thought an overdose of religious education. For years thereafter he was dogged by trouble and frustration. Business failure, insanity, fatal illness, suicide—these calamities in his immediate family embittered and depressed him. Post-war disillusionment, ever more serious alcoholism, impending mental and physical collapse, brought him to the point of self-destruction.

One night, when confined in a hospital, he was approached by an alcoholic who had known a spiritual experience. Our friend's gorge rose as he bitterly cried out: "If there is a God, He certainly hasn't done anything for me." But later, alone in his room, he asked himself this question: "Is it possible that all the religious people I have known are wrong?" While pondering the answer he felt as though he lived in hell. Then, like a thunderbolt, a great thought came. It crowded out all else:

*"WHO ARE YOU TO SAY THERE IS NO GOD?"*

This man recounts that he tumbled out of bed to his knees. In a few seconds he was overwhelmed by a conviction of the Presence of God. It poured over and through him with the certainty and majesty of a great tide at flood. The barriers he had built through the years were swept away. He stood in the Presence of Infinite Power and Love. He had stepped from bridge to shore. For the first time, he lived in conscious companionship with his Creator.

Thus was our friend's cornerstone fixed in place. No later vicissitude has shaken it. His alcoholic problem was taken away. That very night three years ago it disappeared. Save for a few brief moments of temptation the thought of drink has never returned; and at such times a great revulsion has risen up in him. Seemingly he could not drink even if he would. God had restored his sanity.

What is this but a miracle of healing? Yet its elements are simple. Circumstances made him willing to believe. He humbly offered himself to his Maker—then he knew.

Even so has God restored us all to our right minds. To this man, the revelation was sudden. Some of us grow into it more slowly. But He has come to all who have honestly sought Him.

When we drew near to Him He disclosed Himself to us!

CHAPTER 5

# How It Works

Rarely have we seen a person fail who has thoroughly followed our path. Those who do not recover are people who cannot or will not completely give themselves to this simple program, usually men and women who are constitutionally incapable of being honest with themselves. There are such unfortunates. They are not at fault; they seem to have been born that way. They are naturally incapable of grasping and developing a manner of living which demands rigorous honesty. Their chances are less than average. There are those, too, who suffer from grave emotional and mental disorders, but many of them do recover if they have the capacity to be honest.

Our stories disclose in a general way what we used to be like, what happened, and what we are like now. If you have decided you want what we have and are willing to go to any length to get it—then you are ready to take certain steps.

At some of these we balked. We thought we could find an easier, softer way. But we could not. With all the earnestness at our command, we beg of you to be fearless and thorough from the very start. Some of us have tried to hold on to our old ideas and the result was nil until we let go absolutely.

Remember that we deal with alcohol—cunning, baffling, powerful! Without help it is too much for us. But there is One who has all power—That One is God. May you find Him now!

Half measures availed us nothing. We stood at the turning point. We asked His protection and care with complete abandon.

Here are the steps we took, which are suggested as a Program of Recovery:

1. We admitted we were powerless over alcohol—that our lives had become unmanageable.
2. Came to believe that a Power greater than ourselves could restore us to sanity.
3. Made a decision to turn our will and our lives over to the care of God *as we understood Him.*

4. Made a searching and fearless moral inventory of ourselves.
5. Admitted to God, to ourselves, and to another human being the exact nature of our wrongs.
6. Were entirely ready to have God remove all these defects of character.
7. Humbly asked Him to remove our shortcomings.
8. Made a list of all persons we had harmed, and became willing to make amends to them all.
9. Made direct amends to such people wherever possible, except when to do so would injure them or others.
10. Continued to take personal inventory and when we were wrong promptly admitted it.
11. Sought through prayer and meditation to improve our conscious contact with God *as we understood Him* praying only for knowledge of His will for us and the power to carry that out.
12. Having had a spiritual experience as the result of these steps, we tried to carry this message to alcoholics, and to practice these principles in all our affairs.

Many of us exclaimed, "What an order! I can't go through with it." Do not be discouraged. No one among us has been able to maintain anything like perfect adherence to these principles. We are not saints. The point is, that we are willing to grow along spiritual lines. The principles we have set down are guides to progress. We claim spiritual progress rather than spiritual perfection.

Our description of the alcoholic, the chapter to the agnostic, and our personal adventures before and after make clear three pertinent ideas:

(a) That we were alcoholic and could not manage our own lives.
(b) That probably no human power could have relieved our alcoholism.
(c) That God could and would if sought.

Being convinced, *we were at step three*, which is that we decided to turn our will and our life over to God as we understood Him. Just what do we mean by that, and just what do we do?

The first requirement was that we be convinced that any life run on self-will could hardly be a success. On that basis we are almost always in collision with something or somebody, even though our motives are good. Most people try to live by self-propulsion. Each person is like an actor who wants to run the whole show: is forever trying to arrange the lights, the ballet, the scenery and the rest of the players in his own way. If his arrangements would only stay put, if only people would do as he wishes, the show would be great. Everybody, including himself, would be pleased. Life would be wonderful. In trying to make these arrangements our actor may sometimes be quite virtuous. He may be kind, considerate, patient, generous; even modest and self-sacrificing. On the other hand, he may be mean, egotistical, selfish and dishonest. But, as with most humans, he is more likely to have varied traits.

What usually happens? The show doesn't come off very well. He begins to think life doesn't treat him right. He decides to exert himself some more. He becomes, on the next occasion, still more demanding or gracious, as the case may be. Still the play does not suit him. Admitting he may be somewhat at fault, he is sure that other people are more to blame. He becomes angry, indignant, self-pitying. What is his basic trouble? Is he not really a self-seeker even when trying to be kind? Is he not a victim of the delusion that he can wrest satisfaction and happiness out of this world if he only manages well? Is it not evident to all the rest of the players that these are the things he wants? And do not his actions make each of them wish to retaliate, snatching all they can get out of the show? Is he not, even in his best moments, a producer of confusion rather than harmony?

Our actor is self-centered—ego-centric, as people like to call it nowadays. He is like the retired business man who lolls in the Florida sunshine in the winter complaining of the sad state of the nation; the minister who sighs over the sins of the twentieth century; politicians and reformers who are sure all would be Utopia if the rest of the world would only behave; the outlaw safe cracker who thinks society has wronged him; and the alcoholic who has lost all and is locked up. Whatever their protestations, are not most of us concerned with ourselves, our resentments, or our self-pity?

Selfishness—self-centeredness! That, we think, is the root of our troubles. Driven by a hundred forms of fear, self-delusion, self-seeking, and self-pity, we step on the toes of our fellows and they retaliate. Sometimes they hurt us, seemingly, without provocation, but we invariably find that at some time in the past we have made decisions based on self, which later placed us in a position to be hurt.

So our troubles, we think, are basically of our own making. They arise out of ourselves, and the alcoholic is an extreme example of self-will run riot, though he usually doesn't think so. Above everything, we alcoholics must be rid of this selfishness. We must, or it kills us! God makes that possible. And there often seems no way of entirely getting rid of self without Him. Many of us had moral and philosophical convictions galore, but we could not live up to them even though we would have liked to. Neither could we reduce our self-centeredness much by wishing or trying on our own power. We had to have God's help.

This is the how and why of it. First of all, we had to quit playing God. It didn't work. Next, we decided that hereafter in this drama of life, God was going to be our Director. He is the Principal, we are His agent. He is the Father, and we are His children. Most good ideas are simple and this concept was the keystone of the new and triumphant arch through which we passed to freedom.

When we sincerely took such a position, all sorts of remarkable things followed. We had a new Employer. Being all powerful, He provided what we needed, if we kept close to Him and performed His work well. Established on such a footing we became less and less interested in ourselves, our little plans and designs. More and more we became interested in seeing what we could contribute to life. As we felt new power flow in, as we enjoyed peace of mind, as we discovered we could face life successfully, as we became conscious of His presence, we began to lose our fear of today, tomorrow, or the hereafter. We were reborn.

We were now at step three. Many of us said to our Maker, *as we understood Him:* "God, I offer myself to Thee—to build with me and to do with me as Thou wilt. Relieve me of the bondage of self, that I may better do Thy will. Take away my difficulties, that victory over them may bear witness to those I would help of Thy Power, Thy Love, and Thy Way of life. May I do Thy will always!" We thought well before taking this step making sure we were ready; that we could at last abandon ourselves utterly to Him.

We found it very desirable to take this spiritual step with an understanding person, such as our wife, best friend, or spiritual adviser. But it is better to meet God alone than with one who might misunderstand. The wording was, of course, quite optional so long as we expressed the idea, voicing it without reservation. This was only a beginning, though if honestly and humbly made, an effect, sometimes a very great one, was felt at once.

Next we launched out on a course of vigorous action, the first step of which is a personal housecleaning, which many of us had never attempted. Though our decision was a vital and crucial step, it could have little permanent effect unless at once followed by a strenuous effort to face, and to be rid of, the things in ourselves which had been blocking us. Our liquor was but a symptom. So we had to get down to causes and conditions.

Therefore, we started upon a personal inventory. *This was step four.* A business which takes no regular inventory usually goes broke. Taking a commercial inventory is a fact-finding and a fact-facing process. It is an effort to discover the truth about the stock-in-trade. One object is to disclose damaged or unsalable goods, to get rid of them promptly and without regret. If the owner of the business is to be successful, he cannot fool himself about values.

We did exactly the same thing with our lives. We took stock honestly. First, we searched out the flaws in our make-up which caused our failure. Being convinced that self, manifested in various ways, was what had defeated us, we considered its common manifestations.

Resentment is the "number one" offender. It destroys more alcoholics than anything else. From it stem all forms of spiritual disease, for we have been not only mentally and physically ill, we have been spiritually sick. When the spiritual malady is overcome, we straighten out mentally and physically. In dealing with resentments, we set them on paper. We listed people, institutions or principles with whom we were angry. We asked ourselves why we were angry. In most cases it was found that our self-esteem, our pocketbooks, our ambitions, our personal relationships (including sex) were hurt or threatened. So we were sore. We were "burned up."

On our grudge list we set opposite each name our injuries. Was it our self-esteem, our security, our ambitions, our personal, or sex relations, which had been interfered with?

We were usually as definite as this example:

| *I'm resentful at:* | *The Cause* | *Affects my:* |
|---|---|---|
| Mr. Brown | His attention to my wife. | Sex relations<br>Self-esteem (fear) |
| | Told my wife of my mistress. | Sex relations<br>Self-esteem (fear) |
| | Brown may get my job at the office. | Security<br>Self-esteem (fear) |
| Mrs. Jones | She's a nut—she snubbed me. She committed her husband for drinking. He's my friend. She's a gossip. | Personal relationship<br>Self-esteem (fear) |
| My employer | Unreasonable—Unjust —Overbearing— Threatens to fire me for drinking and padding my expense account. | Self-esteem (fear)<br>Security |
| My wife | Misunderstands and nags. Likes Brown. Wants house put in her name. | Pride—Personal and sex relations—Security (fear) |

We went back through our lives. Nothing counted but thoroughness and honesty. When we were finished we considered it carefully. The first thing apparent was that this world and its people were often quite wrong. To conclude that others were wrong was as far as most of us ever got. The usual outcome was that people continued to wrong us and we stayed sore. Sometimes it was remorse and then we were sore at ourselves. But the more we fought and tried to have our way, the worse matters got. As in war, the victor only *seemed* to win. Our moments of triumph were short-lived.

It is plain that a life which includes deep resentment leads only to futility and unhappiness. To the precise extent that we permit these, do we squander the hours that might have been worth while. But with the alcoholic whose hope is the maintenance and growth of a spiritual experience, this business of resentment is infinitely grave. We found that it is fatal. For when harboring such feelings we shut ourselves off from the sunlight of the Spirit. The insanity of alcohol returns and we drink again. And with us, to drink is to die.

If we were to live, we had to be free of anger. The grouch and the brainstorm were not for us. They may be the dubious luxury of normal men, but for alcoholics these things are poison.

We turned back to the list, for it held the key to the future. We were prepared to look at it from an entirely different angle. We began to see that the world and its people really dominated us. In that state, the wrong-doing of others, fancied or real, had power to actually kill. How could we escape? We saw that these resentments must be mastered, but how? We could not wish them away any more than alcohol.

This was our course: we realized that the people who wronged us were perhaps spiritually sick. Though we did not like their symptoms and the way these disturbed us, they, like ourselves were sick, too. We asked God to help us show them the same tolerance, pity, and patience that we would cheerfully grant a sick friend. When a person offended we said to ourselves "This is a sick man. How can I be helpful to him? God save me from being angry. Thy will be done."

We avoid retaliation or argument. We wouldn't treat sick people that way. If we do, we destroy our chance of being helpful. We cannot be helpful to all people, but at least God will show us how to take a kindly and tolerant view of each and every one.

Referring to our list again. Putting out of our minds the wrongs others had done, we resolutely looked for our own mistakes. Where had we been selfish, dishonest, self-seeking and frightened? Though a situation had not been entirely our fault, we tried to disregard the other person involved entirely. Where were we to blame? The inventory was ours, not the other man's. When we saw our faults we listed them. We placed them before us in black and white. We admitted our wrongs honestly and were willing to set these matters straight.

Notice that the word fear is bracketed alongside the difficulties with Mr. Brown, Mrs. Jones, the employer, and the wife. This short word somehow touches about every aspect of our lives. It was an evil and corroding thread; the fabric of our existence was shot through with it. It set in motion trains of circumstances which brought us misfortune we felt we didn't deserve. But did not we, ourselves, set the ball rolling? Sometimes we think fear ought to be classed with stealing. It seems to cause more trouble.

We reviewed our fears thoroughly. We put them on paper, even though we had no resentment in connection with them. We asked ourselves why we had them. Wasn't it because self-reliance failed us? Self-reliance was good as far as it went, but it didn't go far enough. Some of us once had great self-confidence, but it didn't fully solve the fear problem, or any other. When it made us cocky, it was worse.

Perhaps there is a better way—we think so. For we are now on a different basis;

the basis of trusting and relying upon God. We trust infinite God rather than our finite selves. We are in the world to play the role He assigns. Just to the extent that we do as we think He would have us, and humbly rely on Him, does He enable us to match calamity with serenity.

We never apologize to anyone for depending upon our Creator. We can laugh at those who think spirituality the way of weakness. Paradoxically, it is the way of strength. The verdict of the ages is that faith means courage. All men of faith have courage. They trust their God. We never apologize for God. Instead we let Him demonstrate, through us, what He can do. We ask Him to remove our fear and direct our attention to what He would have us be. At once, we commence to outgrow fear.

Now about sex. Many of us needed an overhauling there. But above all, we tried to be sensible on this question. It's so easy to get way off the track. Here we find human opinions running to extremes—absurd extremes, perhaps. One set of voices cry that sex is a lust of our lower nature, a base necessity of procreation. Then we have the voices who cry for sex and more sex; who bewail the institution of marriage; who think that most of the troubles of the race are traceable to sex causes. They think we do not have enough of it, or that it isn't the right kind. They see its significance everywhere. One school would allow man no flavor for his fare and the other would have us all on a straight pepper diet. We want to stay out of this controversy. We do not want to be the arbiter of anyone's sex conduct. We all have sex problems. We'd hardly be human if we didn't. What can we do about them?

We reviewed our own conduct over the years past. Where had we been selfish, dishonest, or inconsiderate? Whom had we hurt? Did we unjustifiably arouse jealousy, suspicion or bitterness? Where were we at fault, what should we have done instead? We got this all down on paper and looked at it.

In this way we tried to shape a sane and sound ideal for our future sex life. We subjected each relation to this test—was it selfish or not? We asked God to mold our ideals and help us to live up to them. We remembered always that our sex powers were God-given, and therefore good, neither to be used lightly or selfishly nor to be despised and loathed.

Whatever our ideal turns out to be, we must be willing to grow toward it. We must be willing to make amends where we have done harm, provided that we do not bring about still more harm in so doing. In other words, we treat sex as we would any other problem. In meditation, we ask God what we should do about each specific matter. The right answer will come, if we want it.

God alone can judge our sex situation. Counsel with persons is often desirable, but we let God be the final judge. We realize that some people are as fanatical about sex as others are loose. We avoid hysterical thinking or advice.

Suppose we fall short of the chosen ideal and stumble? Does this mean we are going to get drunk? Some people tell us so. But this is only a half-truth. It depends on us and our motives. If we are sorry for what we have done, and have the honest desire to let God take us to better things, we believe we will be forgiven and will have learned our lesson. If we are not sorry, and our conduct continues to harm others, we are quite sure to drink. We are not theorizing. These are facts out of our experience.

To sum up about sex: we earnestly pray for the right ideal, for guidance in each questionable situation, for sanity, and for the strength to do the right thing. If sex is very troublesome, we throw ourselves the harder into helping others. We think of their needs and work for them. This takes us out of ourselves. It quiets the imperious urge, when to yield would mean heartache.

If we have been thorough about our personal inventory, we have written down a lot. We have listed and analyzed our resentments. We have begun to comprehend their futility and their fatality. We have commenced to see their terrible destructiveness. We have begun to learn tolerance, patience and good will toward all men, even our enemies, for we look on them as sick people. We have listed the people we have hurt by our conduct, and were willing to straighten out the past if we could.

In this book you read again and again that faith did for us what we could not do for ourselves. We hope you are convinced now that God can remove whatever self-will has blocked you off from Him. If you have already made a decision, and an inventory of your grosser handicaps, you have made a good beginning. That being so you have swallowed and digested some big chunks of truth about yourself.

CHAPTER 6

# Into Action

Having made our personal inventory, what shall we do about it? We have been trying to get a new attitude, a new relationship with our Creator, and to discover the obstacles in our path. We have admitted certain defects; we have ascertained in a rough way what the trouble is; we have put our finger on the weak items in our personal inventory. Now these are about to be cast out. This requires action on our part, which, when completed, will mean that we have admitted to God, to ourselves, and to another human being, the exact nature of our defects. This brings us to *the fifth step* in the Program of Recovery mentioned in the preceding chapter.

This is perhaps difficult—especially discussing our defects with another person. We think we have done well enough in admitting these things to ourselves. There is doubt about that. In actual practice, we usually find a solitary self-appraisal insufficient. Many of us thought it necessary to go much further. We will be more reconciled to discussing ourselves with another person when we see good reasons why we should do so. The best reason first: if we skip this vital step, we may not overcome drinking. Time after time newcomers have tried to keep to themselves certain facts about their lives. Trying to avoid this humbling experience, they have turned to easier methods. Almost invariably they got drunk. Having persevered with the rest of the program, they wondered why they fell. We think the reason is that they never completed their housecleaning. They took inventory all right, but hung on to some of the worst items in stock. They only *thought* they had lost their egoism and fear; they only *thought* they had humbled themselves. But they had not learned enough of humility, fearlessness and honesty, in the sense we find it necessary, until they told someone else *all* their life story.

More than most people, the alcoholic leads a double life. He is very much the actor. To the outer world he presents his stage character. This is the one he likes his fellows to see. He wants to enjoy a certain reputation, but knows in his heart he doesn't deserve it.

The inconsistency is made worse by the things he does on his sprees. Coming to his senses, he is revolted at certain episodes he vaguely remembers. These memories are a nightmare. He trembles to think someone might have observed him. As fast as he can, he pushes these memories far inside himself. He hopes they will never see the light of day. He is under constant fear and tension—that makes for more drinking.

Psychologists are inclined to agree with us. We have spent thousands of dollars for examinations. We know but few instances where we have given these doctors a fair break. We have seldom told them the whole truth, nor have we followed their advice. Unwilling to be honest with these sympathetic men, we were honest with no one else. Small wonder many in the medical profession have a low opinion of alcoholics and their chance for recovery!

We must be entirely honest with somebody if we expect to live long or happily in this world. Rightly and naturally, we think well before we choose the person or persons with whom to take this intimate and confidential step. Those of us belonging to a religious denomination which requires confession, must, and of course, will want to go to the properly appointed authority whose duty it is to receive it. Though we have no religious connection, we may still do well to talk with someone ordained by an established religion. We often find such a person quick to see and understand our problem. Of course, we sometimes encounter people who do not understand alcoholics.

If we cannot, or would rather not do this, we search our acquaintance for a close-mouthed, understanding friend. Perhaps our doctor or psychologist will be the person. It may be one of our own family, but we cannot disclose anything to our wives or our parents which will hurt them and make them unhappy. We have no right to save our own skin at another person's expense. Such parts of our story we tell to someone who will understand, yet be unaffected. The rule is we must be hard on ourself, but always considerate of others.

Notwithstanding the great necessity for discussing ourselves with someone, it may be one is so situated that there is no suitable person available. If that is so, this step may be postponed, only, however, if we hold ourselves in complete readiness to go through with it at the first opportunity. We say this because we are very anxious that we talk to the right person. It is important that he be able to keep a confidence; that he fully understand and approve what we are driving at; that he will not try to change our plan. But we must not use this as a mere excuse to postpone.

When we decide who is to hear our story, we waste no time. We have a written inventory, and we are prepared for a long talk. We explain to our partner what we are about to do, and why we have to do it. He should realize that we are engaged upon a life-and-death errand. Most people approached in this way will be glad to help; they will be honored by our confidence.

We pocket our pride and go to it, illuminating every twist of character, every dark cranny of the past. Once we have taken this step, withholding nothing, we are delighted. We can look the world in the eye. We can be alone at perfect peace and ease. Our fears fall from us. We begin to feel the nearness of our Creator. We may have had certain spiritual beliefs, but now we begin to have a spiritual experience.

The feeling that the drink problem has disappeared will often come strongly. We feel we are on the Broad Highway, walking hand in hand with the Spirit of the Universe.

Returning home we find a place where we can be quiet for an hour, carefully reviewing what we have done. We thank God from the bottom of our heart that we know Him better. Taking this book down from our shelf we turn to the page which contains the twelve steps. Carefully reading the first five proposals we ask if we have omitted anything, for we are building an arch through which we shall walk a free man at last. Is our work solid so far? Are the stones properly in place? Have we skimped on the cement put into the foundation? Have we tried to make mortar without sand?

If we can answer to our satisfaction, we then look at *step six.* We have emphasized willingness as being indispensable. Are we now ready to let God remove from us all the things which we have admitted are objectionable? Can He now take them all—every one? Should we still cling to something we will not let go, we ask God to help us be willing.

When ready, we say something like this: "My Creator, I am now willing that you should have all of me, good and bad. I pray that you now remove from me every single defect of character which stands in the way of my usefulness to you and my fellows. Grant me strength, as I go out from here, to do your bidding. Amen. We have then completed *step seven.*

Now we need more action without which we find that "Faith without works is dead." Let's look at *steps eight and nine.* We have a list of all persons we have harmed and to whom we are willing to make amends. We made it when we took inventory. We subjected ourselves to a drastic self-appraisal. Now we go out to our fellows and repair the damage done in the past. We attempt to sweep away the debris which has accumulated out of our effort to live on self-will and run the show ourselves. If we haven't the will to do this, we ask until it comes. Remember it was agreed at the beginning *we would go to any lengths for victory over alcohol.*

Probably there are still some misgivings. As we look over the list of business acquaintances and friends we have hurt, we may feel diffident about going to some of them on a spiritual basis. Let us be reassured. To some people we need not, and probably should not emphasize the spiritual feature on our first approach. We might prejudice them. At the moment we are trying to put our lives in order. But this is not an end in itself. Our real purpose is to fit ourselves to be of maximum service to God and the people about us. It is seldom wise to approach an individual, who still smarts from our injustice to him, and announce that we have gone religious. In the prize ring, this would be called leading with the chin. Why lay ourselves open to being branded fanatics or religious bores? We may kill a future opportunity to carry a beneficial message. But our man is sure to be impressed with a sincere desire to set right the wrong. He is going to be more interested in a demonstration of good will than in our talk of spiritual discoveries.

We don't use this as an excuse for shying away from the subject of God. When it will serve any good purpose, we are willing to announce our convictions with tact and common sense. The question of how to approach the man we hated will arise. It may be he has done us more harm than we have done him and, though we may have acquired a better attitude toward him, we are still not too keen about admitting our faults. Nevertheless, with a person we dislike, we take the bit in our teeth. It is harder to go to an enemy than to a friend, but we find it much more beneficial to us. We go to him in a helpful and forgiving spirit, confessing our former ill feeling and expressing our regret.

Under no condition do we criticize such a person or argue. Simply we tell him that we will never get over drinking until we have done our utmost to straighten out the past. We are there to sweep off our side of the street, realizing that nothing worth while can be accomplished until we do so, never trying to tell him what he should do. His faults are not discussed. We stick to our own. If our manner is calm, frank, and open, we will be gratified with the result.

In nine cases out of ten the unexpected happens. Sometimes the man we are calling upon admits his own fault; so feuds of years' standing melt away in an hour. Rarely do we fail to make satisfactory progress. Our former enemies sometimes praise what we are doing and wish us well. Occasionally, they will offer assistance. It should not matter, however, if someone does throw us out of his office. We have made our demonstration, done our part. It's water over the dam.

Most alcoholics owe money. We do not dodge our creditors. Telling them what we are trying to do, we make no bones about our drinking; they usually know it anyway, whether we think so or not. Nor are we afraid of disclosing our alcoholism on the theory it may cause financial harm. Approached in this way, the most ruthless creditor will sometimes surprise us. Arranging the best deal we can we let these people know we are sorry. Our drinking has made us slow to pay. We must lose our fear of creditors no matter how far we have to go, for we are liable to drink if we are afraid to face them.

Perhaps we have committed a criminal offense which might land us in jail if known to the authorities. We may be short in our accounts and unable to make good. We have already admitted this in confidence to another person, but we are sure we would be imprisoned or lose our job if it were known. Maybe it's only a petty offense such as padding the expense account. Most of us have done that sort of thing. Maybe we are divorced, and have remarried but haven't kept up the alimony to number one. She is indignant about it, and has a warrant out for our arrest. That's a common form of trouble too.

Although these reparations take innumerable forms, there are some general principles which we find guiding. Reminding ourselves that we have decided to go to any lengths to find a spiritual experience, we ask that we be given strength and direction to do the right thing, no matter what the personal consequences may be. We may lose our position or reputation, or face jail, but are willing. We have to be. We must not shrink at anything.

Usually, however, other people are involved. Therefore, we are not to be the hasty and foolish martyr who would needlessly sacrifice others to save himself from the alcoholic pit. A man we know had remarried. Because of resentment and drinking, he had not paid alimony to his first wife. She was furious. She went to court and got an order for his arrest. He had commenced our way of life, had secured a position, and was getting his head above water. It would have been impressive heroics if he had walked up to the Judge and said, "Here I am."

We thought he ought to be willing to do that if necessary, but if he were in jail, he could provide nothing for either family. We suggested he write his first wife admitting his faults and asking forgiveness. He did, and also sent a small amount of money. He told her what he would try to do in the future. He said he was perfectly willing to go to jail if she insisted. Of course she did not, and the whole situation has long since been adjusted.

Before taking drastic action which might implicate other people we secure their consent. If we have obtained permission, have consulted with others, asked God to help, and the drastic step is indicated we must not shrink.

This brings to mind a story about one of our friends. While drinking, he accepted a sum of money from a bitterly-hated business rival, giving him no receipt for it. He subsequently denied having received the money and used the incident as a basis for discrediting the man. He thus used his own wrong-doing as a means of destroying the reputation of another. In fact, his rival was ruined.

He felt he had done a wrong he could not possibly make right. If he opened that old affair, he was afraid it would destroy the reputation of his partner, disgrace his family and take away his means of livelihood. What right had he to involve those dependent upon him? How could he possibly make a public statement exonerating his rival?

After consulting with his wife and partner he came to the conclusion that it was better to take those risks than to stand before his Creator guilty of such ruinous slander. He saw that he had to place the outcome in God's hands or he would soon start drinking again, and all would be lost anyhow. He attended church for the first time in many years. After the sermon, he quietly got up and made an explanation. His action met widespread approval, and today he is one of the most trusted citizens of his town. This all happened three years ago.

The chances are that we have domestic troubles. Perhaps we are mixed up with women in a fashion we wouldn't care to have advertised. We doubt if, in this respect, alcoholics are fundamentally much worse than other people. But drinking does complicate sex relations in the home. After a few years with an alcoholic, a wife gets worn out, resentful, and uncommunicative. How could she be anything else? The husband begins to feel lonely, sorry for himself. He commences to look around in the night clubs, or their equivalent, for something besides liquor. Perhaps he is having a secret and exciting affair with "the girl who understands." In fairness we must say that she may understand, but what are we going to do about a thing like that? A man so involved often feels very remorseful at times, especially if he is married to a loyal and courageous girl who has literally gone through hell for him.

Whatever the situation, we usually have to do something about it. If we are sure our wife does not know, should we tell her? Not always, we think. If she knows in a general way that we have been wild, should we tell her in detail? Undoubtedly we should admit our fault. She may insist on knowing all the particulars. She will want to know who the woman is and where she is. We feel we ought to say to her that we have no right to involve another person. We are sorry for what we have done, and God willing, it shall not be repeated. More than that we cannot do; we have no right to go further. Though there may be justifiable exceptions, and though we wish to lay down no rule of any sort, we have often found this the best course to take.

Our design for living is not a one-way street. It is as good for the wife as for the husband. If we can forget, so can she. It is better, however, that one does not needlessly name a person upon whom she can vent jealousy.

Perhaps there are some cases where the utmost frankness is demanded. No outsider can appraise such an intimate situation. It may be both will decide that the way of good sense and loving kindness is to let by-gones be by-gones. Each might pray about it, having the other one's happiness uppermost in mind. Keep it always in sight that we deal with that most terrible human emotion—jealousy. Good generalship may decide that the problem be attacked on the flank, rather than risk a face-to-face combat.

Should we have no such complication, there is plenty we should do at home. Sometimes we hear an alcoholic say that the only thing he needs to do is to keep sober. Certainly he must keep sober, for there will be no home if he doesn't. But he is yet a long way from making good to the wife or parents whom for years he has so shockingly treated. Passing all understanding is the patience mothers and wives have had with alcoholics. Had this not been so, many of us would have no homes today, would perhaps be dead.

The alcoholic is like a tornado roaring his way through the lives of others. Hearts are broken. Sweet relationships are dead. Affections have been uprooted. Selfish and inconsiderate habits have kept the home in turmoil. We feel a man is unthinking when he says that sobriety is enough. He is like the farmer who came up out of his cyclone cellar to find his home ruined. To his wife, he remarked, "Don't see anything the matter here, Ma. Ain't it grand the wind stopped blowin'?"

Yes, there is a long period of reconstruction ahead. We must take the lead. A remorseful mumbling that we are sorry won't fill the bill at all. We ought to sit down with the family and frankly analyze the past as we now see it, being very careful not to criticize them. Their defects may be glaring, but the chances are that our own actions are partly responsible. So we clean house with the family, asking each morning in meditation that our Creator show us the way of patience, tolerance, kindliness and love.

The spiritual life is not a theory. *We have to live it.* Unless one's family expresses a desire to live upon spiritual principles we think we ought not to urge them. We should not talk incessantly to them about spiritual matters. They will change in time. Our behavior will convince them more than our words. We must remember that ten or twenty years of drunkenness would make a skeptic out of anyone.

There may be some wrongs we can never fully right. We don't worry about them if we can honestly say to ourselves that we would right them if we could. Some people cannot be seen—we send them an honest letter. And there may be a valid reason for postponement in some cases. But we don't delay if it can be avoided. We should be sensible, tactful, and considerate and humble without being servile or scraping. As God's people we stand on our feet; we don't crawl before anyone.

If we are painstaking about this phase of our development, we will be amazed before half through! We are going to know a new freedom and happiness. We will not regret the past nor wish to shut the door on it. We will comprehend the word serenity and know peace. No matter how far down the scale we have gone, we will see how our experience can benefit others. That feeling of uselessness and self-pity will disappear. We will lose interest in selfish things and gain interest in our fellows. Self-seeking will slip away. Our whole attitude and outlook upon life will change. Fear of people and of economic insecurity will leave us. We will intuitively know how to handle situations which used to baffle us. We will suddenly realize that God is doing for us what we could not do for ourselves.

Are these extravagant promises? We think not. They are being fulfilled among us—sometimes quickly, sometimes slowly. They will always materialize if we work for them.

This thought brings us to *step ten*, which suggests we continue to take personal inventory and continue to set right any new mistakes as we go along. We vigorously commenced this way of living as we cleaned up the past. We have entered the world of Spirit. Our next function is to grow in understanding and effectiveness. This is not an overnight matter. It should continue for our life time. Continue to watch for selfishness, dishonesty, resentment, and fear. When these crop up, we ask God at once to remove them. We discuss them with someone immediately and make amends quickly if we have harmed anyone. Then we resolutely turn our thoughts to someone we can help. Love and tolerance of others is our code.

And we have ceased fighting anything or anyone—even alcohol. For by this time sanity will have returned. We will seldom be interested in liquor. If tempted, we recoil from it as from a hot flame. We react sanely and normally, and will find that this has happened automatically. We see that our new attitude toward liquor has been given us without any thought or effort on our part. It just comes! That is the miracle of it. We are not fighting it, neither are we avoiding temptation. We feel as though we had been placed in a position of neutrality—safe and protected. We have not even sworn off. Instead, the problem has been removed. It does not exist for us. We are neither cocky, nor are we afraid. That is our experience. That is how we react so long as we keep in fit spiritual condition.

It is easy to let up on the spiritual program of action and rest on our laurels. We are headed for trouble if we do, for alcohol is a subtle foe. We are not cured of alcoholism. What we really have is a daily reprieve contingent on the maintenance of our spiritual condition. Every day is a day when we must carry the vision of God's will into all of our activities. "How can I best serve Thee—Thy will (not mine) be done." These are thoughts which must go with us constantly. We can exercise our will power along this line all we wish. It is the proper use of the will.

Much has already been said about receiving strength, inspiration, and direction from Him who has all knowledge and power. If we have carefully followed directions, we have begun to sense the flow of His Spirit into us. To some extent we have become God-conscious. We have begun to develop this vital sixth sense. But we must go further and that means more action.

*Step eleven* suggests prayer and meditation. We shouldn't be shy on this matter of prayer. Better men than we are using it constantly. It works, if we have the proper attitude and work at it. It would be easy to be vague about this matter. Yet, we believe we can make some definite and valuable suggestions.

When we retire at night, we constructively review our day. Were we resentful, selfish, dishonest, or afraid? Do we owe an apology? Have we kept something to ourselves which should be discussed with another person at once? Were we kind and loving toward all? What could we have done better? Were we thinking of ourselves most of the time? Or were we thinking of what we could do for others, of what we could pack into the stream of life? But we must be careful not to drift into worry, remorse or morbid reflection, for that would diminish our usefulness to others. After making our review we ask God's forgiveness and inquire what corrective measures should be taken.

On awakening let us think about the twenty-four hours ahead. We consider our plans for the day. Before we begin, we ask God to direct our thinking, especially asking that it be divorced from self-pity, dishonest or self-seeking motives. Under these conditions we can employ our mental faculties with assurance for after all God gave us brains to use. Our thought life will be placed on a much higher plane when our thinking is cleared of wrong motives.

In thinking about our day we may face indecision. We may not be able to determine which course to take. Here we ask God for inspiration, an intuitive thought or a decision. We relax and take it easy. We don't struggle. We are often surprised how the right answers come after we have tried this a while. What used to be the hunch or the occasional inspiration gradually becomes a working part of the mind. Being still inexperienced and just making conscious contact with God, it is not probable that we are going to be inspired at all times. We might pay for this presumption in all sorts of absurd actions and ideas. Nevertheless we find that our thinking will, as time passes, be more and more on the plane of inspiration. We come to rely upon it.

We usually conclude the period of meditation with a prayer that we be shown all through the day what our next step is to be, that we be given whatever we need to take care of such problems. We ask especially for freedom from self-will, and are careful to make no request for ourselves only. We may ask for ourselves, however, if others will be helped. We are careful never to pray for our own selfish ends. Many of us have wasted a lot of time doing that, and it doesn't work. You can easily see why.

If circumstances warrant, we ask our wives or friends to join us in morning meditation. If we belong to a religious denomination which requires a definite morning devotion, we attend to that also. If not members of religious bodies, we sometimes select and memorize a few set prayers which emphasize the principles we have been discussing. There are many helpful books also. Suggestions about these may be obtained from one's priest, minister, or rabbi. Be quick to see where religious people are right. Make use of what they offer.

As we go through the day, we pause when agitated or doubtful, and ask for the right thought or action. We constantly remind ourselves we are no longer running the show, humbly saying to ourselves many times each day "Thy will be done." We are then in much less danger of excitement, fear, anger, worry, self-pity, or foolish decisions. We become much more efficient. We do not tire so easily, for we are not burning up energy foolishly as we did when trying to arrange life to suit ourselves.

It works—it really does.

We alcoholics are undisciplined. So we let God discipline us in the simple way we have just outlined.

But this is not all. There is action and more action. "Faith without works is dead." The next chapter is entirely devoted to step twelve.

CHAPTER 7

# Working with Others

Practical experience shows that nothing will so much insure immunity from drinking as intensive work with other alcoholics. It works when other activities fail. This is our *twelfth suggestion:* Carry this message to other alcoholics! You can help when no one else can. You can secure their confidence when others fail. Remember they are very ill.

Life will take on new meaning. To watch people recover, to see them help others, to watch loneliness vanish, to see a fellowship grow up about you, to have a host of friends—this is an experience you must not miss. We know you will not want to miss it. Frequent contact with newcomers and with each other is the bright spot of our lives.

Perhaps you are not acquainted with any drinkers who want to recover. You can easily find some by asking a few doctors, ministers, priests and hospitals. They will be only too glad to assist you. Don't start out as an evangelist or reformer. Unfortunately a lot of prejudice exists. You will be handicapped if you arouse it. Ministers and doctors are competent and you can learn much from them if you wish, but it happens that because of your own drinking experience you can be uniquely useful to other alcoholics. So cooperate; never criticize. To be helpful is our only aim.

When you discover a prospect for Alcoholics Anonymous, find out all you can about him. If he does not want to stop drinking, don't waste time trying to persuade him. You may spoil a later opportunity. This advice is given for his family also. They should be patient, realizing they are dealing with a sick person.

If there is any indication that he wants to stop, have a good talk with the person most interested in him—usually his wife. Get an idea of his behavior, his problems, his background, the seriousness of his condition, and his religious leanings. You need this information to put yourself in his place, to see how you would like him to approach you if the tables were turned.

Usually it is wise to wait till he goes on a binge. The family may object to this, but unless he is in a dangerous physical condition, it is better to risk it. Don't deal with him when he is very drunk, unless he is ugly and the family needs your help.

Wait for the end of the spree, or at least for a lucid interval. Then let his family or a friend ask him if he wants to quit for good and if he would go to any extreme to do so. If he says yes, then his attention should be drawn to you as a person who has recovered. You should be described to him as one of a fellowship who, as a part of their own recovery, try to help others, and who will be glad to talk to him if he cares to see you.

If he does not want to see you, never force yourself upon him. Neither should the family hysterically plead with him to do anything, nor should they tell him much about you. They should wait for the end of his next drinking bout. You might place this book where he can see it in the interval. Here no specific rule can be given. The family must decide these things. But urge them not to be over-anxious, for that might spoil matters.

Usually the family should not try to tell your story. When possible, avoid meeting a man through his family. Approach through a doctor or an institution is a better bet. If your man needs hospitalization, he should have it, but not forcibly, unless he is violent. Let the doctor if he will tell him he has something in the way of a solution.

When your man is better, the doctor might suggest a visit from you. Though you have talked with the family, leave them out of the first discussion. Under these conditions your prospect will see he is under no pressure. He will feel he can deal with you without being nagged by his family. Call on him while he is still jittery. He may be more receptive when depressed.

See your man alone, if possible. At first engage in general conversation. After a while, turn the talk to some phase of drinking. Tell him enough about your drinking habits, symptoms, and experiences to encourage him to speak of himself. If he wishes to talk, let him do so. You will thus get a better idea of how you ought to proceed. If he is not communicative, give him a sketch of your drinking career up to the time you quit. But say nothing, for the moment, of how that was accomplished. If he is in a serious mood dwell on the troubles liquor has caused you, being careful not to moralize or lecture. If his mood is light, tell him humorous stories of your escapades. Get him to tell some of his.

When he sees you know all about the drinking game, commence to describe yourself as an alcoholic. Tell him how baffled you were, how you finally learned that you were sick. Give him an account of the struggles you made to stop. Show him the mental twist which leads to the first drink of a spree. We suggest you do this as we have done it in the chapter on alcoholism. If he is alcoholic, he will understand you at once. He will match your mental inconsistencies with some of his own.

If you are satisfied that he is a real alcoholic, begin to dwell on the hopeless feature of the malady. Show him, from your own experience, how the queer mental condition surrounding that first drink prevents normal functioning of the will power. Don't at this stage refer to this book, unless he has seen it and wishes to discuss it. And be careful not to brand him an alcoholic. Let him draw his own conclusion. If he sticks to the idea that he can still control his drinking, tell him that possibly he can—if he is not too alcoholic. But insist that if he is severely afflicted, there may be little chance he can recover by himself.

Continue to speak of alcoholism as a sickness, a fatal malady. Talk about the conditions of body and mind which accompany it. Keep his attention focused mainly on your personal experience. Explain that many are doomed who never realize their predicament. Doctors are rightly loath to tell alcoholic patients the whole story unless it will serve some good purpose. But you may talk to him about the hopelessness of alcoholism, because you offer a solution. You will soon have your friend admitting he has many, if not all, of the traits of the alcoholic. If his own doctor is willing to tell him that he is alcoholic, so much the better. Even though your protegé may not have entirely admitted his condition, he has become very curious to know how you got well. Let him ask you that question, if he will. If he does not ask, proceed with the rest of your story. *Tell him exactly what happened to you.* Stress the spiritual feature freely. If the man be agnostic or atheist, make it emphatic that *he does not have to agree with your conception of God.* He can choose any conception he likes, provided it makes sense to him. *The main thing is that he be willing to believe in a Power greater than himself and that he live by spiritual principles.*

When dealing with such a person, you had better use everyday language to describe spiritual principles. There is no use arousing any prejudice he may have against certain theological terms and conceptions, about which he may already be confused. Don't raise such issues, no matter what your own convictions are.

Your prospect may belong to a religious denomination. His religious education and training may be far superior to yours. In that case he is going to wonder how you can add anything to what he already knows. But he will be curious to learn why his own convictions have not worked, and yours seem to work so well. He may be an example of the truth that faith alone is insufficient. To be vital, faith must be accompanied by self sacrifice and unselfish, constructive action. Let him see that you are not there to instruct him in religion. Admit that he probably knows more about it than you do, but call to his attention the fact that however deep his faith and knowledge, he could not have applied it, or he would not drink. Perhaps your story will help him see where he fails to practice the very precepts he knows so well. We represent no particular faith or denomination. We are dealing only with general principles common to most denominations.

Outline the program of action, explaining how you made a self-appraisal, how you straightened out your past, and why you are now endeavoring to be helpful to him. It is important for him to realize that your attempt to pass this on to him plays a vital part in your own recovery. Actually, he may be helping you more than you are helping him. Make it plain he is under no obligation to you, that you hope only that he will try to help other alcoholics when he escapes his own difficulties. Suggest how important it is that he place the welfare of other people ahead of his own. Make it clear that he is not under pressure, that he needn't see you again, if he doesn't want to. You should not be offended if he wants to call it off, for he has helped you more than you have helped him. If your talk has been sane, quiet and full of human understanding, you have perhaps made a friend. Maybe you have disturbed him about the question of alcoholism. This is all to the good. The more hopeless he feels, the better. He will be more likely to follow your suggestions.

Your candidate may give reasons why he need not follow all of the program. He may rebel at the thought of a drastic housecleaning which requires discussion with other people. Do not contradict such views. Tell him you once felt as he does, but you doubt whether you would have made much progress had you not taken action. On your first visit tell him about the fellowship of Alcoholics Anonymous. If he shows interest, lend him your copy of this book.

Unless your friend wants to talk further about himself, do not wear out your welcome. Give him a chance to think it over. If you do stay, let him steer the conversation in any direction he likes. Sometimes a new man is anxious to proceed at once, and you may be tempted to let him do so. This is sometimes a mistake. If he has trouble later, he is likely to say you rushed him. You will be most successful with alcoholics if you do not exhibit any passion for crusade or reform. Never talk down to an alcoholic from any moral or spiritual hilltop, simply lay out the kit of spiritual tools for his inspection. Show him how they worked with you. Offer him friendship and fellowship. Tell him that if he wants to get well you will do anything to help.

If he is not interested in your solution, if he expects you to act only as a banker for his financial difficulties or a nurse for his sprees, you may have to drop him until he changes his mind. This he may do after he gets hurt some more.

If he is sincerely interested and wants to see you again, ask him to read this book in the interval. After doing that, he must decide for himself whether he wants to go on. He should not be pushed or prodded by you, his wife, or his friends. If he is to find God, the desire must come from within.

If he thinks he can do the job in some other way, or prefers some other spiritual approach, encourage him to follow his own conscience. We have no monopoly on God; we merely have an approach that worked with us. But point out that we alcoholics have much in common and that you would like, in any case, to be friendly. Let it go at that.

Do not be discouraged if your prospect does not respond at once. Search out another alcoholic and try again. You are sure to find someone desperate enough to accept with eagerness what you offer. We find it a waste of time to keep chasing a man who cannot or will not work with you. If you leave such a person alone, he may soon become convinced that he cannot recover by himself. To spend too much time on any one situation is to deny some other alcoholic an opportunity to live and be happy. One of our fellowship failed entirely with his first half dozen prospects. He often says that if he had continued to work on them, he might have deprived many others, who have since recovered, of their chance.

Suppose now you are making your second visit to a man. He has read this volume and says he is prepared to go through with the twelve steps of The Program of Recovery. Having had the experience yourself, you can give him much practical advice. Let him know you are available if he wishes to make a decision and tell his story, but do not insist upon it if he prefers to consult someone else.

He may be broke and homeless. If he is, you might try to help him about getting a job, or give him a little financial assistance. But you should not deprive your family or creditors of money they should have. Perhaps you will want to take the man into your home for a few days. But be sure you use discretion. Be certain he will be welcomed by your family, and that he is not trying to impose upon you for money, connections, or shelter. Permit that and you only harm him. You will be making it possible for him to be insincere. You may be aiding in his destruction, rather than his recovery.

Never avoid these responsibilities, but be sure you are doing the right thing if you assume them. Helping others is the foundation stone of your recovery. A kindly act once in a while isn't enough. You have to act the Good Samaritan every day, if need be. It may mean the loss of many nights' sleep, great interference with your pleasures, interruptions to your business. It may mean sharing your money and your home, counseling frantic wives and relatives, innumerable trips to police courts, sanitariums, hospitals, jails and asylums. Your telephone may jangle at any time of the day or night. Your wife may sometimes say she is neglected. A drunk may smash the furniture in your home, or burn a mattress. You may have to fight with him if he is violent. Sometimes you will have to call a doctor and administer sedatives under his direction. Another time you may have to send for the police or an ambulance. Occasionally you will have to meet such conditions.

We seldom allow an alcoholic to live in our homes for long at a time. It is not good for him, and it sometimes creates serious complications in a family.

Though an alcoholic does not respond, there is no reason why you should neglect his family. You should continue to be friendly to them. The family should be offered your way of life. Should they accept, and practice spiritual principles, there is a much better chance the head of the family will recover. And even though he continues to drink, the family will find life more bearable.

For the type of alcoholic who is able and willing to get well, little charity, in the ordinary sense of the word, is needed or wanted. The men who cry for money and shelter before conquering alcohol, are on the wrong track. Yet we do go to great extremes to provide each other with these very things, when such action is warranted. This may seem inconsistent, but we think it is not.

It is not the matter of giving that is in question, but when and how to give. That often makes the difference between failure and success. The minute we put our work on a service plane, the alcoholic commences to rely upon our assistance rather than upon God. He clamors for this or that, claiming he cannot master alcohol until his material needs are cared for. Nonsense. Some of us have taken very hard knocks to learn this truth: job or no job—wife or no wife—we simply do not stop drinking so long as we place dependence upon other people ahead of dependence on God.

Burn the idea into the consciousness of every man that he can get well regardless of anyone. The only condition is that he trust in God and clean house.

Now, the domestic problem: There may be divorce, separation, or just strained relations. When your prospect has made such reparation as he can to his family, and has thoroughly explained to them the new principles by which he is living, he should proceed to put those principles into action at home. That is, if he is lucky enough to have a home. Though his family be at fault in many respects, he should not be concerned about that. He should concentrate on his own spiritual demonstration. Argument and fault-finding are to be avoided like leprosy. In many homes this is a difficult thing to do, but it must be done if any results are to be expected. If persisted in for a few months, the effect on a man's family is sure to be great. The most incompatible people discover they have a basis upon which they can meet. Little by little the family may see their own defects and admit them. These can then be discussed in an atmosphere of helpfulness and friendliness.

After they have seen tangible results, the family will perhaps want to go along. These things will come to pass naturally and in good time, provided, however, the alcoholic continues to demonstrate that he can be sober, considerate, and helpful, regardless of what anyone says or does. Of course, we all fall much below this standard many times. But we must try to repair the damage immediately lest we pay the penalty by a spree.

If there be divorce or separation, there should be no undue haste for the couple to get together. The man should be sure of his recovery. The wife should fully understand his new way of life. If their old relationship is to be resumed, it must be on a better basis, since the former did not work. This means a new attitude and spirit all around. Sometimes it is to the best interests of all concerned that a couple remain apart. Obviously, no rule can be laid down. Let the alcoholic continue his program day by day. When the time for living together has come, it will be apparent to both parties.

Let no alcoholic say he cannot recover unless he has his family back. This just isn't so. In some cases the wife will never come back for one reason or another. Remind the prospect that his recovery is not dependent upon people. It is dependent upon his relationship with God. We have seen men get well whose families have not returned at all. We have seen others slip when the family came back too soon.

Both you and the new man must walk day by day in the path of spiritual progress. If you persist, remarkable things will happen. When we look back, we realize that the things which came to us when we put ourselves in God's hands were better than anything we could have planned. Follow the dictates of a Higher Power and you will presently live in a new and wonderful world, no matter what your present circumstances!

When working with a man and his family, you should take care not to participate in their quarrels. You may spoil your chance of being helpful if you do. But urge upon a man's family that he has been a very sick person and should be treated accordingly. You should warn against arousing resentment or jealousy. You should point out that his defects of character are not going to disappear over night. Show them that he has entered upon a period of growth. Ask them to remember, when they are impatient, the blessed fact of his sobriety.

If you have been successful in solving your own domestic problems, tell the newcomer's family how that was accomplished. In this way you can set them on the right track without becoming critical of them. The story of how you and your wife settled your difficulties is worth any amount of criticism.

Assuming we are spiritually fit, we can do all sorts of things alcoholics are not supposed to do. People have said we must not go where liquor is served; we must not have it in our homes; we must shun friends who drink; we must avoid moving pictures which show drinking scenes; we must not go into bars; our friends must hide their bottles if we go to their houses; we mustn't think or be reminded about alcohol at all. Our experience shows that this is not necessarily so.

We meet these conditions every day. An alcoholic who cannot meet them, still has an alcoholic mind: there is something the matter with his spiritual status. His only chance for sobriety would be some place like Greenland Ice Cap, and even there an Eskimo might turn up with a bottle of scotch and ruin everything! Ask any woman who has sent her husband to distant places on the theory he would escape the alcohol problem.

In our belief any scheme of combating alcoholism which proposes to shield the sick man from temptation is doomed to failure. If the alcoholic tries to shield himself, he may succeed for a time, but usually winds up with a bigger explosion than ever. We have tried these methods. These attempts to do the impossible have always failed.

So our rule is not to avoid a place where there is drinking, *if we have a legitimate reason for being there.* That includes bars, nightclubs, dances, receptions, weddings, even plain ordinary whoopee parties. To a person who has had experience with an alcoholic, this may seem like tempting Providence, but it isn't.

You will note that we made an important qualification. Therefore, ask yourself on each occasion, "Have I any good social, business, or personal reason for going to this place? Or am I expecting to steal a little vicarious pleasure from the atmosphere of such places?" If you answer these questions satisfactorily, you need have no apprehension. Go or stay away, whatever seems best. But be sure you are on solid spiritual ground before you start and that your motive in going is thoroughly good. Do not think of what you will get out of the occasion. Think of what you can bring to it. But if you are shaky, you had better work with another alcoholic instead!

Why sit with a long face in places where there is drinking, sighing about the good old days. If it is a happy occasion, try to increase the pleasure of those there; if a business occasion, go and attend to your business enthusiastically. If you are with a person who wants to eat in a bar, by all means go along. Let your friends know they are not to change their habits on your account. At a proper time and place explain to all your friends why alcohol disagrees with you. If you do this thoroughly, few people will ask you to drink. While you were drinking, you were withdrawing from life little by little. Now you are getting back into the social life of this world. Don't start to withdraw again just because your friends drink liquor.

Your job now is to be at the place where you may be of maximum helpfulness to others, so never hesitate to go anywhere, if you can be helpful. You should not hesitate to visit the most sordid spot on earth on such an errand. Keep on the firing line of life with these motives, and God will keep you unharmed.

Many of us keep liquor in our homes. We often need it to carry green recruits through a severe hangover. Some of us still serve it to our friends provided they are not alcoholic. But some of us think we should not serve liquor to anyone. We never argue this question. We feel that each family, in the light of their own circumstances, ought to decide for themselves.

We are careful never to show intolerance or hatred of drinking as an institution. Experience shows that such an attitude is not helpful to anyone. Every new alcoholic looks for this spirit among us and is immensely relieved when he finds we are not witch-burners. A spirit of intolerance might repel alcoholics whose lives could have been saved, had it not been for such stupidity. We would not even do the cause of temperate drinking any good, for not one drinker in a thousand likes to be told anything about alcohol by one who hates it.

Someday we hope that Alcoholics Anonymous will help the public to a better realization of the gravity of the alcoholic problem, but we shall be of little use if our attitude is one of bitterness or hostility. Drinkers will not stand for it.

*After all, our problems were of our own making. Bottles were only a symbol. Besides, we have stopped fighting anybody or anything. We have to!*

CHAPTER 8

# To Wives

With few exceptions, our book thus far has spoken of men. But what we have said applies quite as much to women. Our activities in behalf of women who drink are on the increase. There is every evidence that women regain their health as readily as men if they try our suggestions.

But for every man who drinks others are involved—the wife who trembles in fear of the next debauch; the mother and father who see their son wasting away.

Among us are wives, relatives, and friends whose problem has been solved, as well as some who have not yet found a happy solution. We want the wives of Alcoholics Anonymous to address the wives of men who drink too much. What they say will apply to nearly everyone bound by ties of blood or affection to an alcoholic.

As wives of Alcoholics Anonymous, we would like you to feel that we understand as perhaps few can. We want to analyze mistakes we have made. We want to leave you with the feeling that no situation is too difficult and no unhappiness too great to be overcome.

We have traveled a rocky road, there is no mistake about that. We have had long rendezvous with hurt pride, frustration, self-pity, misunderstanding, and fear. These are not pleasant companions. We have been driven to maudlin sympathy, to bitter resentment. Some of us veered from extreme to extreme, ever hoping that one day our loved ones would be themselves once more.

Our loyalty, and the desire that our husbands hold up their heads and be like other men have begotten all sorts of predicaments. We have been unselfish and self-sacrificing. We have told innumerable lies to protect our pride and our husbands' reputations. We have prayed, we have begged, we have been patient. We have struck out viciously. We have run away. We have been hysterical. We have been terror stricken. We have sought sympathy. We have had retaliatory love affairs with other men.

Our homes have been battle-grounds many an evening. In the morning we have kissed and made up. Our friends have counseled chucking the men and we have done so with finality, only to be back in a little while, hoping, always hoping. Our men have sworn great solemn oaths they were through drinking forever. We have believed them when no one else could, or would. Then, in days, weeks, or months, a fresh outburst.

We seldom had friends at our homes, never knowing how or when the men of the house would appear. We could make few social engagements. We came to live almost alone. When we were invited out, our husbands sneaked so many drinks that they spoiled the occasion. If, on the other hand, they took nothing, their self-pity made them killjoys.

There was never financial security. Positions were always in jeopardy or gone. An armored car could not have brought the pay envelopes home. The checking account melted like snow in June.

Sometimes there were other women. How heart breaking was this discovery; how cruel to be told they understood our men as we did not!

The bill collectors; the sheriffs; the angry taxi drivers; the policemen; the bums; the pals; and even the ladies they sometimes brought home—our husbands thought we were so inhospitable. "Joykiller, nag, wet blanket"—that's what they said. Next day they would be themselves again and we would forgive and try to forget.

We have tried to hold the love of our children for their father. We have told small tots that father was sick, which was much nearer the truth than we realized. They struck the children, kicked out door panels, smashed treasured crockery, and ripped the keys out of pianos. In the midst of such pandemonium they may have rushed out threatening to live with the other woman forever. In desperation, we have even got tight ourselves—the drunk to end all drunks. The unexpected result was that our husbands seemed to like it.

Perhaps at this point we got a divorce and took the children home to father and mother. Then we were severely criticized by our husband's parents for desertion. Usually we did not leave. We stayed on and on. We finally sought employment ourselves as destitution faced us and our families.

We began to ask medical advice as the sprees got closer together. The alarming physical and mental symptoms, the deepening pall of remorse, depression and inferiority that settled down on our loved ones—these things terrified and distracted us. As animals on a treadmill, we have patiently and wearily climbed, falling back in exhaustion after each futile effort to reach solid ground. Most of us have entered the final stage with its commitment to health resorts, sanitariums, hospitals, and jails. Sometimes there were screaming delirium and insanity. Death was often near.

Under these conditions we naturally made mistakes. Some of them rose out of ignorance of alcoholism. Sometimes we sensed dimly that we were dealing with sick men. Had we fully understood the nature of the alcoholic illness, we might have behaved differently.

How could men who loved their wives and children be so unthinking, so callous, so cruel? There could be no love in such persons, we thought. And just as we were being convinced of their heartlessness, they would surprise us with fresh resolves and new attentions. For a while they would be their old sweet selves, only to dash the new structure of affection to pieces once more. Asked why they commenced to drink again, they would reply with some silly excuse, or none. It was so baffling, so heartbreaking. Could we have been so mistaken in the men we married? When drinking, they were strangers. Sometimes they were so inaccessible that it seemed as though a great wall had been built around them.

And even if they did not love their families, how could they be so blind about themselves? What had become of their judgment, their common sense, their will power? Why could they not see that drink meant ruin to them? Why was it, when these dangers were pointed out that they agreed and then got drunk again immediately?

These are some of the questions which race through the mind of every girl who has an alcoholic husband. We hope this book has answered some of them. Perhaps your husband has been living in that strange world of alcoholism where everything is distorted and exaggerated. You can see that he really does love you with his better self. Of course, there is such a thing as incompatibility, but in nearly every instance the alcoholic only seems to be unloving and inconsiderate; it is usually because he is warped and sickened that he says and does these appalling things. Today most of our men are better husbands and fathers than ever before.

Try not to condemn your alcoholic husband no matter what he says or does. He is just another very sick, unreasonable person. Treat him, when you can, as though he had pneumonia. When he angers you, remember that he is very ill.

There is an important exception to the foregoing. We realize some men are thoroughly bad-intentioned, that no amount of patience will make any difference. An alcoholic of this temperament may be quick to use this chapter as a club over your head. Don't let him get away with it. If you are positive he is one of this type you may feel you had better leave. Is it right to let him ruin your life and the lives of your children? Especially when he has before him a way to stop his drinking and abuse if he really wants to pay the price.

The problem with which you struggle usually falls within one of four categories:

*One:* Your husband may be only a heavy drinker. His drinking may be constant or it may be heavy only on certain occasions. Perhaps he spends too much money for liquor. It may be slowing him up mentally and physically, but he does not see it. Sometimes he is a source of embarrassment to you and his friends. He is positive he can handle his liquor, that it does him no harm, that drinking is necessary in his business. He would probably be insulted if called an alcoholic. This world is full of people like him. Some will moderate or stop altogether, and some will not. Of those who keep on, a good number will become true alcoholics after a while.

*Two:* Your husband is showing lack of control, for he is unable to stay on the water wagon, even when he wants to. He often gets entirely out of hand when drinking. He admits this is true, but is positive that he will do better. He has begun to try, with or without your cooperation, various means of moderating or staying dry. Maybe he is beginning to lose his friends. His business may suffer somewhat. He is worried at times, and is becoming aware that he cannot drink like other people. He sometimes drinks in the morning, and through the day also, to hold his nervousness in check. He is remorseful after serious drinking bouts and tells you he wants to stop. But when he gets over the spree, he begins to think once more how he can drink moderately next time. We think this person is in danger. These are the earmarks of a real alcoholic. Perhaps he can still tend to business fairly well. He has by no means ruined everything. As we say among ourselves, *"He wants to want to stop."*

*Three:* This husband has gone much further than husband number two. Though once like number two, he became worse. His friends have slipped away, his home is a near-wreck, and he cannot hold a position. Maybe the doctor has been called in, and the weary round of sanitariums and hospitals has begun. He admits he cannot drink like other people, but does not see why. He clings to the notion that he will yet find a way to do so. He may have come to the point where he desperately wants to stop but cannot. His case presents additional questions which we shall try to answer for you. You can be quite hopeful of a situation like this.

*Four:* You may have a husband of whom you completely despair. He has been placed in one institution after another. He is violent, or appears definitely insane, when drunk. Sometimes he drinks on the way home from the hospital. Perhaps he has had delirium tremens. Doctors may shake their heads and advise you to have him committed. Maybe you have already been obliged to put him away. This picture may not be as dark as it looks. Many of our husbands were just as far gone. Yet they got well.

Let's now go back to husband number one. Oddly enough, he is often difficult to deal with. He enjoys drinking. It stirs his imagination. His friends feel closer over a highball. Perhaps you enjoy drinking with him yourself when he doesn't go too far. You have passed happy evenings together chatting and drinking before your fire. Perhaps you both like parties which would be dull without liquor. We have enjoyed such evening ourselves; we had a good time. We know all about liquor as a social lubricant. Some, but not all of us, think it has its advantages when reasonably used.

The first principle of success is that you should never be angry. Even though your husband becomes unbearable, and you have to leave him temporarily, you should, if you can, go without rancor. Patience and good temper are most necessary.

Our next thought is that you should never tell him what he must do about his drinking. If he gets the idea that you are a nag or a killjoy, your chance of accomplishing anything useful may be zero. He will use that as an excuse to drink some more. He will tell you he is misunderstood. This may lead to lonely evenings for you. He may seek someone to console him—not always another man.

Be determined that your husband's drinking is not going to spoil your relation with your children or your friends. They need your companionship and your help. It is possible to have a full and useful life, though your husband continues to drink. We know women who are unafraid, even happy, under these conditions. Do not set your heart on reforming your husband. You may be unable to do so, no matter how hard you try.

We know these suggestions are sometimes difficult to follow, but you will save many a heartbreak if you can succeed in observing them. Your husband may come to appreciate your reasonableness and patience. This may lay the groundwork for a friendly talk about his alcoholic problem. Try to have him bring up the subject himself. Be sure you are not critical during such a discussion. Attempt instead, to put yourself in his place. Let him see that you want to be helpful rather than critical.

When a discussion does arise, you might suggest he read this book, or at least the chapter on alcoholism. Tell him you have been worried, though perhaps needlessly. You think he ought to know the subject better, as everyone should have a clear understanding of the risk he takes if he drinks too much. Show him you have confidence in his power to stop or moderate. Say you do not want to be a wet blanket; that you only want him to take care of his health. Thus you may succeed in interesting him in alcoholism.

He probably has several alcoholics among his own acquaintances. You might suggest that you both take an interest in them. Drinkers like to help other drinkers. Your husband may be willing to talk to one of them.

If this kind of approach does not catch your husband's interest, it may be best to drop the subject, but after a friendly talk your husband will usually revive the topic himself. This may take patient waiting, but it will be worth it. Meanwhile you might try to help the wife of another serious drinker. If you act upon these principles, your husband may stop or moderate.

Suppose, however, that your husband fits the description of number two. The same principles which apply to husband number one should be practiced. But after his next binge, ask him if he would really like to get over drinking for good. Do not ask that he do it for you or anyone else. Just would he *like* to?

The chances are he would. Show him your copy of this book and tell him what you have found out about alcoholism. Show him that as alcoholics, the writers of the book understand. Tell him some of the interesting stories you have read. If you think he will be shy of a spiritual remedy, ask him to look at the chapter on alcoholism. Then perhaps he will be interested enough to continue.

If he is enthusiastic your cooperation will mean a great deal. If he is luke-warm, or thinks he is not an alcoholic, we suggest you leave him alone. Avoid urging him to follow our program. The seed has been planted in his mind. He knows that over a hundred men, much like himself, have recovered. But don't remind him of this after he has been drinking, for he may be angry. Sooner or later, you are likely to find him reading the book once more. Wait until repeated stumbling convinces him he must act, for the more you hurry him, the longer his recovery may be delayed.

If you have a number three husband, you may be in luck. Being certain he wants to stop, you can go to him with this volume as joyfully as though you had struck oil. He may not share your enthusiasm, but he is practically sure to read the book, and he may go for the program at once. If he does not, you will probably not have long to wait. Again, you should not crowd him. Let him decide for himself. Cheerfully see him through more sprees. Talk about his condition or this book only when he raises the issue. In some cases it may be better to let someone outside the family present the book. They can urge action without arousing hostility. If your husband is otherwise a normal individual, your chances are good at this stage.

You would suppose that men in the fourth classification would be quite hopeless; but that is not so. Many of Alcoholics Anonymous were like that. Everybody had given them up. Defeat seemed certain. Yet often such men had spectacular and powerful recoveries.

There are exceptions. Some men have been so impaired by alcohol that they cannot stop. Sometimes there are cases where alcoholism is complicated by other disorders. A good doctor or psychiatrist can tell you whether these complications are serious. In any event, try to have your husband read this book. His reaction may be one of enthusiasm. If he is already committed to an institution but can convince you and your doctor that he means business, give him a chance to try our method, unless the doctor thinks his mental condition too abnormal or dangerous. We make this recommendation with some confidence. About a year ago a certain state institution released four chronic alcoholics. It was fully expected they would all be back in a few weeks. Only one of them has returned. The others had no relapse at all. The power of God goes deep!

You may have the reverse situation on your hands. Perhaps you have a husband who is at large, but who should be committed. Some men cannot, or will not get over alcoholism. When they become too dangerous, we think the kind thing is to lock them up, of course a good doctor should always be consulted. The wives and children of such men suffer horribly, but not less than the men themselves.

But sometimes you must start life anew. We know women who have done it. If such women adopt a spiritual way of life, their road will be smoother.

If your husband is a drinker, you probably worry over what other people are thinking and you hate to meet your friends. You draw more and more into yourself and you think everyone is talking about conditions at your home. You avoid the subject of drinking, even with your own parents. You do not know what to tell the children. When your husband is bad, you become a trembling recluse, wishing the telephone had never been invented.

We find that most of this embarrassment is unnecessary. While you need not discuss your husband at length, you can quietly let your friends know the nature of his illness. But you must be on guard not to embarrass or harm your husband.

When you have carefully explained to such people that he is a sick person, you will have created a new atmosphere. Barriers which have sprung up between you and your friends will disappear with the growth of sympathetic understanding. You will no longer be self-conscious, nor feel that you must apologize as though your husband were a weak character. He may be anything but that. Your new courage, good nature, and lack of self-consciousness will do wonders for you socially.

The same principle applies in dealing with the children. Unless they actually need protection from their father, it is best not to take sides in any argument he has with them while drinking. Use your energies to promote a better understanding all around. Then that terrible tension which grips the home of every problem drinker will be lessened.

Frequently you have felt obliged to tell your husband's employer and his friends that he was sick, when as a matter of fact he was tight. Avoid answering these inquiries as much as you can. Whenever possible, let your husband explain. Your desire to protect him should not cause you to lie to people, when they have a right to know where he is and what he is doing. Discuss this with him when he is sober and in good spirits. Ask him what you should do if he places you in such a position again. But be careful not to be resentful about the last time he did so.

There is another paralyzing fear. You may be afraid your husband will lose his position; you are thinking of the disgrace and hard times which will befall you and the children. This experience may come to you. Or you may already have had it several times. Should it happen again, regard it in a different light. Maybe it will prove a blessing! It may convince your husband he wants to stop drinking forever. And now you know that he can stop if he will! Time after time, this apparent calamity has been a boon to us, for it opened up a path which led to the discovery of God.

We have elsewhere remarked how much better life is when lived on a spiritual plane. If God can solve the age-old riddle of alcoholism, he can solve your problems too. We wives found that, like everybody else, we were afflicted with pride, self-pity, vanity, and all the things which go to make up the self-centered person; and we were not above selfishness or dishonesty. As our husbands began to apply spiritual principles in their lives, we began to see the desirability of doing so too.

At first, some of us did not believe we needed this help. We thought, on the whole, we were pretty good women, capable of being nicer if our husbands stopped drinking. But it was a silly idea that we were too good to need God. Now we try to put spiritual principles to work in every department of our lives. When we do that, we find it solves our problems too: the ensuing lack of fear, worry and hurt feelings is a wonderful thing. We urge you to try our program, for nothing will be so helpful to your husband as the radically changed attitude toward him which God will show you how to have. Go along with your husband if you possibly can.

If you and your husband find a solution for the pressing problem of drink, you are, of course, going to be very happy. But all problems will not be solved at once. Seed has started to sprout in a new soil, but growth has only begun. In spite of your new-found happiness, there will be ups and downs. Many of the old problems will still be with you. This is as it should be.

The faith and sincerity of both you and your husband will be put to the test. These work-outs should be regarded as part of your education, for thus you will be learning to live. You will make mistakes, but if you are in earnest, they will not drag you down. Instead, you will capitalize them. A better way of life will emerge when they are overcome.

Some of the snags you will encounter are irritation, hurt-feelings, and resentments. Your husband will sometimes be unreasonable, and you will want to criticize. Starting from a speck on the domestic horizon, great thunderclouds of dispute may gather. These family dissensions are very dangerous, especially to your husband. Often you must carry the burden of avoiding them or keeping them under control. Never forget that resentment is a deadly hazard to an alcoholic. We do not mean that you have to agree with your husband wherever there is an honest difference of opinion. Just be careful not to disagree in a resentful or critical spirit.

You and your husband will find that you can dispose of serious problems easier than you can the trivial ones. Next time you and he have a heated discussion, no matter what the subject, it should be the privilege of either to smile and say, "This is getting serious. I'm sorry I got disturbed. Let's talk about it later." If your husband is trying to live on a spiritual basis, he will also be doing everything in his power to avoid disagreement or contention.

Your husband knows he owes you more than sobriety. He wants to make good. Yet you must not expect too much. His ways of thinking and doing are the habits of years. Patience, tolerance, understanding, and love are the watchwords. Show him these things in yourself and they will be reflected back to you from him. Live and let live is the rule. If you both show a willingness to remedy your own defects, there will be little need to criticize each other.

We women carry with us a picture of the ideal man, the sort of chap we would like our husbands to be. It is the most natural thing in the world, once his liquor problem is solved, to feel that he will now measure up to that cherished vision. The chances are he will not, for like yourself, he is just beginning his development. Be patient.

Another feeling we are very likely to entertain is one of resentment that love and loyalty could not cure our husbands of alcoholism. We do not like the thought that the contents of a book, or the work of another alcoholic, has accomplished in a few weeks the end for which we struggled for years. At such moments we forget that alcoholism is an illness over which we could not possibly have had any power. Your husband will be the first to say it was your devotion and care which brought him to the point where he could have a spiritual experience. Without you he would have gone to pieces long ago. When resentful thoughts come, try to pause and count your blessings. After all, your family is reunited, alcohol is no longer a problem, and you and your husband are working together toward an undreamed-of future.

Still another difficulty is that you may become jealous of the attention he bestows on other people, especially alcoholics. You have been starving for his companionship, yet he spends long hours helping other men and their families. You feel he should now be yours. The fact is that he should work with other people to maintain his own sobriety. Sometimes he will be so interested that he becomes really neglectful. Your house is filled with strangers. You may not like some of them. He gets stirred up about their troubles, but not at all about yours. It will do little good if you point that out and urge more attention for yourself. We find it a real mistake to dampen his enthusiasm for alcoholic work. You should join in his efforts as much as you possibly can. We suggest you direct some of your thought to the wives of his new alcoholic friends. They need the counsel and love of a woman who has gone through what you have.

It is probably true that you and your husband have been living too much alone, for drinking many times isolates the wife of an alcoholic. Therefore, you probably need fresh interests and a great cause to live for as much as your husband. If you cooperate, rather than complain, you will find that his excess enthusiasm will tone down. Both of you will awaken to a new sense of responsibility for others. You, as well as your husband, ought to think of what you can put into life, instead of how much you can take out. Inevitably your lives will be fuller for doing so. You will lose the old life to find one much better.

Perhaps your husband will make a fair start on the new basis, but just as things are going beautifully, he dismays you by coming home drunk. If you are satisfied he really wants to get over drinking, you need not be alarmed. Though it is infinitely better he have no relapse at all, as has been true with many of our men, it is by no means a bad thing in some cases. Your husband will see at once that he must redouble his spiritual activities if he expects to survive. You need not remind him of his spiritual deficiency—he will know of it. Cheer him up and ask him how you can be still more helpful.

The slightest sign of fear or intolerance may lessen your husband's chance of recovery. In a weak moment he may take your dislike of his high-stepping friends as one of those insanely trivial excuses to drink.

We never, never try to arrange a man's life, so as to shield him from temptation. The slightest disposition on your part to guide his appointments or his affairs so he will not be tempted will be noticed. Make him feel absolutely free to come and go as he likes. This is important. If he gets drunk, don't blame yourself. God has either removed your husband's liquor problem, or He has not. If not, it had better be found out right away. Then you and your husband can get right down to fundamentals. If a repetition is to be prevented, place the problem, along with everything else, in God's hands.

We realize we have been giving you much direction and advice. We may have seemed to lecture. If that is so we are sorry, for we ourselves, don't always care for people who lecture us. But what we have related is based upon experience, some of it painful. We had to learn these things the hard way. That is why we are anxious that you understand, that you avoid these unnecessary difficulties.

So to you out there—who may soon be with us—we say "Good luck and God bless you!"

CHAPTER 9

# The Family Afterward

Our women folk have suggested certain attitudes a wife may take with the husband who is recovering. Perhaps they created the impression that he is to be wrapped in cotton wool and placed on a pedestal. Successful readjustment means the opposite. All members of the family should meet upon the common ground of tolerance, understanding, and love. This involves a process of deflation. The alcoholic, his wife, his children, his "in-laws," each one is likely to have fixed ideas about the family's attitude towards himself or herself. Each is interested in having his or her wishes respected. We find the more one member of a family demands that the others concede to him, the more resentful they become. This makes for discord and unhappiness.

And why? Is it not because each wants to play the lead? Is not each trying to arrange the family show to his liking? Is he not unconsciously trying to see what he can take from the family life, rather than give?

Cessation of drinking is but the first step away from a highly strained, abnormal condition. A doctor said to us, "Years of living with an alcoholic is almost sure to make any wife or child neurotic. The entire family is, to some extent, ill." Let families realize, as they start their journey, that all will not be fair weather. Each in his turn may be footsore and may straggle. There will be alluring shortcuts and by-paths down which they may wander and lose their way.

Suppose we tell you some of the obstacles a family will meet; suppose we suggest how they may be avoided—even converted to good use for others. The family of an alcoholic longs for the return of happiness and security. They remember when father was romantic, thoughtful, and successful. Today's life is measured against that of other years and, when it falls short, the family may be unhappy.

Family confidence in dad is rising high. The good old days will soon be back, they think. Sometimes they demand that dad bring them back instantly! God, they believe, almost owes this recompense on a long overdue account. But the head of the house has spent years in pulling down the structures of business, romance, friendship, health—these things are now ruined or damaged. It will take time to clear away the wreck. Though old buildings will eventually be replaced by finer ones, the new structures will take years to complete.

Father knows he is to blame; it may take him many seasons of hard work to be restored financially, but he shouldn't be reproached. Perhaps he will never have much money again. But the wise family will admire him for what he is trying to be, rather than for what he is trying to get.

Now and then the family will be plagued by spectres from the past, for the drinking career of almost every alcoholic has been marked by escapades, funny, humiliating, shameful, or tragic. The first impulse will be to bury these skeletons in a dark closet and padlock the door. The family may be possessed by the idea that future happiness can be based only upon forgetfulness of the past. We think that such a view is quite self-centered and in direct conflict with the new way of living.

Henry Ford once made a wise remark to the effect that experience is the thing of supreme value in life. That is true only if one is willing to turn the past to good account. We grow by our willingness to face and rectify errors and convert them into assets. The alcoholic's past thus becomes the principal asset of the family, and frequently it is almost the only one!

This painful past may be of infinite value to other families still struggling with their problem. We think each family which has been relieved owes something to those which have not, and when the occasion requires, each member of it, should be only too willing to bring former mistakes, no matter how grievous, out of their hiding places. Showing others who suffer how we were given help, is the very thing which makes life seem so worth while to us now. Cling to the thought that, in God's hands, the dark past is the greatest possession you have—the key to life and happiness for others. With it you can avert death and misery for them.

It is possible to dig up past misdeeds so they become a blight, a veritable plague. For example, we know of situations in which the alcoholic or his wife have had love affairs. In the first flush of spiritual experience they forgave each other and drew closer together. The miracle of reconciliation was at hand. Then, under one provocation or another, the aggrieved one would unearth the old affair and angrily cast its ashes about. A few of us have had these growing pains and they hurt a great deal. Husbands and wives have sometimes been obliged to separate for a time until new perspective, new victory over hurt pride, could be rewon. In most cases, the alcoholic survived this ordeal without relapse, but not always. So we think that unless some good and useful purpose is to be served, past occurrences should not be discussed.

We families of Alcoholics Anonymous keep few skeletons in the closet. Everyone knows about the others' alcoholic troubles. This is a condition which, in ordinary life, would produce untold grief; there might be scandalous gossip, laughter at the expense of other people, and a tendency to take advantage of intimate information. Among us, these are rare occurrences. We do talk about each other a great deal but almost invariably temper such talk by a spirit of love and tolerance.

Another principle we observe carefully is that we do not relate intimate experiences of another person unless we are sure he would approve. We find it better, when possible, to stick to our own stories. A man may criticize or laugh at himself and it will affect others favorably, but criticism or ridicule of him coming from another often produces the contrary effect. Members of a family should watch such matters carefully, for one careless, inconsiderate remark has been known to raise the very devil. We alcoholics are sensitive people. It takes some of us a long time to outgrow that serious handicap.

Many alcoholics are enthusiasts. They run to extremes. At the beginning of recovery a man will take, as a rule, one of two directions. He may either plunge into a frantic attempt to get on his feet in business, or he may be so enthralled by his new life that he talks or thinks of little else. In either case certain family problems will arise. With these we have experience galore.

We think it dangerous if he rushes headlong at his economic problem. The family will be affected also, pleasantly at first, as they feel their money troubles are to be solved, then not so pleasantly as they find themselves neglected. Dad may be tired at night and preoccupied by day. He may take small interest in the· children and may show irritation when reproved for his delinquencies. If not irritable, he may seem dull and boring, not gay and affectionate, as the family would like him to be. Mother may complain of inattention. They are all disappointed, and often let him feel it. Beginning with such complaints, a barrier arises. He is straining every nerve to make up for lost time. He is striving to recover fortune and reputation and feels he is doing very well.

Sometimes mother and children don't think so. Having been neglected and misused in the past, they think father owes them more than they are getting. They want him to make a fuss over them. They expect him to give them the nice times they used to have before he drank so much, and to show his contrition for what they suffered. But dad doesn't give freely of himself. Resentment grows. He becomes still less communicative. Sometimes he explodes over a trifle. The family is mystified. They criticize, pointing out how he is falling down on his spiritual program.

This sort of thing can be avoided. Both father and the family are mistaken, though each side may have some justification. It is of little use to argue and only makes the impasse worse. The family must realize that dad, though marvelously improved, is still convalescing. They should be thankful he is sober and able to be of this world once more. Let them praise his progress. Let them remember that his drinking wrought all kinds of damage that may take long to repair. If they sense these things, they will not take so seriously his periods of crankiness, depression, or apathy, which will disappear when there is tolerance, love, and spiritual understanding.

The head of the house ought to remember that he is mainly to blame for what befell his home. He can scarcely square the account in his lifetime. But he must see the danger of over-concentration on financial success. Although financial recovery is on the way for many of us, we found we could not place money first. For us, material well-being always followed spiritual progress; it never preceded.

Since the home has suffered more than anything else, it is well that a man exert himself there. He is not likely to get far in any direction if he fails to show unselfishness and love under his own roof. We know there are difficult wives and families, but the man who is getting over alcoholism must remember he did much to make them so.

As each member of a resentful family begins to see his shortcomings and admits them to the others, he lays a basis for helpful discussion. These family talks will be constructive if they can be carried on without heated argument, self-pity, self-justification, or resentful criticism. Little by little, mother and children will see they ask too much, and father will see he gives too little. Giving, rather than getting, will become the guiding principle.

Assume on the other hand that father has, at the outset, a stirring spiritual experience. Over-night, as it were, he is a different man. He becomes a religious enthusiast. He is unable to focus on anything else. As soon as his sobriety begins to be taken as a matter of course, the family may look at their strange new dad with apprehension, then with irritation. There is talk about spiritual matters morning, noon and night. He may demand that the family find God in a hurry, or exhibit amazing indifference to them and say he is above worldly considerations. He may tell mother, who has been religious all her life, that she doesn't know what it's all about, and that she had better get his brand of spirituality while there is yet time.

When father takes this tack, the family may react unfavorably. They may be jealous of a God who has stolen dad's affections. While grateful that he drinks no more, they may not like the idea that God has accomplished the miracle where they failed. They often forget father was beyond human aid. They may not see why their love and devotion did not straighten him out. Dad is not so spiritual after all, they say. If he means to right his past wrongs, why all this concern for everyone in the world but his family? What about his talk that God will take care of them? They suspect father is a bit balmy!

He is not so unbalanced as they might think. Many of us have experienced dad's elation. We have indulged in spiritual intoxication. Like a gaunt prospector, belt drawn in over the last ounce of food, our pick struck gold. Joy at our release from a lifetime of frustration knew no bounds. Father feels he has struck something better than gold. For a time he may try to hug the new treasure to himself. He may not see at once that he has barely scratched a limitless lode which will pay dividends only if he mines it for the rest of his life and insists on giving away the entire product.

If the family cooperates, dad will soon see that he is suffering from a distortion of values. He will perceive that his spiritual growth is lopsided, that for an average man like himself, a spiritual life which does not include his family obligations may not be so perfect after all. If the family will appreciate that dad's current behavior is but a phase of his development, all will be well. In the midst of an understanding and sympathetic family, these vagaries of dad's spiritual infancy will quickly disappear.

The opposite may happen should the family condemn and criticize. Dad may feel that for years his drinking has placed him on the wrong side of every argument, but that now he has become a superior person, with God on his side. If the family persists in criticism, this fallacy may take a still greater hold on father. Instead of treating the family as he should, he may retreat further into himself and feel he has spiritual justification for so doing.

Though the family does not fully agree with dad's spiritual activities, they should let him have his head. Even if he displays a certain amount of neglect and irresponsibility towards the family, it is well to let him go as far as he likes in helping other alcoholics. During those first days of convalescence, this will do more to insure his sobriety than anything else. Though some of his manifestations are alarming and disagreeable, we think dad will be on a firmer foundation than the man who is placing business or professional success ahead of spiritual development. He will be less likely to drink again, and anything is preferable to that.

Those of us who have spent much time in the world of spiritual make-believe have eventually seen the childishness of it. This dream world has been replaced by a great sense of purpose, accompanied by a growing consciousness of the power of God in our lives. We have come to believe He would like us to keep our heads in the clouds with Him, but that our feet ought to be firmly planted on earth, nevertheless. That is where our fellow travelers are, and that is where our work must be done. These are the realities for us. We have found nothing incompatible between a powerful spiritual experience, and a life of sane and happy usefulness.

One more suggestion: Whether the family has spiritual convictions or not, they may do well to examine the principles by which the alcoholic member is trying to live. They can hardly fail to approve these simple principles, though the head of the house still fails somewhat in practicing them. Nothing will help the man who is off on a spiritual tangent so much as the wife who adopts a sane spiritual program, making a better practical use of it.

There will be other profound changes in the household. Liquor incapacitated father for so many years that mother became head of the house. She met these responsibilities gallantly. By force of circumstances, she was often obliged to treat father as a sick or wayward child. Even when he wanted to assert himself, he could not, for his drinking placed him constantly in the wrong. Mother made all the plans and gave the directions. When sober, father usually obeyed. Thus mother, through no fault of her own, became accustomed to wearing the family trousers. Father, coming suddenly to life again, often begins to assert himself. This means trouble, unless the family watches for these tendencies in each other and come to a friendly agreement about them.

Drinking isolates most homes from the outside world. Father may have laid aside for years all normal activities—clubs, civic duties, sports. When he renews interest in such things, a feeling of jealousy may arise. The family may feel they hold a mortgage on dad, so big that no equity should be left for outsiders. Instead of developing new channels of activity for themselves, mother and children may demand that he stay home and make up the deficiency.

At the very beginning, the couple ought to frankly face the fact that each will have to yield here and there, if the family is going to play an effective part in the new life. Father will necessarily spend much time with other alcoholics, but this activity should be balanced. New acquaintenances who know nothing of alcoholism might be made and thoughtful consideration given their needs. The problems of the community might engage attention. Though the family has no religious connections, they may wish to make contact with, or take membership in a religious body.

Alcoholics who have derided religious people will be helped by such contacts. Being possessed of a spiritual experience, the alcoholic will find he has much in common with these people, though he may differ with them on many matters. If he does not argue about religion, he will make new friends, and is sure to find new avenues of usefulness and pleasure. He and his family can be a bright spot in such congregations. He may bring new hope and new courage to many a priest, minister, or rabbi, who gives his all to minister to our troubled world. We intend the foregoing as a helpful suggestion only. So far as we are concerned, there is nothing obligatory about it. As non-denominational people, we cannot make up others minds for them. Each individual should consult his own conscience.

We have been speaking to you of serious, sometimes tragic things. We have been dealing with alcohol in its worst aspect. But we aren't a glum lot. If newcomers could see no joy or fun in our existence, they wouldn't want it. We absolutely insist on enjoying life. We try not to indulge in cynicism over the state of the nations, nor do we carry the world's troubles on our shoulders. When we see a man sinking into the mire that is alcoholism, we give him first aid and place what we have at his disposal. For his sake, we do recount and almost relive the horrors of our past. But those of us who have tried to shoulder the entire burden and trouble of others, find we are soon overcome by them.

So we think cheerfulness and laughter make for usefulness. Outsiders are sometimes shocked when we burst into merriment over a seemingly tragic experience out of the past. But why shouldn't we laugh? We have recovered, and have been given the power to help others.

Everybody knows that those in bad health, and those who seldom play, do not laugh much. So let each family play together or separately, as much as their circumstances warrant. We are sure God wants us to be happy, joyous, and free. We cannot subscribe to the belief that this life is a vale of tears, though it once was just that for many of us. But it is clear that we made our own misery. God didn't do it. Avoid then, the deliberate manufacture of misery, but if trouble comes, cheerfully capitalize it as an opportunity to demonstrate His omnipotence.

Now about health: A body badly burned by alcohol does not often recover overnight, nor do twisted thinking and depression vanish in a twinkling. We are convinced that a spiritual mode of living is a most powerful health restorative. We, who have recovered from serious drinking, are miracles of mental health. But we have seen remarkable transformations in our bodies. Hardly one of our crowd now shows any mark of dissipation.

But this does not mean that we disregard human health measures. God has abundantly supplied this world with fine doctors, psychologists, and practitioners of various kinds. Do not hesitate to take your health problems to such persons. Most of them give freely of themselves, that their fellows may enjoy sound minds and bodies. Try to remember that though God has wrought miracles among us, we should never belittle a good doctor or psychiatrist. Their services are often indispensable in treating a newcomer and following his case afterward.

One of the many doctors who had the opportunity of reading this book in manuscript form told us that the use of sweets was often helpful, of course depending upon a doctor's advice. He thought all alcoholics should constantly have chocolate available for its quick energy value at times of fatigue. He added that occasionally in the night a vague craving arose which would be satisfied by candy. Many of us have noticed a tendency to eat sweets and have found this practice beneficial.

A word about sex relations. Alcohol is so sexually stimulating to some men that they have over-indulged. Couples are occasionally dismayed to find that when drinking is stopped, the man tends to be impotent. Unless the reason is understood, there may be an emotional upset. Some of us had this experience, only to enjoy, in a few months, a finer intimacy than ever. There should be no hesitancy in consulting a doctor or psychologist if this condition persists. We do not know of any case where this difficulty lasted long.

The alcoholic may find it hard to re-establish friendly relations with his children. Their young minds were impressionable while he was drinking. Without saying so, they may cordially hate him for what he has done to them and to their mother. The children are sometimes dominated by a pathetic hardness and cynicism. They cannot seem to forgive and forget. This may hang on for months, long after their mother has accepted dad's new way of living and thinking.

In time they will see that he is a new man and in their own way they will let him know it. When this happens, they can be invited to join in morning meditation, then they can take part in the daily discussion without rancor or bias. From that point on, progress will be rapid. Marvelous results often follow such a reunion.

Whether the family goes on a spiritual basis or not, the alcoholic member has to if he would recover. The others must be convinced of his new status beyond a shadow of a doubt. Seeing is believing to most families who have lived with a drinker.

Here is a case in point: One of our friends is a heavy smoker and coffee drinker. There was no doubt he over-indulged. Seeing this, and meaning to be helpful, his wife commenced to admonish him about it. He admitted he was overdoing these things, but frankly said that he was not ready to stop. His wife is one of those persons who really feel there is something rather sinful about these commodities, so she nagged, and her intolerance finally threw him into a fit of anger. He got drunk.

Of course our friend was wrong—dead wrong. He had to painfully admit that and mend his spiritual fences. Though he is now a most effective member of Alcoholics Anonymous, he still smokes and drinks coffee, but neither his wife nor anyone else stands in judgment. She sees she was wrong to make a burning issue out of such a matter when his more serious ailments were being rapidly cured.

We have three little mottoes which are apropos. Here they are: "FIRST THINGS FIRST," "LIVE AND LET LIVE" and "EASY DOES IT."

# CHAPTER 10

# To Employers

One of our friends, whose gripping story you will read, has spent much of his life in the world of big business. He has hired and fired hundreds of men. He knows the alcoholic as the employer sees him. His present views ought to prove exceptionally useful to business men everywhere.

But let him tell you:

I was at one time assistant manager of a corporation department employing sixty-six hundred men. One day my secretary came in saying that Mr. B—— insisted on speaking with me. I told her to say that I was not interested. I had warned him several times that he had but one more chance. Not long afterward he had called me from Hartford on two successive days, so drunk he could hardly speak. I told him he was through—finally and forever.

My secretary returned to say that it was not Mr. B—— on the phone; it was Mr. B——'s brother, and he wished to give me a message. I still expected a plea for clemency, but these words came through the receiver: "I just wanted to tell you Paul jumped from a hotel window in Hartford last Saturday. He left us a note saying you were the best boss he ever had, and that you were not to blame in any way."

Another time, as I opened a letter which lay on my desk, a newspaper clipping fell out. It was the obituary of one of the best salesman I ever had. After two weeks of drinking, he had placed his toe on the trigger of a loaded shotgun—the barrel was in his mouth. I had discharged him for drinking six weeks before.

Still another experience: A woman's voice came faintly over long distance from Virginia. She wanted to know if her husband's company insurance was still in force. Four days before he had hanged himself in his woodshed. I had been obliged to discharge him for drinking, though he was brilliant, alert, and one of the best organizers I have ever known.

Here were three exceptional men lost to this world because I did not understand alcoholism as I do now. What irony—I became an alcoholic myself! And but for the intervention of an understanding person, I might have followed in their footsteps.

My downfall cost the business community unknown thousands of dollars, for it takes real money to train a man for an executive position. This kind of waste goes on unabated. We think the business fabric is shot through with a situation which might be helped by better understanding all around.

Nearly every modern employer feels a moral responsibility for the well-being of his help, and he tries to meet these responsibilities. That he has not always done so for the alcoholic is easily understood. To him the alcoholic has often seemed a fool of the first magnitude. Because of the employee's special ability, or of his own strong personal attachment to him, the employer has sometimes kept such a man at work long beyond a reasonable period. Some employers have tried every known remedy. In only a few instances have there been a lack of patience and tolerance. And we, who have imposed on the best of employers, can scarcely blame them if they have been short with us.

Here, for instance, is a typical example: An officer of one of the largest banking institutions in America knows I no longer drink. One day he told me about an executive of the same bank, who, from his description, was undoubtedly alcoholic. This seemed to me like an opportunity to be helpful, so I spent two hours talking about alcoholism, the malady, and described the symptoms and results as well as I could. His comment was: "Very interesting. But I'm sure this man is done drinking. He has just returned from a three-months' leave of absence, has taken a cure, looks fine, and to clinch the matter, the board of directors told him this was his last chance."

The only answer I could make was that if the man followed the usual pattern, he would go on a bigger bust than ever. I felt this was inevitable and wondered if the bank were doing the man an injustice. Why not bring him in contact with some of our alcoholic crowd? He might have a chance. I pointed out I had had nothing to drink whatever for three years, and this in the face of difficulties that would have made nine out of ten men drink their heads off. Why not at least afford him an opportunity to hear my story? "Oh no," said my friend, "this chap is either through with liquor, or he is minus a job. If he has your will power and guts, he will make the grade."

I wanted to throw up my hands in discouragement, for I saw that I had failed to help my banker friend understand. He simply could not believe that his brother-executive suffered from a serious illness. There was nothing to do but wait.

Presently the man did slip and was fired. Following his discharge, we contacted him. Without much ado, he accepted the principles and procedure that had helped us. He is undoubtedly on the road to recovery. To me, this incident illustrates lack of understanding as to what really ails the alcoholic, and lack of knowledge as to what part employers might profitably take in salvaging their sick employees.

If you desire to help it might be well to disregard your own drinking, or lack of it. Whether you are a hard drinker, a moderate drinker, or a teetotaler, you may have some pretty strong opinions, perhaps prejudices. Those who drink moderately may be more annoyed with an alcoholic than a total abstainer would be. Drinking occasionally, and understanding your own reactions, it is possible for you to become quite sure of many things, which, so far as the alcoholic is concerned, are not always so. As a moderate drinker, you can take your liquor or leave it alone. Whenever you want to, you control your drinking. Of an evening, you can go on a mild bender, get up in the morning, shake your head, and go to business. To you, liquor is no real problem. You cannot see why it should be to anyone else, save the spineless and stupid.

When dealing with an alcoholic, there may be a natural annoyance that a man could be so weak, stupid and irresponsible. Even when you understand the malady better, you may find this feeling rising.

A look at the alcoholic in your organization is many times illuminating. Is he not usually brilliant, fast-thinking, imaginative and likeable? When sober, does he not work hard and have a knack of getting things done? If he had these qualities and did not drink would he be worth retaining? Should he have the same consideration as other ailing employees? Is he worth salvaging? If your decision is yes, whether the reason be humanitarian, or business, or both, then the following suggestions may be helpful.

Can you discard the feeling that you are dealing only with habit, with stubbornness, or a weak will? If this presents difficulty re-reading chapters two and three, where the alcoholic sickness is discussed at length might be worth while. You, as a business man, want to know the necessities before considering the result. If you concede that your employee is ill, can he be forgiven for what he has done in the past? Can his past absurdities be forgotten? Can it be appreciated that he has been a victim of crooked thinking, directly caused by the action of alcohol on his brain?

I well remember the shock I received when a prominent doctor in Chicago told me of cases where pressure of the spinal fluid actually ruptured the brain. No wonder an alcoholic is strangely irrational. Who wouldn't be, with such a fevered brain? Normal drinkers are not so affected, nor can they understand the abberations of the alcoholic.

Your man has probably been trying to conceal a number of scrapes, perhaps pretty messy ones. They may be disgusting. You may be at a loss to understand how such a seemingly above-board chap could be so involved. But these scrapes can generally be charged, no matter how bad, to the abnormal action of alcohol on his mind. When drinking, or getting over a bout, an alcoholic, sometimes the model of honesty when normal, will do incredible things. Afterward, his revulsion will be terrible. Nearly always, these antics indicate nothing more than temporary conditions.

This is not to say that all alcoholics are honest and upright when not drinking. Of course that isn't so, and such people often may impose on you. Seeing your attempt to understand and help, some men will try to take advantage of your kindness. If you are sure your man does not want to stop, he may as well be discharged: the sooner the better. You are not doing him a favor by keeping him on. Firing such an individual may prove a blessing to him. It may be just the jolt he needs. I know, in my own particular case, that nothing my company could have done would have stopped me, for so long as I was able to hold my position, I could not possibly realize how serious my situation was. Had they fired me first, and had they then taken steps to see that I was presented with the solution contained in this book, I might have returned to them six months later, a well man.

But there are many men who want to stop, and with them you can go far. Your understanding treatment of their cases will pay dividends.

Perhaps you have such a man in mind. He wants to quit drinking, and you want to help him, even if it be only a matter of good business. You now know more about alcoholism. You can see that he is mentally and physically sick. You are willing to overlook his past performances. Suppose an approach is made something like this:

State that you know about his drinking, that it must stop. You might say you appreciate his abilities, would like to keep him, but cannot, if he continues to drink. A firm attitude at this point has helped many of us.

Next he can be assured that you do not intend to lecture, moralize, or condemn; that if this was done formerly, it was because of misunderstanding. If possible express a lack of hard feeling toward him. At this point, it might be well to explain alcoholism, the sickness. Say that you believe he is a gravely-ill person, with this qualification—being perhaps fatally ill, does he want to get well immediately? You ask because many alcoholics, being warped and drugged, do not want to quit. But does he? Will he take every necessary step, submit to anything to get well, to stop drinking forever?

If he says yes, does he really mean it, or down inside does he think he is fooling you, and that after rest and treatment he will be able to get away with a few drinks now and then? We believe a man should be thoroughly probed on these points. Be satisfied he is not deceiving himself or you.

Whether you mention this book is a matter for your discretion. If he temporizes and still thinks he can ever drink again, even beer, he might as well be discharged after the next bender which, if an alcoholic, he is almost certain to have. He should understand that emphatically. Either you are dealing with a man who can and will get well, or you are not. If not, why waste time with him? This may seem severe, but it is usually the best course.

After satisfying yourself that your man wants to recover and that he will go to any extreme to do so, you may suggest a definite course of action. For most alcoholics who are drinking, or who are just getting over a spree, a certain amount of physical treatment is desirable, even imperative. The matter of physical treatment should, of course, be referred to your own doctor. Whatever the method, its object is to thoroughly clear mind and body of the effects of alcohol. In competent hands, this seldom takes long, nor is it very expensive. Your man will fare better if placed in such physical condition that he can think straight and no longer craves liquor. If you propose such a procedure to him, it may be necessary to advance the cost of treatment, but we believe it should be made plain that any expense will later be deducted from his pay. It is better for him to feel fully responsible.

If your man accepts your offer, it should be pointed out that physical treatment is but a small part of the picture. Though you are providing him with the best possible medical attention, he should understand that he must undergo a change of heart. To get over drinking will require a transformation of thought and attitude. We all had to place recovery above everything, for without recovery we would have lost both home and business.

Can you have every confidence in his ability to recover? While on the subject of confidence, can you adopt the attitude that so far as you are concerned, this will be a strictly personal matter, that his alcoholic derelictions, the treatment about to be undertaken, will never be discussed without his consent? It might be well to have a long chat with him on his return.

To return to the subject matter of this book: It contains full suggestions by which the employee may solve his problem. To you, some of the ideas which it contains are novel. Perhaps you are not quite in sympathy with the approach we suggest. By no means do we offer it as the last word on this subject, but so far as we are concerned, it has worked with us. After all, are you not looking for results rather than methods? Whether your employee likes it or not, he will learn the grim truth about alcoholism. That won't hurt him a bit, though he does not go for this remedy.

We suggest you draw the book to the attention of the doctor who is to attend your patient during treatment. If the book is read the moment the patient is able, while acutely depressed, realization of his condition may come to him.

We hope the doctor will tell the patient the truth about his condition, whatever that happens to be. When the man is presented with this volume it is best that no one tell him he must abide by its suggestions. The man must decide for himself.

You are betting, of course, that your changed attitude and the contents of this book will turn the trick. In some cases it will, and in others it may not. But we think that if you persevere, the percentage of successes will gratify you. When our work spreads and our numbers increase, we hope your employees may be put in personal contact with some of us. Meanwhile, we are sure a great deal can be accomplished by the use of the book alone.

On your employee's return, talk with him. Ask him if he thinks he has the answer. If he feels free to discuss his problems with you, if he knows you understand, and will not be upset by anything he wishes to say, he will probably be off to a fast start.

In this connection, can you remain undisturbed if the man proceeds to tell you shocking things? He may, for example, reveal that he has padded his expense account, or that he has planned to take your best customers away from you. In fact, he may say almost anything if he has accepted our solution, which, as you know, demands rigorous honesty. Can you charge this off as you would a bad account and start fresh with him? If he owes you money you may wish to make terms.

If he speaks of his home situation, you can undoubtedly make helpful suggestions. Can he talk frankly with you so long as he does not bear business tales or criticize his associates? With this kind of employee such an attitude will command undying loyalty.

The greatest enemies of we alcoholics are resentment, jealousy, envy, frustration, and fear. Wherever men are gathered together in business, there will be rivalries, and, arising out of these, a certain amount of office politics. Sometimes we alcoholics have an idea that people are trying to pull us down. Often this is not so at all. But sometimes our drinking will be used politically.

One instance comes to mind in which a malicious individual was always making friendly little jokes about an alcoholic's drinking exploits. In this way he was slyly carrying tales. In another case, an alcoholic was sent to a hospital for treatment. Only a few knew of it at first, but within a short time, it was bill-boarded throughout the entire company. Naturally this sort of thing decreased the man's chance of recovery. The employer can many times protect the victim from this kind of talk. The employer cannot play favorites, but he can always defend a man from needless provocation and unfair criticism.

As a class, alcoholics are energetic people. They work hard and they play hard. Your man should be on his mettle to make good. Being somewhat weakened, and faced with physical and mental readjustment to a life which knows no alcohol, he may overdo. You may have to curb his desire to work sixteen hours a day. You may need to encourage him to play once in a while. He may wish to do a lot for other alcoholics and something of the sort may come up during business hours. A reasonable amount of latitude will be helpful. This work is necessary to maintain his sobriety.

After your man has gone along without drinking a few months, you may be able to make use of his services with other employees who are giving you the alcoholic run-around—provided, of course, they are willing to have a third party in the picture. An alcoholic who has recovered, but holds a relatively unimportant job, can talk to a man with a better position. Being on radically different basis of life, he will never take advantage of the situation.

Your man may be trusted. Long experience with alcoholic excuses naturally arouses suspicion. When his wife next calls saying he is sick, you might jump to the conclusion he is drunk. If he is, and is still trying to recover, he will tell you about it, even if it means the loss of his job. For he knows he must be honest if he would live at all. He will appreciate knowing you are not bothering your head about him at all, that you are not suspicious, nor are you trying to run his life so he will be shielded from temptation to drink. If he is conscientiously following the Program of Recovery he can go anywhere your business may call him.

In case he does stumble, even once, you will have to decide whether to let him go. If you are sure he doesn't mean business, there is no doubt you should discharge him. If, on the contrary, you are sure he is doing his utmost, you may wish to give him another chance. But you should feel under no obligation to keep him on, for your obligation has been well discharged already.

There is another thing you might wish to do. If your organization is a large one, your junior executives might be provided with this book. You might let them know you have no quarrel with the alcoholics of your organization. These juniors are often in a difficult position. Men under them are frequently their friends. So, for one reason or another, they cover these men, hoping matters will take a turn for the better. They often jeopardize their own positions by trying to help serious drinkers who should have been fired long ago, or else given an opportunity to get well.

After reading this book, a junior executive can go to such a man and say approximately this, "Look here, Ed. Do you want to stop drinking or not? You put me on the spot every time you get drunk. It isn't fair to me or the firm. I have been learning something about alcoholism. If you are an alcoholic, you are a mighty sick man. You act like one. The firm wants to help you get over it, and if you are interested, there is a way out. If you do, your past will be forgotten and the fact that you went away for treatment will not be mentioned. But if you cannot, or will not stop drinking, I think you ought to resign."

Your junior executive may not agree with the contents of our book. He need not, and often should not, show it to his alcoholic prospect. But at least he will understand the problem and will no longer be misled by ordinary promises. He will be able to take a position with such a man which is eminently fair and square. He will have no further reason for covering up an alcoholic employee.

It boils right down to this: No man should be fired just because he is alcoholic. If he wants to stop, he should be afforded a real chance. If he cannot, or does not want to stop, he should be discharged. The exceptions are few.

We think this method of approach will accomplish several things. It will permit the rehabilitation of good men. At the same time you will feel no reluctance to rid yourself of those who cannot, or will not, stop. Alcoholism may be causing your organization considerable damage in its waste of time, men and reputation. We hope our suggestions will help you plug up this sometimes serious leak. We think we are sensible when we urge that you stop this waste and give your worth-while man a chance.

The other day an approach was made to the vice-president of a large industrial concern. He remarked: "I'm mighty glad you fellows got over your drinking. But the policy of this company is not to interfere with the habits of our employees. If a man drinks so much that his job suffers, we fire him. I don't see how you can be of any help to us, for as you see, we don't have any alcoholic problem." This same company spends millions for research every year. Their cost of production is figured to a fine decimal point. They have recreational facilities. There is company insurance. There is a real interest, both humanitarian and business, in the well-being of employees. But alcoholism—well, they just don't believe they have it.

Perhaps this is a typical attitude. We, who have collectively seen a great deal of business life, at least from the alcoholic angle, had to smile at this gentleman's sincere opinion. He might be shocked if he knew how much alcoholism is costing his organization a year. That company may harbor many actual or potential alcoholics.

We believe that managers of large enterprises often have little idea how prevalent this problem is. Even if you feel your organization has no alcoholic problem, it might pay to take another look down the line. You may make some interesting discoveries.

Of course, this chapter refers to alcoholics, sick people, deranged men. What our friend, the vice-president, had in mind, was the habitual or whoopee drinker. As to them, his policy is undoubtedly sound, but he did not distinguish between such people and the alcoholic.

It is not to be expected that an alcoholic employee will receive a disproportionate amount of time and attention. He should not be made a favorite. The right kind of man, the kind who recovers, will not want this sort of thing. He will not impose. Far from it. He will work like the devil, and thank you to his dying day.

Today, I own a little company. There are two alcoholic employees, who produce as much as five normal salesmen. But why not? They have a new attitude, and they have been saved from a living death. I have enjoyed every moment spent in getting them straightened out.

# CHAPTER 11

# A Vision for You

For most normal folks, drinking means conviviality, companionship, and colorful imagination. It means release from care, boredom, and worry. It is joyous intimacy with friends, and a feeling that life is good. But not so with us in those last days of heavy drinking. The old pleasures were gone. They were but memories. Never could we recapture the great moments of the past. There was an insistent yearning to enjoy life as we once did and a heartbreaking obsession that some new miracle of control would enable us to do it. There was always one more attempt—and one more failure.

The less people tolerated us, the more we withdrew from society, from life itself. As we became subjects of King Alcohol, shivering denizens of his mad realm, the chilling vapor that is loneliness settled down. It thickened, ever becoming blacker. Some of us sought out sordid places, hoping to find understanding companionship and approval. Momentarily we did—then would come oblivion and the awful awakening to face the hideous Four Horsemen—Terror, Bewilderment, Frustration, Despair. Unhappy drinkers who read this page will understand!

Now and then a serious drinker, being dry at the moment says, "I don't miss it at all. Feel better. Work better. Having a better time." As ex-alcoholics, we smile at such a sally. We know our friend is like a boy whistling in the dark to keep up his spirits. He fools himself. Inwardly he would give anything to take half a dozen drinks and get away with them. He will presently try the old game again, for he isn't happy about his sobriety. He cannot picture life without alcohol. Some day he will be unable to imagine life either with alcohol or without it. Then he will know loneliness such as few do. He will be at the jumping-off place. He will wish for the end.

We have shown how we got out from under. You say: "Yes, I'm willing. But am I to be consigned to a life where I shall be stupid, boring and glum, like some righteous people I see? I know I must get along without liquor, but how can I? Have you a sufficient substitute?"

Yes, there is a substitute, and it is vastly more than that. It is a Fellowship in Alcoholics Anonymous. There you will find release from care, boredom, and worry. Your imagination will be fired. Life will mean something at last. The most satisfactory years of your existence lie ahead. Thus we find The Fellowship, and so will you.

"How is that to come about?" you ask. "Where am I to find these people?"

You are going to meet these new friends in your own community. Near you alcoholics are dying helplessly like people in a sinking ship. If you live in a large place, there are hundreds. High and low, rich and poor, these are future Fellows of Alcoholics Anonymous. Among them you will make lifelong friends. You will be bound to them with new and wonderful ties, for you will escape disaster together and you will commence shoulder to shoulder your common journey. Then you will know what it means to give of yourself, that others may survive and rediscover life. You will learn the full meaning of "Love they neighbor as thyself."

It may seem incredible that these men are to become happy, respected, and useful once more. How can they rise out of such misery, bad repute and hopelessness? The practical answer is that since these things have happened among us, they can happen with you. Should you wish them above all else, and be willing to make use of our experience, we are sure they will come. The age of miracles is still with us. Our own recovery proves that!

Our hope is that when this ship of a book is launched on the world tide of alcoholism, defeated drinkers will seize upon it, to follow its suggestions. Many, we are sure, will rise to their feet and march on. They will approach still other sick ones and Fellowships of Alcoholics Anonymous may spring up in each city and hamlet, havens for those who must find a way out.

In the chapter "Working with Others" you gathered an idea of how we approach and aid others to health. Suppose now that through you several families have adopted this way of life. You will want to know more of how to proceed from that point. Perhaps the best way of treating you to a glimpse of your future will be to describe the growth of the Fellowship among us. Here is a brief account:

Nearly four years ago, one of our number made a journey to a certain western city. From the business standpoint, his trip came off badly. Had he been successful in his enterprise, he would have been set on his feet financially, which, at the time, seemed vitally important. But his venture wound up in a law suit and bogged down completely. The proceding was shot through with much hard feeling and controversy.

Bitterly discouraged, he found himself in a strange place, discredited and almost broke. Still physically weak, and sober but a few months, he saw that his predicament was dangerous. He wanted so much to talk with someone, but whom?

One dismal afternoon he paced a hotel lobby wondering how his bill was to be paid. At one end of the room stood a glass covered directory of local churches. Down the lobby a door opened into an attractive bar. He could see the gay crowd inside.

In there he would find companionship and release. Unless he took some drinks, he might not have the courage to scrape an acquaintance, and would have a lonely week-end.

Of course, he couldn't drink, but why not sit hopefully at a table, a bottle of ginger ale before him? Then after all, had he not been sober six months now? Perhaps he could handle, say, three drinks—no more! Fear gripped him. He was on thin ice. Again it was the old, insidious insanity—that first drink. With a shiver, he turned away and walked down the lobby to the church directory. Music and gay chatter still floated to him from the bar.

But what about his responsibilities—his family and the men who would die because they would not know how to get well, ah—yes, those other alcoholics? There must be many such in this town. He would phone a clergyman. His sanity returned, and he thanked God. Selecting a church at random from the directory, he stepped into a booth and lifted the receiver.

His call to the clergyman led him presently to a certain resident of the town, who, though formerly able and respected, was then nearing the nadir of alcoholic despair. It was the usual situation: home in jeopardy, wife ill, children distracted, bills in arrears, and standing damaged. He had a desperate desire to stop, but saw no way out; for he had earnestly tried many avenues of escape. Painfully aware of being somehow abnormal, the man did not fully realize what it means to be alcoholic.

When our friend related his experience, the man agreed that no amount of will power he might muster could stop his drinking for long. A spiritual experience, he conceded, was absolutely necessary, but the price seemed high upon the basis suggested. He told how he lived in constant worry about those who might find out about his alcoholism. He had, of course, the familiar alcoholic obsession that few knew of his drinking. Why, he argued, should he lose the remainder of his business, only to bring still more suffering to his family, by foolishly admitting his plight to people from whom he made his livelihood? He would do anything, he said, but that.

Being intrigued, however, he invited our friend to his home. Some time later, and just as he thought he was getting control of his liquor situation, he went on a roaring bender. For him, this was the spree that ended all sprees. He saw that he would have to face his problems squarely, that God might give him mastery.

One morning he took the bull by the horns and set out to tell those he feared what his trouble had been. He found himself surprisingly well received, and learned that many knew of his drinking. Stepping into his car, he made the rounds of people he had hurt. He trembled as he went about, for this might mean ruin, particularly to a person in his line of business.

At midnight he came home exhausted, but very happy. He has not had a drink since. As we shall see, he now means a great deal to his community, and the major liabilities of thirty years of hard drinking have been repaired in four.

But life was not easy for the two friends. Plenty of difficulties presented themselves. Both saw that they must keep spiritually active. One day they called up the head nurse of a local hospital. They explained their need and inquired if she had a first class alcoholic prospect.

She replied, "Yes, we've got a corker. He's just beaten up a couple of nurses. Goes off his head completely when drinking. But he's a grand chap when sober, though he's been in here six times in the last four months. Understand he was once a well-known lawyer in town, but just now we've got him strapped down tight."

Here was a prospect all right, but, by the description, none too promising. The use of spiritual principles in such cases was not so well-understood as it is now. But one of the friends said, "Put him in a private room. We'll be down."

Two days later, a future Fellow of Alcoholics Anonymous stared glassily at the strangers beside his bed. "Who are you fellows, and why this private room? I was always in a ward before."

Said one of the visitors, "We're giving you a treatment for alcoholism."

Hopelessness was written large on the man's face as he replied: "Oh, but that's no use. Nothing would fix me. I'm a goner. The last three times, I got drunk on the way home from here. I'm afraid to go out the door. I can't understand it."

For an hour, the two friends told him about their drinking experiences. Over and over, he would say: "That's me. That's me. I drink like that."

The man in the bed was told of the acute poisoning from which he suffered, how it deteriorates the body of an alcoholic and warps his mind. There was much talk about the mental state preceding the first drink.

"Yes, that's me," said the sick man, "the very image. You fellows know your stuff all right, but I don't see what good it'll do. You fellows are somebody. I was once, but I'm a nobody now. From what you tell me, I know more than ever I can't stop." At this both the visitors burst into a laugh. Said the future Fellow Anonymous: "Damn little to laugh about that I can see."

The two friends spoke of their spiritual experience and told him about the course of action they carried out.

He interrupted: "I used to be strong for the church, but that won't fix it. I've prayed to God on hangover mornings and sworn that I'd never touch another drop but by nine o'clock I'd be boiled as an owl."

Next day found the prospect more receptive. He had been thinking it over. "Maybe you're right," he said. "God ought to be able to do anything." Then he added, "He sure didn't do much for me when I was trying to fight this booze racket alone."

On the third day the lawyer gave his life to the care and direction of his Creator, and said he was perfectly willing to do anything necessary. His wife came, scarcely daring to be hopeful, but she thought she saw something different about her husband already. He had begun to have a spiritual experience.

That afternoon he put on his clothes and walked from the hospital a free man.

He entered a political campaign, making speeches, frequenting men's gathering places of all sorts, often staying up all night. He lost the race by only a narrow margin. But he had found God—and in finding God had found himself.

That was in June, 1935. He never drank again. He too, has become a respected and useful member of his community. He has helped other men recover, and is a power in the church from which he was long absent.

So, you see, there were three alcoholics in that town, who now felt they had to give to others what they had found, or be sunk. After several failures to find others, a fourth turned up. He came through an acquaintance who had heard the good news. He proved to be a devil-may-care young fellow whose parents could not make out whether he wanted to stop drinking or not. They were deeply religious people, much shocked by their son's refusal to have anything to do with the church. He suffered horribly from his sprees, but it seemed as if nothing could be done for him. He consented, however, to go to the hospital, where he occupied the very room recently vacated by the lawyer.

He had three visitors. After a bit, he said: "The way you fellows put this spiritual stuff makes sense. I'm ready to do business. I guess the old folks were right after all." So one more was added to the Fellowship.

All this time our friend of the hotel lobby incident remained in that town. He was there three months. He now returned home, leaving behind his first acquaintance, the lawyer, and the devil-may-care chap. These men had found something brand new in life. Though they knew they must help other alcoholics if they would remain sober, that motive became secondary. It was transcended by the happiness they found in giving themselves for others. They shared their homes, their slender resources, and gladly devoted their spare hours to fellow-sufferers. They were willing, by day or night, to place a new man in the hospital and visit him afterward. They grew in numbers. They experienced a few distressing failures, but in those cases, they made an effort to bring the man's family into a spiritual way of living, thus relieving much worry and suffering.

A year and six months later these three had succeeded with seven more. Seeing much of each other, scarce an evening passed that someone's home did not shelter a little gathering of men and women, happy in their release, and constantly thinking how they might present their discovery to some newcomer. In addition to these casual get-togethers, it became customary to set apart one night a week for a meeting to be attended by anyone or everyone interested in a spiritual way of life. Aside from fellowship and sociability, the prime object was to provide a time and place where new people might bring their problems.

Outsiders became interested. One man and his wife placed their large home at the disposal of this strangely assorted crowd. This couple has since become so fascinated that they have dedicated their home to the work. Many a distracted wife has visited this house to find loving and understanding companionship among women who knew their problem, to hear from the lips of men like their husbands what had happened to them, to be advised how her own wayward mate might be hospitalized and approached when next he stumbled.

Many a man, yet dazed from his hospital experience, has stepped over the threshold of that home into freedom. Many an alcoholic who entered there came away with an answer. He succumbed to that gay crowd inside, who laughed at their misfortune and understood him. Impressed by those who visited him at the hospital, he capitulated entirely, when, later, in an upper room of this house, he heard the story of some man whose experience closely tallied with his own. The expression on the faces of the women, that indefinable something in the eyes of the men, the stimulating and electric atmosphere of the place, conspired to let him know that here was haven at last.

The very practical approach to his problems, the absence of intolerance of any kind, the informality, the genuine democracy, the uncanny understanding which these people had were irresistible. He and his wife would leave elated by the thought of what they could now do for some stricken acquaintance and his family. They knew they had a host of new friends; it seemed they had known these strangers always. They had seen miracles, and one was to come to them. They had visioned The Great Reality—their loving and All Powerful Creator.

Now, this house will hardly accommodate its weekly visitors, for they number sixty or eighty as a rule. Alcoholics are being attracted from far and near. From surrounding towns, families drive long distances to be present. A community thirty miles away has fifteen Fellows of Alcoholics Anonymous. Being a large place, we think that some day its Fellowship will number many hundreds.

But life among Alcoholics Anonymous is more than attending gatherings and visiting hospitals. Cleaning up old scrapes, helping to settle family differences, explaining the disinherited son to his irate parents, lending money and securing jobs for each other, when justified—these are everyday occurrences. No one is too discredited, nor has sunk too low to be welcomed cordially—if he means business. Social distinctions, petty rivalries and jealousies—these are laughed out of countenance. Being wrecked in the same vessel, being restored and united under one God, with hearts and minds attuned to the welfare of others, the things which matter so much to some people no longer signify much to them. How could they?

Under only slightly different conditions, the same thing is taking place in several eastern cities. In one of these there is a well-known hospital for the treatment of alcoholic and drug addiction. Four years ago one of our number was a patient there. Many of us have felt, for the first time, the Presence and Power of God within its walls. We are greatly indebted to the doctor in attendance there, for he, although it might prejudice his own work, has told us his belief in our work.

Every few days this doctor suggests our approach to one of his patients. Understanding our work, he can do this with an eye to selecting those who are willing and able to recover on a spiritual basis. Many of us, former patients, go there to help. Then, in this eastern city, there are informal meetings such as we have described to you, where you may see thirty or forty, there are the same fast friendships, there is the same helpfulness to one another as you find among our western friends. There is a good bit of travel between East and West and we foresee a great increase in this helpful interchange.

Some day we hope that every alcoholic who journeys will find a Fellowship of Alcoholics Anonymous at his destination. To some extent this is already true. Some of us are salesmen and go about. Little clusters of twos and threes and fives of us have sprung up in other communities, through contact with our two larger centers. Those of us who travel drop in as often as we can. This practice enables us to lend a hand, at the same time avoiding certain alluring distractions of the road, about which any traveling man can inform you.

Thus we grow. And so can you, though you be but one man with this book in your hand. We believe and hope it contains all you will need to begin.

We know what you are thinking. You are saying to yourself: "I'm jittery and alone. I couldn't do that." But you can. You forget that you have just now tapped a source of power so much greater than yourself. To duplicate, with such backing, what we have accomplished is only a matter of willingness, patience and labor.

We know a former alcoholic who was living in a large community. He had lived there but a few weeks when he found that the place probably contained more alcoholics per square mile than any city in the country. This was only a few days ago at this writing. The authorities were much concerned. He got in touch with a prominent psychiatrist who has undertaken certain responsibilities for the mental health of the community. The doctor proved to be able and exceedingly anxious to adopt any workable method of handling the situation. So he inquired, what did our friend have on the ball?

Our friend proceeded to tell him. And with such good effect that the doctor agreed to a test among his patients and certain other alcoholics from a clinic which he attends. Arrangements were also made with the chief psychiatrist of a large public hospital to select still others from the stream of misery which flows through that institution.

So our fellow worker will soon have friends galore. Some of them may sink and perhaps never get up, but if our experience is a criterion, more than half of those approached will become Fellows of Alcoholics Anonymous. When a few men in this city have found themselves, and have discovered the joy of helping others to face life again, there will be no stopping until everyone in that town has had his opportunity to recover—if he can and will.

Still you may say: "But I will not have the benefit of contact with you who write this book." We cannot be sure. God will determine that, so you must remember that your real reliance is always upon Him. He will show you how to create the Fellowship you crave.

Our book is meant to be suggestive only. We realize we know only a little. God will constantly disclose more to you and to us. Ask him in your morning meditation what you can do each day for the man who is still sick. The answers will come, if your own house is in order. But obviously you cannot transmit something you haven't got. See to it that your relationship with Him is right, and great events will come to pass for you and countless others This is the Great Fact for us.

Abandon yourself to God as you understand God. Admit your faults to him and your fellows. Clear away the wreckage of your past. Give freely of what you find, and join us. We shall be with you, in the Fellowship of The Spirit, and you will surely meet some of us as you trudge the Road of Happy Destiny.

May God bless you and keep you—until then.

# PERSONAL STORIES

# The Doctor's Nightmare

I was born in a small New England village of about seven thousand souls. The general moral standard was, as I recall it, far above the average. No beer or liquor was sold in the neighborhood, except at the State liquor agency where perhaps one might procure a pint if he could convince the agent that he really needed it. Without this proof the expectant purchaser would be forced to depart empty handed with none of what I later came to believe was the great panacea for all human ills. Men who had liquor shipped in from Boston or New York by express were looked upon with great distrust and disfavor by most of the good townspeople. The town was well supplied with churches and schools in which I pursued my early educational activities.

My father was a professional man of recognized ability and both my father and mother were most active in church affairs. Both father and mother were considerably above the average in intelligence.

Unfortunately for me I was the only child, which perhaps engendered the selfishness which played such an important part in bringing on my alcoholism.

From childhood through high school I was more or less forced to go to church, Sunday School and evening service, Monday night Christian Endeavor and sometimes to Wednesday evening prayer meeting. This had the effect of making me resolve that when I was free from parental domination, I would never again darken the doors of a church. This resolution I kept steadfastly for the next *forty* years, except when circumstances made it seem unwise to absent myself.

After high school came four years in one of the best colleges in the country where drinking seemed to be a major extra-curricular activity. Almost everyone seemed to do it. I did it more and more, and had lots of fun without much grief, either physical or financial. I seemed to be able to snap back the next morning better than most of my fellow drinkers, who were cursed (or perhaps blessed) with a great deal of morning-after nausea. Never once in my life have I had a headache, which fact leads me to believe that I was an alcoholic almost from the start. My whole life seemed to be centered around doing what I wanted to do, without regard for the rights, wishes, or privileges of anyone else; a state of mind which became more and more predominant as the years passed. I was graduated with "summa cum laude" in the eyes of the drinking fraternity, but not in the eyes of the Dean.

The next three years I spent in Boston, Chicago, and Montreal in the employ of a large manufacturing concern, selling railway supplies, gas engines of all sorts, and many other items of heavy hardware. During these years, I drank as much as my purse permitted, still without paying too great a penalty, although I was beginning to have morning "jitters" at times. I lost only a half day's work during these three years.

My next move was to take up the study of medicine, entering one of the largest universities in the country. There I took up the business of drinking with much greater earnestness than I had previously shown. On account of my enormous capacity for beer, I was elected to membership in one of the drinking societies, and soon became one of the leading spirits. Many mornings I have gone to classes, and even though fully prepared, would turn and walk back to the fraternity house because of my jitters, not daring to enter the classroom for fear of making a scene should I be called on for recitation.

This went from bad to worse until sophomore spring when, after a prolonged period of drinking, I made up my mind that I could not complete my course, so I packed my grip and went South and spent a month on a large farm owned by a friend of mine. When I got the fog out of my brain, I decided that quitting school was very foolish and that I had better return and continue my work. When I reached school, I discovered the faculty had other ideas on the subject. After much argument they allowed me to return and take my exams, all of which I passed creditably. But they were much disgusted and told me they would attempt to struggle along without my presence. After many painful discussions, they finally gave me my credits and I migrated to another of the leading universities of the country and entered as a Junior that Fall.

There my drinking became so much worse that the boys in the fraternity house where I lived felt forced to send for my father, who made a long journey in the vain endeavor to get me straightened around. This had little effect however for I kept on drinking and used a great deal more hard liquor than in former years.

Coming up to final exams I went on a particularly strenuous spree. When I went in to write the examinations, my hand trembled so I could not hold a pencil. I passed in at least three absolutely blank books. I was, of course, soon on the carpet and the upshot was that I had to go back for two more quarters and remain absolutely dry, if I wished to graduate. This I did, and proved myself satisfactory to the faculty, both in deportment and scholastically.

I conducted myself so creditably that I was able to secure a much coveted internship in a western city, where I spent two years. During these two years I was kept so busy that I hardly left the hospital at all. Consequently, I could not get into any trouble.

When those two years were up, I opened an office downtown. Then I had some money, all the time in the world, and considerable stomach trouble. I soon discovered that a couple of drinks would alleviate my gastric distress, at least for a few hours at a time, so it was not at all difficult for me to return to my former excessive indulgence.

By this time I was beginning to pay very dearly physically and, in hope of relief, voluntarily incarcerated myself at least a dozen times in one of the local sanitariums. I was between Scylla and Charybdis now, because if I did not drink my stomach tortured me, and if I did, my nerves did the same thing. After three years of this, I wound up in the local hospital where they attempted to help me, but I would get my friends to smuggle me a quart, or I would steal the alcohol about the building, so that I got rapidly worse.

Finally my father had to send a doctor out from my home town who managed to get me back there some way and I was in bed about two months before I could venture out of the house. I stayed about town a couple of months more and returned to resume my practice. I think I must have been thoroughly scared by what had happened, or by the doctor, or probably both, so that I did not touch a drink again until the country went dry.

With the passing of the Eighteenth Amendment I felt quite safe. I knew everyone would buy a few bottles, or cases, of liquor as their exchequers permitted, and it would soon be gone. Therefore it would make no great difference, even if I should do some drinking. At that time I was not aware of the almost unlimited supply the government made it possible for us doctors to obtain, neither had I any knowledge of the bootlegger who soon appeared on the horizon. I drank with moderation at first, but it took me only a relatively short time to drift back into the old habits which had wound up so disastrously before.

During the next few years, I developed two distinct phobias. One was the fear of not sleeping, and the other was the fear of running out of liquor. Not being a man of means, I knew that if I did not stay sober enough to earn money, I would run out of liquor. Most of the time, therefore, I did not take the morning drink which I craved so badly, but instead would fill up on large doses of sedatives to quiet the jitters, which distressed me terribly. Occasionally, I would yield to the morning craving, but if I did, it would be only a few hours before I would be quite unfit for work. This would lessen my chances of smuggling some home that evening, which in turn would mean a night of futile tossing around in bed followed by a morning of unbearable jitters. During the subsequent fifteen years I had sense enough never to go to the hospital if I had been drinking, and very seldom did I receive patients. I would sometimes hide out in one of the clubs of which I was a member, and had the habit at times of registering at a hotel under a fictitious name. But my friends usually found me and I would go home if they promised that I should not be scolded.

If my wife were planning to go out in the afternoon, I would get a large supply of liquor and smuggle it home and hide it in the coal bin, the clothes chute, over door jambs, over beams in the cellar and in cracks in the cellar tile. I also made use of old trunks and chests, the old can container, and even the ash container. The water tank on the toilet I never used, because that looked too easy. I found out later that my wife inspected it frequently. I used to put eight or twelve ounce bottles of alcohol in a fur lined glove and toss it onto the back airing porch when winter days got dark enough. My bootlegger had hidden alcohol at the back steps where I could get it at my convenience. Sometimes I would bring it in my pockets, but they were inspected, and that became too risky. I used also to put it up in four ounce bottles and stick several in my stocking tops. This worked nicely until my wife and I went to see Wallace Beery in "Tugboat Annie," after which the pant-leg and stocking racket were out!

I will not take space to relate all my hospital or sanitarium experiences.

During all this time we became more or less ostracized by our friends. We could not be invited out because I would surely get tight and my wife dared not invite people in for the same reason. My phobia for sleeplessness demanded that I get drunk every night, but in order to get more liquor for the next night, I had to stay sober during the day, at least up to four o'clock. This routine went on with few interruptions for seventeen years. It was really a horrible nightmare, this earning money, getting liquor, smuggling it home, getting drunk, morning jitters, taking large doses of sedatives to make it possible for me to earn more money, and so on ad nauseam. I used to promise my wife, my friends, and my children that I would drink no more—promises which seldom kept me sober even through the day, though I was very sincere when I made them.

For the benefit of those experimentally inclined, I should mention the so-called beer experiment. When beer first came back, I thought that I was safe. I could drink all I wanted of that. It was harmless; nobody ever got drunk on beer. So I filled the cellar full, with the permission of my good wife. It was not long before I was drinking at least a case and a half a day. I put on thirty pounds weight in about two months, looked like a pig, and was uncomfortable from shortness of breath. It then occurred to me that after one was all smelled up with beer nobody could tell what had been drunk, so I began to fortify my beer with straight alcohol. Of course, the result was very bad, and that ended the beer experiment.

About the time of the beer experiment I was thrown in with a crowd of people who attracted me because of their seeming poise, health, and happiness. They spoke with great freedom from embarrassment, which I could never do, and they seemed very much at ease on all occasions and appeared very healthy. More than these attributes, they seemed to be happy. I was self conscious and ill at ease most of the time, my health was at the breaking point, and I was thoroughly miserable. I sensed they had something I did not have, from which I might readily profit. I learned that it was something of a spiritual nature, which did not appeal to me very much, but I thought it could do no harm. I gave the matter much time and study for the next two and a half years, but still got tight every night nevertheless. I read everything I could find, and talked to everyone who I thought knew anything about it.

My good wife became deeply interested and it was her interest that sustained mine, though I at no time sensed that it might be an answer to my liquor problem. How my wife kept her faith and courage during all those years, I'll never know, but she did. If she had not, I know I would have been dead a long time ago. For some reason, we alcoholics seem to have the gift of picking out the world's finest women. Why they should be subjected to the tortures we inflicted upon them, I cannot explain.

About this time a lady called up my wife one Saturday afternoon, saying she wanted me to come over that evening to meet a friend of hers who might help me. It was the day before Mother's Day and I had come home plastered, carrying a big potted plant which I set down on the table and forthwith went upstairs and passed out. The next day she called again. Wishing to be polite, though I felt very badly, I said, "Let's make the call," and extracted from my wife a promise that we would not stay over fifteen minutes.

We entered her house at exactly five o'clock and it was eleven fifteen when we left. I had a couple of shorter talks with this man afterward, and stopped drinking abruptly. This dry spell lasted for about three weeks; Then I went to Atlantic City to attend several days' meeting of a National Society of which I was a member. I drank all the Scotch they had on the train and bought several quarts on my way to the hotel. This was on Sunday. I got tight that night, stayed sober Monday till after the dinner and then proceeded to get tight again. I drank all I dared in the bar, and then went to my room to finish the job. Tuesday I started in the morning, getting well organized by noon. I did not want to disgrace myself, so I then checked out. I bought some more liquor on the way to the depot. I had to wait some time for the train. I remember nothing from then on until I woke up at a friend's house, in a town near home. These good people notified my wife, who sent my newly-made friend over to get me. He came and got me home and to bed, gave me a few drinks that night, and one bottle of beer the next morning.

That was June 10, 1935, and that was my last drink. As I write nearly four years have passed.

The question which might naturally come into your mind would be: "what did the man do or say that was different from what others had done or said?" It must be remembered that I had read a great deal and talked to everyone who knew, or thought they knew, anything about the subject of alcoholism. This man was a man who had experienced many years of frightful drinking, who had had most all the drunkard's experience known to man, but who had been cured by the very means I had been trying to employ, that is to say, the spiritual approach. He gave me information about the subject of alcoholism which was undoubtedly helpful. *Of far more importance was the fact that he was the first living human with whom I had ever talked, who knew what he was talking about in regard to alcoholism from actual experience. In other words, he talked my language.* He knew all the answers, and certainly not because he had picked them up in his reading.

It is a most wonderful blessing to be relieved of the terrible curse with which I was afflicted. My health is good and I have regained my self-respect and the respect of my colleagues. My home life is ideal and my business is as good as can be expected in these uncertain times.

I spend a great deal of time passing on what I learned to others who want and need it badly. I do it for four reasons:

1. Sense of duty.
2. It is a pleasure.
3. Because in so doing I am paying my debt to the man who took time to pass it on to me.
4. Because every time I do it I take out a little more insurance for myself against a possible slip.

Unlike most of our crowd, I did not get over my craving for liquor much during the first two and one-half years of abstinence. It was almost always with me. But at no time have I been anywhere near yielding. I used to get terribly upset when I saw my friends drink and knew I could not, but I schooled myself to believe that though I once had the same privilege, I had abused it so frightfully that it was withdrawn. So it doesn't behoove me to squawk about it, for after all, nobody ever used to throw me down and pour any liquor down my throat.

If you think you are an atheist, an agnostic, a skeptic, or have any other form of intellectual pride which keeps you from accepting what is in this book, I feel sorry for you. If you still think you are strong enough to beat the game alone, that is your affair. But if you really and truly want to quit drinking liquor for good and all, and sincerely feel that you must have some help, we know that we have an answer for you. It never fails if you go about it with one half the zeal you have been in the habit of showing when getting another drink.

Your Heavenly Father will never let you down!

# The Unbeliever

Dull . . . listless . . . semicomatose . . . I lay on my bed in a famous hospital for alcoholics. Death or worse had been my sentence.

What was the difference? What difference did anything make? Why think of those things which were gone—why worry about the results of my drunken escapades? What the hell were the odds if my wife had discovered the mistress situation? Two swell boys . . . sure . . . but what difference would a corpse or an asylum imprisoned father make to them? . . . thoughts stop whirling in my head . . . that's the worst of this sobering-up process . . . the old think tank is geared in high-high . . . what do I mean high-high . . . where did that come from . . . oh yes, that first Cadillac I had, it had four speeds . . . had a high-high gear . . . insane asylum . . . how that bus could scamper . . . yes . . . even then liquor probably poisoned me. What had the little doctor said this morning . . . thoughts hesitate a moment . . . stop your mad turning . . . what was I thinking about . . . oh yes, the doctor.

This morning I reminded Doc this was my tenth visit. I had spent a couple of thousand dollars on these trips and those I had financed for the plastered play girls who also couldn't sober up. Jackie was a honey until she got plastered and then she was a hellion. Wonder what gutter she's in now. Where was I? Oh . . . I asked the doctor to tell me the truth. He owed it to me for the amount of money I had spent. He faltered. Said I'd been drunk that's all. God! Didn't I know that?

But Doc, you're evading. Tell me honestly what is the matter with me. I'll be all right did you say? But Doc, you've said that before. You said once that if I stopped for a year I would be over the habit and would never drink again. I didn't drink for over a year, but I did start to drink again.

Tell me what is the matter with me. I'm an alcoholic? Ha ha and ho ho! As if I didn't know that! But aside from your fancy name for a plain drunk, tell me why I drink. You say a true alcoholic is something different from a plain drunk? What do you mean . . . let me have it cold . . . brief and with no trimmings.

An alcoholic is a person who has an allergy to alcohol? Is poisoned by it? One drink does something to the chemical make-up of the body? That drink effects the nerves and in a certain number of hours another drink is medically demanded? And so the vicious cycle is started? An ever smaller amount of time between drinks to stop those screaming, twitching, invisible wires called nerves?

I know that history Doc . . . how the spiral tightens . . . a drink . . . unconscious . . . awake . . . drink . . . unconscious . . . poured into the hospital . . . suffer the agonies of hell . . . the shakes . . . thoughts running wild . . . brain unleashed . . . engine without a governor. But hell Doc, I don't want to drink! I've got one of the stubbornest will powers known in business. I stick at things. I get them done. I've stuck on the wagon for months. And not been bothered by it . . . and then suddenly, incomprehensibly, an empty glass in my hand and another spiral started. How did the Doc explain that one?

He couldn't. That was one of the mysteries of true alcoholism. A famous medical foundation had spent a fortune trying to segregate the reasons for the alcoholic as compared to the plain hard, heavy drinker. Had tried to find the cause. And all they had been able to determine as a fact was that the majority of the alcohol in every drink taken by the alcoholic went to the fluid in which the brain floated. Why a man ever started when he knew those things was one of the things that could not be fathomed. Only the damn fool public believed it a matter of weak will power. Fear . . . ostracism . . . loss of family . . . loss of position . . . the gutter . . . nothing stopped the alcoholic.

Doc! What do you mean—nothing! What! An incurable disease? Doc, you're kidding me! You're trying to scare me into stopping! What's that you say? You wish you were? What are those tears in your eyes Doc? What's that? Forty years you've spent at this alcoholic business and you have yet to see a true alcoholic cured? Your life defeated and wasted? Oh, come, come Doc . . . what would some of us do without you? If even to only sober up. But Doc . . . let's have it. What is going to be my history from here on out? Some vital organ will stop or the mad house with a wet brain? How soon? Within two years? But, Doc, I've got to do something about it! I'll see doctors . . . I'll go to sanitariums. Surely the medical profession knows something about it. So little, you say? But why? Messy. Yes, I'll admit there is nothing messier than an alcoholic drunk.

What's that Doc? You know a couple of fellows that were steady customers here that haven't been drunk for about ten months? You say they claim they are cured? And they make an avocation of passing it on to others? What have they got? You don't know . . . and you don't believe they are cured . . . well why tell me about it? A fine fellow you say, plenty of money, and you're sure it isn't a racket . . . just wants to be helpful . . . call him up for me will you, Doc?

How Doc had hated to tell me. Thoughts stop knocking at my door. Why can't I get drunk like other people, get up next morning, toss my head a couple of times and go to work? Why do I have to shake so I can't hold the razor? Why does every little muscle inside me have to feel like a crawling worm? Why do even my vocal cords quiver so words are gibberish until I've had a big drink? Poison! Of course! But how could anyone understand such a necessity for a drink that it has to be loaded with pepper to keep it from bouncing? Can any mortal understand such secret shame in having to have a drink as to make a person keep the bottles hidden all over the house. The morning drink . . . shame and necessity . . . weakness . . . remorse. But what do the family know about it? What do doctors know about it? Little Doc was right, they know nothing. They just say "Be strong"—"Don't take that drink"—"Suffer it through."

What the hell do they know about suffering? Not sickness. Not a belly ache—oh yes, your guts get so sore that you cannot place your hands on them . . . oh sure, every time you go you twist and writhe in pain. What the hell does any non-alcoholic know about suffering? Thoughts . . . stop this mad merry-go-round. And worst of all this mental suffering—the hating yourself—the feeling of absurd, irrational weakness—the unworthiness. Out that window! Use the gun in the drawer! What about poison? Go out in a garage and start the car. Yeah, that's the way out . . . but then people'll say "He was plastered." I can't leave that story behind. That's worse than cowardly.

Isn't there some one who understands? Thoughts . . . please, oh please, stop . . . I'm going nuts . . . or am I nuts now? Never . . . never again will I take another drink, not even a glass of beer . . . even that starts it. Never . . . never . . . never again . . . and yet I've said that a dozen times and inexplicably I've found an empty glass in my hand and the whole story repeated.

My Lord, the tragedy that sprang out of her eyes when I came home with a breath on me . . . and fear. The smiles wiped off the kids' faces. Terror stalking through the house. Yes . . . that changed it from a home into a house. Not drunk yet, but they knew what was coming. Mr. Hyde was moving in.

And so I'm going to die. Or a wet brain. What was it that fellow said who was here this afternoon? Damn fool thought . . . get out of my mind. Now I know I'm going nuts. And science knows nothing about it. And psychiatrists. I've spent plenty on them. Thoughts, go away! No . . . I don't want to think about what that fellow said this afternoon.

He's trying . . . idealistic as hell . . . nice fellow, too. Oh, why do I have to suffer with this revolving brain? Why can't I sleep? What was it he said? Oh yes, came in and told about his terrific drunks, his trips up here, this same thing I'm going through. Yes, he's an alcoholic all right. And then he told me he knew he was cured. Told me he was peaceful . . . (I'll never know peace again) . . . that he didn't carry constant fear around with him. Happy because he felt free. But it's screwy. He said so himself. But he did get my confidence when he started to tell what he had gone through. It was so exactly like my case. He knows what this torture is. He raised my hopes so high; it looked as though he had something. I don't know, I guess I was so sold that I expected him to spring some kind of a pill and I asked him desperately what it was.

And he said "God."

And I laughed.

A ball bat across my face would have been no greater shock. I was so high with hope and expectation. How can a man be so heartless? He said that it sounded screwy but it worked, at least it had with him . . . said he was not a religionist . . . in fact didn't go to church much . . . my ears came up at that . . . his unconventionality attracted me . . . said that some approaches to religion were screwy . . . talked about how the simplest truth in the world had been often all balled up by complicating it . . . that attracted me . . . get out of my mind . . . what a fine religious bird I'd be . . . imagine the glee of the gang at me getting religion . . . phooey . . . thoughts, please slow down . . . why don't they give me something to go to sleep . . . lie down in green pastures . . . the guy's nuts . . . forget him.

And so it's the mad house for me . . . glad mother is dead, she won't have to suffer that . . . if I'm going nuts maybe it'd be better to be crazy the way he is . . . at least the kids wouldn't have the insane father whisper to carry through life . . . life's cruel . . . the puny-minded, curtain hiding gossips . . . "didn't you know his father was committed for insanity?" What a sly label that would be to hang on those boys . . . damn the gossiping, reputation-shredding, busybodies who put their noses into other people's business.

He'd laid in this same dump . . . suffered . . . gone through hell . . . made up his mind to get well . . . studied alcoholism . . . Jung . . . Blank Medical Foundation . . . asylums . . . Hopkins . . . many said incurable disease . . . impossible . . . nearly all known cures had been through religion . . . revolted him . . . made a study of religion . . . more he studied the more it was bunk to him . . . not understandable . . . self-hypnotism . . . and then the thought hit him that people had it all twisted up. They were trying to pour everyone into moulds, put a tag on them, tell them what they had to do and how they had to do it, for the salvation of their own souls. When as a matter of fact people were through worrying about their souls, they wanted action right here and now. A lot of tripe was usually built up around the simplest and most beautiful ideas in the world.

And how did he put the idea . . . bunk . . . bunk . . . why in hell am I still thinking about him . . . in hell . . . that's good . . . I am in hell. He said: "I came to the conclusion that there is SOMETHING. I know not what It is, but It is bigger than I. If I will acknowledge It, if I will humble myself, if I will give in and bow in submission to that SOMETHING and then try to lead a life as fully in accord with my idea of good as possible, I will be in tune." And later the word good contracted in his mind to God.

But mister, I can't see any guy with long white whiskers up there just waiting for me to make a plea . . . and what did he answer . . . said I was trying to complicate it . . . why did I insist on making It human . . . all I had to do was believe in some power greater than myself and knuckle down to It . . . and I said maybe, but tell me mister why are you wasting your time up here? Don't hand me any bunk about it being more blessed to give than to receive . . . asked him what this thing cost and he laughed. He said it wasn't a waste of time . . . in doping it out he had thought of something somebody had said. A person never knew a lesson until he tried to pass it on to someone else. And that he had found out every time he tried to pass this on

It became more vivid to him. So if we wanted to get hard boiled about it, he owed me, I didn't owe him. That's a new slant . . . the guy's crazy as a loon . . . get away from him brain . . . picture me going around telling other people how to run their lives . . . if I could only go to sleep . . . that sedative doesn't seem to take hold.

He could visualize a great fellowship of us . . . quietly passing this from alcoholic to alcoholic . . . nothing organized . . . not ministers . . . not missionaries . . . what a story . . . thought we'd have to do it to get well . . . some kind of a miracle had happened in his life . . . common sense guy at that . . . his plan does fire the imagination.

Told him it sounded like self hypnotism to me and he said what of it . . . didn't care if it was yogi-sim, self-hypnotism, or anything else . . . four of them were well. But it's so damn hypocritical . . . I get beat every other way and then I turn around and lay it in God's lap . . . damned if I ever would turn to God . . . what a low-down, cowardly, despicable trick that would be . . . don't believe in God anyway . . . just a lot of hooey to keep the masses in subjugation . . . world's worst inquisitions have been practiced in His name . . . and he said . . . do I have to turn into an inquisitionist . . . if I don't knuckle down, I die . . . why the low-down missionary . . . what a bastardly screw to put on a person . . . a witch burner, that's what he is . . . the hell with him and all his damn theories . . . witch burner.

Sleep, please come to my door . . . that last was the eight hundred and eighty-fifth sheep over the fence . . . guess I'll put in some black ones . . . sheep . . . shepherds . . . wise men . . . what was that story . . . hell there I go back on that same line . . . told him I couldn't understand and I couldn't believe anything I couldn't understand. He said he supposed then that I didn't use electricity. No one actually understood where it came from or what it was. Nuts to him. He's got too many answers. What did he think the nub of the whole thing was? Subjugate self to some power above . . . ask for help . . . mean it . . . try to pass it on. Asked him what he was going to name this? Said it would be fatal to give it any kind of a tag . . . to have any sort of formality.

I'm going nuts . . . tried to get him into an argument about miracles . . . about Immaculate Conception . . . about stars leading three wise men . . . Jonah and the whale. He wanted to know what difference those things made . . . he didn't even bother his head about them . . . if he did, he would get tight again. So I asked him what he thought about the Bible. Said he read it, and used those things he understood. He didn't take the Bible literally as an instruction book, for there was no nonsense you could not make out of it that way.

Thought I had him when I asked about the past sins I had committed. Guess I've done everything in the book . . . I supposed I would have to adopt the attitude that all was forgiven . . . here I am pure and clean as the driven snow . . . or else I was to go through life flogging myself mentally . . . bah. But he had the answer for that one too. Said he couldn't call back the hellish things he had done, but he figured life might be a ledger page. If he did a little good here and there, maybe the score would be evened up some day. On the other hand, if he continued as he had been going there would be nothing but debit items on the sheet. Kind of common sense.

This is ridiculous . . . have I lost all power of logic . . . would I fall for all that religious line . . . let's see if I can't get to thinking straight . . . that's it . . . I'm trying to do too much thinking . . . just calm myself . . . quietly . . . quiet now . . . relax every muscle . . . start at the toes and move up . . . insane . . . wet brain . . . those boys . . . what a mess my life is . . . mistress . . . how I hate her . . . ah . . . I know what's the matter . . . that fellow gave me an emotional upset . . . I'll list every reason I couldn't accept his way of thinking. After laughing at this religious stuff all these years I'd be a hypocrite. That's one. Second, if there was a God, why all this suffering? Wait a minute, he said that was one of the troubles, we tried to give God some form. Make It just a Power that will help. Third, it sounds like the Salvation Army. Told him that and he said he was not going around singing on any street corners but nevertheless the Salvation Army did a great work. Simply, if he heard of a guy suffering the torments, he told him his story and belief.

There I go thinking again . . . just started to get calmed down . . . sleep . . . boys . . . insane . . . death . . . mistress . . . life all messed up . . . business. Now listen, take hold . . . what am I going to do? NEVER . . . that's final and in caps. Never . . . that's net no discount. Never . . . never . . . and my mind is made up. NEVER am I going to be such a cowardly low down dog as to acknowledge God. The two faced, gossiping Babbitts can go around with their sanctimonious mouthings, their miserable worshipping, their Bible quotations, their holier-than-thou attitudes, their nicey-nice, Sunday-worshipping, Monday-robbing actions, but never will they find me acknowledging God. Let me laugh . . . I'd like to shriek with insane glee . . . my mind's made up . . . insane, there it is again.

Brrr, this floor is cold on my knees . . . why are the tears running like a river down my cheeks . . . God, have mercy on my soul!

# The European Drinker

I was born in Europe, in Alsace to be exact, shortly after it had become German and practically grew up with "good Rhine wine" of song and story. My parents had some vague ideas of making a priest out of me and for some years I attended the Franciscan school at Basle, Switzerland, just across the border, about six miles from my home. But, although I was a good Catholic, the monastic life had little appeal for me.

Very early I became apprenticed to harness-making and acquired considerable knowledge of upholstering. My daily consumption of wine was about a quart, but that was common where I lived. Everybody drank wine. And it is true that there was no great amount of drunkenness. But I can remember, in my teens, that there were a few characters who caused the village heads to nod pityingly and sometimes in anger as they paused to say, "That sot, Henri" and "Ce pauvre Jules," who drank too much. They were undoubtedly the alcoholics of our village.

Military service was compulsory and I did my stretch with the class of my age, goose-stepping in German barracks and taking part in the Boxer Rebellion in China, my first time at any great distance from home. In foreign parts many a soldier who has been abstemious at home learns to use new and potent drinks. So I indulged with my comrades in everything the Far East had to offer. I cannot say, however, that I acquired any craving for hard liquor as a result. When I got back to Germany I settled down to finish my apprenticeship, drinking the wine of the country as usual.

Many friends of my family had emigrated to America, so at 24 I decided that the United States offered me the opportunity I was never likely to find in my native land. I came directly to a growing industrial city in the middle west, where I have lived practically ever since. I was warmly welcomed by friends of my youth who had preceded me. For weeks after my arrival I was feted and entertained in the already large colony of Alsatians in the city, among the Germans in their saloons and clubs. I early decided that the wine of America was very inferior stuff and took up beer instead.

I soon found work at my trade in harness-making. It was still an age of horses. But I discovered that harness and saddle-making in America was different than anything I had known. Every man in the shop was a specialist and instead of having a variety of jobs to do every day, I was compelled to sit all day long at a bench doing the same thing endlessly. I found it very monotonous and, wanting a change, I found it when I got work as an upholsterer in a large furniture store.

Fond of singing, I joined a German singing society which had good club headquarters. There I sat in the evenings, enjoying with my friends our memories of the "old country," singing the old songs we all knew, playing simple card games for drinks and consuming great quantities of beer.

At that time I could go into any saloon, have one or two beers, walk out and forget about it. I had no desire whatever to sit down at a table and stay a whole morning or afternoon drinking. Certainly at that time I was one of those who "can take it or leave it alone." There had never been any drunkards in my family. I came of good stock, of men and women who drank wine all their lives as a beverage, and while they occasionally got drunk at special celebrations, they were up and about their business the next day.

Prohibition came. Having regard for the law of the land, I resigned myself to the will of the national legislators and quit drinking altogether, not because I had found it harmful, but because I couldn't get what I was accustomed to drink. You can all remember that in the first few months after the change, a great many men, who had formerly been used to a few beers every day or an occasional drink of whiskey, simply quit all alcoholic drinks. For the great majority of us, however, that condition didn't last. We saw very early that prohibition wasn't going to work. It wasn't very long before home-brewing was an institution and men began to search ferverishly for old recipe books on winemaking.

But I hardly tasted anything for two years and started in business for myself, founding a mattress factory which is today an important industrial enterprise in our city. I was doing very well with that and general upholstering work, and there was every indication that I would be financially independent by the time I reached middle age. By this time I was married and was paying for a home. Like most immigrants I wanted to be somebody and have something and I was very happy and contented as I felt success crown my efforts. I missed the old social times, of course, but had no definite craving even for beer.

Successful home-brewers among my friends began to invite me to their homes. I decided that if these fellows could make it I would try it myself and so I did. It wasn't very long until I had developed a pretty good brew with uniformity and plenty of authority. I knew the stuff I was making was a lot stronger than I had been used to, but never suspected that steady drinking of it might develop a taste for something even stronger.

It wasn't long before the bootlegger was an established institution in this, as in other towns. I was doing well in business and in going around town I was frequently invited to have a drink in a speakeasy. I condoned my domestic brewing and the bootleggers and their business. More and more I formed the habit of doing some of my business in the speakeasy and after a time did not need that as an excuse. The "speaks" usually sold whiskey. Beer was too bulky and it couldn't be kept in a jug under the counter ready to be dumped when John Law would come around. I was now forming an entirely new drinking technique. Before long I had a definite taste for hard liquor, knew nausea and headaches I had never known before, but as in the old days, I suffered them out. Gradually, however, I'd suffer so much that I simply had to have the morning-after drink.

I became what is called a periodical drinker. I was eased out of the business I had founded and was reduced to doing general upholstery in a small shop at the back of my house. My wife upbraided me often and plenty when she saw that my "periodicals" were gradually losing me what business I could get. I began to bring bottles in. I had them hidden away in the house and all over my shop in careful concealment. I had all the usual experiences of the alcoholic for I was certainly one by this time. Sometimes, after sobering up after a bout of several weeks, I would righteously resolve to quit. With a great deal of determination, I would throw out full pints—pour them out and smash the bottles—firmly resolved never to take another drink of the stuff. I was going to straighten up.

In four or five days I would be hunting all over the place, at home and in my workshop for the bottles I had destroyed, cursing myself for being a damned fool. My "periodicals" became more frequent until I reached the point where I wanted to devote all my time to drinking, working as little as possible and then only when the necessity of my family demanded it. As soon as I had satisfied that, what I earned as an upholsterer went for liquor. I would promise to have jobs done and never do them. My customers lost confidence in me to the point where I retained what business I had only because I was a well-trained and reputedly fine craftsman. "Best in the business, when he's sober," my customers would say and I still had a following who would give me work though they deplored my habits because they knew the job would be well done when they eventually got it.

I had always been a good Catholic, possibly not so devoted as I should have been, but fairly regular in my attendance at services. I had never doubted the existence of the Supreme Being but now I began to absent myself from my church where I had formerly been a member of the choir. Unfortunately, I had no desire to consult my priest about my drinking. In fact I was scared to talk to him about it, for I feared the kind of talk he would give me. Unlike many other Catholics who frequently take pledges for definite periods—a year, two years or for good, I never had any desire to "take a pledge" before the priest. And yet, realizing at last that liquor really had me, I wanted to quit. My wife wrote away for advertised cures for the liquor habit and gave them to me in coffee. I even got them myself and tried them. None of the various cures of this kind were any good.

My experiences differ very little from the experiences of other alcoholics but if ever a man was firmly in the grip of a power that could lead only to ruin and disgrace, I was that man.

I had the usual array of friends who tried to stop me in my drinking career. I can hear them yet. Kindly for the most part, yet blind and almost wholly without understanding, they had the approach that every alcoholic knows:

"Can't you be a man?"

"You can cut it out."

"You've got a good wife; you could have the best business in town. What's the matter with you anyway?"

Every alcoholic has heard those familiar phrases from well-meaning friends. And they were my friends, too. In their way they did what they could, helped me at different times to get on my feet after a particularly bad time, aided me in unraveling my tangled business affairs, suggested this and suggested that. They all wanted to help me. But none of them knew how. Not one of them had the answer I wanted.

My wife got talking to a local merchant one day. He was known as a deeply religious man. He was undoubtedly a fundamentalist with strong leanings toward evangelistic preaching. He knew me and something of my reputation. My wife asked him to help her if he could. So he came to see me, bringing a friend along. He found me drunk and in bed. This man had never been an alcoholic and his approach to me was the familiar one of the emotional seeker after souls. Well, there I was, lying in an alcoholic stupor with occasional flashes of emotional self-pity, in pretty much the same condition as the drunk who plunges to the sawdust at the appeal of a religious orator.

Good, honest and sincere man, he prayed at my bedside and I promised to go to church with him to hear an evangelist. He didn't wait for me to come to his office, he came after me. I heard the evangelist but was not impressed. The service was entirely foreign to what I had been accustomed to in my religious observance since childhood. I have no doubt of the preacher's sincerity and seek not at all to belittle his work, but I was unaffected. So I got no answer.

There are alcoholics who have been without any consciousness of God all their lives; there are some who are actual haters of the idea of a Supreme Being; there are others, like myself, who have never given up a belief in the Almighty, but who have always felt that God is far off. And that's the way I felt. I had a closer sense of God during the mass at church, a feeling of His presence, but in everyday life He seemed to be at a distance from me and more as a righteous judge, than an all-wise, pitying Father to the human race.

Then occurred the event that saved me. An alcoholic came to see me who is a doctor. He didn't talk like a preacher at all. In fact his language was perfectly suited to my understanding. He had no desire to know anything except whether I was definite about my desire to quit drinking. I told him with all the sincerity at my command that I did. Even then he went into no great detail about how he and a crowd of alcoholics, with whom he associated, had mastered their difficulty. Instead he told me that some of them wanted to talk to me and would be over to see me.

This doctor had imparted his knowledge to just a few other men at that time—not more than four or five—they now number more than seventy persons. And, because as I have discovered since, it is part of the "treatment" that these men be sent to see and talk with alcoholics who want to quit, he kept them busy. He had already imbued them with his own spirit until they were ready and willing at all times to go where sent, and as a doctor he well knew that this mission and duty would strengthen them as it later helped me. The visits from these men impressed me at once. Where preaching and prayers had touched me very little, I was immediately impressed with desire for further knowledge of these men.

"There must be something to it," I said to myself. "Why would these busy men take the time to come to see me? They understand my problem. Like me, they've tried this remedy and that remedy but never found one that worked. But whatever it is they are using now, it seems to keep them sober."

Certainly I could see they were sober. The third man who came to see me had been one of the greatest business-getters his company had ever employed. From the top of the heap in a few years he had skidded to becoming a shuffling customer, still entering the better barrooms but welcomed by neither mine host nor his patrons. His own business was practically gone, he told me, when he discovered the answer.

"You've been trying man's ways and they always fail," he told me. "You can't win unless you try God's way."

I had never heard of the remedy expressed in just this language. In a few sentences he made God seem personal to me, explained Him as a being who was interested in me, the alcoholic, and that all I needed to do was to be willing to follow His way for me; that as long as I followed it I would be able to overcome my desire for liquor.

Well, there I was, willing to try it, but I didn't know how, except in a vague way. I knew somehow that it meant more than just going to church and living a moral life. If that was all, then I was a little doubtful that it was the answer I was looking for.

He went on talking and told me that he had found the plan has a basis of love and the practice of Christ's injunction, "Love thy neighbor as thyself." Taking that as a foundation, he reasoned that if a man followed that rule he could not be selfish. I could see that. And he further said that God could not accept me as a sincere follower of His Divine Law unless I was ready to be thoroughly honest about it.

That was perfectly logical. My church taught that. I had always known that in theory. We talked, too, about personal morals. Every man has his problem of this kind but we didn't discuss it very much. My visitor well knew, that as I tried to follow God I would get to studying these things out for myself.

We talked things over a long time. I saw readily that I couldn't afford to quibble. I already believed in God, had always done so. Was ready to give my will to Him. That's what it came to.

That day I gave my will to God and asked to be directed. But I have never thought of that as something to do and then forget about. I very early came to see that there had to be a continual renewal of that simple deal with God; that I had perpetually to keep the bargain. So I began to pray; to place my problems in God's hands.

For a long time I kept on trying, in a pretty dumb way at first, I know, but very earnestly. I didn't want to be a fake. And I began putting in practice what I was learning every day. It wasn't very long until my doctor friend sent me to tell another alcoholic what my experience had been. This duty together with my weekly meetings with my fellow alcoholics and my daily renewal of the contract I originally made with God have kept me sober when nothing else ever did.

I have been sober for three years now. The first few months were hard. Many things happened; business trials, little worries, and feelings of general despondency came near driving me to the bottle, but I made progress. As I go along I seem to get strength daily to be able to resist more easily. And when I get upset, cross-grained and out of tune with my fellow man I know that I am out of tune with God. Searching where I have been at fault, it is not hard to discover and get right again, for I have proven to myself and to many others who know me that God can keep a man sober if he will let Him.

Being a Catholic, it is natural that I should attend my own church which I do regularly. I partake of its sacraments which have a new and deeper meaning to me now. I realize what it is to be in the presence of God right in my own home and I realize it deeply when I am at church. For when a man is truly trying to do God's will, instead of his own, he is very conscious of being in the presence of God always, wherever he may be.

# A Feminine Victory

To my lot falls the rather doubtful distinction of being the only "lady" alcoholic in our particular section. Perhaps it is because of a desire for a "supporting cast" of my own sex that I am praying for inspiration to tell my story in a manner that may give other women who have this problem the courage to see it in its true light and seek the help that has given me a new lease on life.

When the idea was first presented to me that *I was an alcoholic*, my mind simply refused to accept it. Horrors! How disgraceful! What humiliation! How preposterous! Why, I loathed the taste of liquor—drinking was simply a means of escape when my sorrows became too great for me to endure. Even after it had been explained to me that alcoholism is a disease, I could not realize that I had it. I was still ashamed, still wanted to hide behind the screen of reasons made up of "unjust treatment," "unhappiness," "tired and dejected," and the dozens of other things that I thought lay at the root of my search for oblivion by means of whiskey or gin.

In any case, I felt quite sure that I was *not* an alcoholic. However, since I have faced the fact, and it surely is a fact, I have been able to use the help that is so freely given when we learn how to be really truthful with ourselves.

The path by which I have come to this blessed help was long and devious. It led through the mazes and perplexities of an unhappy marriage and divorce, and a dark time of separation from my grown children, and a readjustment of life at an age when most women feel pretty sure of a home and security.

But I *have* reached the source of help. I *have* learned to recognize and acknowledge the underlying cause of my disease; selfishness, self-pity and resentment. A few short months ago those three words applied to *me* would have aroused as much indignation in my heart as the word alcoholic. The ability to accept them as my own has been derived from trying, with the un-ending help of God, to live with certain goals in mind.

Coming to the grim fact of alcoholism, I wish I could present the awful reality of its insidiousness in such a way that no one could ever again fail to recognize the comfortable, easy steps that lead down to the edge of the precipice, and show how those steps suddenly disappeared when the great gulf yawned before me. I couldn't possibly turn and get back to solid earth again that way.

The first step is called—"The first drink in the morning to pull you out of a hangover."

I remember so well when I got onto that step—I had been drinking just like most of the young married crowd I knew. For a couple of years it went on, at parties and at "speakeasies," as they were then called, and with cocktails after matinees. Just going the rounds and having a good time.

Then came the morning when I had my first case of jitters. Someone suggested a little of the "hair of the dog that bit me." A half hour after that drink I was sitting on top of the world, thinking how simple it was to cure shaky nerves. How wonderful liquor was, in only a few minutes my head had stopped aching, my spirits were back to normal and all was well in this very fine world.

Unfortunately, there was a catch to it—I was an alcoholic. As time went on the one drink in the morning had to be taken a little earlier—it had to be followed by a second one in an hour or so, before I really felt equal to getting on with the business of living.

Gradually I found at parties the service was a little slow; the rest of the crowd being pretty happy and carefree after the second round. My reaction was inclined to be just the opposite. Something had to be done about that so I'd just help myself to a fast one, sometimes openly, but as time went on and my need became more acute, I often did it on the quiet.

In the meantime, the morning-after treatment was developing into something quite stupendous. The eye-openers were becoming earlier, bigger, more frequent, and suddenly, it was lunch time! Perhaps there was a plan for the afternoon—a bridge or tea, or just callers. My breath had to be accounted for, so along came such alibis as a touch of grippe or some other ailment for which I'd just taken a hot whiskey and lemon. Or "someone" had been in for lunch and we had just had a couple of cocktails. Then came the period of brazening it out—going to social gatherings well fortified against the jitters; next the phone call in the morning—"Terribly sorry that I can't make it this afternoon, I have an awful headache"; then simply forgetting that there were engagements at all; spending two or three days drinking, sleeping it off, and waking to start all over again.

Of course, I had the well known excuses; my husband was failing to come home for dinner or hadn't been home for several days; he was spending money which was needed to pay bills; he had always been a drinker; I had never known anything about it until I was almost thirty years old and he gave me my first drink. Oh, I had them all down, letter perfect—all the excuses, reasons and justifications. What I did not know was that I was being destroyed by selfishness, self-pity and resentment.

There were the swearing-off periods and the "goings on the wagon"—they would last anywhere from two weeks to three or four months. Once, after a very severe illness of six weeks' duration (caused by drinking), I didn't touch anything of an alcoholic nature for almost a year. I thought I had it licked that time, but all of a sudden things were worse than ever. I found fear had no effect.

Next came the hospitalization, not a regular sanitarium, but a local hospital where my doctor would ship me when I'd get where I had to call him in. That poor man—I wish he could read this for he would know then it was no fault of his I wasn't cured.

When I was divorced, I thought the cause had been removed. I felt that being away from what I had considered injustice and ill-treatment would solve the problem of my unhappiness. In a little over a year I was in the alcoholic ward of a public hospital!

It was there that L—— came to me. I had known her very slightly ten years before. My ex-husband brought her to me hoping that she could help. She did. From the hospital I went home with her.

There, her husband told me the secret of his rebirth. It is not really a secret at all, but something free and open to all of us. He asked me if I believed in God or some power greater than myself. Well, I did believe in God, but at that time I hadn't any idea what He is. As a child I had been taught my "Now I lay me's" and "Our Father which art in Heaven." I had been sent to Sunday School and taken to church. I had been baptized and confirmed. I had been taught to realize there is a God and to "love" him. *But though I had been taught all these things, I had never learned them.*

When B—— (L's husband) began to talk about God, I felt pretty low in my mind. I thought God was something that I, and lots of other people like me, had to worry along without. Yet I had always had the "prayer habit." In fact I used to say in my mind "Now, if God answers this prayer, I'll know there *is* a God." It was a great system, only somehow it didn't seem to work!

Finally B—— put it to me this way: "You admit you've made a mess of things trying to run them your way, are you willing to give up? Are you willing to say: "Here it is God, all mixed up. I don't know how to un-mix it, I'll leave it to you." Well, I couldn't quite do that. I wasn't feeling very well, and I was afraid that later when the fog wore off, I'd want to back out. So we let it rest a few days. L and B sent me to stay with some friends of theirs out of town—I'd never seen them before. The man of that house, P—— had given up drinking three months before. After I had been there a few days, I saw that P—— and his wife had something that made them mighty hopeful and happy. But I got a little uneasy going into a perfect stranger's home and staying day after day. I said this to P—— and his reply was: "Why, you don't know how much it is helping me to have you here." Was that a surprise! Always before that when I was recovering from a tailspin I'd been just a pain in the neck to everyone. So, I began to sense in a small way just what these spiritual principles were all about.

Finally I very self-consciously and briefly asked God to show me how to do what He wanted me to do. My prayer was just about as weak and helpless a thing as one could imagine, but it taught me how to open my mouth and pray earnestly and sincerely. However, I had not quite made the grade. I was full of fears, shames, and other "bug-a-boos" and two weeks later an incident occurred that put me on the toboggan again. I seemed to feel that the hurt of that incident was too great to endure without some "release." So I forsook Spirit in favor of "spirits" and that evening I was well on the way to a long session with my old enemy "liquor." I begged the person in whose home I was living not to let anyone know, but she, having good sense, got in touch right away with those who had helped me before and very shortly they had rallied round.

I was eased out of the mess and in a day or two I had a long talk with one of the crowd. I dragged out all my sins of commission and ommission, I told everything I could think of that might be the cause of creating a fear situation, a remorse situation, or a shame situation. It was pretty terrible, I thought then, to lay myself bare that way, but I know now that such is the first step away from the edge of the precipice.

Things went very well for quite a while, then came a dull rainy day. I was alone. The weather and my self-pity began to cook up a nice dish of the blues for me. There was liquor in the house and I found myself suggesting to myself "Just one drink will make me feel so much more cheerful." Well, I got the Bible and "Victorious Living" and sitting down in full view of the bottle of whiskey, I commenced to read. I also prayed. But I didn't say "I must not take that drink because I owe it to so and so not to." I didn't say "I won't take that drink because I'm strong enough to resist temptation." I didn't say "I must not" or "I will not" at all. I simply prayed and read and in half an hour I got up and was absolutely free of the urge for a drink.

It might be very grand to be able to say "Finis" right here, but I see now I hadn't gone all the way I was intended to go. I was still coddling and nursing my two pets, self-pity and resentment. Naturally, I came a cropper once more. This time I went to the telephone (after I had taken about two drinks) and called L to tell her what I had done. She asked me to promise that I would not take another drink before someone came to me. Well, I had learned enough about truthfulness to refuse to give that promise. Had I been living after the old pattern, I would have been ashamed to call for help. In fact I should not have wanted help. I should have tried to hide the fact that I was drinking and continued until I again wound up behind the "eight ball." I was taken back to B's home where I stayed for three weeks. The drinking ended the morning after I got there, but the suffering continued for some time. I felt desperate and I questioned my ability to really avail myself of the help that the others had received and applied so successfully. Gradually, however, God began to clear my channels so that real understanding began to come. Then was the time when full realization and acknowledgement came to me. It was realization and acknowledgement of the fact that I was full of self-pity and resentment, realization of the fact that I had not fully given my problems to God. *I was still trying to do my own fixing.*

That was more than a year ago. Since then, although circumstances are no different, for there are still trials and hardships and hurts and disappointments and disillusionments, self-pity and resentment are being eliminated. In this past year I haven't been tempted once. I have no more idea of taking a drink to aid me through a difficult period than I would if I had never drank. But I know absolutely that the minute I close my channels with sorrow for myself, or being hurt by, or resentful toward anyone, I am in horrible danger.

I know that my victory is none of my human doing. I know that I must keep myself worthy of Divine help. And the glorious thing is this: I am free, I am happy, and perhaps I am going to have the blessed opportunity of "passing it on." I say in all reverence—Amen.

# Our Southern Friend

Two rosy-cheeked children stand at the top of a long hill as the glow of the winter sunset lights up the snow covered country-side. "It's time to go home" says my sister. She is the eldest. After one more exhilarating trip on the sled, we plod homeward through the deep snow. The light from an oil lamp shines from an upstairs window of our home. We stamp the snow from our boots and rush in to the warmth of the coal stove which is supposed to heat upstairs as well. "Hello dearies," calls Mother from above, "get your wet things off."

"Where's Father?" I ask, having gotten a whiff of sausage cooking through the kitchen door and thinking of supper.

"He went down to the swamp," replies Mother. "He should be home soon."

Father is an Episcopal minister and his work takes him over long drives on bad roads. His parishioners are limited in number, but his friends are many, for to him race, creed, or social position make no difference. It is not long before he drives up in the old buggy. Both he and old Maud are glad to get home. The drive was long and cold but he was thankful for the hot bricks which some thoughtful person had given him for his feet. Soon supper is on the table. Father says grace, which delays my attack on the buckwheat cakes and sausage. What an appetite!

A big setter lies asleep near the stove. He begins to make queer sounds and his feet twitch. What is he after in his dreams? More cakes and sausage. At last I am filled. Father goes to his study to write some letters. Mother plays the piano and we sing. Father finishes his letters and we all join in several exciting games of parchesi. Then Father is persuaded to read aloud some more of "The Rose and the Ring."

Bed-time comes. I climb to my room in the attic. It is cold so there is no delay. I crawl under a pile of blankets and blow out the candle. The wind is rising and howls around the house. But I am safe and warm. I fall into a dreamless sleep.

I am in church. Father is delivering his sermon. A wasp is crawling up the back of the lady in front of me. I wonder if it will reach her neck. Shucks! It has flown away.

Ho, hum, maybe the watermelons are ripe in Mr. Jones patch. That's an idea! Benny will know, but Mr. Jones will not know what happened to some of them, if they are. At last! The message has been delivered.

"Let your light so shine before men that they may see your good works—." I hunt for my nickel to drop in the plate so that mine will be seen.

Father comes forward in the chancel of the church. "The peace of God which passes all understanding, keep your hearts and minds—." Hurray! Just a hymn and then church will be over until next week!

I am in another fellow's room at college. "Freshman," said he to me, "do you ever take a drink?" I hesitated. Father had never directly spoken to me about drinking and he never drank any, so far as I knew. Mother hated liquor and feared a drunken man. Her brother had been a drinker and had died in a state hospital for the insane. But his life was unmentionable, so far as I was concerned. I had never had a drink but I had seen enough merriment in the boys who were drinking to be interested. I would never be like the village drunkard at home. How a lot of people despised him! Just a weakling!

"Well," said the older boy. "Do you?"

"Once in a while," I lied. I could not let him think I was a sissy.

He poured out two drinks. "Here's looking at you," said he. I gulped it down and choked. I didn't like it, but I would not say so. No, never! A mellow glow stole over me. Say! This wasn't so bad after all. In fact, it was darn good. Sure I'd have another. The glow increased. Other boys came in. My tongue loosened. Everyone laughed loudly. I was witty. I had no inferiorities. Why, I wasn't even ashamed of my skinny legs! This was the real thing!

A haze filled the room. The electric light began to move. Then two bulbs appeared. The faces of the other boys grew dim. How sick I felt. I staggered to the bathroom—. Shouldn't have drunk so much or so fast. But I knew how to handle it now. I'd drink like a gentleman after this.

And so I met John Barleycorn. The grand fellow who at my call made me "a hale fellow, well met," who gave me such a fine voice, as we sang "Hail, hail, the gang's all here," and "Sweet Adeline," who gave me freedom from fear and feelings of inferiority. Good old John! He was my pal, all right.

Final exams of my senior year and I may somehow graduate. I would never have tried, but Mother counts on it so. A case of measles saved me from being kicked out during my Sophomore year. Bells, bells, bells! Class, library, laboratory! Am I tired!

But the end is in sight. My last exam and an easy one. I gaze at the board with its questions. Can't remember the answer to the first. I'll try the second. No soap there. Say this is getting serious! I don't seem to remember anything. I concentrate on one of the questions. I don't seem to be able to keep my mind on what I am doing. I get uneasy. If I don't get started soon, I won't have time to finish. No use. I can't think.

Oh! An idea! I leave the room, which the honor system allows. I go to my room.

I pour out half a tumbler of grain alcohol and fill it with ginger ale. Oh, boy! Now back to the exam. My pen moves rapidly. I know enough of the answers to get by. Good old John Barleycorn! He can certainly be depended on. What a wonderful power he has over the mind! He has given me my diploma!

Underweight! How I hate that word. Three attempts to enlist in the service, and three failures because of being skinny. True, I have recently recovered from pneumonia and have an alibi, but my friends are in the war, or going, and I am not. To hell with it all! I visit a friend who is awaiting orders. The atmosphere of "eat, drink, and be merry" prevails and I absorb it. I drink a lot every night. I can hold a lot now, more than the others.

I am examined for the draft and pass the physical exam. What a dirty deal! Drafted! The shame of it. I am to go to camp on November 13th. The Armistice is signed on the 11th and the draft is called off. Never in the service! The war leaves me with a pair of blankets, a toilet kit, a sweater knit by my sister, and a still greater inferiority.

It is ten o'clock of a Saturday night. I am working hard on the books of a subsidiary company of a large corporation. I have had experience in selling, collecting, and accounting, and am on my way up the ladder.

Then the crack-up. Cotton struck the skids and collections went cold. A twenty-three million dollar surplus wiped out. Offices closed up and workers discharged. I, and the books of my division have been transferred to the head office. I have no assistance and am working nights, Saturdays and Sundays. My salary has been cut. My wife and new baby are fortunately staying with relatives. What a life! I feel exhausted. The doctor has told me that if I don't give up inside work, I'll have tuberculosis. But what am I to do? I have a family to support and have no time to be looking for another job.

Oh, well. I reach for the bottle which I just got from George, the elevator boy.

I am a traveling salesman. The day is over and business has been not so good. I'll go to bed. I wish I were home with the family and not in this dingy hotel.

Well—well—look who's here! Good old Charlie! It's great to see him. How's the boy? A drink? You bet your life! We buy a gallon of "corn" because it is so cheap. Yet I am fairly steady when I go to bed.

Morning comes. I feel horribly. A little drink will put me on my feet. But it takes others to keep me there.

I see some prospects. I am too miserable to care if they give me an order or not. My breath would knock out a mule, I learn from a friend. Back at the hotel and more to drink. I come to early in the morning. My mind is fairly clear, but inwardly I am undergoing torture. My nerves are screaming in agony. I go to the drug store and it is not open. I wait. Minutes are interminable. Will the store never open? At last! I hurry in. The druggist fixes me up a bromide. I go back to the hotel and lie down. I wait. I am going crazy. The bromides have no effect. I get a doctor. He gives me a hypodermic. Blessed peace!

And I blame this experience on the quality of the liquor.

I am a real estate salesman. "What is the price of that house," I ask the head of the firm I work for. He names me a price. Then he says, "That is what the builders are asking, but we will add on $500.00 and split it, if you can close the deal." The prospect signs the contract for the full amount. My boss buys the property and sells to the prospect. I get my commission and $250.00 extra and everything is Jake. But is it? Something is sour. So let's have a drink!

I become a teacher in a boy's school. I am happy in my work. I like the boys and we have lots of fun, in class and out.

An unhappy mother comes to me about her boy, for she knows I am fond of him. They expected him to get high marks and he has not the ability to do it. So he altered his report card through fear of his father. And his dishonesty has been discovered. Why are there so many foolish parents, and why is there so much unhappiness in these homes?

The doctors bills are heavy and the bank account is low. My wife's parents come to our assistance. I am filled with hurt pride and self-pity. I seem to get no sympathy for my illness and have no appreciation of the love behind the gift.

I call the boot-legger and fill up my charred keg. But I do not wait for the charred keg to work. I get drunk. My wife is extremely unhappy. Her father comes to sit with me. He never says an unkind word. He is a real friend but I do not appreciate him.

We are staying with my wife's father. Her mother is in critical condition at a hospital. The wind is moaning in the pine trees. I cannot sleep. I must get myself together. I sneak down stairs and get a bottle of whiskey from the cellaret. I pour drinks down my throat. My father-in-law appears. "Have a drink?" I ask. He makes no reply, and hardly seems to see me. His wife dies that night.

Mother has been dying of cancer for a long time. She is near the end and now in a hospital. I have been drinking a lot, but never get drunk. Mother must never know. I see her about to go.

I return to the hotel where I am staying and get gin from the bell-boy. I drink and go to bed; I take a few the next morning and go see my mother once more. I cannot stand it. I go back to the hotel and get more gin. I drink steadily. I come to at three in the morning. The indescribable torture has me again. I turn on the light. I must get out of the room or I shall jump out of the window. I walk miles. No use. I go to the hospital, where I have made friends with the night superintendent. She puts me to bed and gives me a hypodermic. Oh, wonderful peace!

Mother and Father die the same year. What is life all about anyway? The world is crazy. Read the newspapers. Everything is a racket. Education is a racket. Medicine is a racket. Religion is a racket. How could there be a loving God who would allow so much suffering and sorrow? Bah! Don't talk to me about religion. For what were my children ever born? I wish I were dead!

I am at the hospital to see my wife. We have another child. But she is not glad to see me. I have been drinking while the baby was arriving. Her father stays with her.

My parents' estates are settled at last. I have some money. I'll try farming. It will be a good life. I'll farm on a large scale and make a good thing of it. But the deluge descends. Lack of judgment, bad management, a hurricane, and the depression create debts in ever-increasing number. But the stills are operating throughout the country-side.

It is a cold, bleak day in November. I have fought hard to stop drinking. Each battle has ended in defeat. I tell my wife I cannot stop drinking. She begs me to go to a hospital for alcoholics which has been recommended. I say I will go. She makes the arrangements, but I will not go. I'll do it all myself. This time I'm off of it for good. I'll just take a few beers now and then.

It is the last day of the following October, a dark, rainy morning. I come to in a pile of hay in a barn. I look for liquor and can't find any. I wander to a stable and drink five bottles of beer. I must get some liquor. Suddenly I feel hopeless, unable to go on. I go home. My wife is in the living room. She had looked for me last evening after I left the car and wandered off into the night. She had looked for me this morning. She has reached the end of her rope. There is no use trying any more, for there is nothing to try. "Don't say anything," I say to her. "I am going to do something."

I am in the hospital for alcoholics. I am an alcoholic. The insane asylum lies ahead. Could I have myself locked up at home? One more foolish idea. I might go out West on a ranch where I couldn't get anything to drink. I might do that. Another foolish idea. I wish I were dead, as I have often wished before. I am too yellow to kill myself. But maybe—. The thought stays in my mind.

Four alcoholics play bridge in a smoke-filled room. Anything to get my mind from myself. The game is over and the other three leave. I start to clean up the debris. One man comes back, closing the door behind him.

He looks at me. "You think you are hopeless, don't you?" he asks.

"I know it," I reply.

"Well, you're not," says the man. "There are men on the streets of New York today who were worse than you, and they don't drink anymore."

"What are you doing here then?" I ask.

"I went out of here nine days ago saying that I was going to be honest, and I wasn't," he answers.

A fanatic, I thought to myself, but I was polite. "What is it?" I enquire.

Then he asks me if I believe in a power greater than myself, whether I call that power God, Allah, Confucius, Prime Cause, Divine Mind, or any other name. I told him that I believe in electricity and other forces of nature, but as for a God, if there is one, He has never done anything for me. Then he asks me if I am willing to right all the wrongs I have ever done to anyone, no matter how wrong I thought they were. Am I willing to be honest with myself about myself and tell someone about myself, and am I willing to think of other people and of their needs instead of myself; to get rid of the drink problem?

"I'll do anything," I reply.

"Then all of your troubles are over" says the man and leaves the room. The man is in bad mental shape certainly. I pick up a book and try to read, but cannot concentrate. I get in bed and turn out the light. But I cannot sleep. Suddenly a thought comes. Can all the worthwhile people I have known be wrong about God? Then I find myself thinking about myself, and a few things that I had wanted to forget. I begin to see I am not the person I had thought myself, that I had judged myself by comparing myself to others, and always to my own advantage. It is a shock.

Then comes a thought that is like A Voice. "Who are you to say there is no God?" It rings in my head, I can't get rid of it.

I get out of bed and go to the man's room. He is reading. "I must ask you a question," I say to the man. "How does prayer fit into this thing?"

"Well," he answers, "you've probably tried praying like I have. When you've been in a jam you've said, 'God, please do this or that' and if it turned out your way that was the last of it and if it didn't you've said 'There isn't any God' or 'He doesn't do anything for me.' Is that right?"

"Yes" I reply.

"That isn't the way" he continued. "The thing I do is to say 'God here I am and here are all my troubles. I've made a mess of things and can't do anything about it. You take me, and all my troubles, and do anything you want with me.' Does that answer your question?"

"Yes, it does" I answer. I return to bed. It doesn't make sense. Suddenly I feel a wave of utter hopelessness sweep over me. I am in the bottom of hell. And there a tremendous hope is born. It might be true.

I tumble out of bed onto my knees. I know not what I say. But slowly a great peace comes to me. I feel lifted up. I believe in God. I crawl back into bed and sleep like a child.

Some men and women come to visit my friend of the night before. He invites me to meet them. They are a joyous crowd. I have never seen people that joyous before. We talk. I tell them of the Peace, and that I believe in God. I think of my wife. I must write her. One girl suggests that I phone her. What a wonderful idea.

My wife hears my voice and knows I have found the answer to life. She comes to New York. I get out of the hospital and we visit some of these new-found friends. What a glorious time we have!

I am home again. I have lost the fellowship. Those that understand me are far away. The same old problems and worries surround me. Members of my family annoy me. Nothing seems to be working out right. I am blue and unhappy. Maybe a drink—I put on my hat and dash off in the car.

Get into the lives of other people, is one thing the fellows in New York had said. I go to see a man I had been asked to visit and tell him my story. I feel much better! I have forgotten about a drink.

I am on a train, headed for a city. I have left my wife at home, sick, and I have been unkind to her in leaving. I am very unhappy. Maybe a few drinks when I get to the city will help. A great fear seizes me. I talk to the stranger in the seat with me. The fear and the insane idea is taken away.

Things are not going so well at home. I am learning that I cannot have my own way as I used to. I blame my wife and children. Anger possesses me, anger such as I have never felt before. I will not stand for it. I pack my bag and leave. I stay with understanding friends.

I see where I have been wrong in some respects. I do not feel angry any more. I return home and say I am sorry for my wrong. I am quiet again. But I have not seen yet that I should do some constructive acts of love without expecting any return. I shall learn this after some more explosions.

I am blue again. I want to sell the place and move away. I want to get where I can find some alcoholics to help, and where I can have some fellowship. A man calls me on the phone. Will I take a young fellow who has been drinking for two weeks to live with me? Soon I have others who are alcoholics and some who have other problems.

I begin to play God. I feel that I can fix them all. I do not fix anyone, but I am getting part of a tremendous education and I have made some new friends.

Nothing is right. Finances are in bad shape. I must find a way to make some money. The family seems to think of nothing but spending. People annoy me. I try to read. I try to pray. Gloom surrounds me. Why has God left me? I mope around the house. I will not go out and I will not enter into anything. What is the matter? I cannot understand. I will not be that way.

I'll get drunk! It is a cold-blooded idea. It is premeditated. I fix up a little apartment over the garage with books and drinking water. I am going to town to get some liquor and food. I shall not drink until I get back to the apartment. Then I shall lock myself in and read. And as I read, I shall take little drinks at long intervals. I shall get myself "mellow" and stay that way.

I get in the car and drive off. Halfway down the driveway a thought strikes me. I'll be honest anyway. I'll tell my wife what I am going to do. I back up to the door and go into the house. I call my wife into a room where we can talk privately. I tell her quietly what I intend to do. She says nothing. She does not get excited. She maintains a perfect calm.

When I am through speaking, the whole idea has become absurd. Not a trace of fear is in me. I laugh at the insanity of it. We talk of other things. Strength has come from weakness.

I cannot see the cause of this temptation now. But I am to learn later that it began with the desire for my own material success becoming greater than the interest in the welfare of my fellow man. I learn more of that foundation stone of character, which is honesty. I learn that when we act upon the highest conception of honesty which is given us, our sense of honesty becomes more acute.

I learn that honesty is truth, and the truth shall make us free!

Sensuality, drunkenness, and worldliness satisfy a man for a time, but their power is a decreasing one. God produces harmony in those who receive His Spirit and follow Its dictates.

Today as I become more harmonized within, I become more in tune with all of God's wonderful creation. The singing of the birds, the sighing of the wind, the patter of raindrops, the roll of thunder, the laughter of happy children, add to the symphony with which I am in tune. The heaving ocean, the driving rain, autumn leaves, the stars of heaven, the perfume of flowers, music, a smile, and a host of other things tell me of the glory of God.

There are periods of darkness, but the stars are shining, no matter how black the night. There are disturbances, but I have learned that if I seek patience and open-mindedness, understanding will come. And with it, direction by the Spirit of God. The dawn comes and with it more understanding, the peace that passes understanding, and the joy of living that is not disturbed by the wildness of circumstances or people around me. Fears, resentments, pride, worldly desires, worry, and self-pity no longer possess me. Ever-increasing are the number of true friends, evergrowing is the capacity for love, ever-widening is the horizon of understanding. And above all else comes a greater thankfulness to, and a greater love for Our Father in heaven.

# A Business Man's Recovery

The S. S. "Falcon" of the Red D. Line, bound from New York to Maracaibo, Venezuela, glided up the bay, and docked at the wharf in the port of La Guayra on a hot tropical afternoon early in 1927. I was a passenger on that boat bound for the oil fields of Maracaibo as an employee of the X Oil Company, under a two year contract at a good salary and maintenance. There I hoped to buckle down to two years of hard work, and save some money, but above all to avoid any long, continued drinking that would interfere with my work, because that had cost me too many jobs in the past.

Not that I was going to give up drinking entirely; no, such a step would be too drastic. But down here in the oil fields with a bunch of hard working, hard drinking good fellows, I, too, would learn how to handle my liquor and not let it get the best of me again. Such an environment would surely do the trick, would surely teach me to drink moderately with the best of them and keep me away from those long, disastrous sprees. I was still young, I could make the grade, and this was my chance to do it. At last I had the real answer, and my troubles were over!

Red and I, who had become bosom shipboard companions on the way down from New York, stood at the rail watching the activity on the dock incident to getting the vessel secured alongside. Red was also on his way to Maracaibo to work for the same company, and we agreed that so long as we were going to be here overnight, we might as well go ashore together and look the town over.

Red was a swell fellow who might take a drink now and then, who might even get drunk once in a while, but he could handle his liquor and did not go to any great excesses. Thousands of other fellows like him, who have been my drinking companions from time to time, were in no way responsible for the way I drank, or what I did, or the way liquor affected me.

So off we went, Red and I, to do the town—and do it we did. After a few drinks we decided there wasn't much else to do in town except to make a round of the "cantinas," have a good time, get back to the ship early and get a good night's rest.

So what harm would a little drinking do now, I reasoned. Especially with one full day and two nights ahead to get over it.

We visited every "cantina" along the straggling main street of La Guayra, and feeling high, wide and handsome, Red and I decided to return to the ship. When we rolled down to the dock we found that our ship had been berthed off from the wharf about thirty feet and that it was necessary to take a tender out to her. No such ordinary method would satisfy Red and myself, so we decided to climb the stern hawser hand over hand to get on board. The flip of a coin decided that I would go first; so off I started, hand over hand, up the hawser.

Now even a good experienced sailor, perfectly sober, would never attempt such a foolhardy feat and, as was to be expected, about half way up the hawser I slipped and fell into the bay with a loud splash. I remember nothing more until next morning. The captain of the boat said to me "Young man, it is true that God looks after drunken fools and little children. You probably don't know it, but this bay is infested with man-eating sharks and usually a man overboard is a goner. How close you were to death, you don't realize, but I do."

Yes, I was lucky to be saved! But it wasn't until ten years later, after I had time and time again tempted Fate by going on protracted benders that I was really saved—not until after I had been fired from job after job, tried the patience of my family to the breaking point, alienated what might have been many, many good, lasting friendships, taken my dear wife through more sorrow and heartaches than any one woman should bear in a lifetime; after doctors, hospitals, psychiatrists, rest cures, changes of scenery and all the other paraphernalia that go with the alcoholic's futile attempts to quit drinking. Finally I dimly began to get the realization that during twenty years of continual drinking every expedient I had tried, (and I had tried them all) had failed me. I hated to admit the fact even to myself, that I just couldn't lick booze. I was licked. I was desperate. I was scared.

I was born in 1900, my father was a hardworking man who did the very best he could to support his family of four on a small income. Mother was very good to us, kind, patient, and loving. As soon as we were old enough my mother sent us to Sunday School and it so happened that as I grew older I took quite an active interest, becoming successively a teacher and later Superintendent of a small Sunday School in uptown New York.

When the United States entered the World War in April 1917, I was under age but, like most other youngsters of that period, wanted very much to get into the fray. My parents, of course, would not hear of this but told me to be sensible and wait until I was eighteen. Being young and restless, however, and fired by the military spirit of the times, I ran away from home to join the Army in another city.

There I joined up. I didn't get into any of the actual hostilities at the front, but later, after the Armistice, served with the United States forces occupying the Rhineland, working my way up to a good non-commissioned rank.

While serving abroad I started to drink. This, of course, was entirely my own choice. Drinking by a soldier during those times was viewed with a degree of indulgence by both superiors and civilians. It seems to me, as I recall it now, that even then I wasn't satisfied to drink like the normal fellow.

Most of the United States Army of Occupation were sent back home in 1921 but my appetite for travel had been whetted, and having heard terrible stories of Prohibition in the United States, I wanted to remain in Europe where "a man could raise a thirst."

Subsequently I went to Russia, then to England, and back to Germany; working in various capacities, my drinking increasing and my drunken escapades getting worse. So back home in 1924 with the sincere desire to stop drinking and the hope that the Prohibition I had heard so much about would enable me to do it—in other words—that it would keep me away from it.

I secured a good position, but it wasn't long before I was initiated into the mysteries of the speakeasy to such an extent that I soon found myself once more jobless. After looking around for some time, I found that my foreign experience would help me in securing work in South America. So, full of hope once more, resolved that at last I was on the wagon to stay, I sailed for the tropics. A little over a year was all the company I then worked for would stand of my continual drinking and ever-lengthening benders. So they had me poured on a boat and shipped back to New York.

This time I was really through. I promised my family and friends, who helped me get along while looking for another job, that I would never take another drink as long as I lived—and I meant it. But alas!

After several successive jobs in and around New York had been lost, and it isn't necessary to tell you the cause, I was sure that the only thing that would enable me to get off the stuff was a change of scenery. With the help of patient, long-suffering friends, I finally persuaded an oil company that I could do a good job for them in the oil fields of Maracaibo.

But it was the same thing all over again!

Back to the United States. I really sobered up for a while—long enough to establish a connection with my present employers. During this time I met the girl who is now my wife. At last here was the real thing—I was in love. I would do anything for her. Yes, I would give up drinking. I would never, never do anything to even remotely affect the happiness that now came into my life. My worries were over, my problem was solved. I had sown my wild oats and now I was going to settle down to be a good husband and live a normal happy life.

And so we were married.

Supported by my new found happiness, my abstinence this time lasted about six months. Then a New Year's party we gave started me off on a long bender. The thing about this episode that is impressed on my mind is how earnestly and sincerely I then promised my wife that I would absolutely and positively this time give up drinking—and again I meant it.

No matter what we tried, and my wife helped me in each new experiment to the best of her ability and understanding, failure was always the result, and each time greater hopelessness.

The next step was doctors, a succession of them, with occasional hospitalization. I remember one doctor who thought a course of seventy-two injections, three a week, after two weeks in a private hospital, would supply the deficiency in my system that would enable me to stop drinking. The night after the seventy-second injection I was paralyzed drunk and a couple of days later talked myself out of being committed to the City Hospital.

My long-suffering employers had a long talk with me and told me that they were only willing to give me one last final chance because during my short periods of sobriety I had shown them that I could do good work. I knew they meant it and that it was the last chance they would ever give me.

I also knew that my wife couldn't stand it much longer.

Somehow or other I felt that I had been cheated—that I had not really been cured at the sanitarium even though I felt good physically. So I talked it over with my wife who said there must be something somewhere that would help me. She persuaded me to go back to the sanitarium and consult Dr. ——, which thank God I did.

He told me everything had been done for me that was medically possible but that unless I decided to quit I was licked. "But doctor," I said, "I have decided time and time again to quit drinking and I was sincere each time, but each time I slipped again and each time it got worse." The doctor smiled and said, "Yes, yes, I've heard that story hundreds of times. You really never made a decision, you just made declarations. You've got to decide and if you really want to quit drinking I know of some fellows who can help you. Would you like to meet them?"

Would a condemned man like a reprieve? Of course I wanted to meet them. I was so scared and so desperate that I was willing to try anything. Thus it was that I met that band of life-savers, Alcoholics Anonymous.

The first thing Bill told me was his own story, which paralleled mine in most respects, and then said that for three years he had had no trouble. It was plain to see that he was a supremely happy man—that he possessed a happiness and peacefulness I had for years envied in men.

What he told me made sense because I knew that everything that I, my wife, my family and my friends had tried had failed. I had always believed in God even though I was not a devout church-goer. Many times in my life I had prayed for the things I wanted God to do for me, but it had never occurred to me that He, in His Infinite Wisdom knew much better than I what I should have, and be, and do, and that if I simply turned the decision over to Him, I would be led along the right path.

At the conclusion of our first interview, Bill suggested that I think it over and come back to see him within a few days if I was interested. Fully realizing the utter futility with which my own efforts had met in the past, and somehow or other sensing that delay might be dangerous, I was back to see him the next day.

At first it seemed a wild, crazy idea to me, but because of the fact that everything else I had tried had failed, because everything seemed so hopeless, and because it worked with these fellows who all had been through the same hell that I had been through, I was willing, at least, to have a try.

To my utter astonishment, when I did give their method a fair trial, it not only worked, but was so amazingly easy and simple that I said to them "Where have you been all my life?"

That was in February, 1937, and life took on an entirely different meaning. It was plain to see that my wife was radiantly happy. All of the differences that we seemed to have been having, all of the tenseness, the worry, confusion, the hectic days and nights that my drinking had poured into our life together, vanished. There was peace. There was real love. There was kindness and consideration. There was everything that goes into the fabric of a happy normal existence together.

My employers, of course, the same as the writers of these stories, must remain anonymous. But I would be very thoughtless if I did not take this opportunity to acknowledge what they did for me. They kept me on, giving me chance after chance, hoping I suppose, that some day I would find the answer, although they themselves did not know what it might be. They do now, however.

A tremendous change took place in my work, in my relationship with my employers, in my association with my co-workers and in my dealings with our customers. Crazy as the idea seemed when broached to me by these men who had found it worked, God did come right into my work when permitted, as He had come into the other activities connected with my life.

With this sort of lubricant the wheels turned so much more smoothly that it seemed as if the whole machine operated on a much better basis than heretofore. Promotion that I had longed for previously, but hadn't deserved, was given to me. Soon another followed; more confidence, more trust, more responsibility and finally a key executive position in that same organization which so charitably kept me on in a minor position through the period of my drunkenness.

You can't laugh that off. Come into my home and see what a happy one it is. Look into my office, it is a happy human beehive of activity. Look into any phase of my life and you will see joy and happiness, a sense of usefulness in the scheme of things, where formerly there was fear, sorrow and utter futility.

# A Different Slant

I probably have one of the shortest stories in this whole volume and it is short because there is one point I wish to get over to an occasional man who may be in my position.

Partner in one of this country's nationally known concerns, happily married with fine children, sufficient income to indulge my whims and future security from the financial standpoint should paint a picture in which there would be no possibility of a man becoming an alcoholic from the psychological standpoint. I had nothing to escape from and I am known as a conservative, sound business man.

I had missed going to my office several times while I tapered off and brought myself to sobriety. This time, though, I found I could not taper off, I could not stop and I had to be hospitalized. That was the greatest shock to my pride I ever had. Such a blow that I made the firm resolve to never again taste as much as one glass of beer. Careful thought and analysis went into that decision.

The doctor at this hospital told me vaguely of the work of men who called themselves Alcoholics Anonymous and asked if I wanted one of them to call upon me. I was sure I needed no outside help, but in order to be polite to the doctor and hoping he would forget it, I assented.

I was embarrassed when a chap called at my house one evening and told me about himself. He quickly sensed my slight resentment and made it plain to me that none of the crowd were missionaries, nor did they feel it their duty to try to help anyone who did not want help. I think I closed the talk by saying I was glad I was not an alcoholic and sorry he had been bothered by me.

Within sixty days, after leaving the hospital the second time, I was pounding at his door, willing to do anything to conquer the vicious thing that had conquered me.

The point I hope I have made is—even a man with everything from the material standpoint, a man with tremendous pride and the will power to function in all ordinary circumstances can become an alcoholic and find himself as hopeless and helpless as the man who has a multitude of worries and troubles.

# Traveler, Editor, Scholar

The annual post-game banquet was winding up. The last rolling "R" of the speaker's hearty Caledonian accent died away sonorously. The company of students and alumni, all Scots, began to adjourn to the spacious bar for stronger stuff than the comparatively innocuous wines on the tables. A goal-scorer in a soccer game between my school and its centuries-old rival, I rated some popularity and the admiration of the moment expressed in famous ales and whiskey and soda. I was the son of a clergyman and just past sixteen years of age.

Waking in my hotel room the next day, I groaned. I didn't want to see or talk to anyone. Then someone raised my head and put a glass to my lips. "What you need is 'a hair of the dog that bit you,' get this into you."

The smell of the stuff sickened me. I grimaced, gulped the draught down and fell back on the bed. Somehow it stayed down and in about fifteen minutes I began to feel better and managed to eat a fair breakfast. That was my first experience of the "morning after" drink.

Back to college and my apprenticeship to a well-known lawyer, the students in their various clubs and societies, tippled enormously. I gave up the law but stayed in school to graduate. Through these college years in a city of well over a million inhabitants I learned all the better barrooms. Burns and Byron and other colorful profligates were the literary idols in the gang of "bloods" with whom I was a popular figure. I thought I was a gay dog and this was the life.

With nothing but a liberal arts education, very definitely estranged from my family and already married, soon after graduation I became a bookmaker's clerk on the British racing circuits, far better off financially than the average professional man. I moved in a gay crowd in the various "pubs" and sporting clubs. My wife traveled with me, but with a baby coming I decided to settle in a large city where I got a job with a commission agent which is a polite term for a hand-book operator. My job was to collect bets and betting-slips in the business section, a lucrative spot. My boss, in his way, was "big business." Drinking was all in the day's work.

One evening, the book, after checking up, was very definitely in the red for plenty through a piece of studied carelessness on my part, and my boss, very shrewd and able, fired me with a parting statement to the effect that once was enough. With a good stake I sailed for New York. I knew I was through among the English "bookies."

Tom Sharkey's brawling bar on 14th Street and the famous wine-room at the back were headquarters for me. I soon ran through my stake. Some college friends got me jobs when I finally had to go to work, but I didn't stick to them. I wanted to travel. Making my way to Pittsburgh, I met other former friends and got a job in a large factory where piecemakers were making good money. My fellow-workers were mostly good Saturday night drinkers and I was right with them. Young and able to travel with the best of them, I managed to hold my job and keep my end up in the barrooms.

One of my keenest memories is of meeting Jack London who came in unannounced one night to our favorite saloon, made a rousing speech, and later set up the drinks all evening.

I quit the factory and got a job on a small newspaper, going from that to a Pittsburgh daily, long ago defunct. Following a big drunk on that sheet where I was doing leg-work and rewrite, a feeling of nostalgia made me buy a ticket for Liverpool and I returned to Britain.

During my visit there, renewing acquaintance with former friends I soon spent most of my money. I wanted to roam again and through relatives got a supercargo job on an Australian packet which allowed me to visit my people in Australia where I was born. But I didn't stay long. I was soon back in Liverpool. Coming out of a pub near the Cunard pier I saw the Lusitania standing out in the middle of the Mersey. She had just come in and was scheduled to sail in two days. In my mind's eye I saw Broadway again and Tom Sharkey's bar; the roar of the subway was in my ears. Saying goodbye to my wife and baby, I was treading Manhattan's streets in a little more than a week. Again I spent my bankroll, by no means as thick as the one I had when I first saw the skyline of Gotham. I was soon broke, this time without trainfare to go anywhere. I got my first introduction to "riding the rods and making a blind."

In my early twenties the hardships of hobo life did not discourage me but I had no wish to become just a tramp. Forced to detrain from an empty gondola on the other side of Chicago by a terrific rainstorm which drenched me to the skin, I hit the first factory building I saw for a job. That job began a series of brief working spells, each one ending in a "drunk" and the urge to travel. My migrations extended for over a year as far west as Omaha. Drifting back to Ohio, I landed on a small newspaper and later was impressed into the direction of boy-welfare work at the local "Y." I stayed sober for four years except for a one-night carousel in Chicago. I stayed so sober that I used to keep a quart of medicinal whiskey in my bureau which I used to taper off the occasional newspaper alcoholics who were sent to see me.

Lots of times, vain-gloriously, I used to take the bottle out, look at it and say, "I've got you licked."

The war was getting along. Curious about it, feeling I was missing something, absolutely without any illusions about the aftermath, with no pronounced feeling of patriotism, I joined up with a Canadian regiment, serving a little over two years. Slight casualties, complicated however by a long and serious illness, were my only mishaps. Remarkably enough, I was a very abstemious soldier. My four years of abstinence had something to do with it, but soldiering is a tough enough game for a sober man, and I had no yen for full-pack slogging through mud with a cognac or vin rouge hangover.

Discharged in 1919, I really made up for my dry spell. Quebec, Toronto, Buffalo, and finally Pittsburgh, were the scenes of man-sized drunks until I had gone through my readjusted discharge pay, a fair sum.

I again became a reporter on a Pittsburgh daily. I applied for a publicity job and got it. My wife came over from Scotland and we started housekeeping in a large Ohio city.

The new job lasted five years. Every encouragement was given me with frequent salary increases, but the sober times between "periods" became shorter. I myself could see deterioration in my work, from being physically and mentally affected by liquor, although I had not yet reached the point where all I wanted was more to drink. Successive Monday morning hangovers, which despite mid-week resolutions to do better, came with unfailing regularity, eventually causing me to quit my job. Washington, D. C. and news-gathering agency work followed with many parties. I couldn't stand the pace. My drinking was never the spaced doses of the careful tippler; it was always gluttonous.

Returning to the town I had left three months before, I became editor of a monthly magazine, soon had additional publicity and advertising accounts and the money rolled in. The strain of overwork soon led me to the bottle again. My wife made several attempts to get me to stop and I had the usual visits from persons who would always ask me "Why?"—as if I knew! Offered the job of advertising manager for an eastern automotive company, I moved to Philadelphia to begin life anew. In three months John Barleycorn had me kicked out.

I did six years of newspaper advertising, and trade journal work with many, many drunks of drab and dreary hue woven into the pattern of my life. I visited my family just once in that time. An old avocation, the collection of first editions, rare books and Americana, fascinated me between times. I had some financial success through no ability of my own, and, when jobless and almost wiped out in 1930, I began to trade and sell my collection and much of the proceeds went to keep my apartment stocked with liquor and almost every night saw me helpless to bed.

I tried to help myself. I even began to go the rounds of the churches. I listened to famous ministers—found nothing. I began to know the inside of jails and workhouses. My family would have nothing to do with me, in fact couldn't, because I couldn't spare any of my money which I needed for drink to support them. My last venture, a book shop, was hastened to closed doors by my steady intoxication. Then I had an idea.

Loading a car with good old books to sell to collectors, librarians, universities and historical societies, I started out to travel the country. I stayed sober during the trip except for an occasional bottle of beer because funds barely met expenses. When I hit Houston, Texas, I found employment in a large bookstore. Need I say here that in a very short time I was walking along a prairie highway with arm extended and thumb pointed? In the two succeeding years I held ten different jobs ranging from newspaper copy-desk and rewrite, to traffic director for an oil field equipment company. Always in between there were intervals of being broke, riding freights and hitch-hiking interminable distances from one big town to another in three states. Now on a new job I was always thinking about payday and how much liquor I could buy and the pleasure I could have.

I knew I was a drunkard. Enduring all the hangover-hells that every alcoholic experiences, I made the usual resolutions. My thoughts sometimes turned to the idea that there must be a remedy. I have stood listening to street-corner preachers tell how they did beat the game. They seemed to be happy in their fashion, they and the little group of supporters, but always pride of intellect stopped me from seeking what they evidently had. Sniffing at emotional religion I walked away. I was an honest agnostic but definitely not a hater of the church or its adherents. What philosophy I had was thoroughly paganistic—all my life was devoted to a search for pleasure. I wanted to do nothing except what it pleased me to do and when I wanted to do it.

Federal Theatre in Texas gave me an administrative job which I held for a year, only because I worked hard and productively when I worked, and because my very tolerant chief ascribed my frequent lapses to a bohemian temperament. When it was closed through Washington edict I began with Federal Writers in San Antonio. In those days my system was always to drink up my last pay check and believe that necessity would bring the next job. A friend who knew I would soon be broke mounted guard over me when I left my job of writing the histories of Texas cities and put me aboard a bus for the town I had left almost five years before.

In five years a good many persons had forgotten that I had been somewhat notorious. I had arrived drunk but promised my wife I would keep sober, and I knew I could get work if I did. Of course, I didn't keep sober. My wife and family stood by me for ten weeks and then, quite justifiably, ejected me. I managed to maintain myself with odd jobs, did ten weeks in a social rescue institution and at length wound up in a second-hand bookstore in an adjacent town as manager. While there I was called to the hospital in my home town to see a former partner who had insisted that I visit him. I found my friend was there for alcoholism and now he was insisting that he had found the only cure. I listened to him, rather tolerantly. I noticed a Bible on his table and it amazed me. I had never known him to be anything but a good healthy pagan with a propensity for getting into liquor jams and scrapes. As he talked I gathered vaguely, (because he was a faltering beginner then just as I am now) that to be relieved of alcoholism I would have to be different.

Some days later, after he had been discharged, a stranger came into my shop in the nearby town. He introduced himself and began to tell me about a bunch of some

60 former drinkers and drunkards who met once a week, and he invited me to go with him to the next meeting. I thanked him, pleaded business engagements and promised I'd go with him at some future date.

"Anyhow, I'm on the wagon now," I said. "I'm doing a job I like and it's quiet where I live, practically no temptations. I don't feel bothered about liquor."

He looked at me quizzically. He knew too well that didn't mean a thing just as I knew in my heart that it would be only a question of time—a few days, a week, or even a month, it was inevitable—till I would be off on another bender. The time came just a week later. And as I look back on the events of two months, I can clearly see that I had been circling around, half-afraid of encountering the remedy for my situation, half-wanting it, deferring fulfillment of my promise to get in touch with the doctor I had heard about. An accident while drunk laid me low for about three weeks. As soon as I could get up and walk I started to drink again and kept it up until my friend of the hospital, who, in his first try at the new way of life had stubbed his toe in Chicago but had come back to the town to take counsel and make a new start, picked me up and got me into a hospital.

I had been drinking heavily from one state of semi-coma to another and it was several days before I got "defogged" but subconsciously I was in earnest about wanting to quit liquor forever. It was no momentary emotionalism born of self-pity in a maudlin condition. I was seeking something and I was ready to learn. I did not need to be told that my efforts were and would be unavailing if I did not get help. The doctor who came to see me almost at once did not assail me with any new doctrines; he made sure that I had a need and that I wanted to have that need filled and little by little I learned how my need could be met. The story of Alcoholics Anonymous fascinated me. Singly and in groups of two or three, they came to visit me. Some of them I had known for years, good two-fisted drinkers who had disappeared from their former haunts. I had missed them myself from the barrooms of the town.

There were business men, professional men, and factory workers. All sorts were represented and their relation of experiences and how they had found the only remedy, added to their human existence as sober men, laid the foundation of a very necessary faith. Indeed, I was beginning to see that I would require implicit faith, like a small child, if I was going to get anywhere or so it appeared as I lay in that hospital. The big thing was that these men were all sober and evidently had something I didn't have. Whatever it was, I wanted it.

I left the hospital on a meeting night. I was greeted warmly, honestly, and with a true ring of sincerity by everyone present. That night I was taken home by a former alcoholic and his wife. They did not show me to my room and wish me a good night's rest. Instead, over coffee cups, this man and his wife told me what had been done for them. They were earnest and obviously trying to help me on the road I had chosen. They will never know how much their talk with me has helped. The hospitality of their home and their fine fellowship were mine freely.

I had never, since the believing days of childhood, been able to conceive an authority directing the universe. But I had never been a flippant, wise-cracking sneerer at the few persons I had met who had impressed me as Christian men and women, or at any institutions whose sincerity of purpose I could see. No conviction was necessary to establish my status as a miserable failure at managing my own life. I began to read the Bible daily and to go over a simple devotional exercise as a way to begin each day. Gradually I began to understand.

I cannot say that my taste for liquor has entirely disappeared. It has been that way with some, but it has not been with me and may never be. Neither can I honestly say that I have forgotten the "fleshpots of Egypt." I haven't. But I can remember the urge of the Prodigal Son to return to his Father that he might taste of the husks that the swine did eat.

Formerly in the acute mental and physical pain during the remorseful periods succeeding each drunk, I found my recollection of the misery I had gone through a bolsterer of resolution and afterward, perhaps, a deterrent for a time. But in those days I had no one to whom I might take my troubles. Today I have. Today I have Someone who will always hear me; I have a warm fellowship among men who understand my problems; I have tasks to do and am glad to do them, to see others who are alcoholics and to help them in any way I can to become sober men.

# The Back-Slider

When I was graduated from high-school the World War was on in full blast. I was too young for the army but old enough to man a machine for the production of the means of wholesale destruction. I became a machine-hand at high wages. Machinery appealed to me anyway, because I had always wanted to be a mechanical engineer. Keen to learn as many different operations as possible, I insisted on being transferred from one operation to another until I had a good practical knowledge of all machines in a standard machine shop. With that equipment I was ready to travel for broader experience and in seven years had worked in the leading industrial centers in the eastern states, supplementing my shop work with night classes in marine engineering.

I had the good times of the period but confined my drinking to weekends, with an occasional party after work in the evenings. But I was unsettled and dissatisfied, and in a sense disgusted with going from job to job and achieving nothing more than a weekly pay envelope. I wasn't particularly interested in making a lot of money, but I wanted to be comfortable and independent as soon as possible.

So I married at that time, and for a while it seemed that I had found the solution to my urge for moving around. Most people settle down when they marry and I thought I'd have the same experience, that my wife and I would choose a place where we could establish a home and bring up a family. I had the dream of wearing carpet slippers in a life of comparative ease by the time I was forty. It didn't work out that way. After the newness of being married had worn off a little the old wander business got me again.

In 1924 I brought my wife to a growing city in the middle west where work was always plentiful. I had been in and out of it several times before and I could always get a job in the engineering department of its largest industrial plant. I early acquired the spirit of the organization which had a real reputation for constructive education of its workers. It encouraged ambition and aided latent talent to develop. I was keen about my work and strove always to place myself in line for promotion.

I had a thorough knowledge of the mechanical needs of the plant and when I was offered a job in the purchasing department's mechanical section I took it.

We were now resident in sort of a workers' paradise, a beautifully landscaped district where employees were encouraged to buy homes from the company. We had a boy about two years after I started with the company and with his advent I began to take marriage seriously. My boy was going to have the best I could give him. He would never have to work through the years as I had done. We had a very nice circle of acquaintance where we lived, nice neighbors and my colleagues in the engineering department and later in purchasing were good people, many of them bent on getting ahead and enjoying the good things of life while they climbed. We had nice parties with very little drinking, just enough to give a little Saturday night glow to things—never enough to get beyond control.

Fateful and fatal came the month of October in the year 1929. Work slowed down. Reassuring statements from financial leaders maintained our confidence that industry would soon be on an even keel again. But the boat kept rocking. In our organization, as in many others, the purchasing department found its work lessened by executive order. Personnel was cut down. Those who were left went around working furiously at whatever there was to do, looking furtively at each other wondering who would be next to go. I wondered if the long hours of overtime with no pay would be recognized in the cutting down program. I lay awake lots of nights just like any other man who sees what he has built up threatened with destruction.

I was laid off. I took it hard for I had been doing a good job and I thought as a man often will, that it might have been somebody else who should get the axe. Yet there was a sense of relief. It had happened. And partly through resentment and partly from a sense of freedom I went out and got pretty well intoxicated. I stayed drunk for three days, something very unusual for me, who had very seldom lost a day's work from drinking.

My experience soon helped me to a fairly important job in the engineering department of another company. My work took me out of town quite a bit, never at any great distance from home, but frequently overnight. Sometimes I wouldn't have to report at the office for a week, but I was always in touch by phone. In a way I was practically my own boss and being away from office discipline I was an easy victim to temptation. And temptation certainly existed. I had a wide acquaintance among the vendors to our company who liked me and were very friendly. At first I turned down the countless offers I had to take a drink, but it wasn't long before I was taking plenty.

I'd get back into town after a trip, pretty well organized from my day's imbibing. It was only a step from this daily drinking to successive bouts with absence from my route. I would phone and my chief couldn't tell from my voice whether I had been drinking or not, but gradually learned of my escapades and warned me of the consequences to myself and my job. Finally when my lapses impaired my efficiency and some pressure was brought to bear on the chief, he let me go. That was in 1932.

I found myself back exactly where I had started when I came to town. I was still a good mechanic and could always get a job as an hourly rated machine operator. This seemed to be the only thing which offered and once more I discarded the white collar for the overalls and canvas gloves. I had spent more than half a dozen good years and had got exactly nowhere, so I did my first really serious drinking. I was good for at least ten days or two weeks off every two months I worked, getting drunk and then half-heartedly sobering up. This went on for almost three years. My wife did the best she could to help me at first, but eventually lost patience and gave up trying to do anything with me at all. I was thrown into one hospital after another, got sobered up, discharged, and ready for another bout. What money I had saved dwindled and I turned everything I had into cash to keep on drinking.

In one hospital, a Catholic Institution, one of the sisters had talked religion to me and had brought a priest in to see me. Both were sorry for me and assured me that I would find relief in Mother Church. I wanted none of it. "If I couldn't stop drinking of my own free will, I was certainly not going to drag God into it," I thought.

During another hospital stay a minister whom I liked and respected came to see me. To me, he was just another non-alcoholic who was unable, even by the added benefit and authority of the cloth, to do anything for an alcoholic.

I sat down one day to figure things out. I was no good to myself, my wife, or my growing boy. My drinking had even affected him; he was a nervous, irritable child, getting along badly at school, making poor grades because the father he knew was a sot and an unpredictable one. My insurance was sufficient to take care of my wife and child for a fresh start by themselves and I decided that I'd simply move out of the world for good. I took a killing dose of bichloride of mercury.

They rushed me to the hospital. The emergency physicians applied the immediate remedies but shook their heads. There wasn't a chance, they said. And for days it was touch and go. One day the chief resident physician came in on his daily rounds. He had often seen me there before for alcoholism.

Standing at my bedside he showed more than professional interest, tried to buoy me up with the desire to live. He asked me if I would really like to quit drinking and have another try at living. One clings to life no matter how miserable. I told him I would and that I would try again. He said he was going to send another doctor to see me, to help me.

This doctor came and sat beside my bed. He tried to cheer me up about my future, pointed out I was still a young man with the world to lick and insisted that I could do it if I really wanted to stop drinking. Without telling me what it was, he said he had an answer to my problem and condition that really worked. Then he told me very simply the story of his own life, a life of generous tippling after professional hours for more than three decades until he had lost almost everything a man can lose, and how he had found and applied the remedy with complete success. He felt sure I could do the same. Day after day he called on me in the hospital and spent hours talking to me.

He simply asked me to make a practical application of beliefs I already held theoretically but had forgotten all my life. I believed in a God who ruled the universe. The doctor submitted to me the idea of God as a father who would not willingly let any of his children perish and suggested that most, if not all of our troubles, come from being completely out of touch with the idea of God, with God Himself. All my life, he said, I had been doing things of my own human will as opposed to God's will and that the only certain way for me to stop drinking was to submit my will to God and let Him handle my difficulties.

I had never looked on my situation in that way, had always felt myself very remote indeed from a Supreme Being. "Doc," as I shall call him hereinafter, was pretty positive that God's law was the Law of Love and that all my resentful feelings which I had fed and cultivated with liquor were the result of either conscious or unconscious, it didn't matter which, disobedience to that law. Was I willing to submit my will? I said I would try to do so. While I was still at the hospital his visits were supplemented by visits from a young fellow who had been a heavy drinker for years but had run into "Doc" and had tried his remedy.

At that time, the ex-alcoholics in this town, who have now grown to considerable proportions, numbered only Doc and two other fellows. To help themselves and compare notes they met once a week in a private house and talked things over. As soon as I came from the hospital I went with them. The meeting was without formality. Taking love as the basic command I discovered that my faithful attempt to practice a law of love led me to clear myself of certain dishonesties.

I went back to my job. New men came and we were glad to visit them. I found that new friends helped me to keep straight and the sight of every new alcoholic in the hospital was a real object lesson to me. I could see in them myself as I had been, something I had never been able to picture before.

Now I come to the hard part of my story. It would be great to say I progressed to a point of splendid fulfillment, but it wouldn't be true. My later experience points a moral derived from a hard and bitter lesson. I went along peacefully for two years after God had helped me quit drinking. And then something happened. I was enjoying the friendship of my ex-alcoholic fellows and getting along quite well in my work and in my small social circle. I had largely won back the respect of my former friends and the confidence of my employer. I was feeling fine—too fine. Gradually I began to take the plan I was trying to follow apart. After all, I asked myself, did I really have to follow any plan at all to stay sober? Here I was, dry for two years and getting along all right. It wouldn't hurt if I just carried on and missed a meeting or two. If not present in the flesh I'd be there in spirit, I said in excuse, for I felt a little bit guilty about staying away.

And I began to neglect my daily communication with God. Nothing happened—not immediately at any rate. Then came the thought that I could stand on my own feet now. When that thought came to mind—that God might have been all very well for the early days or months of my sobriety but I didn't need Him now—I was a gone coon. I got clear away from the life I had been attempting to lead. I was in real danger. It was just a step from that kind of thinking to the idea that my two years training in total abstinence was just what I needed to be able to handle a glass of beer. I began to taste. I became fatalistic about things and soon was drinking deliberately knowing I'd get drunk, stay drunk, and what would inevitably happen.

My friends came to my aid. They tried to help me, but I didn't want help. I was ashamed and preferred not to see them come around. And they knew that as long as I didn't want to quit, as long as I preferred my own will instead of God's will, the remedy simply could not be applied. It is a striking thought that God never forces anyone to do His will, that His help is ever available but has to be sought in all earnestness and humility.

This condition lasted for months, during which time I had voluntarily entered a private institution to get straightened out. On the last occasion when I came out of the fog, I asked God to help me again. Shamefaced as I was, I went back to the fellowship. They made me welcome, offered me collectively and individually all the help I might need. They treated me as though nothing had happened. And I feel that it is the most telling tribute to the efficacy of this remedy that during my period of relapse I still knew this remedy would work with me if I would let it, but I was too stubborn to admit it.

That was a year ago. Depend upon it, I stay mighty close to what has proven to be good for me. I don't dare risk getting very far away. And I have found that in simple faith I get results by placing my life in God's hands every day, by asking Him to keep me a sober man for 24 hours, and trying to do His will. He has never let me down yet.

# Home Brewmeister

Strangely enough, or by some queer quirk, I became acquainted with the "hilarious life" just at the time in my life when I was beginning to really settle down to a common-sense, sane, domestic life. My wife became pregnant and the doctor recommended the use of Porter Ale . . . so . . . I bought a six gallon crock and a few bottles, listened to advice from amateur brewmeisters, and was off on my beer manufacturing career on a small scale (for the time being). Somehow or other, I must have misunderstood the doctor's instructions, for I not only made the beer for my wife, I also drank it for her.

As time went on, I found that it was customary to open a few bottles whenever visitors dropped in. That being the case, it didn't take me long to figure out that my meager manufacturing facilities were entirely inadequate to the manufacture of beer for social and domestic consumption. From that point on, I secured crocks of ten gallon capacity and really took quite an active interest in the manufacture of home brew.

We were having card parties with limburger and beer quite regularly. Eventually, of course, what with all the hilarity that could be provoked with a few gallons of beer, there seemed to be no need of bridge or poker playing for entertainment. Well . . . we all know how those things go. The parties waxed more liquid and hilarious as time went on, and eventually I discovered that a little shot of liquor now and then between beers had the tendency to put me in a whacky mood much quicker than having to down several quarts of beer to obtain the same results. The inevitable result of this discovery was that I soon learned that beer made a very good wash for whiskey. That discovery so intrigued me, that I stayed on that diet almost entirely for the balance of my extended drinking career. Yes sir, the old Boilermaker and his Helper. The last day of my drinking career, I drank 22 of them between 10 and 12 a.m. and I shall never know how many more followed them until I was poured into bed that night.

I was getting along fairly well with my party drinking for quite some time however, but eventually I began to visit beer joints in between parties. A night or so a week in a joint, and a party or so a week at home or with friends, along with a little lone drinking, soon had me preparing for the existence of a top flight drunkard.

Three years after I started on my drinking career, I lost my first job. At that time, I was living out of town, so I moved back to the home town and made a connection in a responsible position with one of the larger companies in the finance business. Up to this point I had spent six years in the business and had enjoyed the reputation of being very successful.

My new duties were extremely confining and my liquor consumption began to increase at this time. Upon leaving the office in the evening, my first stop would be a saloon about a block from the office. However, as there happened to be several saloons within that distance, I didn't find it necessary to patronize the same place each evening. It doesn't pay to be seen in the same place at the same hour every day, you know.

The general procedure was to take 4 or 5 shots in the first place I stopped at. This would get me feeling fit, and then I would start for home and fireside, thirteen miles away. Well . . . on the way home numerous places must be passed. If I were alone I would stop at four or five of them, but only one or two in the event I had my mistrusting wife with me.

Eventually I would arrive home for a late supper, for which, of course, I had absolutely no relish. I would make a feeble attempt at eating supper but never met with any howling success. I never enjoyed any meal, but I ate my lunch at noon for two reasons: first, to help get me out of the fog of the night before, and second, to furnish some measure of nourishment. (My enjoyment of meals now is an added feature to the Seven Wonders of the World to me. I can still hardly believe it). Eventually, the noon meal was also dispensed with.

I cannot remember just when I became the victim of insomnia, but I do know that the last year and a half I never went to bed sober a single night. I couldn't sleep. I had a mortal fear of going to bed and tossing all night. Evenings at home were an ordeal. As a result, I would fall off in a drunken stupor every night.

How I was able to discharge my duties at the office during those horrible mornings, I will never be able to explain. Handling customers, dealers, insurance people, dictation, telephoning, directing new employees, answering to superiors, etc. However, it finally caught up with me, and when it did, I was a mental, physical, and nervous wreck.

I arrived at the stage where I couldn't quite make it to the office some mornings. Then I would send an excuse of illness. But the firm became violently ill with my drunkenness and their course of treatment was to remove their ulcer in the form of me from their payroll, amid much fanfare and very personal and slighting remarks and insinuations.

During this time, I had been threatened, beaten, kissed, praised and damned alternately by relatives, family, friends and strangers, but of course it all went for naught. How many times I swore off in the morning and got drunk before sunset I don't know. I was on the toboggan and really making time.

After being fired, I lined up with a new finance company that was just starting in business, and took the position of business promotion man, contacting automobile dealers. WOW . . . was that something??? While working in an office, there was some semblance of restraint, but, oh boy, when I got on the outside with this new company without supervision, did I go to town???

I really worked for several weeks, and having had a fairly wide acquaintance with the dealer trade, it was not difficult for me to line enough of them up to give me a very substantial volume of business with a minimum of effort.

Now I was getting drunk all the time. It wasn't necessary to report to the office in person every day, and when I did go in, it was just to make an appearance and bounce right out again. Was that a merry-go-round for the eight months that it lasted???

Finally this company also became ill and I was once more looking for a job. Then I learned something else. I learned that a person just can't find a job hanging in a dive or barroom all day and all night, as jobs don't seem to turn up in those places. I became convinced of that because I spent most of my time there and nary a job turned up. By this time, my chances of getting lined up in my chosen business were shot. Everyone had my number and wouldn't hire me at any price.

I have omitted details of transgressions that I made when drunk for several reasons. One is that I don't remember too many of them, as I was one of those drunks who could be on his feet and attend a meeting or a party, engage in a conversation with people and do things that any nearly normal person would do, and the next day, not remember a thing about where I was, what I did, who I saw, or how I got home. (That condition was a distinct handicap to me in trying to vindicate myself with the not so patient wife).

I also committed other indiscretions of which I see no particular point in relating. Anyone who is a rummy or is close to rummies knows what all those things amount to without having to be told about them.

Things eventually came to the point where I had no friends. I didn't care to go visiting unless the parties we might visit had plenty of liquor on hand and I could get stinking drunk. Fact is, that I was always well on my way before I would undertake to go visiting at all. (Naturally, this condition was also a source of great delight to my wife).

After holding good positions, making better than average income for over ten years, I was in debt, had no clothes to speak of, no money, no friends, and no one any longer tolerating me but my wife. My son had absolutely no use for me. Even some of the saloonkeepers where I had spent so much time and money, requested that I stay away from their places. Finally, an old business acquaintance of mine, whom I hadn't seen for several years offered me a job. I was on that job a month and drunk most of the time.

Just at this time my wife heard of a doctor in another city who had been very successful with drunks. She offered me the alternative of going to see him or her leaving me for good and all. Well . . . I had a job, and I really wanted desperately to stop drinking, but couldn't, so I readily agreed to visit the doctor she recommended.

That was the turning point of my life. My wife accompanied me on my visit and the doctor really told me some things that in my state of jitters nearly knocked me out of the chair. He talked about himself, but I was sure it was me. He mentioned lies, deceptions, etc. in the course of his story in the presence of the one person in the world I wouldn't want to know such things. How did he know all this? I had never seen him before, and at the time hoped to hell I would never see him again. However, he explained to me that he had been just such a rummy as I, only for a much longer period of time.

He advised me to enter the particular hospital to which staff he was connected and I readily agreed. In all honesty though, I was skeptical, but I wanted so definitely to quit drinking that I would have welcomed any sort of physical torture or pain to accomplish the result.

I made arrangements to enter the hospital three days later and promptly went out and got stiff for three days. It was with grim foreboding and advanced jitters that I checked in at the hospital. Of course, I had no hint or intimation as to what the treatment was to consist of. Was I to be surprised!

After being in the hospital for several days, a plan of living was outlined to me. A very simple plan that I find much joy and happiness in following. It is impossible to put on paper all the benefits I have derived . . . physical, mental, domestic, spiritual, and monetary.

This is no idle talk. It is the truth.

From a physical standpoint, I gained 16 pounds in the first two months I was off liquor. I eat three good meals a day now, and really enjoy them. I sleep like a baby, and never give a thought to such a thing as insomnia. I feel as I did when I was fifteen years younger.

Mentally . . . I know where I was last night, the night before, and the nights before that. Also, I have no fear of anything. I have self confidence and assurance that cannot be confused with the cockeyness or noise-making I once possessed. I can think clearly and am helped much in my thinking and judgment by my spiritual development which grows daily.

From a domestic standpoint, we really have a home now. I am anxious to get home after dark. My wife is ever glad to see me come in. My youngster has adopted me. Our home is always full of friends and visitors (No home brew as an inducement).

Spiritually . . . I have found a Friend who never lets me down and is ever eager to help. I can actually take my problems to Him and He does give me comfort, peace, and radiant happiness.

From a monetary standpoint . . . in the past nine months, I have reduced my reckless debts to almost nothing, and have had money to get along comfortably. I still have my job, and just prior to the writing of this narrative, I received an advancement.

For all of these blessings, I thank Him.

# The Seven Month Slip

At fourteen years of age, when I should have been at home under the supervision of my parents, I was in the United States army serving a one year enlistment. I found myself with a bunch of men none too good for a fourteen year old kid who passed easily for eighteen. I transferred my hero-worshipping to these men of the world. I suppose the worst damage done in that year in the army barracks was the development of an almost unconscious admiration for their apparently jolly sort of living.

Once out of uniform I went to Mexico where I worked for an oil company. Here I learned to take on a good cargo of beer and hold it. Later I rode the range in the Texas cow country and often went to town with the boys to "whoop it up on payday." By the time I returned to my home in the middle west I had learned several patterns of living, to say nothing of a cock-sure attitude that I needed no advice from anyone.

The next ten years are sketchy. During this time I married and established my own home and everything was lovely for a time. Soon I was having a good time getting around the law in speakeasies. Oh yes, I outsmarted our national laws but I was not quite successful in evading the old moral law.

I was working for a large industrial concern and had been promoted to a supervisional job. In spite of big parties, I was for three or four years able to be on the job the next morning. Then gradually the hangovers became more persistent and I found myself not only needing a few shots of liquor before I could go to work at all, but finally found it advisable to stay at home and sober up by the taper-off method. My bosses tried to give me some good advice. When that didn't help they tried more drastic measures, laying me off without pay. They covered up my too frequent absences many times in order to keep them from the attention of the higher officials in the company.

My attitude was that I could handle my liquor whenever I wanted to go about it seriously, and I considered my absences no worse than those of other employees and officials who were getting away with murder in their drinking.

One does not have to use his imagination much to realize that this sort of drinking is hard on the matrimonial relationship. After proving myself neither faithful nor capable of being temperate, my wife left me and obtained a judicial separation. This gave me a really good excuse to get drunk.

In the years 1933 and 1934 I was fired several times, but always got my job back on my promises to do better. On the last occasion I was reduced to the labor gang in the plant. I made a terrific effort to stay sober and prove myself capable of better things. I succeeded pretty well and one day I was called into the production chief's office and told I had met with the approval of the executive department and to be ready to start on a better job.

This good news seemed to justify a mild celebration with a few beers. Exactly four days later I reported for work only to find that they too knew about the "mild" celebration and that they had decided to check me out altogether. After a time I went back and was assigned to one of the hardest jobs in the factory. I was in bad shape physically and after six months of this, I quit, going on a drunk with my last pay check.

Then I began to find that the friends with whom I had been drinking for some time seemed to disappear. This made me resentful and I found myself many times feeling that everybody was against me. Bootleg joints became my hangouts. I sold my books, car, and even clothing in order to buy a few drinks.

I am certain that my family kept me from gravitating to flophouses and gutters. I am eternally thankful to them that they never threw me out or refused me help when I was drinking. Of course I didn't appreciate their kindness then, and I began to stay away from home on protracted drinking spells.

Somehow my family heard of two men in town who had found a way to quit drinking. They suggested that I contact these men but I retorted "If I can't handle my liquor with my own will power then I had better jump over the viaduct."

Another of my usual drinking spells came on. I drank for about ten days with no food except coffee before I was sick enough to start the battle back to sobriety with the accompanying shakes, night sweats, jittery nerves, and horrible dreams. This time I felt that I really needed some help. I told my mother she could call the doctor who was the center of the little group of former drinkers. She did.

I allowed myself to be taken to a hospital where it took several days for my head to clear and my nerves to settle. Then, one day I had a couple of visitors, one a man from New York and the other a local attorney. During our conversation I learned that they had been as bad as myself in this drinking, and that they had found relief and had been able to make a come-back. Later they went into more detail and put it to me very straight that I'd have to give over my desires and attitudes to a power higher than myself which would give me new desires and attitudes.

Here was religion put to me in a different way and presented by three past-masters in liquor guzzling. On the strength of their stories I decided to give it a try. And it worked, as long as I allowed it to do so.

After a year of learning new ways of living, new attitudes and desires, I became self-confident and then careless. I suppose you would say I got to feeling too sure of myself and Zowie! First it was a beer on Saturday nights and then it was a fine drunk. I knew exactly what I had done to bring myself to this old grief. I had tried to handle my life on the strength of my own ideas and plans instead of looking to God for the inspiration and the strength.

But I didn't do anything about it. I thought "to hell with everybody. I'm going to do as I please." So I floundered around for seven months refusing help from any quarter. But one day I volunteered to take another drunk on a trip to sober him up. When we got back to town we were both drunk and went to a hotel to sober up. Then I began to reason the thing out. I had been a sober, happy man for a year, living decently and trying to follow the will of God. Now I was unshaven, unkept, ill-looking, bleary-eyed. I decided then and there and went back to my friends who offered me help and who never lectured me on my seven month failure.

That was more than a year ago. I don't say now that I can do anything. I only know that as long as I seek God's help to the best of my ability, just so long will liquor never bother me.

# My Wife and I

Coming from a farm boyhood with the common education of the little red schoolhouse, I had worked during the war and afterwards for seven years at high wages in a booming industrial town, had saved considerable money and finally married an able, well-educated woman who had an unusual gift of common sense and far more than the average business vision, a true helpmate in every way.

In our early twenties, we were both ambitious and had boundless faith in our ability to succeed. We talked over the future all the time, exchanged ideas and really planned our way in life. Just working in a factory, even at highly-paid piece work, and saving out of my wages, did not seem to us to be the best way to do. We talked things over and decided to strike out for ourselves. Our first venture, a neighborhood grocery store, prospered. Another neighborhood store, in an ideal location at a nearby summer resort, looked good to us. We bought it and started in to make it go. Then came a business slump affecting the whole country. With fewer customers I had lots of time on my hands and was getting to like high-powered home brew and the potent liquors of prohibition days entirely too well. That didn't help the business. We finally shut up shop.

Jobs were scarce, but by persistence I again found a factory job. In a few months the factory closed down. We had again accumulated a small stake and since the job situation showed no improvement, we thought we would try business again.

This time we opened a restaurant in a semi-rural section and for a time all went well. My wife opened up in the morning, did all the baking and cooking and waited on trade. I relieved her later in the day and stayed open late to catch every possible bit of business. Our place became a regular hang-out for groups of latecomers who showed up with a bottle every now and then.

I told myself that I was one man who could handle my liquor because I was always on my feet at closing time. I talked knowingly about spacing my drinks, about taking only a measured shot, and about the folly of gulping down big drinks. Yes sir, I was never going to be one of those "rummies" who let liquor get the best of them. Young and strong, I could throw off the effects of the previous night's drinking and stand the nausea the following morning, even abstaining from taking a drink until the afternoon. But before long the idea of suffering for a few hours didn't seem so good.

The morning drink became the first act of the daily routine. I had now become a "regular." I had my regular remedy—a stiff shot to start the day and no waiting till a specified time. I used to wait for the need, soon I was craving the stuff so much that I didn't wait for that. My wife could see that it was gripping me. She warned me, gently at first, with quiet seriousness. Was I going to pave the way to losing this business just when it needed to be nursed along? We began to run behind. My wife, anxious for the goal we had set out to reach, and seeing the result if I didn't brace up, talked straight from the shoulder. We had words. I left in a passion.

Our separation lasted a week, I did a lot of thinking, and went back to my wife. Quieter, somewhat remorseful, we talked things over. Our situation was worse than I had anticipated. We got a buyer for the place and sold out. We still had some money left.

I had always been a natural mechanic, handy with tools. We moved back into town with a slim bankroll and, still determined never to be a factory hand again, I looked around and finding a workshop location with a house adjacent I started a sheet-metal shop. I had chosen a very difficult time to start up. My business practically vanished on account of the depression.

There were no jobs of any kind. We fell far behind on our rent and other obligations. Our cupboard was often bare. With every penny needed for food and shelter, and wearing old clothes with nothing new except what our two youngsters needed, I didn't touch a drop for two years. I went after business. I slugged doorbells all over the town asking for jobs. My wife rang bells with me, taking one side of the street while I worked the other. We left nothing undone to keep going, but we were still far behind, so far that at the low point we could see eviction and our belongings in the street.

I braced myself to talk to our landlord who was connected with a large real estate firm managing many properties. We were behind six months in our rent and they saw that the only way to get their back rent was to give me a couple of small jobs. My wife learned to use the tools to shape and fashion material when I was doing the installation work. The real estate firm liked my work and began to give me more jobs. In those grim days, with babies to feed, I couldn't spend what little money came in for drink. I stayed sober. My wife and I even started back to church, began paying our dues.

They were thin years, those depression years. For three years in succession, Christmas in our little family was just the 25th of December. Our customers saw us as two earnest young people trying to get along and as times improved a little we began to get better jobs. Now we could hire some competent workmen and bought a car and a few small trucks. We prospered and moved into a better-equipped house.

My pockets, which hadn't jingled for years, now held folding money. The first greenbacks grew into a roll with a rubber band around it. I became well-known to real estate firms, business men, and politicians. I was well-liked, popular with everyone. Following a prosperous season came a quiet period. With time on our hands I had a drinking spell. It lasted for a month, but with the aid of my wife, I checked myself in time. "Remember how we lost the store! Remember our restaurant!" my wife said. Yes, I could remember. Those times were too recent and their memory too bitter. I solemnly swore off and once more climbed aboard the wagon, this time for nine long months.

Business kept up. It became evident that by careful handling we might eventually have something pretty good, a sufficient income to provide a good living for us all and ensure a good education for our children.

My business is seasonal. Fall and early winter are rush times. The first few months of the year are quiet. But though business slackened, I got around making contracts, lining up future work and meeting people who would be able to put work in my way. Not yet sensing any great danger, in spite of past experiences, I seldom refused the invitations of business friends to have a drink. In a short time I was drinking every day and eventually much more than I had ever done before for I always had a roll in my pocket.

At first I was even more jolly than usual when I came home in the evening to my wife and family. But the joking good fellow who was the husband and father they had known, gave place to a man who slammed the door when he came in. My wife, genuinely alarmed now as week after week went past without any sign that I was going to quit, tried to reason with me, but the old arguments didn't work this time.

Summer came on with its demand for roof repairs and spouting installations. My wife often started the men to work in the morning, did shop jobs, kept the books, and in addition, ran the house and looked after the family.

For eight months my daily routine was steady drinking. Even after slumping in bed late at night in a semi-stupor, I would get up at all hours and drive to some all-night spot where I could get what I wanted. I was going to have a good time in spite of hell and high water.

I became increasingly surly when at home. I was the boss. I was master in my own house, wasn't I? I became morose, with few lucid moments between drinks. I would listen to no arguments and certainly attempts to reason with me were futile. Unknown to me, my wife influenced some of my friends and business associates to drop in casually. They were mostly non-drinkers and generally ended up by mildly upbraiding me.

"A fine lot of Job's comforters," I would say. I felt that everybody was against me, thought bitterly of my wife as being of little help and told myself I wasn't getting the breaks, that everybody was making a mountain out of a molehill and so, to hell with everything! I still had money and with money I could always buy bottled happiness. And still my wife kept trying. She got our pastor to talk to me. It was no good.

Drinking and staying drunk without cessation, even my splendid constitution began to give way. My wife called doctors who gave me temporary relief. Then my wife left me after a bitter quarrel, taking the children with her. My pride was hurt and I began to regard myself as an injured husband and an unappreciated father who, deep in his heart, just doted on his children. I went to see her and demanded to see them. I up and told her that I didn't care whether she came back or not, that I wanted the children. My wife, wise woman, thought she still had a chance to have me, save our home for the children. She threw aside her sense of injury, spoke right up to me and said she was coming back, that forbidding her the house wouldn't work, that she had helped me get what I had and was going to cross its threshold and resume its management. She did just that. When she opened the door she was appalled at the sight of it, curtains down, dishes and utensils unwashed, dirty glasses and empty bottles everywhere.

Every alcoholic reaches the end of the tether some day. For me there came a day when, physically and mentally, I was unable to make my way to a saloon for a drink. I went to bed. I told my wife for the first time that I wanted to quit drinking, but couldn't. I asked her to do something for me; I had never done this before. I realized that I needed help. Somehow in talking with a lady doctor, my wife had heard of another doctor who in some mysterious way had stopped drinking after thirty years and had been successful in helping a few other alcoholics to become sober men. As a last resort, my wife appealed to this doctor, who insisted on a certain situation before he could help; his experience had taught him that unless that situation existed nothing could be done for the alcoholic.

"Does your husband want to stop drinking, or is he merely temporarily uncomfortable? Has he come to the end of the road?" he asked my wife.

She told him that for the first time I had expressed a desire to quit, that I had asked her in desperation to try to do something—anything, to help me stop. He said he would see me the following morning.

With every part of my being craving a drink, I could hardly sit still when I got up to await the visit from the man she had talked to on the phone, but something kept me in the house. I wanted to hear what this fellow had to offer and since he was a medical man I had some preconceived notions ready for him when he came. I was pretty jittery when my wife opened the door to admit a tall, somewhat brusque professional man who, from his speech, was obviously an Easterner. I don't know what I had expected, but his salutation, designed to shake me up, I can now see, had almost the same effect as the hosing with cold water in a turkish bath.

"I hear you're another 'rummy," he said as he smiled and sat down beside me. I let him talk. Gradually he drew me out until what I did tell him gave him a picture of my experience. And then he put it to me plainly. "If you are perfectly sure that you want to quit drinking for good, if you are serious about it, if you don't merely wish to get well so that you can take up drinking again at some future date, you can be relieved," he said.

I told him that I had never wanted anything as much in my life as to be able to quit using liquor, and I meant every word of it.

"The first thing to do with your husband," he said, turning to my wife, "is to get him to a hospital and have him 'defogged.' I'll make the necessary arrangements."

He didn't go into any further explanation, not even to my wife. That evening I was in a hospital bed. The next day the doctor called. He told me that several former alcoholics were now dry as a result of following a certain prescribed course of action and that some of them would be in to see me. My wife came to see me faithfully. She, too, had been learning, perhaps more quickly than I was doing, through talking with the doctor who by this time was getting down to brass tacks with me. My friend was the human agency employed by an all-wise Father to bring me into a pathway of life.

It is an easy matter to repeat and orally affirm a faith. Here were these men who visited me and they, like myself, had tried everything else and although it was plain to be seen none of them were perfect, they were living proof that the sincere attempt to follow the cardinal teachings of Jesus Christ was keeping them sober. If it could do that for others, I was resolved to try it, believing it could do something for me also.

I went home after four days, my mind clear, feeling much better physically and, what was far more important, with something better than just will power to aid me. I got to know others of these alcoholics whose human center was my doctor. They came to our home. I met their wives and families. They invited my wife and myself to their homes. I learned that it would be well to begin the day with morning devotion which is the custom in our house now.

It was almost a year when I began to get a little careless. One day I hoisted a few drinks, arriving home far from sober. My wife and I talked it over, both knowing it had happened because I had stopped following the plan. I acknowledged my fault to God and asked His help to keep to the course I had to follow.

Our home is a happy one. My children no longer hide when they see me coming. My business has improved. And—this is important—I try to do what I can for my fellow alcoholics. In our town there are some 70 of us, ready and willing to spend our time to show the way to sobriety and sanity to men who are like what we used to be.

# A Ward of the Probate Court

At about the time of my graduation from high school, a state university was established in our city. On the call for an office assistant, I was recommended by my superintendent, and got the position. I was rather his choice and pride, but a few years later, I met him in a nearby city and "panhandled" him for two "bucks" for drinks.

I grew with this institution and advanced in position. I took a year off for attendance at an engineering college. At college I refrained from any hilarious celebrating or drinking.

War was declared. I was away from home on business at the State Capitol where my mother couldn't raise objections and I enlisted. Overseas I was on five fronts from Alsace up to the North Sea. Upon relief from the lines—back in the rest-area, "vin rouge" and "cognac" helped in the let down from trying circumstances. I was introduced to the exhilaration of intoxication. The old spirit, "What the hell? Heinie may have you tagged," didn't help toward any moderation in drinking then. We had many casualties but one of the real catastrophies was the loss of a pal, a lieutenant who died from the D.T.'s over there, after it was all over. This didn't slow me up and back in the States I had a big fling before returning home.

My plans were to cover up with my mother and the girl I was to marry, that I had become addicted to alcohol. But I exposed the fact on the day our engagement was announced. On the way I met a training camp buddy, got drunk and missed the party. Booze had got over its first real blow on me. I saw her briefly that night but didn't have the guts to face her people. The romance was over.

To forget, I engaged in a super-active life in social, fraternal, and civic promotion in my community. This all outside my position in the President's Office of the State University. I became a leader—the big flash in the pan. I organized and was first commander of the American Legion Post—raised funds and built a fine memorial Club House. Was Secretary of Elks, Eagles, Chamber of Commerce, City Club, and active as an operator and officer in political circles. I was always a good fellow and controlled my drinking, indulging only in sprees in private clubs or away from home.

I was deposed from the executive position at the college by a political change in the governorship of the State. I knew the sales manager of the Securities Division of a large Utility corporation in Wall Street, and started out to sell securities. The issues and the market were good and I had a fine opportunity. I was away from home and I began to drink heavily. To get away from my drinking associates, I managed to be transferred to another city, but this didn't help. Booze had me, my sales and commissions diminished, I remained almost in a continuous stupor on my drawing account until I was released.

I braced up, got sober, and made a good connection with a steamship agency, a concern promoting European travel and study at most all important universities in Europe. Those were the bath-tub gin days and for drinking in and about my office, I held out in this position for only a year.

I was now engaged to be married and fortunately I got another position as salesman for a large corporation. I worked hard, was successful, and drinking became periodical. I was married and my wife soon learned that I was no social drinker. I tried hard to control it, but could not. There were many separations and she would return home. I would make pledges and a sincere effort and then my top would blow off again. I began here to take sanitarium treatments to satisfy my wife and my folks.

I had a great capacity for drink and work. With the help of turkish baths, bromo-seltzer and aspirin, I held to the job. I became top-notcher in the entire sales force of the country. I was assigned to more special territory and finally into the market of keenest competition. I was top rate in salary, won bonus awards and was bringing in the volume. But there was always the drawback my excessive drinking made at times. I was called in once, twice, and warned. Finally I wasn't to be tolerated any longer, although I was doing a good job. I had lasted five and a half years.

I lost my wife along with my job and fine income. This was a terrible jolt. I tried for a hook-up, but I had a black eye marring a good record. I became discouraged and depressed. I sought relief with booze. There began the four black years of my life.

I had returned home to the community where I had been so prominent. These were dry days still and I hung out at the clubs with bars. I got so I would last on a job but a few days, just until I could get an advance for drinks. I began to get entangled with the law—arrested for driving while intoxicated and drunken and disorderly conduct.

My folks heard of the cure at the State Hospital. I was picked up drunk and sent there by the Probate Court. I was administered paraldehyde and came to in a receiving ward among lunatics. I was transferred to another ward of less violent cases and I found a little group of alcoholics and "junkers" (dope addicts). I learned from them the seriousness of being a ward of the Probate Court. I felt then if I ever got released the old devil alcohol would never get me in a jam like this again. In times of great distress such as this, I would pray to God for help.

I was fortunate and was released after eleven days and nights barred up in the laughing academy—"bug-house." That was enough. I wanted no more of it. I took a job as manager of a club and put myself to the old acid test. I was going to really assert my will power. I even tended bar part of the time, but never imbibed a bit. This lasted about three months.

I went to an annual convention of my overseas division and came to locked up in a cheap hotel room, new shoes, suit coat, hat and purse missing. I must have slipped badly.

Then followed much drinking and trouble. After a few arrests for intoxication, the law decided another sojourn to the State Hospital would tame me. They jumped the stay this time from eleven days to eleven weeks. It was getting tough for me. I came out in good physical condition and held a fear of getting probated again, thinking the seige might be eleven months. I got another job and stayed dry for about two months and off to the races again.

I became terribly weak—couldn't eat and tried to get nourishment from booze and mostly only bootleg at that. One time, I just made it into a hospital and another time a police patrol took me to the hospital instead of the jail. I suffered badly from insomnia. As many as three shots in the arm had no effect.

I would get in shape and back at it again. I was going to battle it to the finish. The time came when I was to be paid my soldier's bonus. I had the limit or maximum coming. Friends advised my folks to send me to a Veterans Hospital before I got this money in my hands. I was probated again, held in a county jail for two weeks and sent again to the asylum. This was my summer resort for three months. I was on the waiting list for the Veterans Hospital but I got into such wonderful physical condition from eating and working out of doors that I was released.

I reached home full of resentment against my folks for their having my money tied up under a guardianship. I went out and got saturated and landed in jail—I had been free from the asylum about eight hours. Behind the bars again so soon—this was bad. However, I was freed again next day and this was my last confinement with the law. I began to use my head, I continued to drink but kept under cover or hid in the "jungles" with the bums.

In a few months an old friend came along. He located me a few times in saloons. We had been drinking pals in the early days, particularly at the club houses. He had heard of my predicament. He himself had quit drinking and looked fine. He encouraged me to visit him in a nearby city.

I wanted to quit drinking, but hadn't much faith in ever getting away from it. I agreed to go into a hospital as the patient of a doctor who had been an alcoholic for many years and was now a new man.

It is almost uncanny—in just eight days I left there a different person. This doctor in plain words was a wonderful guy—he spent many hours with me telling me his experience with alcohol. Others of his band, which was then small, visited me—told me their stories. They were all strangers to me, but treated me as a friend. I was impressed with their interest and fellowship. I learned the secret. They had a religious experience. I was willing, and renewed my acquaintance with God and acknowledged Him as a reality.

I found it easy. I came to life and have been free now for two years. I hope never to take another drink. I am building up a reputation again and nearly every day am complimented on my appearance.

I have a new outlook on life. I look forward to each day with happiness because of the real enjoyment it is to me to be sane, sober, and respectable. I was existing really from one drink until the next, with no perception about circumstances, conditions, or even nature's elements. My acquaintance with God—lost and forgotten when I was a young man—is renewed. God is all-loving and all-forgiving. The memories of my past are being dimmed by the life I now aspire to.

# Riding the Rods

Fourteen years old and strong, I was ready—an American Whittington who knew a better way to get places than by walking. The "clear the way" whistle of a fast freight thundering over the crossing on the tracks a mile away was a siren call. Sneaking away from my farm home one night, I made my way to the distant yards. Ducking along a lane between two made-up trains that seemed endless, I made my way to the edge of the yards. Here and there I passed a silent, waiting figure. Then a little group talking among themselves. Edging in, I listened eagerly. I had met my first hoboes. They talked of places I had never heard of. This town was good. A fellow could get by on the Bowery all winter if he knew the ropes; that other town was "hostile"; thirty days for "vag" awaited you in another if you didn't hit the cinders before the road "bulls" fine-combed the train.

Then they noticed me. Somehow a new kid is always an object of interest to the adventurers of the rails. "Where ye makin' for, Kid?"

I had heard one of them mention "Dee-troit" and it seemed as good an answer as any. I had no plans, just wanted to get away—anywhere—just away!

"That Michigan Manifest will be along any minute now; I think she's moving." The tall hobo who had spoken grabbed me by the arm. "Come on, kid. We'll help you."

Suddenly I felt big. I had gotten away! The two hoboes talked, the tall one about getting work in Detroit, the other arguing for staying on the road. Then the one who had boosted me up began to quiz me. I told him I had run away from the farm. In a sort of halting way he told me not to get the train habit or it would get me until I would always want to be moving. The rocking motion of the car as the train increased speed became a cradle song in my ears. I fell asleep.

It was way past dawn when I awoke. My two companions were already sitting up and talking. The day wore on. We passed through small towns. Soon the train was threading its way between factories and huge warehouses, crossing tracks with brisk clatter, coming into a large railway yard. Brakes went on. They helped me off. We were in Detroit.

My hobo friends parted at a street corner. The tall one took me along right into town and got a room for both of us with "Mother Kelly," a kindly Irish landlady if there ever was one. "Sit tight, kid," he said. "I'll see you through as much as I can. Me to find a job."

He got a job. For almost two years he looked after me. He was always vigilant, steering me past the snares and pitfalls that are always in the path of a growing boy. This hobo, Tom Casey, who never talked much about himself or his experience except as a warning illustration of "What not to do," made me start a bank account and keep it growing. It is to him I owe the fact that I didn't become a "road kid," that I never became a hobo. Came a day when he left me. The road was calling him, he explained, although that never seemed to me to be the reason. I never saw Tom Casey again, but from this man I received my first lesson in the guiding and compelling principle of the Good Life. "Love thy neighbor as thyself."

I was city-wise by this time, uncontaminated to be sure, thanks to my friend. No longer a "boy rube in the big town." I found a job quickly enough but I missed Tom. I began to hang around pool rooms and it was inevitable that I soon learned to handle a schooner of beer and an occasional "shot." Jobs were plentiful. If I didn't feel right in the morning after a night with the "corner gang" I didn't go to work. I lost jobs. My bank account dwindled, disappeared entirely. My new barroom friends were little help. I was broke.

It was summer and the park benches, hard and uncomfortable as they were, appealed to me more than the squalid "flops" of the city's slums. So I slept out a few nights. Young and full of energy, I hunted for work. The war was on and work was easy to get. I became a machine-shop hand, progressing rapidly from drill-press to milling machine to lathe. I could quit a job one day and have a new one the next with more money. Soon I again had a good boarding-house, clothes and money. But I never started another bank account. "Plenty of time for that," I thought. My week-ends were spent in my conception of "a good time," finally becoming regular carousals and debauches over Saturday and Sunday. I had the usual experiences of being slipped a "Mickey Finn" and getting slugged and rolled for my money. These had no deterrent effect. I could always get jobs and live comfortably again in a few weeks. Soon, however, I tired of the weary routine of working and drinking. I began to dislike the city. Somehow my boyhood days on the farm didn't seem to be so bad at a distance.

No, I didn't go home, but found work not too far away. I still drank. I soon got restless and took a freight for a Michigan city, arriving there broke late at night. I set out to look for friends. They helped me find work. Slowly I began to climb the industrial job ladder once more and eventually achieved a responsible position as a machine setter in a large plant. I was sitting on top of the world again. The sense of accomplishment I had now told me that I had earned the right to have enjoyable week-ends once more. The week-ends began to extend to Tuesday and Wednesday until I frequently worked only from Thursday to Saturday with the bottle always in my mind. In a vague sort of way I had set a time to quit drinking but that was at least fifteen years away and "What the hell!" I said to myself. "I'm going to have a good time while I'm young."

Then I was fired. Piqued, I drank up my last pay check and when I got sober again found another job—then another—and another in quick succession. I was soon back on the park benches. And once more I got a break when everything seemed dark. An old friend volunteered to get me a job driving a bus. He said he would buy me a uniform and give me the hospitality of his home if I would promise to quit drinking. Of course I promised. I had been working about three days when the bus line superintendent called me into his office.

"Young fellow," he said, "In your application you state that you don't use alcoholic liquors. Now, we always check a man's references and three of the firms you have worked for say you're a highly capable man, but you have the drink habit."

I looked at him. It was all true, I admitted, but I had been out of work such a long time that I had welcomed this job as an opportunity to redeem myself. I told him what I had promised my friend, that I was sincerely doing my best and not drinking a drop. I asked him to give me a chance.

"Somehow I think you are in earnest," he said. "I believe you mean it. I'll give you a chance and help you to make good."

He shook my hand in friendship and encouragement. I strode from his office with high hope. "John Barleycorn will never make a bum out of me again," I told myself with determination.

For three months I drove my route steadily with never a hitch. My employers were satisfied. I felt pretty good. I was really on the wagon this time, wasn't I?

Yes indeed, I was on the wagon for good.

I soon repaid my debt to my friend for his stake in me and even saved a little money. The feeling of security increased. It was summer and, hot and tired at the end of the day, I began to stop in at a speakeasy on my way home. Detroit beer was good then, almost like old-time pre-prohibition stuff. "This is the way to do it," I would say to myself. "Stick to beer. After all, it's really a food and it sure hits the spot after a trick of wheeling that job around in this man's town. It's the hard liquor that gets a man down. Beer for mine."

Even then with all the hard lessons of bitter experience behind me I did not realize that thinking along that line was a definite red light on my road in life—a real danger signal.

The evening glass of beer led, as usual, to the night when I didn't get away from the bar until midnight. I began to need a bracer in the morning. Beer, I knew from experience was simply no good as a bracer—all right as a thirst quencher perhaps, but lacking action and authority the next morning. I needed a jolt.

The morning jolt became a habit. Then it got to be several jolts until I was generally pretty well organized when I started to work. Spacing my drinks over the day I managed not to appear drunk, just comfortable, as I drove along the crowded thoroughfares of the city. Then came the accident.

On one of the avenues a man darted from between parked cars right in my path.

I swung the bus sharply over to keep from hitting him but couldn't quite make it. He died in the hospital. Passenger and sidewalk witnesses absolved me completely. Even if I had been completely sober I couldn't have cleared him. The company investigation immediately after the accident showed me blameless but my superiors knew I had been drinking. They fired me—not for the accident—but for drinking on the job.

Well, once more I felt I had enough of city life and found a job on an upstate farm. While there I met a young school-teacher, fell in love with her and she with me. We were married. Farm work was not very remunerative for a young couple so we went successively to Pontiac, Michigan, and later to an industrial city in Ohio. For economy's sake we had been living with my wife's people, but somehow we never seemed able to get ahead. I was still drinking but not so much as formerly, or so it seemed to me.

The new location seemed ideal—no acquaintances, no entanglements, no boon companions to entice me. I made up my mind to leave liquor alone and get ahead. But I forgot one boon companion, one who was always at my elbow, one who followed me from city to farm and back to city. I had forgotten about John Barleycorn.

Even so, the good resolutions held for a time—new job, comfortable home, and understanding helpmate, they all helped. We had a son and soon came another. We began to make friends and moved in a small social circle of my fellow-workers and their wives and families. Those were still bootleg days. Drinks were always available but nobody seemed to get very drunk. We just had a good time, welcome surcease after a week of toil. Here were none of the rowdy debauches that I had known, I had discovered "social drinking" how to "drink like a gentleman and hold my liquor." There is no point in reiterating the recurrence of experience already described. The "social drinking" didn't hold up. I became the bootlegger's first morning customer. How I ever managed to hold the job I had I don't know. I began to receive the usual warnings from my superiors. They had no effect. I had now come to an ever-deepening realization that I was a drunkard, that there was no help for me.

I told my wife that. She sought counsel of her friends and my friends. They came and talked with me. Reverend gentlemen, who knew nothing of my problem, pointed me to the age-old religious formula. I would have none of it. It left me cold. Now, with hope gone, I haunted the mean thoroughfares of speakeasy districts, with my mind on nothing but the next drink. I managed to work enough to maintain a slim hold on my job. Then I began to reason with myself.

"What good are you?" I would say. "Your wife and children would be better off if they never saw you again. Why don't you get away and never come back? Let them forget about you. Get away—get away anywhere—that's the thing to do."

That night, coatless and hatless, I hopped a freight for Pittsburgh. The following day I walked the streets of the Smoky City. I offered to work at a roadside stand for a meal. I got the meal, walked on, sat down by the roadside to think.

"What a heel I've turned out to be!" I soliloquized. "My wife and two kids back there—no money—what can they do? I should have another try at it. Maybe I'll never get well, but at least I can earn a dollar or two now and then—for them."

I took another freight back home. Despite my absence, my job was still open. I went to work, but it was no go. I would throw a few dollars at my wife on payday and drink up what was left. I hated my surroundings, hated my job, my fellow-workers—the whole town. I tried Detroit again, landing there with a broken arm. How I got it I'll never know for I was far gone in drink when I left. My wife's relatives returned me to my home in a few days. I became morose, mooning around the house by myself. Seeing me come home, my wife would leave a little money on the table, grab the children and flee. I was increasingly ugly. Now, all hope was gone entirely. I made several attempts on my life. My wife had to hide any knives and hammers. She feared for her own safety. I feared for my mind—feared that I was breaking—that I would end up insane. Finally the fear got so terrible that I asked my wife to have me "put away" legally. There came a morning when, alone in my room, I began to wreck it, breaking the furniture, destroying everything in sight. Desperate, my wife had to employ the means I had suggested to her in the depths of alcoholic despair. Loath to have me committed to the state asylum, still trying to save something from the wreckage of my life and hers, she had me placed in a hospital, hoping against hope to save me.

I was placed under restraint. The treatment was strenuous—no alcohol—just bromides and sleeping potions. The nights were successions of physical and mental agony. It was weeks before I could sit still for any length of time. I didn't want to talk to anyone and cared less to listen. That gradually wore off and one day I fell into casual conversation with another patient—another alcoholic. We began to compare notes. I told him frankly that I was in despair, that no thinking I had ever been able to do had shown me a way of escape, that all my attempts to try will power (well-meaning persons had often said, "Why don't you use your will power?"—as if will power were a faculty one could turn on and off like a faucet!) had been of no avail.

"Being in here and getting fixed up temporarily," I told him bitterly, "is no good. I know that only too well. I can see nothing but the same old story over again. I'm simply unable to quit. When I get out of here I'm going to blow town."

My fellow-patient and new found acquaintance looked at me a long time in silence and finally spoke. From the most unexpected quarter in the world, from a man who was in the same position I was in, from a fellow-alcoholic, came the first ray of hope I had seen.

"Listen fellow," he said, looking at me with ten times the earnestness of the many good citizens and other well-intentioned persons who had tried their best to help me. "Listen to me. I know a way out. I know the only answer. And I know it works."

I stared at him in amazement. There were several mild mental cases in the place and, little as I knew about their exhibitions of tendencies, I knew that even in a normal conversation, strange ideas might be expected. Was this fellow perhaps a little balmy—a wee bit off? Here was a man, an admitted alcoholic like myself, trying to tell me he knew the remedy for my situation. I wanted to hear what he had to suggest but made the reservation that he was probably a little "nutty." At the same time I was ready to listen, like any drowning man, to grasp at even a straw.

My friend smiled, he knew what I was thinking. "Yes," he continued. "Forget that I'm here. Forget that I'm just another 'rummy.' But I had the answer once—the only answer."

He seemed to be recalling his very recent past. Looking at me earnestly, his voice impressive in its sincerity, he went on. "For more than a year before coming here I was a sober man, thoroughly dry. I wasn't just on the wagon. I was dry! And I would still be dry if I had stuck to the plan which kept me sober all that time."

Let me say here that he later went back to the very plan he told me about and has since been sober for more than a year for the second time.

He told me his own story briefly and went on to tell me of a certain cure for alcoholism—the only certain cure. I had anticipated hearing of some new treatment, some newly discovered panacea that I had not heard of, something which no doubt combined drugs and mental healing. But it was neither one nor the other; it was certainly not a mixture of any kind.

He spoke of some 30 men in my town who were ready to take me by the hand and call me by my first name. They would be friends without canting or ranting. He told me they met once a week to talk over their experiences, how they tried to help each other, how they spent their time in helping men like me.

"I know it sounds strange, incredible, maybe," he said. "I slipped, got drunk after being sober for a year, but I'm going back to try again. I know it works."

Helpless, without faith in myself or anyone else, entirely doubtful that the fellow really had something, I began to ask questions. I had to be interested or go crazy.

"How do you go about this—where do I have to go?" I asked.

"You don't have to go anywhere," he said. "Someone will come to you if you want them to." He didn't go into any detail, just told me that much and little more. I did some thinking that afternoon. Calling one of the nurses I asked her to get in touch with my wife and have her come to see me that evening.

She came during visiting hours. She expected, I know, to hear me plead for instant release from the place. I didn't talk about that. In my lame way I told her the story. It made little impression.

"It doesn't sound right," she said. "If this plan—and for the life of me I don't quite get it from what you've told me—if this plan is successful, why is this fellow back here himself?"

I was stumped. I was too ignorant about the thing myself to be capable of explaining it clearly to her. "I don't know," I said. "I'll admit it sounds queer, the way this fellow is and all that, but somehow I feel there's something to it. Anyhow, I want to know more about it."

She went away skeptically. But the next day I had a visitor, a doctor who had been himself an alcoholic. He told me little more about the plan. He was kindly, didn't offer any cut and dried formula to overcome my life-long difficulty. He presented no religious nostrums, suggested no saving rituals. Later he sent some of the other ex-alcoholics to see me.

A few days later my fellow-alcoholic was released, and shortly afterward I was allowed to go home also. Through the man who had first told me of the plan I was introduced to several other former alcoholics. They told me their experiences. Many were men of former affluence and position. Some had hit even lower levels than I had.

The first Wednesday evening after my release found me a somewhat shame-faced but intensely curious attendant at a gathering in a private home in this city. Some forty others were present. For the first time I saw a fellowship I had never known in actual operation. I could actually feel it. I learned that this could be mine, that I could win my way to sobriety and sanity if I would follow a few precepts, simple in statement, but profound and far-reaching in their effect if followed. It penetrated to my inner consciousness that the mere offering of lip-service wasn't enough. Still ignorant, still a little doubting, but in deadly earnest, I made up my mind to make an honest effort to try.

That was two years ago. The way has not been easy. The new way of living was strange at first, but all my thoughts were on it. The going was sometimes slow; halting were my steps among the difficulties of the path. But always, when troubles came, when doubts assailed and temptation was strong and the old desire returned, I knew where to go for aid. Helping others also strengthened me and helped me to grow.

Today I have achieved, through all these things, a measure of happiness and contentment I had never known before. Material success has mattered little. But I know that my wants will be taken care of.

I expect to have difficulties every day of my life, I expect to encounter stops and hindrances, but now there is a difference. I have a new and tried foundation for every new day.

# The Salesman

I learned to drink in a workmanlike manner when the law of the land said I couldn't and what started out as a young man's fun became a habit which in its later existence laid me by the heels many a time and almost finished my career.

'Teen years were uneventful with me. I was raised on a farm but saw little future in farming. I was going to be a business man, took a business college course, acquired a truck and stand in the city market of a nearby town, and started off. I brought produce from my folks' place and sold it to city customers and there were plenty of them with bulging pocketbooks.

Back of me was the normal life of a farmer's son. My parents were unusually understanding people. My father was a life-long comrade till the day of his death. The business theory I had learned in college was now being practiced and I was equipped beyond many of my competitors to be materially successful. Soon I had expanded until I was represented in all the city markets and also in another city. In 1921 we had the forerunner of the later depression and my customers disappeared. Successively I had to close my stands and was finally wiped out altogether. Being a young man of affairs, I had begun to do a little business and social drinking and now with time on my hands, I seemed to do more of it.

Following a year of factory work, during which time I got married, I got a job with a grocer as clerk. My grocer-employer was an expert wine-maker and I had free access to his cellar. The work was monotonous in the extreme, behind a counter all day when I had been used to driving around attending to business, meeting people and building for what I thought was a great future. I mark, too, as a milestone, the death of my father, whom I missed greatly.

I kept hitting the wine, with just occasional use of liquor. Leaving the grocery I went back into the produce business and out among people, went back to liquor again and got my first warning to quit before it got me.

I was anxious to get with a concern which would give me an opportunity to build up again, and landed a job with a nationally known biscuit company. I was assigned to a good business region, covering several important towns, and almost at once began to earn real money. In a very short time I was the star salesman of the company, winning a reputation as a business-getter. Naturally I drank with my better customers for on my route I had many stops where that was good business. But I had things rather well under control and in the early days on this job I seldom wound up my day's work with any visible effects of drinking.

I had a private brewery at home which was now producing 15 gallons a week most of which I drank myself. It is typical of the attitude I had toward alcohol at that time that, when a fire threatened total destruction of my home and garage, I rushed to the cellar and rescued my most precious possessions—a keg of wine and all the beer I could carry, and got pretty indignant when my better half suggested that I had better get some of the needed effects out of the house before it burned down.

My home-brewing gradually became a bore and I began to carry home bottles of powerful bootleg whiskey, starting with half a pint every night and winding up with a quart as my daily after-supper allowance. For a time I kept on the job spacing my drinks en route and very little of them in the morning hours. I just couldn't wait until I got home to drink. In a very short time I became an all-day drinker.

Chain-store managers and quantity buyers were both my guests and hosts and every now and then we had prodigious parties. Finally, in a re-organization shake-up resulting in new district managers with a pretty poor territory deal for me, I gave the company two weeks notice and quit. I had bought a home but in the year and a half following I had little income and finally lost that. I became satisfied with just enough to live on and buy the liquor I wanted. Then I landed in the hospital when my car was hit by a truck. My car was ruined entirely. That loss and my injuries plus the recriminations of my wife sort of sobered me up. When I got out of the hospital I stayed sober for six weeks and had made up my mind to quit.

I went back in the business where I had been a successful salesman, but with another company. When I started with this concern I talked things over with my wife and made her some very solemn promises. I wasn't going to touch another drop of liquor.

By this time prohibition was a thing of the past and saloons and clubs where I was well known as a good customer and a good spender became my patrons. I rolled up business until I was again a star, but after the first four months on the new job I began to slip. It is not unusual in the drinking experience of any man that after a time of sobriety he comes to the conclusion that he "can handle it." In no time at all liquor again became the most important thing in my life and every day became like another, steady drinking in every saloon and club on my route. I would get to headquarters every night in a top-heavy condition, just able to maintain equilibrium. I began to get warnings and was repeatedly fired and taken on again. My wife's parents died about this time in unfortunate circumstances. All my troubles seemed to be piling up on me and liquor was the only refuge I knew.

Some nights I wouldn't go home at all and when I did go home I was displeased when my wife had supper ready and equally angry when she didn't. I didn't want to eat at all and frequently when I underestimated my consumption of the amount of liquor I brought home, I made extra trips back to town to renew the supply. My morning ration when I started out was five double whiskies before I could do any business at all. I would go into a saloon, trembling like a leaf, tired in appearance and deathly sick, I would down two double whiskies, feel the glow and become almost immediately transformed. In half an hour I would be able to navigate pretty well and start out on my route. My daily reports became almost illegible and finally, following arrest for driving while intoxicated and on my job at that, I got scared and stayed sober for several days. Not long afterward I was fired for good.

My wife suggested I go to my old home in the country, which I did. Continued drinking convinced my wife I was a hopeless case and she entered suit for divorce. I got another job, but didn't stop drinking. I kept on working although my physical condition was such as to have required extensive hospitalization. For years I hadn't had a peaceful night's sleep and never knew a clear head in the morning. I had lost my wife, and had become resigned to going to bed some night and never waking again.

Every drunkard has one or two friends who haven't entirely given up hope for him, but I came to the point where I had none. That is, none but my Mother, and she, devoted soul, had tried everything with me. Through her, people came to me and talked, but nothing they said—some were ministers and others good church members—helped me a particle. I would agree with them when they were with me and as fast as they went away, I'd go after my bottle. Nothing suggested to me seemed to offer a way out.

I was getting to a place where I wanted to quit drinking but didn't know how. My Mother heard of a doctor who had been having marked success with alcoholics. She asked me if I'd like to talk to him and I agreed to go with her.

I had known, of course, of the various cures and after we had discussed the matter of my drinking fairly thoroughly, the doctor suggested that I go into the local hospital for a short time. I was very skeptical, even after the doctor hinted there was more to his plan than medical treatment. He told me of several men whom I knew who had been relieved and invited me to meet a few of them who got together every week. I promised I would be on deck at their next meeting but told him I had little faith in any hospital treatments. Meeting night, I was as good as my word and met the small group. The doctor was there but somehow I felt quite outside of the circle. The meeting was informal, nevertheless I was little impressed. It is true they did no psalm singing, nor was there any set ritual, but I just didn't care for anything religious. If I had thought of God at all in the years of drinking, it was with a faint idea that when I came to die I would sort of fix things up with Him.

I say that the meeting did not impress me. However, I could see men whom I had known as good, hard-working drunkards apparently in their right minds, but I just couldn't see where I came into the picture. I went home, stayed sober for a few days, but was soon back to my regular quota of liquor every day.

Some six months later, after a terrific binge, in a maudlin and helpless state, I made my way to the doctor's home. He gave me medical treatment and had me taken to the home of one of my relatives. I told him I had come to the point where I was ready for the remedy, the only remedy. He sent two of the members to see me. They were both kindly to me, told me what they had gone through and how they had overcome their fight with liquor. They made it very plain that I had to seek God, that I had to state my case to Him and ask for help. Prayer was something I had long forgotten. I think my first sincere utterance must have sounded pretty weak. I didn't experience any sudden change, and the desire for liquor wasn't taken away overnight, but I began to enjoy meeting these people and began to exchange the liquor habit for something that has helped me in every way. Every morning I read a part of the Bible and ask God to carry me through the day safely.

There is another part I want to talk about—a very important part. I think I would have had much more difficulty in getting straightened out if I hadn't been almost immediately put to work. I don't mean getting back on my job as salesman. I mean something that is necessary to my continued happiness. While I was still shakily trying to rebuild my job of selling, the doctor sent me to see another alcoholic who was in the hospital. All the doctor asked me to do was tell my story. I told it, not any too well perhaps, but as simply and as earnestly as I knew how.

I've been sober for two years, kept that way by submitting my natural will to the Higher Power and that is all there is to it. That submission wasn't just a single act, however. It became a daily duty; it had to be that. Daily I am renewed in strength and I have never come to the point where I have wanted to say, "Thanks God, I think I can paddle my own canoe now," for which I am thankful.

I have been reunited with my wife, making good in business, and paying off debts as I am able. I wish I could find words to tell my story more graphically. My former friends and employers are amazed and see in me a living proof that the remedy I have used really works. I have been fortunate to be surrounded with friends ever ready to help, but I firmly believe any man can get the same result if he will sincerely work at it God's way.

# Fired Again

It seems to me that I never did do things normally. When I learned to dance I had to go dancing every night in the week if possible; when I worked or studied I wanted no interruptions or distractions. Wherever I worked I wanted to be the highest paid man in the place or I was irritated; and of course when I drank I could never seem to stop until I was saturated. I was usually hard to get along with as a boy; if the others wouldn't play my way I'd go home.

The town we lived in when I was a child was rather new and raw, peopled largely by immigrants who seemed to be constantly getting married with free drinks and eats for anybody who cared to come. We kids usually managed to get to these celebrations, and although supposed to have soda pop we could get ourselves one or two beers. With this sort of background and more money than was good for me, it was fairly easy to start getting drunk before I was sixteen.

After I left home I earned rather decent salaries but was never satisfied with my position, salary, or the treatment accorded me by my employer. I very seldom stayed on one job for more than six months until I was married at the age of 28, at which time I had already begun to lose jobs because of my drinking. Whenever things went wrong I knew that a few drinks would make everything rosy, my fears, doubts and worries would vanish and I would always promise myself that the next time I would stop short of getting plastered. Somehow things seldom worked out that way though.

I was irritated by the efforts of so many doctors, ministers, lawyers, employers, relatives and friends who remonstrated with me, none of whom knew from personal experience what I was up against. I'd fall down, get up, work a while, get my debts paid (at least the most pressing ones) drink moderately for a few days or weeks, but eventually get myself so messed up in tangle-foot that I'd lose another job. In one year (1916) I quit two jobs because I thought I'd be discharged anyhow and was fired outright from five more, which is more jobs than many men have in a lifetime. Had I remained sober, any one of them would have led to advancement because they were with growing companies and in my chosen field of engineering.

After being discharged for the fifth time that year, I drank more than ever, cadging drinks and meals where I could, and running up a large rooming-house account. My brother took me home and my folks talked me into going to a sanitarium for thirty days. This place was operated by a physician who was a personal friend of the family and I was his only patient at the time. The doctor did his best, saw that I got into good physical condition, tried to straighten out the mental quirks he thought partly responsible for my drinking, and I left with the firm resolve never to drink again.

Before I left the sanitarium I answered an advertisement for an engineer in a small Ohio town and after an interview, obtained the position. In three days after leaving the sanitarium I had a job I liked at a satisfactory salary in a small town with basic living costs (board, room and laundry) amounting only to about 15% of my salary. I was all set, sober, working in a congenial atmosphere for a firm that had more profitable business than they knew what to do with. I made some beautiful plans. I could save enough in a few years to complete my formal education and there were no saloons in the town to trip me up. So what? So at the end of the week I was drunk again for no particular reason at all that I could understand. In about three months I was out of a job again, but in the meantime two things of major importance had happened. I had fallen in love and war had been declared.

I had learned my lesson. I knew definitely that I couldn't take even one drink. I wanted to get married so I planned very earnestly to get another job, stay sober, and save some money. I went to Pittsburgh on Sunday, called on a manufacturer of rolling-mill equipment and on Monday, got a position and went to work. I was first paid at the end of the second week, was drunk before the end of the day and couldn't be bothered with going to work the next Monday.

Why did I take that first drink? I honestly don't know. Anyhow I nearly went crazy that summer and really developed some sort of mental disturbance. The night clerk of the small hotel where I was staying saw me go out about three in the morning in pajamas and slippers and had a policeman take me back into my room. I suppose he was used to screwy drunks or he would have taken me to jail instead. I stayed there a few days and sweated the alcohol out of my system, went to the office to collect the balance of my salary, paid my room rent, and found I had just enough money to get home. So home I went, sick, broke, discouraged and despairing of ever attaining a normal, happy life.

After two or three weeks of idleness at home, I obtained a subordinate position with a former employer, doing the lowest grade of drafting work on an hourly basis. I kept reasonably sober for several months, went to see my fiancée one or two weekends, was advanced rapidly in salary and responsibility, had a date set for the wedding and then inadvertently learned that one of the men working under my direction was receiving about forty dollars more per month than I was, which burnt me up to such an extent I quit after an argument, took my money, packed my personal effects, left them at the corner drug store, and went downtown and got plastered. Knowing that I would be greeted with tears, sorrowful sympathy and more grief when I got home, I stayed away until I was again destitute.

I was really worried sick about my drinking so father again advanced the money for treatment. This time I took a three-day cure and left with the firm resolve never to drink again, got a better position than I'd had before and actually did keep sober for several months, saved some money, paid my debts and again made plans to get married. But the desire for a drink was with me constantly after the first week or two, and the memory of how sick I had been from liquor and the agonies of the treatment I had undergone faded into the background. I had only begun to restore the confidence of my associates, family, friends and myself before I was off again, without any excuse this time. The wedding was again postponed and it looked very much as though it would never take place. My employer did not turn me loose but I was in another nice jam nevertheless. After considerable fumbling around mentally as to what to do I went back to the three-day cure for the second time.

After this treatment I got along a little better, was married in the spring of 1919 and did very little drinking for several years. I got along very well with my work, had a happy home life, but when away from home with little likelihood of being caught at it, I'd go on a mild binge. The thought of what would happen if my wife caught me drinking served to keep me reasonably straight for several years. My work became increasingly more important. I had many outside interests and drinking became less of a factor in my life, but I did continue to tipple some during my out-of-town trips and it was because of this tendency that things finally became all snarled up at home.

I was sent to New York on business and later stopped at a night club where I had been drunk before. I certainly must have been very tight and it is quite likely that I was "Mickey Finned" for I woke up about noon the next day in my hotel without a cent. I had to borrow money to get home on but didn't bother to start back till several days later. When I got there I found a sick child, a distracted wife and had lost another job paying $7,000 a year. This, however, was not the worst of it. I must have given my business card to one of the girls at the night club for she started to send me announcements of another clip-joint where she was employed and writing me long hand "come on" notes, one of which fell into my wife's hands. I'll leave what happened after that to the reader's imagination.

I went back into the business of getting and losing jobs and eventually got to the point where I didn't seem to have any sense of responsibility to myself or to my family. I'd miss important family anniversaries, forget to come home for Christmas and in general wouldn't go home until I was exhausted physically and flat broke. About four years ago I didn't come home on Christmas Eve but arrived there about six o'clock on Christmas morning, minus the tree I had promised to get, but with an enormous package of liquor on board. I took the three-day cure again with the usual results but about three weeks later I went to a party and decided a few beers wouldn't hurt me; however I didn't get back to work for three days and a short while later had lost my job and was again at the bottom of things. My wife obtained employment on a relief basis and I finally got straightened out with my employer who placed me in another position in a nearby city which I also lost by the end of the year.

So it went until about a year ago when a neighbor happened to hear me trying to get into the house and asked my wife whether I had been having some drinking difficulties. This, of course, disturbed my wife but our neighbor was not just inquisitive. She had heard of the work of an ex-alcoholic doctor who was busily engaged in passing on the benefits he had received from another who had found the answer to his difficulties with liquor. As a result of this my wife saw the doctor. Then I talked with him, spent a few days in a local hospital and haven't had a drink since.

While in the hospital about twenty men called on me and told me of their experiences and the help they had received. Of the twenty I happened to know five, three of whom I had never seen completely sober. I became convinced then and there that if these men had learned something that could keep them sober, I also could profit from the same knowledge. Before leaving the hospital, two of these men, convinced of my sincerity of purpose, imparted to me the necessary knowledge and mental tools which have resulted in my complete sobriety for thirteen months, and an assurance that I need never, so long as I live, drink anything of an alcoholic nature if I kept on the right track.

My health is better, I enjoy a fellowship which gives me a happier life than I have ever known, and my family joins me in a daily expression of gratitude.

# The Fearful One

When I was 21, I was taken suddenly and violently ill and was ill for seven years. As a result of this illness I was left with a poorish nervous system and a curious phobia. As this has a large place in my story, I will try to explain it clearly. After I had been ill some months, I grew strong enough to get out of doors a little each day, but found I couldn't get farther than the nearest corner without becoming totally panic stricken. As soon as I turned back home the panic would vanish. I gradually overcame this particular phase of the trouble by setting myself longer distances to walk each day. Similarly I learned later to take short street car rides, then longer ones, and so forth, until I appeared to be doing most of the things other people do daily. But the things I did not have to do each day, or at least frequently, remained unconquered and a source of great but secret embarrassment to me.

So I went on for years, planning always to sidestep the things I was afraid of, but concealing my fear from everyone. Those years of illness were not all total invalidism. I made a good living part of the time, but was continually falling down and having to get up and start over again. The whole process gave me a licked feeling, especially when, towards the end of my twenties, I had to give up the presidency of a small company which was just turning the corner to real success. Shortly after this, I was successfully operated on and became a physically well man. But the surgeon did not remove the phobia, that remained with me.

During the period of my illness I was not especially interested in liquor. I was not a teetotaler, but I was just a "social drinker." However, when I was about thirty, my mother died. I went to pieces as I had become very dependent on my parents through my illness. When I began to get on my feet again I discovered that whiskey was a fine relief from the terrific nervous headaches I had developed. Long after the headaches were gone, however, I kept discovering other difficulties for which whiskey was a grand cure. During the ensuing ten years I once, by sheer will power, remained dry for five weeks.

I had many business opportunities during those ten years which, although I tried to keep them in my grasp, slipped through my fingers. A lovely wife came and went. She tried her best and our baby's birth put me on my mettle for all of six months, but after that, worse and more of it. When my wife finally took the baby and left, did I square my shoulders and go to work to prove to her and to the world that I was a man? I did not. I stayed drunk for a solid month.

The next two years were simply a drawn-out process of less and less work and more and more liquor. They ended eventually at the home of a very dear friend whose family were out of town. I had been politely but firmly kicked out of the house where I had been boarding, and although I seemed to be able to find money to buy drinks with, I couldn't find enough to pay advance room rent anywhere.

One night, sure my number was up, I chucked my "pride" and told this friend a good deal of my situation. He was a man of considerable means and he might have done what many men would have done in such a case. He might have handed me fifty dollars and said that I ought to pull myself together and make a new start. I have thanked God more than once that that was just what he did not do.

Instead, he took me out, bought me three more drinks, put me to bed and yanked me bodily out of town the next noon to a city 200 miles away and into the arms of one of the most extraordinary bunch of men in the United States. Here, while in the hospital, men with clear eyes and happy faces came to see me and told me the story of their lives. Some of them were hard to believe, but it didn't take a lot of brain work to see they had something I could use. And it was so simple. The sum and substance of it seemed to be that if I would turn to God, it was very probable that He could do a better job with my life than I had.

When I got out of the hospital, I was invited to stay in the home of one of the fellows. Here I found myself suddenly and uncontrollably seized with the old panic. I was in a strange house, in a strange city, and fear gripped me. I shut myself in my room. I couldn't sit down, I couldn't stand up, I couldn't lie down, couldn't leave because I had nowhere to go and no money to take me. Any attempt at reasoning accomplished nothing.

Suddenly in this maelstrom I grasped at a straw. Maybe God would help me—just maybe, mind you. I was willing to give Him a chance, but with considerable doubt. I got down on my knees—something I hadn't done in thirty years. I asked Him if He would let me hand over all these fears and this panic to Him. I lay down on the bed and went to sleep like a baby. An hour later I awoke to a new world. I could scarcely credit my senses, but that terrible phobia which had wrecked my life for eighteen years, was gone. Utterly gone. And in its place was a power and fearlessness which is a bit hard to get accustomed to.

All that happened nearly six months ago. In those six months a new life has opened before me. It isn't that I have been cured of an ordinarily incurable disease. I have found a joy in living that has nothing to do with money or material success. I know that incomparable happiness that comes from helping some other fellow get straightened out. Don't get me wrong. We are not a bunch of angels. None of us has any notion of becoming such. But we know that we can never go completely back to old ways because we are traveling upward through service to others and in trying to be honest, decent, and loving toward the world, instead of sliding and slipping around in a life of drinking, cheating, lying and doing what we like.

# Truth Freed Me!

In May 1936, after a prolonged period of alcoholism, my friends, my associates, my superiors, and those people who really loved me in spite of embarrassments too numerous to mention, finally left me because they had come to the conclusion that I didn't have any idea of doing or trying to do the right thing.

I was a spineless individual who didn't care a rap for anyone or anything—I was hopeless and knew it—and then in my extremity, The Divine Comforter, "Truth" came to me in a barroom where I had spent the major portion of six weeks.

The Divine Comforter, in my experience, came in the guise of a former drinking companion whom I had assisted home on several occasions. Because of physical infirmities brought about by alcoholic excess, he had been unable to walk a distance of three blocks to his home unassisted, when I last saw him. Now he approached me, and to my amazement he was sober and appeared greatly improved in physical condition.

He induced me to take a ride with him, and as we rode along told me of the marvelous thing that had come into his life. He had more than a practical idea of my difficulties, he also had a logical and practical idea as to how they might be overcome.

He started the conversation by explaining acute alcoholism and stated very bluntly that I was an alcoholic. This was news to me in spite of the fact that I had promised everybody East of the Mississippi, if they would take time to listen, that I was through with drink. At the time I made these promises, I honestly wanted to quit drinking, but for some unknown reason hadn't seemed able to. He told me why I failed.

He then suggested that I accompany him to a local doctor who had been helpful to him. It took forty-eight hours of persuasion and quite a few drinks to fortify myself, but I finally agreed to go. The doctor turned out to be one who had been an alcoholic himself, and in gratitude for the release he had found and because he understood the true meaning of the phrase "Brotherly Love" was spending a great portion of his time helping unfortunate individuals like myself.

With the help and advice of these two individuals and two or three associates, I was able, for the first time in two and a half years, to stay sober for six weeks, and then disastrously tried the beer experiment. For some time I couldn't get hold of myself, but gradually came out of hiding and exposed myself again to this influence which had been so helpful.

July 2, 1936, I again contacted the two individuals, and since that day I have never had a drink. However, because of the difficulties I encountered as the result of the beer experiment, I was unable for some time to find reality in this new way of life. I was doubtful, fearful, full of self-pity, afraid to humiliate myself.

This unreality lasted until December 11th, when I was faced with the absolute necessity of raising a sum of money. For the first time came the realization that I was faced with a difficulty from which I seemed unable to extricate myself. Of course, I took time out to bemoan the fact that "after all I'd done, this had to happen to me" but on the advice of my wife, I reluctantly went to a banker.

I told him my story completely. I went to him believing that my need was money. I went there as a last resort to attempt to pry it loose to meet my needs. My need was not money, but again I had been led to the proper source. After having related my story to the banker, who knew my reputation not only as an alcoholic but as an individual who didn't pay his bills, he said, "I know something of what you are trying to do, and I believe you are on the right track. Are you right with the Father who knows your needs before you ask? If so, you are not dependent upon this bank or any individual in it, or any rules by which we operate, because your help comes from an ever present and all powerful Father. I am going to do everything I can to secure this loan for you. However, I don't want anything that happens here to throw you off the track, I want you to leave here feeling that you have done everything you could to secure these funds, and go about your business. Your business is business with God's work. I don't know whether that calls for you to go and collect a bill, sell some new contract, or to sit quietly and pray, but your Father knows and if you will but permit Him, He will direct you."

I had again found reality. My needs were met from another entirely unexpected source.

The manifestations of this ever present Power in my experience since 1936 are too numerous to mention. Let it suffice to say that I am profoundly grateful for the opportunities I have had of seeing and knowing "TRUTH."

# Smile with Me, At Me

At the age of eighteen I finished high school and during my last year there my studies were dropping away to be replaced by dancing, going out nights, and thinking of a good time as most of the boys of my age did. I secured a job with a well known telegraph company which lasted about a year, due to the fact I thought I was too clever for a $7.00 a week job which did not supply me with enough money for my pleasures, such as taking girls out, etc. I was not at all satisfied with my small wages.

Now, I was a very good violinist at the time and was offered jobs with some well known orchestras, but my parents objected to my being a professional musician although my last year in high school was mostly spent playing for dances and giving exhibition dances at most of the fraternity affairs. Now naturally I was far from satisfied with my seven dollars a week wages, so when I came across a boy neighbor of mine on the subway one night (by the way I read in the newspaper that this same boy died four days ago) he told me he was a host in a celebrated Restaurant and Cabaret, and that his salary ran $14.00 per week and he made $50.00 a week in tips. Well, think of being paid for dancing with the carefree ladies of the afternoon and receiving all that sum, and me working for only $7.00 per. The following day I went straight uptown to Broadway and never did go back to my old job.

This was the beginning of a long stretch of high-flying as I thought, only to find out when I was forty-one years old to be very low-flying. I worked in this restaurant until I was twenty-one, then we went into the world war. I joined the navy. My enlistment pleased the owner of my cabaret so much that he offered me a good job at the end of my federal service.

The day I walked in to his establishment with my release from active duty, he said, "You are my assistant manager from now on." Well, this pleased me as you can imagine and my hat from then on would not fit.

Now, all this time my taste for liquor was constantly growing although it was no habit and I had no craving. In other words, if I had a date and wanted a drink with the girl friend I would, otherwise I would not think of it at all.

In six months time I found I was too good for this job and a competitive restauranteer, or a chain of the best well-known night clubs offered me a better position which I accepted. This night life was starting to tell and show its marks and together with the slump in that sort of business at the time, I decided to apply for a job with a well known ballet master who drilled many choruses for Broadway shows.

I was this man's assistant and I really had to work very hard for the little money I received, sometimes twelve hours or more a day, but I got the experience and honor which was just what I was looking for. This was one time when my work interfered with my drinking. This job came to an end one evening when I was drinking quite heavily. A certain prominent actress inquired of Professor X, my boss, if I would be interested to sign an eighty week contract for a vaudeville tour. It seems she could use me as a partner in her act. Now, a very nice woman, Miss J. who was office clerk and pianist for the boss, overheard the conversation and told both Mr. X and Miss Z that I would not be interested.

On hearing this I went out and drank enough to cause plenty of trouble, slapping Miss J. and doing an all round drunk act in the studio.

This was the end of my high-flying among the white lights. I was only twenty-four years old and I came home to settle down; in fact I had to. I was broke both financially and in spirit.

Being a radio operator in the navy, I became interested in amateur radio. I got a federal license and made a transmitting radio set and would often sit up half the night trying to reach out all over the country. Broadcasting radio was just in its infancy then, so I began to make small receiving sets for my friends and neighbors. Finally I worked up quite a business and opened a store, then two stores, with eleven people working for me.

Now here is where Old Barleycorn showed his hidden strength. I found that in order to have a paying business I had to make friends, not the kind I was used to, but ordinary, sane, hard working people. In order to do this I should not drink, but I found that I could not stop.

I will never forget the first time I realized this. Every Saturday, my wife and I would go to some tavern. I would take a bottle of wine, gin, or the like, and we would spend an evening dancing, drinking, etc. (This was fourteen years ago.)

I was practically a pioneer in the radio business and that must account for people putting up with me as they did. However, within three years time I had lost both stores, I won't say entirely due to my drinking, but at least if I had been physically and mentally fit, I could have survived and kept a small business going.

Now from this time up to about a year ago, I drifted from one job to another. I peddled brushes, did odd jobs such as painting, and finally got established with a well known piano company as assistant service manager.

Then came the big crash of 1929 and this particular company abolished their radio department. For two years I worked for one of my old competitors who owned a radio store. He put up with my drinking until I was in such a physical breakdown that I had to quit.

All this time my troubles at home were getting worse. My whole family blamed my failure on the alcoholic question and so the usual arguments would start the instant I came in the house. This naturally made me go out and drink some more. If I had no money, I would borrow, beg, or even steal enough for a bottle.

My wife fortunately went to business which was our only salvation. Our little boy was six years old at the time and due to the fact we needed someone to care for him during the day we moved in with my family. Now the trouble did start, because I not only had my wife to face every evening, but three of the elders of the family.

My wife did everything for me she possibly could. First she got in touch with a well known psychiatrist and I went faithfully to him for a few months. This particular doctor was such a nervous individual, I thought he had the St. Vitus' dance and I really thought he needed some kind of treatment more than I did. He advised hospitalization from three months to a year.

Well, this was all out of order as far as I was concerned. In the first place I had an idea that my wife wanted to put me away in a state institution where maybe I would be stuck for the rest of my life. In the second place, I wanted to go, if anywhere, to a private institution and that was far beyond our financial means. In the third place, I knew that that would be no cure, because I reasoned that it would be like taking candy out of a young child's reach. The instant I would come out a free man I would go right back to old Alky again. In this one thing I found out later I was perfectly right.

What I thought and wanted at the time was "not to want, to want to take a drink." This phrase is a very important link in my story. I knew this could only be done by myself, but how could I accomplish it? Well, this was the main question.

The point was always that when I did drink, I wanted all the time not to, and that alone wasn't enough. At the time I felt like a drink, I did not want to take it at all, but I had to, it seemed. So if you can grasp what I mean, I wished I would not want that drink. Am I nuts, or do you get me?

To get back to the doctor. If anything, these visits made me worse, and worst of all, everyone told me I wanted to drink and that was all there was to that. After going to as many as six or eight other doctors, some of my own friends advised my wife to make her plans for the future as I was a hopeless case, had no backbone, no will power, and would end up in the gutter.

Well, here I was, a man with much ability, a violinist, a radio engineer, a ballet master, and at this point took up hair dressing, so that added one more to the list. Can you beat it? I knew there must be some way out of all this mess. Everyone told me to stop my drinking, but none could tell me how, until I met a friend and believe me he turned out to be a true friend, something I never had until this past year.

One morning, after one of my escapades, my wife informed me I was to go with her to a public hospital or she would pack up and leave with our boy. My father, being a physician for forty years, put me in a private New York hospital. I was there ten days and was put in physical shape, and above everything else put on the right path to recovery and happiness.

My friend first asked me if I really wanted to stop drinking, and if I did, would I do anything no matter what it was in order to? I knew there was only one thing left to do if I wished to live and not enter an insane asylum where I knew I would eventually wind up.

Making up my mind that I would, he said, "Fine." And went on to explain the simple steps to take. After spending an hour or two with me that day he returned two days later and went into the subject more thoroughly. He explained he had been in the same hospital with the same malady and after taking these steps after his discharge, had not taken a drink in three years and also there were about sixty others that had this same experience. All these fellows got together on Sunday evenings and brought their wives and everybody spent a very pleasant time together.

Well, after I met all these people, I was more than surprised to find a very interesting, sociable, and friendly crowd. They seemed to take more interest in me than all of my old fraternity brothers or Broadway pals had ever done.

There were no dues or expenses whatsoever. I went along for about fourteen weeks, partly keeping these ideas, and so one afternoon I thought it would do no harm to take a couple of drinks and no more. Saying to myself, "I have this thing in hand now, I can be a moderate drinker." Here I made a fatal mistake. After all my past experience, again I thought I could handle the situation only to find out one week later it was the same old thing. I repeated the same thing over again and another week again.

Finally I was back at the hospital, although I went under protest. My wife had expected to take two weeks vacation in the country with me, but instead had to use this money for the hospital expenses. During my one week stay, I held this as a grudge against her. The result was I got drunk three days after I was discharged from the hospital. And she left me for two weeks. During this period of time I drank heavily, being upset not only over her absence, but perfectly at sea as to how I could ever get back on my feet and make a new start again.

There was no mistake about it there was something that I failed to do in those simple steps. So I carefully went over each day as best I could since my first drink after the fourteen weeks of sobriety, and found I had slipped away from quite a few of some of the most important things which I should do in order to keep sober.

Certainly I was down now—ashamed to face my new friends—my own family giving me up as lost and everyone saying, "The system didn't work, did it?"

This last remark was more than too much for me. Why should this fellowship of hard working fellows be jeopardized by me? It worked for them. As a matter of fact, not one who has kept faithfully to it has ever slipped.

One morning, after a sleepless night worrying over what I could do to straighten myself out, I went to my room alone—took my Bible in hand and asked Him, the One Power, that I might open to a good place to read—and I read. "For I delight in the law of God after the inward man. But I see a different law in my members, warring against the law of my mind and bringing me into captivity under the law of sin which is in my members. Wretched man that I am! Who shall deliver me out of the body of this death?"

That was enough for me—I started to understand. Here were the words of Paul a great teacher. When then if I had slipped? Now, I could understand.

From that day I gave and still give and always will, time every day to read the word of God and let Him do all the caring. Who am I to try to run myself or anyone else?

# A Close Shave

The year 1890 witnessed my advent as the youngest of five sons to a fine Christian mother and a hard working blacksmith father. At the age of eight my father used to send me after his pail of beer and it was by lapping the foam off the beer that I first discovered that the taste was much to my liking. By the time I was fourteen, at which time I quit school, I had found that wine and hard cider were also pleasing to my palate. The next six years I spent learning the art of barbering and by the end of this period I had become both a proficient barber and an earnest drinker.

During the next 10 or 12 years I was able to acquire several lucrative shops, some with poolrooms and restaurants attached. It seemed quite impossible however for me to stand prosperity so I would drink myself out of one situation, get myself together a bit, develop another, and then repeat the performance.

The time came when I could no longer refinance myself so I began to float about the country, getting a job here and there as I could, but invariably I got fired in a short time because of my unreliability.

My marriage, which occurred in 1910 about the time I started my successful ownership of shops, resulted in our having a family of ten children who were usually desperately in need because I used my slender income for booze instead of providing for them.

I finally secured a job in a shop in a town of about 4,500 people, where I now live. My reputation for drinking soon became more or less generally known. About this time a deacon and the pastor of one of the local churches used to come in the shop for their work and were constantly inviting me to church and Bible classes, which invitations irritated me very much. I earnestly wished they would mind their own business.

I finally did accept one or two invitations to social functions at the home of one of these men, and was received so cordially that the barrier between us was partially lowered.

I did not stop drinking however, though my feeling toward these men was kindly. They at last persuaded me to go to a nearby town to have a talk with a doctor who had had a great deal of experience with this type of trouble. I listened to the man for two hours, and although my mind was quite foggy I retained a good deal of what he said. I feel that the combined effort of these three Christian gentlemen made it possible for me to have a vital spiritual experience. This occurred in March, 1937.

For about six years previous to this time I was never at any time completely free from the influence of liquor.

Since that time I have regained the love of my family and the respect of the community, and can truthfully say that the past two years have been the happiest of my life.

I have busied myself a great deal during these two years in helping others who were afflicted as I was, and the combined efforts of the deacon, the pastor, and myself, have resulted in nine other men finding a way out of difficulties which were identical with mine. I feel this activity has played an important part in my mastery of this most devastating habit.

# Educated Agnostic

Why go into the drinking pattern that is so much the same with all of us? Three times I had left the hospital with hope that I was saying goodbye forever. And here I was again.

The first day there I told the kindly doctor that I was a thoroughly hopeless case and would probably continue to return as long as I could beg, borrow, or steal the money to get in. On the second day he told me that he knew of something that would keep me off liquor for life. I laughed at him. Yes, indeed, I would do anything or take anything that would produce such results, but there wasn't anything. On the third day a man came to talk with me. He was an alcoholic who had stopped! He talked about alcoholism and a spiritual way of life. I was deeply impressed by his seriousness, but nothing that he said made sense to me. He spoke about God, and a power greater than one's self. I remember being very careful not to say anything that might shake his faith in whatever it was he believed! I was deeply grateful to him for taking the trouble to talk with me, but what he had was not for me. I had thought much about religion and had come to rather definite conclusions. There was no God. The universe was an inexplicable phenomenon. In spite of my sorry state and outlook, there were many beautiful things in life, but no beauty. There were truths discoverable about life, but no truth. There were people who were good, kind, considerate, but no such thing as goodness. I had read rather extensively, but when people began to talk in such ultimates I was lost. I could find in life no eternal purpose nor anything that might be labeled "divine guidance." War, illness, cruelty, stupidity, poverty and greed were not and could not be the product of any purposeful creation. The whole thing simply didn't make sense.

About this I felt no deep emotion. I had struggled with the problem during late adolescence, but had long since ceased to give it anxious thought. Many people believe in a god of some sort and worship him in various ways. That was excellent. I thought it nice that so many people, poor misguided souls, could find so simple a solution to their problems. If this world proved too hopelessly disillusioning they could always seek comfort in a more pleasant existence promised in a world to come, where wrongs would be righted and justice tempered with tender mercy would prevail. But none of that was for me. I had enough courage and intellectual honesty to face life as I saw it without recourse to a self-erected deity.

The next day another man visited me. He, too, had been an alcoholic and stopped drinking. He pointed out that I had found myself unable to handle my liquor problem by myself. He had been in the same position, yet he hadn't had a drink in over three years! He told me of other men who had found sobriety through the recognition of some power beyond themselves. If I cared to I was to consider myself invited to a gathering the following Tuesday where I would meet other alcoholics who had stopped.

With the knowledge I now have, it is hard for me to recall how screwy the whole thing sounded—the blind leading the blind, a union of drunks, all banded together in some kind of a spiritual belief! What could be more idiotic! But . . . these men were sober! Nuts!

I returned to my despairing wife with this incoherent story of a bunch of drunks who had found a cure for their alcoholism through some kind of spiritual exercise and who held regular meetings where, as far as I could figure out, they went through some kind of spiritual exercise! She was very nearly convinced that my mental balance had now been completely and probably permanently destroyed. The only rational support I could find for giving it a try was that it was vouched for by the kindly doctor whom she had met on several occasions at the hospital. That and the fact that nothing else worked.

May I stop at this point and address a few sentences direct to agnostic or atheistically inclined alcoholics: You can't take less stock in the references made to God in this book than I would have if this book had been available to me at that time. To you those references have no meaning. They have simply used a name that people give to a fond delusion. All your life, except possibly in early childhood, when you conceived of an enormous figure with a flowing white beard somewhere beyond the clouds, it has meant nothing. You have now too much intelligence and honesty to allow of such delusions. Even if you could, you are too proud to affirm a belief now that you are in desperate trouble, that you denied when things were rosy. Or, you might possibly persuade yourself to believe in some creative force, or algebraic "X," but what earthly good would an "X" be in solving such a problem as you face? And, even admitting, from your knowledge of psychology, it is possible you might acquire such delusions, how could you possibly believe in them if you recognized them as delusions? Some such thinking must have been going on in your mind as you have weighed these incredible experiences against your own inability to cope with a problem that is gradually destroying your personality. Rest assured that such questions were in my mind. I could see no satisfactory solution to any of them. But I kept hard to the only thing that seemed to hold out any hope, and gradually my difficulties were lessened. I have not given up my intellect for the sake of my soul, nor have I destroyed my integrity to preserve my health and sanity. *All I had feared to lose I have gained and all I feared to gain I have lost.*

But to conclude my story: The following Tuesday, hardly daring to hope and fearful of the worst, my wife and I attended our first gathering with former alcoholic slaves who had been made free through the rediscovery of a power for good, found through a spiritual attitude toward life. I know that I have never before been so inspired. It was not anything that happened. Because nothing happened. Nor yet by anything that was said, but more by an atmosphere created by friendliness, sincerity, honesty, confidence, and good cheer. I couldn't believe that these men could have been drunks, and yet gradually I learned their stories, alcoholics every one!

That was, with me, the beginning of a new life. It would be difficult, if not impossible, for me to put into words the change that has taken place in me, I have since learned that with many members the change has been almost instantaneous. This was not the case with me. I was tremendously inspired at first, but my basic thinking was not altered that evening nor did I expect any profound change. I felt that while the spiritual aspect of what these men had was not for me, I did believe strongly in the emphasis they put on the need to help others. I felt that if I could have the inspiration of these gatherings and if I could have an opportunity to try to help others that the two together would re-enforce my own will-power and thus be of tremendous assistance. But gradually, in a manner I can not explain, I began to re-examine the beliefs I had thought beyond criticism. Almost imperceptibly my whole attitude toward life underwent a silent revolution. I lost many worries and gained confidence. I found myself saying and thinking things that a short time ago I would have condemned as platitudes! A belief in the basic spirituality of life has grown and with it belief in a supreme and guiding power for good.

In the process of this change I can recognize two immensely significant steps for me. The first step I took when I admitted to myself for the first time that all my previous thinking might be wrong. The second step came when I first consciously wished to believe. As a result of this experience I am convinced that to seek is to find, to ask is to be given. The day never passes that I do not silently cry out in thankfulness, not merely for my release from alcohol, but even more for a change that has given life new meaning, dignity, and beauty.

# Another Prodigal Story

"Hello, Pal."

"Hello, Buddy!"

"Have a drink?"

"Got one!"

"Come over on the next stool, I'm lonesome. Hell of a world."

"You said it, brother,—hell of a world."

"You taking rye? Mine's gin. God, I'm up against it now!"

"How's 'at?"

"Oh, same old hell—hell—hell. She's going to leave me now!"

"Your wife?"

"Yeah. How am I going to live? Can't go home like this; too damn drunk to stay out. Can't land in jail—will if I stay out—ruin my business—business going anyway—break her heart. Where is she you ask? She's at the store, working I guess, probably eating her heart out waiting for me. What time is it? Seven o'clock? Store's been closed an hour. She's gone home by now. Well, what the hell. Have one more—then I'll go."

That is a hazy recollection of my last debauch. Nearly a year ago now. By the time my new "bar fly friend" and I had soaked up several more, I was shedding tears and he, in the tender throes of drunken sympathy, was working out a guaranteed plan whereby my wife would greet me with great joy and out-spread arms as soon as "we" got home.

Yes "we" were going to my home. He was the finest fixer in the world. He knew all about how to handle wives. He admitted that!

So, two drunks, now lifetime buddies, stumbled out arm in arm headed up the hill towards home.

A draft of cool air cleared some of the fog away from my befuddled brain. "Wait a minute, what's this so-and-so-plan of yours? I got to know about it," I said. "I got to know what you're going to say and what I say."

The plan was a honey! All he had to do was to lead me up to the apartment, ring the bell, ask my wife if I was her husband, and then tell her he had found me down at the river about to jump from the bridge and had saved my life.

"That's all there is to it," he kept mumbling over and over, "works every time—never fails."

On up the hill we staggered, then my "life saver" got a better idea that would clinch the deal. He'd have to go home first and put on clean linen. Couldn't let the nice lady see a dirty shirt.

That sounded all right. Maybe he'd have a bottle at his home. So we stumbled up to his place, a dreary third floor back room, on a third rate street.

I have a hazy recollection of that place, but have never been able to find it since. There was a photograph of a quite pretty girl on his dresser. He told me it was a picture of his wife and that she had kicked him out because he was drunk. "You know how women are," he said.

Some fixer!

He did put on a clean shirt all right and then reached into a drawer and pulled out a .38 calibre revolver. That gave me quite a sobering shock. I reached for the gun realizing in a hazy way that here was trouble.

He began to pull the trigger and every moment I expected to hear an explosion, but the gun was empty. He proved it!

Then he got a new idea. To reconcile my wife and make her happy, he would tell her the gun was mine, that I stood on the bridge, with the gun at my head and that he snatched it away just in time to save my life.

God Almighty must have, at that moment, granted me a flash of sanity. I quickly excused myself while he was completing his toilet and, on the pretext of phoning my wife, rushed noisily down the stairs and ran down the street with all my might.

Some blocks away I came to a drug store, bought a pint of gin, and drank half it in several large gulps, staggered on up to my apartment, and tumbled into bed, fully dressed and dead drunk.

This wasn't any new terror for my wife. This sort of thing had been going on for several years, only I was getting worse and worse with each drunken spree and more difficult to handle.

Only the previous day I had been in an accident. A Good Samaritan saw my condition and got me away quickly, before the police came, and drove me back to my home.

I was dreadfully drunk that day and my wife consulted a lawyer as preliminary to entering divorce action. I swore to her that I wouldn't drink again and within 24 hours, here I was in bed dead drunk.

Several months previously I had spent a week in a New York hospital for alcoholics and came out feeling that everything would be all right. Then I began to think that I had the thing licked. I could practice a little controlled drinking. I knew I couldn't take much but just one drink before dinner. That went all right, too. Sure I had it licked now! The next step was to take one quick one at noon and cover it up with a milk shake. To make it doubly sure, I'd have ice cream put into the milk shake, and then, so help me, I don't know what the next step down was, but I surely landed at the bottom with an awful, heartbreaking thud.

The next morning was June 7th. I recall the date so well because the sixth is my daughter's birthday. And that, by the grace of God, was my last spree.

That morning I was afraid to open my eyes, surely my wife would have kept her promise and left me. I loved my wife. It is a paradox I know, but I did and do.

When I did stir, there she was sitting at my bedside.

"Come on," she said, "get up, bathe, shave and dress. We're going to New York this morning."

"New York!" I said. "To the hospital?"

"Yes."

"I haven't any money to pay a hospital."

"I know you haven't," she said, "but I arranged it all last night over long distance and I'm going to give you that one chance, once again. If you let me down this time, that's all there is."

Well, I went into that hospital again feeling like a whipped cur. My wife pleaded with the doctor to please do something to save her husband, to save her home, to save our business, and our self-respect.

The doctor assured us that he really had something for me this time that would work and with that faint hope, we separated; she to hurry back home, 150 miles away, and carry on the work of two people and I to sit trembling and fearful there in what seemed to me, a shameful place.

Four days later a man called on me and seemed interested to know how I was coming along. He told me that he, too, had been there several times but had now found relief.

That night another man came. He, too, had suffered the same trouble and told how he and the other fellow and several more had been released from alcohol.

Then the next day a fine fellow came, and in a halting but effective way, told how he had placed himself in God's hand and keeping. Almost before I knew it, I was asking God to clean me up.

I suppose there are many who feel a strong resentment against such a spiritual approach. Some of Alcoholics Anonymous whom I have met since that day tell me they had difficulty in accepting a simple, day to day, plan of faith. In my case I was ripe for such an opportunity, perhaps because of early religious training. I have always, it seems, had a keen sense of the fact and presence of God.

That, too, like loving my wife and at the same time hurting her so dreadfully, is paradoxical, but it's a fact. I knew that God, was there with infinite love and yet, somehow, I kept on drifting further and further away. But now I do feel that my heart and mind are "tuned in" and by His grace there will be no more alcoholic "static."

After making this final agreement (not just another resolution) to let God to be first in my life, the whole outlook and horizon brightened up in a manner which I am unable to describe except to say that it was "glorious."

The following day was Monday and my ex-alcoholic friend insisted that I check out from the hospital and come over to his home in 'Jersey. I did that and there I found a lovely wife and children all so "happy about the whole thing."

The next night I was taken to a meeting, at the home of an ex-alcoholic in Brooklyn, where to my surprise, there were more than 30 men like myself, telling of a liberty of living unmatched by anything I had ever seen.

Since returning to my home, life has been so different. I have paid off the old debts, have money enough now for decent, clothes and some to use in helping others, a thing which I enjoy doing but didn't do when I had to contribute so generously to alcohol.

I am trying to help other alcoholics. At this writing there are four of us working, all of whom have been kicked around dreadfully.

There is no "cocky" feeling about this for me. I know I am an alcoholic and while I used to call on God to help me, my conclusion is that I was simply asking God to help me drink alcohol without its hurting me which is a far different thing than asking him to help me not to drink at all.

So here I stand, living day to day, in His presence, and it is wonderful—This prodigal came home.

# The Car Smasher

During the first week of March, 1937, through the grace of God, I ended 20 years of a life made practically useless because I could not do two things.

First, I was unable to not take a drink.

Second, I was unable to take a drink without getting drunk.

Perhaps a third as important as the other two should be added; my being unwilling to admit either of the first two.

With the result I kept trying to drink without getting drunk, and kept making a nightmare of my life, causing suffering and hardship to all those relatives and friends who tried so hard to help me and whom, when I was sober, I took the greatest pleasure in pleasing.

The first time I drank anything strong, or in greater quantity than a glass of beer, I got disgustingly drunk and missed the dinner which had been arranged for me in honor of my coming marriage.

I had to be taken home and remained in bed the following day; more sick than I thought a human could be and live. Yet, until two years ago I periodically did the same thing.

Making money was always pretty easy when I was sober and worked.

All right when sober—absolutely helpless with a drink aboard. But I seemed to have had the idea that making money or a living was something to take or let alone.

I got into the real estate business—began to neglect business, sometimes with four houses under construction, wouldn't see any of them for a week or even longer—sometimes paid good money for an option, then forgot to exercise it. I made and lost plenty of money in the market.

Understand, I wasn't actually drunk all of this time but there seemed always to be an excuse to have a drink, and this first one, more and more often lead to my becoming drunk. As time went on, periods between drunks got shorter and I was full of fear; fear that I wouldn't be able to do anything I agreed to do; fear of meeting men; worrying about what they might know of my drinking and its results; all of which made me quite useless whether I was sober or drunk.

Thus I drifted. Breaking promises to my wife, my mother, and a host of other relatives and friends who stood more from me and tried harder than humans should be expected to, to help me.

I always seemed to pick the most inopportune time for a binge. An important business deal to be closed might find me in another city. Once when entrusted to purchase for a large customer, I agreed to meet his representative in New York. I spent the time waiting for a train in a bar; arrived in New York tight; stayed tight the week; and came home by a route twice the distance from New York.

Worked weeks, by long distance, wire, letters, and personal calls, to contact possible business connections under proper conditions and finally succeeded, only to show up tight or get tight and insult the man who's friendship, or respect meant so much.

Each time there was the feeling of regret, inability to understand why, but a firm determination that it would never happen again—but it did—in fact the periods between became increasingly shorter, and the duration of each binge longer.

During the aforementioned period, I had spent thousands of dollars, my home was broken up; half a dozen cars smashed up; I had been picked up by police for driving while intoxicated—plain drunk; had sponged and borrowed money; cashed rubber checks; and made such a general nuisance of myself that I lost all the friends I had. At least they felt unwilling to be a party to financing me while I made a more complete ass of myself. And I, on my side was ashamed to face any of them when I was sober.

My friends secured jobs for me; I made good on them for a time. I advanced quickly to night superintendent in a factory but it wasn't long until I was missing, or worse, turning up drunk; was warned—warned again; finally fired. I was later rehired as a factory hand and mighty glad to have it—advance again—then back to the bottom—always the same process.

I drank continuously and when I drank, sooner or later, and generally sooner, I got drunk and threw everything away.

During the early part of 1935 my brother secured my release from the city jail. On that day by sincere but non-alcoholic friends I was shown what might be done about my drinking with the help of God.

I asked for this help, gratefully accepted it, and in addition to losing my desire for drink, asked for and received the same help in other matters. I began to earn my living and in my new found security, was unashamed to meet people I had avoided for years with happy results.

Things continued well, I had two or three advancements to better jobs with greater earning power. My every need was being met as long as I accepted and acknowledged the Divine Help which was so generously given.

I find now, as I look back, that this period covered about six or eight months, then I began to think how smart I was; to wonder if my superiors realized what they had in me; if they were not pretty small about the money they paid me; as these thoughts grew, my feeling of gratefulness grew less. I was neglecting to ask for help—when I received it as I always did, I neglected to acknowledge it. Instead I took great credit for myself. I began to take credit for the non-drinking too—it came to me strongly that I had conquered the drinking habit myself—I became convinced of my great will power.

Then someone suggested a glass of beer—I had one. This was even better than I thought—I could take a drink and not get drunk. So another day, another beer until it was regular every day. Now I was indeed in the saddle concerning drink—could take it or leave it alone. Just to prove it to myself, I decided to march right past the place I usually stopped for beer, and I felt pretty good as I went to the parking lot for my car. The longer I drove the greater was my pride that I had finally licked liquor. I was sure I had—so sure in fact that I stopped and had a beer before I went home. In my smugness I continued to drink beer and began occasionally to drink liquor.

So it went until inevitably, "as darkness follows the sun," I got drunk and was right back where I had been fifteen years before, slipping into a binge every now and then—never knowing when they would come—nor where I would wind up.

This lasted about eight months—I didn't miss much time from work—did spend one ten day stretch in the hospital after a beating I got while drunk—was warned a few times by my superiors—but was "getting by."

In the meantime I had heard of some men who, like myself, were what I had always scoffed at being—alcoholics. I had been invited to see them, but after twenty years of drinking, I felt there was nothing wrong with me. *They* might need it; *they* might be queer; but not me. I wasn't going to get drunk again.

Of course I did, again and again, until these men not only contacted me but took me under their wing.

After a few days of "degoofing" in a hospital, these men came to me one by one and told me of their experiences. They didn't lecture—didn't tell me I should quit. But they did tell me *how* to quit. THAT WAS IMPORTANT and simple too.

Their suggestion was that we simply acknowledge we had made a pretty dismal failure of our lives, that we accept as truth and act upon what we had always been taught and known, that there was a kind and merciful God; that we were His children; and, that if we would let Him, He would help us.

I had certainly made a mess of my life. From the age of 20 I had thrown aside everything God had seen fit to endow me with. Why not avail myself of this all wise, ever-present help?

This I did. I ask for, accept, and acknowledge this help, and know that so long as I do, I shall never take a drink and what is more important, though impossible without the first, all other phases of my life have been helped.

There are, it seems to me, four steps to be taken by one who is a victim of alcoholism.

FIRST: Have a real desire to quit.
SECOND: Admit you can't. (This is hardest.)
THIRD: Ask for His ever present help.
FOURTH: Accept and acknowledge this help.

# Hindsight

Fired! Still, I got a new and better job. One which gave me more time to relax and where drinking was permitted during working hours. People were beginning to criticize my drinking habits and I scoffed at them. Hadn't I earned ten thousand dollars that year? And wasn't this the middle of the depression? Who were they to say that I couldn't handle my liquor? A year of this and I was fired.

Other jobs followed with the same net result. After each experience of this kind I would sit down and figure out the reason why it happened. I always found a good reason, and usually people accepted it and gave me another chance. For weeks, sometimes months, I wouldn't touch a drop and because I could do this, I reasoned that there was a real excuse for that last bender, and since that excuse no longer existed I could start to drink moderately again.

I usually did—for a while. Then I would step up the consumption about one glass per day until I reached the stage where all of the past unhappy experiences associated with drinking were brought back to my mind. Soon I was crying in my beer; full of self-pity, and off again to a flying start toward a floundering finish.

How many times this happened, I don't know. I don't even want to know. I do know that during this period I completely smashed nine new automobiles and was never scratched. Even this didn't convince me that there might be a God who was looking out for me in answer to the prayers of others. I made many friends and abused them terribly. I didn't want to, but when it was a question of a friendship or a drink, I usually took the drink.

In a final effort to escape, I went to New York thinking I could leave my reputation and troubles behind me. It didn't work. I was hired by eight nationally known organizations and fired just as quickly when they had checked my references. The world was against me. They wouldn't give me a chance. So I continued my drinking and took any mediocre job I could get.

Occasionally I dropped into a church half hoping that I might absorb something, anything, that might help a little bit. On one of these visits I saw and met a girl who I felt could be the answer to all of my problems. I told her all about myself and how

I felt sure that with her friendship and love everything could and would be different. Although born in New York she was "from Missouri." I would have to show her first. She had seen other girls try to reform men by marrying them and she knew it didn't work.

She suggested praying and having faith and a lot of things that seemed silly at the time, but I really got down to business and started doing some serious bargaining with God. I prayed and prayed. In all earnestness I said, "If You will get this girl for me then I'll stop drinking for You." And "If You will only get me my original job back, I'll drink moderately for You."

I soon found out that God didn't work that way because I didn't get the girl or the job.

Six months later I was sitting in a small hotel on the west side of New York full of remorse and desperate because I didn't know what would happen next. A middle-aged man approached me and said in a very sincere voice, "Do you really want to stop drinking?" Immediately I answered "Yes," because I knew that was the correct answer. He wrote down a name and address and said "When you are sure you do, go and see this man." He walked away.

I began to think, "Did I really want to quit? Why should I? If I couldn't have this girl and I couldn't ever have a good job again, why in the hell should I quit?" I tucked the address into my pocket along with a nickel for subway fare, just in case I ever decided to really quit. I started drinking again, but could get no happiness or release regardless of the number of drinks.

Occasionally I would check up to see if the address and the nickel were still safe, because I was being tortured with one thought this girl had given to me. "You must be decent for your own sake. And because you want to be decent, not because some one else wants you to be."

A week later I found myself in the presence of the man whose address was in my pocket. His story was incredible. I couldn't believe it, but he had the proof. I met men whose stories convinced me that in the ranks of men who had been heavy drinkers I was an amateur and a sissy.

What I heard was hard to believe but I wanted to believe it. What's more I wanted to try it and see if it wouldn't work for me.

It worked, and is still working. For weeks I was bitter against society. Why didn't some one put me wise to this before? Why did I have to go on like that for years making my parents unhappy, abusing friends, and passing up opportunities? It wasn't fair that I should be the instrument to make people unhappy.

I believe now that I was given this experience so that I might understand and be of use in helping others to find a solution to this and other problems.

When I decided to do something about my problem, I was reconciled to the fact that it might be necessary for me to wash dishes, scrub floors, or do some menial task for possibly many years in order to re-establish myself as a sober, sane, and reliable person. Although I still wanted and hoped for the better things in life, I was prepared to accept whatever was due me.

Once I became sincere, good things began to happen to me. My first experience in overcoming fear was three weeks later when I applied for a position with a national organization. After numerous questions I was finally asked why I had left the company I had been with six years. I replied that I had been fired for being a drunk. The manager was flabbergasted and so completely astounded by the truth that he refused to believe me. I referred him to my former employer but he refused to write him—but he did give me the job.

It has been three and a half years since I made that decision. Those years have been the happiest years of my life. The little girl, who was big enough to tell me the nasty truth when I needed it, is now my wife.

Eight months ago I went to another city to set up a new business. I had sufficient money to last me several months. What I wanted to accomplish could have been done under ordinary circumstances in about two weeks. The obstacles I have encountered and overcome are hard to enumerate. At least twenty times I have been sure that I would be doing business within the next twenty-four hours and at least twenty times something has happened which later made it seem that the business never would get started.

While I am writing this I happen to be at the low point of the twenty-first time. Money is exhausted. All recent developments have been unfavorable, everything seems on the surface to be wrong. Yet I am not discouraged. I am not blue. I feel no bitterness toward these people who have tried to obstruct the progress of the business, and somehow I feel because I have tried hard, played square, and met situations, that something good will come from this whole experience. It may not come the way I want it, but I sincerely believe that it will come the way that it is best.

# On His Way

In early youth I believe I had some of the tendencies which lead to alcoholism. I refer to attempted escapes from reality.

At fifteen and sixteen, although free at home to drink small amounts of beer and wine, I drank considerable quantities of stronger liquors at school and other places. Not enough to cause serious worry, but enough apparently to give me occasionally what I thought I wanted. Escape? A feeling of superiority? I do not know.

I then decided I'd had enough of school, which decision was probably shared by the schools. The next few years were spent in civil engineering work, travel, sports, and a little idleness, and I seem to have avoided alcoholic difficulties of the more pronounced kind.

Immediately before marriage and in the short time before sailing for France, alcohol began to take a real part in my life. A year and a half in war time France postponed the inevitable and the post war period of hopes and plans brought me nearer and nearer to the point where I eventually found myself to be an alcoholic. Not that I would have admitted it then, having the alcoholic's usual facility for deception, both to self and others.

Divorced, sometimes suspecting that drinking was the basis for most of my troubles but never admitting it, I had enough left in health, interests of various kinds, and luck to carry on with considerable success.

About this time I stopped all social drinking. I became a periodical drunkard, the sprees lasting from three days to three weeks and the dry intervals lasting from three weeks to four months.

During one of the best years, I made a happy marriage and the age of thirty-five found me with the following: a beautiful little home presided over by a kind, understanding, and lovely wife; a partnership in a firm I had helped to found years before; more than a comfortable income; many luxuries and many friends; opportunity to follow my interests and hobbies; a love of my work; pride in my success; great health; optimism; and hope on the credit side. On the other hand, I had a growing, gnawing fear of my recurring trouble.

I slipped by far too easy stages to the bottom in less than eight years. Not a pleasant place, the bottom. Sometimes I slept in a cheap hotel or rooming house, sometimes a flop house, sometimes the back room of a police station and once in a doorway; many times in the alcoholic ward at a hospital, and once in a subway toilet. Sometimes decently fed, clothed, and housed, I worked at my business on commission with a large firm; sometimes I dared not appear there cold, hungry, with torn clothes, shaking body and muddled brain advertising what I had become. Helpless, hopeless, bitter.

Sometimes I was apparently on the way back, and sometimes writhing in bed for days at a time, terrorized by the fear of insanity and by the spectres of people without faces, people with horrible faces, people grimacing and laughing at me and my misery. Tortured by dreams from which I would awake with a scream of agony and bathed in cold sweat. Tortured by day dreams of what might have been, dreams of the kindness, faith and love that had been heaped upon me.

Due to this last however, and to what little remained of my former self and perhaps to some lingering power of spiritual faith, I became somewhat better. Not well, but better.

This helped me to take stock and to try to do some clear thinking. I found my inventory somewhat mixed, but as my thoughts became clearer, I grew much better and at last arrived at that point where for the first time in several years I could see some light and hope ahead of me. Through a haze of doubt and skepticism I began to realize, partly at least, many things in myself which had greased the path I had pursued, and some vague thoughts and ideas came to me that are now crystallizing with the help of the men I have been happy to join.

What thoughts and ideas? The answer is short, although the road to it is long and tedious.

My intelligence, instead of drawing me further away from spiritual faith is bringing me closer to it. I no longer react in quite the same way when my will and desires are apparently frustrated.

The simple words "Thy Will Be Done" and the simple ideas of honesty and of helping others are taking on a new meaning for me. I should not be surprised to find myself coming to the astounding conclusion that God, whoever or whatever He may be, is eminently more capable of running this universe than I am. At last I believe I am on my way.

# An Alcoholic's Wife

I have the misfortune, or I should say the good fortune of being an alcoholic's wife. I say misfortune because of the worry and grief that goes with drinking, and good fortune because we found a new way of living.

My husband did not drink, to my knowledge, for several years after we were married. Then we started on an occasional Saturday night party. As I drank nothing except an occasional highball I soon became what was called a "wet blanket." The parties became more frequent and more often I was left at home.

I would sit up and wait for him. As each car passed the house I would return to walking the floor and crying and feeling so sorry for myself, thinking, "Here I am left at home to take care of the baby and him out having a good time."

When he did return sometimes on Sunday and sometimes a week later, it usually called for a scene. If he was still drunk I would put him to bed and cry some more. If he was sober it would mean I would say all the things I had been thinking and cry some more. He usually got drunk again.

I finally went to work as the bills worried me. I thought if I worked and got the bills paid he would quit drinking. He had no money in the bank but would write checks as he knew I would pay them for the boy's sake and in the hopes that each time would be the last.

I thought I should have a lot of credit, as I was paying his bills, taking care of the house and baby, besides my work, making as much money as he was, doing without things I wanted so he could have a good time.

I always went to church and thought I was living a Christian life. After my husband came in contact with Alcoholics Anonymous I thought our troubles were over as I was sure all our trouble was his drinking.

I soon found out that there was a lot wrong with me. I was selfish with my money, time, and thoughts. I was selfish about my time because I was always tired and had no time left for my family's pleasure or to do God's work. All I did was go to Sunday School and Church on Sunday with the boy and thought that was all God wanted me to do. I would be irritable and lose my temper and say all manner of things which usually called for another drunk and me pitying myself all over again.

Since giving my husband's problem to God I have found a peace and happiness. I know that when I try to take care of the problems of my husband I am a stumbling block as my husband has to take his problems to God the same as I do.

My husband and I now talk over our problems and trust in a Divine Power. We have now started to live. When we live with God we want for nothing.

# An Artist's Concept

*"There is a principle which is a bar against all information, which is proof against all arguments and which can not fail to keep a man in everlasting ignorance—that principle is contempt prior to investigation."*

—HERBERT SPENCER

The above quotation is descriptive of the mental attitudes of many alcoholics when the subject of religion, as a cure, is first brought to their attention. It is only when a man has tried everything else, when in utter desperation and terrific need he turns to something bigger than himself, that he gets a glimpse of the way out. It is then that contempt is replaced by hope, and hope by fulfillment.

In this personal story I have endeavored to relate something of my experience in the search for spiritual help rather than a description of the neurotic drinking that made the search necessary. After all, the pattern of most alcoholic experiences fits a pretty general mold. Experiences differ because of circumstances, environment, and temperament, but the after effects, both physical and mental, are almost identical. It makes but little difference how or why a man becomes an alcoholic once this disease manifests itself. The preventive measures adopted for alcoholic tendencies in the future will have to be found in a more progressive program of mental hygiene and medical research than is now obtainable. It is important that at present we believe there is only one sure pathway to recovery for any alcoholic.

In my own case I was not entirely ignorant of the causes that led me into excessive drinking. In a desperate effort to eliminate these causes, to find a means to better mental and physical health, I investigated the alcoholic problem from every angle. Medicine, psychology, psychiatry, and psychoanalysis absorbed my interest and supplied me with a great deal of general and specific information. It led me in the end, however, to the fact that for me here was a mental and physical disease that science had placed in the category of "incurables." Briefly, all that this study and research ever did for me was to show something about WHY I drank. It substantiated a fact I had known all along, that my drinking was symptomatic. It did point out a road to better mental health but it demanded something of me in return that I did not have to give. It asked of me a *power* of self-will but it did not take into consideration that this self-will was already drugged with poison—that it was very sick. Intuitively I also knew that a person constrained to temperance by the domination of will is no more *cured* of his vice than if he were locked up in prison. I knew that somehow, some way, the mental stream, the emotions, must be purified before the right pathway could be followed.

It was about this time that I began "flirting" with religion as a possible way out. I approached the subject in a wary, none too reverent, attitude. I believed in an omnipotent God or Deity, but the orthodox approach through the church, with its dogma and ritual, left me unmoved. The more I struggled to gain an intelligent grasp upon spiritual development, the more confused I became. On the other hand a purely materialistic viewpoint that postulated a "mechanical order of things" seemed too negative even to entertain. As an artist I had spent too much time communing with nature—trying to place upon canvas or paper my emotional feelings, not to know that a tremendous spiritual power was back of the universe. There was, however, so much that seemed illogical or sentimental about religion in general—so many doubts assailed me, so many problems to be confronted—yet there was within myself a strong and urgent desire for spiritual satisfaction. The occasional periods in which I felt a spiritual emotion, I immediately examined with all the ardor of the inveterate analyst. Was this emotion just a form of religious ecstasy? Was it fear? Was it just blind belief or had I tapped something?

"Most men," wrote Thoreau, "lead lives of quiet desperation." It was the articulation of this despair that led to my drinking in the beginning. Religion, so far, had only added to my desperation. I drank more than ever.

A seed had been planted, however, and a short time afterward I met the man who has for the past five years devoted a great deal of time and energy to helping alcoholics. Looking back on that meeting, the simplicity of his talk with me is amazing. He told me very little but what I already knew, in part, but what he did have to say was bereft of all fancy spiritual phraseology—it was simple Christianity imparted with Divine Power. The next day I met over twenty men who had achieved a mental rebirth from alcoholism. Here again it was not so much what these men told me in regard to their experiences that was impressive, as it was a sense or feeling that an invisible influence was at work. What was it this man had and these other men exemplified without their knowing? They were human every-day sort of people. They certainly were not pious. They had no "holier than thou" attitude. They were not reformers, and their concepts of religion in some cases were almost inarticulate. But they had *something!* Was it just their sincerity that was magnetic? Yes, they certainly were sincere, but much more than that emanated from them. Was it their great and terrible need, now being fulfilled, that made me feel a vibratory force that was new and strange? Now I was getting closer and suddenly, it seemed to me, I had the answer. These men were but instruments. Of themselves they were nothing.

Here at last was a demonstration of spiritual law at work. Here was spiritual law working through human lives just as definitely and with the same phenomena expressed in the physical laws that govern the material world.

These men were like lamps supplied with current from a huge spiritual dynamo and controlled by the rheostat of their souls. They burned dim, bright, or brilliant, depending upon the degree and progress of their contact. And this contact could only be maintained just so long as they obeyed that spiritual law.

These men were thinking straight—therefore their actions corresponded to their thoughts. They had given themselves, *their minds*, over to a higher power for *direction.* Here, it seemed to me, in the one word "Thought"—was the crux of the whole spiritual quest. That "As a man thinketh in his heart, so is he" and so is his health, his environment, his failure, or his success in life.

How foolish I had been in my quest for spiritual help. How selfish and egotistical I had been to think that I could approach God *intellectually.* In the very struggle to obtain faith I had lost it. I had given to the term faith a religious significance only. I had failed to see that faith was "our common everyday manner of thinking." That good and evil were but end results of certain uniform and reliable spiritual laws. Obviously, my own thinking had been decidedly wrong. Normal most of the time, it was abnormal at the wrong times. Like everyone's thinking, it was a mixture of good and bad, but mainly it was uncontrolled.

I had been sticking my chin out and getting socked by spiritual law until I was punch drunk. If one could become humble, if he could become *"as a little child"* before this powerful spiritual thought force, the pathway could be discovered.

The day I made my first efforts in this direction an entire new world opened up for me. Drinking as a vicious habit was washed completely out of my consciousness. I have never even been tempted to take a drink since. As a matter of fact there are so many other things within myself that need correction that the drink habit looks silly in comparison. Please do not assume that all this is but an exposition of spiritual pride. A chart of my spiritual progress would look like the "graph" of a business that had been hit by everything but an earthquake. But there has been progress. It has cured me of a vicious habit. Where my life had been full of mental turmoil there is now an ever increasing depth of calmness. Where there was a hit or miss attitude toward living there is now new direction and force.

The approaches of man to God are many and varied. My conception of God as Universal Mind is after all but one man's approach to and concept of the Supreme Being. To me it makes sense, opens up a fascinating field of endeavor and is a challenge, the acceptance of which can make of life the "Adventure Magnificent."

# The Rolling Stone

After the breaking up of our home, my Father went west and took up his work and became fairly successful.

Then it was decided that I should be sent to a preparatory school so to a mid-western school I was sent. It didn't last long for I got into a jam and left.

I went to Chicago, wrote my Father and he sent me fare to come on west, which I did. I started in to High School after I got there, but I had no companionship, for my Father was away most of the day and when he came in he always spent the evenings reading and studying.

This all caused me to become very bitter towards anything religious, because I felt that I was only in his way when he wanted to read his religious books and he took only enough interest in me to leave a dollar on the dresser each morning to buy my meals with. It caused me to become so hostile towards anything religious that I formed a hatred against religion which I was to carry for years.

During the time which I spent by myself, I had found that I could buy wine and loaf around saloons and it wasn't long before I had formed a taste for drink. I was only about fourteen years old then, but I looked eighteen.

When vacation time came I wanted to go to San Francisco. My father willingly let me go and after seeing the sights of that city I decided I wanted to go to sea and see the world, so it was only a short time before I found myself signed as an apprentice at sea and leading a new life.

In the meantime my mother had married again. I knew she was well taken care of so my letters were few and my visits home were years apart, and through the selfish interest I had taken in myself I never gave a thought to how worried she might be over me. I had become· a person wrapped up in my own life only and giving no thought of anyone else.

Starting to sea out of San Francisco brought me in and out of port there a great deal so I considered San Francisco my home, and as I had arrived there about 1905 I knew the old San Francisco of before the earthquake where the lid was off and vice flourished at all times.

In my young life I saw all and knew all and considered myself well able to play the game as others did.

I developed into a steady drinker and, when going to sea, was sure I took enough liquor along to take care of me for the trip. When we arrived at a foreign port we would go ashore and proceed to see the sights which mostly started at the first saloon. If American liquor was not to be had or was too high in cost then we would drink their native drink, and as I look back it hardly seems possible that I have a brain left to remember with for I have done about everything possible to destroy it by over-indulgence in alcohol.

I have been to most of the ports in this world; have stayed in some for some time; have put in a winter in Alaska; lived in the tropics; but no time did I ever find a place where I could not get liquor.

I quit the sea when I was just past 20. I had become interested in construction work, also had studied some art and learned the Freco decorating trade. Eventually I went into the building trade and have followed that ever since.

I had always made good wages or made good at contracting, but was ever a rolling stone, never staying in one place long and drinking just the same as in my seafaring days.

I had always a certain respect for myself and I carried my liquor well for years; knew enough not to make a show of myself and stopped when I had enough.

Then came the war. I was 29 years old and was in Texas when I went into the army and went overseas from there. After leaving Texas I found out that we were stopping in my home town for an hour and I received permission to call my mother when we arrived there, so fortunately I was able to get her down to the train before I left. I had not been home in 11 years and I then told her if I came back alive I would come home to stay.

I had not been in the service long before I was a high ranking non-commissioned officer, for I had learned army discipline years before in the army transport service and while in this country and when behind the lines in France this gave me a chance to get my liquor when my buddies couldn't.

But when we got to the front lines it was the first time in years that I was unable to get my daily share of alcohol but, when it was possible, I never missed.

On into Germany for six months where I made up for lost time. "Schnapps" was barred to American Troops but I got mine. After coming back to the U.S. I received an honorable discharge and came back to my home and mother.

Then I started trying to break away from liquor but it did not last. The last few years found me in all kinds of mixups for I had at last developed into an alcoholic.

When I drank I would get to the state where it required a doctor to straighten me out. The times I have had to rely upon doctors are numerous. I even tried sanitariums for relief. I had plenty of suffering thrown in but still I would drift back again to that first drink and off again I went.

I wanted to quit but each time I drank it was worse than before. The misery that my mother went through was unbelievable for I had become her sole support. I was willing to try anything if I could only get a release from this curse. I knew it was breaking up my home and I was losing everyone that was dear to me.

For a few months I was successful in discontinuing drinking. Then all of a sudden I fell again. I lost my position and thought I was through.

When I was told of a doctor who had been successful in overcoming alcohol and was asked to go and see him in a nearby city, I consented but with a feeling that it was just another cure.

From him and a number of other men, however, I found it was possible to become a man again. He suggested my entrance into a hospital to clear my mind and build me up. Meals had become a thing of the past for me. I had lost all appetite for food but forced myself to eat a little to survive.

This doctor told me that unless I was sincere in wanting to quit drinking, I would be wasting his time and mine and also money in doing this. My answer was I would try anything that would release me.

I went into the hospital and started to build my body up again through proper nourishment, and my mind through a different method than I had ever known of.

A religious awakening was conveyed to me through some unseen force. I at one time would have laughed at such a possibility because I had tried it and failed because I had not applied it properly. I, at last, was shown the way by these men to whom I am now most grateful.

I am now 50 years old, unmarried, have become sane and sensible again, have made my mother happy and brought back those who were dear to me, have made many new friends, mix where I never mixed before, received back my old position. I have the respect of my fellow men and have learned how to actually live and really enjoy life. It has been nearly a year and a half since I have found this new life and I know as long as I do the few things that God requires me to do, I never will take another drink.

# Lone Endeavor

As a mother looked idly through a small medical journal, an article written by a doctor on alcoholism caught her attention. Anything in reference to this subject was worthy of perusal, for her son, an only child, had been drinking uncontrollably for years. Each year of his drinking had added new heartaches, though every small ray of hope had been investigated, and though he had tried desperately to stop. But little had been accomplished. He was occasionally able to remain sober for short periods at a time, but things constantly became worse.

So this mother read the short medical article with a heavy heart, for she was constantly on the alert to find something which might prove helpful to her son.

The article gave only a vague hint of the solution found by many alcoholics, which is fully covered in this book, but the mother immediately wrote to the doctor explaining her heart-breaking problem, and requesting further information. She felt there must be help somewhere, and surely if other men had recovered from alcoholism, her son also had a chance.

The doctor turned her letter over to Alcoholics Anonymous. It ended as follows:

"God knows if you can help my son, it will bring happiness to many of us who love him and ache with him in his futile efforts to overcome his problem. Please accept my gratitude for whatever you may be able to do and let me hear from you."

A few days later the following letter was sent to this mother. It was our initial effort to help others through the book alone.

"About a hundred men, here in the east, have found a solution for alcoholism that really works. We are now preparing a book hoping to help others who suffer in the same way, and are enclosing a rough copy of the first two chapters. As soon as possible we will forward rough copy of the rest of the proposed book."

We received no answer for some time, and later wrote again:

"We are sending you a pre-publication multilith copy of 'ALCOHOLICS ANONYMOUS.' We would appreciate hearing about your son's condition and his reaction to this volume, as this is the first time we have had an opportunity of trying to help an alcoholic at long distance. Won't you please write us?

Sincerely,
Alcoholics Anonymous"

After another period of silence from the far west, during which time we began to think this book was inadequate without personal contact, we received a long letter from the son, himself. A letter which we feel will be of tremendous help to others who live in distant places, who feel alone and totally unable to work this program out by themselves. A letter which encompasses a man's solitary effort to take what we had to offer and carry the program through alone. Alone except for one book and the help which printed pages could give; alone until he had tried our program of recovery and found spiritual comfort and help.

He wrote as follows:

"I want to thank you from the bottom of my heart for your letters and for 'ALCOHOLICS ANONYMOUS.' I have read this book from cover to cover and it is really the first time I have read anything dealing with alcoholism that made sense and showing understanding of the problems of the alcoholic.

I found the personal stories very accurate as pertaining to my own experience; any one of them might have been my own story.

I started drinking in 1917 when I was 18. I enlisted in the army, soon became a non-commissioned officer, went overseas as a sergeant. I associated with older men, drank, gambled, and ran around with them, sampling everything France had to offer.

Upon my return from France I continued drinking. At that time I could get plenty tight at night, get up in the morning and go to work feeling O.K. The following fifteen years were one drunk after another which, of course, as they got worse, meant one job after another. Police Department truck driving, etc. Then in an attempt to get away from it all I enlisted in the U. S. Marine Corps. In 13 months time I drank very little and was promoted to Gunnery Sergeant, a rank that usually takes 10 or 12 years to obtain, if ever. I started drinking again. In six months I was reduced to Line Sergeant. I transferred to get away from my former associates.

Then came several years in China. China of all places for a man who wanted to stay away from booze. My four years over, I did not re-enlist.

Came more jobs selling automobiles, real estate, etc. Then down to odd jobs. I was drinking so much no one could take a chance by giving me a steady job, such as I could easily have handled if I left the liquor alone. I married and the booze split that up. My mother was a nervous wreck. I was getting arrested for drinking three or four times a year. I had myself committed on two different occasions to

State Hospitals, but soon after discharge, I was back at it again. Two years ago I went to a private hospital for a liquor cure. A week after getting out I was curious as to what would happen if I took a drink. I took it—nothing happened. I took another—why go further. I went back to the private hospital, came out and was O.K. for a few months—then at it again.

Now previous to this and at the time of these cures, I was working at a State Hospital for the insane. I saw continually the effects of liquor but did it help me to leave it alone? No—it did not. But it did make me realize that if I did not, I would end up in the "bughouse" and someone else would be carrying the keys. After several years of working at mental institutions always in a violent ward, on account of my six feet 2 inches and 210 lbs., I realized there was too much nervous tension and every couple of months I would "blow up" and be off drunk for a week or ten days.

I left mental work and got a job at the County General Hospital where I am now in a medical ward. We get quite a few patients with D.T.s, all broken out with wine sores, etc. I steadied down a bit, but not enough. I was off "sick" for several days every six or eight weeks.

I married again. A good Catholic girl whose people were used to having liquor, especially wine around the house always. She of course could not understand about my drinking—as far as that's concerned, neither could I. And all this time my poor mother and wife became more and more worried.

Mother had heard of your wonderful work and wrote a doctor. You answered with letters, and finally the book. Before the book arrived and after reading the chapters I knew that the only way to combat this curse was to ask the help of that greater Power, God. I realized it even though I was then on a binge!

I contacted a friend of mine who is liaison officer of the Disabled Veterans of the World War. He made arrangements for my care in a State Sanitarium which specializes in alcoholism. I wanted to get the liquor out of my system and start this new idea right. I explained my absence as "Flu" and under the care of the head psychiatrist spent most of the time from Sept. 1, 1938 till Jan. 15, 1939 at the hospital having my appendix removed and a ventral hernia fixed up.

Six weeks ago I returned from the sanitarium and your book was here waiting for me. I read, more than that I pored over it so as not to miss anything. I thought to myself, yes, this is the only way. God is my only chance. I have prayed before but I guess not the right way. I have followed out the suggestions in the book, I am happier this moment than I have been in years. I'm sure I have found the solution, thanks to ALCOHOLICS ANONYMOUS.

I have had talks with another man, an attorney, who was at the sanitarium when I was. He has my book now and he is very much enthused.

I go down to the sanitarium every week for a check-up and medicine which they give me, just a tonic, no sedatives. The manager has asked me to contact some of his patients along our line. How I told him I would appreciate his letting me do so!

Would you put me in touch with some 'A.A.s' out here? I know it would help me and help me to help others.

I hope you can make sense out of this letter. I could write so much more but this I have written just as it popped into my head.

Please let me hear from you."

This man's lone struggle was impressive. Wouldn't the story of his solitary recovery be helpful to many others who would have to start out by themselves with only this book to aid them?

So we immediately sent him a wire:

> JUST RECEIVED LETTER. MAY WE HAVE YOUR PERMISSION TO USE LETTER ANONYMOUSLY IN BOOK AS FIRST EXAMPLE OF WHAT MIGHT BE ACCOMPLISHED WITHOUT PERSONAL CONTACT. IMPORTANT YOU WIRE THIS PERMISSION AS BOOK IS GOING TO PRINTER.
>
> ALCOHOLICS ANONYMOUS

His wire arrived next day:

> PERMISSION GRANTED WITH PLEASURE. LOTS OF LUCK.

# THE GREATEST THING IN THE WORLD

HENRY DRUMMOND

*1874*

# The Biblical Message

Though I speak with the tongues of men and of angels, and have not Love, I am become as sounding brass, or a tinkling cymbal. And though I have the gift of prophecy, and understand all mysteries, and all knowledge; and though I have all faith, so that I could remove mountains, and have not Love, I am nothing. And though I bestow all my goods to feed the poor, and though I give my body to be burned, and have not Love, it profiteth me nothing.

*Love suffereth long, and is kind;*
*Love envieth not;*
*Love vaunteth not itself, is not puffed up,*
*Doth not behave itself unseemly,*
*Seeketh not her own,*
*Is not easily provoked,*
*Thinketh no evil;*
*Rejoiceth not in iniquity, but rejoiceth in the truth;*
*Beareth all things, believeth all things, hopeth all*
*things, endure all things.*

Love never faileth: but whether there be prophecies, they shall fail; whether there be tongues, they shall cease; whether there be knowledge, it shall vanish away. For we know in part, and we prophesy in part. But when that which is perfect is come, then that which is in part shall be done away. When I was a child, I spake as a child, I understood as a child, I thought as a child: but when I became a man, I put away childish things. For now we see through a glass, darkly; but then face to face: now I know in part; but then shall I know even as also I am known. And now abideth faith, hope, Love, these three; but the greatest of these is Love.—1 Cor. xiii.

# The Supreme Good

Every one has asked himself the great question of antiquity as of the modern world: What is the *summum bonum*—the supreme good? You have life before you. Once only you can live it. What is the noblest object of desire, the supreme gift to covet?

We have been accustomed to be told that the greatest thing in the religious world is Faith. That great word has been the keynote for centuries of the popular religion; and we have easily learned to look upon it as the greatest thing in the world. Well, we are wrong. If we have been told that, we may miss the mark. I have taken you in the chapter which I have just read, to Christianity at its source; and there we have seen, "The greatest of these is love." It is not an oversight. Paul was speaking of faith just a moment before. He says, "If I have all faith, so that I can remove mountains, and have not love; I am nothing." So far from forgetting he deliberately contrasts them, "Now abideth Faith, Hope, Love," and without a moment's hesitation the decision falls, "The greatest of these is Love."

And it is not prejudice. A man is apt to recommend to others his own strong point.

Love was not Paul's strong point. The observing student can detect a beautiful tenderness growing and ripening all through his character as Paul gets old; but the hand that wrote "The greatest of these is love," when we meet it first, is stained with blood.

Nor is this letter to the Corinthians peculiar in singling out love as the *summum bonum.* The masterpieces of Christianity are agreed about it. Peter says, "Above all things have fervent love among yourselves." *Above all things.* And John goes farther, "God is love." And you remember the profound remark which Paul makes elsewhere, "Love is the fulfilling of the law." Did you ever think what he meant by that? In those days men were working their passage to Heaven by keeping the Ten Commandments, and the hundred and ten other commandments which they had manufactured out of them. Christ said, I will show you a more simple way. If you do one thing, you will do these hundred and ten things, without ever thinking about them. If you love, you will unconsciously fulfil the whole law. And you can readily see for yourselves how that must be so. Take any of the commandments. "Thou shalt have no other gods before Me." If a man love God, you will not require to tell him that. Love is the fulfilling of that law. "Take not His name in vain." Would he ever dream of taking His name in vain if he loved Him? "Remember the Sabbath day to keep it holy." Would he not be too glad to have one day in seven to dedicate more exclusively to the object of his affection? Love would fulfil all these laws regarding God. And so, if he loved Man you would never think of telling him to honor his father and mother. He could not do anything else. It would be preposterous to tell him not to kill. You could only insult him if you suggested that he should not steal—how could he steal from those he loved. It would be superfluous to beg him not to bear false witness against his neighbor. If he loved him it would be the last thing he would do.

And you would never dream of urging him not to covet what his neighbors had. He would rather they possessed it than himself. In this way "Love is the fulfilling of the law." It is the rule for fulfilling all rules, the new commandment for keeping all the old commandments, Christ's one secret of the Christian life.

Now Paul had learned that; and in this noble eulogy he has given us the most wonderful and original account extant of the *summum bonum*. We may divide it into three parts. In the beginning of the short chapter, we have Love *contrasted;* in the heart of it, we have Love *analyzed;* toward the end, we have Love *defended* as the supreme gift.

# The Contrast

Paul begins by contrasting Love with other things that men in those days thought much of. I shall not attempt to go over those things in detail. Their inferiority is already obvious.

He contrasts it with eloquence. And what a noble gift it is, the power of playing upon the souls and wills of men, and rousing them to lofty purposes and holy deeds. Paul says, "If I speak with the tongues of men and of angels, and have not love, I am become as sounding brass, or a tinkling cymbal." And we all know why. We have all felt the brazenness of words without emotion, the hollowness, the unaccountable unpersuasiveness, of eloquence behind which lies no Love.

He contrasts it with prophecy. He contrasts it with mysteries. He contrasts it with faith. He contrasts it with charity. Why is Love greater than faith? Because the end is greater than the means. And why is it greater than charity? Because the whole is greater than the part. Love is greater than faith, because the end is greater than the means. What is the use of having faith? It is to connect the soul with God. And what is the object of connecting man with God? That he may become like God. But God is Love. Hence Faith, the means, is in order to Love, the end. Love, therefore, obviously is greater than faith. It is greater than charity, again, because the whole is greater than a part. Charity is only a little bit of Love, one of the innumerable avenues of Love, and there may even be, and there is, a great deal of charity without Love. It is a very easy thing to toss a copper to a beggar on the street; it is generally an easier thing than not to do it. Yet Love is just as often in the withholding. We purchase relief from the sympathetic feelings roused by the spectacle of misery, at the copper's cost. It is too cheap—too cheap for us, and often too dear for the beggar. If we really loved him we would either do more for him, or less.

Then Paul contrasts it with sacrifice and martyrdom. And I beg the little band of would-be missionaries—and I have the honor to call some of you by this name for the first time—to remember that though you give your bodies to be burned, and have not Love, it profits nothing—nothing! You can take nothing greater to the heathen world than the impress and the reflection of the Love of God upon your own character. That is the universal language. It will take you years to speak in Chinese, or in the dialects of India. From the day you land, that language of Love, understood by all, will be pouring forth its unconscious eloquence. It is the man who is the missionary, it is not his words. His character is his message. In the heart of Africa, among the great Lakes, I have come across black men and women who remembered the only white man they ever saw before—David Livingstone; and as you cross his footsteps in that dark continent, men's faces light up as they speak of the kind Doctor who passed there years ago. They could not understand him; but they felt the Love that beat in his heart. Take into your new sphere of labor, where you also mean to lay down your life, that simple charm, and your lifework must succeed. You can take nothing greater, you need take nothing less. It is not worth while going if you take anything less. You may take every accomplishment; you may be braced for every sacrifice; but if you give your body to be burned, and have not Love, it will profit you and the cause of Christ *nothing.*

# The Analysis

After contrasting Love with these things, Paul, in three verses, very short, gives us an amazing analysis of what this supreme thing is. I ask you to look at it. It is a compound thing, he tells us. It is like light. As you have seen a man of science take a beam of light and pass it through a crystal prism, as you have seen it come out on the other side of the prism broken up into its component colors—red, and blue, and yellow, and violet, and orange, and all the colors of the rainbow—so Paul passes this thing, Love, through the magnificent prism of his inspired intellect, and it comes out on the other side broken up into its elements. And in these few words we have what one might call the Spectrum of Love, the analysis of Love. Will you observe what its elements are? Will you notice that they have common names; that they are virtues which we hear about every day; that they are things which can be practiced by every man in every place in life; and how, by a multitude of small things and ordinary virtues, the supreme thing, the *summum bonum* is made up.

The Spectrum of Love has nine ingredients:

Patience .................... "Love suffereth long."
Kindness .................. "And is kind."
Generosity ............... "Love envieth not."
Humility .................. "Love vaunteth not itself, is not puffed up."
Courtesy .................. "Doth not behave itself unseemly."
Unselfishness ........... "Seeketh not her own."
Good Temper........... "Is not easily provoked."
Guilelessness............ "Thinketh no evil."
Sincerity..................... "Rejoiceth not in iniquity, but rejoiceth in the truth."

Patience; kindness; generosity; humility; courtesy; unselfishness; good temper; guilelessness; sincerity—these make up the supreme gift, the stature of the perfect man. You will observe that all are in relation to men, in relation to life, in relation to the known to-day and the near to-morrow, and not to the unknown eternity. We hear much of love to God; Christ spoke much of love to man. We make a great deal of peace with heaven; Christ made much of peace on earth. Religion is not a strange or added thing, but the inspiration of the secular life, the breathing of an eternal spirit through this temporal world. The supreme thing, in short, is not a thing at all, but the giving of a further finish to the multitudinous words and acts which make up the sum of every common day.

There is no time to do more than make a passing note upon each of these ingredients. Love is *Patience.* This is the normal attitude of Love; Love passive, Love waiting to begin; not in a hurry; calm; ready to do its work when the summons comes, but meantime wearing the ornament of a meek and quiet spirit. Love suffers long; beareth all things; believeth all things; hopeth all things. For love understands, and therefore waits.

*Kindness.* Love active. Have you ever noticed how much of Christ's life was spent in doing kind things—in *merely* doing kind things? Run over it with that in view, and you will find that He spent a great proportion of His time simply in making people happy, in doing good turns to people. There is only one thing greater than happiness in the world, and that is holiness; and it is not in our keeping; but what God *has* put in our power is the happiness of those about us, and that is largely to be secured by our being kind to them.

"The greatest thing," says some one, "a man can do for his Heavenly Father is to be kind to some of His other children." I wonder why it is that we are not all kinder than we are? How much the world needs it. How easily it is done. How instantaneously it acts. How infallibly it is remembered. How superabundantly it pays itself back—for there is no debtor in the world so honorable, so superbly honorable, as Love. "Love never faileth." Love is success, Love is happiness, Love is life. "Love I say," with Browning, "is energy of Life."

> *"For life, with all it yields of joy or woe*
> *And hope and fear,*
> *Is just our chance o' the prize of learning love,—*
> *How love might be, hath been indeed, and is."*

Where Love is, God is. He that dwelleth in Love dwelleth in God. God is Love. Therefore *love.* Without distinction, without calculation, without procrastination, love. Lavish it upon the poor, where it is very easy; especially upon the rich, who often need it most; most of all upon our equals, where it is very difficult, and for whom perhaps we each do least of all. There is a difference between *trying to please* and *giving pleasure.* Give pleasure. Lose no chance of giving pleasure. For that is the ceaseless and anonymous triumph of a truly loving spirit. "I shall pass through this world but once. Any good thing therefore that I can do, or any kindness that I can show to any human being, let me do it now. Let me not defer it or neglect it, for I shall not pass this way again."

*Generosity.* "Love envieth not." This is love in competition with others. Whenever you attempt a good work you will find other men doing the same kind of work, and probably doing it better. Envy them not. Envy is a feeling of ill-will to those who are in the same line as ourselves, a spirit of covetousness and detraction. How little Christian work even is a protection against un-Christian feeling. That most despicable of all the unworthy moods which cloud a Christian's soul assuredly waits for us on the threshold of every work, unless we are fortified with this grace of magnanimity. Only one thing truly need the Christian envy, the large, rich, generous soul which "envieth not."

And then, after having learned all that, you have to learn this further thing, *Humility*—to put a seal upon your lips and forget what you have done. After you have been kind, after Love has stolen forth into the world and done its beautiful work, go back into the shade again and say nothing about it. Love hides even from itself. Love waives even self-satisfaction. "Love vaunteth not itself, is not puffed up."

The fifth ingredient is a somewhat strange one to find in this *summum bonum: Courtesy.* This is Love in society, Love in relation to etiquette. "Love doth not behave itself unseemly." Politeness has been defined as love in trifles. Courtesy is said to be love in little things. And the one secret of politeness is to love. Love *cannot* behave itself unseemly. You can put the most untutored persons into the highest society, and if they have a reservoir of Love in their heart, they will not behave themselves unseemly. They simply cannot do it. Carlyle said of Robert Burns that there was no truer gentleman in Europe than the ploughman-poet. It was because he loved everything—the mouse, and the daisy, and all the things, great and small, that God had made. So with this simple passport he could mingle with any society, and enter courts and palaces from his little cottage on the banks of the Ayr. You know the meaning of the word "gentleman." It means a gentle man—a man who does things gently with love. And that is the whole art and mystery of it. The gentle man cannot in the nature of things do an ungentle, and ungentlemanly thing. The ungentle soul, the inconsiderate, unsympathetic nature cannot do anything else. "Love doth not behave itself unseemly."

*Unselfishness.* "Love seeketh not her own." Observe: Seeketh not even that which is her own. In Britain the Englishman is devoted, and rightly, to his rights. But there come times when a man may exercise even the higher right of giving up his rights. Yet Paul does not summon us to give up our rights. Love strikes much deeper. It would have us not seek them at all, ignore them, eliminate the personal element altogether from our calculations. It is not hard to give up our rights. They are often external. The difficult thing is to give up ourselves. The more difficult thing still is not to seek things for ourselves at all. After we have sought them, bought them, won them, deserved them, we have taken the cream off them for ourselves already. Little cross then to give them up. But not to seek them, to look every man not on his own things, but on the things of others—*id opus est.* "Seekest thou great things for thyself?" said the prophet; *"seek them not."* Why? Because there is no greatness in things. Things cannot be great. The only greatness is unselfish love. Even self-denial in itself is nothing, is almost a mistake. Only a great purpose or a mightier love can justify the waste. It is more difficult, I have said, not to seek our own at all, than, having sought it, to give it up. I must take that back. It is only true of a partly selfish heart. Nothing is a hardship to Love, and nothing is hard. I believe that Christ's "yoke" is easy. Christ's "yoke" is just His way of taking life. And I believe it is an easier way than any other. I believe it is a happier way than any other. The most obvious lesson in Christ's teaching is that there is no happiness in having and getting anything, but only in giving. I repeat, *there is no happiness in having or in getting, but only in giving.* And half the world is on the wrong scent in pursuit of happiness. They think it consists in having and getting, and in being served by others. It consists in giving, and in serving others. He that would be great among you, said Christ, let him serve. He that would be happy, let him remember that there is but one way—it is more blessed, it is more happy, to give than to receive.

The next ingredient is a very remarkable one: *Good Temper.* "Love is not easily provoked." Nothing could be more striking than to find this here. We are inclined to look upon bad temper as a very harmless weakness. We speak of it as a mere infirmity of nature, a family failing, a matter of temperament, not a thing to take into very serious account in estimating a man's character. And yet here, right in the heart of this analysis of love, it finds a place; and the Bible again and again returns to condemn it as one of the most destructive elements in human nature.

The peculiarity of ill temper is that it is the vice of the virtuous. It is often the one blot on an otherwise noble character. You know men who are all but perfect, and women who would be entirely perfect, but for an easily ruffled, quick-tempered, or "touchy" disposition. This compatibility of ill temper with high moral character is one of the strangest and saddest problems of ethics. The truth is there are two great classes of sins—sins of the *Body,* and sins of the *Disposition.* The Prodigal Son may be taken as a type of the first, the Elder Brother of the second. Now, society has no doubt whatever as to which of these is the worse. Its brand falls, without a challenge, upon the Prodigal. But are we right? We have no balance to weigh one another's sins, and coarser and finer are but human words; but faults in the higher nature may be less venial than those in the lower, and to the eye of Him who is Love, a sin against Love may seem a hundred times more base. No form of vice, not worldliness, not greed of gold, not drunkenness itself, does more to un-Christianize society than evil temper. For embittering life, for breaking up communities, for destroying the most sacred relationships, for devastating homes, for withering up men and women, for taking the bloom of childhood, in short, for sheer gratuitous misery-producing power, this influence stands alone. Look at the Elder Brother, moral, hard-working, patient, dutiful—let him get all credit for his virtues—look at this man, this baby, sulking outside his own father's door. "He was angry," we read, "and would not go in." Look at the effect upon the father, upon the servants, upon the happiness of the guests. Judge of the effect upon the Prodigal—and how many prodigals are kept out of the Kingdom of God by the unlovely character of those who profess to be inside? Analyze, as a study in Temper, the thunder-cloud as it gathers upon the Elder-Brother's brow. What is it made of? Jealousy, anger, pride, uncharity, cruelty, self-righteousness, touchiness, doggedness, sullenness,—these are the ingredients of this dark and loveless soul. In varying proportions, also, these are the ingredients of all ill temper. Judge if such sins of the disposition are not worse to live in, and for others to live with, than sins of the body. Did Christ indeed not answer the question Himself when He said, "I say unto you, that the publicans and the harlots go into the Kingdom of Heaven before you"? There is really no place in Heaven for a disposition like this. A man with such a mood could only make Heaven miserable for all the people in it. Except, therefore, such a man be born again, he cannot, he simply *cannot*, enter the Kingdom of Heaven. For it is perfectly certain—and you will not misunderstand me—that to enter Heaven a man must take it with him.

You will see then why Temper is significant. It is not in what it is alone, but in what it reveals. This is why I take the liberty now of speaking of it with such unusual plainness. It is a test for love, a symptom, a revelation of an unloving nature at bottom. It is the intermittent fever which bespeaks unintermittent disease within; the occasional bubble escaping to the surface which betrays some rottenness underneath; a sample of the most hidden products of the soul dropped involuntarily when off one's guard; in a word, the lightning form of a hundred hideous and un-Christian sins. For a want of patience, a want of kindness, a want of generosity, a want of courtesy, a want of unselfishness, all are instantaneously symbolized in one flash of Temper.

Hence it is not enough to deal with the Temper. We must go to the source, and change the inmost nature, and the angry humors will die away of themselves. Souls are made sweet not by taking the acid fluids out, but by putting something in—a great Love, a new Spirit, the Spirit of Christ. Christ, the Spirit of Christ, interpenetrating ours, sweetens, purifies, transforms all. This only can eradicate what is wrong, work a chemical change, renovate and regenerate, and rehabilitate the inner man. Will-power does not change men. Time does not change men. Christ does. Therefore "Let that mind be in you which was also in Christ Jesus." Some of us have not much time to lose. Remember, once more, that this is a matter of life or death. I cannot help speaking urgently, for myself, for yourselves. "Whoso shall offend one of these little ones, which believe in me, it were better for him that a millstone were hanged about his neck, and that he were drowned in the depth of the sea." That is to say, it is the deliberate verdict of the Lord Jesus that it is better not to live than not to love. *It is better not to live than not to love.*

*Guilelessness* and *Sincerity* may be dismissed almost with a word. Guilelessness is the grace for suspicious people. And the possession of it is the great secret of personal influence. You will find, if you think for a moment, that the people who influence you are people who believe in you. In an atmosphere of suspicion men shrivel up; but in that atmosphere they expand, and find encouragement and educative fellowship. It is a wonderful thing that here and there in this hard, uncharitable world there should still be left a few rare souls who think no evil. This is the great unworldliness. Love "Thinketh no evil," imputes no motive, sees the bright side, puts the best construction on every action. What a delightful state of mind to live in!

What a stimulus and benediction even to meet with it for a day! To be trusted is to be saved. And if we try to influence or elevate others, we shall soon see that success is in proportion to their belief of our belief in them. For the respect of another is the first restoration of the self-respect a man has lost; our ideal of what he is becomes to him the hope and pattern of what he may become.

"Love rejoiceth not in iniquity, but rejoiceth in the truth." I have called this *Sincerity* from the words rendered in the Authorized Version by "rejoiceth in the truth." And, certainly, were this the real translation, nothing could be more just. For he who loves will love Truth not less than men. He will rejoice in the Truth—rejoice not in what he has been taught to believe; not in this Church's doctrine or in that; not in this ism or in that ism; but "in *the Truth.*" He will accept only what is real; he will strive to get at facts; he will search for *Truth* with a humble and unbiased mind, and cherish whatever he finds at any sacrifice. But the more literal translation of the Revised Version calls for just such a sacrifice for truth's sake here. For what Paul really meant is, as we there read, "Rejoiceth not in unrighteousness, but rejoiceth with the truth," a quality which probably no one English word—and certainly not *Sincerity*—adequately defines. It includes, perhaps more strictly, the self-restraint which refuses to make capital out of others' faults; the charity which delights not in exposing the weakness of others, but "covereth all things"; the sincerity of purpose which endeavors to see things as they are, and rejoices to find them better than suspicion feared or calumny denounced.

So much for the analysis of Love. Now the business of our lives is to have these things fitted into our characters. That is the supreme work to which we need to address ourselves in this world, to learn Love. Is life not full of opportunities for learning Love? Every man and woman every day has a thousand of them. The world is not a playground; it is a schoolroom. Life is not a holiday, but an education. And the one eternal lesson for us all is *how better we can love.* What makes a man a good cricketer? Practice. What makes a man a good artist, a good sculptor, a good musician? Practice. What makes a man a good linguist, a good stenographer? Practice. What makes a man a good man? Practice. Nothing else. There is nothing capricious about religion. We do not get the soul in different ways, under different laws, from those in which we get the body and the mind. If a man does not exercise his arm he develops no biceps muscle; and if a man does not exercise his soul, he acquires no muscle in his soul, no strength of character, no vigor of moral fibre, nor beauty of spiritual growth. Love is not a thing of enthusiastic emotion. It is a rich, strong, manly, vigorous expression of the whole round Christian character—the Christlike nature in its fullest development. And the constituents of this great character are only to be built up by ceaseless practice.

What was Christ doing in the carpenter's shop? Practicing. Though perfect, we read that He *learned* obedience, and grew in wisdom and in favor with God. Do not quarrel therefore with your lot in life. Do not complain of its never ceasing cares, its petty environment, the vexations you have to stand, the small and sordid souls you have to live and work with. Above all, do not resent temptation; do not be perplexed because it seems to thicken round you more and more, and ceases neither for effort nor for agony nor prayer. That is your practice. That is the practice which God appoints you; and it is having its work in making you patient, and humble, and generous, and unselfish, and kind, and courteous. Do not grudge the hand that is moulding the still too shapeless image within you. It is growing more beautiful, though you see it not, and every touch of temptation may add to its perfection. Therefore keep in the midst of life. Do not isolate yourself. Be among men, and among things, and among troubles, and difficulties, and obstacles. You remember Goethe's words: *Es bildet ein Talent sich in der Stille, Doch ein Charakter in dem Strom der Welt.* "Talent develops itself in solitude; character in the stream of life." Talent develops itself in solitude—the talent of prayer, of faith, of meditation, of seeing the unseen; Character grows in the stream of the world's life. That chiefly is where men are to learn love.

How? Now, how? To make it easier, I have named a few of the elements of love. But these are only elements. Love itself can never be defined. Light is something more than the sum of its ingredients—a glowing, dazzling, tremulous ether. And love is something more than all its elements—a palpitating, quivering, sensitive, living thing. By synthesis of all the colors, men can make whiteness, they cannot make light. By synthesis of all the virtues, men can make virtue, they cannot make love. How then are we to have this transcendent living whole conveyed into our souls? We brace our wills to secure it. We try to copy those who have it. We lay down rules about it. We watch. We pray. But these things alone will not bring Love into our nature. Love is an *effect.* And only as we fulfil the right condition can we have the effect produced. Shall I tell you what the *cause* is?

If you turn to the Revised Version of the First Epistle of John you will find these words: "We love because He first loved us." "We love," not "We love *Him.*" That is the way the old version has it, and it is quite wrong. "*We love*—because He first loved us." Look at that word "because." It is the *cause* of which I have spoken. "*Because* He first loved us," the effect follows that we love, we love Him, we love all men. We cannot help it. Because He loved us, we love, we love everybody. Our heart is slowly changed. Contemplate the love of Christ, and you will love. Stand before that mirror, reflect Christ's character and you will be changed into the same image from tenderness to tenderness. There is no other way. You cannot love to order. You can only look at the lovely object, and fall in love with it, and grow into likeness to it. And so look at this Perfect Character, this Perfect Life. Look at the great Sacrifice as He laid down Himself, all through life, and upon the Cross of Calvary, and you must love Him. And loving Him, you must become like Him. Love begets love. It is a process of induction. Put a piece of iron in the presence of an electrified body, and that piece of iron for a time becomes electrified. It is changed into a temporary magnet in the mere presence of a permanent magnet, and as long as you leave the two side by side, they are both magnets alike. Remain side by side with Him who loved us, and gave Himself for us, and you too will become a permanent magnet, a permanently attractive force; and like Him you will draw all men unto you, like Him you will be drawn unto all men. That is the inevitable effect of Love. Any man who fulfils that cause must have that effect produced in him. Try to give up the idea that religion comes to us by chance, or by mystery, or by caprice. It comes to us by natural law, or by supernatural law, for all law is Divine. Edward Irving went to see a dying boy once, and when he entered the room he just put his hand on the sufferer's head, and said, "My boy, God loves you," and went away. And the boy started from his bed, and called out to the people in the house, "God loves me! God loves me!" It changed that boy. The sense that God loved him overpowered him, melted him down, and began the creating of a new heart in him. And that is how the love of God melts down the unlovely heart in man, and begets in him the new creature, who is patient and humble and gentle and unselfish. And there is no other way to get it. There is no mystery about it. We love others, we love everybody, we love our enemies, because He first loved us.

# The Defence

Now I have a closing sentence or two to add about Paul's reason for singling out love as the supreme possession. It is a very remarkable reason. In a single word it is this: *it lasts.* "Love," urges Paul, "never faileth." Then he begins again one of his marvellous lists of the great things of the day, and exposes them one by one. He runs over the things that men thought were going to last, and shows that they are all fleeting, temporary, passing away.

"Whether there be prophecies, they shall fail." It was the mother's ambition for her boy in those days that he should become a prophet. For hundreds of years God had never spoken by means of any prophet, and at that time the prophet was greater than the King. Men waited wistfully for another messenger to come and hung upon his lips when he appeared as upon the very voice of God. Paul says, "Whether there be prophecies, they shall fail." This book is full of prophecies. One by one they have "failed"; that is, having been fulfilled, their work is finished; they have nothing more to do now in the world except to feed a devout man's faith.

Then Paul talks about tongues. That was another thing that was greatly coveted. "Whether there be tongues, they shall cease." As we all know, many, many centuries have passed since tongues have been known in this world. They have ceased. Take it in any sense you like. Take it, for illustration merely, as languages in general—a sense which was not in Paul's mind at all, and which though it cannot give us the specific lesson will point the general truth. Consider the words in which these chapters were written—Greek. It has gone. Take the Latin—the other great tongue of those days. It ceased long ago. Look at the Indian language. It is ceasing. The language of Wales, of Ireland, of the Scottish Highlands, is dying before our eyes. The most popular book in the English tongue at the present time, except the Bible, is one of Dickens's works, his *Pickwick Papers.* It is largely written in the language of London street-life; and experts assure us that in fifty years it will be unintelligible to the average English reader.

Then Paul goes farther, and with even greater boldness adds, "Whether there be knowledge, it shall vanish away." The Wisdom of the ancients, where is it? It is wholly gone. A schoolboy to-day knows more than Sir Isaac Newton knew. His knowledge has vanished away. You put yesterday's newspaper in the fire. Its knowledge has vanished away. You buy the old editions of the great encyclopædias for a few pence. Their knowledge has vanished away. Look how the coach has been superseded by the use of steam. Look how electricity has superseded that, and swept a hundred almost new inventions into oblivion. One of the greatest living authorities, Sir William Thomson, said the other day, "The steam-engine is passing away." "Whether there be knowledge, it shall vanish away." At every workshop you will see, in a back yard, a heap of old iron, a few wheels, a few levers, a few cranks, broken and eaten with rust. Twenty years ago that was the pride of the city. Men flocked in from the country to see the great invention; now it is superseded, its day is done. And all the boasted science and philosophy of this day will soon be old. But yesterday, in the University of Edinburgh, the greatest figure in the faculty was Sir James Simpson, the discoverer of chloroform. The other day his successor and nephew, Professor Simpson, was asked by the librarian of the University to go to the library and pick out the books on his subject that were no longer needed. And his reply to the librarian was this: "Take every textbook that is more than ten years old, and put it down in the cellar." Sir James Simpson was a great authority only a few years ago: men came from all parts of the earth to consult him; and almost the whole teaching of that time is consigned by the science of to-day to oblivion. And in every branch of science it is the same. "Now we know in part. We see through a glass darkly."

Can you tell me anything that is going to last? Many things Paul did not condescend to name. He did not mention money, fortune, fame; but he picked out the great things of his time, the things the best men thought had something in them, and brushed them peremptorily aside. Paul had no charge against these things in themselves. All he said about them was that they would not last. They were great things, but not supreme things. There were things beyond them. What we are stretches past what we do, beyond what we possess. Many things that men denounce as sins are not sins; but they are temporary. And that is a favorite argument of the New Testament. John says of the world, not that it is wrong, but simply that it "passeth away." There is a great deal in the world that is delightful and beautiful; there is a great deal in it that is great and engrossing; but it will not last. All that is in the world, the lust of the eye, the lust of the flesh, and the pride of life, are but for a little while. Love not the world therefore. Nothing that it contains is worth the life and consecration of an immortal soul. The immortal soul must give itself to something that is immortal. And the only immortal things are these: "Now abideth faith, hope, love, but the greatest of these is love."

Some think the time may come when two of these three things will also pass away—faith into sight, hope into fruition. Paul does not say so. We know but little now about the conditions of the life that is to come. But what is certain is that Love must last. God, the Eternal God, is Love. Covet therefore that everlasting gift, that one thing which it is certain is going to stand, that one coinage which will be current in the Universe when all the other coinages of all the nations of the world shall be useless and unhonored. You will give yourselves to many things, give yourself first to Love. Hold things in their proportion. *Hold things in their proportion.* Let at least the first great object of our lives be to achieve the character defended in these words, the character—and it is the character of Christ—which is built round Love.

I have said this thing is eternal. Did you ever notice how continually John associates love and faith with eternal life? I was not told when I was a boy that "God so loved the world that He gave His only-begotten Son, that whosoever believeth in Him should have everlasting life." What I was told, I remember, was, that God so loved the world that, if I trusted in Him, I was to have a thing called peace, or I was to have rest, or I was to have joy, or I was to have safety. But I had to find out for myself that whosoever trusteth in Him—that is, whosoever loveth Him, for trust is only the avenue to Love—hath everlasting *life.* The Gospel offers a man life. Never offer men a thimbleful of Gospel. Do not offer them merely joy, or merely peace, or merely rest, or merely safety; tell them how Christ came to give men a more abundant life than they have, a life abundant in love, and therefore abundant in salvation for themselves, and large in enterprise for the alleviation and redemption of the world. Then only can the Gospel take hold of the whole of a man, body, soul, and spirit, and give to each part of his nature its exercise and reward. Many of the current Gospels are addressed only to a part of man's nature. They offer peace, not life; faith, not Love; justification, not regeneration. And men slip back again from such religion because it has never really held them. Their nature was not all in it. It offered no deeper and gladder life-current than the life that was lived before. Surely it stands to reason that only a fuller love can compete with the love of the world.

To love abundantly is to live abundantly, and to love forever is to live forever. Hence, eternal life is inextricably bound up with love. We want to live forever for the same reason that we want to live to-morrow. Why do you want to live to-morrow? It is because there is some one who loves you, and whom you want to see to-morrow, and be with, and love back. There is no other reason why we should live on than that we love and are beloved. It is when a man has no one to love him that he commits suicide. So long as he has friends, those who love him and whom he loves, he will live, because to live is to love. Be it but the love of a dog, it will keep him in life; but let that go and he has no contact with life, no reason to live. He dies by his own hand. Eternal life also is to know God, and God is love. This is Christ's own definition. Ponder it. "This is life eternal, that they might know Thee the only true God, and Jesus Christ whom Thou hast sent." Love must be eternal. It is what God is. On the last analysis, then, love is life. Love never faileth, and life never faileth, so long as there is love. That is the philosophy of what Paul is showing us; the reason why in the nature of things Love should be the supreme thing—because it is going to last; because in the nature of things it is an Eternal Life. It is a thing that we are living now, not that we get when we die; that we shall have a poor chance of getting when we die unless we are living now. No worse fate can befall a man in this world than to live and grow old alone, unloving and unloved. To be lost is to live in an unregenerate condition, loveless and unloved; and to be saved is to love; and he that dwelleth in love dwelleth already in God. For God is Love.

Now I have all but finished. How many of you will join me in reading this chapter once a week for the next three months? A man did that once and it changed his whole life. Will you do it? It is for the greatest thing in the world. You might begin by reading it every day, especially the verses which describe the perfect character. "Love suffereth long, and is kind; love envieth not; love vaunteth not itself." Get these ingredients into your life. Then everything that you do is eternal. It is worth doing. It is worth giving time to. No man can become a saint in his sleep; and to fulfil the condition required demands a certain amount of prayer and meditation and time, just as improvement in any direction, bodily or mental, requires preparation and care. Address yourselves to that one thing; at any cost have this transcendent character exchanged for yours. You will find as you look back upon your life that the moments that stand out, the moments when you have really lived, are the moments when you have done things in a spirit of love. As memory scans the past, above and beyond all the transitory pleasures of life, there leap forward those supreme hours when you have been enabled to do unnoticed kindnesses to those round about you, things too trifling to speak about, but which you feel have entered into your eternal life. I have seen almost all the beautiful things God has made; I have enjoyed almost every pleasure that He has planned for man; and yet as I look back I see standing out above all the life that has gone four or five short experiences when the love of God reflected itself in some poor imitation, some small act of love of mine, and these seem to be the things which alone of all one's life abide. Everything else in all our lives is transitory. Every other good is visionary. But the acts of love which no man knows about, or can ever know about—they never fail.

In the book of Matthew, where the Judgment Day is depicted for us in the imagery of One seated upon a throne and dividing the sheep from the goats, the test of a man then is not, "How have I believed?" but "How have I loved?" The test of religion, the final test of religion, is not religiousness but Love. I say the final test of religion at that great Day is not religiousness, but Love; not what I have done, not what I have believed, not what I have achieved, but how I have discharged the common charities of life. Sins of commission in that awful indictment are not even referred to. By what we have not done, *by sins of omission*, we are judged. It could not be otherwise. For the withholding of love is the negation of the spirit of Christ, the proof that we never knew Him, that for us He lived in vain. It means that He suggested nothing in all our thoughts, that He inspired nothing in all our lives, that we were not once near enough to Him to be seized with the spell of His compassion for the world. It means that—

*"I lived for myself, I thought for myself,*
*For myself, and none beside—*
*Just as if Jesus had never lived,*
*As if He had never died."*

It is the Son of *Man* before whom the nations of the world shall be gathered. It is in the presence of *Humanity* that we shall be charged. And the spectacle itself, the mere sight of it, will silently judge each one. Those will be there whom we have met and helped; or there, the unpitied multitude whom we neglected or despised. No other Witness need be summoned. No other charge than lovelessness shall be preferred. Be not deceived. The words which all of us shall one Day hear sound not of theology but of life, not of churches and saints but of the hungry and the poor, not of creeds and doctrines but of shelter and clothing, not of Bibles and prayer-books but of cups of cold water in the name of Christ. Thank God the Christianity of today is coming nearer the world's need. Live to help that on. Thank God men know better, by a hair's-breadth, what religion is, what God is, who Christ is, where Christ is. Who is Christ? He who fed the hungry, clothed the naked, visited the sick. And where is Christ? Where?—whoso shall receive a little child in My name receiveth Me. And who are Christ's? Every one that loveth is born of God.

# IN TUNE WITH THE INFINITE

RALPH WALDO TRINE

(1897)

# Contents


Preface 255

1. Fullness of Peace, Power, and Plenty: Prelude 257
2. The Supreme Fact of the Universe 258
3. The Supreme Fact of Human Life 260
4. Fullness of Life—Bodily Health and Vigor 270
5. The Secret, Power, and Effects of Love 288
6. Wisdom and Interior Illumination 296
7. The Realization of Perfect Peace 309
8. Coming into Fullness of Power 316
9. Plenty of All Things—The Law of Prosperity 326
10. How Men Have Become Prophets, Seers, Sages, and Saviours 333
11. The Basic Principle of All Religions—The Universal Religion 337
12. Entering Now into the Realization of the Highest Riches 341
13. "The Way" 346

# Preface

There is a golden thread that runs through every religion in the world. There is a golden thread that runs through the lives and the teachings of all the prophets, seers, sages, and saviours in the world's history, through the lives of all men and women of truly great and lasting power. All that they have ever done or attained to has been done in full accordance with law. What one has done, all may do.

This same golden thread must enter into the lives of all who today, in this busy work-a-day world of ours, would exchange impotence for power, weakness and suffering for abounding health and strength, pain and unrest for perfect peace, poverty of whatever nature for fullness and plenty.

Each is building his own world. We both build from within and attract from without. Thought is the force with which we build, for thoughts are forces. Like builds like and like attracts like. In the degree that thought is spiritualized does it become more subtle and powerful in its workings. This spiritualizing is in accordance with law and is within the power of all.

Everything is first worked out in the unseen before it is manifested in the seen, in the ideal before it is realized in the real, in the spiritual before it shows forth in the material. The realm of the unseen is the realm of cause. The realm of the seen is the realm of effect. The nature of effect is always determined and conditioned by the nature of its cause.

To point out the great facts in connection with, and the great laws underlying the workings of the interior, spiritual, thought forces, to point them out so simply and so clearly that even a child can understand, is the author's aim. To point them out so simply and so clearly that all can grasp them, that all can take them and infuse them into every-day life, so as to mould it in all its details in accordance with what they would have it, is his purpose. That life can be thus moulded by them is not a matter of mere speculation or theory with him, but a matter of positive knowledge.

There is a divine sequence running throughout the universe. Within and above and below the human will incessantly works the Divine will. To come into harmony with it and thereby with all the higher laws and forces, to come then into league and to work in conjunction with them, in order that they can work in league and in conjunction with us, is to come into the chain of this wonderful sequence. This is the secret of all success. This is to come into the possession of unknown riches, into the realization of undreamed-of powers.

R. W. T.

CHAPTER 1

# Fullness of Peace, Power, and Plenty

## PRELUDE

The optimist is right. The pessimist is right. The one differs from the other as the light from the dark. Yet both are right. Each is right from his own particular point of view, and this point of view is the determining factor in the life of each. It determines as to whether it is a life of power or of impotence, of peace or of pain, of success or of failure.

The optimist has the power of seeing things in their entirety and in their right relations. The pessimist looks from a limited and a one-sided point of view. The one has his understanding illumined by wisdom, the understanding of the other is darkened by ignorance. Each is building his world from within, and the result of the building is determined by the point of view of each. The optimist, by his superior wisdom and insight, is making his own heaven, and in the degree that he makes his own heaven is he helping to make one for all the world beside. The pessimist, by virtue of his limitations, is making his own hell, and in the degree that he makes his own hell is he helping to make one for all mankind.

You and I have the predominating characteristics of an optimist or the predominating characteristics of a pessimist. We then are making, hour by hour, our own heaven or our own hell; and in the degree that we are making the one or the other for ourselves are we helping make it for all the world beside.

The word heaven means harmony. The word hell is from the old English *hell*, meaning to build a wall around, to separate; to be *helled* was to be shut off from. Now if there is such a thing as harmony there must be that something one can be in right relations with; for to be in right relations with anything is to be in harmony with it. Again, if there is such a thing as being *helled*, shut off, separated from, there must be that something from which one is held, shut off, or separated.

CHAPTER 2

# The Supreme Fact of the Universe

The great central fact of the universe is that Spirit of Infinite Life and Power that is back of all, that animates all, that manifests itself in and through all; that self-existent principle of life from which all has come, and not only from which all has come, but from which all is continually coming. If there is an individual life, there must of necessity be an infinite source of life from which it comes. If there is a quality or a force of love, there must of necessity be an infinite source of love whence it comes. If there is wisdom, there must be the all-wise source back of it from which it springs. The same is true in regard to peace, the same in regard to power, the same in regard to what we call material things.

There is, then, this Spirit of Infinite Life and Power back of all which is the source of all. This Infinite Power is creating, working, ruling through the agency of great immutable laws and forces that run through all the universe, that surround us on every side. Every act of our every-day lives is governed by these same great laws and forces. Every flower that blooms by the wayside, springs up, grows, blooms, fades, according to certain great immutable laws. Every snowflake that plays between earth and heaven, forms, falls, melts, according to certain great unchangeable laws.

In a sense there is nothing in all the great universe but law. If this is true there must of necessity be a force behind it all that is the maker of these laws and a force greater than the laws that are made. This Spirit of Infinite Life and Power that is back of all is what I call God. I care not what term you may use, be it Kindly Light, Providence, the Over Soul, Omnipotence, or whatever term may be most convenient. I care not what the term may be as long as we are agreed in regard to the great central fact itself.

God, then, is this Infinite Spirit which fills all the universe with Himself alone, so that all is from Him and in Him, and there is nothing that is outside. Indeed and in truth, then, in Him we live and move and have our being. He is the life of our life, our very life itself. We have received, we are continually receiving our life from Him. We are partakers of the life of God: and though we differ from Him in that we are individualized spirits, while He is the Infinite Spirit including us as well as all else beside, yet *in essence the life of God and the life of man are identically the same, and so are one.* They differ not in essence, in quality; they differ in degree.

There have been and are highly illumined souls who believe that we receive our life from God after the manner of a divine inflow. And again, there have been and are those who believe that our life is one with the life of God, and so that God and man are one. Which is right? Both are right; both right when rightly understood.

In regard to the first: if God is the Infinite Spirit of Life back of all, whence all comes, then clearly our life as individualized spirits is continually coming from this Infinite Source by means of this divine inflow. In the second place, if our lives as individualized spirits are directly from, are parts of this Infinite Spirit of Life, then the degree of the Infinite Spirit that is manifested in the life of each must be identical in quality with that Source, the same as a drop of water taken from the ocean is, in nature, in characteristics, identical with that ocean, its source. And how could it be otherwise? The liability to misunderstanding in this latter case, however, is this: in that although the life of God and the life of man in essence are identically the same, the life of God so far transcends the life of individual man that it includes all else beside. In other words, so far as the quality of life is concerned, in essence they are the same; so far as the degree of life is concerned, they are vastly different.

In this light is it not then evident that both conceptions are true? and more, that they are one and the same? Both conceptions may be typified by one and the same illustration.

There is a reservoir in a valley which receives its supply from an inexhaustible reservoir on the mountain side. It is then true that the reservoir in the valley receives its supply by virtue of the inflow of the water from the larger reservoir on the mountain side. It is also true that the water in this smaller reservoir is in nature, in quality, in characteristics identically the same as that in the larger reservoir which is its source. The difference, however, is this: the reservoir on the mountain side, in the *amount* of its water, so far transcends the reservoir in the valley that it can supply an innumerable number of like reservoirs and still be unexhausted.

And so in the life of man. If, as I think we have already agreed, however we may differ in regard to anything else, there is this Infinite Spirit of Life back of all, the life of all, and so, from which all comes, then the life of individual man, your life and mine, must come by a divine inflow from this Infinite Source. And if this is true, then the life that comes by this inflow to man is necessarily the same in essence as is this Infinite Spirit of Life. There is a difference. It is not a difference in essence. It is a difference in degree.

If this is true, does it not then follow that in the degree that man opens himself to this divine inflow does he approach to God? If so, it then necessarily follows that in the degree that he makes this approach does he take on the God-powers. And if the God-powers are without limit, does it not then follow that the only limitations man has are the limitations he sets to himself, by virtue of not knowing himself?

CHAPTER 3

# The Supreme Fact of Human Life

From the great central fact of the universe in regard to which we have agreed, namely, this Spirit of Infinite Life that is back of all and from which all comes, we are led to inquire as to what is the great central fact in human life. From what has gone before, the question almost answers itself.

*The great central fact in human life, in your life and in mine, is the coming into a conscious, vital realization of our oneness with this Infinite Life, and the opening of ourselves fully to this divine inflow.* This is the great central fact in human life, for in this all else is included, all else follows in its train. In just the degree that we come into a conscious realization of our oneness with the Infinite Life, and open ourselves to this divine inflow, do we actualize in ourselves the qualities and powers of the Infinite Life.

And what does this mean? It means simply this: that we are recognizing our true identity, that we are bringing our lives into harmony with the same great laws and forces, and so opening ourselves to the same great inspirations, as have all the prophets, seers, sages, and saviours in the world's history, all men of truly great and mighty power. For in the degree that we come into this realization and connect ourselves with this Infinite Source, do we make it possible for the higher powers to play, to work, to manifest through us.

We can keep closed to this divine inflow, to these higher forces and powers, through ignorance, as most of us do, and thus hinder or even prevent their manifesting through us. Or we can intentionally close ourselves to their operations and thus deprive ourselves of the powers to which, by the very nature of our being, we are rightful heirs. On the other hand, we can come into so vital a realization of the oneness of our real selves with this Infinite Life, and can open ourselves so fully to the incoming of this divine inflow, and so to the operation of these higher forces, inspirations, and powers, that we can indeed and in truth become what we may well term, God-men.

And what is a God-man? One in whom the powers of God are manifesting, though yet a man. No one can set limitations to a man or a woman of this type; for the only limitations he or she can have are those set by the self. Ignorance is the most potent factor in setting limitations to the majority of mankind; and so the great majority of people continue to live their little, dwarfed, and stunted lives simply by virtue of the fact that they do not realize the larger life to which they are heirs. They have never as yet come into a knowledge of the real identity of their true selves.

Mankind has not yet realized that the real self is one with the life of God. Through its ignorance it has never yet opened itself to the divine inflow, and so has never made itself a channel through which the infinite powers and forces can manifest. When we know ourselves merely as men, we live accordingly, and have merely the powers of men. When we come into the realization of the fact that we are God-men, then again we live accordingly, and have the powers of God-men. *In the degree that we open ourselves to this divine inflow are we changed from mere men into God-men.*

A friend has a beautiful lotus pond. A natural basin on his estate—his farm as he always calls it—is supplied with water from a reservoir in the foothills some distance away. A gate regulates the flow of the water from the main that conducts it from the reservoir to the pond. It is a spot of transcendent beauty. There, through the days of the perfect summer weather, the lotus flowers lie full blown upon the surface of the clear, transparent water. The June roses and other wild flowers are continually blooming upon its banks. The birds come here to drink and to bathe, and from early until late one can hear the melody of their song. The bees are continually at work in this garden of wild flowers. A beautiful grove, in which many kinds of wild berries and many varieties of brakes and ferns grow, stretches back of the pond as far as the eye can reach.

Our friend is a man, nay more, a God-man, a lover of his kind, and as a consequence no notice bearing such words as "Private grounds, no trespassing allowed," or "Trespassers will be prosecuted," stands on his estate. But at the end of a beautiful by-way that leads through the wildwood up to this enchanting spot, stands a notice bearing the words "All are welcome to the Lotus Pond." All love our friend. Why? They can't help it. He so loves them, and what is his is theirs.

Here one may often find merry groups of children at play. Here many times tired and weary looking men and women come, and somehow, when they go their faces wear a different expression,—the burden seems to be lifted; and now and then I have heard them when leaving, sometimes in a faint murmur, as if uttering a benediction, say, "God bless our brother-friend." Many speak of this spot as the Garden of God. My friend calls it his Soul Garden, and he spends many hours in quiet here. Often have I seen him after the others have gone, walking to and fro, or sitting quietly in the clear moonlight on an old rustic bench, drinking in the perfume of the wild flowers. He is a man of a beautifully simple nature. He says that here the real things of life come to him, and that here his greatest and most successful plans, many times as by a flash of inspiration, suggest themselves to him.

Everything in the immediate vicinity seems to breathe a spirit of kindliness, comfort, good-will, and good cheer. The very cattle and sheep as they come to the old stone-fence at the edge of the grove and look across to this beautiful spot seem, indeed, to get the same enjoyment that the people are getting. They seem almost to smile in the realization of their contentment and enjoyment; or perhaps it seems so to the looker-on, because he can scarcely help smiling as he sees the manifested evidence of their contentment and pleasure.

The gate of the pond is always open wide enough to admit a supply of water so abundant that it continually overflows a quantity sufficient to feed a stream that runs through the fields below, giving the pure mountain water in drink to the cattle and flocks that are grazing there. The stream then flows on through the neighbors' fields.

Not long ago our friend was absent for a year. He rented his estate during his absence to a man who, as the world goes, was of a very "practical" turn of mind. He had no time for anything that did not bring him direct "practical" returns. The gate connecting the reservoir with the lotus pond was shut down, and no longer had the crystal mountain water the opportunity to feed and overflow it. The notice of our friend, "All are welcome to the Lotus Pond," was removed, and no longer were the gay companies of children and of men and women seen at the pond. A great change came over everything. On account of the lack of the life-giving water the flowers in the pond wilted, and their long stems lay stretched upon the mud in the bottom. The fish that formerly swam in its clear water soon died and gave an offensive odor to all who came near. The flowers no longer bloomed on its banks. The birds no longer came to drink and to bathe. No longer was heard the hum of the bees; and more, the stream that ran through the fields below dried up, so that the cattle and the flocks no longer got their supply of clear mountain water.

The difference between the spot now and the lotus pond when our friend gave it his careful attention was caused, as we readily see, by the shutting of the gate to the pond, thus preventing the water from the reservoir in the hills which was the source of its life, from entering it. And when this, the source of its life, was shut off, not only was the appearance of the lotus pond entirely changed, but the surrounding fields were deprived of the stream to whose banks the flocks and cattle came for drink.

In this do we not see a complete parallel so far as human life is concerned? In the degree that we recognize our oneness, our connection with the Infinite Spirit which is the life of all, and in the degree that we open ourselves to this divine inflow, do we come into harmony with the highest, the most powerful, and the most beautiful everywhere. And in the degree that we do this do we overflow, so that all who come in contact with us receive the effects of this realization on our part. This is the lotus pond of our friend, he who is in love with all that is truest and best in the universe. And in the degree that we fail to recognize our oneness with this Infinite Source, and so close, shut ourselves to this divine inflow, do we come into that state where there seems to be with us nothing of good, nothing of beauty, nothing of power; and when this is true, those who come in contact with us receive not good, but harm. This is the spot of the lotus pond while the farm was in the hands of a renter.

There is this difference between the lotus pond and your life and mine. It has no power in itself of opening the gate to the inflow of the water from the reservoir which is its source. In regard to this it is helpless and dependent upon an outside agency. You and I have the power, the power within us, to open or to close ourselves to this divine inflow exactly as we choose. This we have through the power of mind, through the operation of thought.

There is the soul life, direct from God. This it is that relates us to the Infinite. There is, then, the physical life. This it is that relates us to the material universe about us. The thought life connects the one with the other. It is this that plays between the two.

Before we proceed farther let us consider very briefly the nature of thought. Thought is not, as is many times supposed, a mere indefinite abstraction, or something of a like nature. It is, on the contrary, a vital, living force, the most vital, subtle, and irresistible force there is in the universe.

In our very laboratory experiments we are demonstrating the great fact that thoughts are forces. They have form, and quality, and substance, and power, and we are beginning to find that there is what we may term a *science of thought*. We are beginning also to find that through the instrumentality of our thought forces we have creative power, not merely in a figurative sense, but creative power in reality.

Everything in the material universe about us, everything the universe has ever known, had its origin first in thought. From this it took its form. Every castle, every statue, every painting, every piece of mechanism, everything had its birth, its origin, first in the mind of the one who formed it before it received its material expression or embodiment. The very universe in which we live is the result of the thought energies of God, the Infinite Spirit that is back of all. And if it is true, as we have found, that we in our true selves are in essence the same and in this sense are one with the life of this Infinite Spirit, do we not then see that in the degree that we come into a vital realization of this stupendous fact, *we, through the operation of our interior, spiritual, thought forces, have in like sense creative power?*

Everything exists in the unseen before it is manifested or realized in the seen, and in this sense it is true that the unseen things are the real, while the things that are seen are the unreal. The unseen things are *cause;* the seen things are *effect.* The unseen things are the eternal; the seen things are the changing, the transient.

The *"power of the word"* is a literal scientific fact. Through the operation of our thought forces we have creative power. The spoken word is nothing more nor less than the outward expression of the workings of these interior forces. The spoken word is then, in a sense, the means whereby the thought forces are focused and directed along any particular line; and this concentration, this giving them direction, is necessary before any outward or material manifestation of their power can become evident.

Much is said in regard to "building castles in the air," and one who is given to this building is not always looked upon with favor. But castles in the air are always necessary before we can have castles on the ground, before we can have castles in which to live. The trouble with the one who gives himself to building castles in the air is not that he builds them in the air, but that he does not go farther and actualize in life, in character, in material form, the castles he thus builds. He does a part of the work, a very necessary part; but another equally necessary part remains still undone.

There is in connection with the thought forces what we may term, the drawing power of mind, and the great law operating here is one with that great law of the universe, that like attracts like. We are continually attracting to us from both the seen and the unseen side of life, forces and conditions most akin to those of our own thoughts.

This law is continually operating whether we are conscious of it or not. We are all living, so to speak, in a vast ocean of thought, and the very atmosphere around us is continually filled with the thought forces that are being continually sent or that are continually going out in the form of thought waves. We are all affected, more or less, by these thought forces, either consciously or unconsciously; and in the degree that we are more or less sensitively organized, or in the degree that we are negative and so are open to outside influences, rather than positive, thus determining what influences shall enter into our realm of thought, and hence into our lives.

There are those among us who are much more sensitively organized than others. As an organism their bodies are more finely, more sensitively constructed. These, generally speaking, are people who are always more or less affected by the mentalities of those with whom they come in contact, or in whose company they are. A friend, the editor of one of our great journals, is so sensitively organized that it is impossible for him to attend a gathering, such as a reception, talk and shake hands with a number of people during the course of the evening, without taking on to a greater or lesser extent their various mental and physical conditions. These affect him to such an extent that he is scarcely himself and in his best condition for work until some two or three days afterward.

Some think it unfortunate for one to be sensitively organized. By no means. It is a good thing, for one may thus be more open and receptive to the higher impulses of the soul within, and to all higher forces and influences from without. It may, however, be unfortunate and extremely inconvenient to be so organized unless one recognize and gain the power of closing himself, of making himself positive to all detrimental or undesirable influences. This power every one, however sensitively organized he may be, can acquire.

This he can acquire through the mind's action. And, moreover, there is no habit of more value to anyone, be he sensitively or less sensitively organized, than that of occasionally taking and holding himself continually in the attitude of mind—I close myself, I make myself positive to all things below, and open and receptive to all higher influences, to all things above. By taking this attitude of mind consciously now and then, it soon becomes a habit, and if one is deeply in earnest in regard to it, it puts into operation silent but subtle and powerful influences in effecting the desired results. In this way all lower and undesirable influences from both the seen and the unseen side of life are closed out, while all higher influences are invited, and in the degree that they are invited will they enter.

And what do we mean by the unseen side of life? First, the thought forces, the mental and emotional conditions in the atmosphere about us that are generated by those manifesting on the physical plane through the agency of physical bodies. Second, the same forces generated by those who have dropped the physical body, or from whom it has been struck away, and who are now manifesting through the agency of bodies of a different nature.

"The individual existence of man *begins* on the sense plane of the physical world, but rises through successive gradations of ethereal and celestial spheres, corresponding with his ever unfolding deific life and powers, to a destiny of unspeakable grandeur and glory. Within and above every physical planet is a corresponding ethereal planet, or soul world, as within and above every physical organism is a corresponding ethereal organism, or soul body, of which the physical is but the external counterpart and materialized expression. From this etherealized or soul planet, which is the immediate home of our arisen humanity, there rises or deepens in infinite gradations spheres within and above spheres, to celestial heights of spiritualized existence utterly inconceivable to the sense man. Embodiment, accordingly, is two-fold,—the physical being but the temporary husk, so to speak, in and by which the real and permanent ethereal organism is individualized and perfected, somewhat as 'the full corn in the ear' is reached by means of its husk, for which there is no further use. By means of this indestructible ethereal body and the corresponding ethereal spheres of environment with the social life and relations in the spheres, the individuality and personal life is preserved forever."

The fact of life in whatever form means the continuance of life, even though the form be changed. Life is the one eternal principle of the universe and so always continues, even though the form of the agency through which it manifests be changed. "In my Father's house are many mansions." And surely, because the individual has dropped, has gone out of the physical body, there is no evidence at all that the life does not go right on the same as before, not commencing,—for there is no cessation,—but commencing in the other form, exactly where it has left off here; for all life is a continuous evolution, step by step; there one neither skips nor jumps.

There are in the other form, then, mentalities and hence lives of all grades and influences, the same as there are in the physical form. If, then, the great law that like attracts like is ever operating, we are continually attracting to us from this side of life influences and conditions most akin to those of our own thoughts and lives. A gruesome thought that we should be so influenced, says one. By no means, all life is one; we are all bound together in the one common and universal life, and especially not when we take into consideration the fact that we have it entirely in our own hands to determine the order of thought we entertain, and consequently the order of influences we attract, and are not mere willowy creatures of circumstance, unless indeed we choose to be.

In our mental lives we can either keep hold of the rudder and so determine exactly what course we take, what points we touch, or we can fail to do this, and failing, we drift, and are blown hither and thither by every passing breeze. And so, on the contrary, welcome should be the thought, for thus we may draw to us the influence and the aid of the greatest, the noblest, and the best who have lived on the earth, whatever the time, wherever the place.

We cannot rationally believe other than that those who have labored in love and with uplifting power here are still laboring in the same way, and in all probability with more earnest zeal, and with still greater power.

"And Elisha prayed, and said, Lord, I pray thee, open his eyes, that he may see. And the Lord opened the eyes of the young man; and he saw: and, behold, the mountain *was full of horses and chariots of fire* round about Elisha."

While riding with a friend a few days ago, we were speaking of the great interest people are everywhere taking in the more vital things of life, the eagerness with which they are reaching out for a knowledge of the interior forces, their ever increasing desire to know themselves and to know their true relations with the Infinite. And in speaking of the great spiritual awakening that is so rapidly coming all over the world, the beginnings of which we are so clearly seeing during the closing years of this, and whose ever increasing proportions we are to witness during the early years of the coming century, I said, "How beautiful if Emerson, the illumined one so far in advance of his time, who labored so faithfully and so fearlessly to bring about these very conditions, how beautiful if he were with us today to witness it all! how he would rejoice!" "How do we know," was the reply, "that he is not witnessing it all? and more, that he is not having a hand in it all,—a hand even greater, perhaps, than when we *saw* him here?" Thank you, my friend, for this reminder. And, truly, "are they not all ministering spirits sent forth to minister to those who shall be heirs of salvation?"

As science is so abundantly demonstrating today,—the things that we see are but a very small fraction of the things that are. The real vital forces at work in our own lives and in the world about us are not seen by the ordinary physical eye. Yet they are the causes of which all things we see are merely the effects. Thoughts are forces; like builds like, and like attracts like. For one to govern his thinking, then, is to determine his life.

Says one of deep insight into the nature of things: "The law of correspondences between spiritual and material things is wonderfully exact in its workings. People ruled by the mood of gloom attract to them gloomy things. People always discouraged and despondent do not succeed in anything, and live only by burdening some one else. The hopeful, confident, and cheerful attract the elements of success. A man's front or back yard will advertise that man's ruling mood in the way it is kept. A woman at home shows her state of mind in her dress. A slattern advertises the ruling mood of hopelessness, carelessness, and lack of system. Rags, tatters, and dirt are always in the mind before being on the body. The thought that is most put out brings its corresponding visible element to crystallize about you as surely and literally as the visible bit of copper in solution attracts to it the invisible copper in that solution. A mind always hopeful, confident, courageous, and determined on its set purpose, and keeping itself to that purpose, attracts to itself out of the elements things and powers favorable to that purpose.

"Every thought of yours has a literal value to you in every possible way. The strength of your body, the strength of your mind, your success in business, and the pleasure your company brings others, depends on the nature of your thoughts. . . . In whatever mood you set your mind does your spirit receive of unseen substance in correspondence with that mood. It is as much a chemical law as a spiritual law. Chemistry is not confined to the elements we see. The elements we do not see with the physical eye outnumber ten thousand times those we do see. The Christ injunction, 'Do good to those who hate you,' is based on a scientific fact and a natural law. So, to do good is to bring to yourself all the elements in nature of power and good. To do evil is to bring the contrary destructive elements. When our eyes are opened, self-preservation will make us stop all evil thought. Those who live by hate will die by hate: that is, 'those who live by the sword will die by the sword.' Every evil thought is as a sword drawn on the person to whom it is directed. If a sword is drawn in return, so much the worse for both."

And says another who knows full well whereof he speaks: "The law of attraction works universally on every plane of *action*, and we attract whatever we desire or expect. If we desire one thing and expect another, we become like houses divided against themselves, which are quickly brought to desolation. Determine resolutely to expect only what you desire, then you will attract only what you wish for. . . . Carry any kind of thought you please about with you, and so long as you retain it, no matter how you roam over land or sea, you will unceasingly attract to yourself, knowingly or inadvertently, exactly and only what corresponds to your own dominant quality of thought. Thoughts are our private property, and we can regulate them to suit our taste entirely by steadily recognizing our ability so to do."

We have just spoken of the drawing power of mind. Faith is nothing more nor less than the operation of the *thought forces* in the form of an earnest desire, coupled with expectation as to its fulfillment. And in the degree that faith, the earnest desire thus sent out, is continually held to and watered by firm expectation, in just that degree does it either draw to itself, or does it change from the unseen into the visible, from the spiritual into the material, that for which it is sent.

Let the element of doubt or fear enter in, and what would otherwise be a tremendous force will be so neutralized that it will fail of its realization. Continually held to and continually watered by firm expectation, it becomes a force, a drawing power, that is irresistible and absolute, and the results will be absolute in direct proportion as it is absolute.

We shall find, as we are so rapidly beginning to find today, that the great things said in regard to faith, the great promises made in connection with it, are not mere vague sentimentalities, but are all great scientific facts, and rest upon great immutable laws. Even in our very laboratory experiments we are beginning to discover the laws underlying and governing these forces. We are now beginning, some at least, to use them understandingly and not blindly, as has so often and so long been the case.

Much is said today in regard to the will. It is many times spoken of as if it were a force in itself. But will is a force, a power, only in so far as it is a particular form of the manifestation of the thought forces; for it is by what we call the "will" that thought is focused and given a particular direction, and in the degree that thought is thus focused and given direction, is it effective in the work it is sent out to accomplish.

In a sense there are two kinds of will,—the human and the divine. The human will is the will of what, for convenience' sake, we may term the lower self. It is the will that finds its life merely in the realm of the mental and the physical,—the sense will. It is the will of the one who is not yet awake to the fact that there is a life that far transcends the life of merely the intellect and the physical senses, and which when realized and lived, does not do away with or minify these, but which, on the contrary, brings them to their highest perfection and to their powers of keenest enjoyment. The divine will is the will of the higher self, the will of the one who recognizes his oneness with the Divine, and who consequently brings his will to work in harmony, in conjunction with the divine will. "The Lord thy God *in the midst of thee* is mighty."

The human will has its limitations. So far and no farther, says the law. The divine will has no limitations. It is supreme. All things are open and subject to you, says the law, and so, in the degree that the human will is transmuted into the divine, in the degree that it comes into harmony with and so acts in conjunction with the divine, does it become supreme. Then it is that "thou shalt decree a thing and it shall be established unto thee." The great secret of life and of power, then, is to make and to keep one's conscious connection with this Infinite Source.

The power of every life, the very life itself, is determined by what it relates itself to. God is immanent as well as transcendent. He is creating, working, ruling in the universe today, in your life and in mine, just as much as He ever has been. We are too apt to regard Him after the manner of an absentee landlord, one who has set into operation the forces of this great universe, and then taken Himself away.

In the degree, however, that we recognize Him as immanent as well as transcendent, are we able to partake of His life and power. For in the degree that we recognize Him as the Infinite Spirit of Life and Power that is today, at this very moment, working and manifesting in and through all, and then, in the degree that we come into the realization of our oneness with this life, do we become partakers of, and so do we actualize in ourselves the qualities of His life. *In the degree that we open ourselves to the inflowing tide of this immanent and transcendent life, do we make ourselves channels through which the Infinite Intelligence and Power can work.*

It is through the instrumentality of the mind that we are enabled to connect the real soul life with the physical life, and so enable the soul life to manifest and work through the physical. The thought life needs *continually* to be illumined from within. This illumination can come in just the degree that through the agency of the mind we recognize our oneness with the Divine, of which each soul is an individual form of expression.

This gives us the inner guiding which we call intuition. "Intuition is to the spiritual nature and understanding practically what sense perception is to the sensuous nature and understanding. It is an inner spiritual sense through which man is opened to the direct revelation and knowledge of God, the secrets of nature and life, and through which he is brought into conscious unity and fellowship with God, and made to realize his own deific nature and supremacy of being as the son of God. Spiritual supremacy and illumination thus realized through the development and perfection of intuition under divine inspiration, gives the perfect inner vision and direct insight into the character, properties, and purpose of all things to which the attention and interest are directed. . . . It is, we repeat, a spiritual sense opening inwardly, as the physical senses open outwardly; and because it has the capacity to perceive, grasp, and know the truth at first hand, independent of all external sources of information, we call it intuition. All inspired teaching and spiritual revelations are based upon the recognition of this spiritual faculty of the soul, and its power to receive and appropriate them . . . Conscious unity of man in spirit and purpose with the Father, born out of his supreme desire and trust, opens his soul through this inner sense to immediate inspiration and enlightenment from the Divine Omniscience, and the co-operative energy of the Divine Omnipotence, under which he becomes a seer and a master.

"On this higher plane of realized spiritual life in the flesh the mind holds the impersonal attitude and acts with unfettered freedom and unbiased vision, grasping truth at first hand, independent of all external sources of information. Approaching all beings and things from the divine side, they are seen in the light of the Divine Omniscience. God's purpose in them, and so the truth concerning them, as it rests in the mind of God, are thus revealed by direct illumination from the Divine Mind, to which the soul is opened inwardly through this spiritual sense we call intuition." Some call it the voice of the soul; some call it the voice of God; some call it the sixth sense. It is our inner spiritual sense.

In the degree that we come into the recognition of our own *true* selves, into the realization of the oneness of our life with the Infinite Life, and in the degree that we open ourselves to this divine inflow, does this voice of intuition, this voice of the soul, this voice of God, speak clearly; and in the degree that we recognize, listen to, and obey it, does it speak ever more clearly, until by-and-by there comes the time when it is unerring, *absolutely unerring*, in its guidance.

CHAPTER 4

# Fullness of Life—Bodily Health and Vigor

God is the Spirit of Infinite Life. If we are partakers of this life, and have the power of opening ourselves fully to its divine inflow, it means more, so far as even the physical life is concerned, than we may at first think. For very clearly, the life of this Infinite Spirit, from its very nature, can admit of no disease; and if this is true, no disease can exist in the body where it freely enters, through which it freely flows.

Let us recognize at the outset that, so far as the physical life is concerned, *all life is from within out.* There is an immutable law which says: "As within, so without; cause, effect." In other words, the thought forces, the various mental states and the emotions, all have in time their effects upon the physical body.

Some one says: "I hear a great deal said today in regard to the effects of the mind upon the body, but I don't know as I place very much confidence in this." Don't you? Some one brings you sudden news. You grow pale, you tremble, or perhaps you fall into a faint. It is, however, through the channel of your mind that the news is imparted to you. A friend says something to you, perhaps at the table, something that seems very unkind. You are hurt by it, as we say. You have been enjoying your dinner, but from this moment your appetite is gone. But what was said entered into and affected you through the channel of your mind.

Look! yonder goes a young man, dragging his feet, stumbling over the slightest obstruction in the path. Why is it? Simply that he is weak-minded, an idiot. In other words, *a falling state of mind is productive of a falling condition of the body.* To be sure minded is to be sure footed. To be uncertain in mind is to be uncertain in step.

Again, a sudden emergency arises. You stand trembling and weak with fear. Why are you powerless to move? Why do you tremble? And yet you believe that the mind has but little influence upon the body. You are for a moment dominated by a fit of anger. For a few hours afterwards you complain of a violent headache. And still you do not seem to realize that the thoughts and emotions have an effect upon the body.

A day or two ago, while conversing with a friend, we were speaking of worry. "My father is greatly given to worry," he said. "Your father is not a healthy man," I said. "He is not strong, vigorous, robust, and active." I then went on to describe to him more fully his father's condition and the troubles which afflicted him. He looked at me in surprise and said, "Why, you do not know my father?" "No," I replied. "How then can you describe so accurately the disease with which he is afflicted?" "You have just told me that your father is greatly given to worry. When you told me this you indicated to me cause. In describing your father's condition I simply connected with the cause its own peculiar effects."

Fear and worry have the effect of closing up the channels of the body, so that the life forces flow in a slow and sluggish manner. Hope and tranquillity open the channels of the body, so that the life forces go bounding through it is such a way that disease can rarely get a foothold.

Not long ago a lady was telling a friend of a serious physical trouble. My friend happened to know that between this lady and her sister the most kindly relations did not exist. He listened attentively to her delineation of her troubles, and then, looking her squarely in the face, in a firm but kindly tone said: "Forgive your sister." The woman looked at him in surprise and said: "I can't forgive my sister." "Very well, then," he replied, "keep the stiffness of your joints and your kindred rheumatic troubles."

A few weeks later he saw her again. With a light step she came toward him and said: "I took your advice. I saw my sister and forgave her. We have become good friends again, and I don't know how it is, but somehow or other from the very day, as I remember, that we became reconciled, my troubles seemed to grow less, and today there is not a trace of the old difficulties left; and really, my sister and I have become such good friends that now we can scarcely get along without one another." Again we have effect following cause.

We have several well-authenticated cases of the following nature: A mother has been dominated for a few moments by an intense passion of anger, and the child at her breast has died within an hour's time, so poisoned became the mother's milk by virtue of the poisonous secretions of the system while under the domination of this fit of anger. In other cases it has caused severe illness and convulsions.

The following experiment has been tried a number of times by a well-known scientist. Several men have been put into a heated room. Each man has been dominated for a moment by a particular passion of some kind; one by an intense passion of anger, and others by different other passions. The experimenter has taken a drop of perspiration from the body of each of these men, and by means of a careful chemical analysis he has been able to determine the particular passion by which each has been dominated. Practically the same results revealed themselves in the chemical analysis of the saliva of each of the men.

Says a noted American author, an able graduate of one of our greatest medical schools, and one who has studied deeply into the forces that build the body and the forces that tear it down: "The mind is the natural protector of the body. . . . Every thought tends to reproduce itself, and ghastly mental pictures of disease, sensuality, and vice of all sorts, produce scrofula and leprosy in the soul, which reproduces them in the body. Anger changes the chemical properties of the saliva to a poison dangerous to life. It is well known that sudden and violent emotions have not only weakened the heart in a few hours, but have caused death and insanity. It has been discovered by scientists that there is a chemical difference between that sudden cold exudation of a person under a deep sense of guilt and the ordinary perspiration; and the state of the mind can sometimes be determined by chemical analysis of the perspiration of a criminal, which, when brought into contact with selenic acid, produces a distinctive pink color. It is well known that fear has killed thousands of victims; while, on the other hand, *courage is a great invigorator.*

"Anger in the mother may poison a nursing child. Rarey, the celebrated horse-tamer, said that an angry word would sometimes raise the pulse of a horse ten beats in a minute. If this is true of a beast, what can we say of its power upon human beings, especially upon a child? Strong mental emotion often causes vomiting. Extreme anger or fright may produce jaundice. A violent paroxysm of rage has caused apoplexy and death. Indeed, in more than one instance, a single night of mental agony has wrecked a life. Grief, long-standing jealousy, constant care and corroding anxiety sometimes tend to develop insanity. Sick thoughts and discordant moods are the natural atmosphere of disease, and crime is engendered and thrives in the miasma of the mind."

From all this we get the great fact we are scientifically demonstrating today,—that the various mental states, emotions, and passions have their various peculiar effects upon the body, and each induces in turn, if indulged in to any great extent, its own peculiar forms of disease, and these in time become chronic.

Just a word or two in regard to their mode of operation. If a person is dominated for a moment by, say a passion of anger, there is set up in the physical organism what we might justly term a bodily thunder-storm, which has the effect of souring, or rather of corroding, the normal, healthy, and life-giving secretions of the body, so that instead of performing their natural functions they become poisonous and destructive. And if this goes on to any great extent, by virtue of their cumulative influences, they give rise to a particular form of disease, which in turn becomes chronic. So the emotion opposite to this, that of kindliness, love, benevolence, goodwill, tends to stimulate a healthy, purifying, and life-giving flow of all the bodily secretions. All the channels of the body seem free and open; the life forces go bounding through them. And these very forces, set into a bounding activity, will in time counteract the poisonous and disease-giving effects of their opposites.

A physician goes to see a patient. He gives no medicine this morning. Yet the very fact of his going makes the patient better. He has carried with him the spirit of health; he has carried brightness of tone and disposition; he has carried hope into the sick chamber; he has left it there. In fact, the very hope and good cheer he has carried with him has taken hold of and has had a subtle but powerful influence upon the mind of the patient; and this mental condition imparted by the physician has in turn its effects upon the patient's body, and so through the instrumentality of this mental suggestion the healing goes on.

*Know, then, whatever cheerful and serene*
*Supports the mind, supports the body, too.*
*Hence the most vital movement mortals feel*
*Is hope; the balm and life-blood of the soul.*

We sometimes hear a person in weak health say to another, "I always feel better when you come." There is a deep scientific reason underlying the statement. "The tongue of the wise is health." The power of suggestion so far as the human mind is concerned is a most wonderful and interesting field of study. Most wonderful and powerful forces can be set into operation through this agency. One of the world's most noted scientists, recognized everywhere as one of the most eminent anatomists living, tells us that he has proven from laboratory experiments that the entire human structure can be completely changed, made over, within a period of less than one year, and that some portions can be entirely remade within a period of a very few weeks.

"Do you mean to say," I hear it asked, "that the body can be changed from a diseased to a healthy condition through the operation of the interior forces?" Most certainly; and more, this is the natural method of cure. The method that has as its work the application of drugs, medicines and external agencies is the artificial method. The only thing that any drug or any medicine can do is to remove obstructions, that the life forces may have simply a better chance to do their work. *The real healing process must be performed by the operation of the life forces within.* A surgeon and physician of world-wide fame recently made to his medical associates the following declaration: "For generations past the most important influence that plays upon nutrition, the *life principle* itself, has remained an unconsidered element in the medical profession, and the almost exclusive drift of its studies and remedial paraphernalia has been confined to the action of matter over mind. This has seriously interfered with the evolutionary tendencies of the doctors themselves, and consequently the psychic factor in professional life is still in a rudimentary or comparatively undeveloped state. But the light of the nineteenth century has dawned, and so the march of mankind in general is taken in the direction of the hidden forces of nature. Doctors are now compelled to join the ranks of students in psychology and follow their patrons into the broader field of mental therapeutics. There is no time for lingering, no time for skepticism or doubt or hesitation. *He who lingers is lost, for the entire race is enlisted in the movement.*"

I am aware of the fact that in connection with the matter we are now considering there has been a great deal of foolishness during the past few years. Many absurd and foolish things have been claimed and done; but this says nothing against, and it has absolutely nothing to do with the great underlying laws themselves. The same has been true of the early days of practically every system of ethics or philosophy or religion the world has ever known. But as time has passed, these foolish, absurd things have fallen away, and the great eternal principles have stood out ever more and more clearly defined.

I know *personally* of many cases where an entire and permanent cure has been effected, in some within a remarkably short period of time, through the operation of these forces. Some of them are cases that had been entirely given up by the regular practice, *materia medica*. We have numerous accounts of such cases in all times and in connection with all religions. And why should not the power of effecting such cures exist among us today? The *power does exist*, and it will be actualized in just the degree that we recognize the same great laws that were recognized in times past.

One person may do a very great deal in connection with the healing of another, but this almost invariably implies co-operation on the part of the one who is thus treated. In the cures that Christ performed he most always needed the co-operation of the one who appealed to him. His question almost invariably was, "Dost thou believe?" He thus stimulated into activity the life-giving forces within the one cured. If one is in a very weak condition, or if his nervous system is exhausted, or if his mind through the influence of the disease is not so strong in its workings, it may be well for him for a time to seek the aid and co-operation of another. But it would be far better for such a one could he bring himself to a vital realization of the omnipotence of his own interior powers.

One may cure another, but to be *permanently healed* one must do it himself. In this way another may be most valuable as a teacher by bringing one to a clear realization of the power of the forces within, but in every case, in order to have a permanent cure, the work of the self is necessary. Christ's words were almost invariably,—Go and sin no more, or, thy sins are forgiven thee, thus pointing out the one eternal and never-changing fact,—that all disease and its consequent suffering is the direct or the indirect result of the violation of law, either consciously or unconsciously, either intentionally or unintentionally.

Suffering is designed to continue only so long as sin continues, sin not necessarily in the theological, but always in the philosophical sense, though many times in the sense of both. The moment the violation ceases, the moment one comes into perfect harmony with the law, the cause of the suffering ceases; and though there may be residing within the cumulative effects of past violation, the cause is removed, and consequently there can be no more effects in the form of additions, and even the diseased condition that has been induced from past violation will begin to disappear as soon as the right forces are set into activity.

There is nothing that will more quickly and more completely bring one into harmony with the laws under which he lives than this vital realization of his oneness with the Infinite Spirit, which is the life of all life. In this there can be no disease, and nothing will more readily remove from the organism the obstructions that have accumulated there, or in other words, the disease that resides there, than this full realization and the complete opening of one's self to this divine inflow. "I shall put my spirit in you, and ye shall live."

The moment a person realizes his oneness with the Infinite Spirit he recognizes himself as a spiritual being, and no longer as a mere physical, material being. He then no longer makes the mistake of regarding himself as body, subject to ills and diseases, but he realizes the fact that he is spirit, spirit now as much as he ever will or can be, and that he is the builder and so the master of the body, the house in which he lives; and the moment he thus recognizes his power as master he ceases in any way to allow it the mastery over him. He no longer fears the elements or any of the forces that he now in his ignorance allows to take hold of and affect the body. The moment he realizes his own supremacy, instead of fearing them as he did when he was out of harmony with them, he learns to love them. He thus comes into harmony with them; or rather, he so orders them that they come into harmony with him. He who formerly was the slave has now become the master. The moment we come to love a thing it no longer carries harm for us.

There are almost countless numbers today, weak and suffering in body, who would become strong and healthy if they would only give God an opportunity to do His work. To such I would say, *Don't shut out the divine inflow.* Do anything else rather than this. Open yourselves to it. Invite it. In the degree that you open yourselves to it, its inflowing tide will course through your bodies a force so vital that the old obstructions that are dominating them today will be driven out before it. "My words are life to them that find them, and health to all their flesh."

There is a trough through which a stream of muddy water has been flowing for many days. The dirt has gradually collected on its sides and bottom, and it continues to collect as long as the muddy water flows through it. Change this. Open the trough to a swift-flowing stream of clear, crystal water, and in a very little while even the very dirt that has collected on its sides and bottom will be carried away. The trough will be entirely cleansed. It will present an aspect of beauty and no longer an aspect of ugliness. And more, the water that now courses through it will be of value; it will be an agent of refreshment, of health and of strength to those who use it.

Yes, in just the degree that you realize your oneness with this Infinite Spirit of Life, and thus actualize your latent possibilities and powers, you will exchange disease for ease, inharmony for harmony, suffering and pain for abounding health and strength. And in the degree that you realize this wholeness, this abounding health and strength in yourself, will you carry it to all with whom you come in contact; for *we must remember that health is contagious as well as disease.*

I hear it asked, What can be said in a concrete way in regard to the practical application of these truths, so that one can hold himself in the enjoyment of perfect bodily health; and more, that one may heal himself of any existing disease? In reply, let it be said that the chief thing that can be done is to point out the great underlying principle, and that each individual must make his own application; one person cannot well make this for another.

First let it be said, that the very fact of one's holding the thought of perfect health sets into operation vital forces which will in time be more or less productive of the effect,—perfect health. Then speaking more directly in regard to the great principle itself, from its very nature, it is clear that more can be accomplished through the process of realization than through the process of affirmation, though for some affirmation may be a help, an aid to realization.

In the degree, however, that you come into a vital realization of your oneness with the Infinite Spirit of Life, whence all life in individual form has come and is continually coming, and in the degree that through this realization you open yourself to its divine inflow, do you set into operation forces that will sooner or later bring even the physical body into a state of abounding health and strength. For to realize that this Infinite Spirit of Life can from its very nature admit of no disease, and to realize that this, then, is the life in you, by realizing your oneness with it, you can so open yourself to its more abundant entrance that the diseased bodily conditions—effects—will respond to the influences of its all-perfect power, this either quickly or more tardily, depending entirely upon yourself.

There have been those who have been able to open themselves so fully to this realization that the healing has been instantaneous and permanent. The degree of intensity always eliminates in like degree the element of time. *It must, however, be a calm, quiet, and expectant intensity, rather than an intensity that is fearing, disturbed, and non-expectant.* Then there are others who have come to this realization by degrees.

Many will receive great help, and many will be entirely healed by a practice somewhat after the following nature: With a mind at peace, and with a heart going out in love to all, go into the quiet of your own interior self, holding the thought,—I am one with the Infinite Spirit of Life, the life of my life. I then as spirit, I a spiritual being, can in my own real nature admit of no disease. I now open my body, in which disease has gotten a foothold, I open it fully to the inflowing tide of this Infinite Life, and it now, even now, is pouring in and coursing through my body, and the healing process is going on. Realize this so fully that you begin to feel a quickening and a warming glow imparted by the life forces to the body. Believe the healing process is going on. Believe in and hold continually to it. Many people greatly desire a certain thing, but expect something else. They have greater faith in the power of evil than in the power of good, and hence remain ill.

If one will give himself to this meditation, realization, treatment, or whatever term it may seem best to use, at stated times, as often as he may choose, and then *continually hold himself in the same attitude of mind,* thus allowing the force to work continually, he will be surprised how rapidly the body will be exchanging conditions of disease and inharmony for health and harmony. There is no particular reason, however, for this surprise, for in this way he is simply allowing the Omnipotent Power to do the work, which will have to do it ultimately in any case.

If there is a local difficulty, and one wants to open this particular portion, in addition to the entire body, to this inflowing life, he can hold this particular portion in thought, for to fix the thought in this way upon any particular portion of the body stimulates or increases the flow of the life forces in that portion. It must always be borne in mind, however, that whatever healing may be thus accomplished, effects will not permanently cease until causes have been removed. In other words, *as long as there is the violation of law, so long disease and suffering will result.*

This realization that we are considering will have an influence not only where there is a diseased condition of the body, but even where there is not this condition it will give an increased bodily life, vigor, and power.

We have had many cases, in all times and in all countries, of healing through the operation of the interior forces, entirely independent of external agencies. Various have been the methods, or rather, various have been the names applied to them, but the great law underlying all is one and the same, and the same today. When the Master sent his followers forth, his injunction to them was to heal the sick and the afflicted, as well as to teach the people. The early church fathers had the power of healing, in short, it was a part of their work.

And why should we not have the power today, the same as they had it then? Are the laws at all different? Identically the same. Why, then? Simply because, with a few rare exceptions here and there, we are unable to get beyond the mere letter of the law into its real vital spirit and power. It is the letter that killeth, it is the spirit that giveth life and power. Every soul who becomes so individualized that he breaks through the mere letter and enters into the real vital spirit, *will have the power*, as have all who have gone before, and when he does, he will also be the means of imparting it to others, for he will be one who will move and who will speak with authority.

We are rapidly finding today, and we shall find even more and more, as time passes, that practically all disease, with its consequent suffering, has its origin in perverted mental and emotional states and conditions. *The mental attitude we take toward anything determines to a greater or lesser extent its effects upon us.* If we fear it, or if we antagonize it, the chances are that it will have detrimental or even disastrous effects upon us. If we come into harmony with it by quietly recognizing and inwardly asserting our superiority over it, in the degree that we are able successfully to do this, in that degree will it carry with it no injury for us.

No disease can enter into or take hold of our bodies unless it find therein something corresponding to itself which makes it possible. And in the same way, no evil or undesirable condition of any kind can come into our lives unless there is already in them that which invites it and so makes it possible for it to come. The sooner we begin to look within ourselves for the cause of whatever comes to us, the better it will be, for so much the sooner will we begin to make conditions within ourselves such that only *good* may enter.

We, who from our very natures should be masters of all conditions, by virtue of our ignorance are mastered by almost numberless conditions of every description.

Do I fear a draft? There is nothing in the draft—a little purifying current of God's pure air—to cause me trouble, to bring on a cold, perhaps an illness. The draft can affect me only in the degree that *I myself* make it possible, only in the degree that I allow it to affect me. We must distinguish between causes and mere occasions. The draft is not cause, nor does it carry cause with it.

Two persons are sitting in the same draft. The one is injuriously affected by it, the other experiences not even an inconvenience, but he rather enjoys it. The one is a creature of circumstances; he fears the draft, cringes before it, continually thinks of the harm it is doing him. In other words, he opens every avenue for it to enter and take hold of him, and so it—harmless and beneficent in itself—brings to him exactly what he has empowered it to bring. The other recognizes himself as the master over and not the creature of circumstances. He is not concerned about the draft. He puts himself into harmony with it, makes himself positive to it, and instead of experiencing any discomfort, he enjoys it, and in addition to its doing him a service by bringing the pure fresh air from without to him, it does him the additional service of hardening him even more to any future conditions of a like nature. But if the draft was cause, it would bring the same results to both. The fact that it does not, shows that it is not a cause, but a condition, and it brings to each, effects which correspond to the conditions it finds within each.

Poor draft! How many thousands, nay millions of times it is made the scapegoat by those who are too ignorant or too unfair to look their own weaknesses square in the face, and who instead of becoming imperial masters, remain cringing slaves. Think of it, what it means! A man created in the image of the eternal God, sharer of His life and power, born to have dominion, fearing, shaking, cringing before a little draft of pure life-giving air. But scapegoats are convenient things, even if the only thing they do for us is to aid us in our constant efforts at self-delusion.

The best way to disarm a draft of the bad effects it has been accustomed to bring one, is first to bring about a pure and healthy set of conditions within, then, to change one's mental attitude toward it. Recognize the fact that of itself it has no power, it has only the power you invest it with. Thus you will put yourself into harmony with it, and will no longer sit in fear of it. Then sit in a draft a few times and get hardened to it, as every one, by going at it judiciously, can readily do. "But suppose one is in delicate health, or especially subject to drafts?" Then be simply a little judicious at first; don't seek the strongest that can be found, especially if you do not as yet in your own mind feel equal to it, for if you do not, it signifies that you still fear it. That supreme regulator of all life, *good common sense,* must be used here, the same as elsewhere.

If we are born to have dominion, and that we are is demonstrated by the fact that some have attained to it,—and what one *has* done, soon or late all *can* do,—then it is not necessary that we live under the domination of any physical agent. In the degree that we recognize our own interior powers, then are we rulers and able to dictate; in the degree that we fail to recognize them, we are slaves, and are dictated to. We build whatever we find within us; we attract whatever comes to us, and all in accordance with spiritual law, for all natural law is spiritual law.

The whole of human life is cause and effect; there is no such thing in it as chance, nor is there even in all the wide universe. Are we not satisfied with whatever comes into our lives? The thing to do, then, is not to spend time in railing against the imaginary something we create and call fate, but to look to the within, and change the causes at work there, in order that things of a different nature may come, for there will come exactly what we cause to come. This is true not only of the physical body, but of all phases and conditions of life. We invite whatever comes, and did we not invite it, either consciously or unconsciously, it could not and it would not come. This may undoubtedly be hard for some to believe, or even to see, at first. But in the degree that one candidly and open-mindedly looks at it, and then studies into the silent, but subtle and, so to speak, omnipotent workings of the thought forces, and as he traces their effects within him and about him, it becomes clearly evident, and easy to understand.

And then whatever does come to one depends for its effects entirely upon his mental attitude toward it. Does this or that occurrence or condition cause you annoyance? Very well; it causes you annoyance, and so disturbs your peace merely because you allow it to. You are born to have absolute control over your own dominion, but if you voluntarily hand over this power, even if for a little while, to some one or to some thing else, then you of course become the creature, the one controlled.

To live undisturbed by passing occurrences you must first find your own centre. You must then be firm in your own centre, and so rule the world from within. He who does not himself condition circumstances allows the process to be reversed, and become a conditioned circumstance. Find your centre and live in it. Surrender it to no person, to no thing. In the degree that you do this will you find yourself growing stronger and stronger in it. And how can one find his centre? By realizing his oneness with the Infinite Power, and by living continually in this realization.

But if you do not rule from your own centre, if you invest this or that with the power of bringing you annoyance, or evil, or harm, then take what it brings, but cease your railing against the eternal goodness and beneficence of all things.

*I swear the earth shall surely be complete*
*To him or her who shall be complete;*
*The earth remains jagged and broken*
*Only to him who remains jagged and broken.*

If the windows of your soul are dirty and streaked, covered with matter foreign to them, then the world as you look out of them will be to you dirty and streaked and out of order. Cease your complainings, however; keep your pessimism, your "poor, unfortunate me" to yourself, lest you betray the fact that your windows are badly in need of something. But know that your friend, who keeps his windows clean, that the Eternal Sun may illumine all within and make visible all without,—know that he lives in a different world from yours.

Then, go wash your windows, and instead of longing for some other world, you will discover the wonderful beauties of this world; and if you don't find transcendent beauties on every hand here, the chances are that you will never find them anywhere.

*The poem hangs on the berry-bush*
*When comes the poet's eye,*
*And the whole street is a masquerade*
*When Shakespeare passes by.*

This same Shakespeare, whose mere passing causes all this commotion, is the one who put into the mouth of one of his creations the words: "The fault, dear Brutus, is not in our stars, but in ourselves, that we are underlings." And the great work of his own life is right good evidence that he realized full well the truth of the facts we are considering. And again he gave us a great truth in keeping with what we are considering when he said:

*Our doubts are traitors,*
*And make us lose the good we oft might win*
*By fearing to attempt.*

There is probably no agent that brings us more undesirable conditions than fear. We should live in fear of nothing, nor will we when we come fully to know ourselves. An old French proverb runs:

*Some of your griefs you have cured,*
*And the sharpest you still have survived;*
*But what torments of pain you endured*
*From evils that never arrived.*

Fear and lack of faith go hand in hand. The one is born of the other. Tell me how much one is given to fear, and I will tell you how much he lacks in faith. Fear is a most expensive guest to entertain, the same as worry is: so expensive are they that no one can afford to entertain them. *We invite what we fear, the same as, by a different attitude of mind, we invite and attract the influences and conditions we desire.* The mind dominated by fear opens the door for the entrance of the very things, for the actualization of the very conditions it fears.

"Where are you going?" asked an Eastern pilgrim on meeting the plague one day. "I am going to Bagdad to kill five thousand people," was the reply. A few days later the same pilgrim met the plague returning. "You told me you were going to Bagdad to kill five thousand people," said he, "but instead, you killed fifty thousand." "No," said the plague. "*I killed only five thousand*, as I told you I would: *the others died of fright.*"

Fear can paralyze every muscle in the body. Fear affects the flow of the blood, likewise the normal and healthy action of all the life forces. Fear can make the body rigid, motionless, and powerless to move.

Not only do we attract to ourselves the things we fear, but we also aid in attracting to others the conditions we in our own minds hold them in fear of. This we do in proportion to the strength of our own thought, and in the degree that they are sensitively organized and so influenced by our thought, and this, although it be unconscious both on their part and on ours.

Children, and especially when very young, are, generally speaking, more sensitive to their surrounding influences than grown people are. Some are veritable little sensitive plates, registering the influences about them, and embodying them as they grow. How careful in their prevailing mental states then should be those who have them in charge, and especially how careful should a mother be during the time she is carrying the child, and when every thought, every mental as well as emotional state has its direct influence upon the life of the unborn child. Let parents be careful how they hold a child, either younger or older, in the thought of fear. This is many times done, unwittingly on their part, through anxiety, and at times through what might well be termed over-care, which is fully as bad as under-care.

I know of a number of cases where a child has been so continually held in the thought of fear lest this or that condition come upon him, that the very things that were feared have been drawn to him, which probably otherwise never would have come at all. Many times there has been no adequate basis for the fear. In case there is a basis, then far wiser is it to take exactly the opposite attitude, so as to neutralize the force at work, and then to hold the child in the thought of wisdom and strength that it may be able to meet the condition and master it, instead of being mastered by it.

But a day or two ago a friend was telling me of an experience of his own life in this connection. At a period when he was having a terrific struggle with a certain habit, he was so continually held in the thought of fear by his mother and the young lady to whom he was engaged,—the engagement to be consummated at the end of a certain period, the time depending on his proving his mastery,—that he, very sensitively organized, *continually* felt the depressing and weakening effects of their negative thoughts. He could always tell exactly how they felt toward him; he was continually influenced and weakened by their fear, by their questionings, by their suspicions, all of which had the effect of lessening the sense of his own power, all of which had an endeavor-paralyzing influence upon him. And so instead of their begetting courage and strength in him, they brought him to a still greater realization of his own weakness and the almost worthless use of struggle.

Here were two who loved him dearly, and who would have done anything and everything to help him gain the mastery, but who, ignorant of the silent, subtle, ever-working and all-telling power of the thought forces, instead of imparting to him courage, instead of adding to his strength, disarmed him of this, and then added an additional weakness from without. In this way the battle for him was made harder in a three-fold degree.

Fear and worry and all kindred mental states are too expensive for any person, man, woman, or child, to entertain or indulge in. Fear paralyzes healthy action, worry corrodes and pulls down the organism, and will finally tear it to pieces. Nothing is to be gained by it, but everything to be lost. Long-continued grief at any loss will do the same. Each brings its own peculiar type of ailment. An inordinate love of gain, a close-fisted, hoarding disposition will have kindred effects. Anger, jealousy, malice, continual fault-finding, lust, has each its own peculiar corroding, weakening, tearing-down effects.

We shall find that not only are happiness and prosperity concomitants of righteousness,—living in harmony with the higher laws, but bodily health as well. The great Hebrew seer enunciated a wonderful chemistry of life when he said,—"As righteousness tendeth to life, so he that pursueth evil, pursueth it to his own death." On the other hand, "In the way of righteousness is life; and in the pathway thereof there is no death." The time will come when it will be seen that this means far more than most people dare *even to think as yet.* "It rests with man to say whether his soul shall be housed in a stately mansion of ever-growing splendor and beauty, or in a hovel of his own building,—a hovel at last ruined and abandoned to decay."

The bodies of almost untold numbers, living their one-sided, unbalanced lives, are every year, through these influences, weakening and falling by the wayside long before their time. Poor, poor houses! Intended to be beautiful temples, brought to desolation by their ignorant, reckless deluded tenants. Poor houses!

A close observer, a careful student of the power of the thought forces, will soon be able to read in the voice, in the movements, in the features, the effects registered by the prevailing mental states and conditions. Or, if he is told the prevailing mental states and conditions, he can describe the voice, the movements, the features, as well as describe, in a general way, the peculiar physical ailments their possessor is heir to.

We are told by good authority that a study of the human body, its structure, and the length of time it takes it to come to maturity, in comparison with the time it takes the bodies of various animals and their corresponding longevity, reveals the fact that its natural age should be nearer a hundred and twenty years than what we commonly find it today. But think of the multitudes all about us whose bodies are aging, weakening, breaking, so that they have to abandon them long before they reach what ought to be a long period of strong, vigorous middle life.

Then, the natural length of life being thus shortened, it comes to be what we might term a race belief that this shortened period is the natural period. And as a consequence many, when they approach a certain age, seeing that as a rule people at this period of life begin to show signs of age, to break and go down hill as we say, they, thinking it a matter of course and that it must be the same with them, by taking this attitude of mind, many times bring upon themselves these very conditions long before it is necessary. Subtle and powerful are the influences of the mind in the building and rebuilding of the body. As we understand them better it may become the custom for people to look forward with pleasure to the teens of their second century.

There comes to mind at this moment a friend, a lady well on to eighty years of age. An old lady, some, most people in fact, would call her, especially those who measure age by the number of the seasons that have come and gone since one's birth. But to call our friend old, would be to call black white. She is no older than a girl of twenty-five, and indeed younger, I am glad to say, or I am sorry to say, depending upon the point of view, than *many* a girl of this age. Seeking for the good in all people and in all things, she has found the good everywhere. The brightness of disposition and of voice that is hers today, that attracts all people to her and that makes her so beautifully attractive to all people, has characterized her all through life. It has in turn carried brightness and hope and courage and strength to hundreds and thousands of people through all these years, and will continue to do so, apparently, for many years yet to come.

No fears, no worryings, no hatreds, no jealousies, no sorrowings, no grievings, no sordid graspings after inordinant gain, have found entrance into her realm of thought. As a consequence her mind, free from these abnormal states and conditions, has not externalized in her body the various physical ailments that the great majority of people are lugging about with them, thinking in their ignorance, that they are natural, and that it is all in accordance with the "eternal order of things" that they should have them. Her life has been one of varied experiences, so that all these things would have found ready entrance into the realm of her mind and so into her life were she ignorant enough to allow them entrance. On the contrary she has been wise enough to recognize the fact that in one kingdom at least she is ruler,—the kingdom of her mind, and that it is hers to dictate as to what shall and what shall not enter there. She knows, moreover, that in determining this she is determining all the conditions of her life. It is indeed a pleasure as well as an inspiration to see her as she goes here and there, to see her sunny disposition, her youthful step, to hear her joyous laughter. Indeed and in truth, Shakespeare knew whereof he spoke when he said,—"It is the mind that makes the body rich."

With great pleasure I watched her but recently as she was walking along the street, stopping to have a word and so a part in the lives of a group of children at play by the wayside, hastening her step a little to have a word with a washerwoman toting her bundle of clothes, stopping for a word with a laboring man returning with dinner pail in hand from his work, returning the recognition from the lady in her carriage, and so imparting some of her own rich life to all with whom she came in contact.

And as good fortune would have it, while still watching her, an old lady passed her,—really old, this one, though at least ten or fifteen years younger, so far as the count by the seasons is concerned. Nevertheless she was bent in form and apparently stiff in joint and muscle. Silent in mood, she wore a countenance of long-faced sadness, which was intensified surely several fold by a black, sombre headgear with an immense heavy veil still more sombre looking if possible. Her entire dress was of this description. By this relic-of-barbarism garb, combined with her own mood and expression, she continually proclaimed to the world two things,—her own personal sorrows and woes, which by this very method she kept continually fresh in her mind, and also her lack of faith in the eternal goodness of things, her lack of faith in the love and eternal goodness of the Infinite Father.

Wrapped only in the thoughts of her own ailments, and sorrows, and woes, she received and she gave nothing of joy, nothing of hope, nothing of courage, nothing of value to those whom she passed or with whom she came in contact. But on the contrary she suggested to all and helped to intensify in many, those mental states all too prevalent in our common human life. And as she passed our friend one could notice a slight turn of the head which, coupled with the expression in her face, seemed to indicate this as her thought,—Your dress and your conduct are not wholly in keeping with a lady of your years. Thank God, then, thank God they are not. And may He in His great goodness and love send us an innumerable company of the same rare type; and may they live a thousand years to bless mankind, to impart the life-giving influences of their own royal lives to the numerous ones all about us who stand so much in need of them.

Would you remain always young, and would you carry all the joyousness and buoyancy of youth into your maturer years? Then have care concerning but one thing,—how you live in your thought world. This will determine all. It was the inspired one, Gautama, the Buddha, who said,—"The mind is everything; what you think you become." And the same thing had Ruskin in mind when he said,—"Make yourself nests of pleasant thoughts. None of us as yet know, for none of us have been taught in early youth, what fairy palaces we may build of beautiful thought,—*proof against all adversity*." And would you have in your body all the elasticity, all the strength, all the beauty of your younger years? Then live these in your mind, making no room for unclean thought, and you will externalize them in your body. In the degree that you keep young in thought will you remain young in body. And you will find that your body will in turn aid your mind, for body helps mind the same as mind builds body.

You are continually building, and so externalizing in your body conditions most akin to the thoughts and emotions you entertain. And not only are you so building from within, but you are also continually drawing from without, forces of a kindred nature. Your particular kind of thought connects you with a similar order of thought from without. If it is bright, hopeful, cheerful, you connect yourself with a current of thought of this nature. If it is sad, fearing, despondent, then this is the order of thought you connect yourself with.

If the latter is the order of your thought, then perhaps unconsciously and by degrees you have been connecting yourself with it. You need to go back and pick up again a part of your child nature, with its careless and cheerful type of thought. "The minds of the group of children at play are unconsciously concentrated in drawing to their bodies a current of playful thought. Place a child by itself, deprive it of its companions, and soon it will mope and become slow of movement. It is cut off from that peculiar thought current and is literally "out of its element."

"You need to bring again this current of playful thought to you which has gradually been turned off. You are too serious or sad, or absorbed in the serious affairs of life. You can be playful and cheerful without being puerile or silly. You can carry on business all the better for being in the playful mood when your mind is off your business. There is nothing but ill resulting from the permanent mood of sadness and seriousness,—the mood which by many so long maintained makes it actually difficult for them to smile at all.

"At eighteen or twenty you commenced growing out of the more playful tendency of early youth. You took hold of the more serious side of life. You went into some business. You became more or less involved in its cares, perplexities and responsibilities. Or, as man or woman, you entered on some phase of life involving care or trouble. Or you became absorbed in some game of business which, as you followed it, left no time for play. Then as you associated with older people you absorbed their old ideas, their mechanical methods of thinking, their acceptance of errors without question or thought of question. In all this you opened your mind to a heavy, care-laden current of thought. Into this you glided unconsciously. That thought is materialized in your blood and flesh. The seen of your body is a deposit or crystallization of the unseen element ever flowing to your body from your mind. Years pass on and you find that your movements are stiff and cumbrous,—that you can with difficulty climb a tree as at fourteen. Your mind has all this time been sending to your body these heavy, inelastic elements, making your body what now it is. . . .

"Your change for the better must be gradual and can only be accomplished by bringing the thought current of an all-round symmetrical strength to bear on it,—by demanding of the Supreme Power to be led in the best way, by diverting your mind from the many unhealthy thoughts which habitually have been flowing into it without your knowing it, to healthier ones. . . .

"Like the beast, the bodies of those of our race have in the past weakened and decayed. This will not always be. Increase of spiritual knowledge will show the cause of such decay, and will show, also, how to take advantage of a Law or Force to build us up, renew ever the body and give it greater and greater strength, instead of blindly using that Law or Force, as has been done in the past, to weaken our bodies and finally destroy them."

Full, rich, and abounding health is the normal and the natural condition of life. Anything else is an abnormal condition, and abnormal conditions as a rule come through perversions. God never created sickness, suffering, and disease; they are man's own creations. They come through his violating the laws under which he lives. So used are we to seeing them that we come gradually, if not to think of them as natural, then to look upon them as a matter of course.

The time will come when the work of the physician will not be to treat and attempt to heal the body, but to heal the mind, which in turn will heal the body. In other words, the true physician will be a teacher; his work will be to keep people well, instead of attempting to make them well after sickness and disease comes on;

and still beyond this there will come a time when each will be his own physician. In the degree that we live in harmony with the higher laws of our being, and so, in the degree that we become better acquainted with the powers of the mind and spirit, will we give less attention to the body,—no less *care*, but less *attention*.

The bodies of thousands today would be much better cared for if their owners gave them less thought and attention. As a rule, those who think least of their bodies enjoy the best health. Many are kept in continual ill health by the abnormal thought and attention they give them.

Give the body the nourishment, the exercise, the fresh air, the sunlight it requires, keep it clean, and then think of it as little as possible. In your thoughts, and in your conversation never dwell upon the negative side. Don't talk of sickness and disease. By talking of these you do yourself harm and you do harm to those who listen to you. Talk of those things that will make people the better for listening to you. Thus you will infect them with health and strength and not with weakness and disease.

To dwell upon the negative side is always destructive. This is true of the body the same as it is true of all other things. The following from one whose thorough training as a physician has been supplemented by extensive study and observations along the lines of the powers of the interior forces, are of special significance and value in this connection: "We can never gain health by contemplating disease, any more than we can reach perfection by dwelling upon imperfection, or harmony through discord. We should keep a high ideal of health and harmony constantly before the mind. . . .

"Never affirm or repeat about your health what you do not wish to be true. Do not dwell upon your ailments, nor study your symptoms. Never allow yourself to be convinced that you are not complete master of yourself. Stoutly affirm your superiority over bodily ills, and do not acknowledge yourself the slave of any inferior power. . . . I would teach children early to build a strong barrier between themselves and disease, by healthy habits of thought, high thinking, and purity of life. I would teach them to expel all thoughts of death, all images of disease, all discordant emotions, like hatred, malice, revenge, envy, and sensuality, as they would banish a temptation to do evil. I would teach them that bad food, bad drink, or bad air makes bad blood; that bad blood makes bad tissue, and bad flesh bad morals. I would teach them that healthy thoughts are as essential to healthy bodies as pure thoughts to a clean life. I would teach them to cultivate a strong will power, and to brace themselves against life's enemies in every possible way. I would teach the sick to have hope, confidence, cheer. Our thoughts and imaginations are the only real limits to our possibilities. No man's success or health will ever reach beyond his own confidence; as a rule, we erect our own barriers.

"Like produces like the universe through. Hatred, envy, malice, jealousy, and revenge all have children. Every bad thought breeds others, and each of these goes on and on, ever reproducing itself, until our world is peopled with their offspring. The true physician and parent of the future will not medicate the body with drugs so much as the mind with principles. The coming mother will teach her child to assuage the fever of anger, hatred, malice, with the great panacea of the world,— Love. The coming physician will teach the people to cultivate cheerfulness, good-will, and noble deeds for a health tonic as well as a heart tonic; and that a merry heart doeth good like a medicine."

The health of your body, the same as the health and strength of your mind, depends upon what you relate yourself with. This Infinite Spirit of Life, this Source of all Life, can from its very nature, we have found, admit of no weakness, no disease. Come then into the full, conscious, vital realization of your oneness with this Infinite Life, open yourself to its more abundant entrance, and full and ever-renewing bodily health and strength will be yours.

*And good may ever conquer ill,*
*Health walk where pain has trod;*
*"As a man thinketh, so is he,"*
*Rise, then, and think with God.*

The whole matter may then be summed up in the one sentence, "God is well and so are you." You must awaken to the knowledge of your *real being.* When this awakening comes, you will have, and you will see that you have, the power to determine what conditions are externalized in your body. You must recognize, you must realize yourself, as one with Infinite Spirit. God's will is then your will; your will is God's will, and "with God all things are possible." When we are able to do away with all sense of separateness by living continually in the realization of this oneness, not only will our bodily ills and weaknesses vanish, but all limitations along all lines.

Then "delight thyself in the Lord, and He shall give thee the desires of thine heart." Then will you feel like crying all the day long, "The lines are fallen unto me in pleasant places; yea, I have a goodly heritage." Drop out of mind your belief in good things and good events coming to you in the future. Come *now* into the real life, and coming, appropriate and actualize them *now.* Remember that only the best is good enough for one with a heritage so royal as yours.

*We buy ashes for bread;*
*We buy diluted wine;*
*Give me the true,—*
*Whose ample leaves and tendrils curled*
*Among the silver hills of heaven,*
*Draw everlasting dew.*

CHAPTER 5

# The Secret, Power, and Effects of Love

This is the Spirit of Infinite Love. The moment we recognize ourselves as one with it we become so filled with love that we see only the good in all. And when we realize that we are all one with this Infinite Spirit, then we realize that in a sense we are all one with each other. When we come into a recognition of this fact, we can then do no harm to any one, to any thing. We find that we are all members of the one great body, and that no portion of the body can be harmed without all the other portions suffering thereby.

When we fully realize the great fact of the oneness of all life,—that all are partakers from this one Infinite Source, and so that the same life is the life in each individual,—then prejudices go and hatreds cease. Love grows and reigns supreme. Then, wherever we go, whenever we come in contact with the fellow-man, we are able to recognize the God within. We thus look only for the good, and we find it. It always pays.

There is a deep scientific fact underlying the great truth, "He that takes the sword shall perish by the sword." The moment we come into a realization of the subtle powers of the thought forces, we can quickly see that the moment we entertain any thoughts of hatred toward another, he gets the effects of these diabolical forces that go out from us, and has the same thoughts of hatred aroused in him, which in turn return to the sender. Then when we understand the effects of the passion, hatred or anger, even upon the physical body, we can see how detrimental, how expensive this is. The same is true in regard to all kindred thoughts or passions, envy, criticism, jealousy, scorn. In the ultimate we shall find that in entertaining feelings of this nature toward another, we always suffer far more than the one toward whom we entertain them.

And then when we fully realize the fact that selfishness is at the root of all error, sin, and crime, and that ignorance is the basis of all selfishness, with what charity we come to look upon the acts of all. It is the ignorant man who seeks his own ends at the expense of the greater whole. It is the ignorant man, therefore, who is the selfish man. The truly wise man is never selfish. He is a seer, and recognizes the fact that he, a single member of the one great body, is benefited in just the degree that the entire body is benefited, and so he seeks nothing for himself that he would not equally seek for all mankind.

If selfishness is at the bottom of all error, sin, and crime, and ignorance is the basis of all selfishness, then when we see a manifestation of either of these qualities, if we are true to the highest within us, we will look for and will see to call forth the good in each individual with whom we come in contact. When God speaks to God, then God responds, and shows forth as God. But when devil speaks to devil, then devil responds, and the devil is always to pay.

I sometimes hear a person say, "I don't see any good in him." No? Then you are no seer. Look deeper and you will find the very God in every human soul. But remember it takes a God to recognize a God. Christ always spoke to the highest, the truest, and the best in men. He knew and he recognized the God in each because he had first realized it in himself. He ate with publicans and sinners. Abominable, the Scribes and Pharisees said. They were so wrapped up in their own conceits, their own self-centredness, hence their own ignorance, that they had never found the God in themselves, and so they never dreamed that it was the real life of even publicans and sinners.

In the degree that we hold a person in the thought of evil or of error, do we suggest evil and error to him. In the degree that he is sensitively organized, or not well individualized, and so, subject to the suggestions of the thought forces from others, will he be influenced; and so in this way we may be sharers in the very evil-doing in which we hold another in thought. In the same way when we hold a person in the thought of the right, the good, and the true, righteousness, goodness, and truth are suggested to him, and thus we have a most beneficent influence on his life and conduct. If our hearts go out in love to all with whom we come in contact, we inspire love, and the same ennobling and warming influences of love always return to us from those in whom we inspire them. There is a deep scientific principle underlying the precept—If you would have all the world love you, you must first love all the world.

In the degree that we love will we be loved. Thoughts are forces. Each creates of its kind. Each comes back laden with the effect that corresponds to itself and of which it is the cause.

*Then let your secret thoughts be fair—*
*They have a vital part, and share*
*In shaping words and moulding fate;*
*God's system is so intricate.*

I know of no better practice than that of a friend who continually holds himself in an attitude of mind that he continually sends out his love in the form of the thought,—"Dear everybody, I love you." And when we realize the fact that a thought invariably produces its effect before it returns, or before it ceases, we can see how he is continually breathing out a blessing not only upon all with whom he comes in contact, but upon all the world. These same thoughts of love, moreover, tokened in various ways, are continually coming to him from all quarters.

Even animals feel the effects of these forces. Some animals are much more sensitively organized than many people are, and consequently they get the effects of our thoughts, our mental states, and emotions much more readily than many people do. Therefore whenever we meet an animal we can do it good by sending out to it these thoughts of love. It will feel the effects whether we simply entertain or whether we voice them. And it is often interesting to note how quickly it responds, and how readily it gives evidence of its appreciation of this love and consideration on our part.

What a privilege and how enjoyable it would be to live and walk in a world where we meet only Gods. In such a world you can live. In such a world I can live. For in the degree that we come into this higher realization do we see only the God in each human soul; and when we are thus able to see Him in every one we meet, we then live in such a world.

And when we thus recognize the God in every one, we by this recognition help to call it forth ever more and more. What a privilege,—this privilege of yours, this privilege of mine! That hypocritical judging of another is something then with which we can have nothing to do; for we have the power of looking beyond the evolving, changing, error-making self, and seeing the real, the changeless, the eternal self which by and by will show forth in the full beauty of holiness. We are then large enough also to realize the fact that when we condemn another, by that very act we condemn ourselves.

This realization so fills us with love that we continually overflow it, and all with whom we come in contact feel its warming and life-giving power. These in turn send back the same feeling of love to us, and so we continually attract love from all quarters. Tell me how much one loves and I will tell you how much he has seen of God. Tell me how much he loves and I will tell you how much he lives with God. Tell me how much he loves and I will tell you how far into the Kingdom of Heaven,—the kingdom of harmony, he has entered, for "love is the fulfilling of the law."

And in a sense love is everything. It is the key to life, and its influences are those that move the world. Live only in the thought of love for all and you will draw love to you from all. Live in the thought of malice or hatred, and malice and hatred will come back to you.

*For evil poisons; malice shafts*
*Like boomerangs return,*
*Inflicting wounds that will not heal*
*While rage and anger burn.*

Every thought you entertain is a force that goes out, and every thought comes back laden with its kind. This is an immutable law. Every thought you entertain has moreover a direct effect upon your body. Love and its kindred emotions are the normal and the natural, those in accordance with the eternal order of the universe, for "God is love." These have a life-giving, health-engendering influence upon your body, besides beautifying your countenance, enriching your voice, and making you ever more attractive in every way. And as it is true that in the degree that you hold thoughts of love for all, you call the same from them in return, and as these have a direct effect upon your mind, and through your mind upon your body, it is as so much life force added to your own from without. You are then continually building this into both your mental and your physical life, and so your life is enriched by its influence.

Hatred and all its kindred emotions are the unnatural, the abnormal, the perversions, and so, out of harmony with the eternal order of the universe. For if love is the fulfilling of the law, then these, its opposites, are direct violations of law, and there can never be a violation of law without its attendant pain and suffering in one form or another. There is no escape from this. And what is the result of this particular form of violation? When you allow thoughts of anger, hatred, malice, jealousy, envy, criticism, or scorn to exercise sway, they have a corroding and poisoning effect upon the organism; they pull it down, and if allowed to continue will eventually tear it to pieces by externalizing themselves in the particular forms of disease they give rise to. And then in addition to the destructive influences from your own mind you are continually calling the same influences from other minds, and these come as destructive forces augmenting your own, thus aiding in the tearing down process.

And so love inspires love; hatred breeds hatred. Love and good-will stimulate and build up the body; hatred and malice corrode and tear it down. Love is a savor of life unto life; hatred is a savor of death unto death.

*There are loyal hearts, there are spirits brave,*
*There are souls that are pure and true;*
*Then give to the world the best you have,*
*And the best will come back to you,*

*Give love, and love to your heart will flow,*
*A strength in your utmost need;*
*Have faith, and a score of hearts will show*
*Their faith in your word and deed.*

I hear it said,—How in regard to one who bears me hatred, towards whom I have entertained no such thoughts and feelings, and so have not been the cause of his becoming my enemy? This may be true, but the chances are that you will have but few enemies if there is nothing of an antagonistic nature in your own mind and heart. Be sure there is nothing of this nature. But if hatred should come from another without apparent cause on your part, then meet it from first to last with thoughts of love and good-will. In this way you can, so to speak, so neutralize its effects that it cannot reach you and so cannot harm you. Love is positive, and stronger than hatred. Hatred can always be conquered by love.

On the other hand, if you meet hatred with hatred, you simply intensify it. You add fuel to the flame already kindled, upon which it will feed and grow, and so you increase and intensify the evil conditions. Nothing is to be gained by it, everything is to be lost. By sending love for hatred you will be able so to neutralize it that it will not only have no effect upon you, but will not be able even to reach you. But more than this, you will by this course sooner or later be able literally to transmute the enemy into the friend. Meet hatred with hatred and you degrade yourself. Meet hatred with love and you elevate not only yourself but also the one who bears you hatred.

The Persian sage has said, "Always meet petulance with gentleness, and perverseness with kindness. A gentle hand can lead even an elephant by a hair. Reply to thine enemy with gentleness. Opposition to peace is sin." The Buddhist says, "If a man foolishly does me wrong I will return him the protection of my ungrudging love. The more evil comes from him, the more good shall go from me." "The wise man avenges injuries by benefits," says the Chinese. "Return good for evil, overcome anger by love; hatred never ceases by hatred, but by love," says the Hindu.

The truly wise man or woman will recognize no one as an enemy. Occasionally we hear the expression, "Never mind; I'll get even with him." Will you? And how will you do it? You can do it in one of two ways. You can, as you have in mind, deal with him as he deals, or apparently deals, with you,—pay him, as we say, in his own coin. If you do this you will get even with him by sinking yourself to his level, and both of you will suffer by it. Or, you can show yourself the larger, you can send him love for hatred, kindness for ill-treatment, and so get even with him by raising him to the higher level. But remember that you can never help another without by that very act helping yourself; and if forgetful of self, then in most all cases the value to you is greater than the service you render another. If you are ready to treat him as he treats you, then you show clearly that there is in you that which draws the hatred and ill-treatment to you; you deserve what you are getting and should not complain, nor would you complain if you were wise. By following the other course you most effectually accomplish your purpose,—you gain a victory for yourself, and at the same time you do a great service for him; for which it is evident he stands greatly in need.

Thus you may become his saviour. He in turn may become the saviour of other error-making, and consequently care-encumbered men and women. Many times the struggles are greater than we can ever know. We need more gentleness and sympathy and compassion in our common human life. Then we will neither blame nor condemn. Instead of blaming or condemning we will sympathize, and all the more we will

*Comfort one another,*
*For the way is often dreary,*

*And the feet are often weary,*
*And the heart is very sad.*
*There is a heavy burden bearing,*
*When it seems that none are caring,*
*And we half forget that ever we were glad.*

*Comfort one another*
*With the hand-clasp close and tender,*
*With the sweetness love can render,*
*And the looks of friendly eyes.*
*Do not wait with grace unspoken,*
*While life's daily bread is broken—*
*Gentle speech is oft like manna from the skies.*

When we come fully to realize the great fact that all evil and error and sin with all their consequent sufferings come through ignorance, then wherever we see a manifestation of these in whatever form, if our hearts are right, we will have compassion, sympathy and compassion for the one in whom we see them. Compassion will then change itself into love, and love will manifest itself in kindly service. Such is the divine method. And so instead of aiding in trampling and keeping a weaker one down, we will hold him up until he can stand alone and become the master. But all life-growth is from within out, and one becomes a true master in the degree that the knowledge of the divinity of his own nature dawns upon his inner consciousness and so brings him to a knowledge of the higher laws; and in no way can we so effectually hasten this dawning in the inner consciousness of another, as by showing forth the divinity within ourselves simply by the way we live.

By example and not by precept. By living, not by preaching. By doing, not by professing. By living the life, not by dogmatizing as to how it should be lived. There is no contagion equal to the contagion of life. Whatever we sow, that shall we also reap, and each thing sown produces of its kind. We can kill not only by doing another bodily injury directly, but we can and we do kill by every antagonistic thought.

Not only do we thus kill, but while we kill we suicide. Many a man has been made sick by having the ill thoughts of a number of people centred upon him; some have been actually killed. Put hatred into the world and we make it a literal hell. Put love into the world and heaven with all its beauties and glories becomes a reality.

Not to love is not to live, or it is to live a living death. The life that goes out in love to all is the life that is full, and rich, and continually expanding in beauty and in power. Such is the life that becomes ever more inclusive, and hence larger in its scope and influence. The larger the man and the woman, the more inclusive they are in their love and their friendships. The smaller the man and the woman, the more dwarfed and dwindling their natures, the more they pride themselves upon their "exclusiveness." Any one—a fool or an idiot—can be exclusive. It comes easy. It takes and it signifies a large nature to be universal, to be inclusive. Only the man or the woman of a small, personal, self-centred, self-seeking nature is exclusive. The man or the woman of a large, royal, unself-centred nature never is. The small nature is the one that continually strives for effect. The larger nature never does. The one goes here and there in order to gain recognition, in order to attach himself to the world. The other stays at home and draws the world *to him*. The one loves merely himself. The other loves all the world; but in his larger love for all the world he finds himself included.

Verily, then, the more one loves the nearer he approaches to God, for God is the spirit of infinite love. And when we come into the realization of our oneness with this Infinite Spirit, then divine love so fills us that, enriching and enrapturing our own lives, from them it flows out to enrich the life of all the world.

In coming into the realization of our oneness with the Infinite Life, we are brought at once into right relations with our fellow-men. We are brought into harmony with the great law, that we find our own lives in losing them in the service of others. We are brought to a knowledge of the fact that all life is one, and so that we are all parts of the one great whole. We then realize that we can't do for another without at the same time doing for ourselves. We also realize that we cannot do harm to another without by that very act doing harm to ourselves. We realize that the man who lives to himself alone lives a little, dwarfed, and stunted life, because he has no part in this larger life of humanity. But the one who in service loses his own life in this larger life, has his own life increased and enriched a thousand or a million fold, and every joy, every happiness, everything of value coming to each member of this greater whole comes as such to him, for he has a part in the life of each and all.

And here let a word be said in regard to true service. Peter and John were one day going up to the temple, and as they were entering the gate they were met by a poor cripple who asked them for alms. Instead of giving him something to supply the day's needs and then leaving him in the same dependent condition for the morrow and the morrow, Peter did him a real service, and a real service for all mankind by saying, Silver and gold have I none, but such as I have I give unto thee. *And then he made him whole.* He thus brought him into the condition where he could help himself. In other words, the greatest service we can do for another is to help him to help himself. To help him directly might be weakening, though not necessarily. It depends entirely upon circumstances. But to help one to help himself is never weakening, but always encouraging and strengthening, because it leads him to a larger and stronger life.

There is no better way to help one to help himself than to bring him to a knowledge of himself. There is no better way to bring one to a knowledge of himself than to lead him to a knowledge of the powers that are lying dormant within his own soul. There is nothing that will enable him to come more readily or more completely into an awakened knowledge of the powers that are lying dormant within his own soul, than to bring him into the conscious, vital realization of his oneness with the

Infinite Life and Power, so that he may open himself to it in order that it may work and manifest through him.

We will find that these same great truths lie at the very bottom of the solution of our social situation; and we will also find that we will never have a full and permanent solution of it until they are fully recognized and built upon.

CHAPTER 6

# Wisdom and Interior Illumination

This is the Spirit of Infinite Wisdom, and in the degree that we open ourselves to it does the highest wisdom manifest itself to and through us. We can in this way go to the very heart of the universe itself and find the mysteries hidden to the majority of mankind,—hidden to them, though not hidden of themselves.

In order for the highest wisdom and insight we must have absolute confidence in the Divine guiding us, but not through the channel of some one else. And why should we go to another for knowledge and wisdom? With God is no respect of persons. Why should we seek these things second hand? Why should we thus stultify our own innate powers? Why should we not go direct to the Infinite Source itself? "If any man lack wisdom let him ask of God." "Before they call I will answer, and while they are yet speaking, I will hear."

When we thus go directly to the Infinite Source itself we are no longer slaves to personalities, institutions, or books. We should always keep ourselves open to suggestions of truth from these agencies. We should always regard them as agencies, however, and *never as sources.* We should never recognize them as masters, but simply as teachers. With Browning, we must recognize the great fact that—

*Truth is within ourselves; it takes no rise*
*From outward things, whate'er you may believe.*
*There is an inmost centre in us all,*
*Where truth abides in fullness.*

There is no more important injunction in all the world, nor one with a deeper interior meaning, than "To thine own self be true." In other words, be true to your own soul, for it is through your own soul that the voice of God speaks to you. This is the interior guide. This is the light that lighteth every man that cometh into the world. This is conscience. This is intuition. This is the voice of the higher self, the voice of the soul, the voice of God. "Thou shalt hear a voice behind thee, saying: This is the way, walk ye in it."

When Elijah was on the mountain it was after the various physical commotions and manifestations that he heard the "still, small voice," the voice of his own soul, through which the Infinite God was speaking. If we will but follow this voice of intuition, it will speak ever more clearly and more plainly, until by and by it will be absolute and unerring in its guidance. The great trouble with us is that we do not listen to and do not follow this voice within our own souls, and so we become as a house divided against itself. We are pulled this way and that, and we are never *certain* of anything. I have a friend who listens so carefully to this inner voice, who, in other words, always acts so quickly and so fully in accordance with his intuitions, and whose life as a consequence is so absolutely guided by them, that he always does the right thing at the right time and in the right way. He always knows when to act and how to act, and he is never in the condition of a house divided against itself.

But some one says, "May it not be dangerous for us to act always upon our intuitions? Suppose we should have an intuition to do harm to some one?" We need not be afraid of this, however, for the voice of the soul, this voice of God speaking through the soul, will never direct one to do harm to another, nor to do anything that is not in accordance with the highest standards. of right, and truth, and justice. And if you at any time have a prompting of this kind, know that it is not the voice of intuition; it is some characteristic of your lower self that is prompting you.

Reason is not to be set aside, but it is to be continually illumined by this higher spiritual perception, and in the degree that it is thus illumined will it become an agent of light and power. When one becomes thoroughly individualized he enters into the realm of all knowledge and wisdom; and to be individualized is to recognize no power outside of the Infinite Power that is back of all. When one recognizes this great fact and opens himself to this Spirit of Infinite Wisdom, he then enters upon the road to the true education, and mysteries that before were closed now reveal themselves to him. This must indeed be the foundation of all true education, this evolving from within, this evolving of what has been involved by the Infinite Power.

All things that it is valuable for us to know will come to us if we will but open ourselves to the voice of this Infinite Spirit. It is thus that we become seers and have the power of seeing into the very heart of things. There are no new stars, there are no new laws or forces, but we can so open ourselves to this Spirit of Infinite Wisdom that we can discover and recognize those that have not been known before; and in this way they become new to us. When in this way we come into a knowledge of truth we no longer need facts that are continually changing. We can then enter into the quiet of our own interior selves. We can open the window and look out, and thus gather the facts as we choose. This is true wisdom. "Wisdom is the knowledge of God." Wisdom comes by intuition. It far transcends knowledge. Great knowledge, knowledge of many things, may be had by virtue simply of a very retentive memory. It comes by tuition. But wisdom far transcends knowledge, in that knowledge is a mere incident of this deeper wisdom.

He who would enter into the realm of wisdom must first divest himself of all intellectual pride. He must become as a little child. Prejudices, preconceived opinions and beliefs always stand in the way of true wisdom. Conceited opinions are always suicidal in their influences. They bar the door to the entrance of truth.

All about us we see men in the religious world, in the world of science, in the political, in the social world, who through intellectual pride are so wrapped in their own conceits and prejudices that larger and later revelations of truth can find no entrance to them; and instead of growing and expanding, they are becoming dwarfed and stunted and still more incapable of receiving truth. Instead of actively aiding in the progress of the world, they are as so many dead sticks in the way that would retard the wheels of progress. This, however, they can never do. Such always in time get bruised, broken, and left behind, while God's triumphal car of truth moves steadily onward.

When the steam engine was still being experimented with, and before it was perfected sufficiently to come into practical use, a well-known Englishman—well known then in scientific circles—wrote an extended pamphlet proving that it would be impossible for it *ever* to be used in ocean navigation, that is, in a trip involving the crossing of the ocean, because it would be utterly impossible for any vessel to carry with it sufficient coal for the use of its furnace. And the interesting feature of the whole matter was that the very first steam vessel that made the trip from England to America, had among its cargo a part of the first edition of this carefully prepared pamphlet. There was only the one edition. Many editions might be sold now.

This seems indeed an amusing fact; but far more amusing is the man who voluntarily closes himself to truth because, forsooth, it does not come through conventional, or orthodox, or heretofore accepted channels; or because it may not be in full accord with, or possibly may be opposed to, established usages or beliefs. On the contrary—

*Let there be many windows in your soul,*
*That all the glory of the universe*
*May beautify it. Not the narrow pane*
*Of one poor creed can catch the radiant rays*
*That shine from countless sources. Tear away*
*The blinds of superstition: let the light*
*Pour through fair windows, broad as truth itself*
*And high as heaven. . . . Tune your ear*
*To all the worldless music of the stars*
*And to the voice of nature, and your heart*
*Shall turn to truth and goodness as the plant*
*Turns to the sun. A thousand unseen hands*
*Reach down to help you to their peace-crowned heights*
*And all the forces of the firmament*
*Shall fortify your strength. Be not afraid*
*To thrust aside half-truths and grasp the whole.*

There is a great law in connection with the coming of truth. It is this: Whenever a man or a woman shuts himself or herself to the entrance of truth on account of intellectual pride, preconceived opinions, prejudices, or for whatever reason, there is a great law which says that truth *in its fullness* will come to that one from no source. And on the other hand, when a man or a woman opens himself or herself fully to the entrance of truth from *whatever* source it may come, there is an equally great law which says that truth will flow in to him or to her from all sources, from all quarters. Such becomes the free man, the free woman, for it is the truth that makes us free. The other remains in bondage, for truth has had no invitation and will not enter where it is not fully and freely welcomed.

And where truth is denied entrance the rich blessings it carries with it cannot take up their abode. On the contrary, when this is the case, it sends an envoy carrying with it atrophy, disease, death, physically and spiritually as well as intellectually. And the man who would rob another of his free and unfettered search for truth, who would stand as the interpreter of truth for another, with the intent of remaining in this position, rather than endeavoring to lead him to the place where he can be his own interpreter, is more to be shunned than a thief and a robber. The injury he works is far greater, for he is doing direct and positive injury to the very life of the one he thus holds.

Who has ever appointed any man, whoever he may be, as the keeper, the custodian, the dispenser of God's illimitable truth? Many indeed are moved and so are called to be teachers of truth; but the true teacher will never stand as the interpreter of truth for another. The *true teacher* is the one whose endeavor is to bring the one he teaches to a true knowledge of himself and hence of his own interior powers, that he may become his own interpreter. All others are, generally speaking, those animated by purely personal motives, self-aggrandizement, or personal gain. Moreover, he who would claim to have all truth and the only truth, is a bigot, a fool, or a knave.

In the Eastern literature is a fable of a frog. The frog lived in a well, and out of his little well he had never been. One day a frog whose home was in the sea came to his well. Interested in all things, he went in. "Who are you? Where do you live?" said the frog in the well. "I am so and so, and my home is in the sea." "The sea? What is that? Where is that?" "It is a very large body of water, and not far away." "How big is your sea?" "Oh, very big." "As big as this?" pointing to a little stone lying near. "Oh, much bigger." "As big as this?" pointing to the board upon which they were sitting. "Oh, much bigger." "How much bigger, then?" "Why, the sea in which I live is bigger than your entire well; it would make millions of wells such as yours." "Nonsense, nonsense; you are a deceiver and a falsifier. Get out of my well. Get out of my well. I want nothing to do with any such frogs as you."

"Ye shall know the truth and the truth shall make you free," is the promise. Ye shall close yourselves to truth, ye shall live in your own conceits, and your own conceits shall make fools and idiots of you, would be a statement applicable to not a few, and to not a few who pride themselves upon their superior intellectual attainments. Idiocy is arrested mental growth. Closing one's self for whatever reason to truth and hence to growth, brings a certain type of idiocy, though it may not be called by this name. And on the other hand, another type is that arrested growth caused by taking all things for granted, without proving them for one's self, merely because they come from a particular person, a particular book, a particular institution. This is caused by one's always looking without instead of being true to the light within, and carefully tending it that it may give an ever clearer light.

With brave and intrepid Walt Whitman, we should all be able to say—

*From this hour I ordain myself loos'd of limits and imaginary lines,*
*Going where I list, my own master total and absolute,*
*Listening to others, considering well what they say,*
*Pausing, searching, receiving, contemplating,*
*Gently, but with undeniable will divesting myself of the holds that would hold me.*

Great should be the joy that God's boundless truth is open to all, open *equally* to all, and that it will make each one its dwelling place in proportion as he earnestly desires it and opens himself to it.

And in regard to the wisdom that guides us in our daily life, there is nothing that it is right and well for us to know that may not be known when we recognize the law of its coming, and are able wisely to use it. Let us know that all things are ours as soon as we know how to appropriate them.

*I hold it as a changeless law,*
*From which no soul can sway or swerve,*
*We have that in us which will draw*
*Whate'er we need or most deserve.*

If the times come when we know not what course to pursue, when we know not which way to turn, the fault lies in ourselves. If the fault lies in ourselves then the correction of this unnatural condition lies also in ourselves. It is never necessary to come into such a state if we are awake and remain awake to the light and the powers within us. The light is ever shining, and the only thing that it is necessary for us diligently to see to is that we permit neither this thing nor that to come between us and the light.

"With Thee is the fountain of life; in Thy light shall we see light."

Let us hear the words of one of the most highly illumined men I have ever known, and one who as a consequence is never in the dark, when the time comes, as to what to do and how to do it. "Whenever you are in doubt as to the course you should pursue, after you have turned to every outward means of guidance, *let the inward eye see, let the inward ear hear,* and allow this simple, natural, beautiful process to go on unimpeded by questionings or doubts. . . . In all dark hours and times of unwonted perplexity we need to follow one simple direction, found, as all needed directions can be found, in the dear old gospel, which so many read, but alas, *so few interpret.* "Enter into thine inner chamber and shut the door." Does this mean that we must literally betake ourselves to a private closet with a key in the door? If it did, then the command could never be obeyed in the open air, on land or sea, and the Christ loved the lakes and the forests far better than the cramping rooms of city dwelling houses; still his counsels are so wide-reaching that there is no spot on earth and no conceivable situation in which any of us may be placed where we cannot follow them.

"One of the most intuitive men we ever met had a desk in a city office where several other gentlemen were doing business constantly and often talking loudly. Entirely undisturbed by the many various sounds about him, this self-centred, faithful man would, in any moment of perplexity, draw the curtains of privacy so completely about him that he would be as fully enclosed in his own psychic aura, and thereby as effectually removed from all distractions as though he were alone in some primeval wood. Taking his difficulty with him into the mystic silence in the form of a direct question, to which he expected a certain answer, he would remain utterly passive until the reply came, and never once through many years' experience did he find himself disappointed or misled. Intuitive perceptions of truth are the daily bread to satisfy our daily hunger; they come like the manna in the desert day by day; each day brings adequate supply for that day's need only. They must be followed instantly, for dalliance with them means their obscuration, and the more we dally the more we invite erroneous impressions to cover intuition with a pall of conflicting moral phantasy born of illusions of the terrence will.

"One condition is imposed by *universal law,* and this we must obey. Put all wishes aside save the one desire to know *truth;* couple with this one demand the fully consecrated determination to follow what is distinctly perceived as truth immediately it is revealed. No other affection must be permitted to share the field with this all-absorbing love of *truth* for its own sake. Obey this one direction and never forget that expectation and desire are bride and bridegroom and forever inseparable, and you will soon find your hitherto darkened way grow luminous with celestial radiance, for with the heaven within, all heavens without incessantly co-operate." This may be termed going into the "silence." This it is to perceive and to be guided by the light that lighteth every man that cometh into the world. This it is to listen to and be guided by the voice of your own soul, the voice of your higher self.

The soul is divine and in allowing it to become translucent to the Infinite Spirit it reveals all things to us. As man turns away from the Divine Light do all things become hidden. There is nothing hidden of itself. When the spiritual sense is opened, then it transcends all the limitations of the physical senses and the intellect. And in the degree that we are able to get away from the limitations set by them, and realize that so far as the real life is concerned it is one with the Infinite Life, then we begin to reach the place where this voice will always speak, where it will never fail us, if we follow it, and as a consequence where we will always have the divine illumination and guidance. To know this and to live in this realization is not to live in heaven hereafter, but to live in heaven here and now, *today and every day.*

No human soul need be without it. When we turn our face in the right direction it comes as simply and as naturally as the flower blooms and with winds blow. It is not to be bought with money or with price. It is a condition waiting simply to be realized, by rich and by poor, by king and by peasant, by master and by servant the world over. All are equal heirs to it. And so the peasant, if he find it first, lives a life far transcending in beauty and in real power the life of his king. The servant, if he finds it first, lives a life surpassing the life of his master.

If you would find the highest, the fullest, and the richest life that not only this world but that any world can know, then do away with the sense of the separateness of your life from the life of God. Hold to the thought of your oneness. In the degree that you do this you will find yourself realizing it more and more, and as this life of realization is lived, you will find that no good thing will be withheld, for all things are included in this. Then it will be yours, without fears or forebodings, simply to do today what your hands find to do, and so be ready for tomorrow, *when it comes,* knowing that tomorrow will bring tomorrow's supplies for the mental, the spiritual, and the physical life. Remember, however, that tomorrow's supplies are not needed until tomorrow comes.

If one is willing to trust himself *fully* to the Law, the Law will never fail him. It is the half-hearted trusting to it that brings uncertain, and so, unsatisfactory results. Nothing is firmer and surer than Deity. It will never fail the one who throws himself wholly upon it. The secret of life then, is to live continually in this realization, whatever one may be doing, wherever one may be, by day and by night, both waking and sleeping. It can be lived in while we are sleeping no less than when we are awake. And here shall we consider a few facts in connection with sleep, in connection with receiving instruction and illumination while asleep?

During the process of sleep it is merely the physical body that is at rest and in quiet; the soul life with all its activities goes right on. Sleep is nature's provision for the recuperation of the body, for the rebuilding and hence the replacing of the waste that is continually going on during the waking hours. It is nature's great restorer. If sufficient sleep is not allowed the body, so that the rebuilding may equalize the wasting process, the body is gradually depleted and weakened, and any ailment or malady, when it is in this condition, is able to find a more ready entrance. It is for this reason that those who are subject to it will take a cold, as we term it, more readily when the body is tired or exhausted through loss of sleep than at most any other time. The body is in that condition where outside influences can have a more ready effect upon it, than when it is in its normal condition. And when they do have an effect they always go to the weaker portions first.

Our bodies are given us to serve far higher purposes than we ordinarily use them for. Especially is this true in the numerous cases where the body is master of its owner. In the degree that we come into the realization of the higher powers of the mind and spirit, in that degree does the body, through their influence upon it, become less gross and heavy, finer in its texture and form. And then, because the mind finds a kingdom of enjoyment in itself, and in all the higher things it becomes related to, *excesses* in eating and drinking, as well as all others, naturally and of their own accord fall away. Then also falls away the desire for the heavier, grosser, less valuable kinds of food and drink, such as the flesh of animals, alcoholic drinks, and all things of the class that stimulate the body and the passions rather than build the body and the brain into a strong, clean, well-nourished, enduring, and fibrous condition. In the degree that the body thus becomes less gross and heavy, finer in its texture and form, is there less waste, and what there is is more easily replaced, so that it keeps in a more regular and even condition. When this is true, less sleep is actually required. And even the amount that is taken does more for a body of this finer type than it can do for one of the other nature.

As the body in this way grows finer, in other words, as the process of its evolution is thus accelerated, it in turn helps the mind and the soul in the realization of ever higher perceptions, and thus body helps mind the same as mind builds body. It was undoubtedly this fact that Browning had in mind when he said:

*Let us cry "All good things*
*Are ours, nor soul helps flesh, more now*
*Than flesh helps soul."*

Sleep, then, is for the resting and the rebuilding of the body. The soul needs no rest, and while the body is at rest in sleep the soul life is active the same as when the body is in activity.

There are some, having a deep insight into the soul's activities, who say that we travel when we sleep. Some are able to recall and bring over into the conscious, waking life the scenes visited, the information gained, and the events that have transpired. Most people are not able to do this and so much that might otherwise be gained is lost. They say, however, that it is in our power, in proportion as we understand the laws, to go where we will, and to bring over into the conscious, waking life all the experiences thus gained. Be this, however, as it may, it certainly is true that while sleeping we have the power, in a perfectly normal and natural way, to get much of value by way of light, instruction, and growth that the majority of people now miss.

If the soul life, that which relates us to Infinite Spirit, is always active, even while the body is at rest, why may not the mind so direct conditions as one falls asleep, that while the body is at rest, it may continually receive illumination from the soul and bring what it thus receives over into the conscious, waking life? This, indeed, can be done, and is done by some to great advantage; and many times the highest inspirations from the soul come in this way, as would seem most natural, since at this time all communications from the outer, material world no longer enter. I know those who do much work during sleep, the same as they get much light along desired lines. By charging the mind on going to sleep as to a particular time for waking, it is possible, as many of us know, to wake on the very minute. Not infrequently we have examples of difficult problems, problems that defied solution during waking hours, being solved during sleep.

A friend, a well-known journalist, had an extended newspaper article clearly and completely worked out for her in this way. She frequently calls this agency to her aid. She was notified by the managing editor one evening to have the article ready in the morning,—an article requiring more than ordinary care, and one in which quite a knowledge of facts was required. It was a matter in connection with which she knew scarcely anything, and all her efforts at finding information regarding it seemed to be of no avail.

She set to work, but it seemed as if even her own powers defied her. Failure seemed imminent. Almost in desperation she decided to retire, and putting the matter into her mind in such a way that she would be able to receive the greatest amount of aid while asleep, she fell asleep and slept soundly until morning. When she awoke her work of the previous evening was the first thing that came into her mind. She lay quietly for a few minutes, and as she lay there, the article, completely written, seemed to stand before her mind. She ran through it, arose, and without dressing took her pen and transcribed it on to paper, literally acting simply as her own amanuensis.

The mind acting intently along a particular line will continue so to act until some other object of thought carries it along another line. And since in sleep only the body is in quiet while the mind and soul are active, then the mind on being given a certain direction when one drops off to sleep, will take up the line along which it is directed, and can be made, in time, to bring over into consciousness the results of its activities. Some will be able very soon to get results of this kind; for some it will take longer. Quiet and continued effort will increase the faculty.

Then by virtue of the law of the drawing power of mind, since the mind is always active, we are drawing to us even while sleeping, influences from the realms kindred to those in which we in our thoughts are living before we fall asleep. In this way we can put ourselves into relation with what ever kinds of influence we choose and accordingly gain much during the process of sleep. In many ways the interior faculties are more open and receptive while we are in sleep than while we are awake. Hence the necessity of exercising even greater care as to the nature of the thoughts that occupy the mind as we enter into sleep, for there can come to us only what we by our own order of thought attract. We have it entirely in our own hands.

And for the same reason,—this greater degree of receptivity during this period,—we are able by understanding and using the law, to gain much of value more readily in this way than when the physical senses are fully open to the material world about us. Many will find a practice somewhat after the following nature of value: When light or information is desired along any particular line, light or information you feel it is right and wise for you to have, as, for example, light in regard to an uncertain course of action, then as you retire, first bring your mind into the attitude of peace and good-will for all. You in this way bring yourself into an harmonious condition, and in turn attract to yourself these same peaceful conditions from without.

Then resting in this sense of peace, quietly and calmly send out your earnest desire for the needed light or information; cast out of your mind all fears or forebodings lest it come not, for "in quietness and in confidence shall be your strength." Take the expectant attitude of mind, firmly believing and expecting that when you awake the desired results will be with you. Then on awaking, before any thoughts or activities from the outside world come in to absorb the attention, remain for a little while receptive to the intuitions or the impressions that come. When they come, when they manifest themselves clearly, then act upon them without delay. In the degree that you do this, in that degree will the power of doing it ever more effectively grow.

Or, if for unselfish purposes you desire to grow and develop any of your faculties, or to increase the health and strength of your body, take a corresponding attitude of mind, the form of which will readily suggest itself in accordance with your particular needs or desires. In this way you will open yourself to, you will connect yourself with, and you will set into operation within yourself, the particular order of forces that will make for these results. Don't be afraid to voice your desires. In this way you set into operation vibratory forces which go out and which make their impress felt somewhere, and which, arousing into activity or uniting with other forces, set about to actualize your desires. No good thing shall be withheld from him who lives in harmony with the higher laws and forces. There are no desires that shall not be satisfied to the one who knows and who wisely uses the powers with which he or she is endowed.

Your sleep will be more quiet, and peaceful, and refreshing, and so your power increased mentally, physically, and spiritually, simply by sending out as you fall asleep, thoughts of love and good-will, thoughts of peace and harmony for all. In this way you are connecting yourself with all the forces in the universe that make for peace and harmony.

A friend who is known the world over through his work along humane lines, has told me that many times in the middle of the night he is awakened suddenly and there comes to his mind, as a flash of inspiration, a certain plan in connection with his work. And as he lies there quietly and opens himself to it, the methods for its successful carrying out all reveal themselves to him clearly. In this way many plans are entered upon and brought to a successful culmination that otherwise would never be thought of, plans that seem, indeed, marvelous to the world at large. He is a man with a sensitive organism, his life in thorough harmony with the higher laws, and given wholly and unreservedly to the work to which he has dedicated it. Just how and from what source these inspirations come he does not fully know. Possibly no one does, though each may have his theory. But this we do know, and it is all we need to know now, at least,—that to the one who lives in harmony with the higher laws of his being, and who opens himself to them, they come.

Visions and inspirations of the highest order will come in the degree that we make for them the right conditions. One who has studied deeply into the subject in hand has said: "To receive education spiritually while the body is resting in sleep is a perfectly normal and orderly experience, and would occur definitely and satisfactorily in the lives of all of us, if we paid more attention to internal and consequently less to external states with their supposed but unreal necessities. . . . Our thoughts make us what we are here and hereafter, and our thoughts are often busier by night than by day, for when we are asleep to the exterior we can be wide awake to the interior world; and the unseen world is a substantial place, the conditions of which are entirely regulated by mental and moral attainments. When we are not deriving information through outward avenues of sensation, we are receiving instruction through interior channels of perception, and when this fact is understood for what it is worth, it will become a universal custom for persons to take to sleep with them the special subject on which they most earnestly desire particular instruction. The Pharaoh type of person dreams, and so does his butler and baker; but the Joseph type, which is that of the truly gifted seer, both dreams and interprets."

But why had not Pharaoh the power of interpreting his dreams? Why was Joseph the type of the "truly gifted seer?" Why did he not only dream, but had also the power to interpret both his own dreams and the dreams of others? Simply read the lives of the two. He who runs may read. In all true power it is, after all, living the life that tells. And in proportion as one lives the life does he not only attain to the highest power and joy for himself, but he also becomes of ever greater service to all the world. One need remain in no hell longer than he himself chooses to; and the moment he chooses not to remain longer, not all the powers in the universe can prevent his leaving it. One can rise to any heaven he himself chooses; and when he chooses so to rise, all the higher powers of the universe combine to help him heavenward.

When one awakes from sleep and so returns to conscious life, he is in a peculiarly receptive and impressionable state. All relations with the material world have for a time been shut off, the mind is in a freer and more natural state, resembling somewhat a sensitive plate, where impressions can readily leave their traces. This is why many times the highest and truest impressions come to one in the early morning hours, before the activities of the day and their attendant distractions have exerted an influence. This is one reason why many people can do their best work in the early hours of the day.

But this fact is also a most valuable one in connection with the moulding of every-day life. The mind is at this time as a clean sheet of paper. We can most valuably use this quiet, receptive, impressionable period by wisely directing the activities of the mind along the highest and most desirable paths, and thus, so to speak, set the pace for the day.

Each morning is a fresh beginning. We are as it were, just beginning life. We have it *entirely* in our own hands. And when the morning with its fresh beginning comes, all yesterdays should be yesterdays, with which we have nothing to do. Sufficient is it to know that the way we lived our yesterday has determined for us our today. And, again, when the morning with its fresh beginning comes, all tomorrows should be tomorrows, with which we have nothing to do. Sufficient to know that the way we live our today determines our tomorrow.

*Every day is a fresh beginning,*
*Every morn is the world made new;*
*You who are weary of sorrow and sinning,*
*Here is a beautiful hope for you,*
*A hope for me and a hope for you.*

*All the past things are past and over,*
*The tasks are done, and the tears are shed.*
*Yesterday's errors let yesterday cover;*
*Yesterday's wounds, which smarted and bled,*
*Are healed with the healing which night has shed*

. . . . . .

*Let them go, since we cannot relieve them,*
*Cannot undo and cannot atone.*
*God in His mercy receive, forgive them!*
*Only the new days are our own.*
*Today is ours, and today alone.*

*Here are the skies all burnished brightly;*
*Here is the spent earth all reborn;*
*Here are the tired limbs springing lightly*
*To face the sun and to share with the morn*
*In the chrism of dew and the cool of dawn.*

*Every day is a fresh beginning,*
*Listen, my soul, to the glad refrain,*
*And, spite of old sorrow and older sinning,*
*And puzzles forecasted, and possible pain,*
*Take heart with the day and begin again.*

Simply the first hour of this new day, with all its richness and glory, with all its sublime and eternity-determining possibilities, and each succeeding hour as it comes, but *not before* it comes. This is the secret of character building. This simple method will bring any one to the realization of the highest life that can be even conceived of, and there is nothing in this connection that can be conceived of that cannot be realized somehow, somewhen, somewhere.

This brings such a life within the possibilities of *all,* for there is *no one,* if really in earnest and if he really desires it, who cannot live to his highest for a single hour. But even though there should be, if he is *only earnest in his endeavor,* then, through the law that like builds like, he will be able to come a little nearer to it the next hour, and still nearer the next, and the next, until sooner or later comes the time when it becomes the natural, and any other would require the effort.

In this way one becomes in love and in league with the highest and best in the universe, and as a consequence, the highest and best in the universe becomes in love and in league with him. They aid him at every turn; they seem literally to move all things his way, because forsooth, he has first moved their way.

CHAPTER 7

# The Realization of Perfect Peace

This is the Spirit of Infinite Peace, and the moment we come into harmony with it there comes to us an inflowing tide of peace, for peace is harmony. A deep interior meaning underlies the great truth, "To be spiritually minded is life and peace." To recognize the fact that we are spirit, and to live in this thought, is to be spiritually minded, and so to be in harmony and peace. Oh, the thousands of men and women all about us weary with care, troubled and ill at ease, running hither and thither to find peace, weary in body, soul, and mind; going to other countries, traveling the world over, coming back, and still not finding it. Of course they have not found it and they never will find it in this way, because they are looking for it where it is not. They are looking for it without when they should look within. Peace is to be found only within, and unless one find it there he will never find it at all.

Peace lies not in the external world. It lies within one's own soul. We may travel over many different avenues in pursuit of it, we may seek it through the channels of the bodily appetites and passions, we may seek it through all the channels of the external, we may chase for it hither and thither, but it will always be just beyond our grasp, because we are searching for it where it is not. In the degree, however, that we order the bodily appetites and passions in accordance with the promptings of the soul within will the higher forms of happiness and peace enter our lives; but in the degree that we fail in doing this will disease, suffering, and discontent enter in.

To be at one with God is to be at peace. The child simplicity is the greatest agency in bringing this full and complete realization, the child simplicity that recognizes its true relations with the Father's life. There are people I know who have come into such a conscious realization of their oneness with this Infinite Life, this Spirit of Infinite Peace, that their lives are fairly bubbling over with joy. I have particularly in mind at this moment a comparatively young man who was an invalid for several years, his health completely broken with nervous exhaustion, who thought there was nothing in life worth living for, to whom everything and everybody presented a gloomy aspect, and he in turn presented a gloomy aspect to all with whom he came in contact. Not long ago he came into such a vital realization of his oneness with this Infinite Power, he opened himself so completely to its divine inflow, that today he is in perfect health, and frequently as I meet him now he cannot resist the impulse to cry out, "Oh, it is a joy to be alive."

I know an officer on our police force who has told me that many times when off duty and on his way home in the evening, there comes to him such a vivid and vital realization of his oneness with this Infinite Power, and this Spirit of Infinite Peace so takes hold of and so fills him, that it seems as if his feet could scarcely keep to the pavement, so buoyant and so exhilarated does he become by reason of this inflowing tide.

He who comes into this higher realization never has any fear, for he has always with him a sense of protection, and the very realization of this makes his protection complete. Of him it is true,—"No weapon that is formed against thee shall prosper"; "There shall no ill come nigh thy dwelling"; "Thou shalt be in league with the stones of the field, and the beasts of the field shall be at peace with thee."

These are the men and the women who seem to live charmed lives. The moment we fear anything we open the door for the entrance of the actualization of the very thing we fear. An animal will never harm a person who is absolutely fearless in regard to it. The instant he fears he opens himself to danger; and some animals, the dog for example, can instantly detect the element of fear, and this gives them the courage to do harm. In the degree that we come into a full realization of our oneness with this Infinite Power do we become calm and quiet, undisturbed by the little occurrences that before so vex and annoy us. We are no longer disappointed in people, for we always read them aright. We have the power of penetrating into their very souls and seeing the underlying motives that are at work there.

A gentleman approached a friend the other day, and with great show of cordiality grasped him by the hand and said, "Why, Mr.——, I am so glad to see you." Quick as a flash my friend read him, and looking him steadily in the eye, replied, "No, you are mistaken, you are not glad to see me; but you are very much disconcerted, so much so that you are now blushing in evidence of it." The gentleman replied, "Well, you know in this day and age of conventionality and form we have to put on the show and sometimes make believe what we do not really feel." My friend once more looked him in the face and said, "Again you are mistaken. Let me give you one little word of advice: You will always fare better and will think far more of yourself, always to recognize and to tell the truth rather than to give yourself to any semblance of it."

As soon as we are able to read people aright we will then cease to be disappointed in them, we will cease to place them on pedestals, for this can never be done without some attendant disappointment. The fall will necessarily come, sooner or later, and moreover, we are thus many times unfair to our friends. When we come into harmony with this Spirit of Peace, evil reports and apparent bad treatment, either at the hands of friends or of enemies, will no longer disturb us. When we are conscious of the fact that in our life and our work we are true to that eternal principle of right, of truth, of justice that runs through all the universe, that unites and governs all, that always eventually prevails, then nothing of this kind can come nigh us, and come what may we will always be tranquil and undisturbed.

The things that cause sorrow, and pain, and bereavement will not be able to take the hold of as they now take, for true wisdom will enable us to see the proper place and know the right relations of all things. The loss of friends by the transition we call death will not cause sorrow to the soul that has come into this higher realization, for he knows that there is no such thing as death, for each one is not only a partaker, but an eternal partaker, of this Infinite Life. He knows that the mere falling away of the physical body by no means affects the real soul life. With a tranquil spirit born of a higher faith he can realize for himself, and to those less strong he can say—

*Loving friends! be wise and dry*
*Straightway every weeping eye;*
*What you left upon the bier*
*Is not worth a single tear;*
*'Tis a simple sea-shell, one*
*Out of which the pearl has gone.*
*The shell was nothing, leave it there;*
*The pearl—the soul—was all, is here.*

And so far as the element of separation is concerned, he realizes that to spirit there are no bounds, and that spiritual communion, whether between two persons in the body, or two persons, one in the body and one out of the body, is within the reach of all. In the degree that the higher spiritual life is realized can there be this higher spiritual communion.

The things that we open ourselves to always come to us. People in the olden times expected to see angels and they saw them; but there is no more reason why they should have seen them than that we should see them now; no more reason why they should come and dwell with them than that they should come and dwell with us, for the great laws governing all things are the same today as they were then. If angels come not to minister unto us it is because we do not invite them, it is because we keep the door closed through which they otherwise might enter.

In the degree that we are filled with this Spirit of Peace by thus opening ourselves to its inflow does it pour through us, so that we carry it with us wherever we go. In the degree that we thus open ourselves do we become magnets to attract peace from all sources; and in the degree that we attract and embody it in ourselves are we able to give it forth to others. We can in this way become such perfect embodiments of peace that wherever we go we are continually shedding benedictions. But a day or two ago I saw a woman grasp the hand of a man (his face showed the indwelling God), saying, "Oh, it does me so much good to see you. I have been in anxiety and almost in despair during the past few hours, but the very sight of you has rolled the burden entirely away." There are people all around us who are continually giving out blessings and comfort, persons whose mere presence seems to change sorrow into joy, fear into courage, despair into hope, weakness into power.

It is the one who has come into the realization of his own true self who carries this power with him and who radiates it wherever he goes,—the one who, as we say, has found his centre. And in all the great universe there is but one centre,—the Infinite Power that is working in and through all. The one who then has found his centre is the one who has come into the realization of his oneness with this Infinite Power, the one who recognizes himself as a spiritual being, for God is spirit.

Such is the man of power. Centred in the Infinite, he has thereby, so to speak, connected himself with, he has attached his belts to, the great power-house of the universe. He is constantly drawing power to himself from all sources. For, thus centred, knowing himself, conscious of his own power, the thoughts that go from his mind are thoughts of strength; and by virtue of the law that like attracts like, he by his thoughts is continually attracting to himself from all quarters the aid of all whose thoughts are thoughts of strength, and in this way he is linking himself with this order of thought in the universe.

And so to him that hath, to him shall be given. This is simply the working of a natural law. His strong, positive, and hence constructive thought is continually working success for him along all lines, and continually bringing to him help from all directions. The things that he sees, that he creates in the ideal, are through the agency of this strong constructive thought continually clothing themselves, taking form, manifesting themselves in the material. Silent, unseen forces are at work which will sooner or later be made manifest in the visible.

Fear and all thoughts of failure never suggest themselves to such a man; or if they do, they are immediately sent out of his mind, and so he is not influenced by this order of thought from without. He does not attract it to him. He is in another current of thought. Consequently the weakening, failure-bringing thoughts of the fearing, the vacillating, the pessimistic about him, have no influence upon him. The one who is of the negative, fearing kind not only has his energies and his physical agents weakened, or even paralyzed through the influence of this kind of thought that is born within him, but he also in this way connects himself with this order of thought in the world about him. And in the degree that he does this does he become a victim to the weak, fearing, negative minds all around him. Instead of growing in power, he increases in weakness. He is in the same order of thought with those of whom it is true,—and even that which they have shall be taken away from them. This again is simply the working of a natural law, the same as is its opposite. Fearing lest I lose even what I have I hide it away in a napkin. Very well. I must then pay the price of my "fearing lest I lose."

Thoughts of strength both build strength from within and attract it from without. Thoughts of weakness actualize weakness from within and attract it from without. Courage begets strength, fear begets weakness. And so courage begets success, fear begets failure. It is the man or the woman of faith, and hence of courage, who is the master of circumstances, and who makes his or her power felt in the world.

It is the man or the woman who lacks faith and who as a consequence is weakened and crippled by fears and forebodings, who is the creature of all passing occurrences.

Within each one lies the cause of whatever comes to him. Each has it in his own hands to determine what comes. Everything in the visible, material world has its origin in the unseen, the spiritual, the thought world. This is the world of cause, the former is the world of effect. The nature of the effect is always in accordance with the nature of the cause. What one lives in his invisible, thought world, he is continually actualizing in his visible, material world. If he would have any conditions different in the latter he must make the necessary change in the former. A clear realization of this great fact would bring success to thousands of men and women who all about us are now in the depths of despair. It would bring health, abounding health and strength to thousands now diseased and suffering. It would bring peace and joy to thousands now unhappy and ill at ease.

And oh, the thousands all about us who are continually living in the slavery of fear. The spirits within that should be strong and powerful, are rendered weak and impotent. Their energies are crippled, their efforts are paralyzed. "Fear is everywhere,—fear of want, fear of starvation, fear of public opinion, fear of private opinion, fear that what we own today may not be ours tomorrow, fear of sickness, fear of death. Fear has become with millions a fixed habit. The thought is everywhere. The thought is thrown upon us from every direction. . . . To live in continual dread, continual cringing, continual fear of anything, be it loss of love, loss of money, loss of position or situation, is to take the readiest means to lose what we fear we shall."

By fear nothing is to be gained, but on the contrary, everything is to be lost. "I know this is true," says one, "but I am given to fear; it's natural to me and I can't help it." Can't help it! In saying this you indicate one great reason of your fear by showing that you do not even know yourself as yet. You must know yourself in order to know your powers, and not until you know them can you use them wisely and fully. Don't say you can't help it. If you think you can't, the chances are that you can't. If you think you can, and act in accordance with this thought, then not only are the chances that you can, but if you act fully in accordance with it, that you can and that you will is an absolute certainty. It was Virgil who in describing the crew which in his mind would win the race, said of them,—They can because they think they can. In other words, this very attitude of mind on their part will infuse a spiritual power into their bodies that will give them the strength and endurance which will enable them to win.

Then take the thought that you *can;* take it merely as a seed-thought, if need be, plant it in your consciousness, tend it, cultivate it, and it will gradually reach out and gather strength from all quarters. It will focus and make positive and active the spiritual force within you that is now scattered and of little avail. It will draw to itself force from without. It will draw to your aid the influence of other minds of its own nature, minds that are fearless, strong, courageous. You will thus draw to yourself and connect yourself with this order of thought. If earnest and faithful, the time will soon come when all fear will loose its hold; and instead of being an embodiment of weakness and a creature of circumstances, you will find yourself a tower of strength and a master of circumstances.

We need more faith in every-day life,—faith in the power that works for good, faith in the Infinite God, and hence faith in ourselves created in His image. And however things at times may seem to go, however dark at times appearances may be, the knowledge of the fact that "the Supreme Power has us in its charge as it has the suns and endless systems of worlds in space," will give us the supreme faith that all is well with us, the same as all is well with the world. "Thou wilt keep him in perfect peace whose mind is stayed on Thee."

There is nothing firmer, and safer, and surer than Deity. Then, as we recognize the fact that we have it in our own hands to open ourselves ever more fully to this Infinite Power, and call upon it to manifest itself in and through us, we will find in ourselves an ever increasing sense of power. For in this way we are working in conjunction with it, and it in turn is working in conjunction with us. We are then led into the full realization of the fact that all things work together for good to those that love the good. Then the fears and forebodings that have dominated us in the past will be transmuted into faith, and faith when rightly understood and rightly used is a force before which nothing can stand.

Materialism leads naturally to pessimism. And how could it do otherwise? A knowledge of the Spiritual Power working in and through us as well as in and through all things, a power that works for righteousness, leads to optimism. Pessimism leads to weakness. Optimism leads to power. The one who is centred in Deity is the one who not only outrides every storm, but who through the faith, and so, the conscious power that is in him, faces storm with the same calmness and serenity that he faces fair weather; for he knows well beforehand what the outcome will be. He knows that underneath are the everlasting arms. He it is who realizes the truth of the injunction, "Rest in the Lord, wait patiently for Him and He shall give thee thy heart's desire." All shall be given, simply given, to him who is ready to accept it. Can anything be clearer than this?

In the degree, then, that we work in conjunction with the Supreme Power do we need the less to concern ourselves about results. To live in the full realization of this fact and all that attends it brings peace, a full, rich, abiding peace,—a peace that makes the present complete, and that, going on before, brings back the assurance that as our days, so shall our strength be. The one who is thus centred, even in the face of all the unrest and the turmoil about us, can realize and say—

*I stay my haste, I make delays,*
*For what avails this eager pace?*
*I stand amid eternal ways,*
*And what is mine shall know my face.*

*Asleep, awake, by night or day,*
*The friends I seek are seeking me;*

*No wind can drive my bark astray,*
*Nor change the tide of destiny.*

. . . . .

*The waters know their own, and draw*
*The brooks that spring in yonder height;*
*So flows the good with equal law*
*Unto the soul of pure delight.*

*The stars come nightly to the sky;*
*The tidal wave unto the sea;*
*Nor time, nor space, nor deep, nor high,*
*Can keep my own away from me.*

CHAPTER 8

# Coming into Fullness of Power

This is the Spirit of Infinite Power, and in the degree that we open ourselves to it does power become manifest in us. With God all things are possible,—that is, in conjunction with God all things are possible. The true secret of power lies in keeping one's connection with the God who worketh all things; and in the degree that we keep this connection are we able literally to rise above every conceivable limitation.

Why, then, waste time in running hither and thither to acquire power? Why waste time with this practice or that practice? Why not go directly to the mountain-top itself, instead of wandering through the by-ways, in the valleys, and on the mountain sides? That man has absolute dominion, as taught in all the scriptures of the world, is true not of physical man, but of *spiritual man*. There are many animals, for example, larger and stronger, over which from a physical standpoint he would not have dominion, but he can gain supremacy over even these by calling into activity the higher mental, psychic, and spiritual forces with which he is endowed.

Whatever can't be done in the physical can be done in the spiritual. And in direct proportion as a man recognizes himself as spirit, and lives accordingly, is he able to transcend in power the man who recognizes himself merely as material. All the sacred literature of the world is teeming with examples of what we call miracles. They are not confined to any particular times or places. There is no age of miracles in distinction from any other period that may be an age of miracles. Whatever has been done in the world's history can be done again through the operation of the same laws and forces. These miracles were performed not by those who were more than men, but by those who through the recognition of their oneness with God became God-men, so that the higher forces and powers worked through them.

For what, let us ask, is a miracle? Is it something supernatural? Supernatural only in the sense of being above the natural, or rather, above that which is natural to man in his ordinary state. A miracle is nothing more nor less than this. One who has come into a knowledge of his true identity, of his oneness with the all-pervading

Wisdom and Power, thus makes it possible for laws higher than the ordinary mind knows of to be revealed to him. These laws he makes use of; the people see the results, and by virtue of their own limitations, call them miracles and speak of the person who performs these apparently supernatural works as a supernatural being. But they as supernatural beings could themselves perform these supernatural works if they would open themselves to the recognition of the same laws, and consequently to the realization of the same possibilities and powers. And let us also remember that the supernatural of yesterday becomes, as in the process of evolution we advance from the lower to the higher, from the more material to the more spiritual, the common and the natural of today, and what seems to be the supernatural of today becomes in the same way the natural of tomorrow, and so on through the ages. Yes, it is the God-man who does the things that appear supernatural, the man who by virtue of his realization of the higher powers transcends the majority and so stands out among them. But any power that is possible to one human soul is possible to another. The same laws operate in every life. We can be men and women of power or we can be men and women of impotence. The moment one vitally grasps the fact that he can rise he will rise, and he can have absolutely no limitations other than the limitations he sets to himself. Cream always rises to the top. It rises simply because *it is the nature of cream to rise.*

We hear much said of "environment." We need to realize that environment should never be allowed to make the man, but that man should always, *and always can,* condition the environment. When we realize this we will find that many times it is not necessary to take ourselves out of any particular environment, because we may yet have a work to do there; but by the very force we carry with us we can so affect and change matters that we will have an entirely new set of conditions in an old environment.

The same is true in regard to "hereditary" traits and influences. We sometimes hear the question asked, "Can they be overcome?" Only the one who doesn't yet know himself can ask a question such as this. If we entertain and live in the belief that they cannot be overcome, then the chances are that they will always remain. The moment, however, that we come into a realization of our true selves, and so of the tremendous powers and forces within,—the powers and forces of the mind and spirit,—hereditary traits and influences that are harmful in nature will begin to lessen, and will disappear with a rapidity directly in proportion to the completeness of this realization.

*There is no thing we cannot overcome;*
*Say not thy evil instinct is inherited,*
*Or that some trait inborn makes thy whole life forlorn,*
*And calls down punishment that is not merited.*

*Back of thy parents and grandparents lies*
*The Great Eternal Will! That too is thine*

*Inheritance,—strong, beautiful, divine,*
*Sure lever of success for one who tries.*

. . . .

*There is no noble height thou canst not climb;*
*All triumphs may be thine in Time's futurity,*
*If, whatso'er thy fault, thou dost not faint or halt;*
*But lean upon the staff of God's security.*

*Earth has no claim the soul cannot contest;*
*Know thyself part of the Eternal Source;*
*Naught can stand before thy spirit's force:*
*The soul's Divine Inheritance is best.*

Again there are many who are living far below their possibilities because they are continually handing over their individualities to others. Do you want to be a power in the world? Then be yourself. Don't class yourself, don't allow yourself to be classed among the *second-hand*, among the *they-say* people. Be true to the highest within your own soul, and then allow yourself to be governed by no customs or conventionalities or arbitrary man-made rules that are not founded upon *principle.* Those things that are founded upon principle will be observed by the right-minded, the right-hearted man or woman, in any case.

Don't surrender your individuality, which is your greatest agent of power, to the customs and conventionalities that have gotten their life from the great mass of those who haven't enough force to preserve their individualities,—those who in other words have given them over as ingredients to the "mush of concession" which one of our greatest writers has said characterizes our modern society. If you do surrender your individuality in this way, you simply aid in increasing the undesirable conditions; in payment for this you become a slave, and the chances are that in time you will be unable to hold even the respect of those whom you in this way try to please.

If you preserve your individuality then you become a master, and if wise and discreet, your influence and power will be an aid in bringing about a higher, a better, and a more healthy set of conditions in the world. All people, moreover, will think more of you, will honor you more highly for doing this than if you show your weakness by contributing yourself to the same "mush of concession" that so many of them are contributing themselves to. With all classes of people you will then have an influence. "A great style of hero draws equally all classes, all extremes of society to him, till we say the very dogs believe in him."

To be one's self is the only worthy, and by all means the only satisfactory, thing to be. "May it not be good policy," says one, "to be governed sometimes by one's surroundings?" What is good policy? To be yourself, first, last and always.

*This above all,—to thine own self be true;*
*And it must follow, as the night the day,*
*Thou canst not then be false to any man.*

"When we appeal to the Supreme and our life is governed by a principle, we are not governed either by fear of public opinion or loss of others' approbation, and we may be sure that the Supreme will sustain us. If in any way we try to live to suit others we never shall suit them, and the more we try the more unreasonable and exacting do they become. The government of your life is a matter that lies entirely between God and yourself, and when your life is swayed and influenced from any other source you are on the wrong path." When we find the kingdom within and become centred in the Infinite, then we become a law unto ourselves. When we become a law unto ourselves, then we are able to bring others to a knowledge of laws higher than they are governed or many times even enslaved by.

When we have found this centre, then that beautiful simplicity, at once the charm and the power of a truly great personality, enters into our lives. Then all striving for effect,—that sure indicator of weakness and a lack of genuine power,—is absent. This striving for effect that is so common is always an indicator of a lack of something. It brings to mind the man who rides behind a dock-tailed horse. Conscious of the fact that there is not enough in *himself* to attract attention, in common with a number of other weaklings, he adopts the brutal method of having his horse's tail sawed off, that its unnatural, odd appearance may attract from people the attention that he of himself is unable to secure.

But the one who strives for effect is always fooled more than he succeeds in fooling others. The man and the woman of true wisdom and insight can always see the causes that prompt, the motives that underlie the acts of all with whom he or she comes in contact. "He is great who is what he is from nature and who never reminds us of others."

The men and the women who are truly awake to the real powers within are the men and women who seem to be doing so little, yet who in reality are doing so much. They seem to be doing so little because they are working with higher agencies, and yet are doing so much because of this very fact. They do their work on the higher plane. They keep so completely their connection with the Infinite Power that *It* does the work for them and they are relieved of the responsibility. They are the care-less people. They are care-less because it is the Infinite Power that is working through them, and with this Infinite Power they are simply cooperating.

*The secret of the highest power is simply the uniting of the outer agencies of expression with the Power that works from within.* Are you a painter? Then in the degree that you open yourself to the power of the forces within will you become great instead of mediocre. You can never put into permanent form inspirations higher than those that come through your own soul. In order for the higher inspirations to come through it, you must open your soul, you must open it fully to the Supreme Source of all inspiration. Are you an orator? In the degree that you come into harmony and work in conjunction with the higher powers that will speak through you will you have the real power of moulding and of moving men. If you use merely your physical agents, you will be simply a demagogue. If you open yourself so that the voice of God can speak through and use your physical agents, you will become a great and true orator, great and true in just the degree that you so open yourself.

Are you a singer? Then open yourself and let the God within pour forth in the spirit of song. You will find it a thousand times easier than all your long and studied practice without this, and other things being equal, there will come to you a power of song so enchanting and so enrapturing that its influence upon all who hear will be irresistible.

When my cabin or tent has been pitched during the summer on the edge or in the midst of a forest, I have sometimes lain awake on my cot in the early morning, just as the day was beginning to break. Silence at first. Then an intermittent chirp here and there. And as the unfolding tints of the dawn became faintly perceptible, these grew more and more frequent, until by and by the whole forest seemed to burst forth in one grand chorus of song. Wonderful! wonderful! It seemed as if the very trees, as if every grass-blade, as if the bushes, the very sky above, and the earth beneath, had part in this wonderful symphony. Then, as I have listened as it went on and on, I have thought, What a study in the matter of song! If we could but learn from the birds. If we could but open ourselves to the same powers and allow them to pour forth in us, what singers, what movers of men we might have! Nay, what singers and what movers of men *we would have!*

Do you know the circumstances under which Mr. Sankey sang for the first time "The Ninety and Nine?" Says one of our able journals: "At a great meeting recently in Denver, Mr. Ira W. Sankey, before singing 'The Ninety and Nine,' which, perhaps, of all his compositions is the one that has brought him the most fame, gave an account of its birth. Leaving Glasgow for Edinburg with Mr. Moody, he stopped at a news-stand and bought a penny religious paper. Glancing over it as they rode on the cars, his eye fell on a few little verses in the corner of the page. Turning to Mr. Moody he said, 'I've found my hymn.' But Mr. Moody was busily engaged and did not hear a word. Mr. Sankey did not find time to make a tune for the verses, so he pasted them in his music scrapbook.

"One day they had an unusually impressive meeting in Edinburg, in which Dr. Bonar had spoken with great effect on 'The Good Shepherd.' At the close of the address Mr. Moody beckoned to his partner to sing. He thought of nothing but the Twenty-third Psalm, but that he had sung so often. His second thought was to sing the verses he had found in the newspaper, but the third thought was, how could it be done when he had no tune. Then a fourth thought came, and that was to sing them *anyway.* He put the verses before him, touched the keys of the organ, opened his mouth and sang, not knowing where he was going to come out. He finished the first verse amid profound silence. He took a long breath and wondered if he could sing the second the same way. He tried and succeeded; after that it was easy to sing it. When he finished the hymn the meeting was all broken down and the throngs were crying. Mr. Sankey says it was the most intense moment of his life. Mr. Moody said he never heard a song like it. It was sung at every meeting, and was soon going over the world."

When we open ourselves to the highest inspirations they never fail us. When we fail to do this we fail in attaining the highest results, whatever the undertaking.

Are you a writer? Then remember that the one great precept underlying all successful literary work is, *Look into thine own heart and write. Be true. Be fearless. Be loyal to the promptings of your own soul.* Remember that an author can never write more than he himself is. If he would write more, then he must be more. He is simply his own amanuensis. He in a sense writes himself into his book. He can put no more into it than he himself is.

If he is one of a great personality, strong in purpose, deep in feeling, open always to the highest inspirations, a certain indefinable something gets into his pages that makes them breathe forth a vital, living power, a power so great that each reader gets the same inspirations as those that spoke through the author. That that's written between the lines is many times more than that that's written in the lines. It is the spirit of the author that engenders this power. It is this that gives that extra twenty-five or thirty per cent that takes a book out of the class called medium and lifts it into the class called superior,—that extra per cent that makes it the one of the hundred that is truly successful, while the ninety-nine never see more than their first edition.

It is this same spiritual power that the author of a great personality puts into his work, that causes it to go so rapidly from reader to reader, for the only way that any book circulates in the ultimate is from mouth to mouth, any book that reaches a large circulation. It is this that many times causes a single reader, in view of its value to himself, to purchase numbers of copies for others. "A good poem," says Emerson, "goes about the world offering itself to reasonable men, who read it with joy and carry it to their reasonable neighbors. Thus it draws to it the *wise and generous souls,* confirming their secret thoughts, and through their sympathy *really publishing itself.*"

This is the type of author who writes not with the thought of having what he writes become literature, but he writes with the sole thought of reaching the hearts of the people, giving them something of vital value, something that will broaden, sweeten, enrich, and beautify their lives; that will lead them to the finding of the higher life and with it the higher powers and the higher joys. It most always happens, however, that if he succeeds in thus reaching the people, the becoming literature part somehow takes care of itself, and far better than if he aimed for it directly.

The one, on the other hand, who fears to depart from beaten paths, who allows himself to be bound by arbitrary rules, limits his own creative powers in just the degree that he allows himself so to be bound. "My book," says one of the greatest of modern authors, "shall smell of the pines and resound with the hum of insects. The swallow over my window shall interweave that thread or straw he carries in his bill into my web also." Far better, gentle sage, to have it smell of the pines and resound with the hum of insects than to have it sound of the rules that a smaller type of man gets by studying the works of a few great, fearless writers like yourself, and formulating from what he thus gains a handbook of rhetoric. "Of no use are the men who study to do exactly as was done before, who can never understand that *today is a new day.*"

When Shakespeare is charged with debts to his authors, Landor replies: "Yet he was more original than his originals. He breathed upon dead bodies and brought them into life." This is the type of man who doesn't move the world's way, but who moves the world his way.

I had rather be an amanuensis of the Infinite God, as it is my privilege literally to be, than a slave to the formulated rules of any rhetorician, or to the opinions of any critic. Oh, the people, the people over and over! Let me give something to them that will lighten the every-day struggles of our common life, something that will add a little sweetness here, a little hope there, something that will make more thoughtful, kind, and gentle this thoughtless, animal-natured man, something that will awaken into activity the dormant powers of this timid, shrinking little woman, powers that when awakened will be irresistible in their influence and that will surprise even herself. Let me give something that will lead each one to the knowledge of the divinity of every human soul, something that will lead each one to the conscious realization of *his own divinity,* with all its attendant riches, and glories, and powers,—let me succeed in doing this, and I can then well afford to be careless as to whether the critics praise or whether they blame. If it is blame, then under these circumstances it is as the cracking of a few dead sticks on the ground below, compared to the matchless music that the soft spring gale is breathing through the great pine forest.

Are you a minister, or a religious teacher of any kind? Then in the degree that you free yourself from the man-made theological dogmas that have held and that are holding and limiting so many, and in the degree that you open yourself to the Divine Breath, will you be one who will speak with authority. In the degree that you do this will you study the prophets less and be in the way of becoming a prophet yourself. The way is open for you exactly the same as it has ever been open for anyone.

If when born into the world you came into a family of the English-speaking race, then in all probability you are a Christian. To be a Christian is to be a follower of the *teachings* of Jesus, the Christ; to live in harmony with the same laws he lived in harmony with: in brief, *to live his life.* The great central fact of his teaching was this conscious union of man with the Father. It was the complete realization of this oneness with the Father on his part that made Jesus the Christ. It was through this that he attained to the power he attained to, that he spake as never man spake.

He never claimed for himself anything that he did not claim equally for all mankind. "The mighty works performed by Jesus were not exceptional, they were the natural and necessary concomitants of his state; he declared them to be in accordance with unvarying order; he spoke of them as no unique performances, but as the outcome of a state to which all might attain if they chose. As a teacher and demonstrator of truth, according to his own confession, he did nothing for the purpose of proving his solitary divinity. . . . The life and triumph of Jesus formed an epoch in the history of the race. His coming and victory marked a new era in human affairs; he introduced a new because a more complete ideal to the earth, and when his three most intimate companions saw in some measure what the new life really signified, they fell to the earth, speechless with awe and admiration."

By coming into this complete realization of his oneness with the Father, by mastering, absolutely mastering every circumstance that crossed his path through life, even to the death of the body, and by pointing out to us the great laws which are the same for us as they were to him, he has given us an ideal of life, an ideal for us to attain to *here and now,* that we could not have without him. *One has conquered first; all may conquer afterward.* By completely realizing it first for himself, and then by pointing out to others this great law of the at-one-ment with the Father, he has become probably the world's greatest saviour.

Don't mistake his mere person for his life and his teachings, an error that has been made in connection with most all great teachers by their disciples over and over again. And if you have been among the number who have been preaching a dead Christ, then for humanity's sake, for Christ's sake, for God's sake, and I speak most reverently, don't steal the people's time any longer, don't waste your own time more, in giving them stones in place of bread, dead form for the spirit of living truth. In his own words, "let the dead bury their dead." Come out from among them. Teach as did Jesus, *the living Christ.* Teach as did Jesus, *the Christ within.* Find this in all its transcendent beauty and power,—find it as Jesus found it, then you also will be one who will speak with authority. Then you will be able to lead large numbers of others to its finding. This is the pearl of great price.

It is the type of preacher whose soul has never as yet even perceived the *vital spirit* of the teachings of Jesus, and who as a consequence instead of giving this to the people, is giving them old forms and dogmas and speculations, who is emptying our churches. This is the type whose chief efforts seem to be in getting men ready to die. The Germans have a saying, Never go to the second thing first. We need men who will teach us first how to live. Living quite invariably precedes dying. This also is true, that when we once know how to live, and live in accordance with what we know, then the dying, as we term it, will in a wonderfully beautiful manner take care of itself. It is in fact the only way in which it can be taken care of.

It is on account of this emptying of our churches, for the reason that the people are tiring of mere husks, that many short-sighted people are frequently heard to say that religion is dying out. Religion dying out? How can anything die before it is really born? And so far as the people are concerned, religion is just being born, or rather they are just awaking to a vital, every-day religion. We are just beginning to get beyond the mere letter into its real, vital spirit. Religion dying out? Impossible even to conceive of. Religion is as much a part of the human soul as the human soul is a part of God. And as long as God and the human soul exist, religion will never die.

Much of the dogma, the form, the ceremony, the mere letter that has stood as religion,—and honestly, many times, let us be fair enough to say,—this, thank God, is rapidly dying out, and never so rapidly as it is today. By two methods it is dying. There is, first, a large class of people tired of or even nauseated with it all, who conscientiously prefer to have nothing rather than this. They are simply abandoning it, the same as a tree abandons its leaves when the early winter comes. There is, second, a large class in whom the Divine Breath is stirring, who are finding the Christ within in all its matchless beauty and redeeming power. And this new life is pushing off the old, the same as in the spring the newly awakened life in the tree pushes off the old, lifeless leaves that have clung on during the winter, to make place for the new ones. And the way this old dead leaf religion is being pushed off on every hand is indeed most interesting and inspiring to witness.

Let the places of those who have been emptying our churches by reason of their attempts to give stones for bread, husks and chaff for the life-giving grain, let their places be taken even for but a few times by those who are open and alive to these higher inspirations, and then let us again question those who feel that religion is dying out. "It is the live coal that kindles others, not the dead." Let their places be taken by those who have caught the inspiration of the Divine Breath, who as a consequence have a message of mighty value and import for the people, who by virtue of this same fact are able to present it with a beauty and a power so enrapturing that it takes captive the soul. Then we will find that the churches that today are dotted here and there with a few dozen people will be filled to overflowing, and there will not be even room enough for all who would enter. "Let the shell perish that the pearl may appear." We need no new revelations as yet. We need simply to find the vital spirit of those we already have. Then in due time, when we are ready for them, new ones will come, but not before.

"What the human soul, all the world over, needs," says John Pulsford, "is not to be harangued, however eloquently, about the old, accepted religion, but to be permeated, charmed, and taken captive by *a warmer and more potent Breath of God than they ever felt before.* And I should not be true to my personal experience if I did not bear testimony that this Divine Breath is as exquisitely adapted to the requirements of the soul's nature as a June morning to the plant. Nor does the morning breath leave the trees freer to delight themselves and develop themselves under its influence than the Breath of God allows each human mind to unfold according to its genius. Nothing stirs the central wheel of the soul like the Breath of God. The whole man is quickened, his senses are new senses, his emotions new emotions; his reason, his affections, his imagination, are all new-born. The change is greater than he knows; he marvels at the powers in himself which the Breath is opening and calling forth. He finds his nature to be an unutterable thing; he is sure therefore that the future must have inconceivable surprises in store. And herein lies the evidence, which I commend to my readers, of the existence of God, and of the Eternal human Hope. Let God's Breath kindle new spring-time in the soul, start into life its deeply buried germs, lead in heaven's summer; you will then have as clear evidence of God from within as you have of the universe from without. Indeed, your internal experience of life, and illimitable Hope in God will be nearer to you, and more prevailing, than all your external and superficial experience of nature and the world."

There is but one source of power in the universe. Whatever then you are, painter, orator, musician, writer, religious teacher, or whatever it may be, know that to catch and take captive the secret of power is so to work in conjunction with the Infinite Power, in order that it may continually work and manifest through you. If you fail in doing this, you fail in everything. If you fail in doing this, your work, whatever it may be, will be third or fourth rate, possibly at times second rate, but it positively never can be first rate. Absolutely impossible will it be for you ever to become a master.

Whatever estimate you put upon yourself will determine the effectiveness of your work along any line. As long as you live merely in the physical and the intellectual, you set limitations to yourself that will hold you as long as you so live. When, however, you come into the realization of your oneness with the Infinite Life and Power, and open yourself that it may work through you, you will find that you have entered upon an entirely new phase of life, and that an ever increasing power will be yours. Then it will be true that your strength will be as the strength of ten because your heart is pure.

*O God! I am one forever*
*With Thee by the glory of birth;*
*The celestial powers proclaim it*
*To the utmost bounds of the earth.*

*I think of this birthright immortal,*
*And my being expands like a rose,*
*As an odorous cloud of incense*
*Around and above me flows.*

*A glorious song of rejoicing*
*In an innermost spirit I hear,*
*And it sounds like heavenly voices,*
*In a chorus divine and clear.*

*And I feel a power uprising,*
*Like the power of an embryo god;*
*With a glorious wall it surrounds me,*
*And lifts me up from the sod.*

CHAPTER 9

# Plenty of All Things—The Law of Prosperity

This is the Spirit of Infinite Plenty, the Power that has brought, that is continually bringing, all things into expression in material form. He who lives in the realization of his oneness with this Infinite Power becomes a magnet to attract to himself a continual supply of whatsoever things he desires.

If one hold himself in the thought of poverty, he will be poor, and the chances are that he will remain in poverty. If he hold himself, whatever present conditions may be, continually in the thought of prosperity, he sets into operation forces that will sooner or later bring him into prosperous conditions. The law of attraction works unceasingly throughout the universe, and the one great and never changing fact in connection with it is, as we have found, that like attracts like. If we are one with this Infinite Power, this source of all things, then in the degree that we live in the realization of this oneness, in that degree do we actualize in ourselves a power that will bring to us an abundance of all things that it is desirable for us to have. In this way we come into possession of a power whereby we can actualize at all times those conditions that we desire.

As all truth exists *now,* and awaits simply our perception of it, so all things necessary for present needs exist *now,* and await simply the power in us to appropriate them. God holds all things in His hands. His constant word is, My child, acknowledge me in all your ways, and in the degree that you do this, in the degree that you live this, then what is mine is yours. Jehovah-jireh,—the Lord will provide. "He giveth to all men liberally and upbraideth not." He giveth liberally to all men who put themselves in the right attitude to receive from Him. He forces no good things upon any one.

The old and somewhat prevalent idea of godliness and poverty has absolutely no basis for its existence, and the sooner we get away from it the better. It had its birth in the same way that the idea of asceticism came into existence, when the idea prevailed that there was necessarily a warfare between the flesh and the spirit. It had its origin therefore in the minds of those who had a distorted, a one-sided view of life. True godliness is in a sense the same as true wisdom. The one who is truly wise, and who uses the forces and powers with which he is endowed, to him the great universe always opens her treasure house. The supply is always equal to the demand,—equal to the demand when the demand is rightly, wisely made. When one comes into the realization of these higher laws, then the fear of want ceases to tyrannize over him.

Are you out of a situation? Let the fear that you will not get another take hold of and *dominate* you, and the chances are that it may be a long time before you will get another, or the one that you do get may be a very poor one indeed. Whatever the circumstances, you must realize that you have within you forces and powers that you can set into operation that will triumph over any and all apparent or temporary losses. Set these forces into operation and you will then be placing a magnet that will draw to you a situation that may be far better than the one you have lost, and the time may soon come when you will be even thankful that you lost the old one.

Recognize, working in and through you, the same Infinite Power that creates and governs all things in the universe, the same Infinite Power that governs the endless systems of worlds in space. Send out your thought,—thought is a force, and it has occult power of unknown proportions when rightly used and wisely directed,—send out your thought that the right situation or the right work will come to you at the right time, in the right way, and that you will recognize it when it comes. Hold to this thought, never allow it to weaken, hold to it, and continually water it with firm expectation. You in this way put your advertisement into a psychical, a spiritual newspaper, a paper that has not a limited circulation, but one that will make its way not only to the utmost bounds of the earth, but of the very universe itself. It is an advertisement, moreover, which if rightly placed on your part, will be far more effective than any advertisement you could possibly put into any printed sheet, no matter what claims are made in regard to its being "the great advertising medium." In the degree that you come into this realization and live in harmony with the higher laws and forces, in that degree will you be able to do this effectively.

If you wish to look through the "want" columns of the newspapers, then do it not in the ordinary way. Put the higher forces into operation and thus place it on a higher basis. As you take up the paper, take this attitude of mind: If there is here an advertisement that it will be well for me to reply to, the moment I come to it I will recognize it. Affirm this, believe it, expect it. If you do this in full faith you will somehow feel the intuition the moment you come to the right one, and this intuition will be nothing more nor less than your own soul speaking to you. When it speaks then act at once.

If you get the situation and it does not prove to be exactly what you want, if you feel that you are capable of filling a better one, then the moment you enter upon it take the attitude of mind that this situation is the stepping-stone that will lead you to one that will be still better. Hold this thought steadily, affirm it, believe it, expect it, and all the time be faithful, *absolutely faithful* to the situation in which you are at present placed. If you are *not* faithful to it then the chances are that it will not be the stepping-stone to something better, but to something poorer. If you are faithful to it, the time may soon come when you will be glad and thankful, when you will rejoice, that you lost your old position.

This is the law of prosperity: When apparent adversity comes, be not cast down by it, but make the best of it, and always look forward for better things, for conditions more prosperous. To hold yourself in this attitude of mind is to set into operation subtle, silent, and irresistible forces that sooner or later will actualize in material form that which is today merely an idea. But ideas have occult power, and ideas, when rightly planted and rightly tended, are the seeds that actualize material conditions.

Never give a moment to complaint, but utilize the time that would otherwise be spent in this way in looking forward and actualizing the conditions you desire. Suggest prosperity to yourself. See yourself in a prosperous condition. Affirm that you will before long be in a prosperous condition. Affirm it calmly and quietly, but strongly and confidently. Believe it, believe it absolutely. Expect it,—keep it continually watered with expectation. You thus make yourself a magnet to attract the things that you desire. Don't be afraid to suggest, to affirm these things, for by so doing you put forth an ideal which will begin to clothe itself in material form. In this way you are utilizing agents among the most subtle and powerful in the universe. If you are particularly desirous for anything that you feel it is good and right for you to have, something that will broaden your life or that will increase your usefulness to others, simply hold the thought that at the right time, in the right way, and through the right instrumentality, there will come to you or there will open up for you the way whereby you can attain what you desire.

I know of a young lady who a short time ago wanted some money very badly. She wanted it for a good purpose; she saw no reason why she shouldn't have it. She is one who has come into an understanding of the power of the interior forces. She took and held herself in the attitude of mind we have just pointed out. In the morning she entered into the silence for a few moments. In this way she brought herself into a more complete harmony with the higher powers. Before the day closed a gentleman called, a member of a family with which she was acquainted. He asked her if she would do for the family some work that they wanted done. She was a little surprised that they should ask her to do this particular kind of work, but she said to herself, "Here is a call. I will respond and see what it will lead to." She undertook the work. *She did it well.* When she had completed it there was put into her hands an amount of money far beyond what she had expected. She felt that it was an amount too large for the work she had done. She protested. They replied, "No; you have done us a service that transcends in value the amount we offer to pay you." The sum thus received was more than sufficient for the work she wished to accomplish.

This is but one of many instances in connection with the wise and effective use of the higher powers. It also carries a lesson,—Don't fold your hands and expect to see things drop into your lap, but set into operation the higher forces and then take hold of the first thing that offers itself. Do what your hands find to do, *and do it well.* If this work is not thoroughly satisfactory to you, then affirm, believe, and expect that it is the agency that will lead you to something better. "The basis for attracting the best of all the world can give to you is to first surround, own, and live in these things in mind, or what is falsely called imagination. All so-called imaginings are realities and forces of unseen element. Live in mind in a palace and gradually palatial surroundings will gravitate to you. But so living is *not* pining, or longing, or complainingly wishing. It is when you are 'down in the world,' calmly and persistently seeing yourself as up. It is when you are now compelled to eat from a tin plate, regarding that tin plate as only the certain step to one of silver. It is *not* envying and growling at other people who have silver plate. That growling is just so much capital stock taken from the bank account of mental force."

A friend who knows the power of the interior forces, and whose life is guided in every detail by them, has given a suggestion in this form: When you are in the arms of the bear, even though he is hugging you, look him in the face and laugh, but all the time keep your eye on the bull. If you allow all of your attention to be given to the work of the bear, the bull may get entirely out of your sight. In other words, if you yield to adversity the chances are that it will master you, but if you recognize in yourself the power of mastery over conditions then adversity will yield to you, and will be changed into prosperity. If when it comes you calmly and quietly recognize it, and use the time that might otherwise be spent in regrets, and fears, and forebodings, in setting into operation the powerful forces within you, it will soon take its leave.

Faith, absolute dogmatic faith, is the only law of true success. When we recognize the fact that a man carries his success or his failure with him, and that it does not depend upon outside conditions, we will come into the possession of powers that will quickly change outside conditions into agencies that make for success. When we come into this higher realization and bring our lives into complete harmony with the higher laws, we will then be able so to focus and direct the awakened interior forces, that they will go out and return laden with that for which they are sent. We will then be great enough to attract success, and it will not always be apparently just a little ways ahead. We can then establish in ourselves a centre so strong that instead of running hither and thither for this or that, we can stay at home and draw to us the conditions we desire. If we firmly establish and hold to this centre, things will seem continually to come our way.

The majority of people of the modern world are looking for things that are practical and that can be utilized in every-day life. The more carefully we examine into the laws underlying the great truths we are considering, the more we will find that they are not only eminently practical, but in a sense, and in the deepest and truest sense, they are the only practical things there are.

There are people who continually pride themselves upon being exceedingly "practical"; but many times those who of themselves think nothing about this are the most practical people the world knows. And, on the other hand, those who take great pride in speaking of their own practicality are many times the least practical. Or again, in some ways they may be practical, but so far as life in its totality is concerned, they are absurdly impractical.

What profit, for example, can there be for the man who, materially speaking, though he has gained the whole world, has never yet become acquainted with his own soul? There are multitudes of men all about us who are entirely missing the real life, men who have not learned even the a, b, c of true living. Slaves they are, abject slaves to their temporary material accumulations. Men who thinking they possess their wealth are on the contrary completely possessed by it. Men whose lives are comparatively barren in service to those about them and to the world at large. Men who when they can no longer hold the body,—the agency by means of which they are related to the material world,—will go out poor indeed, pitiably poor. Unable to take even the smallest particle of their accumulations with them, they will enter upon the other form of life naked and destitute.

The kindly deeds, the developed traits of character, the realized powers of the soul, the real riches of the inner life and unfoldment, all those things that become our real and eternal possessions, have been given no place in their lives, and so of the real things of life they are destitute. Nay, many times worse than destitute. We must not suppose that habits once formed are any more easily broken off in the other form of life than they are in this. If one voluntarily grows a certain mania here, we must not suppose that the mere dropping of the body makes all conditions perfect. All is law, all is cause and effect. As we sow, so shall we also reap, not only in this life but in all lives.

He who is enslaved with the sole desire for material possessions here will continue to be enslaved even after he can no longer retain his body. Then, moreover, he will have not even the means of gratifying his desires. Dominated by this habit, he will be unable to set his affections, for a time at least, upon other things, and the desire, without the means of gratifying it will be doubly torturing to him. Perchance this torture may be increased by his seeing the accumulations he thought were his now being scattered and wasted by spendthrifts. He wills his property, as we say, to others, but he can have no word as to its use.

How foolish, then, for us to think that any material possessions *are ours.* How absurd, for example, for one to fence off a number of acres of God's earth and say they are *his.* Nothing is ours that we cannot retain. The things that come into our hands come not for the purpose of being possessed, as we say, much less for the purpose of being hoarded. They come into our hands to be used, to be wisely used. We are stewards merely, and as stewards we shall be held accountable for the way we use whatever is entrusted to us. That great law of compensation that runs through all life is wonderfully exact in its workings, although we may not always fully comprehend it, or even recognize it when it operates in connection with ourselves.

The one who has come into the realization of the higher life no longer has a desire for the accumulation of enormous wealth, any more than he has a desire for any other *excess.* In the degree that he comes into the recognition of the fact that he is wealthy within, external wealth becomes less important in his estimation. When he comes into the realization of the fact that there is a source within from which he can put forth a power to call to him and actualize in his hands at any time a sufficient supply for all his needs, he no longer burdens himself with vast material accumulations that require his constant care and attention, and thus take his time and his thought from the real things of life. In other words, he first finds the *kingdom,* and he realizes that when he has found this, all other things follow in full measure.

It is as hard for a rich man to enter into the kingdom of heaven, said the Master,—he who having nothing had everything,—as it is for a camel to pass through the eye of a needle. In other words, if a man give all his time to the accumulation, the hoarding of outward material possessions far beyond what he can possibly ever use, what time has he for the finding of that wonderful kingdom, which when found, brings all else with it. Which is better, to have millions of dollars, and to have the burden of taking care of it all,—for the one always involves the other,—or to come into the knowledge of such laws and forces that every need will be supplied in good time, to know that no good thing shall be withheld, to know that we have it in our power to make the supply always equal to the demand?

The one who enters into the realm of this higher knowledge, never cares to bring upon himself the species of insanity that has such a firm hold upon so many in the world today. He avoids it as he would avoid any loathsome disease of the body. When we come into the realization of the higher powers, we will then be able to give more attention to the real life, instead of giving so much to the piling up of vast possessions that hamper rather than help. It is the medium ground that brings the true solution here, the same as it is in all phases of life.

Wealth beyond a certain amount cannot be used, and when it cannot be used it then becomes a hindrance rather than an aid, a curse rather than a blessing. All about us are persons with lives now stunted and dwarfed who could make them rich and beautiful, filled with a perennial joy, if they would begin wisely to use that which they have spent the greater portion of their lives in accumulating.

The man who accumulates during his entire life, and who leaves even all when he goes out for "benevolent purposes," comes far short of the ideal life. It is but a poor excuse of a life. It is not especially commendable in me to give a pair of old, worn-out shoes that I shall never use again to another who is in need of shoes. But it is commendable, if indeed doing anything we ought to do can be spoken of as being commendable, it is commendable for me to give a good pair of strong shoes to the man who in the midst of a severe winter is practically shoeless, the man who is exerting every effort to earn an honest living and thereby take care of his family's needs. And if in giving the shoes I also give myself, he then has a double gift, and I a double blessing.

There is no wiser use that those who have great accumulations can make of them than wisely to put them into life, into character, *day by day while they live.* In this way their lives will be continually enriched and increased. The time will come when it will be regarded as a disgrace for a man to die and leave vast accumulations behind him.

Many a person is living in a palace today who in the real life is poorer than many a one who has not even a roof to cover him. A man may own and live in a palace, but the palace for him may be a poorhouse still.

Moth and rust are nature's wise provisions—God's methods—for disintegrating and scattering, in this way getting ready for use in new forms, that which is hoarded and consequently serving no use. There is also a great law continually operating whose effects are to dwarf and deaden the powers of true enjoyment, as well as all the higher faculties of the one who hoards.

Multitudes of people are continually keeping away from them higher and better things because they are forever clinging on to the old. If they would use and pass on the old, room would be made for new things to come. Hoarding always brings loss in one form or another. Using, wisely using, brings an ever renewing gain.

If the tree should as ignorantly and as greedily hold on to this year's leaves when they have served their purpose, where would be the full and beautiful new life that will be put forth in the spring? Gradual decay and finally death would be the result. If the tree is already dead, then it may perhaps be well enough for it to cling on to the old, for no new leaves will come. But as long as the life in the tree is active, it is *necessary* that it rid itself of the old ones, that room may be made for the new.

Opulence is the law of the universe, an abundant supply for every need if nothing is put in the way of its coming. The natural and the normal life for us is this,—To have such a fullness of life and power by living so continually in the realization of our oneness with the Infinite Life and Power that we find ourselves in the constant possession of an abundant supply of all things needed.

Then not by hoarding but by wisely using and ridding ourselves of things as they come, an ever renewing supply will be ours, a supply far better adapted to present needs than the old could possibly be. In this way we not only come into possession of the richest treasures of the Infinite Good ourselves, but we also become open channels through which they can flow to others.

## CHAPTER 10

# How Men Have Become Prophets, Seers, Sages, and Saviours

I have tried thus far to deal fairly with you in presenting these vital truths, and have spoken of everything on the basis of our own reason and insight. It has been my aim to base nothing on the teachings of others, though they may be the teachings of those inspired. Let us now look for a moment at these same great truths in the light of the thoughts and the teachings as put forth by some of the world's great thinkers and inspired teachers.

The sum and substance of the thought presented in these pages is, you will remember, that the great central fact in human life is the coming into a conscious, vital realization of our oneness with the Infinite Life, and the opening of ourselves fully to this divine inflow. I and the Father are one, said the Master. In this we see how he recognized his oneness with the Father's life. Again he said, The words that I speak unto you I speak not of myself: but the Father that dwelleth in me, He doeth the works. In this we see how clearly he recognized the fact that he of himself could do nothing, only as he worked in conjunction with the Father. Again, my Father works and I work. In other words, my Father sends the power, I open myself to it, and work in conjunction with it.

Again he said, Seek ye first the kingdom of God and His righteousness, and all these things shall be added unto you. And he left us not in the dark as to exactly what he meant by this, for again he said, Say not Lo here nor lo there, know ye not that the kingdom of heaven is within you? According to his teaching, the kingdom of God and the kingdom of heaven were one and the same. If, then, his teaching is that the kingdom of heaven is within us, do we not clearly see that, putting it in other words, his injunction is nothing more nor less than, Come ye into a conscious realization of your oneness with the Father's life. As you realize this oneness you find the kingdom, and when you find this, all things else shall follow.

The story of the prodigal son is another beautiful illustration of this same great teaching of the Master. After the prodigal had spent everything, after he had wandered in all the realms of the physical senses in the pursuit of happiness and pleasure, and found that this did not satisfy but only brought him to the level of the animal creation, he then came to his senses and said, I will arise and go to my Father. In other words, after all these wanderings, his own soul at length spoke to him and said, You are not a mere animal. You are your Father's child. Arise and go to your Father, who holds all things in His hands. Again, the Master said, Call no man your Father upon the earth: for one is your Father, which is in heaven. Here he recognized the fact that the real life is direct from the life of God. Our fathers and our mothers are the agents that give us the bodies, the houses in which we live, but the real life comes from the Infinite Source of Life, God, who is our Father.

One day word was brought to the Master that his mother and his brethren were without, wishing to speak with him. Who is my mother and who are my brethren? said he. Whosoever shall do the will of my Father which is in heaven, the same is my brother, and my sister, and mother.

Many people are greatly enslaved by what we term ties of relationship. It is well, however, for us to remember that our true relatives are not necessarily those who are connected with us by ties of blood. Our truest relatives are those who are nearest akin to us in mind, in soul, in spirit. Our nearest relatives may be those living on the opposite side of the globe,—people whom we may never have seen as yet, but to whom we will yet be drawn, either in this form of life or in another, through that ever working and never failing law of attraction.

When the Master gave the injunction, Call no man your father upon the earth: for one is your Father, which is in heaven, he here gave us the basis for that grand conception of the fatherhood of God. And if God is equally the Father of all, then we have here the basis for the brotherhood of man. But there is, in a sense, a conception still higher than this, namely, the oneness of man and God, and hence the oneness of the whole human race. When we realize this fact, then we clearly see how in the degree that we come into the realization of our oneness with the Infinite Life, and so, every step that we make God-ward, we aid in lifting all mankind up to this realization, and enable them, in turn, to make a step Godward.

The Master again pointed out our true relations with the Infinite Life when he said, Except ye become as little children ye shall not enter into the kingdom of heaven. When he said, Man shall not live by bread alone, but by every word that proceedeth out of the mouth of God, he gave utterance to a truth of far greater import than we have as yet commenced fully to grasp. Here he taught that even the physical life can not be maintained by material food alone, but that one's connection with this Infinite Source determines to a very great extent the condition of even the bodily structure and activities. Blessed are the pure in heart for they shall see God. In other words, blessed are they who in all the universe recognize only God, for by such God shall be seen.

Said the great Hindu sage, Manu, He who in his own soul perceives the Supreme Soul in all beings, and acquires equanimity toward them all, attains the highest bliss. It was Athanasius who said, Even we may become Gods walking about in the flesh. The same great truth we are considering is the one that runs through the life and the teachings of Gautama, he who became the Buddha. People are in bondage, said he, because they have not yet removed the idea of *I*. To do away with all sense of separateness, and to recognize the oneness of the self with the Infinite, is the spirit that breathes through all his teachings. Running through the lives of all the mediæval mystics was this same great truth,—union with God.

Then, coming nearer to our own time, we find the highly illumined seer, Emanuel Swedenborg, pointing out the great laws in connection with what he termed, the divine influx, and how we may open ourselves more fully to its operations. The great central fact in the religion and worship of the Friends is, the inner light,—God in the soul of man speaking directly in just the degree that the soul is opened to Him. The inspired one, the seer who when with us lived at Concord, recognized the same great truth when he said, We are all inlets to the great sea of life. And it was by opening himself so fully to its inflow that he became one inspired.

All through the world's history we find that the men and the women who have entered into the realm of true wisdom and power, and hence into the realm of true peace and joy, have lived in harmony with this Higher Power. David was strong and powerful and his soul burst forth in praise and adoration in just the degree that he listened to the voice of God and lived in accordance with his higher promptings. Whenever he failed to do this we hear his soul crying out in anguish and lamentation. The same is true of every nation or people. When the Israelites acknowledged God and followed according to His leadings they were prosperous, contented, and powerful, and nothing could prevail against them. When they depended upon their own strength alone and failed to recognize God as the source of their strength, we find them overcome, in bondage, or despair.

A great immutable law underlies the truth, Blessed are they that hear the word of God and do it. Then follows all. We are wise in the degree that we live according to the higher light.

All the prophets, seers, sages, and saviours in the world's history became what they became, and consequently had the powers they had, through an entirely natural process. They all recognized and came into the conscious realization of their oneness with the Infinite Life. God is no respecter of persons. He doesn't create prophets, seers, sages, and saviours as such. He creates men. But here and there one recognizes his true identity, recognizes the oneness of his life with the Source whence it came. He lives in the realization of this oneness, and in turn becomes a prophet, seer, sage, or saviour. Neither is God a respecter of races or of nations. He has no chosen people; but here and there a race or nation becomes a respecter of God and hence lives the life of a chosen people.

There has been no age or place of miracles in distinction from any other age or place. What we term miracles have abounded in all places and at all times where conditions have been made for them. They are being performed today just as much as they ever have been when the laws governing them are respected. Mighty men, we are told they were, mighty men who walked with God; and in the words "who walked with God" lies the secret of the words "mighty men." Cause, effect.

The Lord never prospers any man, but the man prospers because he acknowledges the Lord, and lives in accordance with the higher laws. Solomon was given the opportunity of choosing whatever he desired; his better judgment prevailed and he chose wisdom. But when he chose wisdom he found that it included all else beside. We are told that God hardened Pharaoh's heart. I don't believe it. God never hardens any one's heart. Pharaoh hardened his own heart and God was blamed for it. But when Pharaoh hardened his heart and disobeyed the voice of God, the plagues came. Again, cause, effect. Had he, on the contrary, listened,—in other words, had he opened himself to and obeyed the voice of God, the plagues would not have come.

We can be our own best friends or we can be our own worst enemies. In the degree that we become friends to the highest and best within us, we become friends to all; and in the degree that we become enemies to the highest and best within us, do we become enemies to all. In the degree that we open ourselves to the higher powers and let them manifest through us, then by the very inspirations we carry with us do we become in a sense the saviours of our fellow-men, and in this way we all are, or may become, the saviours one of another. In this way you may become, indeed, one of the world's redeemers.

CHAPTER 11

# The Basic Principle of All Religions—The Universal Religion

The great truth we are considering is the fundamental principle running through all religions. We find it in every one. In regard to it all agree. It is, moreover, a great truth in regard to which all people can agree, whether they belong to the same or to different religions. People always quarrel about the trifles, about their personal views of minor insignificant points. They always come together in the presence of great fundamental truths, the threads of which run through all. The quarrels are in connection with the lower self, the agreements are in connection with the higher self.

A place may have its factions that quarrel and fight among themselves, but let a great calamity come upon the land, flood, famine, pestilence, and these little personal differences are entirely forgotten and all work shoulder to shoulder in the one great cause. The changing, the evolving self gives rise to quarrels; the permanent, the soul self unites all in the highest efforts of love and service.

Patriotism is a beautiful thing; it is well for me to love my country, but why should I love my own country more than I love all others? If I love my own and hate others, I then show my limitations, and my patriotism will stand the test not even for my own. If I love my own country and in the same way love all other countries, then I show the largeness of my nature, and a patriotism of this kind is noble and always to be relied upon.

The view of God in regard to which we are agreed, that He is the Infinite Spirit of Life and Power that is back of all, that is working in and through all, that is the life of all, is a matter in regard to which all men, all religions can agree. With this view there can be no infidels or atheists. There are atheists and infidels in connection with many views that are held concerning God, and thank God there are. Even devout and earnest people among us attribute things to God that no respectable men or women would permit to be attributed to themselves. This view is satisfying to those who cannot see how God can be angry with his children, jealous, vindictive. A display of these qualities always lessens our respect for men and women, and still we attribute them to God.

The earnest, sincere heretic is one of the greatest friends true religion can have. Heretics are among God's greatest servants. They are among the true servants of mankind. Christ was one of the greatest heretics the world has ever known. He allowed himself to be bound by no established or orthodox teachings or beliefs. Christ is preeminently a type of the universal. John the Baptist is a type of the personal. John dressed in a particular way, ate a particular kind of food, belonged to a particular order, lived and taught in a particular locality, and he himself recognized the fact that he must decrease while Christ must increase. Christ, on the other hand, gave himself absolutely no limitations. He allowed himself to be bound by nothing. He was absolutely universal and as a consequence taught not for his own particular day, but for all time.

This mighty truth which we have agreed upon as the great central fact of human life is the golden thread that runs through all religions. When we make it the paramount fact in our lives we will find that minor differences, narrow prejudices, and all these laughable absurdities will so fall away by virtue of their very insignificance, that a Jew can worship equally as well in a Catholic cathedral, a Catholic in a Jewish synagogue, a Buddhist in a Christian church, a Christian in a Buddhist temple. Or all can worship equally well about their own hearth-stones, or out on the hillside, or while pursuing the avocations of every-day life. For true worship, only God and the human soul are necessary. It does not depend upon times, or seasons, or occasions. Anywhere and at any time God and man in the bush may meet.

This is the great fundamental principle of the universal religion upon which all can agree. This is the great fact that is permanent. There are many things in regard to which all cannot agree. These are the things that are personal, non-essential, and so as time passes they gradually fall away. One who doesn't grasp this great truth, a Christian, for example, asks, "But was not Christ inspired?" Yes, but he was not the only one inspired. Another who is a Buddhist asks, "Was not Buddha inspired?" Yes, but he was not the only one inspired. A Christian asks, "But is not our Christian Bible inspired?" Yes, but there are other inspired scriptures. A Brahmin or a Buddhist asks, "Are not the Vedas inspired?" Yes, but there are other inspired sacred books. Your error is not in believing that your particular scriptures are inspired, but your error is—and you show your absurdly laughable limitations by it—your inability to see that other scriptures are also inspired.

The sacred books, the inspired writings, all come from the same source,—God, God speaking through the souls of those who open themselves that He may thus speak. Some may be more inspired than others. It depends entirely on the relative degree that this one or that one opens himself to the Divine voice. Says one of the inspired writers in the Hebrew scriptures, Wisdom is the breath of the power of God, and *in all ages* entering into holy souls she maketh them friends of God and prophets.

Let us not be among the number so dwarfed, so limited, so bigoted as to think that the Infinite God has revealed Himself to one little handful of His children, in one little quarter of the globe, and at one particular period of time. This isn't the pattern by which God works. Of a truth I perceive that God is no respecter of persons, but in every nation he that revereth God and worketh righteousness is accepted of Him, says the Christian Bible.

When we fully realize this truth we will then see that it makes but little difference what particular form of religion one holds to, but it does make a tremendous difference how true he is to the *vital* principles of this one. In the degree that we love self less and love truth more, in that degree will we care less about converting people to our particular way of thinking, but all the more will we care to aid them in coming into the full realization of truth through the channels best adapted to them. The doctrine of our master, says the Chinese, consisted solely in integrity of heart. We will find as we search that this is the doctrine of every one who is at all worthy of the name of master.

The great fundamental principles of all religions are the same. They differ only in their minor details according to the various degrees of unfoldment of different people. I am sometimes asked, "To what religion do you belong?" What religion? Why, bless you, there is only one religion,—the religion of the living God. There are, of course, the various creeds of the same religion arising from the various interpretations of different people, but they are all of minor importance. The more unfolded the soul the less important do these minor differences become. There are also, of course, the various so-called religions. There is in reality, however, but one religion.

The moment we lose sight of this great fact we depart from the real, vital spirit of true religion and allow ourselves to be limited and bound by form. In the degree that we do this we build fences around ourselves which keep others away from us, and which also prevent our coming into the realization of universal truth; there is nothing worthy the name of truth that is not universal.

There is only one religion. "Whatever road I take joins the highway that leads to Thee," says the inspired writer in the Persian scriptures. "Broad is the carpet God has spread, and beautiful the colors he has given it." "The pure man respects every form of faith," says the Buddhist. "My doctrine makes no difference between high and low, rich and poor; like the sky, it has room for all, and like the water, it washes all alike." "The broad minded see the truth in different religions; the narrow minded see only the differences," says the Chinese. The Hindu has said, "The narrow minded ask, 'Is this man a stranger, or is he of our tribe?' But to those in whom love dwells, the whole world is but one family." "Altar flowers are of many species, but all worship is one." "Heaven is a palace with many doors, and each may enter in his own way." "Are we not all children of one Father?" says the Christian. "God has made of one blood all nations, to dwell on the face of the earth." It was a latter-day seer who said, "That which was profitable to the soul of man the Father revealed to the ancients; that which is profitable to the soul of man today revealeth He this day."

It was Tennyson who said, "I dreamed that stone by stone I reared a sacred fane, a temple, neither pagoda, mosque, nor church, but loftier, simpler, always open-doored to every breath from heaven, and Truth and Peace and Love and Justice came and dwelt therein."

Religion in its true sense is the most joyous thing the human soul can know, and when the real religion is realized, we will find that it will be an agent of peace, of joy, and of happiness, and never an agent of gloomy, long-faced sadness. It will then be attractive to all and repulsive to none. Let our churches grasp these great truths, let them give their time and attention to bringing people into a knowledge of their true selves, into a knowledge of their relations, of their oneness, with the Infinite God, and such joy will be the result, and such crowds will flock to them, that their very walls will seem almost to burst, and such songs of joy will continually pour forth as will make all people in love with the religion that makes for every-day life, and hence the religion that is true and vital. Adequacy for life, adequacy for every-day life here and now, must be the test of all true religion. If it does not bear this test, then it simply is not religion. We need an every-day, a this-world religion. All time spent in connection with any other is worse than wasted. The eternal life that we are now living will be well lived if we take good care of each little period of time as it presents itself day after day. If we fail in doing this, we fail in everything.

CHAPTER 12

# Entering Now into the Realization of the Highest Riches

I hear the question, What can be said in a concrete way in regard to the method of coming into this realization? The facts underlying it are, indeed, most beautiful and true, but how can we actualize in ourselves the realization that carries with it such wonderful results?

The method is not difficult if we do not of ourselves make it difficult. The principal word to be used is the word,—Open. Simply to open your mind and heart to this divine inflow which is waiting only for the opening of the gate, that it may enter. It is like opening the gate of the trough which conducts the water from the reservoir above into the field below. The water, by virtue of its very nature, will rush in and irrigate the field if the gate is but opened. As to the realization of our oneness with this Infinite Life and Power, after seeing, as I think we have clearly seen by this time, the relations it bears to us and we to it, the chief thing to be said is simply,—Realize your oneness with it. The open mind and heart whereby one is brought into the receptive attitude is the first thing necessary. Then the earnest, sincere desire.

It may be an aid at first to take yourself for a few moments each day into the quiet, into the silence, where you will not be agitated by the disturbances that enter in through the avenues of the physical senses. There in the quiet alone with God, put yourself into the receptive attitude. Calmly, quietly, and expectantly desire that this realization break in upon and take possession of your soul. As it breaks in upon and takes possession of the soul, it will manifest itself to your mind, and from this you will feel its manifestations in every part of your body. Then in the degree that you open yourself to it you will feel a quiet, peaceful, illuminating power that will harmonize body, soul, and mind, and that will then harmonize these with all the world. You are now on the mountain top and the voice of God is speaking to you. *Then, as you descend, carry this realization with you.* Live in it, waking, working, thinking, walking, sleeping. In this way, although you may not be continually on the mountain top, you will nevertheless be continually living in the realization of all the beauty, and inspiration, and power you have felt there.

Moreover, the time will come when in the busy office or on the noisy street you can enter into the silence by simply drawing the mantle of your own thoughts about you and realizing that there and everywhere the Spirit of Infinite Life, Love, Wisdom, Peace, Power, and Plenty is guiding, keeping, protecting, leading you. This is the spirit of continual prayer. This it is to pray without ceasing. This it is to know and to walk with God. *This it is to find the Christ within.* This is the new birth, the second birth. First that which is natural, then that which is spiritual. It is thus that the old man Adam is put off and the new man Christ is put on. This it is to be saved unto life eternal, whatever one's form of belief or faith may be; for it is life eternal to know God. "The Sweet By and By" will be a song of the past. We will create a new song —"The Beautiful Eternal Now."

This is the realization that you and I can come into this very day, this very hour, this very minute, if we desire and if we will it. And if now we merely set our faces in the right direction, it is then but a matter of time until we come into the full splendors of this complete realization. To set one's face in the direction of the mountain and then simply to journey on, whether rapidly or more slowly, will bring him to it. But unless one set his face in the right direction and make the start, he will not reach it. It was Goethe who said:

> *Are you in earnest? Seize this very minute:*
> *What you can do, or dream you can, begin it;*
> *Boldness has genius, power, and magic in it.*
> *Only engage and then the mind grows heated;*
> *Begin and then the work will be completed.*

Said the young man, Gautama Siddhaˆrtha, I have awakened to the truth and I am resolved to accomplish my purpose,—Verily I shall become a Buddha. It was this that brought him into the life of the Enlightened One, and so into the realization of Nirvana right here in this life. That this same realization and life is within the possibilities of all here and now was his teaching. It was this that has made him the Light Bearer to millions of people.

Said the young man, Jesus, Know ye not that I must be about my Father's business? Making this the one great purpose of his life he came into the full and complete realization,—I and the Father are one. He thus came into the full realization of the Kingdom of Heaven right here in this life. That all could come into this same realization and life here and now was his teaching. It was this that has made him the Light Bearer to millions of people.

And so far as practical things are concerned, we may hunt the wide universe through and we shall find that there is no injunction more practical than, Seek ye first the kingdom of God and His righteousness and all other things shall be added unto you. And in the light of what has gone before, I think there is no one who is open to truth and honest with himself who will fail to grasp the underlying reason and see the great laws upon which it is based.

Personally I know lives that have so fully entered into the kingdom through the realization of their oneness with the Infinite Life and through the opening of themselves so fully to its divine guidance, that they are most wonderful concrete examples of the reality of this great and all-important truth. They are people whose lives are in this way guided not only in a general way, but literally in every detail. They simply live in the realization of their oneness with this Infinite Power, continually in harmony with it, and so continually in the realization of the kingdom of heaven. An abundance of all things is theirs. They are never at a loss for anything. The supply seems always equal to the demand. They never seem at a loss in regard to what to do or how to do it. Their lives are care-less lives. They are lives free from care because they are continually conscious of the fact that the higher powers are doing the guiding, and they are relieved of the responsibility. To enter into detail in connection with some of these lives, and particularly with two or three that come to my mind at this moment, would reveal facts that no doubt to some would seem almost incredible if not miraculous. But let us remember that what is possible for one life to realize is possible for all. This is indeed the natural and the normal life, that which will be the every-day life of every one who comes into and who lives in this higher realization and so in harmony with the higher laws. This is simply getting into the current of that divine sequence running throughout the universe; and when once in it, life then ceases to be a plodding and moves along day after day much as the tides flow, much as the planets move in their courses, much as the seasons come and go.

All the frictions, all the uncertainties, all the ills, the sufferings, the fears, the forebodings, the perplexities of life come to us because we are out of harmony with the divine order of things. They will continue to come as long as we so live. Rowing against the tide is hard and uncertain. To go with the tide and thus to take advantage of the working of a great natural force is safe and easy. To come into the conscious, vital realization of our oneness with the Infinite Life and Power is to come into the current of this divine sequence. Coming thus into harmony with the Infinite, brings us in turn into harmony with all about us, into harmony with the life of the heavens, into harmony with all the universe. And above all, it brings us into harmony with ourselves, so that body, soul, and mind become perfectly harmonized, and when this is so, life becomes full and complete.

The sense life then no longer masters and enslaves us. The physical is subordinated to and ruled by the mental; this in turn is subordinated to and continually illumined by the spiritual. Life is then no longer the poor, one-sided thing it is in so many cases; but the threefold, the all-round life with all its beauties and ever increasing joys and powers is entered upon. Thus it is that we are brought to realize that the middle path is the great solution of life; neither asceticism on the one hand nor license and perverted use on the other. Everything is for use, but all must be wisely used in order to be fully enjoyed.

As we live in these higher realizations the senses are not ignored but are ever more fully perfected. As the body becomes less gross and heavy, finer in its texture and form, all the senses become finer, so that powers we do not now realize as belonging to us gradually develop. Thus we come, in a perfectly natural and normal way, into the super-conscious realms whereby we make it possible for the higher laws and truths to be revealed to us. As we enter into these realms we are then not among those who give their time in speculating as to whether this one or that one had the insight and the powers attributed to him, but we are able *to know* for ourselves. Neither are we among those who attempt to lead the people upon the hearsay of some one else, but we know whereof we speak, and only thus can we speak with authority. There are many things that we cannot know until by living the life we bring ourselves into that state where it is possible for them to be revealed to us. "If any man will do His will, he shall know of the doctrine." It was Plotinus who said, The mind that wishes to behold God must itself become God. As we thus make it possible for these higher laws and truths to be revealed to us, we will in turn become enlightened ones, channels through which they may be revealed to others.

When one is fully alive to the possibilities that come with this higher awakening, as he goes here and there, as he mingles with his fellow-men, he imparts to all an inspiration that kindles in them a feeling of power kindred to his own. We are all continually giving out influences similar to those that are playing in our own lives. We do this in the same way that each flower emits its own peculiar odor. The rose breathes out its fragrance upon the air and all who come near it are refreshed and inspired by this emanation from the soul of the rose. A poisonous weed sends out its obnoxious odor; it is neither refreshing nor inspiring in its effects, and if one remain near it long he may be so unpleasantly affected as to be made even ill by it.

The higher the life the more inspiring and helpful are the emanations that it is continually sending out. The lower the life the more harmful is the influence it continually sends out to all who come in contact with it. Each one is continually radiating an atmosphere of one kind or the other.

We are told by the mariners who sail on the Indian Seas, that many times they are able to tell their approach to certain islands long before they can see them by the sweet fragrance of the sandalwood that is wafted far out upon the deep. Do you not see how it would serve to have such a soul playing through such a body that as you go here and there a subtle, silent force goes out from you that all feel and are influenced by; so that you carry with you an inspiration and continually shed a benediction wherever you go; so that your friends and all people will say,—His coming brings peace and joy into our homes, welcome his coming; so that as you pass along the street, tired, and weary, and even sin-sick men and women will feel a certain divine touch that will awaken new desires and a new life in them; that will make the very horse as you pass him turn his head with a strange, half-human, longing look? Such are the subtle powers of the human soul when it makes itself translucent to the Divine. To know that such a life is within our living here and now is enough to make one burst forth with songs of joy. And when the life itself is entered upon, the sentiment of at least one song will be:

*Oh! I stand in the Great Forever,*
*All things to me are divine;*
*I eat of the heavenly manna,*
*I drink of the heavenly wine.*

*In the gleam of the shining rainbow*
*The Father's Love I behold,*
*As I gaze on its radiant blending*
*Of crimson and blue and gold.*

*In all the bright birds that are singing,*
*In all the fair flowers that bloom,*
*Whose welcome aromas are bringing*
*Their blessings of sweet perfume;*

*In the glorious tint of the morning,*
*In the gorgeous sheen of the night,*
*Oh! my soul is lost in rapture,*
*My senses are lost in sight.*

As one comes into and lives continually in the full, conscious realization of his oneness with the Infinite Life and Power, then all else follows. This it is that brings the realization of such splendors, and beauties, and joys as a life that is thus related with the Infinite Power alone can know. This it is to come into the realization of heaven's richest treasures while walking the earth. This it is to bring heaven down to earth, or rather to bring earth up to heaven. This it is to exchange weakness and impotence for strength; sorrows and sighings for joy; fears and forebodings for faith; longings for realizations. This it is to come into fullness of peace, power, and plenty. This it is to be in tune with the Infinite.

CHAPTER 13

# "The Way"

Life is not so complex if we do not so persistently make it so. We accept the results or the effects; but we concern ourselves all too little with the realm of cause. The springs of life are all from within. Invariably it is true—as is the inner so always and inevitably will be the outer.

There is a Divine current that will bear us with peace and safety on its bosom if we are sufficiently alert and determined to find it—and go with it. The natural, normal life is by a law divine under the guidance of the Spirit.

There is a mystic force that transcends the powers of the intellect and likewise of the body. There are certain faculties that we have that are not a part of the active, thinking mind; they transcend any possible activities of the active thinking mind. Through them we have intuitions, impulses, leadings, that instead of being merely the occasional, *should be the normal and habitual.*

They would be if we understood better the laws that pertain to them and observe them; for here, as in connection with everything in the universe and everything in human life, all is governed by law—the Elemental law of cause and effect. Supreme Intelligence, Creative Power, works only through law. There is an inner spirit or guide that rules and regulates the life when the life is brought into that state or condition whereby it can make itself known, and in turn, dominate the life.

Jesus, Master of the laws of life, and supreme revealer of them to men, had a full and practical knowledge of it. He not only abundantly demonstrated it in his own life, but he made clear the way whereby it may become the common possession of other lives; for—do not worry about your life—was his clear-cut and repeated command. He not only gave the injunction or command, but he demonstrated the method whereby the fears and forebodings and uncertainties of life, can be displaced by a force or a power that will bring them to an end.

It was embodied in his other injunction or command that he gave utterance to so repeatedly: "Seek ye first the Kingdom of God and His righteousness and all these things shall be added to you." And by all these things, he meant, all of the common needs and necessities of the daily life.

The finding of the Kingdom of God is the recognition of the indwelling Divine Life as the source and therefore as the Essence of our own lives. It is the bringing of men's minds and therefore acts into harmony with the Divine will and purpose. It is the saving of men from their lower conceptions and selves, and a lifting them up to a realization of their higher selves, which as he taught, is eternally one with God, the Father; and which, when realized, lifts a man's thoughts, acts, purposes and conduct—his entire life—up to that pattern or standard.

It was not merely a poetic fancy, but the recognition of a fundamental law, as well-known laws of modern psychology, mental and spiritual science, are now clearly demonstrating, that induced the Prophet to say: "And thine ears shall hear a word behind thee, saying, This is the way, walk ye in it, when ye turn to the right-hand and when ye turn to the left." And again: "The Lord in the midst of thee is mighty." And still again: "He that dwelleth in the secret place of the Most High shall abide under the shadow of the Almighty."

How often do the meagre accounts of the Master's life tell us of his going up to the mountain to pray—*for communion with the Father.* And then we find him invariably down among men, always where the need for help and for human service was the greatest.

This habit of taking a little time daily, alone in the quiet, in communion with one's Source, that the illumination and guidance of the Holy Spirit may become alive and active in the life, and going then about one's daily work ever open to and conscious of this Divine guidance, trusting and resting it in, strengthened and sustained always by this Divine power, will bring definiteness and direction, will bring hope and courage, will bring peace and power to every one who will heed the Master's injunction and will follow his example. These it has brought to great numbers to whom before, life was an enigma; and this because the life had been lived entirely from the outside.

The higher forces and powers of the inner life, those of the mind and spirit, always potential within, become of actual value only as they are recognized, realized, and used.

The Master's *Way of the Spirit,* the finding of the Kingdom within, leads into no blind alley. It leads out and triumphantly out onto the great plain of clear vision, of unself-centred activity, of heroic endeavor and accomplishment.

If we would spend a fraction of the time that we spend in needless anxiety, in definite constructive thought, in "silent demand," visualizing the conditions that we would have, with faith in their fulfillment, we would soon know that the Master's illustration of the care-free bird is fact and not fancy—It is, he said, what life should be.

The little time spent in the quiet each day—alone with one's God—that we may make and keep our connection with the Infinite Source—our source and our life—

will be a boon to any life. It will prove, if we are faithful, to be the most priceless possession that we have.

While it is impossible for one to make a formula for another that one should follow, the following may perchance contain some little suggestions—each must follow his or her own leading and therefore method:

My Father in Heaven, Infinite Spirit of life and love and wisdom and power, in whom I live and move and have my being, whence cometh my help, manifest Thyself in me.

Help me to open myself to the highest wisdom and insight and love and power, that I may serve Thee and my fellow-men, and all my fellow-creatures faithfully, and that I may have the Divine guidance and care, and that all my needs be supplied.

Oh *Christ within,* enfold and lead me and reign supreme, that the One Life that is my life, I may realize and manifest ever more fully.

I am strong in the Infinite Spirit of life and love and wisdom and power. I have and shall have the Divine guidance and care; for it is the Father that worketh in me—My Father works and I work.

The following little motto—A resolve for today—may contain a little aid for the following of the *Way:*

### I AM RESOLVED

I believe that my Brother intended that I take his teachings in the simple, frank, and open manner in which he gave them, out on the hill-side, by the calm blue waters of the Galilean sea, and out under the stars of heaven.

I believe that he knew what he meant, and that he meant what he said, when he gave the substance of all religion and the duty of man, as love to God, and love and service for his fellow-men.

I am therefore resolved at this, the beginning of another day, this fresh beginning of life, to go forth eager and happy and unafraid, in that I can come into the same filial relations of love and guidance and care with my Father in Heaven, that my Elder Brother realized and lived, and going before revealed to me.

I shall listen intently to know, and shall run with eager feet to do my Father's will, calm and quiet within, knowing that I shall have the Divine guidance and care, and that no harm therefore shall befall me; for I am now living in God's life and there I shall live forever.

I am resolved in all human contact to meet petulance with patience, questionings with kindness, hatred with love, eager always to do the kindly deed that brings the joy of service—and that alone makes human life truly human.

I shall seek no advantage for myself to the detriment or the harm of my neighbor, knowing that it is only through the law of mutuality that I can fully enjoy what I gain—or can even be a man.

I am resolved therefore so to live this day, that when the twilight comes and the night falls, I shall be not only another day's journey nearer home; but I shall have lived a man's part and done a man's work in the world—and shall indeed deserve my Father's love and care.

# THE MENTAL EQUIVALENT

EMMET FOX

(1943)

This booklet is the substance of two lectures
delivered by Emmet Fox at Unity School of Christianity,
Kansas City, Mo.

We are all supremely interested in one subject. There is one thing that means more to us than all the other things in the world put together, and that is our search for God and the understanding of His nature. The aim of the metaphysical movement is to teach the practice of the presence of God.

We practice the presence of God by seeing Him everywhere, in all things and in all people, despite any appearances to the contrary. As we look about the world with the eyes of the flesh, we see inharmony, fear, and all sorts of difficulties; but our leader Jesus Christ taught us, saying, "Judge not according to appearance, but judge righteous judgment." So when we see the appearance of evil we look through it to the truth that lies back of it. As soon as we see this truth, and see it spiritually, the appearance changes, because this is a mental world. Now most people do not know this: they think it is a material world, and that is why humanity has so many problems. After nineteen centuries of formal Christianity the world is passing through desperate difficulties. But we know the Truth; we do not judge by appearances. We know that we live in a mental world, and to know that is the key to life.

If a child could be taught only one thing, it should be taught that this is a mental world. I would let all the other things go and teach him that.

Whatever enters into your life is but the material expression of some belief in your own mind. The kind of body you have, the kind of home you have, the kind of work you do, the kind of people you meet, are all conditioned by and correspond to the mental concepts you are holding. The Bible teaches that from beginning to end. I am putting it in the language of metaphysics; the Bible gives it in the language of religion, but it is the same Truth.

About twenty years ago I coined the phrase "mental equivalent." And now I want to say that for anything that you want in your life—a healthy body, a satisfactory vocation, friends, opportunities, and above all the understanding of God—you must furnish a mental equivalent. Supply yourself with a mental equivalent, and the thing must come to you. Without a mental equivalent it cannot come. Now as to the things in your life that you would like to be rid of, (everyone has such things in his life). Perhaps bodily difficulties or faults of character are the most important. We all have habits of thought and action, and we all have business, family, and personal conditions we would like to be rid of. If we rid our mind of the mental equivalent of them, they must go.

Everything that you see or feel on the material plane, whether it is your body, your home, your business, or your city, is but the expression in the concrete of a mental equivalent held by you. Everything in your city is the embodiment of mental equivalents held by the citizens. Everything in your country is the embodiment of mental equivalents held by the people of the country; and the state of the world embodies the mental equivalent of the two thousand million people who make up the world.

What about war? That is the physical expression of a mental equivalent held by the human race. The human race has believed in the old bogey of fear. It has believed that you can enrich yourself by taking something belonging to someone else. It has believed in death. It has believed in lack. It has believed that aggression pays and that helping yourself to other people's things is a good policy. We have all believed this in some degree. The natural result of this has been to precipitate in the outer a picture of war, death, suffering, and so on. Because humanity had the mental equivalent of war the war came.

Today the world is beginning to get the mental equivalent of peace, and that is why peace will come. A new world will come. The new world will be worth living in. In the great new world that is going to come a little later on—and it will come sooner than some people think—there will be peace, harmony, and understanding between man and man and between nation and nation; but *always the thing you see in the outer is the precipitation on the physical plane of a mental equivalent held by one or more people.*

Now of course I borrowed this expression "mental equivalent" from physics and chemistry. We speak of the mechanical equivalent of heat, for example, and engineers constantly have to work out the equivalent of one kind of energy in another kind of energy. They have to discover how much electricity they will need to do certain mechanical work, such as driving a compressor. They have to find out how much coal will be needed to produce so much electricity, and so on. In like manner *there is a mental equivalent of every object or occurrence on the physical plane.*

The secret of successful living is to build up the mental equivalent that you want; and to get rid of, to expunge, the mental equivalent that you do not want.

Suppose you have rheumatism. I have friends in London who have it all the time; in fact, rheumatism used to be called the national British disease. Some people there have it beginning in October and lasting until March; others only have it until Christmas; others do not get it before Christmas and then have it until February. Of two men living in the same town, doing the same work, eating the same food, drinking the same water, why does one have to have rheumatism from October until February and the other does not have it at all or has it at a different time? Why? Because they have furnished the mental equivalent for what they get. Why is a quarrelsome person always in trouble? He makes New York too hot to hold him, so he goes to Chicago. He thinks he will like it in Chicago; but pretty soon he has enemies in Chicago, so he goes down to Kansas City. He has heard there are nice people there. But soon he is in trouble again. Why? He has what we call a quarrelsome disposition. He has the mental equivalent of strife.

There is another man, and wherever he goes there is peace. If there is a quarrelsome family and he visits them, there is peace while he is there. He has the mental equivalent of peace and true divine love.

So the key to life is to build in the mental equivalents of what you want and to expunge the equivalents of what you do not want. How do you do it? You build in the mental equivalents by thinking quietly, constantly, and persistently of the kind of thing you want, and by thinking that has two qualities: *clearness* or definiteness, and *interest.* If you want to build anything into your life—if you want to bring health, right activity, your true place, inspiration; if you want to bring right companionship, and above all if you want understanding of God—form a mental equivalent of the thing which you want by thinking about it a great deal, by thinking clearly and with interest. Remember *clarity* and *interest;* those are the two poles.

# Universal Polarity

The law of polarity is of course a cosmic law. Everything is produced by two other things. Anything that is ever produced anywhere in the universe is produced by two other things. That is the law of polarity. In the organic world we see it as parenthood. In the inorganic world, the world of physics and chemistry, we see it as the protons and electrons. That is how the material universe is built up; it always takes two things to produce a third. And that is the real ultimate meaning back of the Trinity.

There were Trinitarian doctrines before the time of Christ. They had trinities in ancient Egypt and India and in Chaldea and Babylonia—always there is the trinity: father, mother, child: activity, material, production. Go where you like, seek where you will, you find the Trinity.

In the building up of thought the two poles are clarity of thought and warmth of feeling; the knowledge and the feeling. Ninety-nine times in a hundred the reason why metaphysical students do not demonstrate is that they lack the feeling in their treatments. They speak the Truth, oh, yes! "I am divine Spirit. I am one with God." But they do not feel it. The second pole is missing. When they talk about their troubles they are full of feeling, but when they speak of Truth they are about as cold as a dead fish; and I cannot think of anything chillier than a cold fish unless it is a metaphysician who has lost his contact with God. They say, "I am divine Spirit," and they say it with no feeling; but when they say, "I have a terrible pain!" it is loaded with feeling, and so the pain they get and the pain they keep.

A man is out of work and he says: "God is my infinite supply. Man is always in his true place." It is said perfunctorily, with no feeling. But if someone asks him whether he has found work, he says: "I have been out of work two years. I wrote letters. I went after that job, but they were prejudiced against me. They wouldn't give me a chance." As soon as he gets on the negative side, the feeling comes in, and he demonstrates that—he remains unemployed. To think clearly and with feeling leads to demonstration, because you have then built a *mental equivalent.*

Think of the conditions you want to produce. If you want to be healthy, happy, prosperous, doing a constructive work, having a continuous understanding of God, you do not picture it necessarily, but you think it, feel it, and get interested in it. What we call "feeling" in connection with thought is really interest. Feeling is not excitement. Did you ever hear of anything coming from excitement except apoplexy? True "feeling" in thought is *interest.*

You cannot show me any man or woman who is successful in his field, from president down to shoeblack, who is not interested in his work; nor can you show me any man who has his heart in his work who is not successful. The most successful shoeblack you have in town here is vitally interested in his work. He has his heart in it. He is a colored boy, and he loves his work. He did such good work that I gave him an extra tip when he finished polishing my shoes, but no money could really pay him for his work. He was so tickled as he did his work, he loved it so much, that I did not really pay him. He paid himself. He enjoyed it. And he had a line of people waiting for him.

You build a mental equivalent for what you want by getting interested in it. That is the way you create feeling. If you want health, get interested in health. If you want the right place, get interested in service, doing something that is really serving your fellow man.

The reason people do not get ahead in business is that they try to think up schemes to get their fellow men's money instead of thinking up opportunities for service. The successful man gets interested in what he wants to do, and gets rid of things he is not interested in.

How are you going to expunge the wrong mental equivalents? Suppose you have a mental equivalent of resentment, or unemployment, or criticism, or not understanding God. When somebody talks about God, it does not interest you much, you get sleepy or bored. Perhaps you do not get along with people—not that you quarrel with them, but they quarrel with you—the quarrel happens! What is to be done?

The only way to expunge a wrong mental equivalent is to supply the opposite. Think the right thing. The right thought automatically expunges the wrong thought. If you say: "I am not going to think resentment any more. I don't believe in it. There is nothing to it. I am not going to think of it any more," what are you thinking about except resentment? You are still thinking resentment all the time and strengthening the mental equivalent of resentment. Forget it! Think of health and bodily ease and peace and harmony and speak the word for it. Then you are building up a mental equivalent of health. If you want your true place—if your problem is unemployment, no job, the wrong job, or a job you do not like—if you say, "I am not going to think unemployment any more," you are wrong. That is thinking "unemployment," is it not? Think "true place."

If I say to you, "Don't think of the Statue of Liberty in New York," you know what you are thinking about. You are not thinking of anything except the Statue of Liberty. There she is, complete with torch in her hand! I said, "Don't think of her," but you do.

Now I am going to say that some time ago I visited, near Springfield, Illinois, a perfect reproduction of the village of New Salem as it was in the days of Abraham Lincoln. Even the log cabin is furnished as it was in his day. The National Park Commission has done it all.

Now you have forgotten the Statue of Liberty for a few seconds, haven't you? You have been thinking of New Salem. I gave you a different idea. That is the key to the management of your mind, the management of your thinking, and therefore the key to the management of your destiny.

Do not dwell on negative things but replace them, supplant them, with the right, constructive things. The law of mind is that you can only get rid of one thought by substituting another. If a carpenter drives a nail into a wooden wall or into a beam, there it is. Now if he takes a second nail and drives it against the first, the first is driven out and falls on the floor and the second one takes the place of the first one. That is what happens in the mind when you substitute one image for another. For everything in life there has to be a mental equivalent.

If you will start in this very day and refuse to think of your mistakes—and of course that includes the mistakes of other people—if you will cease to think of mistakes and hold the right concepts instead, cease to think fear and think of divine love instead, cease to think lack and think prosperity and the presence of God's abundance instead—and then if you will think as clearly as possible and get *interested;* you will be building a mental equivalent of happiness and prosperity.

If your thought is very vague, you do not build a mental equivalent. If your thought is lacking in interest, you do not build a mental equivalent. So make your thoughts as clear and definite as possible. Never strain. As soon as you start straining, taking the clenching-the-fist attitude, saying, "I am going to get what I want; I am going to get it if it kills me," all mental building stops.

We have all been told to relax. I have seen people tense up as soon as they were told to relax. They were going to relax if it killed them; and of course they missed the whole point.

Get the thought of what you want as clear as you can. Be definite but not too specific.

If you live in an apartment and say, "I want a house in the country or in the suburbs, and I want it to have a porch and a large yard with trees and flowers," that is all right. But do not say, "I must have a certain house—the one at 257 Ninth Street or 21 Fifth Avenue."

Suppose you go shopping. Well, you should know what you are shopping for. You should have some definite idea. If you say, "I want something, I don't know what—I will leave it to God"; if you say, "I want a business, it may be a farm or a shop I want—I will leave it to Divine Mind," you are foolish. What are you here for? You must have some desires and wishes, because you represent God here. So you must say, "Yes, I want a shop; and I know the kind of shop I want."

I know a woman who demonstrated a hat shop. She had no capital, but she wanted to go into business. She wanted a hat shop. She loves to make hats. She has a natural flair for it. She can make hats that look well on the homeliest people; and this is the art of millinery, isn't it? She was a good businesswoman, so she built the mental equivalent of a hat shop. She did not say, "I must be in a certain block on a certain street." She did not say, "I am going to get a hat shop if it kills me" or "I am going to get a hat shop, and I want Jane Smith's hat shop." She built a definite mental equivalent, and that is the right way. If you say, "I want a strong, healthy body," and build up a mental equivalent for it by constantly thinking of your body as perfect, that is fine. Do not think of details very much. Do not say, "First of all I'm going to get my teeth fixed up with right thought, and I'll let my bald head wait" or "Maybe I should get my bald head fixed up first, because my teeth can wait." It is the details that are wrong. The evil of outlining lies in going into small details and in saying, "I want it in my time, in my way, whether God wants it or not." Apart from that (going too much into small details) you must have definite ideas.

Do not strain to get your ideas clear. They will be clearer the second day or the fifty-second day. If you have a pair of field glasses and you look at something and want the focus clearer, you slowly turn the wheel until the focus is clear.

Getting your mental equivalent may take you a week or a month or a year. *Charge it with interest*, like an electric charge, or it is dead. Love is the only way. You cannot be interested in a thing unless you love it. If you love it, it is filled with interest, it is filled with energy and life, and it comes true.

There is an interesting story about Napoleon. He thought a big nose was a sign of strong character. He said, "Give me a man with plenty of nose." If someone came to him and said that a certain officer ought to be promoted, he would say: "Has he got plenty of nose? Give me a man with a big nose." If an officer was killed, he replaced him with someone with a big nose. You know what happened. The law sent him Wellington, and Wellington destroyed him. Wellington had the largest nose in English history. He said himself it was more of a handle than a nose. Take that as a joke if you like, but it does carry an important lesson.

The doctrine of the mental equivalent is the essence of the metaphysical teaching; the doctrine that you will get whatever you provide the mental equivalent for.

I have known some very, very remarkable cases where people furnished the mental equivalent and out of the blue came things they never could have hoped for in the ordinary way. I know many men and women in London and New York and other places who seemingly had no human chance to attain success; but they got hold of this knowledge of mental equivalents, they quietly and faithfully applied this knowledge; and sometime sooner or later the thing they wanted came to them, without any help from anything outside; and it stayed with them and brought a blessing.

# Building a New Mental Equivalent

It is your bounden duty to demonstrate, and in order to do so successfully you need to know why you should do so. Why should you demonstrate at all? Some people say, "Since God is all, and everything is perfect, why should I seek to demonstrate His law?" Because you have to prove the harmony of being in your own life. That is why. If there were no need to demonstrate, one might just as well go to bed and stay there or, more simply still, stroll around to the nearest undertaker.

Of course we are here on earth to express God, and true expression is what we call demonstration, because it demonstrates the law of Being. It is your duty to be healthy, prosperous, and free. It is your duty to express God to the utmost of your power; and you have no right to relinquish your efforts until you have accomplished this. Until you have excellent health and are visibly regenerating, until you have found your true place and right activity, until you are free from conscious fear, anxiety, and criticism, you are not demonstrating, and you must find out why and correct the error, whatever it is.

Jesus has told us that we always demonstrate our consciousness, and Unity is teaching the same truth today. You always demonstrate what you habitually have in your mind. What sort of mind have you? I am not going to tell you—and do not let anyone else tell you either, because they do not know. People who like you will think your mentality is better than it is; those who do not like you will think it is worse. So do not ask anybody about your mentality; but examine your conditions and see what you are demonstrating. This method is scientific and infallible.

If an automobile engineer is working out a new design for an engine, if he is going to do something different about the valves, for instance, he doesn't say: "I wonder what Smith thinks about this. I like Smith. If Smith is against this I won't try it." Nor does he say, "I won't try this idea because it comes from France, and I don't like those people." He is impersonal and perfectly unemotional about it. He says, "I will test it out, and decide by the results I obtain."

Then he tries it out, measuring the results carefully, and decides accordingly. He does not laugh, or cry, or get excited, or bang the table; but he tests out the idea scientifically and judges only by results.

That is how you should handle your mentality. That is how you should practice the metaphysical teaching. You demonstrate the state of your mind at any given time. You experience in the outer what you really think in the inner. This is the meaning of the old saying "As within so without." Note carefully that in the Bible the word "within" always means thought and the word "without" means manifestation or experience. That is why Jesus said that the kingdom of heaven (health, harmony, and freedom) is within. Harmonious thought means harmonious experience. Fear thought or anger thought means suffering or frustration.

This brings me to the most important thing I want to say, namely that if you want to change your life; if you want to be healthier, happier, younger, more prosperous; above all, if you want to get nearer to God—and I know that you do—*you must change your thought and keep it changed.* That is the secret of controlling your life, and there is no other way. Jesus Himself could not have done it in any other way, because this is a cosmic law. Change your thought and keep it changed. We have all been taught this very thing since the metaphysical movement began. I heard it stated in those very words many times nearly forty years ago in London; but most of us are slow to realize the importance of it. If you want to change some condition in your life, you must change your thought about it and keep it changed. Then the condition will change accordingly. All that anyone else can do for you is to help you change your thought. That is what a metaphysician can do for you, but you yourself must keep it changed. No one else can think for you. "No man can save his brother's soul or pay his brother's debt."

To change your thought and keep it changed is the way to build a new mental equivalent; it is the secret of accomplishment. You already have a mental equivalent for everything that is in your life today; and you must destroy the patterns for the things you do not want, and then they will disappear. You must build a new pattern or mental equivalent for the things you want, and then they will come into your life.

Of course changing your thought for a short time is the easiest thing in the world. Everyone does this when he goes to a metaphysical meeting. The beautiful atmosphere and the positive instruction make people feel optimistic. The teacher reminds the audience of the Truth of Being, and they think, "I believe that, and I am going to practice it." But five minutes after they have left the meeting they forget about it, perhaps for hours. The trouble with most students is not that they do not change their thought but that they do not keep it changed.

If you want health you must cease to think sickness and fear, and you must get the habit of thinking health and harmony. There can be no sickness without fear. You cannot be adversely affected by anything if you really have no fear concerning it. Everyone has many fears in the subconscious mind that he is not consciously aware of, but they are operating just the same.

A man said: "I entered a town in a foreign country in the east of Europe during a typhoid epidemic. I did not know there was any typhoid. I never thought about it.

I didn't know the language and couldn't read the papers. They were printed in Greek. Yet I got typhoid and had quite a siege. How do you account for that?"

The explanation is that he believed in typhoid fever. He believed one can catch it from others, and that it makes one very ill, for so many days, and therefore he had a subconscious fear of it. He subconsciously knew there was typhoid around, and as it always does, the subconscious enacted or dramatized his real beliefs and fears, and presented him with a good hearty case of typhoid.

If he had really believed that he was a child of God who could not be hurt by anything, he would not have had typhoid.

Change your thought and keep it changed, not for ten seconds or even ten days but steadily and permanently. Then you will build a new mental equivalent, and *a mental equivalent is always demonstrated.*

The secret of harmony and success is to concentrate your thought upon harmony and success. That is why I teach that attention is the key to life. What you attend to or concentrate upon you bring into your life, because you are building a mental equivalent.

Many people fail to concentrate successfully because they think that concentration means will power. They actually try to concentrate with their muscles and blood vessels. They frown. They clench their hands. Unwittingly they are thinking of an engineer's drill or a carpenter's bit and brace. They suppose that the harder you press the faster you get through. But all this is quite wrong.

Forget the drill and think of a photographic camera. In a camera there is of course no question of pressure. There the secret lies in *focus.* If you want to photograph something you focus your camera lens quietly, steadily, and persistently on it for the necessary length of time. Suppose I want to photograph a vase of flowers. What do I do? Well, I do not press it violently against the lens of the camera. That would be silly. I place the vase in front of the camera and keep it there. But suppose that after a few moments I snatch away the vase and hold a book in front of the camera, and then snatch that away, and hold up a chair, and then put the flowers back for a few moments, and so forth. You know what will happen to my photograph. It will be a crazy blur. Is not that what people do to their minds when they cannot keep their thoughts concentrated for any length of time? They think health for a few minutes and then they think sickness or fear. They think prosperity and then they think depression. They think about bodily perfection and then they think about old age and their pains and aches. Is it any wonder that man is so apt to demonstrate the "marred image"?

Note carefully that I did not advocate taking one thought and trying to hold it by will power. That is bad. You must allow a train of *relevant* thoughts to have free play in your mind, one leading naturally to the next, but they must all be positive, constructive, and harmonious, and appertaining to your desire; and you must think quietly and without effort. Then you will get the mental equivalent of all-round success, and then success itself will follow; success in health, in social relationships, in your work, in your spiritual development.

# Maintaining the New Equivalent

It is always good to make a practical experiment, so I advise you to take a single problem in your life—something you want to get rid of or something you want to obtain—and change your thought about this thing, and keep it changed. Do not be in a hurry to select your problem; take your time.

Do not tell anyone you are doing this. If you tell a friend about it you are thereby strongly affirming the existence of the problem, which is the very thing you are trying to get rid of. If you tell your friend that you are going to work on your rheumatism or on lack, you are making these things very real to your subconscious mind. Also your spiritual energy is leaking away, as electricity does in what we call a "ground."

Take your problem and change your mind concerning it, and keep it changed for a month, and you will be astonished at the results you will get. If you really do keep your thought changed you will not have to wait a month. If you really change your thought and keep it changed, the demonstration may come in a few hours. But to keep tensely looking for the demonstration is really affirming the existence of the problem, is it not? The secret is to keep your thought changed into the new condition. So keep your thought carefully, quietly expressive of the new condition that you want to produce. Believe what you are thinking, and to prove that you believe it you must act the part.

By changing your mind about your problem in this way and keeping it changed, you are building a new mental equivalent, a mental equivalent of harmony and success, and that mental equivalent, as we know, must be outpictured in your experience.

For a while you will find that your thought will keep slipping back into the old rut. Such is the force of habit. But if you are quietly persistent you will gain the victory. It is always a little difficult to change a habit, but it can be done, and then the new right habit becomes easier than the old wrong habit, and that is how a new mental equivalent is built.

*Change your mind and keep it changed.*

Do not talk about the negative thing or act as if it were there. Act your part as though the new condition were already in being in the outer. If you will do this, the new condition will presently appear in the outer, because the outer is always but the projection or outpicturing of the inner.

We project our own belief and call it experience, and this gives us the clue to the difference between a true action and a false or unreal action.

What is true action? A true action is one that really changes things, that gets you somewhere. A false action does not. For example, if your car has traction it is moving. That is a true action, and you will presently reach your destination; but if it does not have traction there will be movement, vibration, but you will not get anywhere. You are wearing out the engine and perhaps the tires, but you do not get anywhere. The same thing happens when a soldier is "marking time" as we say. He is tiring himself and wearing out his shoes but not getting anywhere. These are examples of false action.

Suppose you have a difficult letter to write or a sermon or a lecture to prepare. Suppose you sit in front of a sheet of paper and draw curlicues or cut the pencil to pieces or tear your hair. These would be false actions, and many people do just that. Such actions get you nowhere. To decide what you are going to say, to start a current of thought and then write it down, is true action. You will note that the difference is that in the false action you begin from the outside. You had not prepared your thoughts. You tried to begin by writing. With the true action you got your thoughts in order first and then the writing or outer activity followed. A false action means deadlock; a true action is always fruitful.

True activity is always from within outward. False activity tries to work from without inward. One is centrifugal and the other centripetal, if you want to be technical. If you are working from within out, your work is alive and will be productive. If you are working from outside inward, your work is dead, and it will have a bad effect on you.

Artists and literary people speak of "potboilers." You know what a potboiler is. It is a picture that you paint or a story that you write, not because you are interested but just to keep the monetary returns coming in. It is never good, because it is not the result of inspiration. It is done from the outside and is a false action. It is a common saying among writers that three potboilers will kill any talent; and that is true. The proper way to paint a picture is to see beauty somewhere, in a landscape or in a beautiful face, or wherever you please. You thrill to that beauty, and then you go to the canvas and express your inspiration there. That is art, and that is true action. It inspires other people and it helps and develops you yourself.

If you write a story or a novel because you have observed life, because you have seen certain things happen and studied certain people, and write it all down because you are alive with it, that is a true action and you write a great book. Dickens, George Eliot, Balzac, and all the great authors wrote in that way. But if you say, "I will do fifteen hundred words a day and give my publishers the 'mixture as before' and that will secure my income," your work will be dead. And this policy will kill any talent that you may have.

If you are in business and you are interested in your job and love it, your work is a positive action and must ultimately bring you success. Even if the work is uncongenial but nevertheless you say, "This is my job for the moment; I am going to do it as well as I can, and then something better will open up," you are working from within outward. Your work is a positive action, and before long something really congenial will come to you.

Most people know that these things are true. They know that they are true for pictures and stories and business life, but they do not realize that they are equally true for the things of the soul. Yet such is the case. If you pray and meditate from the outside just because you think it is a duty or because you will feel guilty if you do not, your prayers will be dead. You will get no demonstration and make no spiritual progress, and you will get no joy. But if you feel that when you are praying and meditating you are visiting with God, and that these moments are the happiest in the twenty-four hours, then you are working from within outward. Your spiritual growth will be fruitful, and you will grow very rapidly in spiritual understanding. When you pray in this way there is no strain and your soul is filled with peace.

The great enemy of prayer is a sense of tension. When you are tense you are always working from the outside inward. Tension in prayer is probably the greatest cause of failure to demonstrate. Remember that the mind always stops working when you are tense. When you think, "I must demonstrate this" or "I must get that in three days," you are tense; you are using your will power, and you will do more harm than good.

Remember this: The door of the soul opens inward. If you will remember this it will save you years and years of waiting for demonstrations. Write in your notebook, the one you carry in your pocket—not the notebook you keep locked in your desk, because that is a mausoleum—or better still, write it on a card, and place it on your dresser: "The door of the soul opens inward." And pray to God that you may remember that truth every time you turn to Him in prayer. You know what it means when a door opens inward: the harder you push against it the tighter you close it. When you press or force or hurl yourself against it you only close it on yourself. When you relax and draw back, you give it a chance to open. In all theaters and other public buildings the doors open outward. The law insists upon this because crowds are apt to become panic-stricken and then they push, and if the doors opened inward the people would imprison themselves and be killed. *The door of the soul opens inward!* That is the law. Relax mentally, draw away from your problem spiritually, and the action of God will open the door for you and you will be free.

There is an old legend of the Middle Ages that is very instructive. It seems that a citizen was arrested by one of the Barons and shut up in a dungeon in his castle. He was taken down dark stairs, down, down, down, by a ferocious-looking jailer who carried a great key a foot long. The door of a cell was opened, and he was thrust into a dark hole. The door shut with a bang, and there he was.

He lay in that dark dungeon for twenty years. Each day the jailer would come, the big door would be opened with a great creaking and groaning, a pitcher of water and a loaf of bread would be thrust in and the door closed again.

Well, after twenty years the prisoner decided that he could not stand it any longer. He wanted to die but he did not want to commit suicide, so he decided that the next day when the jailer came he would attack him. The jailer would then kill him in self-defense, and thus his misery would be at an end. He thought he would examine the door carefully so as to be ready for tomorrow and, going over, he caught the handle and turned it. To his amazement the door opened, and upon investigation he found that there was no lock upon it and never had been, and that for all those twenty years he had not been locked in, except in belief.

At any time in that period he could have opened the door if only he had known it. He thought it was locked, but it was not. He groped along the corridor and felt his way upstairs. At the top of the stairs two soldiers were chatting, and they made no attempt to stop him. He crossed the great yard without attracting attention. There was an armed guard on the drawbridge at the great gate, but they paid no attention to him, and he walked out a free man.

He went home unmolested and lived happily ever after. He could have done this any time through those long years since his arrest if he had known enough, but he did not. He was a captive, not of stone and iron but of false belief. He was not locked in; he only thought he was. Of course this is only a legend, but it is an extremely instructive one.

We are all living in some kind of prison, some of us in one kind, some in another; some in a prison of lack, some in a prison of remorse and resentment, some in a prison of blind, unintelligent fear, some in a prison of sickness. But always the prison is in our thought and not in the nature of things.

There is no truth in our seeming troubles. There is no reality in lack. There is no power in time or conditions to make us old or tired or sick.

The Jesus Christ teaching, and the Unity movement in particular, comes to us and says: "You are not locked in a prison of circumstances. You are not chained in any dungeon. In the name of God, turn the handle, walk out, and be free."

Build a mental equivalent of freedom, of vibrant physical health, of true prosperity, of increasing understanding and achievement for God. Build it by thinking of it, having faith in it and acting the part, and the old limitation equivalent will gradually fade out, for the door is unlocked and the voice of God in your heart says, "Be free."

# AS A MAN THINKETH

JAMES ALLEN

(1903)

*"Mind is the Master power that moulds and makes,*
*And Man is Mind, and evermore he takes*
*The tool of Thought, and, shaping what he wills,*
*Brings forth a thousand joys, a thousand ills:—*
*He thinks in secret, and it comes to pass:*
*Environment is but his looking-glass."*

# Foreword

This little volume (the result of meditation and experience) is not intended as an exhaustive treatise on the much-written-upon subject of the power of thought. It is suggestive rather than explanatory, its object being to stimulate men and women to the discovery and perception of the truth that—

"They themselves are makers of themselves"

by virtue of the thoughts which they choose and encourage; that mind is the master weaver, both of the inner garment of character and the outer garment of circumstance, and that, as they may have hitherto woven in ignorance and pain they may now weave in enlightenment and happiness.

JAMES ALLEN
*Broad Park Avenue,*
*Ilfracombe,*
*England.*

# Contents

1. Thought and Character 375
2. Effect of Thought on Circumstances 377
3. Effect of Thought on Health and the Body 383
4. Thought and Purpose 384
5. The Thought-Factor in Achievement 386
6. Visions and Ideals 388
7. Serenity 391

# Thought and Character

The aphorism, "As a man thinketh in his heart so is he," not only embraces the whole of a man's being, but is so comprehensive as to reach out to every condition and circumstance of his life. A man is literally *what he thinks*, his character being the complete sum of all his thoughts.

As the plant springs from, and could not be without, the seed, so every act of a man springs from the hidden seeds of thought, and could not have appeared without them. This applies equally to those acts called "spontaneous" and "unpremeditated" as to those which are deliberately executed.

Act is the blossom of thought, and joy and suffering are its fruits; thus does a man garner in the sweet and bitter fruitage of his own husbandry.

> "Thought in the mind hath made us. What we are
> By thought was wrought and built. If a man's mind
> Hath evil thoughts, pain comes on him as comes
> The wheel the ox behind. . . .
>                 If one endure
> In purity of thought, joy follows him
> As his own shadow—sure."

Man is a growth by law, and not a creation by artifice, and cause and effect is as absolute and undeviating in the hidden realm of thought as in the world of visible and material things. A noble and Godlike character is not a thing of favor or chance, but is the natural result of continued effort in right thinking, the effect of long-cherished association with Godlike thoughts. An ignoble and bestial character, by the same process, is the result of the continued harboring of groveling thoughts.

Man is made or unmade by himself; in the armory of thought he forges the weapons by which he destroys himself; he also fashions the tools with which he builds for himself heavenly mansions of joy and strength and peace. By the right choice and true application of thought, man ascends to the Divine Perfection; by the abuse and wrong application of thought, he descends below the level of the beast. Between these two extremes are all the grades of character, and man is their maker and master.

Of all the beautiful truths pertaining to the soul which have been restored and brought to light in this age, none is more gladdening or fruitful of divine promise and confidence than this—that man is the master of thought, the molder of character, and the maker and shaper of condition, environment, and destiny.

As a being of Power, Intelligence, and Love, and the lord of his own thoughts, man holds the key to every situation, and contains within himself that transforming and regenerative agency by which he may make himself what he wills.

Man is always the master, even in his weakest and most abandoned state; but in his weakness and degradation he is the foolish master who misgoverns his "household." When he begins to reflect upon his condition, and to search diligently for the Law upon which his being is established, he then becomes the wise master, directing his energies with intelligence, and fashioning his thoughts to fruitful issues. Such is the *conscious* master, and man can only thus become by discovering *within himself* the laws of thought; which discovery is totally a matter of application, self-analysis, and experience.

Only by much searching and mining are gold and diamonds obtained, and man can find every truth connected with his being if he will dig deep into the mine of his soul; and that he is the maker of his character, the molder of his life, and the builder of his destiny, he may unerringly prove, if he will watch, control, and alter his thoughts, tracing their effects upon himself, upon others, and upon his life and circumstances, linking cause and effect by patient practice and investigation, and utilizing his every experience, even to the most trivial, everyday occurrence, as a means of obtaining that knowledge of himself which is Understanding, Wisdom, Power. In this direction, as in no other, is the law absolute that "He that seeketh findeth; and to him that knocketh it shall be opened"; for only by patience, practice, and ceaseless importunity can a man enter the Door of the Temple of Knowledge.

# Effect of Thought on Circumstances

A man's mind may be likened to a garden, which may be intelligently cultivated or allowed to run wild; but whether cultivated or neglected, it must, and will, *bring forth*. If no useful seeds are *put* into it, then an abundance of useless weed seeds will *fall* therein, and will continue to produce their kind.

Just as a gardener cultivates his plot, keeping it free from weeds, and growing the flowers and fruits which he requires, so may a man tend the garden of his mind, weeding out all the wrong, useless, and impure thoughts, and cultivating toward perfection the flowers and fruits of right, useful, and pure thoughts. By pursuing this process, a man sooner or later discovers that he is the master gardener of his soul, the director of his life. He also reveals, within himself, the laws of thought, and understands, with ever-increasing accuracy, how the thought forces and mind elements operate in the shaping of his character, circumstances, and destiny.

Thought and character are one, and as character can only manifest and discover itself through environment and circumstance, the outer conditions of a person's life will always be found to be harmoniously related to his inner state. This does not mean that a man's circumstances at any given time are an indication of his *entire* character, but that those circumstances are so intimately connected with some vital thought element within himself that, for the time being, they are indispensable to his development.

Every man is where he is by the law of his being; the thoughts which he has built into his character have brought him there, and in the arrangement of his life there is no element of chance, but all is the result of a law which cannot err. This is just as true of those who feel "out of harmony" with their surroundings as of those who are contented with them.

As a progressive and evolving being, man is where he is that he may learn that he may grow; and as he learns the spiritual lesson which any circumstance contains for him, it passes away and gives place to other circumstances.

Man is buffeted by circumstances so long as he believes himself to be the creature of outside conditions, but when he realizes that he is a creative power, and that he may command the hidden soil and seeds of his being out of which circumstances grow, he then becomes the rightful master of himself.

That circumstances *grow* out of thought every man knows who has for any length of time practiced self-control and self-purification, for he will have noticed that the alteration in his circumstances has been in exact ratio with his altered mental condition. So true is this that when a man earnestly applies himself to remedy the defects in his character, and makes swift and marked progress, he passes rapidly through a succession of vicissitudes.

The soul attracts that which it secretly harbors; that which it loves, and also that which it fears; it reaches the height of its cherished aspirations; it falls to the level of its unchastened desires—and circumstances are the means by which the soul receives its own.

Every thought seed sown or allowed to fall into the mind, and to take root there, produces its own, blossoming sooner or later into act, and bearing its own fruitage of opportunity and circumstance. Good thoughts bear good fruit, bad thoughts bad fruit.

The outer world of circumstance shapes itself to the inner world of thought, and both pleasant and unpleasant external conditions are factors which make for the ultimate good of the individual. As the reaper of his own harvest, man learns both by suffering and bliss.

Following the inmost desires, aspirations, thoughts, by which he allows himself to be dominated (pursuing the will-o'-the-wisps of impure imaginings or steadfastly walking the highway of strong and high endeavor), a man at last arrives at their fruition and fulfillment in the outer conditions of his life. The laws of growth and adjustment everywhere obtain.

A man does not come to the almshouse or the jail by the tyranny of fate or circumstance, but by the pathway of groveling thoughts and base desires. Nor does a pure-minded man fall suddenly into crime by stress of any mere external force; the criminal thought had long been secretly fostered in the heart, and the hour of opportunity revealed its gathered power. Circumstance does not make the man; it reveals him to himself. No such conditions can exist as descending into vice and its attendant sufferings apart from vicious inclinations, or ascending into virtue and its pure happiness without the continued cultivation of virtuous aspirations; and man, therefore, as the lord and master of thought, is the maker of himself, the shaper and author of environment. Even at birth the soul comes to its own, and through every step of its earthly pilgrimage it attracts those combinations of conditions which reveal itself, which are the reflections of its own purity and impurity, its strength and weakness.

Men do not attract that which they *want*, but that which they *are*. Their whims, fancies, and ambitions are thwarted at every step, but their inmost thoughts and desires are fed with their own food, be it foul or clean. The "divinity that shapes our ends" is in ourselves; it is our very self. Man is manacled only by himself: thought and action are the jailers of Fate—they imprison, being base; they are also the angels of Freedom—they liberate, being noble. Not what he wishes and prays for does a man get, but what he justly earns. His wishes and prayers are only gratified and answered when they harmonize with his thoughts and actions.

In the light of this truth, what, then, is the meaning of "fighting against circumstances"? It means that a man is continually revolting against an *effect* without, while all the time he is nourishing and preserving its *cause* in his heart. That cause may take the form of a conscious vice or an unconscious weakness; but whatever it is, it stubbornly retards the efforts of its possessor, and thus calls aloud for remedy.

Men are anxious to improve their circumstances, but are unwilling to improve themselves; they therefore remain bound. The man who does not shrink from self-crucifixion can never fail to accomplish the object upon which his heart is set. This is as true of earthly as of heavenly things. Even the man whose sole object is to acquire wealth must be prepared to make great personal sacrifices before he can accomplish his object; and how much more so he who would realize a strong and well-poised life?

Here is a man who is wretchedly poor. He is extremely anxious that his surroundings and home comforts should be improved, yet all the time he shirks his work, and considers he is justified in trying to deceive his employer on the ground of the insufficiency of his wages. Such a man does not understand the simplest rudiments of those principles which are the basis of true prosperity, and is not only totally unfitted to rise out of his wretchedness, but is actually attracting to himself a still deeper wretchedness by dwelling in, and acting out, indolent, deceptive, and unmanly thoughts.

Here is a rich man who is the victim of a painful and persistent disease as the result of gluttony. He is willing to give large sums of money to get rid of it, but he will not sacrifice his gluttonous desires. He wants to gratify his taste for rich and unnatural viands and have his health as well. Such a man is totally unfit to have health, because he has not yet learned the first principles of a healthy life.

Here is an employer of labor who adopts crooked measures to avoid paying the regulation wage, and, in the hope of making larger profits, reduces the wages of his workpeople. Such a man is altogether unfitted for prosperity, and when he finds himself bankrupt, both as regards reputation and riches, he blames circumstances, not knowing that he is the sole author of his condition.

I have introduced these three cases merely as illustrative of the truth that man is the causer (though nearly always unconsciously) of his circumstances, and that, while aiming at a good end, he is continually frustrating its accomplishment by encouraging thoughts and desires which cannot possibly harmonize with that end. Such cases could be multiplied and varied almost indefinitely, but this is not necessary, as the reader can, if he so resolves, trace the action of the laws of thought in his own mind and life, and until this is done, mere external facts cannot serve as a ground of reasoning.

Circumstances, however, are so complicated, thought is so deeply rooted, and the conditions of happiness vary so vastly with individuals, that a man's *entire* soul condition (although it may be known to himself) cannot be judged by another from the external aspect of his life alone. A man may be honest in certain directions, yet suffer privations; a man may be dishonest in certain directions, yet acquire wealth; but the conclusion usually formed that the one man fails *because of his particular honesty*, and that the other prospers *because of his particular dishonesty*, is the result of a superficial judgment, which assumes that the dishonest man is almost totally corrupt, and the honest man almost entirely virtuous. In the light of a deeper knowledge and wider experience, such judgment is found to be erroneous. The dishonest man may have some admirable virtues which the other does not possess; and the honest man obnoxious vices which are absent in the other. The honest man reaps the good results of his honest thoughts and acts; he also brings upon himself the sufferings which his vices produce. The dishonest man likewise garners his own suffering and happiness.

It is pleasing to human vanity to believe that one suffers because of one's virtue; but not until a man has extirpated every sickly, bitter, and impure thought from his mind, and washed every sinful stain from his soul, can he be in a position to know and declare that his sufferings are the result of his good, and not of his bad qualities; and on the way to, yet long before he has reached, that supreme perfection, he will have found, working in his mind and life, the Great Law which is absolutely just, and which cannot, therefore, give good for evil, evil for good. Possessed of such knowledge, he will then know, looking back upon his past ignorance and blindness, that his life is, and always was, justly ordered, and that all his past experiences, good and bad, were the equitable outworking of his evolving, yet unevolved self.

Good thoughts and actions can never produce bad results; bad thoughts and actions can never produce good results. This is but saying that nothing can come from corn but corn, nothing from nettles but nettles. Men understand this law in the natural world, and work with it; but few understand it in the mental and moral world (though its operation there is just as simple and undeviating), and they, therefore, do not coöperate with it.

Suffering is *always* the effect of wrong thought in some direction. It is an indication that the individual is out of harmony with himself, with the Law of his being. The sole and supreme use of suffering is to purify, to burn out all that is useless and impure. Suffering ceases for him who is pure. There could be no object in burning gold after the dross had been removed, and a perfectly pure and enlightened being could not suffer.

The circumstances which a man encounters with suffering are the result of his own mental inharmony. The circumstances which a man encounters with blessedness are the result of his own mental harmony. Blessedness, not material possessions, is the measure of right thought; wretchedness, not lack of material possessions, is the measure of wrong thought. A man may be cursed and rich; he may be blessed and poor. Blessedness and riches are only joined together when the riches are rightly and wisely used; and the poor man only descends into wretchedness when he regards his lot as a burden unjustly imposed.

Indigence and indulgence are the two extremes of wretchedness. They are both equally unnatural and the result of mental disorder. A man is not rightly conditioned until he is a happy, healthy, and prosperous being; and happiness, health, and prosperity are the result of a harmonious adjustment of the inner with the outer, of the man with his surroundings.

A man only begins to be a man when he ceases to whine and revile, and commences to search for the hidden justice which regulates his life. And as he adapts his mind to that regulating factor, he ceases to accuse others as the cause of his condition, and builds himself up in strong and noble thoughts; ceases to kick against circumstances, but begins to *use* them as aids to his more rapid progress, and as a means of discovering the hidden powers and possibilities within himself.

Law, not confusion, is the dominating principle in the universe; justice, not injustice, is the soul and substance of life; and righteousness, not corruption, is the molding and moving force in the spiritual government of the world. This being so, man has but to right himself to find that the universe is right; and during the process of putting himself right, he will find that as he alters his thoughts toward things, and other people, things and other people will alter toward him.

The proof of this truth is in every person, and it therefore admits of easy investigation by systematic introspection and self-analysis. Let a man radically alter his thoughts, and he will be astonished at the rapid transformation it will effect in the material conditions of his life. Men imagine that thought can be kept secret, but it cannot; it rapidly crystallizes into habit and habit solidifies into circumstance. Bestial thoughts crystallize into habits of drunkenness and sensuality, which solidify into circumstances of destitution and disease: impure thoughts of every kind crystallize into enervating and confusing habits, which solidify into distracting and adverse circumstances: thoughts of fear, doubt, and indecision crystallize into weak, unmanly, and irresolute habits, which solidify into circumstances of failure, indigence, and slavish dependence: lazy thoughts crystallize into habits of uncleanliness and dishonesty, which solidify into circumstances of foulness and beggary: hateful and condemnatory thoughts crystallize into habits of accusation and violence, which solidify into circumstances of injury and persecution: selfish thoughts of all kinds crystallize into habits of self-seeking, which solidify into circumstances more or less distressing. On the other hand, beautiful thoughts of all kinds crystallize into habits of grace and kindliness, which solidify into genial and sunny circumstances: pure thoughts crystallize into habits of temperance and self-control, which solidify into circumstances of repose and peace: thoughts of courage, self-reliance, and decision crystallize into manly habits, which solidify into circumstances of success, plenty, and freedom: energetic thoughts crystallize into habits of cleanliness and industry, which solidify into circumstances of pleasantness: gentle and forgiving thoughts crystallize into habits of gentleness, which solidify into protective and preservative circumstances: loving and unselfish thoughts crystallize into habits of self-forgetfulness for others, which solidify into circumstances of sure and abiding prosperity and true riches.

A particular train of thought persisted in, be it good or bad, cannot fail to produce its results on the character and circumstances. A man cannot *directly* choose his circumstances, but he can choose his thoughts, and so indirectly, yet surely, shape his circumstances.

Nature helps every man to the gratification of the thoughts which he most encourages, and opportunities are presented which will most speedily bring to the surface both the good and evil thoughts.

Let a man cease from his sinful thoughts, and all the world will soften toward him, and be ready to help him; let him put away his weakly and sickly thoughts, and lo! opportunities will spring up on every hand to aid his strong resolves; let him encourage good thoughts, and no hard fate shall bind him down to wretchedness and shame. The world is your kaleidoscope, and the varying combinations of colors which at every succeeding moment it presents to you are the exquisitely adjusted pictures of your evermoving thoughts.

*"You will be what you will to be;*
*Let failure find its false content*
*In that poor word, 'environment,'*
*But spirit scorns it, and is free.*

*"It masters time, it conquers space;*
*It cows that boastful trickster, Chance,*
*And bids the tyrant Circumstance*
*Uncrown, and fill a servant's place.*

*"The human Will, that force unseen,*
*The offspring of a deathless Soul,*
*Can hew a way to any goal.*
*Though walls of granite intervene,*

*"Be not impatient in delay.*
*But wait as one who understands;*
*When spirit rises and commands,*
*The gods are ready to obey."*

# Effect of Thought on Health and the Body

The body is the servant of the mind. It obeys the operations of the mind, whether they be deliberately chosen or automatically expressed. At the bidding of unlawful thoughts the body sinks rapidly into disease and decay; at the command of glad and beautiful thoughts it becomes clothed with youthfulness and beauty.

Disease and health, like circumstances, are rooted in thought. Sickly thoughts will express themselves through a sickly body. Thoughts of fear have been known to kill a man as speedily as a bullet, and they are continually killing thousands of people just as surely though less rapidly. The people who live in fear of disease are the people who get it. Anxiety quickly demoralizes the whole body, and lays it open to the entrance of disease; while impure thoughts, even if not physically indulged, will soon shatter the nervous system.

Strong, pure, and happy thoughts build up the body in vigor and grace. The body is a delicate and plastic instrument, which responds readily to the thoughts by which it is impressed, and habits of thought will produce their own effects, good or bad, upon it.

Men will continue to have impure and poisoned blood so long as they propagate unclean thoughts. Out of a clean heart comes a clean life and a clean body. Out of a defiled mind proceeds a defiled life and a corrupt body. Thought is the font of action, life, and manifestation; make the fountain pure, and all will be pure.

Change of diet will not help a man who will not change his thoughts. When a man makes his thoughts pure, he no longer desires impure food.

Clean thoughts make clean habits. The so-called saint who does not wash his body is not a saint. He who has strengthened and purified his thoughts does not need to consider the malevolent microbe.

If you would perfect your body, guard your mind. If you would renew your body, beautify your mind. Thoughts of malice, envy, disappointment, despondency, rob the body of its health and grace. A sour face does not come by chance; it is made by sour thoughts. Wrinkles that mar are drawn by folly, passion, pride.

# Thought and Purpose

Until thought is linked with purpose there is no intelligent accomplishment. With the majority the bark of thought is allowed to "drift" upon the ocean of life. Aimlessness is a vice, and such drifting must not continue for him who would steer clear of catastrophe and destruction.

They who have no central purpose in their life fall an easy prey to petty worries, fears, troubles, and self-pityings, all of which are indications of weakness, which lead, just as surely as deliberately planned sins (though by a different route), to failure, unhappiness, and loss, for weakness cannot persist in a power-evolving universe.

A man should conceive of a legitimate purpose in his heart, and set out to accomplish it. He should make this purpose the centralizing point of his thoughts. It may take the form of a spiritual ideal, or it may be a worldly object, according to his nature at the time being; but whichever it is, he should steadily focus his thought forces upon the object which he has set before him. He should make this purpose his supreme duty, and should devote himself to its attainment, not allowing his thoughts to wander away into ephemeral fancies, longings, and imaginings. This is the royal road to self-control and true concentration of thought. Even if he fails again and again to accomplish his purpose (as he necessarily must until weakness is overcome), the *strength of character gained* will be the measure of his *true* success, and this will form a new starting point for future power and triumph.

Those who are not prepared for the apprehension of a *great* purpose, should fix the thoughts upon the faultless performance of their duty, no matter how insignificant their task may appear. Only in this way can the thoughts be gathered and focused, and resolution and energy be developed, which being done, there is nothing which may not be accomplished.

The weakest soul, knowing its own weakness, and believing this truth—*that strength can only be developed by effort and practice,* will, thus believing, at once begin to exert itself, and, adding effort to effort, patience to patience, and strength to strength, will never cease to develop, and will at last grow divinely strong.

As the physically weak man can make himself strong by careful and patient training, so the man of weak thoughts can make them strong by exercising himself in right thinking.

To put away aimlessness and weakness, and to begin to think with purpose, is to enter the ranks of those strong ones who only recognize failure as one of the pathways to attainment; who make all conditions serve them, and who think strongly, attempt fearlessly, and accomplish masterfully.

Having conceived of his purpose, a man should mentally mark out a *straight* pathway to its achievement, looking neither to the right nor the left. Doubts and fears should be rigorously excluded; they are disintegrating elements which break up the straight line of effort, rendering it crooked, ineffectual, useless. Thoughts of doubt and fear never accomplish anything, and never can. They always lead to failure. Purpose, energy, power to do, and all strong thoughts cease when doubt and fear creep in.

The will to do springs from the knowledge that we *can* do. Doubt and fear are the great enemies of knowledge, and he who encourages them, who does not slay them, thwarts himself at every step.

He who has conquered doubt and fear has conquered failure. His every thought is allied with power, and all difficulties are bravely met and wisely overcome. His purposes are seasonably planted, and they bloom and bring forth fruit which does not fall prematurely to the ground.

Thought allied fearlessly to purpose becomes creative force: he who *knows* this is ready to become something higher and stronger than a mere bundle of wavering thoughts and fluctuating sensations; he who *does* this has become the conscious and intelligent wielder of his mental powers.

# The Thought-Factor in Achievement

All that a man achieves and all that he fails to achieve is the direct result of his own thoughts. In a justly ordered universe, where loss of equipoise would mean total destruction, individual responsibility must be absolute. A man's weakness and strength, purity and impurity, are his own, and not another man's; they are brought about by himself, and not by another; and they can only be altered by himself, never by another. His condition is also his own, and not another man's. His suffering and his happiness are evolved from within. As he thinks, so he is; as he continues to think, so he remains.

A strong man cannot help a weaker unless that weaker is *willing* to be helped, and even then the weak man must become strong of himself; he must, by his own efforts, develop the strength which he admires in another. None but himself can alter his condition.

It has been usual for men to think and to say, "Many men are slaves because one is an oppressor; let us hate the oppressor." Now, however, there is among an increasing few a tendency to reverse this judgment, and to say, "One man is an oppressor because many are slaves; let us despise the slaves." The truth is that oppressor and slave are cooperators in ignorance, and, while seeming to afflict each other, are in reality afflicting themselves. A perfect Knowledge perceives the action of law in the weakness of the oppressed and the misapplied power of the oppressor; a perfect Love, seeing the suffering which both states entail, condemns neither; a perfect Compassion embraces both oppressor and oppressed.

He who has conquered weakness, and has put away all selfish thoughts, belongs neither to oppressor nor oppressed. He is free.

A man can only rise, conquer, and achieve by lifting up his thoughts. He can only remain weak, and abject, and miserable by refusing to lift up his thoughts.

Before a man can achieve anything, even in worldly things, he must lift his thoughts above slavish animal indulgence. He may not, in order to succeed, give up *all* animality and selfishness, by any means; but a portion of it must, at least, be sacrificed. A man whose first thought is bestial indulgence could neither think clearly nor plan methodically; he could not find and develop his latent resources, and would fail in any undertaking. Not having commenced manfully to control his thoughts, he is not in a position to control affairs and to adopt serious responsibilities. He is not fit to act independently and stand alone. But he is limited only by the thoughts which he chooses.

There can be no progress, no achievement without sacrifice, and a man's worldly success will be in the measure that he sacrifices his confused animal thoughts, and fixes his mind on the development of his plans, and the strengthening of his resolution and self-reliance. And the higher he lifts his thoughts, the more manly, upright, and righteous he becomes, the greater will be his success, the more blessed and enduring will be his achievements.

The universe does not favor the greedy, the dishonest, the vicious, although on the mere surface it may sometimes appear to do so; it helps the honest, the magnanimous, the virtuous. All the great Teachers of the ages have declared this in varying forms, and to prove and know it a man has but to persist in making himself more and more virtuous by lifting up his thoughts.

Intellectual achievements are the result of thought consecrated to the search for knowledge, or for the beautiful and true in life and nature. Such achievements may be sometimes connected with vanity and ambition, but they are not the outcome of those characteristics; they are the natural outgrowth of long and arduous effort, and of pure and unselfish thoughts.

Spiritual achievements are the consummation of holy aspirations. He who lives constantly in the conception of noble and lofty thoughts, who dwells upon all that is pure and unselfish, will, as surely as the sun reaches its zenith and the moon its full, become wise and noble in character, and rise into a position of influence and blessedness.

Achievement, of whatever kind, is the crown of effort, the diadem of thought. By the aid of self-control, resolution, purity, righteousness, and well-directed thought a man ascends; by the aid of animality, indolence, impurity, corruption, and confusion of thought a man descends.

A man may rise to high success in the world, and even to lofty altitudes in the spiritual realm, and again descend into weakness and wretchedness by allowing arrogant, selfish, and corrupt thoughts to take possession of him.

Victories attained by right thought can only be maintained by watchfulness. Many give way when success is assured, and rapidly fall back into failure.

All achievements, whether in the business, intellectual, or spiritual world, are the result of definitely directed thought, are governed by the same law and are of the same method; the only difference lies in *the object of attainment.*

He who would accomplish little must sacrifice little; he who would achieve much must sacrifice much; he who would attain highly must sacrifice greatly.

# Visions and Ideals

The dreamers are the saviors of the world. As the visible world is sustained by the invisible, so men, through all their trials and sins and sordid vocations, are nourished by the beautiful visions of their solitary dreamers. Humanity cannot forget its dreamers; it cannot let their ideals fade and die; it lives in them; it knows them as the *realities* which it shall one day see and know.

Composer, sculptor, painter, poet, prophet, sage, these are the makers of the afterworld, the architects of heaven. The world is beautiful because they have lived; without them, laboring humanity would perish.

He who cherishes a beautiful vision, a lofty ideal in his heart, will one day realize it. Columbus cherished a vision of another world, and he discovered it; Copernicus fostered the vision of a multiplicity of worlds and a wider universe, and he revealed it; Buddha beheld the vision of a spiritual world of stainless beauty and perfect peace, and he entered into it.

Cherish your visions; cherish your, ideals; cherish the music that stirs in your heart, the beauty that forms in your mind, the loveliness that drapes your purest thoughts, for out of them will grow all delightful conditions, all heavenly environment; of these, if you but remain true to them, your world will at last be built.

To desire is to obtain; to aspire is to achieve. Shall man's basest desires receive the fullest measure of gratification, and his purest aspirations starve for lack of sustenance? Such is not the Law: such a condition of things can never obtain: "Ask and receive."

Dream lofty dreams, and as you dream, so shall you become. Your Vision is the promise of what you shall one day be; your Ideal is the prophecy of what you shall at last unveil.

The greatest achievement was at first and for a time a dream. The oak sleeps in the acorn; the bird waits in the egg; and in the highest vision of the soul a waking angel stirs. Dreams are the seedlings of realities.

Your circumstances may be uncongenial, but they shall not long remain so if you but perceive an Ideal and strive to reach it. You cannot travel *within* and stand still *without*. Here is a youth hard pressed by poverty and labor; confined hours in an unhealthy workshop; unschooled, and lacking all the arts of refinement. But he dreams of better things: he thinks of intelligence, of refinement, of grace and beauty. He conceives of, mentally builds up, an ideal condition of life; the vision of a wider liberty and a larger scope takes possession of him; unrest urges him to action, and he utilizes all his spare time and means, small though they are, to the development of his latent powers and resources. Very soon so altered has his mind become that the workshop can no longer hold him. It has become so out of harmony with his mentality that it falls out of his life as a garment is cast aside, and, with the growth of opportunities which fit the scope of his expanding powers, he passes out of it forever. Years later we see this youth as a full-grown man. We find him a master of certain forces of the mind which he wields with world-wide influence and almost unequaled power. In his hands he holds the cords of gigantic responsibilities; he speaks, and lo! lives are changed; men and women hang upon his words and remold their characters, and, sunlike, he becomes the fixed and luminous center around which innumerable destinies revolve. He has realized the Vision of his youth. He has become one with his Ideal.

And you, too, youthful reader, will realize the Vision (not the idle wish) of your heart, be it base or beautiful, or a mixture of both, for you will always gravitate toward that which you, secretly, most love. Into your hands will be placed the exact results of your own thoughts; you will receive that which you earn; no more, no less. Whatever your present environment may be, you will fall, remain, or rise with your thoughts, your Vision, your Ideal.

You will become as small as your controlling desire; as great as your dominant aspiration: in the beautiful words of Stanton Kirkham Davis, "You may be keeping accounts, and presently you shall walk out of the door that for so long has seemed to you the barrier of your ideals, and shall find yourself before an audience—the pen still behind your ear, the ink stains on your fingers—and then and there shall pour out the torrent of your inspiration. You may be driving sheep, and you shall wander to the city—bucolic and open mouthed; shall wander under the intrepid guidance of the spirit into the studio of the master, and after a time he shall say, 'I have nothing more to teach you.' And now you have become the master who did so recently dream of great things while driving sheep. You shall lay down the saw and the plane to take upon yourself the regeneration of the world."

The thoughtless, the ignorant, and the indolent, seeing only the apparent effects of things and not the things themselves, talk of luck, of fortune, and chance. Seeing a man grow rich, they say, "How lucky he is!" Observing another become intellectual, they exclaim, "How highly favored he is!" And noting the saintly character and wide influence of another, they remark, "How chance aids him at every turn!" They do not see the trials and failures and struggles which these men have voluntarily encountered in order to gain their experience; have no knowledge of the sacrifices they have made, of the undaunted efforts they have put forth, of the faith they have exercised, that they might overcome the apparently insurmountable, and realize the

Vision of their heart. They do not know the darkness and the heartaches; they only see the light and joy, and call it "luck"; do not see the long and arduous journey, but only behold the pleasant goal, and call it "good fortune"; do not understand the process, but only perceive the result, and call it "chance."

In all human affairs there are *efforts*, and there are *results*, and the strength of the effort is the measure of the result. Chance is not. "Gifts," powers, material, intellectual, and spiritual possessions are the fruits of effort; they are thoughts completed, objects accomplished, visions realized.

The Vision that you glorify in your mind, the Ideal that you enthrone in your heart—this you will build your life by, this you will become.

# Serenity

Calmness of mind is one of the beautiful jewels of wisdom. It is the result of long and patient effort in self-control. Its presence is an indication of ripened experience, and of a more than ordinary knowledge of the laws and operations of thought.

A man becomes calm in the measure that he understands himself as a thought-evolved being, for such knowledge necessitates the understanding of others as the result of thought, and as he develops a right understanding, and sees more and more clearly the internal relations of things by the action of cause and effect, he ceases to fuss and fume and worry and grieve, and remains poised, steadfast, serene.

The calm man, having learned how to govern himself, knows how to adapt himself to others; and they, in turn, reverence his spiritual strength, and feel that they can learn of him and rely upon him. The more tranquil a man becomes, the greater is his success, his influence, his power for good. Even the ordinary trader will find his business prosperity increase as he develops a greater self-control and equanimity, for people will always prefer to deal with a man whose demeanor is strongly equable.

The strong, calm man is always loved and revered. He is like a shade-giving tree in a thirsty land, or a sheltering rock in a storm. "Who does not love a tranquil heart, a sweet-tempered, balanced life? It does not matter whether it rains or shines, or what changes come to those possessing these blessings, for they are always sweet, serene, and calm. That exquisite poise of character which we call serenity is the last lesson of culture; it is the flowering of life, the fruitage of the soul. It is precious as wisdom, more to be desired than gold—yea, than even fine gold. How insignificant mere money-seeking looks in comparison with a serene life—a life that dwells in the ocean of Truth, beneath the waves, beyond the reach of tempests, in the Eternal Calm!

"How many people we know who sour their lives, who ruin all that is sweet and beautiful by explosive tempers, who destroy their poise of character, and make bad blood! It is a question whether the great majority of people do not ruin their lives and mar their happiness by lack of self-control. How few people we meet in life who are well-balanced, who have that exquisite poise which is characteristic of the finished character!"

Yes, humanity surges with uncontrolled passion, is tumultuous with ungoverned grief, is blown about by anxiety and doubt. Only the wise man, only he whose thoughts are controlled and purified, makes the winds and the storms of the soul obey him.

Tempest-tossed souls, wherever ye may be, under whatsoever conditions ye may live, know this—in the ocean of life the isles of Blessedness are smiling, and the sunny shore of your ideal awaits your coming. Keep your hand firmly upon the helm of thought. In the bark of your soul reclines the commanding Master; He does but sleep; wake Him. Self-control is strength; Right Thought is mastery; Calmness is power. Say unto your heart, "Peace, be still!"

# RELIGION THAT WORKS

THE REV. SAM SHOEMAKER

*1928*

*To*
*A. S. R.*

# Introduction

I am not fond of reading sermons. Most of those which live in speech die in print; many more have never lived at all. But all the addresses, contained in this volume, I have read with profit and two of them, at least, I shall always remember.

For here are genuine convictions set forth with clarity and vigor. Here are the words of one who has found, for himself and others, the dynamic of a personal religion. On the basis of that experience he speaks to the world of here and now as we find it in our own American life in a great city. He puts down what one man thinks we ought to know about God and Man and Sin and the Gospel of Jesus Christ.

There is life in these pages. May they bring life to those who read them.

ALBERT PARKER FITCH.

*Park Avenue Presbyterian Church Manse,*
*New York City.*

# Contents


I. What If I Had But One Sermon to Preach? 401

II. The Necessity of Christ 407

III. What Is Unbelief? 412

IV. The Meaning of Self-Surrender 418

V. How to Know the Will of God 424

VI. The Fellowship of the Holy Ghost 430

VII. The Importance of Individuals 436

VIII. Isaiah's Vision of God 442

IX. What Shall We Do with Trouble? 448

X. Undistracted Loyalty to Christ 453

XI. The Higher Reaches of Christian Experience 459

I

# What If I Had But One Sermon to Preach?

*"This is life eternal, that they should know thee the only true God, and him whom thou didst send, even Jesus Christ."*
—JOHN 17:3.

It is a moving and sobering experience to try to make ready a sermon in which one attempts to say out the core of what one has found really important, really vital, in what one has learned about life, and the place of Christianity in it—to cut down the trivial and incidental, and to say the things one feels sure about, and believes everlastingly to matter to human beings.

If I had but one sermon to preach, I should first want to take a fresh look into the revealed heart of God. I believe the greatest window ever opened on the Eternal is the seventeenth chapter of St. John. There you will find set out before you the things Jesus thought about in the hour of His crisis: His faith and His fears, His values and His aims. He sees life in terms of a network of relationships between His Father, Himself, and those who have been given Him out of the world. That chapter is filled with personal pronouns. And in one great sentence He seems to give to us the sum and heart of the whole matter: "This is life eternal, that they should know thee the only true God, and him whom thou didst send, even Jesus Christ."

Now I should want to speak first about the homesickness of the human soul for God. Life does not furnish its own interpretation, the world does not provide its own meaning. The world of sense is well enough until our spirit is awake: but the moment we awake, we feel a lonely sense of uneasiness. The wider awake we become, the sharper is the sense of incompleteness. Within myself, within all men who have revealed to me their own real interior life, I find a spiritual instinct, buried as deep within our natures as any physical instinct can ever possibly be. The life of sense cannot satisfy it, the glare of education cannot reason it out for us. My work has carried me behind the scenes in a good many lives, back into the recesses where men really live: and I never come back from that kind of an excursion without a profounder conviction that I do not need to create spiritual interest and craving—that has been cared for long before.

There is a great phrase for this, early in the fourth Gospel, where it is written, "That was the true light that lighteth every man." That light may shine in conscience, intuition, imagination, beauty, the sense of the "numinous" or divine in the world. This interpretation means that there is a connection between the historic Christ and a man's interior longing and aspiration: a practical working identity between Him and our enlightened consciences. If we were what that interior incompleteness craves for, we should be like Christ. And the nearer we become like Him, and through Him reach the Father, the more fully is that intense and invisible longing satisfied and completed, so that whatever happens to the outward life, the inward life is rich and vivid and believing. St. Augustine's great saying for this is familiar to you all: "Thou hast made us for Thyself, and our hearts are restless till they find rest in Thee." The admission of that fact is the first step, I think, to a genuine solution of the problem of life. We are homesick as we stand.

If I had but one sermon to preach, I should want to say also that all of us at one time or other thwart and disobey that spiritual nature within us. We sin. We live in a generation that loves to feed itself on cheerful evasions of so sharp and condemning a word as sin—which calls our misdoings by nicer, softer words, explaining them by psychological processes and names which take all the responsibility out of our actions. To call those acts, and the condition of mind out of which they spring, by the name of sin is to say that we are free and independent moral beings, that we did not have to act thus and could have done otherwise. I want an explanation of why it is that after I have disobeyed the call of God within me, there comes an immediate self-judgment and self-reproach which is not scared off because somebody tells me I have merely inherited a moral taboo: and why it is that when I have sinned, prayer and peace are both impossible.

Now, there has got to be some provision for that fact in us, and some solution of the problem raised by it. I don't only want a way of life: there have been a thousand sages to say things that correspond with my inner ethical sense. If Jesus could provide only a way of life, He would stand on a level with Confucius and Moses and Socrates. I need redemption, not maxims. There is a rift through my soul because of sin—a split, a division in my nature. He who denies that for me is like a doctor who denies mortal sickness when it is there. It wants a tremendous cure. The more one thinks about sin, the more absurdly inadequate appear the current philosophies with their foolish faith in our power to pull ourselves up, by our own boot-straps. I need help from without. I need salvation. I need the Cross. And "the Cross is the medicine of the world."

Now, there is another fact as inescapable as the fact of sin, though our generation needs to learn it over again, and that is the fact of conversion. It is possible for a human soul to be lifted into a region hitherto undiscovered, where the rift is healed, where the disunity is harmonized, where peace takes the place of pain, and strength of weakness, and where one begins to live Life with a capital L. The kind of thing that happened to St. Paul is happening still. Divided and unhappy people are constantly being unified by what we call conversion. The blessed news of the Christian Gospel is that nobody needs to rest content with being what he is. Utterly without regard for anybody's gifts or limitations, Jesus held out to us a Gospel that begins, "Whosoever . . ."

Now, you know as well as I do, that we have left conversion, on the whole, to the rescue missions and the Salvation Army. God be praised for all they are doing. But it is one of the deepest convictions of my life that conversion needs to be put within reach of privileged and educated people, that Park Avenue needs it as badly as the Bowery, and that thousands upon thousands of ordinary church-people have been kept outside the real joy and power of the Christian religion because the Christian Church has been too ready to accept them as they are, and has hardly believed its own Invincible Christ is strong enough to convert the complacent and the prosperous and the intelligent. I am through catering to the intellectual vanity of this generation, and I am through being satisfied with lip-service in well-to-do church members.

Last night I was called to a hotel in this city, where a young man who had made wreck of his life had been drinking steadily for a week. In despair about himself, he asked for help. And from ten-thirty to one we talked. I told him of the Christ who could save men like himself: and hungrily and eagerly he listened. But years back a clergyman had failed him in the hour of his need: he had made a serious mistake in school, and the clergyman shut his door on him as a protest. And he carried in his heart a raging hatred for church-hypocrisy, which had kept him from Holy Communion and any church service since he was a boy. He was persuaded to come to Holy Communion this morning at the early service, and it was the first time in fifteen years. And as his soul wrestled in a life and death struggle, some woman kneeling piously behind him was talking to her neighbour about whether she had gone to such and such a show last night! I don't know who that woman is, and I don't want to know. But it is a sad pass when a human soul coming to Christ for rescue from sin and self, must be interrupted by that kind of a Christian.

The world does not need an awakening any more than the Church does. It was to an educated religious gentleman that Jesus said, "Ye must be born again." That imperative is a judgment against those who withstand conversion. But it is a hope held out to those fearful and self-depreciating people who do not think themselves capable of conversion. The new life begins by utter self-dedication to the will of God. All of us can do that, and must.

If I had but one sermon to preach, I should want to say to you all that I believe enormously in the possibility of a guided life, influenced and led at every step by the Holy Spirit. Conversion is the beginning, not the ending, of an experience of God. That experience continues when we use all the means Jesus put at our disposal for continuation—prayer, the Scriptures, the Church and the Sacraments, Christian fellowship and worship. There is a kind of Christianity which sticks faithfully by the precepts, a kind of new legalism, and good so far as it goes. But I believe God meant each one of us to experience a fresh and personal relationship to Him which becomes creative and original. Many situations in my life are not covered by the Sermon on the Mount. I need special guidance and illumination. The prophets of Israel had it. The apostles had it. Where is it gone to in this age? We believe in the Holy Spirit as we believe in some dead human character: he was once, but he is gone. The deepest need of our age, the cure for most of our back-door attempts to establish communication with the other world, is a rediscovery of the Holy Spirit.

What infinite possibilities of learning the will of God, through communion with Him, may lie ahead of us, who can dare to imagine? Here, surely, is the realm in which unbelievable development is still possible. Science, with a long face, says, "Man is done evolving physically and intellectually: we have not gone beyond the Greeks in body or brain." And religion, scanning a far horizon with hope in her eyes, says, "Man has scarcely begun to evolve spiritually: he is to-day spiritually where he was physically when his eyes were light-spots and his spine a piece of gristle. And beyond him stretch unseen and unimagined capacities for traffic with the other world." It is not the scientists who deny, but the spiritual experimenters who believe in first-hand touch with God, who are the real progressives in our world. The most advanced type of human being I know is represented by this sentence from a friend, just put, into my hands: "I feel the beginning of the experience of a day when prayer runs under and through everything."

If this were the last sermon I were going to preach, I should lay upon you all your duty to cry out to men in darkness that this is The Way. Because it has been done badly, because some have been offended by it, we have tended to forget and omit evangelism altogether. In the days of religion's youth and vigour and health, when it is potent enough to form men's minds and transform their lives, you will find it carrying them far out beyond self-conscious concern about what others will say or think of them: they have found the Messiah, and it is heavy upon their hearts that they must call out to the world, "Come and see!" that they may find Him also. It would not be an intrusion to call to a caravan in the desert that you know where water is: and we are here as in a desert, where the souls of men shrivel and go to dust for lack of the Water of Life. Let it be done with wisdom and tact, with sympathy and good humour and seasoned with salt—but let it be done!

I suspect that if you and I knew that our end were near, we should regret nothing so much as to look back upon the lost opportunities of hungry human souls to whom we might have spoken of the all-satisfyingness of the Christ, but to whom we did not speak because we were afraid. Touching lives one by one is fascinating business, and involves some of the most rewarding and beautiful human relationships that can possibly arise. But its motive does not lie in its interest or its reward, but in its urgent need. We may think we are emancipated in this generation; but for all our freedom, we are making a worse fist of life than men made when they believed in God. And we need a host of men and women who believe that, to go forth and say it in the highways and byways of the earth. If you have found The Way, tell men so—otherwise they will probably never find it.

And I should want to say a particular word about the amazing adequacy of Christ. He is alive, and He is a Person, and He is within reach of you and me. Of the best life that has been lived for twenty centuries, He is the author. The best men and women I know owe everything to Him. He does not save them from the hard knocks that life brings to us all, surely by some design: but He saves them from bitterness, from rebelliousness, from the feeling of destitution and futility. When trouble comes, they do not worry, but rather wait for His full purpose to emerge through the trial. That much I see in others. And what I see for them, that I have experienced for myself. I am not old, and outwardly life has slipped along smoothly and happily for me: but you know that no man can live at all, in his own or others' experience, without inward struggle, battle, temptation, suffering. I can say to you without reserve or quibbling, that Jesus Christ satisfies. He puts a purpose into life it never had before. He shares all its loads and its perplexities. He literally and actually stoops into my life to give me help in the hour of temptation, as often as I let Him come. He makes people happy, not with the hard indifference to trouble of the Stoic, not with the soft indifference of the professional optimist, but with that joy of His own which caused Him to cry out, "Be of good cheer—I have overcome the world."

And because of His adequacy here, I trust Him in what He says of all that lies before. I find Him mistaken in nothing He said about this life: I trust Him about the next. I believe that one day I shall face Him, and give account to Him of the deeds done in the body. And if that be so, it is going to alter all my way of travelling through this world. If I had but this one sermon to preach, I think I should surely want to warn against the prevalent view of life which makes this world the centre. Life is short, and quantitatively unimportant. But life is decisive, and qualitatively immensely important. For there takes place in this life a set of character, a drift of spirit, which there is no good ground for believing will cease to obtain when the last river is crossed. We shall be when we land yonder what we were when we left this shore. Through unending ages, I believe, the love of God will pursue a soul to the utmost confines of this universe to fetch it back to Him: but souls are free to choose, and free to refuse. They miss God here, and they may reject Him forever. The soul that permanently refuses God chooses hell instead.

I believe that hell is the lasting absence of God—that is what I understand by it, and I see no Christian warrant for a sentimental evasion of believing in it. It is the natural evolution of a rebellious soul. We want everything else to go according to strict law, but we want God to intervene suddenly when we see where the path we have been treading leads us, and to save everybody regardless. We are tampering with spiritual laws in our easy modern forgetfulness of the wages of sin. God is not pitchforking souls into hell—they are pitchforking themselves when they refuse His salvation from themselves and their sin. You don't grow hyacinths out of onions: and souls are not born into the presence of God in heaven who have all their lives fled His presence on earth. I am not commending a religion of fear, but simply a religion of fact, and not of fancy, as too many choose for themselves to-day. This world is the brief schooltime of an everlasting spirit: and we need to take it seriously for the training, but not as if it were the world which matters most.

But that "eternal life" which goes on in the infinite ages of God does not begin with death, it begins with the acceptance of God in Jesus Christ. "This is life eternal, that they should know thee, the only true God, and him whom thou didst send, even Jesus Christ." God is knowable in Christ: and what that acquaintance brings to us is a present sense of our immortality, in a life which is so good that we feel within us it is indestructible.

There is but one final thing I would want to say. To some of us that relationship is an aspiration unrealized. We do not know Him, nor have we really found Him. And I believe the trouble lies here: we have not surrendered ourselves to Him. There is something within us He hates, and we will not let it go. There is a plan He has for us bigger than our own plan, and we are afraid of it. Somewhere we hold back. Somewhere we keep control of our own destiny. Let go! Abandon yourself to Him. Say to Him, "Not my will but Thine be done." Live it. Pray for it. Put yourself at His disposal for time and for eternity. And if your experience is anything like mine has been, you will find that Jesus gives to life a zest and a glory, a peace and a purpose, which He only can give. If these glimpses of eternal life which come to us through Him are pledges of what we may know perpetually when the shadows flee away, I want to live forever. And by the mercy of God in Christ by His gift of eternal life, by the atoning sacrifice of His Cross, I believe I shall.

Let us pray:

O God, who didst send Thy Son into the world to make Thyself known to us in ways we could understand: Lay upon us a sense of urgency about our religion, lest in apathy and dull acceptance we miss the best Thou hast for us. Waken all the spiritual possibilities within us. Help us to give all we have to Thee, and to help. Thee build the Kingdom. And in Thy mercy bring us at the last into Thy presence, to worship and enjoy Thee forever. Through the merits of Thy Son, Jesus Christ our Saviour. Amen.

II

# The Necessity of Christ

*"No man hath seen God at any time; the only begotten Son, who is in the bosom of the Father, he hath declared him."*

—JOHN 1:18.

I speak to you to-day upon the Necessity of Christ.

One may believe that the reason why Christ came was the sin of man. God had tried all through the long path of human history to make Himself known. Through dim heathen ceremonies, through the haunting fears of animism, through pagan mythology; and then through the law and the prophets of the Hebrews, through Abraham and Moses, through Isaiah and Hosea, God had been sending out reminders to the human race. But all failed because of the stubbornness of man, his wilfulness and his independence. And "Christ Jesus came into the world to save sinners"—there is scriptural authority for this view, and it commends itself to every man's common sense.

But I do not believe that is the *only* reason for the coming of Christ. It is quite possible that, even if we had done what we should and been what we ought, Christ would nevertheless have come. For all we know, it may have been part of the eternal purpose of God that, "in the fullness of time," He should send forth His Son into the world. I believe that there are things which God wanted to say to us human beings which could not be said save through such an one as Christ, and that He was necessary in God's whole scheme, and not merely a remedy for the apparent failure of God to make men remember Him.

I want to take up with you certain points which seem to me to necessitate a human revelation of God, a historic expression of God in terms of human life. There are facts in our experience which, without Christ, seem to me to remain unsolved and insoluble problems.

In the first place, God is hard to know. There is a widely-known preacher of very liberal thinking who has said recently that it is presumptuous of Christians to think that they can know God. This gentleman has turned agnostic, and feels that we cannot know. But I would like to remind him that Christianity itself is agnostic about God, apart from the revelation of Christ. "No man hath seen God at any time," says St. John—and I take it that he means something more than physical sight which could have no application here: he means, I believe, that in His final nature, apart from authentic revelation of Himself, God is obscure and unknowable. The mystery of life lies too heavy upon us all not to know how desolate a mood that sentence may express: "No man hath seen God at any time." There is ruthlessness in natural creation which is hard to reconcile with a good God. There is impersonality in the laws of the natural world to which we are all made subject. The mechanism of the modern is only the fatalism of the ancient in a different dress, the Anangke of the Greek, the Kismet of the Mohammedan. There are times when we seem to be caught as a wild thing in a trap. Little children suffer for others' sins, and men hate and fight, and there is the everlasting problem of the dreadfully poor. What kind of a God is God? That is the ever-present problem of life.

And even if you say that the force of the universe is personal, in the sense that there is intelligence and will in that Force, how much does He care for us, whether we rise or sink? What communication is possible between us? Are there secrets in His keeping which I may learn if I listen? Is He force, or is He Father? Those questions, without Christ, are left permanently unanswered. But if Christ is the revelation of God, if God feels towards us as Christ does; if He represents the perfect character of God completely expressed in human and understandable terms, then, for all that our liberal friend may say, we do know God. Him whom we have been ignorantly worshipping, Him Christ declares unto us. The perfection of Christ's own life and character is the best seal that He is the revelation of God. What can you think of God as being, which Christ is not? What further perfection does your imagination glimpse which is not in Christ? And can you not say, with St. John, that "the only begotten Son, who is in the bosom of the Father, he hath declared Him"?

Not only is God hard to know, but life is hard to meet successfully. People are always at sea about what they shall love most: and from that comes the perplexity of mind which does not know how to act. We have no basic values, therefore we have no standards, therefore we have no principle of living and acting. How many people have you known who, with a gesture of new-won freedom, have flung religion to the winds, and for a few months or years gone along without it? And then comes wonder. What *is* right? What *is* worth working for? What meaning *has* life, after all?

I talked but this week with a man who was long ago a member of this church, and now feels no need to go anywhere. Yet he spends much time away from his wife and children because of small irritation. And he talked to me shyly about his own "confusion of mind." Life *is* confusing without Christ: for we know neither what to believe in nor what principle to act upon. There are mysterious and seemingly contradictory experiences which come to all of us: and we do not know our way through them. And I suppose that what we do at a time like that is to look about to those who seem to be meeting life more successfully than we are. We see through the failures of nine-tenths of what people call life: and in the other tenth we see a glimmer of meaning. From them we seek sympathy, or advice, or just strength to lean on. But there is no permanent cure here. For we shall be again in trouble. Must we be everlastingly restless, always turning to someone else for a second-hand solution? What makes us turn to those other people? It is generally that, as we say, they have "got something." That is an evasive phrase for saying they believe in and trust God. They generally trust God as they have come to know Him in Christ. Why not go direct to the Source? Why not say that Christ offers the only ideal for man that fits in this world and covers all the cases that can arise?

And it is not enough merely to *tell* about an ideal. The world's sages from the beginning have done that. But Christ also embodies that ideal perfectly in Himself. He is not pointing to a distant height while He stands Himself just where we stand. He began just where we are and made the climb: but He stands upon that height and calls down to us to come up, for He knows the ascent is possible, because He has made it. That is the only kind of an ideal that is worth much to us—not only a realizeable ideal, but a realized ideal, embodied in a perfect life. I say that Christ is utterly necessary to give mankind light on his path.

Third, sin is hard to overcome. For there are times when I see light on my path, and know just where I ought to go: but I do not go. I wilfully go in another direction. And when I know the will of God and choose my own instead, that is sin.

The world has its cheap solutions. One of them is that everybody else sins, too. And that is a lying solution, for some have found the path: and even if the majority have not, there is no more peace in herd-sin than in individual sin.

Another solution is that we do enough good to make up for it in the long run: John may get drunk, but John is good-hearted, and God will forget the getting drunk. It is the solution of a morally foggy mind. It is ethically no solution at all. For when we sit down alone and face ourselves as we really are, we know that sin is a barrier between us and our own best, and between us and God. It is a definite problem which we consider as a problem except when we are trying to evade it for self-justification. And we need a solution for it.

Christ offers us three things. The first is *forgiveness* for the past. He holds out the heart of God as willing to forgive anyone who comes in honest penitence and says he is sorry and means to stop. He makes matters right between us and Him. As a friend said to me this week, "The past is *gone*."

The second is power to stop sinning. None of us does very well at overcoming sin, but when we do, we know that it has not been all our own doing. Co-operation, yes, but not our own sole effort. For "every virtue we possess, and every victory won, and every thought of holiness, are His alone."

And the third is, the *Cross* to make up for the mass of unatoned, unforgiven, unwashed sin. There is a heap of it. Some I have not recognized. Some I have not had heart to confront and deal with. Some I committed with Christ almost standing by. I can do nothing about it. There is absolutely no excuse for it. I cannot honestly say I tried not to do it. Nothing in me can handle that sin. Only the stooping and infinite mercy of God, taking my sin upon Him, can deal with it, shrive it, obliterate it. The Cross is the only solution. And without it the revelation of God in Christ and the Ideal of man in Christ would leave a terrible incompleteness. Christ alone holds in His hand the key and the cure for sin. Plenty of sages, with ideals to offer. Plenty of good people, with advice. But only one Saviour, to offer a solution for human sin.

And finally, death looks like the end. It is all very well for people to talk about caterpillars turning into butterflies: and the return of the springtime, with the sprouting leaves upon the trees. But butterflies die, and trees die: and while the energy may go off into some other sphere, according to some law of the conservation of energy, that is not much comfort. People may talk about living on in posterity, or the fame of a good name: but that is a pale immortality, a substitute and cheat for eternal life. We belong to the animal kingdom: and it looks as though dead things stay dead. We shall never know again, I suppose, the withering devastation of death in the ancient pagan world. I have seen some of it remaining in China and India. Whatever survival was believed in in the pagan world was shadowy and filmy existence, the spawn of a hopeless hope. There was nothing whatever to authenticate it but the wish of men. And for most of us, it is not a cheerful prospect that death is the end of all things. A few people with more bravado than brains talk about meeting it philosophically and the rest, but normal human beings wish for immortality, and crave it as deeply as they crave anything in life.

Now, Christ brings a solution here. He sets going in men's lives here a quality which He called "eternal life," which was the product of a relationship between us and His Father through Him. He believed that that life went on in the infinite ages of God unbroken and ever unfolding in new riches. This might be merely a hope also, except for one fact: and that fact is His own death and resurrection. Lord Acton, the British historian, said that the resurrection of Christ was one of the best-authenticated facts in history. Never mind now whether body rose with spirit: the indubitable fact is that the apostles were in touch afresh with the Personality which had left them, to all physical appearance, on the Cross. They gathered together again, picked up the bits of a movement shattered by His two days in the grave, and set out to conquer the world with the faith in life after death. And that was the sure part of their creed which utterly swept the pagan world, long dark with despair about the future. I do not want a hope, I want a well-authenticated assurance of life to come. Anybody can wish: but I want evidence. And Christ brought that evidence and laid it before me, woven into the very vitals of the early Church, by His own presence and risen power in their midst. Death is not the end, but the beginning. Christ alone is our final witness.

I hope that what I have said may help to convince you of the central necessity of Christ in faith. There are those who say that Christ did not think of Himself except as a way to God, and that He put God in the first place. So, I think, He did; but He also said that He was one with His Father, and that He was Way and Truth and Life, and Bread of Life, and Door, and Good Shepherd, and Resurrection and Life, and Son of God. "No man cometh unto the Father but by me" lays an emphasis upon

Christ as great as that upon God. If God cannot be fully known and approached apart from Christ, which I believe is not a dogma but an experience, then there is not much difference between Them. When learned modern theologians say they are baffled by the Nicene Creed with its outworn metaphysics, "begotten of the Father before all worlds, God of God, light of light, very God of very God, begotten not made, being of one substance with the Father by whom all things were made," I should like to presume to tell them that it means one very great big thing, and that is, that there is not much difference between God and Christ. Now, if they do not believe that, let them come out and say so. But let them be honest, and stop talking about creedal obscurity, when the fog is in their own minds. The kind of Christianity which has captured the world has not been a Christianity of ethics, or of faith in God, or of social righteousness alone—it has been a Christianity which emphasized Christ and exalted Him and prayed to Him and found Him a living Lord of present experience, and sought to have the kind of experiences reproduced in them which He had in His own life.

And so I ask you to focus your minds, not so much upon His philosophy or His view of God, or even His teachings, but rather upon Christ Himself. We cannot be too much concerned with Him. The greatest servants the world has ever seen have been those whose minds revolve round Him with a kind of holy pre-occupation, who cannot let Him alone, whose gaze always comes to a full stop when their eyes meet Him. From that creative relationship arises more kindness, more ingenious human service, more moral power, more spiritual insight, and more sweetness of life, than from anywhere else in all the world.

It is not enough to know the centrality of Christ in Christian thinking; we must make Him central in our planning and our working and our spending. He is not necessary to the wide world unless He is necessary to us. It is a dangerous thing to put Him at the centre of history and not put Him also at the centre of our lives.

Let us to-day, in thankfulness for what He has done for us and for all men, enthrone Him again in the high place of our hearts.

III

# What Is Unbelief?

*"And he marvelled because of their unbelief."*
—MARK 6:6.

Probably no generation ever paid such high honour to unbelief as our own. There are a great many people to-day who almost automatically think better of the intellectual integrity of the man who disbelieves than of the man who believes. Since Tennyson said:

*"There lives more faith in honest doubt,*
*Believe me, than in half the creeds,"*

every little two-by-four sceptic has taken it to apply to himself, and set his faithlessness upon a higher pinnacle for admiration than the faith of Isaiah or of St. John the Divine. Unbelief is a very popular personage today, and I think we may do well to look a little into his ancestry and his character.

Go back in your imagination to a scene outside the village church in the city of Nazareth. A young Man of this town has just come back from a preaching and healing journey by the Lake of Galilee. Word has been brought back to the village of the extraordinary influence this Man has exerted, healing the sick, even raising the dead, calling men away from their livelihood to follow Him in His mission. These stories spread like wildfire in an oriental village: and they are added to, and distorted and seen out of focus. A little family, without too much imagination, is a bit embarrassed at the fame of this Eldest Son; and they wish He would come home and let His mission alone—there is plenty of hard work to be done in Nazareth.

And on this Saturday morning a crowd of chatterers gather just after church, the village gossips, the half-sentimental, half-cruel group that makes up a popular crowd. The young Man has come home and preached in the village church. And because He was wise without being learned, and because He was spiritually powerful without being recognized before He left the village, and because He was nobody but one of themselves, "the carpenter, the Son of Mary," they were scandalized about Him. And there emanated from that crowd a cloud, a mist of unbelief as palpable as poison gas, an atmosphere of scepticism and devastating misgiving, so that all He would do was to heal a few sick folk—presumably in some quarter of the town where the air was clear, where those fumes of withering rejection had not been able to come.

But for those few unspoiled spots, where a green blade of unwithered faith stood upright, all Nazareth lay under a miasma of unbelief in the only Person that keeps Nazareth from oblivion. The words, the gestures, the silences of the muttering little crowd of gossipers spread like an unholy gas, from the very door of the village church.

"And he marvelled because of their unbelief."

What is unbelief? We think to-day that it means intellectual unwillingness to swallow ancient doctrines. But there was no doctrine here. We think that it means the dark conclusion of men who have looked life square in the face and say that it is insensate and meaningless. But here was no hard philosophical reasoning. We think that unbelief is the attitude of a proud Hindu or Confucianist towards Christianity, for which, with perverted tolerance, we admire him and in which we encourage him. But here was no comparison, and no judgment laid against far-distant men. We like to keep unbelief in the upper story of our natures, and to think that it is the product of reason alone: because that feeds our pride just where this generation most wants it to be fed. But this unbelief had other factors in it than sound reasoning.

Now, I want to stop long enough to pay my respects to all those who have genuine intellectual difficulty with Christianity. The new world has created new problems. We cannot, if we would, look out on life with the outlook which men had half a century ago. Let me say that I have no fear for Christianity if you will make a complete intellectual investigation of it, historically, philosophically, psychologically and, above all, practically. But I have a great many fears that you will be deceived about your own intellectuality, as thousands are to-day deceived about theirs. There is more in the make-up of common human unbelief than pure and honest reasoning.

What was the unbelief of that crowd in Nazareth? *Unbelief was the rejection of spiritual power in the plain face of that power.* It didn't come out of their heads, but out of their hearts and their attitudes and their customs and their purses, and right up out of the inward vitals of them. There was mighty little that was intellectual in it: but all the rest of a wrongly-based nature rose up to stand against this Man. Unbelief was the refusal to recognize and to accept a spiritual power whose force was manifested to them where they could all see it. This was not something which their minds forced them to reject: it was something their consciences forced them to receive, but they would not. Faith would not have meant believing in something they could not see, but accepting something they *could* see.

The primary factor in their unbelief was moral. Be sure of this: that what Jesus "marvelled at" you may put down for an unnecessary and an unnatural thing. Do you remember when Jesus appeared to the eleven, after His resurrection, and "upbraided them with their unbelief and hardness of heart"? You may be sure that Jesus would not rebuke an honest intellectual dissent. He must have felt in them some quality for which they were responsible, some moral obtuseness which kept them from recognizing Him in the plain manifestation of His resurrection-power. It was no paltry intellectual questioning which He felt, either after the resurrection, or way back there in Nazareth: He felt that the moral stubbornness and unreceptiveness of these men was the predominant quality of their unbelief. I shall never forget studying the eighth chapter of St. John with a man whom I believe to be the most gifted preacher of this generation: and he called that chapter "a supernaturally acute analysis of the ultimate moral origin of unbelief." It is a striking and terrible phrase—"the ultimate moral origin of unbelief."

But the more I come into touch with unbelief, and see round it, and see behind it, the more do I believe in the judgment which lies wrapped in that phrase. I believe that all intellectual doubt is alloyed with moral factors. We do not come to any conclusions merely with our minds. The rest of our nature casts its vote in every decision. Sin is always calling to doubt, "Come over and help us." These two together will rob a man of all the spiritual conviction he has, if they can bind him between them. I have never met a perfect man, nor a man without some kind of moral twist in him. I believe that when a man's mind comes to deal with religion, it cannot suddenly slough off all the rest of him and become naked and honest mentality all at once. No—the rest of his nature will have its vote. And by as much as I have never found a *man* whose *life* was not alloyed with sin, by so much have I never found a man whose *mind* was not alloyed with sin in making its decisions. The profoundest scientist has prejudices, loves, temperament, dispositional tendencies, which affect all his work; and enter especially into all large judgments which he makes of life as a whole. All men sin.

Therefore, into the doubt of every man comes the weight of sin, pulling the scales towards unbelief. For unbelief and sin are sworn and congenital allies. If sin can make a man lose faith in God, it can have its own way with him. If doubt can make sin its ally, together they can rob him of God and wreck his life. There is a subtle and inevitable co-operation between these two. Unbelief may be honest, intellectually considered: but search your unbelief with honest scrutiny, and see what else you find tied to it, beside scrupulous intellectual fidelity to the facts!

Similarly, the way out of unbelief is moral as well as intellectual. Jesus said, "If any man willeth to do his will, he shall know." That is to say, "If any man will begin by living up to as much as he understands of the moral requisites of God, he will later, in the light of his experience, come to see straight intellectually." That is an experimental challenge, and it has been the experience of thousands upon thousands that it is an experiment which leads to truth for life. I may be quite unable to convince a man he is wrong in not believing in God or in the divinity of Christ: if I can get him to live according to the revealed will of the God in whom as yet he cannot believe, time will come when he will believe in that God and understand with his mind. A moral experiment is worth ten times an intellectual investigation in apprehending spiritual truth. Obedience is as much the organ of spiritual understanding as reason. Many people have come into a personal and living faith by trying the experiment which is implied in: "If any man willeth to do his will, he shall know."

Unbelief, therefore, is not naked intellectual doubt: it is compounded with moral refusal to proceed upon the evidence of the experience of others. It is as much a matter of temperament, oftentimes, as of reason. And it often has its seat more in the will than in the mind. Unbelief is the negative atmosphere, the unexpectant, unhopeful attitude. Christian Science is right so far: we do create an atmosphere conducive to creative progress, or hostile to it. The root of some unbelief is the spirit of "It can't be done."

It is unbelief to treat an old situation as though it could never be remedied. We are always thinking people cannot be changed—especially the people we know best, and whose qualities seem to be so rooted that they can never be altered. Frequently I come upon young men whose families have never given them any religion to speak of. They have gone off to school and heard about Christ as a new experience. Because it is new, it is sometimes more interesting to them than to those families who have been long exposed to it. Such a boy comes home, and wonders what would happen if his family should really understand about Christ. I talked with such a boy last week. And it was hard for him to realize that his father is plastic and changeable still. He is not the immovably set and unalterable human being he thinks of as his father—but is probably unsatisfied underneath a kind of success. But it is hard for that boy to think of his father in new ways. And it is hard to escape the binding and killing effect of that kind of unbelief. We all succumb to it whenever we regard anybody as hopeless and impossible to touch. God can touch anybody. Our own unfaith may make it impossible for God to do the work He wants to do through us.

It is unbelief when you are called upon to assume a larger responsibility which is offered to you by others who know your capacity: and something within you quails and shivers and says: "No. I am not capable of it. I will fail." The very willingness to tackle it might have distended your own capacity. Many a man seems to undergo a fresh accession of ability when he begins a piece of work which is too large for him.

And it is unbelief when we are called to go through something, and we begin to waver and fear. We may know that we are going to lose someone who is very dear to us, or that we must face a long period of suffering, or separation. Something inside us crumples up and goes dead. We all know the sensation. And yet that very fear may paralyze the power which would have made it possible to go through with it. Unbelief isn't doubting some fact of long ago—unbelief is acting and feeling as though there were no God in the daily conduct of our lives. You can believe in miracles in the New Testament and the Old: but if you cannot believe in miracles in your own life, your faith is cold, intellectual assent; and not the warm and vibrant thing Christ meant faith to be.

It is unbelief when we are satisfied with second-best when we can aim at first. The kind of unbelief, which is my problem, is to think there are people who really cannot grasp or undergo the thing I mean by an experience of Christ. When I put anyone—old, conventional Christian, or weak, unconvinced unbeliever—outside the actual possibility of as deep an experience of Christ as I have known, that is unbelief.

When I am sometimes dreaming great things for this parish, and seeing in it potentially a great spiritual centre, where men and women may find held up the living Christ, and feel His Spirit amongst us, and find Him and be forever changed, and go forth bearing His message to the world, something whispers in my ear, "That's a day-dream. They will not really get what you mean. They will be just like every other crowd of church-people—no friendlier, no deeper, no realer than any others. Do not expect too much. Give them as much religion as will keep them coming to church and being decent citizens, but do not expect to make prophets out of them; for you cannot hope to do it." *That* is unbelief for me.

There *have* been congregations that have radiated the Spirit of Christ so that any chance comer felt it the moment he came in the door—congregations filled with real spiritual power. Against the evidence of facts rises up this mood, this misgiving, this fear out of some dark place in my own heart. And that doubt for me is sin—sin against which I have to fight as against any other sin. It is not a reasonable conclusion: faith enough on my part and on yours might achieve the miracle of an entirely Christian local church. When I doubt it, the fear arises, not from outside myself where I cannot control it, but from inside myself where I can.

It is unbelief when we see the power of Christ come wonderfully down into the life of another, and they say, "But that never can come to me." How do you know? Do you not close the door in the face of Christ when you say a thing like that, and lock it when you persist in saying that the other person is better equipped by temperament than you, or does not have the baffling questions arise that come to you? How do you know? Most honest people have intellectual difficulties with religion. You are not alone. They have fought through their doubts—why shouldn't you fight through yours?

I say that Jesus would not marvel at unbelief unless unbelief were something which could be dealt with as a problem, and did not need to be accepted as a fate. Unbelief may be a way-station, but it is not meant for a destination. There are other factors in most of it than pure reason. And by its own unwillingness to die, like a dead leaf, and let a live thing come and take its place—by its persistent demand to monopolize life, doubt usurps the direction of life which ought to belong, until God is found, to the conscience; and after God is found, to Him.

It is no good being general. Let us come to grips with the unbelief in our own lives—not the questioning of this or that miracle or point of theology—those may need to wait till larger matters are settled. I mean unbelief about God and life and the goodness of the universe and the worthwhileness of life. If you question here, ask yourself very honestly how much sin enters into your doubt—sin of intellectual pride, sin of self-pity which loves to think itself injured in an unjust cosmos, sin of laziness which will not really investigate, sin of fear which will not face God lest He ask of us that which we are unwilling to grant. I do not say this to condemn you, but to reveal you to yourselves. Be quite honest whether this seems to you a wholly reasonable way to look at religion—or whether you are more like the crowd at Nazareth, whose unbelief was born and spread in the very place where Christ's power could have been proved and demonstrated. They would not give Him the chance to prove Himself. Is that what you are doing? Have you sought out people He has helped, and found out how it came? Or have you gone off skulking and said religion was all humbug and emotion?

Are you afraid of the demands of Christ? "Cold feet" have kept more people away from Christ than cold logic. It was that moral, responsible element in unbelief which Christ detected and despised in the crowd at Nazareth, and despises still. He says to our age, as He said to His own, with terrible exposure of sin as the root of unbelief: "Why do ye not understand my speech? Even because ye cannot hear my word. Ye are of your father the devil, and the lusts of your father it is your will to do. He was a murderer from the beginning, and standeth not in the truth because there is no truth in him." "Because there is no truth in him"—there stands Christ's exposure of the root and cause for much in us which masquerades as intellectual integrity. Somebody needs to take down this generation in the pride of its intellect, and humble it before God. This world is the small end of life. Knowledge of God is worth more than all the wisdom of the world. This age needs to know how much of its unbelief is conceit at the bottom.

Let us, then, lift up our eyes to the Christ, and lay hold of every meaning we can find in Him. In Him are gathered up all the values which our best selves understand. Let us put aside abstract intellectual difficulties, and seek first a personal relationship to Him, in the light of which truth may break. Let us bring to Him, not only ourselves but our problems, not only our faith but our unbelief as well, saying with the centurion of old: "Lord, I believe. Help thou"—for there is none other to help—"mine unbelief."

Let us pray:

O God, who in all ages hast imparted Thyself to man and set alight the fire of faith in his heart: Grant to us the faith which comes from search. Cleanse our lives from all that negates and crushes out faith: fill them with the purity and honesty which fosters it. Search us for the evil which makes unbelief its friend, and drive it far from us. So that being willing, in all things, to do Thy will, we may know the truth which shall set us free, by the light of the Holy Spirit. Through Jesus Christ our Lord. Amen.

IV

# The Meaning of Self-Surrender

*"Who then offereth willingly to consecrate himself this day unto Jehovah?"*
—I CHRONICLES 29:5.

The meaning of self-surrender to God is the deepest meaning in all the experience of religion. There is something deep-hidden within us which makes us feel that, whatever God is, He is more ideal than we are, and that we shall tend to find our life by yielding it, in as nearly an absolute sense as possible, to the Ideal Power which we call God. The very earliest stirrings of faith in God at all carry with them some natural response of this sort. It is hard for us to think of God without thinking also of our duty towards Him, and it is impossible to conceive that duty in any vitally personal sense without the consciousness that we cannot begin to do it until we have first offered the whole of ourselves to God. Like human love, religion is impossible without the maximum of self-giving.

I am perfectly sure that self-surrender is for most people an unrealized aspiration. They feel the edges of it in great moments of joy or of sadness. Music stirs it in them, if they be susceptible to music. Art may do it, or a sunset sky. A great spoken word, or the convincing life of a saint—there are a thousand possible stimuli to the thought of self-surrender to the Power of the universe. But this generally goes off into diffuse ether. The thing is mostly emotion which does not harness itself to something that needs to be done. It is fitful and unsustained. It is a glimpse we get into reality, that does not last long enough to become an abiding possession, a permanent attitude of obedience and trust and loving co-operation.

If I can to-day, I want to draw this thing out of the vague region where for most of us it resides, only occasionally invading our minds, and put it where it may become actual for us all. May I say to you, frankly and personally, that I was a missionary on foreign soil, with a Christian home, confirmation, many student conferences, and a decision to enter the ministry, behind me, before I ever saw the luminous depths, the liberating power, of the experience of self-surrender? My brethren, these things ought not so to be; and it is one of the great resolves of my ministry that they shall not be where, by preaching and talking in season and out of season, upon the reality of this experience, I can prevent them from being. It is a lamentable thing that in our religious instruction, and our preaching, we can hit upon so many peripheral and secondary things, while Christian people go through their lives without knowing that this central experience is possible for them.

William James has told us that people belong to one of two types, the once-born, or the twice-born type. Emerson was a type of the first, a mind always at unity with itself, with little consciousness of duality or division, which holds communion with the Absolute as with a familiar Friend, and which finds harmony and peace by falling naturally into step with the purposes of Providence. The twice-born type is aware of disunity, division, a rift at the centre of being, something in oneself that is out of gear and out of step and needs righting. St. Paul is the great type of it, and the heart of the need for second birth is his cry: "Wretched man that I am! Who shall deliver me from the body of this death?" The once-born type takes naturally to goodness and elevated activity which makes for happiness and peace. The twice-born type is beset with anxieties and inward friction which can only find happy activity after an inward readjustment has taken place.

A great many of us belong to the twice-born group, or ought to belong to it, who need to find it out. We like to think we are once-born, and all right as we are. We have glossed over the division and disunity within us by a fictitious outward self-possession and quietness. But the rift can only be fully healed when we have given ourselves over to God.

Now, for this twice-born type, there are two possible ways of surrendering. A surrender may be largely a deliberate act of will. A man having seen the issue of surrender, and knowing that God wants the whole of his life unreservedly, may make the plunge and throw himself utterly upon God to do with as He will. Such a surrender is that described in the *Life of Prof. Henry B. Wright*,[1] of Yale, where he says, of a meeting he attended at Northfield: "I was afraid I should be asked to go as a foreign missionary, but I went down. There, seated in an armchair at one end of the room, was the greatest human I have ever known, Dwight L. Moody. He spoke to us simply and briefly about the issues of life, using John 7:17 as his theme: 'If any man willeth to do his will, he shall know of the teaching, whether it be of God, or whether I speak from myself.' There in the quiet, without anyone knowing what was going on, I gave myself to God, my whole mind, heart and body: and I meant it." Those of you who know of Henry Wright's profound influence for more than twenty years upon student life in this country, and the emphasis he always put on the need for absolute surrender to God's will, will not ask whether such an experience is lasting; you will know that it is both lasting and widely multiplying.

I could give you a hundred instances of men and women whom I have known,

1 By George Stewart, p. 18.

who have, at a critical place in their lives, made this momentous turning and have never retraced their steps or gone back on their decision. You may be the kind of person who, having seen the choice, must deliberately, coolly, sanely and with resolve, hand yourself to God by making a deed of trust for your life, disposing of yourself to Him so that you can never take yourself back again.

There are others of this twice-born type who cannot thus take the kingdom of heaven by force. There are two elements in the complete experience of which I speak, if surrender grows into conversion: man's turn, and God's search. For some of us, the critical element is the dedication of our own wills. For others it is the moment of God's invasion. Surrender is, then, not so much effort as is required in throwing ourselves over upon the mercy of God, but only so much effort as is needed to open the door of our life to Him. We must all know that what God does for us in a conversion is the great matter, and not what we do for ourselves: but there are natures in which this is the supreme part, in the sense that surrender is a passive thing rather than an active one. I am not now talking about resignation under pain and trouble, which is quite another question. I am speaking of the need for an open and relaxed and unstruggling mind as the medium through which God can alone come into the lives of some people. Possibly there is an element of each emphasis needed in us all, so that we both make the effort of deliberate self-surrender and also cease from all effort, so that no exertion on our part may interfere with God's dealing with us. We may not be able to tell which is to be our particular means of surrendering, until we try it.

One is bound to be asked the question whether this is a sudden or a gradual matter. I believe that it is a relatively sudden matter for many, and a combination of suddenness and gradualness for others. For the person who wakes up to the fact that they are matured in every other way, but babes in their spiritual development, so that the great experience of religion has yet to come, I believe that it is likely to be an experience which takes place at a definite and recognized time. It is significant that James wrote: "Self-surrender has been and always must be regarded as the vital turning-point of the religious life. . . . One may say that the development of Christianity in inwardness has consisted in little more than the greater and greater emphasis attached to this crisis of self-surrender." Crisis, mark you, not process.

The process which comes before the act of surrender is the long discovery that the way of self is no way at all, and leads nowhither—the lonely, despairing, feverish desire to be rid of oneself. And the process which comes after the act of surrender is the steady matching-up of the actual with the ideal, the rethinking and remoulding life in accordance with the great decision. Both processes may take time, much time. But the decision itself has the definiteness about it which any decision has: you may prepare long for a decision, you may work long to carry it out. But when you decide, the hammer falls, and there cannot be delay.

Now I want to speak of four immediate results of surrender, when one has wholly let go of one's life, and is living continually with reference to God. By these I think it fair to test whether we have surrendered or not.

The first is a wide sense of liberation. The queer thing about self-will is that it kills the very thing it wants, freedom. If you know any more abject slave than the man or woman who has throughout his life had his own way, I would like to know where you find one. One of my friends tells me, when I talk to him along these lines: "I feel as if you were trying to put a big, black overcoat on me, and button it tight." But it is precisely his own complete control of the issues of his life which is, year after year, buttoning the overcoat tighter and tighter; and it is the very surrender which he fears that alone can bring him liberty. There is no freedom under God's wide heaven like the freedom of having committed yourself, lock, stock and barrel, to the will of God. The joy of it is an unearthly thing, which follows you and grows greater with the years.

The next result is an inquiry into one's life-plans in the large, to see if they be such as God would choose as His first, best plan for us. For younger people this is bound to concern their life-work and their marriage, and to demand that these great choices be made upon a basis of honest search for God's will. There are in the world a great many empty places, hard places, thrilling places which the world cannot see as thrilling. God wants workers there. There is a lot He wants done in this world, and there are very few who will lay themselves open to His plan, and promise to fit in wherever He says. Here, again, many a man or woman fears he must become a missionary, or give up what promises to be a successful worldly marriage to wait for one with better foundations; and it seems a heavy cross. Yet when one makes the commitment with regard to these larger life-plans, he finds that God makes no mistakes, and the thing he thought he could never do may be the very thing he loves to do most.

There is a retroactive element in a genuine surrender, too. You cannot give your life to God without being willing to turn back into the past, and there make right the things you know to have been wrong. Past wrong leaves its roots in our subconscious minds, and if you dig below the soil you will find the old foundations just as they were left. Personal relationships which have been filled with misunderstandings and irritation, business deals which have compromised with principle, injustice which calls for the fairness to reopen the question, rudeness or criticism or talebearing which only honest apology and confession will make right—these things feel the change in the atmosphere when we have genuinely surrendered, and they must be acclimatized to the new life. Nobody has really given in to God who leaves untouched the unforgiven grudge, or the unrighted wrong. The new life demands a clean slate.

And then there must be growing victory over sin. Deliverance!—that was the cry of victory of Christianity to the first century. St. Paul went into a rotten port-city like Corinth, infested with all the degradation of the worst of Greek degeneracy, and told his people he was determined to know nothing among them but Jesus Christ. Real Christianity has always been able to save men from sin. And when I find people who have all their lives been coming to church, and have never mastered a quick tongue, a disagreeable spirit, the touchiness which resents the slightest interference with one's own desires, and which makes one hard to get along with, I do not say that Christianity has failed, I say that we Christians have simply not surrendered our whole hearts to the Lord Jesus Christ.

For two nights of this past week my work has carried me to the Jerry McAuley Water Street Mission.[2] I heard there the vivid and simple and unostentatious testimonies of men who had been redeemed from all kinds of sin. They said they had been kept for two days, several weeks, twenty years, by the power of Christ. There is a difference between that happy and vivid and unashamed religion, and our decent and reticent and less effective kind: the difference isn't in the amount of decency nearly so much as it is in the amount of power. I would to God the churches of this city had in them the power that is there, that we expected people to be converted as they do, expected them to witness as they do. And back of that power over broken sin there lies a great yielding, a deep surrender to the love and will of God.

Now, my friends, I always want to say a special word in a sermon like this to those whose major choices seem to have been made, and who feel it is now a question of making the best of it because it is too late to change. It is never too late. When you miss God's first best plan for you, He has a second, and if you miss that, a third. Your situation is always new to God. He can and will always begin over again to deal with you, and give you another chance. It is a great thing to surrender to God in the fulness of youth, but it is also a great thing to surrender at any time. I beg you not to think of yourselves as too far along the way to change.

Let us to-day ask ourselves with complete candour whether we ever have surrendered everything to His will. Did we miss His whole plan for us years ago by taking a turn we knew was wrong?

Have we felt the pressure of His love all these years, and feared to respond to it, as Francis Thompson did, "lest having Him, I should have naught beside"?

Have we let sin creep in somewhere till we take it for part of us which we cannot strip away and get free from?

Have we given Him our homes, our money, our ambition, our joy, our suffering, our human ties, our characters, our hearts? Is there somewhere a conscious withholding?—for if there is, there is so much less of that freedom and joy and peace in believing which comes alone when we give all.

It is one of the dearest hopes of my life that this congregation will learn the art of winning lives to Jesus Christ: the beginning is with ourselves. No man can give what he does not possess. You cannot ask another to give himself to Christ till you have given yourself. This is no academic self-examination. Something is desperately wrong with our modern version of Christianity, and I suspect that it is the want of just this surrender amongst us. I believe you are in or out. Henry Wright startled some people once by saying: "No man or woman oozes unconsciously into the kingdom of God. In the final analysis, all enlist, and every soldier knows when he en-

2 Since this was written, Calvary Church has opened its own Rescue Mission at 346 East Twenty-third Street, New York City.

listed." But I believe he was right. Have you ever enlisted? Or have you all your life hung around the recruiting station, and thought about it? God has a place for you, a work for you to do. You will do it, or it will go undone.

"Who then offereth willingly to consecrate himself this day unto Jehovah?"

Let us pray:

O God our Father, it is so easy for us to drift along, and say our prayers and sing our worship as though with all our hearts we loved to do Thy will. Thou knowest us better than we know ourselves, and in Thy presence we see how much of our life is outside Thy control. Grant us grace to give Thee everything we have and are, and use us for Thy glory. For the sake of Jesus Christ our Lord. Amen.

V

# How to Know the Will of God

Thirty-five years ago a lithe and well-dressed Scotsman of middle age was visiting American universities and conferences. He was making public addresses and holding private interviews everywhere he went. He was a scientist of considerable reputation, and he was one of the first men to see his way through the problem of adopting a modern viewpoint towards history and science, while he kept hold of a vital and personal evangelical Christianity. That man's name was Henry Drummond. They were widely different, but he was a close and understanding friend of D. L. Moody's, and they worked together here, as they had worked together in England when Mr. Moody had been there years before.

Henry Drummond was a marvellous combination of analyst and partisan, scientist and enthusiast, investigator and propagandist. To many men is it given to be onlookers of life, who dissect it and anatomize it. And to many more is it given to throw themselves headlong into the thick of life as participants. But Henry Drummond mixed those two elements in his personality in such a way as to make him of peculiar service to our generation. He was possessed of a wide knowledge of science, and he loved the search for truth in scientific regions. But he loved men as well as truth; and the passion of his life was the winning of young men for Christ. He knew intimately well the hearts of thousands of men. I do not much listen to the pronouncements of men whose minds smell of books, when they come to practical matters of religion; for I do not trust them unless they also know life. Henry Drummond knew life, and lived it richly.

Now, anyone who knows much about people spiritually comes to feel, sooner or later, that the greatest problem any of us face is the problem of what we shall do about the will of God. When we come to believe in God at all, we come to believe in Him as having something definite to say about our lives. To believe in the fact of the will of God is only to believe in God in the concrete. As you cannot pray without words, so you cannot imagine God apart from His desires which touch us. There is at the heart of religion this marriage between the mystical and the moral. And Henry Drummond, with inerrant insight, went often into this great problem. It was the love of his life to do the will of God. He was no glib and facile interpreter of what it was: he spent long hours searching his Bible for light on the question. And when he had finished his study, this scholar seeking a truth of metaphysics, this devoted Christian trying to know the heart and mind of his God, he wrote down in the flyleaf of his Bible these eight points:

1. Pray.
2. Think.
3. Talk to wise people, but do not regard their decision as final.
4. Beware of the bias of your own will, but do not be too much afraid of it (God never unnecessarily thwarts a man's nature and likings, and it is a mistake to think that His will is in the line of the disagreeable).
5. Meantime, do the next thing, for doing God's will in small things is the best preparation for knowing it in great things.
6. When decision and action are necessary, go ahead.
7. Never reconsider your decision when it is finally acted upon; and—
8. You will probably not find out till afterwards, perhaps long afterwards, that you were led at all.

Now, let me take these steps one at a time, and embroider them a little in detail, reminding you first that I am not sure I have in everything caught the sense of Henry Drummond, and that I am packing my own meaning into his phrases.

1. "Pray." It is a common thing to run to God in petulant and frantic demand, asking Him to tell us what to do. This may be the sudden reversal of a life of self-seeking and self-guidance; and it is not to be wondered at if not much guidance comes from Him. What we often seek is His approval, not His will. When we come in a great honesty, having put our own wills behind us, seeking candidly the mind of the Lord, it is generally rather plain sailing: a mood or disposition comes upon us with light in it, or a direct thought flits across our mind with illumination. These experiences are too common amongst Christians for any of you to pooh-pooh them until you have tried honestly. But when we come only in curiosity, merely wondering what God might like us to do, quite different is the result. We get nowhere, prayer is a fog, we get up anxious and fretful and in a stew. To find God's will in prayer demands a colossal honesty in our minds. A man recently disputed my use of the word honesty in this connection: he said willingness and unselfishness I might use, but honesty implied dishonesty in coming to God with our minds made up. Yet this is precisely what we are; we are dishonest when we prejudice the will of God by trying to twist it into our own will: we are not honest with facts, especially the great fact that God's plan may not be our plan. "My thoughts are not your thoughts" is true more often than we care to remember. So that to pray for God's will to be revealed we must be ready and willing to have it revealed, and come to Him with an open mind.

There is in the city of New York the president of a great company. He is a devoted

Christian, and it has been his practise to bring up his sons to attend church regularly on Sunday mornings till they are twenty-one; after that they are free to choose for themselves. One Sunday one of his sons came to him and said: "Father, there is a house party over in —— to-day, and if you don't mind I shall take the car and go over." The father said: "Yes, son, you can go, under one condition." "What is that?" the son asked. "That you will go up-stairs and talk to God about it for fifteen minutes." And the son said: "Well, dad, I guess I won't go." That boy had learned already that in the realized presence of God, one sees things as they really are, if one is only honest and willing to see them.

Yet I recall a friend of mine speaking of his desire to know what he ought to do with his life. I asked if he had prayed about it. He said that he had, and he asked God what to do: but that if God had said certain things, he would not have been willing to do them. That is not prayer: it is a kind of blasphemy instead. It points the truth that no man can see the will of God who is not willing to see it. One of Drummond's favourite verses in this connection was John 7:17: "If any man *willeth* to do his will, he shall know." And wrapped up in that little verse there lies more empirical spiritual experience than almost anywhere else I know. This, then, is the first guide—to pray.

2. "Think." There is a moral obligation to be as intelligent as you can. Turn over the possibilities in your mind. Face all the facts you can find, honestly and fearlessly, I am not afraid of too much thought in religion, I am only afraid of too little of it. It is not sound reasoning which steals men's religion, it is half-baked rationalizing. Some people use their brains to convince themselves they ought to do what they want to do. Jesus says, against this kind of thing: "Judge not according to appearance, but judge righteous judgment." It may be a good thing to put down the pros and cons in two written columns, and weigh one against the other. If the decision concerns your life-work, face the needs of the world frankly, as well as your own qualifications. We are apt to be too subjective in some of these questions. I believe we do well to look out on the world, and ask what it is which that world needs most, and then ask ourselves how we can best supply that need—rather than to turn in upon ourselves and ask what riches and talents lie hidden within us which we must find a way to turn loose upon the world. Look out, and assemble all the facts you can. There is nothing the matter with using human brains, so long as an honest character lies behind them. But this is an age of more self-deception, under the guise of intellectual honesty, than any I know about. Remember that, when all is said and done, God may communicate His wish to you, and knock your thinking endwise. To be thoroughgoingly, intellectually honest, you will consider as the greatest factor of all the will of God.

3. "Talk to wise people, but do not regard their decision as final." That is, don't expect them to make up your mind for you. Consult them for what they are worth. But make the decision your own. There are always a lot of people in the world who like to talk to ministers, as if we knew it all: they run to us to settle things they ought to be close enough to God to settle for themselves. And we are always in danger of

priding ourselves upon our influence, and handing out packages of advice, when as a matter of fact we ought to be dealing with a larger issue, the issue of their surrender to God's will, and their own search for what it is. Now, don't discuss this with just anybody you happen to think about, but with people who love God and His will and are themselves putting the kingdom of heaven first.

A friend of mine went to a business man in Philadelphia who had asked him to come into business with him: and when he told him he had decided for the ministry, and asked what he thought of it, the business man said: "You d——— f———." Now, a man like that forfeits his right ever to advise anybody. A man who will drench a young man's aspirations with that kind of materialistic cold water is not fit to make suggestions to a pig. Go to really wise people, wise with God's wisdom: and He will often speak to you through them, as generally He does speak through others. But let this talk be for a *clearing* of the issue, not for a *settlement* of it. What they say to you is valid only insofar as it rings a bell in your own heart.

4. "Beware of the bias of your own will, but do not be too much afraid of it (God never unnecessarily thwarts a man's nature and likings, and it is a mistake to think that His will is in the line of the disagreeable)." Drummond was talking to Scotsmen with consciences a yard long when he added to his universal warning: "Beware of the bias of your own will," the balance, "But do not be too much afraid of it." I think the first half of it is probably more applicable to us. We are not likely to err on the side of interpreting God's will hardly, but softly. When you consult God and your mind is already partially made up, you need very seriously to beware of that bias, for it will throw out all the calculations. Left to ourselves, we are very likely to please ourselves.

And yet we need the postscript, too: "Do not be too much afraid of it. God never unnecessarily thwarts a man's nature and likings, and it is a mistake to think that His will is in the line of the disagreeable." It is a mistake, and a great one. I heard a woman say within a week that whatever was the hardest thing to do was probably God's will: but I do not believe that. Some people think God goes around hunting up hard and unhappy jobs, and then trailing them down and loading the jobs off on them. To make God that kind of a supernatural taskmaster is to be unchristian in our thought of Him. There are hard jobs to be done, and somebody has got to do them. But I feel sure that God made us for a particular piece of work, and that we shall never be fully happy until we find that work. You may not think it looks like you would enjoy it: but if it is His place you will, and you will never really be happy anywhere else.

5. "Meantime, do the next thing, for doing God's will in small things is the best preparation for knowing it in great things." Some are so preoccupied with the obvious that they never get above it to take a look at the whole: but some also are so busy with the abstract they never see the concrete, nor complete the ordinary duty which stares them in the face. A man who is honestly living up to the light he has, to-day, will have more light to-morrow, when he needs it. Sometimes God makes us wait for the full emergence of His plan. If we have been faithful in a few things, He will

make us master of many things, revealing as much truth as we can live up to. I know a man in business in downtown New York. He has been soundly changed in his own life, and he loves to bring Christ into the lives of men. He does not know whether God wants him to go into the ministry or not. Meanwhile he is doing a fine job in an insurance office, and working there until or unless he is guided to go elsewhere. There is an enormous amount of common sense about real religion which we miss sometimes because it is not exactly the common sense of the world at large.

6. "When decision and action are necessary, go ahead." Go ahead fearlessly. God will give you for each step as much light as you really need, and perhaps no more. You may see from here to the next corner, and there the path seems to turn down into the dark. Go that far, and more light will come. Do not wait till you see light on all the road before you: most of us never do see it. The Greeks used to wear lanterns on their shoes: it would throw light about three feet ahead of them, and then they had to take one more step to get three feet more of light. So it is with finding the will of God. You may not see all the sides of a question of importance, yet you must decide it. God will give you *enough* light. Do not rush Him, or the situation; but when you must, let the hammer fall, act on all the light you have, and you will make no mistake. The more you trust God in critical situations, the more you will learn that you can trust Him: and that if you will throw the onus of decision off yourself and on to Him, giving Him only a ready and obedient will, you will be amazed at the way things work out for you.

7. "Never reconsider the decision when it is finally acted upon." That is of immense importance. Every thoughtful person, every conscientious person, wonders again and again about an old decision; wants to go back and tear it up by the roots and ask again why it was ever made. Some people do that about marriage, many do it about their life's work. They acted in all good faith at the time: but later they question their own decision. It is a fatal thing to do. Now, if the decision was made selfishly, we may have to make the best of a bad margin; remembering that God has always a substitute will which goes into the game when the first-string will is put out. But if they acted under God so far as they understood, it was the best they could do. If trial and difficulty has come since, that was meant to have its place. We should spend our lives on regrets, and many do so spend them, if we spent much time reconsidering decisions that have been already acted upon. *Until* a decision is acted upon, reconsider as much as you like. But afterwards, go forward and banish fear.

8. "You will probably not find out till afterwards, perhaps long afterwards, that you were led at all." I should not put so much of an interval as Drummond implies; for I believe that we often know we acted rightly by a very quick sense of being right, and sometimes by the manifest outworking of God's plan which shows itself quickly. And yet there is an immense truth here. He is talking about totals and broad outlines. And one finds that the great compensation for the steady fleeing-away of the years is a larger and longer look at one's own life, and a clearer view of the path by which he has come. One sees here just the right person coming across one's path to point a truth, or to enlarge a horizon. There we came across that great book that

turned us upward. In another place a great sorrow made us tender and kinder. And the map of the will of God is not the track of a railway stretching away before us, but rather the wake of a ship lying white behind us. We see best how clear that path is as we look back upon it over a long period of time. I ask you to-day to look back across your own life—not somebody's else, for we never know all the factors anywhere but in our own—look at your own life, and see whether, if you have acted according to your best, and interpreted events with a will to find God's purpose, things have not marvellously worked together for good.

But we end where we began. Prayer is the heart of the discovery of the will of God. I will defend it against all comers that something happens when a man lays his life open before God, and asks Him to make known His will, which cannot happen by any amount of uninspired thought or human direction. We see into the heart of things in prayer like that. But that kind of prayer is impossible without radical and basic surrender to the will of God first. "If any man willeth to do his will"—this means, no grudging concession to God, but whole-hearted allegiance and the co-operation of one's whole self—"he shall know." The man who knows God's will is the man who loves it. The man who finds out what God wants is the man who cares what God wants, who feels upon him the same kind of burdens God feels and carries. If God can count on you, He can commit His secrets to you. We have got to get on God's side before it's any use to ask what is God's plan.

As Drummond finished his address in Appleton Chapel, at Harvard, thirty-five years ago, he said: "Above all things, do not touch Christianity unless you are willing to seek the kingdom of God first. I promise you a miserable existence if you seek it second." That is true. And the matter with many who call themselves Christians, and have never found any thrill and power in their religion, lies just there: they are not seeking the kingdom first.

But when you do come out on that side with all your heart, and seek the kingdom first, I can promise you not a miserable existence, but the only thing that satisfies on this side of eternity. I say to you that it will be the tragedy of your life to miss the will of God, and the standing and crowning success of your life to find it. There is no other success than to do what God wants you to do.

"Not every one that saith unto me, Lord, Lord, shall enter into the kingdom of heaven; but he that doeth the will of my Father who is in heaven."

God give us the grace to ask: "Lord, what wilt thou have me to do?"

Let us pray:

O God, who in Thy love for us dost plan for us a way far better than our own: Grant us to desire Thy will above all things, and desiring it, to seek it; and seeking it, to find it; and finding it, to serve Thee faithfully and to make Thee known to men. Through Jesus Christ our Lord.

VI

# The Fellowship of the Holy Ghost

*". . . The fellowship of the Holy Ghost."*
—II CORINTHIANS 13:14.

This is Whitsunday. The derivation is apparently from White-Sunday, the day when the catechumens were dressed in white for confirmation, a custom begun some time during the Middle Ages. It is the Church's yearly memorial of the great event of Pentecost, when the disciples were gathered "with one accord in one place," and the Holy Spirit came upon them.

There are many thoughts which stir in one's mind when one comes to this great day of Pentecost, about which one would like to have the time to preach. There is that in a genuine experience of the Holy Spirit which would solve a great many of our typical problems and our tragic ills. It would solve the problem of "spiritualism" which seeks, by an unauthentic route, to find contact with the other world: it would do away with the uncertainty which is poisoning so much of modern life: it might even cure our inflated intellectualism by the manifestation of a greater wisdom than this world can offer.

But I have chosen one thought, one very great thought, connected with the Pentecost experience: and that is "the fellowship of the Holy Ghost." You all recognize it as a phrase from our most familiar benediction, which closes the Second Epistle to the Corinthians.

I have generally understood that phrase, I suspect in company with most of you, to mean something which I find a closer study discards. I have been accustomed to think that the beloved benediction which begins "The grace of our Lord Jesus Christ . . .," prays for a special attachment on our part to each Person of the Trinity—so that "the fellowship of the Holy Ghost" would mean "the companionship of the Holy Ghost" severally in our own hearts.

This is probably a false interpretation. The phrase refers to something which seems to have been a very definite apostolic concept; namely, the fellowship of believing people which was created by the Holy Ghost, rather than fellowship individually with the Holy Ghost Himself. You will readily see that these are two very different ideas: one is an individual, the other is a corporate experience. One finds the Holy Spirit unmediated: the other finds Him through the group-experience of men and women like-minded.

Now, when one leaves behind the immediate results of the coming of the Spirit at Pentecost, this fellowship is the great residuum. We all remember the tongues of fire, and the speaking with tongues, and St. Peter's interpretation of what happened as the fulfilment of God's promise to pour out His Spirit upon all flesh—the way the crowd who heard him were convicted and subsequently baptized into the Church. Those were the mode of the experience: but the thing which was left was what they called "the Fellowship." There is a verse later in the same account which says: "They continued steadfastly in the apostles' teaching, and fellowship, in the breaking of bread and the prayers." But in the Greek there is an article before the word for fellowship, *koinonia*, which makes the phrase an independent one, as most modern commentators recognize. It was not just "fellowship," it was a particular one, "*the* fellowship." It means they continued, not in the apostles' teaching and fellowship, but in the apostles' teaching, and the fellowship.

This was a new thing. And to it was given its distinctive name. As this word for fellowship is used through the Acts and the Epistles, it makes us feel that it is not a common word in its common usage, it is a common word lifted from common usage into special. They looked for some language of earth in which to express a heavenly experience of being spiritually welded, as they found they were by Pentecost. This was not, mark you again, merely a fellowship of the believers amongst themselves, nor yet a fellowship of men and women each of whom was linked individually with the Holy Spirit: it is the much profounder experience of fellowship between those who had found the Holy Spirit together, and were still understanding Him with a corporate understanding. It was such an experience as made them aware of the third side of the triangle in every relationship which they had. When they were with another believer they were experiencing his experience of the Holy Spirit—when they were individually linked with the Holy Spirit, in prayer and inspiration, they were bound to recognize that they first knew Him through the body of other believers. This was, I say, a wholly new thing, requiring a new name, "The Fellowship"—and as I study it, it seems to me perhaps the most significant bearing which Pentecost has upon the life of the Church to-day. It preceded and moulded the "organization" of the Church—it was the vital spiritually creative urge which later took the form of the organized "ecclesia."

The symbol of that fellowship was the broken loaf, or bread, as we translate it. In the verse where we read of the after-life of those Pentecostconverts: "They continued in the apostles' teaching, and the fellowship, and the breaking of bread, and the prayers." There seems to have been more symbolic meaning attached to the breaking of the bread, to its brokenness, than came later to be the case. And it stood, not only for the broken body of Christ, but also for the body of believers, broken, as they were, through giving up their own wills for Christ's, broken by persecution also, and then the mingled particles kneaded into one Christian body.

The outward character of the fellowship was actual brotherhood and "togetherness" of the very most profound and intense kind. We read that "all that believed were together." It was as though a corporate personality had been developed, a group becoming almost a spiritual individual, thinking and experiencing and understanding together. We read also that they "had all things common: and they sold their possessions and goods, and parted them to all, according as any man had need." It is too absurd for denial to call this, as it frequently has been called, "an experiment in communism": they cared nothing for the economics of the matter, it was a spontaneous expression of spiritual fellowship, equalizing the material inequalities of the believers, and giving simply because a spiritual brother had need. Ananias' sin of withholding was not only the sin of falsehood, but the sin of treason and disloyalty.

The pledge to the outside world of the reality of this fellowship was in its ethical results. To the believers were given exceptional and miraculous powers for the lifting and strengthening of life: there were the gifts of tongues, breaking down walls between differing nationalities, and obscure men found themselves integral parts of a movement tremendous with meaning, so that one lofty purpose held them continuously. The great word for the centre of the fellowship was *agape*, love: and this was no sentimental and effusive matter, it was genuine understanding and self-giving so great that all barriers went down before it, even the age-old barrier between Jew and Gentile. There is sarcasm when we say to-day: "See how these Christians love one another!"—but it was sober fact then. And with this went the quieter powers for living all of life with sweetness and kindness of spirit—what St. Paul called "the fruit of the Spirit, love, joy, peace, longsuffering, kindness, goodness, faithfulness, meekness, self-control." This was not the cooling-down of great powers to small, that men who had had part in miracles became interested in the gentle art of getting along with other people; but rather the permeation by religion of the whole of life—its long quiet stretches as well as its high moments and crises.

But I believe that neither complete community of thought and possession, nor elevation of moral life, can account for the amazing effect of this fellowship upon the world. There is a deeper cause. And it lies in the common discovery of spiritual truth, the insight which came from "the fellowship of the Holy Ghost." There is about the apostolic company of disciples an unmistakable mark of sheer vitality, of heightened powers and amplified possibilities which means they have struck a whole new vein of truth about life. What St. Paul called *epignosis*, knowledge, was far beyond anything we find in ordinary education, or any collection of facts, or any human body of truth: it was the window into ultimate reality, the knowledge of this world which comes from being closely acquainted with the other.

Consider what it did for those who set down our Gospels and Epistles, the most immortal literature of the ages, coming forth from the minds of simple men, "trailing clouds of glory" because they had been touched with the inspiration of the Holy Spirit. Consider the effect upon the mind of St. Paul: admittedly he would have been a great mind anyway, he was thus endowed. But under the dominance of the Spirit he became more than the philosopher he would have been in any case, more than sage or poet, he became seer and prophet, revealer of the hidden things of God, so that we forget the gigantic intellectual faculties of St. Paul in wonder at the contemplation of his spiritual intuition. All this literary output came forth through the experiences of the fellowship: they shared often in its writing and composition, they shared always in the life out of which it was produced.

But there is a still more remarkable phase of spiritual understanding than the heightening of what we should call intellectual faculties. I mean the group-experience of being led by the Holy Spirit, both in their own daily walk and conversation, and particularly in their conquest of the world about them. Not only were they set apart from the paganism round about by purity and elevation of life, but they became ingenious in their witness to that same paganism, and turned it by hundreds into their own fellowship. This implies a surefootedness, a continuous inspiration, a group-guidance which was the great effective element in the beginnings of Christianity. They were melted down into such a spiritual unity amongst themselves, born of love and of honesty and of spiritual fellowship, that they stood and thought and attacked like one living individual.

This was not conformity and imitation; it was the highest form of individualism and liberty, the liberty which has learned perfect loyalty. The Spirit can communicate His truth to a spiritual fellowship of believers in ways He cannot communicate it to individuals: it is another phase of Christ's meaning when He said that "where two or three are gathered together in my name, there am I in the midst of them." He is wherever a believer is: but He is present in heightened reality in the fellowship. And His will is clarified by the corrective and perspective which one derives from the experience, not of general humanity, but of his brothers in the faith. This was what bound into unbreakable unity the disciples of the early Church, and what made the early Church the superb and supreme example in all history of what a little group of entirely consecrated and indivisibly united people can do against the world.

You will not have followed me thus far without realizing that I have much more in mind than a historic study of one result of Pentecost. You have been all along conscious of how far our own church, and our contemporaneous Christianity, falls short of even a parallel or analogous experience to this which we have been considering. Pentecost was not an isolated event: soon after it there followed another time when the disciples were praying for strength to withstand their persecutors and to witness bravely, and "the place was shaken wherein they were gathered together; and they were all filled with the Holy Spirit, and they spake the word of God with boldness." And down through the history of the Church there have been many times when a group of believers stepped out boldly upon God's promises, dared to take Him at His word, dared to break with the world and then turn round to capture it for Christ: and to them the daring Spirit of God could entrust Himself with special revealing and guiding power, making of the group of believers a channel of God into the world, the pattern of a new order of social relationships, and a phalanx almost military in unity and power, for conquest of the world without. There have been repetitions of Pentecost. Great spiritual movements, gathering about such names as Francis and Tauler and Wesley and Loyola, have always been group-movements.

Is it day-dreaming to believe that such a movement might come in our time, in our world? God does not give Himself by accident. There is always a time of testing, and proof of dependability; then comes the great revelation. There was a moral and a spiritual basis for Pentecost: it came to disciplined, dedicated, self-forgetful lives, centred in Jesus Christ as Lord and Saviour, as Master and Friend. It came when they needed it, and when they were gathered together for inner strengthening, to do their great work in the world of standing for the Gospel and spreading it. If God found a group of us, each committed beyond recall in his own soul to Jesus Christ, paying the price of Christian fellowship one with another, burdened to make Christ effective in New York as He began to be effective in Jerusalem—forgetting our conventional little fears and hesitancies—leaving behind us the icy formality of our religion which extends even towards those who come with us into God's house, seeking this same supreme thing as we ourselves—a group made up of every human type differing in the outward things of taste and talent, but all the more united because superficial dissimilarities were forgotten through the one great possession of Christ—God might again break through, and astonish the world through a brotherhood of His transfigured lives.

Dead Christians and half-dead Christians short-circuit that kind of power. There are groups of nominal Christian people amongst whom Pentecost is forever out of the question. I suspect prosperity is inimical to it in a church, I know that complacency and coldness of spirit are. There is not even common, human friendliness in some churches: how can there ever be spiritual fellowship? And there are other churches where all direct action of the Spirit of God upon human souls is explained away by natural and psychological processes: you will not find Pentecost repeated where men no longer believe in Pentecost, but name it some variety of social emotion.

But the field is whitening to a harvest. New York needs Pentecost. A young business man of wealth and culture, with all that belongs to this world and little that belongs to the other, said to me this week: "Don't you think the time is ripe for a big evangelistic push right here in New York?" It was a significant and revealing question from that kind of a man. I believe he spoke for thousands who want an authentic reinterpretation of Gospel and apostolic Christianity to-day. There are sections of New York that *want* Pentecost. They are not the conventionally religious sections. If one church found "the fellowship of the Holy Ghost," and let loose through this city a group of inspired individuals with a message from on high—and one day that group were found "with one accord in one place," coming together for fresh fire, for more life, thrust together by the persecution of one part of the world without, and by the spiritual hunger of the other part, bound to one another in this closest of all ties—God might choose so to manifest Himself again to men.

Let us search our hearts for what in us would hinder such an event from taking place right here. Let us be conscious again of our weakness by ourselves. And then let us dare to look up into the face of God, and pray with humility and with boldness:

"Come, Holy Ghost, *our* souls inspire."

In the stillness, let us pray to the Lord of Pentecost.

Silent Prayer.

O Holy Ghost, Lord and Giver of Life: Grant unto the Church such fellowship through Thee as made her powerful and invincible at the beginning. Come again with great might into our midst, and fill us with the fire of cleansing and illumination: and send us forth aflame with Thee into the world. Through Jesus Christ our Lord. Amen.

VII

# The Importance of Individuals

*"Jesus saw Nathanael . . ."*
—JOHN 1:47.

Jesus had been talking with a new disciple, named Philip. In the brief period of his discipleship, Philip had caught the infection with which Jesus filled His followers, the redemptive infection, the passion to bring men to God. And, moving off from Jesus a little, Philip spoke to a friend of his named Nathanael. Philip made a great announcement to him. He said that the great expectation of Moses and the prophets was here, Jesus of Nazareth. And as they talked together, reasoning whether the Messiah should spring from so unlikely a village as Nazareth, they were moving towards Jesus.

Jesus stood watching this action—watching it, I suspect, with the most tremendous kind of excitement, and the profoundest kind of joy, that ever gladdened His heart while He lived in our world. To see another take fire at one's own highest enthusiasm is joy beyond joy. He was taking it all in, missing nothing of its import and incident. He called Nathanael by name, greatly to his surprise; and then He complimented the spiritual sincerity of his life. Nathanael was astonished: "Whence knowest thou me?" And Jesus told him that He had seen him under the fig tree, before Philip called him. The amazed man said: "Rabbi, thou art the Son of God; thou art the King of Israel!" And Jesus said: "Do you believe in me just because I saw you under the fig tree? You will see greater things than that!"

I want to ask you to attempt to understand something of the consciousness of a Man who, while talking with a friend, was also taking in a stranger—seeing in the friend a roadway into the life of the stranger—studying the posture, the face, the probable tastes, the aspirations of the stranger, whom most men would have missed by the roadside as he sat under a fig tree. There was in Jesus such a preoccupation with individuals, such a knowledge of "what was in man," as I think never anywhere else existed on this planet.

When Jesus "saw" Nathanael, much more was involved than being aware of a man moving towards Him. This was not only eyesight: it was insight. He not only beheld the presence of a man, but He saw through into the heart and meaning of that man. He took in Nathanael's spirituality of nature, calling him "an Israelite indeed, in whom is no guile"—a sincere man, that is; not a sinless man, but a man in spiritual earnest—one of those whose faith He came "not to destroy but to fulfil." Probably Nathanael was one of those spiritually refined and reticent people who must be carefully drawn out by sympathy, or they will close up entirely. This word of commendation was like a warm sun to draw a bud into bloom. Jesus understood much more about Nathanael than Nathanael was aware of. He "saw" his sincerity, his aspiration, his shyness perhaps, his spiritual hunger, perhaps his need, though He said nothing of it so early in the conversation. Next time you "see" somebody, ask yourself whether you "see" them with any vestige of the comprehension with which Jesus saw Nathanael.

And He says that He was watching him before Philip called him, while he was under the fig tree. What was happening while he was under the fig tree? He may have closed his eyes in prayer, and Jesus saw that. He may have had on his face the strain and anguish of temptation, and Jesus saw that. He may have been looking off into the heavens, waiting for Messiah in company with that devout segment of Judaism which waited for Him, and Jesus saw that. Nathanael under the fig tree. Jesus had nothing else and nothing more to go on. Yet He read that hint as though it had been an exposition. From that detail He built up a careful analysis of a man. It led to Nathanael's discipleship. He is an obscure person, never again mentioned in the gospels, until he stands by the lakeside in the dawn of a morning after the resurrection, where Jesus reveals Himself. But the fact is, Nathanael began his discipleship on the day when he was understood—understood by Jesus, who had a genius for understanding individuals.

One of the very greatest needs of our day is a reawakening of the consciousness of the individual. All through our life we need to learn the wonderful art of Jesus, the art of seeing people.

It is needed in business. We have heard a great deal about welfare and safety devices in business—about better housing and recreational facilities and trained psychiatrists to watch the health of the workers. And it is all good, very good. Would God we had more of it, and every business were progressive enough to include it. But there is one danger in it all, the danger of doing all this simply to increase the efficiency of the men, simply to fill the coffers of the business. And there is another danger, that it may all be mass-welfare which forgets the individual. The business which sees men, not as economic units to be made efficient, but as human individualities and souls to be developed and enriched through their work—that is the only kind of business which can have Jesus' approval. And wherever any of us are employing people in order to grind out of them what we can, without concerning ourselves with their own highest and best life, we are so far not Christians at all. I heard a Christian business-woman this week tell of her firm voluntarily raising the pay to a truckman who was losing money at the rates he asked, but who had made no request of them whatever: and of paying for him a debt he had contracted. That kind of thing must be well-pleasing to our Father in heaven: and it makes for bonds of loyalty which strengthen all human efforts.

It is needed in medicine. I am sometimes frightened at the sheer magnitude of the schemes and the institutions we are making for the prevention and relief of human sickness. There is no more merciful, Christlike work in the world than the work of doctors and nurses: no more gloriously Christian building on earth than a hospital. But I believe the restoration of health has in it an infinite number of non-material factors—factors which can only be dealt with by the most delicate impingement of personality upon personality. We all know how needed is confidence in the nurse and doctor, if a patient is to recover to maximum. But there are yet more spiritual factors necessary. A psychiatrist said to me a few weeks ago that ninety per cent of the people who came to him needed to have restored their faith in the worthwhileness of living. That is not a material matter, it is profoundly a spiritual matter. No man can manage that in crowds: it requires intimate, personal concern. It was said that Dr. Osler could almost tell what a man needed the moment he walked in the office. God give us doctors who are spiritual diagnosticians as well—and we shall scotch bad-health off the face of the earth!

We need the consciousness of individuals in education. The tendency in education to-day seems to be towards maximum scientific efficiency: and that means the intellectual survival of the fittest. There are hordes of college professors to-day who consider that they have no responsibility whatever beyond the transfer of certain collections of information from their heads to the heads of their students. I believe that real education means helping people to find the best that as been thought and said in the world, and then to act upon it. It is no easy thing to get from twelve to twenty: and to be herded according to mental tests, without regard for those intricacies of personality which differentiate us one from the other, produces disastrous moral and psychological results. I dare to say that the profoundest understanding of human beings is impossible except upon a basis of personal acquaintance and sympathy; and that without religion, and the peculiar insight into life which genuine religion brings, the highest kind of sympathy cannot be developed.

The story is told of an old professor at Princeton, many years ago, who learned from another student that something he had said in his philosophy lecture had upset the mind of one of his Freshmen. That evening this old man, whom I remember and who was very fat, went up five flights of stairs to the room of this Freshman, rapped at his door and went into his room, saying: "I understand something I said this morning bothered your faith: and I want to come round and talk about it." That Freshman is the Secretary for Home Missions in one of the great churches of this country. And he will never forget the reverence for his own soul of that professor of philosophy. God send us teachers like that!

But perhaps it comes back more to our churches than to anything else. Theoretically we stand for a consciousness of the individual, because theoretically we stand for Christ. Again and again, when I speak with Christians and Christian workers about work for individuals, they say to me: “Of course—that is what I have always emphasized. The individual is the only thing that matters.” But, my friends, the most dangerous things for religion are always the things to which religion says: “Of course.” We have said, “Of course,” to the creeds, till the life has gone out of them. We have said, “Of course,” to making a more fraternal world, till we no longer stop to ask whether we ourselves are brotherly. We have said, “Of course,” to the Sermon on the Mount, till its terrible demands roll off us like so much water from a roof. Sometimes I see a safe and complacent kind of Christian carrying a Bible in his hand: and I wonder the dynamite in that old Book doesn’t go off in his hands, and blow his safety to pieces! That’s not a book for cautious and unadventurous people: it is the record of lives who, when they found God, found themselves in conflict with most of what the world about them stood for. Beware of saying, “Of course,” lest you should not mean what you say!

I say that the Church of Christ needs an awakening of the consciousness of the individual. We need a Church which “sees” people, as Jesus saw Nathanael. It is possible to go to a great many churches and never hear a word of welcome, nor find the slightest opportunity for Christian friendship. If we are to go further with “seeing” individuals, we must begin upon the simplest level of common human friendliness. We’ve got to drop the pious discourtesy inside God’s house which has driven so many from us forever.

But it goes deeper than this. We must gauge our whole work for Christ to the needs of individuals, as I believe He gauged His. Our organizations are, on the whole, adapted for the group and not the individual: we think more in terms of clubs and committees than we do in terms of people. Our sermons are aimed at congregations, and they ought to be aimed at individual lives, at the problems and sorrows and interests which hold the attention of people individually. We ministers need much more definite training in dealing with individuals than we usually get in theological seminaries. I was with a group of twenty ministers recently, and I went round the circle asking how many of them, while in seminary, had had any real training in meeting the needs of individuals, in going out to capture unredeemed lives for Jesus Christ—and, of the lot, one man said that there was one hour in his three-year course when somebody had talked about work like that! That is a shame and a scandal, and you laypeople ought to rise up and demand something better—for your own spiritual lives suffer from the lack in your ministers.

It is a monstrous spectacle to see an average church, say, of two or three hundred people, with one minister expected single-handed to care for the spiritual life of those people; and yet forced to carry the thousand fretful details of administration and executive work, when he ought to be steeping his mind in good reading, and his soul in prayer and meditation, and his life in the common life of his people. My own situation is so happily different from this that I can speak about it for some of my brothers. But I think it is no wonder many a minister gives up hope of reaching many individuals and settles down to meeting you in the mass.

We need to expect a great deal more of our people in actual spiritual experience. I am sometimes appalled at how little difference religion can make in a human life where, possibly for years, for half a lifetime, the formalities and outwardnesses of religion have been practiced: and yet the quality of that life—its timidity, its defeat, its moral mediocrity—has never been perceptibly changed. I say that no amount of organization can ever remedy things like that. The only cure there, is for a man of God, be he layman or minister, to begin to pray, and to go to that person willing to give, as St. Paul said, "Not the gospel of God only, but also our own souls," and lead that person into a profounder experience of God through Christ. We need a Church and a ministry that sees people "under the fig tree," in the time of crises, in the hour of need; sees them as they are, sees them also as they might be; turns the sceptic into the disciple, as Jesus and Philip turned Nathanael.

What might not come if a church should develop such a consciousness of the importance of the individual, that all its work, even its group-work, was arranged for the individual? Suppose some church began by being friendly and welcoming, and went on to train a group of people who could actually meet the needs of individuals, who knew how to carry unconvinced people into a genuine experience of Christ—so that a congregation became, not a lot of disjointed individuals, but a brotherhood shot through with human links—what might not that church do in a great city? Someone asked a friend of mine for his creed awhile ago, and he said: "People are more important than things, and God can guide."

I confess that my hopes for this parish Church of Calvary lie in this very direction. We are off the beaten track, thank God. People come to us because they want to, not because it is convenient or conventional. We are given the chance to do a qualitative as against a quantitative work, an individual as against a mass-work. I wish with all my heart that this might come to be known as the church of the individual, where we "see" people with a fragment of the same understanding with which Jesus "saw" Nathanael. The great Dr. Alexander Whyte, of Free St. George's, Edinburgh, was once called "a specialist in sin": he profoundly understood the subtleties of sin, and its ravages in human personality. In the same spirit, I wish that this church might be known as a specialist in the individual, as a place where there is always time for everybody who wants help, where the importance of the individual is never forgotten, for the Lord Jesus Christ never forgot it.

Will you not, good Christian people, carry more of that spirit of the consciousness of individuality with you wherever you go? As I walked down the street one afternoon this week, I was aware that I "saw" almost nobody—*like* the blind man in the Bible, when he was only half-cured, they were "men as trees walking." That's not good enough. Let us pray for more of Christ's understanding and insight, just in our ordinary way of taking people day by day. Let us see spiritual possibilities where we saw only scepticism or indifference before, disciples in strangers. Let us pray that Christ will touch our eyes afresh, till as individuals and as a church we "see every man clearly,"—and so fulfil the law of the love of Christ.

Let us pray:

O God, our Father, who beholdest each one of us as though we were an only child: Help us to look upon others with the love wherewith Thou lookest upon us. Grant to us something of the beautiful sympathy and understanding of Christ. Keep us from ever passing over anybody as though they did not matter. Fill our churches and fill our hearts with real love for people: and help us to serve them and to reveal Thee to them. Through Jesus Christ our Lord. Amen.

VIII

# Isaiah's Vision of God

*"Here am I: send me."*
—ISAIAH 6:8.

This is Trinity Sunday. It is ordinarily a time when we give ourselves to thinking about the nature of God. I am an ardent Trinitarian. I do not believe that the Trinity is a matter only of abstract metaphysical speculation: I believe that the doctrine grew out of authentic spiritual discoveries which had their origin in no less august a source than the very being of the Godhead Himself. Generally I am disposed, on Trinity Sunday, to try to defend the ancient belief of Christendom against the very easy and superficial criticism which would throw it into the discard.

But to-day I want instead to deal with the vision one man had of God, and what it did for his life. I shall be at pains to show you that it makes a difference whether a man believes in God, and what it will do to transform the whole course of his subsequent existence if he catches a genuine vision of the reality of God in this universe. Here, let me say, I am not using "vision" in the technical sense of spiritual appearance to the eye of the inward soul: I mean rather some experience, of hearing, seeing, feeling or discovering which causes a man to acquire an absolute faith "that God is, and that he is the rewarder of them that seek him."

The vision of Isaiah took place "in the year that King Uzziah died." This is not historical detail: it is spiritual setting. Made king at sixteen, reigning for fifty-two years, Uzziah had taken land from the Philistines, and been a patron of agriculture, and been rich in flocks and herds. He was a great king. But he began to feel his own powers. He grew proud and haughty, and one day he went into the temple and with his own hands offered incense which only the priests could offer; and for his proud impiety leprosy broke out upon his forehead at once—and, chased by the priests—he ran out of the temple, and was a leper till he died. The palace changed to the lazar-house. And in the year when this wretched man died, Isaiah saw God.

I expect that Isaiah saw in the sacrilege of the king the representative desecration of the people, and even his own sin. A man given the liberty of a great opportunity, stretching himself to the fulness of his possibility, and then destroying himself by the very freedom which made him great—here was technical dramatic tragedy—here was Adam, and Israel, and all humanity pictured to the life: and because even prophecy itself may be heavily compounded of pride, Isaiah knew by a fearful insight that perhaps he was found in the picture, too. And above the strutting of ostentatious and ephemeral man, above the long panorama of human egotism and impudence, the everlasting Onlooker kept His watch. In the year that leprosy dug a grave for the king's glory, and the greatest human achievement was proved with terrible proof to be temporal, Isaiah the prophet caught a vision of the Eternal.

"I saw the Lord sitting upon a throne, high and lifted up; and his train filled the temple." It does not mean "temple" literally, but "palace." Isaiah may have been standing in the temple, perhaps on the spot where Uzziah sinned; but the vision is of the throne of heaven, and the robes of God fill the spacious courts about Him. The foreground is the Jerusalem temple, fading and shading off into the eternal dwelling of God Himself. In the temple the king had sinned. In the temple Isaiah's conscience had been roused and stirred. Naturally in the temple, with his feet standing upon its rock while his mind scaled the heights of heaven, came the vision of God.

And there is a choir of heavenly beings round about Him, crying: "Holy, holy, holy is the Lord of hosts: the whole earth is full of his glory." We think of the meaning of holiness to-day, and we intend by it great purity or goodness or active loving-kindness. And that is because the Holy Spirit has been working these two thousand years, changing not only our lives but our language. Holiness originally was not positive but negative: it means only separateness, distinctness and difference from man. It was the function of Israel to clean the idea of God: to purge it of heathen attritions; to lift it above moral imperfections. Just where representative man had sinned, Isaiah beheld Him who is of purer eyes than to behold iniquity. Do not suppose that there is any suggestion of a Trinity in the Trisagion, "Holy, Holy, Holy." The repetition is not theological differentiation, it is religious intensification by emphasis. "The whole earth is full of his glory." Glory is the outwardness of holiness, as Jesus' face shone at the transfiguration.

And at this vision of unseen things, this sight behind the veil, what wonder the rocks beneath his feet seemed to shake at the voices of those heavenly beings, and the house filled with smoke? Let no one think that this is the smoke of the incense of worship—it is the smoke which means the meeting of incompatibles, like fire and water, like sin and holiness. It was smoke which hid sinful man from the sin-scorching presence of the All-holy. He stood embarrassed, abashed, at the personal encounter of God.

And from this holiness he recoiled, saying: "Woe is me! for I am undone: because I am a man of unclean lips, and I dwell in the midst of a people of unclean lips: for mine eyes have seen the king, Jehovah of hosts." Sin always focuses for each of us in the place where we sin characteristically: and as for a prophet speech is the purest of all occupations, so uncleanness of lips, dishonesty or vileness, is the focus of all sin. And then he thought of all the blasphemy and low talking and profaneness of speech the whole length and breadth of the land—and then of all the other sin that held the people—and he confessed for himself and for them, saying that his confession was pressed from him because he had looked into the face of God.

Then comes a picture of the profoundest spiritual significance. One of the seraphim flew towards him with a "live coal "in his hand, which he had taken with tongs from off the altar: the meaning is a "glowing stone," such as was the ordinary means for carrying fire in common homes, the fire that warmed the water or cooked the meal or heated the house. Notice this: there is no temple paraphernalia here, no mediatorial apparatus nor ritual. It is as simple a form of sacrament as when our Lord took bread and wine: Isaiah saw the angel take common fire from off an altar of coals before the Lord. And, as in all true sacraments, there accompanied the outward gesture and act a rational and intelligible word: "Lo, this hath touched thy lips; and thine iniquity is taken away, and thy sin forgiven."

Isaiah belonged to a people who believed passionately in physical sacrifice, he stood on a temple-floor where every suggestion of it was made to him: but the only sacrifice he offered was the sacrifice of a broken spirit, a broken and a contrite heart, and the expression of it in confession. Seven hundred years later another Member of his inspired race by one great act of atonement did away with all physical sacrifice forever, One "who needeth not daily, like those high priests, to offer up sacrifices, first for his own sins, and then for the sins of the people: for this he did once for all, when he offered up himself." But the genius of the spiritual insight of Isaiah foresaw in his vision a day of free and unbought grace, which he had for standing abashed in confession, and waiting upon God.

Now, there are some of you here who by now are saying to yourselves, This man is talking unadulterated mysticism: he is dwelling upon the pious imagination of a man long dead, concerning a fancy which came into his head one day as he stood in the court of the temple after the king had died. Let us come into close grips with something modern and near and pertinent!

And to you I should like to say that the things we have been dealing with thus far are neither ancient nor modern, but eternal. For we have seen a man lift up his head to behold the chaos called life. The human reformer was dead in shameful disease. The people were disorganized and rebellious. A catastrophe lay on Isaiah's hands. He could find no solution upon the face of the earth, and he turned up to God. And looking into the face of God he saw against God's holiness his own sin, against God's perfection his own shame. And he felt abysmally unfit to do anything to retrieve the failure men had made of life. And here are the materials for a single human tragedy upon the profoundest scale. Here is where faith is born, or scepticism. This is where a man turns back to life with the power of the everlasting in his bosom, or the desolation of hell in his heart. The bitter satirists of modern life have gone wrong here where they were baffled in the problem of human reconstruction. Some of our most thorny literary critics were really meant for Isaiahs and Ezekiels and St. Pauls. They are ill-content with life as they find it. They crawl away into their libraries to snarl and carp and bite, because they did not, at some crucial moment in their careers, learn to worship and confess and transform the life about them with spiritual forces. You want something modern, do you? The problem of what to do with a chaotic world ought to be modern enough for you!

And the first thing to do for a chaotic modern world is to get some order in your own chaotic souls. Isaiah stood there in the presence of God long enough to let God sink in. He confessed his own utter need, his desperate guilt and shame. And to such honesty God can respond with the gift of grace, with the helping hand of His extended power. You may think it is mystical moonshine we have been engaged with this last fifteen minutes: but it has been an attempt to traverse with a human soul its turmoil of concern about itself and about mankind, and to show that what a man shall do and be forever is dependent upon how he meets that concern, and whether God, the All-holy, the Eternal, is admitted into the innermost recesses of his life. Nothing can happen through you, modern seeker after human betterment, until something has happened to you and in you. The anarchy of your own spirit must give place to a divine obedience. The first problem in all Israel for Isaiah was Isaiah. And the first problem in all modern America for you is you.

Now, when Isaiah's sin is forgiven, he can discern the deep concerns of God Himself. "And I heard the voice of the Lord, saying, Whom shall I send, and who will go for us?" A man has always a false experience of God who has a solitary experience of Him. Come close enough to God to know the sureness of His touch upon your life, and you will feel, with Isaiah, the throb of infinite and indiscriminate outgoing anxiety for all the whole family of earth. "Whom shall I send?" There is a message for the comfortless and hopeless in the earth, a message for the proud and the self-sufficient—who will carry it? For God has chosen to speak His greatest messages through others, not through the thunders out of the blue of heaven, but through the voices of rational and intelligible men.

"Then said I, Here am I." A man who has just looked Almighty God in the face is not in a presumptuous mood. This is not spoken from self-assurance, it is spoken from desire to co-operate with God and fulfil His will. It is an awesome thing to be volunteer messenger for God. But Isaiah will dare to try it, in the power of the grace that has come to him. It was not the mood of a moment, it was the hue and resolution of a lifetime. Whether he deals politically with Egyptian and Assyrian intrigue: or morally with the king or the unsettled people, there is written forever across his life: "Here am I." It is the offer of a self.

And having offered himself, seen himself in relation to God's plan, he definitely asks God for a commission. "Send me." Dare you look into God's heart, and discern all His infinite compassion towards the children of men, and then think of the rebellion of men's hearts, their stony indifference, their calculating and devilish sin, and offering your life for a bridge say with him: "Send me"?

And swiftly comes the commission: "Go and tell this people, Listen and listen—but never understand! Look and look—but never see! Make their mind dull, make their ears heavy and close up their eyes, lest their eyes see, and their ears heat, lest their minds understand and their health be restored." How shall we interpret this hard saying? Plainly this is not a picture of God's will, but it is a picture of how men act. A genuine message from God does one of two things: it captures and subdues, or it hardens and enrages. If I stand here in Christ's pulpit and say smooth things to you, nobody will be any the worse or any the better: but if God gives me an authentic message from Himself, and I say the truth to you in all its naked power, it will help some people immensely, and it will anger some people furiously. We are not plastic to anybody's hand, nor was Israel: we come into God's house full of predispositions and already twisted in one direction or the other. Real preaching is not presentation, it is strife: it is warfare with sin and the devil for the lives of men. Isaiah knew what the people would do: he was warned of God, that he might not be surprised when it came to pass.

And for the sin of the people, the sin of disobedience, Isaiah promises judgment. God will make a clean sweep. The land will be desolate and forsaken: it will be repeatedly withered for its sin. But hope lay in a minority: there was a remnant—a few true and faithful and inspired souls who would keep the torch burning, and transmit God's light unimpaired to fresh generations. These are two cornerstones of Isaiah's teaching: destruction of the mass, preservation of what was worth preserving. And it all means one thing: God's own self-vindication through human history. He is not mocked. The nation that tries to do without Him shall surely fall. Prosperity may be but the cloak for rottenness. Let us beware, we who are at ease in Zion, lest such a fate come upon us here in our own beloved and foolish land, so rich, so heedless, so restless for God.

So far as Isaiah was concerned, there was one possible prevention of that judgment having full course: and that was that he could get Israel to listen to him when he told them what God wanted. Isaiah stood between Israel and destruction, if they only knew it. He had the solution in his hands. He was the key to the situation, but whether he could unlock doors with it was dependent upon his own powers of persuasion backed by the grace which found him. It was a situation to make a man quail and run with craven fear. But he did not run. He stood in the breach. He tried to make Israel listen to God. Israel was destroyed, as he said they would be when they did not obey: but the remnant was saved according to his prophecy—and the true remnant of Israel was Christ.

That man was in the thick of the politics of his day. He knew them better than king or people. He saw through events to principles, through practical exigencies to eternal falsehoods and truths. Isaiah's vision of God did not send him into an eremite's cell, it sent him into the market-place and the temple and the gatherings of the people. He was one of the great forces of his time. But it came, not from the pleasure of playing politics, not from the love of harangue or being talked about: it came from catching from God, in his vision, the concern of God for mankind. And that is what a genuine vision of God always does for any man: it sends him into the world to remake life to the best of his ability in accordance with what he has learned of God.

Now what about ourselves? We come into God's house this Trinity Sunday, and sing hymns of praise and say prayers of petition and thanksgiving. If we are: simple enough, real enough, we may with the insight of the prophet see the Lord high and lifted up here in His own house. It will comfort us. It will inspire us. What else will it do? O my friends, let it stir us and awaken us and disturb us with anxiety for His other children! We say we are only one. So we are. But one may be enough, where we are, to save the day.

The other afternoon I was walking through the Metropolitan Arcade, and a man had in his hand a great bunch of daisies: and he was giving one to the elevator man, and one to the watchman, and one to the policeman. It seemed a very little gift. But I remembered a field of daisies, standing thick with flowers somewhere in the country: and this nosegay for a buttonhole in the city came from the country, it was a real daisy; and they eagerly seized them, because they wanted that touch of the country in the town! So is a genuine Christian wherever you put him—just one just a unit, just one man to stand in the gap. But back of him lie the armies of the Christians: he stands not alone; but backed by all Christ's fields of Christians.

And the heart of the meaning of Isaiah's vision is perhaps the heart of the meaning of the Christian Gospel: that God needs men and cannot do without them. And that when a man dares to put aside, not the pride of presumption so much as the pride of false humility, and say to God, "Here am I: send me," God says: "Go!"

Let us pray:

O God, whom in all ages men have sought and found, and who hast made Thyself known to us through Thy Son and Thy Holy Spirit: Grant us this day a genuine vision of Thee, that beholding Thee we may understand Thee, and understanding, may obey Thee, and being obedient unto Thee may fulfil Thy will and have some share in Thy redemptive purpose towards all men. Through Jesus Christ our Lord, whom with the Father and the Holy Spirit we worship as one God, world without end. Amen.

# IX

# What Shall We Do with Trouble?

*"Blessed is the man whose strength is in thee: in whose heart are thy ways. Who going through the vale of misery use it for a well: and the pools are filled with water."*
—PSALM 84:5, 6 (PRAYER BOOK).

Besides what religion has to give to human beings of intellectual and philosophical interpretations of life, it has two plain and practical problems which are always facing it. It has got to give men some power by which to get the mastery over sin, and it has got to help them when they are in trouble to find peace and comfort. Religion is both a strenuous and a soothing thing: and much of our difficulty has arisen from our being strenuous when we should have been comforting, and perhaps more often-from our being soothing when we should have been drastic instead. We are to think this morning of religion in its power to tide us over the places of sorrow in our life.

I suppose that no man or woman gets past thirty years of age, who lives and thinks at all, who does not have to reckon with sorrow and trouble. We all have our early years of easy optimism, when things are going well with us, and the sky is full of sunlight. We ought to be glad for those years, for sometimes they are the years in which we form our great resolves and set out, with magnificent hope, toward great goals. But the time will come when something flings itself across our path which seems to chill our hope and put out the fires of our hearts.

We set upon a plan of work, with that mixture of motives, selfish and altruistic, which is so nearly universal. And we put our heart into it, and work for all we are worth, but, do what we will, the thing begins to drag. It does not seem to: be altogether our fault, but a combination of forces some of which we cannot control. And one day we must face it bravely but honestly—*we have failed.*

Or a young man undertakes a large piece of work, which is going to demand of him the maximum of intellectual and physical energy. And one day he begins to feel bad, and a doctor tells him that he must pull out of it all, and go into a high atmosphere, for he finds a spot in his lung: and that man turns from all that he hoped to do, and packs himself off to the country to try to regain his health: and the things he dreams there are full of fear and sadness. Or a family watches two beautiful children grow up, amid every opportunity they can provide, and gives them all the world's best: and finds that they only expect more. One makes a good marriage which does not last very long, because it has got no foundations of religion. The other turns hard as flint, and has no human concern for anything but pleasure. And these two children, who began with so much promise, and still in the eyes of the world appear so well, are disappointments to their parents, who carry in their hearts heavy misgivings whether it would not have been better if the kindness had been tempered with less of the selfish joy of giving to one's own, and more of the iron that makes for character. What sadder thing is there in this world than to be disappointed in those God has given us to be our very own?

Or we see a family, happy in its full circle, each contributing something to the whole life—and then, one by one, they fall sick and wither and drop away like the leaves off a tree, until one alone is left, to try to go on and make the best of it when the world no longer holds much of interest.

It is of no good to keep on with the list. We could picture a thousand such instances, and every one of then I would evoke the response of someone in this congregation who had "been there." We live in a lonely and terrifying world. Men seem sometimes to be the playthings of a fortune which has in it neither reason to explain it, nor rhyme to soften it. You have not lived at all if you have come to the conclusion that all is well with the world. You have been sitting back in pudgy comfort where you do not see life as it is, if you do not know what tragedies fasten upon human beings. I wish that you could all see what a minister sees in the course of a week, if he is on his job. The reason we have got such shallow views of what Christ did for the world, and the reason we make Him to be such a smiling cheer-monger is that we do not reckon with the exceeding sinfulness of sin, and the exceeding sorrowfulness of sorrow.

I am not given much to sentimentalizing about trouble, and you will generally hear me say things in this pulpit which imply that most of man's difficulty is of his own making and can be of his own unmaking. I say those things because they are the zone of hope in human life, and because I believe infinitely in man, in his freedom to choose and to carve out a wide destiny for himself if he seek the will of God. But I have seen too much of life not to know that sadness and sorrow are not to be dismissed by any facile gesture of hard-hearted optimism, such as parades all round us these days in a hundred self-deceived cults. Evil is serious business in all its aspects: and sorrow is one of them. You will not glorify God, nor better understand the Christian religion, by minimizing the reality of trouble in this world, for the New Testament nowhere does any such thing. "In the world ye shall have tribulation"—that is the verdict. Now what are we going to do about it?

Everything depends upon how you take it and what you make of it. I am not attempting now any guesses at the question of why sorrow is here, but only into the practical question of what to do with it now we've got it. The whole solution is not a theoretical one, but a practical one. Trouble crushes one life, and softens another: embitters one, and makes another sympathetic, because of the different ways in which it is regarded and handled. I will make a few suggestions which have helped me when trouble was present.

In the first place, see your own trouble in its setting as part of the long tragedy which has everywhere accompanied human life. You are not alone in it. Your age is not alone in its sorrows. I remember going up on a hill beside the Bosphorus one afternoon in considerable distress of mind. And I began to think of the infinite pain which had been suffered in that region where I stood. I thought of Roman legions giving themselves that Constantine might build his capital; I thought of the workmen who toiled to build St. Sophia, and of Justinian's vain cry when the church was completed, "I have conquered thee, O Solomon"; of the splendid folly of the Crusaders, crossing this strait into Asia Minor, never to return again to Europe. Gallipoli was a few hundred miles down the narrows, and the bones of English lads filled a gigantic graveyard, not far from the sea. Across the water lay Asia Minor, where Paul had laboured and preached and worn himself out, more Mohammedan than Christian to-day. Possibly there were more Christians in Asia Minor at the end of his life than there are now. And I began to realize that my own trouble was very small, and must be looked at in the light of all this pageant of pain down the ages, which must have some meaning for human life. Sorrow, like sin, isolates its victims, and makes them believe they are alone in their suffering. I think it is a considerable help to make ourselves conscious of the conspicuous place which trouble and sorrow have been given in human experience. If you believe life is explainable at all, you must dignify the experience of trouble by granting that it has its place and carries meaning.

Second, set your trouble in the light of the Cross of Christ. The best the world ever saw came to this. He did not move serenely and indifferently across the stage of human affairs, scattering roses and smiling His way into men's protecting affections. The closer He got to meeting the world's need by showing the world where it stood in its relation to God, the closer did He come to treading upon the toes of men who would not stand for it, and who finally brought Him to a criminal death. It would have been a mockery and a joke on us if He had come into the world in luxury, when men are in want; slipped through the world in success, when men fail; and lived to enjoy the full fruit of His labours, when men are cut off in the bitterness of disappointment. If He be God, this had to happen. I should have no use for a God who would not share this colossal tragedy by coming into it and bearing it. I should deny Him a fraction of homage. But He *did* share it, shared the extreme of it, in ignominy and disappointment and physical pain. The simplest meaning of the Cross is that God suffered, and in the end that may be for us, while here below, the profoundest meaning. When you suffer, remember that God suffered, and suffers still.

Third, share your trouble. I do not mean share it for the relief it brings to you to talk about it, for that may be, after a time, a very selfish thing to do. I mean, share it where it will create an atmosphere in which someone else in trouble can share that trouble with you, so that *they* may find relief. There are gushing people, moist with piety and dripping with sentimentality, who find dissipation in unburdening their troubles on others—plainly they must learn how to be unselfish with sorrow, so that they do not force it on all, but also do not withhold it from those whom it will help. The sun alone can set free a ship caught in frozen ice-fields; and you may keep a heart from breaking if you can start an ice-floe. The sharing of trouble which is for our own relief is selfish and sentimental, the sharing which builds a bridge across into the heart of another is one of God's benedictions let into the world.

And, fourth, try to find the meaning in your trouble. Perhaps at the very beginning of trouble, you may be expected only to hold on tenaciously to old moorings—to stand it. But as the time runs on, and pain gives place to peace, you will find that God has not left you at any time, but has been leading you through the darkness as well as through the day. You may find a harshness has been melted out of you forever because of the sorrow you have suffered. You may find that your absurd trust in yourself, and your pride in prosperity or pleasure in success, has given way to dependence upon God, and reliance upon Him for all your needs. You may find that when someone you loved was withdrawn from you, for the first time you learned to love humanity: and now you see *your* child in every child, *your* brother in every man, *your* sister in every woman. I have seen women left alone in the world who became mothers and sisters to the world; and men who became its fathers and its brothers. There is always a hopeful way of taking trouble: a dear old saint of God, not far from this church, said to me, in her illness and weakness a little time ago: "Now I have time to pray as long as I want for everybody I want to pray for." You may discover that, since you have been in trouble, for the first time in your life you can exercise genuine sympathy: it is easy to coin smooth words to say to people when they suffer, but no word at all is better if they know that you have been through what they are going through, and this alone is to "suffer with" anyone.

I do not believe, my friends, that God sends trouble, or deliberately wills the trouble which comes upon the children of men. Much of it is of our own making, some is due to natural forces in the physical universe to which we belong, some of it I give up trying to understand. But I believe that God *uses* that trouble, turns it to good account, works it into the whole fabric of our lives, and gives meaning to it. When I find a person, as occasionally one does, who still is rebellious after years have passed, still grudges the loss of her child or her husband, still reproaches God for a sorrow He did not will, but is anxious to guide and use, I believe that this person is nursing a sorrow for a kind of morbid joy which comes from the clinging to it. You cannot seek the meaning of a sorrow; while you hug it to yourself, and will not give it to God to shed His light upon. You must let Him make something of it, or you have yourself been guilty of causing yourself injury, and cannot blame Him if you turn sour and grow hard. You have done it because you refused to find the meaning for yourself. You remember in *Pilgrim's Progress*, where Christian goes through the Valley of Humiliation: and the story says: "This Valley of Humiliation is of itself as fruitful a place as any the crow flies over: and I am persuaded, if we could hit upon it, we might find somewhere hereabouts something that might give us an account why Christian was so hardly beset in this place."

Thus to read sorrow in the light of the sorrows of others, and of our Lord Himself—to allow sorrow to make us more sympathetic than we could have been without it—to see what may "give us an account why we were so beset in this place"—is to go through the vale of misery and use it for a well. The kind of faith which interprets experience in this fashion finds that the "pools *are* filled with water," water enough for us to bear out and give to a thirsty world full of men who are like as in a desert. It looks back upon all the events of life and says that God has wondrously led, and that all things do work together for good to them that love Him. It is no Christianity which tries to make good out of evil, and says that sorrow does not exist: neither is it Christianity which is overwhelmed and crushed by sorrow. It *is* Christianity which finds the hand of God in all experience. It was Jesus who said: "In the world ye shall have tribulation." But He also said: "Be of good cheer; I have overcome the world."

Let us pray:

Father, who dealest gently with Thy children, even when we know it not; teach us to know that nothing but our own disobedience can take us out of Thy hand, and help us to trust ourselves and those we love to Thy loving care at all times. Be thou for us a light in the darkness and joy in all our grief. Through Him who giveth us the victory, our Lord Jesus Christ.

X

# Undistracted Loyalty to Christ

*"If I will that he tarry till I come, what is that to thee? Follow thou me."*

—JOHN 21:22.

No character more steadily maintains throughout the gospels his clear-cut, dominant traits than Simon Peter. From the beginning to the end he is the same impulsive, generous, independent, strong-headed, meddlesome nature. And in the last chapter of St. John all those characteristics are recapitulated.

You are all familiar with the story. Simon, consulting no one, announces that he is going fishing—and the rest follow. In the morning, after a night without success, Jesus standing on the shore calls to them to cast their nets on the right side of the ship This they do, and they take in a large catch—they counted them, and there were a hundred and fifty-three. Simon plunges into the water, unable to get to the Master quickly enough, and to show Him their success.

Possibly there was something a little breathless and unsubstantial about all this protestation of loyalty and attention. After breakfast, He took Simon alone, and pressed three times upon him that earnest question, whether he really loved Him—and three times told him what he did would speak louder than what he said.

Then, turning quickly to the future which they should soon face without His visible presence, He warned Simon what should come: "When thou wast young, thou girdest thyself, and walkedst whither thou wouldest: but when thou shalt be old, thou shalt stretch forth thy hands, and another shall gird thee, and carry thee whither thou wouldest not."

There is hardly any young man who has had any slight experience of religion at all, and who considers the future calmly, who does not realize that matters may look differently when health begins to wane, when obligations begin to tie him hand and foot, when the undeveloped sides of his nature will stick out like a clay-pit in a meadow, and circumstances envelop him in an unbreakable clutch. Perhaps there is no more sobering thought in the world than to wonder whether the religion of our youth is dependent upon happy activity, upon favouring circumstance, upon the buoyancy of first enthusiasm,—whether in the grey days of decline our soul will still travel lightly when our limbs grow stiff.

Yet it is in the midst of this solemn conversation, directed at him alone, a man whose imagination must have seen in a quick flash what Jesus warned him of—it is here that Simon Peter, with consummate spiritual impropriety, looks round and catches sight of the Beloved Disciple, and says to Jesus: "What about him, Lord?" And Jesus comes back with a swift reply to that inquisitive and impertinent question: "If I will that he tarry till I come, what is that to thee? Follow thou me."

There lies profound meaning in Jesus' ready rebuke to the spiritual woolgathering and preoccupation involved in Simon's question. The meaning is that there is no more insidious enemy to Christian discipleship than idle curiosity and inquisitiveness into questions which are suggested by discipleship but have no direct relation to it. There is a place in the Christian religion for thought, for the intellectual faculties to play across the whole complex experience of life, to recognize fact as fact, to cut away superstition which always lies near to the truest religion, and to prevent us from accepting with the intuitive part of us something which the reasonable part of us must reject. But there is no place in the Christian religion for perpetual quibbling about questions which do not bear upon the major and immediate issues of life.

Jesus sends down His command, through the centuries, to go into the ends of the earth and preach His Gospel to every creature. In our souls we know that there is no other religion so good as His, because there is no other life so good as His. But we begin wondering about all the Mohammedans and Hindus and Confucianists and Buddhists that ever lived in ages gone, and our response to His practical command is an abstract question: "Lord, what is going to happen to the souls of all these people in kingdom come? There are good people amongst them. Surely you will not consign the whole lot of them to brimstone and perdition. What will you do with them?" And Jesus says: "All souls are mine. I know where men have been true to the flicker of light that was given them. You stand in the blaze of the Light of the World, wondering whether their light is as great as Mine. What is that to thee? Follow thou Me."

Jesus calls to men to group themselves together in His fellowship, the Church. It is the body of Christ. It is the brotherhood of believers, and ideally the only genuine brotherhood in the world. And we say: "But, Lord, the Church is full of hypocrites. I know a man who made a great profession of Christ, and then took what didn't belong to him, and then lied to get out of it. Is that religion? I know people that go to church, and come out no better than they went in: is that religion?" And Jesus says: "What is that to thee? Follow thou Me."

Someone sets out to live a Christian life. And, for all the joy and adventure of it, there is a good deal that is hard about it, too. And the long process of sanctification, the toning-up of the whole of life in accord with the Spirit of Christ, begins to wear on us and tire us out. And then joking round, like Simon, we see another disciple who just takes to religion like a duck to water: things seem to go well, his life looks like a steady crescendo and progress, he is not devilled as we are by inner misgivings and haunting fears, and we begin to say: "Lord, why does this person get along so much more easily than I? Why do others have a fortunate temperament, while I worry? Why am I tried by sorrow and suffering, while hey go free?" And Jesus says: "What do you know of all the inward struggles of another life? What business is it of yours to complain against God, about the fortune of another? What is that to thee? Follow thou Me."

Or we grow worried about someone we love. Let us say that a younger member of our family gets tremendously interested in Christ and His work. We pine and sigh about the youth of to-day being irreligious—and then in the next breath we lament that our youth has gotten *too* religious. And we wonder what will happen to them if they keep on with this thing. Thy may give their lives to it, and have very little to live on. They may give up the advantageous marriage we had hoped for, and go and be single, or marry some consecrated soul we never heard of. A number of parents that I know are in a stew over what vital religion may do to their children. And to them Jesus is saying: "The tenderest human ties are yet tenderer to Me. I know every need of your child. Your very worry may break the stream of power by which I can reach that child through every hour of need. What is all that to thee? Follow thou Me."

Now and then I come across someone who is terribly concerned at what is happening to Christianity in our day. They do not lay the emphasis where it ought to be laid—on the undistracted loyalty of every man and woman to Christ—and work towards that—but they go trotting about spreading a miasma of fear and distrust and prejudice against some section of Christians, or some development with which they are not in sympathy. How often does one hear from some distressed soul about the harm the Roman Catholics are doing, their political activities, and their unbreakable system. Or some very clever intellectual spends any amount of powder blowing up the position of the Fundamentalists. Or some conservative soul ties up the atheists and the communists and the Bolshevists and the liberal Christians in one big bundle, and wants both Church and state to cart them out into the harbour and throw them overboard. Jesus did not attack the dangers of His day in that fashion. He sought the undivided loyalty of converted hearts to Himself. He never worried where He could not help. And He says to you: "Do not deal with symptoms, but with causes. Get to men's hearts, and change them, and your society will clear up. Give over your atheistic fears and anxieties about other people's errors. What is that to thee? Follow thou Me."

How many people, as they contemplate the possibility of starting to live the Christian life, want to see the end from the beginning, want to know at the outset just what will be the cost and the outcome. Will this inevitably bring me happiness? May I have to cut my connections with my friends? Would I have to pull out of the business, if I found something shady in its operations? May I hold on to the minor self-indulgence which I love?

Or again, how often they ward off the fundamental issue of deciding for Christ by running up numberless bypaths which lead nowhere. Many a man sits opposite to me in conversation, asking vague questions about Christianity which if they were answered would not alter by a fraction the smallest detail of his life, trifling over irrelevant abstractions while Christ stands in the midst waiting for his choice. And I believe Jesus says to men like that: "I chose a path which began on the bright slopes of Galilee, and closed on a dark hill outside Jerusalem. Shall not the servant tread it still? Leave off your fears for your own future, and your footless questions about interesting spiritual abstractions. What are they to thee? Follow thou Me."

One of the commonest questionings which arise in connection with religion is the question of why some good life is plagued with sorrow. A saint lies stricken on a bed of pain. An upright man and woman lose their child, and life goes out with the loss. A fine young spirit, with infinite possibilities, is snuffed out in a motor accident. The mother of young children goes out of her mind, and leaves a home behind her withdrawal more desolate than if she were dead. I do not believe Jesus could wish us never to ask, "Why?" He asked His own Father, "Why?" from the Cross. But He did not spend His life in futile quibbling and questioning about evil: He did His best to do away with evil and supplant it by good. I think it is true that we do not know the *whole* story of anybody's life but our own: they may need chastening, reminding, softening, testing in ways we know nothing of. We generally can account for the events in our own life, if we wait long enough for God to work through His whole plan. But it is idle to speculate and wonder, where we cannot know all the facts. We may destroy the very faith which would help another to interpret his sorrow helpfully, if we ourselves are unbelieving about it. And Jesus says to us: "What is that to thee? Follow thou Me."

One could go on with instances like these for half a day. I know many a half-convinced life that will never get any further conviction while these purely external matters of curiosity hold sway over their minds. No sooner does a green blade of faith spring up in their souls, than one of these extraneous questions stands ready with the shears to cut it down. Even when a believing human soul can give good reason in reply to the question, that kind of a mind retreats to take up, another question, forever asking and never deciding.

I want to say to you again, I am not pleading for irrational faith. A faith without intellectual foundation is not going to stand for long: and a faith you can't look at honestly is superstition. But I am saying that there are moods of distracting inquisitiveness and curiosity in which, if they are persisted in, it is easy to pull up the roots of the firmest faith. There are many questions of interest, questions which whet our wits and feed our imaginations, questions the philosophers have left unanswered, and which yet have nothing to do with the immediate business of living well.

The Christian solution to these questions, or to the deeper problem of existence out of which they all arise, is a unique one. Jesus says that all knowledge of this interior, spiritual world is best had through first forming a loyalty to Himself which is undistracted by any prior considerations whatever: and that in the attachment with Him there comes a kind of understanding in which the questions which really matter in life are made clear. "I am the light of the world," is His claim, "he that followeth me shall not walk in the darkness, but shall have the light of life." There is a loyalty, there is a holy preoccupation with Jesus Himself, which becomes a climate in which irrelevant questions no longer clamour for solution, and in which the questions which concern the practical prosecution of life find answer. That is one of the deepest and one of the most blessed of the experiences of religion.

Jesus asks from us an attachment us like anything else on this earth. There is no human being to whom we can give ourselves with the utter certainty that in the very giving there is sure illumination and blessing. He says to all the ages, "Follow Me," with the imperiousness of certain authority. He will not brook any turning aside to consider any lesser issues: that attachment is primary, and all else must find its place in subservience to it. Jesus asks you to "go it blind" with Him. He asks it because He knows that only so will you ever gain your sight.

There lie a thousand questions in the minds of people in this church this morning, questions bearing upon religion if not arising out of it. Many of you wonder what God can do with your own futile past, and others look into the future with fear. Another is bothered with the wages of sin, or the dread of age, or the approach of sickness, or the possibility of enormous disappointment, or the obligation to a distasteful duty—or just the age-old everlasting and ever-present problem of the evil in the world, which no religious man can blink without nursing a lie in his soul. It is a temptation for us all to muse and fret about these things, all the while that Jesus is laying upon us the command to follow. Like Simon, we are ever looking over our shoulder at these things, and so drawing away our attention from Him to them.

But it has been the cumulative experience of the finest spirits who have ever crossed this earth that when they turn back to Christ from these distracting and upsetting and irrelevant questions, and concentrate their attention upon the one gigantic attachment to Christ, living all their lives upon this straight-line loyalty to Him, there is guidance and grace for each separate problem which arises, the tangled skeins of life come straight, and there hovers about that one tremendous loyalty itself such radiance of illumination as can never be found elsewhere on this planet.

Give over, then, I ask you, your secondary questionings and your irrelevant inquisitiveness into matters which are not pertinent to what you ought to do next. Foster and encourage the spirit to follow Christ, at all costs, whithersoever He leads. And you will find, what many more of us have found, that "in his light we shall see light," and in His straight path we shall not stumble.

**Let us pray:**

**O Master of the world: who art still lovingly and imperiously calling us away from all the distractions of sin and curiosity which divide our loyalty to Thee: Keep us from the sin of idle questioning and help us so to put our trust in Thee that we may learn by following, and see, by utter surrender, all of the truth which we need. We ask it in Thy Name. Amen.**

XI

# The Higher Reaches of Christian Experience

*"I will lift up mine eyes unto the hills."*

**—PSALM 121:1.**

Probably the most difficult problem which any idealistic way of taking life must encounter is the problem of where to adapt, and where to refuse to adapt, to that mixture of sordidness and possibility which we call human nature. Religion is dedicated to the proposition that there is a spirit in man: and that however strong or evil his instincts may be, they can be brought into line with the high desires of the spirit.

Christianity passionately believes that. And yet again and again our religion has suffered the same decline to which all our human affairs are subject. We let it slip down into comfortable counterfeits. We tend—the best of us—to compromise with human nature. We say, with our lives if not with our mouths, that human nature is too weak a thing to expect that it can be lifted up to the level of New Testament Christianity: so we had better adapt Christianity till it better fits human-nature. We conform to our surroundings, we compare our religion with the rest of the congregation, we take colour from our companions who belong to the world, we keep up with the neighbours in clothes and houses. In the very solitude of our own hearts, we admit to ourselves that we "cannot always live on the heights." How many times have you heard people say that?

Yes, we succumb to our own human nature. David Harum says some folks have more human nature than others—and we belong to the some that are afflicted with lots of it.

To-day, as we look into the archways of a fresh year of life, perhaps it will help us to get above the common levels of Christianity as we know and live it, and to think about the high places where we may still climb in the year that opens before us and the time that is left to us. Few of us would venture to say that the past year did not contain great spiritual neglects and even great spiritual failures. One feels something close to fear as he considers the cycle of the years, running swiftly on, and sees what a short distance he has moved since he passed the last milestone.

I know that for myself I feel there are whole great areas where my own Christianity is weak, and where I want to lift and deepen my own experience. I always try to preach to myself when I am speaking aloud to you, but especially to-day I shall be talking of levels of spiritual living far above those to which I have grown accustomed in the touch-and-go of ordinary living. I shall speak, not so much of places where I have been, as of places where I should like to be, and where I should like to go in your company through this next year of spiritual pilgrimage. Let us this morning "lift up our eyes unto the hills," and consider several of the high places of the spirit.

I should like to live always in the high place of *faith*. I do not mean the low hills of assent to inherited theological propositions, but the high hill of such trust in God as literally transfigures the earth. I mean the faith which refuses ever to consider any situation a trap, but views each one as a crucible in which some creative event may take place—the kind of faith which set St. Paul to work in prison as gaily as in the market-place, which sees advantages wrapped in limitations, and man's extremity as God's opportunity which He will not fail to improve.

I mean the faith which sees through the outwardness of sorrow to its inwardness, and finds a meaning for the deepest loss: as a friend wrote to me but this week of the death of her husband, "I think I have got to the point of realizing *why* the person I loved most in the world had to go. With him alive I was too happy and too contented. I'm afraid I should never have made any *real* effort after truth. It was one of those instances where the 'good' (and oh, how good it was!) was the enemy of the best." I mean the faith that cannot be shaken out of its inward harmony and tranquility by any outward misfortune or neglect or hostility: but that has a foundation in another world, utterly independent of what man can do unto it.

I mean the faith which is sure of the final conquest of good over evil—sure of it because the quantity of evil is outweighed by the quality of good, and because God is God. And the faith which sees in immortality the inevitable outgrowth of the kind of life which Jesus Christ makes possible in this world.

I should like always to live in the high places of *love*. Love that allows nobody to stand outside its view, builds no artificial fences between people, sees men's hearts and not their clothes or their colour, and looks on them somewhat as God looks on them. Love that is never uncomfortable in the presence of incompatibles, but with ingenuity brings together into fellowship divers kinds of people who would usually not understand each other, love which is a great reconciler of those whom the crusty custom of the world has divided. Love that rejoices in the success of those who are our rivals, is fair to the truth of those who are our critics, is patient of those who wilfully misunderstand us.

Love that is brave enough to call sin sin, and to conclude all men under sin: and then to refuse to believe that there is a soul anywhere that cannot be saved. Love for those that irritate us, foolishly take our time, needlessly harry us about trifles, are stupid about taking a hint. Love that always sees people and situations as they lie in the mind of God, big with potentiality, no matter what the situation be. I am convinced that love like that will wear some of us out, and tax us beyond human power: it crucified Christ, but it set going a new force in human life.

And humility—the high place of *humility.* Someone will say it ought to be a low place for humility: but I think not. Genuine humility cannot be attained by avoiding pride: it can only be attained by discovering gratitude. The truest humility in the world is that of the man who has been lifted up by God, carried above his sins, given peace for his pain and joy for his crying; and who, standing on the strong rock, thinks not of the security of his own position but of the mercy of God for putting him there. Yes, humility is a high place—a very high place indeed. There are human door-mats who feign humility but do not have it. They are cultivating it as a virtue: and the cultivation of humility as a virtue is almost a vice. Let them experience a great deliverance, or really know the salvation of God in their souls, and their humility will grow out of their sense of obligation and gratitude.

Let us all try this coming year to dwell so much upon what God has done for us that we may develop an ever-present thankfulness to Him. And then we shall refer all the joy and success of our life to Him and not to ourselves. And that is humbleness. I do not want mock-humbleness, the obsequious and snivelling kind: but the humility which is born of meditating upon that great thought, "What hast thou that thou didst not receive?"

Another high place where I would like to live always. I should like always to make an *impression for Christ,* and not for myself, upon every life I meet. There are lives in the world obviously possessed. One feels in them both the constraint and the liberty of a great Other, with them at all times. That impression would be made often by words, for what a man loves most, that he talks about. But it will be made, too, by the subtlest attitudes, by the things he reads and doesn't read in the newspapers, by the books on his table, by the recreation he chooses, by the way he talks to the telephone operator, and says good-morning to the elevator man in his office. You know as well as I do that there are people who live that way twenty-four hours in the day, and they are not saccharine and effusive people, they are as often quiet and restrained people.

Christ works through us according to the nature He has given to us. One of us will touch people by buoyancy and enthusiasm: another will touch them by the possession of evident inward peace. One will witness for Christ by radiant health and happiness: and another will show Him forth by patience in illness. It is possible, when we meet people, to be relaxed, sensitive, generous of time, responsive, ready to change our plans to meet their needs: and through a life thus ready and at liberty from itself Christ can and does shine. Surely it would be to live on the heights if we could succeed in never giving a misimpression for Him: if we could literally reflect Him in every word and act and thought.

And then there is another high place of Christian experience. It is the height a man reaches when *prayer becomes the climate of its life.* Not a ritual, not a habit, not a last resort, but a climate wherein a man's soul draws breath. One comes increasingly to believe in the reality of a spiritual kingdom, as high above the animal kingdom as the animal is above the inanimate—a kingdom with its own laws which supersede the laws that science understands in the two lower kingdoms. When a human soul lives continually in that kingdom, the common events of life are seen in a glow of significance, coincidences turn into Providences, frustrations into opportunity, and miracle becomes the order of the day. There is a higher ether which if a man breathe, all his normal gifts are lifted into superhuman power, as unlettered men were empowered to write the most immortal books in the world.

There is nothing to be wondered at if some who make this kingdom their home, see beyond into the World of Reality at times through the eyes of their souls, and come back to say that they have seen a vision of Christ and eternity. From the height of that mountain, many things are visible beyond which are hidden from our eyes as we walk below in the valley. And in that kingdom, the communication of the will of God to our finite minds becomes, in the truest sense, natural: it is expected, we are quiet enough to hear, and obedient enough to understand; our wills slip over into God's will and become one with it. This is not an unscalable height: I know lives that live there, and would God we might all join them and dwell with them "in heavenly places by Christ Jesus."

Now, it will do us only harm if we are content to look up to these high places from a distance, and then stay where we are. I think that it was Chesterton who once described the mood of most of us with comic accuracy: "I will lift up mine eyes unto the hills, but I will not drag my carcase thither." We need to stake fresh claims for ourselves on those high places during this new year, and to take new ground. And we had better begin to make the ascent by roads which are accessible to us.

Let us determine at all costs that we shall master our besetting sin this year, and put its domination behind us. What holds us back from faith and love and living for Christ and communion with God? Generally the thought of our utter unworthiness, which is another way of saying our sin. To each of us there is a familiar form of it; that besets and tortures and bedevils us: and which is the gateway to a train of discouragement and loneliness and more sin. And the reason we fail with the mastery of it is usually that we do not definitely give it up, or believe that we can give it up: but when we break it, keep the memory of its possibility in one corner of our minds, remembering that we can always go back to it. Let us claim for ourselves that great promise, in the fourteenth of Romans, "Sin shall have no more dominion over you."

Let us anew turn over to God all our possessions for His use. The only possible excuse for our being well cared for is that what we have we really share with those in need. It is easy to have a comfortable house which we meant to use that way, and then to draw into its quietness and enjoy its peace for ourselves. The last thing most

Christian people ever surrender to God's immediate guidance is their bank-account: they will not dare to let the Holy Spirit preside while they are writing checks. They will even be humanly generous, but to allow God complete control in what they do with what they possess requires an absoluteness of dedication which they will not make. Let us at least be tithers, but let us not be content until God has it all. For Jesus knew the opportunity of possessions, but He knew their danger, too, to wall the life away from the very need it ought to satisfy. We cannot live on the high places without committing all our possessions to God.

Let us stake a claim in Bible study this year. Let us resolve that next New Year's will find us thoroughly familiar with one great book—say Isaiah, or St. John's Gospel, or Romans. The depth of spiritual life is partly measured by our understanding of the Word of God. Modern Christianity is full of good works, but we are weak on scholarship and on deep Bible study.

Also, let us do some real spiritual reading this year. Get hold of Dick Sheppard's *Impatience of a Parson*, and you will find, not I think an adequate solution but a very acute diagnosis of the present state of religion. Bishop Temple's *Christ the Truth* is solid reading but illuminating: so is Hocking's *Human Nature and Its Remaking*. One of the profoundest books that has appeared in recent years is Rudolph Otto's *Idea of the Holy*—not light reading, but a deep shaft sunk into spiritual truth. Our Christianity is shallow for the most part. Let us deepen it with knowledge.

And then let us take another road—a hard road for many. Let us promise God that we shall choose a group of people, and do our best, by prayer, by the gifts of books, by influence, to reach them decisively for Christ this next year. I mean that for every one of you, no matter what predilections or prejudice you may have about "personal work." Do it as you choose, so you do it with the help of God. But do not do it slip-shod. Do not leave it till next December. Do not complain about your shyness: forget it in the urgency of the love of God. Get them on your hearts and in your prayers. Pray for God's solution to all their problems, for God to open the door to you. It is wonderful how prayer changes the face of a relationship.

I am convinced that many a Christian will never walk on the high places of his faith just because he will not learn how to share his faith with others. I know you weren't brought up that way, some of you: neither was I. I had to learn it. But I would not go back to that old buttoned-up religion, when I was afraid to say a word for Christ, not for anything. This city is ripe for a great awakening. Your friends, who say little, think much. Get busy. Determine that you will be of some use to God through this coming year, or find out what is the matter.

Yes, the hills are high, but they are nearer than we thought, because there are roadways that lead up to the top. Some of you have never seriously thought of changing your comfortable religion, and going up higher. God give us all this New Year's Day the mind to forsake the compromises of the years that are flown, and to seek the heights with Christ.

Let us. pray:

Father, forgive the cold love of the years. Our souls have always looked up to the high places, and known that they were our rightful home. But we have been tied and bound by fear to change our ways. Lift us up by the glory of Christ's hope for us, and help us to make the ascent to the life Thou wouldest have us to live. Through Jesus Christ our Lord.

# THE VARIETIES OF RELIGIOUS EXPERIENCE

WILLIAM JAMES

*1902*

To

E. P. G.

IN FILIAL GRATITUDE AND LOVE

# Contents

**LECTURE I**

Religion and Neurology 477

*Introduction: the course is not anthropological, but deals with personal documents—Questions of fact and questions of value—In point of fact, the religious are often neurotic—Criticism of medical materialism, which condemns religion on that account—Theory that religion has a sexual origin refuted—All states of mind are neurally conditioned—Their significance must be tested not by their origin but by the value of their fruits—Three criteria of value; origin useless as a criterion—Advantages of the psychopathic temperament when a superior intellect goes with it—especially for the religious life.*

**LECTURE II**

Circumscription of the Topic 492

*Futility of simple definitions of religion—No one specific "religious sentiment"—Institutional and personal religion—We confine ourselves to the personal branch—Definition of religion for the purpose of these lectures—Meaning of the term "divine"—The divine is what prompts* solemn *reactions—Impossible to make our definitions sharp—We must study the more extreme cases—Two ways of accepting the universe—Religion is more enthusiastic than philosophy—Its characteristic is enthusiasm in solemn emotion—Its ability to overcome unhappiness—Need of such a faculty from the biological point of view.*

**LECTURE III**

The Reality of the Unseen 508

*Percepts* versus *abstract concepts—Influence of the latter on belief—Kant's theological Ideas—We have a sense of reality other than that given by the special senses—Examples of "sense of presence"—The feeling of unreality—Sense of a divine presence: examples—Mystical experiences: examples—Other cases of sense of God's presence—Convincingness of unreasoned experience—Inferiority of rationalism in establishing belief—*

*Either enthusiasm or solemnity may preponderate in the religious attitude of individuals.*

**LECTURES IV AND V**

The Religion of Healthy-Mindedness 524
*Happiness is man's chief concern—"Once-born" and "twice-born" characters—Walt Whitman—Mixed nature of Greek feeling—Systematic healthy-mindedness—Its reasonableness—Liberal Christianity shows it—Optimism as encouraged by Popular Science—The "Mind-cure" movement—Its creed—Cases—Its doctrine of evil—Its analogy to Lutheran theology—Salvation by relaxation—Its methods: suggestion—meditation—"recollection"—verification—Diversity of possible schemes of adaptation to the universe—Appendix: Two mind-cure cases.*

**LECTURES VI AND VII**

The Sick Soul 555
*Healthy-mindedness and repentance—Essential pluralism of the healthy-minded philosophy—Morbid-mindedness: its two degrees—The pain-threshold varies in individuals—Insecurity of natural goods—Failure, or vain success of every life—Pessimism of all pure naturalism—Hopelessness of Greek and Roman view—Pathological unhappiness—"Anhedonia"—Querulous melancholy—Vital zest is a pure gift—Loss of it makes physical world look different—Tolstoy—Bunyan—Alline—Morbid fear—Such cases need a supernatural religion for relief—Antagonism of healthy-mindedness and morbidness—The problem of evil cannot be escaped.*

**LECTURE VIII**

The Divided Self, and the Process of Its Unification 579
*Heterogeneous personality—Character gradually attains unity—Examples of divided self—The unity attained need not be religious—"Counter conversion" cases—Other cases—Gradual and sudden unification—Tolstoy's recovery—Bunyan's.*

**LECTURE IX**

Conversion 594
*Case of Stephen Bradley—The psychology of character-changes—Emotional excitements make new centres of personal energy—Schematic ways of representing this—Starbuck likens conversion to normal moral ripening—Leuba's ideas—Seemingly unconvertible persons—Two types of conversion—Subconscious incubation of motives—Self-surrender—Its importance in religious history—Cases.*

**LECTURE X**

Conversion—*Concluded* 611
*Cases of sudden conversion—Is suddenness essential?—No, it depends on psychological idiosyncrasy—Proved existence of transmarginal, or subliminal, consciousness—"Automatisms"—Instantaneous conversions seem due to the possession of an active subconscious self by the subject—The value of conversion depends not on the process, but on the fruits—These are not superior in sudden conversion—Professor Coe's views—Sanctification as a result—Our psychological account does not exclude direct presence of the Deity—Sense of higher control—Relations of the emotional "faith-state" to intellectual beliefs—Leuba quoted—Characteristics of the faith state: sense of truth; the world appears new—Sensory and motor automatisms—Permanency of conversions.*

**LECTURES XI, XII, AND XIII**

Saintliness 637
*Sainte-Beuve on the State of Grace—Types of character as due to the balance of impulses and inhibitions—Sovereign excitements—Irascibility—Effects of higher excitement in general—The saintly life is ruled by spiritual excitement—This may annul sensual impulses permanently—Probable subconscious influences involved—Mechanical scheme for representing permanent alteration in character—Characteristics of saintliness—Sense of reality of a higher power—Peace of mind, charity—Equanimity, fortitude, etc.—Connection of this with relaxation—Purity of life—Asceticism—Obedience—Poverty—The sentiments of democracy and of humanity—General effects of higher excitements.*

**LECTURES XIV AND XV**

The Value of Saintliness 679
*It must be tested by the human value of its fruits—The reality of the God must, however, also be judged—"Unfit" religions get eliminated by "experience"—Empiricism is not skepticism—Individual and tribal religion—Loneliness of religious originators—Corruption follows success—Extravagances—Excessive devoutness, as fanaticism—As theopathic absorption—Excessive purity—Excessive charity—The perfect man is adapted only to the perfect environment—Saints are leavens—Excesses of asceticism—Asceticism symbolically stands for the heroic life—Militarism and voluntary poverty as possible equivalents—*Pros and cons *of the saintly character—Saints* versus *"strong" men—Their social function must be considered—Abstractly the saint is the highest type, but in the present environment it may fail, so we make ourselves saints at our peril—The question of theological truth.*

**LECTURES XVI AND XVII**

Mysticism 709

*Mysticism defined—Four marks of mystic states—They form a distinct region of consciousness—Examples of their lower grades—Mysticism and alcohol—"The anæsthetic revelation"—Religious mysticism—Aspects of Nature—Consciousness of God—"Cosmic consciousness"—Yoga—Buddhistic mysticism—Sufism—Christian mystics—Their sense of revelation—Tonic effects of mystic states—They describe by negatives—Sense of union with the Absolute—Mysticism and music—Three conclusions—(1) Mystical states carry authority for him who has them—(2) But for no one else—(3) Nevertheless, they break down the exclusive authority of rationalistic states—They strengthen monistic and optimistic hypotheses.*

**LECTURE XVIII**

Philosophy 741

*Primacy of feeling in religion, philosophy being a secondary function—Intellectualism professes to escape subjective standards in her theological constructions "Dogmatic theology"—Criticism of its account of God's attributes—"Pragmatism" as a test of the value of conceptions—God's metaphysical attributes have no practical significance—His moral attributes are proved by bad arguments; collapse of systematic theology—Does transcendental idealism fare better? Its principles—Quotations from John Caird—They are good as restatements of religious experience, but uncoercive as reasoned proof—What philosophy* can *do for religion by transforming herself into "science of religions."*

**LECTURE XIX**

Other Characteristics 758

*Æsthetic elements in religion—Contrast of Catholicism and Protestantism—Sacrifice and Confession—Prayer—Religion holds that spiritual work is really effected in prayer—Three degrees of opinion as to what is effected—First degree—Second degree—Third degree—Automatisms, their frequency among religious leaders—Jewish cases—Mohammed—Joseph Smith—Religion and the subconscious region in general.*

**LECTURE XX**

Conclusions 775

*Summary of religious characteristics—Men's religions need not be identical—"The science of religions" can only suggest, not proclaim, a religious creed—Is religion a "survival" of primitive thought?—Modern science rules out the concept of personality—Anthropomorphism and belief in the personal characterized pre-scientific thought—Personal forces are real, in spite of this—*

*Scientific objects are abstractions, only individualized experiences are concrete—Religion holds by the concrete—Primarily religion is a biological reaction—Its simplest terms are an uneasiness and a deliverance; description of the deliverance—Question of the reality of the higher power—The author's hypotheses: 1. The subconscious self as intermediating between nature and the higher region—2. The higher region, or "God"—3. He produces real effects in nature.*

Postscript 796

*Philosophic position of the present work defined as piecemeal supernaturalism—Criticism of universalistic supernaturalism—Different principles must occasion differences in fact—What differences in fact can God's existence occasion?—The question of immortality—Question of God's uniqueness and infinity: religious experience does not settle this question in the affirmative—The pluralistic hypothesis is more conformed to common sense.*

# Preface

This book would never have been written had I not been honored with an appointment as Gifford Lecturer on Natural Religion at the University of Edinburgh. In casting about me for subjects of the two courses of ten lectures each for which I thus became responsible, it seemed to me that the first course might well be a descriptive one on "Man's Religious Appetites," and the second a metaphyical one on "Their Satisfaction through Philosophy." But the unexpected growth of the psychological matter as I came to write it out has resulted in the second subject being postponed entirely, and the description of man's religious constitution now fills the twenty lectures. In Lecture XX I have suggested rather than stated my own philosophic conclusions, and the reader who desires immediately to know them should turn to pages 507–515, and to the "Postscript" of the book. I hope to be able at some later day to express them in more explicit form.

In my belief that a large acquaintance with particulars often makes us wiser than the possession of abstract formulas, however deep, I have loaded the lectures with concrete examples, and I have chosen these among the extremer expressions of the religious temperament. To some readers I may consequently seem, before they get beyond the middle of the book, to offer a caricature of the subject. Such convulsions of piety, they will say, are not sane. If, however, they will have the patience to read to the end, I believe that this unfavorable impression will disappear; for I there combine the religious impulses with other principles of common sense which serve as correctives of exaggeration, and allow the individual reader to draw as moderate conclusions as he will.

My thanks for help in writing these lectures are due to Edwin D. Starbuck, of Stanford University, who made over to me his large collection of manuscript material; to Henry W. Rankin, of East Northfield, a friend unseen but proved, to whom I owe precious information; to Theodore Flournoy, of Geneva, to Canning Schiller of Oxford, and to my colleague Benjamin Rand, for documents; to my colleague Dickinson S. Miller, and to my friends, Thomas Wren Ward, of New York, and Wincenty Lutoslawski, late of Cracow, for important suggestions and advice.

Finally, to conversations with the lamented Thomas Davidson and to the use of his books, at Glenmore, above Keene Valley, I owe more obligations than I can well express.

HARVARD UNIVERSITY,
March, 1902.

## LECTURE I

# Religion and Neurology

It is with no small amount of trepidation that I take my place behind this desk, and face this learned audience. To us Americans, the experience of receiving instruction from the living voice, as well as from the books, of European scholars, is very familiar. At my own University of Harvard, not a winter passes without its harvest, large or small, of lectures from Scottish, English, French, or German representatives of the science or literature of their respective countries whom we have either induced to cross the ocean to address us, or captured on the wing as they were visiting our land. It seems the natural thing for us to listen whilst the Europeans talk. The contrary habit, of talking whilst the Europeans listen, we have not yet acquired; and in him who first makes the adventure it begets a certain sense of apology being due for so presumptuous an act. Particularly must this be the case on a soil as sacred to the American imagination as that of Edinburgh. The glories of the philosophic chair of this university were deeply impressed on my imagination in boyhood. Professor Fraser's Essays in Philosophy, then just published, was the first philosophic book I ever looked into, and I well remember the awestruck feeling I received from the account of Sir William Hamilton's classroom therein contained. Hamilton's own lectures were the first philosophic writings I ever forced myself to study, and after that I was immersed in Dugald Stewart and Thomas Brown. Such juvenile emotions of reverence never get outgrown; and I confess that to find my humble self promoted from my native wilderness to be actually for the time an official here, and transmuted into a colleague of these illustrious names, carries with it a sense of dreamland quite as much as of reality.

But since I have received the honor of this appointment I have felt that it would never do to decline. The academic career also has its heroic obligations, so I stand here without further deprecatory words. Let me say only this, that now that the current, here and at Aberdeen, has begun to run from west to east, I hope it may continue to do so. As the years go by, I hope that many of my countrymen may be asked to lecture in the Scottish universities, changing places with Scotsmen lecturing in the United States; I hope that our people may become in all these higher matters even as one people; and that the peculiar philosophic temperament, as well as the peculiar political temperament, that goes with our English speech may more and more pervade and influence the world.

As regards the manner in which I shall have to administer this lectureship, I am neither a theologian, nor a scholar learned in the history of religions, nor an anthropologist. Psychology is the only branch of learning in which I am particularly versed. To the psychologist the religious propensities of man must be at least as interesting as any other of the facts pertaining to his mental constitution. It would seem, therefore, that, as a psychologist, the natural thing for me would be to invite you to a descriptive survey of those religious propensities.

If the inquiry be psychological, not religious institutions, but rather religious feelings and religious impulses must be its subject, and I must confine myself to those more developed subjective phenomena recorded in literature produced by articulate and fully self-conscious men, in works of piety and autobiography. Interesting as the origins and early stages of a subject always are, yet when one seeks earnestly for its full significance, one must always look to its more completely evolved and perfect forms. It follows from this that the documents that will most concern us will be those of the men who were most accomplished in the religious life and best able to give an intelligible account of their ideas and motives. These men, of course, are either comparatively modern writers, or else such earlier ones as have become religious classics. The *documents humains* which we shall find most instructive need not then be sought for in the haunts of special erudition—they lie along the beaten highway; and this circumstance, which flows so naturally from the character of our problem, suits admirably also your lecturer's lack of special theological learning. I may take my citations, my sentences and paragraphs of personal confession, from books that most of you at some time will have had already in your hands, and yet this will be no detriment to the value of my conclusions. It is true that some more adventurous reader and investigator, lecturing here in future, may unearth from the shelves of libraries documents that will make a more delectable and curious entertainment to listen to than mine. Yet I doubt whether he will necessarily, by his control of so much more out-of-the-way material, get much closer to the essence of the matter in hand.

The question, What are the religious propensities? and the question, What is their philosophic significance? are two entirely different orders of question from the logical point of view; and, as a failure to recognize this fact distinctly may breed confusion, I wish to insist upon the point a little before we enter into the documents and materials to which I have referred.

In recent books on logic, distinction is made between two orders of inquiry concerning anything. First, what is the nature of it? how did it come about? what is its constitution, origin, and history? And second, What is its importance, meaning, or significance, now that it is once here? The answer to the one question is given in an *existential judgment* or proposition. The answer to the other is a *proposition of value*, what the Germans call a *Werthurtheil*, or what we may, if we like, denominate a *spiritual judgment*. Neither judgment can be deduced immediately from the other. They proceed from diverse intellectual preoccupations, and the mind combines them only by making them first separately, and then adding them together.

In the matter of religions it is particularly easy to distinguish the two orders of question. Every religious phenomenon has its history and its derivation from natural antecedents. What is nowadays called the higher criticism of the Bible is only a study of the Bible from this existential point of view, neglected too much by the earlier church. Under just what biographic conditions did the sacred writers bring forth their various contributions to the holy volume? And what had they exactly in their several individual minds, when they delivered their utterances? These are manifestly questions of historical fact, and one does not see how the answer to them can decide offhand the still further question: of what use should such a volume, with its manner of coming into existence so defined, be to us as a guide to life and a revelation? To answer this other question we must have already in our mind some sort of a general theory as to what the peculiarities in a thing should be which give it value for purposes of revelation; and this theory itself would be what I just called a spiritual judgment. Combining it with our existential judgment, we might indeed deduce another spiritual judgment as to the Bible's worth. Thus if our theory of revelation-value were to affirm that any book, to possess it, must have been composed automatically or not by the free caprice of the writer, or that it must exhibit no scientific and historic errors and express no local or personal passions, the Bible would probably fare ill at our hands. But if, on the other hand, our theory should allow that a book may well be a revelation in spite of errors and passions and deliberate human composition, if only it be a true record of the inner experiences of great-souled persons wrestling with the crises of their fate, then the verdict would be much more favorable. You see that the existential facts by themselves are insufficient for determining the value; and the best adepts of the higher criticism accordingly never confound the existential with the spiritual problem. With the same conclusions of fact before them, some take one view, and some another, of the Bible's value as a revelation, according as their spiritual judgment as to the foundation of values differs.

I make these general remarks about the two sorts of judgment, because there are many religious persons—some of you now present, possibly, are among them—who do not yet make a working use of the distinction, and who may therefore feel first a little startled at the purely existential point of view from which in the following lectures the phenomena of religious experience must be considered. When I handle them biologically and psychologically as if they were mere curious facts of individual history, some of you may think it a degradation of so sublime a subject, and may even suspect me, until my purpose gets more fully expressed, of deliberately seeking to discredit the religious side of life.

Such a result is of course absolutely alien to my intention; and since such a prejudice on your part would seriously obstruct the due effect of much of what I have to relate, I will devote a few more words to the point.

There can be no doubt that as a matter of fact a religious life, exclusively pursued, does tend to make the person exceptional and eccentric. I speak not now of your ordinary religious believer, who follows the conventional observances of his country, whether it be Buddhist, Christian, or Mohammedan. His religion has been made for him by others, communicated to him by tradition, determined to fixed forms by imitation, and retained by habit. It would profit us little to study this second-hand religious life. We must make search rather for the original experiences which were the pattern-setters to all this mass of suggested feeling and imitated conduct. These experiences we can only find in individuals for whom religion exists not as a dull habit, but as an acute fever rather. But such individuals are "geniuses" in the religious line; and like many other geniuses who have brought forth fruits effective enough for commemoration in the pages of biography, such religious geniuses have often shown symptoms of nervous instability. Even more perhaps than other kinds of genius, religious leaders have been subject to abnormal psychical visitations. Invariably they have been creatures of exalted emotional sensibility. Often they have led a discordant inner life, and had melancholy during a part of their career. They have known no measure, been liable to obsessions and fixed ideas; and frequently they have fallen into trances, heard voices, seen visions, and presented all sorts of peculiarities which are ordinarily classed as pathological. Often, moreover, these pathological features in their career have helped to give them their religious authority and influence.

If you ask for a concrete example, there can be no better one than is furnished by the person of George Fox. The Quaker religion which he founded is something which it is impossible to overpraise. In a day of shams, it was a religion of veracity rooted in spiritual inwardness, and a return to something more like the original gospel truth than men had ever known in England. So far as our Christian sects today are evolving into liberality, they are simply reverting in essence to the position which Fox and the early Quakers so long ago assumed. No one can pretend for a moment that in point of spiritual sagacity and capacity, Fox's mind was unsound. Everyone who confronted him personally, from Oliver Cromwell down to county magistrates and jailers, seems to have acknowledged his superior power. Yet from the point of view of his nervous constitution, Fox was a psychopath or *détraqué* of the deepest dye. His Journal abounds in entries of this sort:—

> "As I was walking with several friends, I lifted up my head, and saw three steeple-house spires, and they struck at my life. I asked them what place that was? They said, Lichfield. Immediately the word of the Lord came to me, that I must go thither. Being come to the house we were going to, I wished the friends to walk into the house, saying nothing to them of whither I was to go. As soon as they were gone I stept away, and went by my eye over hedge and ditch till I came within a mile of Lichfield; where, in a great field, shepherds were keeping their sheep. Then was I commanded by the Lord to pull off my shoes. I stood still, for

it was winter: but the word of the Lord was like a fire in me. So I put off my shoes and left them with the shepherds; and the poor shepherds trembled, and were astonished. Then I walked on about a mile, and as soon as I was got within the city, the word of the Lord came to me again, saying: Cry, 'Wo to the bloody city of Lichfield!' So I went up and down the streets, crying with a loud voice, Wo to the bloody city of Lichfield! It being market day, I went into the market-place, and to and fro in the several parts of it, and made stands, crying as before, Wo to the bloody city of Lichfield! And no one laid hands on me. As I went thus crying through the streets, there seemed to me to be a channel of blood running down the streets, and the market-place appeared like a pool of blood. When I had declared what was upon me, and felt myself clear, I went out of the town in peace; and returning to the shepherds gave them some money, and took my shoes of them again. But the fire of the Lord was so on my feet, and all over me, that I did not matter to put on my shoes again, and was at a stand whether I should or no, till I felt freedom from the Lord so to do: then, after I had washed my feet, I put on my shoes again. After this a deep consideration came upon me, for what reason I should be sent to cry against that city, and call it The bloody city! For though the parliament had the minister one while, and the king another, and much blood had been shed in the town during the wars between them, yet there was no more than had befallen many other places. But afterwards I came to understand, that in the Emperor Diocletian's time a thousand Christians were martyr'd in Lichfield. So I was to go, without my shoes, through the channel of their blood, and into the pool of their blood in the market-place, that I might raise up the memorial of the blood of those martyrs, which had been shed above a thousand years before, and lay cold in their streets. So the sense of this blood was upon me, and I obeyed the word of the Lord."

Bent as we are on studying religion's existential conditions, we cannot possibly ignore these pathological aspects of the subject. We must describe and name them just as if they occurred in non-religious men. It is true that we instinctively recoil from seeing an object to which our emotions and affections are committed handled by the intellect as any other object is handled. The first thing the intellect does with an object is to class it along with something else. But any object that is infinitely important to us and awakens our devotion feels to us also as if it must be *sui generis* and unique. Probably a crab would be filled with a sense of personal outrage if it could hear us class it without ado or apology as a crustacean, and thus dispose of it. "I am no such thing," it would say; I am MYSELF, MYSELF alone."

The next thing the intellect does is to lay bare the causes in which the thing originates. Spinoza says: "I will analyze the actions and appetites of men as if it were a question of lines, of planes, and of solids." And elsewhere he remarks that he will consider our passions and their properties with the same eye with which he looks on all other natural things, since the consequences of our affections flow from their nature with the same necessity as it results from the nature of a triangle that its three angles should be equal to two right angles. Similarly M. Taine, in the introduction to his history of English literature, has written: "Whether facts be moral or physical, it makes no matter. They always have their causes. There are causes for ambition, courage, veracity, just as there are for digestion, muscular movement, animal heat. Vice and virtue are products like vitriol and sugar." When we read such proclamations of the intellect bent on showing the existential conditions of absolutely everything, we feel—quite apart from our legitimate impatience at the somewhat ridiculous swagger of the program, in view of what the authors are actually able to perform—menaced and negated in the springs of our innermost life. Such cold-blooded assimilations threaten, we think, to undo our soul's vital secrets, as if the same breath which should succeed in explaining their origin would simultaneously explain away their significance, and make them appear of no more preciousness, either, than the useful groceries of which M. Taine speaks.

Perhaps the commonest expression of this assumption that spiritual value is undone if lowly origin be asserted is seen in those comments which unsentimental people so often pass on their more sentimental acquaintances. Alfred believes in immortality so strongly because his temperament is so emotional. Fanny's extraordinary conscientiousness is merely a matter of overinstigated nerves. William's melancholy about the universe is due to bad digestion—probably his liver is torpid. Eliza's delight in her church is a symptom of her hysterical constitution. Peter would be less troubled about his soul if he would take more exercise in the open air, etc. A more fully developed example of the same kind of reasoning is the fashion, quite common nowadays among certain writers, of criticizing the religious emotions by showing a connection between them and the sexual life. Conversion is a crisis of puberty and adolescence. The macerations of saints, and the devotion of missionaries, are only instances of the parental instinct of self-sacrifice gone astray. For the hysterical nun, starving for natural life, Christ is but an imaginary substitute for a more earthly object of affection. And the like.[1]

1 As with many ideas that float in the air of one's time, this notion shrinks from dogmatic general statement and expresses itself only partially and by innuendo. It seems to me that few conceptions are less instructive than this re-interpretation of religion as perverted sexuality. It reminds one, so crudely is it often employed, of the famous Catholic taunt, that the Reformation may be best understood by remembering that its *fons et origo* was Luther's wish to marry a nun:—the effects are infinitely wider than the alleged causes, and for the most part opposite in nature. It is true that in the vast collection of religious phenomena, some are undisguisedly amatory—e. g., sex-deities and obscene rites in polytheism, and ecstatic feelings of union with the Savior in a few Christian mystics. But then why not equally call religion an aberration of the digestive function, and prove one's point by the worship of Bacchus and Ceres, or by the ecstatic feelings of some other saints about the Eucharist? Religious language clothes itself in such poor symbols as our life affords, and the whole organism gives overtones of comment whenever the mind is strongly stirred to expression. Language drawn from eating and drinking is probably as common in religious literature as is language drawn from the sexual life. We "hunger and thirst" after righteousness; we "find the Lord a sweet savor;" we "taste and see that he is good." "Spiritual milk for American babes, drawn from the breasts of both testaments," is a sub-title of the once famous New England Primer, and Christian devotional literature indeed quite floats in milk, thought of from the point of view, not of the mother, but of the greedy babe.

Saint Francois de Sales, for instance, thus describes the "orison of quietude": "In this state the soul

We are surely all familiar in a general way with this method of discrediting states of mind for which we have an antipathy. We all use it to some degree in criticizing persons whose states of mind we regard as overstrained. But when other people criticize our own more exalted soul-flights by calling them "nothing but" expressions of our organic disposition, we feel outraged and hurt, for we know that, whatever be our organism's peculiarities, our mental states have their substantive value as revelations of the living truth; and we wish that all this medical materialism could be made to hold its tongue.

Medical materialism seems indeed a good appellation for the too simple-minded system of thought which we are considering. Medical materialism finishes up Saint Paul by calling his vision on the road to Damascus a discharging lesion of the oc-

---

is like a little child still at the breast, whose mother, to caress him whilst he is still in her arms, makes her milk distill into his mouth without his even moving his lips. So it is here. . . . Our Lord desires that our will should be satisfied with sucking the milk which His Majesty pours into our mouth, and that we should relish the sweetness without even knowing that it cometh from the Lord." And again: "Consider the little infants, united and joined to the breasts of their nursing mothers, you will see that from time to time they press themselves closer by little starts to which the pleasure of sucking prompts them. Even so, during its orison, the heart united to its God oftentimes makes attempts at closer union by movements during which it presses closer upon the divine sweetness." Chemin de la Perfection, ch. xxxi.; Amour de Dieu, vii. ch. i.

In fact, one might almost as well interpret religion as a perversion of the respiratory function. The Bible is full of the language of respiratory oppression: "Hide not thine ear at my breathing; my groaning is not hid from thee; my heart panteth, my strength faileth me; my bones are hot with my roaring all the night long; as the hart panteth after the water-brooks, so my soul panteth after thee, O my God." *God's Breath in Man* is the title of the chief work of our best known American mystic (Thomas Lake Harris); and in certain non-Christian countries the foundation of all religious discipline consists in regulation of the inspiration and expiration.

These arguments are as good as much of the reasoning one hears in favor of the sexual theory. But the champions of the latter will then say that their chief argument has no analogue elsewhere. The two main phenomena of religion, namely, melancholy and conversion, they will say, are essentially phenomena of adolescence, and therefore synchronous with the development of sexual life. To which the retort again is easy. Even were the asserted synchrony unrestrictedly true as a fact (which it is not), it is not only the sexual life, but the entire higher mental life which awakens during adolescence. One might then as well set up the thesis that the interest in mechanics, physics, chemistry, logic, philosophy, and sociology, which springs up during adolescent years along with that in poetry and religion, is also a perversion of the sexual instinct:—but that would be too absurd. Moreover, if the argument from synchrony is to decide, what is to be done with the fact that the religious age *par excellence* would seem to be old age, when the uproar of the sexual life is past?

The plain truth is that to interpret religion one must in the end look at the immediate content of the religious consciousness. The moment one does this, one sees how wholly disconnected it is in the main from the content of the sexual consciousness. Everything about the two things differs, objects, moods, faculties concerned, and acts impelled to. Any *general* assimilation is simply impossible: what we find most often is complete hostility and contrast. If now the defenders of the sex-theory say that this makes no difference to their thesis; that without the chemical contributions which the sex-organs make to the blood, the brain would not be nourished so as to carry on religious activities, this final proposition may be true or not true; but at any rate it has become profoundly uninstructive: we can deduce no consequences from it which help us to interpret religion's meaning or value. In this sense the religious life depends just as much upon the spleen, the pancreas, and the kidneys as on the sexual apparatus, and the whole theory has lost its point in evaporating into a vague general assertion of the dependence, *somehow*, of the mind upon the body.

cipital cortex, he being an epileptic. It snuffs out Saint Teresa as an hysteric, Saint Francis of Assisi as an hereditary degenerate. George Fox's discontent with the shams of his age, and his pining for spiritual veracity, it treats as a symptom of a disordered colon. Carlyle's organtones of misery it accounts for by a gastro-duodenal catarrh. All such mental overtensions, it says, are, when you come to the bottom of the matter, mere affairs of diathesis (auto-intoxications most probably), due to the perverted action of various glands which physiology will yet discover.

And medical materialism then thinks that the spiritual authority of all such personages is successfully undermined.[2]

Let us ourselves look at the matter in the largest possible way. Modern psychology, finding definite psycho-physical connections to hold good, assumes as a convenient hypothesis that the dependence of mental states upon bodily conditions must be thoroughgoing and complete. If we adopt the assumption, then of course what medical materialism insists on must be true in a general way, if not in every detail: Saint Paul certainly had once an epileptoid, if not an epileptic seizure; George Fox was an hereditary degenerate; Carlyle was undoubtedly auto-intoxicated by some organ or other, no matter which—and the rest. But now, I ask you, how can such an existential account of facts of mental history decide in one way or another upon their spiritual significance? According to the general postulate of psychology just referred to, there is not a single one of our states of mind, high or low, healthy or morbid, that has not some organic process as its condition. Scientific theories are organically conditioned just as much as religious emotions are; and if we only knew the facts intimately enough, we should doubtless see "the liver" determining the dicta of the sturdy atheist as decisively as it does those of the Methodist under conviction anxious about his soul. When it alters in one way the blood that percolates it, we get the methodist, when in another way, we get the atheist form of mind. So of all our raptures and our drynesses, our longings and pantings, our questions and beliefs. They are equally organically founded, be they religious or of non-religious content.

To plead the organic causation of a religious state of mind, then, in refutation of its claim to possess superior spiritual value, is quite illogical and arbitrary, unless one has already worked out in advance some psycho-physical theory connecting spiritual values in general with determinate sorts of physiological change. Otherwise none of our thoughts and feelings, not even our scientific doctrines, not even our *dis*-beliefs, could retain any value as revelations of the truth, for every one of them without exception flows from the state of its possessor's body at the time.

It is needless to say that medical materialism draws in point of fact no such sweeping skeptical conclusion. It is sure, just as every simple man is sure, that some states of mind are inwardly superior to others, and reveal to us more truth, and in this it simply makes use of an ordinary spiritual judgment. It has no physiological

2 For a first-rate example of medical-materialist reasoning, see an article on "les Variétés du Type dévot," by Dr. Binet-Sanglé, in the Revue de l'Hypnotisme, xiv. 161.

theory of the production of these its favorite states, by which it may accredit them; and its attempt to discredit the states which it dislikes, by vaguely associating them with nerves and liver, and connecting them with names connoting bodily affliction, is altogether illogical and inconsistent.

Let us play fair in this whole matter, and be quite candid with ourselves and with the facts. When we think certain states of mind superior to others, is it ever because of what we know concerning their organic antecedents? No! it is always for two entirely different reasons. It is either because we take an immediate delight in them; or else it is because we believe them to bring us good consequential fruits for life. When we speak disparagingly of "feverish fancies," surely the fever-process as such is not the ground of our disesteem—for aught we know to the contrary, 103° or 104° Fahrenheit might be a much more favorable temperature for truths to germinate and sprout in, than the more ordinary blood-heat of 97 or 98 degrees. It is either the disagreeableness itself of the fancies, or their inability to bear the criticisms of the convalescent hour. When we praise the thoughts which health brings, health's peculiar chemical metabolisms have nothing to do with determining our judgment. We know in fact almost nothing about these metabolisms. It is the character of inner happiness in the thoughts which stamps them as good, or else their consistency with our other opinions and their serviceability for our needs, which make them pass for true in our esteem.

Now the more intrinsic and the more remote of these criteria do not always hang together. Inner happiness and serviceability do not always agree. What immediately feels most "good" is not always most "true," when measured by the verdict of the rest of experience. The difference between Philip drunk and Philip sober is the classic instance in corroboration. If merely "feeling good" could decide, drunkenness would be the supremely valid human experience. But its revelations, however acutely satisfying at the moment, are inserted into an environment which refuses to bear them out for any length of time. The consequence of this discrepancy of the two criteria is the uncertainty which still prevails over so many of our spiritual judgments. There are moments of sentimental and mystical experience—we shall hereafter hear much of them—that carry an enormous sense of inner authority and illumination with them when they come. But they come seldom, and they do not come to everyone; and the rest of life makes either no connection with them, or tends to contradict them more than it confirms them. Some persons follow more the voice of the moment in these cases, some prefer to be guided by the average results. Hence the sad discordancy of so many of the spiritual judgments of human beings; a discordancy which will be brought home to us acutely enough before these lectures end.

It is, however, a discordancy that can never be resolved by any merely medical test. A good example of the impossibility of holding strictly to the medical tests is seen in the theory of the pathological causation of genius promulgated by recent authors. "Genius," said Dr. Moreau, "is but one of the many branches of the neuropathic tree." "Genius," says Dr. Lombroso, "is a symptom of hereditary degeneration of the epileptoid variety, and is allied to moral insanity." "Whenever a man's life," writes Mr. Nisbet, "is at once sufficiently illustrious and recorded with sufficient fullness to be a subject of profitable study, he inevitably falls into the morbid category. . . . And it is worthy of remark that, as a rule, the greater the genius, the greater the unsoundness."[3]

Now do these authors, after having succeeded in establishing to their own satisfaction that the works of genius are fruits of disease, consistently proceed thereupon to impugn the *value* of the fruits? Do they deduce a new spiritual judgment from their new doctrine of existential conditions? Do they frankly forbid us to admire the productions of genius from now onwards? and say outright that no neuropath can ever be a revealer of new truth?

No! their immediate spiritual instincts are too strong for them here, and hold their own against inferences which, in mere love of logical consistency, medical materialism ought to be only too glad to draw. One disciple of the school, indeed, has striven to impugn the value of works of genius in a wholesale way (such works of contemporary art, namely, as he himself is unable to enjoy, and they are many) by using medical arguments.[4] But for the most part the masterpieces are left unchallenged; and the medical line of attack either confines itself to such secular productions as everyone admits to be intrinsically eccentric, or else addresses itself exclusively to religious manifestations. And then it is because the religious manifestations have been already condemned because the critic dislikes them on internal or spiritual grounds.

In the natural sciences and industrial arts it never occurs to anyone to try to refute opinions by showing up their author's neurotic constitution. Opinions here are invariably tested by logic and by experiment, no matter what may be their author's neurological type. It should be no otherwise with religious opinions. Their value can only be ascertained by spiritual judgments directly passed upon them, judgments based on our own immediate feeling primarily; and secondarily on what we can ascertain of their experiential relations to our moral needs and to the rest of what we hold as true.

*Immediate luminousness, in short, philosophical reasonableness*, and *moral helpfulness* are the only available criteria. Saint Teresa might have had the nervous system of the placidest cow, and it would not now save her theology, if the trial of the theology by these other tests should show it to be contemptible. And conversely if her theology can stand these other tests, it will make no difference how hysterical or nervously off her balance Saint Teresa may have been when she was with us here below.

You see that at bottom we are thrown back upon the general principles by which the empirical philosophy has always contended that we must be guided in our search

3 J. F. Nisbet: The Insanity of Genius, 3d ed., London, 1893, pp. xvi., xxiv.

4 Max Nordau, in his bulky book entitled *Degeneration*.

for truth. Dogmatic philosophies have sought for tests for truth which might dispense us from appealing to the future. Some direct mark, by noting which we can be protected immediately and absolutely, now and forever, against all mistake—such has been the darling dream of philosophic dogmatists. It is clear that the origin of the truth would be an admirable criterion of this sort, if only the various origins could be discriminated from one another from this point of view, and the history of dogmatic opinion shows that origin has always been a favorite test. Origin in immediate intuition; origin in pontifical authority; origin in supernatural revelation, as by vision, hearing, or unaccountable impression; origin in direct possession by a higher spirit, expressing itself in prophecy and warning; origin in automatic utterance generally—these origins have been stock warrants for the truth of one opinion after another which we find represented in religious history. The medical materialists are therefore only so many belated dogmatists, neatly turning the tables on their predecessors by using the criterion of origin in a destructive instead of an accreditive way.

They are effective with their talk of pathological origin only so long as supernatural origin is pleaded by the other side, and nothing but the argument from origin is under discussion. But the argument from origin has seldom been used alone, for it is too obviously insufficient. Dr. Maudsley is perhaps the cleverest of the rebutters of supernatural religion on grounds of origin. Yet he finds himself forced to write:—

"What right have we to believe Nature under any obligation to do her work by means of complete minds only? She may find an incomplete mind a more suitable instrument for a particular purpose. It is the work that is done, and the quality in the worker by which it was done, that is alone of moment; and it may be no great matter from a cosmical standpoint, if in other qualities of character he was singularly defective—if indeed he were hypocrite, adulterer, eccentric, or lunatic. . . . Home we come again, then, to the old and last resort of certitude—namely the common assent of mankind, or of the competent by instruction and training among mankind."[5]

In other words, not its origin, but *the way in which it works on the whole*, is Dr. Maudsley's final test of a belief. This is our own empiricist criterion; and this criterion the stoutest insisters on supernatural origin have also been forced to use in the end. Among the visions and messages some have always been too patently silly, among the trances and convulsive seizures some have been too fruitless for conduct and character, to pass themselves off as significant, still less as divine. In the history of Christian mysticism the problem how to discriminate between such messages and experiences as were really divine miracles, and such others as the demon in his malice was able to counterfeit, thus making the religious person twofold more the child of hell he was before, has always been a difficult one to solve, needing all the

5 H. Maudsley: Natural Causes and Supernatural Seemings, 1886, pp. 257, 256.

sagacity and experience of the best directors of conscience. In the end it had to come to our empiricist criterion: By their fruits ye shall know them, not by their roots. Jonathan Edwards's Treatise on Religious Affections is an elaborate working out of this thesis. The *roots* of a man's virtue are inaccessible to us. No appearances whatever are infallible proofs of grace. Our practice is the only sure evidence, even to ourselves, that we are genuinely Christians.

> "In forming a judgment of ourselves now," Edwards writes, "we should certainly adopt that evidence which our supreme Judge will chiefly make use of when we come to stand before him at the last day. . . . There is not one grace of the Spirit of God, of the existence of which, in any professor of religion, Christian practice is not the most decisive evidence. . . . The degree in which our experience is productive of practice shows the degree in which our experience is spiritual and divine."

Catholic writers are equally emphatic. The good dispositions which a vision, or voice, or other apparent heavenly favor leave behind them are the only marks by which we may be sure they are not possible deceptions of the tempter. Says Saint Teresa:—

> "Like imperfect sleep which, instead of giving more strength to the head, doth but leave it the more exhausted, the result of mere operations of the imagination is but to weaken the soul. Instead of nourishment and energy she reaps only lassitude and disgust: whereas a genuine heavenly vision yields to her a harvest of ineffable spiritual riches, and an admirable renewal of bodily strength. I alleged these reasons to those who so often accused my visions of being the work of the enemy of mankind and the sport of my imagination. . . . I showed them the jewels which the divine hand had left with me:—they were my actual dispositions. All those who knew me saw that I was changed; my confessor bore witness to the fact; this improvement, palpable in all respects, far from being hidden, was brilliantly evident to all men. As for myself, it was impossible to believe that if the demon were its author, he could have used, in order to lose me and lead me to hell, an expedient so contrary to his own interests as that of uprooting my vices, and filling me with masculine courage and other virtues instead, for I saw clearly that a single one of these visions was enough to enrich me with all that wealth."[6]

I fear I may have made a longer excursus than was necessary, and that fewer words would have dispelled the uneasiness which may have arisen among some of you as I announced my pathological programme. At any rate you must all be ready now to judge the religious life by its results exclusively, and I shall assume that the bugaboo of morbid origin will scandalize your piety no more.

---

6 Autobiography, ch. xxviii.

Still, you may ask me, if its results are to be the ground of our final spiritual estimate of a religious phenomenon, why threaten us at all with so much existential study of its conditions? Why not simply leave pathological questions out?

To this I reply in two ways: First, I say, irrepressible curiosity imperiously leads one on; and I say, secondly, that it always leads to a better understanding of a thing's significance to consider its exaggerations and perversions, its equivalents and substitutes and nearest relatives elsewhere. Not that we may thereby swamp the thing in the wholesale condemnation which we pass on its inferior congeners, but rather that we may by contrast ascertain the more precisely in what its merits consist, by learning at the same time to what particular dangers of corruption it may also be exposed.

Insane conditions have this advantage, that they isolate special factors of the mental life, and enable us to inspect them unmasked by their more usual surroundings. They play the part in mental anatomy which the scalpel and the microscope play in the anatomy of the body. To understand a thing rightly we need to see it both out of its environment and in it, and to have acquaintance with the whole range of its variations. The study of hallucinations has in this way been for psychologists the key to their comprehension of normal sensation, that of illusions has been the key to the right comprehension of perception. Morbid impulses and imperative conceptions, "fixed ideas," so called, have thrown a flood of light on the psychology of the normal will; and obsessions and delusions have performed the same service for that of the normal faculty of belief.

Similarly, the nature of genius has been illuminated by the attempts, of which I already made mention, to class it with psychopathical phenomena. Borderland insanity, crankiness, insane temperament, loss of mental balance, psycopathic degeneration (to use a few of the many synonyms by which it has been called), has certain peculiarities and liabilities which, when combined with a superior quality of intellect in an individual, make it more probable that he will make his mark and affect his age, than if his temperament were less neurotic. There is of course no special affinity between crankiness as such and superior intellect,[7] for most psychopaths have feeble intellects, and superior intellects more commonly have normal nervous systems. But the pyschopathic temperament, whatever be the intellect with which it finds itself paired, often brings with it ardor and excitability of character. The cranky person has extraordinary emotional susceptibility. He is liable to fixed ideas and obsessions. His conceptions tend to pass immediately into belief and action; and when he gets a new idea, he has no rest till he proclaims it, or in some way "works it off." "What shall I think of it?" a common person says to himself about a vexed question; but in a "cranky" mind "What must I do about it?" is the form the question tends to take. In the autobiography of that high-souled woman, Mrs. Annie Besant, I read the following passage: "Plenty of people wish well to any good cause, but very

7 Superior intellect, as Professor Bain has admirably shown, seems to consist in nothing so much as in a large development of the faculty of association by similarity.

few care to exert themselves to help it, and still fewer will risk anything in its support. 'Someone ought to do it, but why should I?' is the ever reëchoed phrase of weak-kneed amiability. 'Someone ought to do it, so why not I?' is the cry of some earnest servant of man, eagerly forward springing to face some perilous duty. Between these two sentences lie whole centuries of moral evolution." True enough! and between these two sentences lie also the different destinies of the ordinary sluggard and the psychopathic man. Thus, when a superior intellect and a psychopathic temperament coalesce—as in the endless permutations and combinations of human faculty, they are bound to coalesce often enough—in the same individual, we have the best possible condition for the kind of effective genius that gets into the biographical dictionaries. Such men do not remain mere critics and understanders with their intellect. Their ideas possess them, they inflict them, for better or worse, upon their companions or their age. It is they who get counted when Messrs. Lombroso, Nisbet, and others invoke statistics to defend their paradox.

To pass now to religious phenomena, take the melancholy which, as we shall see, constitutes an essential moment in every complete religious evolution. Take the happiness which achieved religious belief confers. Take the trancelike states of insight into truth which all religious mystics report.[8] These are each and all of them special cases of kinds of human experience of much wider scope. Religious melancholy, whatever peculiarities it may have *qua* religious, is at any rate melancholy. Religious happiness is happiness. Religious trance is trance. And the moment we renounce the absurd notion that a thing is exploded away as soon as it is classed with others, or its origin is shown; the moment we agree to stand by experimental results and inner quality, in judging of values—who does not see that we are likely to ascertain the distinctive significance of religious melancholy and happiness, or of religious trances, far better by comparing them as conscientiously as we can with other varieties of melancholy, happiness, and trance, than by refusing to consider their place in any more general series, and treating them as if they were outside of nature's order altogether?

I hope that the course of these lectures will confirm us in this supposition. As regards the psychopathic origin of so many religious phenomena, that would not be in the least surprising or disconcerting, even were such phenomena certified from on high to be the most precious of human experiences. No one organism can possibly yield to its owner the whole body of truth. Few of us are not in some way infirm, or even diseased; and our very infirmities help us unexpectedly. In the psychopathic temperament we have the emotionality which is the *sine qua non* of moral perception; we have the intensity and tendency to emphasis which are the essence of practical moral vigor; and we have the love of metaphysics and mysticism which carry one's interests beyond the surface of the sensible world. What, then, is more natural than that this temperament should introduce one to regions of religious truth, to

8 I may refer to a criticism of the insanity theory of genius in the Psychological Review, ii. 287 (1895).

corners of the universe, which your robust Philistine type of nervous system, forever offering its biceps to be felt, thumping its breast, and thanking Heaven that it hasn't a single morbid fiber in its composition, would be sure to hide forever from its self-satisfied possessors?

If there were such a thing as inspiration from a higher realm, it might well be that the neurotic temperament would furnish the chief condition of the requisite receptivity. And having said thus much, I think that I may let the matter of religion and neuroticism drop.

The mass of collateral phenomena, morbid or healthy, with which the various religious phenomena must be compared in order to understand them better, forms what in the slang of pedagogics is termed "the apperceiving mass" by which we comprehend them. The only novelty that I can imagine this course of lectures to possess lies in the breadth of the apperceiving mass. I may succeed in discussing religious experiences in a wider context than has been usual in university courses.

LECTURE II

# Circumscription of the Topic

Most books on the philosophy of religion try to begin with a precise definition of what its essence consists of. Some of these would-be definitions may possibly come before us in later portions of this course, and I shall not be pedantic enough to enumerate any of them to you now. Meanwhile the very fact that they are so many and so different from one another is enough to prove that the word "religion" cannot stand for any single principle or essence, but is rather a collective name. The theorizing mind tends always to the oversimplification of its materials. This is the root of all that absolutism and one-sided dogmatism by which both philosophy and religion have been infested. Let us not fall immediately into a one-sided view of our subject, but let us rather admit freely at the outset that we may very likely find no one essence, but many characters which may alternately be equally important to religion. If we should inquire for the essence of "government," for example, one man might tell us it was authority, another submission, another police, another an army, another an assembly, another a system of laws; yet all the while it would be true that no concrete government can exist without all these things, one of which is more important at one moment and others at another. The man who knows governments most completely is he who troubles himself least about a definition which shall give their essence. Enjoying an intimate acquaintance with all their particularities in turn, he would naturally regard an abstract conception in which these were unified as a thing more misleading than enlightening. And why may not religion be a conception equally complex?[9]

Consider also the "religious sentiment" which we see referred to in so many books, as if it were a single sort of mental entity.

In the psychologies and in the philosophies of religion, we find the authors at-

9 I can do no better here than refer my readers to the extended and admirable remarks on the futility of all these definitions of religion, in an article by Professor Leuba, published in the Monist for January, 1901, after my own text was written.

tempting to specify just what entity it is. One man allies it to the feeling of dependence; one makes it a derivative from fear; others connect it with the sexual life; others still identify it with the feeling of the infinite; and so on. Such different ways of conceiving it ought of themselves to arouse doubt as to whether it possibly can be one specific thing; and the moment we are willing to treat the term "religious sentiment" as a collective name for the many sentiments which religious objects may arouse in alternation, we see that it probably contains nothing whatever of a psychologically specific nature. There is religious fear, religious love, religious awe, religious joy, and so forth. But religious love is only man's natural emotion of love directed to a religious object; religious fear is only the ordinary fear of commerce, so to speak, the common quaking of the human breast, in so far as the notion of divine retribution may arouse it; religious awe is the same organic thrill which we feel in a forest at twilight, or in a mountain gorge; only this time it comes over us at the thought of our supernatural relations; and similarly of all the various sentiments which may be called into play in the lives of religious persons. As concrete states of mind, made up of a feeling *plus* a specific sort of object, religious emotions of course are psychic entities distinguishable from other concrete emotions; but there is no ground for assuming a simple abstract "religious emotion" to exist as a distinct elementary mental affection by itself, present in every religious experience without exception.

As there thus seems to be no one elementary religious emotion, but only a common storehouse of emotions upon which religious objects may draw, so there might conceivably also prove to be no one specific and essential kind of religious object, and no one specific and essential kind of religious act.

The field of religion being as wide as this, it is manifestly impossible that I should pretend to cover it. My lectures must be limited to a fraction of the subject. And, although it would indeed be foolish to set up an abstract definition of religion's essence, and then proceed to defend that definition against all comers, yet this need not prevent me from taking my own narrow view of what religion shall consist in *for the purpose of these lectures*, or, out of the many meanings of the word, from choosing the one meaning in which I wish to interest you particularly, and proclaiming arbitrarily that when I say "religion" I mean that. This, in fact, is what I must do, and I will now preliminarily seek to mark out the field I choose.

One way to mark it out easily is to say what aspects of the subject we leave out. At the outset we are struck by one great partition which divides the religious field. On the one side of it lies institutional, on the other personal religion. As M. P. Sabatier says, one branch of religion keeps the divinity, another keeps man most in view. Worship and sacrifice, procedures for working on the dispositions of the deity, theology and ceremony and ecclesiastical organization, are the essentials of religion in the institutional branch. Were we to limit our view to it, we should have to define religion as an external art, the art of winning the favor of the gods. In the more personal branch of religion it is on the contrary the inner dispositions of man himself which form the center of interest, his conscience, his deserts, his helplessness, his incompleteness. And although the favor of the God, as forfeited or gained, is still an essential feature of the story, and theology plays a vital part therein, yet the acts to which this sort of religion prompts are personal not ritual acts, the individual transacts the business by himself alone, and the ecclesiastical organization, with its priests and sacraments and other go-betweens, sinks to an altogether secondary place. The relation goes direct from heart to heart, from soul to soul, between man and his maker.

Now in these lectures I propose to ignore the institutional branch entirely, to say nothing of the ecclesiastical organization, to consider as little as possible the systematic theology and the ideas about the gods themselves, and to confine myself as far as I can to personal religion pure and simple. To some of you personal religion, thus nakedly considered, will no doubt seem too incomplete a thing to wear the general name. "It is a part of religion," you will say, "but only its unorganized rudiment; if we are to name it by itself, we had better call it man's conscience or morality than his religion. The name 'religion' should be reserved for the fully organized system of feeling, thought, and institution, for the Church, in short, of which this personal religion, so called, is but a fractional element."

But if you say this, it will only show the more plainly how much the question of definition tends to become a dispute about names. Rather than prolong such a dispute, I am willing to accept almost any name for the personal religion of which I propose to treat. Call it conscience or morality, if you yourselves prefer, and not religion—under either name it will be equally worthy of our study. As for myself, I think it will prove to contain some elements which morality pure and simple does not contain, and these elements I shall soon seek to point out; so I will myself continue to apply the word "religion" to it; and in the last lecture of all, I will bring in the theologies and the ecclesiasticisms, and say something of its relation to them.

In one sense at least the personal religion will prove itself more fundamental than either theology or ecclesiasticism. Churches, when once established, live at second-hand upon tradition; but the *founders* of every church owed their power originally to the fact of their direct personal communion with the divine. Not only the superhuman founders, the Christ, the Buddha, Mahomet, but all the originators of Christian sects have been in this case;—so personal religion should still seem the primordial thing, even to those who continue to esteem it incomplete.

There are, it is true, other things in religion chronologically more primordial than personal devoutness in the moral sense. Fetishism and magic seem to have preceded inward piety historically—at least our records of inward piety do not reach back so far. And if fetishism and magic be regarded as stages of religion, one may say that personal religion in the inward sense and the genuinely spiritual ecclesiasticisms which it founds are phenomena of secondary or even tertiary order. But, quite apart from the fact that many anthropologists—for instance, Jevons and Frazer—expressly oppose "religion" and "magic" to each other, it is certain that the whole system of thought which leads to magic, fetishism, and the lower superstitions may just as well be called primitive science as called primitive religion. The question thus becomes a verbal one again; and our knowledge of all these early stages of thought and feeling is in any case so conjectural and imperfect that farther discussion would not be worth while.

Religion, therefore, as I now ask you arbitrarily to take it, shall mean for us *the feelings, acts, and experiences of individual men in their solitude, so far as they apprehend themselves to stand in relation to whatever they may consider the divine.* Since the relation may be either moral, physical, or ritual, it is evident that out of religion in the sense in which we take it, theologies, philosophies, and ecclesiastical organizations may secondarily grow. In these lectures, however, as I have already said, the immediate personal experiences will amply fill our time, and we shall hardly consider theology or ecclesiasticism at all.

We escape much controversial matter by this arbitrary definition of our field. But, still, a chance of controversy comes up over the word "divine," if we take the definition in too narrow a sense. There are systems of thought which the world usually calls religious, and yet which do not positively assume a God. Buddhism is in this case. Popularly, of course, the Buddha himself stands in place of a God; but in strictness the Buddhistic system is atheistic. Modern transcendental idealism, Emersonianism, for instance, also seems to let God evaporate into abstract Ideality. Not a deity *in concreto*, not a superhuman person, but the immanent divinity in things, the essentially spiritual structure of the universe, is the object of the transcendentalist cult. In that address to the graduating class at Divinity College in 1838 which made Emerson famous, the frank expression of this worship of mere abstract laws was what made the scandal of the performance.

> "These laws," said the speaker, "execute themselves. They are out of time, out of space, and not subject to circumstance: Thus, in the soul of man there is a justice whose retributions are instant and entire. He who does a good deed is instantly ennobled. He who does a mean deed is by the action itself contracted. He who puts off impurity thereby puts on purity. If a man is at heart just, then in so far is he God; the safety of God, the immortality of God, the majesty of God, do enter into that man with justice. If a man dissemble, deceive, he deceives himself, and goes out of acquaintance with his own being. Character is always known. Thefts never enrich; alms never impoverish; murder will speak out of stone walls. The least admixture of a lie—for example, the taint of vanity, any attempt to make a good impression, a favorable appearance—will instantly vitiate the effect. But speak the truth, and all things alive or brute are vouchers, and the very roots of the grass underground there do seem to stir and move to bear your witness. For all things proceed out of the same spirit, which is differently named love, justice, temperance, in its different applications, just as the ocean receives different names on the several shores which it washes. In so far as he roves from these ends, a man bereaves himself of power, of auxiliaries. His being shrinks... he becomes less and less, a mote, a point, until absolute badness is absolute death. The perception of this law awakens in the mind a sentiment which we call the religious sentiment, and which makes our highest happiness. Wonderful is

its power to charm and to command. It is a mountain air. It is the embalmer of the world. It makes the sky and the hills sublime, and the silent song of the stars is it. It is the beatitude of man. It makes him illimitable. When he says 'I ought'; when love warns him; when he chooses, warned from on high, the good and great deed; then, deep melodies wander through his soul from supreme wisdom. Then he can worship, and be enlarged by his worship; for he can never go behind this sentiment. All the expressions of this sentiment are sacred and permanent in proportion to their purity. [They] affect us more than all other compositions. The sentences of the olden time, which ejaculate this piety, are still fresh and fragrant. And the unique impression of Jesus upon mankind, whose name is not so much written as ploughed into the history of this world, is proof of the subtle virtue of this infusion."[10]

Such is the Emersonian religion. The universe has a divine soul of order, which soul is moral, being also the soul within the soul of man. But whether this soul of the universe be a mere quality like the eye's brilliancy or the skin's softness, or whether it be a self-conscious life like the eye's seeing or the skin's feeling, is a decision that never unmistakably appears in Emerson's pages. It quivers on the boundary of these things, sometimes leaning one way sometimes the other, to suit the literary rather than the philosophic need. Whatever it is, though, it is active. As much as if it were a God, we can trust it to protect all ideal interests and keep the world's balance straight. The sentences in which Emerson, to the very end, gave utterance to this faith are as fine as anything in literature: "If you love and serve men, you cannot by any hiding or stratagem escape the remuneration. Secret retributions are always restoring the level, when disturbed, of the divine justice. It is impossible to tilt the beam. All the tyrants and proprietors and monopolists of the world in vain set their shoulders to heave the bar. Settles forevermore the ponderous equator to its line, and man and mote, and star and sun, must range to it, or be pulverized by the recoil."[11]

Now it would be too absurd to say that the inner experiences that underlie such expressions of faith as this and impel the writer to their utterance are quite unworthy to be called religious experiences. The sort of appeal that Emersonian optimism, on the one hand, and Buddhistic pessimism, on the other, make to the individual and the son of response which he makes to them in his life are in fact indistinguishable from, and in many respects identical with, the best Christian appeal and response. We must therefore, from the experiential point of view, call these godless or quasi-godless creeds "religions"; and accordingly when in our definition of religion we speak of the individual's relation to "what he considers the divine," we must interpret the term "divine" very broadly, as denoting any object that is god*like*, whether it be a concrete deity or not.

But the term "godlike," if thus treated as a floating general quality, becomes

10 Miscellanies, 1868, p. 120 (abridged).

11 Lectures and Biographical Sketches, 1868, p. 186.

exceedingly vague, for many gods have flourished in religious history, and their attributes have been discrepant enough. What then is that essentially godlike quality—be it embodied in a concrete deity or not—our relation to which determines our character as religious men? It will repay us to seek some answer to this question before we proceed farther.

For one thing, gods are conceived to be first things in the way of being and power. They overarch and envelop, and from them there is no escape. What relates to them is the first and last word in the way of truth. Whatever then were most primal and enveloping and deeply true might at this rate be treated as godlike, and a man's religion might thus be identified with his attitude, whatever it might be, toward what he felt to be the primal truth.

Such a definition as this would in a way be defensible. Religion, whatever it is, is a man's total reaction upon life, so why not say that any total reaction upon life is a religion? Total reactions are different from casual reactions, and total attitudes are different from usual or professional attitudes. To get at them you must go behind the foreground of existence and reach down to that curious sense of the whole residual cosmos as an everlasting presence, intimate or alien, terrible or amusing, lovable or odious, which in some degree everyone possesses. This sense of the world's presence, appealing as it does to our peculiar individual temperament, makes us either strenuous or careless, devout or blasphemous, gloomy or exultant, about life at large; and our reaction, involuntary and inarticulate and often half unconscious as it is, is the completest of all our answers to the question, "What is the character of this universe in which we dwell?" It expresses our individual sense of it in the most definite way. Why then not call these reactions our religion, no matter what specific character they may have? Non-religious as some of these reactions may be, in one sense of the word "religious," they yet belong to *the general sphere of the religious life*, and so should generically be classed as religious reactions. "He believes in No-God, and he worships him," said a colleague of mine of a student who was manifesting a fine atheistic ardor; and the more fervent opponents of Christian doctrine have often enough shown a temper which, psychologically considered, is indistinguishable from religious zeal.

But so very broad a use of the word "religion" would be inconvenient, however defensible it might remain on logical grounds. There are trifling, sneering attitudes even toward the whole of life; and in some men these attitudes are final and systematic. It would strain the ordinary use of language too much to call such attitudes religious, even though, from the point of view of an unbiased critical philosophy, they might conceivably be perfectly reasonable ways of looking upon life. Voltaire, for example, writes thus to a friend, at the age of seventy-three: "As for myself," he says, "weak as I am, I carry on the war to the last moment, I get a hundred pike-thrusts, I return two hundred, and I laugh. I see near my door Geneva on fire with quarrels over nothing, and I laugh again; and, thank God, I can look upon the world as a farce even when it becomes as tragic as it sometimes does. All comes out even at the end of the day, and all comes out still more even when all the days are over."

Much as we may admire such a robust old gamecock spirit in a valetudinarian, to call it a religious spirit would be odd. Yet it is for the moment Voltaire's reaction on the whole of life. *Je m'en fiche* is the vulgar French equivalent for our English ejaculation "Who cares?" And the happy term *je me'n fichisme* recently has been invented to designate the systematic determination not to take anything in life too solemnly. "All is vanity" is the relieving word in all difficult crises for this mode of thought, which that exquisite literary genius Renan took pleasure, in his later days of sweet decay, in putting into coquettishly sacrilegious forms which remain to us as excellent expressions of the "all is vanity" state of mind. Take the following passage, for example—we must hold to duty, even against the evidence, Renan says—but he then goes on:—

> "There are many chances that the world may be nothing but a fairy pantomime of which no God has care. We must therefore arrange ourselves so that on neither hypothesis we shall be completely wrong. We must listen to the superior voices, but in such a way that if the second hypothesis were true we should not have been too completely duped. If in effect the world be not a serious thing, it is the dogmatic people who will be the shallow ones, and the worldly minded whom the theologians now call frivolous will be those who are really wise.
>
> "*In utrumque paratus*, then. Be ready for anything—that perhaps is wisdom. Give ourselves up, according to the hour, to confidence, to skepticism, to optimism, to irony, and we may be sure that at certain moments at least we shall be with the truth. . . . Good-humor is a philosophic state of mind; it seems to say to Nature that we take her no more seriously than she takes us. I maintain that one should always talk of philosophy with a smile. We owe it to the Eternal to be virtuous; but we have the right to add to this tribute our irony as a sort of personal reprisal. In this way we return to the right quarter jest for jest; we play the trick that has been played on us. Saint Augustine's phrase: *Lord, if we are deceived, it is by thee!* remains a fine one, well suited to our modern feeling. Only we wish the Eternal to know that if we accept the fraud, we accept it knowingly and willingly. We are resigned in advance to losing the interest on our investments of virtue, but we wish not to appear ridiculous by having counted on them too securely."[12]

Surely all the usual associations of the word "religion" would have to be stripped away if such a systematic *parti pris* of irony were also to be denoted by the name. For common men "religion," whatever more special meanings it may have, signifies always a *serious* state of mind. If any one phrase could gather its universal message, that phrase would be, "All is *not* vanity in this Universe, whatever the appearances may suggest." If it can stop anything, religion as commonly apprehended can stop just such chaffing talk as Renan's. It favors gravity, not pertness; it says "hush" to all vain chatter and smart wit.

12 Feuilles détachées, pp. 394–398 (abridged).

But if hostile to light irony, religion is equally hostile to heavy grumbling and complaint. The world appears tragic enough in some religions, but the tragedy is realized as purging, and a way of deliverance is held to exist. We shall see enough of the religious melancholy in a future lecture; but melancholy, according to our ordinary use of language, forfeits all title to be called religious when, in Marcus Aurelius's racy words, the sufferer simply lies kicking and screaming after the fashion of a sacrificed pig. The mood of a Schopenhauer or a Nietzsche—and in a less degree one may sometimes say the same of our own sad Carlyle—though often an ennobling sadness, is almost as often only peevishness running away with the bit between its teeth. The sallies of the two German authors remind one, half the time, of the sick shriekings of two dying rats. They lack the purgatorial note which religious sadness gives forth.

There must be something solemn, serious, and tender about any attitude which we denominate religious. If glad, it must not grin or snicker; if sad, it must not scream or curse. It is precisely as being *solemn* experiences that I wish to interest you in religious experiences. So I propose—arbitrarily again, if you please—to narrow our definition once more by saying that the word "divine," as employed therein, shall mean for us not merely the primal and enveloping and real, for that meaning if taken without restriction might prove too broad. The divine shall mean for us only such a primal reality as the individual feels impelled to respond to solemnly and gravely, and neither by a curse nor a jest.

But solemnity, and gravity, and all such emotional attributes, admit of various shades; and, do what we will with our defining, the truth must at last be confronted that we are dealing with a field of experience where there is not a single conception that can be sharply drawn. The pretension, under such conditions, to be rigorously "scientific" or "exact" in our terms would only stamp us as lacking in understanding of our task. Things are more or less divine, states of mind are more or less religious, reactions are more or less total, but the boundaries are always misty, and it is everywhere a question of amount and degree. Nevertheless, at their extreme of development, there can never be any question as to what experiences are religious. The divinity of the object and the solemnity of the reaction are too well marked for doubt. Hesitation as to whether a state of mind is "religious," or "irreligious," or "moral," or "philosophical," is only likely to arise when the state of mind is weakly characterized, but in that case it will be hardly worthy of our study at all. With states that can only by courtesy be called religious we need have nothing to do, our only profitable business being with what nobody can possibly feel tempted to call anything else. I said in my former lecture that we learn most about a thing when we view it under a microscope, as it were, or in its most exaggerated form. This is as true of religious phenomena as of any other kind of fact. The only cases likely to be profitable enough to repay our attention will therefore be cases where the religious spirit is unmistakable and extreme. Its fainter manifestations we may tranquilly pass by. Here, for example, is the total reaction upon life of Frederick Locker Lampson, whose autobiography, entitled "Confidences," proves him to have been a most amiable man.

"I am so far resigned to my lot that I feel small pain at the thought of having to part from what has been called the pleasant habit of existence, the sweet fable of life. I would not care to live my wasted life over again, and so to prolong my span. Strange to say, I have but little wish to be younger. I submit with a chill at my heart. I humbly submit because it is the Divine Will, and my appointed destiny. I dread the increase of infirmities that will make me a burden to those around me, those dear to me. No! let me slip away as quietly and comfortably as I can. Let the end come, if peace come with it.

"I do not know that there is a great deal to be said for this world, or our sojourn here upon it; but it has pleased God so to place us, and it must please me also. I ask you, what is human life? Is not it a maimed happiness—care and weariness, weariness and care, with the baseless expectation, the strange cozenage of a brighter to-morrow? At best it is but a froward child, that must be played with and humored, to keep it quiet till it falls asleep, and then the care is over."[13]

This is a complex, a tender, a submissive, and a graceful state of mind. For myself, I should have no objection to calling it on the whole a religious state of mind, although I dare say that to many of you it may seem too listless and half-hearted to merit so good a name. But what matters it in the end whether we call such a state of mind religious or not? It is too insignificant for our instruction in any case; and its very possessor wrote it down in terms which he would not have used unless he had been thinking of more energetically religious moods in others, with which he found himself unable to compete. It is with these more energetic states that our sole business lies, and we can perfectly well afford to let the minor notes and the uncertain border go.

It was the extremer cases that I had in mind a little while ago when I said that personal religion, even without theology or ritual, would prove to embody some elements that morality pure and simple does not contain. You may remember that I promised shortly to point out what those elements were. In a general way I can now say what I had in mind.

"I accept the universe" is reported to have been a favorite utterance of our New England transcendentalist, Margaret Fuller; and when some one repeated this phrase to Thomas Carlyle, his sardonic comment is said to have been: "Gad! she'd better!" At bottom the whole concern of both morality and religion is with the manner of our acceptance of the universe. Do we accept it only in part and grudgingly, or heartily and altogether? Shall our protests against certain things in it be radical and unforgiving, or shall we think that, even with evil, there are ways of living that must lead to good? If we accept the whole, shall we do so as if stunned into submission—as Carlyle would have us—"Gad! we'd better!"—or shall we do so with enthusiastic

13 Op. cit., pp. 314, 313.

assent? Morality pure and simple accepts the law of the whole which it finds reigning, so far as to acknowledge and obey it, but it may obey it with the heaviest and coldest heart, and never cease to feel it as a yoke. But for religion, in its strong and fully developed manifestations, the service of the highest never is felt as a yoke. Dull submission is left far behind, and a mood of welcome, which may fill any place on the scale between cheerful serenity and enthusiastic gladness, has taken its place.

It makes a tremendous emotional and practical difference to one whether one accept the universe in the drab discolored way of stoic resignation to necessity, or with the passionate happiness of Christian saints. The difference is as great as that between passivity and activity, as that between the defensive and the aggressive mood. Gradual as are the steps by which an individual may grow from one state into the other, many as are the intermediate stages which different individuals represent, yet when you place the typical extremes beside each other for comparison, you feel that two discontinuous psychological universes confront you, and that in passing from one to the other a "critical point" has been overcome.

If we compare stoic with Christian ejaculations we see much more than a difference of doctrine; rather is it a difference of emotional mood that parts them. When Marcus Aurelius reflects on the eternal reason that has ordered things, there is a frosty chill about his words which you rarely find in a Jewish, and never in a Christian piece of religious writing. The universe is "accepted" by all these writers; but how devoid of passion or exultation the spirit of the Roman Emperor is! Compare his fine sentence: "If gods care not for me or my children, here is a reason for it," with Job's cry: "Though he slay me, yet will I trust in him!" and you immediately see the difference I mean. The *anima mundi*, to whose disposal of his own personal destiny the Stoic consents, is there to be respected and submitted to, but the Christian God is there to be loved; and the difference of emotional atmosphere is like that between an arctic climate and the tropics, though the outcome in the way of accepting actual conditions uncomplainingly may seem in abstract terms to be much the same.

> "It is a man's duty," says Marcus Aurelius, "to comfort himself and wait for the natural dissolution, and not to be vexed, but to find refreshment solely in these thoughts—first that nothing will happen to me which is not conformable to the nature of the universe; and secondly that I need do nothing contrary to the God and deity within me; for there is no man who can compel me to transgress. He is an abscess on the universe who withdraws and separates himself from the reason of our common nature, through being displeased with the things which happen. For the same nature produces these, and has produced thee too. And so accept everything which happens, even if it seem disagreeable, because it leads to this, the health of the universe and to the prosperity and felicity of Zeus. For he would not have brought on any man what he has brought, if it were not useful for the whole. The integrity of the whole is

mutilated if thou cuttest off anything. And thou dost cut off, as far as it is in thy power, when thou art dissatisfied, and in a manner triest to put anything out of the way."[14]

Compare now this mood with that of the old Christian author of the Theologia Germanica:—

"Where men are enlightened with the true light, they renounce all desire and choice, and commit and commend themselves and all things to the eternal Goodness, so that every enlightened man could say: 'I would fain be to the Eternal Goodness what his own hand is to a man.' Such men are in a state of freedom, because they have lost the fear of pain or hell, and the hope of reward or heaven, and are living in pure submission to the eternal Goodness, in the perfect freedom of fervent love. When a man truly perceiveth and considereth himself, who and what he is, and findeth himself utterly vile and wicked and unworthy, he falleth into such a deep abasement that it seemeth to him reasonable that all creatures in heaven and earth should rise up against him. And therefore he will not and dare not desire any consolation and release; but he is willing to be unconsoled and unreleased; and he doth not grieve over his sufferings, for they are right in his eyes, and he hath nothing to say against them. This is what is meant by true repentance for sin; and he who in this present time entereth into this hell, none may console him. Now God hath not forsaken a man in this hell, but He is laying his hand upon him, that the man may not desire nor regard anything but the eternal Good only. And then, when the man neither careth for nor desireth anything but the eternal Good alone, and seeketh not himself nor his own things, but the honour of God only, he is made a partaker of all manner of joy, bliss, peace, rest, and consolation, and so the man is henceforth in the kingdom of heaven. This hell and this heaven are two good safe ways for a man, and happy is he who truly findeth them."[15]

How much more active and positive the impulse of the Christian writer to accept his place in the universe is! Marcus Aurelius agrees *to* the scheme—the German theologian agrees *with* it. He literally *abounds* in agreement, he runs out to embrace the divine decrees.

Occasionally, it is true, the stoic rises to something like a Christian warmth of sentiment, as in the often quoted passage of Marcus Aurelius:—

"Everything harmonizes with me which is harmonious to thee, O Universe. Nothing for me is too early nor too late, which is in due time for thee. Everything is fruit to me which thy seasons bring, O Nature: from thee are all things, in thee

14 Book V., ch. ix. (abridged).
15 Chaps. x., xi. (abridged): Winkworth's translation.

are all things, to thee all things return. The poet says, Dear City of Cecrops; and wilt thou not say, Dear City of Zeus?"[16]

But compare even as devout a passage as this with a genuine Christian outpouring, and it seems a little cold. Turn, for instance, to the Imitation of Christ:—

"Lord, thou knowest what is best; let this or that be according as thou wilt. Give what thou wilt, so much as thou wilt, when thou wilt. Do with me as thou knowest best, and as shall be most to thine honour. Place me where thou wilt, and freely work thy will with me in all things.... When could it be evil when thou wert near? I had rather be poor for thy sake than rich without thee. I choose rather to be a pilgrim upon the earth with thee, than without thee to possess heaven. Where thou art, there is heaven; and where thou art not, behold there death and hell."[17]

It is a good rule in physiology, when we are studying the meaning of an organ, to ask after its most peculiar and characteristic sort of performance, and to seek its office in that one of its functions which no other organ can possibly exert. Surely the same maxim holds good in our present quest. The essence of religious experiences, the thing by which we finally must judge them, must be that element or quality in them which we can meet nowhere else. And such a quality will be of course most prominent and easy to notice in those religious experiences which are most one-sided, exaggerated, and intense.

Now when we compare these intenser experiences with the experiences of tamer minds, so cool and reasonable that we are tempted to call them philosophical rather than religious, we find a character that is perfectly distinct. That character, it seems to me, should be regarded as the practically important *differentia* of religion for our purpose; and just what it is can easily be brought out by comparing the mind of an abstractly conceived Christian with that of a moralist similarly conceived.

A life is manly, stoical, moral, or philosophical, we say, in proportion as it is less swayed by paltry personal considerations and more by objective ends that call for energy, even though that energy bring personal loss and pain. This is the good side of war, in so far as it calls for "volunteers." And for morality life is a war, and the service of the highest is a sort of cosmic patriotism which also calls for volunteers. Even a sick man, unable to be militant outwardly, can carry on the moral warfare. He can willfully turn his attention away from his own future, whether in this world or the next. He can train himself to indifference to his present drawbacks and im-

16 Book IV., §23.

17 Benham's translation: Book III., chaps. xv., lix. Compare Mary Moody Emerson: "Let me be a blot on this fair world, the obscurest, the loneliest sufferer, with one proviso—that I know it is His agency. I will love Him though He shed frost and darkness on every way of mine." R. W. Emerson: Lectures and Biographical Sketches, p. 188.

merse himself in whatever objective interests still remain accessible. He can follow public news, and sympathize with other people's affairs. He can cultivate cheerful manners, and be silent about his miseries. He can contemplate whatever ideal aspects of existence his philosophy is able to present to him, and practice whatever duties, such as patience, resignation, trust, his ethical system requires. Such a man lives on his loftiest, largest plane. He is a high-hearted freeman and no pining slave. And yet he lacks something which the Christian *par excellence*, the mystic and ascetic saint, for example, has in abundant measure, and which makes of him a human being of an altogether different denomination.

The Christian also spurns the pinched and mumping sick-room attitude, and the lives of saints are full of a kind of callousness to diseased conditions of body which probably no other human records show. But whereas the merely moralistic spurning takes an effort of volition, the Christian spurning is the result of the excitement of a higher kind of emotion, in the presence of which no exertion of volition is required. The moralist must hold his breath and keep his muscles tense; and so long as this athletic attitude is possible all goes well—morality suffices. But the athletic attitude tends ever to break down, and it inevitably does break down even in the most stalwart when the organism begins to decay, or when morbid fears invade the mind. To suggest personal will and effort to one all sicklied o'er with the sense of irremediable impotence is to suggest the most impossible of things. What he craves is to be consoled in his very powerlessness, to feel that the spirit of the universe recognizes and secures him, all decaying and failing as he is. Well, we are all such helpless failures in the last resort. The sanest and best of us are of one clay with lunatics and prison inmates, and death finally runs the robustest of us down. And whenever we feel this, such a sense of the vanity and provisionality of our voluntary career comes over us that all our morality appears but as a plaster hiding a sore it can never cure, and all our well-doing as the hollowest substitute for that well-*being* that our lives ought to be grounded in, but, alas! are not.

And here religion comes to our rescue and takes our fate into her hands. There is a state of mind, known to religious men, but to no others, in which the will to assert ourselves and hold our own has been displaced by a willingness to close our mouths and be as nothing in the floods and waterspouts of God. In this state of mind, what we most dreaded has become the habitation of our safety, and the hour of our moral death has turned into our spiritual birthday. The time for tension in our soul is over, and that of happy relaxation, of calm deep breathing, of an eternal present, with no discordant future to be anxious about, has arrived. Fear is not held in abeyance as it is by mere morality, it is positively expunged and washed away.

We shall see abundant examples of this happy state of mind in later lectures of this course. We shall see how infinitely passionate a thing religion at its highest flights can be. Like love, like wrath, like hope, ambition, jealousy, like every other instinctive eagerness and impulse, it adds to life an enchantment which is not rationally or logically deducible from anything else. This enchantment, coming as a gift when it does come—a gift of our organism, the physiologists will tell us, a gift of God's grace, the theologians say—is either there or not there for us, and there are persons who can no more become possessed by it than they can fall in love with a given woman by mere word of command. Religious feeling is thus an absolute addition to the Subject's range of life. It gives him a new sphere of power. When the outward battle is lost, and the outer world disowns him, it redeems and vivifies an interior world which otherwise would be an empty waste.

If religion is to mean anything definite for us, it seems to me that we ought to take it as meaning this added dimension of emotion, this enthusiastic temper of espousal, in regions where morality strictly so called can at best but bow its head and acquiesce. It ought to mean nothing short of this new reach of freedom for us, with the struggle over, the keynote of the universe sounding in our ears, and everlasting possession spread before our eyes.[18]

This sort of happiness in the absolute and everlasting is what we find nowhere but in religion. It is parted off from all mere animal happiness, all mere enjoyment of the present, by that element of solemnity of which I have already made so much account. Solemnity is a hard thing to define abstractly, but certain of its marks are patent enough. A solemn state of mind is never crude or simple—it seems to contain a certain measure of its own opposite in solution. A solemn joy preserves a sort of bitter in its sweetness; a solemn sorrow is one to which we intimately consent. But there are writers who, realizing that happiness of a supreme sort is the prerogative of religion, forget this complication, and call all happiness, as such, religious. Mr. Havelock Ellis, for example, identifies religion with the entire field of the soul's liberation from oppressive moods.

> "The simplest functions of physiological life," he writes, "may be its ministers. Every one who is at all acquainted with the Persian mystics knows how wine may be regarded as an instrument of religion. Indeed, in all countries and in all ages, some form of physical enlargement—singing, dancing, drinking, sexual excitement—has been intimately associated with worship. Even the momentary expansion of the soul in laughter is, to however slight an extent, a religious exercise. . . . Whenever an impulse from the world strikes against the organism, and the resultant is not discomfort or pain, not even the muscular contraction of strenuous manhood, but a joyous expansion or aspiration of the whole soul—there is religion. It is the infinite for which we hunger, and we ride gladly on every little wave that promises to bear us towards it."[19]

18 Once more, there are plenty of men, constitutionally sombre men, in whose religious life this rapturousness is lacking. They are religious in the wider sense; yet in this acutest of all senses they are not so, and it is religion in the acutest sense that I wish, without disputing about words, to study first, so as to get at its typical *differentia*.

19 The New Spirit, p. 232.

But such a straight identification of religion with any and every form of happiness leaves the essential peculiarity of religious happiness out. The more commonplace happinesses which we get are "reliefs," occasioned by our momentary escapes from evils either experienced or threatened. But in its most characteristic embodiments, religious happiness is no mere feeling of escape. It cares no longer to escape. It consents to the evil outwardly as a form of sacrifice—inwardly it knows it to be permanently overcome. If you ask *how* religion thus falls on the thorns and faces death, and in the very act annuls annihilation, I cannot explain the matter, for it is religion's secret, and to understand it you must yourself have been a religious man of the extremer type. In our future examples, even of the simplest and healthiest-minded type of religious consciousness, we shall find this complex sacrificial constitution, in which a higher happiness holds a lower unhappiness in check. In the Louvre there is a picture, by Guido Reni, of St. Michael with his foot on Satan's neck. The richness of the picture is in large part due to the fiend's figure being there. The richness of its allegorical meaning also is due to his being there—that is, the world is all the richer for having a devil in it, *so long as we keep our foot upon his neck.* In the religious consciousness, that is just the position in which the fiend, the negative or tragic principle, is found; and for that very reason the religious consciousness is so rich from the emotional point of view.[20] We shall see how in certain men and women it takes on a monstrously ascetic form. There are saints who have literally fed on the negative principle, on humiliation and privation, and the thought of suffering and death—their souls growing in happiness just in proportion as their outward state grew more intolerable. No other emotion than religious emotion can bring a man to this peculiar pass. And it is for that reason that when we ask our question about the value of religion for human life, I think we ought to look for the answer among these violenter examples rather than among those of a more moderate hue.

Having the phenomenon of our study in its acutest possible form to start with, we can shade down as much as we please later. And if in these cases, repulsive as they are to our ordinary worldly way of judging, we find ourselves compelled to acknowledge religion's value and treat it with respect, it will have proved in some way its value for life at large. By subtracting and toning down extravagances we may thereupon proceed to trace the boundaries of its legitimate sway.

To be sure, it makes our task difficult to have to deal so much with eccentricities and extremes. "How *can* religion on the whole be the most important of all human functions," you may ask, "if every several manifestation of it in turn have to be corrected and sobered down and pruned away?" Such a thesis seems a paradox impossible to sustain reasonably—yet I believe that something like it will have to be our final contention. That personal attitude which the individual finds himself impelled

20 I owe this allegorical illustration to my lamented colleague and friend, Charles Carroll Everett.

to take up towards what he apprehends to be the divine—and you will remember that this was our definition—will prove to be both a helpless and a sacrificial attitude. That is, we shall have to confess to at least some amount of dependence on sheer mercy, and to practice some amount of renunciation, great or small, to save our souls alive. The constitution of the world we live in requires it:—

> *"Entbehren sollst du! sollst entbehren!*
> *Das ist der ewige Gesang*
> *Der jedem an die Ohren klingt,*
> *Den, unser ganzes Leben lang*
> *Uns heiser jede Stunde singt."*

For when all is said and done, we are in the end absolutely dependent on the universe; and into sacrifices and surrenders of some sort, deliberately looked at and accepted, we are drawn and pressed as into our only permanent positions of repose. Now in those states of mind which fall short of religion, the surrender is submitted to as an imposition of necessity, and the sacrifice is undergone at the very best without complaint. In the religious life, on the contrary, surrender and sacrifice are positively espoused: even unnecessary givings-up are added in order that the happiness may increase. *Religion thus makes easy and felicitous what in any case is necessary;* and if it be the only agency that can accomplish this result, its vital importance as a human faculty stands vindicated beyond dispute. It becomes an essential organ of our life, performing a function which no other portion of our nature can so successfully fulfill. From the merely biological point of view, so to call it, this is a conclusion to which, so far as I can now see, we shall inevitably be led, and led moreover by following the purely empirical method of demonstration which I sketched to you in the first lecture. Of the farther office of religion as a metaphysical revelation I will say nothing now.

But to foreshadow the terminus of one's investigations is one thing, and to arrive there safely is another. In the next lecture, abandoning the extreme generalities which have engrossed us hitherto, I propose that we begin our actual journey by addressing ourselves directly to the concrete facts.

LECTURE III

# The Reality of the Unseen

Were one asked to characterize the life of religion in the broadest and most general terms possible, one might say that it consists of the belief that there is an unseen order, and that our supreme good lies in harmoniously adjusting ourselves thereto. This belief and this adjustment are the religious attitude in the soul. I wish during this hour to call your attention to some of the psychological peculiarities of such an attitude as this, or belief in an object which we cannot see. All our attitudes, moral, practical, or emotional, as well as religious, are due to the "objects" of our consciousness, the things which we believe to exist, whether really or ideally, along with ourselves. Such objects may be present to our senses, or they may be present only to our thought. In either case they elicit from us a *reaction;* and the reaction due to things of thought is notoriously in many cases as strong as that due to sensible presences. It may be even stronger. The memory of an insult may make us angrier than the insult did when we received it. We are frequently more ashamed of our blunders afterwards than we were at the moment of making them; and in general our whole higher prudential and moral life is based on the fact that material sensations actually present may have a weaker influence on our action than ideas of remoter facts.

The more concrete objects of most men's religion, the deities whom they worship, are known to them only in idea. It has been vouchsafed, for example, to very few Christian believers to have had a sensible vision of their Saviour; though enough appearances of this sort are on record, by way of miraculous exception, to merit our attention later. The whole force of the Christian religion, therefore, so far as belief in the divine personages determines the prevalent attitude of the believer, is in general exerted by the instrumentality of pure ideas, of which nothing in the individual's past experience directly serves as a model.

But in addition to these ideas of the more concrete religious objects, religion is full of abstract objects which prove to have an equal power. God's attributes as such, his holiness, his justice, his mercy, his absoluteness, his infinity, his omniscience, his tri-unity, the various mysteries of the redemptive process, the operation of the sacraments, etc., have proved fertile wells of inspiring meditation for Christian believers.[21] We shall see later that the absence of definite sensible images is positively insisted on by the mystical authorities in all religions as the *sine qua non* of a successful orison, or contemplation of the higher divine truths. Such contemplations are expected (and abundantly verify the expectation, as we shall also see) to influence the believer's subsequent attitude very powerfully for good.

Immanuel Kant held a curious doctrine about such objects of belief as God, the design of creation, the soul, its freedom, and the life hereafter. These things, he said, are properly not objects of knowledge at all. Our conceptions always require a sense-content to work with, and as the words soul," "God," "immortality," cover no distinctive sense-content whatever, it follows that theoretically speaking they are words devoid of any significance. Yet strangely enough they have a definite meaning *for our practice.* We can act *as if* there were a God; feel *as if* we were free; consider Nature *as if* she were full of special designs; lay plans *as if* we were to be immortal; and we find then that these words do make a genuine difference in our moral life. Our faith *that* these unintelligible objects actually exist proves thus to be a full equivalent in *praktischer Hinsicht*, as Kant calls it, or from the point of view of our action, for a knowledge of *what* they might be, in case we were permitted positively to conceive them. So we have the strange phenomenon, as Kant assures us, of a mind believing with all its strength in the real presence of a set of things of no one of which it can form any notion whatsoever.

My object in thus recalling Kant's doctrine to your mind is not to express any opinion as to the accuracy of this particularly uncouth part of his philosophy, but only to illustrate the characteristic of human nature which we are considering, by an example so classical in its exaggeration. The sentiment of reality can indeed attach itself so strongly to our object of belief that our whole life is polarized through and through, so to speak, by its sense of the existence of the thing believed in, and yet that thing, for purpose of definite description, can hardly be said to be present to our mind at all. It is as if a bar of iron, without touch or sight, with no representative faculty whatever, might nevertheless be strongly endowed with an inner capacity for magnetic feeling; and as if, through the various arousals of its magnetism by magnets coming and going in its neighborhood, it might be consciously determined to different attitudes and tendencies. Such a bar of iron could never give you an outward description of the agencies that had the power of stirring it so strongly; yet of their presence, and of their significance for its life, it would be intensely aware through every fibre of its being.

It is not only the Ideas of pure Reason as Kant styled them, that have this power

21 Example: "I have had much comfort lately in meditating on the passages which show the personality of the Holy Ghost, and his distinctness from the Father and the Son. It is a subject that requires searching into to find out, but, when realized, gives one so much more true and lively a sense of the fullness of the Godhead, and its work in us and to us, than when only thinking of the Spirit in its effect on us." Augustus Hare: Memorials, i. 244, Maria Hare to Lucy H. Hare.

of making us vitally feel presences that we are impotent articulately to describe. All sorts of higher abstractions bring with them the same kind of impalpable appeal. Remember those passages from Emerson which I read at my last lecture. The whole universe of concrete objects, as we know them, swims, not only for such a transcendentalist writer, but for all of us, in a wider and higher universe of abstract ideas, that lend it its significance. As time, space, and the ether soak through all things so (we feel) do abstract and essential goodness, beauty, strength, significance, justice, soak through all things good, strong, significant, and just.

Such ideas, and others equally abstract, form the background for all our facts, the fountain-head of all the possibilities we conceive of. They give its "nature," as we call it, to every special thing. Everything we know is "what" it is by sharing in the nature of one of these abstractions. We can never look directly at them, for they are bodiless and featureless and footless, but we grasp all other things by their means, and in handling the real world we should be stricken with helplessness in just so far forth as we might lose these mental objects, these adjectives and adverbs and predicates and heads of classification and conception.

This absolute determinability of our mind by abstractions is one of the cardinal facts in our human constitution. Polarizing and magnetizing us as they do, we turn towards them and from them, we seek them, hold them, hate them, bless them, just as if they were so many concrete beings. And beings they are, beings as real in the realm which they inhabit as the changing things of sense are in the realm of space.

Plato gave so brilliant and impressive a defense of this common human feeling, that the doctrine of the reality of abstract objects has been known as the platonic theory of ideas ever since. Abstract Beauty, for example, is for Plato a perfectly definite individual being, of which the intellect is aware as of something additional to all the perishing beauties of the earth. "The true order of going," he says, in the often quoted passage in his "Banquet," "is to use the beauties of earth as steps along which one mounts upwards for the sake of that other Beauty, going from one to two, and from two to all fair forms, and from fair forms to fair actions, and from fair actions to fair notions, until from fair notions, he arrives at the notion of absolute Beauty, and at last knows what the essence of Beauty is."[22] In our last lecture we had a glimpse of the way in which a platonizing writer like Emerson may treat the abstract divineness of things, the moral structure of the universe, as a fact worthy of worship. In those various churches without a God which to-day are spreading through the world under the name of ethical societies, we have a similar worship of the abstract divine, the moral law believed in as an ultimate object. "Science" in many minds is genuinely taking the place of a religion. Where this is so, the scientist treats the "Laws of Nature" as objective facts to be revered. A brilliant school of interpretation of Greek mythology would have it that in their origin the Greek gods were only half-metaphoric personifications of those great spheres of abstract law and

22 Symposium, Jowett, 1871, i. 527.

order into which the natural world falls apart—the sky-sphere, the ocean-sphere, the earth-sphere, and the like; just as even now we may speak of the smile of the morning, the kiss of the breeze, or the bite of the cold, without really meaning that these phenomena of nature actually wear a human face.[23]

As regards the origin of the Greek gods, we need not at present seek an opinion. But the whole array of our instances leads to a conclusion something like this: It is as if there were in the human consciousness a *sense of reality, a feeling of objective presence, a perception* of what we may call "something there," more deep and more general than any of the special and particular "senses" by which the current psychology supposes existent realities to be originally revealed. If this were so, we might suppose the senses to waken our attitudes and conduct as they so habitually do, by first exciting this sense of reality; but anything else, any idea, for example, that might similarly excite it, would have that same prerogative of appearing real which objects of sense normally possess. So far as religious conceptions were able to touch this reality-feeling, they would be believed in in spite of criticism, even though they might be so vague and remote as to be almost unimaginable, even though they might be such non-entities in point of *whatness*, as Kant makes the objects of his moral theology to be.

The most curious proofs of the existence of such an undifferentiated sense of reality as this are found in experiences of hallucination. It often happens that an hallucination is imperfectly developed: the person affected will feel a "presence" in the room, definitely localized, facing in one word, often coming suddenly, and as suddenly gone; and yet neither seen, heard, touched, nor cognized in any of the usual "sensible" ways. Let me give you an example of this, before I pass to the objects with whose presence religion is more peculiarly concerned.

An intimate friend of mine, one of the keenest intellects I know, has had several experiences of this sort. He writes as follows in response to my inquiries:—

> "I have several times within the past few years felt the so-called 'consciousness of a presence.' The experiences which I have in mind are clearly distinguishable from another kind of experience which I have had very frequently, and which I fancy many persons would also call the 'consciousness of a presence.' But the difference for me between the two sets of experience is as great as the difference between feeling a slight warmth originating I know not where, and standing in the midst of a conflagration with all the ordinary senses alert.
>
> "It was about September, 1884, when I had the first experience. On the previous night I had had, after getting into bed at my rooms in College, a vivid tactile hallucination of being grasped by the arm, which made me get up and search the room for an intruder; but the sense of presence properly so called came on the next night. After I had got into bed and blown out the candle, I lay awake

23 Example: "Nature is always so interesting, under whatever aspect she shows herself, that when it rains, I seem to see a beautiful woman weeping. She appears the more beautiful, the more afflicted she is." B. de St. Pierre.

> awhile thinking on the previous night's experience, when suddenly I *felt* something come into the room and stay close to my bed. It remained only a minute or two. I did not recognize it by any ordinary sense, and yet there was a horribly unpleasant 'sensation' connected with it. It stirred something more at the roots of my being than any ordinary perception. The feeling had something of the quality of a very large tearing vital pain spreading chiefly over the chest, but within the organism—and yet the feeling was not *pain* so much as *abhorrence.* At all events, something was present with me, and I knew its presence far more surely than I have ever known the presence of any fleshly living creature. I was conscious of its departure as of its coming: an almost instantaneously swift going through the door, and the 'horrible sensation' disappeared.
>
> "On the third night when I retired my mind was absorbed in some lectures which I was preparing, and I was still absorbed in these when I became aware of the actual presence (though not of the *coming*) of the thing that was there the night before, and of the 'horrible sensation.' I then mentally concentrated all my effort to charge this 'thing,' if it was evil, to depart, if it was *not* evil, to tell me who or what it was, and if it could not explain itself, to go, and that I would compel it to go. It went as on the previous night, and my body quickly recovered its normal state.
>
> "On two other occasions in my life I have had precisely the same 'horrible sensation.' Once it lasted a full quarter of an hour. In all three instances the certainty that there in outward space there stood *something* was indescribably *stronger* than the ordinary certainty of companionship when we are in the close presence of ordinary living people. The something seemed close to me, and intensely more real than any ordinary perception. Although I felt it to be like unto myself, so to speak, or finite, small, and distressful, as it were, I didn't recognize it as any individual being or person."

Of course such an experience as this does not connect itself with the religious sphere. Yet it may upon occasion do so; and the same correspondent informs me that at more than one other conjuncture he had the sense of presence developed with equal intensity and abruptness, only then it was filled with a quality of joy.

> "There was not a mere consciousness of something there, but fused in the central happiness of it, a startling awareness of some ineffable good. Not vague either, not like the emotional effect of some poem, or scene, or blossom, of music, but the sure knowledge of the close presence of a sort of mighty person, and after it went, the memory persisted as the one perception of reality. Everything else might be a dream, but not that."

My friend, as it oddly happens, does not interpret these latter experiences theistically, as signifying the presence of God. But it would clearly not have been unnatural to interpret them as a revelation of the deity's existence. When we reach the subject of mysticism, we shall have much more to say upon this head.

Lest the oddity of these phenomena should disconcert you, I will venture to read you a couple of similar narratives, much shorter, merely to show that we are dealing with a well-marked natural kind of fact. In the first case, which I take from the Journal of the Society for Psychical Research, the sense of presence developed in a few moments into a distinctly visualized hallucination—but I leave that part of the story out.

"I had read," the narrator says, "some twenty minutes or so, was thoroughly absorbed in the book, my mind was perfectly quiet, and for the time being my friends were quite forgotten, when suddenly without a moment's warning my whole being seemed roused to the highest state of tension or aliveness, and I was aware, with an intenseness not easily imagined by those who had never experienced it, that another being or presence was not only in the room, but quite close to me. I put my book down, and although my excitement was great, I felt quite collected, and not conscious of any sense of fear. Without changing my position, and looking straight at the fire, I knew somehow that my friend A. H. was standing at my left elbow, but so far behind me as to be hidden by the armchair in which I was leaning back. Moving my eyes round slightly without otherwise changing my position, the lower portion of one leg became visible, and I instantly recognized the gray-blue material of trousers he often wore, but the stuff appeared semitransparent, reminding me of tobacco smoke in consistency,"[24]—and hereupon the visual hallucination came.

Another informant writes:—

"Quite early in the night I was awakened. . . . I felt as if I had been aroused intentionally, and at first thought some one was breaking into the house. . . . I then turned on my side to go to sleep again, and immediately felt a consciousness of a presence in the room, and singular to state, it was not the consciousness of a live person, but of a spiritual presence. This may provoke a smile, but I can only tell you the facts as they occurred to me. I do not know how to better describe my sensations than by simply stating that I felt a consciousness of a spiritual presence. . . . I felt also at the same time a strong feeling of superstitious dread, as if something strange and fearful were about to happen."[25]

Professor Flournoy of Geneva gives me the following testimony of a friend of his, a lady, who has the gift of automatic or involuntary writing:—

"Whenever I practice automatic writing, what makes me feel that it is not due to a subconscious self is the feeling I always have of a foreign presence, external to my body. It is sometimes so definitely characterized that I could point to its exact position. This impression of presence is impossible to describe. It varies in intensity and clearness according to the personality from whom the writing pro-

24 Journal of the S. P. R., February, 1895, p. 26.

25 E. Gurney: Phantasms of the Living, i. 384.

fesses to come. If it is some one whom I love, I feel it immediately, before any writing has come. My heart seems to recognize it."

In an earlier book of mine I have cited at full length a curious case of presence felt by a blind man. The presence was that of the figure of a gray-bearded man dressed in a pepper and salt suit, squeezing himself under the crack of the door and moving across the floor of the room towards a sofa. The blind subject of this quasi-hallucination is an exceptionally intelligent reporter. He is entirely without internal visual imagery and cannot represent light or colors to himself, and is positive that his other senses, hearing, etc., were not involved in this false perception. It seems to have been an abstract conception rather, with the feelings of reality and spatial outwardness directly attached to it—in other words, a fully objectified and exteriorized *idea*.

Such cases, taken along with others which would be too tedious for quotation, seem sufficiently to prove the existence in our mental machinery of a sense of present reality more diffused and general than that which our special senses yield. For the pyschologists the tracing of the organic seat of such a feeling would form a pretty problem—nothing could be more natural than to connect it with the muscular sense, with the feeling that our muscles were innervating themselves for action. Whatsoever thus innervated our activity, or "made our flesh creep"—our senses are what do so oftenest—might then appear real and present, even though it were but an abstract idea. But with such vague conjectures we have no concern at present, for our interest lies with the faculty rather than with its organic seat.

Like all positive affections of consciousness, the sense of reality has its negative counterpart in the shape of a feeling of unreality by which persons may be haunted, and of which one sometimes hears complaint:—

> "When I reflect on the fact that I have made my appearance by accident upon a globe itself whirled through space as the sport of the catastrophes of the heavens," says Madame Ackermann; "when I see myself surrounded by beings as ephemeral and incomprehensible as I am myself, and all excitedly pursuing pure chimeras, I experience a strange feeling of being in a dream. It seems to me as if I have loved and suffered and that erelong I shall die, in a dream. My last word will be, 'I have been dreaming.' "[26]

In another lecture we shall see how in morbid melancholy this sense of the unreality of things may become a carking pain, and even lead to suicide.

We may now lay it down as certain that in the distinctively religious sphere of experience, many persons (how many we cannot tell) possess the objects of their belief, not in the form of mere conceptions which their intellect accepts as true, but rather in the form of quasi-sensible realities directly apprehended. As his sense of

26 Pensées d'un Solitaire, p. 66.

the real presence of these objects fluctuates, so the believer alternates between warmth and coldness in his faith. Other examples will bring this home to one better than abstract description, so I proceed immediately to cite some. The first example is a negative one, deploring the loss of the sense in question. I have extracted it from an account given me by a scientific man of my acquaintance, of his religious life. It seems to me to show clearly that the feeling of reality may be something more like a sensation than an intellectual operation properly so-called.

> "Between twenty and thirty I gradually became more and more agnostic and irreligious, yet I cannot say that I ever lost that 'indefinite consciousness' which Herbert Spencer describes so well, of an Absolute Reality behind phenomena. For me this Reality was not the pure Unknowable of Spencer's philosophy, for although I had ceased my childish prayers to God, and never prayed to *It* in a formal manner, yet my more recent experience shows me to have been in a relation to *It* which practically was the same thing as prayer. Whenever I had any trouble, especially when I had conflict with other people, either domestically or in the way of business, or when I was depressed in spirits or anxious about affairs, I now recognize that I used to fall back for support upon this curious relation I felt myself to be in to this fundamental cosmical *It*. It was on my side, or I was on Its side, however you please to term it, in the particular trouble, and it always strengthened me and seemed to give me endless vitality to feel its underlying and supporting presence. In fact, it was an unfailing fountain of living justice, truth, and strength, to which I instinctively turned at times of weakness, and it always brought me out. I know now that it was a personal relation I was in to it, because of late years the power of communicating with it has left me, and I am conscious of a perfectly definite loss. I used never to fail to find it when I turned to it. Then came a set of years when sometimes I found it, and then again I would be wholly unable to make connection with it. I remember many occasions on which at night in bed, I would be unable to get to sleep on account of worry. I turned this way and that in the darkness, and groped mentally for the familiar sense of that higher mind of my mind which had always seemed to be close at hand as it were, closing the passage, and yielding support, but there was no electric current. A blank was there instead of *It*: I couldn't find anything. Now, at the age of nearly fifty, my power of getting into connection with it has entirely left me; and I have to confess that a great help has gone out of my life. Life has become curiously dead and indifferent; and I can now see that my old experience was probably exactly the same thing as the prayers of the orthodox, only I did not call them by that name. What I have spoken of as 'It' was practically not Spencer's Unknowable, but just my own instinctive and individual God, whom I relied upon for higher sympathy, but whom somehow I have lost."

Nothing is more common in the pages of religious biography than the way in which seasons of lively and of difficult faith are described as alternating. Probably every religious person has the recollection of particular crisis in which a directer vision of the truth, a direct perception, perhaps, of a living God's existence, swept in and overwhelmed the languor of the more ordinary belief. In James Russell Lowell's correspondence there is a brief memorandum of an experience of this kind:—

"I had a revelation last Friday evening. I was at Mary's, and happening to say something of the presence of spirits (of whom, I said, I was often dimly aware), Mr. Putnam entered into an argument with me on spiritual matters. As I was speaking, the whole system rose up before me like a vague destiny looming from the Abyss. I never before so clearly felt the Spirit of God in me and around me. The whole room seemed to me full of God. The air seemed to waver to and fro with the presence of Something I knew not what. I spoke with the calmness and clearness of a prophet. I cannot tell you what this revelation was. I have not yet studied it enough. But I shall perfect it one day, and then you shall hear it and acknowledge its grandeur."[27]

Here is a longer and more developed experience from a manuscript communication by a clergyman—I take it from Starbuck's manuscript collection:—

"I remember the night, and almost the very spot on the hilltop, where my soul opened out, as it were, into the Infinite, and there was a rushing together of the two worlds, the inner and the outer. It was deep calling unto deep—the deep that my own struggle had opened up within being answered by the unfathomable deep without, reaching beyond the stars. I stood alone with Him who had made me, and all the beauty of the world, and love, and sorrow, and even temptation. I did not seek Him, but felt the perfect unison of my spirit with His. The ordinary sense of things around me faded. For the moment nothing but an ineffable joy and exultation remained. It is impossible fully to describe the experience. It was like the effect of some great orchestra when all the separate notes have melted into one swelling harmony that leaves the listener conscious of nothing save that his soul is being wafted upwards, and almost bursting with its own emotion. The perfect stillness of the night was thrilled by a more solemn silence. The darkness held a presence that was all the more felt because it was not seen. I could not any more have doubted that *He* was there than that I was. Indeed, I felt myself to be, if possible, the less real of the two.

"My highest faith in God and truest idea of him were then born in me. I have stood upon the Mount of Vision since, and felt the Eternal round about me. But never since has there come quite the same stirring of the heart. Then, if ever, I believe, I stood face to face with God, and was born anew of his spirit. There was, as I recall it, no sudden change of thought or of belief, except that my early crude conception, had, as it were, burst into flower. There was no destruction of the old, but a rapid, wonderful unfolding. Since that time no discussion that I have heard of the proofs of God's existence has been able to shake my faith. Having once felt the presence of God's spirit, I have never lost it again for long. My most assuring evidence of his existence is deeply rooted in that hour of vision, in the

27 Letters of Lowell. i. 75.

memory of that supreme experience, and in the conviction, gained from reading and reflection, that something the same has come to all who have found God. I am aware that it may justly be called mystical. I am not enough acquainted with philosophy to defend it from that or any other charge. I feel that in writing of it I have overlaid it with words rather than put it clearly to your thought. But, such as it is, I have described it as carefully as I now am able to do."

Here is another document, even more definite in character, which, the writer being a Swiss, I translate from the French original.[28]

"I was in perfect health: we were on our sixth day of tramping, and in good training. We had come the day before from Sixt to Trient by Buet. I felt neither fatigue, hunger, nor thirst, and my state of mind was equally healthy. I had had at Forlaz good news from home; I was subject to no anxiety, either near or remote, for we had a good guide, and there was not a shadow of uncertainty about the road we should follow. I can best describe the condition in which I was by calling it a state of equilibrium. When all at once I experienced a feeling of being raised above myself, I felt the presence of God—I tell of the thing just as I was conscious of it—as if his goodness and his power were penetrating me altogether. The throb of emotion was so violent that I could barely tell the boys to pass on and not wait for me. I then sat down on a stone, unable to stand any longer, and my eyes overflowed with tears. I thanked God that in the course of my life he had taught me to know him, that he sustained my life and took pity both on the insignificant creature and on the sinner that I was. I begged him ardently that my life might be consecrated to the doing of his will. I felt his reply, which was that I should do his will from day to day, in humility and poverty, leaving him, the Almighty God, to be judge of whether I should some time be called to bear witness more conspicuously. Then, slowly, the ecstasy left my heart; that is, I felt that God had withdrawn the communion which he had granted, and I was able to walk on, but very slowly, so strongly was I still possessed by the interior emotion. Besides, I had wept uninterruptedly for several minutes, my eyes were swollen, and I did not wish my companions to see me. The state of ecstasy may have lasted four or five minutes, although it seemed at the time to last much longer. My comrades waited for me ten minutes at the cross of Barine, but I took about twenty-five or thirty minutes to join them, for as well as I can remember, they said that I had kept them back for about half an hour. The impression had been so profound that in climbing slowly the slope I asked myself if it were possible that Moses on Sinai could have had a more intimate communication with God. I think it well to add that in this ecstasy of mine God had neither form, color, odor, nor taste; moreover, that the feeling of his presence was accompanied with no determinate localization. It was rather as if my personality had been transformed by the presence of a *spiritual spirit*. But the more I seek words to express this intimate intercourse, the more I feel the impossibility of describing the thing

28 I borrow it, with Professor Flournoy's permission, from his rich collection of psychological documents.

by any of our usual images. At bottom the expression most apt to render what I felt is this: God was present, though invisible; he fell under no one of my senses, yet my consciousness perceived him."

The adjective "mystical" is technically applied, most often, to states that are of brief duration. Of course such hours of rapture as the last two persons describe are mystical experiences, of which in a later lecture I shall have much to say. Meanwhile here is the abridged record of another mystical or semi-mystical experience, in a mind evidently framed by nature for ardent piety. I owe it to Starbuck's collection. The lady who gives the account is the daughter of a man well known in his time as a writer against Christianity. The suddenness of her conversion shows well how native the sense of God's presence must be to certain minds. She relates that she was brought up in entire ignorance of Christian doctrine, but, when in Germany, after being talked to by Christian friends, she read the Bible and prayed, and finally the plan of salvation flashed upon her like a stream of light.

"To this day," she writes, "I cannot understand dallying with religion and the commands of God. The very instant I heard my Father's cry calling unto me, my heart bounded in recognition. I ran, I stretched forth my arms, I cried aloud, 'Here, here I am, my Father.' Oh, happy child, what should I do? 'Love me,' answered my God. 'I do, I do,' I cried passionately. 'Come unto me,' called my Father. 'I will,' my heart panted. Did I stop to ask a single question? Not one. It never occurred to me to ask whether I was good enough, or to hesitate over my unfitness, or to find out what I thought of his church, or . . . to wait until I should be satisfied. Satisfied! I was satisfied. Had I not found my God and my Father? Did he not love me? Had he not called me? Was there not a Church into which I might enter? . . . Since then I have had direct answers to prayer—so significant as to be almost like talking with God and hearing his answer. The idea of God's reality has never left me for one moment."

Here is still another case, the writer being a man aged twenty-seven, in which the experience, probably almost as characteristic, is less vividly described:—

"I have on a number of occasions felt that I had enjoyed a period of intimate communion with the divine. These meetings came unasked and unexpected, and seemed to consist merely in the temporary obliteration of the conventionalities which usually surround and cover my life. . . . Once it was when from the summit of a high mountain I looked over a gashed and corrugated landscape extending to a long convex of ocean that ascended to the horizon, and again from the same point when I could see nothing beneath me but a boundless expanse of white cloud, on the blown surface of which a few high peaks, including the one I was on, seemed plunging about as if they were dragging their anchors. What I felt on these occasions was a temporary loss of my own identity, accompanied by an illumination which revealed to me a deeper significance than I had been wont to attach to life. It is in this that I find my justification for saying that

I have enjoyed communication with God. Of course the absence of such a being as this would be chaos. I cannot conceive of life without its presence."

Of the more habitual and so to speak chronic sense of God's presence the following sample from Professor Starbuck's manuscript collection may serve to give an idea. It is from a man aged forty-nine—probably thousands of unpretending Christians would write an almost identical account.

"God is more real to me than any thought or thing or person. I feel his presence positively, and the more as I live in closer harmony with his laws as written in my body and mind. I feel him in the sunshine or rain; and awe mingled with a delicious restfulness most nearly describes my feelings. I talk to him as to a companion in prayer and praise, and our communion is delightful. He answers me again and again, often in words so clearly spoken that it seems my outer ear must have carried the tone, but generally in strong mental impressions. Usually a text of Scripture, unfolding some new view of him and his love for me, and care for my safety. I could give hundreds of instances, in school matters, social problems, financial difficulties, etc. That he is mine and I am his never leaves me, it is an abiding joy. Without it life would be a blank, a desert, a shoreless, trackless waste."

I subjoin some more examples from writers of different ages and sexes. They are also from Professor Starbuck's collection, and their number might be greatly multiplied. The first is from a man twenty-seven years old:—

"God is quite real to me. I talk to him and often get answers. Thoughts sudden and distinct from any I have been entertaining come to my mind after asking God for his direction. Something over a year ago I was for some weeks in the direst perplexity. When the trouble first appeared before me I was dazed, but before long (two or three hours) I could hear distinctly a passage of Scripture: 'My grace is sufficient for thee.' Every time my thoughts turned to the trouble I could hear this quotation. I don't think I ever doubted the existence of God, or had him drop out of my consciousness. God has frequently stepped into my affairs very perceptibly, and I feel that he directs many little details all the time. But on two or three occasions he has ordered ways for me very contrary to my ambitions and plans."

Another statement (none the less valuable psychologically for being so decidedly childish) is that of a boy of seventeen:—

"Sometimes as I go to church, I sit down, join in the service, and before I go out I feel as if God was with me, right side of me, singing and reading the Psalms with me. . . . And then again I feel as if I could sit beside him, and put my arms around him, kiss him, etc. When I am taking Holy Communion at the altar, I try to get with him and generally feel his presence."

I let a few other cases follow at random:—

"God surrounds me like the physical atmosphere. He is closer to me than my own breath. In him literally I live and move and have my being."—

"There are times when I seem to stand in his very presence, to talk with him. Answers to prayer have come, sometimes direct and overwhelming in their revelation of his presence and powers. There are times when God seems far off, but this is always my own fault."—

"I have the sense of a presence, strong, and at the same time soothing, which hovers over me. Sometimes it seems to enwrap me with sustaining arms."

Such is the human ontological imagination, and such is the convincingness of what it brings to birth. Unpicturable beings are realized, and realized with an intensity almost like that of an hallucination. They determine our vital attitude as decisively as the vital attitude of lovers is determined by the habitual sense, by which each is haunted, of the other being in the world. A lover has notoriously this sense of the continuous being of his idol, even when his attention is addressed to other matters and he no longer represents her features. He cannot forget her; she uninterruptedly affects him through and through.

I spoke of the convincingness of these feelings of reality, and I must dwell a moment longer on that point. They are as convincing to those who have them as any direct sensible experiences can be, and they are, as a rule, much more convincing than results established by mere logic ever are. One may indeed be entirely without them; probably more than one of you here present is without them in any marked degree; but if you do have them, and have them at all strongly, the probability is that you cannot help regarding them as genuine perceptions of truth, as revelations of a kind of reality which no adverse argument, however unanswerable by you in words, can expel from your belief. The opinion opposed to mysticism in philosophy is sometimes spoken of as *rationalism*. Rationalism insists that all our beliefs ought ultimately to find for themselves articulate grounds. Such grounds, for rationalism, must consist of four things: (1) definitely statable abstract principles; (2) definite facts of sensation; (3) definite hypotheses based on such facts; and (4) definite inferences logically drawn. Vague impressions of something indefinable have no place in the rationalistic system, which on its positive side is surely a splendid intellectual tendency, for not only are all our philosophies fruits of it, but physical science (amongst other good things) is its result.

Nevertheless, if we look on man's whole mental life as it exists, on the life of men that lies in them apart from their learning and science, and that they inwardly and privately follow, we have to confess that the part of it of which rationalism can give an account is relatively superficial. It is the part that has the *prestige* undoubtedly, for it has the loquacity, it can challenge you for proofs, and chop logic, and put you down with words. But it will fail to convince or convert you all the same, if your dumb intuitions are opposed to its conclusions. If you have intuitions at all, they come from a deeper level of your nature than the loquacious level which rationalism inhabits. Your whole subconscious life, your impulses, your faiths, your needs, your divinations, have prepared the premises, of which your consciousness now feels the weight of the result; and something in you absolutely *knows* that that result must be truer than any logic-chopping rationalistic talk, however clever, that may contradict it. This inferiority of the rationalistic level in founding belief is just as manifest when rationalism argues for religion as when it argues against it. That vast literature of proofs of God's existence drawn from the order of nature, which a century ago seemed so overwhelmingly convincing, to-day does little more than gather dust in libraries, for the simple reason that our generation has ceased to believe in the kind of God it argued for. Whatever sort of a being God may be, we *know* to-day that he is nevermore that mere external inventor of "contrivances" intended to make manifest his "glory" in which our great-grandfathers took such satisfaction, though just how we know this we cannot possibly make clear by words either to others or to ourselves. I defy any of you here fully to account for your persuasion that if a God exist he must be a more cosmic and tragic personage than that Being.

The truth is that in the metaphysical and religious sphere, articulate reasons are cogent for us only when our inarticulate feelings of reality have already been impressed in favor of the same conclusion. Then, indeed, our intuitions and our reason work together, and great world-ruling systems, like that of the Buddhist or of the Catholic philosophy, may grow up. Our impulsive belief is here always what sets up the original body of truth, and our articulately verbalized philosophy is but its showy translation into formulas. The unreasoned and immediate assurance is the deep thing in us, the reasoned argument is but a surface exhibition. Instinct leads, intelligence does but follow. If a person feels the presence of a living God after the fashion shown by my quotations, your critical arguments, be they never so superior, will vainly set themselves to change his faith.

Please observe, however, that I do not yet say that it is *better* that the subconscious and non-rational should thus hold primacy in the religious realm. I confine myself to simply pointing out that they do so hold it as a matter of fact.

So much for our sense of the reality of the religious objects. Let me now say a brief word more about the attitudes they characteristically awaken.

We have already agreed that they are *solemn;* and we have seen reason to think that the most distinctive of them is the sort of joy which may result in extreme cases from absolute self-surrender. The sense of the kind of object to which the surrender is made has much to do with determining the precise complexion of the joy; and the whole phenomenon is more complex than any simple formula allows. In the literature of the subject, sadness and gladness have each been emphasized in turn. The ancient saying that the first maker of the Gods was fear receives voluminous corroboration from every age of religious history; but none the less does religious history show the part which joy has evermore tended to play. Sometimes the joy has been primary; sometimes secondary, being the gladness of deliverance from the fear. This latter state of things, being the more complex, is also the more complete; and as we proceed, I think we shall have abundant reason for refusing to leave out either the sadness or the gladness, if we look at religion with the breadth of view which it demands. Stated in the completest possible terms, a man's religion involves both moods of contraction and moods of expansion of his being. But the quantitative mixture and order of these moods vary so much from one age of the world, from one system of thought, and from one individual to another, that you may insist either on the dread and the submission, or on the peace and the freedom as the essence of the matter, and still remain materially within the limits of the truth. The constitutionally sombre and the constitutionally sanguine onlooker are bound to emphasize opposite aspects of what lies before their eyes.

The constitutionally sombre religious person makes even of his religious peace a very sober thing. Danger still hovers in the air about it. Flexion and contraction are not wholly checked. It were sparrowlike and childish after our deliverance to explode into twittering laughter and caper-cutting, and utterly to forget the imminent hawk on bough. Lie low, rather, lie low; for you are in the hands of a living God. In the Book of Job, for example, the impotence of man and the omnipotence of God is the exclusive burden of its author's mind. "It is as high as heaven; what canst thou do?—deeper than hell; what canst thou know?" There is an astringent relish about the truth of this conviction which some men can feel, and which for them is as near an approach as can be made to the feeling of religious joy.

> "In Job," says that coldly truthful writer, the author of Mark Rutherford, "God reminds us that man is not the measure of his creation. The world is immense, constructed on no plan or theory which the intellect of man can grasp. It is *transcendent* everywhere. This is the burden of every verse, and is the secret, if there be one, of the poem. Sufficient or insufficient, there is nothing more. . . . God is great, we know not his ways. He takes from us all we nave, but yet if we possess our souls in patience, we *may* pass the valley of the shadow, and come out in sunlight again. We may or we may not! . . . What more have we to say now than God said from the whirlwind over two thousand five hundred years ago?"[29]

If we turn to the sanguine onlooker, on the other hand, we find that deliverance is felt as incomplete unless the burden be altogether overcome and the danger forgotten. Such onlookers give us definitions that seem to the sombre minds of whom we have just been speaking to leave out all the solemnity that makes religious peace so different from merely animal joys. In the opinion of some writers an attitude might be called religious, though no touch were left in it of sacrifice or submission, no tendency to flexion, no bowing of the head. Any "habitual and regulated admiration," says Professor J. R. Seeley,[30] "is worthy to be called a religion"; and accordingly he thinks that our Music, our Science, and our so-called "Civilization," as these things are now organized and admiringly believed in, form the more genuine reli-

29 Mark Rutherford's Deliverance, London, 1885, pp. 196, 198.

30 In his book (too little read, I fear), Natural Religion, 3d edition, Boston, 1886, pp. 91, 122.

gions of our time. Certainly the unhesitating and unreasoning way in which we feel that we must inflict our civilization upon "lower" races, by means of Hotchkiss guns, etc., reminds one of nothing so much as of the early spirit of Islam spreading its religion by the sword.

In my last lecture I quoted to you the ultra-radical opinion of Mr. Havelock Ellis, that laughter of any sort may be considered a religious exercise, for it bears witness to the soul's emancipation. I quoted this opinion in order to deny its adequacy. But we must now settle our scores more carefully with this whole optimistic way of thinking. It is far too complex to be decided off-hand. I propose accordingly that we make of religious optimism the theme of the next two lectures.

LECTURES IV AND V

# The Religion of Healthy-Mindedness

If we were to ask the question: "What is human life's chief concern?" one of the answers we should receive would be: "It is happiness." How to gain, how to keep, how to recover happiness, is in fact for most men at all times the secret motive of all they do, and of all they are willing to endure. The hedonistic school in ethics deduces the moral life wholly from the experiences of happiness and unhappiness which different kinds of conduct bring; and, even more in the religious life than in the moral life, happiness and unhappiness seem to be the poles round which the interest revolves. We need not go so far as to say with the author whom I lately quoted that any persistent enthusiasm is, as such, religion, nor need we call mere laughter a religious exercise; but we must admit that any persistent enjoyment may *produce* the sort of religion which consists in a grateful admiration of the gift of so happy an existence; and we must also acknowledge that the more complex ways of experiencing religion are new manners of producing happiness, wonderful inner paths to a supernatural kind of happiness, when the first gift of natural existence is unhappy, as it so often proves itself to be.

With such relations between religion and happiness, it is perhaps not surprising that men come to regard the happiness which a religious belief affords as a proof of its truth. If a creed makes a man feel happy, he almost inevitably adopts it. Such a belief ought to be true; therefore it is true—such, rightly or wrongly, is one of the "immediate inferences" of the religious logic used by ordinary men.

> "The near presence of God's spirit," says a German writer,[31] "may be experienced in its reality—indeed *only* experienced. And the mark by which the spirit's existence and nearness are made irrefutably clear to those who have ever had the experience is the utterly incomparable *feeling of happiness* which is connected with the nearness, and which is therefore not only a possible and altogether proper feeling for us to have here below, but is the best and most indispensable

31 C. Hilty: Glück, dritter Theil, 1900, p. 18.

proof of God's reality. No other proof is equally convincing, and therefore happiness is the point from which every efficacious new theology should start."

In the hour immediately before us, I shall invite you to consider the simpler kinds of religious happiness, leaving the more complex sorts to be treated on a later day.

In many persons, happiness is congenital and irreclaimable. "Cosmic emotion" inevitably takes in them the form of enthusiasm and freedom. I speak not only of those who are animally happy. I mean those who, when unhappiness is offered or proposed to them, positively refuse to feel it, as if it were something mean and wrong. We find such persons in every age, passionately flinging themselves upon their sense of the goodness of life, in spite of the hardships of their own condition, and in spite of the sinister theologies into which they may be born. From the outset their religion is one of union with the divine. The heretics who went before the reformation are lavishly accused by the church writers of antinomian practices, just as the first Christians were accused of indulgence in orgies by the Romans. It is probable that there never has been a century in which the deliberate refusal to think ill of life has not been idealized by a sufficient number of persons to form sects, open or secret, who claimed all natural things to be permitted. Saint Augustine's maxim, *Dilige et quod vis fac*—if you but love [God], you may do as you incline—is morally one of the profoundest of observations, yet it is pregnant, for such persons, with passports beyond the bounds of conventional morality. According to their characters they have been refined or gross; but their belief has been at all times systematic enough to constitute a definite religious attitude. God was for them a giver of freedom, and the sting of evil was overcome. Saint Francis and his immediate disciples were, on the whole, of this company of spirits, of which there are of course infinite varieties. Rousseau in the earlier years of his writing, Diderot, B. de Saint Pierre, and many of the leaders of the eighteenth century anti-christian movement were of this optimistic type. They owed their influence to a certain authoritativeness in their feeling that Nature, if you will only trust her sufficiently, is absolutely good.

It is to be hoped that we all have some friend, perhaps more often feminine than masculine, and young than old, whose soul is of this sky-blue tint, whose affinities are rather with flowers and birds and all enchanting innocencies than with dark human passions, who can think no ill of man or God, and in whom religious gladness, being in possession from the outset, needs no deliverance from any antecedent burden.

"God has two families of children on this earth," says Francis W. Newman,[32] "*the once-born and the twice-born,*" and the once-born he describes as follows: "They see God, not as a strict Judge, not as a Glorious Potentate; but as the animating Spirit of a beautiful harmonious world, Beneficent and Kind, Merciful as well as

32 The Soul; its Sorrows and its Aspirations, 3d edition, 1852, pp. 89, 91.

Pure. The same characters generally have no metaphysical tendencies: they do not look back into themselves. Hence they are not distressed by their own imperfections: yet it would be absurd to call them self-righteous; for they hardly think of themselves *at all*. This childlike quality of their nature makes the opening of religion very happy to them: for they no more shrink from God, than a child from an emperor, before whom the parent trembles: in fact, they have no vivid conception of *any* of the qualities in which the severer Majesty of God consists.[33] He is to them the impersonation of Kindness and Beauty. They read his character, not in the disordered world of man, but in romantic and harmonious nature. Of human sin they know perhaps little in their own hearts and not very much in the world; and human suffering does but melt them to tenderness. Thus, when they approach God, no inward disturbance ensues; and without being as yet spiritual, they have a certain complacency and perhaps romantic sense of excitement in their simple worship."

In the Romish Church such characters find a more congenial soil to grow in than in Protestantism, whose fashions of feeling have been set by minds of a decidedly pessimistic order. But even in Protestantism they have been abundant enough; and in its recent "liberal" developments of Unitarianism and latitudinarianism generally, minds of this order have played and still are playing leading and constructive parts. Emerson himself is an admirable example. Theodore Parker is another—here are a couple of characteristic passages from Parker's correspondence.[34]

"Orthodox scholars say: 'In the heathen classics you find no consciousness of sin.' It is very true—God be thanked for it. They were conscious of wrath, of cruelty, avarice, drunkenness, lust, sloth, cowardice, and other actual vices, and struggled and got rid of the deformities, but they were not conscious of 'enmity against God,' and didn't sit down and whine and groan against non-existent evil. I have done wrong things enough in my life, and do them now; I miss the mark, draw bow, and try again. But I am not conscious of hating God, or man, or right, or love, and I know there is much 'health in me'; and in my body, even now, there dwelleth many a good thing, spite of consumption and Saint Paul." In another letter Parker writes: "I have swum in clear sweet waters all my days; and if sometimes they were a little cold, and the stream ran adverse and something rough, it was never too strong to be breasted and swum through. From the days of earliest boyhood, when I went stumbling through the grass, . . . up to the gray-bearded manhood of this time, there is none but has left me honey in the hive of memory that I now feed on for present delight. When I recall the years . . . I am filled with a sense of sweetness and wonder that such little things can make a mortal so exceedingly rich. But I must confess that the chiefest of all my delights is still the religious."

33 I once heard a lady describe the pleasure it gave her to think that she "could always cuddle up to God."

34 John Weiss: Life of Theodore Parker, i. 152, 32.

Another good expression of the "once-born" type of consciousness, developing straight and natural, with no element of morbid compunction or crisis, is contained in the answer of Dr. Edward Everett Hale, the eminent Unitarian preacher and writer, to one of Dr. Starbuck's circulars. I quote a part of it:—

> "I observe, with profound regret, the religious struggles which come into many biographies, as if almost essential to the formation of the hero. I ought to speak of these, to say that any man has an advantage, not to be estimated, who is born, as I was, into a family where the religion is simple and rational; who is trained in the theory of such a religion, so that he never knows, for an hour, what these religious or irreligious struggles are. I always knew God loved me, and I was always grateful to him for the world he placed me in. I always liked to tell him so, and was always glad to receive his suggestions to me. . . . I can remember perfectly that when I was coming to manhood, the half-philosophical novels of the time had a deal to say about the young men and maidens who were facing the 'problem of life.' I had no idea whatever what the problem of life was. To live with all my might seemed to me easy; to learn where there was so much to learn seemed pleasant and almost of course; to lend a hand, if one had a chance, natural; and if one did this, why, he enjoyed life because he could not help it, and without proving to himself that he ought to enjoy it. . . . A child who is early taught that he is God's child, that he may live and move and have his being in God, and that he has, therefore, infinite strength at hand for the conquering of any difficulty, will take life more easily, and probably will make more of it, than one who is told that he is born the child of wrath and wholly incapable of good."[35]

One can but recognize in such writers as these the presence of a temperament organically weighted on the side of cheer and fatally forbidden to linger, as those of opposite temperament linger, over the darker aspects of the universe. In some individuals optimism may become quasi-pathological. The capacity for even a transient sadness or a momentary humility seems cut off from them as by a kind of congenital anæsthesia.[36]

---

35 Starbuck: Psychology of Religion, pp. 305, 306.

36 "I know not to what physical laws philosophers will some day refer the feelings of melancholy. For myself, I find that they are the most voluptuous of all sensations," writes Saint Pierre, and accordingly he devotes a series of sections of his work on Nature to the Plaisirs de la Ruine, Plaisirs des Tombeaux, Ruines de la Nature, Plaisirs de la Solitude—each of them more optimistic than the last.

This finding of a luxury in woe is very common during adolescence. The truth-telling Marie Bashkirtseff expresses it well:—

"In this depression and dreadful uninterrupted suffering, I don't condemn life. On the contrary, I like it and find it good. Can you believe it? I find everything good and pleasant, even my tears, my grief. I enjoy weeping, I enjoy my despair. I enjoy being exasperated and sad. I feel as if these were so many diversions, and I love life in spite of them all. I want to live on. It would be cruel to have me die when I am so accommodating. I cry, I grieve, and at the same time I am pleased—no, not exactly that—I know not how to express it. But everything in life pleases me. I find everything agreeable, and in the very midst of my prayers for happiness, I find myself happy at being miserable. It is not I who undergo all this—my body weeps and cries; but something inside of me which is above me is glad of it all."

The supreme contemporary example of such an inability to feel evil is of course Walt Whitman.

> "His favorite occupation," writes his disciple, Dr. Bucke, "seemed to be strolling or sauntering about outdoors by himself, looking at the grass, the trees, the flowers, the vistas of light, the varying aspects of the sky, and listening to the birds, the crickets, the tree frogs, and all the hundreds of natural sounds. It was evident that these things gave him a pleasure far beyond what they give to ordinary people. Until I knew the man," continues Dr. Bucke, "it had not occurred to me that any one could derive so much absolute happiness from these things as he did. He was very fond of flowers, either wild or cultivated; liked all sorts. I think he admired lilacs and sunflowers just as much as roses. Perhaps, indeed, no man who ever lived liked so many things and disliked so few as Walt Whitman. All natural objects seemed to have a charm for him. All sights and sounds seemed to please him. He appeared to like (and I believe he did like) all the men, women, and children he saw (though I never knew him to say that he liked any one), but each who knew him felt that he liked him or her, and that he liked others also. I never knew him to argue or dispute, and he never spoke about money. He always justified, sometimes playfully, sometimes quite seriously, those who spoke harshly of himself or his writings, and I often thought he even took pleasure in the opposition of enemies. When I first knew [him], I used to think that he watched himself, and would not allow his tongue to give expression to fretfulness, antipathy, complaint, and remonstrance. It did not occur to me as possible that these mental states could be absent in him. After long observation, however, I satisfied myself that such absence or unconsciousness was entirely real. He never spoke deprecatingly of any nationality or class of men, or time in the world's history, or against any trades or occupations—not even against any animals, insects, or inanimate things, nor any of the laws of nature, nor any of the results of those laws, such as illness, deformity, and death. He never complained or grumbled either at the weather, pain, illness, or anything else. He never swore. He could not very well, since he never spoke in anger and apparently never was angry. He never exhibited fear, and I do not believe he ever felt it."[37]

Walt Whitman owes his importance in literature to the systematic expulsion from his writings of all contractile elements. The only sentiments he allowed himself to express were of the expansive order; and he expressed these in the first person, not as your mere monstrously conceited individual might so express them, but vicariously for all men, so that a passionate and mystic ontological emotion suffuses his words, and ends by persuading the reader that men and women, life and death, and all things are divinely good.

Thus it has come about that many persons to-day regard Walt Whitman as the restorer of the eternal natural religion. He has infected them with his own love of

---

Journal de Marie Bashkirtseff, i. 67.

37 R. M. Bucke: Cosmic Consciousness, pp. 182–186, abridged.

comrades, with his own gladness that he and they exist. Societies are actually formed for his cult; a periodical organ exists for its propagation, in which the lines of orthodoxy and heterodoxy are already beginning to be drawn;[38] hymns are written by others in his peculiar prosody; and he is even explicitly compared with the founder of the Christian religion, not altogether to the advantage of the latter.

Whitman is often spoken of as a "pagan." The word nowadays means sometimes the mere natural animal man without a sense of sin; sometimes it means a Greek or Roman with his own peculiar religious consciousness. In neither of these senses does it fitly define this poet. He is more than your mere animal man who has not tasted of the tree of good and evil. He is aware enough of sin for a swagger to be present in his indifference towards it, a conscious pride in his freedom from flexions and contractions, which your genuine pagan in the first sense of the word would never show.

*"I could turn and live with animals, they are so placid and self-contained,*
*I stand and look at them long and long;*
*They do not sweat and whine about their condition.*
*They do not lie awake in the dark and weep for their sins.*
*Not one is dissatisfied, not one is demented with the mania of owning things,*
*Not one kneels to another, nor to his kind that lived thousands of years ago,*
*Not one is respectable or unhappy over the whole earth."*[39]

No natural pagan could have written these well-known lines. But on the other hand Whitman is less than a Greek or Roman; for their consciousness, even in Homeric times, was full to the brim of the sad mortality of this sunlit world, and such a consciousness Walt Whitman resolutely refuses to adopt. When, for example, Achilles, about to slay Lycaon, Priam's young son, hears him sue for mercy, he stops to say:—

"Ah, friend, thou too must die: why thus lamentest thou? Patroclos too is dead, who was better far than thou.... Over me too hang death and forceful fate. There cometh morn or eve or some noonday when my life too some man shall take in battle, whether with spear he smite, or arrow from the string."[40]

Then Achilles savagely severs the poor boy's neck with his sword, heaves him by the foot into the Scamander, and calls to the fishes of the river to eat the white fat of Lycaon. Just as here the cruelty and the sympathy each ring true, and do not mix or interfere with one another, so did the Greeks and Romans keep all their sadnesses and gladnesses unmingled and entire. Instinctive good they did not reckon sin; nor

38 I refer to The Conservator, edited by Horace Traubel, and published monthly at Philadelphia.
39 Song of Myself, 32.
40 Iliad, XXI., E. Myers's translation.

had they any such desire to save the credit of the universe as to make them insist, as so many of *us* insist, that what immediately appears as evil must be "good in the making," or something equally ingenious. Good was good, and bad just bad, for the earlier Greeks. They neither denied the ills of nature—Walt Whitman's verse, "What is called good is perfect and what is called bad is just as perfect," would have been mere silliness to them—nor did they, in order to escape from those ills, invent "another and a better world" of the imagination, in which, along with the ills, the innocent goods of sense would also find no place. This integrity of the instinctive reactions, this freedom from all moral sophistry and strain, gives a pathetic dignity to ancient pagan feeling. And this quality Whitman's outpourings have not got. His optimism is too voluntary and defiant; his gospel has a touch of bravado and an affected twist,[41] and this diminishes its effect on many readers who yet are well disposed towards optimism, and on the whole quite willing to admit that in important respects Whitman is of the genuine lineage of the prophets.

If, then, we give the name of healthy-mindedness to the tendency which looks on all things and sees that they are good, we find that we must distinguish between a more involuntary and a more voluntary or systematic way of being healthy-minded. In its involuntary variety, healthy-mindedness is a way of feeling happy about things immediately. In its systematical variety, it is an abstract way of conceiving things as good. Every abstract way of conceiving things selects some one aspect of them as their essence for the time being, and disregards the other aspects. Systematic healthy-mindedness, conceiving good as the essential and universal aspect of being, deliberately excludes evil from its field of vision; and although, when thus nakedly stated, this might seem a difficult feat to perform for one who is intellectually sincere with himself and honest about facts, a little reflection shows that the situation is too complex to lie open to so simple a criticism.

In the first place, happiness, like every other emotional state, has blindness and insensibility to opposing facts given it as its instinctive weapon for self-protection against disturbance. When happiness is actually in possession, the thought of evil can no more acquire the feeling of reality than the thought of good can gain reality when melancholy rules. To the man actively happy, from whatever cause, evil simply cannot then and there be believed in. He must ignore it; and to the bystander he may then seem perversely to shut his eyes to it and hush it up.

But more than this: the hushing of it up may, in a perfectly candid and honest mind, grow into a deliberate religious policy, or *parti pris*. Much of what we call evil is due entirely to the way men take the phenomenon. It can so often be converted into a bracing and tonic good by a simple change of the sufferer's inner attitude from one of fear to one of fight; its sting so often departs and turns into a relish when,

41 "God is afraid of me!" remarked such a titanic-optimistic friend in my presence one morning when he was feeling particularly hearty and cannibalistic. The defiance of the phrase showed that a Christian education in humility still rankled in his breast.

after vainly seeking to shun it, we agree to face about and bear it cheerfully, that a man is simply bound in honor, with reference to many of the facts that seem at first to disconcert his peace, to adopt this way of escape. Refuse to admit their badness; despise their power; ignore their presence; turn your attention the other way; and so far as you yourself are concerned at any rate, though the facts may still exist, their evil character exists no longer. Since you make them evil or good by your own thoughts about them, it is the ruling of your thoughts which proves to be your principal concern.

The deliberate adoption of an optimistic turn of mind thus makes its entrance into philosophy. And once in, it is hard to trace its lawful bounds. Not only does the human instinct for happiness, bent on self-protection by ignoring, keep working in its favor, but higher inner ideals have weighty words to say. The attitude of unhappiness is not only painful, it is mean and ugly. What can be more base and unworthy than the pining, puling, mumping mood, no matter by what outward ills it may have been engendered? What is more injurious to others? What less helpful as a way out of the difficulty? It but fastens and perpetuates the trouble which occasioned it, and increases the total evil of the situation. At all costs, then, we ought to reduce the sway of that mood; we ought to scout it in ourselves and others, and never show it tolerance. But it is impossible to carry on this discipline in the subjective sphere without zealously emphasizing the brighter and minimizing the darker aspects of the objective sphere of things at the same time. And thus our resolution not to indulge in misery, beginning at a comparatively small point within ourselves, may not stop until it has brought the entire frame of reality under a systematic conception optimistic enough to be congenial with its needs.

In all this I say nothing of any mystical insight or persuasion that the total frame of things absolutely must be good. Such mystical persuasion plays an enormous part in the history of the religious consciousness, and we must look at it later with some care. But we need not go so far at present. More ordinary non-mystical conditions of rapture suffice for my immediate contention. All invasive moral states and passionate enthusiasms make one feelingless to evil in some direction. The common penalties cease to deter the patriot, the usual prudences are flung by the lover to the winds. When the passion is extreme, suffering may actually be gloried in, provided it be for the ideal cause, death may lose its sting, the grave its victory. In these states, the ordinary contrast of good and ill seems to be swallowed up in a higher denomination, an omnipotent excitement which engulfs the evil, and which the human being welcomes as the crowning experience of his life. This, he says, is truly to live, and I exult in the heroic opportunity and adventure.

The systematic cultivation of healthy-mindedness as a religious attitude is therefore consonant with important currents in human nature, and is anything but absurd. In fact, we all do cultivate it more or less, even when our professed theology should in consistency forbid it. We divert our attention from disease and death as much as we can; and the slaughter-houses and indecencies without end on which our life is founded are huddled out of sight and never mentioned, so that the world we recognize officially in literature and in society is a poetic fiction far handsomer and cleaner and better than the world that really is.[42]

The advance of liberalism, so-called, in Christianity, during the past fifty years, may fairly be called a victory of healthy-mindedness within the church over the morbidness with which the old hell-fire theology was more harmoniously related. We have now whole congregations whose preachers, far from magnifying our consciousness of sin, seem devoted rather to making little of it. They ignore, or even deny, eternal punishment, and insist on the dignity rather than on the depravity of man. They look at the continual preoccupation of the old-fashioned Christian with the salvation of his soul as something sickly and reprehensible rather than admirable; and a sanguine and "muscular" attitude, which to our forefathers would have seemed purely heathen, has become in their eyes an ideal element of Christian character. I am not asking whether or not they are right, I am only pointing out the change.

The persons to whom I refer have still retained for the most part their nominal connection with Christianity, in spite of their discarding of its more pessimistic theological elements. But in that "theory of evolution" which, gathering momentum for a century, has within the past twenty-five years swept so rapidly over Europe and America, we see the ground laid for a new sort of religion of Nature, which has entirely displaced Christianity from the thought of a large part of our generation. The idea of a universal evolution lends itself to a doctrine of general meliorism and progress which fits the religious needs of the healthy-minded so well that it seems almost as if it might have been created for their use. Accordingly we find "evolutionism" interpreted thus optimistically and embraced as a substitute for the religion they were born in, by a multitude of our contemporaries who have either been trained scientifically, or been fond of reading popular science, and who had already begun to be inwardly dissatisfied with what seemed to them the harshness and irrationality of the orthodox Christian scheme. As examples are better than descriptions, I will quote a document received in answer to Professor Starbuck's circular of questions. The writer's state of mind may by courtesy be called a religion, for it is his reaction on the whole nature of things, it is systematic and reflective, and it loyally binds him to certain inner ideals. I think you will recognize in him, coarse-meated and incapable of wounded spirit as he is, a sufficiently familiar contemporary type.

Q. *What does Religion mean to you?*

A. It means nothing; and it seems, so far as I can observe, useless to others. I am sixty-seven years of age and have resided in X. fifty years, and have been in business forty-five, consequently I have some little experience of life and men, and some

42 "As I go on in this life, day by day, I become more of a bewildered child; I cannot get used to this world, to procreation, to heredity, to sight, to hearing; the commonest things are a burthen. The prim, obliterated, polite surface of life, and the broad, bawdy, and orgiastic—or mænadic—foundations, form a spectacle to which no habit reconciles me." R. L. Stevenson: Letters, ii. 355.

women too, and I find that the most religious and pious people are as a rule those most lacking in uprightness and morality. The men who do not go to church or have any religious convictions are the best. Praying, singing of hymns, and sermonizing are pernicious—they teach us to rely on some supernatural power, when we ought to rely on ourselves. I *tee*totally disbelieve in a God. The God-idea was begotten in ignorance, fear, and a general lack of any knowledge of Nature. If I were to die now, being in a healthy condition for my age, both mentally and physically, I would just as lief, yes, rather, die with a hearty enjoyment of music, sport, or any other rational pastime. As a timepiece stops, we die—there being no immortality in either case.

Q. *What comes before your mind corresponding to the words God, Heaven, Angels, etc?*

A. Nothing whatever. I am a man without a religion. These words mean so much mythic bosh.

Q. *Have you had any experiences which appeared providential?*

A. None whatever. There is no agency of the superintending kind. A little judicious observation as well as knowledge of scientific law will convince any one of this fact.

Q. *What things work most strongly on your emotions?*

A. Lively songs and music; Pinafore instead of an Oratorio. I like Scott, Burns, Byron, Longfellow, especially Shakespeare, etc., etc. Of songs, the Star-Spangled Banner, America, Marseillaise, and all moral and soul-stirring songs, but wishy-washy hymns are my detestation. I greatly enjoy nature, especially fine weather, and until within a few years used to walk Sundays into the country, twelve miles often, with no fatigue, and bicycle forty or fifty. I have dropped the bicycle. I never go to church, but attend lectures when there are any good ones. All of my thoughts and cogitations have been of a healthy and cheerful kind, for instead of doubts and fears I see things as they are, for I endeavor to adjust myself to my environment. This I regard as the deepest law. Mankind is a progressive animal. I am satisfied he will have made a great advance over his present status a thousand years hence.

Q. *What is your notion of sin?*

A. It seems to me that sin is a condition, a disease, incidental to man's development not being yet advanced enough. Morbidness over it increases the disease. We should think that a million of years hence equity, justice, and mental and physical good order will be so fixed and organized that no one will have any idea of evil or sin.

Q. *What is your temperament?*

A. Nervous, active, wide-awake, mentally and physically. Sorry that Nature compels us to sleep at all.

If we are in search of a broken and a contrite heart, clearly we need not look to this brother. His contentment with the finite incases him like a lobster-shell and shields him from all morbid repining at his distance from the infinite. We have in him an excellent example of the optimism which may be encouraged by popular science.

To my mind a current far more important and interesting religiously than that which sets in from natural science towards healthy-mindedness is that which has recently poured over America and seems to be gathering force every day—I am ignorant what foothold it may yet have acquired in Great Britain—and to which, for the sake of having a brief designation, I will give the title of the "Mind-cure movement." There are various sects of this "New Thought," to use another of the names by which it calls itself; but their agreements are so profound that their differences may be neglected for my present purpose, and I will treat the movement, without apology, as if it were a simple thing.

It is a deliberately optimistic scheme of life, with both a speculative and a practical side. In its gradual development during the last quarter of a century, it has taken up into itself a number of contributory elements, and it must now be reckoned with as a genuine religious power. It has reached the stage, for example, when the demand for its literature is great enough for insincere stuff, mechanically produced for the market, to be to a certain extent supplied by publishers—a phenomenon never observed, I imagine, until a religion has got well past its earliest insecure beginnings.

One of the doctrinal sources of Mind-cure is the four Gospels; another is Emersonianism or New England transcendentalism; another is Berkeleyan idealism; another is spiritism, with its messages of "law" and "progress" and "development"; another the optimistic popular science evolutionism of which I have recently spoken; and, finally, Hinduism has contributed a strain. But the most characteristic feature of the mind-cure movement is an inspiration much more direct. The leaders in this faith have had an intuitive belief in the all-saving power of healthy-minded attitudes as such, in the conquering efficacy of courage, hope, and trust, and a correlative contempt for doubt, fear, worry, and all nervously precautionary states of mind.[43] Their belief has in a general way been corroborated by the practical experience of their disciples; and this experience forms to-day a mass imposing in amount.

The blind have been made to see, the halt to walk; lifelong invalids have had their health restored. The moral fruits have been no less remarkable. The deliberate adoption of a healthy-minded attitude has proved possible to many who never supposed they had it in them; regeneration of character has gone on on an extensive scale; and cheerfulness has been restored to countless homes. The indirect influence of this has been great. The mind-cure principles are beginning so to pervade the air that one catches their spirit at second-hand. One hears of the "Gospel of Relaxation," of the "Don't Worry Movement," of people who repeat to themselves, "Youth, health,

43 "Cautionary Verses for Children": this title of a much used work, published early in the nineteenth century, shows how far the muse of evangelical protestantism in England, with her mind fixed on the idea of danger, had at last drifted away from the original gospel freedom. Mind-cure might be briefly called a reaction against all that religion of chronic anxiety which marked the earlier part of our century in the evangelical circles of England and America.

vigor!" when dressing in the morning, as their motto for the day. Complaints of the weather are getting to be forbidden in many households; and more and more people are recognizing it to be bad form to speak of disagreeable sensations, or to make much of the ordinary inconveniences and ailments of life. These general tonic effects on public opinion would be good even if the more striking results were non-existent. But the latter abound so that we can afford to overlook the innumerable failures and self-deceptions that are mixed in with them (for in everything human failure is a matter of course), and we can also overlook the verbiage of a good deal of the mind-cure literature, some of which is so moonstruck with optimism and so vaguely expressed that an academically trained intellect finds it almost impossible to read it at all.

The plain fact remains that the spread of the movement has been due to practical fruits, and the extremely practical turn of character of the American people has never been better shown than by the fact that this, their only decidedly original contribution to the systematic philosophy of life, should be so intimately knit up with concrete therapeutics. To the importance of mind-cure the medical and clerical professions in the United States are beginning, though with much recalcitrancy and protesting, to open their eyes. It is evidently bound to develop still farther, both speculatively and practically, and its latest writers are far and away the ablest of the group.[44] It matters nothing that, just as there are hosts of persons who cannot pray, so there are greater hosts who cannot by any possibility be influenced by the mind-curers' ideas. For our immediate purpose, the important point is that so large a number should exist who *can* be so influenced. They form a psychic type to be studied with respect.[45]

---

44 I refer to Mr. Horatio W. Dresser and Mr. Henry Wood, especially the former. Mr. Dresser's works are published by G. P. Putnam's Sons, New York and London; Mr. Wood's by Lee & Shepard, Boston.

45 Lest my own testimony be suspected, I will quote another reporter, Dr. H. H. Goddard, of Clark University, whose thesis on "the Effects of Mind on Body as evidenced by Faith Cures" is published in the American Journal of Psychology for 1899 (vol. x.). This critic, after a wide study of the facts, concludes that the cures by mind-cure exist, but are in no respect different from those now officially recognized in medicine as cures by suggestion; and the end of his essay contains an interesting physiological speculation as to the way in which the suggestive ideas may work (p. 67 of the reprint). As regards the general phenomenon of mental cure itself, Dr. Goddard writes: "In spite of the severe criticism we have made of reports of cure, there still remains a vast amount of material, showing a powerful influence of the mind in disease. Many cases are of diseases that have been diagnosed and treated by the best physicians of the country, or which prominent hospitals have tried their hand at curing, but without success. People of culture and education have been treated by this method with satisfactory results. Diseases of long standing have been ameliorated, and even cured. . . . We have traced the mental element through primitive medicine and folk-medicine of to-day, patent medicine, and witchcraft. We are convinced that it is impossible to account for the existence of these practices, if they did not cure disease, and that if they cured disease, it must have been the mental element that was effective. The same argument applies to those modern schools of mental therapeutics—Divine Healing and Christian Science. It is hardly conceivable that the large body of intelligent people who comprise the body known distinctively as Mental Scientists should continue to exist if the whole thing were a delusion. It is not a thing of a day; it is not confined to a few; it is not local. It is true that many failures are recorded, but that only adds to the argument. There must be many and striking successes to

To come now to a little closer quarters with their creed. The fundamental pillar on which it rests is nothing more than the general basis of all religious experience, the fact that man has a dual nature, and is connected with two spheres of thought, a shallower and a profounder sphere, in either of which he may learn to live more habitually. The shallower and lower sphere is that of the fleshly sensations, instincts, and desires, of egotism, doubt, and the lower personal interests. But whereas Christian theology has always considered *frowardness* to be the essential vice of this part of human nature, the mind-curers say that the mark of the beast in it is *fear;* and this is what gives such an entirely new religious turn to their persuasion.

"Fear," to quote a writer of the school, "has had its uses in the evolutionary process, and seems to constitute the whole of forethought in most animals; but that it should remain any part of the mental equipment of human civilized life is an absurdity. I find that the fear element of forethought is not stimulating to those more civilized persons to whom duty and attraction are the natural motives, but is weakening and deterrent. As soon as it becomes unnecessary, fear becomes a positive deterrent, and should be entirely removed, as dead flesh is removed from living tissue. To assist in the analysis of fear, and in the denunciation of its expressions, I have coined the word *fearthought* to stand for the unprofitable element of forethought, and have defined the word 'worry' as *fearthought in contradistinction to forethought.* I have also defined fearthought as the *self-imposed or self-permitted suggestion of inferiority,* in order to place it where it really belongs, in the category of harmful, unnecessary, and therefore not respectable things."[46]

The "misery-habit," the "martyr-habit," engendered by the prevalent "fearthought," get pungent criticism from the mind-cure writers:—

> "Consider for a moment the habits of life into which we are born. There are certain social conventions or customs and alleged requirements, there is a theological bias, a general view of the world. There are conservative ideas in regard to our early training, our education, marriage, and occupation in life. Following close upon this, there is a long series of anticipations, namely, that we shall suffer certain children's diseases, diseases of middle life, and of old age; the thought that we shall grow old, lose our faculties, and again become childlike; while crowning all is the fear of death. Then there is a long line of particular fears and

counterbalance the failures, otherwise the failures would have ended the delusion. . . . Christian Science, Divine Healing, or Mental Science do not, and never can in the very nature of things, cure all diseases; nevertheless, the practical applications of the general principles of the broadest mental science will tend to prevent disease. . . . We do find sufficient evidence to convince us that the proper reform in mental attitude would relieve many a sufferer of ills that the ordinary physician cannot touch; would even delay the approach of death to many a victim beyond the power of absolute cure, and the faithful adherence to a truer philosophy of life will keep many a man well, and give the doctor time to devote to alleviating ills that are unpreventable" (pp. 33, 34 of reprint).

46 Horace Fletcher: Happiness as found in Forethought *minus* Fearthought, Menticulture Series, ii. Chicago and New York, Stone. 1897, pp. 21–25, abridged.

trouble-bearing expectations, such, for example, as ideas associated with certain articles of food, the dread of the east wind, the terrors of hot weather, the aches and pains associated with cold weather, the fear of catching cold if one sits in a draught, the coming of hay-fever upon the 14th of August in the middle of the day, and so on through a long list of fears, dreads, worriments, anxieties, anticipations, expectations, pessimisms, morbidities, and the whole ghostly train of fateful shapes which our fellow-men, and especially physicians, are ready to help us conjure up, an array worthy to rank with Bradley's 'unearthly ballet of bloodless categories.'

"Yet this is not all. This vast array is swelled by innumerable volunteers from daily life—the fear of accident, the possibility of calamity, the loss of property, the chance of robbery, of fire, or the outbreak of war. And it is not deemed sufficient to fear for ourselves. When a friend is taken ill, we must forthwith fear the worst and apprehend death. If one meets with sorrow . . . sympathy means to enter into and increase the suffering."[47]

"Man," to quote another writer, "often has fear stamped upon him before his entrance into the outer world; he is reared in fear; all his life is passed in bondage to fear of disease and death, and thus his whole mentality becomes cramped, limited, and depressed, and his body follows its shrunken pattern and specification. . . . Think of the millions of sensitive and responsive souls among our ancestors who have been under the dominion of such a perpetual nightmare! Is it not surprising that health exists at all? Nothing but the boundless divine love, exuberance, and vitality, constantly poured in, even though unconsciously to us, could in some degree neutralize such an ocean of morbidity."[48]

Although the disciples of the mind-cure often use Christian terminology, one sees from such quotations how widely their notion of the fall of man diverges from that of ordinary Christians.[49]

Their notion of man's higher nature is hardly less divergent, being decidedly pantheistic. The spiritual in man appears in the mind-cure philosophy as partly

47 H. W. Dresser: Voices of Freedom, New York, 1899, p. 38.

48 Henry Wood: Ideal Suggestion through Mental Photography, Boston, 1899, p. 54.

49 Whether it differs so much from Christ's own notion is for the exegetists to decide. According to Harnack, Jesus felt about evil and disease much as our mind-curers do. "What is the answer which Jesus sends to John the Baptist?" asks Harnack, and says it is this: "'The blind see, and the lame walk, the lepers are cleansed, and the deaf hear, the dead rise up, and the gospel is preached to the poor.' That is the 'coming of the kingdom,' or rather in these saving works the kingdom is already there. By the overcoming and removal of misery, of need, of sickness, by these actual effects John is to see that the new time has arrived. The casting out of devils is only a part of this work of redemption, *but Jesus points to that as the sense and seal of his mission*. Thus to the wretched, sick, and poor did he address himself, but not as a moralist, and without a trace of sentimentalism. He never makes groups and departments of the ills; he never spends time in asking whether the sick one 'deserves' to be cured; and it never occurs to him to sympathize with the pain or the death. He nowhere says that sickness is a beneficent infliction, and that evil has a healthy use. No, he calls sickness sickness and health health. All evil, all wretchedness, is for him something dreadful; it is of the great kingdom of Satan; but he feels the power of the Saviour within him. He knows that advance is possible only when weakness is overcome, when sickness is made well." Das Wesen des Christenthums, 1900, p. 39.

conscious, but chiefly subconscious; and through the subconscious part of it we are already one with the Divine without any miracle of grace, or abrupt creation of a new inner man. As this view is variously expressed by different writers, we find in it traces of Christian mysticism, of transcendental idealism, of vedantism, and of the modern psychology of the subliminal self. A quotation or two will put us at the central point of view:—

> "The great central fact of the universe is that spirit of infinite life and power that is back of all, that manifests itself in and through all. This spirit of infinite life and power that is back of all is what I call God. I care not what term you may use, be it Kindly Light, Providence, the Over-Soul, Omnipotence, or whatever term may be most convenient, so long as we are agreed in regard to the great central fact itself. God then fills the universe alone, so that all is from Him and in Him, and there is nothing that is outside. He is the life of our life, our very life itself. We are partakers of the life of God; and though we differ from Him in that we are individualized spirits, while He is the Infinite Spirit, including us, as well as all else beside, yet in essence the life of God and the life of man are identically the same, and so are one. They differ not in essence or quality; they differ in degree.
>
> "The great central fact in human life is the coming into a conscious vital realization of our oneness with this Infinite Life, and the opening of ourselves fully to this divine inflow. In just the degree that we come into a conscious realization of our oneness with the Infinite Life, and open ourselves to this divine inflow, do we actualize in ourselves the qualities and powers of the Infinite Life, do we make ourselves channels through which the Infinite Intelligence and Power can work. In just the degree in which you realize your oneness with the Infinite Spirit, you will exchange dis-ease for ease, inharmony for harmony, suffering and pain for abounding health and strength. To recognize our own divinity, and our intimate relation to the Universal, is to attach the belts of our machinery to the powerhouse of the Universe. One need remain in hell no longer than one chooses to; we can rise to any heaven we ourselves choose: and when we choose so to rise, all the higher powers of the Universe combine to help us heavenward."[50]

Let me now pass from these abstracter statements to some more concrete accounts of experience with the mind-cure religion. I have many answers from correspondents—the only difficulty is to choose. The first two whom I shall quote are my personal friends. One of them, a woman, writing as follows, expresses well the feeling of continuity with the Infinite Power, by which all mind-cure disciples are inspired.

"The first underlying cause of all sickness, weakness, or depression is the *human sense of separateness* from that Divine Energy which we call God. The soul which

---

50 R. W. Trine: In Tune with the Infinite, 26th thousand, N. Y., 1899. I have strung scattered passages together.

can feel and affirm in serene but jubilant confidence, as did the Nazarene: 'I and my Father are one,' has no further need of healer, or of healing. This is the whole truth in a nutshell, and other foundation for wholeness can no man lay than this fact of impregnable divine union. Disease can no longer attack one whose feet are planted on this rock, who feels hourly, momently, the influx of the Deific Breath. If one with Omnipotence, how can weariness enter the consciousness, how illness assail that indomitable spark?

"This possibility of annulling forever the law of fatigue has been abundantly proven in my own case; for my earlier life bears a record of many, many years of bedridden invalidism, with spine and lower limbs paralyzed. My thoughts were no more impute than they are to-day, although my belief in the necessity of illness was dense and unenlightened; but since my resurrection in the flesh, I have worked as a healer unceasingly for fourteen years without a vacation, and can truthfully assert that I have never known a moment of fatigue or pain, although coming in touch constantly with excessive weakness, illness, and disease of all kinds. For how can a conscious part of Deity be sick?—since 'Greater is he that is *with* us than all that can strive against us.'"

My second correspondent, also a woman, sends me the following statement:—

> "Life seemed difficult to me at one time. I was always breaking down, and had several attacks of what is called nervous prostration, with terrible insomnia, being on the verge of insanity; besides having many other troubles, especially of the digestive organs. I had been sent away from home in charge of doctors, had taken all the narcotics, stopped all work, been fed up, and in fact knew all the doctors within reach. But I never recovered permanently till this New Thought took possession of me.
>
> "I think that the one thing which impressed me most was learning the fact that we must be in absolutely constant relation or mental touch (this word is to me very expressive) with that essence of life which permeates all and which we call God. This is almost unrecognizable unless we live it into ourselves *actually*, that is, by a constant turning to the very innermost, deepest consciousness of our real selves or of God in us, for illumination from within, just as we turn to the sun for light, warmth, and invigoration without. When you do this consciously, realizing that to turn inward to the light within you is to live in the presence of God or your divine self, you soon discover the unreality of the objects to which you have hitherto been turning and which have engrossed you without.
>
> "I have come to disregard the meaning of this attitude for bodily health *as such*, because that comes of itself, as an incidental result, and cannot be found by any special mental act or desire to have it, beyond that general attitude of mind I have referred to above. That which we usually make the object of life, those outer things we are all so wildly seeking, which we so often live and die for, but which then do not give us peace and happiness, they should all come of themselves as accessory, and as the mere outcome or natural result of a far higher life sunk deep in the bosom of the spirit. This life is the real seeking of

the kingdom of God, the desire for his supremacy in our hearts, so that all else comes as that which shall be 'added unto you'—as quite incidental and as a surprise to us, perhaps; and yet it is the proof of the reality of the perfect poise in the very centre of our being.

"When I say that we commonly make the object of our life that which we should not work for primarily, I mean many things which the world considers praiseworthy and excellent, such as success in business, fame as author or artist, physician or lawyer, or renown in philanthropic undertakings. Such things should be results, not objects. I would also include pleasures of many kinds which seem harmless and good at the time, and are pursued because many accept them—I mean conventionalities, sociabilities, and fashions in their various development, these being mostly approved by the masses, although they may be unreal, and even unhealthy superfluities."

Here is another case, more concrete, also that of a woman. I read you these cases without comment—they express so many varieties of the state of mind we are studying.

"I had been a sufferer from my childhood till my fortieth year. [Details of ill-health are given which I omit.] I had been in Vermont several months hoping for good from the change of air, but steadily growing weaker, when one day during the latter part of October, while resting in the afternoon, I suddenly heard as it were these words: 'You will be healed and do a work you never dreamed of.' These words were impressed upon my mind with such power I said at once that only God could have put them there. I believed them in spite of myself and of my suffering and weakness, which continued until Christmas, when I returned to Boston. Within two days a young friend offered to take me to a mental healer (this was January 7, 1881). The healer said: 'There is nothing but Mind; we are expressions of the One Mind; body is only a mortal belief; as a man thinketh so is he.' I could not accept all she said, but I translated all that was there for *me* in this way: 'There is nothing but God; I am created by Him, and am absolutely dependent upon Him; mind is given me to use; and by just so much of it as I will put upon the thought of right action in body I shall be lifted out of bondage to my ignorance and fear and past experience.' That day I commenced accordingly to take a little of every food provided for the family, constantly saying to myself: 'The Power that created the stomach must take care of what I have eaten.' By holding these suggestions through the evening I went to bed and fell asleep, saying: 'I am soul, spirit, just one with God's Thought of me,' and slept all night without waking, for the first time in several years [the distress-turns had usually recurred about two o'clock in the night]. I felt the next day like an escaped prisoner, and believed I had found the secret that would in time give me perfect health. Within ten days I was able to eat anything provided for others, and after two weeks I began to have my own positive mental suggestions of Truth, which were to me like stepping-stones. I will note a few of them; they came about two weeks apart.

"1st. I am Soul, therefore it is well with me.

"2d. I am Soul, therefore I *am* well.

"3d. A sort of inner vision of myself as a four-footed beast with a protuberance on every part of my body where I had suffering, with my own face, begging me to acknowledge it as myself. I resolutely fixed my attention on being well, and refused to even look at my old self in this form.

"4th. Again the vision of the beast far in the background, with faint voice. Again refusal to acknowledge.

"5th. Once more the vision, but only of my eyes with the longing look; and again the refusal. Then came the conviction, the inner consciousness, that I was perfectly well and always had been, for I was Soul, an expression of God's Perfect Thought. That was to me the perfect and completed separation between what I was and what I appeared to be. I succeeded in never losing sight after this of my real being, by constantly affirming this truth, and by degrees (though it took me two years of hard work to get there) *I expressed health continuously throughout my whole body.*

"In my subsequent nineteen years' experience I have never known this Truth to fail when I applied it, though in my ignorance I have often failed to apply it, but through my failures I have learned the simplicity and trustfulness of the little child."

But I fear that I risk tiring you by so many examples, and I must lead you back to philosophic generalities again. You see already by such records of experience how impossible it is not to class mind-cure as primarily a religious movement. Its doctrine of the oneness of our life with God's life is in fact quite indistinguishable from an interpretation of Christ's message which in these very Gifford lectures has been defended by some of your very ablest Scottish religious philosophers.[51]

But philosophers usually profess to give a quasi-logical explanation of the existence of evil, whereas of the general fact of evil in the world, the existence of the

51 The Cairds, for example. In Edward Caird's Glasgow Lectures of 1890–92 passages like this abound:—

"The declaration made in the beginning of the ministry of Jesus that 'the time is fulfilled, and the kingdom of heaven is at hand,' passes with scarce a break into the announcement that 'the kingdom of God is among you'; and the importance of this announcement is asserted to be such that it makes, so to speak, a difference *in kind* between the greatest saints and prophets who lived under the previous reign of division, and 'the least in the kingdom of heaven.' The highest ideal is brought close to men and declared to be within their reach, they are called on to be 'perfect as their Father in heaven is perfect.' The sense of alienation and distance from God which had grown upon the pious in Israel just in proportion as they had learned to look upon Him as no mere national divinity, but as a God of justice who would punish Israel for its sin as certainly as Edom or Moab, is declared to be no longer in place; and the typical form of Christian prayer points to the abolition of the contrast between this world and the next which through all the history of the Jews had continually been growing wider: 'As in heaven, so on earth.' The sense of the division of man from God, as a finite being from the Infinite, as weak and sinful from the Omnipotent Goodness, is not indeed lost; but it can no longer overpower the consciousness of oneness. The terms 'Son' and 'Father' at once state the opposition and mark its limit. They show that it is not an absolute opposition, but one which presupposes an indestructible principle of unity, that can and must become a principle of reconciliation." The Evolution of Religion, ii. pp. 146, 147.

selfish, suffering, timorous finite consciousness, the mind-curers, so far as I am acquainted with them, profess to give no speculative explanation. Evil is empirically there for them as it is for everybody, but the practical point of view predominates, and it would ill agree with the spirit of their system to spend time in worrying over it as a "mystery" or "problem," or in "laying to heart" the lesson of its experience, after the manner of the Evangelicals. Don't reason about it, as Dante says, but give a glance and pass beyond! It is Avidhya, ignorance! something merely to be outgrown and left behind, transcended and forgotten. Christian Science so-called, the sect of Mrs. Eddy, is the most radical branch of mind-cure in its dealings with evil. For it evil is simply a *lie*, and any one who mentions it is a liar. The optimistic ideal of duty forbids us to pay it the compliment even of explicit attention. Of course, as our next lectures will show us, this is a bad speculative omission, but it is intimately linked with the practical merits of the system we are examining. Why regret a philosophy of evil, a mind-curer would ask us, if I can put you in possession of a life of good?

After all, it is the life that tells; and mind-cure has developed a living system of mental hygiene which may well claim to have thrown all previous literature of the *Diätetik der Seele* into the shade. This system is wholly and exclusively compacted of optimism: "Pessimism leads to weakness. Optimism leads to power." "Thoughts are things," as one of the most vigorous mind-cure writers prints in bold type at the bottom of each of his pages; and if your thoughts are of health, youth, vigor, and success, before you know it these things will also be your outward portion. No one can fail of the regenerative influence of optimistic thinking, pertinaciously pursued. Every man owns indefeasibly this inlet to the divine. Fear, on the contrary, and all the contracted and egoistic modes of thought, are inlets to destruction. Most mind-curers here bring in a doctrine that thoughts are "forces," and that, by virtue of a law that like attracts like, one man's thoughts draw to themselves as allies all the thoughts of the same character that exist the world over. Thus one gets, by one's thinking, reinforcements from elsewhere for the realization of one's desires; and the great point in the conduct of life is to get the heavenly forces on one's side by opening one's own mind to their influx.

On the whole, one is struck by a psychological similarity between the mind-cure movement and the Lutheran and Wesleyan movements. To the believer in moralism and works, with his anxious query, "What shall I do to be saved?" Luther and Wesley replied: "You are saved now, if you would but believe it." And the mind-curers come with precisely similar words of emancipation. They speak, it is true, to persons for whom the conception of salvation has lost its ancient theological meaning, but who labor nevertheless with the same eternal human difficulty. *Things are wrong with them;* and "What shall I do to be clear, right, sound, whole, well?" is the form of their question. And the answer is: "You *are* well, sound, and clear already, if you did but know it." "The whole matter may be summed up in one sentence," says one of the authors whom I have already quoted, *"God is well, and so are you.* You must awaken to the knowledge of your real being."

The adequacy of their message to the mental needs of a large fraction of mankind is what gave force to those earlier gospels. Exactly the same adequacy holds in the case of the mind-cure message, foolish as it may sound upon its surface; and seeing its rapid growth in influence, and its therapeutic triumphs, one is tempted to ask whether it may not be destined (probably by very reason of the crudity and extravagance of many of its manifestations[52]) to play a part almost as great in the evolution of the popular religion of the future as did those earlier movements in their day.

But I here fear that I may begin to "jar upon the nerves" of some of the members of this academic audience. Such contemporary vagaries, you may think, should hardly take so large a place in dignified Gifford lectures. I can only beseech you to have patience. The whole outcome of these lectures will, I imagine, be the emphasizing to your mind of the enormous diversities which the spiritual lives of different men exhibit. Their wants, their susceptibilities, and their capacities all vary and must be classed under different heads. The result is that we have really different types of religious experience; and, seeking in these lectures closer acquaintance with the healthy-minded type, we must take it where we find it in most radical form. The psychology of individual types of character has hardly begun even to be sketched as yet—our lectures may possibly serve as a crumb-like contribution to the structure. The first thing to bear in mind (especially if we ourselves belong to the clerico-academic-scientific type, the officially and conventionally "correct" type, "the deadly respectable" type, for which to ignore others is a besetting temptation) is that nothing can be more stupid than to bar out phenomena from our notice, merely because we are incapable of taking part in anything like them ourselves.

Now the history of Lutheran salvation by faith, of methodistic conversions, and of what I call the mind-cure movement seems to prove the existence of numerous persons in whom—at any rate at a certain stage in their development—a change of character for the better, so far from being facilitated by the rules laid down by official moralists, will take place all the more successfully if those rules be exactly reversed. Official moralists advise us never to relax our strenuousness. "Be vigilant, day and night," they adjure us; "hold your passive tendencies in check; shrink from no effort; keep your will like a bow always bent." But the persons I speak of find that all this conscious effort leads to nothing but failure and vexation in their hands, and only makes them twofold more the children of hell they were before. The tense and voluntary attitude becomes in them an impossible fever and torment. Their machinery refuses to run at all when the bearings are made so hot and the belts so tight.

Under these circumstances the way to success, as vouched for by innumerable authentic personal narrations, is by an anti-moralistic method, by the "surrender"

52 It remains to be seen whether the school of Mr. Dresser, which assumes more and more the form of mind-cure experience and academic philosophy mutually impregnating each other, will score the practical triumphs of the less critical and rational sects.

of which I spoke in my second lecture. Passivity, not activity; relaxation, not intentness, should be now the rule. Give up the feeling of responsibility, let go your hold, resign the care of your destiny to higher powers, be genuinely indifferent as to what becomes of it all, and you will find not only that you gain a perfect inward relief, but often also, in addition, the particular goods you sincerely thought you were renouncing. This is the salvation through self-despair, the dying to be truly born, of Lutheran theology, the passage into *nothing* of which Jacob Behmen writes. To get to it, a critical point must usually be passed, a corner turned within one. Something must give way, a native hardness must break down and liquefy; and this event (as we shall abundantly see hereafter) is frequently sudden and automatic, and leaves on the Subject an impression that he has been wrought on by an external power.

Whatever its ultimate significance may prove to be, this is certainly one fundamental form of human experience. Some say that the capacity or incapacity for it is what divides the religious from the merely moralistic character. With those who undergo it in its fullness, no criticism avails to cast doubt on its reality. They *know;* for they have actually *felt* the higher powers, in giving up the tension of their personal will.

A story which revivalist preachers often tell is that of a man who found himself at night slipping down the side of a precipice. At last he caught a branch which stopped his fall, and remained clinging to it in misery for hours. But finally his fingers had to loose their hold, and with a despairing farewell to life, he let himself drop. He fell just six inches. If he had given up the struggle earlier, his agony would have been spared. As the mother earth received him, so, the preachers tell us, will the everlasting arms receive *us* if we confide absolutely in them, and give up the hereditary habit of relying on our personal strength, with its precautions that cannot shelter and safeguards that never save.

The mind-curers have given the widest scope to this sort of experience. They have demonstrated that a form of regeneration by relaxing, by letting go, psychologically indistinguishable from the Lutheran justification by faith and the Wesleyan acceptance of free grace, is within the reach of persons who have no conviction of sin and care nothing for the Lutheran theology. It is but giving your little private convulsive self a rest, and finding that a greater Self is there. The results, slow or sudden, or great or small, of the combined optimism and expectancy, the regenerative phenomena which ensue on the abandonment of effort, remain firm facts of human nature, no matter whether we adopt a theistic, a pantheistic-idealistic, or a medical-materialistic view of their ultimate causal explanation.[53]

---

53 The theistic explanation is by divine grace, which creates a new nature within one the moment the old nature is sincerely given up. The pantheistic explanation (which is that of most mind-curers) is by the merging of the narrower private self into the wider or greater self, the spirit of the universe (which is your own "subconscious" self), the moment the isolating barriers of mistrust and anxiety are removed. The medico-materialistic explanation is that simpler cerebral processes act more freely where they are left to act automatically by the shunting-out of physiologically (though in this instance not spiritually) "higher" ones which, seeking to regulate, only succeed in inhibiting results.—Whether this

When we take up the phenomena of revivalistic conversion, we shall learn something more about all this. Meanwhile I will say a brief word about the mind-curer's *methods.*

They are of course largely suggestive. The suggestive influence of environment plays an enormous part in all spiritual education. But the word "suggestion," having acquired official status, is unfortunately already beginning to play in many quarters the part of a wet blanket upon investigation, being used to fend off all inquiry into the varying susceptibilities of individual cases. "Suggestion" is only another name for the power of ideas, *so far as they prove efficacious over belief and conduct.* Ideas efficacious over some people prove inefficacious over others. Ideas efficacious at some times and in some human surroundings are not so at other times and elsewhere. The ideas of Christian churches are not efficacious in the therapeutic direction to-day, whatever they may have been in earlier centuries; and when the whole question is as to why the salt has lost its savor here or gained it there, the mere blank waving of the word "suggestion" as if it were a banner gives no light. Dr. Goddard, whose candid psychological essay on Faith Cures ascribes them to nothing but ordinary suggestion, concludes by saying that "Religion [and by this he seems to mean our popular Christianity] has in it all there is in mental therapeutics, and has it in its best form. Living up to [our religious] ideas will do anything for us that can be done." And this in spite of the actual fact that the popular Christianity does absolutely *nothing*, or did nothing until mind-cure came to the rescue.[54]

---

third explanation might, in a psycho-physical account of the universe, be combined with either of the others may be left an open question here.

54 Within the churches a disposition has always prevailed to regard sickness as a visitation; something sent by God for our good, either as chastisement, as warning, or as opportunity for exercising virtue, and, in the Catholic Church, of earning "merit." "Illness," says a good Catholic writer P. Lejeune: Introd. à la Vie Mystique, 1899, p. 218), "is the most excellent corporeal mortifications, the mortification which one has not one's self chosen, which is imposed directly by God, and is the direct expression of his will. 'If other mortifications are of silver,' Mgr. Gay says, 'this one is of gold; since although it comes of ourselves, coming as it does of original sin, still on its greater side, as coming (like all that happens) from the providence of God, it is of divine manufacture. And how just are its blows! And how efficacious it is! . . . I do not hesitate to say that patience in a long illness is mortification's very masterpiece, and consequently the triumph of mortified souls.' " According to this view, disease should in any case be submissively accepted, and it might under certain circumstances even be blasphemous to wish it away.

Of course there have been exceptions to this, and cures by special miracle have at all times been recognized within the church's pale, almost all the great saints having more or less performed them. It was one of the heresies of Edward Irving, to maintain them still to be possible. An extremely pure faculty of healing after confession and conversion on the patient's part, and prayer on the priest's, was quite spontaneously developed in the German pastor, Joh. Christoph Blumhardt, in the early forties and exerted during nearly thirty years. Blumhardt's Life by Zündel (5th edition, Zurich, 1887) gives in chapters ix., x., xi., and xvii. a pretty full account of his healing activity, which he invariably ascribed to direct divine interposition. Blumhardt was a singularly pure, simple, and non-fanatical character, and in this part of his work followed no previous model. In Chicago to-day we have the case of Dr. J. A. Dowie, a Scottish Baptist preacher, whose weekly "Leaves of Healing" were in the year of grace 1900 in their sixth volume, and who, although he denounces the cures wrought in other sects as "diabolical counterfeits" of his own exclusively "Divine Healing," must on the whole be counted into the mind-cure

An idea, to be suggestive, must come to the individual with the force of a revelation. The mind-cure with its gospel of healthy-mindedness has come as a revelation to many whose hearts the church Christianity had left hardened. It has let loose their springs of higher life. In what can the originality of any religious movement consist, save in finding a channel, until then sealed up, through which those springs may be set free in some group of human beings?

The force of personal faith, enthusiasm, and example, and above all the force of novelty, are always the prime suggestive agency in this kind of success. If mind-cure should ever become official, respectable, and intrenched, these elements of suggestive efficacy will be lost. In its acuter stages every religion must be a homeless Arab of the desert. The church knows this well enough, with its everlasting inner struggle of the acute religion of the few against the chronic religion of the many, indurated into an obstructiveness worse than that which irreligion opposes to the movings of the Spirit. "We may pray," says Jonathan Edwards, "concerning all those saints that are not lively Christians, that they may either be enlivened, or taken away; if that be true that is often said by some at this day, that these cold dead saints do more hurt than natural men, and lead more souls to hell, and that it would be well for mankind if they were all dead."[55]

The next condition of success is the apparent existence, in large numbers, of minds who unite healthy-mindedness with readiness for regeneration by letting go. Protestantism has been too pessimistic as regards the natural man, Catholicism has been too legalistic and moralistic, for either the one or the other to appeal in any generous way to the type of character formed of this peculiar mingling of elements. However few of us here present may belong to such a type, it is now evident that it forms a specific moral combination, well represented in the world.

Finally, mind-cure has made what in our protestant countries is an unprecedentedly great use of the subconscious life. To their reasoned advice and dogmatic assertion, its founders have added systematic exercise in passive relaxation, concentration, and meditation, and have even invoked something like hypnotic practice. I quote some passages at random:—

> "The value, the potency of ideals is the great practical truth on which the New Thought most strongly insists—the development namely from within outward, from small to great.[56] Consequently one's thought should be centred on the ideal outcome, even though this trust be literally like a step in the dark.[57] To attain the ability thus effectively to direct the mind, the New Thought advises the practice

---

movement. In mind-cure circles the fundamental article of faith is that disease should never be accepted. It is wholly of the pit. God wants us to be absolutely healthy, and we should not tolerate ourselves on any lower terms.

55 Edwards, from whose book on the Revival in New England I quote these words, dissuades from such a use of prayer, but it is easy to see that he enjoys making his thrust at the cold dead church members.

56 H. W. Dresser: Voices of Freedom, 46.

57 Dresser: Living by the Spirit, 58.

of concentration, or in other words, the attainment of self-control. One is to learn to marshal the tendencies of the mind, so that they may be held together as a unit by the chosen ideal. To this end, one should set apart times for silent meditation, by one's self, preferably in a room where the surroundings are favorable to spiritual thought. In New Thought terms, this is called 'entering the silence.'"[58]

"The time will come when in the busy office or on the noisy street you can enter into the silence by simply drawing the mantle of your own thoughts about you and realizing that there and everywhere the Spirit of Infinite Life, Love, Wisdom, Peace, Power, and Plenty is guiding, keeping, protecting, leading you. This is the spirit of continual prayer.[59] One of the most intuitive men we ever met had a desk at a city office where several other gentlemen were doing business constantly, and often talking loudly. Entirely undisturbed by the many various sounds about him, this self-centred faithful man would, in any moment of perplexity, draw the curtains of privacy so completely about him that he would be as fully inclosed in his own psychic aura, and thereby as effectually removed from all distractions, as though he were alone in some primeval wood. Taking his difficulty with him into the mystic silence in the form of a direct question, to which he expected a certain answer, he would remain utterly passive until the reply came, and never once through many years' experience did he find himself disappointed or misled."[60]

Wherein, I should like to know, does this *intrinsically* differ from the practice of "recollection" which plays so great a part in Catholic discipline? Otherwise called the practice of the presence of God (and so known among ourselves, as for instance in Jeremy Taylor), it is thus defined by the eminent teacher Alvarez de Paz in his work on Contemplation.

"It is the recollection of God, the thought of God, which in all places and circumstances makes us see him present, lets us commune respectfully and lovingly with him, and fills us with desire and affection for him. . . . Would you escape from every ill? Never lose this recollection of God, neither in prosperity nor in adversity, nor on any occasion whichsoever it be. Invoke not, to excuse yourself from this duty, either the difficulty or the importance of your business, for you can always remember that God sees you, that you are under his eye. If a thousand times an hour you forget him, reanimate a thousand times the recollection. If you cannot practice this exercise continuously, at least make yourself as familiar with it as possible; and, like unto those who in a rigorous winter draw near the fire as often as they can, go as often as you can to that ardent fire which will warm your soul."[61]

58 Dresser: Voices of Freedom, 33.

59 Trine: In Tune with the Infinite, p. 214.

60 Trine: p. 117.

61 Quoted by Lejeune: Introd. à la Vie Mystique, 1899, p. 66.

All the external associations of the Catholic discipline are of course unlike anything in mind-cure thought, but the purely spiritual part of the exercise is identical in both communions, and in both communions those who urge it write with authority, for they have evidently experienced in their own persons that whereof they tell. Compare again some mind-cure utterances:—

"High, healthful, pure thinking can be encouraged, promoted, and strengthened. Its current can be turned upon grand ideals until it forms a habit and wears a channel. By means of such discipline the mental horizon can be flooded with the sunshine of beauty, wholeness, and harmony. To inaugurate pure and lofty thinking may at first seem difficult, even almost mechanical, but perseverance will at length render it easy, then pleasant, and finally delightful.

"The soul's real world is that which it has built of its thoughts, mental states, and imaginations. If we *will*, we can turn our backs upon the lower and sensuous plane, and lift ourselves into the realm of the spiritual and Real, and there gain a residence. The assumption of states of expectancy and receptivity will attract spiritual sunshine, and it will flow in as naturally as air inclines to a vacuum.... Whenever the thought is not occupied with one's daily duty or profession, it should be sent aloft into the spiritual atmosphere. There are quiet leisure moments by day, and wakeful hours at night, when this wholesome and delightful exercise may be engaged in to great advantage. If one who has never made any systematic effort to lift and control the thought-forces will, for a single month, earnestly pursue the course here suggested, he will be surprised and delighted at the result, and nothing will induce him to go back to careless, aimless, and superficial thinking. At such favorable seasons the outside world, with all its current of daily events, is barred out, and one goes into the silent sanctuary of the inner temple of soul to commune and aspire. The spiritual hearing becomes delicately sensitive, so that the 'still, small voice' is audible, the tumultuous waves of external sense are hushed, and there is a great calm. The ego gradually becomes conscious that it is face to face with the Divine Presence; that mighty, healing, loving, Fatherly life which is nearer to us than we are to ourselves. There is soul contact with the Parent-Soul, and an influx of life, love, virtue, health, and happiness from the Inexhaustible Fountain."[62]

When we reach the subject of mysticism, you will undergo so deep an immersion into these exalted states of consciousness as to be wet all over, if I may so express myself; and the cold shiver of doubt with which this little sprinkling may affect you will have long since passed away—doubt, I mean, as to whether all such writing be not mere abstract talk and rhetoric set down *pour encourager les autres*. You will then be convinced, I trust, that these states of consciousness of "union" form a perfectly definite class of experiences, of which the soul may occasionally partake, and which certain persons may live by in a deeper sense than they live by anything else

62 Henry Wood: Ideal Suggestion through Mental Photography, pp. 51, 70 (abridged).

with which they have acquaintance. This brings me to a general philosophical reflection with which I should like to pass from the subject of healthy-mindedness, and close a topic which I fear is already only too long drawn out. It concerns the relation of all this systematized healthy-mindedness and mind-cure religion to scientific method and the scientific life.

In a later lecture I shall have to treat explicitly of the relation of religion to science on the one hand, and to primeval savage thought on the other. There are plenty of persons to-day—"scientists" or "positivists," they are fond of calling themselves—who will tell you that religious thought is a mere survival, an atavistic reversion to a type of consciousness which humanity in its more enlightened examples has long since left behind and out-grown. If you ask them to explain themselves more fully, they will probably say that for primitive thought everything is conceived of under the form of personality. The savage thinks that things operate by personal forces, and for the sake of individual ends. For him, even external nature obeys individual needs and claims, just as if these were so many elementary powers. Now science, on the other hand, these positivists say, has proved that personality, so far from being an elementary force in nature, is but a passive resultant of the really elementary forces, physical, chemical, physiological, and psycho-physical, which are all impersonal and general in character. Nothing individual accomplishes anything in the universe save in so far as it obeys and exemplifies some universal law. Should you then inquire of them by what means science has thus supplanted primitive thought, and discredited its personal way of looking at things, they would undoubtedly say it has been by the strict use of the method of experimental verification. Follow out science's conceptions practically, they will say, the conceptions that ignore personality altogether, and you will always be corroborated. The world is so made that all your expectations will be experientially verified so long, and only so long, as you keep the terms from which you infer them impersonal and universal.

But here we have mind-cure, with her diametrically opposite philosophy, setting up an exactly identical claim. Live as if I were true, she says, and every day will practically prove you right. That the controlling energies of nature are personal, that your own personal thoughts are forces, that the powers of the universe will directly respond to your individual appeals and needs, are propositions which your whole bodily and mental experience will verify. And that experience does largely verify these primeval religious ideas is proved by the fact that the mind-cure movement spreads as it does, not by proclamation and assertion simply, but by palpable experiential results. Here, in the very heyday of science's authority, it carries on an aggressive warfare against the scientific philosophy, and succeeds by using science's own peculiar methods and weapons. Believing that a higher power will take care of us in certain ways better than we can take care of ourselves, if we only genuinely throw ourselves upon it and consent to use it, it finds the belief, not only not impugned, but corroborated by its observation.

How conversions are thus made, and converts confirmed, is evident enough from the narratives which I have quoted. I will quote yet another couple of shorter ones to give the matter a perfectly concrete turn. Here is one:—

> "One of my first experiences in applying my teaching was two months after I first saw the healer. I fell, spraining my right ankle, which I had done once four years before, having then had to use a crutch and elastic anklet for some months, and carefully guarding it ever since. As soon as I was on my feet I made the positive suggestion (and felt it through all my being): 'There is nothing but God, and all life comes from him perfectly. I cannot be sprained or hurt, I will let him take care of it.' Well, I never had a sensation in it, and I walked two miles that day."

The next case not only illustrates experiment and verification, but also the element of passivity and surrender of which awhile ago I made such account.

> "I went into town to do some shopping one morning, and I had not been gone long before I began to feel ill. The ill feeling increased rapidly, until I had pains in all my bones, nausea and faintness, headache, all the symptoms in short that precede an attack of influenza. I thought that I was going to have the grippe, epidemic then in Boston, or something worse. The mind-cure teachings that I had been listening to all the winter thereupon came into my mind, and I thought that here was an opportunity to test myself, on my way home I met a friend, and I refrained with some effort from telling her how I felt. That was the first step gained. I went to bed immediately, and my husband wished to send for the doctor. But I told him that I would rather wait until morning and see how I felt. Then followed one of the most beautiful experiences of my life.
>
> "I cannot express it in any other way than to say that I did 'lie down in the stream of life and let it flow over me.' I gave up all fear of any impending disease; I was perfectly willing and obedient. There was no intellectual effort, or train of thought. My dominant idea was: 'Behold the handmaid of the Lord: be it unto me even as thou wilt,' and a perfect confidence that all would be well, that all *was* well. The creative life was flowing into me every instant, and I felt myself allied with the Infinite, in harmony, and full of the peace that passeth understanding. There was no place in my mind for a jarring body. I had no consciousness of time or space or persons; but only of love and happiness and faith.
>
> "I do not know how long this state lasted, nor when I fell asleep; but when I woke up in the morning, *I was well.*"

These are exceedingly trivial instances,[63] but in them, if we have anything at all, we have the method of experiment and verification. For the point I am driving at now, it makes no difference whether you consider the patients to be deluded victims of their imagination or not. That they seemed to *themselves* to have been cured by

63 See Appendix to this lecture for two other cases furnished me by friends.

the experiments tried was enough to make them converts to the system. And although it is evident that one must be of a certain mental mould to get such results (for not every one can get thus cured to his own satisfaction any more than every one can be cured by the first regular practitioner whom he calls in), yet it would surely be pedantic and over-scrupulous for those who *can* get their savage and primitive philosophy of mental healing verified in such experimental ways as this, to give them up at word of command for more scientific therapeutics. What are we to think of all this? Has science made too wide a claim?

I believe that the claims of the sectarian scientist are, to say the least, premature. The experiences which we have been studying during this hour (and a great many other kinds of religious experiences are like them) plainly show the universe to be a more many-sided affair than any sect, even the scientific sect, allows for. What, in the end, are all our verifications but experiences that agree with more or less isolated systems of ideas (conceptual systems) that our minds have framed? But why in the name of common sense need we assume that only one such system of ideas can be true? The obvious outcome of our total experience is that the world can be handled according to many systems of ideas, and is so handled by different men, and will each time give some characteristic kind of profit, for which he cares, to the handler, while at the same time some other kind of profit has to be omitted or postponed. Science gives to all of us telegraphy, electric lighting, and diagnosis, and succeeds in preventing and curing a certain amount of disease. Religion in the shape of mind-cure gives to some of us serenity, moral poise, and happiness, and prevents certain forms of disease as well as science does, or even better in a certain class of persons. Evidently, then, the science and the religion are both of them genuine keys for unlocking the world's treasure-house to him who can use either of them practically. Just as evidently neither is exhaustive or exclusive of the other's simultaneous use. And why, after all, may not the world be so complex as to consist of many interpenetrating spheres of reality, which we can thus approach in alternation by using different conceptions and assuming different attitudes, just as mathematicians handle the same numerical and spatial facts by geometry, by analytical geometry, by algebra, by the calculus, or by quaternions, and each time come out right? On this view religion and science, each verified in its own way from hour to hour and from life to life, would be co-eternal. Primitive thought, with its belief in individualized personal forces, seems at any rate as far as ever from being driven by science from the field to-day. Numbers of educated people still find it the directest experimental channel by which to carry on their intercourse with reality.[64]

The case of mind-cure lay so ready to my hand that I could not resist the tempta-

64 Whether the various spheres or systems are ever to fuse integrally into one absolute conception, as most philosophers assume that they must, and how, if so, that conception may best be reached, are questions that only the future can answer. What is certain now is the fact of lines of disparate conception, each corresponding to some part of the world's truth, each verified in some degree, each leaving out some part of real experience.

tion of using it to bring these last truths home to your attention, but I must content myself to-day with this very brief indication. In a later lecture the relations of religion both to science and to primitive thought will have to receive much more explicit attention.

## *Appendix*

CASE I. "My own experience is this: I had long been ill, and one of the first results of my illness, a dozen years before, had been a diplopia which deprived me of the use of my eyes for reading and writing almost entirely, while a later one had been to shut me out from exercise of any kind under penalty of immediate and great exhaustion. I had been under the care of doctors of the highest standing both in Europe and America, men in whose power to help me I had had great faith, with no or ill result. Then, at a time when I seemed to be rather rapidly losing ground, I heard some things that gave me interest enough in mental healing to make me try it; I had no great hope of getting any good from it—it was a *chance* I tried, partly because my thought was interested by the new possibility it seemed to open, partly because it was the only chance I then could see. I went to X. in Boston, from whom some friends of mine had got, or thought they had got, great help; the treatment was a silent one; little was said, and that little carried no conviction to my mind; whatever influence was exerted was that of another person's thought or feeling silently projected on to my unconscious mind, into my nervous system as it were, as we sat still together. I believed from the start in the *possibility* of such action, for I knew the power of the mind to shape, helping or hindering, the body's nerve-activities, and I thought telepathy probable, although unproved, but I had no belief in it as more than a possibility, and no strong conviction nor any mystic or religious faith connected with my thought of it that might have brought imagination strongly into play.

"I sat quietly with the healer for half an hour each day, at first with no result; then, after ten days or so, I became quite suddenly and swiftly conscious of a tide of new energy rising within me, a sense of power to pass beyond old halting-places, of power to break the bounds that, though often tried before, had long been veritable walls about my life, too high to climb. I began to read and walk as I had not done for years, and the change was sudden, marked, and unmistakable. This tide seemed to mount for some weeks, three or four perhaps, when, summer having come, I came away, taking the treatment up again a few months later. The lift I got proved permanent, and left me slowly gaining ground instead of losing, it but with this lift the influence seemed in a way to have spent itself, and, though my confidence in the reality of the power had gained immensely from this first experience, and should have helped me to make further gain in health and strength if my belief in it had been the potent factor there, I never after this got any result at all as striking or as clearly marked as this which came when I made trial of it first, with little faith and doubtful expectation. It is difficult to put all the evidence in such a matter into words, to gather up into a distinct statement all that one bases one's conclusions on, but I have always felt that I had abundant evidence to justify (to myself, at least) the conclusion that I came to then, and since have held to, that the physical change which came at that time was, first, the result of a change wrought within me by a change of mental state; and secondly, that that change of mental state was not, save in a very secondary way, brought about through the influence of an excited imagination, or a *consciously* received suggestion of an hypnotic sort. Lastly, I believe that this change was the result of my receiving telephathically, and upon a mental stratum quite below the level of immediate consciousness, a healthier and more energetic attitude, receiving it from another person whose thought was directed upon me with the intention of impressing the idea of this attitude upon me. In my case the disease was distinctly what would be classed as nervous, not organic; but from such opportunities as I have had of observing, I have come to the conclusion that the dividing line that has been drawn is an arbitrary one, the nerves controlling the internal activities and the nutrition of the body throughout; and I believe that the central nervous system, by starting and inhibiting local centres, can exercise a vast influence upon disease of any kind, if it can be brought to bear. In my judgment the question is simply how to bring it to bear, and I think that the uncertainty and remarkable differences in the results obtained through mental healing do but show how ignorant we are as yet of the forces at work and of the means we should take to make them effective. That these results are not due to chance coincidences my observation of myself and others makes me sure; that the conscious mind, the imagination, enters into them as a factor in many cases is doubtless true, but in many others, and sometimes very extraordinary ones, it hardly seems to enter in at all. On the whole I am inclined to think that as the healing action, like the morbid one, springs from the plane of the normally *un*conscious mind, so the strongest and most effective impressions are those which *it* receives, in some as yet unknown, subtle way, *directly* from a healthier mind whose state, through a hidden law of sympathy, it reproduces."

Case ii. "At the urgent request of friends, and with no faith and hardly any hope (possibly owing to a previous unsuccessful experience with a Christian Scientist), our little daughter was placed under the care of a healer, and cured of a trouble about which the physician had been very discouraging in his diagnosis. This interested me, and I began studying earnestly the method and philosophy of this method of healing. Gradually an inner peace and tranquillity came to me in so positive a way that my manner changed greatly. My children and friends noticed the change and commented upon it. All feelings of irritability disappeared. Even the expression of my face changed noticeably.

"I had been bigoted, aggressive, and intolerant in discussion, both in public and private. I grew broadly tolerant and receptive toward the views of others. I had been nervous and irritable, coming home two or three times a week with a sick headache induced, as I then supposed, by dyspepsia and catarrh. I grew serene and gentle, and the physical troubles entirely disappeared. I had been in the habit of approaching every business interview with an almost morbid dread. I now meet every one with confidence and inner calm.

"I may say that the growth has all been toward the elimination of selfishness. I do not mean simply the grosser, more sensual forms, but those subtler and generally unrecognized kinds, such as express themselves in sorrow, grief, regret, envy, etc. It has been in the direction of a practical, working realization of the immanence of God and the Divinity of man's true, inner self.

# The Sick Soul

At our last meeting, we considered the healthy-minded temperament, the temperament which has a constitutional incapacity for prolonged suffering, and in which the tendency to see things optimistically is like a water of crystallization in which the individual's character is set. We saw how this temperament may become the basis for a peculiar type of religion, a religion in which good, even the good of this world's life, is regarded as the essential thing for a rational being to attend to. This religion directs him to settle his scores with the more evil aspects of the universe by systematically declining to lay them to heart or make much of them, by ignoring them in his reflective calculations, or even, on occasion, by denying outright that they exist. Evil is a disease; and worry over disease is itself an additional form of disease, which only adds to the original complaint. Even repentance and remorse, affections which come in the character of ministers of good, may be but sickly and relaxing impulses. The best repentance is to up and act for righteousness, and forget that you ever had relations with sin.

Spinoza's philosophy has this sort of healthy-mindedness woven into the heart of it, and this has been one secret of its fascination. He whom Reason leads, according to Spinoza, is led altogether by the influence over his mind of good. Knowledge of evil is an "inadequate" knowledge, fit only for slavish minds. So Spinoza categorically condemns repentance. When men make mistakes, he says—

> "One might perhaps expect gnawings of conscience and repentance to help to bring them on the right path, and might thereupon conclude (as every one does conclude) that these affections are good things. Yet when we look at the matter closely, we shall find that not only are they not good, but on the contrary deleterious and evil passions. For it is manifest that we can always get along better by reason and love of truth than by worry of conscience and remorse. Harmful are these and evil, inasmuch as they form a particular kind of sadness; and the disadvantages of sadness," he continues, "I have already proved, and shown that we should strive to keep it from our life. Just so we should endeavor, since uneasi-

ness of conscience and remorse are of this kind of complexion, to flee and shun these states of mind."[65]

Within the Christian body, for which repentance of sins has from the beginning been the critical religious act, healthy-mindedness has always come forward with its milder interpretation. Repentance according to such healthy-minded Christians means *getting away from* the sin, not groaning and writhing over its commission. The Catholic practice of confession and absolution is in one of its aspects little more than a systematic method of keeping healthy-mindedness on top. By it a man's accounts with evil are periodically squared and audited, so that he may start the clean page with no old debts inscribed. Any Catholic will tell us how clean and fresh and free he feels after the purging operation. Martin Luther by no means belonged to the healthy-minded type in the radical sense in which we have discussed it, and he repudiated priestly absolution for sin. Yet in this matter of repentance he had some very healthy-minded ideas, due in the main to the largeness of his conception of God.

"When I was a monk," he says, "I thought that I was utterly cast away, if at any time I felt the lust of the flesh: that is to say, if I felt any evil motion, fleshly lust, wrath, hatred, or envy against any brother. I assayed many ways to help to quiet my conscience, but it would not be; for the concupiscence and lust of my flesh did always return, so that I could not rest, but was continually vexed with these thoughts: This or that sin thou hast committed: thou art infected with envy, with impatiency, and such other sins: therefore thou art entered into this holy order in vain, and all thy good works are unprofitable. But if then I had rightly understood these sentences of Paul: 'The flesh lusteth contrary to the Spirit, and the Spirit contrary to the flesh; and these two are one against another, so that ye cannot do the things that ye would do,' I should not have so miserably tormented myself, but should have thought and said to myself, as now commonly I do, 'Martin, thou shalt not utterly be without sin, for thou hast flesh; thou shalt therefore feel the battle thereof.' I remember that Staupitz was wont to say, 'I have vowed unto God above a thousand times that I would become a better man: but I never performed that which I vowed. Hereafter I will make no such vow: for I have now learned by experience that I am not able to perform it. Unless, therefore, God be favorable and merciful unto me for Christ's sake, I shall not be able, with all my vows and all my good deeds, to stand before him.' This (of Staupitz's) was not only a true, but also a godly and a holy desperation; and this must they all confess, both with mouth and heart, who will be saved. For the godly trust not to their own righteousness. They look unto Christ their reconciler, who gave his life for their sins. Moreover, they know that the remnant of sin which is in their flesh is not laid to their charge, but freely pardoned. Notwithstanding, in the mean while they fight in spirit against the flesh, lest they should *fulfill* the lusts thereof; and although they feel the flesh to rage and rebel, and themselves

65 Tract on God, Man, and Happiness, Book ii. ch. x.

also do fall sometimes into sin through infirmity, yet are they not discouraged, nor think therefore that their state and kind of life, and the works which are done according to their calling, displease God; but they raise up themselves by faith."[66]

One of the heresies for which the Jesuits got that spiritual genius, Molinos, the founder of Quietism, so abominably condemned was his healthy-minded opinion of repentance:—

"When thou fallest into a fault, in what matter soever it be, do not trouble nor afflict thyself for it. For they are effects of our frail Nature, stained by Original Sin. The common enemy will make thee believe, as soon as thou fallest into any fault, that thou walkest in error, and therefore art out of God and his favor, and herewith would he make thee distrust of the divine Grace, telling thee of thy misery, and making a giant of it; and putting it into thy head that every day thy soul grows worse instead of better, whilst it so often repeats these failings. O blessed Soul, open thine eyes; and shut the gate against these diabolical suggestions, knowing thy misery, and trusting in the mercy divine. Would not he be a mere fool who, running at tournament with others, and falling in the best of the career, should lie weeping on the ground and afflicting himself with discourses upon his fall? Man (they would tell him), lose no time, get up and take the course again, for he that rises again quickly and continues his race is as if he had never fallen. If thou seest thyself fallen once and a thousand times, thou oughtest to make use of the remedy which I have given thee, that is, a loving confidence in the divine mercy. These are the weapons with which thou must fight and conquer cowardice and vain thoughts. This is the means thou oughtest to use—not to lose time, not to disturb thyself, and reap no good."[67]

Now in contrast with such healthy-minded views as these, if we treat them as a way of deliberately minimizing evil, stands a radically opposite view, a way of maximizing evil, if you please so to call it, based on the persuasion that the evil aspects of our life are of its very essence, and that the world's meaning most comes home to us when we lay them most to heart. We have now to address ourselves to this more morbid way of looking at the situation. But as I closed our last hour with a general philosophical reflection on the healthy-minded way of taking life, I should like at this point to make another philosophical reflection upon it before turning to that heavier task. You will excuse the brief delay.

If we admit that evil is an essential part of our being and the key to the interpretation of our life, we load ourselves down with a difficulty that has always proved burdensome in philosophies of religion. Theism, whenever it has erected itself into a systematic philosophy of the universe, has shown a reluctance to let God be anything less than All-in-All. In other words, philosophic theism has always shown a

66 Commentary on Galatians, Philadelphia, 1891, pp. 510–514 (abridged).

67 Molinos: Spiritual Guide, Book II., chaps. xvii., xviii. (abridged).

tendency to become pantheistic and monistic, and to consider the world as one unit of absolute fact; and this has been at variance with popular or practical theism, which latter has ever been more or less frankly pluralistic, not to say polytheistic, and shown itself perfectly well satisfied with a universe composed of many original principles, provided we be only allowed to believe that the divine principle remains supreme, and that the others are subordinate. In this latter case God is not necessarily responsible for the existence of evil; he would only be responsible if it were not finally overcome. But on the monistic or pantheistic view, evil, like everything else, must have its foundation in God; and the difficulty is to see how this can possibly be the case if God be absolutely good. This difficulty faces us in every form of philosophy in which the world appears as one flawless unit of fact. Such a unit is an *Individual*, and in it the worst parts must be as essential as the best, must be as necessary to make the individual what he is; since if any part whatever in an individual were to vanish or alter, it would no longer be *that* individual at all. The philosophy of absolute idealism, so vigorously represented both in Scotland and America to-day, has to struggle with this difficulty quite as much as scholastic theism struggled in its time; and although it would be premature to say that there is no speculative issue whatever from the puzzle, it is perfectly fair to say that there is no clear or easy issue, and that the only *obvious* escape from paradox here is to cut loose from the monistic assumption altogether, and to allow the world to have existed from its origin in pluralistic form, as an aggregate or collection of higher and lower things and principles, rather than an absolutely unitary fact. For then evil would not need to be essential; it might be, and may always have been, an independent portion that had no rational or absolute right to live with the rest, and which we might conceivably hope to see got rid of at last.

Now the gospel of healthy-mindedness, as we have described it, casts its vote distinctly for this pluralistic view. Whereas the monistic philosopher finds himself more or less bound to say, as Hegel said, that everything actual is rational, and that evil, as an element dialectically required, must be pinned in and kept and consecrated and have a function awarded to it in the final system of truth, healthy-mindedness refuses to say anything of the sort.[68] Evil, it says, is emphatically irrational, and *not* to be pinned in, or preserved, or consecrated in any final system of truth. It is a pure abomination to the Lord, an alien unreality, a waste element, to be sloughed off and negated, and the very memory of it, if possible, wiped out and forgotten. The ideal, so far from being co-extensive with the whole actual, is a mere *extract* from the actual, marked by its deliverance from all contact with this diseased, inferior, and excrementitious stuff.

68 I say this in spite of the monistic utterances of many mind-cure writers; for these utterances are really inconsistent with their attitude towards disease, and can easily be shown not to be logically involved in the experiences of union with a higher Presence with which they connect themselves. The higher Presence, namely, need not be the absolute whole of things, it is quite sufficient for the life of religious experience to regard it as a part, if only it be the most ideal part.

Here we have the interesting notion fairly and squarely presented to us, of there being elements of the universe which may make no rational whole in conjunction with the other elements, and which, from the point of view of any system which those other elements make up, can only be considered so much irrelevance and accident—so much "dirt," as it were, and matter out of place. I ask you now not to forget this notion; for although most philosophers seem either to forget it or to disdain it too much ever to mention it, I believe that we shall have to admit it ourselves in the end as containing an element of truth. The mind-cure gospel thus once more appears to us as having dignity and importance. We have seen it to be a genuine religion, and no mere silly appeal to imagination to cure disease; we have seen its method of experimental verification to be not unlike the method of all science; and now here we find mind-cure as the champion of a perfectly definite conception of the metaphysical structure of the world. I hope that, in view of all this, you will not regret my having pressed it upon your attention at such length.

Let us now say good-by for a while to all this way of thinking, and turn towards those persons who cannot so swiftly throw off the burden of the consciousness of evil, but are congenitally fated to suffer from its presence. Just as we saw that in healthy-mindedness there are shallower and profounder levels, happiness like that of the mere animal, and more regenerate sorts of happiness, so also are there different levels of the morbid mind, and the one is much more formidable than the other. There are people for whom evil means only a mal-adjustment with *things*, a wrong correspondence of one's life with the environment. Such evil as this is curable, in principle at least, upon the natural plane, for merely by modifying either the self or the things, or both at once, the two terms may be made to fit, and all go merry as a marriage bell again. But there are others for whom evil is no mere relation of the subject to particular outer things, but something more radical and general, a wrongness or vice in his essential nature, which no alteration of the environment, or any superficial rearrangement of the inner self, can cure, and which requires a supernatural remedy. On the whole, the Latin races have leaned more towards the former way of looking upon evil, as made up of ills and sins in the plural, removable in detail; while the Germanic races have tended rather to think of Sin in the singular, and with a capital S, as of something ineradicably ingrained in our natural subjectivity, and never to be removed by any superficial piecemeal operations.[69] These comparisons of races are always open to exception, but undoubtedly the northern tone in religion has inclined to the more intimately pessimistic persuasion, and this way of feeling, being the more extreme, we shall find by far the more instructive for our study.

Recent psychology has found great use for the word "threshold" as a symbolic designation for the point at which one state of mind passes into another. Thus we

69 Cf. J. Milsand: Luther et le Serf-Arbitre, 1884, *passim*.

speak of the threshold of a man's consciousness in general, to indicate the amount of noise, pressure, or other outer stimulus which it takes to arouse his attention at all. One with a high threshold will doze through an amount of racket by which one with a low threshold would be immediately waked. Similarly, when one is sensitive to small differences in any order of sensation, we say he has a low "difference-threshold"—his mind easily steps over it into the consciousness of the differences in question. And just so we might speak of a "pain-threshold," a "fear-threshold," a "misery-threshold," and find it quickly overpassed by the consciousness of some individuals, but lying too high in others to be often reached by their consciousness. The sanguine and healthy-minded live habitually on the sunny side of their misery-line, the depressed and melancholy live beyond it, in darkness and apprehension. There are men who seem to have started in life with a bottle or two of champagne inscribed to their credit; whilst others seem to have been born close to the pain-threshold, which the slightest irritants fatally send them over.

Does it not appear as if one who lived more habitually on one side of the pain-threshold might need a different sort of religion from one who habitually lived on the other? This question, of the relativity of different types of religion to different types of need, arises naturally at this point, and will became a serious problem ere we have done. But before we confront it in general terms, we must address ourselves to the unpleasant task of hearing what the sick souls, as we may call them in contrast to the healthy-minded, have to say of the secrets of their prison-house, their own peculiar form of consciousness. Let us then resolutely turn our backs on the once-born and their sky-blue optimistic gospel; let us not simply cry out, in spite of all appearances, "Hurrah for the Universe!—God's in his Heaven, all's right with the world." Let us see rather whether pity, pain, and fear, and the sentiment of human helplessness may not open a profounder view and put into our hands a more complicated key to the meaning of the situation.

To begin with, how *can* things so insecure as the successful experiences of this world afford a stable anchorage? A chain is no stronger than its weakest link, and life is after all a chain. In the healthiest and most prosperous existence, how many links of illness, danger, and disaster are always interposed? Unsuspectedly from the bottom of every fountain of pleasure, as the old poet said, something bitter rises up: a touch of nausea, a falling dead of the delight, a whiff of melancholy, things that sound a knell, for fugitive as they may be, they bring a feeling of coming from a deeper region and often have an appalling convincingness. The buzz of life ceases at their touch as a piano-string stops sounding when the damper falls upon it.

Of course the music can commence again;—and again and again—at intervals. But with this the healthy-minded consciousness is left with an irremediable sense of precariousness. It is a bell with a crack; it draws its breath on sufferance and by an accident.

Even if we suppose a man so packed with healthy-mindedness as never to have experienced in his own person any of these sobering intervals, still, if he is a reflecting being, he must generalize and class his own lot with that of others; and, doing so, he must see that his escape is just a lucky chance and no essential difference. He might just as well have been born to an entirely different fortune. And then indeed the hollow security! What kind of a frame of things is it of which the best you can say is, "Thank God, it has let me off clear this time!" Is not its blessedness a fragile fiction? Is not your joy in it a very vulgar glee, not much unlike the snicker of any rogue at his success? If indeed it were all success, even on such terms as that! But take the happiest man, the one most envied by the world, and in nine cases out of ten his inmost consciousness is one of failure. Either his ideals in the line of his achievements are pitched far higher than the achievements themselves, or else he has secret ideals of which the world knows nothing, and in regard to which he inwardly knows himself to be found wanting.

When such a conquering optimist as Goethe can express himself in this wise, how must it be with less successful men?

> "I will say nothing," writes Goethe in 1824, "against the course of my existence. But at bottom it has been nothing but pain and burden, and I can affirm that during the whole of my 75 years, I have not had four weeks of genuine well-being. It is but the perpetual rolling of a rock that must be raised up again forever."

What single-handed man was ever on the whole as successful as Luther? yet when he had grown old, he looked back on his life as if it were an absolute failure.

> "I am utterly weary of life. I pray the Lord will come forthwith and carry me hence. Let him come, above all, with his last Judgment: I will stretch out my neck, the thunder will burst forth, and I shall be at rest."—And having a necklace of white agates in his hand at the time he added: "O God, grant that it may come without delay. I would readily eat up this necklace to-day, for the Judgment to come to-morrow."—The Electress Dowager, one day when Luther was dining with her, said to him: "Doctor, I wish you may live forty years to come." "Madam," replied he, "rather than live forty years more, I would give up my chance of Paradise."

Failure, then, failure! so the world stamps us at every turn. We strew it with our blunders, our misdeeds, our lost opportunities, with all the memorials of our inadequacy to our vocation. And with what a damning emphasis does it then blot us out! No easy fine, no mere apology or formal expiation, will satisfy the world's demands, but every pound of flesh exacted is soaked with all its blood. The subtlest forms of suffering known to man are connected with the poisonous humiliations incidental to these results.

And they are pivotal human experiences. A process so ubiquitous and everlasting is evidently an integral part of life. "There is indeed one element in human destiny," Robert Louis Stevenson writes, "that not blindness itself can controvert. Whatever else we are intended to do, we are not intended to succeed; failure is the fate allotted."[70] And our nature being thus rooted in failure, is it any wonder that theologians should have held it to be essential, and thought that only through the personal experience of humiliation which it engenders the deeper sense of life's significance is reached?[71]

But this is only the first stage of the world-sickness. Make the human being's sensitiveness a little greater, carry him a little farther over the misery-threshold, and the good quality of the successful moments themselves when they occur is spoiled and vitiated. All natural goods perish. Riches take wings; fame is a breath; love is a cheat; youth and health and pleasure vanish. Can things whose end is always dust and disappointment be the real goods which our souls require? Back of everything is the great spectre of universal death, the all-encompassing blackness:—

> "What profit hath a man of all his labour which he taketh under the Sun? I looked on all the works that my hands had wrought, and behold, all was vanity and vexation of spirit. For that which befalleth the sons of men befalleth beasts; as the one dieth, so dieth the other; all are of the dust, and all turn to dust again. . . . The dead know not anything, neither have they any more a reward; for the memory of them is forgotten. Also their love and their hatred and their envy is now perished; neither have they any more a portion for ever in anything that is done under the Sun. . . . Truly the light is sweet, and a pleasant thing it is for the eyes to behold the Sun: but if a man live many years and rejoice in them all, yet let him remember the days of darkness; for they shall be many."

In short, life and its negation are beaten up inextricably together. But if the life be good, the negation of it must be bad. Yet the two are equally essential facts of existence; and all natural happiness thus seems infected with a contradiction. The breath of the sepulchre surrounds it.

To a mind attentive to this state of things and rightly subject to the joy-destroying chill which such a contemplation engenders, the only relief that healthy-mindedness can give is by saying: "Stuff and nonsense, get out into the open air!" or "Cheer up, old fellow, you'll be all right erelong, if you will only drop your morbidness!" But in all seriousness, can such bald animal talk as that be treated as a rational answer? To ascribe religious value to mere happy-go-lucky contentment with one's brief chance at natural good is but the very consecration of forgetfulness and superficiality. Our troubles lie indeed too deep for *that* cure. The fact that we *can* die, that we *can* be ill

---

70 He adds with characteristic healthy-mindedness: "Our business is to continue to fail in good spirits."
71 The God of many men is little more than their court of appeal against the damnatory judgment passed on their failures by the opinion of this world. To our own consciousness there is usually a residuum of worth left over after our sins and errors have been told off—our capacity of acknowledging and regretting them is the germ of a better self *in posse* at least. But the world deals with us *in actu* and not *in posse*: and of this hidden germ, not to be guessed at from without, it never takes account. Then we turn to the All-knower, who knows our bad, but knows this good in us also, and who is just. We cast ourselves with our repentance on his mercy: only by an All-knower can we finally be judged. So the need of a God very definitely emerges from this sort of experience of life.

at all, is what perplexes us; the fact that we now for a moment live and are well is irrelevant to that perplexity. We need a life not correlated with death, a health not liable to illness, a kind of good that will not perish, a good in fact that flies beyond the Goods of nature.

It all depends on how sensitive the soul may become to discords. "The trouble with me is that I believe too much in common happiness and goodness," said a friend of mine whose consciousness was of this sort, "and nothing can console me for their transiency. I am appalled and disconcerted at its being possible." And so with most of us: a little cooling down of animal excitability and instinct, a little loss of animal toughness, a little irritable weakness and descent of the pain-threshold, will bring the worm at the core of all our usual springs of delight into full view, and turn us into melancholy metaphysicians. The pride of life and glory of the world will shrivel. It is after all but the standing quarrel of hot youth and hoary eld. Old age has the last word: the purely naturalistic look at life, however enthusiastically it may begin, is sure to end in sadness.

This sadness lies at the heart of every merely positivistic, agnostic, or naturalistic scheme of philosophy. Let sanguine healthy-mindedness do its best with its strange power of living in the moment and ignoring and forgetting, still the evil background is really there to be thought of, and the skull will grin in at the banquet. In the practical life of the individual, we know how his whole gloom or glee about any present fact depends on the remoter schemes and hopes with which it stands related. Its significance and framing give it the chief part of its value. Let it be known to lead nowhere, and however agreeable it may be in its immediacy, its glow and gilding vanish. The old man, sick with an insidious internal disease, may laugh and quaff his wine at first as well as ever, but he knows his fate now, for the doctors have revealed it; and the knowledge knocks the satisfaction out of all these functions. They are partners of death and the worm is their brother, and they turn to a mere flatness.

The lustre of the present hour is always borrowed from the background of possibilities it goes with. Let our common experiences be enveloped in an eternal moral order; let our suffering have an immortal significance; let Heaven smile upon the earth, and deities pay their visits; let faith and hope be the atmosphere which man breathes in;—and his days pass by with zest; they stir with prospects, they thrill with remoter values. Place round them on the contrary the curdling cold and gloom and absence of all permanent meaning which for pure naturalism and the popular science evolutionism of our time are all that is visible ultimately, and the thrill stops short, or turns rather to an anxious trembling.

For naturalism, fed on recent cosmological speculations, mankind is in a position similar to that of a set of people living on a frozen lake, surrounded by cliffs over which there is no escape, yet knowing that little by little the ice is melting, and the inevitable day drawing near when the last film of it will disappear, and to be drowned ignominiously will be the human creature's portion. The merrier the skating, the warmer and more sparkling the sun by day, and the ruddier the bonfires at night, the more poignant the sadness with which one must take in the meaning of the total situation.

The early Greeks are continually held up to us in literary works as models of the healthy-minded joyousness which the religion of nature may engender. There was indeed much joyousness among the Greeks—Homer's flow of enthusiasm for most things that the sun shines upon is steady. But even in Homer the reflective passages are cheerless,[72] and the moment the Greeks grew systematically pensive and thought of ultimates, they became unmitigated pessimists.[73] The jealousy of the gods, the nemesis that follows too much happiness, the all-encompassing death, fate's dark opacity, the ultimate and unintelligible cruelty, were the fixed background of their imagination. The beautiful joyousness of their polytheism is only a poetic modern fiction. They knew no joys comparable in quality of preciousness to those which we shall erelong see that Brahmans, Buddhists, Christians, Mohammedans, twice-born people whose religion is non-naturalistic, get from their several creeds of mysticism and renunciation.

Stoic insensibility and Epicurean resignation were the farthest advance which the Greek mind made in that direction. The Epicurean said: "Seek not to be happy, but rather to escape unhappiness; strong happiness is always linked with pain; therefore hug the safe shore, and do not tempt the deeper raptures. Avoid disappointment by expecting little, and by aiming low; and above all do not fret." The Stoic said: "The only genuine good that life can yield a man is the free possession of his own soul; all other goods are lies." Each of these philosophies is in its degree a philosophy of despair in nature's boons. Trustful self-abandonment to the joys that freely offer has entirely departed from both Epicurean and Stoic; and what each proposes is a way of rescue from the resultant dust-and-ashes state of mind. The Epicurean still awaits results from economy of indulgence and damping of desire. The Stoic hopes for no results, and gives up natural good altogether. There is dignity in both these forms

---

72 E.g., Iliad XVII. 446: "Nothing then is more wretched anywhere than man of all that breathes and creeps upon this earth."

73 E.g., Theognis, 425–428: "Best of all for all things upon earth is it not to be born nor to behold the splendors of the Sun; next best to traverse as soon as possible the gates of Hades." See also the almost identical passage in Œdipus in Colonus, 1225.—The Anthology is full of pessimistic utterances: "Naked came I upon the earth, naked I go below the ground—why then do I vainly toil when I see the end naked before me?"—"How did I come to be? Whence am I? Wherefore did I come? To pass away. How can I learn aught when naught I know? Being naught I came to life: once more shall I be what I was. Nothing and nothingness is the whole race of mortals."—"For death we are all cherished and fattened like a herd of hogs that is wantonly butchered."

The difference between Greek pessimism and the oriental and modern variety is that the Greeks had not made the discovery that the pathetic mood may be idealized, and figure as a higher form of sensibility. Their spirit was still too essentially masculine for pessimism to be elaborated or lengthily dwelt on in their classic literature. They would have despised a life set wholly in a minor key, and summoned it to keep within the proper bounds of lachrymosity. The discovery that the enduring emphasis, so far as this world goes, may be laid on its pain and failure, was reserved for races more complex, and (so to speak) more feminine than the Hellenes had attained to being in the classic period. But all the same was the outlook of those Hellenes blackly pessimistic.

of resignation. They represent distinct stages in the sobering process which man's primitive intoxication with sense-happiness is sure to undergo. In the one the hot blood has grown cool, in the other it has become quite cold; and although I have spoken of them in the past tense, as if they were merely historic, yet Stoicism and Epicureanism will probably be to all time typical attitudes, marking a certain definite stage accomplished in the evolution of the world-sick soul.[74] They mark the conclusion of what we call the once-born period, and represent the highest flights of what twice-born religion would call the purely natural man—Epicureanism, which can only by great courtesy be called a religion, showing his refinement, and Stoicism exhibiting his moral will. They leave the world in the shape of an unreconciled contradiction, and seek no higher unity. Compared with the complex ecstasies which the supernaturally regenerated Christian may enjoy, or the oriental pantheist indulge in, their receipts for equanimity are expedients which seem almost crude in their simplicity.

Please observe, however, that I am not yet pretending finally to *judge* any of these attitudes. I am only describing their variety.

The securest way to the rapturous sorts of happiness of which the twice-born make report has as an historic matter of fact been through a more radical pessimism than anything that we have yet considered. We have seen how the lustre and enchantment may be rubbed off from the goods of nature. But there is a pitch of unhappiness so great that the goods of nature may be entirely forgotten, and all sentiment of their existence vanish from the mental field. For this extremity of pessimism to be reached, something more is needed than observation of life and reflection upon death. The individual must in his own person become the prey of a pathological melancholy. As the healthy-minded enthusiast succeeds in ignoring evil's very existence, so the subject of melancholy is forced in spite of himself to ignore that of all good whatever: for him it may no longer have the least reality. Such sensitiveness and susceptibility to mental pain is a rare occurrence where the nervous constitution is entirely normal; one seldom finds it in a healthy subject even where he is the victim of the most atrocious cruelties of outward fortune. So we note here the neurotic constitution, of which I said so much in my first lecture, making its active entrance on our scene, and destined to play a part in much that follows. Since these experiences of melancholy are in the first instance absolutely private and individual, I can now help myself out with personal documents. Painful indeed they will be to listen to, and there is almost an indecency in handling them in public. Yet

---

74 For instance, on the very day on which I write this page, the post brings me some aphorisms from a worldly-wise old friend in Heidelberg which may serve as a good contemporaneous expression of Epicureanism: "By the word 'happiness' every human being understands something different. It is a phantom pursued only by weaker minds. The wise man is satisfied with the more modest but much more definite term *contentment*. What education should chiefly aim at is to save us from a discontented life. Health is one favoring condition, but by no means an indispensable one, of contentment. Woman's heart and love are a shrewd device of Nature, a trap which she sets for the average man, to force him into working. But the wise man will always prefer work chosen by himself."

they lie right in the middle of our path; and if we are to touch the psychology of religion at all seriously, we must be willing to forget conventionalities, and dive below the smooth and lying official conversational surface.

One can distinguish many kinds of pathological depression. Sometimes it is mere passive joylessness and dreariness, discouragement, dejection; lack of taste and zest and spring. Professor Ribot has proposed the name *anhedonia* to designate this condition.

> "The state of *anhedonia*, if I may coin a new word to pair off with analgesia," he writes, "has been very little studied, but it exists. A young girl was smitten with a liver disease which for some time altered her constitution. She felt no longer any affection for her father and mother. She would have played with her doll, but it was impossible to find the least pleasure in the act. The same things which formerly convulsed her with laughter entirely failed to interest her now. Esquirol observed the case of a very intelligent magistrate who was also a prey to hepatic disease. Every emotion appeared dead within him. He manifested neither perversion nor violence, but complete absence of emotional reaction. If he went to the theatre, which he did out of habit, he could find no pleasure there. The thought of his house, of his home, of his wife, and of his absent children moved him as little, he said, as a theorem of Euclid."[75]

Prolonged seasickness will in most persons produce a temporary condition of anhedonia. Every good, terrestrial or celestial, is imagined only to be turned from with disgust. A temporary condition of this sort, connected with the religious evolution of a singularly lofty character, both intellectual and moral, is well described by the Catholic philosopher, Father Gratry, in his autobiographical recollections. In consequence of mental isolation and excessive study at the Polytechnic school, young Gratry fell into a state of nervous exhaustion with symptoms which he thus describes:—

> "I had such a universal terror that I woke at night with a start, thinking that the Pantheon was tumbling on the Polytechnic school, or that the school was in flames, or that the Seine was pouring into the Catacombs, and that Paris was being swallowed up. And when these impressions were past, all day long without respite I suffered an incurable and intolerable desolation, verging on despair. I thought myself, in fact, rejected by God, lost, damned! I felt something like the suffering of hell. Before that I had never even thought of hell. My mind had never turned in that direction. Neither discourses nor reflections had impressed me in that way. I took no account of hell. Now, and all at once, I suffered in a measure what is suffered there.
>
> "But what was perhaps still more dreadful is that every idea of heaven was taken away from me: I could no longer conceive of anything of the sort. Heaven

75 Ribot: Psychologie des sentiments, p. 54.

did not seem to me worth going to. It was like a vacuum; a mythological elysium, an abode of shadows less real than the earth. I could conceive no joy, no pleasure in inhabiting it. Happiness, joy, light, affection, love—all these words were now devoid of sense. Without doubt I could still have talked of all these things, but I had become incapable of feeling anything in them, of understanding anything about them, of hoping anything from them, or of believing them to exist. There was my great and inconsolable grief! I neither perceived nor conceived any longer the existence of happiness or perfection. An abstract heaven over a naked rock. Such was my present abode for eternity."[76]

So much for melancholy in the sense of incapacity for joyous feeling. A much worse form of it is positive and active anguish, a sort of psychical neuralgia wholly unknown to healthy life. Such anguish may partake of various characters, having sometimes more the quality of loathing; sometimes that of irritation and exasperation; or again of self-mistrust and self-despair; or of suspicion, anxiety, trepidation, fear. The patient may rebel or submit; may accuse himself, or accuse outside powers; and he may or he may not be tormented by the theoretical mystery of why he should so have to suffer. Most cases are mixed cases, and we should not treat our classifications with too much respect. Moreover, it is only a relatively small proportion of cases that connect themselves with the religious sphere of experience at all. Exasperated cases, for instance, as a rule do not. I quote now literally from the first case of melancholy on which I lay my hand. It is a letter from a patient in a French asylum.

"I suffer too much in this hospital, both physically and morally. Besides the burnings and the sleeplessness (for I no longer sleep since I am shut up here, and the little rest I get is broken by bad dreams, and I am waked with a jump by night mares, dreadful visions, lightning, thunder, and the rest), fear, atrocious fear, presses me down, holds me without respite, never lets me go. Where is the justice in it all! What have I done to deserve this excess of severity? Under what form will this fear crush me? What would I not owe to any one who would rid me of my life! Eat, drink, lie awake all night, suffer without interruption—such is the fine legacy I have received from my mother! What I fail to understand is this

---

76 A. GRATRY: Souvenirs de ma jeunesse, 1880, pp. 119–121, abridged. Some persons are affected with anhedonia permanently, or at any rate with a loss of the usual appetite for life. The annals of suicide supply such examples as the following:—

An uneducated domestic servant, aged nineteen, poisons herself, and leaves two letters expressing her motive for the act. To her parents she writes:—

"Life is sweet perhaps to some, but I prefer what is sweeter than life, and that is death. So good-by forever, my dear parents. It is nobody's fault, but a strong desire of my own which I have longed to fulfill for three or four years. I have always had a hope that some day I might have an opportunity of fulfilling it, and now it has come. . . . It is a wonder I have put this off so long, but I thought perhaps I should cheer up a bit and put all thought out of my head." To her brother she writes: "Good-by forever, my own dearest brother. By the time you get this I shall be gone forever. I know, dear love, there is no forgiveness for what I am going to do. . . . I am tired of living, so am willing to die. . . . Life may be sweet to some, but death to me is sweeter." S. A. K. STRAHAN: Suicide and Insanity, 2d edition, London, 1894, p. 131.

abuse of power. There are limits to everything, there is a middle way. But God knows neither middle way nor limits. I say God, but why? All I have known so far has been the devil. After all, I am afraid of God as much as of the devil, so I drift along, thinking of nothing but suicide, but with neither courage nor means here to execute the act. As you read this, it will easily prove to you my insanity. The style and the ideas are incoherent enough—I can see that myself. But I cannot keep myself from being either crazy or an idiot; and, as things are, from whom should I ask pity? I am defenseless against the invisible enemy who is tightening his coils around me. I should be no better armed against him even if I saw him, or had seen him. Oh, if he would but kill me, devil take him! Death, death, once for all! But I stop. I have raved to you long enough. I say raved, for I can write no otherwise, having neither brain nor thoughts left. O God! what a misfortune to be born! Born like a mushroom, doubtless between an evening and a morning; and how true and right I was when in our philosophy-year in college I chewed the cud of bitterness with the pessimists. Yes, indeed, there is more pain in life than gladness—it is one long agony until the grave. Think how gay it makes me to remember that this horrible misery of mine, coupled with this unspeakable fear, may last fifty, one hundred, who knows how many more years!"[77]

This letter shows two things. First, you see how the entire consciousness of the poor man is so choked with the feeling of evil that the sense of there being any good in the world is lost for him altogether. His attention excludes it, cannot admit it: the sun has left his heaven. And secondly you see how the querulous temper of his misery keeps his mind from taking a religious direction. Querulousness of mind tends in fact rather towards irreligion; and it has played, so far as I know, no part whatever in the construction of religious systems.

Religious melancholy must be cast in a more melting mood. Tolstoy has left us, in his book called My Confession, a wonderful account of the attack of melancholy which led him to his own religious conclusions. The latter in some respects are peculiar; but the melancholy presents two characters which make it a typical document for our present purpose. First it is a well-marked case of anhedonia, of passive loss of appetite for all life's values; and second, it shows how the altered and estranged aspect which the world assumed in consequence of this stimulated Tolstoy's intellect to a gnawing, carking questioning and effort for philosophic relief. I mean to quote Tolstoy at some length; but before doing so, I will make a general remark on each of these two points.

First on our spiritual judgments and the sense of value in general.

It is notorious that facts are compatible with opposite emotional comments, since the same fact will inspire entirely different feelings in different persons, and at different times in the same person; and there is no rationally deducible connection

77 Roubinovitch et Toulouse: La Mélancolie, 1897, p. 170, abridged.

between any outer fact and the sentiments it may happen to provoke. These have their source in another sphere of existence altogether, in the animal and spiritual region of the subject's being. Conceive yourself, if possible, suddenly stripped of all the emotion with which your world now inspires you, and try to imagine it *as it exists*, purely by itself, without your favorable or unfavorable, hopeful or apprehensive comment. It will be almost impossible for you to realize such a condition of negativity and deadness. No one portion of the universe would then have importance beyond another; and the whole collection of its things and series of its events would be without significance, character, expression, or perspective. Whatever of value, interest, or meaning our respective worlds may appear endued with are thus pure gifts of the spectator's mind. The passion of love is the most familiar and extreme example of this fact. If it comes, it comes; if it does not come, no process of reasoning can force it. Yet it transforms the value of the creature loved as utterly as the sunrise transforms Mont Blanc from a corpse-like gray to a rosy enchantment; and it sets the whole world to a new tune for the lover and gives a new issue to his life. So with fear, with indignation, jealousy, ambition, worship. If they are there, life changes. And whether they shall be there or not depends almost always upon non-logical, often on organic conditions. And as the excited interest which these passions put into the world is our gift to the world, just so are the passions themselves gifts—gifts to us, from sources sometimes low and sometimes high; but almost always non-logical and beyond our control. How can the moribund old man reason back to himself the romance, the mystery, the imminence of great things with which our old earth tingled for him in the days when he was young and well? Gifts, either of the flesh or of the spirit; and the spirit bloweth where it listeth; and the world's materials lend their surface passively to all the gifts alike, as the stage-setting receives indifferently whatever alternating colored lights may be shed upon it from the optical apparatus in the gallery.

Meanwhile the practically real world for each one of us, the effective world of the individual, is the compound world, the physical facts and emotional values in indistinguishable combination. Withdraw or pervert either factor of this complex resultant, and the kind of experience we call pathological ensues.

In Tolstoy's case the sense that life had any meaning whatever was for a time wholly withdrawn. The result was a transformation in the whole expression of reality. When we come to study the phenomenon of conversion or religious regeneration, we shall see that a not infrequent consequence of the change operated in the subject is a transfiguration of the face of nature in his eyes. A new heaven seems to shine upon a new earth. In melancholiacs there is usually a similar change, only it is in the reverse direction. The world now looks remote, strange, sinister, uncanny. Its color is gone, its breath is cold, there is no speculation in the eyes it glares with. "It is as if I lived in another century," says one asylum patient.—"I see everything through a cloud," says another, "things are not as they were, and I am changed."—"I see," says a third, "I touch, but the things do not come near me, a thick veil alters the hue and look of everything."—"Persons move like shadows, and sounds seem to come from a distant world."—"There is no longer any past for me; people appear so strange; it is as if I could not see any reality, as if I were in a theatre; as if people were actors, and everything were scenery; I can no longer find myself; I walk, but why? Everything floats before my eyes, but leaves no impression."—"I weep false tears, I have unreal hands: the things I see are not real things."—Such are expressions that naturally rise to the lips of melancholy subjects describing their changed state.[78]

Now there are some subjects whom all this leaves a prey to the profoundest astonishment. The strangeness is wrong. The unreality cannot be. A mystery is concealed, and a metaphysical solution must exist. If the natural world is so double-faced and unhomelike, what world, what thing is real? An urgent wondering and questioning is set up, a poring theoretic activity, and in the desperate effort to get into right relations with the matter, the sufferer is often led to what becomes for him a satisfying religious solution.

At about the age of fifty, Tolstoy relates that he began to have moments of perplexity, of what he calls arrest, as if he knew not "how to live," or what to do. It is obvious that these were moments in which the excitement and interest which our functions naturally bring had ceased. Life had been enchanting, it was now flat sober, more than sober, dead. Things were meaningless whose meaning had always been self-evident. The questions "Why?" and "What next?" began to beset him more and more frequently. At first it seemed as if such questions must be answerable, and as if he could easily find the answers if he would take the time; but as they ever became more urgent, he perceived that it was like those first discomforts of a sick man, to which he pays but little attention till they run into one continuous suffering, and then he realizes that what he took for a passing disorder means the most momentous thing in the world for him, means his death.

These questions "Why?" "Wherefore?" "What for?" found no response.

> "I felt," says Tolstoy, "that something had broken within me on which my life had always rested, that I had nothing left to hold on to, and that morally my life had stopped. An invincible force impelled me to get rid of my existence, in one way or another. It cannot be said exactly that I *wished* to kill myself, for the force which drew me away from life was fuller, more powerful, more general than any mere desire. It was a force like my old aspiration to live, only it impelled me in the opposite direction. It was an aspiration of my whole being to get out of life.
>
> "Behold me then, a man happy and in good health, hiding the rope in order not to hang myself to the rafters of the room where every night I went to sleep alone; behold me no longer going shooting, lest I should yield to the too easy temptation of putting an end to myself with my gun.
>
> "I did not know what I wanted. I was afraid of life; I was driven to leave it; and in spite of that I still hoped something from it.
>
> "All this took place at a time when so far as all my outer circumstances went,

78 I cull these examples from the work of G. Dumas: La Tristesse et la Joie, 1900.

I ought to have been completely happy. I had a good wife who loved me and whom I loved; good children and a large property which was increasing with no pains taken on my part. I was more respected by my kinsfolk and acquaintance than I had ever been; I was loaded with praise by strangers; and without exaggeration I could believe my name already famous. Moreover I was neither insane nor ill. On the contrary, I possessed a physical and mental strength which I have rarely met in persons of my age. I could mow as well as the peasants, I could work with my brain eight hours uninterruptedly and feel no bad effects.

"And yet I could give no reasonable meaning to any actions of my life. And I was surprised that I had not understood this from the very beginning. My state of mind was as if some wicked and stupid jest was being played upon me by some one. One can live only so long as one is intoxicated, drunk with life; but when one grows sober one cannot fail to see that it is all a stupid cheat. What is truest about it is that there is nothing even funny or silly in it; it is cruel and stupid, purely and simply.

"The oriental fable of the traveler surprised in the desert by a wild beast is very old.

"Seeking to save himself from the fierce animal, the traveler jumps into a well with no water in it; but at the bottom of this well he sees a dragon waiting with open mouth to devour him. And the unhappy man, not daring to go out lest he should be the prey of the beast, not daring to jump to the bottom lest he should be devoured by the dragon, clings to the branches of a wild bush which grows out of one of the cracks of the well. His hands weaken, and he feels that he must soon give way to certain fate; but still he clings, and see two mice, one white, the other black, evenly moving round the bush to which he hangs, and gnawing off its roots.

"The traveler sees this and knows that he must inevitably perish; but while thus hanging he looks about him and finds on the leaves of the bush some drops of honey. These he reaches with his tongue and licks them off with rapture.

"Thus I hang upon the boughs of life, knowing that the inevitable dragon of death is waiting ready to tear me, and I cannot comprehend why I am thus made a martyr. I try to suck the honey which formerly consoled me; but the honey pleases me no longer, and day and night the white mouse and the black mouse gnaw the branch to which I cling. I can see but one thing: the inevitable dragon and the mice—I cannot turn my gaze away from them.

"This is no fable, but the literal incontestable truth which every one may understand. What will be the outcome of what I do to-day? Of what I shall do to-morrow? What will be the outcome of all my life? Why should I live? Why should I do anything? Is there in life any purpose which the inevitable death which awaits me does not undo and destroy?

"These questions are the simplest in the world. From the stupid child to the wisest old man, they are in the soul of every human being. Without an answer to them, it is impossible, as I experienced, for life to go on.

"'But perhaps,' I often said to myself, 'there may be something I have failed to notice or to comprehend. It is not possible that this condition of despair should be natural to mankind.' And I sought for an explanation in all the

> branches of knowledge acquired by men. I questioned painfully and protractedly and with no idle curiosity. I sought, not with indolence, but laboriously and obstinately for days and nights together. I sought like a man who is lost and seeks to save himself—and I found nothing. I became convinced, moreover, that all those who before me had sought for an answer in the sciences have also found nothing. And not only this, but that they have recognized that the very thing which was leading me to despair—the meaningless absurdity of life—is the only incontestable knowledge accessible to man."

To prove this point, Tolstoy quotes the Buddha, Solomon, and Schopenhauer. And he finds only four ways in which men of his own class and society are accustomed to meet the situation. Either mere animal blindness, sucking the honey without seeing the dragon or the mice—"and from such a way," he says, "I can learn nothing, after what I now know;" or reflective epicureanism, snatching what it can while the day lasts—which is only a more deliberate sort of stupefaction than the first; or manly suicide; or seeing the mice and dragon and yet weakly and plaintively clinging to the bush of life.

Suicide was naturally the consistent course dictated by the logical intellect.

> "Yet," says Tolstoy, "whilst my intellect was working, something else in me was working too, and kept me from the deed—a consciousness of life, as I may call it, which was like a force that obliged my mind to fix itself in another direction and draw me out of my situation of despair. . . . During the whole course of this year, when I almost unceasingly kept asking myself how to end the business, whether by the rope or by the bullet, during all that time, alongside of all those movements of my ideas and observations, my heart kept languishing with another pining emotion. I can call this by no other name than that of a thirst for God. This craving for God had nothing to do with the movement of my ideas—in fact, it was the direct contrary of that movement—but it came from my heart. It was like a feeling of dread that made me seem like an orphan and isolated in the midst of all these things that were so foreign. And this feeling of dread was mitigated by the hope of finding the assistance of some one."[79]

Of the process, intellectual as well as emotional, which, starting from this idea of God, led to Tolstoy's recovery, I will say nothing in this lecture, reserving it for a later hour. The only thing that need interest us now is the phenomenon of his absolute disenchantment with ordinary life, and the fact that the whole range of habitual values may, to a man as powerful and full of faculty as he was, come to appear so ghastly a mockery.

When disillusionment has gone as far as this, there is seldom a *restitutio ad integrum*. One has tasted of the fruit of the tree, and the happiness of Eden never comes again. The happiness that comes, when any does come—and often enough it

79 My extracts are from the French translation by "Zonia." In abridging I have taken the liberty of transposing one passage.

fails to return in an acute form, though its form is sometimes very acute—is not the simple, ignorance of ill, but something vastly more complex, including natural evil as one of its elements, but finding natural evil no such stumbling-block and terror because it now sees it swallowed up in supernatural good. The process is one of redemption, not of mere reversion to natural health, and the sufferer, when saved, is saved by what seems to him a second birth, a deeper kind of conscious being than he could enjoy before.

We find a somewhat different type of religious melancholy enshrined in literature in John Bunyan's autobiography. Tolstoy's preoccupations were largely objective, for the purpose and meaning of life in general was what so troubled him; but poor Bunyan's troubles were over the condition of his own personal self. He was a typical case of the psychopathic temperament, sensitive of conscience to a diseased degree, beset by doubts, fears and insistent ideas, and a victim of verbal automatisms, both motor and sensory. These were usually texts of Scripture which, sometimes damnatory and sometimes favorable, would come in a half-hallucinatory form as if they were voices, and fasten on his mind and buffet it between them like a shuttlecock. Added to this were a fearful melancholy self-contempt and despair:

> "Nay, thought I, now I grow worse and worse; now I am farther from conversion than ever I was before. If now I should have burned at the stake, I could not believe that Christ had love for me; alas, I could neither hear him, nor see him, nor feel him, nor savor any of his things. Sometimes I would tell my condition to the people of God, which, when they heard, they would pity me, and would tell of the Promises. But they had as good have told me that I must reach the Sun with my finger as have bidden me receive or rely upon the Promise [Yet] all this while as to the act of sinning, I never was more tender than now; I durst not take a pin or stick, though but so big as a straw, for my conscience now was sore, and would smart at every touch; I could not tell how to speak my words, for fear I should misplace them. Oh, how gingerly did I then go, in all I did or said! I found myself as on a miry bog that shook if I did but stir; and was as there left both by God and Christ, and the spirit, and all good things.
>
> "But my original and inward pollution, that was my plague and my affliction. By reason of that, I was more loathsome in my own eyes than was a toad; and I thought I was so in God's eyes too. Sin and corruption, I said, would as naturally bubble out of my heart as water would bubble out of a fountain. I could have changed heart with anybody. I thought none but the Devil himself could equal me for inward wickedness and pollution of mind. Sure, thought I, I am forsaken of God; and thus I continued a long while, even for some years together.
>
> "And now I was sorry that God had made me a man. The beasts, birds, fishes, etc., I blessed their condition, for they had not a sinful nature; they were not obnoxious to the wrath of God; they were not to go to hell-fire after death. I could therefore have rejoiced, had my condition been as any of theirs. Now I blessed the condition of the dog and toad, yea, gladly would I have been in the condition of the dog or horse, for I knew they had no soul to perish under the

everlasting weight of Hell or Sin, as mine was like to do. Nay, and though I saw this, felt this, and was broken to pieces with it, yet that which added to my sorrow was, that I could not find with all my soul that I did desire deliverance. My heart was at times exceedingly hard. If I would have given a thousand pounds for a tear, I could not shed one; no, nor sometimes scarce desire to shed one.

"I was both a burthen and a terror to myself; nor did I ever so know, as now, what it was to be weary of my life, and yet afraid to die. How gladly would I have been anything but myself! Anything but a man! and in any condition but my own."[80]

Poor patient Bunyan, like Tolstoy, saw the light again, but we must also postpone that part of his story to another hour. In a later lecture I will also give the end of the experience of Henry Alline, a devoted evangelist who worked in Nova Scotia a hundred years ago, and who thus vividly describes the high-water mark of the religious melancholy which formed its beginning. The type was not unlike Bunyan's.

"Everything I saw seemed to be a burden to me; the earth seemed accursed for my sake: all trees, plants, rocks, hills, and vales seemed to be dressed in mourning and groaning, under the weight of the curse, and everything around me seemed to be conspiring my ruin. My sins seemed to be laid open; so that I thought that every one I saw knew them, and sometimes I was almost ready to acknowledge many things, which I thought they knew: yea sometimes it seemed to me as if every one was pointing me out as the most guilty wretch upon earth. I had now so great a sense of the vanity and emptiness of all things here below, that I knew the whole world could not possibly make me happy, no, nor the whole system of creation. When I waked in the morning, the first thought would be, Oh, my wretched soul, what shall I do, where shall I go? And when I laid down, would say, I shall be perhaps in hell before morning. I would many times look on the beasts with envy, wishing with all my heart I was in their place, that I might have no soul to lose; and when I have seen birds flying over my head, have often thought within myself, Oh, that I could fly away from my danger and distress! Oh, how happy should I be, if I were in their place!"[81]

Envy of the placid beasts seems to be a very widespread affection in this type of sadness.

The worst kind of melancholy is that which takes the form of panic fear. Here is an excellent example, for permission to print which I have to thank the sufferer. The original is in French, and though the subject was evidently in a bad nervous condition at the time of which he writes, his case has otherwise the merit of extreme simplicity. I translate freely.

---

80 Grace abounding to the Chief of Sinners: I have printed a number of detached passages continuously.

81 The Life and Journal of the Rev. Mr. Henry Alline, Boston, 1806, pp. 25, 26. I owe my acquaintance with this book to my colleague, Dr. Benjamin Rand.

"Whilst in this state of philosophic pessimism and general depression of spirits about my prospects, I went one evening into a dressing-room in the twilight to procure some article that was there; when suddenly there fell upon me without any warning, just as if it came out of the darkness, a horrible fear of my own existence. Simultaneously there arose in my mind the image of an epileptic patient whom I had seen in the asylum, a black-haired youth with greenish skin, entirely idiotic, who used to sit all day on one of the benches, or rather shelves against the wall, with his knees drawn up against his chin, and the coarse gray undershirt, which was his only garment, drawn over them inclosing his entire figure. He sat there like a sort of sculptured Egyptian cat or Peruvian mummy, moving nothing but his black eyes and looking absolutely non-human. This image and my fear entered into a species of combination with each other. *That shape am I*, I felt, potentially. Nothing that I possess can defend me against that fate, if the hour for it should strike for me as it struck for him. There was such a horror of him, and such a perception of my own merely momentary discrepancy from him, that it was as if something hitherto solid within my breast gave way entirely, and I became a mass of quivering fear. After this the universe was changed for me altogether. I awoke morning after morning with a horrible dread at the pit of my stomach, and with a sense of the insecurity of life that I never knew before, and that I have never felt since.[82] It was like a revelation; and although the immediate feelings passed away, the experience has made me sympathetic with the morbid feelings of others ever since. It gradually faded, but for months I was unable to go out into the dark alone.

"In general I dreaded to be left alone. I remember wondering how other people could live, how I myself had ever lived, so unconscious of that pit of insecurity beneath the surface of life. My mother in particular, a very cheerful person, seemed to me a perfect paradox in her unconsciousness of danger, which you may well believe I was very careful not to disturb by revelations of my own state of mind. I have always thought that this experience of melancholia of mine had a religious bearing."

On asking this correspondent to explain more fully what he meant by these last words, the answer he wrote was this:—

"I mean that the fear was so invasive and powerful that if I had not clung to scripture-texts like 'The eternal God is my refuge,' etc., 'Come unto me, all ye

82 Compare Bunyan: "There was I struck into a very great trembling, insomuch that at some times I could, for days together, feel my very body, as well as my mind, to shake and totter under the sense of the dreadful judgment of God, that should fall on those that have sinned that most fearful and unpardonable sin. I felt also such clogging and heat at my stomach, by reason of this my terror, that I was, especially at some times, as if my breast-bone would have split asunder. . . . Thus did I wind, and twine, and shrink, undo the burden that was upon me; which burden also did so oppress me that I could neither stand, nor go, nor lie, either at rest or quiet."

that labor and are heavy-laden,' etc., 'I am the resurrection and the life,' etc., I think I should have grown really insane."[83]

There is no need of more examples. The cases we have looked at are enough. One of them gives us the vanity of mortal things; another the sense of sin; and the remaining one describes the fear of the universe;—and in one or other of these three ways it always is that man's original optimism and self-satisfaction get leveled with the dust.

In none of these cases was there any intellectual insanity or delusion about matters of fact; but were we disposed to open the chapter of really insane melancholia, with its hallucinations and delusions, it would be a worse story still-desperation absolute and complete, the whole universe coagulating about the sufferer into a material of overwhelming horror, surrounding him without opening or end. Not the conception or intellectual perception of evil, but the grisly blood-freezing heart-palsying sensation of it close upon one, and no other conception or sensation able to live for a moment in its presence. How irrelevantly remote seem all our usual refined optimisms and intellectual and moral consolations in presence of a need of help like this! Here is the real core of the religious problem: Help! help! No prophet can claim to bring a final message unless he says things that will have a sound of reality in the ears of victims such as these. But the deliverance must come in as strong a form as the complaint, if it is to take effect; and that seems a reason why the coarser religions, revivalistic, orgiastic, with blood and miracles and supernatural operations, may possibly never be displaced. Some constitutions need them too much.

Arrived at this point, we can see how great an antagonism may naturally arise between the healthy-minded way of viewing life and the way that takes all this experience of evil as something essential. To this latter way, the morbid-minded way, as we might call it, healthy-mindedness pure and simple seems unspeakably blind and shallow. To the healthy-minded way, on the other hand, the way of the sick soul seems unmanly and diseased. With their grubbing in rat-holes instead of living in the light; with their manufacture of fears, and preoccupation with every unwholesome kind of misery, there is something almost obscene about these children of wrath and cravers of a second birth. If religious intolerance and hanging and burning could again become the order of the day, there is little doubt that, however it may have been in the past, the healthy-minded would at present show themselves the less indulgent party of the two.

In our own attitude, not yet abandoned, of impartial onlookers, what are we to say of this quarrel? It seems to me that we are bound to say that morbid-mindedness ranges over the wider scale of experience, and that its survey is the one that overlaps.

83 For another case of fear equally sudden, see Henry James: Society the Redeemed Form of Man, Boston, 1879, pp. 43 ff.

The method of averting one's attention from evil, and living simply in the light of good is splendid as long as it will work. It will work with many persons; it will work far more generally than most of us are ready to suppose; and within the sphere of its successful operation there is nothing to be said against it as a religious solution. But it breaks down impotently as soon as melancholy comes; and even though one be quite free from melancholy one's self, there is no doubt that healthy-mindedness is inadequate as a philosophical doctrine, because the evil facts which it refuses positively to account for are a genuine portion of reality; and they may after all be the best key to life's significance, and possibly the only openers of our eyes to the deepest levels of truth.

The normal process of life contains moments as bad as any of those which insane melancholy is filled with, moments in which radical evil gets its innings and takes its solid turn. The lunatic's visions of horror are all drawn from the material of daily fact. Our civilization is founded on the shambles, and every individual existence goes out in a lonely spasm of helpless agony. If you protest, my friend, wait till you arrive there yourself! To believe in the carnivorous reptiles of geologic times is hard for our imagination—they seem too much like mere museum specimens. Yet there is no tooth in any one of those museum-skulls that did not daily through long years of the foretime hold fast to the body struggling in despair of some fated living victim. Forms of horror just as dreadful to the victims, if on a smaller spatial scale, fill the world about us to-day. Here on our very hearths and in our gardens the infernal cat plays with the panting mouse, or holds the hot bird fluttering in her jaws. Crocodiles and rattlesnakes and pythons are at this moment vessels of life as real as we are; their loathsome existence fills every minute of every day that drags its length along; and whenever they or other wild beasts clutch their living prey, the deadly horror which an agitated melancholiac feels is the literally right reaction on the situation.[84]

It may indeed be that no religious reconciliation with the absolute totality of things is possible. Some evils, indeed, are ministerial to higher forms of good; but it may be that there are forms of evil so extreme as to enter into no good system whatsoever, and that, in respect of such evil, dumb submission or neglect to notice

---

84 Example: "It was about eleven o'clock at night . . . but I strolled on still with the people. . . . Suddenly upon the left side of our road, a crackling was heard among the bushes; all of us were alarmed, and in an instant a tiger, rushing out of the jungle, pounced upon the one of the party that was foremost, and carried him off in the twinkling of an eye. The rush of the animal, and the crush of the poor victim's bones in his mouth, and his last cry of distress, 'Ho hai!' involuntarily reëchoed by all of us, was over in three seconds; and then I know not what happened till I returned to my senses, when I found myself and companions lying down on the ground as if prepared to be devoured by our enemy, the sovereign of the forest. I find my pen incapable of describing the terror of that dreadful moment. Our limbs stiffened, our power of speech ceased, and our hearts beat violently, and only a whisper of the same 'Ho hai!' was heard from us. In this state we crept on all fours for some distance back, and then ran for life with the speed of an Arab horse for about half an hour, and fortunately happened to come to a small village. . . . After this every one of us was attacked with fever, attended with shivering, in which deplorable state we remained till morning."—Autobiography of Lutfullah, a Mohammedan Gentleman, Leipzig, 1857, p. 112.

is the only practical resource. This question must confront us on a later day. But provisionally, and as a mere matter of program and method, since the evil facts are as genuine parts of nature as the good ones, the philosophic presumption should be that they have some rational significance, and that systematic healthy-mindedness, failing as it does to accord to sorrow, pain, and death any positive and active attention whatever, is formally less complete than systems that try at least to include these elements in their scope.

The completest religions would therefore seem to be those in which the pessimistic elements are best developed. Buddhism, of course, and Christianity are the best known to us of these. They are essentially religions of deliverance: the man must die to an unreal life before he can be born into the real life. In my next lecture, I will try to discuss some of the psychological conditions of this second birth. Fortunately from now onward we shall have to deal with more cheerful subjects than those which we have recently been dwelling on.

## LECTURE VIII

# The Divided Self, and the Process of Its Unification

The last lecture was a painful one, dealing as it did with evil as a pervasive element of the world we live in. At the close of it we were brought into full view of the contrast between the two ways of looking at life which are characteristic respectively of what we called the healthy-minded, who need to be born only once, and of the sick souls, who must be twice-born in order to be happy. The result is two different conceptions of the universe of our experience. In the religion of the once-born the world is a sort of rectilinear or one-storied affair, whose accounts are kept in one denomination, whose parts have just the values which naturally they appear to have, and of which a simple algebraic sum of pluses and minuses will give the total worth. Happiness and religious peace consist in living on the plus side of the account. In the religion of the twice-born, on the other hand, the world is a double-storied mystery. Peace cannot be reached by the simple addition of pluses and elimination of minuses from life. Natural good is not simply insufficient in amount and transient, there lurks a falsity in its very being. Cancelled as it all is by death if not by earlier enemies, it gives no final balance, and can never be the thing intended for our lasting worship. It keeps us from our real good, rather; and renunciation and despair of it are our first step in the direction of the truth. There are two lives, the natural and the spiritual, and we must lose the one before we can participate in the other.

In their extreme forms, of pure naturalism and pure salvationism, the two types are violently contrasted; though here as in most other current classifications, the radical extremes are somewhat ideal abstractions, and the concrete human beings whom we oftenest meet are intermediate varieties and mixtures. Practically, however, you all recognize the difference: you understand, for example, the disdain of the methodist convert for the mere sky-blue healthy-minded moralist; and you likewise enter into the aversion of the latter to what seems to him the diseased subjectivism of the Methodist, dying to live, as he calls it, and making of paradox and the inversion of natural appearances the essence of God's truth.[85]

85 E.g., "Our young people are diseased with the theological problems of original sin, origin of evil, predestination, and the like. These never presented a practical difficulty to any man—never darkened

The psychological basis of the twice-born character seems to be a certain discordancy or heterogeneity in the native temperament of the subject, an incompletely unified moral and intellectual constitution.

> "Homo duplex, homo duplex!" writes Alphonse Daudet. "The first time that I perceived that I was two was at the death of my brother Henri, when my father cried out so dramatically, 'He is dead, he is dead!' While my first self wept, my second self thought, 'How truly given was that cry, how fine it would be at the theatre.' I was then fourteen years old.
>
> "This horrible duality has often given me matter for reflection. Oh, this terrible second me, always seated whilst the other is on foot, acting, living, suffering, bestirring itself. This second me that I have never been able to intoxicate, to make shed tears, or put to sleep. And how it sees into things, and how it mocks!"[86]

Recent works on the psychology of character have had much to say upon this point.[87] Some persons are born with an inner constitution which is harmonious and well balanced from the outset. Their impulses are consistent with one another, their will follows without trouble the guidance of their intellect, their passions are not excessive, and their lives are little haunted by regrets. Others are oppositely constituted; and are so in degrees which may vary from something so slight as to result in a merely odd or whimsical inconsistency, to a discordancy of which the consequences may be inconvenient in the extreme. Of the more innocent kinds of heterogeneity I find a good example in Mrs. Annie Besant's autobiography.

> "I have ever been the queerest mixture of weakness and strength, and have paid heavily for the weakness. As a child I used to suffer tortures of shyness, and if my shoe-lace was untied would feel shamefacedly that every eye was fixed on the unlucky string; as a girl I would shrink away from strangers and think myself unwanted and unliked, so that I was full of eager gratitude to any one who noticed me kindly; as the young mistress of a house I was afraid of my servants, and would let careless work pass rather than bear the pain of reproving the ill-doer; when I have been lecturing and debating with no lack of spirit on the platform, I have preferred to go without what I wanted at the hotel rather than to ring and make the waiter fetch it. Combative on the platform in defense of any cause I cared for, I shrink from quarrel or disapproval in the house, and am a coward at heart in private while a good fighter in public. How often have I passed unhappy quarters of an hour screwing up my courage to find fault with

---

across any man's road, who did not go out of his way to seek them. These are the soul's mumps, and measles, and whooping-coughs," etc. Emerson: "Spiritual Laws."

86 Notes sur la Vie, p. 1.

87 See, for example, F. Paulhan, in his book Les Caractères, 1894, who contrasts les Equilibrés, les Unifiés, with les Inquiets, les Contrariants, les Incohérents, les Emiettés, as so many diverse psychic types.

some subordinate whom my duty compelled me to reprove, and how often have I jeered myself for a fraud as the doughty platform combatant, when shrinking from blaming some lad or lass for doing their work badly. An unkind look or word has availed to make me shrink into myself as a snail into its shell, while, on the platform, opposition makes me speak my best."[88]

This amount of inconsistency will only count as amiable weakness; but a stronger degree of heterogeneity may make havoc of the subject's life. There are persons whose existence is little more than a series of zig-zags, as now one tendency and now another gets the upper hand. Their spirit wars with their flesh, they wish for incompatibles, wayward impulses interrupt their most deliberate plans, and their lives are one long drama of repentance and of effort to repair misdemeanors and mistakes.

Heterogeneous personality has been explained as the result of inheritance—the traits of character of incompatible and antagonistic ancestors are supposed to be preserved alongside of each other.[89] This explanation may pass for what it is worth—it certainly needs corroboration. But whatever the cause of heterogeneous personality may be, we find the extreme examples of it in the psychopathic temperament, of which I spoke in my first lecture. All writers about that temperament make the inner heterogeneity prominent in their descriptions. Frequently, indeed, it is only this trait that leads us to ascribe that temperament to a man at all. A "dégénéré supérieur" is simply a man of sensibility in many directions, who finds more difficulty than is common in keeping his spiritual house in order and running his furrow straight, because his feelings and impulses are too keen and too discrepant mutually. In the haunting and insistent ideas, in the irrational impulses, the morbid scruples, dreads, and inhibitions which beset the psychopathic temperament when it is thoroughly pronounced, we have exquisite examples of heterogeneous personality. Bunyan had an obsession of the words, "Sell Christ for this, sell him for that, sell him, sell him!" which would run through his mind a hundred times together, until one day out of breath with retorting, "I will not, I will not," he impulsively said, "Let him go if he will," and this loss of the battle kept him in despair for over a year. The lives of the saints are full of such blasphemous obsessions, ascribed invariably to the direct agency of Satan. The phenomenon connects itself with the life of the subconscious self, so-called, of which we must erelong speak more directly.

Now in all of us, however constituted, but to a degree the greater in proportion as we are intense and sensitive and subject to diversified temptations, and to the greatest possible degree if we are decidedly psychopathic, does the normal evolution of character chiefly consist in the straightening out and unifying of the inner self. The higher and the lower feelings, the useful and the erring impulses, begin by being a comparative chaos within us—they must end by forming a stable system of functions in right subordination. Unhappiness is apt to characterize the period of order-

---

88 Annie Besant: an Autobiography, p. 82.

89 Smith Baker, in Journal of Nervous and Mental Diseases, September, 1893.

making and struggle. If the individual be of tender conscience and religiously quickened, the unhappiness will take the form of moral remorse and compunction, of feeling inwardly vile and wrong, and of standing in false relations to the author of one's being and appointer of one's spiritual fate. This is the religious melancholy and "conviction of sin" that have played so large a part in the history of Protestant Christianity. The man's interior is a battle-ground for what he feels to be two deadly hostile selves, one actual, the other ideal. As Victor Hugo makes his Mahomet say:—

> *"Je suis le champ vil des sublimes combats:*
> *Tantôt l'homme d'en haut, et tantôt l'homme d'en bas;*
> *Et le mal dans ma bouche avec le bien alterne,*
> *Comme dans le désert le sable et la citerne."*

Wrong living, impotent aspirations; "What I would, that do I not; but what I hate, that do I," as Saint Paul says; self-loathing, self-despair; an unintelligible and intolerable burden to which one is mysteriously the heir.

Let me quote from some typical cases of discordant personality, with melancholy in the form of self-condemnation and sense of sin. Saint Augustine's case is a classic example. You all remember his half-pagan, half-Christian bringing up at Carthage, his emigration to Rome and Milan, his adoption of Manicheism and subsequent skepticism, and his restless search for truth and purity of life; and finally how, distracted by the struggle between the two souls in his breast and ashamed of his own weakness of will, when so many others whom he knew and knew of had thrown off the shackles of sensuality and dedicated themselves to chastity and the higher life, he heard a voice in the garden say, "*Sume, lege*" (take and read), and opening the Bible at random, saw the text, "not in chambering and wantonness," etc., which seemed directly sent to his address, and laid the inner storm to rest forever.[90] Augustine's psychological genius has given an account of the trouble of having a divided self which has never been surpassed.

> "The new will which I began to have was not yet strong enough to overcome that other will, strengthened by long indulgence. So these two wills, one old, one new, one carnal, the other spiritual, contended with each other and disturbed my soul. I understood by my own experience what I had read, 'flesh lusteth against spirit, and spirit against flesh.' It was myself indeed in both the wills, yet more myself in that which I approved in myself than in that which I disapproved in myself. Yet it was through myself that habit had attained so fierce a mastery over

90 Louis Gourdon (Essai sur la Conversion de Saint Augustine, Paris, Fischbacher, 1900) has shown by an analysis of Augustine's writings immediately after the date of his conversion (a. d. 386) that the account he gives in the Confessions is premature. The crisis in the garden marked a definitive conversion from his former life, but it was to the neo-platonic spiritualism and only a halfway stage toward Christianity. The latter he appears not fully and radically to have embraced until four years more had passed.

me, because I had willingly come whither I willed not. Still bound to earth, I refused, O God, to fight on thy side, as much afraid to be freed from all bonds, as I ought to have feared being trammeled by them.

"Thus the thoughts by which I meditated upon thee were like the efforts of one who would awake, but being overpowered with sleepiness is soon asleep again. Often does a man when heavy sleepiness is on his limbs defer to shake it off, and though not approving it, encourage it; even so I was sure it was better to surrender to thy love than to yield to my own lusts, yet, though the former course convinced me, the latter pleased and held me bound. There was naught in me to answer thy call, 'Awake, thou sleeper,' but only drawling, drowsy words, 'Presently; yes, presently; wait a little while.' But the 'presently' had no 'present,' and the 'little while' grew long. . . . For I was afraid thou wouldst hear me too soon, and heal me at once of my disease of lust, which I wished to satiate rather than to see extinguished. With what lashes of words did I not scourge my own soul. Yet it shrank back; it refused, though it had no excuse to offer. . . . I said within myself: 'Come, let it be done now,' and as I said it, I was on the point of the resolve. I all but did it, yet I did not do it. And I made another effort, and almost succeeded, yet I did not reach it, and did not grasp it, hesitating to die to death, and live to life; and the evil to which I was so wonted held me more than the better life I had not tried."[91]

There could be no more perfect description of the divided will, when the higher wishes lack just that last acuteness, that touch of explosive intensity, of dynamogenic quality (to use the slang of the psychologists), that enables them to burst their shell, and make irruption efficaciously into life and quell the lower tendencies forever. In a later lecture we shall have much to say about this higher excitability.

I find another good description of the divided will in the autobiography of Henry Alline, the Nova Scotian evangelist, of whose melancholy I read a brief account in my last lecture. The poor youth's sins were, as you will see, of the most harmless order, yet they interfered with what proved to be his truest vocation, so they gave him great distress.

"I was now very moral in my life, but found no rest of conscience. I now began to be esteemed in young company, who knew nothing of my mind all this while, and their esteem began to be a snare to my soul, for I soon began to be fond of carnal mirth, though I still flattered myself that if I did not get drunk, nor curse, nor swear, there would be no sin in frolicking and carnal mirth, and I thought God would indulge young people with some (what I called simple or civil) recreation. I still kept a round of duties, and would not suffer myself to run into any open vices, and so got along very well in time of health and prosperity, but when I was distressed or threatened by sickness, death, or heavy storms of thunder, my religion would not do, and I found there was something wanting, and would

91 Confessions, Book VIII., chaps. v., vii., xi., abridged.

begin to repent my going so much to frolics, but when the distress was over, the devil and my own wicked heart, with the solicitations of my associates, and my fondness for young company, were such strong allurements, I would again give way, and thus I got to be very wild and rude, at the same time kept up my rounds of secret prayer and reading; but God, not willing I should destroy myself, still followed me with his calls, and moved with such power upon my conscience, that I could not satisfy myself with my diversions, and in the midst of my mirth sometimes would have such a sense of my lost and undone condition, that I would wish myself from the company, and after it was over, when I went home, would make many promises that I would attend no more on these frolics, and would beg forgiveness for hours and hours; but when I came to have the temptation again, I would give way: no sooner would I hear the music and drink a glass of wine, but I would find my mind elevated and soon proceed to any sort of merriment or diversion, that I thought was not debauched or openly vicious; but when I returned from my carnal mirth I felt as guilty as ever, and could sometimes not close my eyes for some hours after I had gone to my bed. I was one of the most unhappy creatures on earth.

"Sometimes I would leave the company (often speaking to the fiddler to cease from playing, as if I was tired), and go out and walk about crying and praying, as if my very heart would break, and beseeching God that he would not cut me off, nor give me up to hardness of heart. Oh, what unhappy hours and nights I thus wore away! When I met sometimes with merry companions, and my heart was ready to sink, I would labor to put on as cheerful a countenance as possible, that they might not distrust anything, and sometimes would begin some discourse with young men or young women on purpose, or propose a merry song, lest the distress of my soul would be discovered, or mistrusted, when at the same time I would then rather have been in a wilderness in exile, than with them or any of their pleasures or enjoyments. Thus for many months when I was in company, I would act the hypocrite and feign a merry heart, but at the same time would endeavor as much as I could to shun their company, oh wretched and unhappy mortal that I was! Everything I did, and wherever I went, I was still in a storm, and yet I continued to be the chief contriver and ringleader of the frolics for many months after; though it was a toil and torment to attend them; but the devil and my own wicked heart drove me about like a slave, telling me that I must do this and do that, and bear this and bear that, and turn here and turn there, to keep my credit up, and retain the esteem of my associates: and all this while I continued as strict as possible in my duties, and left no stone unturned to pacify my conscience, watching even against my thoughts, and praying continually wherever I went: for I did not think there was any sin in my conduct, when I was among carnal company, because I did not take any satisfaction there, but only followed it, I thought, for sufficient reasons.

"But still, all that I did or could do, conscience would roar night and day."

Saint Augustine and Alline both emerged into the smooth waters of inner unity and peace, and I shall next ask you to consider more closely some of the peculiarities of the process of unification, when it occurs. It may come gradually, or it may occur abruptly; it may come through altered feelings, or through altered powers of action; or it may come through new intellectual insights, or through experiences which we shall later have to designate as "mystical." However it come, it brings a characteristic sort of relief; and never such extreme relief as when it is cast into the religious mould. Happiness! happiness! religion is only one of the ways in which men gain that gift. Easily, permanently, and successfully, it often transforms the most intolerable misery into the profoundest and most enduring happiness.

But to find religion is only one out of many ways of reaching unity; and the process of remedying inner incompleteness and reducing inner discord is a general psychological process, which may take place with any sort of mental material, and need not necessarily assume the religious form. In judging of the religious types of regeneration which we are about to study, it is important to recognize that they are only one species of a genus that contains other types as well. For example, the new birth may be away from religion into incredulity; or it may be from moral scrupulosity into freedom and license; or it may be produced by the irruption into the individual's life of some new stimulus or passion, such as love, ambition, cupidity, revenge, or patriotic devotion. In all these instances we have precisely the same psychological form of event,—a firmness, stability, and equilibrium succeeding a period of storm and stress and inconsistency. In these non-religious cases the new man may also be born either gradually or suddenly.

The French philosopher Jouffroy has left an eloquent memorial of his own "counter-conversion," as the transition from orthodoxy to infidelity has been well styled by Mr. Starbuck. Jouffroy's doubts had long harassed him; but he dates his final crisis from a certain night when his disbelief grew fixed and stable, and where the immediate result was sadness at the illusions he had lost.

> "I shall never forget that night of December," writes Jouffroy, "in which the veil that concealed from me my own incredulity was torn. I hear again my steps in that narrow naked chamber where long after the hour of sleep had come I had the habit of walking up and down. I see again that moon, halfveiled by clouds, which now and again illuminated the frigid window-panes. The hours of the night flowed on and I did not note their passage. Anxiously I followed my thoughts, as from layer to layer they descended towards the foundation of my consciousness, and, scattering one by one all the illusions which until then had screened its windings from my view, made them every moment more clearly visible.
>
> "Vainly I clung to these last beliefs as a shipwrecked sailor clings to the fragments of his vessel; vainly, frightened at the unknown void in which I was about to float, I turned with them towards my childhood, my family, my country, all that was dear and sacred to me: the inflexible current of my thought was too strong—parents, family, memory, beliefs, it forced me to let go of everything. The investigation went on more obstinate and more severe as it drew near its term, and did not stop until the end was reached. I knew then that in the depth of my mind nothing was left that stood erect.

"This moment was a frightful one; and when towards morning I threw myself exhausted on my bed, I seemed to feel my earlier life, so smiling and so full, go out like a fire, and before me another life opened, sombre and unpeopled, where in future I must live alone, alone with my fatal thought which had exiled me thither, and which I was tempted to curse. The days which followed this discovery were the saddest of my life."[92]

---

92 Th. Jouffroy: Nouveaux Mélanges philosophiques, 2me edition, p. 83. I add two other cases of counter-conversion dating from a certain moment. The first is from Professor Starbuck's manuscript collection, and the narrator is a woman.

"Away down in the bottom of my heart, I believe I was always more or less skeptical about 'God;' skepticism grew as an undercurrent, all through my early youth, but it was controlled and covered by the emotional elements in my religious growth. When I was sixteen I joined the church and was asked if I loved God. I replied 'Yes,' as was customary and expected. But instantly with a flash something spoke within me, 'No, you do not.' I was haunted for a long time with shame and remorse for my falsehood and for my wickedness in not loving God, mingled with fear that there might be an avenging God who would punish me in some terrible way.... At nineteen, I had an attack of tonsilitis. Before I had quite recovered, I heard told a story of a brute who had kicked his wife down-stairs, and then continued the operation until she became insensible. I felt the horror of the thing keenly. Instantly this thought flashed through my mind: 'I have no use for a God who permits such things.' This experience was followed by months of stoical indifference to the God of my previous life, mingled with feelings of positive dislike and a somewhat proud defiance of him. I still thought there might be a God. If so he would probably damn me, but I should have to stand it. I felt very little fear and no desire to propitiate him. I have never had any personal relations with him since this painful experience."

The second case exemplifies how small an additional stimulus will overthrow the mind into a new state of equilibrium when the process of preparation and incubation has proceeded far enough. It is like the proverbial last straw added to the camel's burden, or that touch of a needle which makes the salt in a supersaturated fluid suddenly begin to crystallize out.

Tolstoy writes: "S., a frank and intelligent man, told me as follows how he ceased to believe:—

"He was twenty-six years old when one day on a hunting expedition, the time for sleep having come, he set himself to pray according to the custom he had held from childhood.

"His brother, who was hunting with him, lay upon the hay and looked at him. When S. had finished his prayer and was turning to sleep, the brother said, 'Do you still keep up that thing?' Nothing more was said. But since that day, now more than thirty years ago, S. has never prayed again; he never takes communion, and does not go to church. All this, not because he became acquainted with convictions of his brother which he then and there adopted; not because he made any new resolution in his soul, but merely because the words spoken by his brother were like the light push of a finger against a leaning wall already about to tumble by its own weight. These words but showed him that the place wherein he supposed religion dwelt in him had long been empty, and that the sentences he uttered, the crosses and bows which he made during his prayer, were actions with no inner sense. Having once seized their absurdity, he could no longer keep them up." Ma Confession, p. 8.

I subjoin an additional document which has come into my possession, and which represents in a vivid way what is probably a very frequent sort of conversion, if the opposite of 'falling in love,' falling out of love, may be so termed. Falling in love also conforms frequently to this type, a latent process of unconscious preparation often preceding a sudden awakening to the fact that the mischief is irretrievably done. The free and easy tone in this narrative gives it a sincerity that speaks for itself.

"For two years of this time I went through a very bad experience, which almost drove me mad. I had fallen violently in love with a girl who, young as she was, had a spirit of coquetry like a cat. As I look back on her now, I hate her, and wonder how I could ever have fallen so low as to be worked upon to such an extent by her attractions. Nevertheless, I fell into a regular fever, could think of nothing else; whenever I was alone, I pictured her attractions, and spent most of the time when I should have been working, in recalling our previous interviews, and imagining future conversations. She was very pretty,

In John Foster's Essay on Decision of Character, there is an account of a case of sudden conversion to avarice, which is illustrative enough to quote:—

> A young man, it appears, "wasted, in two or three years, a large patrimony in profligate revels with a number of worthless associates who called themselves his friends, and who, when his last means were exhausted, treated him of course with neglect or contempt. Reduced to absolute want, he one day went out of the house with an intention to put an end to his life; but wandering awhile almost unconsciously, he came to the brow of an eminence which overlooked what were lately his estates. Here he sat down, and remained fixed in thought a number of hours, at the end of which he sprang from the ground with a vehement, exulting emotion. He had formed his resolution, which was, that all these estates should be his again; he had formed his plan, too, which he instantly began to execute. He walked hastily forward, determined to seize the first opportunity, of however humble a kind, to gain any money, though it were ever so despicable a trifle, and resolved absolutely not to spend, if he could help it, a farthing of whatever he might obtain. The first thing that drew his attention was a heap of coals shot out of carts on the pavement before a house. He offered himself to shovel or wheel

---

good humored, and jolly to the last degree, and intensely pleased with my admiration. Would give me no decided answer yes or no, and the queer thing about it was that whilst pursuing her for her hand, I secretly knew all along that she was unfit to be a wife for me, and that she never would say yes. Although for a year we took our meals at the same boarding-house, so that I saw her continually and familiarly, our closer relations had to be largely on the sly, and this fact, together with my jealousy of another one of her male admirers, and my own conscience despising me for my uncontrollable weakness, made me so nervous and sleepless that I really thought I should become insane. I understand well those young men murdering their sweethearts, which appear so often in the papers. Nevertheless I did love her passionately, and in some ways she did deserve it.

"The queer thing was the sudden and unexpected way in which it all stopped. I was going to my work after breakfast one morning, thinking as usual of her and of my misery, when, just as if some outside power laid hold of me, I found myself turning round and almost running to my room, where I immediately got out all the relics of her which I possessed, including some hair, all her notes and letters, and ambrotypes on glass. The former I made a fire of, the latter I actually crushed beneath my heel, in a sort of fierce joy of revenge and punishment. I now loathed and despised her altogether, and as for myself I felt as if a load of disease had suddenly been removed from me. That was the end. I never spoke to her or wrote to her again in all the subsequent years, and I have never had a single moment of loving thought towards one for so many months entirely filled my heart. In fact, I have always rather hated her memory, though now I can see that I had gone unnecessarily far in that direction. At any rate, from that happy morning onward I regained possession of my own proper soul, and have never since fallen into any similar trap."

This seems to me an unusually clear example of two different levels of personality, inconsistent in their dictates, yet so well balanced against each other as for a long time to fill the life with discord and dissatisfaction. At last, not gradually, but in a sudden crisis, the unstable equilibrium is resolved, and this happens so unexpectedly that it is as if, to use the writer's words, "some outside power laid hold." Professor Starbuck gives an analogous case, and a converse case of hatred suddenly turning into love, in his Psychology of Religion, p. 141. Compare the other highly curious instances which he gives on pp. 137–144, of sudden non-religious alterations of habit or character. He seems right in conceiving all such sudden changes as results of special cerebral functions unconsciously developing until they are ready to play a controlling part when they make irruption into the conscious life. When we treat of sudden "conversion," I shall make as much use as I can of this hypothesis of subconscious incubation.

them into the place where they were to be laid, and was employed. He received a few pence for the labor; and then, in pursuance of the saving part of his plan, requested some small gratuity of meat and drink, which was given him. He then looked out for the next thing that might chance; and went, with indefatigable industry, through a succession of servile employments in different places, of longer and shorter duration, still scrupulous in avoiding, as far as possible, the expense of a penny. He promptly seized every opportunity which could advance his design, without regarding the meanness of occupation or appearance. By this method he had gained, after a considerable time, money enough to purchase in order to sell again a few cattle, of which he had taken pains to understand the value. He speedily but cautiously turned his first gains into second advantages; retained without a single deviation his extreme parsimony; and thus advanced by degrees into larger transactions and incipient wealth. I did not hear, or have forgotten, the continued course of his life, but the final result was, that he more than recovered his lost possessions, and died an inveterate miser, worth £60,000."[93]

Let me turn now to the kind of case, the religious case, namely, that immediately concerns us. Here is one of the simplest possible type, an account of the conversion to the systematic religion of healthy-mindedness of a man who must already have been naturally of the healthy-minded type. It shows how, when the fruit is ripe, a touch will make it fall.

Mr. Horace Fletcher, in his little book called Menticulture, relates that a friend with whom he was talking of the self-control attained by the Japanese through their practice of the Buddhist discipline said:—

"'You must first get rid of anger and worry.' 'But,' said I, 'is that possible?' 'Yes,' replied he; 'it is possible to the Japanese, and ought to be possible to us.'

"On my way back I could think of nothing else but the words 'get rid, get rid'; and the idea must have continued to possess me during my sleeping hours, for the first consciousness in the morning brought back the same thought, with the revelation of a discovery, which framed itself into the reasoning, 'If it is possible to get rid of anger and worry, why is it necessary to have them at all?' I felt the strength of the argument, and at once accepted the reasoning. The baby had discovered that it could walk. It would scorn to creep any longer.

"From the instant I realized that these cancer spots of worry and anger were removable, they left me. With the discovery of their weakness they were exorcised. From that time life has had an entirely different aspect.

"Although from that moment the possibility and desirability of freedom from the depressing passions has been a reality to me, it took me some months to feel absolute security in my new position; but, as the usual occasions for worry and anger have presented themselves over and over again, and I have been unable to feel them in the slightest degree, I no longer dread or guard against them,

93 Op. cit., Letter III., abridged.

and I am amazed at my increased energy and vigor of mind; at my strength to meet situations of all kinds, and at my disposition to love and appreciate everything.

"I have had occasion to travel more than ten thousand miles by rail since that morning. The same Pullman porter, conductor, hotel-waiter, peddler, book-agent, cabman, and others who were formerly a source of annoyance and irritation have been met, but I am not conscious of a single incivility. All at once the whole world has turned good to me. I have become, as it were, sensitive only to the rays of good.

"I could recount many experiences which prove a brand-new condition of mind, but one will be sufficient. Without the slightest feeling of annoyance or impatience, I have seen a train that I had planned to take with a good deal of interested and pleasurable anticipation move out of the station without me, because my baggage did not arrive. The porter from the hotel came running and panting into the station just as the train pulled out of sight. When he saw me, he looked as if he feared a scolding, and began to tell of being blocked in a crowded street and unable to get out. When he had finished, I said to him: 'It doesn't matter at all, you couldn't help it, so we will try again to-morrow. Here is your fee, I am sorry you had all this trouble in earning it.' The look of surprise that came over his face was so filled with pleasure that I was repaid on the spot for the delay in my departure. Next day he would not accept a cent for the service, and he and I are friends for life.

"During the first weeks of my experience I was on guard only against worry and anger; but, in the mean time, having noticed the absence of the other depressing and dwarfing passions, I began to trace a relationship, until I was convinced that they are all growths from the two roots I have specified. I have felt the freedom now for so long a time that I am sure of my relation toward it; and I could no more harbor any of the thieving and depressing influences that once I nursed as a heritage of humanity than a fop would voluntarily wallow in a filthy gutter.

"There is no doubt in my mind that pure Christianity and pure Buddhism, and the Mental Sciences and all Religions, fundamentally teach what has been a discovery to me; but none of them have presented it in the light of a simple and easy process of elimination. At one time I wondered if the elimination would not yield to indifference and sloth. In my experience, the contrary is the result. I feel such an increased desire to do something useful that it seems as if I were a boy again and the energy for play had returned. I could fight as readily as (and better than) ever, if there were occasion for it. It does not make one a coward. It can't, since fear is one of the things eliminated. I notice the absence of timidity in the presence of any audience. When a boy, I was standing under a tree which was struck by lightning, and received a shock from the effects of which I never knew exemption until I had dissolved partnership with worry. Since then, lightning and thunder have been encountered under conditions which would formerly have caused great depression and discomfort, without [my] experiencing a trace of either. Surprise is also greatly modified, and one is less liable to become startled by unexpected sights or noises.

"As far as I am individually concerned, I am not bothering myself at present as to what the results of this emancipated condition may be. I have no doubt that the perfect health aimed at by Christian Science may be one of the possibilities, for I note a marked improvement in the way my stomach does its duty in assimilating the food I give it to handle, and I am sure it works better to the sound of a song than under the friction of a frown. Neither am I wasting any of this precious time formulating an idea of a future existence or a future Heaven. The Heaven that I have within myself is as attractive as any that has been promised or that I can imagine; and I am willing to let the growth lead where it will, as long as the anger and their brood have no part in misguiding it."[94]

The older medicine used to speak of two ways, *lysis* and *crisis*, one gradual, the other abrupt, in which one might recover from a bodily disease. In the spiritual realm there are also two ways, one gradual, the other sudden, in which inner unification may occur. Tolstoy and Bunyan may again serve us as examples, examples, as it happens, of the gradual way, though it must be confessed at the outset that it is hard to follow these windings of the hearts of others, and one feels that their words do not reveal their total secret.

Howe'er this be, Tolstoy, pursuing his unending questioning, seemed to come to one insight after another. First he perceived that his conviction that life was meaningless took only this finite life into account. He was looking for the value of one finite term in that of another, and the whole result could only be one of those indeterminate equations in mathematics which end with o=o. Yet this is as far as the reasoning intellect by itself can go, unless irrational sentiment or faith brings in the infinite. Believe in the infinite as common people do, and life grows possible again.

"Since mankind has existed, wherever life has been, there also has been the faith that gave the possibility of living. Faith is the sense of life, that sense by virtue of which man does not destroy himself, but continues to live on. It is the force whereby we live. If Man did not believe that he must live for something, he would not live at all. The idea of an infinite God, of the divinity of the soul, of the union of men's actions with God—these are ideas elaborated in the infinite secret depths of human thought. They are ideas without which there would be no life, without which I myself," said Tolstoy, "would not exist. I began to see that I had no right to rely on my individual reasoning and neglect these answers given by faith, for they are the only answers to the question."

Yet how believe as the common people believe, steeped as they are in grossest superstition? It is impossible—but yet their life! their life! It is normal. It is happy! It is an answer to the question!

94 H. Fletcher: Menticulture, or the A-B-C of True Living, New York and Chicago, 1899, pp. 26–36, abridged.

Little by little, Tolstoy came to the settled conviction—he says it took him two years to arrive there—that his trouble had not been with life in general, not with the common life of common men, but with the life of the upper, intellectual, artistic classes, the life which he had personally always led, the cerebral life, the life of conventionality, artificiality, and personal ambition. He had been living wrongly and must change. To work for animal needs, to abjure lies and vanities, to relieve common wants, to be simple, to believe in God, therein lay happiness again.

> "I remember," he says, "one day in early spring, I was alone in the forest, lending my ear to its mysterious noises. I listened, and my thought went back to what for these three years it always was busy with—the quest of God. But the idea of him, I said, how did I ever come by the idea?
>
> "And again there arose in me, with this thought, glad aspirations towards life. Everything in me awoke and received a meaning. . . . Why do I look farther? a voice within me asked. He is there: he, without whom one cannot live. To acknowledge God and to live are one and the same thing. God is what life is. Well, then! live, seek God, and there will be no life without him. . . .
>
> "After this, things cleared up within me and about me better than ever, and the light has never wholly died away. I was saved from suicide. Just how or when the change took place I cannot tell. But as insensibly and gradually as the force of life had been annulled within me, and I had reached my moral death-bed, just as gradually and imperceptibly did the energy of life come back. And what was strange was that this energy that came back was nothing new. It was my ancient juvenile force of faith, the belief that the sole purpose of my life was to be *better*. I gave up the life of the conventional world, recognizing it to be no life, but a parody on life, which its superfluities simply keep us from comprehending,"—and Tolstoy thereupon embraced the life of the peasants, and has felt right and happy, or at least relatively so, ever since.[95]

As I interpret his melancholy, then, it was not merely an accidental vitiation of his humors, though it was doubtless also that. It was logically called for by the clash between his inner character and his outer activities and aims. Although a literary artist, Tolstoy was one of those primitive oaks of men to whom the superfluities and insincerities, the cupidities, complications, and cruelties of our polite civilization are profoundly unsatisfying, and for whom the eternal veracities lie with more natural and animal things. His crisis was the getting of his soul in order, the discovery of its genuine habitat and vocation, the escape from falsehoods into what for him were ways of truth. It was a case of heterogeneous personality tardily and slowly finding its unity and level. And though not many of us can imitate Tolstoy, not having enough, perhaps, of the aboriginal human marrow in our bones, most of us may at least feel as if it might be better for us if we could.

Bunyan's recovery seems to have been even slower. For years together he was

95 I have considerably abridged Tolstoy's words in my translation.

alternately haunted with texts of Scripture, now up and now down, but at last with an ever growing relief in his salvation through the blood of Christ.

> "My peace would be in and out twenty times a day; comfort now and trouble presently; peace now and before I could go a furlong as full of guilt and fear as ever heart could hold." When a good text comes home to him, "This," he writes, "gave me good encouragement for the space of two or three hours"; or "This was a good day to me, I hope I shall not forget it"; or "The glory of these words was then so weighty on me that I was ready to swoon as I sat; yet, not with grief and trouble, but with solid joy and peace"; or "This made a strange seizure on my spirit; it brought light with it, and commanded a silence in my heart of all those tumultuous thoughts that before did use, like masterless hell-hounds, to roar and bellow and make a hideous noise within me. It showed me that Jesus Christ had not quite forsaken and cast off my Soul."
>
> Such periods accumulate until he can write: "And now remained only the hinder part of the tempest, for the thunder was gone beyond me, only some drops would still remain, that now and then would fall upon me";—and at last: "Now did my chains fall off my legs indeed; I was loosed from my afflictions and irons; my temptations also fled away; so that from that time, those dreadful Scriptures of God left off to trouble me; now went I also home rejoicing, for the grace and love of God. . . . Now could I see myself in Heaven and Earth at once; in Heaven by my Christ, by my Head, by my Righteousness and Life, though on Earth by my body or person. . . . Christ was a precious Christ to my soul that night; I could scarce lie in my bed for joy and peace and triumph through Christ."

Bunyan became a minister of the gospel, and in spite of his neurotic constitution, and of the twelve years he lay in prison for his non-conformity, his life was turned to active use. He was a peacemaker and doer of good, and the immortal Allegory which he wrote has brought the very spirit of religious patience home to English hearts.

But neither Bunyan nor Tolstoy could become what we have called healthy-minded. They had drunk too deeply of the cup of bitterness ever to forget its taste, and their redemption is into a universe two stories deep. Each of them realized a good which broke the effective edge of his sadness; yet the sadness was preserved as a minor ingredient in the heart of the faith by which it was overcome. The fact of interest for us is that as a matter of fact they could and did find *something* welling up in the inner reaches of their consciousness, by which such extreme sadness could be overcome. Tolstoy does well to talk of it as *that by which men live;* for that is exactly what it is, a stimulus, an excitement, a faith, a force that re-infuses the positive willingness to live, even in full presence of the evil perceptions that erewhile made life seem unbearable. For Tolstoy's perceptions of evil appear within their sphere to have remained unmodified. His later works show him implacable to the whole system of official values: the ignobility of fashionable life; the infamies of empire; the spuriousness of the church, the vain conceit of the professions; the meannesses and cruelties that go with great success; and every other pompous crime and lying institution of this world. To all patience with such things his experience has been for him a permanent ministry of death.

Bunyan also leaves this world to the enemy.

> "I must first pass a sentence of death," he says, "upon everything that can properly be called a thing of this life, even to reckon myself, my wife, my children, my health, my enjoyments, and all, as dead to me, and myself as dead to them; to trust in God through Christ, as touching the world to come; and as touching this world, to count the grave my house, to make my bed in darkness, and to say to corruption, Thou art my father, and to the worm, Thou art my mother and sister. . . . The parting with my wife and my poor children hath often been to me as the pulling of my flesh from my bones, especially my poor blind child who lay nearer my heart than all I had besides. Poor child, thought I, what sorrow art thou like to have for thy portion in this world! Thou must be beaten, must beg, suffer hunger, cold, nakedness, and a thousand calamities, though I cannot now endure that the wind should blow upon thee. But yet I must venture you all with God, though it goeth to the quick to leave you."[96]

The "hue of resolution" is there, but the full flood of ecstatic liberation seems never to have poured over poor John Bunyan's soul.

These examples may suffice to acquaint us in a general way with the phenomenon technically called "Conversion." In the next lecture I shall invite you to study its peculiarities and concomitants in some detail.

96 In my quotations from Bunyan I have omitted certain intervening portions of the text.

## LECTURE IX

# Conversion

To be converted, to be regenerated, to receive grace, to experience religion, to gain an assurance, are so many phrases which denote the process, gradual or sudden, by which a self-hitherto divided, and consciously wrong inferior and unhappy, becomes unified and consciously right superior and happy, in consequence of its firmer hold upon religious realities. This at least is what conversion signifies in general terms, whether or not we believe that a direct divine operation is needed to bring such a moral change about.

Before entering upon a minuter study of the process, let me enliven our understanding of the definition by a concrete example. I choose the quaint case of an unlettered man, Stephen H. Bradley, whose experience is related in a scarce American pamphlet.[97]

I select this case because it shows how in these inner alterations one may find one unsuspected depth below another, as if the possibilities of character lay disposed in a series of layers or shells, of whose existence we have no premonitory knowledge.

Bradley thought that he had been already fully converted at the age of fourteen.

> "I thought I saw the Saviour, by faith, in human shape, for about one second in the room, with arms extended, appearing to say to me, Come. The next day I rejoiced with trembling; soon after, my happiness was so great that I said that I wanted to die; this world had no place in my affections, as I knew of, and every day appeared as solemn to me as the Sabbath. I had an ardent desire that all mankind might feel as I did; I wanted to have them all love God supremely. Previous to this time I was very selfish and self-righteous; but now I desired the welfare of all mankind, and could with a feeling heart forgive my worst enemies, and I felt as if I should be willing to bear the scoffs and sneers of any person, and

97 A sketch of the life of Stephen H. Bradley, from the age of five to twenty-four years, including his remarkable experience of the power of the Holy Spirit on the second evening of November, 1829. Madison, Connecticut, 1830.

suffer anything for His sake, if I could be the means in the hands of God, of the conversion of one soul."

Nine years later, in 1829, Mr. Bradley heard of a revival of religion that had begun in his neighborhood. "Many of the young converts," he says, "would come to me when in meeting and ask me if I had religion, and my reply generally was, I hope I have. This did not appear to satisfy them; they said they *knew they* had it. I requested them to pray for me, thinking with myself, that if I had not got religion now, after so long a time professing to be a Christian, that it was time I had, and hoped their prayers would be answered in my behalf.

"One Sabbath, I went to hear the Methodist at the Academy. He spoke of the ushering in of the day of general judgment; and he set it forth in such a solemn and terrible manner as I never heard before. The scene of that day appeared to be taking place, and so awakened were all the powers of my mind that, like Felix, I trembled involuntarily on the bench where I was sitting, though I felt nothing at heart. The next day evening I went to hear him again. He took his text from Revelation: 'And I saw the dead, small and great, stand before God.' And he represented the terrors of that day in such a manner that it appeared as if it would melt the heart of stone. When he finished his discourse, an old gentleman turned to me and said, 'This is what I call preaching.' I thought the same; but my feelings were still unmoved by what he said, and I did not enjoy religion, but I believe he did.

"I will now relate my experience of the power of the Holy Spirit which took place on the same night. Had any person told me previous to this that I could have experienced the power of the Holy Spirit in the manner which I did, I could not have believed it, and should have thought the person deluded that told me so. I went directly home after the meeting, and when I got home I wondered what made me feel so stupid. I retired to rest soon after I got home, and felt indifferent to the things of religion until I began to be exercised by the Holy Spirit, which began in about five minutes after, in the following manner:—

"At first, I began to feel my heart beat very quick all on a sudden, which made me at first think that perhaps something is going to ail me, though I was not alarmed, for I felt no pain. My heart increased in its beating, which soon convinced me that it was the Holy Spirit from the effect it had on me. I began to feel exceedingly happy and humble, and such a sense of unworthiness as I never felt before. I could not very well help speaking out, which I did, and said, Lord, I do not deserve this happiness, or words to that effect, while there was a stream (resembling air in feeling) came into my mouth and heart in a more sensible manner than that of drinking anything, which continued, as near as I could judge, five minutes or more, which appeared to be the cause of such a palpitation of my heart. It took complete possession of my soul, and I am certain that I desired the Lord, while in the midst of it, not to give me any more happiness, for it seemed as if I could not contain what I had got. My heart seemed as if it would burst, but it did not stop until I felt as if I was unutterably full of the love and grace of God. In the mean time while thus exercised, a thought arose in my mind, what can it mean? and all at once, as if to answer it, my memory became exceedingly clear, and it appeared to me just as if the New Testament was placed open before me, eighth chapter of Romans, and as light as if some candle lighted was held for me to read the 26th and 27th verses of that chapter, and I read these words: 'The Spirit helpeth our infirmities with groanings which cannot be uttered.' And all the time that my heart was a-beating, it made me groan like a person in distress, which was not very easy to stop, though I was in no pain at all, and my brother being in bed in another room came and opened the door, and asked me if I had got the toothache. I told him no, and that he might get to sleep. I tried to stop. I felt unwilling to go to sleep myself, I was so happy, fearing I should lose it—thinking within myself

*'My willing soul would stay*
*In such a frame as this.'*

And while I lay reflecting, after my heart stopped beating, feeling as if my soul was full of the Holy Spirit, I thought that perhaps there might be angels hovering round my bed. I felt just as if I wanted to converse with them, and finally I spoke, saying, 'O ye affectionate angels! how is it that ye can take so much interest in our welfare, and we take so little interest in our own.' After this, with difficulty I got to sleep; and when I awoke in the morning my first thoughts were: What has become of my happiness? and, feeling a degree of it in my heart, I asked for more, which was given to me as quick as thought. I then got up to dress myself, and found to my surprise that I could but just stand. It appeared to me as if it was a little heaven upon earth. My soul felt as completely raised above the fears of death as of going to sleep; and like a bird in a cage, I had a desire, if it was the will of God, to get released from my body and to dwell with Christ, though willing to live to do good to others, and to warn sinners to repent. I went downstairs feeling as solemn as if I had lost all my friends, and thinking with myself, that I would not let my parents know it until I had first looked into the Testament. I went directly to the shelf and looked into it, at the eighth of Romans, and every verse seemed to almost speak and to confirm it to be truly the Word of God, and as if my feelings corresponded with the meaning of the word. I then told my parents of it, and told them that I thought that they must see that when I spoke, that it was not my own voice, for it appeared so to me. My speech seemed entirely under the control of the Spirit within me; I do not mean that the words which I spoke were not my own, for they were. I thought that I was influenced similar to the Apostles on the day of Pentecost (with the exception of having power to give it to others, and doing what they did). After breakfast I went round to converse with my neighbors on religion, which I could not have been hired to have done before this, and at their request I prayed with them, though I had never prayed in public before.

"I now feel as if I had discharged my duty by telling the truth, and hope by the blessing of God, it may do some good to all who shall read it. He has fulfilled his promise in sending the Holy Spirit down into our hearts, or mine at least, and I now defy all the Deists and Atheists in the world to shake my faith in Christ."

So much for Mr. Bradley and his conversion, of the effect of which upon his later life we gain no information. Now for a minuter survey of the constituent elements of the conversion process.

If you open the chapter on Association, of any treatise on Psychology, you will read that a man's ideas, aims, and objects form diverse internal groups and systems, relatively independent of one another. Each "aim" which he follows awakens a certain specific kind of interested excitement, and gathers a certain group of ideas together in subordination to it as its associates; and if the aims and excitements are distinct in kind, their groups of ideas may have little in common. When one group is present and engrosses the interest, all the ideas connected with other groups may be excluded from the mental field. The President of the United States when, with paddle, gun, and fishing-rod, he goes camping in the wilderness for a vacation, changes his system of ideas from top to bottom. The presidential anxieties have lapsed into the background entirely; the official habits are replaced by the habits of a son of nature, and those who knew the man only as the strenuous magistrate would not "know him for the same person" if they saw him as the camper.

If now he should never go back, and never again suffer political interests to gain dominion over him, he would be for practical intents and purposes a permanently transformed being. Our ordinary alterations of character, as we pass from one of our aims to another, are not commonly called transformations, because each of them is so rapidly succeeded by another in the reverse direction; but whenever one aim grows so stable as to expel definitively its previous rivals from the individual's life, we tend to speak of the phenomenon, and perhaps to wonder at it, as a "transformation."

These alternations are the completest of the ways in which a self may be divided. A less complete way is the simultaneous coexistence of two or more different groups of aims, of which one practically holds the right of way and instigates activity, whilst the others are only pious wishes, and never practically come to anything. Saint Augustine's aspirations to a purer life, in our last lecture, were for a while an example. Another would be the President in his full pride of office, wondering whether it were not all vanity, and whether the life of a wood-chopper were not the wholesomer destiny. Such fleeting aspirations are mere *velleitates*, whimsies. They exist on the remoter outskirts of the mind, and the real self of the man, the centre of his energies, is occupied with an entirely different system. As life goes on, there is a constant change of our interests, and a consequent change of place in our systems of ideas, from more central to more peripheral, and from more peripheral to more central parts of consciousness. I remember, for instance, that one evening when I was a youth, my father read aloud from a Boston newspaper that part of Lord Gifford's will which founded these four lectureships. At that time I did not think of being a teacher of philosophy, and what I listened to was as remote from my own life as if it related to the planet Mars. Yet here I am, with the Gifford system part and parcel of my very self, and all my energies, for the time being, devoted to successfully identifying myself with it. My soul stands now planted in what once was for it a practically unreal object, and speaks from it as from its proper habitat and centre.

When I say "Soul," you need not take me in the ontological sense unless you prefer to; for although ontological language is instinctive in such matters, yet Buddhists or Humians can perfectly well describe the facts in the phenomenal terms which are their favorites. For them the soul is only a succession of fields of consciousness: yet there is found in each field a part, or sub-field, which figures as focal and contains the excitement, and from which, as from a centre, the aim seems to be taken. Talking of this part, we involuntarily apply words of perspective to distinguish it from the rest, words like "here," "this," "now," "mine," or "me"; and we ascribe to the other parts the positions "there," "then," "that," "his" or "thine," "it," "not me." But a "here" can change to a "there," and a "there" become a "here," and what was "mine" and what was "not mine" change their places.

What brings such changes about is the way in which emotional excitement alters. Things hot and vital to us to-day are cold to-morrow. It is as if seen from the hot parts of the field that the other parts appear to us, and from these hot parts personal desire and volition make their sallies. They are in short the centres of our dynamic energy, whereas the cold parts leave us indifferent and passive in proportion to their coldness.

Whether such language be rigorously exact is for the present of no importance. It is exact enough, if you recognize from your own experience the facts which I seek to designate by it.

Now there may be great oscillation in the emotional interest, and the hot places may shift before one almost as rapidly as the sparks that run through burnt-up paper. Then we have the wavering and divided self we heard so much of in the previous lecture. Or the focus of excitement and heat, the point of view from which the aim is taken, may come to lie permanently within a certain system; and then, if the change be a religious one, we call it a *conversion*, especially if it be by crisis, or sudden.

Let us hereafter, in speaking of the hot place in a man's consciousness, the group of ideas to which he devotes himself, and from which he works, call it *the habitual centre of his personal energy*. It makes a great difference to a man whether one set of his ideas, or another, be the centre of his energy; and it makes a great difference, as regards any set of ideas which he may possess, whether they become central or remain peripheral in him. To say that a man is "converted" means, in these terms, that religious ideas, previously peripheral in his consciousness, now take a central place, and that religious aims form the habitual centre of his energy.

Now if you ask of psychology just *how* the excitement shifts in a man's mental system, and *why* aims that were peripheral become at a certain moment central, psychology has to reply that although she can give a general description of what happens, she is unable in a given case to account accurately for all the single forces at work. Neither an outside observer nor the Subject who undergoes the process can explain fully how particular experiences are able to change one's centre of energy so decisively, or why they so often have to bide their hour to do so. We have a thought, or we perform an act, repeatedly, but on a certain day the real meaning of the thought peals through us for the first time, or the act has suddenly turned into a moral impossibility. All we know is that there are dead feelings, dead ideas, and cold beliefs, and there are hot and live ones; and when one grows hot and alive within us, everything has to re-crystallize about it. We may say that the heat and liveliness mean only the "motor efficacy," long deferred but now operative, of the idea; but such talk itself is only circumlocution, for whence the sudden motor efficacy? And our explanations then get so vague and general that one realizes all the more the intense individuality of the whole phenomenon.

In the end we fall back on the hackneyed symbolism of a mechanical equilibrium. A mind is a system of ideas, each with the excitement it arouses, and with tendencies impulsive and inhibitive, which mutually check or reinforce one another. The collection of ideas alters by subtraction or by addition in the course of experience, and the tendencies alter as the organism gets more aged. A mental system may be undermined or weakened by this interstitial alteration just as a building is, and yet for a time keep upright by dead habit. But a new perception, a sudden emotional shock, or an occasion which lays bare the organic alteration, will make the whole fabric fall together; and then the centre of gravity sinks into an attitude more stable, for the new ideas that reach the centre in the rearrangement seem now to be locked there, and the new structure remains permanent.

Formed associations of ideas and habits are usually factors of retardation in such changes of equilibrium. New information, however acquired, plays an accelerating part in the changes; and the slow mutation of our instincts and propensities, under the "unimaginable touch of time" has an enormous influence. Moreover, all these influences may work subconsciously or half unconsciously.[98] And when you get a Subject in whom the subconscious life—of which I must speak more fully soon—is largely developed, and in whom motives habitually ripen in silence, you get a case of which you can never give a full account, and in which, both to the Subject and the onlookers, there may appear an element of marvel. Emotional occasions, especially violent ones, are extremely potent in precipitating mental rearrangements. The sudden and explosive ways in which love, jealousy, guilt, fear, remorse, or anger can seize upon one are known to everybody.[99] Hope, happiness, security, resolve, emo-

98 Jouffroy is an example: "Down this slope it was that my intelligence had glided, and little by little it had got far from its first faith. But this melancholy revolution had not taken place in the broad daylight of my consciousness; too many scruples, too many guides and sacred affections had made it dreadful to me, so that I was far from avowing to myself the progress it had made. It had gone on in silence, by an involuntary elaboration of which I was not the accomplice; and although I had in reality long ceased to be a Christian, yet, in the innocence of my intention, I should have shuddered to suspect it, and thought it calumny had I been accused of such a falling away." Then follows Jouffroy's account of his counter-conversion, quoted above on p. 585.

99 One hardly needs examples; but for remorse, see Othello after the murder; for anger, see Lear after Cordelia's first speech to him; for resolve, see p. 587 (J. Foster case). Here is a pathological case in which *guilt* was the feeling that suddenly exploded: "One night I was seized on entering bed with a rigor, such

tions characteristic of conversion, can be equally explosive. And emotions that come in this explosive way seldom leave things as they found them.

In his recent work on the Psychology of Religion, Professor Starbuck of California has shown by a statistical inquiry how closely parallel in its manifestations the ordinary "conversion" which occurs in young people brought up in evangelical circles is to that growth into a larger spiritual life which is a normal phase of adolescence in every class of human beings. The age is the same, falling usually between fourteen and seventeen. The symptoms are the same,—sense of incompleteness and imperfection; brooding, depression, morbid introspection, and sense of sin; anxiety about the hereafter; distress over doubts, and the like. And the result is the same—a happy relief and objectivity, as the confidence in self gets greater through the adjustment of the faculties to the wider outlook. In spontaneous religious awakening, apart from revivalistic examples, and in the ordinary storm and stress and moulting-time of adolescence, we also may meet with mystical experiences, astonishing the subjects by their suddenness, just as in revivalistic conversion. The analogy, in fact, is complete; and Starbuck's conclusion as to these ordinary youthful conversions would seem to be the only sound one: Conversion is in its essence a normal adolescent phenomenon, incidental to the passage from the child's small universe to the wider intellectual and spiritual life of maturity.

"Theology," says Dr. Starbuck, "takes the adolescent tendencies and builds upon them; it sees that the essential thing in adolescent growth is bringing the person out of childhood into the new life of maturity and personal insight. It accordingly brings those means to bear which will intensify the normal tendencies. It shortens up the period of duration of storm and stress." The conversion phenomena of "conviction of sin" last, by this investigator's statistics, about one fifth as long as the periods of adolescent storm and stress phenomena of which he also got statistics, but they are very much more intense. Bodily accompaniments, loss of sleep and appetite, for example, are much more frequent in them. "The essential distinction appears to be that conversion intensifies but shortens the period by bringing the person to a definite crisis."[100]

The conversions which Dr. Starbuck here has in mind are of course mainly those of very commonplace persons, kept true to a pre-appointed type by instruction, appeal, and example. The particular form which they affect is the result of suggestion and imitation.[101] If they went through their growth-crisis in other faiths and

---

as Swedenborg describes as coming over him with a sense of holiness, but over me with a sense of *guilt*. During that whole night I lay under the influence of the rigor, and from its inception I felt that I was under the curse of God. I have never done one act of duty in my life—sins against God and man, beginning as far as my memory goes back—a wildcat in human shape."

100 E. D. Starbuck: The Psychology of Religion, pp. 224, 262.

101 No one understands this better than Jonathan Edwards understood it already. Conversion narratives of the more commonplace sort must always be taken with the allowances which he suggests: "A rule received and established by common consent has a very great, though to many persons an insensible influence in forming their notions of the process of their own experience. I know very well how

other countries, although the essence of the change would be the same (since it is one in the main so inevitable), its accidents would be different. In Catholic lands, for example, and in our own Episcopalian sects, no such anxiety and conviction of sin is usual as in sects that encourage revivals. The sacraments being more relied on in these more strictly ecclesiastical bodies, the individual's personal acceptance of salvation needs less to be accentuated and led up to.

But every imitative phenomenon must once have had its original, and I propose that for the future we keep as close as may be to the more first-hand and original forms of experience. These are more likely to be found in sporadic adult cases.

Professor Leuba, in a valuable article on the psychology of conversion,[102] subordinates the theological aspect of the religious life almost entirely to its moral aspect. The religious sense he defines as "the feeling of unwholeness, of moral imperfection, of sin, to use the technical word, accompanied by the yearning after the peace of unity." "The word 'religion,'" he says, "is getting more and more to signify the conglomerate of desires and emotions springing from the sense of sin and its release"; and he gives a large number of examples, in which the sin ranges from drunkenness to spiritual pride, to show that the sense of it may beset one and crave relief as urgently as does the anguish of the sickened flesh or any form of physical misery.

Undoubtedly this conception covers an immense number of cases. A good one to use as an example is that of Mr. S. H. Hadley, who after his conversion became an active and useful rescuer of drunkards in New York. His experience runs as follows:—

> "One Tuesday evening I sat in a saloon in Harlem, a homeless, friendless, dying drunkard. I had pawned or sold everything that would bring a drink. I could not sleep unless I was dead drunk. I had not eaten for days, and for four nights preceding I had suffered with delirium tremens, or the horrors, from midnight till morning. I had often said, 'I will never be a tramp. I will never be cornered, for when that time comes, if ever it comes, I will find a home in the bottom of the river.' But the Lord so ordered it that when that time did come I was not able to walk one quarter of the way to the river. As I sat there thinking, I seemed to feel some great and mighty presence. I did not know then what it was. I did learn afterwards that it was Jesus, the sinner's friend. I walked up to the bar and pounded it with my fist till I made the glasses rattle. Those who stood by drinking looked on with scornful curiosity. I said I would never take another drink,

they proceed as to this matter, for I have had frequent opportunities of observing their conduct. Very often their experience at first appears like a confused chaos, but then those parts are selected which bear the nearest resemblance to such particular steps as are insisted on; and these are dwelt upon in their thoughts, and spoken of from time to time, till they grow more and more conspicuous in their view, and other parts which are neglected grow more and more obscure. Thus what they have experienced is insensibly strained, so as to bring it to an exact conformity to the scheme already established in their minds. And it becomes natural also for ministers, who have to deal with those who insist upon distinctness and clearness of method, to do so too." Treatise on Religious Affections.

102 Studies in the Psychology of Religious Phenomena, American Journal of Psychology, vii. 309 (1896).

if I died on the street, and really I felt as though that would happen before morning. Something said, 'If you want to keep this promise, go and have yourself locked up.' I went to the nearest station-house and had myself locked up.

"I was placed in a narrow cell, and it seemed as though all the demons that could find room came in that place with me. This was not all the company I had, either. No, praise the Lord: that dear Spirit that came to me in the saloon was present, and said, Pray. I did pray, and though I did not feel any great help, I kept on praying. As soon as I was able to leave my cell I was taken to the police court and remanded back to the cell. I was finally released, and found my way to my brother's house, where every care was given me. While lying in bed the admonishing Spirit never left me, and when I arose the following Sabbath morning I felt that day would decide my fate, and toward evening it came into my head to go to Jerry M'Auley's Mission. I went. The house was packed, and with great difficulty I made my way to the space near the platform. There I saw the apostle to the drunkard and the outcast—that man of God, Jerry M'Auley. He rose, and amid deep silence told his experience. There was a sincerity about this man that carried conviction with it, and I found myself saying, 'I wonder if God can save *me*?' I listened to the testimony of twenty-five or thirty persons, every one of whom had been saved from rum, and I made up my mind that I would be saved or die right there. When the invitation was given, I knelt down with a crowd of drunkards. Jerry made the first prayer. Then Mrs. M'Auley prayed fervently for us. Oh, what a conflict was going on for my poor soul! A blessed whisper said, 'Come'; the devil said, 'Be careful.' I halted but a moment, and then, with a breaking heart, I said, 'Dear Jesus, can you help me?' Never with mortal tongue can I describe that moment. Although up to that moment my soul had been filled with indescribable gloom, I felt the glorious brightness of the noonday sun shine into my heart. I felt I was a free man. Oh, the precious feeling of safety, of freedom, of resting on Jesus! I felt that Christ with all his brightness and power had come into my life; that, indeed, old things had passed away and all things had become new.

"From that moment till now I have never wanted a drink of whiskey, and I have never seen money enough to make me take one. I promised God that night that if he would take away the appetite for strong drink, I would work for him all my life. He has done his part, and I have been trying to do mine."[103]

Dr. Leuba rightly remarks that there is little doctrinal theology in such an experience, which starts with the absolute need of a higher helper, and ends with the sense that he has helped us. He gives other cases of drunkards' conversions which are purely ethical, containing, as recorded, no theological beliefs whatever. John B. Gough's case, for instance, is practically, says Dr. Leuba, the conversion of an athe-

103 I have abridged Mr. Hadley's account. For other conversions of drunkards, see his pamphlet, Rescue Mission Work, published at the Old Jerry M'Auley Water Street Mission, New York City. A striking collection of cases also appears in the appendix to Professor Leuba's article.

ist—neither God nor Jesus being mentioned.[104] But in spite of the importance of this type of regeneration, with little or no intellectual readjustment, this writer surely makes it too exclusive. It corresponds to the subjectively centered form of morbid melancholy, of which Bunyan and Alline were examples. But we saw in our seventh lecture that there are objective forms of melancholy also, in which the lack of rational meaning of the universe, and of life anyhow, is the burden that weighs upon one—you remember Tolstoy's case.[105] So there are distinct elements in conversion, and their relations to individual lives deserve to be discriminated.[106]

Some persons, for instance, never are, and possibly never under any circumstances could be, converted. Religious ideas cannot become the centre of their spiritual energy. They may be excellent persons, servants of God in practical ways, but they are not children of his kingdom. They are either incapable of imagining the invisible; or else, in the language of devotion, they are life-long subjects of "barrenness" and "dryness." Such inaptitude for religious faith may in some cases be intellectual in its origin. Their religious faculties may be checked in their natural tendency to expand, by beliefs about the world that are inhibitive, the pessimistic and materialistic beliefs, for example, within which so many good souls, who in former times would have freely indulged their religious propensities, find themselves nowadays, as it were, frozen; or the agnostic vetoes upon faith as something weak and shameful, under which so many of us today lie cowering, afraid to use our instincts. In many persons such inhibitions are never overcome. To the end of their days they refuse to believe, their personal energy never gets to its religious centre, and the latter remains inactive in perpetuity.

In other persons the trouble is profounder. There are men anæsthetic on the religious side, deficient in that category of sensibility. Just as a bloodless organism can never, in spite of all its goodwill, attain to the reckless "animal spirits" enjoyed by those of sanguine temperament; so the nature which is spiritually barren may admire and envy faith in others, but can never compass the enthusiasm and peace which those who are temperamentally qualified for faith enjoy. All this may, however, turn out eventually to have been a matter of temporary inhibition. Even late in life some thaw, some release may take place, some bolt be shot back in the barrenest breast, and the man's hard heart may soften and break into religious feeling. Such cases more than any others suggest the idea that sudden conversion is by miracle.

---

104 A restaurant waiter served provisionally as Gough's "Saviour." General Booth, the founder of the Salvation Army, considers that the first vital step in saving outcasts consists in making them feel that some decent human being cares enough for them to take an interest in the question whether they are to rise or sink.

105 The crisis of apathetic melancholy—no use in life—into which J. S. Mill records that he fell, from which he emerged by the reading of Marmontel's Memoirs (Heaven save the mark!) and Wordsworth's poetry, is another intellectual and general metaphysical case. See Mill's Autobiography, New York, 1873, pp. 141, 148.

106 Starbuck, in addition to "escape from sin," discriminates "spiritual illumination" as a distinct type of conversion experience. Psychology of Religion, p. 85.

So long as they exist, we must not imagine ourselves to deal with irretrievably fixed classes.

Now there are two forms of mental occurrence in human beings, which lead to a striking difference in the conversion process, a difference to which Professor Starbuck has called attention. You know how it is when you try to recollect a forgotten name. Usually you help the recall by working for it, by mentally running over the places, persons, and things with which the word was connected. But sometimes this effort fails: you feel then as if the harder you tried the less hope there would be, as though the name were *jammed*, and pressure in its direction only kept it all the more from rising. And then the opposite expedient often succeeds. Give up the effort entirely; think of something altogether different, and in half an hour the lost name comes sauntering into your mind, as Emerson says, as carelessly as if it had never been invited. Some hidden process was started in you by the effort, which went on after the effort ceased, and made the result come as if it came spontaneously. A certain music teacher, says Dr. Starbuck, says to her pupils after the thing to be done has been clearly pointed out, and unsuccessfully attempted: "Stop trying and it will do itself!"[107]

There is thus a conscious and voluntary way and an involuntary and unconscious way in which mental results may get accomplished; and we find both ways exemplified in the history of conversion, giving us two types, which Starbuck calls the *volitional type* and the *type by self-surrender* respectively.

In the volitional type the regenerative change is usually gradual, and consists in the building up, piece by piece, of a new set of moral and spiritual habits. But there are always critical points here at which the movement forward seems much more rapid. This psychological fact is abundantly illustrated by Dr. Starbuck. Our education in any practical accomplishment proceeds apparently by jerks and starts, just as the growth of our physical bodies does.

"An athlete . . . sometimes awakens suddenly to an understanding of the fine points of the game and to a real enjoyment of it, just as the convert awakens to an appreciation of religion. If he keeps on engaging in the sport, there may come a day when all at once the game plays itself through him—when he loses himself in some great contest. In the same way, a musician may suddenly reach a point at which pleasure in the technique of the art entirely falls away, and in some moment of inspiration he becomes the instrument through which music flows. The writer has chanced to hear two different married persons, both of whose wedded lives had been beautiful from the beginning, relate that not until a year or more after marriage did they awake to the full blessedness of married life. So it is with the religious experience of these persons we are studying."[108]

We shall erelong hear still more remarkable illustrations of subconsciously maturing processes eventuating in results of which we suddenly grow conscious. Sir William

107 Psychology of Religion, p. 117.

108 Psychology of Religion, p. 385. Compare, also, pp. 137–144 and 262.

Hamilton and Professor Laycock of Edinburgh were among the first to call attention to this class of effects; but Dr. Carpenter first, unless I am mistaken, introduced the term "unconscious cerebration," which has since then been a popular phrase of explanation. The facts are now known to us far more extensively than he could know them, and the adjective "unconscious," being for many of them almost certainly a misnomer, is better replaced by the vaguer term "subconscious" or "subliminal."

Of the volitional type of conversion it would be easy to give examples,[109] but they are as a rule less interesting than those of the self-surrender type, in which the subconscious effects are more abundant and often startling. I will therefore hurry to the latter, the more so because the difference between the two types is after all not radical. Even in the most voluntarily built-up sort of regeneration there are passages of partial self-surrender interposed; and in the great majority of all cases, when the will had done its uttermost towards bringing one close to the complete unification aspired after, it seems that the very last step must be left to other forces and performed without the help of its activity. In other words, self-surrender becomes then indispensable. "The personal will," says Dr. Starbuck, "must be given up. In many cases relief persistently refuses to come until the person ceases to resist, or to make an effort in the direction he desires to go."

> "I had said I would not give up; but when my will was broken, it was all over," writes one of Starbuck's correspondents.—Another says: "I simply said: 'Lord, I have done all I can; I leave the whole matter with Thee;' and immediately there came to me a great peace."—Another: "All at once it occurred to me that I might be saved, too, if I would stop trying to do it all myself, and follow Jesus: somehow I lost my load."—Another: "I finally ceased to resist, and gave myself up, though

109 For instance, C. G. Finney italicizes the volitional element: "Just at this point the whole question of Gospel salvation opened to my mind in a manner most marvelous to me at the time. I think I then saw, as clearly as I ever have in my life, the reality and fullness of the atonement of Christ. Gospel salvation seemed to me to be an offer of something to be accepted, and all that was necessary on my part to get my own consent to give up my sins and accept Christ. After this distinct revelation had stood for some little time before my mind, the question seemed to be put, 'Will you accept it now, to-day?' I replied, 'Yes; *I will accept it to-day, or I will die in the attempt!*' " He then went into the woods, where he describes his struggles. He could not pray, his heart was hardened in its pride. "I then reproached myself for having promised to give my heart to God before I left the woods. When I came to try, I found I could not. . . . My inward soul hung back, and there was no going out of my heart to God. The thought was pressing me, of the rashness of my promise that I would give my heart to God that day, or die in the attempt. It seemed to me as if that was binding on my soul; and yet I was going to break my vow. A great sinking and discouragement came over me, and I felt almost too weak to stand upon my knees. Just at this moment I again thought I heard some one approach me, and I opened my eyes to see whether it were so. But right there the revelation of my pride of heart, as the great difficulty that stood in the way, was distinctly shown to me. An overwhelming sense of my wickedness in being ashamed to have a human being see me on my knees before God took such powerful possession of me, that I *cried at the top of my voice, and exclaimed that I would not leave that place if all the men on earth and all the devils in hell surrounded me.* 'What!' I said, 'such a degraded sinner as I am, on my knees confessing my sins to the great and holy God; and ashamed to have any human being, and a sinner like myself, find me on my knees endeavoring to make my peace with my offended God!' The sin appeared awful, infinite. It broke me down before the Lord." Memoirs, pp. 14–16, abridged.

it was a hard struggle. Gradually the feeling came over me that I had done my part, and God was willing to do his."[110]—"Lord, Thy will be done; damn or save!" cries John Nelson,[111] exhausted with the anxious struggle to escape damnation; and at that moment his soul was filled with peace.

Dr. Starbuck gives an interesting, and it seems to me a true, account—so far as conceptions so schematic can claim truth at all—of the reasons why self-surrender at the last moment should be so indispensable. To begin with, there are two things in the mind of the candidate for conversion: first, the present incompleteness or wrongness, the "sin" which he is eager to escape from; and, second, the positive ideal which he longs to compass. Now with most of us the sense of our present wrongness is a far more distinct piece of our consciousness than is the imagination of any positive ideal we can aim at. In a majority of cases, indeed, the "sin" almost exclusively engrosses the attention, so that conversion is *"a process of struggling away from sin rather than of striving towards righteousness."*[112] *A man's conscious wit and will, so far as they strain towards the ideal, are aiming at something only dimly and inaccurately imagined. Yet all the while the forces of mere organic ripening within him are going on towards their own prefigured result, and his conscious strainings are letting loose subconscious allies behind the scenes, which in their way work towards rearrangement; and the rearrangement towards which all these deeper forces tend is pretty surely definite, and definitely different from what he consciously conceives and determines. It may consequently be actually interfered with (jammed*, as it were, like the lost word when we seek too energetically to recall it), by his voluntary efforts slanting from the true direction.

Starbuck seems to put his finger on the root of the matter when he says that to exercise the personal will is still to live in the region where the imperfect self is the thing most emphasized. Where, on the contrary, the subconscious forces take the lead, it is more probably the better self *in posse* which directs the operation. Instead of being clumsily and vaguely aimed at from without, it is then itself the organizing centre. What then must the person do? "He must relax," says Dr. Starbuck—"that is, he must fall back on the larger Power that makes for righteousness, which has been welling up in his own being, and let it finish in its own way the work it has begun.... The act of yielding, in this point of view, is giving one's self over to the new life, making it the centre of a new personality, and living, from within, the truth of it which had before been viewed objectively."[113]

"Man's extremity is God's opportunity" is the theological way of putting this fact of the need of self-surrender; whilst the physiological way of stating it would be, "Let

110 Starbuck: Op. cit., pp. 91, 114.
111 Extracts from the Journal of Mr. John Nelson, London, no date, p. 24.
112 Starbuck, p. 64.
113 Starbuck, p. 115.

one do all in one's power, and one's nervous system will do the rest." Both statements acknowledge the same fact.[114]

To state it in terms of our own symbolism: When the new centre of personal energy has been subconsciously incubated so long as to be just ready to open into flower, "hands off" is the only word for us, it must burst forth unaided!

We have used the vague and abstract language of psychology. But since, in any terms, the crisis described is the throwing of our conscious selves upon the mercy of powers which, whatever they may be, are more ideal than we are actually, and make for our redemption, you see why self-surrender has been and always must be regarded as the vital turning-point of the religious life, so far as the religious life is spiritual and no affair of outer works and ritual and sacraments. One may say that the whole development of Christianity in inwardness has consisted in little more than the greater and greater emphasis attached to this crisis of self-surrender. From Catholicism to Lutheranism, and then to Calvinism; from that to Wesleyanism; and from this, outside of technical Christianity altogether, to pure "liberalism" or transcendental idealism, whether or not of the mind-cure type, taking in the mediæval mystics, the quietists, the pietists, and quakers by the way, we can trace the stages of progress towards the idea of an immediate spiritual help, experienced by the individual in his forlornness and standing in no essential need of doctrinal apparatus or propitiatory machinery.

Psychology and religion are thus in perfect harmony up to this point, since both admit that there are forces seemingly outside of the conscious individual that bring redemption to his life. Nevertheless psychology, defining these forces as "subconscious," and speaking of their effects, as due to "incubation," or "cerebration," implies that they do not transcend the individual's personality; and herein she diverges from Christian theology, which insists that they are direct supernatural operations of the Deity. I propose to you that we do not yet consider this divergence final, but leave the question for a while in abeyance—continued inquiry may enable us to get rid of some of the apparent discord.

Revert, then, for a moment more to the psychology of self-surrender.

When you find a man living on the ragged edge of his consciousness, pent in to his sin and want and incompleteness, and consequently inconsolable, and then simply tell him that all is well with him, that he must stop his worry, break with his discontent, and give up his anxiety, you seem to him to come with pure absurdities. The only positive consciousness he has tells him that all is *not* well, and the better way you offer sounds simply as if you proposed to him to assert cold-blooded falsehoods. "The will to believe" cannot be stretched as far as that. We can make ourselves more faithful to a belief of which we have the rudiments, but we cannot create a belief out of whole cloth when our perception actively assures us of its opposite.

114 Starbuck, p. 113.

The better mind proposed to us comes in that case in the form of a pure negation of the only mind we have, and we cannot actively will a pure negation.

There are only two ways in which it is possible to get rid of anger, worry, fear, despair, or other undesirable affections. One is that an opposite affection should overpoweringly break over us, and the other is by getting so exhausted with the struggle that we have to stop—so we drop down, give up, and *don't care* any longer. Our emotional brain-centres strike work, and we lapse into a temporary apathy. Now there is documentary proof that this state of temporary exhaustion not infrequently forms part of the conversion crisis. So long as the egoistic worry of the sick soul guards the door, the expansive confidence of the soul of faith gains no presence. But let the former faint away, even but for a moment, and the latter can profit by the opportunity, and, having once acquired possession, may retain it. Carlyle's Teufelsdröckh passes from the everlasting No to the everlasting Yes through a "Centre of Indifference."

Let me give you a good illustration of this feature in the conversion process. That genuine saint, David Brainerd, describes his own crisis in the following words:—

> "One morning, while I was walking in a solitary place as usual, I at once saw that all my contrivances and projects to effect or procure deliverance and salvation for myself were utterly in vain; I was brought quite to a stand, as finding myself totally lost. I saw that it was forever impossible for me to do anything towards helping or delivering myself, that I had made all the pleas I ever could have made to all eternity; and that all my pleas were vain, for I saw that self-interest had led me to pray, and that I had never once prayed from any respect to the glory of God. I saw that there was no necessary connection between my prayers and the bestowment of divine mercy; that they laid not the least obligation upon God to bestow his grace upon me; and that there was no more virtue or goodness in them than there would be in my paddling with my hand in the water. I saw that I had been heaping up my devotions before God, fasting, praying, etc., pretending, and indeed really thinking sometimes that I was aiming at the glory of God; whereas I never once truly intended it, but only my own happiness. I saw that as I had never done anything for God, I had no claim on anything from him but perdition, on account of my hypocrisy and mockery. When I saw evidently that I had regard to nothing but self-interest, then my duties appeared a vile mockery and a continual course of lies, for the whole was nothing but self-worship, and an horrid abuse of God.
>
> "I continued, as I remember, in this state of mind, from Friday morning till the Sabbath evening following (July 12, 1739), when I was walking again in the same solitary place. Here, in a mournful melancholy state *I was attempting to pray; but found no heart to engage in that or any other duty; my former concern, exercise, and religious affections were now gone. I thought that the Spirit of God had quite left me; but still was not distressed; yet disconsolate, as if there was nothing in heaven or earth could make me happy. Having been thus endeavoring to pray—though, as I thought, very stupid and senseless*—for near half an hour; then, as I was walking in a thick grove, unspeakable glory seemed to open to the

apprehension of my soul. I do not mean any external brightness, nor any imagination of a body of light, but it was a new inward apprehension or view that I had of God, such as I never had before, nor anything which had the least resemblance to it. I had no particular apprehension of any one person in the Trinity, either the Father, the Son, or the Holy Ghost; but it appeared to be Divine glory. My soul rejoiced with joy unspeakable, to see such a God, such a glorious Divine Being; and I was inwardly pleased and satisfied that he should be God over all for ever and ever. My soul was so captivated and delighted with the excellency of God that I was even swallowed up in him; at least to that degree that I had no thought about my own salvation, and scarce reflected that there was such a creature as myself. I continued in this state of inward joy, peace, and astonishing, till near dark without any sensible abatement; and then began to think and examine what I had seen; and felt sweetly composed in my mind all the evening following. I felt myself in a new world, and everything about me appeared with a different aspect from what it was wont to do. At this time, the way of salvation opened to me with such infinite wisdom, suitableness, and excellency, that I wondered I should ever think of any other way of salvation; was amazed that I had not dropped my own contrivances, and complied with this lovely, blessed, and excellent way before. If I could have been saved by my own duties or any other way that I had formerly contrived, my whole soul would now have refused it. I wondered that all the world did not see and comply with this way of salvation, entirely by the righteousness of Christ."[115]

I have italicized the passage which records the exhaustion of the anxious emotion hitherto habitual. In a large proportion, perhaps the majority, of reports, the writers speak as if the exhaustion of the lower and the entrance of the higher emotion were simultaneous,[116] yet often again they speak as if the higher actively drove the lower out. This is undoubtedly true in a great many instances, as we shall presently see. But often there seems little doubt that both conditions—subconscious ripening of the one affection and exhaustion of the other—must simultaneously have conspired, in order to produce the result.

T. W. B., a convert of Nettleton's, being brought to an acute paroxysm of conviction of sin, ate nothing all day, locked himself in his room in the evening in complete despair, crying aloud, "How long, O Lord, how long?" "After repeating this and similar language," he says, "several times, *I seemed to sink away into a state of insensibility.* When I came to myself again I was on my knees, praying

---

115 Edward's and Dwight's Life of Brainerd, New Haven, 1822, pp. 45–47, abridged.

116 Describing the whole phenomenon as a change of equilibrium, we might say that the movement of new psychic energies towards the personal centre and the recession of old ones towards the margin (or the rising of some objects above, and the sinking of others below the conscious threshold) were only two ways of describing an indivisible event. Doubtless this is often absolutely true, and Starbuck is right when he says that "self-surrender" and "new determination," though seeming at first sight to be such different experiences, are "really the same thing. Self-surrender sees the change in terms of the old self; determination sees it in terms of the new." Op. cit., p. 160.

not for myself but for others. I felt submission to the will of God, willing that he should do with me as should seem good in his sight. My concern seemed all lost in concern for others."[117]

Our great American revivalist Finney writes: "I said to myself: 'What is this? I must have grieved the Holy Ghost entirely away. I have lost all my conviction. I have not a particle of concern about my soul; and it must be that the Spirit has left me.' 'Why!' thought I, 'I never was so far from being concerned about my own salvation in my life.' . . . I tried to recall my convictions, to get back again the load of sin under which I had been laboring. I tried in vain to make myself anxious. I was so quiet and peaceful that I tried to feel concerned about that, lest it should be the result of my having grieved the Spirit away."[118]

But beyond all question there are persons in whom, quite independently of any exhaustion in the Subject's capacity for feeling, or even in the absence of any acute previous feeling, the higher condition, having reached the due degree of energy, bursts through all barriers and sweeps in like a sudden flood. These are the most striking and memorable cases, the cases of instantaneous conversion to which the conception of divine grace has been most peculiarly attached. I have given one of them at length—the case of Mr. Bradley. But I had better reserve the other cases and my comments on the rest of the subject for the following lecture.

117 A. A. Bonar: Nettleton and his Labors, Edinburgh, 1854, p. 261.
118 Charles G. Finney: Memoirs written by Himself, 1876, pp. 17, 18.

## LECTURE X

# Conversion—*Concluded*

In this lecture we have to finish the subject of Conversion, considering at first those striking instantaneous instances of which Saint Paul's is the most eminent, and in which, often amid tremendous emotional excitement or perturbation of the senses, a complete division is established in the twinkling of an eye between the old life and the new. Conversion of this type is an important phase of religious experience, owing to the part which it has played in Protestant theology, and it behooves us to study it conscientiously on that account.

I think I had better cite two or three of these cases before proceeding to a more generalized account. One must know concrete instances first; for, as Professor Agassiz used to say, one can see no farther into a generalization than just so far as one's previous acquaintance with particulars enables one to take it in. I will go back, then, to the case of our friend Henry Alline, and quote his report of the 26th of March, 1775, on which his poor divided mind became unified for good.

> "As I was about sunset wandering in the fields lamenting my miserable lost and undone condition, and almost ready to sink under my burden, I thought I was in such a miserable case as never any man was before. I returned to the house, and when I got to the door, just as I was stepping off the threshold, the following impressions came into my mind like a powerful but small still voice. You have been seeking, praying, reforming, laboring, reading, hearing, and meditating, and what have you done by it towards your salvation? Are you any nearer to conversion now than when you first began? Are you any more prepared for heaven, or fitter to appear before the impartial bar of God, than when you first began to seek?
>
> "It brought such conviction on me that I was obliged to say that I did not think I was one step nearer than at first, but as much condemned, as much exposed, and as miserable as before. I cried out within myself, O Lord God, I am lost, and if thou, O Lord, dost not find out some new way, I know nothing of, I shall never be saved, for the ways and methods I have prescribed to myself have

all failed me, and I am willing they should fail. O Lord, have mercy! O Lord, have mercy!

"These discoveries continued until I went into the house and sat down. After I sat down, being all in confusion, like a drowning man that was just giving up to sink, and almost in an agony, I turned very suddenly round in my chair, and seeing part of an old Bible lying in one of the chairs, I caught hold of it in great haste; and opening it without any premeditation, cast my eyes on the 38th Psalm, which was the first time I ever saw the word of God: it took hold of me with such power that it seemed to go through my whole soul, so that it seemed as if God was praying in, with, and for me. About this time my father called the family to attend prayers; I attended, but paid no regard to what he said in his prayer, but continued praying in those words of the Psalm. Oh, help me, help me! cried I, thou Redeemer of souls, and save me, or I am gone forever; thou canst this night, if thou pleasest, with one drop of thy blood atone for my sins, and appease the wrath of an angry God. At that instant of time when I gave all up to him to do with me as he pleased, and was willing that God should rule over me at his pleasure, redeeming love broke into my soul with repeated scriptures, with such power that my whole soul seemed to be melted down with love; the burden of guilt and condemnation was gone, darkness was expelled, my heart humbled and filled with gratitude, and my whole soul, that was a few minutes ago groaning under mountains of death, and crying to an unknown God for help, was now filled with immortal love, soaring on the wings of faith, freed from the chains of death and darkness, and crying out, My Lord and my God; thou art my rock and my fortress, my shield and my high tower, my life, my joy, my present and my everlasting portion. Looking up, I thought I saw that same light [he had on more than one previous occasion seen subjectively a bright blaze of light], though it appeared different; and as soon as I saw it, the design was opened to me, according to his promise, and I was obliged to cry out: Enough, enough, O blessed God! The work of conversion, the change, and the manifestations of it are no more disputable than that light which I see, or anything that ever I saw.

"In the midst of all my joys, in less than half an hour after my soul was set at liberty, the Lord discovered to me my labor in the ministry and call to preach the gospel. I cried out, Amen, Lord, I'll go; send me, send me. I spent the greatest part of the night in ecstasies of joy, praising and adoring the Ancient of Days for his free and unbounded grace. After I had been so long in this transport and heavenly frame that my nature seemed to require sleep, I thought to close my eyes for a few moments; then the devil stepped in, and told me that if I went to sleep, I should lose it all, and when I should awake in the morning I would find it to be nothing but a fancy and delusion. I immediately cried out, O Lord God, if I am deceived, undeceive me.

"I then closed my eyes for a few minutes, and seemed to be refreshed with sleep; and when I awoke, the first inquiry was, Where is my God? And in an instant of time, my soul seemed awake in and with God, and surrounded by the arms of everlasting love. About sunrise I arose with joy to relate to my parents what God had done for my soul, and declared to them the miracle of God's unbounded grace. I took a Bible to show them the words that were impressed by

God on my soul the evening before; but when I came to open the Bible, it appeared all new to me.

"I so longed to be useful in the cause of Christ, in preaching the gospel, that it seemed as if I could not rest any longer, but go I must and tell the wonders of redeeming love. I lost all taste for carnal pleasures, and carnal company, and was enabled to forsake them."[119]

Young Mr. Alline, after the briefest of delays, and with no book-learning but his Bible, and no teaching save that of his own experience, became a Christian minister, and thenceforward his life was fit to rank, for its austerity and single-mindedness, with that of the most devoted saints. But happy as he became in his strenuous way, he never got his taste for even the most innocent carnal pleasures back. We must class him, like Bunyan and Tolstoy, amongst those upon whose soul the iron of melancholy left a permanent imprint. His redemption was into another universe than this mere natural world, and life remained for him a sad and patient trial. Years later we can find him making such an entry as this in his diary: "On Wednesday the 12th I preached at a wedding, and had the happiness thereby to be the means of excluding carnal mirth."

The next case I will give is that of a correspondent of Professor Leuba, printed in the latter's article, already cited, in vol. vi. of the American Journal of Psychology. This subject was an Oxford graduate, the son of a clergyman, and the story resembles in many points the classic case of Colonel Gardiner, which everybody may be supposed to know. Here it is, somewhat abridged:—

"Between the period of leaving Oxford and my conversion I never darkened the door of my father's church, although I lived with him for eight years, making what money I wanted by journalism, and spending it in high carousal with any one who would sit with me and drink it away. So I lived, sometimes drunk for a week together, and then a terrible repentance, and would not touch a drop for a whole month.

"In all this period, that is, up to thirty-three years of age, I never had a desire to reform on religious grounds. But all my pangs were due to some terrible remorse I used to feel after a heavy carousal, the remorse taking the shape of regret after my folly in wasting my life in such a way—a man of superior talents and education. This terrible remorse turned me gray in one night, and whenever it came upon me I was perceptibly grayer the next morning. What I suffered in this way is beyond the expression of words. It was hell-fire in all its most dreadful tortures. Often did I vow that if I got over 'this time' I would reform. Alas, in about three days I fully recovered, and was as happy as ever. So it went on for years, but, with a physique like a rhinoceros, I always recovered, and as long as I let drink alone, no man was as capable of enjoying life as I was.

"I was converted in my own bedroom in my father's rectory house at pre-

119 Life and Journals, Boston, 1806, pp. 31–40, abridged.

cisely three o'clock in the afternoon of a hot July day (July 13, 1886). I was in perfect health, having been off from the drink for nearly a month. I was in no way troubled about my soul. In fact, God was not in my thoughts that day. A young lady friend sent me a copy of Professor Drummond's Natural Law in the Spiritual World, asking me my opinion of it as a literary work only. Being proud of my critical talents and wishing to enhance myself in my new friend's esteem, I took the book to my bedroom for quiet, intending to give it a thorough study, and then write her what I thought of it. It was here that God met me face to face, and I shall never forget the meeting. 'He that hath the Son hath life eternal, he that hath not the Son hath not life.' I had read this scores of times before, but this made all the difference. I was now in God's presence and my attention was absolutely 'soldered' on to this verse, and I was not allowed to proceed with the book till I had fairly considered what these words really involved. Only then was I allowed to proceed, feeling all the while that there was another being in my bedroom, though not seen by me. The stillness was very marvelous, and I felt supremely happy. It was most unquestionably shown me, in one second of time, that I had never touched the Eternal: and that if I died then, I must inevitably be lost. I was undone. I knew it as well as I now know I am saved. The Spirit of God showed it me in ineffable love; there was no terror in it; I felt God's love so powerfully upon me that only a mighty sorrow crept over me that I had lost all through my own folly; and what was I to do? What could I do? I did not repent even; God never asked me to repent. All I felt was 'I am undone,' and God cannot help it, although he loves me. No fault on the part of the Almighty. All the time I was supremely happy: I felt like a little child before his father. I had done wrong, but my Father did not scold me, but loved me most wondrously. Still my doom was sealed. I was lost to a certainty, and being naturally of a brave disposition I did not quail under it, but deep sorrow for the past, mixed with regret for what I had lost, took hold upon me, and my soul thrilled within me to think it was all over. Then there crept in upon me so gently, so lovingly, so unmistakably, a way of escape, and what was it after all? The old, old story over again, told in the simplest way: 'There is no name under heaven whereby ye can be saved except that of the Lord Jesus Christ.' No words were spoken to me; my soul seemed to see my Saviour in the spirit, and from that hour to this, nearly nine years now, there has never been in my life one doubt that the Lord Jesus Christ and God the Father both worked upon me that afternoon in July, both differently, and both in the most perfect love conceivable, and I rejoiced there and then in a conversion so astounding that the whole village heard of it in less than twenty-four hours.

"But a time of trouble was yet to come. The day after my conversion I went into the hay-field to lend a hand with the harvest, and not having made any promise to God to abstain or drink in moderation only, I took too much and came home drunk. My poor sister was heart-broken; and I felt ashamed of myself and got to my bedroom at once, where she followed me, weeping copiously. She said I had been converted and fallen away instantly. But although I was quite full of drink (not muddled, however), I knew that God's work begun in me was not going to be wasted. About midday I made on my knees the first prayer before

God for twenty years. I did not ask to be forgiven; I felt that was no good, for I would be sure to fall again. Well, what did I do? I committed myself to him in the profoundest belief that my individuality was going to be destroyed, that he would take all from me, and I was willing. In such a surrender lies the secret of a holy life. From that hour drink has had no terrors for me: I never touch it, never want it. The same thing occurred with my pipe: after being a regular smoker from my twelfth year the desire for it went at once, and has never returned. So with every known sin, the deliverance in each case being permanent and complete. I have had no temptation since conversion, God seemingly having shut out Satan from that course with me. He gets a free hand in other ways, but never on sins of the flesh. Since I gave up to God all ownership in my own life, he has guided me in a thousand ways, and has opened my path in a way almost incredible to those who do not enjoy the blessing of a truly surrendered life."

So much for our graduate of Oxford, in whom you notice the complete abolition of an ancient appetite as one of the conversion's fruits.

The most curious record of sudden conversion with which I am acquainted is that of M. Alphonse Ratisbonne, a freethinking French Jew, to Catholicism, at Rome in 1842. In a letter to a clerical friend, written a few months later, the convert gives a palpitating account of the circumstances.[120] The predisposing conditions appear to have been slight. He had an elder brother who had been converted and was a Catholic priest. He was himself irreligious, and nourished an antipathy to the apostate brother and generally to his "cloth." Finding himself at Rome in his twenty-ninth year, he fell in with a French gentleman who tried to make a proselyte of him, but who succeeded no farther after two or three conversations than to get him to hang (half jocosely) a religious medal round his neck, and to accept and read a copy of a short prayer to the Virgin. M. Ratisbonne represents his own part in the conversations as having been of a light and chaffing order; but he notes the fact that for some days he was unable to banish the words of the prayer from his mind, and that the night before the crisis he had a sort of nightmare, in the imagery of which a black cross with no Christ upon it figured. Nevertheless, until noon of the next day he was free in mind and spent the time in trivial conversations. I now give his own words.

"If at this time any one had accosted me, saying: 'Alphonse, in a quarter of an hour you shall be adoring Jesus Christ as your God and Saviour; you shall lie prostrate with your face upon the ground in a humble church; you shall be smiting your breast at the foot of a priest; you shall pass the carnival in a college of Jesuits to prepare yourself to receive baptism, ready to give your life for the Catholic faith; you shall renounce the world and its pomps and pleasures; renounce your fortune, your hopes, and if need be, your betrothed; the affections

120 My quotations are made from an Italian translation of this letter in the Biografia del Sig. M. A. Ratisbonne, Ferrara, 1843, which I have to thank Monsignore D. O'Connell of Rome for bringing to my notice. I abridge the original.

of your family, the esteem of your friends, and your attachment to the Jewish people; you shall have no other aspiration than to follow Christ and bear his cross till death';—if, I say, a prophet had come to me with such a prediction, I should have judged that only one person could be more mad than he—whosoever, namely, might believe in the possibility of such senseless folly becoming true. And yet that folly is at present my only wisdom, my sole happiness.

"Coming out of the café I met the carriage of Monsieur B. [the proselyting friend]. He stopped and invited me in for a drive, but first asked me to wait for a few minutes whilst he attended to some duty at the church of San Andrea delle Fratte. Instead of waiting in the carriage, I entered the church myself to look at it. The church of San Andrea was poor, small, and empty; I believe that I found myself there almost alone. No work of art attracted my attention; and I passed my eyes mechanically over its interior without being arrested by any particular thought. I can only remember an entirely black dog which went trotting and turning before me as I mused. In an instant the dog had disappeared, the whole church had vanished, I no longer saw anything, . . . or more truly I saw, O my God, one thing alone.

"Heavens, how can I speak of it? Oh no! human words cannot attain to expressing the inexpressible. Any description, however sublime it might be, could be but a profanation of the unspeakable truth.

"I was there prostrate on the ground, bathed in my tears, with my heart beside itself, when M. B. called me back to life. I could not reply to the questions which followed from him one upon the other. But finally I took the medal which I had on my breast, and with all the effusion of my soul I kissed the image of the Virgin, radiant with grace, which it bore. Oh, indeed, it was She! It was indeed She! [What he had seen had been a vision of the Virgin.]

"I did not know where I was: I did not know whether I was Alphonse or another. I only felt myself changed and believed myself another me; I looked for myself in myself and did not find myself. In the bottom of my soul I felt an explosion of the most ardent joy; I could not speak; I had no wish to reveal what had happened. But I felt something solemn and sacred within me which made me ask for a priest. I was led to one; and there, alone, after he had given me the positive order, I spoke as best I could, kneeling, and with my heart still trembling. I could give no account to myself of the truth of which I had acquired a knowledge and a faith. All that I can say is that in an instant the bandage had fallen from my eyes; and not one bandage only, but the whole manifold of bandages in which I had been brought up. One after another they rapidly disappeared, even as the mud and ice disappear under the rays of the burning sun.

"I came out as from a sepulchre, from an abyss of darkness; and I was living, perfectly living. But I wept, for at the bottom of that gulf I saw the extreme of misery from which I had been saved by an infinite mercy; and I shuddered at the sight of my iniquities, stupefied, melted, overwhelmed with wonder and with gratitude. You may ask me how I came to this new insight, for truly I had never opened a book of religion nor even read a single page of the Bible, and the dogma of original sin is either entirely denied or forgotten by the Hebrews of to-day, so that I had thought so little about it that I doubt whether I ever knew its name.

But how came I, then, to this perception of it? I can answer nothing save this, that on entering that church I was in darkness altogether, and on coming out of it I saw the fullness of the light. I can explain the change no better than by the simile of a profound sleep or the analogy of one born blind who should suddenly open his eyes to the day. He sees, but cannot define the light which bathes him and by means of which he sees the objects which excite his wonder. If we cannot explain physical light, how can we explain the light which is the truth itself? And I think I remain within the limits of veracity when I say that without having any knowledge of the letter of religious doctrine, I now intuitively perceived its sense and spirit. Better than if I saw them, I *felt* those hidden things; I felt them by the inexplicable effects they produced in me. It all happened in my interior mind; and those impressions, more rapid than thought, shook my soul, revolved and turned it, as it were, in another direction, towards other aims, by other paths. I express myself badly. But do you wish, Lord, that I should inclose in poor and barren words sentiments which the heart alone can understand?"

I might multiply cases almost indefinitely, but these will suffice to show you how real, definite, and memorable an event a sudden conversion may be to him who has the experience. Throughout the height of it he undoubtedly seems to himself a passive spectator or undergoer of an astounding process performed upon him from above. There is too much evidence of this for any doubt of it to be possible. Theology, combining this fact with the doctrines of election and grace, has concluded that the spirit of God is with us at these dramatic moments in a peculiarly miraculous way, unlike what happens at any other juncture of our lives. At that moment, it believes, an absolutely new nature is breathed into us, and we become partakers of the very substance of the Deity.

That the conversion should be instantaneous seems called for on this view, and the Moravian Protestants appear to have been the first to see this logical consequence. The Methodists soon followed suit, practically if not dogmatically, and a short time ere his death, John Wesley wrote:—

"In London alone I found 652 members of our Society who were exceeding clear in their experience, and whose testimony I could see no reason to doubt. And every one of these (without a single exception) has declared that his deliverance from sin was instantaneous; that the change was wrought in a moment. Had half of these, or one third, or one in twenty, declared it was *gradually* wrought in *them*, I should have believed this, with regard to *them*, and thought that *some* were gradually sanctified and some instantaneously. But as I have not found, in so long a space of time, a single person speaking thus, I cannot but believe that sanctification is commonly, if not always, an instantaneous work." Tyerman's Life of Wesley, i. 463.

All this while the more usual sects of Protestantism have set no such store by instantaneous conversion. For them as for the Catholic Church, Christ's blood, the sacraments, and the individual's ordinary religious duties are practically supposed to suffice to his salvation, even though no acute crisis of self-despair and surrender followed by relief should be experienced. For Methodism, on the contrary, unless there have been a crisis of this sort, salvation is only offered, not effectively received, and Christ's sacrifice in so far forth is incomplete. Methodism surely here follows, if not the healthier-minded, yet on the whole the profounder spiritual instinct. The individual models which it has set up as typical and worthy of imitation are not only the more interesting dramatically, but psychologically they have been the more complete.

In the fully evolved Revivalism of Great Britain and America we have, so to speak, the codified and stereotyped procedure to which this way of thinking has led. In spite of the unquestionable fact that saints of the once-born type exist, that there may be a gradual growth in holiness without a cataclysm; in spite of the obvious leakage (as one may say) of much mere natural goodness into the scheme of salvation; revivalism has always assumed that only its own type of religious experience can be perfect; you must first be nailed on the cross of natural despair and agony, and then in the twinkling of an eye be miraculously released.

It is natural that those who personally have traversed such an experience should carry away a feeling of its being a miracle rather than a natural process. Voices are often heard, lights seen, or visions witnessed; automatic motor phenomena occur; and it always seems, after the surrender of the personal will, as if an extraneous higher power had flooded in and taken possession. Moreover the sense of renovation, safety, cleanness, rightness, can be so marvelous and jubilant as well to warrant one's belief in a radically new substantial nature.

> "Conversion," writes the New England Puritan, Joseph Alleine, "is not the putting in a patch of holiness; but with the true convert holiness is woven into all his powers, principles, and practice. The sincere Christian is quite a new fabric, from the foundation to the top-stone. He is a new man, a new creature."
>
> And Jonathan Edwards says in the same strain: "Those gracious influences which are the effects of the Spirit of God are altogether supernatural—are quite different from anything that unregenerate men experience. They are what no improvement, or composition of natural qualifications or principles will ever produce; because they not only differ from what is natural, and from everything that natural men experience in degree and circumstances, but also in kind, and are of a nature far more excellent. From hence it follows that in gracious affections there are [also] new perceptions and sensations entirely different in their nature and kind from anything experienced by the [same] saints before they were sanctified. . . . The conceptions which the saints have of the loveliness of God, and that kind of delight which they experience in it, are quite peculiar, and entirely different from anything which a natural man can possess, or of which he can form any proper notion."

And that such a glorious transformation as this ought of necessity to be preceded by despair is shown by Edwards in another passage.

> "Surely it cannot be unreasonable," he says, "that before God delivers us from a state of sin and liability to everlasting woe, he should give us some considerable sense of the evil from which he delivers us, in order that we may know and feel the importance of salvation, and be enabled to appreciate the value of what God is pleased to do for us. As those who are saved are successively in two extremely different states—first in a state of condemnation and then in a state of justification and blessedness—and as God, in the salvation of men, deals with them as rational and intelligent creatures, it appears agreeable to this wisdom, that those who are saved should be made sensible of their Being, in those two different states. In the first place, that they should be made sensible of their state of condemnation; and afterwards, of their state of deliverance and happiness."

Such quotations express sufficiently well for our purpose the doctrinal interpretation of these changes. Whatever part suggestion and imitation may have played in producing them in men and women in excited assemblies, they have at any rate been in countless individual instances an original and unborrowed experience. Were we writing the story of the mind from the purely natural-history point of view, with no religious interest whatever, we should still have to write down man's liability to sudden and complete conversion as one of his most curious peculiarities.

What, now, must we ourselves think of this question? Is an instantaneous conversion a miracle in which God is present as he is present in no change of heart less strikingly abrupt? Are there two classes of human beings, even among the apparently regenerate, of which the one class really partakes of Christ's nature while the other merely seems to do so? Or, on the contrary, may the whole phenomenon of regeneration, even in these startling instantaneous examples, possibly be a strictly natural process, divine in its fruits, of course, but in one case more and in another less so, and neither more nor less divine in its mere causation and mechanism than any other process, high or low, of man's interior life?

Before proceeding to answer this question, I must ask you to listen to some more psychological remarks. At our last lecture, I explained the shifting of men's centres of personal energy within them and the lighting up of new crises of emotion. I explained the phenomena as partly due to explicitly conscious processes of thought and will, but as due largely also to the subconscious incubation and maturing of motives deposited by the experiences of life. When ripe, the results hatch out, or burst into flower. I have now to speak of the subconscious region, in which such processes of flowering may occur, in a somewhat less vague way. I only regret that my limits of time here force me to be so short.

The expression "field of consciousness" has but recently come into vogue in the psychology books. Until quite lately the unit of mental life which figured most was the single "idea," supposed to be a definitely outlined thing. But at present psychologists are tending, first, to admit that the actual unit is more probably the total mental state, the entire wave of consciousness or field of objects present to the thought at any time; and, second, to see that it is impossible to outline this wave, this field, with any definiteness.

As our mental fields succeed one another, each has its centre of interest, around which the objects of which we are less and less attentively conscious fade to a margin so faint that its limits are unassignable. Some fields are narrow fields and some are wide fields. Usually when we have a wide field we rejoice, for we then see masses of truth together, and often get glimpses of relations which we divine rather than see, for they shoot beyond the field into still remoter regions of objectivity, regions which we seem rather to be about to perceive than to perceive actually. At other times, of drowsiness, illness, or fatigue, our fields may narrow almost to a point, and we find ourselves correspondingly oppressed and contracted.

Different individuals present constitutional differences in this matter of width of field. Your great organizing geniuses are men with habitually vast fields of mental vision, in which a whole programme of future operations will appear dotted out at once, the rays shooting far ahead into definite directions of advance. In common people there is never this magnificent inclusive view of a topic. They stumble along, feeling their way, as it were, from point to point, and often stop entirely. In certain diseased conditions consciousness is a mere spark, without memory of the past or thought of the future, and with the present narrowed down to some one simple emotion or sensation of the body.

The important fact which this "field" formula commemorates is the indetermination of the margin. Inattentively realized as is the matter which the margin contains, it is nevertheless there, and helps both to guide our behavior and to determine the next movement of our attention. It lies around us like a "magnetic field," inside of which our centre of energy turns like a compass-needle, as the present phase of consciousness alters into its successor. Our whole past store of memories floats beyond this margin, ready at a touch to come in; and the entire mass of residual powers, impulses, and knowledges that constitute our empirical self stretches continuously beyond it. So vaguely drawn are the outlines between what is actual and what is only potential at any moment of our conscious life, that it is always hard to say of certain mental elements whether we are conscious of them or not.

The ordinary psychology, admitting fully the difficulty of tracing the marginal outline, has nevertheless taken for granted, first, that all the consciousness the person now has, be the same focal or marginal, inattentive or attentive, is there in the "field" of the moment, all dim and impossible to assign as the latter's outline may be; and, second, that what is absolutely extra-marginal is absolutely non-existent, and cannot be a fact of consciousness at all.

And having reached this point, I must now ask you to recall what I said in my last lecture about the subconscious life. I said, as you may recollect, that those who first laid stress upon these phenomena could not know the facts as we now know them. My first duty now is to tell you what I meant by such a statement.

I cannot but think that the most important step forward that has occurred in psychology since I have been a student of that science is the discovery, first made in

1886, that, in certain subjects at least, there is not only the consciousness of the ordinary field, with its usual centre and margin, but an addition thereto in the shape of a set of memories, thoughts, and feelings which are extra-marginal and outside of the primary consciousness altogether, but yet must be classed as conscious facts of some sort, able to reveal their presence by unmistakable signs. I call this the most important step forward because, unlike the other advances which psychology has made, this discovery has revealed to us an entirely unsuspected peculiarity in the constitution of human nature. No other step forward which psychology has made can proffer any such claim as this.

In particular this discovery of a consciousness existing beyond the field, or subliminally as Mr. Myers terms it, casts light on many phenomena of religious biography. That is why I have to advert to it now, although it is naturally impossible for me in this place to give you any account of the evidence on which the admission of such a consciousness is based. You will find it set forth in many recent books, Binet's Alterations of Personality[121] being perhaps as good a one as any to recommend.

The human material on which the demonstration has been made has so far been rather limited and, in part at least, eccentric, consisting of unusually suggestible hypnotic subjects, and of hysteric patients. Yet the elementary mechanisms of our life are presumably so uniform that what is shown to be true in a marked degree of some persons is probably true in some degree of all, and may in a few be true in an extraordinarily high degree.

The most important consequence of having a strongly developed ultra-marginal life of this sort is that one's ordinary fields of consciousness are liable to incursions from it of which the subject does not guess the source, and which, therefore, take for him the form of unaccountable impulses to act, or inhibitions of action, of obsessive ideas, or even of hallucinations of sight or hearing. The impulses may take the direction of automatic speech or writing, the meaning of which the subject himself may not understand even while he utters it; and generalizing this phenomenon, Mr. Myers has given the name of *automatism*, sensory or motor, emotional or intellectual, to this whole sphere of effects, due to "up-rushes" into the ordinary consciousness of energies originating in the subliminal parts of the mind.

The simplest instance of an automatism is the phenomenon of post-hypnotic suggestion, so-called. You give to a hypnotized subject, adequately susceptible, an order to perform some designated act—usual or eccentric, it makes no difference—after he wakes from his hypnotic sleep. Punctually, when the signal comes or the time elapses upon which you have told him that the act must ensue, he performs it;—but in so doing he has no recollection of your suggestion, and he always trumps up an improvised pretext for his behavior if the act be of an eccentric kind. It may even be suggested to a subject to have a vision or to hear a voice at a certain interval after waking, and when the time comes the vision is seen or the voice heard, with

121 Published in the International Scientific Series.

no inkling on the subject's part of its source. In the wonderful explorations by Binet, Janet, Breuer, Freud, Mason, Prince, and others, of the subliminal consciousness of patients with hysteria, we have revealed to us whole systems of underground life, in the shape of memories of a painful sort which lead a parasitic existence, buried outside of the primary fields of consciousness, and making irruptions thereinto with hallucinations, pains, convulsions, paralyses of feeling and of motion, and the whole procession of symptoms of hysteric disease of body and of mind. Alter or abolish by suggestion these subconscious memories, and the patient immediately gets well. His symptoms were automatisms, in Mr. Myers's sense of the word. These clinical records sound like fairy-tales when one first reads them, yet it is impossible to doubt their accuracy; and, the path having been once opened by these first observers, similar observations have been made elsewhere. They throw, as I said, a wholly new light upon our natural constitution.

And it seems to me that they make a farther step inevitable. Interpreting the unknown after the analogy of the known, it seems to me that hereafter, wherever we meet with a phenomenon of automatism, be it motor impulses, or obsessive idea, or unaccountable caprice, or delusion, or hallucination, we are bound first of all to make search whether it be not an explosion, into the fields of ordinary consciousness, of ideas elaborated outside of those fields in subliminal regions of the mind. We should look, therefore, for its source in the Subject's subconscious life. In the hypnotic cases, we ourselves create the source by our suggestion, so we know it directly. In the hysteric cases, the lost memories which are the source have to be extracted from the patient's Subliminal by a number of ingenious methods, for an account of which you must consult the books. In other pathological cases, insane delusions, for example, or psychopathic obsessions, the source is yet to seek, but by analogy it also should be in subliminal regions which improvements in our methods may yet conceivably put on tap. There lies the mechanism logically to be assumed—but the assumption involves a vast program of work to be done in the way of verification, in which the religious experiences of man must play their part.[122]

122 The reader will here please notice that in my exclusive reliance in the last lecture on the subconscious "incubation" of motives deposited by a growing experience, I followed the method of employing accepted principles of explanation as far as one can. The subliminal region, whatever else it may be, is at any rate a place now admitted by psychologists to exist for the accumulation of vestiges of sensible experience (whether inattentively or attentively registered), and for their elaboration according to ordinary psychological or logical laws into results that end by attaining such a "tension" that they may at times enter consciousness with something like a burst. It thus is "scientific" to interpret all otherwise unaccountable invasive alterations of consciousness as results of the tension of subliminal memories reaching the bursting-point. But candor obliges me to confess that there are occasional bursts into consciousness of results of which it is not easy to demonstrate any prolonged subconscious incubation. Some of the cases I used to illustrate the sense of presence of the unseen in Lecture III were of this order; and we shall see other experiences of the kind when we come to the subject of mysticism. The case of Mr. Bradley, that of M. Ratisbonne, possibly that of Colonel Gardiner, possibly that of Saint Paul, might not be so easily explained in this simple way. The result, then, would have to be ascribed either to a merely physiological nerve storm, a "discharging lesion" like that of epilepsy; or, in case it were useful and rational, as in the two latter cases named, to some more mystical or theological hy-

And thus I return to our own specific subject of instantaneous conversions. You remember the cases of Alline, Bradley, Brainerd, and the graduate of Oxford converted at three in the afternoon. Similar occurrences abound, some with and some without luminous visions, all with a sense of astonished happiness, and of being wrought on by a higher control. If, abstracting altogether from the question of their value for the future spiritual life of the individual, we take them on their psychological side exclusively, so many peculiarities in them remind us of what we find outside of conversion that we are tempted to class them along with other automatisms, and to suspect that what makes the difference between a sudden and a gradual convert is not necessarily the presence of divine miracle in the case of one and of something less divine in that of the other, but rather a simple psychological peculiarity, the fact, namely, that in the recipient of the more instantaneous grace we have one of those Subjects who are in possession of a large region in which mental work can go on subliminally, and from which invasive experiences, abruptly upsetting the equilibrium of the primary consciousness, may come.

I do not see why Methodists need object to such a view. Pray go back and recollect one of the conclusions to which I sought to lead you in my very first lecture. You may remember how I there argued against the notion that the worth of a thing can be decided by its origin. Our spiritual judgment, I said, our opinion of the significance and value of a human event or condition, must be decided on empirical grounds exclusively. If the *fruits for life* of the state of conversion are good, we ought to idealize and venerate it, even though it be a piece of natural psychology; if not, we ought to make short work with it, no matter what supernatural being may have infused it.

Well, how is it with these fruits? If we except the class of preëminent saints of whom the names illumine history, and consider only the usual run of "saints," the shopkeeping church-members and ordinary youthful or middle-aged recipients of instantaneous conversion, whether at revivals or in the spontaneous course of methodistic growth, you will probably agree that no splendor worthy of a wholly supernatural creature fulgurates from them, or sets them apart from the mortals who have never experienced that favor. Were it true that a suddenly converted man as such is, as Edwards says,[123] of an entirely different kind from a natural man, partaking as he does directly of Christ's substance, there surely ought to be some exquisite class-mark, some distinctive radiance attaching even to the lowliest specimen of this genus, to which no one of us could remain insensible, and which, so far as it went, would prove him more excellent than ever the most highly gifted among mere nat-

pothesis. I make this remark in order that the reader may realize that the subject is really complex. But I shall keep myself as far as possible at present to the more "scientific" view; and only as the plot thickens in subsequent lectures shall I consider the question of its absolute sufficiency as an explanation of all the facts. That subconscious incubation explains a great number of them, there can be no doubt.

123 Edwards says elsewhere: "I am bold to say that the work of God in the conversion of one soul, considered together with the source, foundation, and purchase of it, and also the benefit, end, and eternal issue of it, is a more glorious work of God than the creation of the whole material universe."

ural men. But notoriously there is no such radiance. Converted men as a class are indistinguishable from natural men; some natural men even excel some converted men in their fruits; and no one ignorant of doctrinal theology could guess by mere every-day inspection of the "accidents" of the two groups of persons before him, that their substance differed as much as divine differs from human substance.

The believers in the non-natural character of sudden conversion have had practically to admit that there is no unmistakable class-mark distinctive of all true converts. The super-normal incidents, such as voices and visions and overpowering impressions of the meaning of suddenly presented scripture texts, the melting emotions and tumultuous affections connected with the crisis of change, may all come by way of nature, or worse still, be counterfeited by Satan. The real witness of the spirit to the second birth is to be found only in the disposition of the genuine child of God, the permanently patient heart, the love of self eradicated. And this, it has to be admitted, is also found in those who pass no crisis, and may even be found outside of Christianity altogether.

Throughout Jonathan Edwards's admirably rich and delicate description of the supernaturally infused condition, in his Treatise on Religious Affections, there is not one decisive trait, not one mark, that unmistakably parts it off from what may possibly be only an exceptionally high degree of natural goodness. In fact, one could hardly read a clearer argument than this book unwittingly offers in favor of the thesis that no chasm exists between the orders of human excellence, but that here as elsewhere, nature shows continuous differences, and generation and regeneration are matters of degree.

All which denial of two objective classes of human beings separated by a chasm must not leave us blind to the extraordinary momentousness of the fact of his conversion to the individual himself who gets converted. There are higher and lower limits of possibility set to each personal life. If a flood but goes above one's head, its absolute elevation becomes a matter of small importance; and when we touch our own upper limit and live in our own highest centre of energy, we may call ourselves saved, no matter how much higher some one else's centre may be. A small man's salvation will always be a great salvation and the greatest of all facts *for him*, and we should remember this when the fruits of our ordinary evangelicism look discouraging. Who knows how much less ideal still the lives of these spiritual grubs and earthworms, these Crumps and Stigginses, might have been, if such poor grace as they have received had never touched them at all?[124]

---

124 Emerson writes: "When we see a soul whose acts are regal, graceful and pleasant as roses, we must thank God that such things can be and are, and not turn sourly on the angel and say: Crump is a better man, with his grunting resistance to all his native devils." True enough. Yet Crump may really be the better *Crump*, for his inner discords and second birth; and your once-born "regal" character, though indeed always better than poor Crump, may fall far short of what he individually might be had he only some Crump-like capacity for compunction over his own peculiar diabolisms, graceful and pleasant and invariably gentlemanly as these may be.

If we roughly arrange human beings in classes, each class standing for a grade of spiritual excellence, I believe we shall find natural men and converts both sudden and gradual in all the classes. The forms which regenerative change effects have, then, no general spiritual significance, but only a psychological significance. We have seen how Starbuck's laborious statistical studies tend to assimilate conversion to ordinary spiritual growth. Another American psychologist, Prof. George A. Coe,[125] has analyzed the cases of seventy-seven converts or ex-candidates for conversion, known to him, and the results strikingly confirm the view that sudden conversion is connected with the possession of an active subliminal self. Examining his subjects with reference to their hypnotic sensibility and to such automatisms as hypnagogic hallucinations, odd impulses, religious dreams about the time of their conversion, etc., he found these relatively much more frequent in the group of converts whose transformation had been "striking," "striking" transformation being defined as a change which, though not necessarily instantaneous, seems to the subject of it to be distinctly different from a process of growth, however rapid."[126] Candidates for conversion at revivals are, as you know, often disappointed: they experience nothing striking. Professor Coe had a number of persons of this class among his seventy-seven subjects, and they almost all, when tested by hypnotism, proved to belong to a subclass which he calls "spontaneous," that is, fertile in self-suggestions, as distinguished from a "passive" subclass, to which most of the subjects of striking transformation belonged. His inference is that self-suggestion of impossibility had prevented the influence upon these persons of an environment which, on the more "passive" subjects, had easily brought forth the effects they looked for. Sharp distinctions are difficult in these regions, and Professor Coe's numbers are small. But his methods were careful, and the results tally with what one might expect; and they seem, on the whole, to justify his practical conclusion, which is that if you should expose to a converting influence a subject in whom three factors unite: first, pronounced emotional sensibility; second, tendency to automatisms; and third, suggestibility of the passive type; you might then safely predict the result: there would be a sudden conversion, a transformation of the striking kind.

Does this temperamental origin diminish the significance of the sudden conversion when it has occurred? Not in the least, as Professor Coe well says; for "the ultimate test of religious values is nothing psychological, nothing definable in terms of *how it happens*, but something ethical, definable only in terms of *what is attained*."[127]

As we proceed farther in our inquiry we shall see that what is attained is often an altogether new level of spiritual vitality, a relatively heroic level, in which impossible things have become possible, and new energies and endurances are shown.

125 In his book, The Spiritual Life, New York, 1900.
126 Op. cit., p. 112.
127 Op. cit., p. 144.

The personality is changed, the man *is* born anew, whether or not his psychological idiosyncrasies are what give the particular shape to his metamorphosis. "Sanctification" is the technical name of this result; and erelong examples of it shall be brought before you. In this lecture I have still only to add a few remarks on the assurance and peace which fill the hour of change itself.

One word more, though, before proceeding to that point, lest the final purpose of my explanation of suddenness by subliminal activity be misunderstood. I do indeed believe that if the Subject have no liability to such subconscious activity, or if his conscious fields have a hard rind of a margin that resists incursions from beyond it, his conversion must be gradual if it occur, and must resemble any simple growth into new habits. His possession of a developed subliminal self, and of a leaky or pervious margin, is thus a *conditio sine qua non* of the Subject's becoming converted in the instantaneous way. But if you, being orthodox Christians, ask me as a psychologist whether the reference of a phenomenon to a subliminal self does not exclude the notion of the direct presence of the Deity altogether, I have to say frankly that as a psychologist I do not see why it necessarily should. The lower manifestations of the Subliminal, indeed, fall within the resources of the personal subject: his ordinary sense-material, inattentively taken in and subconsciously remembered and combined, will account for all his usual automatisms. But just as our primary wide-awake consciousness throws open our senses to the touch of things material, so it is logically conceivable that *if there be* higher spiritual agencies that can directly touch us, the psychological condition of their doing so *might be* our possession of a subconscious region which alone should yield access to them. The hubbub of the waking life might close a door which in the dreamy Subliminal might remain ajar or open.

Thus that perception of external control which is so essential a feature in conversion might, in some cases at any rate, be interpreted as the orthodox interpret it: forces transcending the finite individual might impress him, on condition of his being what we may call a subliminal human specimen. But in any case the *value* of these forces would have to be determined by their effects, and the mere fact of their transcendency would of itself establish no presumption that they were more divine than diabolical.

I confess that this is the way in which I should rather see the topic left lying in your minds until I come to a much later lecture, when I hope once more to gather these dropped threads together into more definitive conclusions. The notion of a subconscious self certainly ought not at this point of our inquiry to be held to *exclude* all notion of a higher penetration. If there be higher powers able to impress us, they may get access to us only through the subliminal door.

Let us turn now to the feelings which immediately fill the hour of the conversion experience. The first one to be noted is just this sense of higher control. It is not always, but it is very often present. We saw examples of it in Alline, Bradley, Brainerd, and elsewhere. The need of such a higher controlling agency is well expressed in the short reference which the eminent French Protestant Adolphe Monod makes to the crisis of his own conversion. It was at Naples in his early manhood, in the summer of 1827.

> "My sadness," he says, "was without limit, and having got entire possession of me, it filled my life from the most indifferent external acts to the most secret thoughts, and corrupted at their source my feelings, my judgment, and my happiness. It was then that I saw that to expect to put a stop to this disorder by my reason and my will, which were themselves diseased, would be to act like a blind man who should pretend to correct one of his eyes by the aid of the other equally blind one. I had then no resource save in *some influence from without.* I remembered the promise of the Holy Ghost; and what the positive declarations of the Gospel had never succeeded in bringing home to me, I learned at last from necessity, and believed, for the first time in my life, in this promise, in the only sense in which it answered the needs of my soul, in that, namely, of a real external supernatural action, capable of giving me thoughts, and taking them away from me, and exerted on me by a God as truly master of my heart as he is of the rest of nature. Renouncing then all merit, all strength, abandoning all my personal resources, and acknowledging no other title to his mercy than my own utter misery, I went home and threw myself on my knees, and prayed as I never yet prayed in my life. From this day onwards a new interior life began for me: not that my melancholy had disappeared, but it had lost its sting. Hope had entered into my heart, and once entered on the path, the God of Jesus Christ, to whom I then had learned to give myself up, little by little did the rest."[128]

It is needless to remind you once more of the admirable congruity of Protestant theology with the structure of the mind as shown in such experiences. In the extreme of melancholy the self that consciously *is* can do absolutely nothing. It is completely bankrupt and without resource, and no works it can accomplish will avail. Redemption from such subjective conditions must be a free gift or nothing, and grace through Christ's accomplished sacrifice is such a gift.

> "God," says Luther, "is the God of the humble, the miserable, the oppressed, and the desperate, and of those that are brought even to nothing; and his nature is to give sight to the blind, to comfort the broken-hearted, to justify sinners, to save the very desperate and damned. Now that pernicious and pestilent opinion of man's own righteousness, which will not be a sinner, unclean, miserable, and damnable, but righteous and holy, suffereth not God to come to his own natural and proper work. Therefore God must take this maul in hand (the law, I mean) to beat in pieces and bring to nothing this beast with her vain confidence, that she may so learn at length by her own misery that she is utterly forlorn and damned. But here lieth the difficulty, that when a man is terrified and cast down, he is so little able to raise himself up again and say, 'Now I am bruised and af-

128 I piece together a quotation made by W. Monod, in his book la Vie, and a letter printed in the work: Adolphe Monod: L. Souvenirs de sa Vie, 1885, p. 433.

flicted enough; now is the time of grace; now is the time to hear Christ.' The foolishness of man's heart is so great that then he rather seeketh to himself more laws to satisfy his conscience. 'If I live,' saith he, 'I will amend my life: I will do this, I will do that.' But here, except thou do the quite contrary, except thou send Moses away with his law, and in these terrors and this anguish lay hold upon Christ who died for thy sins, look for no salvation. Thy cowl, thy shaven crown, thy chastity, thy obedience, thy poverty, thy works, thy merits? what shall all these do? what shall the law of Moses avail? If I, wretched and damnable sinner, through works or merits could have loved the Son of God, and so come to him, what needed he to deliver himself for me? If I, being a wretch and damned sinner, could be redeemed by any other price, what needed the Son of God to be given? But because there was no other price, therefore he delivered neither sheep, ox, gold, nor silver, but even God himself, entirely and wholly 'for me,' even 'for me,' I say, a miserable, wretched sinner. Now, therefore, I take comfort and apply this to *myself*. And this manner of applying is the very true force and power of faith. For he died *not* to justify the righteous, but the *un*-righteous, and to make *them* the children of God."[129]

That is, the more literally lost you are, the more literally you are the very being whom Christ's sacrifice has already saved. Nothing in Catholic theology, I imagine, has ever spoken to sick souls as straight as this message from Luther's personal experience. As Protestants are not all sick souls, of course reliance on what Luther exults in calling the dung of one's merits, the filthy puddle of one's own righteousness, has come to the front again in their religion; but the adequacy of his view of Christianity to the deeper parts of our human mental structure is shown by its wildfire contagiousness when it was a new and quickening thing.

Faith that Christ has genuinely done his work was part of what Luther meant by faith, which so far is faith in a fact intellectually conceived of. But this is only one part of Luther's faith, the other part being far more vital. This other part is something not intellectual but immediate and intuitive, the assurance, namely, that I, this individual I, just as I stand, without one plea, etc., am saved now and forever.[130]

Professor Leuba is undoubtedly right in contending that the conceptual belief about Christ's work, although so often efficacious and antecedent, is really accessory

---

129 Commentary on Galatians, ch. iii. verse 19, and ch. ii. verse 20, abridged.

130 In some conversions, both steps are distinct; in this one, for example:—

"Whilst I was reading the evangelical treatise, I was soon struck by an expression: 'the finished work of Christ.' 'Why,' I asked of myself, 'does the author use these terms? Why does he not say "the atoning work"?' Then these words, 'It is finished,' presented themselves to my mind. 'What is it that is finished?' I asked, and in an instant my mind replied: 'A perfect expiation for sin; entire satisfaction has been given; the debt has been paid by the Substitute. Christ has died for our sins; not for ours only, but for those of all men. If, then, the entire work is finished, all the debt paid, what remains for me to do?' In another instant the light was shed through my mind by the Holy Ghost, and the joyous conviction was given me that nothing more was to be done, save to fall on my knees, to accept this Saviour and his love, to praise God forever." Autobiography of Hudson Taylor. I translate back into English from the French translation of Challand (Geneva, no date), the original not being accessible.

and non-essential, and that the "joyous conviction" can also come by far other channels than this conception. It is to the joyous conviction itself, the assurance that all is well with one, that he would give the name of faith *par excellence.*

> "When the sense of estrangement," he writes, "fencing man about in a narrowly limited ego, breaks down, the individual finds himself 'at one with all creation.' He lives in the universal life; he and man, he and nature, he and God, are one. That state of confidence, trust, union with all things, following upon the achievement of moral unity, is the *Faith-state.* Various dogmatic beliefs suddenly, on the advent of the faith-state, acquire a character of certainty, assume a new reality, become an object of faith. As the ground of assurance here is not rational, argumentation is irrelevant. But such conviction being a mere casual offshoot of the faith-state, it is a gross error to imagine that the chief practical value of the faith-state is its power to stamp with the seal of reality certain particular theological conceptions.[131] On the contrary, its value lies solely in the fact that it is the psychic correlate of a biological growth reducing contending desires to one direction; a growth which expresses itself in new affective states and new reactions; in larger, nobler, more Christ-like activities. The ground of the specific assurance in religious dogmas is then an affective experience. The objects of faith may even be preposterous; the affective stream will float them along, and invest them with unshakable certitude. The more startling the affective experience, the less explicable it seems, the easier it is to make it the carrier of unsubstantiated notions."[132]

The characteristics of the affective experience which, to avoid ambiguity, should, I think, be called the state of assurance rather than the faith-state, can be easily enumerated, though it is probably difficult to realize their intensity, unless one has been through the experience one's self.

The central one is the loss of all the worry, the sense that all is ultimately well with one, the peace, the harmony, the *willingness to be,* even though the outer conditions should remain the same. The certainty of God's "grace," of "justification," "salvation," is an objective belief that usually accompanies the change in Christians; but this may be entirely lacking and yet the affective peace remain the same—you will recollect the case of the Oxford graduate: and many might be given where the assurance of personal salvation was only a later result. A passion of willingness, of acquiescence, of admiration, is the glowing centre of this state of mind.

The second feature is the sense of perceiving truths not known before. The mysteries of life become lucid, as Professor Leuba says; and often, nay usually, the solution is more or less unutterable in words. But these more intellectual phenomena may be postponed until we treat of mysticism.

A third peculiarity of the assurance state is the objective change which the world

131 Tolstoy's case was a good comment on those words. There was almost no theology in his conversion. His faith-state was the sense come back that life was infinite in its moral significance.
132 American Journal of Psychology, vii. 345–347, abridged.

often appears to undergo. "An appearance of newness beautifies every object," the precise opposite of that other sort of newness, that dreadful unreality and strangeness in the appearance of the world, which is experienced by melancholy patients, and of which you may recall my relating some examples. This sense of clean and beautiful newness within and without is one of the commonest entries in conversion records. Jonathan Edwards thus describes it in himself:—

"After this my sense of divine things gradually increased, and became more and more lively, and had more of that inward sweetness. The appearance of everything was altered; there seemed to be, as it were, a calm, sweet cast, or appearance of divine glory, in almost everything. God's excellency, his wisdom, his purity and love, seemed to appear in everything; in the sun, moon, and stars; in the clouds and blue sky; in the grass, flowers, and trees; in the water and all nature; which used greatly to fix my mind. And scarce anything, among all the works of nature, was so sweet to me as thunder and lightning; formerly nothing had been so terrible to me. Before, I used to be uncommonly terrified with thunder, and to be struck with terror when I saw a thunderstorm rising; but now, on the contrary, it rejoices me."[133]

Billy Bray, an excellent little illiterate English evangelist, records his sense of newness thus:—

"I said to the Lord: 'Thou hast said, they that ask shall receive, they that seek shall find, and to them that knock the door shall be opened, and I have faith to believe it.' In an instant the Lord made me so happy that I cannot express what I felt. I shouted for joy. I praised God with my whole heart. . . . I think this was in November, 1823, but what day of the month I do not know. I remember this, that everything looked new to me, the people, the fields, the cattle, the trees. I was like a new man in a new world. I spent the greater part of my time in praising the Lord."[134]

Starbuck and Leuba both illustrate this sense of newness by quotations. I take the two following from Starbuck's manuscript collection. One, a woman, says:—

"I was taken to a camp-meeting, mother and religious friends seeking and praying for my conversion. My emotional nature was stirred to its depths; confessions of depravity and pleading with God for salvation from sin made me oblivious of all surroundings. I plead for mercy, and had a vivid realization of forgiveness and renewal of my nature. When rising from my knees I exclaimed, 'Old things have passed away, all things have become new.' It was like entering another world, a new state of existence. Natural objects were glorified, my spiritual vision was so clarified that I saw beauty in every material object in the

133 Dwight: Life of Edwards, New York, 1830, p. 61, abridged.
134 W. F. Bourne: The King's Son, a Memoir of Billy Bray, London, Hamilton, Adams & Co., 1887, p. 9.

universe, the woods were vocal with heavenly music; my soul exulted in the love of God, and I wanted everybody to share in my joy."

The next case is that of a man:—

"I know not how I got back into the encampment, but found myself staggering up to Rev. ——'s Holiness tent—and as it was full of seekers and a terrible noise inside, some groaning, some laughing, and some shouting, and by a large oak, ten feet from the tent, I fell on my face by a bench, and tried to pray, and every time I would call on God, something like a man's hand would strangle me by choking. I don't know whether there were any one around or near me or not. I thought I should surely die if I did not get help, but just as often as I would pray, that unseen hand was felt on my throat and my breath squeezed off. Finally something said: 'Venture on the atonement, for you will die anyway if you don't.' So I made one final struggle to call on God for mercy, with the same choking and strangling, determined to finish the sentence of prayer for Mercy, if I did strangle and die, and the last I remember that time was falling back on the ground with the same unseen hand on my throat. I don't know how long I lay there or what was going on. None of my folks were present. When I came to myself, there were a crowd around me praising God. The very heavens seemed to open and pour down rays of light and glory. Not for a moment only, but all day and night, floods of light and glory seemed to pour through my soul, and oh, how I was changed, and everything became new. My horses and hogs and even everybody seemed changed."

This man's case introduces the feature of automatisms, which in suggestible subjects have been so startling a feature at revivals since, in Edwards's, Wesley's and Whitfield's time, these became a regular means of gospel-propagation. They were at first supposed to be semi-miraculous proofs of "power" on the part of the Holy Ghost; but great divergence of opinion quickly arose concerning them. Edwards, in his Thoughts on the Revival of Religion in New England, has to defend them against their critics; and their value has long been matter of debate even within the revivalistic denominations.[135] They undoubtedly have no essential spiritual significance, and although their presence makes his conversion more memorable to the convert, it has never been proved that converts who show them are more persevering or fertile in good fruits than those whose change of heart has had less violent accompaniments. On the whole, unconsciousness, convulsions, visions, involuntary vocal utterances, and suffocation, must be simply ascribed to the subject's having a large subliminal region, involving nervous instability. This is often the subject's own view of the matter afterwards. One of Starbuck's correspondents writes, for instance:—

135 Consult WILLIAM B. SPRAGUE: Lectures on Revivals of Religion, New York, 1832, in the long Appendix to which the opinions of a large number of ministers are given.

"I have been through the experience which is known as conversion. My explanation of it is this: the subject works his emotions up to the breaking point, at the same time resisting their physical manifestations, such as quickened pulse, etc., and then suddenly lets them have their full sway over his body. The relief is something wonderful, and the pleasurable effects of the emotions are experienced to the highest degree."

There is one form of sensory automatism which possibly deserves special notice on account of its frequency. I refer to hallucinatory or pseudo-hallucinatory luminous phenomena, *photisms*, to use the term of the psychologists. Saint Paul's blinding heavenly vision seems to have been a phenomenon of this sort; so does Constantine's cross in the sky. The last case but one which I quoted mentions floods of light and glory. Henry Alline mentions a light, about whose externality he seems uncertain. Colonel Gardiner sees a blazing light. President Finney writes:—

"All at once the glory of God shone upon and round about me in a manner almost marvelous. . . . A light perfectly ineffable shone in my soul, that almost prostrated me on the ground. . . . This light seemed like the brightness of the sun in every direction. It was too intense for the eyes. . . . I think I knew something then, by actual experience, of that light that prostrated Paul on the way to Damascus. It was surely a light such as I could not have endured long."[136]

Such reports of photisms are indeed far from uncommon. Here is another from Starbuck's collection, where the light appeared evidently external:—

"I had attended a series of revival services for about two weeks off and on. Had been invited to the altar several times, all the time becoming more deeply impressed, when finally I decided I must do this, or I should be lost. Realization of conversion was very vivid, like a ton's weight being lifted from my heart; a strange light which seemed to light up the whole room (for it was dark); a conscious supreme bliss which caused me to repeat 'Glory to God' for a long time. Decided to be God's child for life, and to give up my pet ambition, wealth and social position. My former habits of life hindered my growth somewhat, but I set about overcoming these systematically, and in one year my whole nature was changed, i. e., my ambitions were of a different order."

Here is another one of Starbuck's cases, involving a luminous element:—

"I had been clearly converted twenty-three years before, or rather reclaimed. My experience in regeneration was then clear and spiritual, and I had not backslidden. But I experienced entire sanctification on the 15th day of March, 1893, about eleven o'clock in the morning. The particular accompaniments of the experience

136 Memoirs, p. 34.

were entirely unexpected. I was quietly sitting at home singing selections out of Pentecostal Hymns. Suddenly there seemed to be a something sweeping into me and inflating my entire being—such a sensation as I had never experienced before. When this experience came, I seemed to be conducted around a large, capacious, well-lighted room. As I walked with my invisible conductor and looked around, a clear thought was coined in my mind, 'They are not here, they are gone.' As soon as the thought was definitely formed in my mind, though no word was spoken, the Holy Spirit impressed me that I was surveying my own soul. Then, for the first time in all my life, did I know that I was cleansed from all sin, and filled with the fullness of God."

Leuba quotes the case of a Mr. Peek, where the luminous affection reminds one of the chromatic hallucinations produced by the intoxicant cactus buds called mescal by the Mexicans:—

"When I went in the morning into the fields to work, the glory of God appeared in all his visible creation. I well remember we reaped oats, and how every straw and head of the oats seemed, as it were, arrayed in a kind of rainbow glory, or to glow, if I may so express it, in the glory of God."[137]

---

137 These reports of sensorial photism shade off into what are evidently only metaphorical accounts of the sense of new spiritual illumination, as, for instance, in Brainerd's statement: "As I was walking in a thick grove, unspeakable glory seemed to open to the apprehension of my soul. I do not mean any external brightness, for I saw no such thing, nor any imagination of a body of light in the third heavens, or anything of that nature, but it was a new inward apprehension or view that I had of God."

In a case like this next one from Starbuck's manuscript collection, the lighting up of the darkness is probably also metaphorical:—

"One Sunday night, I resolved that when I got home to the ranch where I was working, I would offer myself with my faculties and all to God to be used only by and for him. . . . It was raining and the roads were muddy; but this desire grew so strong that I kneeled down by the side of the road and told God all about it, intending then to get up and go on. Such a thing as any special answer to my prayer never entered my mind, having been converted by faith, but still being most undoubtedly saved. Well, while I was praying, I remember holding out my hands to God and telling him they should work for him, my feet walk for him, my tongue speak for him, etc., etc., if he would only use me as his instrument and give me a satisfying experience—when suddenly the darkness of the night seemed lit up—I felt, realized, knew, that God heard and answered my prayer. Deep happiness came over me; I felt I was accepted into the inner circle of God's loved ones."

In the following case also the flash of light is metaphorical:—

"A prayer meeting had been called for at close of evening service. The minister supposed me impressed by his discourse (a mistake—he was dull). He came and, placing his hand upon my shoulder, said: 'Do you not want to give your heart to God?' I replied in the affirmative. Then said he, 'Come to the front seat.' They sang and prayed and talked with me. I experienced nothing but unaccountable wretchedness. They declared that the reason why I did not 'obtain peace' was because I was not willing to give up all to God. After about two hours the minister said we would go home. As usual, on retiring, I prayed. In great distress, I at this time simply said, 'Lord, I have done all I can, I leave the whole matter with thee.' Immediately, like a flash of light, there came to me a great peace, and I arose and went into my parents' bedroom and said, 'I do feel so wonderfully happy.' This I regard as the hour of conversion. It was the hour in which I became assured of divine acceptance and favor. So far as my life was concerned, it made little immediate change."

The most characteristic of all the elements of the conversion crisis, and the last one of which I shall speak, is the ecstasy of happiness produced. We have already heard several accounts of it, but I will add a couple more. President Finney's is so vivid that I give it at length:—

> "All my feelings seemed to rise and flow out; and the utterance of my heart was, 'I want to pour my whole soul out to God.' The rising of my soul was so great that I rushed into the back room of the front office, to pray. There was no fire and no light in the room; nevertheless it appeared to me as if it were perfectly light. As I went in and shut the door after me, it seemed as if I met the Lord Jesus Christ face to face. It did not occur to me then, nor did it for some time afterwards, that it was wholly a mental state. On the contrary, it seemed to me that I saw him as I would see any other man. He said nothing, but looked at me in such a manner as to break me right down at his feet. I have always since regarded this as a most remarkable state of mind; for it seemed to me a reality that he stood before me, and I fell down at his feet and poured out my soul to him. I wept aloud like a child, and made such confessions as I could with my choked utterance. It seemed to me that I bathed his feet with my tears; and yet I had no distinct impression that I touched him, that I recollect. I must have continued in this state for a good while; but my mind was too absorbed with the interview to recollect anything that I said. But I know, as soon as my mind became calm enough to break off from the interview, I returned to the front office, and found that the fire that I had made of large wood was nearly burned out. But as I turned and was about to take a seat by the fire, I received a mighty baptism of the Holy Ghost. Without any expectation of it, without ever having the thought in my mind that there was any such thing for me, without any recollection that I had ever heard the thing mentioned by any person in the world, the Holy Spirit descended upon me in a manner that seemed to go through me, body and soul. I could feel the impression, like a wave of electricity, going through and through me. Indeed, it seemed to come in waves and waves of liquid love; for I could not express it in any other way. It seemed like the very breath of God. I can recollect distinctly that it seemed to fan me, like immense wings.
>
> "No words can express the wonderful love that was shed abroad in my heart. I wept aloud with joy and love; and I do not know but I should say I literally bellowed out the unutterable gushings of my heart. These waves came over me, and over me, and over me, one after the other, until I recollect I cried out, 'I shall die if these waves continue to pass over me.' I said, 'Lord, I cannot bear any more;' yet I had no fear of death.
>
> "How long I continued in this state, with this baptism continuing to roll over me and go through me, I do not know. But I know it was late in the evening when a member of my choir—for I was the leader of the choir—came into the office to see me. He was a member of the church. He found me in this state of loud weeping, and said to me, 'Mr. Finney, what ails you?' I could make him no answer for some time. He then said, 'Are you in pain?' I gathered myself up as best I could, and replied, 'No, but so happy that I cannot live.' "

I just now quoted Billy Bray; I cannot do better than give his own brief account of his post-conversion feelings:—

"I can't help praising the Lord. As I go along the street, I lift up one foot, and it seems to say 'Glory'; and I lift up the other, and it seems to say 'Amen'; and so they keep up like that all the time I am walking."[138]

One word, before I close this lecture, on the question of the transiency or permanence of these abrupt conversions. Some of you, I feel sure, knowing that numerous backslidings and relapses take place, make of these their apperceiving mass for interpreting the whole subject, and dismiss it with a pitying smile at so much "hysterics." Psychologically, as well as religiously, however, this is shallow. It misses the point of serious interest, which is not so much the duration as the nature and quality of these shiftings of character to higher levels. Men lapse from every level—we need no statistics to tell us that. Love is, for instance, well known not to be irrevocable, yet, constant or inconstant, it reveals new flights and reaches of ideality while it lasts. These revelations form its significance to men and women, whatever be its duration. So with the conversion experience: that it should for even a short time show a human being what the high-water mark of his spiritual capacity is, this is what constitutes its importance—an importance which backsliding cannot diminish, although persistence might increase it. As a matter of fact, all the more striking instances of conversion, all those, for instance, which I have quoted, *have* been permanent. The case of which there might be most doubt, on account of its suggesting so strongly an epileptoid seizure, was the case of M. Ratisbonne. Yet I am informed that Ratisbonne's whole future was shaped by those few minutes. He gave up his project of marriage, became a priest, founded at Jerusalem, where he went to dwell, a mission of nuns for the conversion of the Jews, showed no tendency to use for

---

138 I add in a note a few more records:—

"One morning, being in deep distress, fearing every moment I should drop into hell, I was constrained to cry in earnest for mercy, and the Lord came to my relief, and delivered my soul from the burden and guilt of sin. My whole frame was in a tremor from head to foot, and my soul enjoyed sweet peace. The pleasure I then felt was indescribable. The happiness lasted about three days, during which time I never spoke to any person about my feelings." Autobiography of Dan Young, edited by W. P. Strickland, New York, 1860.

"In an instant there rose up in me such a sense of God's taking care of those who put their trust in him that for an hour all the world was crystalline, the heavens were lucid, and I sprang to my feet and began to cry and laugh." H. W. Beecher, quoted by Leuba.

"My tears of sorrow changed to joy, and I lay there praising God in such ecstasy of joy as only the soul who experiences it can realize."—"I cannot express how I felt. It was as if I had been in a dark dungeon and lifted into the light of the sun. I shouted and I sang praise unto him who loved me and washed me from my sins. I was forced to retire into a secret place, for the tears did flow, and I did not wish my shopmates to see me, and yet I could not keep it a secret."—"I experienced joy almost to weeping."—"I felt my face must have shone like that of Moses. I had a general feeling of buoyancy. It was the greatest joy it was ever my lot to experience."—"I wept and laughed alternately. I was as light as if walking on air. I felt as if I had gained greater peace and happiness than I had ever expected to experience." Starbuck's correspondents.

egotistic purposes the notoriety given him by the peculiar circumstances of his conversion—which, for the rest, he could seldom refer to without tears—and in short remained an exemplary son of the Church until he died, late in the 80's, if I remember rightly.

The only statistics I know of, on the subject of the duration of conversions, are those collected for Professor Starbuck by Miss Johnston. They embrace only a hundred persons, evangelical church-members, more than half being Methodists. According to the statement of the subjects themselves, there had been backsliding of some sort in nearly all the cases, 93 per cent of the women, 77 per cent of the men. Discussing the returns more minutely, Starbuck finds that only 6 per cent are relapses from the religious faith which the conversion confirmed, and that the backsliding complained of is in most only a fluctuation in the ardor of sentiment. Only six of the hundred cases report a change of faith. Starbuck's conclusion is that the effect of conversion is to bring with it "a changed attitude towards life, which is fairly constant and permanent, although the feelings fluctuate. . . . In other words, the persons who have passed through conversion, having once taken a stand for the religious life, tend to feel themselves identified with it, no matter how much their religious enthusiasm declines."[139]

139 Psychology of Religion, pp. 360, 357.

LECTURES XI, XII, AND XIII

# Saintliness

The last lecture left us in a state of expectancy. What may the practical fruits for life have been, of such movingly happy conversions as those we heard of? With this question the really important part of our task opens, for you remember that we began all this empirical inquiry not merely to open a curious chapter in the natural history of human consciousness, but rather to attain a spiritual judgment as to the total value and positive meaning of all the religious trouble and happiness which we have seen. We must, therefore, first describe the fruits of the religious life, and then we must judge them. This divides our inquiry into two distinct parts. Let us without further preamble proceed to the descriptive task.

It ought to be the pleasantest portion of our business in these lectures. Some small pieces of it, it is true, may be painful, or may show human nature in a pathetic light, but it will be mainly pleasant, because the best fruits of religious experience are the best things that history has to show. They have always been esteemed so; here if anywhere is the genuinely strenuous life; and to call to mind a succession of such examples as I have lately had to wander through, though it has been only in the reading of them, is to feel encouraged and uplifted and washed in better moral air.

The highest flights of charity, devotion, trust, patience, bravery to which the wings of human nature have spread themselves have been flown for religious ideals. I can do no better than quote, as to this, some remarks which Sainte-Beuve in his History of Port-Royal makes on the results of conversion or the state of grace.

"Even from the purely human point of view," Sainte-Beuve says, "the phenomenon of grace must still appear sufficiently extraordinary, eminent, and rare, both in its nature and in its effects, to deserve a closer study. For the soul arrives thereby at a certain fixed and invincible state, a state which is genuinely heroic, and from out of which the greatest deeds which it ever performs are executed. Through all the different forms of communion, and all the diversity of the means which help to produce this state, whether it be reached by a jubilee, by a general confession, by a solitary prayer and effusion, whatever in short to be the place and the occasion, it is easy to recognize that it is fundamentally one state in spirit and fruits. Penetrate a little beneath the diversity of circumstances, and it becomes evident that in Christians of different epochs it is always one and the same modification by which they are affected: there is veritably a single fundamental and identical spirit of piety and charity, common to those who have received grace; an inner state which before all things is one of love and humility, of infinite confidence in God, and of severity for one's self, accompanied with tenderness for others. The fruits peculiar to this condition of the soul have the same savor in all, under distant suns and in different surroundings, in Saint Teresa of Avila just as in any Moravian brother of Herrnhut."[140]

Sainte-Beuve has here only the more eminent instances of regeneration in mind, and these are of course the instructive ones for us also to consider. These devotees have often laid their course so differently from other men that, judging them by worldly law, we might be tempted to call them monstrous aberrations from the path of nature. I begin, therefore, by asking a general psychological question as to what the inner conditions are which may make one human character differ so extremely from another.

I reply at once that where the character, as something distinguished from the intellect, is concerned, the causes of human diversity lie chiefly in our *differing susceptibilities of emotional excitement*, and in the *different impulses and inhibitions* which these bring in their train. Let me make this more clear.

Speaking generally, our moral and practical attitude, at any given time, is always a resultant of two sets of forces within us, impulses pushing us one way and obstructions and inhibitions holding us back. "Yes! yes!" say the impulses; "No! no!" say the inhibitions. Few people who have not expressly reflected on the matter realize how constantly this factor of inhibition is upon us, how it contains and moulds us by its restrictive pressure almost as if we were fluids pent within the cavity of a jar. The influence is so incessant that it becomes subconscious. All of you, for example, sit here with a certain constraint at this moment, and entirely without express consciousness of the fact, because of the influence of the occasion. If left alone in the room, each of you would probably involuntarily rearrange himself, and make his attitude more "free and easy." But proprieties and their inhibitions snap like cobwebs if any great emotional excitement supervenes. I have seen a dandy appear in the street with his face covered with shaving-lather because a house across the way was on fire; and a woman will run among strangers in her nightgown if it be a question of saving her baby's life or her own. Take a self-indulgent woman's life in general. She will yield to every inhibition set by her disagreeable sensations, lie late in bed, live upon tea or bromides, keep indoors from the cold. Every difficulty finds her obedient to its "no." But make a mother of her, and what have you? Possessed by maternal excitement, she now confronts wakefulness, weariness, and toil without an instant of hesitation or a word of complaint. The inhibitive power of pain

140 Sainte-Beuve: Port-Royal, vol. i. pp. 95 and 106, abridged.

over her is extinguished wherever the baby's interests are at stake. The inconveniences which this creature occasions have become, as James Hinton says, the glowing heart of a great joy, and indeed are now the very conditions whereby the joy becomes most deep.

This is an example of what you have already heard of as the "expulsive power of a higher affection." But be the affection high or low, it makes no difference, so long as the excitement it brings be strong enough. In one of Henry Drummond's discourses he tells of an inundation in India where an eminence with a bungalow upon it remained unsubmerged, and became the refuge of a number of wild animals and reptiles in addition to the human beings who were there. At a certain moment a royal Bengal tiger appeared swimming towards it, reached it, and lay panting like a dog upon the ground in the midst of the people, still possessed by such an agony of terror that one of the Englishmen could calmly step up with a rifle and blow out its brains. The tiger's habitual ferocity was temporarily quelled by the emotion of fear, which became sovereign, and formed a new centre for his character.

Sometimes no emotional state is sovereign, but many contrary ones are mixed together. In that case one hears both "yeses" and "noes," and the "will" is called on then to solve the conflict. Take a soldier, for example, with his dread of cowardice impelling him to advance, his fears impelling him to run, and his propensities to imitation pushing him towards various courses if his comrades offer various examples. His person becomes the seat of a mass of interferences; and he may for a time simply waver, because no one emotion prevails. There is a pitch of intensity, though, which, if any emotion reach it, enthrones that one as alone effective and sweeps its antagonists and all their inhibitions away. The fury of his comrades' charge, once entered on, will give this pitch of courage to the soldier; the panic of their rout will give this pitch of fear. In these sovereign excitements, things ordinarily impossible, grow natural because the Inhibitions are annulled. Their "no! no!" not only is not heard, it does not exist. Obstacles are then like tissue-paper hoops to the circus rider—no impediment; the flood is higher than the dam they make. "Lass sie betteln gehn wenn sie hungrig sind!" cries the grenadier, frantic over his Emperor's capture, when his wife and babes are suggested; and men pent into a burning theatre have been known to cut their way through the crowd with knives.[141]

141 " 'Love would not be love,' says Bourget, 'unless it could carry one to crime.' And so one may say that no passion would be a veritable passion unless it could carry one to crime." (Sighele: Psychologie des Sectes, p. 136.) In other words, great passions annual the ordinary inhibitions set by "conscience." And conversely, of all the criminal human beings, the false, cowardly, sensual, or cruel persons who actually live, there is perhaps not one whose criminal impulse may not be at some moment overpowered by the presence of some other emotion to which his character is also potentially liable, provided that other emotion be only made intense enough. Fear is usually the most available emotion for this result in this particular class of persons. It stands for conscience, and may here be classed appropriately as a "higher affection." If we are soon to die, or if we believe a day of judgment to be near at hand, how quickly do we put our moral house in order—we do not see how sin can evermore exert temptation over us! Old-fashioned hell-fire Christianity well knew how to extract from fear its full equivalent in the way of fruits for repentance, and its full conversion value.

One mode of emotional excitability is exceedingly, important in the composition of the energetic character, from its peculiarly destructive power over inhibitions. I mean what in its lower form is mere irascibility, susceptibility to wrath, the fighting temper; and what in subtler ways manifests itself as impatience, grimness, earnestness, severity of character. Earnestness means willingness to live with energy, though energy bring pain. The pain may be pain to other people or pain to one's self—it makes little difference; for when the strenuous mood is on one, the aim is to break something, no matter whose or what. Nothing annihilates an inhibition as irresistibly as anger does it; for, as Moltke says of war, destruction pure and simple is its essence. This is what makes it so invaluable an ally of every other passion. The sweetest delights are trampled on with a ferocious pleasure the moment they offer themselves as checks to a cause by which our higher indignations are elicited. It costs then nothing to drop friendships, to renounce long-rooted privileges and possessions, to break with social ties. Rather do we take a stern joy in the astringency and desolation; and what is called weakness of character seems in most cases to consist in the inaptitude for these sacrificial moods, of which one's own inferior self and its pet softnesses must often be the targets and the victims.[142]

So far I have spoken of temporary alterations produced by shifting excitements in the same person. But the relatively fixed differences of character of different persons are explained in a precisely similar way. In a man with a liability to a special sort of emotion, whole ranges of inhibition habitually vanish, which in other men remain effective, and other sorts of inhibition take their place. When a person has an inborn genius for certain emotions, his life differs strangely from that of ordinary people, for none of their usual deterrents check him. Your mere aspirant to a type of character, on the contrary, only shows, when your natural lover, fighter, or reformer, with whom the passion is a gift of nature, comes along, the hopeless inferiority of voluntary to instinctive action. He has deliberately to overcome his inhibitions; the genius with the inborn passion seems not to feel them at all; he is free of all that inner friction and nervous waste. To a Fox, a Garibaldi, a General Booth, a John Brown, a Louise Michel, a Bradlaugh, the obstacles omnipotent over those around them are as if non-existent. Should the rest of us so disregard them, there might be many such heroes, for many have the wish to live for similar ideals, and only the adequate degree of inhibition-quenching fury is lacking.[143]

---

142 Example: Benjamin Constant was often marveled at as an extraordinary instance of superior intelligence with inferior character. He writes (Journal, Paris, 1895, p. 56), "I am tossed and dragged about by my miserable weakness. Never was anything so ridiculous as my indecision. Now marriage, now solitude; now Germany, now France, hesitation upon hesitation, and all because at bottom I am *unable to give up anything.*" He can't "get mad" at any of his alternatives; and the career of a man beset by such an all-round amiability is hopeless.

143 The great thing which the higher excitabilities give is *courage;* and the addition or subtraction of a certain amount of this quality makes a different man, a different life. Various excitements let the courage loose. Trustful hope will do it; inspiring example will do it; love will do it; wrath will do it. In some people it is natively so high that the mere touch of danger does it, though danger is for most men the great inhibitor of action. "Love of adventure" becomes in such persons a ruling passion. "I believe,"

The difference between willing and merely wishing, between having ideals that are creative and ideals that are but pinings and regrets, thus depends solely either on the amount of steam-pressure chronically driving the character in the ideal direction, or on the amount of ideal excitement transiently acquired. Given a certain amount of love, indignation, generosity, magnanimity, admiration, loyalty, or enthusiasm of self-surrender, the result is always the same. That whole raft of cowardly obstructions, which in tame persons and dull moods are sovereign impediments to action, sinks away at once. Our conventionality, our shyness, laziness, and stinginess, our demands for precedent and permission, for guarantee and surety, our small suspicions, timidities, despairs, where are they now? Severed like cobwebs, broken like bubbles in the sun—

> *"Wo sind die Sorge nun und Noth*
> *Die mich noch gestern wollt' erschlaffen?*
> *Ich schäm' mich dess' im Morgenroth."*

The flood we are borne on rolls them so lightly under that their very contact is unfelt. Set free of them, we float and soar and sing. This auroral openness and uplift gives to all creative ideal levels a bright and caroling quality, which is nowhere more marked than where the controlling emotion is religious. "The true monk," writes an Italian mystic, "takes nothing with him but his lyre."

We may now turn from these psychological generalities to those fruits of the religious state which form the special subject of our present lecture. The man who lives in his religious centre of personal energy, and is actuated by spiritual enthusiasms, differs from his previous carnal self in perfectly definite ways. The new ardor which burns in his breast consumes in its glow the lower "noes" which formerly beset him, and keeps him immune against infection from the entire groveling portion of his nature. Magnanimities once impossible are now easy; paltry conventionalities and mean incentives once tyrannical hold no sway. The stone wall inside of him has fallen, the hardness in his heart has broken down. The rest of us can, I think, imagine this by recalling our state of feeling in those temporary "melting moods" into

says General Skobeleff, "that my bravery is simply the passion and at the same time the contempt of danger. The risk of life fills me with an exaggerated rapture. The fewer there are to share it, the more I like it. The participation of my body in the event is required to furnish me an adequate excitement. Everything intellectual appears to me to be reflex; but a meeting of man to man, a duel, a danger into which I can throw myself head-foremost, attracts me, moves me, intoxicates me. I am crazy for it, I love it, I adore it. I run after danger as one runs after women; I wish it never to stop. Were it always the same, it would always bring me a new pleasure. When I throw myself into an adventure in which I hope to find it, my heart palpitates with the uncertainty; I could wish at once to have it appear and yet to delay. A sort of painful and delicious shiver shakes me; my entire nature runs to meet the peril with an impetus that my will would in vain try to resist" (Juliette Adam: Le Général Skobeleff, Nouvelle Revue, 1886, abridged.) Skobeleff seems to have been a cruel egoist; but the disinterested Garibaldi, if one may judge by his "Memorie," lived in an unflagging emotion of similar danger-seeking excitement.

which either the trials of real life, or the theatre, or a novel sometimes throws us. Especially if we weep! For it is then as if our tears broke through an inveterate inner dam, and let all sorts of ancient peccancies and moral stagnancies drain away, leaving us now washed and soft of heart and open to every nobler leading. With most of us the customary hardness quickly returns, but not so with saintly persons. Many saints, even as energetic ones as Teresa and Loyola, have possessed what the church traditionally reveres as a special grace, the so-called gift of tears. In these persons the melting mood seems to have held almost uninterrupted control. And as it is with tears and melting moods, so it is with other exalted affections. Their reign may come by gradual growth or by a crisis; but in either case it may have "come to stay."

At the end of the last lecture we saw this permanence to be true of the general paramountcy of the higher insight, even though in the ebbs of emotional excitement meaner motives might temporarily prevail and backsliding might occur. But that lower temptations may remain completely annulled, apart from transient emotion and as if by alteration of the man's habitual nature, is also proved by documentary evidence in certain cases. Before embarking on the general natural history of the regenerate character, let me convince you of this curious fact by one or two examples. The most numerous are those of reformed drunkards. You recollect the case of Mr. Hadley in the last lecture; the Jerry McAuley Water Street Mission abounds in similar instances. You also remember the graduate of Oxford, converted at three in the afternoon, and getting drunk in the hay-field the next day, but after that permanently cured of his appetite. "From that hour drink has had no terrors for me: I never touch it, never want it. The same thing occurred with my pipe. . . . the desire for it went at once and has never returned. So with every known sin, the deliverance in each case being permanent and complete. I have had no temptations since conversion."

Here is an analogous case from Starbuck's manuscript collection:—

> "I went into the old Adelphi Theatre, where there was a Holiness meeting, . . . and I began saying, 'Lord, Lord, I must have this blessing.' Then what was to me an audible voice said: 'Are you willing to give up everything to the Lord?' and question after question kept coming up, to all of which I said: 'Yes, Lord; yes, Lord!' until this came: 'Why do you not accept it *now?*' and I said: 'I do, Lord.'—I felt no particular joy, only a trust. Just then the meeting closed, and, as I went out on the street, I met a gentleman smoking a fine cigar, and a cloud of smoke came into my face, and I took a long, deep breath of it, and praise the Lord, all my appetite for it was gone. Then as I walked along the street, passing saloons where the fumes of liquor came out, I found that all my taste and longing for that accursed stuff was gone. Glory to God! . . . [But] for ten or eleven long years [after that] I was in the wilderness with its ups and downs. My appetite for liquor never came back."

The classic case of Colonel Gardiner is that of a man cured of sexual temptation in a single hour. To Mr. Spears the colonel said, "I was effectually cured of all inclination to that sin I was so strongly addicted to that I thought nothing but shooting me through the head could have cured me of it; and all desire and inclination to it was removed, as entirely as if I had been a sucking child; nor did the temptation return to this day." Mr. Webster's words on the same subject are these: "One thing I have heard the colonel frequently say, that he was much addicted to impurity before his acquaintance with religion; but that, so soon as he was enlightened from above, he felt the power of the Holy Ghost changing his nature so wonderfully that his sanctification in this respect seemed more remarkable than in any other."[144]

Such rapid abolition of ancient impulses and propensities reminds us so strongly of what has been observed as the result of hypnotic suggestion that it is difficult not to believe that subliminal influences play the decisive part in these abrupt changes of heart, just as they do in hypnotism.[145] Suggestive therapeutics abound in records of cure, after a few sittings, of inveterate bad habits with which the patient, left to ordinary moral and physical influences, had struggled in vain. Both drunkenness and sexual vice have been cured in this way, action through the subliminal seeming thus in many individuals to have the prerogative of inducing relatively stable change. If the grace of God miraculously operates, it probably operates through the subliminal door, then. But just *how* anything operates in this region is still unexplained, and we shall do well now to say good-by to the *process* of transformation altogether—leaving it, if you like, a good deal of a psychological or theological mystery—and to turn our attention to the fruits of the religious condition, no matter in what way they may have been produced.[146]

---

144 Doddridge's Life of Colonel James Gardiner, London Religious Tract Society, pp. 23–32.

145 Here, for example, is a case, from Starbuck's book, in which a "sensory automatism" brought about quickly what prayers and resolves had been unable to effect. The subject is a woman. She writes:—

"When I was about forty I tried to quit smoking, but the desire was on me, and had me in its power. I cried and prayed and promised God to quit, but could not. I had smoked for fifteen years. When I was fifty-three, as I sat by the fire one day smoking, a voice came to me. I did not hear it with my ears, but more as a dream or sort of double think. It said, 'Louisa, lay down smoking.' At once I replied. 'Will you take the desire away?' But it only kept saying: 'Louisa, lay down smoking.' Then I got up, laid my pipe on the mantel-shelf, and never smoked again or had any desire to. The desire was gone as though I had never known it or touched tobacco. The sight of others smoking and the smell of smoke never gave me the least wish to touch it again." The Psychology of Religion, p. 142.

146 Professor Starbuck expresses the radical destruction of old influences physiologically, as a cutting off of the connection between higher and lower cerebral centres. "This condition," he says, "in which the association-centres connected with the spiritual life are cut off from the lower, is often reflected in the way correspondents describe their experiences. . . . For example: 'Temptations from without still assail me, but there is nothing *within* to respond to them.' The ego [here] is wholly identified with the higher centres, whose quality of feeling is that of withinness. Another of the respondents says: 'Since then, although Satan tempts me, there is as it were a wall of brass around me, so that his darts cannot touch me.' "—Unquestionably, functional exclusions of this sort must occur in the cerebral organ. But on the side accessible to introspection, their causal condition is nothing but the degree of spiritual excitement, getting at last so high and strong as to be sovereign; and it must be frankly confessed that we do not know just why or how such sovereignty comes about in one person and not in another. We can only give our imagination a certain delusive help by mechanical analogies.

If we should conceive, for example, that the human mind, with its different possibilities of equilibrium, might be like a many-sided solid with different surfaces on which it could lie flat, we might

The collective name for the ripe fruits of religion in a character is Saintliness.[147] The saintly character is the character for which spiritual emotions are the habitual centre of the personal energy; and there is a certain composite photograph of universal saintliness, the same in all religions, of which the features can easily be traced.[148]

They are these:—

1. A feeling of being in a wider life than that of this world's selfish little interests; and a conviction, not merely intellectual, but as it were sensible, of the existence of an Ideal Power. In Christian saintliness this power is always personified as God; but abstract moral ideals, civic or patriotic utopias, or inner versions of holiness or right may also be felt as the true lords and enlargers of our life, in ways which I described in the lecture on the Reality of the Unseen.[149]

---

liken mental revolutions to the spatial revolutions of such a body. As it is pried up, say by a lever, from a position in which it lies on surface A, for instance, it will linger for a time unstably halfway up, and if the lever cease to urge it, it will tumble back or "relapse" under the continued pull of gravity. But if at last it rotate far enough for its centre of gravity to pass beyond surface A altogether, the body will fall over, on surface B, say, and abide there permanently. The pulls of gravity towards A have vanished, and may now be disregarded. The polyhedron has become immune against farther attraction from their direction.

In this figure of speech the lever may correspond to the emotional influences making for a new life, and the initial pull of gravity to the ancient drawbacks and inhibitions. So long as the emotional influence fails to reach a certain pitch of efficacy, the changes it produces are unstable, and the man relapses into his original attitude. But when a certain intensity is attained by the new emotion, a critical point is passed, and there then ensues an irreversible revolution, equivalent to the production of a new nature.

147 I use this word in spite of a certain flavor of "sanctimoniousness" which sometimes clings to it, because no other word suggests as well the exact combination of affections which the text goes on to describe.

148 "It will be found," says Dr. W. R. Inge (in his lectures on Christian Mysticism, London, 1899, p. 326), "that men of preeminent saintliness agree very closely in what they tell us. They tell us that they have arrived at an unshakable conviction, not based on inference but on immediate experience, that God is a spirit with whom the human spirit can hold intercourse; that in him meet all that they can imagine of goodness, truth, and beauty; that they can see his footprints everywhere in nature, and feel his presence within them as the very life of their life, so that in proportion as they come to themselves they come to him. They tell us what separates us from him and from happiness is, first, self-seeking in all its forms; and, secondly, sensuality in all its forms; that these are the ways of darkness and death, which hide from us the face of God; while the path of the just is like a shining light, which shineth more and more unto the perfect day."

149 The "enthusiasm of humanity" may lead to a life which coalesces in many respects with that of Christian saintliness. Take the following rules proposed to members of the Union pour l'Action morale, in the Bulletin de l'Union, April 1–15, 1894. See, also, Revue Bleue, August 13, 1892.

"We would make known in our own persons the usefulness of rule, of discipline, of resignation and renunciation; we would teach the necessary perpetuity of suffering, and explain the creative part which it plays. We would wage war upon false optimism; on the base hope of happiness coming to us ready made; on the notion of a salvation by knowledge alone, or by material civilization alone, vain symbol as this is of civilization, precarious external arrangement, ill-fitted to replace the intimate union and consent of souls. We would wage war also on bad morals, whether in public or in private life; on luxury, fastidiousness, and over-refinement; on all that tends to increase the painful, immoral,

2. A sense of the friendly continuity of the ideal power with our own life, and a willing self-surrender to its control.

3. An immense elation and freedom, as the outlines of the confining selfhood melt down.

4. A shifting of the emotional centre towards loving and harmonious affections, towards "yes, yes," and away from "no," where the claims of the non-ego are concerned.

These fundamental inner conditions have characteristic practical consequences, as follows:—

*a. Asceticism.*—The self-surrender may become so passionate as to turn into self-immolation. It may then so overrule the ordinary inhibitions of the flesh that the saint finds positive pleasure in sacrifice and asceticism, measuring and expressing as they do the degree of his loyalty to the higher power.

*b. Strength of Soul.*—The sense of enlargement of life may be so uplifting that personal motives and inhibitions, commonly omnipotent, become too insignificant for notice, and new reaches of patience and fortitude open out. Fears and anxieties go, and blissful equanimity takes their place. Come heaven, come hell, it makes no difference now!

> "We forbid ourselves all seeking after popularity, all ambition to appear important. We pledge ourselves to abstain from falsehood, in all its degrees. We promise not to create or encourage illusions as to what is possible, by what we say or write. We promise to one another active sincerity, which strives to see truth clearly, and which never fears to declare what it sees.
>
> "We promise deliberate resistance to the tidal waves of fashion, to the 'booms' and panics of the public mind, to all the forms of weakness and of fear.
>
> "We forbid ourselves the use of sarcasm. Of serious things we will speak seriously and unsmilingly, without banter and without the appearance of banter;—and even so of all things, for there are serious ways of being light of heart.
>
> "We will put ourselves forward always for what we are simply and without false humility, as well as without pedantry, affectation, or pride."

*c. Purity.*—The shifting of the emotional centre brings with it, first, increase of purity. The sensitiveness to spiritual discords is enhanced, and the cleansing of existence from brutal and sensual elements becomes imperative. Occasions of contact with such elements are avoided: the saintly life must deepen its spiritual con-

---

and anti-social multiplications of our wants; on all that excites envy and dislike in the soul of the common people, and confirms the notion that the chief end of life is freedom to enjoy. We would preach by our example the respect of superiors and equals, the respect of all men; affectionate simplicity in our relations with inferiors and insignificant persons; indulgence where our own claims only are concerned, but firmness in our demands where they relate to duties towards others or towards the public.

"For the common people are what we help them to become; their vices are our vices, gazed upon, envied, and imitated; and if they come back with all their weight upon us, it is but just.

sistency and keep unspotted from the world. In some temperaments this need of purity of spirit takes an ascetic turn, and weaknesses of the flesh are treated with relentless severity.

*d. Charity.*—The shifting of the emotional centre brings, secondly, increase of charity, tenderness for fellow-creatures. The ordinary motives to antipathy, which usually set such close bounds to tenderness among human beings, are inhibited. The saint loves his enemies, and treats loathsome beggars as his brothers.

I now have to give some concrete illustrations of these fruits of the spiritual tree. The only difficulty is to choose, for they are so abundant.

Since the sense of Presence of a higher and friendly power seems to be the fundamental feature in the spiritual life, I will begin with that.

In our narratives of conversion we saw how the world might look shining and transfigured to the convert, and, apart from anything acutely religious, we all have moments when the universal life seems to wrap us round with friendliness. In youth and health, in summer, in the woods or on the mountains, there come days when the weather seems all whispering with peace, hours when the goodness and beauty of existence enfold us like a dry warm climate, or chime through us as if our inner ears were subtly ringing with the world's security. Thoreau writes:—

> "Once, a few weeks after I came to the woods, for an hour I doubted whether the near neighborhood of man was not essential to a serene and healthy life. To be alone was somewhat unpleasant. But, in the midst of a gentle rain, while these thoughts prevailed, I was suddenly sensible of such sweet and beneficent society in Nature, in the very pattering of the drops, and in every sight and sound around my house, an infinite and unaccountable friendliness all at once, like an atmosphere, sustaining me, as made the fancied advantages of human neighborhood insignificant, and I have never thought of them since. Every little pine-needle expanded and swelled with sympathy and befriended me. I was so distinctly made aware of the presence of something kindred to me, that I thought no place could ever be strange to me again."[150]

In the Christian consciousness this sense of the enveloping friendliness becomes most personal and definite. "The compensation," writes a German author, "for the loss of that sense of personal independence which man so unwillingly gives up, is the disappearance of all *fear* from one's life, the quite indescribable and inexplicable feeling of an inner *security*, which one can only experience, but which, once it has been experienced, one can never forget."[151]

I find an excellent description of this state of mind in a sermon by Mr. Voysey:—

---

150 H. Thoreau: Walden, Riverside edition, p. 206, abridged.

151 C. H. Hilty: Glück, vol. i. p. 85.

"It is the experience of myriads of trustful souls, that this sense of God's unfailing presence with them in their going out and in their coming in, and by night and day, is a source of absolute repose and confident calmness. It drives away all fear of what may befall them. That nearness of God is a constant security against terror and anxiety. It is not that they are at all assured of physical safety, or deem themselves protected by a love which is denied to others, but that they are in a state of mind equally ready to be safe or to meet with injury. If injury befall them, they will be content to bear it because the Lord is their keeper, and nothing can befall them without his will. If it be his will, then injury is for them a blessing and no calamity at all. Thus and thus only is the trustful man protected and shielded from harm. And I for one—by no means a thick-skinned or hard-nerved man—am absolutely satisfied with this arrangement, and do not wish for any other kind of immunity from danger and catastrophe. Quite as sensitive to pain as the most highly strung organism, I yet feel that the worst of it is conquered, and the sting taken out of it altogether, by the thought that God is our loving and sleepless keeper, and that nothing can hurt us without his will."[152]

More excited expressions of this condition are abundant in religious literature. I could easily weary you with their monotony. Here is an account from Mrs. Jonathan Edwards:—

"Last night," Mrs. Edwards writes, "was the sweetest night I ever had in my life. I never before, for so long a time together, enjoyed so much of the light and rest and sweetness of heaven in my soul, but without the least agitation of body during the whole time. Part of the night I lay awake, sometimes asleep, and sometimes between sleeping and waking. But all night I continued in a constant, clear, and lively sense of the heavenly sweetness of Christ's excellent love, of his nearness to me, and of my dearness to him; with an inexpressibly sweet calmness of soul in an entire rest in him. I seemed to myself to perceive a glow of divine love come down from the heart of Christ in heaven into my heart in a constant stream, like a stream or pencil of sweet light. At the same time my heart and soul all flowed out in love to Christ, so that there seemed to be a constant flowing and reflowing of heavenly love, and I appeared to myself to float or swim, in these bright, sweet beams, like the motes swimming in the beams of the sun, or the streams of his light which come in at the window. I think that what I felt each minute was worth more than all the outward comfort and pleasure which I had enjoyed in my whole life put together. It was pleasure, without the least sting, or any interruption. It was a sweetness, which my soul was lost in; it seemed to be all that my feeble frame could sustain. There was but little difference, whether I was asleep or awake, but if there was any difference, the sweetness was greatest while I was asleep.[153] As I awoke early the next morning, it seemed to me that I

152 The Mystery of Pain and Death, London, 1892, p. 258.

153 Compare Madame Guyon: "It was my practice to arise at midnight for purposes of devotion. . . . It seemed to me that God came at the precise time and woke me from sleep in order that I might enjoy

had entirely done with myself. I felt that the opinions of the world concerning me were nothing, and that I had no more to do with any outward interest of my own than with that of a person whom I never saw. The glory of God seemed to swallow up every wish and desire of my heart. . . . After retiring to rest and sleeping a little while, I awoke, and was led to reflect on God's mercy to me, in giving me, for many years, a willingness to die; and after that, in making me willing to live, that I might do and suffer whatever he called me to here. I also thought how God had graciously given me an entire resignation to his will, with respect to the kind and manner of death that I should die; having been made willing to die on the rack, or at the stake, and if it were God's will, to die in darkness. But now it occurred to me, I used to think of living no longer than to the ordinary age of man. Upon this I was led to ask myself, whether I was not willing to be kept out of heaven even longer; and my whole heart seemed immediately to reply: Yes, a thousand years, and a thousand in horror, if it be most for the honor of God, the torment of my body being so great, awful, and overwhelming that none could bear to live in the country where the spectacle was seen, and the torment of my mind being vastly greater. And it seemed to me that I found a perfect willingness, quietness, and alacrity of soul in consenting that it should be so, if it were most for the glory of God, so that there was no hesitation, doubt, or darkness in my mind. The glory of God seemed to overcome me and swallow me up, and every conceivable suffering, and everything that was terrible to my nature, seemed to shrink to nothing before it. This resignation continued in its clearness and brightness the rest of the night, and all the next day, and the night following, and on Monday in the forenoon, without interruption or abatement."[154]

The annals of Catholic saintship abound in records as ecstatic or more ecstatic than this. "Often the assaults of the divine love," it is said of the Sister Séraphique de la Martinière, "reduced her almost to the point of death. She used tenderly to complain of this to God. 'I cannot support it,' she used to say. 'Bear gently with my weakness, or I shall expire under the violence of your love.' "[155]

Let me pass next to the Charity and Brotherly Love which are a usual fruit of saintliness, and have always been reckoned essential theological virtues, however limited may have been the kinds of service which the particular theology enjoined. Brotherly love would follow logically from the assurance of God's friendly presence, the notion of our brotherhood as men being an immediate inference from that of God's fatherhood of us all. When Christ utters the precepts: "Love your enemies,

---

him. When I was out of health or greatly fatigued, he did not awake me, but at such times I felt, even in my sleep, a singular possession of God. He loved me so much that he seemed to pervade my being, at a time when I could be only imperfectly conscious of his presence. My sleep is sometimes broken—a sort of half sleep; but my soul seems to be awake enough to know God, when it is hardly capable of knowing anything else." T. C. Upham: The Life and Religious Experiences of Madame de la Mothe Guyon, New York, 1877, vol. i., p. 260.

154 I have considerably abridged the words of the original, which is given in Edwards's Narrative of the Revival in New England.

155 Bougaud: Hist. de la Bienheureuse Marguerite Marie, 1894, p. 125.

bless them that curse you, do good to them that hate you, and pray for them which despitefully use you, and persecute you," he gives for a reason: "That ye may be the children of your Father which is in heaven: for he maketh his sun to rise on the evil and on the good, and sendeth rain on the just and on the unjust." One might therefore be tempted to explain both the humility as to one's self and the charity towards others which characterize spiritual excitement, as results of the all-leveling character of theistic belief. But these affections are certainly not mere derivatives of theism. We find them in Stoicism, in Hinduism, and in Buddhism in the highest possible degree. They *harmonize* with paternal theism beautifully; but they harmonize with all reflection whatever upon the dependence of mankind on general causes; and we must, I think, consider them not subordinate but coördinate parts of that great complex excitement in the study of which we are engaged. Religious rapture, moral enthusiasm, ontological wonder, cosmic emotion, are all unifying states of mind, in which the sand and grit of the selfhood incline to disappear, and tenderness to rule. The best thing is to describe the condition integrally as a characteristic affection to which our nature is liable, a region in which we find ourselves at home, a sea in which we swim; but not to pretend to explain its parts by deriving them too cleverly from one another. Like love or fear, the faith-state is a natural psychic complex, and carries charity with it by organic consequence. Jubilation is an expansive affection, and all expansive affections are self-forgetful and kindly so long as they endure.

We find this the case even when they are pathological in origin. In his instructive work, la Tristesse et la Joie,[156] M. Georges Dumas compares together the melancholy and the joyous phase of circular insanity, and shows that, while selfishness characterizes the one, the other is marked by altruistic impulses. No human being so stingy and useless as was Marie in her melancholy period! But the moment the happy period begins, "sympathy and kindness become her characteristic sentiments. She displays a universal goodwill, not only of intention, but in act. . . . She becomes solicitous of the health of other patients, interested in getting them out, desirous to procure wool to knit socks for some of them. Never since she has been under my observation have I heard her in her joyous period utter any but charitable opinions."[157] And later, Dr. Dumas says of all such joyous conditions that "unselfish sentiments and tender emotions are the only affective states to be found in them. The subject's mind is closed against envy, hatred, and vindictiveness, and wholly transformed into benevolence, indulgence, and mercy."[158]

There is thus an organic affinity between joyousness and tenderness, and their companionship in the saintly life need in no way occasion surprise. Along with the happiness, this increase of tenderness is often noted in narratives of conversion. "I began to work for others";—"I had more tender feeling for my family and friends";—"I spoke at once to a person with whom I had been angry";—"I felt for

156 Paris, 1900.
157 Page 130.
158 Page 167.

every one, and loved my friends better";—"I felt every one to be my friend";—these are so many expressions from the records collected by Professor Starbuck.[159]

> "When," says Mrs. Edwards, continuing the narrative from which I made quotation a moment ago, "I arose on the morning of the Sabbath, I felt a love to all mankind, wholly peculiar in its strength and sweetness, far beyond all that I had ever felt before. The power of that love seemed inexpressible. I thought, if I were surrounded by enemies, who were venting their malice and cruelty upon me, in tormenting me, it would still be impossible that I should cherish any feelings towards them but those of love, and pity, and ardent desires for their happiness. I never before felt so far from a disposition to judge and censure others, as I did that morning. I realized also, in an unusual and very lively manner, how great a part of Christianity lies in the performance of our social and relative duties to one another. The same joyful sense continued throughout the day—a sweet love to God and all mankind."

Whatever be the explanation of the charity, it may efface all usual human barriers.[160]

Here, for instance, is an example of Christian non-resistance from Richard Weaver's autobiography. Weaver was a collier, a semi-professional pugilist in his younger days, who became a much beloved evangelist. Fighting, after drinking, seems to have been the sin to which he originally felt his flesh most perversely inclined. After his first conversion he had a backsliding, which consisted in pounding a man who had insulted a girl. Feeling that, having once fallen, he might as well be hanged for a sheep as for a lamb, he got drunk and went and broke the jaw of another man who had lately challenged him to fight and taunted him with cowardice for refusing as a Christian man;—I mention these incidents to show how genuine a change of heart is implied in the later conduct which he describes as follows:—

> "I went down the drift and found the boy crying because a fellow-workman was trying to take the wagon from him by force. I said to him:—
>
> " 'Tom, you mustn't take that wagon.'

159 Op. cit., p. 127.

160 The barrier between men and animals also. We read of Towianski, an eminent Polish patriot and mystic, that "one day one of his friends met him in the rain, caressing a big dog which was jumping upon him and covering him horribly with mud. On being asked why he permitted the animal thus to dirty his clothes, Towianski replied: 'This dog, whom I am now meeting for the first time, has shown a great fellow-feeling for me, and a great joy in my recognition and acceptance of his greetings. Were I to drive him off, I should wound his feelings and do him a moral injury. It would be an offense not only to him, but to all the spirits of the other world who are on the same level with him. The damage which he does to my coat is as nothing in comparison with the wrong which I should inflict upon him, in case I were to remain indifferent to the manifestations of his friendship. We ought,' he added, 'both to lighten the condition of animals, whenever we can, and at the same time to facilitate in ourselves that union of the world of all spirits, which the sacrifice of Christ has made possible.' " André Towianski, Traduction de l'Italien, Turin, 1897 (privately printed). I owe my knowledge of this book and of Towianski to my friend Professor W. Lutoslawski, author of "Plato's Logic."

"He swore at me, and called me a Methodist devil. I told him that God did not tell me to let him rob me. He cursed again, and said he would push the wagon over me.

" 'Well,' I said, 'let us see whether the devil and thee are stronger than the Lord and me.'

"And the Lord and I proving stronger than the devil and he, he had to get out of the way, or the wagon would have gone over him. So I gave the wagon to the boy. Then said Tom:—

" 'I've a good mind to smack thee on the face.'

" 'Well,' I said, 'if that will do thee any good, thou canst do it.' So he struck me on the face.

"I turned the other cheek to him, and said, 'Strike again.'

"He struck again and again, till he had struck me five times. I turned my cheek for the sixth stroke; but he turned away cursing. I shouted after him: 'The Lord forgive thee, for I do, and the Lord save thee.'

"This was on a Saturday; and when I went home from the coal-pit my wife saw my face was swollen, and asked what was the matter with it. I said: 'I've been fighting, and I've given a man a good thrashing.'

"She burst out weeping, and said, 'O Richard, what made you fight?' Then I told her all about it; and she thanked the Lord I had not struck back.

"But the Lord had struck, and his blows have more effect than man's. Monday came. The devil began to tempt me, saying: 'The other men will laugh at thee for allowing Tom to treat thee as he did on Saturday.' I cried, 'Get thee behind me, Satan;'—and went on my way to the coal-pit.

"Tom was the first man I saw. I said 'Good-morning,' but got no reply.

"He went down first. When I got down, I was surprised to see him sitting on the wagon-road waiting for me. When I came to him he burst into tears and said: 'Richard, will you forgive me for striking you?'

" 'I have forgiven thee,' said I; 'ask God to forgive thee. The Lord bless thee.' I gave him my hand, and we went each to his work."[161]

"Love your enemies!" Mark you, not simply those who happen not to be your friends, but your *enemies*, your positive and active enemies. Either this is a mere Oriental hyperbole, a bit of verbal extravagance, meaning only that we should, as far as we can, abate our animosities, or else it is sincere and literal. Outside of certain cases of intimate individual relation, it seldom has been taken literally. Yet it makes one ask the question: Can there in general be a level of emotion so unifying, so obliterative of differences between man and man, that even enmity may come to be an irrelevant circumstance and fail to inhibit the friendlier interests aroused? If positive well-wishing could attain so supreme a degree of excitement, those who were swayed by it might well seem superhuman beings. Their life would be morally discrete from the life of other men, and there is no saying, in the absence of positive experience of an authentic kind—for there are few active examples in our scriptures,

161 J. Patterson's Life of Richard Weaver, pp. 66–68, abridged.

and the Buddhistic examples are legendary,[162]—what the effects might be: they might conceivably transform the world.

Psychologically and in principle, the precept "Love your enemies" is not self-contradictory. It is merely the extreme limit of a kind of magnanimity with which, in the shape of pitying tolerance of our oppressors, we are fairly familiar. Yet if radically followed, it would involve such a breach with our instinctive springs of action as a whole, and with the present world's arrangements, that a critical point would practically be passed, and we should be born into another kingdom of being. Religious emotion makes us feel that other kingdom to be close at hand, within our reach.

The inhibition of instinctive repugnance is proved not only by the showing of love to enemies, but by the showing of it to any one who is personally loathsome. In the annals of saintliness we find a curious mixture of motives impelling in this direction. Asceticism plays its part; and along with charity pure and simple, we find humility or the desire to disclaim distinction and to grovel on the common level before God. Certainly all three principles were at work when Francis of Assisi and Ignatius Loyola exchanged their garments with those of filthy beggars. All three are at work when religious persons consecrate their lives to the care of leprosy or other peculiarly unpleasant diseases. The nursing of the sick is a function to which the religious seem strongly drawn, even apart from the fact that church traditions set that way. But in the annals of this sort of charity we find fantastic excesses of devotion recorded which are only explicable by the frenzy of self-immolation simultaneously aroused. Francis of Assisi kisses his lepers; Margaret Mary Alacoque, Francis Xavier, St. John of God, and others are said to have cleansed the sores and ulcers of their patients with their respective tongues; and the lives of such saints as Elizabeth of Hungary and Madame de Chantal are full of a sort of reveling in hospital purulence, disagreeable to read of, and which makes us admire and shudder at the same time.

So much for the human love aroused by the faith-state. Let me next speak of the Equanimity, Resignation, Fortitude, and Patience which it brings.

"A paradise of inward tranquillity" seems to be faith's usual result; and it is easy, even without being religious one's self, to understand this. A moment back, in treating of the sense of God's presence, I spoke of the unaccountable feeling of safety which one may then have. And, indeed, how can it possibly fail to steady the nerves, to cool the fever, and appease the fret, if one be sensibly conscious that, no matter what one's difficulties for the moment may appear to be, one's life as a whole is in the keeping of a power whom one can absolutely trust? In deeply religious men the abandonment of self to this power is passionate. Whoever not only says, but *feels*,

162 As where the future Buddha, incarnated as a hare, jumps into the fire to cook himself for a meal for a beggar—having previously shaken himself three times, so that none of the insects in his fur should perish with him.

"God's will be done," is mailed against every weakness; and the whole historic array of martyrs, missionaries, and religious reformers is there to prove the tranquil-mindedness, under naturally agitating or distressing circumstances, which self-surrender brings.

The temper of the tranquil-mindedness differs, of course, according as the person is of a constitutionally sombre or of a constitutionally cheerful cast of mind. In the sombre it partakes more of resignation and submission; in the cheerful it is a joyous consent. As an example of the former temper, I quote part of a letter from Professor Lagneau, a venerated teacher of philosophy who lately died, a great invalid, at Paris:—

> "My life, for the success of which you send good wishes, will be what it is able to be. I ask nothing from it, I expect nothing from it. For long years now I exist, think, and act, and am worth what I am worth, only through the despair which is my sole strength and my sole foundation. May it preserve for me, even in these last trials to which I am coming, the courage to do without the desire of deliverance. I ask nothing more from the source whence all strength cometh, and if that is granted, your wishes will have been accomplished."[163]

There is something pathetic and fatalistic about this, but the power of such a tone as a protection against outward shocks is manifest. Pascal is another Frenchman of pessimistic natural temperament. He expresses still more amply the temper of self-surrendering submissiveness:—

> "Deliver me, Lord," he writes in his prayers, "from the sadness at my proper suffering which self-love might give, but put into me a sadness like your own. Let my sufferings appease your choler. Make them an occasion for my conversion and salvation. I ask you neither for health nor for sickness, for life nor for death; but that you may dispose of my health and my sickness, my life and my death, for your glory, for my salvation, and for the use of the Church and of your saints, of whom I would by your grace be one. You alone know what is expedient for me; you are the sovereign master; do with me according to your will. Give to me, or take away from me, only conform my will to yours. I know but one thing, Lord, that it is good to follow you, and bad to offend you. Apart from that, I know not what is good or bad in anything. I know not which is most profitable to me, health or sickness, wealth or poverty, nor anything else in the world. That discernment is beyond the power of men or angels, and is hidden among the secrets of your Providence, which I adore, but do not seek to fathom."[164]

When we reach more optimistic temperaments, the resignation grows less passive. Examples are sown so broadcast throughout history that I might well pass on

163 Bulletin de l'Union pour l'Action Morale, September, 1894.

164 B. Pascal: Prières pour lea Maladies, §§ xiii., xiv., abridged.

without citation. As it is, I snatch at the first that occurs to my mind. Madame Guyon, a frail creature physically, was yet of a happy native disposition. She went through many perils with admirable serenity of soul. After being sent to prison for heresy—

> "Some of my friends," she writes, "wept bitterly at the hearing of it, but such was my state of acquiescence and resignation that it failed to draw any tears from me. . . . There appeared to be in me then, as I find it to be in me now, such an entire loss of what regards myself, that any of my own interests gave me little pain or pleasure; ever wanting to will or wish for myself only the very thing which God does." In another place she writes: "We all of us came near perishing in a river which we found it necessary to pass. The carriage sank in the quicksand. Others who were with us threw themselves out in excessive fright. But I found my thoughts so much taken up with God that I had no distinct sense of danger. It is true that the thought of being drowned passed across my mind, but it cost no other sensation or reflection in me than this—that I felt quite contented and willing it were so, if it were my heavenly Father's choice." Sailing from Nice to Genoa, a storm keeps her eleven days at sea. "As the irritated waves dashed round us," she writes, "I could not help experiencing a certain degree of satisfaction in my mind. I pleased myself with thinking that those mutinous billows, under the command of Him who does all things rightly, might probably furnish me with a watery grave. Perhaps I carried the point too far, in the pleasure which I took in thus seeing myself beaten and bandied by the swelling waters. Those who were with me took notice of my intrepidity."[165]

The contempt of danger which religious enthusiasm produces may be even more buoyant still. I take an example from that charming recent autobiography, "With Christ at Sea," by Frank Bullen. A couple of days after he went through the conversion on shipboard of which he there gives an account—

> "It was blowing stiffly," he writes, "and we were carrying a press of canvas to get north out of the bad weather. Shortly after four bells we hauled down the flying-jib, and I sprang out astride the boom to furl it. I was sitting astride the boom when suddenly it gave way with me. The sail slipped through my fingers, and I fell backwards, hanging head downwards over the seething tumult of shining foam under the ship's bows, suspended by one foot. But I felt only high exultation in my certainty of eternal life. Although death was divided from me by a hair's breadth, and I was acutely conscious of the fact, it gave me no sensation but joy. I suppose I could have hung there no longer than five seconds, but in that time I lived a whole age of delight. But my body asserted itself, and with a desperate gymnastic effort I regained the boom. How I furled the sail I don't know, but

165 From THOMAS C. UPHAM's Life and Religious Opinions and Experiences of Madame de la Mothe Guyon, New York, 1877, ii. 48, i. 141, 413, abridged.

I sang at the utmost pitch of my voice praises to God that went pealing out over the dark waste of waters."[166]

The annals of martyrdom are of course the signal field of triumph for religious imperturbability. Let me cite as an example the statement of a humble sufferer, persecuted as a Huguenot under Louis XIV:—

"They shut all the doors," Blanche Gamond writes, "and I saw six women, each with a bunch of willow rods as thick as the hand could hold, and a yard long. He gave me the order, 'Undress yourself,' which I did. He said, 'You are leaving on your shift; you must take it off.' They had so little patience that they took it off themselves, and I was naked from the waist up. They brought a cord with which they tied me to a beam in the kitchen. They drew the cord tight with all their strength and asked me, 'Does it hurt you?' and then they discharged their fury upon me, exclaiming as they struck me, 'Pray now to your God.' It was the Roulette woman who held this language. But at this moment I received the greatest consolation that I can ever receive in my life, since I had the honor of being whipped for the name of Christ, and in addition of being crowned with his mercy and his consolations. Why can I not write down the inconceivable influences, consolations, and peace which I felt interiorly? To understand them one must have passed by the same trial; they were so great that I was ravished, for there where afflictions abound grace is given superabundantly. In vain the women cried, 'We must double our blows; she does not feel them, for she neither speaks nor cries.' And how should I have cried, since I was swooning with happiness within?"[167]

The transition from tenseness, self-responsibility, and worry, to equanimity, receptivity, and peace, is the most wonderful of all those shiftings of inner equilibrium, those changes of the personal centre of energy, which I have analyzed so often; and the chief wonder of it is that it so often comes about, not by doing, but by simply relaxing and throwing the burden down. This abandonment of self-responsibility seems to be the fundamental act in specifically religious, as distinguished from moral practice. It antedates theologies and is independent of philosophies. Mind-cure, theosophy, stoicism, ordinary neurological hygiene, insist on it as emphatically as Christianity does, and it is capable of entering into closest marriage with every speculative creed.[168] Christians who have it strongly live in what is called "recollection," and are never anxious about the future, nor worry over the outcome of the day. Of Saint Catharine of Genoa it is said that "she took cognizance of things, only

166 Op. cit., London, 1901, p. 130.

167 Claparède et Goty: Deuz Héroines de la Foi, Paris, 1880, p. 112.

168 Compare these three different statements of it: A. P. Call: As a Matter of Course, Boston, 1894; H. W. Dresser: Living by the Spirit, New York and London, 1900; H. W. Smith: The Christian's Secret of a Happy Life, published by the Willard Tract Repository, and now in thousands of hands.

as they were presented to her in succession, *moment by moment*." To her holy soul, "the divine moment was the present moment, . . . and when the present moment was estimated in itself and in its relations, and when the duty that was involved in it was accomplished, it was permitted to pass away as if it had never been, and to give way to the facts and duties of the moment which came after."[169] Hinduism, mind-cure, and theosophy all lay great emphasis upon this concentration of the consciousness upon the moment at hand.

The next religious symptom which I will note is what I have called Purity of Life. The saintly person becomes exceedingly sensitive to inner inconsistency or discord, and mixture and confusion grow intolerable. All the mind's objects and occupations must be ordered with reference to the special spiritual excitement which is now its keynote. Whatever is unspiritual taints the pure water of the soul and is repugnant. Mixed with this exaltation of the moral sensibilities there is also an ardor of sacrifice, for the beloved deity's sake, of everything unworthy of him. Sometimes the spiritual ardor is so sovereign that purity is achieved at a stroke—we have seen examples. Usually it is a more gradual conquest. Billy Bray's account of his abandonment of tobacco is a good example of the latter form of achievement.

> "I had been a smoker as well as a drunkard, and I used to love my tobacco as much as I loved my meat, and I would rather go down into the mine without my dinner than without my pipe. In the days of old, the Lord spoke by the mouths of his servants, the prophets; now he speaks to us by the spirit of his Son. I had not only the feeling part of religion, but I could hear the small, still voice within speaking to me. When I took the pipe to smoke, it would be applied within, 'It is an idol, a lust; worship the Lord with clean lips.' So, I felt it was not right to smoke. The Lord also sent a woman to convince me. I was one day in a house, and I took out my pipe to light it at the fire, and Mary Hawke—for that was the woman's name—said, 'Do you not feel it is wrong to smoke?' I said that I felt something inside telling me that it was an idol, a lust, and she said that was the Lord. Then I said, 'Now, I must give it up, for the Lord is telling me of it inside, and the woman outside, so the tobacco must go, love it as I may.' There and then I took the tobacco out of my pocket, and threw it into the fire, and put the pipe under my foot, 'ashes to ashes, dust to dust.' And I have not smoked since. I found it hard to break off old habits, but I cried to the Lord for help, and he gave me strength, for he has said, 'Call upon me in the day of trouble, and I will deliver thee.' The day after I gave up smoking I had the toothache so bad that I did not know what to do. I thought this was owing to giving up the pipe, but I said I would never smoke again, if I lost every tooth in my head. I said, 'Lord, thou hast told us My yoke is easy and my burden is light,' and when I said that, all the pain left me. Sometimes the thought of the pipe would come back to me very strong; but the Lord strengthened me against the habit, and, bless his name, I have not smoked since."

169 T. C. UPHAM: Life of Madame Catharine Adorna, 3d ed., New York, 1864, pp. 158, 172–74.

> Bray's biographer writes that after he had given up smoking, he thought that he would chew a little, but he conquered this dirty habit, too. "On one occasion," Bray said, "when at a prayer-meeting at Hicks Mill, I heard the Lord say to me, 'Worship me with clean lips.' So, when we got up from our knees, I took the quid out of my mouth and 'whipped 'en' [threw it] under the form. But, when we got on our knees again, I put another quid into my mouth. Then the Lord said to me again, 'Worship me with clean lips.' So I took the quid out of my mouth, and whipped 'en under the form again, and said, 'Yes, Lord, I will.' From that time I gave up chewing as well as smoking, and have been a free man."

The ascetic forms which the impulse for veracity and purity of life may take are often pathetic enough. The early Quakers, for example, had hard battles to wage against the worldliness and insincerity of the ecclesiastical Christianity of their time. Yet the battle that cost them most wounds was probably that which they fought in defense of their own right to social veracity and sincerity in their thee-ing and thou-ing, in not doffing the hat or giving titles of respect. It was laid on George Fox that these conventional customs were a lie and a sham, and the whole body of his followers thereupon renounced them, as a sacrifice to truth, and so that their acts and the spirit they professed might be more in accord.

> "When the Lord sent me into the world," says Fox in his journal, "he forbade me to put off my hat to any, high or low: and I was required to 'thee' and 'thou' all men and women, without any respect to rich or poor, great or small. And as I traveled up and down, I was not to bid people Good-morning, or Good-evening, neither might I bow or scrape with my leg to any one. This made the sects and professions rage. Oh! the rage that was in the priests, magistrates, professors, and people of all sorts: and especially in priests and professors: for though 'thou' to a single person was according to their accidence and grammar rules, and according to the Bible, yet they could not bear to hear it: and because I could not put off my hat to them, it set them all into a rage. . . . Oh! the scorn, heat, and fury that arose! Oh! the blows, punchings, beatings, and imprisonments that we underwent for not putting off our hats to men! Some had their hats violently plucked off and thrown away, so that they quite lost them. The bad language and evil usage we received on this account is hard to be expressed, besides the danger we were sometimes in of losing our lives for this matter, and that by the great professors of Christianity, who thereby discovered they were not true believers. And though it was but a small thing in the eye of man, yet a wonderful confusion it brought among all professors and priests: but, blessed be the Lord, many came to see the vanity of that custom of putting off hats to men, and felt the weight of Truth's testimony against it."

In the autobiography of Thomas Elwood, an early Quaker, who at one time was secretary to John Milton, we find an exquisitely quaint and candid account of the trials he underwent both at home and abroad, in following Fox's canons of sincerity. The anecdotes are too lengthy for citation; but Elwood sets down his manner of feeling about these things in a shorter passage, which I will quote as a characteristic utterance of spiritual sensibility:—

"By this divine light, then," says Elwood, "I saw that though I had not the evil of the common uncleanliness, debauchery, profaneness, and pollutions of the world to put away, because I had, through the great goodness of God and a civil education, been preserved out of those grosser evils, yet I had many other evils to put away and to cease from; some of which were not by the world, which lies in wickedness (1 John v. 19), accounted evils, but by the light of Christ were made manifest to me to be evils, and as such condemned in me.

"As particularly those fruits and effects of pride that discover themselves in the vanity and superfluity of apparel; which I took too much delight in. This evil of my doings I was required to put away and cease from; and judgment lay upon me till I did so.

"I took off from my apparel those unnecessary trimmings of lace, ribbons, and useless buttons, which had no real service, but were set on only for that which was by mistake called ornament; and I ceased to wear rings.

"Again, the giving of flattering titles to men between whom and me there was not any relation to which such titles could be pretended to belong. This was an evil I had been much addicted to, and was accounted a ready artist in; therefore this evil also was I required to put away and cease from. So that thenceforward I durst not say, Sir, Master, My Lord, Madam (or My Dame); or say Your Servant to any one to whom I did not stand in the real relation of a servant, which I had never done to any.

"Again, respect of persons, in uncovering the head and bowing the knee or body in salutation, was a practice I had been much in the use of; and this, being one of the vain customs of the world, introduced by the spirit of the world, instead of the true honor which this is a false representation of, and used in deceit as a token of respect by persons one to another, who bear no real respect one to another; and besides this, being a type and a proper emblem of that divine honor which all ought to pay to Almighty God, and which all of all sorts, who take upon them the Christian name, appear in when they offer their prayers to him, and therefore should not be given to men;—I found this to be one of those evils which I had been too long doing; therefore I was now required to put it away and cease from it.

"Again, the corrupt and unsound form of speaking in the plural number to a single person, *you* to one, instead of *thou*, contrary to the pure, plain, and single language of truth, *thou* to one, and you to more than one, which had always been used by God to men, and men to God, as well as one to another, from the oldest record of time till corrupt men, for corrupt ends, in later and corrupt times, to flatter, fawn, and work upon the corrupt nature in men, brought in that false and senseless way of speaking you to one, which has since corrupted the modern languages, and hath greatly debased the spirits and depraved the manners of men;—this evil custom I had been as forward in as others, and this I was now called out of and required to cease from.

"These and many more evil customs which had sprung up in the night of darkness and general apostasy from the truth and true religion were now, by the inshining of this pure ray of divine light in my conscience, gradually discovered to me to be what I ought to cease from, shun, and stand a witness against."[170]

These early Quakers were Puritans indeed. The slightest inconsistency between profession and deed jarred some of them to active protest. John Woolman writes in his diary:—

"In these journeys I have been where much cloth hath been dyed; and have at sundry times walked over ground where much of their dyestuffs has drained away. This hath produced a longing in my mind that people might come into cleanness of spirit, cleanness of person, and cleanness about their houses and garments. Dyes being invented partly to please the eye, and partly to hide dirt, I have felt in this weak state, when traveling in dirtiness, and affected with unwholesome scents, a strong desire that the nature of dyeing cloth to hide dirt may be more fully considered.

"Washing our garments to keep them sweet is cleanly, but it is the opposite to real cleanliness to hide dirt in them. Through giving way to hiding dirt in our garments a spirit which would conceal that which is disagreeable is strengthened. Real cleanliness becometh a holy people; but hiding that which is not clean by coloring our garments seems contrary to the sweetness of sincerity. Through some sorts of dyes cloth is rendered less useful. And if the value of dyestuffs, and expense of dyeing, and the damage done to cloth, were all added together, and that cost applied to keeping all sweet and clean, how much more would real cleanliness prevail.

"Thinking often on these things, the use of hats and garments dyed with a dye hurtful to them, and wearing more clothes in summer than are useful, grew more uneasy to me; believing them to be customs which have not their foundation in pure wisdom. The apprehension of being singular from my beloved friends was a strait upon me; and thus I continued in the use of some things, contrary to my judgment, about nine months. Then I thought of getting a hat the natural color of the fur, but the apprehension of being looked upon as one affecting singularity felt uneasy to me. On this account I was under close exercise of mind in the time of our general spring meeting in 1762, greatly desiring to be rightly directed; when, being deeply bowed in spirit before the Lord, I was made willing to submit to what I apprehended was required of me; and when I returned home, got a hat of the natural color of the fur.

"In attending meetings, this singularity was a trial to me, and more especially at this time, as white hats were used by some who were fond of following the changeable modes of dress, and as some friends, who knew not from what motives I wore it, grew shy of me, I felt my way for a time shut up in the exercise of the ministry. Some friends were apprehensive that my wearing such a hat savored of an affected singularity: those who spoke with me in a friendly way, I

170 The History of Thomas Elwood, written by Himself, London, 1885, pp. 32–34.

generally informed in a few words, that I believed my wearing it was not in my own will."

When the craving for moral consistency and purity is developed to this degree, the subject may well find the outer world too full of shocks to dwell in, and can unify his life and keep his soul unspotted only by withdrawing from it. That law which impels the artist to achieve harmony in his composition by simply dropping out whatever jars, or suggests a discord, rules also in the spiritual life. To omit, says Stevenson, is the one art in literature: "If I knew how to omit, I should ask no other knowledge." And life, when full of disorder and slackness and vague superfluity, can no more have what we call character than literature can have it under similar conditions. So monasteries and communities of sympathetic devotees open their doors, and in their changeless order, characterized by omissions quite as much as constituted of actions, the holy-minded person finds that inner smoothness and cleanness which it is torture to him to feel violated at every turn by the discordancy and brutality of secular existence.

That the scrupulosity of purity may be carried to a fantastic extreme must be admitted. In this it resembles Asceticism, to which further symptom of saintliness we had better turn next. The adjective "ascetic" is applied to conduct originating on diverse psychological levels, which I might as well begin by distinguishing from one another.

1. Asceticism may be a mere expression of organic hardihood, disgusted with too much ease.
2. Temperance in meat and drink, simplicity of apparel, chastity, and non-pampering of the body generally, may be fruits of the love of purity, shocked by whatever savors of the sensual.
3. They may also be fruits of love, that is, they may appeal to the subject in the light of sacrifices which he is happy in making to the Deity whom he acknowledges.
4. Again, ascetic mortifications and torments may be due to pessimistic feelings about the self, combined with theological beliefs concerning expiation. The devotee may feel that he is buying himself free, or escaping worse sufferings hereafter, by doing penance now.
5. In psychopathic persons, mortifications may be entered on irrationally, by a sort of obsession or fixed idea which comes as a challenge and must be worked off, because only thus does the subject get his interior consciousness feeling right again.
6. Finally, ascetic exercises may in rarer instances be prompted by genuine perversions of the bodily sensibility, in consequence of which normally pain-giving stimuli are actually felt as pleasures.

I will try to give an instance under each of these heads in turn; but it is not easy to get them pure, for in cases pronounced enough to be immediately classed as ascetic, several of the assigned motives usually work together. Moreover, before citing any examples at all, I must invite you to some general pyschological considerations which apply to all of them alike.

A strange moral transformation has within the past century swept over our Western world. We no longer think that we are called on to face physical pain with equanimity. It is not expected of a man that he should either endure it or inflict much of it, and to listen to the recital of cases of it makes our flesh creep morally as well as physically. The way in which our ancestors looked upon pain as an eternal ingredient of the world's order, and both caused and suffered it as a matter-of-course portion of their day's work, fills us with amazement. We wonder that any human beings could have been so callous. The result of this historic alteration is that even in the Mother Church herself, where ascetic discipline has such a fixed traditional prestige as a factor of merit, it has largely come into desuetude, if not discredit. A believer who flagellates or "macerates" himself today arouses more wonder and fear than emulation. Many Catholic writers who admit that the times have changed in this respect do so resignedly; and even add that perhaps it is as well not to waste feelings in regretting the matter, for to return to the heroic corporeal discipline of ancient days might be an extravagance.

Where to seek the easy and the pleasant seems instinctive—and instinctive it appears to be in man; any deliberate tendency to pursue the hard and painful as such and for their own sakes might well strike one as purely abnormal. Nevertheless, in moderate degrees it is natural and even usual to human nature to court the arduous. It is only the extreme manifestations of the tendency that can be regarded as a paradox.

The psychological reasons for this lie near the surface. When we drop abstractions and take what we call our will in the act, we see that it is a very complex function. It involves both stimulations and inhibitions; it follows generalized habits; it is escorted by reflective criticisms; and it leaves a good or a bad taste of itself behind, according to the manner of the performance. The result is that, quite apart from the immediate pleasure which any sensible experience may give us, our own general moral attitude in procuring or undergoing the experience brings with it a secondary satisfaction or distaste. Some men and women, indeed, there are who can live on smiles and the word "yes" forever. But for others (indeed for most), this is too tepid and relaxed a moral climate. Passive happiness is slack and insipid, and soon grows mawkish and intolerable. Some austerity and wintry negativity, some roughness, danger, stringency, and effort, some "no! no!" must be mixed in, to produce the sense of an existence with character and texture and power. The range of individual differences in this respect is enormous; but whatever the mixture of yeses and noes may be, the person is infallibly aware when he has struck it in the right proportion *for him*. This, he feels, is my proper vocation, this is the *optimum*, the law, the life for me to live. Here I find the degree of equilibrium, safety, calm, and leisure which I need, or here I find the challenge, passion, fight, and hardship without which my soul's energy expires.

Every individual soul, in short, like every individual machine or organism, has its own best conditions of efficiency. A given machine will run best under a certain steam-pressure, a certain amperage; an organism under a certain diet, weight, or exercise. You seem to do best, I heard a doctor say to a patient, at about 140 millimeters of arterial tension. And it is just so with our sundry souls: some are happiest in calm weather; some need the sense of tension, of strong volition, to make them feel alive and well. For these latter souls, whatever is gained from day to day must be paid for by sacrifice and inhibition, or else it comes too cheap and has no zest.

Now when characters of this latter sort become religious, they are apt to turn the edge of their need of effort and negativity against their natural self; and the ascetic life gets evolved as a consequence.

When Professor Tyndall in one of his lectures tells us that Thomas Carlyle put him into his bath-tub every morning of a freezing Berlin winter, he proclaimed one of the lowest grades of asceticism. Even without Carlyle, most of us find it necessary to our soul's health to start the day with a rather cool immersion. A little farther along the scale we get such statements as this, from one of my correspondents, an agnostic:—

> "Often at night in my warm bed I would feel ashamed to depend so on the warmth, and whenever the thought would come over me I would have to get up, no matter what time of night it was, and stand for a minute in the cold, just so as to prove my manhood."

Such cases as these belong simply to our head 1. In the next case we probably have a mixture of heads 2 and 3—the asceticism becomes far more systematic and pronounced. The writer is a Protestant, whose sense of moral energy could doubtless be gratified on no lower terms, and I take his case from Starbuck's manuscript collection.

> "I practiced fasting and mortification of the flesh. I secretly made burlap shirts, and put the burrs next the skin, and wore pebbles in my shoes. I would spend nights flat on my back on the floor without any covering."

The Roman Church has organized and codified all this sort of thing, and given it a market-value in the shape of "merit." But we see the cultivation of hardship cropping out under every sky and in every faith, as a spontaneous need of character. Thus we read of Channing, when first settled as a Unitarian minister, that—

> "He was now more simple than ever, and seemed to have become incapable of any form of self-indulgence. He took the smallest room in the house for his study, though he might easily have commanded one more light, airy, and in

every way more suitable; and chose for his sleeping chamber an attic which he shared with a younger brother. The furniture of the latter might have answered for the cell of an anchorite, and consisted of a hard mattress on a cot-bedstead, plain wooden chairs and table, with matting on the floor. It was without fire, and to cold he was throughout life extremely sensitive; but he never complained or appeared in any way to be conscious of inconvenience. 'I recollect,' says his brother, 'after one most severe night, that in the morning he sportively thus alluded to his suffering: "If my bed were my country, I should be somewhat like Bonaparte: I have no control except over the part which I occupy; the instant I move, frost takes possession." ' In sickness only would he change for the time his apartment and accept a few comforts. The dress too that he habitually adopted was of most inferior quality; and garments were constantly worn which the world would call mean, though an almost feminine neatness preserved him from the least appearance of neglect."[171]

Channing's asceticism, such as it was, was evidently a compound of hardihood and love of purity. The democracy which is an offshoot of the enthusiasm of humanity, and of which I will speak later under the head of the cult of poverty, doubtless bore also a share. Certainly there was no pessimistic element in his case. In the next case we have a strongly pessimistic element, so that it belongs under head 4. John Cennick was Methodism's first lay preacher. In 1735 he was convicted of sin, while walking in Cheapside—

"And at once left off sing-singing, card-playing, and attending theatres. Sometimes he wished to go to a popish monastery, to spend his life in devout retirement. At other times he longed to live in a cave, sleeping on fallen leaves, and feeding on forest fruits. He fasted long and often, and prayed nine times a day.... Fancying dry bread too great an indulgence for so great a sinner as himself, he began to feed on potatoes, acorns, crabs, and grass; and often wished that he could live on roots and herbs. At length, in 1737, he found peace with God, and went on his way rejoicing."[172]

In this poor man we have morbid melancholy and fear, and the sacrifices made are to purge out sin, and to buy safety. The hopelessness of Christian theology in respect of the flesh and the natural man generally has, in systematizing fear, made of it one tremendous incentive to self-mortification. It would be quite unfair, however, in spite of the fact that this incentive has often been worked in a mercenary way for hortatory purposes, to call it a mercenary incentive. The impulse to expiate and do penance is, in its first intention, far too immediate and spontaneous an expression of self-despair and anxiety to be obnoxious to any such reproach. In the

171 Memoirs of W. E. Channing, Boston, 1840, i. 196.

172 L. Tyerman: The Life and Times of the Rev. John Wesley, i. 274.

form of loving sacrifice, of spending all we have to show our devotion, ascetic discipline of the severest sort may be the fruit of highly optimistic religious feeling.

M. Vianney, the curé of Ars, was a French country priest, whose holiness was exemplary. We read in his life the following account of his inner need of sacrifice:—

> "'On this path,' M. Vianney said, 'it is only the first step that costs. There is in mortification a balm and a savor without which one cannot live when once one has made their acquaintance. There is but one way in which to give one's self to God—that is, to give one's self entirely, and to keep nothing for one's self. The little that one keeps is only good to trouble one and make one suffer.' Accordingly he imposed it on himself that he should never smell a flower, never drink when parched with thirst, never drive away a fly, never show disgust before a repugnant object, never complain of anything that had to do with his personal comfort, never sit down, never lean upon his elbows when he was kneeling. The Curé of Ars was very sensitive to cold, but he would never take means to protect himself against it. During a very severe winter, one of his missionaries contrived a false floor to his confessional and placed a metal case of hot water beneath. The trick succeeded, and the Saint was deceived: 'God is very good,' he said with emotion. 'This year, through all the cold, my feet have always been warm.' "[173]

In this case the spontaneous impulse to make sacrifices for the pure love of God was probably the uppermost conscious motive. We may class it, then, under our head 3. Some authors think that the impulse to sacrifice is the main religious phenomenon. It is a prominent, a universal phenomenon certainly, and lies deeper than any special creed. Here, for instance, is what seems to be a spontaneous example of it, simply expressing what seemed right at the time between the individual and his Maker. Cotton Mather, the New England Puritan divine, is generally reputed a rather grotesque pedant; yet what is more touchingly simple than his relation of what happened when his wife came to die?

> "When I saw to what a point of resignation I was now called of the Lord," he says, "I resolved, with his help, therein to glorify him. So, two hours before my lovely consort expired, I kneeled by her bedside, and I took into my two hands a dear hand, the dearest in the world. With her thus in my hands, solemnly and sincerely gave her up unto the Lord: and in token of my real *Resignation*, I gently put her out of my hands, and laid away a most lovely hand, resolving that I would never touch it more. This was the hardest, and perhaps the bravest action that ever I did. She . . . told me that she signed and sealed my act of resignation. And though before that she called for me continually, she after this never asked for me any more."[174]

Father Vianney's asceticism taken in its totality was simply the result of a permanent flood of high spiritual enthusiasm, longing to make proof of itself. The

173 A. Mounin: Le Curé d'Ars, Vie de M. J. B. M. Vianney, 1864, p. 545, abridged.
174 B. Wendell: Cotton Mather, New York, no date, p. 198.

Roman Church has, in its incomparable fashion, collected all the motives towards asceticism together, and so codified them that any one wishing to pursue Christian perfection may find a practical system mapped out for him in any one of a number of ready-made manuals.[175] The dominant Church notion of perfection is of course the negative one of avoidance of sin. Sin proceeds from concupiscence, and concupiscence from our carnal passions and temptations, chief of which are pride, sensuality in all its forms, and the loves of worldly excitement and possession. All these sources of sin must be resisted; and discipline and austerities are a most efficacious mode of meeting them. Hence there are always in these books chapters on self-mortification. But whenever a procedure is codified, the more delicate spirit of it evaporates, and if we wish the undiluted ascetic spirit—the passion of self-contempt wreaking itself on the poor flesh, the divine irrationality of devotion making a sacrificial gift of all it has (its sensibilities, namely) to the object of its adoration—we must go to autobiographies, or other individual documents.

Saint John of the Cross, a Spanish mystic who flourished—or rather who existed, for there was little that suggested flourishing about him—in the sixteenth century, will supply a passage suitable for our purpose.

> "First of all, carefully excite in yourself an habitual affectionate will in all things to imitate Jesus Christ. If anything agreeable offers itself to your senses, yet does not at the same time tend purely to the honor and glory of God, renounce it and separate yourself from it for the love of Christ, who all his life long had no other taste or wish than to do the will of his Father whom he called his meat and nourishment. For example, you take satisfaction in *hearing* of things in which the glory of God bears no part. Deny yourself this satisfaction, mortify your wish to listen. You take pleasure in *seeing* objects which do not raise your mind to God: refuse yourself this pleasure, and turn away your eyes. The same with conversations and all other things. Act similarly, so far as you are able, with all the operations of the senses, striving to make yourself free from their yokes.
>
> "The radical remedy lies in the mortification of the four great natural passions, joy, hope, fear, and grief. You must seek to deprive these of every satisfaction and leave them as it were in darkness and the void. Let your soul therefore turn always:
>
> "Not to what is most easy, but to what is hardest;
> "Not to what tastes best, but to what is most distasteful;
> "Not to what most pleases, but to what disgusts;
> "Not to matter of consolation, but to matter for desolation rather;
> "Not to rest, but to labor;
> "Not to desire the more, but the less;
> "Not to aspire to what is highest and most precious, but to what is lowest and most contemptible;

175 That of the earlier Jesuit, Rodriguez, which has been translated into all languages, is one of the best known. A convenient modern manual, very well put together, is L'Ascétique Chrétienne, by M. J. Ribet, Paris, Poussielgue, nouvelle édition, 1898.

"Not to will anything, but to will nothing;

"Not to seek the best in everything, but to seek the worst, so that you may enter for the love of Christ into a complete destitution, a perfect poverty of spirit, and an absolute renunciation of everything in this world.

"Embrace these practices with all the energy of your soul and you will find in a short time great delights and unspeakable consolations.

"Despise yourself, and wish that others should despise you;

"Speak to your own disadvantage, and desire others to do the same;

"Conceive a low opinion of yourself, and find it good when others hold the same;

"To enjoy the taste of all things, have no taste for anything.

"To know all things, learn to know nothing.

"To possess all things, resolve to possess nothing.

"To be all things, be willing to be nothing.

"To get to where you have no taste for anything, go through whatever experiences you have no taste for.

"To learn to know nothing, go whither you are ignorant.

"To reach what you possess not, go whithersoever you own nothing.

"To be what you are not, experience what you are not.

These later verses play with that vertigo of self-contradiction which is so dear to mysticism. Those that come next are completely mystical, for in them Saint John passes from God to the more metaphysical notion of the All.

"When you stop at one thing, you cease to open yourself to the All.

"For to come to the All you must give up the All.

"And if you should attain to owning the All, you must own it, desiring Nothing.

"In this spoliation, the soul finds its tranquillity and rest. Profoundly established in the centre of its own nothingness, it can be assailed by naught that comes from below; and since it no longer desires anything, what comes from above cannot depress it; for its desires alone are the causes of its woes."[176]

And now, as a more concrete example of heads 4 and 5, in fact of all our heads together, and of the irrational extreme to which a psychopathic individual may go in the line of bodily austerity, I will quote the sincere Suso's account of his own self-tortures. Suso, you will remember, was one of the fourteenth century German mystics; his autobiography, written in the third person, is a classic religious document.

"He was in his youth of a temperament full of fire and life; and when this began to make itself felt, it was very grievous to him; and he sought by many devices how he might bring his body into subjection. He wore for a long time a hair shirt and an iron chain, until the blood ran from him, so that he was obliged to leave

176 SAINT JEAN DE LA Croix, Vie et Œuvres, Paris, 1893, ii. 94, 99, abridged.

them off. He secretly caused an undergarment to be made for him; and in the undergarment he had strips of leather fixed, into which a hundred and fifty brass nails, pointed and filed sharp, were driven, and the points of the nails were always turned towards the flesh. He had this garment made very tight, and so arranged as to go round him and fasten in front, in order that it might fit the closer to his body, and the pointed nails might be driven into his flesh; and it was high enough to reach upwards to his navel. In this he used to sleep at night. Now in summer, when it was hot, and he was very tired and ill from his journeyings, or when he held the office of lecturer, he would sometimes, as he lay thus in bonds, and oppressed with toil, and tormented also by noxious insects, cry aloud and give way to fretfulness, and twist round and round in agony, as a worm does when run through with a pointed needle. It often seemed to him as if he were lying upon an ant-hill, from the torture caused by the insects; for if he wished to sleep, or when he had fallen asleep, they vied with one another.[177] Sometimes he cried to Almighty God in the fullness of his heart: Alas! Gentle God, what a dying is this! When a man is killed by murderers or strong beasts of prey it is soon over; but I lie dying here under the cruel insects, and yet cannot die. The nights in winter were never so long, nor was the summer so hot, as to make him leave off this exercise. On the contrary, he devised something farther—two leathern loops into which he put his hands, and fastened one on each side his throat, and made the fastenings so secure that even if his cell had been on fire about him, he could not have helped himself. This he continued until his hands and arms had become almost tremulous with the strain, and then he devised something else: two leather gloves; and he caused a brazier to fit them all over with sharp-pointed brass tacks, and he used to put them on at night, in order that if he should try while asleep to throw off the hair undergarment, or relieve himself from the gnawings of the vile insects, the tacks might then stick into his body. And so it came to pass. If ever he sought to help himself with his hands in his sleep, he drove the sharp tacks into his breast, and tore himself, so that his flesh festered. When after many weeks the wounds had healed, he tore himself again and made fresh wounds.

"He continued this tormenting exercise for about sixteen years. At the end of this time, when his blood was now chilled, and the fire of his temperament destroyed, there appeared to him in a vision on Whitsunday, a messenger from heaven, who told him that God required this of him no longer. Whereupon he discontinued it, and threw all these things away into a running stream."

Suso then tells how, to emulate the sorrows of his crucified Lord, he made himself a cross with thirty protruding iron needles and nails. This he bore on his bare back between his shoulders day and night. "The first time that he stretched out this cross upon his back his tender frame was struck with terror at

---

177 "Insects," i.e. lice, were an unfailing token of mediæval sainthood. We read of Francis of Assisi's sheepskin that "often a companion of the saint would take it to the fire to clean and *dispediculate* it, doing so, as he said, because the seraphic father himself was no enemy of *pedocchi*, but on the contrary kept them on him (le portava adosso), and held it for an honor and a glory to wear these celestial pearls in his habit." Quoted by P. Sabatier: Speculum Perfectionis, etc., Paris, 1898, p. 231, note.

it, and blunted the sharp nails slightly against a stone. But soon, repenting of this womanly cowardice, he pointed them all again with a file, and placed once more the cross upon him. It made his back, where the bones are, bloody and seared. Whenever he sat down or stood up, it was as if a hedgehog-skin were on him. If any one touched him unawares, or pushed against his clothes, it tore him."

Suso next tells of his penitences by means of striking this cross and forcing the nails deeper into the flesh, and likewise of his self-scourgings—a dreadful story—and then goes on as follows: "At this same period the Servitor procured an old castaway door, and he used to lie upon it at night without any bedclothes to make him comfortable, except that he took off his shoes and wrapped a thick cloak round him. He thus secured for himself a most miserable bed; for hard pea-stalks lay in humps under his head, the cross with the sharp nails stuck into his back, his arms were locked fast in bonds, the horsehair undergarment was round his loins, and the cloak too was heavy and the door hard. Thus he lay in wretchedness, afraid to stir, just like a log, and he would send up many a sigh to God.

"In winter he suffered very much from the frost. If he stretched out his feet they lay bare on the floor and froze, if he gathered them up the blood became all on fire in his legs, and this was great pain. His feet were full of sores, his legs dropsical, his knees bloody and seared, his loins covered with scars from the horsehair, his body wasted, his mouth parched with intense thirst, and his hands tremulous from weakness. Amid these torments he spent his nights and days; and he endured them all out of the greatness of the love which he bore in his heart to the Divine and Eternal Wisdom, our Lord Jesus Christ, whose agonizing sufferings he sought to imitate. After a time he gave up this penitential exercise of the door, and instead of it he took up his abode in a very small cell, and used the bench, which was so narrow and short that he could not stretch himself upon it, as his bed. In this hole, or upon the door, he lay at night in his usual bonds, for about eight years. It was also his custom, during the space of twenty-five years, provided he was staying in the convent, never to go after compline in winter into any warm room, or to the convent stove to warm himself, no matter how cold it might be, unless he was obliged to do so for other reasons. Throughout all these years he never took a bath, either a water or a sweating bath; and this he did in order to mortify his comfort-seeking body. He practiced during a long time such rigid poverty that he would neither receive nor touch a penny, either with leave or without it. For a considerable time he strove to attain such a high degree of purity that he would neither scratch nor touch any part of his body, save only his hands and feet."[178]

I spare you the recital of poor Suso's self-inflicted tortures from thirst. It is pleasant to know that after his fortieth year, God showed him by a series of visions that he had sufficiently broken down the natural man, and that he might leave these

178 The Life of the Blessed Henry Suso, by Himself, translated by T. F. Knox, London, 1865, pp. 56–80, abridged.

exercises off. His case is distinctly pathological, but he does not seem to have had the alleviation, which some ascetics have enjoyed, of an alteration of sensibility capable of actually turning torment into a perverse kind of pleasure. Of the founder of the Sacred Heart order, for example, we read that

> "Her love of pain and suffering was insatiable. . . . She said that she could cheerfully live till the day of judgment, provided she might always have matter for suffering for God; but that to live a single day without suffering would be intolerable. She said again that she was devoured with two unassuageable fevers, one for the holy communion, the other for suffering, humiliation, and annihilation. 'Nothing but pain,' she continually said in her letters, 'makes my life supportable.' "[179]

So much for the phenomena to which the ascetic impulse will in certain persons give rise. In the ecclesiastically consecrated character three minor branches of self-mortification have been recognized as indispensable pathways to perfection. I refer to the chastity, obedience, and poverty which the monk vows to observe; and upon the heads of obedience and poverty I will make a few remarks.

First, of Obedience. The secular life of our twentieth century opens with this virtue held in no high esteem. The duty of the individual to determine his own conduct and profit or suffer by the consequences seems, on the contrary, to be one of our best rooted contemporary Protestant social ideals. So much so that it is difficult even imaginatively to comprehend how men possessed of an inner life of their own could ever have come to think the subjection of its will to that of other finite creatures recommendable. I confess that to myself it seems something of a mystery. Yet it evidently corresponds to a profound interior need of many persons, and we must do our best to understand it.

On the lowest possible plane, one sees how the expediency of obedience in a firm ecclesiastical organization must have led to its being viewed as meritorious. Next, experience shows that there are times in every one's life when one can be better counseled by others than by one's self. Inability to decide is one of the commonest symptoms of fatigued nerves; friends who see our troubles more broadly, often see them more wisely than we do; so it is frequently an act of excellent virtue to consult and obey a doctor, a partner, or a wife. But, leaving these lower prudential regions, we find, in the nature of some of the spiritual excitements which we have been studying, good reasons for idealizing obedience. Obedience may spring from the general religious phenomenon of inner softening and self-surrender and throwing one's self on higher powers. So saving are these attitudes felt to be that in themselves, apart from utility, they become ideally consecrated; and in obeying a man whose fallibility we see through thoroughly, we, nevertheless, may feel much as we do when we

179 Bougaud: Hist. de la bienheureuse Marguerite Marie, Paris, 1894, pp. 265, 171. Compare, also, pp. 386, 387.

resign our will to that of infinite wisdom. Add self-despair and the passion of self-crucifixion to this, and obedience becomes an ascetic sacrifice, agreeable quite irrespective of whatever prudential uses it might have.

It is as a sacrifice, a mode of "mortification," that obedience is primarily conceived by Catholic writers, a "sacrifice which man offers to God, and of which he is himself both the priest and the victim. By poverty he immolates his exterior possessions; by chastity he immolates his body; by obedience he completes the sacrifice, and gives to God all that he yet holds as his own, his two most precious goods, his intellect and his will. The sacrifice is then complete and unreserved, a genuine holocaust, for the entire victim is now consumed for the honor of God."[180] Accordingly, in Catholic discipline, we obey our superior not as mere man, but as the representative of Christ. Obeying God in him by our intention, obedience is easy. But when the text-book theologians marshal collectively all their reasons for recommending it, the mixture sounds to our ears rather odd.

> "One of the great consolations of the monastic life," says a Jesuit authority, "is the assurance we have that in obeying we can commit no fault. The Superior may commit a fault in commanding you to do this thing or that, but you are certain that you commit no fault so long as you obey, because God will only ask you if you have duly performed what orders you received, and if you can furnish a clear account in that respect, you are absolved entirely. Whether the things you did were opportune, or whether there were not something better that might have been done, these are questions not asked of you, but rather of your Superior. The moment what you did was done obediently, God wipes it out of your account, and charges it to the Superior. So that Saint Jerome well exclaimed, in celebrating the advantages of obedience, 'Oh, sovereign liberty! Oh, holy and blessed security by which one become almost impeccable!'
>
> "Saint John Climachus is of the same sentiment when he calls obedience an excuse before God. In fact, when God asks why you have done this or that, and you reply, it is because I was so ordered by my Superiors, God will ask for no other excuse. As a passenger in a good vessel with a good pilot need give himself no farther concern, but may go to sleep in peace, because the pilot has charge over all, and 'watches for him'; so a religious person who lives under the yoke of obedience goes to heaven as if while sleeping, that is, while leaning entirely on the conduct of his Superiors, who are the pilots of his vessel, and keep watch for him continually. It is no small thing, of a truth, to be able to cross the stormy sea of life on the shoulders and in the arms of another, yet that is just the grace which God accords to those who live under the yoke of obedience. Their Superior bears all their burdens. . . . A certain grave doctor said that he would rather spend his life in picking up straws by obedience, than by his own responsible choice busy himself with the loftiest works of charity, because one is certain of following the will of God in whatever one may do from obedience, but never

---

180 Lejuene: Introduction à la Vie Mystique, 1899, p. 277. The holocaust simile goes back at least as far as Ignatius Loyola.

certain in the same degree of anything which we may do of our own proper movement."[181]

One should read the letters in which Ignatius Loyola recommends obedience as the backbone of his order, if one would gain insight into the full spirit of its cult.[182] They are too long to quote; but Ignatius's belief is so vividly expressed in a couple of sayings reported by companions that, though they have been so often cited, I will ask your permission to copy them once more:—

> "I ought," an early biographer reports him as saying, "on entering religion, and thereafter, to place myself entirely in the hands of God, and of him who takes His place by His authority. I ought to desire that my Superior should oblige me to give up my own judgment, and conquer my own mind. I ought to set up no difference between one Superior and another, . . . but recognize them all as equal before God, whose place they fill. For if I distinguish persons, I weaken the spirit of obedience. In the hands of my Superior, I must be a soft wax, a thing, from which he is to require whatever pleases him, be it to write or receive letters, to speak or not to speak to such a person, or the like; and I must put all my fervor in executing zealously and exactly what I am ordered. I must consider myself as a corpse which has neither intelligence nor will; be like a mass of matter which without resistance lets itself be placed wherever it may please any one; like a stick in the hand of an old man, who uses it according to his needs and places it where it suits him. So must I be under the hands of the Order, to serve it in the way it judges most useful.
>
> "I must never ask of the Superior to be sent to a particular place, to be employed in a particular duty. . . . I must consider nothing as belonging to me personally, and as regards the things I use, be like a statue which lets itself be stripped and never opposes resistance."[183]

The other saying is reported by Rodriguez in the chapter from which I a moment ago made quotations. When speaking of the Pope's authority, Rodriguez writes:—

> "Saint Ignatius said, when general of his company, that if the Holy Father were to order him to set sail in the first bark which he might find in the port of Ostia, near Rome, and to abandon himself to the sea, without a mast, without sails, without oars or rudder or any of the things that are needful for navigation or subsistence, he would obey not only with alacrity, but without anxiety or repugnance, and even with a great internal satisfaction."[184]

With a solitary concrete example of the extravagance to which the virtue we are considering has been carried, I will pass to the topic next in order.

---

181 ALFONSO RODRIGUEZ, S. J.: Pratique de la Perfection Chrétienne, Part iii., Treatise v., ch. x.

182 Letters li. and cxx. of the collection translated into French by Bouix, Paris, 1870.

183 BARTOLI-MICHEL, ii. 13.

184 RODRIGUEZ: Op. cit., Part iii., Treatise v., ch. vi

"Sister Marie Claire [of Port Royal] had been greatly imbued with the holiness and excellence of M. de Langres. This prelate, soon after he came to Port Royal, said to her one day, seeing her so tenderly attached to Mother Angélique, that it would perhaps be better not to speak to her again. Marie Claire, greedy of obedience, took this inconsiderate word for an oracle of God, and from that day forward remained for several years without once speaking to her sister."[185]

Our next topic shall be Poverty, felt at all times and under all creeds as one adornment of a saintly life. Since the instinct of ownership is fundamental in man's nature, this is one more example of the ascetic paradox. Yet it appears no paradox at all, but perfectly reasonable, the moment one recollects how easily higher excitements hold lower cupidities in check. Having just quoted the Jesuit Rodriguez on the subject of obedience, I will, to give immediately a concrete turn to our discussion of poverty, also read you a page from his chapter on this latter virtue. You must remember that he is writing instructions for monks of his own order, and bases them all on the text, "Blessed are the poor in spirit."

"If any one of you," he says, "will know whether or not he is really poor in spirit, let him consider whether he loves the ordinary consequences and effects of poverty, which are hunger, thirst, cold, fatigue, and the denudation of all conveniences. See if you are glad to wear a worn-out habit full of patches. See if you are glad when something is lacking to your meal, when you are passed by in serving it, when what you receive is distasteful to you, when your cell is out of repair. If you are not glad of these things, if instead of loving them you avoid them, then there is proof that you have not attained the perfection of poverty of spirit." Rodriguez then goes on to describe the practice of poverty in more detail. "The first point is that which Saint Ignatius proposes in his constitutions, when he says, 'Let no one use anything as if it were his private possession.' 'A religious person,' he says, 'ought in respect to all the things that he uses, to be like a statue which one may drape with clothing, but which feels no grief and makes no resistance when one strips it again. It is in this way that you should feel towards your clothes, your books, your cell, and everything else that you make use of; if ordered to quit them, or to exchange them for others, have no more sorrow than if you were a statue being uncovered. In this way you will avoid using them as if they were your private possession. But if, when you give up your cell, or yield possession of this or that object or exchange it for another, you feel repugnance and are not like a statue, that shows that you view these things as if they were your private property.'

"And this is why our holy founder wished the superiors to test their monks somewhat as God tested Abraham, and to put their poverty and their obedience to trial, that by this means they may become acquainted with the degree of their virtue, and gain a chance to make ever farther progress in perfection, . . . making the one move out of his room when he finds it comfortable and is attached to it;

185 SAINTE-BEUVE: Histoire de Port Royal, i. 346.

taking away from another a book of which he is fond; or obliging a third to exchange his garment for a worse one. Otherwise we should end by acquiring a species of property in all these several objects, and little by little the wall of poverty that surrounds us and constitutes our principal defense would be thrown down. The ancient fathers of the desert used often thus to treat their companions. . . . Saint Dositheus, being sick-nurse, desired a certain knife, and asked Saint Dorotheus for it, not for his private use, but for employment in the infirmary of which he had charge. Whereupon Saint Dorotheus answered him: 'Ha!' Dositheus, so that knife pleases you so much! Will you be the slave of a knife or the slave of Jesus Christ! Do you not blush with shame at wishing that a knife should be your master? I will not let you touch it.' Which reproach and refusal had such an effect upon the holy disciple that since that time he never touched the knife again.' . . .

"Therefore, in our rooms," Father Rodriguez continues, "there must be no other furniture than a bed, a table, a bench, and a candlestick, things purely necessary, and nothing more. It is not allowed among us that our cells should be ornamented with pictures or aught else, neither armchairs, carpets, curtains, nor any sort of cabinet or bureau of any elegance. Neither is it allowed us to keep anything to eat, either for ourselves or for those who may come to visit us. We must ask permission to go to the refectory even for a glass of water; and finally we may not keep a book in which we can write a line, or which we may take away with us. One cannot deny that thus we are in great poverty. But this poverty is at the same time a great repose and a great perfection. For it would be inevitable, in case a religious person were allowed to own superfluous possessions, that these things would greatly occupy his mind, be it to acquire them, to preserve them, or to increase them; so that in not permitting us at all to own them, all these inconveniences are remedied. Among the various good reasons why the company forbids secular persons to enter our cells, the principal one is that thus we may the easier be kept in poverty. After all, we are all men, and if we were to receive people of the world into our rooms, we should not have the strength to remain within the bounds prescribed, but should at least wish to adorn them with some books to give the visitors a better opinion of our scholarship."[186]

Since Hindu fakirs, Buddhist monks, and Mohammedan dervishes unite with Jesuits and Franciscans in idealizing poverty as the loftiest individual state, it is worth while to examine into the spiritual grounds for such a seemingly unnatural opinion. And first, of those which lie closest to common human nature.

The opposition between the men who *have* and the men who *are* is immemorial. Though the gentleman, in the old-fashioned sense of the man who is well born, has usually in point of fact been predaceous and reveled in lands and goods, yet he has never identified his essence with these possessions, but rather with the personal superiorities, the courage, generosity, and pride supposed to be his birthright. To certain huckstering kinds of consideration he thanked God he was forever inacces-

186 Rodriguez: Op. cit., Part iii, Treatise iii., chaps. vi., vii.

sible, and if in life's vicissitudes he should become destitute through their lack, he was glad to think that with his sheer valor he was all the freer to work out his salvation. "Wer nur selbst was hätte," says Lessing's Tempelherr, in Nathan the Wise, "mein Gott, mein Gott, ich habe nichts!" This ideal of the well-born man without possessions was embodied in knight-errantry and templardom; and, hideously corrupted as it has always been, it still dominates sentimentally, if not practically, the military and aristocratic view of life. We glorify the soldier as the man absolutely unincumbered. Owning nothing but his bare life, and willing to toss that up at any moment when the cause commands him, he is the representative of unhampered freedom in ideal directions. The laborer who pays with his person day by day, and has no rights invested in the future, offers also much of this ideal detachment. Like the savage, he may make his bed wherever his right arm can support him, and from his simple and athletic attitude of observation, the property-owner seems buried and smothered in ignoble externalities and trammels, "wading in straw and rubbish to his knees." The claims which *things* make are corrupters of manhood, mortgages on the soul, and a drag anchor on our progress towards the empyrean.

> "Everything I meet with," writes Whitefield, "seems to carry this voice with it—'Go thou and preach the Gospel; be a pilgrim on earth; have no party or certain dwelling place.' My heart echoes back, 'Lord Jesus, help me to do or suffer thy will. When thou seest me in danger of *nestling*—in pity—in tender pity—put a *thorn* in my nest to prevent me from it.' "[187]

The loathing of "capital" with which our laboring classes today are growing more and more infected seems largely composed of this sound sentiment of antipathy for lives based on mere having. As an anarchist poet writes:—

> "Not by accumulating riches, but by giving away that which you have,
> "Shall you become beautiful;
> "You must undo the wrappings, not case yourself in fresh ones;
> "Not by multiplying clothes shall you make your body sound and healthy, but rather by discarding them . . .
> "For a soldier who is going on a campaign does not seek what fresh furniture he can carry on his back, but rather what he can leave behind;
> "Knowing well that every additional thing which he cannot freely use and handle is an impediment."[188]

In short, lives based on having are less free than lives based either on doing or on being, and in the interest of action people subject to spiritual excitement throw away possessions as so many clogs. Only those who have no private interests can follow an ideal straight away. Sloth and cowardice creep in with every dollar or

187 R. Philip: The Life and Times of George Whitefield, London, 1842, p. 366.
188 Edward Carpenter: Towards Democracy, p. 362, abridged.

guinea we have to guard. When a brother novice came to Saint Francis, saying: "Father, it would be a great consolation to me to own a psalter, but even supposing that our general should concede to me this indulgence, still I should like also to have your consent," Francis put him off with the examples of Charlemagne, Roland, and Oliver, pursuing the infidels in sweat and labor, and finally dying on the field of battle. "So care not," he said, "for owning books and knowledge, but care rather for works of goodness." And when some weeks later the novice came again to talk of his craving for the psalter, Francis said: "After you have got your psalter you will crave a breviary; and after you have got your breviary you will sit in your stall like a grand prelate, and will say to your brother: "Hand me my breviary."... And thenceforward he denied all such requests, saying: A man possesses of learning only so much as comes out of him in action, and a monk is a good preacher only so far as his deeds proclaim him such, for every tree is known by its fruits."[189]

But beyond this more worthily athletic attitude involved in doing and being, there is, in the desire of not having, something profounder still, something related to that fundamental mystery of religious experience, the satisfaction found in absolute surrender to the larger power. So long as any secular safeguard is retained, so long as any residual prudential guarantee is clung to, so long the surrender is incomplete, the vital crisis is not passed, fear still stands sentinel, and mistrust of the divine obtains: we hold by two anchors, looking to God, it is true, after a fashion, but also holding by our proper machinations. In certain medical experiences we have the same critical point to overcome. A drunkard, or a morphine or cocaine maniac, offers himself to be cured. He appeals to the doctor to wean him from his enemy, but he dares not face blank abstinence. The tyrannical drug is still an anchor to windward: he hides supplies of it among his clothing; arranges secretly to have it smuggled in in case of need. Even so an incompletely regenerate man still trusts in his own expedients. His money is like the sleeping potion which the chronically wakeful patient keeps beside his bed; he throws himself on God, but *if* he should need the other help, there it will be also. Every one knows cases of this incomplete and ineffective desire for reform—drunkards whom, with all their self-reproaches and resolves, one perceives to be quite unwilling seriously to contemplate *never* being drunk again! Really to give up anything on which we have relied, to give it up definitely, "for good and all" and forever, signifies one of those radical alterations of character which came under our notice in the lectures on conversion. In it the inner man rolls over into an entirely different position of equilibrium, lives in a new centre of energy from this time on, and the turning-point and hinge of all such operations seems usually to involve the sincere acceptance of certain nakednesses and destitutions.

Accordingly, throughout the annals of the saintly life, we find this ever-recurring note: Fling yourself upon God's providence without making any reserve whatever—

189 Speculum Perfectionis, ed. P. Sabatier, Paris, 1898, pp. 10, 13.

take no thought for the morrow—sell all you have and give it to the poor—only when the sacrifice is ruthless and reckless will the higher safety really arrive. As a concrete example let me read a page from the biography of Antoinette Bourignon, a good woman, much persecuted in her day by both Protestants and Catholics, because she would not take her religion at second hand. When a young girl, in her father's house—

> "She spent whole nights in prayer, off repeating: *Lord, what wilt thou have me to do?* And being one night in a most profound penitence, she said from the bottom of her heart: 'O my Lord! What must I do to please thee? For I have nobody to teach me. Speak to my soul and it will hear thee.' At that instant she heard, as if another had spoke within her: *Forsake all earthly things. Separate thyself from the love of the creatures. Deny thyself.* She was quite astonished, not understanding this language, and mused long on these three points, thinking how she could fulfill them. She thought she could not live without earthly things, nor without loving the creatures, nor without loving herself. Yet she said, 'By thy Grace I will do it, Lord!' But when she would perform her promise, she knew not where to begin. Having thought on the religious in monasteries, that they forsook all earthly things by being shut up in a cloister, and the love of themselves by subjecting of their wills, she asked leave of her father to enter into a cloister of the barefoot Carmelites, but he would not permit it, saying he would rather see her laid in her grave. This seemed to her a great cruelty, for she thought to find in the cloister the true Christians she had been seeking, but she found afterwards that he knew the cloisters better than she; for after he had forbidden her, and told her he would never permit her to be a religious, nor give her any money to enter there, yet she went to Father Laurens, the Director, and offered to serve in the monastery and work hard for her bread, and be content with little, if he would receive her. At which he smiled and said: *That cannot be. We must have money to build; we take no maids without money; you must find the way to get it, else there is no entry here.*
>
> "This astonished her greatly, and she was thereby undeceived as to the cloisters, resolving to forsake all company and live alone till it should please God to show her what she ought to do and whither to go. She asked always earnestly, 'When shall I be perfectly thine, O my God?' And she thought he still answered her, *When thou shalt no longer possess anything, and shalt die to thyself.* 'And where shall I do that, Lord?' He answered her, *In the desert.* This made so strong an impression on her soul that she aspired after this; but being a maid of eighteen years only, she was afraid of unlucky chances, and was never used to travel, and knew no way. She laid aside all these doubts and said, 'Lord, thou wilt guide me how and where it shall please thee. It is for thee that I do it. I will lay aside my habit of a maid, and will take that of a hermit that I may pass unknown.' Having then secretly made ready this habit, while her parents thought to have married her, her father having promised her to a rich French merchant, she prevented the time, and on Easter evening, having cut her hair, put on the habit, and slept a little, she went out of her chamber about four in the morning, taking nothing but one penny to buy bread for that day. And it being said to her in going out,

*Where is thy faith? in a penny?* she threw it away, begging pardon of God for her fault, and saying, 'No, Lord, my faith is not in a penny, but in thee alone.' Thus she went away wholly delivered from the heavy burthen of the cares and good things of this world, and found her soul so satisfied that she no longer wished for anything upon earth, resting entirely upon God, with this only fear lest she should be discovered and be obliged to return home; for she felt already more content in this poverty than she had done for all her life in all the delights of the world."[190]

The penny was a small financial safeguard, but an effective spiritual obstacle. Not till it was thrown away could the character settle into the new equilibrium completely.

Over and above the mystery of self-surrender, there are in the cult of poverty other religious mysteries. There is the mystery of veracity: "Naked came I into the world," etc.—whoever first said that, possessed this mystery. My own bare entity must fight the battle—shams cannot save me. There is also the mystery of democracy, or sentiment of the equality before God of all his creatures. This sentiment (which seems in general to have been more widespread in Mohammedan than in Christian lands) tends to nullify man's usual acquisitiveness. Those who have it spurn dignities and honors, privileges and advantages, preferring, as I said in a former lecture, to grovel on the common level before the face of God. It is not exactly the sentiment of humility, though it comes so close to it in practice. It is *humanity*, rather, refusing to enjoy anything that others do not share. A profound moralist, writing of Christ's saying, "Sell all thou hast and follow me," proceeds as follows:—

"Christ may have meant: If you love mankind absolutely you will as a result not care for any possessions whatever, and this seems a very likely proposition. But it is one thing to believe that a proposition is probably true; it is another thing to see it as a fact. If you loved mankind as Christ loved them, you would see his conclusion as a fact. It would be obvious. You would sell your goods, and they

190 An Apology for M. Antonia Bourignon, London, 1699, pp. 269, 270, abridged.

Another example from Starbuck's MS. collection:—

"At a meeting held at six the next morning, I heard a man relate his experience. He said: The Lord asked him if he would confess Christ among the quarrymen with whom he worked, and he said he would. Then he asked him if he would give up to be used of the Lord the four hundred dollars he had laid up, and he said he would, and thus the Lord saved him. The thought came to me at once that I had never made a real consecration either of myself or of my property to the Lord, but had always tried to serve the Lord in *my* way. Now the Lord asked me if I would serve him in *his* way, and go out alone and penniless if he so ordered. The question was pressed home, and I must decide: To forsake all and have him, or have all and lose him! I soon decided to take him; and the blessed assurance came, that he had taken me for his own, and my joy was full. I returned home from the meeting with feelings as simple as a child. I thought all would be glad to hear of the joy of the Lord that possessed me, and so I began to tell the simple story. But to my great surprise, the pastors (for I attended meetings in three churches) opposed the experience and said it was fanaticism, and one told the members of his church to shun those that professed it, and I soon found that my foes were those of my own household."

would be no loss to you. These truths, while literal to Christ, and to any mind that has Christ's love for mankind, become parables to lesser natures. There are in every generation people who, beginning innocently, with no predetermined intention of becoming saints, find themselves drawn into the vortex by their interest in helping mankind, and by the understanding that comes from actually doing it. The abandonment of their old mode of life is like dust in the balance. It is done gradually, incidentally, imperceptibly. Thus the whole question of the abandonment of luxury is no question at all, but a mere incident to another question, namely, the degree to which we abandon ourselves to the remorseless logic of our love for others."[191]

But in all these matters of sentiment one must have "been there" one's self in order to understand them. No American can ever attain to understanding the loyalty of a Briton towards his king, of a German towards his emperor; nor can a Briton or German ever understand the peace of heart of an American in having no king, no Kaiser, no spurious nonsense, between him and the common God of all. If sentiments as simple as these are mysteries which one must receive as gifts of birth, how much more is this the case with those subtler religious sentiments which we have been considering! One can never fathom an emotion or divine its dictates by standing outside of it. In the glowing hour of excitement, however, all incomprehensibilities are solved, and what was so enigmatical from without becomes transparently obvious. Each emotion obeys a logic of its own, and makes deductions which no other logic can draw. Piety and charity live in a different universe from worldly lusts and fears, and form another centre of energy altogether. As in a supreme sorrow lesser vexations may become a consolation; as a supreme love may turn minor sacrifices into gain; so a supreme trust may render common safeguards odious, and in certain glows of generous excitement it may appear unspeakably mean to retain one's hold of personal possessions. The only sound plan, if we are ourselves outside the pale of such emotions, is to observe as well as we are able those who feel them, and to record faithfully what we observe; and this, I need hardly say, is what I have striven to do in these last two descriptive lectures, which I now hope will have covered the ground sufficiently for our present needs.

191 J. J. CHAPMAN, in the Political Nursery, vol. iv. p. 4, April, 1900, abridged.

## LECTURES XIV AND XV

# The Value of Saintliness

We have now passed in review the more important of the phenomena which are regarded as fruits of genuine religion and characteristics of men who are devout. Today we have to change our attitude from that of description to that of appreciation; we have to ask whether the fruits in question can help us to judge the absolute value of what religion adds to human life. Were I to parody Kant, I should say that a "Critique of pure Saintliness" must be our theme.

If, in turning to this theme, we could descend upon our subject from above like Catholic theologians, with our fixed definitions of man and man's perfection and our positive dogmas about God, we should have an easy time of it. Man's perfection would be the fulfillment of his end; and his end would be union with his Maker. That union could be pursued by him along three paths, active, purgative, and contemplative, respectively; and progress along either path would be a simple matter to measure by the application of a limited number of theological and moral conceptions and definitions. The absolute significance and value of any bit of religious experience we might hear of would thus be given almost mathematically into our hands.

If convenience were everything, we ought now to grieve at finding ourselves cut off from so admirably convenient a method as this. But we did cut ourselves off from it deliberately in those remarks which you remember we made, in our first lecture, about the empirical method; and it must be confessed that after that act of renunciation we can never hope for clean-cut and scholastic results. *We* cannot divide man sharply into an animal and a rational part. *We* cannot distinguish natural from supernatural effects; nor among the latter know which are favors of God, and which are counterfeit operations of the demon. We have merely to collect things together without any special *a priori* theological system, and out of an aggregate of piecemeal judgments as to the value of this and that experience—judgments in which our general philosophic prejudices, our instincts, and our common sense are our only guides—decide that *on the whole* one type of religion is approved by its fruits, and another type condemned. "On the whole"—I fear we shall never escape complicity with that qualification, so dear to your practical man, so repugnant to your systematizer!

I also fear that as I make this frank confession, I may seem to some of you to throw our compass overboard, and to adopt caprice as our pilot. Skepticism or wayward choice, you may think, can be the only results of such a formless method as I have taken up. A few remarks in deprecation of such an opinion, and in farther explanation of the empiricist principles which I profess, may therefore appear at this point to be in place.

Abstractly, it would seem illogical to try to measure the worth of a religion's fruits in merely human terms of value. How *can* you measure their worth without considering whether the God really exists who is supposed to inspire them? If he really exists, then all the conduct instituted by men to meet his wants must necessarily be a reasonable fruit of his religion—it would be unreasonable only in case he did not exist. If, for instance, you were to condemn a religion of human or animal sacrifices by virtue of your subjective sentiments, and if all the while a deity were really there demanding such sacrifices, you would be making a theoretical mistake by tacitly assuming that the deity must be non-existent; you would be setting up a theology of your own as much as if you were a scholastic philosopher.

To this extent, to the extent of disbelieving peremptorily in certain types of deity, I frankly confess that we must be theologians. If disbeliefs can be said to constitute a theology, then the prejudices, instincts, and common sense which I chose as our guides make theological partisans of us whenever they make certain beliefs abhorrent.

But such common-sense prejudices and instincts are themselves the fruit of an empirical evolution. Nothing is more striking than the secular alteration that goes on in the moral and religious tone of men, as their insight into nature and their social arrangements progressively develop. After an interval of a few generations the mental climate proves unfavorable to notions of the deity which at an earlier date were perfectly satisfactory: the older gods have fallen below the common secular level, and can no longer be believed in. Today a deity who should require bleeding sacrifices to placate him would be too sanguinary to be taken seriously. Even if powerful historical credentials were put forward in his favor, we would not look at them. Once, on the contrary, his cruel appetites were of themselves credentials. They positively recommended him to men's imaginations in ages when such coarse signs of power were respected and no others could be understood. Such deities then were worshiped because such fruits were relished.

Doubtless historic accidents always played some later part, but the original factor in fixing the figure of the gods must always have been psychological. The deity to whom the prophets, seers, and devotees who founded the particular cult bore witness was worth something to them personally. They could use him. He guided their imagination, warranted their hopes, and controlled their will—or else they required him as a safeguard against the demon and a curber of other people's crimes.

In any case, they chose him for the value of the fruits he seemed to them to yield. So soon as the fruits began to seem quite worthless; so soon as they conflicted with indispensable human ideals, or thwarted too extensively other values; so soon as they appeared childish, contemptible, or immoral when reflected on, the deity grew discredited, and was erelong neglected and forgotten. It was in this way that the Greek and Roman gods ceased to be believed in by educated pagans; it is thus that we ourselves judge of the Hindu, Buddhist, and Mohammedan theologies; Protestants have so dealt with the Catholic notions of deity, and liberal Protestants with older Protestant notions; it is thus that Chinamen judge of us, and that all of us now living will be judged by our descendants. When we cease to admire or approve what the definition of a deity implies, we end by deeming that deity incredible.

Few historic changes are more curious than these mutations of theological opinion. The monarchical type of sovereignty was, for example, so ineradicably planted in the mind of our own forefathers that a dose of cruelty and arbitrariness in their deity seems positively to have been required by their imagination. They called the cruelty "retributive justice," and a God without it would certainly have struck them as not "sovereign" enough. But today we abhor the very notion of eternal suffering inflicted; and that arbitrary dealing-out of salvation and damnation to selected individuals, of which Jonathan Edwards could persuade himself that he had not only a conviction, but a "delightful conviction," as of a doctrine "exceeding pleasant, bright, and sweet," appears to us, if sovereignly anything, sovereignly irrational and mean. Not only the cruelty, but the paltriness of character of the gods believed in by earlier centuries also strikes later centuries with surprise. We shall see examples of it from the annals of Catholic saintship which makes us rub our Protestant eyes. Ritual worship in general appears to the modern transcendentalist, as well as to the ultra-puritanic type of mind, as if addressed to a deity of an almost absurdly childish character, taking delight in toy-shop furniture, tapers and tinsel, costume and mumbling and mummery, and finding his "glory" incomprehensibly enhanced thereby:—just as on the other hand the formless spaciousness of pantheism appears quite empty to ritualistic natures, and the gaunt theism of evangelical sects seems intolerably bald and chalky and bleak. Luther, says Emerson, would have cut off his right hand rather than nail his theses to the door at Wittenberg, if he had supposed that they were destined to lead to the pale negations of Boston Unitarianism.

So far, then, although we are compelled, whatever may be our pretensions to empiricism, to employ some sort of a standard of theological probability of our own whenever we assume to estimate the fruits of other men's religion, yet this very standard has been begotten out of the drift of common life. It is the voice of human experience within us, judging and condemning all gods that stand athwart the pathway along which it feels itself to be advancing. Experience, if we take it in the largest sense, is thus the parent of those disbeliefs which, it was charged, were inconsistent with the experiential method. The inconsistency, you see, is immaterial, and the charge may be neglected.

If we pass from disbeliefs to positive beliefs, it seems to me that there is not even a formal inconsistency to be laid against our method. The gods we stand by are the gods we need and can use, the gods whose demands on us are reinforcements of our demands on ourselves and on one another. What I then propose to do is, briefly stated, to test saintliness by common sense, to use human standards to help us decide how far the religious life commends itself as an ideal kind of human activity. If it commends itself, then any theological beliefs that may inspire it, in so far forth will stand accredited. If not, then they will be discredited, and all without reference to anything but human working principles. It is but the elimination of the humanly unfit, and the survival of the humanly fittest, applied to religious beliefs; and if we look at history candidly and without prejudice, we have to admit that no religion has ever in the long run established or proved itself in any other way. Religions have *approved* themselves; they have ministered to sundry vital needs which they found reigning. When they violated other needs too strongly, or when other faiths came which served the same needs better, the first religions were supplanted.

The needs were always many, and the tests were never sharp. So the reproach of vagueness and subjectivity and "on the whole"-ness, which can with perfect legitimacy be addressed to the empirical method as we are forced to use it, is after all a reproach to which the entire life of man in dealing with these matters is obnoxious. No religion has ever yet owed its prevalence to "apodictic certainty." In a later lecture I will ask whether objective certainty can ever be added by theological reasoning to a religion that already empirically prevails.

One word, also, about the reproach that in following this sort of an empirical method we are handing ourselves over to systematic skepticism.

Since it is impossible to deny secular alterations in our sentiments and needs, it would be absurd to affirm that one's own age of the world can be beyond correction by the next age. Skepticism cannot, therefore, be ruled out by any set of thinkers as a possibility against which their conclusions are secure; and no empiricist ought to claim exemption from this universal liability. But to admit one's liability to correction is one thing, and to embark upon a sea of wanton doubt is another. Of willfully playing into the hands of skepticism we cannot be accused. He who acknowledges the imperfectness of his instrument, and makes allowance for it in discussing his observations, is in a much better position for gaining truth than if he claimed his instrument to be infallible. Or is dogmatic or scholastic theology less doubted in point of fact for claiming, as it does, to be in point of right undoubtable? And if not, what command over truth would this kind of theology really lose if, instead of absolute certainty, she only claimed reasonable probability for her conclusions? If *we* claim only reasonable probability, it will be as much as men who love the truth can ever at any given moment hope to have within their grasp. Pretty surely it will be more than we could have had, if we were unconscious of our liability to err.

Nevertheless, dogmatism will doubtless continue to condemn us for this confession. The mere outward form of inalterable certainty is so precious to some minds that to renounce it explicitly is for them out of the question. They will claim it even where the facts most patently pronounce its folly. But the safe thing is surely to recognize that all the insights of creatures of a day like ourselves must be provisional. The wisest of critics is an altering being, subject to the better insight of the morrow, and right at any moment, only "up to date" and "on the whole." When larger ranges of truth open, it is surely best to be able to open ourselves to their reception, unfettered by our previous pretensions. "Heartily know, when half-gods go, the gods arrive."

The fact of diverse judgments about religious phenomena is therefore entirely unescapable, whatever may be one's own desire to attain the irreversible. But apart from that fact, a more fundamental question awaits us, the question whether men's opinions ought to be expected to be absolutely uniform in this field. Ought all men to have the same religion? Ought they to approve the same fruits and follow the same leadings? Are they so like in their inner needs that, for hard and soft, for proud and humble, for strenuous and lazy, for healthy-minded and despairing, exactly the same religious incentives are required? Or are different functions in the organism of humanity allotted to different types of man, so that some may really be the better for a religion of consolation and reassurance, whilst others are better for one of terror and reproof? It might conceivably be so; and we shall, I think, more and more suspect it to be so as we go on. And if it be so, how can any possible judge or critic help being biased in favor of the religion by which his own needs are best met? He aspires to impartiality; but he is too close to the struggle not to be to some degree a participant, and he is sure to approve most warmly those fruits of piety in others which taste most good and prove most nourishing to *him*.

I am well aware of how anarchic much of what I say may sound. Expressing myself thus abstractly and briefly, I may seem to despair of the very notion of truth. But I beseech you to reserve your judgment until we see it applied to the details which lie before us. I do indeed disbelieve that we or any other mortal men can attain on a given day to absolutely incorrigible and unimprovable truth about such matters of fact as those with which religions deal. But I reject this dogmatic ideal not out of a perverse delight in intellectual instability. I am no lover of disorder and doubt as such. Rather do I fear to lose truth by this pretension to possess it already wholly. That we can gain more and more of it by moving always in the right direction, I believe as much as any one, and I hope to bring you all to my way of thinking before the termination of these lectures. Till then, do not, I pray you, harden your minds irrevocably against the empiricism which I profess.

I will waste no more words, then, in abstract justification of my method, but seek immediately to use it upon the facts.

In critically judging of the value of religious phenomena, it is very important to insist on the distinction between religion as an individual personal function, and religion as an institutional, corporate, or tribal product. I drew this distinction, you may remember, in my second lecture. The word "religion," as ordinarily used, is equivocal. A survey of history shows us that, as a rule, religious geniuses attract disciples, and produce groups of sympathizers. When these groups get strong enough to "organize" themselves, they become ecclesiastical institutions with corporate ambitions of their own. The spirit of politics and the lust of dogmatic rule are then apt to enter and to contaminate the originally innocent thing; so that when we hear the word "religion" nowadays, we think inevitably of some "church" or other; and to some persons the word "church" suggests so much hypocrisy and tyranny and meanness and tenacity of superstition that in a wholesale undiscerning way they glory in saying that they are "down" on religion altogether. Even we who belong to churches do not exempt other churches than our own from the general condemnation.

But in this course of lectures ecclesiastical institutions hardly concern us at all. The religious experience which we are studying is that which lives itself out within the private breast. First-hand individual experience of this kind has always appeared as a heretical sort of innovation to those who witnessed its birth. Naked comes it into the world and lonely; and it has always, for a time at least, driven him who had it into the wilderness, often into the literal wilderness out of doors, where the Buddha, Jesus, Mohammed, St. Francis, George Fox, and so many others had to go. George Fox expresses well this isolation; and I can do no better at this point than read to you a page from his Journal, referring to the period of his youth when religion began to ferment within him seriously.

> "I fasted much," Fox says, "walked abroad in solitary places many days, and often took my Bible, and sat in hollow trees and lonesome places until night came on; and frequently in the night walked mournfully about by myself; for I was a man of sorrows in the time of the first workings of the Lord in me.
>
> "During all this time I was never joined in profession of religion with any, but gave up myself to the Lord, having forsaken all evil company, taking leave of father and mother, and all other relations, and traveled up and down as a stranger on the earth, which way the Lord inclined my heart; taking a chamber to myself in the town where I came, and tarrying sometimes more, sometimes less in a place: for I durst not stay long in a place, being afraid both of professor and profane, lest, being a tender young man, I should be hurt by conversing much with either. For which reason I kept much as a stranger, seeking heavenly wisdom and getting knowledge from the Lord; and was brought off from outward things, to rely on the Lord alone. As I had forsaken the priests, so I left the separate preachers also, and those called the most experienced people; for I saw there was none among them all that could speak to my condition. And when all my hopes in them and in all men were gone so that I had nothing outwardly to help me, nor could tell what to do; then, oh then, I heard a voice which said, 'There is one, even Jesus Christ, that can speak to thy condition.' When I heard it, my heart did leap for joy. Then the Lord let me see why there was none upon the earth that could speak to my condition. I had not fellowship with any people, priests, nor professors, nor any sort of separated people. I was afraid of all carnal talk and talkers, for I could see nothing but corruptions. When I was in the deep,

under all shut up, I could not believe that I should ever overcome; my troubles, my sorrows, and my temptations were so great that I often thought I should have despaired, I was so tempted. But when Christ opened to me how he was tempted by the same devil, and had overcome him, and had bruised his head; and that through him and his power, life, grace, and spirit, I should overcome also, I had confidence in him. If I had had a king's diet, palace, and attendance, all would have been as nothing; for nothing gave me comfort but the Lord by his power. I saw professors, priests, and people were whole and at ease in that condition which was my misery, and they loved that which I would have been rid of. But the Lord did stay my desires upon himself, and my care was cast upon him alone."[192]

A genuine first-hand religious experience like this is bound to be a heterodoxy to its witnesses, the prophet appearing as a mere lonely madman. If his doctrine prove contagious enough to spread to any others, it becomes a definite and labeled heresy. But if it then still prove contagious enough to triumph over persecution, it becomes itself an orthodoxy; and when a religion has become an orthodoxy, its day of inwardness is over: the spring is dry; the faithful live at second hand exclusively and stone the prophets in their turn. The new church, in spite of whatever human goodness it may foster, can be henceforth counted on as a staunch ally in every attempt to stifle the spontaneous religious spirit, and to stop all later bubblings of the fountain from which in purer days it drew its own supply of inspiration. Unless, indeed, by adopting new movements of the spirit it can make capital out of them and use them for its selfish corporate designs! Of protective action of this politic sort, promptly or tardily decided on, the dealings of the Roman ecclesiasticism with many individual saints and prophets yield examples enough for our instruction.

The plain fact is that men's minds are built, as has been often said, in water-tight compartments. Religious after a fashion, they yet have many other things in them beside their religion, and unholy entanglements and associations inevitably obtain. The basenesses so commonly charged to religion's account are thus, almost all of them, not chargeable at all to religion proper, but rather to religion's wicked practical partner, the spirit of corporate dominion. And the bigotries are most of them in their turn chargeable to religion's wicked intellectual partner, the spirit of dogmatic dominion, the passion for laying down the law in the form of an absolutely closed-in theoretic system. The ecclesiastical spirit in general is the sum of these two spirits of dominion; and I beseech you never to confound the phenomena of mere tribal or corporate psychology which it presents with those manifestations of the purely interior life which are the exclusive object of our study. The baiting of Jews, the hunting of Albigenses and Waldenses, the stoning of Quakers and ducking of Methodists, the murdering of Mormons and the massacring of Armenians, express much rather that aboriginal human neophobia, that pugnacity of which we all share the vestiges,

192 George Fox: Journal, Philadelphia, 1800, pp. 59–61, abridged.

and that inborn hatred of the alien and of eccentric and non-conforming men as aliens, than they express the positive piety of the various perpetrators. Piety is the mask, the inner force is tribal instinct. You believe as little as I do, in spite of the Christian unction with which the German emperor addressed his troops upon their way to China, that the conduct which he suggested, and in which other Christian armies went beyond them, had anything whatever to do with the interior religious life of those concerned in the performance.

Well, no more for past atrocities than for this atrocity should we make piety responsible. At most we may blame piety for not availing to check our natural passions, and sometimes for supplying them with hypocritical pretexts. But hypocrisy also imposes obligations, and with the pretext usually couples some restriction; and when the passion gust is over, the piety may bring a reaction of repentance which the irreligious natural man would not have shown.

For many of the historic aberrations which have been laid to her charge, religion as such, then, is not to blame. Yet of the charge that over-zealousness or fanaticism is one of her liabilities we cannot wholly acquit her, so I will next make a remark upon that point. But I will preface it by a preliminary remark which connects itself with much that follows.

Our survey of the phenomena of saintliness has unquestionably produced in your minds an impression of extravagance. Is it necessary, some of you have asked, as one example after another came before us, to be quite so fantastically good as that? We who have no vocation for the extremer ranges of sanctity will surely be let off at the last day if our humility, asceticism, and devoutness prove of a less convulsive sort. This practically amounts to saying that much that it is legitimate to admire in this field need nevertheless not be imitated, and that religious phenomena, like all other human phenomena, are subject to the law of the golden mean. Political reformers accomplish their successive tasks in the history of nations by being blind for the time to other causes. Great schools of art work out the effects which it is their mission to reveal, at the cost of a one-sidedness for which other schools must make amends. We accept a John Howard, a Mazzini, a Botticelli, a Michael Angelo, with a kind of indulgence. We are glad they existed to show us that way, but we are glad there are also other ways of seeing and taking life. So of many of the saints whom we have looked at. We are proud of a human nature that could be so passionately extreme, but we shrink from advising others to follow the example. The conduct we blame ourselves for not following lies nearer to the middle line of human effort. It is less dependent on particular beliefs and doctrines. It is such as wears well in different ages, such as under different skies all judges are able to commend.

The fruits of religion, in other words, are, like all human products, liable to corruption by excess. Common sense must judge them. It need not blame the votary; but it may be able to praise him only conditionally, as one who acts faithfully according to his lights. He shows us heroism in one way, but the unconditionally good way is that for which no indulgence need be asked.

We find that error by excess is exemplified by every saintly virtue. Excess, in human faculties, means usually one-sidedness or want of balance; for it is hard to imagine an essential faculty too strong, if only other faculties equally strong be there to coöperate with it in action. Strong affections need a strong will; strong active powers need a strong intellect; strong intellect needs strong sympathies, to keep life steady. If the balance exist, no one faculty can possibly be too strong—we only get the stronger all-round character. In the life of saints, technically so called, the spiritual faculties are strong, but what gives the impression of extravagance proves usually on examination to be a relative deficiency of intellect. Spiritual excitement takes pathological forms whenever other interests are too few and the intellect too narrow. We find this exemplified by all the saintly attributes in turn—devout love of God, purity, charity, asceticism, all may lead astray. I will run over these virtues in succession.

First of all let us take Devoutness. When unbalanced, one of its vices is called Fanaticism. Fanaticism (when not a mere expression of ecclesiastical ambition) is only loyalty carried to a convulsive extreme. When an intensely loyal and narrow mind is once grasped by the feeling that a certain superhuman person is worthy of its exclusive devotion, one of the first things that happens is that it idealizes the devotion itself. To adequately realize the merits of the idol gets to be considered the one great merit of the worshiper; and the sacrifices and servilities by which savage tribesmen have from time immemorial exhibited their faithfulness to chieftains are now outbid in favor of the deity. Vocabularies are exhausted and languages altered in the attempt to praise him enough; death is looked on as gain if it attract his grateful notice; and the personal attitude of being his devotee becomes what one might almost call a new and exalted kind of professional specialty within the tribe.[193] The legends that gather round the lives of holy persons are fruits of this impulse to celebrate and glorify. The Buddha[194] and Mohammed[195] and their companions and

193 Christian saints have had their specialties of devotion, Saint Francis to Christ's wounds; Saint Anthony of Padua to Christ's childhood; Saint Bernard to his humanity; Saint Teresa to Saint Joseph, etc. The Shi-ite Mohammedans venerate Ali, the Prophet's son-in-law, instead of Abu-bekr, his brother-in-law. Vambéry describes a dervish whom he met in Persia, "who had solemnly vowed, thirty years before, that he would never employ his organs of speech otherwise but in uttering, everlastingly, the name of his favorite, *Ali, Ali*. He thus wished to signify to the world that he was the most devoted partisan of that Ali who had been dead a thousand years. In his own home, speaking with his wife, children, and friends, no other word but 'Ali!' ever passed his lips. If he wanted food or drink or anything else, he expressed his wants still by repeating 'Ali!' Begging or buying at the bazaar, it was always 'Ali!' Treated ill or generously, he would still harp on his monotonous 'Ali!' Latterly his zeal assumed such tremendous proportions that, like a madman, he would race, the whole day, up and down the streets of the town, throwing his stick high up into the air, and shriek out, all the while, at the top of his voice, 'Ali!' This dervish was venerated by everybody as a saint, and received everywhere with the greatest distinction." Arminius Vambéry, his Life and Adventures, written by Himself, London, 1889, p. 69. On the anniversary of the death of Hussein, Ali's son, the Shi-ite Moslems still make the air resound with cries of his name and Ali's.

194 Compare H. C. Warren: Buddhism in Translation, Cambridge, U.S., 1898, passim.

195 Compare J. L. Merrick: The Life and Religion of Mohammed, as contained in the Sheeah traditions of the Hyat-ul-Kuloob, Boston. 1850, passim.

many Christian saints are incrusted with a heavy jewelry of anecdotes which are meant to be honorific, but are simply *abgeschmackt* and silly, and form a touching expression of man's misguided propensity to praise.

An immediate consequence of this condition of mind is jealousy for the deity's honor. How can the devotee show his loyalty better than by sensitiveness in this regard? The slightest affront or neglect must be resented, the deity's enemies must be put to shame. In exceedingly narrow minds and active wills, such a care may become an engrossing preoccupation; and crusades have been preached and massacres instigated for no other reason than to remove a fancied slight upon the God. Theologies representing the gods as mindful of their glory, and churches with imperialistic policies, have conspired to fan this temper to a glow, so that intolerance and persecution have come to be vices associated by some of us inseparably with the saintly mind. They are unquestionably its besetting sins. The saintly temper is a moral temper, and a moral temper has often to be cruel. It is a partisan temper, and that is cruel. Between his own and Jehovah's enemies a David knows no difference; a Catherine of Siena, panting to stop the warfare among Christians which was the scandal of her epoch, can think of no better method of union among them than a crusade to massacre the Turks; Luther finds no word of protest or regret over the atrocious tortures with which the Anabaptist leaders were put to death; and a Cromwell praises the Lord for delivering his enemies into his hands for "execution." Politics come in in all such cases; but piety finds the partnership not quite unnatural. So, when "freethinkers" tell us that religion and fanaticism are twins, we cannot make an unqualified denial of the charge.

Fanaticism must then be inscribed on the wrong side of religion's account, so long as the religious person's intellect is on the stage which the despotic kind of God satisfies. But as soon as the God is represented as less intent on his own honor and glory, it ceases to be a danger.

Fanaticism is found only where the character is masterful and aggressive. In gentle characters, where devoutness is intense and the intellect feeble, we have an imaginative absorption in the love of God to the exclusion of all practical human interests, which, though innocent enough, is too one-sided to be admirable. A mind too narrow has room but for one kind of affection. When the love of God takes possession of such a mind, it expels all human loves and human uses. There is no English name for such a sweet excess of devotion, so I will refer to it as a *theopathic* condition.

The blessed Margaret Mary Alacoque may serve as an example.

> "To be loved here upon the earth," her recent biographer exclaims: "to be loved by a noble, elevated, distinguished being; to be loved with fidelity, with devotion—what enchantment! But to be loved by God! and loved by him to distraction [aimé jusqu'à la folie]!—Margaret melted away with love at the thought of such a thing. Like Saint Philip of Neri in former times, or like Saint Francis

Xavier, she said to God: 'Hold back, O my God, these torrents which overwhelm me, or else enlarge my capacity for their reception.' "[196]

The most signal proofs of God's love which Margaret Mary received were her hallucinations of sight, touch, and hearing, and the most signal in turn of these were the revelations of Christ's sacred heart, "surrounded with rays more brilliant than the Sun, and transparent like a crystal. The wound which he received on the cross visibly appeared upon it. There was a crown of thorns round about this divine Heart, and a cross above it." At the same time Christ's voice told her that, unable longer to contain the flames of his love for mankind, he had chosen her by a miracle to spread the knowledge of them. He thereupon took out her mortal heart, placed it inside of his own and inflamed it, and then replaced it in her breast, adding: "Hitherto thou hast taken the name of my slave, hereafter thou shalt be called the well-beloved disciple of my Sacred Heart."

In a later vision the Saviour revealed to her in detail the "great design" which he wished to establish through her instrumentality. "I ask of thee to bring it about that every first Friday after the week of holy Sacrament shall be made into a special holy day for honoring my Heart by a general communion and by services intended to make honorable amends for the indignities which it has received. And I promise thee that my Heart will dilate to shed with abundance the influences of its love upon all those who pay to it these honors, or who bring it about that others do the same."

"This revelation," says Mgr. Bougaud, "is unquestionably the most important of all the revelations which have illumined the Church since that of the Incarnation and of the Lord's Supper. . . . After the Eucharist, the supreme effort of the Sacred Heart."[197] Well, what were its good fruits for Margaret Mary's life? Apparently little else but sufferings and prayers and absences of mind and swoons and ecstasies. She became increasingly useless about the convent, her absorption in Christ's love—

"which grew upon her daily, rendering her more and more incapable of attending to external duties. They tried her in the infirmary, but without much success, although her kindness, zeal, and devotion were without bounds, and her charity rose to acts of such a heroism that our readers would not bear the recital of them. They tried her in the kitchen, but were forced to give it up as hopeless—everything dropped out of her hands. The admirable humility with which she made amends for her clumsiness could not prevent this from being prejudicial to the order and regularity which must always reign in a community. They put her in the school, where the little girls cherished her, and cut pieces out of her clothes [for relics] as if she were already a saint, but where she was too absorbed inwardly to pay the necessary attention. Poor dear sister, even less after her vi-

196 Bougaud: Hist. de la bienheureuse Marguerite Marie, Paris, 1894, p. 145.

197 Bougaud: Hist. de la bienheureuse Marguerite Marie, Paris, 1894, pp. 365, 241.

sions than before them was she a denizen of earth, and they had to leave her in her heaven."[198]

Poor dear sister, indeed! Amiable and good, but so feeble of intellectual outlook that it would be too much to ask of us, with our Protestant and modern education, to feel anything but indulgent pity for the kind of saintship which she embodies. A lower example still of theopathic saintliness is that of Saint Gertrude, a Benedictine nun of the thirteenth century, whose "Revelations," a well-known mystical authority, consist mainly of proofs of Christ's partiality for her undeserving person. Assurances of his love, intimacies and caresses and compliments of the most absurd and puerile sort, addressed by Christ to Gertrude as an individual, form the tissue of this paltry-minded recital.[199] In reading such a narrative, we realize the gap between the thirteenth and the twentieth century, and we feel that saintliness of character may yield almost absolutely worthless fruits if it be associated with such inferior intellectual sympathies. What with science, idealism, and democracy, our own imagination has grown to need a God of an entirely different temperament from that Being interested exclusively in dealing out personal favors, with whom our ancestors were so contented. Smitten as we are with the vision of social righteousness, a God indifferent to everything but adulation, and full of partiality for his individual favorites, lacks an essential element of largeness; and even the best professional sainthood of former centuries, pent in as it is to such a conception, seems to us curiously shallow and unedifying.

Take Saint Teresa, for example, one of the ablest women, in many respects, of whose life we have the record. She had a powerful intellect of the practical order. She wrote admirable descriptive psychology, possessed a will equal to any emergency, great talent for politics and business, a buoyant disposition, and a first-rate literary style. She was tenaciously aspiring, and put her whole life at the service of her reli-

---

198 Bougaud: Op. cit., p. 267.

199 Examples: "Suffering from a headache, she sought, for the glory of God, to relieve herself by holding certain odoriferous substances in her mouth, when the Lord appeared to her to lean over towards her lovingly, and to find comfort Himself in these odors. After having gently breathed them in, He arose, and said with a gratified air to the Saints, as if contented with what He had done: 'See the new present which my betrothed has given Me!'

"One day, at chapel, she heard supernaturally sung the words, *'Sanctus, Sanctus, Sanctus.'* The Son of God leaning towards her like a sweet lover, and giving to her soul the softest kiss, said to her at the second Sanctus: 'In this *Sanctus* addressed to my person, receive with this kiss all the sanctity of my divinity and of my humanity, and let it be to thee a sufficient preparation for approaching the communion table.' And the next following Sunday, while she was thanking God for this favor, behold the Son of God, more beauteous than thousands of angels, takes her in His arms as if He were proud of her, and presents her to God the Father, in that perfection of sanctity with which He had dowered her. And the Father took such delight in this soul thus presented by His only Son, that, as if unable longer to restrain Himself, He gave her, and the Holy Ghost gave her also, the Sanctity attributed to each by His own *Sanctus*—and thus she remained endowed with the plenary fullness of the blessing of *Sanctity*, bestowed on her by Omnipotence, by Wisdom, and by Love." Révélations de Sainte Gertrude, Paris, 1898, i. 44, 186.

gious ideals. Yet so paltry were these, according to our present way of thinking, that (although I know that others have been moved differently) I confess that my only feeling in reading her has been pity that so much vitality of soul should have found such poor employment.

In spite of the sufferings which she endured, there is a curious flavor of superficiality about her genius. A Birmingham anthropologist, Dr. Jordan, has divided the human race into two types, whom he calls "shrews" and "non-shrews" respectively.[200] The shrew-type is defined as possessing an "active unimpassioned temperament." In other words, shrews are the "motors," rather than the "sensories,"[201] and their expressions are as a rule more energetic than the feelings which appear to prompt them. Saint Teresa, paradoxical as such a judgment may sound, was a typical shrew, in this sense of the term. The bustle of her style, as well as of her life, proves it. Not only must she receive unheard-of personal favors and spiritual graces from her Saviour, but she must immediately write about them and *exploiter* them professionally, and use her expertness to give instruction to those less privileged. Her voluble egotism; her sense, not of radical bad being, as the really contrite have it, but of her "faults" and "imperfections" in the plural; her stereotyped humility and return upon herself, as covered with "confusion" at each new manifestation of God's singular partiality for a person so unworthy, are typical of shrewdom: a paramountly feeling nature would be objectively lost in gratitude, and silent. She had some public instincts, it is true; she hated the Lutherans, and longed for the church's triumph over them; but in the main her idea of religion seems to have been that of an endless amatory flirtation—if one may say so without irreverence—between the devotee and the deity; and apart from helping younger nuns to go in this direction by the inspiration of her example and instruction, there is absolutely no human use in her, or sign of any general human interest. Yet the spirit of her age, far from rebuking her, exalted her as superhuman.

We have to pass a similar judgment on the whole notion of saintship based on merits. Any God who, on the one hand, can care to keep a pedantically minute account of individual shortcomings, and on the other can feel such partialities, and load particular creatures with such insipid marks of favor, is too small-minded a God for our credence. When Luther, in his immense manly way, swept off by a stroke of his hand the very notion of a debit and credit account kept with individuals by the Almighty, he stretched the soul's imagination and saved theology from puerility.

So much for mere devotion, divorced from the intellectual conceptions which might guide it towards bearing useful human fruit.

---

200 FURNEAUX JORDAN: Character in Birth and Parentage, first edition. Later editions change the nomenclature.

201 As to this distinction, see the admirably practical account in J. M. BALDWIN's little book, The Story of the Mind, 1898.

The next saintly virtue in which we find excess is Purity. In theopathic characters, like those whom we have just considered, the love of God must not be mixed with any other love. Father and mother, sisters, brothers, and friends are felt as interfering distractions; for sensitiveness and narrowness, when they occur together, as they often do, require above all things a simplified world to dwell in. Variety and confusion are too much for their powers of comfortable adaptation. But whereas your aggressive pietist reaches his unity objectively, by forcibly stamping disorder and divergence out, your retiring pietist reaches his subjectively, leaving disorder in the world at large, but making a smaller world in which he dwells himself and from which he eliminates it altogether. Thus, alongside of the church militant with its prisons, dragonnades, and inquisition methods, we have the church *fugient*, as one might call it, with its hermitages, monasteries, and sectarian organizations, both churches pursuing the same object—to unify the life,[202] and simplify the spectacle presented to the soul. A mind extremely sensitive to inner discords will drop one external relation after another, as interfering with the absorption of consciousness in spiritual things. Amusements must go first, then conventional "society," then business, then family duties, until at last seclusion, with a subdivision of the day into hours for stated religious acts, is the only thing that can be borne. The lives of saints are a history of successive renunciations of complication, one form of contact with the outer life being dropped after another, to save the purity of inner tone.[203] "Is it not better," a young sister asks her Superior, "that I should not speak at all during the hour of recreation, so as not to run the risk, by speaking, of falling into some sin of which I might not be conscious?"[204] If the life remains a social one at all, those who take part in it must follow one identical rule. Embosomed in this monotony, the zealot for purity feels clean and free once more. The minuteness of uniformity

202 On this subject I refer to the work of M. Murisier (Les Maladies du Sentiment Religieux, Paris, 1901), who makes inner unification the mainspring of the whole religious life. But *all* strongly ideal interests, religious or irreligious, unify the mind and tend to subordinate everything to themselves. One would infer from M. Murisier's pages that this formal condition was peculiarly characteristic of religion, and that one might in comparison almost neglect material content, in studying the latter. I trust that the present work will convince the reader that religion has plenty of material content which is characteristic, and which is more important by far than any general psychological form. In spite of this criticism, I find M. Murisier's book highly instructive.

203 Example: "At the first beginning of the Servitor's [Suso's] interior life, after he had purified his soul properly by confession, he marked out for himself, in thought, three circles, within which he shut himself up, as in a spiritual intrenchment. The first circle was his cell, his chapel, and the choir. When he was within this circle, he seemed to himself in complete security. The second circle was the whole monastery as far as the outer gate. The third and outermost circle was the gate itself, and here it was necessary for him to stand well upon his guard. When he went outside these circles, it seemed to him that he was in the plight of some wild animal which is outside its hole, and surrounded by the hunt, and therefore in need of all its cunning and watchfulness." The Life of the Blessed Henry Suso, by Himself, translated by Knox, London, 1865, p. 168.

204 Vie des premières Religieuses Dominicaines de la Congrégation de St. Dominique, à Nancy; Nancy, 1896, p. 129.

maintained in certain sectarian communities, whether monastic or not, is something almost inconceivable to a man of the world. Costume, phraseology, hours, and habits are absolutely stereotyped, and there is no doubt that some persons are so made as to find in this stability an incomparable kind of mental rest.

We have no time to multiply examples, so I will let the case of Saint Louis of Gonzaga serve as a type of excess in purification. I think you will agree that this youth carried the elimination of the external and discordant to a point which we cannot unreservedly admire. At the age of ten, his biographer says:—

> "The inspiration came to him to consecrate to the Mother of God his own virginity—that being to her the most agreeable of possible presents. Without delay, then, and with all the fervor there was in him, joyous of heart, and burning with love, he made his vow of perpetual chastity. Mary accepted the offering of his innocent heart, and obtained for him from God, as a recompense, the extraordinary grace of never feeling during his entire life the slightest touch of temptation against the virtue of purity. This was an altogether exceptional favor, rarely accorded even to Saints themselves, and all the more marvelous in that Louis dwelt always in courts and among great folks, where danger and opportunity are so unusually frequent. It is true that Louis from his earliest childhood had shown a natural repugnance for whatever might be impure or unvirginal, and even for relations of any sort whatever between persons of opposite sex. But this made it all the more surprising that he should, especially since this vow, feel it necessary to have recourse to such a number of expedients for protecting against even the shadow of danger the virginity which he had thus consecrated. One might suppose that if any one could have contented himself with the ordinary precautions, prescribed for all Christians, it would assuredly have been he. But no! In the use of preservatives and means of defense, in flight from the most insignificant occasions, from every possibility of peril, just as in the mortification of his flesh, he went farther than the majority of saints. He, who by an extraordinary protection of God's grace was never tempted, measured all his steps as if he were threatened on every side by particular dangers. Thenceforward he never raised his eyes, either when walking in the streets, or when in society. Not only did he avoid all business with females even more scrupulously than before, but he renounced all conversation and every kind of social recreation with them, although his father tried to make him take part; and he commenced only too early to deliver his innocent body to austerities of every kind."[205]

At the age of twelve, we read of this young man that "if by chance his mother sent one of her maids of honor to him with a message, he never allowed her to come in, but listened to her through the barely opened door, and dismissed her immediately. He did not like to be alone with his own mother, whether at table or in conversation; and when the rest of the company withdrew, he sought also a pretext for retiring. . . . Several great ladies, relatives of his, he avoided learning to know even

205 Meschler's Life of Saint Louis of Gonzaga, French translation by Lebréquier, 1891, p. 40.

by sight; and he made a sort of treaty with his father, engaging promptly and readily to accede to all his wishes, if he might only be excused from all visits to ladies." (Ibid., p. 71.)

When he was seventeen years old Louis joined the Jesuit order,[206] against his father's passionate entreaties, for he was heir of a princely house; and when a year later the father died, he took the loss as a "particular attention" to himself on God's part, and wrote letters of stilted good advice, as from a spiritual superior, to his grieving mother. He soon became so good a monk that if any one asked him the number of his brothers and sisters, he had to reflect and count them over before replying. A Father asked him one day if he were never troubled by the thought of his family, to which, "I never think of them except when praying for them," was his only answer. Never was he seen to hold in his hand a flower or anything perfumed, that he might take pleasure in it. On the contrary, in the hospital, he used to seek for whatever was most disgusting, and eagerly snatch the bandages of ulcers, etc., from the hands of his companions. He avoided worldly talk, and immediately tried to turn every conversation on to pious subjects, or else he remained silent. He systematically refused to notice his surroundings. Being ordered one day to bring a book from the rector's seat in the refectory, he had to ask where the rector sat, for in the three months he had eaten bread there, so carefully did he guard his eyes that he had not noticed the place. One day, during recess, having looked by chance on one of his companions, he reproached himself as for a grave sin against modesty. He cultivated silence, as preserving from sins of the tongue; and his greatest penance was the limit which his superiors set to his bodily penances. He sought after false accusations and unjust reprimands as opportunities of humility; and such was his obedience that, when a room-mate, having no more paper, asked him for a sheet, he did not feel free to give it to him without first obtaining the permission of the superior, who, as such, stood in the place of God, and transmitted his orders.

I can find no other sorts of fruit than these of Louis's saintship. He died in 1591, in his twenty-ninth year, and is known in the Church as the patron of all young people. On his festival, the altar in the chapel devoted to him in a certain church in Rome "is embosomed in flowers, arranged with exquisite taste; and a pile of letters may be seen at its foot, written to the Saint by young men and women, and directed to 'Paradiso.' They are supposed to be burnt unread except by San Luigi, who must find singular petitions in these pretty little missives, tied up now with a green ribbon, expressive of hope, now with a red one, emblematic of love," etc.[207]

---

206 In his boyish note-book he praises the monastic life for its freedom from sin, and for the imperishable treasures, which it enables us to store up, "of merit in God's eyes which makes of Him our debtor for all Eternity." Loc. cit., p. 62.

207 Mademoiselle Mori, a novel quoted in Hare's Walks in Rome, 1900, i. 55.

I cannot resist the temptation to quote from Starbuck's book, p. 388, another case of purification by elimination. It runs as follows:—

"The signs of abnormality which sanctified persons show are of frequent occurrence. They get out of tune with other people; often they will have nothing to do with churches, which they regard as

Our final judgment of the worth of such a life as this will depend largely on our conception of God, and of the sort of conduct he is best pleased with in his creatures. The Catholicism of the sixteenth century paid little heed to social righteousness; and to leave the world to the devil whilst saving one's own soul was then accounted no discreditable scheme. To-day, rightly or wrongly, helpfulness in general human affairs is, in consequence of one of those secular mutations in moral sentiment of which I spoke, deemed an essential element of worth in character; and to be of some public or private use is also reckoned as a species of divine service. Other early Jesuits, especially the missionaries among them, the Xaviers, Brébeufs, Jogues, were objective minds, and fought in their way for the world's welfare; so their lives to-day inspire us. But when the intellect, as in this Louis, is originally no larger than a pin's head, and cherishes ideas of God of corresponding smallness, the result, notwithstanding the heroism put forth, is on the whole repulsive. Purity, we see in the object-lesson, is *not* the one thing needful; and it is better that a life should contract many a dirt-mark, than forfeit usefulness in its efforts to remain unspotted.

Proceeding onwards in our search of religious extravagance, we next come upon excesses of Tenderness and Charity. Here saintliness has to face the charge of preserving the unfit, and breeding parasites and beggars. "Resist not evil," "Love your enemies," these are saintly maxims of which men of this world find it hard to speak without impatience. Are the men of this world right, or are the saints in possession of the deeper range of truth?

No simple answer is possible. Here, if anywhere, one feels the complexity of the moral life, and the mysteriousness of the way in which facts and ideals are interwoven.

Perfect conduct is a relation between three terms: the actor, the objects for which he acts, and the recipients of the action. In order that conduct should be abstractly

worldly; they become hypercritical towards others; they grow careless of their social, political, and financial obligations. As an instance of this type may be mentioned a woman of sixty-eight of whom the writer made a special study. She had been a member of one of the most active and progressive churches in a busy part of a large city. Her pastor described her as having reached the censorious stage. She had grown more and more out of sympathy with the church; her connection with it finally consisted simply in attendance at prayer-meeting, at which her only message was that of reproof and condemnation of the others for living on a low plane. At last she withdrew from fellowship with any church. The writer found her living alone in a little room on the top story of a cheap boarding-house, quite out of touch with all human relations, but apparently happy in the enjoyment of her own spiritual blessings. Her time was occupied in writing booklets on sanctification—page after page of dreamy rhapsody. She proved to be one of a small group of persons who claim that entire salvation involves three steps instead of two; not only must there be conversion and sanctification, but a third, which they call 'crucifixion' or 'perfect redemption,' and which seems to bear the same relation to sanctification that this bears to conversion. She related how the Spirit had said to her, 'Stop going to church. Stop going to holiness meetings. Go to your own room and I will teach you.' She professes to care nothing for colleges, or preachers, or churches, but only cares to listen to what God says to her. Her description of her experience seemed entirely consistent; she is happy and contented, and her life is entirely satisfactory to herself. While listening to her own story, one was tempted to forget that it was from the life of a person who could not live by it in conjunction with her fellows."

perfect, all three terms, intention, execution, and reception, should be suited to one another. The best intention will fail if it either work by false means or address itself to the wrong recipient. Thus no critic or estimator of the value of conduct can confine himself to the actor's animus alone, apart from the other elements of the performance. As there is no worse lie than a truth misunderstood by those who hear it, so reasonable arguments, challenges to magnanimity, and appeals to sympathy or justice, are folly when we are dealing with human crocodiles and boa-constrictors. The saint may simply give the universe into the hands of the enemy by his trustfulness. He may by non-resistance cut off his own survival.

Herbert Spencer tells us that the perfect man's conduct will appear perfect only when the environment is perfect: to no inferior environment is it suitably adapted. We may paraphrase this by cordially admitting that saintly conduct would be the most perfect conduct conceivable in an environment where all were saints already; but by adding that in an environment where few are saints, and many the exact reverse of saints, it must be ill adapted. We must frankly confess, then, using our empirical common sense and ordinary practical prejudices, that in the world that actually is, the virtues of sympathy, charity, and non-resistance may be, and often have been, manifested in excess. The powers of darkness have systematically taken advantage of them. The whole modern scientific organization of charity is a consequence of the failure of simply giving alms. The whole history of constitutional government is a commentary on the excellence of resisting evil, and when one cheek is smitten, of smiting back and not turning the other cheek also.

You will agree to this in general, for in spite of the Gospel, in spite of Quakerism, in spite of Tolstoi, you believe in fighting fire with fire, in shooting down usurpers, locking up thieves, and freezing out vagabonds and swindlers.

And yet you are sure, as I am sure, that were the world confined to these hard-headed, hard-hearted, and hard-fisted methods exclusively, were there no one prompt to help a brother first, and find out afterwards whether he were worthy; no one willing to drown his private wrongs in pity for the wronger's person; no one ready to be duped many a time rather than live always on suspicion; no one glad to treat individuals passionately and impulsively rather than by general rules of prudence; the world would be an infinitely worse place than it is now to live in. The tender grace, not of a day that is dead, but of a day yet to be born somehow, with the golden rule grown natural, would be cut out from the perspective of our imaginations.

The saints, existing in this way, may, with their extravagances of human tenderness, be prophetic. Nay, innumerable times they have proved themselves prophetic. Treating those whom they met, in spite of the past, in spite of all appearances, as worthy, they have stimulated them to *be* worthy, miraculously transformed them by their radiant example and by the challenge of their expectation.

From this point of view we may admit the human charity which we find in all saints, and the great excess of it which we find in some saints, to be a genuinely creative social force, tending to make real a degree of virtue which it alone is ready to assume as possible. The saints are authors, *auctores*, increasers, of goodness. The potentialities of development in human souls are unfathomable. So many who seemed irretrievably hardened have in point of fact been softened, converted, regenerated, in ways that amazed the subjects even more than they surprised the spectators, that we never can be sure in advance of any man that his salvation by the way of love is hopeless. We have no right to speak of human crocodiles and boa-constrictors as of fixedly incurable beings. We know not the complexities of personality, the smouldering emotional fires, the other facets of the character-polyhedron, the resources of the subliminal region. St. Paul long ago made our ancestors familiar with the idea that every soul is virtually sacred. Since Christ died for us all without exception, St. Paul said, we must despair of no one. This belief in the essential sacredness of every one expresses itself to-day in all sorts of humane customs and reformatory institutions, and in a growing aversion to the death penalty and to brutality in punishment. The saints, with their extravagance of human tenderness, are the great torch-bearers of this belief, the tip of the wedge, the clearers of the darkness. Like the single drops which sparkle in the sun as they are flung far ahead of the advancing edge of a wave-crest or of a flood, they show the way and are forerunners. The world is not yet with them, so they often seem in the midst of the world's affairs to be preposterous. Yet they are impregnators of the world, vivifiers and animaters of potentialities of goodness which but for them would lie forever dormant. It is not possible to be quite as mean as we naturally are, when they have passed before us. One fire kindles another; and without that over-trust in human worth which they show, the rest of us would lie in spiritual stagnancy.

Momentarily considered, then, the saint may waste his tenderness and be the dupe and victim of his charitable fever, but the general function of his charity in social evolution is vital and essential. If things are ever to move upward, some one must be ready to take the first step, and assume the risk of it. No one who is not willing to try charity, to try non-resistance as the saint is always willing, can tell whether these methods will or will not succeed. When they do succeed, they are far more powerfully successful than force or worldly prudence. Force destroys enemies; and the best that can be said of prudence is that it keeps what we already have in safety. But non-resistance, when successful, turns enemies into friends; and charity regenerates its objects. These saintly methods are, as I said, creative energies; and genuine saints find in the elevated excitement with which their faith endows them an authority and impressiveness which makes them irresistible in situations where men of shallower nature cannot get on at all without the use of worldly prudence. This practical proof that worldly wisdom may be safely transcended is the saint's magic gift to mankind.[208] Not only does his vision of a better world console us for

208 The best missionary lives abound in the victorious combination of non-resistance with personal authority. John G. Paton, for example, in the New Hebrides, among brutish Melanesian cannibals, preserves a charmed life by dint of it. When it comes to the point, no one ever dares actually to strike him. Native converts, inspired by him, showed analogous virtue. "One of our chiefs, full of the Christ-

the generally prevailing prose and barrenness; but even when on the whole we have to confess him ill adapted, he makes some converts, and the environment gets better for his ministry. He is an effective ferment of goodness, a slow transmuter of the earthly into a more heavenly order.

In this respect the Utopian dreams of social justice in which many contemporary socialists and anarchists indulge are, in spite of their impracticability and non-adaptation to present environmental conditions, analogous to the saint's belief in an existent kingdom of heaven. They help to break the edge of the general reign of hardness and are slow leavens of a better order.

The next topic in order is Asceticism, which I fancy you are all ready to consider without argument a virtue liable to extravagance and excess. The optimism and refinement of the modern imagination has, as I have already said elsewhere, changed the attitude of the church towards corporeal mortification, and a Suso or a Saint Peter of Alcantara[209] appear to us to-day rather in the light of tragic mountebanks

---

kindled desire to seek and to save, sent a message to an inland chief, that he and four attendants would come on Sabbath and tell them the gospel of Jehovah God. The reply came back sternly forbidding their visit, and threatening with death any Christian that approached their village. Our chief sent in response a loving message, telling them that Jehovah had taught the Christians to return good for evil, and that they would come unarmed to tell them the story of how the Son of God came into the world and died in order to bless and save his enemies. The heathen chief sent back a stern and prompt reply once more: 'If you come, you will be killed.' On Sabbath morn the Christian chief and his four companions were met outside the village by the heathen chief, who implored and threatened them once more. But the former said:—

" 'We come to you without weapons of war! We come only to tell you about Jesus. We believe that He will protect us to-day.'

"As they pressed steadily forward towards the village, spears began to be thrown at them. Some they evaded, being all except one dexterous warriors; and others they literally received with their bare hands, and turned them aside in an incredible manner. The heathen, apparently thunderstruck at these men thus approaching them without weapons of war, and not even flinging back their own spears which they had caught, after having thrown what the old chief called 'a shower of spears,' desisted from mere surprise. Our Christian chief called out, as he and his companions drew up in the midst of them on the village public ground:—

" 'Jehovah thus protects us. He has given us all your spears! Once we would have thrown them back at you and killed you. But now we come, not to fight but to tell you about Jesus. He has changed our dark hearts. He asks you now to lay down all these your other weapons of war, and to hear what we can tell you about the love of God, our great Father, the only living God.'

"The heathen were perfectly overawed. They manifestly looked on these Christians as protected by some Invisible One. They listened for the first time to the story of the Gospel and of the Cross. We lived to see that chief and all his tribe sitting in the school of Christ. And there is perhaps not an island in these southern seas, amongst all those won for Christ, where similar acts of heroism on the part of converts cannot be recited." JOHN G. PATON, Missionary to the New Hebrides, An Autobiography, second part, London, 1890, p. 243.

209 Saint Peter, Saint Teresa tells us in her autobiography (French translation, p. 333), "had passed forty years without ever sleeping more than an hour and a half a day. Of all his mortifications, this was the one that had cost him the most. To compass it, he kept always on his knees or on his feet. The little sleep he allowed nature to take was snatched in a sitting posture, his head leaning against a piece of wood fixed in the wall. Even had he wished to lie down, it would have been impossible, because his cell was only four feet and a half long. In the course of all these years he never raised his hood, no matter what

than of sane men inspiring us with respect. If the inner dispositions are right, we ask, what need of all this torment, this violation of the outer nature? It keeps the outer nature too important. Any one who is genuinely emancipated from the flesh will look on pleasures and pains, abundance and privation, as alike irrelevant and indifferent. He can engage in actions and experience enjoyments without fear of corruption or enslavement. As the Bhagavad-Gita says, only those need renounce worldly actions who are still inwardly attached thereto. If one be really unattached to the fruits of action, one may mix in the world with equanimity. I quoted in a former lecture Saint Augustine's antinomian saying: If you only love God enough, you may safely follow all your inclinations. "He needs no devotional practices," is one of Ramakrishna's maxims, "whose heart is moved to tears at the mere mention of the name of Hari."[210] And the Buddha, in pointing out what he called "the middle way" to his disciples, told them to abstain from both extremes, excessive mortification being as unreal and unworthy as mere desire and pleasure. The only perfect life, he said, is that of inner wisdom, which makes one thing as indifferent to us as another, and thus leads to rest, to peace, and to Nirvâna.[211]

We find accordingly that as ascetic saints have grown older, and directors of conscience more experienced, they usually have shown a tendency to lay less stress on special bodily mortifications. Catholic teachers have always professed the rule that, since health is needed for efficiency in God's service, health must not be sacrificed to mortification. The general optimism and healthy-mindedness of liberal Protestant circles to-day makes mortification for mortification's sake repugnant to us. We can no longer sympathize with cruel deities, and the notion that God can take delight in the spectacle of sufferings self-inflicted in his honor is abhorrent. In consequence of all these motives you probably are disposed, unless some special utility can be shown in some individual's discipline, to treat the general tendency to asceticism as pathological.

---

the ardor of the sun or the rain's strength. He never put on a shoe. He wore a garment of coarse sackcloth, with nothing else upon his skin. This garment was as scant as possible, and over it a little cloak of the same stuff. When the cold was great he took off the cloak and opened for a while the door and little window of his cell. Then he closed them and resumed the mantle—his way, as he told us, of warming himself, and making his body feel a better temperature. It was a frequent thing with him to eat once only in three days; and when I expressed my surprise, he said that it was very easy if one once had acquired the habit. One of his companions has assured me that he has gone sometimes eight days without food. . . . His poverty was extreme; and his mortification, even in his youth, was such that he told me he had passed three years in a house of his order without knowing any of the monks otherwise than by the sound of their voice, for he never raised his eyes, and only found his way about by following the others. He showed this same modesty on public highways. He spent many years without ever laying eyes upon a woman; but he confessed to me that at the age he had reached it was indifferent to him whether he laid eyes on them or not. He was very old when I first came to know him, and his body so attenuated that it seemed formed of nothing so much as of so many roots of trees. With all this sanctity he was very affable. He never spoke unless he was questioned, but his intellectual right-mindedness and grace gave to all his words an irresistible charm."

210 F. Max Müller: Ramakrishna, his Life and Sayings, 1899, p. 180.

211 Oldenberg: Buddha; translated by W. Hoey, London, 1882, p. 127.

Yet I believe that a more careful consideration of the whole matter, distinguishing between the general good intention of asceticism and the uselessness of some of the particular acts of which it may be guilty, ought to rehabilitate it in our esteem. For in its spiritual meaning asceticism stands for nothing less than for the essence of the twice-born philosophy. It symbolizes, lamely enough no doubt, but sincerely, the belief that there is an element of real wrongness in this world, which is neither to be ignored nor evaded, but which must be squarely met and overcome by an appeal to the soul's heroic resources, and neutralized and cleansed away by suffering. As against this view, the ultra-optimistic form of the once-born philosophy thinks we may treat evil by the method of ignoring. Let a man who, by fortunate health and circumstances, escapes the suffering of any great amount of evil in his own person, also close his eyes to it as it exists in the wider universe outside his private experience, and he will be quit of it altogether, and can sail through life happily on a healthy-minded basis. But we saw in our lectures on melancholy how precarious this attempt necessarily is. Moreover it is but for the individual; and leaves the evil outside of him, unredeemed and unprovided for in his philosophy.

No such attempt can be a *general* solution of the problem; and to minds of sombre tinge, who naturally feel life as a tragic mystery, such optimism is a shallow dodge or mean evasion. It accepts, in lieu of a real deliverance, what is a lucky personal accident merely, a cranny to escape by. It leaves the general world unhelped and still in the clutch of Satan. The real deliverance, the twice-born folk insist, must be of universal application. Pain and wrong and death must be fairly met and overcome in higher excitement, or else their sting remains essentially unbroken. If one has ever taken the fact of the prevalence of tragic death in this world's history fairly into his mind—freezing, drowning, entombment alive, wild beasts, worse men, and hideous diseases—he can with difficulty, it seems to me, continue his own career of worldly prosperity without suspecting that he may all the while not be really inside the game, that he may lack the great initiation.

Well, this is exactly what asceticism thinks; and it voluntarily takes the initiation. Life is neither farce nor genteel comedy, it says, but something we must sit at in mourning garments, hoping its bitter taste will purge us of our folly. The wild and the heroic are indeed such rooted parts of it that healthy-mindedness pure and simple, with its sentimental optimism, can hardly be regarded by any thinking man as a serious solution. Phrases of neatness, cosiness, and comfort can never be an answer to the sphinx's riddle.

In these remarks I am leaning only upon mankind's common instinct for reality, which in point of fact has always held the world to be essentially a theatre for heroism. In heroism, we feel, life's supreme mystery is hidden. We tolerate no one who has no capacity whatever for it in any direction. On the other hand, no matter what a man's frailties otherwise may be, if he be willing to risk death, and still more if he suffer it heroically, in the service he has chosen, the fact consecrates him forever. Inferior to ourselves in this or that way, if yet we cling to life, and he is able "to fling it away like a flower" as caring nothing for it, we account him in the deepest way our born superior. Each of us in his own person feels that a high-hearted indifference to life would expiate all his shortcomings.

The metaphysical mystery, thus recognized by common sense, that he who feeds on death that feeds on men possesses life supereminently and excellently, and meets best the secret demands of the universe, is the truth of which asceticism has been the faithful champion. The folly of the cross, so inexplicable by the intellect, has yet its indestructible vital meaning.

Representatively, then, and symbolically, and apart from the vagaries into which the unenlightened intellect of former times may have let it wander, asceticism must, I believe, be acknowledged to go with the profounder way of handling the gift of existence. Naturalistic optimism is mere syllabub and flattery and sponge-cake in comparison. The practical course of action for us, as religious men, would therefore, it seems to me, not be simply to turn our backs upon the ascetic impulse, as most of us to-day turn them, but rather to discover some outlet for it of which the fruits in the way of privation and hardship might be objectively useful. The older monastic asceticism occupied itself with pathetic futilities, or terminated in the mere egotism of the individual, increasing his own perfection.[212] But is it not possible for us to discard most of these older forms of mortification, and yet find saner channels for the heroism which inspired them?

Does not, for example, the worship of material luxury and wealth, which constitutes so large a portion of the "spirit" of our age, make somewhat for effeminacy and unmanliness? Is not the exclusively sympathetic and facetious way in which most children are brought up to-day—so different from the education of a hundred years ago, especially in evangelical circles—in danger, in spite of its many advantages, of developing a certain trashiness of fibre? Are there not hereabouts some points of application for a renovated and revised ascetic discipline?

Many of you would recognize such dangers, but would point to athletics, militarism, and individual and national enterprise and adventure as the remedies. These contemporary ideals are quite as remarkable for the energy with which they make for heroic standards of life, as contemporary religion is remarkable for the way in which it neglects them.[213] War and adventure assuredly keep all who engage in them from treating themselves too tenderly. They demand such incredible efforts, depth beyond depth of exertion, both in degree and in duration, that the whole scale of motivation alters. Discomfort and annoyance, hunger and wet, pain and cold, squalor and filth, cease to have any deterrent operation whatever. Death turns into a

212 "The vanities of all others may die out, but the vanity of a saint as regards his sainthood is hard indeed to wear away." Ramakrishna, his Life and Sayings, 1899, p. 172.

213 "When a church has to be run by oysters, ice-cream, and fun," I read in an American religious paper, "you may be sure that it is running away from Christ." Such, if one may judge by appearances, is the present plight of many of our churches.

commonplace matter, and its usual power to check our action vanishes. With the annulling of these customary inhibitions, ranges of new energy are set free, and life seems cast upon a higher plane of power.

The beauty of war in this respect is that it is so congruous with ordinary human nature. Ancestral evolution has made us all potential warriors; so the most insignificant individual, when thrown into an army in the field, is weaned from whatever excess of tenderness toward his precious person he may bring with him, and may easily develop into a monster of insensibility.

But when we compare the military type of self-severity with that of the ascetic saint, we find a world-wide difference in all their spiritual concomitants.

" 'Live and let live,' " writes a clear-headed Austrian officer, "is no device for an army. Contempt for one's own comrades, for the troops of the enemy, and, above all, fierce contempt for one's own person, are what war demands of every one. Far better is it for an army to be too savage, too cruel, too barbarous, than to possess too much sentimentality and human reasonableness. If the soldier is to be good for anything as a soldier, he must be exactly the opposite of a reasoning and thinking man. The measure of goodness in him is his possible use in war. War, and even peace, require of the soldier absolutely peculiar standards of morality. The recruit brings with him common moral notions, of which he must seek immediately to get rid. For him victory, success, must be *everything.* The most barbaric tendencies in men come to life again in war, and for war's uses they are incommensurably good."[214]

These words are of course literally true. The immediate aim of the soldier's life is, as Moltke said, destruction, and nothing but destruction; and whatever constructions wars result in are remote and non-military. Consequently the soldier cannot train himself to be too feelingless to all those usual sympathies and respects, whether for persons or for things, that make for conservation. Yet the fact remains that war is a school of strenuous life and heroism; and, being in the line of aboriginal instinct, is the only school that as yet is universally available. But when we gravely ask ourselves whether this wholesale organization of irrationality and crime be our only bulwark against effeminacy, we stand aghast at the thought, and think more kindly of ascetic religion. One hears of the mechanical equivalent of heat. What we now need to discover in the social realm is the moral equivalent of war: something heroic that will speak to men as universally as war does, and yet will be as compatible with their spiritual selves as war has proved itself to be incompatible. I have often thought that in the old monkish poverty-worship, in spite of the pedantry which infested it, there might be something like that moral equivalent of war which we are seeking. May not voluntarily accepted poverty be "the strenuous life," without the need of crushing weaker peoples?

Poverty indeed *is* the strenuous life—without brass bands or uniforms or hysteric popular applause or lies or circumlocutions; and when one sees the way in

214 C. V. B. K.: Friedens- und Kriegs-moral der Heere. Quoted by Hamon: Psychologie du Militaire professional, 1895, p. xli.

which wealth-getting enters as an ideal into the very bone and marrow of our generation, one wonders whether a revival of the belief that poverty is a worthy religious vocation may not be "the transformation of military courage," and the spiritual reform which our time stands most in need of.

Among us English-speaking peoples especially do the praises of poverty need once more to be boldly sung. We have grown literally afraid to be poor. We despise any one who elects to be poor in order to simplify and save his inner life. If he does not join the general scramble and pant with the money-making street, we deem him spiritless and lacking in ambition. We have lost the power even of imagining what the ancient idealization of poverty could have meant: the liberation from material attachments, the unbribed soul, the manlier indifference, the paying our way by what we are or do and not by what we have, the right to fling away our life at any moment irresponsibly—the more athletic trim, in short, the moral fighting shape. When we of the so-called better classes are scared as men were never scared in history at material ugliness and hardship; when we put off marriage until our house can be artistic, and quake at the thought of having a child without a bank-account and doomed to manual labor, it is time for thinking men to protest against so unmanly and irreligious a state of opinion.

It is true that so far as wealth gives time for ideal ends and exercise to ideal energies, wealth is better than poverty and ought to be chosen. But wealth does this in only a portion of the actual cases. Elsewhere the desire to gain wealth and the fear to lose it are our chief breeders of cowardice and propagators of corruption. There are thousands of conjunctures in which a wealth-bound man must be a slave, whilst a man for whom poverty has no terrors becomes a freeman. Think of the strength which personal indifference to poverty would give us if we were devoted to unpopular causes. We need no longer hold our tongues or fear to vote the revolutionary or reformatory ticket. Our stocks might fall, our hopes of promotion vanish, our salaries stop, our club doors close in our faces; yet, while we lived, we would imperturbably bear witness to the spirit, and our example would help to set free our generation. The cause would need its funds, but we its servants would be potent in proportion as we personally were contented with our poverty.

I recommend this matter to your serious pondering, for it is certain that the prevalent fear of poverty among the educated classes is the worst moral disease from which our civilization suffers.

I have now said all that I can usefully say about the several fruits of religion as they are manifested in saintly lives, so I will make a brief review and pass to my more general conclusions.

Our question, you will remember, is as to whether religion stands approved by its fruits, as these are exhibited in the saintly type of character. Single attributes of saintliness may, it is true, be temperamental endowments, found in non-religious individuals. But the whole group of them forms a combination which, as such, is religious, for it seems to flow from the sense of the divine as from its psychological centre. Whoever possesses strongly this sense comes naturally to think that the smallest details of this world derive infinite significance from their relation to an unseen divine order. The thought of this order yields him a superior denomination of happiness, and a steadfastness of soul with which no other can compare. In social relations his service-ability is exemplary; he abounds in impulses to help. His help is inward as well as outward, for his sympathy reaches souls as well as bodies, and kindles unsuspected faculties therein. Instead of placing happiness where common men place it, in comfort, he places it in a higher kind of inner excitement, which converts discomforts into sources of cheer and annuls unhappiness. So he turns his back upon no duty, however thankless; and when we are in need of assistance, we can count upon the saint lending his hand with more certainty than we can count upon any other person. Finally, his humble-mindedness and his ascetic tendencies save him from the petty personal pretensions which so obstruct our ordinary social intercourse, and his purity gives us in him a clean man for a companion. Felicity, purity, charity, patience, self-severity—these are splendid excellencies, and the saint of all men shows them in the completest possible measure.

But, as we saw, all these things together do not make saints infallible. When their intellectual outlook is narrow, they fall into all sorts of holy excesses, fanaticism or theopathic absorption, self-torment, prudery, scrupulosity, gullibility, and morbid inability to meet the world. By the very intensity of his fidelity to the paltry ideals with which an inferior intellect may inspire him, a saint can be even more objectionable and damnable than a superficial carnal man would be in the same situation. We must judge him not sentimentally only, and not in isolation, but using our own intellectual standards, placing him in his environment, and estimating his total function.

Now in the matter of intellectual standards, we must bear in mind that it is unfair, where we find narrowness of mind, always to impute it as a vice to the individual, for in religious and theological matters he probably absorbs his narrowness from his generation. Moreover, we must not confound the essentials of saintliness, which are those general passions of which I have spoken, with its accidents, which are the special determinations of these passions at any historical moment. In these determinations the saints will usually be loyal to the temporary idols of their tribe. Taking refuge in monasteries was as much an idol of the tribe in the middle ages, as bearing a hand in the world's work is to-day. Saint Francis or Saint Bernard, were they living to-day, would undoubtedly be leading consecrated lives of some sort, but quite as undoubtedly they would not lead them in retirement. Our animosity to special historic manifestations must not lead us to give away the saintly impulses in their essential nature to the tender mercies of inimical critics.

The most inimical critic of the saintly impulses whom I know is Nietzsche. He contrasts them with the worldly passions as we find these embodied in the predaceous military character, altogether to the advantage of the latter. Your born saint, it must be confessed, has something about him which often makes the gorge of a carnal man rise, so it will be worth while to consider the contrast in question more fully.

Dislike of the saintly nature seems to be a negative result of the biologically useful instinct of welcoming leadership, and glorifying the chief of the tribe. The chief is the potential, if not the actual tyrant, the masterful, overpowering man of prey. We confess our inferiority and grovel before him. We quail under his glance, and are at the same time proud of owning so dangerous a lord. Such instinctive and submissive hero-worship must have been indispensable in primeval tribal life. In the endless wars of those times, leaders were absolutely needed for the tribe's survival. If there were any tribes who owned no leaders, they can have left no issue to narrate their doom. The leaders always had good consciences, for conscience in them coalesced with will, and those who looked on their face were as much smitten with wonder at their freedom from inner restraint as with awe at the energy of their outward performances.

Compared with these beaked and taloned graspers of the world, saints are herbivorous animals, tame and harmless barn-yard poultry. There are saints whose beard you may, if you ever care to, pull with impunity. Such a man excites no thrills of wonder veiled in terror; his conscience is full of scruples and returns; he stuns us neither by his inward freedom nor his outward power; and unless he found within us an altogether different faculty of admiration to appeal to, we should pass him by with contempt.

In point of fact, he does appeal to a different faculty. Reënacted in human nature is the fable of the wind, the sun, and the traveler. The sexes embody the discrepancy. The woman loves the man the more admiringly the stormier he shows himself, and the world deifies its rulers the more for being willful and unaccountable. But the woman in turn subjugates the man by the mystery of gentleness in beauty, and the saint has always charmed the world by something similar. Mankind is susceptible and suggestible in opposite directions, and the rivalry of influences is unsleeping. The saintly and the worldly ideal pursue their feud in literature as much as in real life.

For Nietzsche the saint represents little but sneakingness and slavishness. He is the sophisticated invalid, the degenerate *par excellence*, the man of insufficient vitality. His prevalence would put the human type in danger.

> "The sick are the greatest danger for the well. The weaker, not the stronger, are the strong's undoing. It is not *fear* of our fellow-man, which we should wish to see diminished; for fear rouses those who are strong to become terrible in turn themselves, and preserves the hard-earned and successful type of humanity. What is to be dreaded by us more than any other doom is not fear, but rather the great disgust, not fear, but rather the great pity—disgust and pity for our human fellows. . . . The *morbid* are our greatest peril—not the 'bad' men, not the predatory beings. Those born wrong, the miscarried, the broken—they it is, the *weakest*, who are undermining the vitality of the race, poisoning our trust in life, and

putting humanity in question. Every look of them is a sighs—'Would I were something other! I am sick and tired of what I am.' In this swamp-soil of self-contempt, every poisonous weed flourishes, and all so small, so secret, so dishonest, and so sweetly rotten. Here swarm the worms of sensitiveness and resentment; here the air smells odious with secrecy, with what is not to be acknowledged; here is woven endlessly the net of the meanest of conspiracies, the conspiracy of those who suffer against those who succeed and are victorious; here the very aspect of the victorious is hated—as if health, success, strength, pride, and the sense of power were in themselves things vicious, for which one ought eventually to make bitter expiation. Oh, how these people would themselves like to inflict the expiation, how they thirst to be the hangmen! And all the while their duplicity never confesses their hatred to be hatred."[215]

Poor Nietzsche's antipathy is itself sickly enough, but we all know what he means, and he expresses well the clash between the two ideals. The carnivorous-minded "strong man," the adult male and cannibal, can see nothing but mouldiness and morbidness in the saint's gentleness and self-severity, and regards him with pure loathing. The whole feud revolves essentially upon two pivots: Shall the seen world or the unseen world be our chief sphere of adaptation? and must our means of adaptation in this seen world be aggressiveness or non-resistance?

The debate is serious. In some sense and to some degree both worlds must be acknowledged and taken account of; and in the seen world both aggressiveness and non-resistance are needful. It is a question of emphasis, of more or less. Is the saint's type or the strong-man's type the more ideal?

It has often been supposed, and even now, I think, it is supposed by most persons, that there can be one intrinsically ideal type of human character. A certain kind of man, it is imagined, must be the best man absolutely and apart from the utility of his function, apart from economical considerations. The saint's type, and the knight's or gentleman's type, have always been rival claimants of this absolute ideality; and in the ideal of military religious orders both types were in a manner blended. According to the empirical philosophy, however, all ideals are matters of relation. It would be absurd, for example, to ask for a definition of "the ideal horse," so long as dragging drays and running races, bearing children, and jogging about with tradesmen's packages all remain as indispensable differentiations of equine function. You may take what you call a general all-round animal as a compromise, but he will be inferior to any horse of a more specialized type, in some one particular direction. We must not forget this now when, in discussing saintliness, we ask if it be an ideal type of manhood. We must test it by its economical relations.

I think that the method which Mr. Spencer uses in his Data of Ethics will help to fix our opinion. Ideality in conduct is altogether a matter of adaptation. A society where all were invariably aggressive would destroy itself by inner friction, and in a

215 Zur Genealogie der Moral, Dritte Abhandlung, § 14. I have abridged, and in one place transposed, a sentence.

society where some are aggressive, others must be non-resistant, if there is to be any kind of order. This is the present constitution of society, and to the mixture we owe many of our blessings. But the aggressive members of society are always tending to become bullies, robbers, and swindlers; and no one believes that such a state of things as we now live in is the millennium. It is meanwhile quite possible to conceive an imaginary society in which there should be no aggressiveness, but only sympathy and fairness—any small community of true friends now realizes such a society. Abstractly considered, such a society on a large scale would be the millennium, for every good thing might be realized there with no expense of friction. To such a millennial society the saint would be entirely adapted. His peaceful modes of appeal would be efficacious over his companions, and there would be no one extant to take advantage of his non-resistance. The saint is therefore abstractly a higher type of man than the "strong man," because he is adapted to the highest society conceivable, whether that society ever be concretely possible or not. The strong man would immediately tend by his presence to make that society deteriorate. It would become inferior in everything save in a certain kind of bellicose excitement, dear to men as they now are.

But if we turn from the abstract question to the actual situation, we find that the individual saint may be well or ill adapted, according to particular circumstances. There is, in short, no absoluteness in the excellence of sainthood. It must be confessed that as far as this world goes, anyone who makes an out-and-out saint of himself does so at his peril. If he is not a large enough man, he may appear more insignificant and contemptible, for all his saintship, than if he had remained a worldling.[216] Accordingly religion has seldom been so radically taken in our Western world that the devotee could not mix it with some worldly temper. It has always found good men who could follow most of its impulses, but who stopped short when it came to non-resistance. Christ himself was fierce upon occasion. Cromwells, Stonewall Jacksons, Gordons, show that Christians can be strong men also.

How is success to be absolutely measured when there are so many environments and so many ways of looking at the adaptation? It cannot be measured absolutely; the verdict will vary according to the point of view adopted. From the biological point of view Saint Paul was a failure, because he was beheaded. Yet he was magnificently adapted to the larger environment of history; and so far as any saint's example is a leaven of righteousness in the world, and draws it in the direction of more prevalent habits of saintliness, he is a success, no matter what his immediate bad fortune may be. The greatest saints, the spiritual heroes whom every one acknowledges, the Francises, Bernards, Luthers, Loyolas, Wesleys, Channings, Moodys, Gratrys, the Phillips Brookses, the Agnes Joneses, Margaret Hallahans,

216 We all know *daft* saints, and they inspire a queer kind of aversion. But in comparing saints with strong men we must choose individuals on the same intellectual level. The under-witted strong man, homologous in his sphere with the under-witted saint, is the bully of that slums, the hooligan or rowdy. Surely on this level also the saint preserves a certain superiority.

and Dora Pattisons, are successes from the outset. They show themselves, and there is no question; every one perceives their strength and stature. Their sense of mystery in things, their passion, their goodness, irradiate about them and enlarge their outlines while they soften them. They are like pictures with an atmosphere and background; and, placed alongside of them, the strong men of this world and no other seem as dry as sticks, as hard and crude as blocks of stone or brickbats.

In a general way, then, and "on the whole," our abandonment of theological criteria, and our testing of religion by practical common sense and the empirical method, leave it in possession of its towering place in history. Economically, the saintly group of qualities is indispensable to the world's welfare. The great saints are immediate successes; the smaller ones are at least heralds and harbingers, and they may be leavens also, of a better mundane order. Let us be saints, then, if we can, whether or not we succeed visibly and temporally. But in our Father's house are many mansions, and each of us must discover for himself the kind of religion and the amount of saintship which best comports with what he believes to be his powers and feels to be his truest mission and vocation. There are no successes to be guaranteed and no set orders to be given to individuals, so long as we follow the methods of empirical philosophy.

This is my conclusion so far. I know that on some of your minds it leaves a feeling of wonder that such a method should have been applied to such a subject, and this in spite of all those remarks about empiricism which I made at the beginning of Lecture XIII. How, you say, can religion, which believes in two worlds and an invisible order, be estimated by the adaptation of its fruits to this world's order alone? It is its *truth*, not its utility, you insist, upon which our verdict ought to depend. If religion is true, its fruits are good fruits, even though in this world they should prove uniformly ill adapted and full of naught but pathos. It goes back, then, after all, to the question of the truth of theology. The plot inevitably thickens upon us; we cannot escape theoretical considerations. I propose, then, that to some degree we face the responsibility. Religious persons have often, though not uniformly, professed to see truth in a special manner. That manner is known as mysticism. I will consequently now proceed to treat at some length of mystical phenomena, and after that, though more briefly, I will consider religious philosophy.

# LECTURES XVI AND XVII

## Mysticism

Over and over again in these lectures I have raised points and left them open and unfinished until we should have come to the subject of Mysticism. Some of you, I fear, may have smiled as you noted my reiterated postponements. But now the hour has come when mysticism must be faced in good earnest, and those broken threads wound up together. One may say truly, I think, that personal religious experience has its root and centre in mystical states of consciousness; so for us, who in these lectures are treating personal experience as the exclusive subject of our study, such states of consciousness ought to form the vital chapter from which the other chapters get their light. Whether my treatment of mystical states will shed more light or darkness, I do not know, for my own constitution shuts me out from their enjoyment almost entirely, and I can speak of them only at second hand. But though forced to look upon the subject so externally, I will be as objective and receptive as I can; and I think I shall at least succeed in convincing you of the reality of the states in question, and of the paramount importance of their function.

First of all, then, I ask, What does the expression "mystical states of consciousness" mean? How do we part off mystical states from other states?

The words "mysticism" and "mystical" are often used as terms of mere reproach, to throw at any opinion which we regard as vague and vast and sentimental, and without a base in either facts or logic. For some writers a "mystic" is any person who believes in thought-transference, or spirit-return. Employed in this way the word has little value: there are too many less ambiguous synonyms. So, to keep it useful by restricting it, I will do what I did in the case of the word "religion," and simply propose to you four marks which, when an experience has them, may justify us in calling it mystical for the purpose of the present lectures. In this way we shall save verbal disputation, and the recriminations that generally go therewith.

1. *Ineffability.*—The handiest of the marks by which I classify a state of mind as mystical is negative. The subject of it immediately says that it defies expression, that no adequate report of its contents can be given in words. It follows from this that its quality must be directly experienced; it cannot be imparted or transferred to others.

In this peculiarity mystical states are more like states of feeling than like states of intellect. No one can make clear to another who has never had a certain feeling, in what the quality or worth of it consists. One must have musical ears to know the value of a symphony; one must have been in love one's self to understand a lover's state of mind. Lacking the heart or ear, we cannot interpret the musician or the lover justly, and are even likely to consider him weak-minded or absurd. The mystic finds that most of us accord to his experiences an equally incompetent treatment.

2. *Noetic quality.*—Although so similar to states of feeling, mystical states seem to those who experience them to be also states of knowledge. They are states of insight into depths of truth unplumbed by the discursive intellect. They are illuminations, revelations, full of significance and importance, all inarticulate though they remain; and as a rule they carry with them a curious sense of authority for aftertime.

These two characters will entitle any state to be called mystical, in the sense in which I use the word. Two other qualities are less sharply marked, but are usually found. These are:—

3. *Transiency.*—Mystical states cannot be sustained for long. Except in rare instances, half an hour, or at most an hour or two, seems to be the limit beyond which they fade into the light of common day. Often, when faded, their quality can but imperfectly be reproduced in memory; but when they recur it is recognized; and from one recurrence to another it is susceptible of continuous development in what is felt as inner richness and importance.

4. *Passivity.*—Although the oncoming of mystical states may be facilitated by preliminary voluntary operations, as by fixing the attention, or going through certain bodily performances, or in other ways which manuals of mysticism prescribe; yet when the characteristic sort of consciousness once has set in, the mystic feels as if his own will were in abeyance, and indeed sometimes as if he were grasped and held by a superior power. This latter peculiarity connects mystical states with certain definite phenomena of secondary or alternative personality, such as prophetic speech, automatic writing, or the mediumistic trance. When these latter conditions are well pronounced, however, there may be no recollection whatever of the phenomenon, and it may have no significance for the subject's usual inner life, to which, as it were, it makes a mere interruption. Mystical states, strictly so-called, are never merely interruptive. Some memory of their content always remains, and a profound sense of their importance. They modify the inner life of the subject between the times of their recurrence. Sharp divisions in this region are, however, difficult to make, and we find all sorts of gradations and mixtures.

These four characteristics are sufficient to mark out a group of states of consciousness peculiar enough to deserve a special name and to call for careful study. Let it then be called the mystical group.

Our next step should be to gain acquaintance with some typical examples. Professional mystics at the height of their development have often elaborately organized experiences and a philosophy based thereupon. But you remember what I said in my first lecture: phenomena are best understood when placed within their series, studied in their germ and in their over-ripe decay, and compared with their exaggerated and degenerated kindred. The range of mystical experience is very wide, much too wide for us to cover in the time at our disposal. Yet the method of serial study is so essential for interpretation that if we really wish to reach conclusions we must use it. I will begin, therefore, with phenomena which claim no special religious significance, and end with those of which the religious pretensions are extreme.

The simplest rudiment of mystical experience would seem to be that deepened sense of the significance of a maxim or formula which occasionally sweeps over one. "I've heard that said all my life," we exclaim, "but I never realized its full meaning until now." "When a fellow-monk," said Luther, "one day repeated the words of the Creed: 'I believe in the forgiveness of sins,' I saw the Scripture in an entirely new light; and straightway I felt as if I were born anew. It was as if I had found the door of paradise thrown wide open."[217] This sense of deeper significance is not confined to rational propositions. Single words,[218] and conjunctions of words, effects of light on land and sea, odors and musical sounds, all bring it when the mind is tuned aright. Most of us can remember the strangely moving power of passages in certain poems read when we were young, irrational doorways as they were through which the mystery of fact, the wildness and the pang of life, stole into our hearts and thrilled them. The words have now perhaps become mere polished surfaces for us; but lyric poetry and music are alive and significant only in proportion as they fetch these vague vistas of a life continuous with our own, beckoning and inviting, yet ever eluding our pursuit. We are alive or dead to the eternal inner message of the arts according as we have kept or lost this mystical susceptibility.

A more pronounced step forward on the mystical ladder is found in an extremely frequent phenomenon, that sudden feeling, namely, which sometimes sweeps over us, of having "been here before," as if at some indefinite past time, in just this place, with just these people, we were already saying just these things. As Tennyson writes:

*"Moreover, something is or seems*
*That touches me with mystic gleams,*
*Like glimpses of forgotten dreams—*

*"Of something felt, like something here;*
*Of something done, I know not where;*
*Such as no language may declare."*[219]

217 Newman's *Securus iudicat orbis terrarum* is another instance.

218 "Mesopotamia" is the stock comic instance.—An excellent old German lady, who had done some traveling in her day, used to describe to me her *Sehnsucht* that she might yet visit "Phīladelphiā," whose wondrous name had always haunted her imagination. Of John Foster it is said that "single words (as *chalcedony*), or the names of ancient heroes, had a mighty fascination over him. 'At any time the word *hermit* was enough to transport him.' The words *woods* and *forests* would produce the most powerful emotion." Foster's Life, by RYLAND, New York, 1846, p. 3.

219 The Two Voices. In a letter to Mr. B. P. Blood, Tennyson reports of himself as follows:—

Sir James Crichton-Browne has given the technical name of "dreamy states" to these sudden invasions of vaguely reminiscent consciousness.[220] They bring a sense of mystery and of the metaphysical duality of things, and the feeling of an enlargement of perception which seems imminent but which never completes itself. In Dr. Crichton-Browne's opinion they connect themselves with the perplexed and scared disturbances of self-consciousness which occasionally precede epileptic attacks. I think that this learned alienist takes a rather absurdly alarmist view of an intrinsically insignificant phenomenon. He follows it along the downward ladder, to insanity; our path pursues the upward ladder chiefly. The divergence shows how important it is to neglect no part of a phenomenon's connections, for we make it appear admirable or dreadful according to the context by which we set it off.

Somewhat deeper plunges into mystical consciousness are met with in yet other dreamy states. Such feelings as these which Charles Kingsley describes are surely far from being uncommon, especially in youth:—

"When I walk the fields, I am oppressed now and then with an innate feeling that everything I see has a meaning, if I could but understand it. And this feeling of being surrounded with truths which I cannot grasp amounts to indescribable awe sometimes. . . . Have you not felt that your real soul was imperceptible to your mental vision, except in a few hallowed moments?"[221]

A much more extreme state of mystical consciousness is described by J. A. Symonds; and probably more persons than we suspect could give parallels to it from their own experience.

> "Suddenly," writes Symonds, "at church, or in company, or when I was reading, and always, I think, when my muscles were at rest, I felt the approach of the mood. Irresistibly it took possession of my mind and will, lasted what seemed an eternity, and disappeared in a series of rapid sensations which resembled the awakening from anæsthetic influence. One reason why I disliked this kind of trance was that I could not describe it to myself. I cannot even now find words

---

"I have never had any revelations through anæsthetics, but a kind of waking trance—this for lack of a better word—I have frequently had, quite up from boyhood, when I have been all alone. This has come upon me through repeating my own name to myself silently, till all at once, as it were out of the intensity of the consciousness of individuality, individuality itself seemed to dissolve and fade away into boundless being, and this not a confused state but the clearest, the surest of the surest, utterly beyond words—where death was an almost laughable impossibility—the loss of personality (if so it were) seeming no extinction, but the only true life. I am ashamed of my feeble description. Have I not said the state is utterly beyond words?"

Professor Tyndall, in a letter, recalls Tennyson saying of this condition: "By God Almighty! there is no delusion in the matter! It is no nebulous ecstasy, but a state of transcendent wonder, associated with absolute clearness of mind." Memoirs of Alfred Tennyson, ii. 473.

220 The Lancet, July 6 and 13, 1895, reprinted as the Cavendish Lecture, on Dreamy Mental States, London, Baillière, 1895. They have been a good deal discussed of late by psychologists. See, for example, Bernard-Leroy: L'Illusion de Fausse Reconnaissance, Paris, 1898.

221 Charles Kingsley's Life, i. 55, quoted by Inge: Christian Mysticism, London, 1899, p. 341.

to render it intelligible. It consisted in a gradual but swiftly progressive obliteration of space, time, sensation, and the multitudinous factors of experience which seem to qualify what we are pleased to call our Self. In proportion as these conditions of ordinary consciousness were subtracted, the sense of an underlying or essential consciousness acquired intensity. At last nothing remained but a pure, absolute, abstract Self. The universe became without form and void of content. But Self persisted, formidable in its vivid keenness, feeling the most poignant doubt about reality, ready, as it seemed, to find existence break as breaks a bubble round about it. And what then? The apprehension of a coming dissolution, the grim conviction that this state was the last state of the conscious Self, the sense that I had followed the last thread of being to the verge of the abyss, and had arrived at demonstration of eternal Maya or illusion, stirred or seemed to stir me up again. The return to ordinary conditions of sentient existence began by my first recovering the power of touch, and then by the gradual though rapid influx of familiar impressions and diurnal interests. At last I felt myself once more a human being; and though the riddle of what is meant by life remained unsolved, I was thankful for this return from the abyss—this deliverance from so awful an initiation into the mysteries of skepticism.

"This trance recurred with diminishing frequency until I reached the age of twenty-eight. It served to impress upon my growing nature the phantasmal unreality of all the circumstances which contribute to a merely phenomenal consciousness. Often have I asked myself with anguish, on waking from that formless state of denuded, keenly sentient being, Which is the unreality—the trance of fiery, vacant, apprehensive, skeptical Self from which I issue, or these surrounding phenomena and habits which veil that inner Self and build a self of flesh-and-blood conventionality? Again, are men the factors of some dream, the dream-like unsubstantiality of which they comprehend at such eventful moments? What would happen if the final stage of the trance were reached?"[222]

In a recital like this there is certainly something suggestive of pathology.[223] The next step into mystical states carries us into a realm that public opinion and ethical philosophy have long since branded as pathological, though private practice and certain lyric strains of poetry seem still to bear witness to its ideality. I refer to the consciousness produced by intoxicants and anæsthetics, especially by alcohol. The sway of alcohol over mankind is unquestionably due to its power to stimulate the mystical faculties of human nature, usually crushed to earth by the cold facts and dry criticisms of the sober hour. Sobriety diminishes, discriminates, and says no; drunkenness expands, unites, and says yes. It is in fact the great exciter of the *Yes* function in man. It brings its votary from the chill periphery of things to the radiant

222 H. F. Brown: J. A. Symonds, a Biography, London, 1895, pp. 29–31, abridged.

223 Crichton-Browne expressly says that Symonds's "highest nerve centres were in some degree enfeebled or damaged by these dreamy mental states which afflicted him so grievously." Symonds was, however, a perfect monster of many-sided cerebral efficiency, and his critic gives no objective grounds whatever for his strange opinion, save that Symonds complained occasionally, as all susceptible and ambitious men complain, of lassitude and uncertainty as to his life's mission.

core. It makes him for the moment one with truth. Not through mere perversity do men run after it. To the poor and the unlettered it stands in the place of symphony concerts and of literature; and it is part of the deeper mystery and tragedy of life that whiffs and gleams of something that we immediately recognize as excellent should be vouchsafed to so many of us only in the fleeting earlier phases of what in its totality is so degrading a poisoning. The drunken consciousness is one bit of the mystic consciousness, and our total opinion of it must find its place in our opinion of that larger whole.

Nitrous oxide and ether, especially nitrous oxide, when sufficiently diluted with air, stimulate the mystical consciousness in an extraordinary degree. Depth beyond depth of truth seems revealed to the inhaler. This truth fades out, however, or escapes, at the moment of coming to; and if any words remain over in which it seemed to clothe itself, they prove to be the veriest nonsense. Nevertheless, the sense of a profound meaning having been there persists; and I know more than one person who is persuaded that in the nitrous oxide trance we have a genuine metaphysical revelation.

Some years ago I myself made some observations on this aspect of nitrous oxide intoxication, and reported them in print. One conclusion was forced upon my mind at that time, and my impression of its truth has ever since remained unshaken. It is that our normal waking consciousness, rational consciousness as we call it, is but one special type of consciousness, whilst all about it, parted from it by the filmiest of screens, there lie potential forms of consciousness entirely different. We may go through life without suspecting their existence; but apply the requisite stimulus, and at a touch they are there in all their completeness, definite types of mentality which probably somewhere have their field of application and adaptation. No account of the universe in its totality can be final which leaves these other forms of consciousness quite disregarded. How to regard them is the question—for they are so discontinuous with ordinary consciousness. Yet they may determine attitudes though they cannot furnish formulas, and open a region though they fail to give a map. At any rate, they forbid a premature closing of our accounts with reality. Looking back on my own experiences, they all converge towards a kind of insight to which I cannot help ascribing some metaphysical significance. The keynote of it is invariably a reconciliation. It is as if the opposites of the world, whose contradictoriness and conflict make all our difficulties and troubles, were melted into unity. Not only do they, as contrasted species, belong to one and the same genus, but *one of the species*, the nobler and better one, *is itself the genus, and so soaks up and absorbs its opposite into itself.* This is a dark saying, I know, when thus expressed in terms of common logic, but I cannot wholly escape from its authority. I feel as if it must mean something, something like what the hegelian philosophy means, if one could only lay hold of it more clearly. Those who have ears to hear, let them hear; to me the living sense of its reality only comes in the artificial mystic state of mind.[224]

224 What reader of Hegel can doubt that that sense of a perfected Being with all its otherness soaked

I just now spoke of friends who believe in the anæsthetic revelation. For them too it is a monistic insight, in which the *other* in its various forms appears absorbed into the One.

"Into this pervading genius," writes one of them, "we pass, forgetting and forgotten, and thenceforth each is all, in God. There is no higher, no deeper, no other, than the life in which we are founded, 'The One remains, the many change and pass;' and each and every one of us *is* the One that remains. . . . This is the ultimatum. . . . As sure as being—whence is all our care—so sure is content, beyond duplexity, antithesis, or trouble, where I have triumphed in a solitude that God is not above."[225]

---

up into itself, which dominates his whole philosophy, must have come from the prominence in his consciousness of mystical moods like this, in most persons kept subliminal? The notion is thoroughly characteristic of the mystical level, and the *Aufgabe* of making it articulate was surely set to Hegel's intellect by mystical feeling.

225 Benjamin Paul Blood: The Anæsthetic Revelation and the Gist of Philosophy, Amsterdam, N. Y., 1874, pp. 35, 36. Mr. Blood has made several attempts to adumbrate the anæsthetic revelation, in pamphlets of rare literary distinction, privately printed and distributed by himself at Amsterdam. Xenos Clark, a philosopher, who died young at Amherst in the '80's, much lamented by those who knew him, was also impressed by the revelation. "In the first place," he once wrote to me, "Mr. Blood and I agree that the revelation is, if anything, non-emotional. It is utterly flat. It is, as Mr. Blood says, 'the one sole and sufficient insight why, or not why, but how, the present is pushed on by the past, and sucked forward by the vacuity of the future. Its inevitableness defeats all attempts at stopping or accounting for it. It is all precedence and presupposition, and questioning is in regard to it forever too late. It is an *initiation of the past.*' The real secret would be the formula by which the 'now' keeps exfoliating out of itself, yet never escapes. What is it, indeed, that keeps existence exfoliating? The formal being of anything, the logical definition of it, is static. For mere logic every question contains its own answer—we simply fill the hole with the dirt we dug out. Why are twice two four? Because, in fact, four is twice two. Thus logic finds in life no propulsion, only a momentum. It goes because it is a-going. But the revelation adds: it goes because it is and *was* a-going. You walk, as it were, round yourself in the revelation. Ordinary philosophy is like a hound hunting his own tail. The more he hunts the farther he has to go, and his nose never catches up with his heels, because it is forever ahead of them. So the present is already a foregone conclusion, and I am ever too late to understand it. But at the moment of recovery from anæsthesis, just then, *before starting on life*, I catch, so to speak, a glimpse of my heels, a glimpse of the eternal process just in the act of starting. The truth is that we travel on a journey that was accomplished before we set out; and the real end of philosophy is accomplished, not when we arrive at, but when we remain in, our destination (being already there)—which may occur vicariously in this life when we cease our intellectual questioning. That is why there is a smile upon the face of the revelation, as we view it. It tells us that we are forever half a second too late—that's all. 'You could kiss your own lips, and have all the fun to yourself,' it says, if you only knew the trick. It would be perfectly easy if they would just stay there till you got round to them. Why don't you manage it somehow?"

Dialectically minded readers of this farrago will at least recognize the region of thought of which Mr. Clark writes, as familiar. In his latest pamphlet, "Tennyson's Trances and the Anæsthetic Revelation," Mr. Blood describes its value for life as follows:—

"The Anæsthetic Revelation is the Initiation of Man into the Immemorial Mystery of the Open Secret of Being, revealed as the Inevitable Vortex of Continuity. Inevitable is the word. Its motive is inherent—it is what has to be. It is not for any love or hate, nor for joy nor sorrow, nor good nor ill. End, beginning, or purpose, it knows not of.

"It affords no particular of the multiplicity and variety of things; but it fills appreciation of the historical and the sacred with a secular and intimately personal illumination of the nature and motive of existence, which then seems reminiscent—as if it should have appeared, or shall yet appear, to every participant thereof.

This has the genuine religious mystic ring! I just now quoted J. A. Symonds. He also records a mystical experience with chloroform, as follows:—

> "After the choking and stifling had passed away, I seemed at first in a state of utter blankness; then came flashes of intense light, alternating with blackness, and with a keen vision of what was going on in the room around me, but no sensation of touch. I thought that I was near death; when, suddenly, my soul became aware of God, who was manifestly dealing with me, handling me, so to speak, in an intense personal present reality. I felt him streaming in like light upon me.... I cannot describe the ecstasy I felt. Then, as I gradually awoke from the influence of the anæsthetics, the old sense of my relation to the world began to return, the new sense of my relation to God began to fade. I suddenly leapt to my feet on the chair where I was sitting, and shrieked out, 'It is too horrible, it is too horrible, it is too horrible,' meaning that I could not bear this disillusionment. Then I flung myself on the ground, and at last awoke covered with blood, calling to the two surgeons (who were frightened), 'Why did you not kill me? Why would you not let me die?' Only think of it. To have felt for that long dateless ecstasy of vision the very God, in all purity and tenderness and truth and absolute love, and then to find that I had after all had no revelation, but that I had been tricked by the abnormal excitement of my brain.
>
> "Yet, this question remains, Is it possible that the inner sense of reality which succeeded, when my flesh was dead to impressions from without, to the ordinary sense of physical relations, was not a delusion but an actual experience? Is it possible that I, in that moment, felt what some of the saints have said they always felt, the undemonstrable but, irrefragable certainty of God?"[226]

---

"Although it is at first startling in its solemnity, it becomes directly such a matter of course—so old-fashioned, and so akin to proverbs, that it inspires exultation rather than fear, and a sense of safety, as identified with the aboriginal and the universal. But no words may express the imposing certainty of the patient that he is realizing the primordial, Adamic surprise of Life.

"Repetition of the experience finds it ever the same, and as if it could not possibly be otherwise. The subject resumes his normal consciousness only to partially and fitfully remember its occurrence, and to try to formulate its baffling import—with only this consolatory afterthought: that he has known the oldest truth, and that he has done with human theories as to the origin, meaning, or destiny of the race. He is beyond instruction in 'spiritual things.'

"The lesson is one of central safety: the Kingdom is within. All days are judgment days: but there can be no climacteric purpose of eternity, nor any scheme of the whole. The astronomer abridges the row of bewildering figures by increasing his unit of measurement: so may we reduce the distracting multiplicity of things to the unity for which each of us stands.

"This has been my moral sustenance since I have known of it. In my first printed mention of it I declared: 'The world is no more the alien terror that was taught me. Spurning the cloud-grimed and still sultry battlements whence so lately Jehovan thunders boomed, my gray gull lifts her wing against the nightfall, and takes the dim leagues with a fearless eye.' And now, after twenty-seven years of this experience, the wing is grayer, but the eye is fearless still, while I renew and doubly emphasize that declaration. I know—as having known—the meaning of Existence: the sane centre of the universe—at once the wonder and the assurance of the soul—for which the speech of reason has as yet no name but the Anæsthetic Revelation."—I have considerably abridged the quotation.

226 Op. cit., pp. 78–80, abridged. I subjoin, also abridging it, another interesting anæsthetic revelation

With this we make connection with religious mysticism pure and simple. Symonds's question takes us back to those examples which you will remember my quoting in the lecture on the Reality of the Unseen, of sudden realization of the immediate presence of God. The phenomenon in one shape or another is not uncommon.

---

communicated to me in manuscript by a friend in England. The subject, a gifted woman, was taking ether for a surgical operation.

"I wondered if I was in a prison being tortured, and why I remembered having heard it said that people 'learn through suffering,' and in view of what I was seeing, the inadequacy of this saying struck me so much that I said, aloud, 'to suffer *is* to learn.'

"With that I became unconscious again, and my last dream immediately preceded my real coming to. It only lasted a few seconds, and was most vivid and real to me, though it may not be clear in words.

"A great Being or Power was traveling through the sky, his foot was on a kind of lightning as a wheel is on a rail, it was his pathway. The lightning was made entirely of the spirits of innumerable people close to one another, and I was one of them. He moved in a straight line, and each part of the streak or flash came into its short conscious existence only that he might travel. I seemed to be directly under the foot of God, and I thought he was grinding his own life up out of my pain. Then I saw that what he had been trying with all his might to do was to *change his course*, to *bend* the line of lightning to which he was tied, in the direction in which he wanted to go. I felt my flexibility and helplessness, and knew that he would succeed. He bended me, turning his corner by means of my hurt, hurting me more than I had ever been hurt in my life, and at the acutest point of this, as he passed, I *saw*. I understood for a moment things that I have now forgotten, things that no one could remember while retaining sanity. The angle was an obtuse angle, and I remember thinking as I woke that had he made it a right or acute angle, I should have both suffered and 'seen' still more, and should probably have died.

"He went on and I came to. In that moment the whole of my life passed before me, including each little meaningless piece of distress, and I *understood* them. *This* was what it had all meant, *this* was the piece of work it had all been contributing to do. I did not see God's purpose, I only saw his intentness and his entire relentlessness towards his means. He thought no more of me than a man thinks of hurting a cork when he is opening wine, or hurting a cartridge when he is firing. And yet, on waking, my first feeling was, and it came with tears, 'Domine non sum digna,' for I had been lifted into a position for which I was too small. I realized that in that half hour under ether I had served God more distinctly and purely than I had ever done in my life before, or than I am capable of desiring to do. I was the means of his achieving and revealing something, I know not what or to whom, and that, to the exact extent of my capacity for suffering.

"While regaining consciousness, I wondered why, since I had gone so deep, I had seen nothing of what the saints call the *love* of God, nothing but his relentlessness. And then I heard an answer, which I could only just catch, saying, 'Knowledge and Love are One, and the *measure* is suffering'—I give the words as they came to me. With that I came finally to (into what seemed a dream world compared with the reality of what I was leaving), and I saw that what would be called the 'cause' of my experience was a slight operation under insufficient ether, in a bed pushed up against a window, a common city window in a common city street. If I had to formulate a few of the things I then caught a glimpse of, they would run somewhat as follows:—

"The eternal necessity of suffering and its eternal vicariousness. The veiled and incommunicable nature of the worst sufferings;—the passivity of genius, how it is essentially instrumental and defenseless, moved, not moving, it must do what it does;—the impossibility of discovery without its price;—finally, the excess of what the suffering 'seer' or genius pays over what his generation gains. (He seems like one who sweats his life out to earn enough to save a district from famine, and just as he staggers back, dying and satisfied, bringing a lac of rupees to buy grain with, God lifts the lac away, dropping *one* rupee, and says, 'That you may give them. That you have earned for them. The rest is for ME.') I perceived also in a way never to be forgotten, the excess of what we see over what we can demonstrate. "And so on!—these things may seem to you delusions, or truisms; but for me they are dark truths, and the power to put them into even such words as these has been given me by an ether dream."

"I know," writes Mr. Trine, "an officer on our police force who has told me that many times when off duty, and on his way home in the evening, there comes to him such a vivid and vital realization of his oneness with this Infinite Power, and this Spirit of Infinite Peace so takes hold of and so fills him, that it seems as if his feet could hardly keep to the pavement, so buoyant and so exhilarated does he become by reason of this inflowing tide."[227]

Certain aspects of nature seem to have a peculiar power of awakening such mystical moods.[228] Most of the striking cases which I have collected have occurred out of doors. Literature has commemorated this fact in many passages of great beauty—this extract, for example, from Amiel's Journal Intime:—

> "Shall I ever again have any of those prodigious reveries which sometimes came to me in former days? One day, in youth, at sunrise, sitting in the ruins of the castle of Faucigny; and again in the mountains, under the noonday sun, above Lavey, lying at the foot of a tree and visited by three butterflies; once more at night upon the shingly shore of the Northern Ocean, my back upon the sand and my vision ranging through the milky way;—such grand and spacious, immortal, cosmogonic reveries, when one reaches to the stars, when one owns the infinite! Moments divine, ecstatic hours; in which our thought flies from world to world, pierces the great enigma, breathes with a respiration broad, tranquil, and deep as the respiration of the ocean, serene and limitless as the blue firmament; . . . instants of irresistible intuition in which one feels one's self great as the universe, and calm as a god. . . . What hours, what memories! The vestiges

227 In Tune with the Infinite, p. 137.

228 The larger God may then swallow up the smaller one. I take this from Starbuck's manuscript collection:—

"I never lost the consciousness of the presence of God until I stood at the foot of the Horseshoe Falls, Niagara. Then I lost him in the immensity of what I saw. I also lost myself, feeling that I was an atom too small for the notice of Almighty God."

I subjoin another similar case from Starbuck's collection:—

"In that time the consciousness of God's nearness came to me sometimes. I say God, to describe what is indescribable. A presence, I might say, yet that is too suggestive of personality, and the moments of which I speak did not hold the consciousness of a personality, but something in myself made me feel myself a part of something bigger than I, that was controlling. I felt myself one with the grass, the trees, birds, insects, everything in Nature. I exulted in the mere fact of existence, of being a part of it all—the drizzling rain, the shadows of the clouds, the tree-trunks, and so on. In the years following, such moments continued to come, but I wanted them constantly. I knew so well the satisfaction of losing self in a perception of supreme power and love, that I was unhappy because that perception was not constant." The cases quoted in my third lecture are still better ones of this type. In her essay, The Loss of Personality, in The Atlantic Monthly (vol. lxxxv, p. 195), Miss Ethel D. Puffer explains that the vanishing of the sense of self, and the feeling of immediate unity with the object, is due to the disappearance, in these rapturous experiences, of the motor adjustments which habitually intermediate between the constant background of consciousness (which is the Self) and the object in the foreground, whatever it may be. I must refer the reader to the highly instructive article, which seems to me to throw light upon the psychological conditions, though it fails to account for the rapture or the revelation-value of the experience in the Subject's eyes.

they leave behind are enough to fill us with belief and enthusiasm, as if they were visits of the Holy Ghost."[229]

Here is a similar record from the memoirs of that interesting German idealist, Malwida von Meysenbug:—

"I was alone upon the seashore as all these thoughts flowed over me, liberating and reconciling; and now again, as once before in distant days in the Alps of Dauphiné, I was impelled to kneel down, this time before the illimitable ocean, symbol of the Infinite. I felt that I prayed as I had never prayed before, and knew now what prayer really is: to return from the solitude of individuation into the consciousness of unity with all that is, to kneel down as one that passes away, and to rise up as one imperishable. Earth, heaven, and sea resounded as in one vast world-encircling harmony. It was as if the chorus of all the great who had ever lived were about me. I felt myself one with them, and it appeared as if I heard their greeting: 'Thou too belongest to the company of those who overcome.'"[230]

The well known passage from Walt Whitman is a classical expression of this sporadic type of mystical experience.

"I believe in you, my Soul . . .
Loaf with me on the grass, loose the stop from your throat; . . .
Only the lull I like, the hum of your valved voice.
I mind how once we lay, such a transparent summer morning.
Swiftly arose and spread around me the peace and knowledge that pass all the argument of the earth,
And I know that the hand of God is the promise of my own,
And I know that the spirit of God is the brother of my own,
And that all the men ever born are also my brothers and the women my sisters and lovers,
And that a kelson of the creation is love."[231]

---

229 Op. cit., i. 43–44.

230 Memoiren einer Idealistin, 5te Auflage, 1900, iii. 166. For years she had been unable to pray, owing to materialistic belief.

231 Whitman in another place expresses in a quieter way what was probably with him a chronic mystical perception: "There is," he writes, "apart from mere intellect, in the make-up of every superior human identity, a wondrous something that realizes without argument, frequently without what is called education (though I think it the goal and apex of all education deserving the name), an intuition of the absolute balance, in time and space, of the whole of this multifariousness, this revel of fools, and incredible make-believe and general unsettledness, we call *the world;* a soul-sight of that divine clue and unseen thread which holds the whole congeries of things, all history and time, and all events, however trivial, however momentous, like a leashed dog in the hand of the hunter. [Of] such soul-sight and root-centre for the mind mere optimism explains only the surface." Whitman charges it against Carlyle that he lacked this perception. Specimen Days and Collect, Philadelphia, 1882, p. 174.

I could easily give more instances, but one will suffice. I take it from the Autobiography of J. Trevor.[232]

"One brilliant Sunday morning, my wife and boys went to the Unitarian Chapel in Macclesfield. I felt it impossible to accompany them—as though to leave the sunshine on the hills, and go down there to the chapel, would be for the time an act of spiritual suicide. And I felt such need for new inspiration and expansion in my life. So, very reluctantly and sadly, I left my wife and boys to go down into the town, while I went further up into the hills with my stick and my dog. In the loveliness of the morning, and the beauty of the hills and valleys, I soon lost my sense of sadness and regret. For nearly an hour I walked along the road to the 'Cat and Fiddle,' and then returned. On the way back, suddenly, without warning, I felt that I was in Heaven—an inward state of peace and joy and assurance indescribably intense, accompanied with a sense of being bathed in a warm glow of light, as though the external condition had brought about the internal effect— a feeling of having passed beyond the body, though the scene around me stood out more clearly and as if nearer to me than before, by reason of the illumination in the midst of which I seemed to be placed. This deep emotion lasted, though with decreasing strength, until I reached home, and for some time after, only gradually passing away.

The writer adds that having had further experiences of a similar sort, he now knows them well.

"The spiritual life," he writes, "justifies itself to those who live it; but what can we say to those who do not understand? This, at least, we can say, that it is a life whose experiences are proved real to their possessor, because they remain with him when brought closest into contact with the objective realities of life. Dreams cannot stand this test. We wake from them to find that they are but dreams. Wanderings of an overwrought brain do not stand this test. These highest experiences that I have had of God's presence have been rare and brief—flashes of consciousness which have compelled me to exclaim with surprise—God is *here*!—or conditions of exaltation and insight, less intense, and only gradually passing away. I have severely questioned the worth of these moments. To no soul have I named them, lest I should be building my life and work on mere phantasies of the brain. But I find that, after every questioning and test, they stand out to-day as the most real experiences of my life, and experiences which have explained and justified and unified all past experiences and all past growth. Indeed, their reality and their far-reaching significance are ever becoming more clear and evident. When they came, I was living the fullest, strongest, sanest, deepest life. I was not seeking them. What I was seeking, with resolute determination, was to live more intensely my own life, as against what I knew would be the adverse judgment of the world. It was in the most real seasons that the Real

232 My Quest for God, London, 1897, pp. 268, 269, abridged.

Presence came, and I was aware that I was immersed in the infinite ocean of God."[233]

Even the least mystical of you must by this time be convinced of the existence of mystical moments as states of consciousness of an entirely specific quality, and of the deep impression which they make on those who have them. A Canadian psychiatrist, Dr. R. M. Bucke, gives to the more distinctly characterized of these phenomena the name of cosmic consciousness. "Cosmic consciousness in its more striking instances is not," Dr. Bucke says, "simply an expansion or extension of the self-conscious mind with which we are all familiar, but the superaddition of a function as distinct from any possessed by the average man as *self*-consciousness is distinct from any function possessed by one of the higher animals."

> "The prime characteristic of cosmic consciousness is a consciousness of the cosmos, that is, of the life and order of the universe. Along with the consciousness of the cosmos there occurs an intellectual enlightenment which alone would place the individual on a new plane of existence—would make him almost a member of a new species. To this is added a state of moral exaltation, an indescribable feeling of elevation, elation, and joyousness, and a quickening of the moral sense, which is fully as striking, and more important than is the enhanced intellectual power. With these come what may be called a sense of immortality, a consciousness of eternal life, not a conviction that he shall have this, but the consciousness that he has it already."[234]

It was Dr. Bucke's own experience of a typical onset of cosmic consciousness in his own person which led him to investigate it in others. He has printed his conclusions in a highly interesting volume, from which I take the following account of what occurred to him:—

> "I had spent the evening in a great city, with two friends, reading and discussing poetry and philosophy. We parted at midnight. I had a long drive in a hansom to my lodging. My mind, deeply under the influence of the ideas, images, and emotions called up by the reading and talk, was calm and peaceful. I was in a state of quiet, almost passive enjoyment, not actually thinking, but letting ideas, images, and emotions flow of themselves, as it were, through my mind. All at once, without warning of any kind, I found myself wrapped in a flame-colored cloud. For an instant I thought of fire, an immense conflagration somewhere close by in that great city; the next, I knew that the fire was within myself. Directly afterward there came upon me a sense of exultation, of immense joyousness accompanied or immediately followed by an intellectual illumination impossible to describe. Among other things, I did not merely come to believe, but I saw that the universe is not composed of dead matter, but is, on the contrary,

233 Op. cit., pp. 256, 257, abridged.

234 Cosmic Consciousness: a study in the evolution of the human Mind, Philadelphia, 1901, p. 2.

a living Presence; I became conscious in myself of eternal life. It was not a conviction that I would have eternal life, but a consciousness that I possessed eternal life then; I saw that all men are immortal; that the cosmic order is such that without any peradventure all things work together for the good of each and all; that the foundation principle of the world, of all the worlds, is what we call love, and that the happiness of each and all is in the long run absolutely certain. The vision lasted a few seconds and was gone; but the memory of it and the sense of the reality of what it taught has remained during the quarter of a century which has since elapsed. I knew that what the vision showed was true. I had attained to a point of view from which I saw that it must be true. That view, that conviction, I may say that consciousness, has never, even during periods of the deepest depression, been lost."[235]

We have now seen enough of this cosmic or mystic consciousness, as it comes sporadically. We must next pass to its methodical cultivation as an element of the religious life. Hindus, Buddhists, Mohammedans, and Christians all have cultivated it methodically.

In India, training in mystical insight has been known from time immemorial under the name of yoga. Yoga means the experimental union of the individual with the divine. It is based on persevering exercise; and the diet, posture, breathing, intellectual concentration, and moral discipline vary slightly in the different systems which teach it. The yogi, or disciple, who has by these means overcome the obscurations of his lower nature sufficiently, enters into the condition termed *samâdhi*, "and comes face to face with facts which no instinct or reason can ever know." He learns—

"That the mind itself has a higher state of existence, beyond reason, a superconscious state, and that when the mind gets to that higher state, then this knowledge beyond reasoning comes. . . . All the different steps in yoga are intended to bring us scientifically to the superconscious state or Samâdhi. . . . Just as unconscious work is beneath consciousness, so there is another work which is above consciousness, and which, also, is not accompanied with the feeling of egoism. . . . There is no feeling *I*, and yet the mind works, desireless, free from restlessness, objectless, bodiless. Then the Truth shines in its full effulgence, and we know ourselves—for Samâdhi lies potential in us all—for what we truly are, free, immortal, omnipotent, loosed from the finite, and its contrasts of good and evil altogether, and identical with the Atman or Universal Soul."[236]

The Vedantists say that one may stumble into superconsciousness sporadically, without the previous discipline, but it is then impure. Their test of its purity, like our

235 Loc. cit., pp. 7, 8. My quotation follows the privately printed pamphlet which preceded Dr. Bucke's larger work, and differs verbally a little from the text of the latter.

236 My quotations are from Vivekananda, Raja Yoga, London, 1896. The completest source of information on Yoga is the work translated by Vihari Lala Mitra: Yoga Vasishta Maha Ramayana, 4 vols. Calcutta, 1891–99.

test of religion's value, is empirical: its fruits must be good for life. When a man comes out of Samâdhi, they assure us that he remains "enlightened, a sage, a prophet, a saint, his whole character changed, his life changed, illumined."[237]

The Buddhists used the word "samâdhi" as well as the Hindus; but "dhyâna" is their special word for higher states of contemplation. There seem to be four stages recognized in dhyâna. The first stage comes through concentration of the mind upon one point. It excludes desire, but not discernment or judgment: it is still intellectual. In the second stage the intellectual functions drop off, and the satisfied sense of unity remains. In the third stage the satisfaction departs, and indifference begins, along with memory and self-consciousness. In the fourth stage the indifference, memory, and self-consciousness are perfected. [Just what "memory" and "self-consciousness" mean in this connection is doubtful. They cannot be the faculties familiar to us in the lower life.] Higher stages still of contemplation are mentioned—a region where there exists nothing, and where the mediator says: "There exists absolutely nothing," and stops. Then he reaches another region where he says: "There are neither ideas nor absence of ideas," and stops again. Then another region where, "having reached the end of both idea and perception, he stops finally." This would seem to be, not yet Nirvâna, but as close an approach to it as this life affords.[238]

In the Mohammedan world the Sufi sect and various dervish bodies are the possessors of the mystical tradition. The Sufis have existed in Persia from the earliest times, and as their pantheism is so at variance with the hot and rigid monotheism of the Arab mind, it has been suggested that Sufism must have been inoculated into Islam by Hindu influences. We Christians know little of Sufism, for its secrets are disclosed only to those initiated. To give its existence a certain liveliness in your minds, I will quote a Moslem document, and pass away from the subject.

Al-Ghazzali, a Persian philosopher and theologian, who flourished in the eleventh century, and ranks as one of the greatest doctors of the Moslem church, has left us one of the few autobiographies to be found outside of Christian literature. Strange that a species of book so abundant among ourselves should be so little represented elsewhere—the absence of strictly personal confessions is the chief difficulty to the purely literary student who would like to become acquainted with the inwardness of religions other than the Christian.

M. Schmölders has translated a part of Al-Ghazzali's autobiography into French:[239]—

237 A European witness, after carefully comparing the results of Yoga with those of the hypnotic or dreamy states artificially producible by us, says: "It makes of its true disciples good, healthy, and happy men. . . . Through the mastery which the yogi attains over his thoughts and his body, he grows into a 'character.' By the subjection of his impulses and propensities to his will, and the fixing of the latter upon the ideal of goodness, he becomes a 'personality' hard to influence by others, and thus almost the opposite of what we usually imagine a 'medium' so-called, or 'psychic subject' to be." Karl Kellner: Yoga: Eine Skizze, München, 1896, p. 21.

238 I follow the account in C. F. Koeppen: Die Religion des Buddha, Berlin, 1857, i. 585 ff.

239 For a full account of him, see D. B. Macdonald: The Life of Al-Ghazzali, in the Journal of the

"The Science of the Sufis," says the Moslem author, "aims at detaching the heart from all that is not God, and at giving to it for sole occupation the meditation of the divine being. Theory being more easy for me than practice, I read [certain books] until I understood all that can be learned by study and hearsay. Then I recognized that what pertains most exclusively to their method is just what no study can grasp, but only transport, ecstasy, and the transformation of the soul. How great, for example, is the difference between knowing the definitions of health, of satiety, with their causes and conditions, and being really healthy or filled. How different to know in what drunkenness consists—as being a state occasioned by a vapor that rises from the stomach—and *being* drunk effectively. Without doubt, the drunken man knows neither the definition of drunkenness nor what makes it interesting for science. Being drunk, he knows nothing; whilst the physician, although not drunk, knows well in what drunkenness consists, and what are its predisposing conditions. Similarly there is a difference between knowing the nature of abstinence, and *being* abstinent or having one's soul detached from the world.—Thus I had learned what words could teach of Sufism, but what was left could be learned neither by study nor through the ears, but solely by giving one's self up to ecstasy and leading a pious life.

"Reflecting on my situation, I found myself tied down by a multitude of bonds—temptations on every side. Considering my teaching, I found it was impure before God. I saw myself struggling with all my might to achieve glory and to spread my name. [Here follows an account of his six months' hesitation to break away from the conditions of his life at Bagdad, at the end of which he fell ill with a paralysis of the tongue.] Then, feeling my own weakness, and having entirely given up my own will, I repaired to God like a man in distress who has no more resources. He answered, as he answers the wretch who invokes him. My heart no longer felt any difficulty in renouncing glory, wealth, and my children. So I quitted Bagdad, and reserving from my fortune only what was indispensable for my subsistence, I distributed the rest. I went to Syria, where I remained about two years, with no other occupation than living in retreat and solitude, conquering my desires, combating my passions, training myself to purify my soul, to make my character perfect, to prepare my heart for meditating on God—all according to the methods of the Sufis, as I had read of them.

"This retreat only increased my desire to live in solitude, and to complete the purification of my heart and fit it for meditation. But the vicissitudes of the times, the affairs of the family, the need of subsistence, changed in some respects my primitive resolve, and interfered with my plans for a purely solitary life. I had never yet found myself completely in ecstasy, save in a few single hours; nevertheless, I kept the hope of attaining this state. Every time that the accidents led me astray, I sought to return; and in this situation I spent ten years. During this solitary state things were revealed to me which it is impossible either to describe or to point out. I recognized for certain that the Sufis are assuredly walking in the path of God. Both in their acts and in their inaction, whether internal or external, they are illumined by the light which proceeds from the prophetic

American Oriental Society, 1899, vol. xx., p. 71.

source. The first condition for a Sufi is to purge his heart entirely of all that is not God. The next key of the contemplative life consists in the humble prayers which escape from the fervent soul, and in the meditations on God in which the heart is swallowed up entirely. But in reality this is only the beginning of the Sufi life, the end of Sufism being total absorption in God. The intuitions and all that precede are, so to speak, only the threshold for those who enter. From the beginning, revelations take place in so flagrant a shape that the Sufis see before them, whilst wide awake, the angels and the souls of the prophets. They hear their voices and obtain their favors. Then the transport rises from the perception of forms and figures to a degree which escapes all expression, and which no man may seek to give an account of without his words involving sin.

"Whosoever has had no experience of the transport knows of the true nature of prophetism nothing but the name. He may meanwhile be sure of its existence, both by experience and by what he hears the Sufis say. As there are men endowed only with the sensitive faculty who reject what is offered them in the way of objects of the pure understanding, so there are intellectual men who reject and avoid the things perceived by the prophetic faculty. A blind man can understand nothing of colors save what he has learned by narration and hearsay. Yet God has brought prophetism near to men in giving them all a state analogous to it in its principal characters. This state is sleep. If you were to tell a man who was himself without experience of such a phenomenon that there are people who at times swoon away so as to resemble dead men, and who [in dreams] yet perceive things that are hidden, he would deny it [and give his reasons]. Nevertheless, his arguments would be refuted by actual experience. Wherefore, just as the understanding is a stage of human life in which an eye opens to discern various intellectual objects uncomprehended by sensation; just so in the prophetic the sight is illumined by a light which uncovers hidden things and objects which the intellect fails to reach. The chief properties of prophetism are perceptible only during the transport, by those who embrace the Sufi life. The prophet is endowed with qualities to which you possess nothing analogous, and which consequently you cannot possibly understand. How should you know their true nature, since one knows only what one can comprehend? But the transport which one attains by the method of the Sufis is like an immediate perception, as if one touched the objects with one's hand."[240]

This incommunicableness of the transport is the keynote of all mysticism. Mystical truth exists for the individual who has the transport, but for no one else. In this, as I have said, it resembles the knowledge given to us in sensations more than that given by conceptual thought. Thought, with its remoteness and abstractness, has often enough in the history of philosophy been contrasted unfavorably with sensation. It is a commonplace of metaphysics that God's knowledge cannot be discursive but must be intuitive, that is, must be constructed more after the pattern

240 A. Schmölders: Essai sur les écoles philosophiques chez les Arabes, Paris, 1842, pp. 54–68, abridged.

of what in ourselves is called immediate feeling, than after that of proposition and judgment. But *our* immediate feelings have no content but what the five senses supply; and we have seen and shall see again that mystics may emphatically deny that the senses play any part in the very highest type of knowledge which their transports yield.

In the Christian church there have always been mystics. Although many of them have been viewed with suspicion, some have gained favor in the eyes of the authorities. The experiences of these have been treated as precedents, and a codified system of mystical theology has been based upon them, in which everything legitimate finds its place.[241] The basis of the system is "orison" or meditation, the methodical elevation of the soul towards God. Through the practice of orison the higher levels of mystical experience may be attained. It is odd that Protestantism, especially evangelical Protestantism, should seemingly have abandoned everything methodical in this line. Apart from what prayer may lead to, Protestant mystical experience appears to have been almost exclusively sporadic. It has been left to our mind-curers to reintroduce methodical meditation into our religious life.

The first thing to be aimed at in orison is the mind's detachment from outer sensations, for these interfere with its concentration upon ideal things. Such manuals as Saint Ignatius's Spiritual Exercises recommend the disciple to expel sensation by a graduated series of efforts to imagine holy scenes. The acme of this kind of discipline would be a semi-hallucinatory mono-ideism—an imaginary figure of Christ, for example, coming fully to occupy the mind. Sensorial images of this sort, whether literal or symbolic, play an enormous part in mysticism.[242] But in certain cases imagery may fall away entirely, and in the very highest raptures it tends to do so. The state of consciousness becomes then insusceptible of any verbal description. Mystical teachers are unanimous as to this. Saint John of the Cross, for instance, one of the best of them, thus describes the condition called the "union of love," which, he says, is reached by "dark contemplation." In this the Deity compenetrates the soul, but in such a hidden way that the soul—

> "finds no terms, no means, no comparison whereby to render the sublimity of the wisdom and the delicacy of the spiritual feeling with which she is filled.... We receive this mystical knowledge of God clothed in none of the kinds of images, in none of the sensible representations, which our mind makes use of in other circumstances. Accordingly in this knowledge, since the senses and the

---

241 GÖRRES's Christliche Mystik gives a full account of the facts. So does RIBET's Mystique Divine, 2 vols., Paris, 1890. A still more methodical modern work is the Mystica Theologia of Vallgornera, 2 vols., Turin, 1890.

242 M. RÉCÉJAC, in a recent volume, makes them essential. Mysticism he defines as "the tendency to draw near to the Absolute morally, *and by the aid of Symbols.*" See his Fondements de la Connaissance mystique, Paris, 1897, p. 66. But there are unquestionably mystical conditions in which sensible symbols play no part.

imagination are not employed, we get neither form nor impression, nor can we give any account or furnish any likeness, although the mysterious and sweet-tasting wisdom comes home so clearly to the inmost parts of our soul. Fancy a man seeing a certain kind of thing for the first time in his life. He can understand it, use and enjoy it, but he cannot apply a name to it, nor communicate any idea of it, even though all the while it be a mere thing of sense. How much greater will be his powerlessness when it goes beyond the senses! This is the peculiarity of the divine language. The more infused, intimate, spiritual, and supersensible it is, the more does it exceed the senses, both inner and outer, and impose silence upon them. . . . The soul then feels as if placed in a vast and profound solitude, to which no created thing has access, in an immense and boundless desert, desert the more delicious the more solitary it is. There, in this abyss of wisdom, the soul grows by what it drinks in from the well-springs of the comprehension of love, . . . and recognizes, however sublime and learned may be the terms we employ, how utterly vile, insignificant, and improper they are, when we seek to discourse of divine things by their means."[243]

I cannot pretend to detail to you the sundry stages of the Christian mystical life.[244] Our time would not suffice, for one thing; and moreover, I confess that the subdivisions and names which we find in the Catholic books seem to me to represent nothing objectively distinct. So many men, so many minds: I imagine that these experiences can be as infinitely varied as are the idiosyncrasies of individuals.

The cognitive aspects of them, their value in the way of revelation, is what we are directly concerned with, and it is easy to show by citation how strong an impression they leave of being revelations of new depths of truth. Saint Teresa is the expert of experts in describing such conditions, so I will turn immediately to what she says of one of the highest of them, the "orison of union."

"In the orison of union," says Saint Teresa, "the soul is fully awake as regards God, but wholly asleep as regards things of this world and in respect of herself. During the short time the union lasts, she is as it were deprived of every feeling, and even if she would, she could not think of any single thing. Thus she needs to employ no artifice in order to arrest the use of her understanding: it remains so stricken with inactivity that she neither knows what she loves, nor in what manner she loves, nor what she wills. In short, she is utterly dead to the things of the world and lives solely in God. . . . I do not even know whether in this state

243 Saint John of the Cross: The Dark Night of the Soul, book ii. ch. xvii., in Vie et Œuvres, 3me édition, Paris, 1893, iii. 428–432. Chapter xi. of book ii. of Saint John's Ascent of Carmel is devoted to showing the harmfulness for the mystical life of the use of sensible imagery.

244 In particular I omit mention of visual and auditory hallucinations, verbal and graphic automatisms, and such marvels as "levitation," stigmatization, and the healing of disease. These phenomena, which mystics have often presented (or are believed to have presented), have no essential mystical significance, for they occur with no consciousness of illumination whatever, when they occur, as they often do, in persons of non-mystical mind. Consciousness of illumination is for us the essential mark of "mystical" states.

she has enough life left to breathe. It seems to me she has not; or at least that if she does breathe, she is unaware of it. Her intellect would fain understand something of what is going on within her, but it has so little force now that it can act in no way whatsoever. So a person who falls into a deep faint appears as if dead. . . .

"Thus does God, when he raises a soul to union with himself, suspend the natural action of all her faculties. She neither sees, hears, nor understands, so long as she is united with God. But this time is always short, and it seems even shorter than it is. God establishes himself in the interior of this soul in such a way, that when she returns to herself, it is wholly impossible for her to doubt that she has been in God, and God in her. This truth remains so strongly impressed on her that, even though many years should pass without the condition returning, she can neither forget the favor she received, nor doubt of its reality. If you, nevertheless, ask how it is possible that the soul can see and understand that she has been in God, since during the union she has neither sight nor understanding, I reply that she does not see it then, but that she sees it clearly later, after she has returned to herself, not by any vision, but by a certitude which abides with her and which God alone can give her. I knew a person who was ignorant of the truth that God's mode of being in everything must be either by presence, by power, or by essence, but who, after having received the grace of which I am speaking, believed this truth in the most unshakable manner. So much so that, having consulted a half-learned man who was as ignorant on this point as she had been before she was enlightened, when he replied that God is in us only by 'grace,' she disbelieved his reply, so sure she was of the true answer: and when she came to ask wiser doctors, they confirmed her in her belief, which much consoled her.

"But how, you will repeat, *can* one have such certainty in respect to what one does not see? This question, I am powerless to answer. These are secrets of God's omnipotence which it does not appertain to me to penetrate. All that I know is that I tell the truth; and I shall never believe that any soul who does not possess this certainty has ever been really united to God."[245]

The kinds of truth communicable in mystical ways, whether these be sensible or supersensible, are various. Some of them relate to this world—visions of the future, the reading of hearts, the sudden understanding of texts, the knowledge of distant events, for example; but the most important revelations are theological or metaphysical.

"Saint Ignatius confessed one day to Father Laynez that a single hour of meditation at Manresa had taught him more truths about heavenly things than all the teachings of all the doctors put together could have taught him. . . . One day in orison, on the steps of the choir of the Dominican church, he saw in a distinct manner the plan of divine wisdom in the creation of the world. On another

245 The Interior Castle, Fifth Abode, ch. i., in Œuvres, translated by Bouix, iii. 421–424.

occasion, during a procession, his spirit was ravished in God, and it was given him to contemplate, in a form and images fitted to the weak understanding of a dweller on the earth, the deep mystery of the holy Trinity. This last vision flooded his heart with such sweetness, that the mere memory of it in after times made him shed abundant tears."[246]

Similarly with Saint Teresa. "One day, being in orison," she writes, "it was granted me to perceive in one instant how all things are seen and contained in God. I did not perceive them in their proper form, and nevertheless the view I had of them was of a sovereign clearness, and has remained vividly impressed upon my soul. It is one of the most signal of all the graces which the Lord has granted me. . . . The view was so subtile and delicate that the understanding cannot grasp it."[247]

She goes on to tell how it was as if the Deity were an enormous and sovereignly limpid diamond, in which all our actions were contained in such a way that their full sinfulness appeared evident as never before. On another day, she relates, while she was reciting the Athanasian Creed—

"Our Lord made me comprehend in what way it is that one God can be in three persons. He made me see it so clearly that I remained as extremely surprised as I was comforted, . . . and now, when I think of the holy Trinity, or hear It spoken of, I understand how the three adorable Persons form only one God and I experience an unspeakable happiness."

---

246 BARTOLI-MICHEL: Vie de Saint Ignace de Loyola, i. 34–36. Others have had illuminations about the created world, Jacob Boehme, for instance. At the age of twenty-five he was "surrounded by the divine light, and replenished with the heavenly knowledge; insomuch as going abroad into the fields to a green, at Görlitz, he there sat down, and viewing the herbs and grass of the field, in his inward light he saw into their essences, use, and properties, which was discovered to him by their lineaments, figures, and signatures." Of a later period of experience he writes: "In one quarter of an hour I saw and knew more than if I had been many years together at an university. For I saw and knew the being of all things, the Byss and the Abyss, and the eternal generation of the holy Trinity, the descent and original of the world and of all creatures through the divine wisdom. I knew and saw in myself all the three worlds, the external and visible world being of a procreation or extern birth from both the internal and spiritual worlds; and I saw and knew the whole working essence, in the evil and in the good, and the mutual original and existence; and likewise how the fruitful bearing womb of eternity brought forth. So that I did not only greatly wonder at it, but did also exceedingly rejoice, albeit I could very hardly apprehend the same in my external man and set it down with the pen. For I had a thorough view of the universe as in a chaos, wherein all things are couched and wrapt up, but it was impossible for me to explicate the same." Jacob Behmen's Theosophic Philosophy, etc., by Edward Taylor, London, 1691, pp. 425, 427, abridged. So George Fox: "I was come up to the state of Adam in which he was before he fell. The creation was opened to me; and it was showed me, how all things had their names given to them, according to their nature and virtue. I was at a stand in my mind, whether I should practice physic for the good of mankind, seeing the nature and virtues of the creatures were so opened to me by the Lord." Journal, Philadelphia, no date, p. 69. Contemporary "Clairvoyance" abounds in similar revelations. Andrew Jackson Davis's cosmogonies, for example, or certain experiences related in the delectable "Reminiscences and Memories of Henry Thomas Butterworth," Lebanon, Ohio, 1886.

247 Vie, pp. 581, 582.

On still another occasion, it was given to Saint Teresa to see and understand in what wise the Mother of God had been assumed into her place in Heaven.[248]

The deliciousness of some of these states seems to be beyond anything known in ordinary consciousness. It evidently involves organic sensibilities, for it is spoken of as something too extreme to be borne, and as verging on bodily pain.[249] But it is too subtle and piercing a delight for ordinary words to denote. God's touches, the wounds of his spear, references to ebriety and to nuptial union have to figure in the phraseology by which it is shadowed forth. Intellect and senses both swoon away in these highest states of ecstasy. "If our understanding comprehends," says Saint Teresa, "it is in a mode which remains unknown to it, and it can understand nothing of what it comprehends. For my own part, I do not believe that it does comprehend, because, as I said, it does not understand itself to do so. I confess that it is all a mystery in which I am lost."[250] In the condition called *raptus* or ravishment by theologians, breathing and circulation are so depressed that it is a question among the doctors whether the soul be or be not temporarily dissevered from the body. One must read Saint Teresa's descriptions and the very exact distinctions which she makes, to persuade one's self that one is dealing, not with imaginary experiences, but with phenomena which, however rare, follow perfectly definite psychological types.

To the medical mind these ecstasies signify nothing but suggested and imitated hypnoid states, on an intellectual basis of superstition, and a corporeal one of degeneration and hysteria. Undoubtedly these pathological conditions have existed in many and possibly in all the cases, but that fact tells us nothing about the value for knowledge of the consciousness which they induce. To pass a spiritual judgment upon these states, we must not content ourselves with superficial medical talk, but inquire into their fruits for life.

Their fruits appear to have been various. Stupefaction, for one thing, seems not to have been altogether absent as a result. You may remember the helplessness in the kitchen and schoolroom of poor Margaret Mary Alacoque. Many other ecstatics would have perished but for the care taken of them by admiring followers. The "otherworldliness" encouraged by the mystical consciousness makes this over-abstraction from practical life peculiarly liable to befall mystics in whom the character is naturally passive and the intellect feeble; but in natively strong minds and characters we find quite opposite results. The great Spanish mystics, who carried the habit of ecstasy as far as it has often been carried, appear for the most part to have shown indomitable spirit and energy, and all the more so for the trances in which they indulged.

248 Loc. cit., p. 574.
249 Saint Teresa discriminates between pain in which the body has a part and pure spiritual pain (Interior Castle, 6th Abode, ch. xi.). As for the bodily part in these celestial joys, she speaks of it as "penetrating to the marrow of the bones, whilst earthly pleasures affect only the surface of the senses. I think," she adds, "that this is a just description, and I cannot make it better." Ibid., 5th Abode, ch. i.
250 Vie, p. 198.

Saint Ignatius was a mystic, but his mysticism made him assuredly one of the most powerfully practical human engines that ever lived. Saint John of the Cross, writing of the intuitions and "touches" by which God reaches the substance of the soul, tells us that—

> "They enrich it marvelously. A single one of them may be sufficient to abolish at a stroke certain imperfections of which the soul during its whole life had vainly tried to rid itself, and to leave it adorned with virtues and loaded with supernatural gifts. A single one of these intoxicating consolations may reward it for all the labors undergone in its life—even were they numberless. Invested with an invincible courage, filled with an impassioned desire to suffer for its God, the soul then is seized with a strange torment—that of not being allowed to suffer enough."[251]

Saint Teresa is as emphatic, and much more detailed. You may perhaps remember a passage I quoted from her in my first lecture. There are many similar pages in her autobiography. Where in literature is a more evidently veracious account of the formation of a new centre of spiritual energy, than is given in her description of the effects of certain ecstasies which in departing leave the soul upon a higher level of emotional excitement?

> "Often, infirm and wrought upon with dreadful pains before the ecstasy, the soul emerges from it full of health and admirably disposed for action . . . as if God had willed that the body itself, already obedient to the soul's desires, should share in the soul's happiness. . . . The soul after such a favor is animated with a degree of courage so great that if at that moment its body should be torn to pieces for the cause of God, it would feel nothing but the liveliest comfort. Then it is that promises and heroic resolutions spring up in profusion in us, soaring desires, horror of the world, and the clear perception of our proper nothingness. . . . What empire is comparable to that of a soul who, from this sublime summit to which God has raised her, sees all the things of earth beneath her feet, and is captivated by no one of them? How ashamed she is of her former attachments! How amazed at her blindness! What lively pity she feels for those whom she recognizes still shrouded in the darkness! . . . She groans at having ever been sensitive to points of honor, at the illusion that made her ever see as honor what the world calls by that name. Now she sees in this name nothing more than an immense lie of which the world remains a victim. She discovers, in the new light from above, that in genuine honor there is nothing spurious, that to be faithful to this honor is to give our respect to what deserves to be respected really, and to consider as nothing, or as less than nothing, whatsoever perishes and is not agreeable to God. . . . She laughs when she sees grave persons, persons of orison, caring for points of honor for which she now feels profoundest contempt. It is suitable to the dignity of their rank to act thus, they pretend, and it makes them

251 Œuvres, ii. 320.

more useful to others. But she knows that in despising the dignity of their rank for the pure love of God they would do more good in a single day than they would effect in ten years by preserving it. . . . She laughs at herself that there should ever have been a time in her life when she made any case of money, when she ever desired it. . . . Oh! if human beings might only agree together to regard it as so much useless mud, what harmony would then reign in the world! With what friendship we would all treat each other if our interest in honor and in money could but disappear from earth! For my own part, I feel as if it would be a remedy for all our ills."[252]

Mystical conditions may, therefore, render the soul more energetic in the lines which their inspiration favors. But this could be reckoned an advantage only in case the inspiration were a true one. If the inspiration were erroneous, the energy would be all the more mistaken and misbegotten. So we stand once more before that problem of truth which confronted us at the end of the lectures on saintliness. You will remember that we turned to mysticism precisely to get some light on truth. Do mystical states establish the truth of those theological affections in which the saintly life has its root?

In spite of their repudiation of articulate self-description, mystical states in general assert a pretty distinct theoretic drift. It is possible to give the outcome of the majority of them in terms that point in definite philosophical directions. One of these directions is optimism, and the other is monism. We pass into mystical states from out of ordinary consciousness as from a less into a more, as from a smallness into a vastness, and at the same time as from an unrest to a rest. We feel them as reconciling, unifying states. They appeal to the yes-function more than to the no-function in us. In them the unlimited absorbs the limits and peacefully closes the account. Their very denial of every adjective you may propose as applicable to the ultimate truth—He, the Self, the Atman, is to be described by "No! no!" only, say the Upanishads[253]—though it seems on the surface to be a no-function, is a denial made on behalf of a deeper yes. Whoso calls the Absolute anything in particular, or says that it is *this*, seems implicitly to shut it off from being *that*—it is as if he lessened it. So we deny the "this," negating the negation which it seems to us to imply, in the interests of the higher affirmative attitude by which we are possessed. The fountain-head of Christian mysticism is Dionysius the Areopagite. He describes the absolute truth by negatives exclusively.

"The cause of all things is neither soul nor intellect; nor has it imagination, opinion, or reason, or intelligence; nor is it reason or intelligence; nor is it spoken or thought. It is neither number, nor order, nor magnitude, nor littleness, nor equality, nor inequality, nor similarity, nor dissimilarity. It neither stands, nor moves, nor rests. . . . It is neither essence, nor eternity, nor time. Even intel-

252 Vie, pp. 229, 200, 231–233, 243.

253 MÜLLER's translation, part ii. p. 180.

lectual contact does not belong to it. It is neither science nor truth. It is not even royalty or wisdom; not one; not unity; not divinity or goodness; nor even spirit as we know it," etc., *ad libitum*.[254]

But these qualifications are denied by Dionysius, not because the truth falls short of them, but because it so infinitely excels them. It is above them. It is *super*-lucent, *super*-splendent, *super*-essential, *super*-sublime, *super everything* that can be named. Like Hegel in his logic, mystics journey towards the positive pole of truth only by the "Methode der Absoluten Negativität."[255]

Thus come the paradoxical expressions that so abound in mystical writings. As when Eckhart tells of the still desert of the Godhead, "where never was seen difference, neither Father, Son, nor Holy Ghost, where there is no one at home, yet where the spark of the soul is more at peace than in itself."[256] As when Boehme writes of the Primal Love, that "it may fitly be compared to Nothing, for it is deeper than any Thing, and is as nothing with respect to all things, forasmuch as it is not comprehensible by any of them. And because it is nothing respectively, it is therefore free from all things, and is that only good, which a man cannot express or utter what it is, there being nothing to which it may be compared, to express it by."[257] Or as when Angelus Silesius sings:—

"Gott ist ein lauter Nichts, ihn rührt kein Nun noch Hier;
Je mehr du nach ihm greiffst, je mehr entwind er dir."[258]

To this dialectical use, by the intellect, of negation as a mode of passage towards a higher kind of affirmation, there is correlated the subtlest of moral counterparts in the sphere of the personal will. Since denial of the finite self and its wants, since asceticism of some sort, is found in religious experience to be the only doorway to the larger and more blessed life, this moral mystery intertwines and combines with the intellectual mystery in all mystical writings.

"Love," continues Behmen, is Nothing, for "when thou art gone forth wholly from the Creature and from that which is visible, and art become Nothing to all that is Nature and Creature, then thou art in that eternal One, which is God himself, and then thou shalt feel within thee the highest virtue of Love. . . . The treasure of treasures for the soul is where she goeth out of the Somewhat into that Nothing out of which all things may be made. The soul here saith, *I have nothing*, for I am utterly stripped and naked; *I can do nothing*, for I have no man-

254 T. Davidson's translation, in Journal of Speculative Philosophy, 1893, vol. xxii., p. 399.
255 "Deus propter excellentiam non immerito Nihil vocatur." Scotus Erigena, quoted by Andrew Seth: Two Lectures on Theism, New York, 1897, p. 55.
256 J. Royce: Studies in Good and Evil, p. 282.
257 Jacob Behmen's Dialogues on the Supersensual Life, translated by Bernard Holland, London, 1901, p. 48.
258 Cherubinischer Wandersmann, Strophe 25.

ner of power, but am as water poured out; *I am nothing*, for all that I am is no more than an image of Being, and only God is to me I AM; and so, sitting down in my own Nothingness, I give glory to the eternal Being, and *will nothing* of myself, that so God may will all in me, being unto me my God and all things."[259]

In Paul's language, I live, yet not I, but Christ liveth in me. Only when I become as nothing can God enter in and no difference between his life and mine remain outstanding.[260]

This overcoming of all the usual barriers between the individual and the Absolute is the great mystic achievement. In mystic states we both become one with the Absolute and we become aware of our oneness. This is the everlasting and triumphant mystical tradition, hardly altered by differences of clime or creed. In Hinduism, in Neoplatonism, in Sufism, in Christian mysticism, in Whitmanism, we find the same recurring note, so that there is about mystical utterances an eternal unanimity which ought to make a critic stop and think, and which brings it about that the mystical classics have, as has been said, neither birthday nor native land. Perpetually telling of the unity of man with God, their speech antedates languages, and they do not grow old.[261]

"That art Thou!" say the Upanishads, and the Vedantists add: "Not a part, not a mode of That, but identically That, that absolute Spirit of the World." "As pure water poured into pure water remains the same, thus, O Gautama, is the Self of a thinker who knows. Water in water, fire in fire, ether in ether, no one can distinguish them: likewise a man whose mind has entered into the Self."[262] " 'Every man,' says the Sufi Gulshan-Râz, whose heart is no longer shaken by any doubt, knows with certainty

259 Op. cit., pp. 42, 74, abridged.

260 From a French book I take this mystical expression of happiness in God's indwelling presence:—

"Jesus has come to take up his abode in my heart. It is not so much a habitation, an association, as a sort of fusion. Oh, new and blessed life! life which becomes each day more luminous. . . . The wall before me, dark a few moments since, is splendid at this hour because the sun shines on it. Wherever its rays fall they light up a conflagration of glory; the smallest speck of glass sparkles, each grain of sand emits fire; even so there is a royal song of triumph in my heart because the Lord is there. My days succeed each other; yesterday a blue sky; to-day a clouded sun; a night filled with strange dreams; but as soon as the eyes open, and I regain consciousness and seem to begin life again, it is always the same figure before me, always the same presence filling my heart. . . . Formerly the day was dulled by the absence of the Lord. I used to wake invaded by all sorts of sad impressions, and I did not find him on my path. To-day he is with me; and the light cloudiness which covers things is not an obstacle to my communion with him. I feel the pressure of his hand, I feel something else which fills me with a serene joy; shall I dare to speak it out? Yes, for it is the true expression of what I experience. The Holy Spirit is not merely making me a visit; it is no mere dazzling apparition which may from one moment to another spread its wings and leave me in my night, it is a permanent habitation. He can depart only if he takes me with him. More than that; he is not other than myself: he is one with me. It is not a juxtaposition, it is a penetration, a profound modification of my nature, a new manner of my being." Quoted from the MS. "of an old man" by WILFRED MONOD: Il Vit: six méditations sur le mystère chrétien, pp. 280–283.

261 Compare M. MAETERLINCK: L'Ornement des Noces spirituelles de Ruysbroeck, Bruxelles, 1891, Introduction, p. xix.

262 Upanishads, M. MÜLLER's translation, ii. 17, 334.

that there is no being save only One. . . . In his divine majesty the *me,* and *we,* the *thou,* are not found, for in the One there can be no distinction. Every being who is annulled and entirely separated from himself, hears resound outside of him this voice and this echo: *I am God:* he has an eternal way of existing, and is no longer subject to death.' "[263] In the vision of God, says Plotinus, "what sees is not our reason, but something prior and superior to our reason. . . . He who thus sees does not properly see, does not distinguish or imagine two things. He changes, he ceases to be himself, preserves nothing of himself. Absorbed in God, he makes but one with him, like a centre of a circle coinciding with another centre."[264] "Here," writes Suso, "the spirit dies, and yet is all alive in the marvels of the Godhead . . . and is lost in the stillness of the glorious dazzling obscurity and of the naked simple unity. It is in this modeless *where* that the highest bliss is to be found."[265] "Ich bin so gross als Gott," sings Angelus Silesius again, "Er ist als ich so klein; Er kann nicht über mich, ich unter ihm nicht sein."[266]

In mystical literature such self-contradictory phrases as "dazzling obscurity," "whispering silence," "teeming desert," are continually met with. They prove that not conceptual speech, but music rather, is the element through which we are best spoken to by mystical truth. Many mystical scriptures are indeed little more than musical compositions.

> "He who would hear the voice of Nada, 'the Soundless Sound,' and comprehend it, he has to learn the nature of Dhâranâ. . . . When to himself his form appears unreal, as do on waking all the forms he sees in dreams; when he has ceased to hear the many, he may discern the ONE—the inner sound which kills the outer. . . . For then the soul will hear, and will remember. And then to the inner ear will speak the voice of the silence. . . . And now thy *Self* is lost in self, *thyself* unto thyself, merged in that self from which thou first didst radiate. . . . Behold! thou hast become the Light, thou hast become the Sound, thou art thy Master and thy God. Thou art thyself the object of thy search: the Voice unbroken, that resounds throughout eternities, exempt from change, from sin exempt, the seven sounds in one, the voice of the silence. *Om tat Sat.*"[267]

These words, if they do not awaken laughter as you receive them, probably stir chords within you which music and language touch in common. Music gives us ontological messages which non-musical criticism is unable to contradict, though it may laugh at our foolishness in minding them. There is a verge of the mind which these things haunt; and whispers therefrom mingle with the operations of our

---

263 Schmölders: Op. cit., p. 210.

264 Enneads, Bouillier's translation. Paris, 1861, iii. 561. Compare pp. 473–477, and vol. i. p. 27.

265 Autobiography, pp. 309, 310.

266 Op. cit., Strophe 10.

267 H. P. Blavatsky: The Voice of the Silence.

understanding, even as the waters of the infinite ocean send their waves to break among the pebbles that lie upon our shores.

"Here begins the sea that ends not till the world's end. Where we stand,
Could we know the next high sea-mark set beyond these wave, that gleam,
We should know what never man hath known, nor eye of man hath scanned. . . .
Ah, but here man's heart leaps, yearning towards the gloom with venturous glee,
From the shore that hath no shore beyond it, set in all the sea."[268]

That doctrine, for example, that eternity is timeless, that our "immortality," if we live in the eternal, is not so much future as already now and here, which we find so often expressed to-day in certain philosophic circles, finds its support in a "hear, hear!" or an "amen," which floats up from that mysteriously deeper level.[269] We recognize the passwords to the mystical region as we hear them, but we cannot use them ourselves; it alone has the keeping of "the password primeval."[270]

I have now sketched with extreme brevity and insufficiency, but as fairly as I am able in the time allowed, the general traits of the mystic range of consciousness. *It is on the whole pantheistic and optimistic, or at least the opposite of pessimistic. It is anti-naturalistic, and harmonizes best with twice-bornness and so-called other-worldly states of mind.*

My next task is to inquire whether we can invoke it as authoritative. Does it furnish any *warrant for the truth* of the twice-bornness and supernaturality and pantheism which it favors? I must give my answer to this question as concisely as I can.

In brief my answer is this—and I will divide it into three parts:—

(1) Mystical states, when well developed, usually are, and have the right to be, absolutely authoritative over the individuals to whom they come.

(2) No authority emanates from them which should make it a duty for those who stand outside of them to accept their revelations uncritically.

(3) They break down the authority of the non-mystical or rationalistic consciousness, based upon the understanding and the senses alone. They show it to be only one kind of consciousness. They open out the possibility of other orders of truth, in which, so far as anything in us vitally responds to them, we may freely continue to have faith.

I will take up these points one by one.

268 Swinburne: On the Verge, in "A Midsummer Vacation."

269 Compare the extracts from Dr. Bucke, quoted on pp. 398, 399.

270 As serious an attempt as I know to mediate between the mystical region and the discursive life is contained in an article on Aristotle's Unmoved Mover, by F. C. S. Schiller, in Mind, vol. ix., 1900.

1.

As a matter of psychological fact, mystical states of a well-pronounced and emphatic sort *are* usually authoritative over those who have them.[271] They have been "there," and know. It is vain for rationalism to grumble about this. If the mystical truth that comes to a man proves to be a force that he can live by, what mandate have we of the majority to order him to live in another way? We can throw him into a prison or a madhouse, but we cannot change his mind—we commonly attach it only the more stubbornly to its beliefs.[272] It mocks our utmost efforts, as a matter of fact, and in point of logic it absolutely escapes our jurisdiction. Our own more "rational" beliefs are based on evidence exactly similar in nature to that which mystics quote for theirs. Our senses, namely, have assured us of certain states of fact; but mystical experiences are as direct perceptions of fact for those who have them as any sensations ever were for us. The records show that even though the five senses be in abeyance in them, they are absolutely sensational in their epistemological quality, if I may be pardoned the barbarous expression—that is, they are face to face presentations of what seems immediately to exist.

The mystic is, in short, *invulnerable*, and must be left, whether we relish it or not, in undisturbed enjoyment of his creed. Faith, says Tolstoy, is that by which men live. And faith-state and mystic state are practically convertible terms.

2.

But I now proceed to add that mystics have no right to claim that we ought to accept the deliverance of their peculiar experiences, if we are ourselves outsiders and feel no private call thereto. The utmost they can ever ask of us in this life is to admit that they establish a presumption. They form a consensus and have an unequivocal outcome; and it would be odd, mystics might say, if such a unanimous type of experience should prove to be altogether wrong. At bottom, however, this would only be an appeal to numbers, like the appeal of rationalism the other way; and the appeal to numbers has no logical force. If we acknowledge it, it is for "suggestive," not for logical reasons: we follow the majority because to do so suits our life.

But even this presumption from the unanimity of mystics is far from being strong. In characterizing mystic states an pantheistic, optimistic, etc., I am afraid I

271 I abstract from weaker states, and from those cases of which the books are full, where the director (but usually not the subject) remains in doubt whether the experience may not have proceeded from the demon.

272 Example: Mr. John Nelson writes of his imprisonment for preaching Methodism: "My soul was as a watered garden, and I could sing praises to God all day long; for he turned my captivity into joy, and gave me to rest as well on the boards, as if I had been on a bed of down. Now could I say, 'God's service is perfect freedom,' and I was carried out much in prayer that my enemies might drink of the same river of peace which my God gave so largely to me." Journal, London, no date, p. 172.

over-simplified the truth. I did so for expository reasons, and to keep the closer to the classic mystical tradition. The classic religious mysticism, it now must be confessed, is only a "privileged case." It is an *extract*, kept true to type by the selection of the fittest specimens and their preservation in "schools." It is carved out from a much larger mass; and if we take the larger mass as seriously as religious mysticism has historically taken itself, we find that the supposed unanimity largely disappears. To begin with, even religious mysticism itself, the kind that accumulates traditions and makes schools, is much less unanimous than I have allowed. It has been both ascetic and antinomianly self-indulgent within the Christian church.[273] It is dualistic in Sankhya, and monistic in Vedanta philosophy. I called it pantheistic; but the great Spanish mystics are anything but pantheists. They are with few exceptions non-metaphysical minds, for whom "the category of personality" is absolute. The "union" of man with God is for them much more like an occasional miracle than like an original identity.[274] How different again, apart from the happiness common to all, is the mysticism of Walt Whitman, Edward Carpenter, Richard Jefferies, and other naturalistic pantheists, from the more distinctively Christian sort.[275] The fact is that the mystical feeling of enlargement, union, and emancipation has no specific intellectual content whatever of its own. It is capable of forming matrimonial alliances with material furnished by the most diverse philosophies and theologies, provided only they can find a place in their framework for its peculiar emotional mood. We have no right, therefore, to invoke its prestige as distinctively in favor of any special belief, such as that in absolute idealism, or in the absolute monistic identity, or in the absolute goodness, of the world. It is only relatively in favor of all these things—it passes out of common human consciousness in the direction in which they lie.

So much for religious mysticism proper. But more remains to be told, for religious mysticism is only one half of mysticism. The other half has no accumulated traditions except those which the text-books on insanity supply. Open any one of these, and you will find abundant cases in which "mystical ideas" are cited as characteristic symptoms of enfeebled or deluded states of mind. In delusional insanity, paranoia, as they sometimes call it, we may have a *diabolical* mysticism, a sort of religious mysticism turned upside down. The same sense of ineffable importance in the smallest events, the same texts and words coming with new meanings, the same voices and visions and leadings and missions, the same controlling by extraneous powers; only this time the emotion is pessimistic: instead of consolations we have desolations; the meanings are dreadful; and the powers are enemies to life. It is

---

273 Ruysbroeck, in the work which Maeterlinck has translated, has a chapter against the antinomianism of disciples. H. Delacroix's book (Essai. sur le mysticisme spéculatif en Allemagne au XIVme Siècle, Paris, 1900) is full of antinomian material. Compare also A. Jundt: Les Amis de Dieu au XIV Siécle, These de Strasbourg, 1879.

274 Compare Paul Rousselot: Les Mystiques Espagnols, Paris, 1869, ch. xii.

275 See Carpenter's Towards Democracy, especially the latter parts, and Jefferies's wonderful and splendid mystic rhapsody, The Story of my Heart.

evident that from the point of view of their psychological mechanism, the classic mysticism and these lower mysticisms spring from the same mental level, from that great subliminal or transmarginal region of which science is beginning to admit the existence, but of which so little is really known. That region contains every kind of matter: "seraph and snake" abide there side by side. To come from thence is no infallible credential. What comes must be sifted and tested, and run the gauntlet of confrontation with the total context of experience, just like what comes from the outer world of sense. Its value must be ascertained by empirical methods, so long as we are not mystics ourselves.

Once more, then, I repeat that non-mystics are under no obligation to acknowledge in mystical states a superior authority conferred on them by their intrinsic nature.[276]

3.

Yet, I repeat once more, the existence of mystical states absolutely overthrows the pretension of non-mystical states to be the sole and ultimate dictators of what we may believe. As a rule, mystical states merely add a supersensuous meaning to the ordinary outward data of consciousness. They are excitements like the emotions of love or ambition, gifts to our spirit by means of which facts already objectively before us fall into a new expressiveness and make a new connection with our active life. They do not contradict these facts as such, or deny anything that our senses have immediately seized.[277] It is the rationalistic critic rather who plays the part of denier in the controversy, and his denials have no strength, for there never can be a state of facts to which new meaning may not truthfully be added, provided the mind ascend to a more enveloping point of view. It must always remain an open question whether mystical states may not possibly be such superior points of view, windows through which the mind looks out upon a more extensive and inclusive world. The difference of the views seen from the different mystical windows need not prevent us from entertaining this supposition. The wider world would in that case prove to have a mixed constitution like that of this world, that is all. It would have its celestial

---

276 In chapter i. of book ii. of his work Degeneration, "MAX NORDAU" seeks to undermine all mysticism by exposing the weakness of the lower kinds. Mysticism for him means any sudden perception of hidden significance in things. He explains such perception by the abundant uncompleted associations which experiences may arouse in a degenerate brain. These give to him who has the experience a vague and vast sense of its leading further, yet they awaken no definite or useful consequent in his thought. The explanation is a plausible one for certain sorts of feeling of significance; and other alienists (Wernicke, for example, in his Grundriss der Psychiatrie, Theil ii., Leipzig, 1896) have explained "paranoiac" conditions by a laming of the association-organ. But the higher mystical flights, with their positiveness and abruptness, are surely products of no such merely negative condition. It seems far more reasonable to ascribe them to inroads from the subconscious life, of the cerebral activity correlative to which we as yet know nothing.

277 They sometimes add subjective *audita et visa* to the facts, but as these are usually interpreted as transmundane, they oblige no alteration in the facts of sense.

and its infernal regions, its tempting and its saving moments, its valid experiences and its counterfeit ones, just as our world has them; but it would be a wider world all the same. We should have to use its experiences by selecting and subordinating and substituting just as is our custom in this ordinary naturalistic world; we should be liable to error just as we are now; yet the counting in of that wider world of meanings, and the serious dealing with it, might, in spite of all the perplexity, be indispensable stages in our approach to the final fullness of the truth.

In this shape, I think, we have to leave the subject. Mystical states indeed wield no authority due simply to their being mystical states. But the higher ones among them point in directions to which the religious sentiments even of non-mystical men incline. They tell of the supremacy of the ideal, of vastness, of union, of safety, and of rest. They offer us *hypotheses*, hypotheses which we may voluntarily ignore, but which as thinkers we cannot possibly upset. The supernaturalism and optimism to which they would persuade us may, interpreted in one way or another, be after all the truest of insights into the meaning of this life.

"Oh, the little more, and how much it is; and the little less, and what worlds away!" It may be that possibility and permission of this sort are all that are religious consciousness requires to live on. In my last lecture I shall have to try to persuade you that this is the case. Meanwhile, however, I am sure that for many of my readers this diet is too slender. If supernaturalism and inner union with the divine are true, you think, then not so much permission, as compulsion to believe, ought to be found. Philosophy has always professed to prove religious truth by coercive argument; and the construction of philosophies of this kind has always been one favorite function of the religious life, if we use this term in the large historic sense. But religious philosophy is an enormous subject, and in my next lecture I can only give that brief glance at it which my limits will allow.

## LECTURE XVIII

# Philosophy

The subject of Saintliness left us face to face with the question, Is the sense of divine presence a sense of anything objectively true? We turned first to mysticism for an answer, and found that although mysticism is entirely willing to corroborate religion, it is too private (and also too various) in its utterances to be able to claim a universal authority. But philosophy publishes results which claim to be universally valid if they are valid at all, so we now turn with our question to philosophy. Can philosophy stamp a warrant of veracity upon the religious man's sense of the divine?

I imagine that many of you at this point begin to indulge in guesses at the goal to which I am tending. I have undermined the authority of mysticism, you say, and the next thing I shall probably do is to seek to discredit that of philosophy. Religion, you expect to hear me conclude, is nothing but an affair of faith, based either on vague sentiment, or on that vivid sense of the reality of things unseen of which in my second lecture and in the lecture on Mysticism I gave so many examples. It is essentially private and individualistic; it always exceeds our powers of formulation; and although attempts to pour its contents into a philosophic mould will probably always go on, men being what they are, yet these attempts are always secondary processes which in no way add to the authority, or warrant the veracity, of the sentiments from which they derive their own stimulus and borrow whatever glow of conviction they may themselves possess. In short, you suspect that I am planning to defend feeling at the expense of reason, to rehabilitate the primitive and unreflective, and to dissuade you from the hope of any Theology worthy of the name.

To a certain extent I have to admit that you guess rightly. I do believe that feeling is the deeper source of religion, and that philosophic and theological formulas are secondary products, like translations of a text into another tongue. But all such statements are misleading from their brevity, and it will take the whole hour for me to explain to you exactly what I mean.

When I call theological formulas secondary products, I mean that in a world in which no religious feeling had ever existed, I doubt whether any philosophic theology could ever have been framed. I doubt if dispassionate intellectual contemplation of the universe, apart from inner unhappiness and need of deliverance on the one hand and mystical emotion on the other, would ever have resulted in religious philosophies such as we now possess. Men would have begun with animistic explanations of natural fact, and criticised these away into scientific ones, as they actually have done. In the science they would have left a certain amount of "psychical research," even as they now will probably have to re-admit a certain amount. But high-flying speculations like those of either dogmatic or idealistic theology, these they would have had no motive to venture on, feeling no need of commerce with such deities. These speculations must, it seems to me, be classed as over-beliefs, buildings-out performed by the intellect into directions of which feeling originally supplied the hint.

But even if religious philosophy had to have its first hint supplied by feeling, may it not have dealt in a superior way with the matter which feeling suggested? Feeling is private and dumb, and unable to give an account of itself. It allows that its results are mysteries and enigmas, declines to justify them rationally, and on occasion is willing that they should even pass for paradoxical and absurd. Philosophy takes just the opposite attitude. Her aspiration is to reclaim from mystery and paradox whatever territory she touches. To find an escape from obscure and wayward personal persuasion to truth objectively valid for all thinking men has ever been the intellect's most cherished ideal. To redeem religion from unwholesome privacy, and to give public status and universal right of way to its deliverances, has been reason's task.

I believe that philosophy will always have opportunity to labor at this task.[278] We are thinking beings, and we cannot exclude the intellect from participating in any of our functions. Even in soliloquizing with ourselves, we construe our feelings intellectually. Both our personal ideals and our religious and mystical experiences must be interpreted congruously with the kind of scenery which our thinking mind inhabits. The philosophic climate of our time inevitably forces its own clothing on us. Moreover, we must exchange our feelings with one another, and in doing so we have to speak, and to use general and abstract verbal formulas. Conceptions and constructions are thus a necessary part of our religion; and as moderator amid the clash of hypotheses, and mediator among the criticisms of one man's constructions by another, philosophy will always have much to do. It would be strange if I disputed this, when these very lectures which I am giving are (as you will see more clearly from now onwards) a laborious attempt to extract from the privacies of religious experience some general facts which can be defined in formulas upon which everybody may agree.

Religious experience, in other words, spontaneously and inevitably engenders myths, superstitions, dogmas, creeds, and metaphysical theologies, and criticisms of one set of these by the adherents of another. Of late, impartial classifications and

278 Compare Professor W. WALLACE's Gifford Lectures, in Lectures and Essays, Oxford, 1898, pp. 17 ff.

comparisons have become possible, alongside of the denunciations and anathemas by which the commerce between creeds used exclusively to be carried on. We have the beginnings of a "Science of Religions," so-called; and if these lectures could ever be accounted a crumb-like contribution to such a science, I should be made very happy.

But all these intellectual operations, whether they be constructive or comparative and critical, presuppose immediate experiences as their subject-matter. They are interpretative and inductive operations, operations after the fact, consequent upon religious feeling, not coordinate with it, not independent of what it ascertains.

The intellectualism in religion which I wish to discredit pretends to be something altogether different from this. It assumes to construct religious objects out of the resources of logical reason alone, or of logical reason drawing rigorous inference from non-subjective facts. It calls its conclusions dogmatic theology, or philosophy of the absolute, as the case may be; it does not call them science of religions. It reaches them in an *a priori* way, and warrants their veracity.

Warranted systems have ever been the idols of aspiring souls. All-inclusive, yet simple; noble, clean, luminous, stable, rigorous, true;—what more ideal refuge could there be than such a system would offer to spirits vexed by the muddiness and accidentality of the world of sensible things? Accordingly, we find inculcated in the theological schools of to-day, almost as much as in those of the fore-time, a disdain for merely possible or probable truth, and of results that only private assurance can grasp. Scholastics and idealists both express this disdain. Principal John Caird, for example, writes as follows in his Introduction to the Philosophy of Religion:—

"Religion must indeed be a thing of the heart; but in order to elevate it from the region of subjective caprice and waywardness, and to distinguish between that which is true and false in religion, we must appeal to an objective standard. That which enters the heart must first be discerned by the intelligence to be *true.* It must be seen as having in its own nature a *right* to dominate feeling, and as constituting the principle by which feeling must be judged.[279] In estimating the religious character of individuals, nations, or races, the first question is, not how they feel, but what they think and believe—not whether their religion is one which manifests itself in emotions, more or less vehement and enthusiastic, but what are the *conceptions* of God and divine things by which these emotions are called forth. Feeling is necessary in religion, but it is by the *content* or intelligent basis of a religion, and not by feeling, that its character and worth are to be determined."[280]

Cardinal Newman, in his work, The Idea of a University, gives more emphatic expression still to this disdain for sentiment.[281] Theology, he says, is a science in the

279 Op. cit., p. 174, abridged.
280 Ibid., p. 186, abridged and italicized.
281 Discourse II. § 7.

strictest sense of the word. I will tell you, he says, what it is not—not "physical evidences" for God, not "natural religion," for these are but vague subjective interpretations:—

> "If," he continues, "the Supreme Being is powerful or skillful, just so far as the telescope shows power, or the microscope shows skill, if his moral law is to be ascertained simply by the physical processes of the animal frame, or his will gathered from the immediate issues of human affairs, if his Essence is just as high and deep and broad as the universe and no more; if this be the fact, then will I confess that there is no specific science about God, that theology is but a name, and a protest in its behalf an hypocrisy. Then, pious as it is to think of Him, while the pageant of experiment or abstract reasoning passes by, still such piety is nothing more than a poetry of thought, or an ornament of language, a certain view taken of Nature which one man has and another has not, which gifted minds strike out, which others see to be admirable and ingenious, and which all would be the better for adopting. It is but the theology of Nature, just as we talk of the *philosophy* or the *romance* of history, or the *poetry* of childhood, or the picturesque or the sentimental or the humorous, or any other abstract quality which the genius or the caprice of the individual, or the fashion of the day, or the consent of the world, recognizes in any set of objects which are subjected to its contemplation. I do not see much difference between avowing that there is no God, and implying that nothing definite can be known for certain about Him."
>
> What I mean by Theology, continues Newman, is none of these things: "I simply mean the *Science of God*, or the truths we know about God, put into a system, just as we have a science of the stars and call it astronomy, or of the crust of the earth and call it geology."

In both these extracts we have the issue clearly set before us: Feeling valid only for the individual is pitted against reason valid universally. The test is a perfectly plain one of fact. Theology based on pure reason must in point of fact convince men universally. If it did not, wherein would its superiority consist? If it only formed sects and schools, even as sentiment and mysticism form them, how would it fulfill its programme of freeing us from personal caprice and waywardness? This perfectly definite practical test of the pretensions of philosophy to found religion on universal reason simplifies my procedure to-day. I need not discredit philosophy by laborious criticism of its arguments. It will suffice if I show that as a matter of history it fails to prove its pretension to be "objectively" convincing. In fact, philosophy does so fail. It does not banish differences; it founds schools and sects just as feeling does. I believe, in fact, that the logical reason of man operates in this field of divinity exactly as it has always operated in love, or in patriotism, or in politics, or in any other of the wider affairs of life, in which our passions or our mystical intuitions fix our beliefs beforehand. It finds arguments for our conviction, for indeed it *has* to find them. It amplifies and defines our faith, and dignifies it and lends it words and plausibility. It hardly ever engenders it; it cannot now secure it.[282]

Lend me your attention while I run through some of the points of the older systematic theology. You find them in both Protestant and Catholic manuals, best of all in the innumerable text-books published since Pope Leo's Encyclical recommending the study of Saint Thomas. I glance first at the arguments by which dogmatic theology establishes God's existence, after that at those by which it establishes his nature.[283]

The arguments for God's existence have stood for hundreds of years with the waves of unbelieving criticism breaking against them, never totally discrediting them in the ears of the faithful, but on the whole slowly and surely washing out the mortar from between their joints. If you have a God already whom you believe in, these arguments confirm you. If you are atheistic, they fail to set you right. The proofs are various. The "cosmological" one, so-called, reasons from the contingence of the world to a First Cause which must contain whatever perfections the world itself contains. The "argument from design" reasons, from the fact that Nature's laws are mathematical, and her parts benevolently adapted to each other, that this cause is both intellectual and benevolent. The "moral argument" is that the moral law presupposes a lawgiver. The "argument *ex consensu gentium*" is that the belief in God is so widespread as to be grounded in the rational nature of man, and should therefore carry authority with it.

As I just said, I will not discuss these arguments technically. The bare fact that all idealists since Kant have felt entitled either to scout or to neglect them shows that they are not solid enough to serve as religion's all-sufficient foundation. Absolutely impersonal reasons would be in duty bound to show more general convincingness. Causation is indeed too obscure a principle to bear the weight of the whole structure of theology. As for the argument from design, see how Darwinian ideas have revolutionized it. Conceived as we now conceive them, as so many fortunate escapes from almost limitless processes of destruction, the benevolent adaptations which we find in Nature suggest a deity very different from the one who figured in the earlier

282 As regards the secondary character of intellectual constructions, and the primacy of feeling and instinct in founding religious beliefs, see the striking work of H. Fielding, The Hearts of Men, London, 1902, which came into my hands after my text was written. "Creeds," says the author, "are the grammar of religion, they are to religion what grammar is to speech. Words are the expression of our wants; grammar is the theory formed afterwards. Speech never proceeded from grammar, but the reverse. As speech progresses and changes from unknown causes, grammar must follow" (p. 313). The whole book, which keeps unusually close to concrete facts, is little more than an amplification of this text.

283 For convenience' sake, I follow the order of A. Stöckl's Lehrbuch der Philosophie, 5te Auflage, Mainz, 1881, Band ii. B. Boedder's Natural Theology, London, 1891, is a handy English Catholic Manual; but an almost identical doctrine is given by such Protestant theologians as C. Hodge: Systematic Theology, New York, 1873, or A. H. Strong: Systematic Theology, 5th edition, New York, 1896.

versions of the argument.[284] The fact is that these arguments do but follow the combined suggestions of the facts and of our feeling. They prove nothing rigorously. They only corroborate our preëxistent partialities.

If philosophy can do so little to establish God's existence, how stands it with her efforts to define his attributes? It is worth while to look at the attempts of systematic theology in this direction.

> Since God is First Cause, this science of sciences says, he differs from all his creatures in possessing existence *a se*. From this "a-se-ity" on God's part, theology deduces by mere logic most of his other perfections. For instance, he must be both *necessary* and *absolute*, cannot not be, and cannot in any way be determined by anything else. This makes Him absolutely unlimited from without, and unlimited also from within; for limitation is non-being; and God is being

284 It must not be forgotten that any form of *dis*order in the world might, by the design argument, suggest a God for just that kind of disorder. The truth is that any state of things whatever that can be named is logically susceptible of teleological interpretation. The ruins of the earthquake at Lisbon, for example: the whole of past history had to be planned exactly as it was to bring about in the fullness of time just that particular arrangement of debris of masonry, furniture, and once living bodies. No other train of causes would have been sufficient. And so of any other arrangement, bad or good, which might as a matter of fact be found resulting anywhere from previous conditions. To avoid such pessimistic consequences and save its beneficent designer, the design argument accordingly invokes two other principles, restrictive in their operation. The first is physical: Nature's forces tend of their own accord only to disorder and destruction, to heaps of ruins, not to architecture. This principle, though plausible at first sight, seems, in the light of recent biology, to be more and more improbable. The second principle is one of anthropomorphic interpretation. No arrangement that for *us* is "disorderly" can possibly have been an object of design at all. This principle is of course a mere assumption in the interests of anthropomorphic Theism.

When one views the world with no definite theological bias one way or the other, one sees that order and disorder, as we now recognize them, are purely human inventions. We are interested in certain types of arrangement, useful, æsthetic, or moral—so interested that whenever we find them realized, the fact emphatically rivets our attention. The result is that we work over the contents of the world selectively. It is overflowing with disorderly arrangements from our point of view, but order is the only thing we care for and look at, and by choosing, one can always find some sort of orderly arrangement in the midst of any chaos. If I should throw down a thousand beans at random upon a table, I could doubtless, by eliminating a sufficient number of them, leave the rest in almost any geometrical pattern you might propose to me, and you might then say that that pattern was the thing prefigured beforehand, and that the other beans were mere irrelevance and packing material. Our dealings with Nature are just like this. She is a vast *plenum* in which our attention draws capricious lines in innumerable directions. We count and name whatever lies upon the special lines we trace, whilst the other things and the untraced lines are neither named nor counted. There are in reality infinitely more things "unadapted" to each other in this world than there are things "adapted"; infinitely more things with irregular relations than with regular relations between them. But we look for the regular kind of thing exclusively, and ingeniously discover and preserve it in our memory. It accumulates with other regular kinds, until the collection of them fills our encyclopædias. Yet all the while between and around them lies an infinite anonymous chaos of objects that no one ever thought of together, of relations that never yet attracted our attention.

The facts of order from which the physico-theological argument starts are thus easily susceptible of interpretation as arbitrary human products. So long as this is the case, although of course no argument against God follows, it follows that the argument for him will fail to constitute a knockdown proof of his existence. It will be convincing only to those who on other grounds believe in him already.

itself. This unlimitedness makes God infinitely perfect. Moreover, God is *One*, and *Only*, for the infinitely perfect can admit no peer. He is *Spiritual*, for were He composed of physical parts, some other power would have to combine them into the total, and his aseity would thus be contradicted. He is therefore both simple and non-physical in nature. He is *simple metaphysically* also, that is to say, his nature and his existence cannot be distinct, as they are in finite substances which share their formal natures with one another, and are individual only in their material aspect. Since God is one and only, his *essentia* and his *esse* must be given at one stroke. This excludes from his being all those distinctions, so familiar in the world of finite things, between potentiality and actuality, substance and accidents, being and activity, existence and attributes. We can talk, it is true, of God's powers, acts, and attributes, but these discriminations are only "virtual," and made from the human point of view. In God all these points of view fall into an absolute identity of being.

This absence of all potentiality in God obliges Him to be *immutable*. He is actuality, through and through. Were there anything potential about Him, He would either lose or gain by its actualization, and either loss or gain would contradict his perfection. He cannot, therefore, change. Furthermore, He is *immense, boundless;* for could He be outlined in space, He would be composite, and this would contradict his indivisibility. He is therefore *omnipresent*, indivisibly there, at every point of space. He is similarly wholly present at every point of time—in other words *eternal*. For if He began in time, He would need a prior cause, and that would contradict his aseity. If He ended, it would contradict his necessity. If He went through any succession, it would contradict his immutability.

He has *intelligence* and *will* and every other creature-perfection, for *we* have them, and *effectus nequit superare causam*. In Him, however, they are absolutely and eternally in act, and their *object*, since God can be bounded by naught that is external, can primarily be nothing else than God himself. He knows himself, then, in one eternal indivisible act, and wills himself with an infinite self-pleasure.[285] Since He must of logical necessity thus love and will himself, He cannot be called "free" *ad intra*, with the freedom of contrarieties that characterizes finite creatures. *Ad extra*, however, or with respect to his creation, God is free. He cannot *need* to create, being perfect in being and in happiness already. He *wills* to create, then, by an absolute freedom.

Being thus a substance endowed with intellect and will and freedom, God is a *person;* and a *living* person also, for He is both object and subject of his own activity, and to be this distinguishes the living from the lifeless. He is thus absolutely *self-sufficient:* his *self-knowledge* and *self-love* are both of them infinite and adequate, and need no extraneous conditions to perfect them.

He is *omniscient*, for in knowing himself as Cause He knows all creature things and events by implication. His knowledge is *previsive*, for He is present to all time.

285 For the scholastics the *facultas appetendi* embraces feeling, desire, and will.

Even our free acts are known beforehand to Him, for otherwise his wisdom would admit of successive moments of enrichment, and this would contradict his immutability. He is *omnipotent* for everything that does not involve logical contradiction. He can make *being*—in other words his power includes *creation*. If what He creates were made of his own substance, it would have to be infinite in essence, as that substance is; but it is finite; so it must be non-divine in substance. If it were made of a substance, an eternally existing matter, for example, which God found there to his hand, and to which He simply gave its form, that would contradict God's definition as First Cause, and make Him a mere mover of something caused already. The things he creates, then, He creates *ex nihilo*, and gives them absolute being as so many finite substances additional to himself. The forms which he imprints upon them have their prototypes in his ideas. But as in God there is no such thing as multiplicity, and as these ideas for us are manifold, we must distinguish the ideas as they are in God and the way in which our minds externally imitate them. We must attribute them to Him only in a *terminative* sense, as differing aspects, from the finite point of view, of his unique essence.

God of course is holy, good, and just. He can do no evil, for He is positive being's fullness, and evil is negation. It is true that He has created physical evil in places, but only as a means of wider good, for *bonum totius præeminet bonum partis*. Moral evil He cannot will, either as end or means, for that would contradict his holiness. By creating free beings He *permits* it only, neither his justice nor his goodness obliging Him to prevent the recipients of freedom from misusing the gift.

As regards God's purpose in creating, primarily it can only have been to exercise his absolute freedom by the manifestation to others of his glory. From this it follows that the others must be rational beings, capable in the first place of knowledge, love, and honor, and in the second place of happiness, for the knowledge and love of God is the mainspring of felicity. In so far forth one may say that God's secondary purpose in creating is *love*.

I will not weary you by pursuing these metaphysical determinations farther, into the mysteries of God's Trinity, for example. What I have given will serve as a specimen of the orthodox philosophical theology of both Catholics and Protestants. Newman, filled with enthusiasm at God's list of perfections, continues the passage which I began to quote to you by a couple of pages of a rhetoric so magnificent that I can hardly refrain from adding them, in spite of the inroad they would make upon our time.[286] He first enumerates God's attributes sonorously, then celebrates his ownership of everything in earth and Heaven, and the dependence of all that happens upon his permissive will. He gives us scholastic philosophy "touched with emotion," and every philosophy should be touched with emotion to be rightly understood. Emotionally, then, dogmatic theology is worth something to minds of

286 Op. cit., Discourse III. § 7.

the type of Newman's. It will aid us to estimate what it is worth intellectually, if at this point I make a short digression.

What God hath joined together, let no man put asunder. The Continental schools of philosophy have too often overlooked the fact that man's thinking is organically connected with his conduct. It seems to me to be the chief glory of English and Scottish thinkers to have kept the organic connection in view. The guiding principle of British philosophy has in fact been that every difference must *make* a difference, every theoretical difference somewhere issue in a practical difference, and that the best method of discussing points of theory is to begin by ascertaining what practical difference would result from one alternative or the other being true. What is the particular truth in question *known as?* In what facts does it result? What is its cash-value in terms of particular experience? This is the characteristic English way of taking up a question. In this way, you remember, Locke takes up the question of personal identity. What you mean by it is just your chain of particular memories, says he. That is the only concretely verifiable part of its significance. All further ideas about it, such as the oneness or manyness of the spiritual substance on which it is based, are therefore void of intelligible meaning; and propositions touching such ideas may be indifferently affirmed or denied. So Berkeley with his "matter." The cash-value of matter is our physical sensations. That is what it is known as, all that we concretely verify of its conception. That, therefore, is the whole meaning of the term "matter"—any other pretended meaning is mere wind of words. Hume does the same thing with causation. It is known as habitual antecedence, and as tendency on our part to look for something definite to come. Apart from this practical meaning it has no significance whatever, and books about it may be committed to the flames, says Hume. Dugald Stewart and Thomas Brown, James Mill, John Mill, and Professor Bain, have followed more or less consistently the same method; and Shadworth Hodgson has used the principle with full explicitness. When all is said and done, it was English and Scotch writers, and not Kant, who introduced "the critical method" into philosophy, the one method fitted to make philosophy a study worthy of serious men. For what seriousness can possibly remain in debating philosophic propositions that will never make an appreciable difference to us in action? And what could it matter, if all propositions were practically indifferent, which of them we should agree to call true or which false?

An American philosopher of eminent originality, Mr. Charles Sanders Peirce, has rendered thought a service by disentangling from the particulars of its application the principle by which these men were instinctively guided, and by singling it out as fundamental and giving to it a Greek name. He calls it the principle of *pragmatism*, and he defends it somewhat as follows:[287]—

287 In an article, How to make our Ideas Clear, in the Popular Science Monthly for January, 1878, vol. xii, p. 286.

Thought in movement has for its only conceivable motive the attainment of belief, or thought at rest. Only when our thought about a subject has found its rest in belief can our action on the subject firmly and safely begin. Beliefs, in short, are rules for action; and the whole function of thinking is but one step in the production of active habits. If there were any part of a thought that made no difference in the thought's practical consequences, then that part would be no proper element of the thought's significance. To develop a thought's meaning we need therefore only determine what conduct it is fitted to produce; that conduct is for us its sole significance; and the tangible fact at the root of all our thought-distinctions is that there is no one of them so fine as to consist in anything but a possible difference of practice. To attain perfect clearness in our thoughts of an object, we need then only consider what sensations, immediate or remote, we are conceivably to expect from it, and what conduct we must prepare in case the object should be true. Our conception of these practical consequences is for us the whole of our conception of the object, so far as that conception has positive significance at all.

This is the principle of Peirce, the principle of pragmatism. Such a principle will help us on this occasion to decide, among the various attributes set down in the scholastic inventory of God's perfections, whether some be not far less significant than others.

If, namely, we apply the principle of pragmatism to God's metaphysical attributes, strictly so called, as distinguished from his moral attributes, I think that, even were we forced by a coercive logic to believe them, we still should have to confess them to be destitute of all intelligible significance. Take God's aseity, for example; or his necessariness; his immateriality; his "simplicity" or superiority to the kind of inner variety and succession which we find in finite beings, his indivisibility, and lack of the inner distinctions of being and activity, substance and accident, potentiality and actuality, and the rest; his repudiation of inclusion in a genus; his actualized infinity; his "personality," apart from the moral qualities which it may comport; his relations to evil being permissive and not positive; his self-sufficiency, self-love, and absolute felicity in himself:—candidly speaking, how do such qualities as these make any definite connection with our life? And if they severally call for no distinctive adaptations of our conduct, what vital difference can it possibly make to a man's religion whether they be true or false?

For my own part, although I dislike to say aught that may grate upon tender associations, I must frankly confess that even though these attributes were faultlessly deduced, I cannot conceive of its being of the smallest consequence to us religiously that any one of them should be true. Pray, what specific act can I perform in order to adapt myself the better to God's simplicity? Or how does it assist me to plan my behavior, to know that his happiness is anyhow absolutely complete? In the middle of the century just past, Mayne Reid was the great writer of books of out-of-door adventure. He was forever extolling the hunters and field-observers of living animals' habits, and keeping up a fire of invective against the "closet-naturalists," as he called them, the collectors and classifiers, and handlers of skeletons and skins. When I was a boy, I used to think that a closet-naturalist must be the vilest type of wretch under the sun. But surely the systematic theologians are the closet-naturalists of the deity, even in Captain Mayne Reid's sense. What is their deduction of metaphysical attributes but a shuffling and matching of pedantic dictionary-adjectives, aloof from morals, aloof from human needs, something that might be worked out from the mere word "God" by one of those logical machines of wood and brass which recent ingenuity has contrived as well as by a man of flesh and blood. They have the trail of the serpent over them. One feels that in the theologians' hands, they are only a set of titles obtained by a mechanical manipulation of synonyms; verbality has stepped into the place of vision, professionalism into that of life. Instead of bread we have a stone; instead of a fish, a serpent. Did such a conglomeration of abstract terms give really the gist of our knowledge of the deity, schools of theology might indeed continue to flourish, but religion, vital religion, would have taken its flight from this world. What keeps religion going is something else than abstract definitions and systems of concatenated adjectives, and something different from faculties of theology and their professors. All these things are after-effects, secondary accretions upon those phenomena of vital conversation with the unseen divine, of which I have shown you so many instances, renewing themselves *in sæcula sæculorum* in the lives of humble private men.

So much for the metaphysical attributes of God! From the point of view of practical religion, the metaphysical monster which they offer to our worship is an absolutely worthless invention of the scholarly mind.

What shall we now say of the attributes called moral? Pragmatically, they stand on an entirely different footing. They positively determine fear and hope and expectation, and are foundations for the saintly life. It needs but a glance at them to show how great is their significance.

God's holiness, for example: being holy, God can will nothing but the good. Being omnipotent, he can secure its triumph. Being omniscient, he can see us in the dark. Being just, he can punish us for what he sees. Being loving, he can pardon too. Being unalterable, we can count on him securely. These qualities enter into connection with our life, it is highly important that we should be informed concerning them. That God's purpose in creation should be the manifestation of his glory is also an attribute which has definite relations to our practical life. Among other things it has given a definite character to worship in all Christian countries. If dogmatic theology really does prove beyond dispute that a God with characters like these exists, she may well claim to give a solid basis to religious sentiment. But verily, how stands it with her arguments?

It stands with them as ill as with the arguments for his existence. Not only do post-Kantian idealists reject them root and branch, but it is a plain historic fact that they never have converted any one who has found in the moral complexion of the world, as he experienced it, reasons for doubting that a good God can have framed it. To prove God's goodness by the scholastic argument that there is no nonbeing in his essence would sound to such a witness simply silly.

No! the book of Job went over this whole matter once for all and definitively. Ratiocination is a relatively superficial and unreal path to the deity: "I will lay mine hand upon my mouth; I have heard of Thee by the hearing of the ear, but now mine eye seeth Thee." An intellect perplexed and baffled, yet a trustful sense of presence—such is the situation of the man who is sincere with himself and with the facts, but who remains religious still.[288]

We must therefore, I think, bid a definitive good-by to dogmatic theology. In all sincerity our faith must do without that warrant. Modern idealism, I repeat, has said good-by to this theology forever. Can modern idealism give faith a better warrant, or must she still rely on her poor self for witness?

The basis of modern idealism is Kant's doctrine of the Transcendental Ego of Apperception. By this formidable term Kant merely meant the fact that the consciousness "I think them" must (potentially or actually) accompany all our objects. Former skeptics had said as much, but the "I" in question had remained for them identified with the personal individual. Kant abstracted and depersonalized it, and made it the most universal of all his categories, although for Kant himself the Transcendental Ego had no theological implications.

It was reserved for his successors to convert Kant's notion of *Bewusstsein überhaupt*, or abstract consciousness, into an infinite concrete self-consciousness which is the soul of the world, and in which our sundry personal self-consciousnesses have their being. It would lead me into technicalities to show you even briefly how this transformation was in point of fact effected. Suffice it to say that in the Hegelian school, which to-day so deeply influences both British and American thinking, two principles have borne the brunt of the operation.

The first of these principles is that the old logic of identity never gives us more than a post-mortem dissection of *disjecta membra*, and that the fullness of life can be construed to thought only by recognizing that every object which our thought may propose to itself involves the notion of some other object which seems at first to negate the first one.

The second principle is that to be conscious of a negation is already virtually to be beyond it. The mere asking of a question or expression of a dissatisfaction proves

288 Pragmatically, the most important attribute of God is his punitive justice. But who, in the present state of theological opinion on that point, will dare maintain that hell fire or its equivalent in some shape is rendered certain by pure logic? Theology herself has largely based this doctrine upon revelation; and, in discussing it, has tended more and more to substitute conventional ideas of criminal law for *a priori* principles of reason. But the very notion that this glorious universe, with planets and winds, and laughing sky and ocean, should have been conceived and had its beams and rafters laid in technicalities of criminality, is incredible to our modern imagination. It weakens a religion to hear it argued upon such a basis.

that the answer or the satisfaction is already imminent; the finite, realized as such, is already the infinite *in posse*.

Applying these principles, we seem to get a propulsive force into our logic which the ordinary logic of a bare, stark self-identity in each thing never attains to. The objects of our thought now *act* within our thought, act as objects act when given in experience. They change and develop. They introduce something other than themselves along with them; and this other, at first only ideal or potential, presently proves itself also to be actual. It supersedes the thing at first supposed, and both verifies and corrects it, in developing the fullness of its meaning.

The program is excellent; the universe *is* a place where things are followed by other things that both correct and fulfill them; and a logic which gave us something like this movement of fact would express truth far better than the traditional school-logic, which never gets of its own accord from anything to anything else, and registers only predictions and subsumptions, or static resemblances and differences. Nothing could be more unlike the methods of dogmatic theology than those of this new logic. Let me quote in illustration some passages from the Scottish transcendentalist whom I have already named.

> "How are we to conceive," Principal Caird writes, "of the reality in which all intelligence rests?" He replies: "Two things may without difficulty be proved, viz., that this reality is an absolute Spirit, and conversely that it is only in communion with this absolute Spirit or Intelligence that the finite Spirit can realize itself. It is absolute; for the faintest movement of human intelligence would be arrested, if it did not presuppose the absolute reality of intelligence, of thought itself. Doubt or denial themselves presuppose and indirectly affirm it. When I pronounce anything to be true, I pronounce it, indeed, to be relative to thought, but not to be relative to my thought, or to the thought of any other individual mind. From the existence of all individual minds as such I can abstract; I can think them away. But that which I cannot think away is thought or self-consciousness itself, in its independence and absoluteness, or, in other words, an Absolute Thought or Self-Consciousness."

Here, you see, Principal Caird makes the transition which Kant did not make: he converts the omnipresence of consciousness in general as a condition of "truth" being anywhere possible, into an omnipresent universal consciousness, which he identifies with God in his concreteness. He next proceeds to use the principle that to acknowledge your limits is in essence to be beyond them; and makes the transition to the religious experience of individuals in the following words:—

> "If [Man] were only a creature of transient sensations and impulses, of an ever coming and going succession of intuitions, fancies, feelings, then nothing could ever have for him the character of objective truth or reality. But it is the prerogative of man's spiritual nature that he can yield himself up to a thought and will that are infinitely larger than his own. As a thinking, self-conscious being,

indeed, he may be said, by his very nature, to live in the atmosphere of the Universal Life. As a thinking being, it is possible for me to suppress and quell in my consciousness every movement of self-assertion, every notion and opinion that is merely mine, every desire that belongs to me as this particular Self, and to become the pure medium of a thought that is universal—in one word, to live no more my own life, but let my consciousness be possessed and suffused by the Infinite and Eternal life of spirit. And yet it is just in this renunciation of self that I truly gain myself, or realize the highest possibilities of my own nature. For whilst in one sense we give up self to live the universal and absolute life of reason, yet that to which we thus surrender ourselves is in reality our truer self. The life of absolute reason is not a life that is foreign to us."

Nevertheless, Principal Caird goes on to say, so far as we are able outwardly to realize this doctrine, the balm it offers remains incomplete. Whatever we may be *in posse*, the very best of us *in actu* falls very short of being absolutely divine. Social morality, love, and self-sacrifice even, merge our Self only in some other finite self or selves. They do not quite identify it with the Infinite. Man's ideal destiny, infinite in abstract logic, might thus seem in practice forever unrealizable.

"Is there, then," our author continues, "no solution of the contradiction between the ideal and the actual? We answer, There is such a solution, but in order to reach it we are carried beyond the sphere of morality into that of religion. It may be said to be the essential characteristic of religion as contrasted with morality, that it changes aspiration into fruition, anticipation into realization; that instead of leaving man in the interminable pursuit of a vanishing ideal, it makes him the actual partaker of a divine or infinite life. Whether we view religion from the human side or the divine—as the surrender of the soul to God, or as the life of God in the soul—in either aspect it is of its very essence that the Infinite has ceased to be a far-off vision, and has become a present reality. The very first pulsation of the spiritual life, when we rightly apprehend its significance, is the indication that the division between the Spirit and its object has vanished, that the ideal has become real, that the finite has reached its goal and become suffused with the presence and life of the Infinite.

"Oneness of mind and will with the divine mind and will is not the future hope and aim of religion, but its very beginning and birth in the soul. To enter on the religious life is to terminate the struggle. In that act which constitutes the beginning of the religious life—call it faith, or trust, or self-surrender, or by whatever name you will—there is involved the identification of the finite with a life which is eternally realized. It is true indeed that the religious life is progressive; but understood in the light of the foregoing idea, religious progress is not progress *towards*, but *within* the sphere of the Infinite. It is not the vain attempt by endless finite additions or increments to become possessed of infinite wealth, but it is the endeavor, by the constant exercise of spiritual activity, to appropriate that infinite inheritance of which we are already in possession. The whole future of the religious life is given in its beginning, but it is given implicitly. The position of the man who has entered on the religious life is that evil, error, imperfection, do not really belong to him: they are excrescences which have no organic relation to his true nature: they are already virtually, as they will be actually, suppressed and annulled, and in the very process of being annulled they become the means of spiritual progress. Though he is not exempt from temptation and conflict, [yet] in that inner sphere in which his true life lies, the struggle is over, the victory already achieved. It is not a finite but an infinite life which the spirit lives. Every pulse-beat of its [existence] is the expression and realization of the life of God."[289]

You will readily admit that no description of the phenomena of the religious consciousness could be better than these words of your lamented preacher and philosopher. They reproduce the very rapture of those crises of conversion of which we have been hearing; they utter what the mystic felt but was unable to communicate; and the saint, in hearing them, recognizes his own experience. It is indeed gratifying to find the content of religion reported so unanimously. But when all is said and done, has Principal Caird—and I only use him as an example of that whole mode of thinking—transcended the sphere of feeling and of the direct experience of the individual, and laid the foundations of religion in impartial reason? Has he made religion universal by coercive reasoning, transformed it from a private faith into a public certainty? Has he rescued its affirmations from obscurity and mystery?

I believe that he has done nothing of the kind, but that he has simply reaffirmed the individual's experiences in a more generalized vocabulary. And again, I can be excused from proving technically that the transcendentalist reasonings fail to make religion universal, for I can point to the plain fact that a majority of scholars, even religiously disposed ones, stubbornly refuse to treat them as convincing. The whole of Germany, one may say, has positively rejected the Hegelian argumentation. As for Scotland, I need only mention Professor Fraser's and Professor Pringle-Pattison's memorable criticisms, with which so many of you are familiar.[290] Once more, I ask,

---

289 John Caird: An Introduction to the Philosophy of Religion, London and New York, 1880, pp. 243–250, and 291–299, much abridged.

290 A. C. Fraser: Philosophy of Theism, second edition, Edinburgh and London, 1899, especially part ii, chaps. vii and viii.; A. Seth [Pringle-Pattison]: Hegelianism and Personality, Ibid., 1890, passim. The most persuasive arguments in favor of a concrete individual Soul of the world, with which I am acquainted, are those of my colleague, Josiah Royce, in his Religious Aspect of Philosophy, Boston, 1885; in his Conception of God, New York and London, 1897; and lately in his Aberdeen Gifford Lectures, The World and the Individual, 2 vols., New York and London, 1901–02. I doubtless seem to some of my readers to evade the philosophic duty which my thesis in this lecture imposes on me, by not even attempting to meet Professor Royce's arguments articulately. I admit the momentary evasion. In the present lectures, which are cast throughout in a popular mould, there seemed no room for subtle metaphysical discussion, and for tactical purposes it was sufficient, the contention of philosophy being what it is (namely, that religion can be transformed into a universally convincing science), to point to the fact that no religious philosophy has actually convinced the mass of thinkers. Meanwhile let me say that I hope that the present volume may be followed by another, if I am spared to write it, in which not only Professor Royce's arguments, but others for monistic absolutism shall be considered with all the technical fullness which their great importance calls for. At present I resign myself to lying passive under the reproach of superficiality.

if transcendental idealism were as objectively and absolutely rational as it pretends to be, could it possibly fail so egregiously to be persuasive?

What religion reports, you must remember, always purports to be a fact of experience: the divine is actually present, religion says, and between it and ourselves relations of give and take are actual. If definite perceptions of fact like this cannot stand upon their own feet, surely abstract reasoning cannot give them the support they are in need of. Conceptual processes can class facts, define them, interpret them; but they do not produce them, nor can they reproduce their individuality. There is always a *plus*, a *thisness*, which feeling alone can answer for. Philosophy in this sphere is thus a secondary function, unable to warrant faith's veracity, and so I revert to the thesis which I announced at the beginning of this lecture.

In all sad sincerity I think we must conclude that the attempt to demonstrate by purely intellectual processes the truth of the deliverances of direct religious experience is absolutely hopeless.

It would be unfair to philosophy, however, to leave her under this negative sentence. Let me close, then, by briefly enumerating what she *can* do for religion. If she will abandon metaphysics and deduction for criticism and induction, and frankly transform herself from theology into science of religions, she can make herself enormously useful.

The spontaneous intellect of man always defines the divine which it feels in ways that harmonize with its temporary intellectual prepossessions. Philosophy can by comparison eliminate the local and the accidental from these definitions. Both from dogma and from worship she can remove historic incrustations. By confronting the spontaneous religious constructions with the results of natural science, philosophy can also eliminate doctrines that are now known to be scientifically absurd or incongruous.

Sifting out in this way unworthy formulations, she can leave a residuum of conceptions that at least are possible. With these she can deal as *hypotheses*, testing them in all the manners, whether negative or positive, by which hypotheses are ever tested. She can reduce their number, as some are found more open to objection. She can perhaps become the champion of one which she picks out as being the most closely verified or verifiable. She can refine upon the definition of this hypothesis, distinguishing between what is innocent over-belief and symbolism in the expression of it, and what is to be literally taken. As a result, she can offer mediation between different believers, and help to bring about consensus of opinion. She can do this the more successfully, the better she discriminates the common and essential from the individual and local elements of the religious beliefs which she compares.

I do not see why a critical Science of Religions of this sort might not eventually command as general a public adhesion as is commanded by a physical science. Even the personally non-religious might accept its conclusions on trust, much as blind persons now accept the facts of optics—it might appear as foolish to refuse them. Yet as the science of optics has to be fed in the first instance, and continually verified later, by facts experienced by seeing persons; so the science of religions would depend for its original material on facts of personal experience, and would have to square itself with personal experience through all its critical reconstructions. It could never get away from concrete life, or work in a conceptual vacuum. It would forever have to confess, as every science confesses, that the subtlety of nature flies beyond it, and that its formulas are but approximations. Philosophy lives in words, but truth and fact well up into our lives in ways that exceed verbal formulation. There is in the living act of perception always something that glimmers and twinkles and will not be caught, and for which reflection comes too late. No one knows this as well as the philosopher. He must fire his volley of new vocables out of his conceptual shotgun, for his profession condemns him to this industry, but he secretly knows the hollowness and irrelevancy. His formulas are like stereoscopic or kinetoscopic photographs seen outside the instrument; they lack the depth, the motion, the vitality. In the religious sphere, in particular, belief that formulas are true can never wholly take the place of personal experience.

In my next lecture I will try to complete my rough description of religious experience; and in the lecture after that, which is the last one, I will try my hand at formulating conceptually the truth to which it is a witness.

LECTURE XIX

# Other Characteristics

We have wound our way back, after our excursion through mysticism and philosophy, to where we were before: the uses of religion, its uses to the individual who has it, and the uses of the individual himself to the world, are the best arguments that truth is in it. We return to the empirical philosophy: the true is what works well, even though the qualification "on the whole" may always have to be added. In this lecture we must revert to description again, and finish our picture of the religious consciousness by a word about some of its other characteristic elements. Then, in a final lecture, we shall be free to make a general review and draw our independent conclusions.

The first point I will speak of is the part which the æsthetic life plays in determining one's choice of a religion. Men, I said awhile ago, involuntarily intellectualize their religious experience. They need formulas, just as they need fellowship in worship. I spoke, therefore, too contemptuously of the pragmatic uselessness of the famous scholastic list of attributes of the deity, for they have one use which I neglected to consider. The eloquent passage in which Newman enumerates them[291] puts us on the track of it. Intoning them as he would intone a cathedral service, he shows how high is their æsthetic value. It enriches our bare piety to carry these exalted and mysterious verbal additions just as it enriches a church to have an organ and old brasses, marbles and frescoes and stained windows. Epithets lend an atmosphere and overtones to our devotion. They are like a hymn of praise and service of glory, and may sound the more sublime for being incomprehensible. Minds like Newman's[292] grow as jealous of their credit as heathen priests are of that of the jewelry and ornaments that blaze upon their idols.

291 Idea of a University, Discourse III. § 7.

292 Newman's imagination so innately craved an ecclesiastical system that he can write: "From the age of fifteen, dogma has been the fundamental principle of my religion: I know no other religion; I cannot enter into the idea of any other sort of religion." And again, speaking of himself about the age of thirty, he writes: "I loved to act as feeling myself in my Bishop's sight, as if it were the sight of God." Apologia, 1897, pp. 48, 50.

Among the buildings-out of religion which the mind spontaneously indulges in, the æsthetic motive must never be forgotten. I promised to say nothing of ecclesiastical systems in these lectures. I may be allowed, however, to put in a word at this point on the way in which their satisfaction of certain æsthetic needs contributes to their hold on human nature. Although some persons aim most at intellectual purity and simplification, for others *richness* is the supreme imaginative requirement.[293] When one's mind is strongly of this type, an individual religion will hardly serve the purpose. The inner need is rather of something institutional and complex, majestic in the hierarchic interrelatedness of its parts, with authority descending from stage to stage, and at every stage objects for adjectives of mystery and splendor, derived in the last resort from the Godhead who is the fountain and culmination of the system. One feels then as if in presence of some vast incrusted work of jewelry or architecture; one hears the multitudinous liturgical appeal; one gets the honorific vibration coming from every quarter. Compared with such a noble complexity, in which ascending and descending movements seem in no way to jar upon stability, in which no single item, however humble, is insignificant, because so many august institutions hold it in its place, how flat does evangelical Protestantism appear, how bare the atmosphere of those isolated religious lives whose boast it is that "man in the bush with God may meet."[294] What a pulverization and leveling of what a gloriously piled-up structure! To an imagination used to the perspectives of dignity and glory, the naked gospel scheme seems to offer an almshouse for a palace.

It is much like the patriotic sentiment of those brought up in ancient empires. How many emotions must be frustrated of their object, when one gives up the titles of dignity, the crimson lights and blare of brass, the gold embroidery, the plumed troops, the fear and trembling, and puts up with a president in a black coat who shakes hands with you, and comes, it may be, from a "home" upon a veldt or prairie with one sitting-room and a Bible on its centre-table. It pauperizes the monarchical imagination!

The strength of these æsthetic sentiments makes it rigorously impossible, it seems to me, that Protestantism, however superior in spiritual profundity it may be to Catholicism, should at the present day succeed in making many converts from the more venerable ecclesiasticism. The latter offers a so much richer pasturage and

---

293 The intellectual difference is quite on a par in practical importance with the analogous difference in character. We saw, under the head of Saintliness, how some characters resent confusion and must live in purity, consistency, simplicity (above, p. 275 ff.). For others, on the contrary, superabundance, over-pressure, stimulation, lots of superficial relations, are indispensable. There are men who would suffer a very syncope if you should pay all their debts, bring it about that their engagements had been kept, their letters answered, their perplexities relieved, and their duties fulfilled, down to one which lay on a clean table under their eyes with nothing to interfere with its immediate performance. A day stripped so staringly bare would be for them appalling. So with ease, elegance, tributes of affection, social recognitions—some of us require amounts of these things which to others would appear a mass of lying and sophistication.

294 In Newman's Lectures on Justification, Lecture VIII. § 6, there is a splendid passage expressive of this æsthetic way of feeling the Christian scheme. It is unfortunately too long to quote.

shade to the fancy, has so many cells with so many different kinds of honey, is so indulgent in its multiform appeals to human nature, that Protestantism will always show to Catholic eyes the almshouse physiognomy. The bitter negativity of it is to the Catholic mind incomprehensible. To intellectual Catholics many of the antiquated beliefs and practices to which the Church gives countenance are, if taken literally, as childish as they are to Protestants. But they are childish in the pleasing sense of "childlike"—innocent and amiable, and worthy to be smiled on in consideration of the undeveloped condition of the dear people's intellects. To the Protestant, on the contrary, they are childish in the sense of being idiotic falsehoods. He must stamp out their delicate and lovable redundancy, leaving the Catholic to shudder at his literalness. He appears to the latter as morose as if he were some hard-eyed, numb, monotonous kind of reptile. The two will never understand each other—their centres of emotional energy are too different. Rigorous truth and human nature's intricacies are always in need of a mutual interpreter.[295] So much for the æsthetic diversities in the religious consciousness.

In most books on religion, three things are represented as its most essential elements. These are Sacrifice, Confession, and Prayer. I must say a word in turn of each of these elements, though briefly. First of Sacrifice.

Sacrifices to gods are omnipresent in primeval worship; but, as cults have grown refined, burnt offerings and the blood of he-goats have been superseded by sacrifices more spiritual in their nature. Judaism, Islam, and Buddhism get along without ritual sacrifice; so does Christianity, save in so far as the notion is preserved in transfigured form in the mystery of Christ's atonement. These religions substitute offerings of the heart, renunciations of the inner self, for all those vain oblations. In the ascetic practices which Islam, Buddhism, and the older Christianity encourage we see how indestructible is the idea that sacrifice of some sort is a religious exercise. In lecturing on asceticism I spoke of its significance as symbolic of the sacrifices which life, whenever it is taken strenuously, calls for. But, as I said my say about those, and as these lectures expressly avoid earlier religious usages and questions of derivation, I will pass from the subject of Sacrifice altogether and turn to that of Confession.

In regard to Confession I will also be most brief, saying my word about it psychologically, not historically. Not nearly as widespread as sacrifice, it corresponds to a more inward and moral stage of sentiment. It is part of the general system of purgation and cleansing which one feels one's self in need of, in order to be in right relations to one's deity. For him who confesses, shams are over and realities have

295 Compare the informality of Protestantism, where the "meek lover of the good," alone with his God, visits the sick, etc., for their own sakes, with the elaborate "business" that goes on in Catholic devotion, and carries with it the social excitement of all more complex businesses. An essentially worldly-minded Catholic woman can become a visitor of the sick on purely coquettish principles, with her confessor and director, her "merit" storing up, her patron saints, her privileged relation to the Almighty, drawing his attention as a professional *devote*, her definite "exercises," and her definitely recognized social *pose* in the organization.

begun; he has exteriorized his rottenness. If he has not actually got rid of it, he at least no longer smears it over with a hypocritical show of virtue—he lives at least upon a basis of veracity. The complete decay of the practice of confession in Anglo-Saxon communities is a little hard to account for. Reaction against popery is of course the historic explanation, for in popery confession went with penances and absolution, and other inadmissible practices. But on the side of the sinner himself it seems as if the need ought to have been too great to accept so summary a refusal of its satisfaction. One would think that in more men the shell of secrecy would have had to open, the pent-in abscess to burst and gain relief, even though the ear that heard the confession were unworthy. The Catholic church, for obvious utilitarian reasons, has substituted auricular confession to one priest for the more radical act of public confession. We English-speaking Protestants, in the general self-reliance and unsociability of our nature, seem to find it enough if we take God alone into our confidence.[296]

The next topic on which I must comment is Prayer—and this time it must be less briefly. We have heard much talk of late against prayer, especially against prayers for better weather and for the recovery of sick people. As regards prayers for the sick, if any medical fact can be considered to stand firm, it is that in certain environments prayer may contribute to recovery, and should be encouraged as a therapeutic measure. Being a normal factor of moral health in the person, its omission would be deleterious. The case of the weather is different. Notwithstanding the recency of the opposite belief,[297] every one now knows that droughts and storms follow from physical antecedents, and that moral appeals cannot avert them. But petitional prayer is only one department of prayer; and if we take the word in the wider sense as meaning every kind of inward communion or conversation with the power recognized as divine, we can easily see that scientific criticism leaves it untouched.

Prayer in this wide sense is the very soul and essence of religion. "Religion," says a liberal French theologian, "is an intercourse, a conscious and voluntary relation, entered into by a soul in distress with the mysterious power upon which it feels itself to depend, and upon which its fate is contingent. This intercourse with God is realized by prayer. Prayer is religion in act; that is, prayer is real religion. It is prayer that distinguishes the religious phenomenon from such similar or neighboring phenomena as purely moral or æsthetic sentiment. Religion is nothing if it be not the vital act by which the entire mind seeks to save itself by clinging to the principle from which it draws its life. This act is prayer, by which term I understand no vain exercise of words, no mere repetition of certain sacred formulæ, but the very movement it-

296 A fuller discussion of confession is contained in the excellent work by FRANK GRANGER: The Soul of a Christian, London, 1900, ch. xii.

297 Example: "The minister at Sudbury, being at the Thursday lecture in Boston, heard the officiating clergyman praying for rain. As soon as the service was over, he went to the petitioner and said, 'You Boston ministers, as soon as a tulip wilts under your windows, go to church and pray for rain, until all Concord and Sudbury are under water.' " R. W. EMERSON: Lectures and Biographical Sketches, p. 363.

self of the soul, putting itself in a personal relation of contact with the mysterious power of which it feels the presence—it may be even before it has a name by which to call it. Wherever this interior prayer is lacking, there is no religion; wherever, on the other hand, this prayer rises and stirs the soul, even in the absence of forms or of doctrines, we have living religion. One sees from this why "natural religion, so-called, is not properly a religion. It cuts man off from prayer. It leaves him and God in mutual remoteness, with no intimate commerce, no interior dialogue, no interchange, no action of God in man, no return of man to God. At bottom this pretended religion is only a philosophy. Born at epochs of rationalism, of critical investigations, it never was anything but an abstraction. An artificial and dead creation, it reveals to its examiner hardly one of the characters proper to religion."[298]

It seems to me that the entire series of our lectures proves the truth of M. Sabatier's contention. The religious phenomenon, studied as in inner fact, and apart from ecclesiastical or theological complications, has shown itself to consist everywhere, and at all its stages, in the consciousness which individuals have of an intercourse between themselves and higher powers with which they feel themselves to be related. This intercourse is realized at the time as being both active and mutual. If it be not effective; if it be not a give and take relation; if nothing be really transacted while it lasts; if the world is in no whit different for its having taken place; then prayer, taken in this wide meaning of a sense that *something is transacting*, is of course a feeling of what is illusory, and religion must on the whole be classed, not simply as containing elements of delusion—these undoubtedly everywhere exist—but as being rooted in delusion altogether, just as materialists and atheists have always said it was. At most there might remain, when the direct experiences of prayer were ruled out as false witnesses, some inferential belief that the whole order of existence must have a divine cause. But this way of contemplating nature, pleasing as it would doubtless be to persons of a pious taste, would leave to them but the spectators' part at a play, whereas in experimental religion and the prayerful life, we seem ourselves to be actors, and not in a play, but in a very serious reality.

The genuineness of religion is thus indissolubly bound up with the question whether the prayerful consciousness be or be not deceitful. The conviction that something is genuinely transacted in this consciousness is the very core of living religion. As to what is transacted, great differences of opinion have prevailed. The unseen powers have been supposed, and are yet supposed, to do things which no enlightened man can nowadays believe in. It may well prove that the sphere of influence in prayer is subjective exclusively, and that what is immediately changed is only the mind of the praying person. But however our opinion of prayer's effects may come to be limited by criticism, religion, in the vital sense in which these lec-

---

298 AUGUSTE SABATIER: Esquisse d'une Philosophie de la Religion. 2me éd., 1897, pp. 24–26, abridged.

tures study it, must stand or fall by the persuasion that effects of some sort genuinely do occur. Through prayer, religion insists, things which cannot be realized in any other manner come about: energy which but for prayer would be bound is by prayer set free and operates in some part, be it objective or subjective, of the world of facts.

This postulate is strikingly expressed in a letter written by the late Frederic W. H. Myers to a friend, who allows me to quote from it. It shows how independent the prayer-instinct is of usual doctrinal complications. Mr. Myers writes:—

> "I am glad that you have asked me about prayer, because I have rather strong ideas on the subject. First consider what are the facts. There exists around us a spiritual universe, and that universe is in actual relation with the material. From the spiritual universe comes the energy which maintains the material; the energy which makes the life of each individual spirit. Our spirits are supported by a perpetual indrawal of this energy, and the vigor of that indrawal is perpetually changing, much as the vigor of our absorption of material nutriment changes from hour to hour.
>
> "I call these 'facts' because I think that some scheme of this kind is the only one consistent with our actual evidence; too complex to summarize here. How, then, should we *act* on these facts? Plainly we must endeavor to draw in as much spiritual life as possible, and we must place our minds in any attitude which experience shows to be favorable to such indrawal. *Prayer* is the general name for that attitude of open and earnest expectancy. If we then ask to *whom* to pray, the answer (strangely enough) must be that *that* does not much matter. The prayer is not indeed a purely subjective thing;—it means a real increase in intensity of absorption of spiritual power or grace;—but we do not know enough of what takes place in the spiritual world to know how the prayer operates;—*who* is cognizant of it, or through what channel the grace is given. Better let children pray to Christ, who is at any rate the highest individual spirit of whom we have any knowledge. But it would be rash to say that Christ himself *hears us;* while to say that *God* hears us is merely to restate the first principle—that grace flows in from the infinite spiritual world."

Let us reserve the question of the truth or falsehood of the belief that power is absorbed until the next lecture, when our dogmatic conclusions, if we have any, must be reached. Let this lecture still confine itself to the description of phenomena; and as a concrete example of an extreme sort, of the way in which the prayerful life may still be led, let me take a case with which most of you must be acquainted, that of George Müller of Bristol, who died in 1898. Müller's prayers were of the crassest petitional order. Early in life he resolved on taking certain Bible promises in literal sincerity, and on letting himself be fed, not by his own worldly foresight, but by the Lord's hand. He had an extraordinarily active and successful career, among the fruits of which were the distribution of over two million copies of the Scripture text, in different languages; the equipment of several hundred missionaries; the circulation of more than a hundred and eleven million of scriptural books, pamphlets, and tracts; the building of five large orphanages, and the keeping and educating of thousands of orphans; finally, the establishment of schools in which over a hundred and twenty-one thousand youthful and adult pupils were taught. In the course of this work Mr. Müller received and administered nearly a million and a half of pounds sterling, and traveled over two hundred thousand miles of sea and land.[299] During the sixty-eight years of his ministry, he never owned any property except his clothes and furniture, and cash in hand; and he left, at the age of eighty-six, an estate worth only a hundred and sixty pounds.

> His method was to let his general wants be publicly known, but not to acquaint other people with the details of his temporary necessities. For the relief of the latter, he prayed directly to the Lord, believing that sooner or later prayers are always answered if one have trust enough. "When I lose such a thing as a key," he writes, "I ask the Lord to direct me to it, and I look for an answer to my prayer; when a person with whom I have made an appointment does not come, according to the fixed time, and I begin to be inconvenienced by it, I ask the Lord to be pleased to hasten him to me, and I look for an answer; when I do not understand a passage of the word of God, I lift up my heart to the Lord that he would be pleased by his Holy Spirit to instruct me, and I expect to be taught, though I do not fix the time when, and the manner how it should be; when I am going to minister in the Word, I seek help from the Lord, and . . . am not cast down, but of good cheer because I look for his assistance."
>
> Müller's custom was to never run up bills, not even for a week. "As the Lord deals out to us by the day, . . . the week's payment might become due and we have no money to meet it; and thus those with whom we deal might be inconvenienced by us, and we be found acting against the commandment of the Lord: 'Owe no man anything.' From this day and henceforward whilst the Lord gives to us our supplies by the day, we purpose to pay at once for every article as it is purchased, and never to buy anything except we can pay for it at once, however much it may seem to be needed, and however much those with whom we deal may wish to be paid only by the week."
>
> The articles needed of which Müller speaks were the food, fuel, etc., of his orphanages. Somehow, near as they often come to going without a meal, they hardly ever seem actually to have done so. "Greater and more manifest nearness of the Lord's presence I have never had than when after breakfast there were no means for dinner for more than a hundred persons; or when after dinner there were no means for the tea, and yet the Lord provided the tea; and all this without one single human being having been informed about our need. . . . Through Grace my mind is so fully assured of the faithfulness of the Lord, that in the midst of the greatest need, I am enabled in peace to go about my other work. Indeed, did not the Lord give me this, which is the result of trusting in him, I

299 My authority for these statistics is the little work on Müller, by FREDERIC G. WARNE, New York, 1898.

should scarcely be able to work at all; for it is now comparatively a rare thing that a day comes when I am not in need for one or another part of the work."[300]

In building his orphanages simply by prayer and faith, Müller affirms that his prime motive was "to have something to point to as a visible proof that our God and Father is the same faithful God that he ever was—as willing as ever to prove himself the living God, in our day as formerly, to all that put their trust in him."[301] For this reason he refused to borrow money for any of his enterprises. "How does it work when we thus anticipate God by going our own way? We certainly weaken faith instead of increasing it; and each time we work thus a deliverance of our own we find it more and more difficult to trust in God, till at last we give way entirely to our natural fallen reason and unbelief prevails. How different if one is enabled to wait God's own time, and to look alone to him for help and deliverance! When at last help comes, after many seasons of prayer it may be, how sweet it is, and what a present recompense! Dear Christian reader, if you have never walked in this path of obedience before, do so now, and you will then know experimentally the sweetness of the joy which results from it."[302]

When the supplies came in but slowly, Müller always considered that this was for the trial of his faith and patience. When his faith and patience had been sufficiently tried, the Lord would send more means. "And thus it has proved,"—I quote from his diary—"for to-day was given me the sum of 2050 pounds, of which 2000 are for the building fund [of a certain house], and 50 for present necessities. It is impossible to describe my joy in God when I received this donation. I was neither excited nor surprised; for I *look out* for answers to my prayers. *I believe that God hears me.* Yet my heart was so full of joy that I could only *sit* before God, and admire him, like David in 2 Samuel vii. At last I cast myself flat down upon my face and burst forth in thanksgiving to God and in surrendering my heart afresh to him for his blessed service."[303]

George Müller's is a case extreme in every respect, and in no respect more so than in the extraordinary narrowness of the man's intellectual horizon. His God was, as he often said, his business partner. He seems to have been for Müller little more than a sort of supernatural clergyman interested in the congregation of tradesmen and others in Bristol who were his saints, and in the orphanages and other enterprises, but unpossessed of any of those vaster and wilder and more ideal attributes with which the human imagination elsewhere has invested him. Müller, in short, was absolutely unphilosophical. His intensely private and practical conception of his relations with the Deity continued the traditions of the most primitive human thought.[304] When we compare a mind like his with such a mind as, for ex-

300 The Life of Trust; Being a Narrative of the Lord's Dealings with George Müller, New American edition, N. Y., Crowell, pp. 228, 194, 219.

301 Ibid., p. 126.

302 Op. cit., p. 383, abridged.

303 Ibid., p. 323.

304 I cannot resist the temptation of quoting an expression of an even more primitive style of religious thought, which I find in Arber's English Garland, vol. vii, p. 440. Robert Lyde, an English sailor, along

ample, Emerson's or Phillips Brooks's, we see the range which the religious consciousness covers.

There is an immense literature relating to answers to petitional prayer. The evangelical journals are filled with such answers, and books are devoted to the subject,[305] but for us Müller's case will suffice.

A less sturdy beggar-like fashion of leading the prayerful life is followed by innumerable other Christians. Persistence in leaning on the Almighty for support and guidance will, such persons say, bring with it proofs, palpable but much more subtle, of his presence and active influence. The following description of a "led" life, by a German writer whom I have already quoted, would no doubt appear to countless Christians in every country as if transcribed from their own personal experience. One finds in this guided sort of life, says Dr. Hilty—

> "That books and words (and sometimes people) come to one's cognizance just at the very moment in which one needs them; that one glides over great dangers as if with shut eyes, remaining ignorant of what would have terrified one or led one astray, until the peril is past—this being especially the case with temptations to vanity and sensuality; that paths on which one ought not to wander are, as it were, hedged off with thorns; but that on the other side great obstacles are suddenly removed; that when the time has come for something, one suddenly receives a courage that formerly failed, or perceives the root of a matter that until then was concealed, or discovers thoughts, talents, yea, even pieces of knowledge and insight, in one's self, of which it is impossible to say whence they come; finally, that persons help us or decline to help us, favor us or refuse us, as if they

---

with an English boy, being prisoners on a French ship in 1689, set upon the crew, of seven Frenchmen, killed two, made the other five prisoners, and brought home the ship. Lyde thus describes how in this feat he found his God a very present help in time of trouble:—

"With the assistance of God I kept my feet when they three and one more did strive to throw me down. Feeling the Frenchman which hung about my middle hang very heavy, I said to the boy, 'Go round the binnacle, and knock down that man that hangeth on my back.' So the boy did strike him one blow on the head which made him fall. . . . Then I looked about for a marlin spike or anything else to strike them withal. But seeing nothing, I said, 'Lord! what shall I do?' Then casting up my eye upon my left side, and seeing a marlin spike hanging, I jerked my right arm and took hold, and struck the point four times about a quarter of an inch deep into the skull of that man that had hold of my left arm. [One of the Frenchmen then hauled the marlin spike away from him.] But through God's wonderful providence! it either fell out of his hand, or else he threw it down, and at this time the Almighty God gave me strength enough to take one man in one hand, and throw at the other's head: and looking about again to see anything to strike them withal, but seeing nothing, I said, 'Lord! what shall I do now?' And then it pleased God to put me in mind of my knife in my pocket. And although two of the men had hold of my right arm, yet God Almighty strengthened me so that I put my right hand into my right pocket, drew out the knife and sheath, . . . put it between my legs and drew it out, and then cut the man's throat with it that had his back to my breast: and he immediately dropt down, and scarce ever stirred after."—I have slightly abridged Lyde's narrative.

305 As, for instance, In Answer to Prayer, by the Bishop of Ripon and others, London, 1898; Touching Incidents and Remarkable Answers to Prayer, Harrisburg, Pa., 1898 (?); H. L. Hastings: The Guiding Hand, or Providential Direction, illustrated by Authentic Instances, Boston, 1898 (?).

had to do so against their will, so that often those indifferent or even unfriendly to us yield us the greatest service and furtherance. (God takes often their worldly goods, from those whom he leads, at just the right moment, when they threaten to impede the effort after higher interests.)

"Besides all this, other noteworthy things come to pass, of which it is not easy to give account. There is no doubt whatever that now one walks continually through 'open doors' and on the easiest roads, with as little care and trouble as it is possible to imagine.

"Furthermore one finds one's self settling one's affairs neither too early nor too late, whereas they were wont to be spoiled by untimeliness, even when the preparations had been well laid. In addition to this, one does them with perfect tranquillity of mind, almost as if they were matters of no consequence, like errands done by us for another person, in which case we usually act more calmly than when we act in our own concerns. Again, one finds that one can *wait* for everything patiently, and that is one of life's great arts. One finds also that each thing comes duly, one thing after the other, so that one gains time to make one's footing sure before advancing farther. And then every thing occurs to us at the right moment, just what we ought to do, etc., and often in a very striking way, just as if a third person were keeping watch over those things which we are in easy danger of forgetting.

"Often, too, persons are sent to us at the right time, to offer or ask for what is needed, and what we should never have had the courage or resolution to undertake of our own accord.

"Through all these experiences one finds that one is kindly and tolerant of other people, even of such as are repulsive, negligent, or ill-willed, for they also are instruments of good in God's hand, and often most efficient ones. Without these thoughts it would be hard for even the best of us always to keep our equanimity. But with the consciousness of divine guidance, one sees many a thing in life quite differently from what would otherwise be possible.

"All these are things that every human being *knows*, who has had experience of them; and of which the most speaking examples could be brought forward. The highest resources of worldly wisdom are unable to attain that which, under divine leading, comes to us of its own accord."[306]

Such accounts as this shade away into others where the belief is, not that particular events are tempered more towardly to us by a superintending providence, as a reward for our reliance, but that by cultivating the continuous sense of our connection with the power that made things as they are, we are tempered more towardly for their reception. The outward face of nature need not alter, but the expressions of meaning in it alter. It was dead and is alive again. It is like the difference between looking on a person without love, or upon the same person with love. In the latter case intercourse springs into new vitality. So when one's affections keep in touch with the divinity of the world's authorship, fear and egotism fall away; and in the

306 C. Hilty: Glück, Dritter Theil, 1900, pp. 92 ff.

equanimity that follows, one finds in the hours, as they succeed each other, a series of purely benignant opportunities. It is as if all doors were opened, and all paths freshly smoothed. We meet a new world when we meet the old world in the spirit which this kind of prayer infuses.

Such a spirit was that of Marcus Aurelius and Epictetus.[307] It is that of mind-curers, of the transcendentalists, and of the so-called "liberal" Christians. As an expression of it, I will quote a page from one of Martineau's sermons:—

> "The universe, open to the eye to-day, looks as it did a thousand years ago: and the morning hymn of Milton does but tell the beauty with which our own familiar sun dressed the earliest fields and gardens of the world. We see what all our fathers saw. And if we cannot find God in your house or in mine, upon the roadside or the margin of the sea; in the bursting seed or opening flower; in the day duty or the night musing; in the general laugh and the secret grief; in the procession of life, ever entering afresh, and solemnly passing by and dropping off; I do not think we should discern him any more on the grass of Eden, or beneath the moonlight of Gethsemane. Depend upon it, it is not the want of greater miracles, but of the soul to perceive such as are allowed us still, that makes us push all the sanctities into the far spaces we cannot reach. The devout feel that wherever God's hand is, *there* is miracle: and it is simply an indevoutness which imagines that only where miracle is, can there be the real hand of God. The customs of Heaven ought surely to be more sacred in our eyes than its anomalies; the dear old ways, of which the Most High is never tired, than the strange things which he does not love well enough ever to repeat. And he who will but discern beneath the sun, as he rises any morning, the supporting finger of the Almighty, may recover the sweet and reverent surprise with which Adam gazed on the first dawn in Paradise. It is no outward change, no shifting in time or place; but only the loving meditation of the pure in heart, that can reawaken the Eternal from the sleep within our souls: that can render him a reality again, and reassert for him once more his ancient name of 'the Living God.' "[308]

When we see all things in God, and refer all things to him, we read in common

307 "Good Heaven!" says Epictetus, "any one thing in the creation is sufficient to demonstrate a Providence, to a humble and grateful mind. The mere possibility of producing milk from grass, cheese from milk, and wool from skins; who formed and planned it? Ought we not, whether we dig or plough or eat, to sing this hymn to God? Great is God, who has supplied us with these instruments to till the ground; great is God, who has given us hands and instruments of digestion; who has given us to grow insensibly and to breathe in sleep. These things we ought forever to celebrate. . . . But because the most of you are blind and insensible, there must be some one to fill this station, and lead, in behalf of all men, the hymn to God; for what else can I do, a lame old man, but sing hymns to God? Were I a nightingale, I would act the part of a nightingale; were I a swan, the part of a swan. But since I am a reasonable creature, it is my duty to praise God . . . and I call on you to join the same song." Works, book i. ch. xvi., Carter-Higginson translation, abridged.

308 James Martineau: end of the sermon "Help Thou Mine Unbelief," in Endeavours after a Christian Life, 2d series. Compare with this page the extract from Voysey on p. 270, above, and those from Pascal and Madame Guyon on p. 281.

matters superior expressions of meaning. The deadness with which custom invests the familiar vanishes, and existence as a whole appears transfigured. The state of a mind thus awakened from torpor is well expressed in these words, which I take from a friend's letter:—

> "If we occupy ourselves in summing up all the mercies and bounties we are privileged to have, we are overwhelmed by their number (so great that we can imagine ourselves unable to give ourselves time even to begin to review the things we may imagine *we have not*). We sum them and realize that *we are actually killed with God's kindness;* that we are surrounded by bounties upon bounties, without which all would fall. Should we not love it; should we not feel buoyed up by the Eternal Arms?"

Sometimes this realization that facts are of divine sending, instead of being habitual, is casual, like a mystical experience. Father Gratry gives this instance from his youthful melancholy period:—

> "One day I had a moment of consolation, because I met with something which seemed to me ideally perfect. It was a poor drummer beating the tattoo in the streets of Paris. I walked behind him in returning to the school on the evening of a holiday. His drum gave out the tattoo in such a way that, at that moment at least, however peevish I were, I could find no pretext for fault-finding. It was impossible to conceive more nerve or spirit, better time or measure, more clearness or richness, than were in this drumming. Ideal desire could go no farther in that direction. I was enchanted and consoled; the perfection of this wretched act did me good. Good is at least possible, I said, since the ideal can thus sometimes get embodied."[309]

In Sénancour's novel of Obermann a similar transient lifting of the veil is recorded. In Paris streets, on a March day, he comes across a flower in bloom, a jonquil:

> "It was the strongest expression of desire: it was the first perfume of the year. I felt all the happiness destined for man. This unutterable harmony of souls, the phantom of the ideal world, arose in me complete. I never felt anything so great or so instantaneous. I know not what shape, what analogy, what secret of relation it was that made me see in this flower a limitless beauty. . . . I shall never inclose in a conception this power, this immensity that nothing will express; this form that nothing will contain; this ideal of a better world which one feels, but which, it seems, nature has not made actual."[310]

We heard in previous lectures of the vivified face of the world as it may appear

309 Souvenirs de ma Jeunesse, 1897, p. 122.

310 Op. cit., Letter XXX.

to converts after their awakening. As a rule, religious persons generally assume that whatever natural facts connect themselves in any way with their destiny are significant of the divine purposes with them. Through prayer the purpose, often far from obvious, comes home to them, and if it be "trial," strength to endure the trial is given. Thus at all stages of the prayerful life we find the persuasion that in the process of communion energy from on high flows in to meet demand, and becomes operative within the phenomenal world. So long as this operativeness is admitted to be real, it makes no essential difference whether its immediate effects be subjective or objective. The fundamental religious point is that in prayer, spiritual energy, which otherwise would slumber, does become active, and spiritual work of some kind is effected really.

So much for Prayer, taken in the wide sense of any kind of communion. As the core of religion, we must return to it in the next lecture.

The last aspect of the religious life which remains for me to touch upon is the fact that its manifestations so frequently connect themselves with the subconscious part of our existence. You may remember what I said in my opening lecture about the prevalence of the psychopathic temperament in religious biography. You will in point of fact hardly find a religious leader of any kind in whose life there is no record of automatisms. I speak not merely of savage priests and prophets, whose followers regard automatic utterance and action as by itself tantamount to inspiration, I speak of leaders of thought and subjects of intellectualized experience. Saint Paul had his visions, his ecstasies, his gift of tongues, small as was the importance he attached to the latter. The whole array of Christian saints and heresiarchs, including the greatest, the Barnards, the Loyolas, the Luthers, the Foxes, the Wesleys, had their visions, voices, rapt conditions, guiding impressions, and "openings." They had these things, because they had exalted sensibility, and to such things persons of exalted sensibility are liable. In such liability there lie, however, consequences for theology. Beliefs are strengthened wherever automatisms corroborate them. Incursions from beyond the transmarginal region have a peculiar power to increase conviction. The inchoate sense of presence is infinitely stronger than conception, but strong as it may be, it is seldom equal to the evidence of hallucination. Saints who actually see or hear their Saviour reach the acme of assurance. Motor automatisms, though rarer, are, if possible, even more convincing than sensations. The subjects here actually feel themselves played upon by powers beyond their will. The evidence is dynamic; the God or spirit moves the very organs of their body.[311]

---

311 A friend of mine, a first-rate psychologist, who is a subject of graphic automatism, tells me that the appearance of independent actuation in the movements of his arm, when he writes automatically, is so distinct that it obliges him to abandon a psychophysical theory which he had previously believed in, the theory, namely, that we have no feeling of the discharge downwards of our voluntary motor-centres. We must normally have such a feeling, he thinks, or the *sense of an absence* would not be so striking as it is in these experiences. Graphic automatism of a fully developed kind is rare in religious history,

The great field for this sense of being the instrument of a higher power is of course "inspiration." It is easy to discriminate between the religious leaders who have been habitually subject to inspiration and those who have not. In the teachings of the Buddha, of Jesus, of Saint Paul (apart from his gift of tongues), of Saint Augustine, of Huss, of Luther, of Wesley, automatic or semi-automatic composition appears to have been only occasional. In the Hebrew prophets, on the contrary, in Mohammed, in some of the Alexandrians, in many minor Catholic saints, in Fox, in Joseph Smith, something like it appears to have been frequent, sometimes habitual. We have distinct professions of being under the direction of a foreign power, and serving as its mouthpiece. As regards the Hebrew prophets, it is extraordinary, writes an author who has made a careful study of them, to see—

> "How, one after another, the same features are reproduced in the prophetic books. The process is always extremely different from what it would be if the prophet arrived at his insight into spiritual things by the tentative efforts of his own genius. There is something sharp and sudden about it. He can lay his finger, so to speak, on the moment when it came. And it always comes in the form of an overpowering force from without, against which he struggles, but in vain. Listen, for instance, [to] the opening of the book of Jeremiah. Read through in like manner the first two chapters of the prophecy of Ezekiel.
>
> "It is not, however, only at the beginning of his career that the prophet passes through a crisis which is clearly not self-caused. Scattered all through the prophetic writings are expressions which speak of some strong and irresistible impulse coming down upon the prophet, determining his attitude to the events of his time, constraining his utterance, making his words the vehicle of a higher meaning than their own. For instance, this of Isaiah's: 'The Lord spake thus to me with a strong hand,'—an emphatic phrase which denotes the overmastering nature of the impulse—'and instructed me that I should not walk in the way of this people.' . . . Or passages like this from Ezekiel: 'The hand of the Lord God fell upon me,' 'The hand of the Lord was strong upon me.' The one standing characteristic of the prophet is that he speaks with the authority of Jehovah himself. Hence it is that the prophets one and all preface their addresses so confidently, 'The Word of the Lord,' or 'Thus saith the Lord.' They have even the audacity to speak in the first person, as if Jehovah himself were speaking. As in Isaiah: 'Hearken unto me, O Jacob, and Israel my called; I am He, I am the First, I also am the last,'—and so on. The personality Of the prophet sinks entirely into

---

so far as my knowledge goes. Such statements as Antonia Bourignon's, that "I do nothing but lend my hand and spirit to another power than mine," is shown by the context to indicate inspiration rather than directly automatic writing. In some eccentric sects this latter occurs. The most striking instance of it is probably the bulky volume called, "Oahspe, a new Bible in the Words of Jehovah and his angel ambassadors," Boston and London, 1891, written and illustrated automatically by Dr. NEWBROUGH of New York, whom I understand to be now, or to have been lately, at the head of the spiritistic community of Shalam in New Mexico. The latest automatically written book which has come under my notice is "Zertoulem's Wisdom of the Ages,' by GEORGE A. FULLER, Boston, 1901.

the background; he feels himself for the time being the mouthpiece of the Almighty."[312]

"We need to remember that prophecy was a profession, and that the prophets formed a professional class. There were schools of the prophets, in which the gift was regularly cultivated. A group of young men would gather round some commanding figure—a Samuel or an Elisha—and would not only record or spread the knowledge of his sayings and doings, but seek to catch themselves something of his inspiration. It seems that music played its part in their exercises.... It is perfectly clear that by no means all of these Sons of the prophets ever succeeded in acquiring more than a very small share in the gift which they sought. It was clearly possible to 'counterfeit' prophecy. Sometimes this was done deliberately.... But it by no means follows that in all cases where a false message was given, the giver of it was altogether conscious of what he was doing."[313]

Here, to take another Jewish case, is the way in which Philo of Alexandria describes his inspiration:—

"Sometimes, when I have come to my work empty, I have suddenly become full; ideas being in an invisible manner showered upon me, and implanted in me from on high; so that through the influence of divine inspiration, I have become greatly excited, and have known neither the place in which I was, nor those who were present, nor myself, nor what I was saying, nor what I was writing; for then I have been conscious of a richness of interpretation, an enjoyment of light, a most penetrating insight, a most manifest energy in all that was to be done; having such effect on my mind as the clearest ocular demonstration would have on the eyes."[314]

If we turn to Islam, we find that Mohammed's revelations all came from the subconscious sphere. To the question in what way he got them—

"Mohammed is said to have answered that sometimes he heard a knell as from a bell, and that this had the strongest effect on him; and when the angel went away, he had received the revelation. Sometimes again he held converse with the angel as with a man, so as easily to understand his words. The later authorities, however, ... distinguish still other kinds. In the Itqân (103) the following are enumerated: 1, revelations with sound of bell, 2, by inspiration of the holy spirit in M.'s heart, 3, by Gabriel in human form, 4, by God immediately, either when awake (as in his journey to heaven) or in dream.... In Almawâhib alladunîya the kinds are thus given: 1, Dream, 2, Inspiration of Gabriel in the Prophet's

312 W. Sanday: The Oracles of God, London, 1892, pp. 49–56, abridged.

313 Op. cit., p. 91. This author also cites Moses's and Isaiah's commissions, as given in Exodus, chaps. iii. and iv., and Isaiah, chap. vi.

314 Quoted by Augustus Clissold: The Prophetic Spirit in Genius and Madness, 1870, p. 67. Mr. Clissold is a Swedenborgian. Swedenborg's case is of course the palmary one of *audita et visa*, serving as a basis of religious revelation.

heart, 3, Gabriel taking Dahya's form, 4, with the bell-sound, etc., 5, Gabriel in propriâ personâ (only twice), 6, revelation in heaven, 7, God appearing in person, but veiled, 8, God revealing himself immediately without veil. Others add two other stages, namely: I, Gabriel in the form of still another man, 2, God showing himself personally in dream."[315]

In none of these cases is the revelation distinctly motor. In the case of Joseph Smith (who had prophetic revelations innumerable in addition to the revealed translation of the gold plates which resulted in the Book of Mormon), although there may have been a motor element, the inspiration seems to have been predominantly sensorial. He began his translation by the aid of the "peep-stones" which he found, or thought or said that he found, with the gold plates—apparently a case of "crystal gazing." For some of the other revelations he used the peep-stones, but seems generally to have asked the Lord for more direct instruction.[316]

Other revelations are described as "openings"—Fox's, for example, were evidently of the kind known in spiritistic circles of to-day as "impressions." As all effective initiators of change must needs live to some degree upon this psychopathic level of sudden perception or conviction of new truth, or of impulse to action so obsessive that it must be worked off, I will say nothing more about so very common a phenomenon.

When, in addition to these phenomena of inspiration, we take religious mysticism into the account, when we recall the striking and sudden unifications of a discordant self which we saw in conversion, and when we review the extravagant obsessions of tenderness, purity, and self-severity met with in saintliness, we cannot, I think, avoid the conclusion that in religion we have a department of human nature with unusually close relations to the transmarginal or subliminal region. If the word "subliminal" is offensive to any of you, as smelling too much of psychical research or other aberrations, call it by any other name you please, to distinguish it from the level of full sunlit consciousness. Call this latter the A-region of personality, if you care to, and call the other the B-region. The B-region, then, is obviously the larger part of each of us, for it is the abode of everything that is latent and the reservoir of

315 Nöldeke, Geschichte des Qorâns, 1860, p. 16. Compare the fuller account in Sir William Muir's: Life of Mahomet, 3d ed., 1894, ch. iii.

316 The Mormon theocracy has always been governed, by direct revelations accorded to the President of the Church and its Apostles. From an obliging letter written to me in 1899 by an eminent Mormon, I quote the following extract:—

"It may be very interesting for you to know that the President [Mr. Snow] of the Mormon Church claims to have had a number of revelations very recently from heaven. To explain fully what these revelations are, it is necessary to know that we, as a people, believe that the Church of Jesus Christ has again been established through messengers sent from heaven. This Church has at its head a prophet, seer, and revelator, who gives to man God's holy will. Revelation is the means through which the will of God is declared directly and in fullness to man. These revelations are got through dreams of sleep or in waking visions of the mind, by voices without visional appearance, or by actual manifestations of the Holy Presence before the eye. We believe that God has come in person and spoken to our prophet and revelator."

everything that passes unrecorded or unobserved. It contains, for example, such things as all our momentarily inactive memories, and it harbors the springs of all our obscurely motived passions, impulses, likes, dislikes, and prejudices. Our intuitions, hypotheses, fancies, superstitions, persuasions, convictions, and in general all our non-rational operations, come from it. It is the source of our dreams, and apparently they may return to it. In it arise whatever mystical experiences we may have, and our automatisms, sensory or motor; our life in hypnotic and "hypnoid" conditions, if we are subjects to such conditions; our delusions, fixed ideas, and hysterical accidents, if we are hysteric subjects; our supra-normal cognitions, if such there be, and if we are telepathic subjects. It is also the fountain-head of much that feeds our religion. In persons deep in the religious life, as we have now abundantly seen—and this is my conclusion—the door into this region seems unusually wide open; at any rate, experiences making their entrance through that door have had emphatic influence in shaping religious history.

With this conclusion I turn back and close the circle which I opened in my first lecture, terminating thus the review which I then announced of inner religious phenomena as we find them in developed and articulate human individuals. I might easily, if the time allowed, multiply both my documents and my discriminations, but a broad treatment is, I believe, in itself better, and the most important characteristics of the subject lie, I think, before us already. In the next lecture, which is also the last one, we must try to draw the critical conclusions which so much material may suggest.

LECTURE XX

# Conclusions

The material of our study of human nature is now spread before us; and in this parting hour, set free from the duty of description, we can draw our theoretical and practical conclusions. In my first lecture, defending the empirical method, I foretold that whatever conclusions we might come to could be reached by spiritual judgments only, appreciations of the significance for life of religion, taken "on the whole." Our conclusions cannot be as sharp as dogmatic conclusions would be, but I will formulate them, when the time comes, as sharply as I can.

Summing up in the broadest possible way the characteristics of the religious life, as we have found them, it includes the following beliefs:—

1. That the visible world is part of a more spiritual universe from which it draws its chief significance;
2. That union or harmonious relation with that higher universe is our true end;
3. That prayer or inner communion with the spirit thereof—be that spirit "God" or "law"—is a process wherein work is really done, and spiritual energy flows in and produces effects, psychological or material, within the phenomenal world.

Religion includes also the following psychological characteristics:—

4. A new zest which adds itself like a gift to life, and takes the form either of lyrical enchantment or of appeal to earnestness and heroism.
5. An assurance of safety and a temper of peace, and, in relation to others, a preponderance of loving affections.

In illustrating these characteristics by documents, we have been literally bathed in sentiment. In re-reading my manuscript, I am almost appalled at the amount of emotionality which I find in it. After so much of this, we can afford to be dryer and less sympathetic in the rest of the work that lies before us.

The sentimentality of many of my documents is a consequence of the fact that I sought them among the extravagances of the subject. If any of you are enemies of what our ancestors used to brand as enthusiasm, and are, nevertheless, still listening to me now, you have probably felt my selection to have been sometimes almost perverse, and have wished I might have stuck to soberer examples. I reply that I took these extremer examples as yielding the profounder information. To learn the secrets of any science, we go to expert specialists, even though they may be eccentric persons, and not to commonplace pupils. We combine what they tell us with the rest of our wisdom, and form our final judgment independently. Even so with religion. We who have pursued such radical expressions of it may now be sure that we know its secrets as authentically as anyone can know them who learns them from another; and we have next to answer, each of us for himself, the practical question: what are the dangers in this element of life? and in what proportion may it need to be restrained by other elements, to give the proper balance?

But this question suggests another one which I will answer immediately and get it out of the way, for it has more than once already vexed us. Ought it to be assumed that in all men the mixture of religion with other elements should be identical? Ought it, indeed, to be assumed that the lives of all men should show identical religious elements? In other words, is the existence of so many religious types and sects and creeds regrettable?

To these questions I answer "No" emphatically. And my reason is that I do not see how it is possible that creatures in such different positions and with such different powers as human individuals are, should have exactly the same functions and the same duties. No two of us have identical difficulties, nor should we be expected to work out identical solutions. Each, from his peculiar angle of observation, takes in a certain sphere of fact and trouble, which each must deal with in a unique manner. One of us must soften himself, another must harden himself; one must yield a point, another must stand firm—in order the better to defend the position assigned him. If an Emerson were forced to be a Wesley, or a Moody forced to be a Whitman, the total human consciousness of the divine would suffer. The divine can mean no single quality, it must mean a group of qualities, by being champions of which in alternation, different men may all find worthy missions. Each attitude being a syllable in human nature's total message, it takes the whole of us to spell the meaning out completely. So a "god of battles" must be allowed to be the god for one kind of person, a god of peace and heaven and home, the god for another. We must frankly recognize the fact that we live in partial systems, and that parts are not interchangeable in the spiritual life. If we are peevish and jealous, destruction of the self must be an element of our religion; why need it be one if we are good and sympathetic from the outset? If we are sick souls, we require a religion of deliverance; but why think so much of deliverance, if we are healthy-minded?[317] Unquestionably, some

317 From this point of view, the contrasts between the healthy and the morbid mind, and between the once-born and the twice-born types, of which I spoke in earlier lectures, cease to be the radical an-

men have the completer experience and the higher vocation, here just as in the social world; but for each man to stay in his own experience, whate'er it be, and for others to tolerate him there, is surely best.

But, you may now ask, would not this one-sidedness be cured if we should all espouse the science of religions as our own religion? In answering this question I must open again the general relations of the theoretic to the active life.

Knowledge about a thing is not the thing itself. You remember what Al-Ghazzali told us in the Lecture on Mysticism—that to understand the causes of drunkenness, as a physician understands them, is not to be drunk. A science might come to understand everything about the causes and elements of religion, and might even decide which elements were qualified, by their general harmony with other branches of knowledge, to be considered true; and yet the best man at this science might be the man who found it hardest to be personally devout. *Tout savoir c'est tout pardonner.* The name of Renan would doubtless occur to many persons as an example of the way in which breadth of knowledge may make one only a dilettante in possibilities, and blunt the acuteness of one's living faith.[318] If religion be a function by which either God's cause or man's cause is to be really advanced, then he who lives the life of it, however narrowly, is a better servant than he who merely knows about it, however much. Knowledge about life is one thing; effective occupation of a place in life, with its dynamic currents passing through your being, is another.

For this reason, the science of religions may not be an equivalent for living religion; and if we turn to the inner difficulties of such a science, we see that a point comes when she must drop the purely theoretic attitude, and either let her knots remain uncut, or have them cut by active faith. To see this, suppose that we have our science of religions constituted as a matter of fact. Suppose that she has assimilated all the necessary historical material and distilled out of it as its essence the same conclusions which I myself a few moments ago pronounced. Suppose that she agrees that religion, wherever it is an active thing, involves a belief in ideal presences, and

---

tagonisms which many think them. The twice-born look down upon the rectilinear consciousness of life of the once-born as being "mere morality," and not properly religion. "Dr. Channing," an orthodox minister is reported to have said, "is excluded from the highest form of religious life by the extraordinary rectitude of his character." It is indeed true that the outlook upon life of the twice-born—holding as it does more of the element of evil in solution—is the wider and completer. The "heroic" or "solemn" way in which life comes to them is a "higher synthesis" into which healthy-mindedness and morbidness both enter and combine. Evil is not evaded, but sublated in the higher religious cheer of these persons. But the final consciousness which each type reaches of union with the divine has the same practical significance for the individual; and individuals may well be allowed to get to it by the channels which lie most open to their several temperaments. In the cases which were quoted in Lecture IV, of the mind-cure form of healthy-mindedness, we found abundant examples of regenerative process. The severity of the crisis in this process is a matter of degree. How long one shall continue to drink the consciousness of evil, and when one shall begin to short-circuit and get rid of it, are also matters of amount and degree, so that in many instances it is quite arbitrary whether we class the individual as a once-born or a twice-born subject.

318 Compare, e. g., the quotation from Renan on p. 37, above.

a belief that in our prayerful communion with them,[319] work is done, and something real comes to pass. She has now to exert her critical activity, and to decide how far, in the light of other sciences and in that of general philosophy, such beliefs can be considered *true.*

Dogmatically to decide this is an impossible task. Not only are the other sciences and the philosophy still far from being completed, but in their present state we find them full of conflicts. The sciences of nature know nothing of spiritual presences, and on the whole hold no practical commerce whatever with the idealistic conceptions towards which general philosophy inclines. The scientist, so-called, is, during his scientific hours at least, so materialistic that one may well say that on the whole the influence of science goes against the notion that religion should be recognized at all. And this antipathy to religion finds an echo within the very science of religions itself. The cultivator of this science has to become acquainted with so many groveling and horrible superstitions that a presumption easily arises in his mind that any belief that is religious probably is false. In the "prayerful communion" of savages with such mumbo-jumbos of deities as they acknowledge, it is hard for us to see what genuine spiritual work—even though it were work relative only to their dark savage obligations—can possibly be done.

The consequence is that the conclusions of the science of religions are as likely to be adverse as they are to be favorable to the claim that the essence of religion is true. There is a notion in the air about us that religion is probably only an anachronism, a case of "survival," an atavistic relapse into a mode of thought which humanity in its more enlightened examples has outgrown; and this notion our religious anthropologists at present do little to counteract.

This view is so widespread at the present day that I must consider it with some explicitness before I pass to my own conclusions. Let me call it the "Survival theory," for brevity's sake.

The pivot round which the religious life, as we have traced it, revolves, is the interest of the individual in his private personal destiny. Religion, in short, is a monumental chapter in the history of human egotism. The gods believed in—whether by crude savages or by men disciplined intellectually—agree with each other in recognizing personal calls. Religious thought is carried on in terms of personality, this being, in the world of religion, the one fundamental fact. To-day, quite as much as at any previous age, the religious individual tells you that the divine meets him on the basis of his personal concerns.

Science, on the other hand, has ended by utterly repudiating the personal point of view. She catalogues her elements and records her laws indifferent as to what purpose may be shown forth by them, and constructs her theories quite careless of their bearing on human anxieties and fates. Though the scientist may individually nourish a religion, and be a theist in his irresponsible hours, the days are over when

319 "Prayerful" taken in the broader sense explained above on pp. 453 ff.

it could be said that for Science herself the heavens declare the glory of God and the firmament showeth his handiwork. Our solar system, with its harmonies, is seen now as but one passing case of a certain sort of moving equilibrium in the heavens, realized by a local accident in an appalling wilderness of worlds where no life can exist. In a span of time which as a cosmic interval will count but as an hour, it will have ceased to be. The Darwinian notion of chance production, and subsequent destruction, speedy or deferred, applies to the largest as well as to the smallest facts. It is impossible, in the present temper of the scientific imagination, to find in the driftings of the cosmic atoms, whether they work on the universal or on the particular scale, anything but a kind of aimless weather, doing and undoing, achieving no proper history, and leaving no result. Nature has no one distinguishable ultimate tendency with which it is possible to feel a sympathy. In the vast rhythm of her processes, as the scientific mind now follows them, she appears to cancel herself. The books of natural theology which satisfied the intellects of our grandfathers seem to us quite grotesque,[320] representing, as they did, a God who conformed the largest

320 How was it ever conceivable, we ask, that a man like Christian Wolff, in whose dry-as-dust head all the learning of the early eighteenth century was concentrated, should have preserved such a baby-like faith in the personal and human character of Nature as to expound her operations as he did in his work on the uses of natural things? This, for example, is the account he gives of the sun and its utility:—

"We see that God has created the sun to keep the changeable conditions on the earth in such an order that living creatures, men and beasts, may inhabit its surface. Since men are the most reasonable of creatures, and able to infer God's invisible being from the contemplation of the world, the sun in so far forth contributes to the primary purpose of creation: without it the race of man could not be preserved or continued. . . . The sun makes daylight, not only on our earth, but also on the other planets; and daylight is of the utmost utility to us; for by its means we can commodiously carry on those occupations which in the night-time would either be quite impossible or at any rate impossible without our going to the expense of artificial light. The beasts of the field can find food by day which they would not be able to find at night. Moreover we owe it to the sunlight that we are able to see everything that is on the earth's surface, not only near by, but also at a distance, and to recognize both near and far things according to their species, which again is of manifold use to us not only in the business necessary to human life, and when we are traveling, but also for the scientific knowledge of Nature, which knowledge for the most part depends on observations made with the help of sight, and, without the sunshine, would have been impossible. If any one would rightly impress on his mind the great advantages which he derives from the sun, let him imagine himself living through only one month, and see how it would be with all his undertakings, if it were not day but night. He would then be sufficiently convinced out of his own experience, especially if he had much work to carry on in the street or in the fields. . . . From the sun we learn to recognize when it is midday, and by knowing this point of time exactly, we can set our clocks right, on which account astronomy owes much to the sun. . . . By help of the sun one can find the meridian. . . . But the meridian is the basis of our sun-dials, and generally speaking, we should have no sun-dials if we had no sun." Ver nünftige Gedanken von den Absichter der natürlichen Dinge, 1782. pp. 74–84.

Or read the account of God's beneficence in the institution of "the great variety throughout the world of men's faces, voices, and handwriting," given in Derham's Physico-theology, a book that had much vogue in the eighteenth century. "Had Man's body," says Dr. Derham, "been made according to any of the Atheistical Schemes, or any other Method than that of the infinite Lord of the World, this wise Variety would never have been: but Men's Faces would have been cast in the same, or not a very different Mould, their Organs of Speech would have sounded the same or not so great a Variety of Notes; and the same Structure of Muscles and Nerves would have given the Hand the same Direction in Writing. And in this Case, what Confusion, what Disturbance, what Mischiefs would the world eternally have lain under! No Security could have been to our persons; no Certainty, no Enjoyment of our Possessions; no

things of nature to the paltriest of our private wants. The God whom science recognizes must be a God of universal laws exclusively, a God who does a wholesale, not a retail business. He cannot accommodate his processes to the convenience of indi-

Justice between Man and Man; no Distinction between Good and Bad, between Friends and Foes, between Father and Child, Husband and Wife, Male or Female; but all would have been turned topsy-turvy, by being exposed to the Malice of the Envious and ill-Natured, to the Fraud and Violence of Knaves and Robbers, to the Forgeries of the crafty Cheat, to the Lusts of the Effeminate and Debauched, and what not! Our Courts of Justice can abundantly testify the dire Effects of Mistaking Men's Faces, of counterfeiting their Hands, and forging Writings. But now as the infinitely wise Creator and Ruler hath ordered the Matter, every man's Face can distinguish him in the Light, and his Voice in the Dark; his Handwriting can speak for him though absent, and be his Witness, and secure his Contracts in future Generations. A manifest as well as admirable Indication of the divine Superintendence and Management."

A God so careful as to make provision even for the unmistakable signing of bank checks and deeds was a deity truly after the heart of eighteenth century Anglicanism.

I subjoin, omitting the capitals, Derham's "Vindication of God by the Institution of Hills and Valleys," and Wolff's altogether culinary account of the institution of Water:—

"The uses," says Wolff, "which water serves in human life are plain to see and need not be described at length. Water is a universal drink of man and beasts. Even though men have made themselves drinks that are artificial, they could not do this without water. Beer is brewed of water and malt, and it is the water in it which quenches thirst. Wine is prepared from grapes, which could never have grown without the help of water; and the same is true of those drinks which in England and other places they produce from fruit.... Therefore since God so planned the world that men and beasts should live upon it and find there everything required for their necessity and convenience, he also made water as one means whereby to make the earth into so excellent a dwelling. And this is all the more manifest when we consider the advantages which we obtain from this same water for the cleaning of our household utensils, of our clothing, and of other matters.... When one goes into a grinding-mill one sees that the grindstone must always be kept wet and then one will get a still greater idea of the use of water."

Of the hills and valleys, Derham, after praising their beauty, discourses as follows: "Some constitutions are indeed of so happy a strength, and so confirmed an health, as to be indifferent to almost any place or temperature of the air. But then others are so weakly and feeble, as not to be able to bear one, but can live comfortably in another place. With some the more subtle and finer air of the hills doth best agree, who are languishing and dying in the feculent and grosser air of great towns, or even the warmer and vaporous air of the valleys and waters. But contrariwise, others languish on the hills, and grow lusty and strong in the warmer air of the valleys.

"So that this opportunity of shifting our abode from the hills to the vales, is an admirable easement, refreshment, and great benefit to the valetudinarian, feeble part of mankind; affording those an easy and comfortable life, who would otherwise live miserably, languish, and pine away.

"To this salutary conformation of the earth we may add another great convenience of the hills, and that is affording commodious places for habitation, serving (as an eminent author wordeth it) as screens to keep off the cold and nipping blasts of the northern and easterly winds, and reflecting the benign and cherishing sunbeams, and so rendering our habitations both more comfortable and more cheerly in winter.

"Lastly, it is to the hills that the fountains owe their rise and the rivers their conveyance, and consequently those vast masses and lofty piles are not, as they are charged, such rude and useless excrescences of our ill-formed globe; but the admirable tools of nature, contrived and ordered by the infinite Creator, to do one of its most useful works. For, was the surface of the earth even and level, and the middle parts of its islands and continents not mountainous and high as now it is, it is most certain there could be no descent for the rivers, no conveyance for the waters; but, instead of gliding along those gentle declivities which the higher lands now afford them quite down to the sea, they would stagnate and perhaps stink, and also drown large tracts of land.

"[Thus] the hills and vales, though to a peevish and weary traveler they may seem incommodious and troublesome, yet are a noble work of the great Creator, and wisely appointed by him for the good of our sublunary world."

viduals. The bubbles on the foam which coats a stormy sea are floating episodes, made and unmade by the forces of the wind and water. Our private selves are like those bubbles—epiphenomena, as Clifford, I believe, ingeniously called them; their destinies weigh nothing and determine nothing in the world's irremediable currents of events.

You see how natural it is, from this point of view, to treat religion as a mere survival, for religion does in fact perpetuate the traditions of the most primeval thought. To coerce the spiritual powers, or to square them and get them on our side, was, during enormous tracts of time, the one great object in our dealings with the natural world. For our ancestors, dreams, hallucinations, revelations, and cock-and-bull stories were inextricably mixed with facts. Up to a comparatively recent date such distinctions as those between what has been verified and what is only conjectured, between the impersonal and the personal aspects of existence, were hardly suspected or conceived. Whatever you imagined in a lively manner, whatever you thought fit to be true, you affirmed confidently; and whatever you affirmed, your comrades believed. Truth was what had not yet been contradicted, most things were taken into the mind from the point of view of their human suggestiveness, and the attention confined itself exclusively to the æsthetic and dramatic aspects of events.[321]

---

321 Until the seventeenth century this mode of thought prevailed. One need only recall the dramatic treatment even of mechanical questions by Aristotle, as, for example, his explanation of the power of the lever to make a small weight raise a larger one. This is due, according to Aristotle, to the generally miraculous character of the circle and of all circular movement. The circle is both convex and concave; it is made by a fixed point and a moving line, which contradict each other; and whatever moves in a circle moves in opposite directions. Nevertheless, movement in a circle is the most "natural" movement; and the long arm of the lever, moving, as it does, in the larger circle, has the greater amount of this natural motion, and consequently requires the lesser force. Or recall the explanation by Herodotus of the position of the sun in winter: It moves to the south because of the cold which drives it into the warm parts of the heavens over Libya. Or listen to Saint Augustine's speculations: "Who gave to chaff such power to freeze that it preserves snow buried under it, and such power to warm that it ripens green fruit? Who can explain the strange properties of fire itself, which blackens all that it burns, though itself bright, and which, though of the most beautiful colors, discolors almost all that it touches and feeds upon, and turns blazing fuel into grimy cinders? . . . Then what wonderful properties do we find in charcoal, which is so brittle that a light tap breaks it, and a slight pressure pulverizes it, and yet is so strong that no moisture rots it, nor any time causes it to decay." City of God, book xxi, ch. iv.

Such aspects of things as these, their naturalness and unnaturalness, the sympathies and antipathies of their superficial qualities, their eccentricities, their brightness and strength and destructiveness, were inevitably the ways in which they originally fastened our attention.

If you open early medical books, you will find sympathetic magic invoked on every page. Take, for example, the famous vulnerary ointment attributed to Paracelsus. For this there were a variety of receipts, including usually human fat, the fat of either a bull, a wild boar, or a bear; powdered earthworms, the *usnia*, or mossy growth on the weathered skull of a hanged criminal, and other materials equally unpleasant—the whole prepared under the planet Venus if possible, but never under Mars or Saturn. Then, if a splinter of wood, dipped in the patient's blood, or the bloodstained weapon that wounded him, be immersed in this ointment, the wound itself being tightly bound up, the latter infallibly gets well—I quote now Van Helmont's account—for the blood on the weapon or splinter, containing in it the spirit of the wounded man, is roused to active excitement by the contact of the ointment, whence there results to it a full commission or power to cure its cousin-german, the blood in the patient's body. This it does by sucking out the dolorous and exotic impression from the wounded

How indeed could it be otherwise? The extraordinary value, for explanation and prevision, of those mathematical and mechanical modes of conception which science uses, was a result that could not possibly have been expected in advance. Weight, movement, velocity, direction, position, what thin, pallid, uninteresting ideas! How could the richer animistic aspects of Nature, the peculiarities and oddities that make phenomena picturesquely striking or expressive, fail to have been first singled out and followed by philosophy as the more promising avenue to the knowledge of Nature's life? Well, it is still in these richer animistic and dramatic aspects that religion delights to dwell. It is the terror and beauty of phenomena, the "promise" of the dawn and of the rainbow, the "voice" of the thunder, the "gentleness" of the summer rain, the "sublimity" of the stars, and not the physical laws which these things follow, by which the religious mind still continues to be most impressed; and just as of yore, the devout man tells you that in the solitude of his room or of the fields he still feels the divine presence, that inflowings of help come in reply to his prayers, and that sacrifices to this unseen reality fill him with security and peace.

Pure anachronism! says the survival-theory;—anachronism for which deanthropomorphization of the imagination is the remedy required. The less we mix the

---

part. But to do this it has to implore the aid of the bull's fat, and other portions of the unguent. The reason why bull's fat is so powerful is that the bull at the time of slaughter is full of secret reluctancy and vindictive murmurs, and therefore dies with a higher flame of revenge about him than any other animal. And thus we have made it out, says this author, that the admirable efficacy of the ointment ought to be imputed, not to any auxiliary concurrence of Satan, but simply to the energy of the *posthumous character of Revenge* remaining firmly impressed upon the blood and concreted fat in the unguent. J. B. Van Helmont: A Ternary of Paradoxes, translated by Walter Charleton, London, 1650.—I much abridge the original in my citations.

The author goes on to prove by the analogy of many other natural facts that this sympathetic action between things at a distance is the true rationale of the case. "If," he says, "the heart of a horse, slain by a witch, taken out of the yet reeking carcase, be impaled upon an arrow and roasted, immediately the whole witch becomes tormented with the insufferable pains and cruelty of the fire, which could by no means happen unless there preceded a conjunction of the spirit of the witch with the spirit of the horse. In the reeking and yet panting heart, the spirit of the witch is kept captive, and the retreat of it prevented by the arrow transfixed. Similarly hath not many a murdered carcase at the coroner's inquest suffered a fresh hæmorrhage or cruentation at the presence of the assassin?—the blood being, as in a furious fit of anger, enraged and agitated by the impress of revenge conceived against the murderer, at the instant of the soul's compulsive exile from the body. So, if you have dropsy, gout, or jaundice, by including some of your warm blood in the shell and white of an egg, which, exposed to a gentle heat, and mixed with a bait of flesh, you shall give to a hungry dog or hog, the disease shall instantly pass from you into the animal, and leave you entirely. And similarly again, if you burn some of the milk either of a cow or of a woman, the gland from which it issued will dry up. A gentleman at Brussels had his nose mowed off in a combat, but the celebrated surgeon Tagliacozzus digged a new nose for him out of the skin of the arm of a porter at Bologna. About thirteen months after his return to his own country, the engrafted nose grew cold, putrefied, and in a few days dropped off, and it was then discovered that the porter had expired, near about the same punctilio of time. There are still at Brussels eye-witnesses of this occurrence," says Van Helmont; and adds, "I pray what is there in this of superstition or of exalted imagination?"

Modern mind-cure literature—the works of Prentice Mulford, for example—is full of sympathetic magic.

private with the cosmic, the more we dwell in universal and impersonal terms, the truer heirs of Science we become.

In spite of the appeal which this impersonality of the scientific attitude makes to a certain magnanimity of temper, I believe it to be shallow, and I can now state my reason in comparatively few words. That reason is that, so long as we deal with the cosmic and the general, we deal only with the symbols of reality, but *as soon as we deal with private and personal phenomena as such, we deal with realities in the completest sense of the term.* I think I can easily make clear what I mean by these words.

The world of our experience consists at all times of two parts, an objective and a subjective part, of which the former may be incalculably more extensive than the latter, and yet the latter can never be omitted or suppressed. The objective part is the sum total of whatsoever at any given time we may be thinking of, the subjective part is the inner "state" in which the thinking comes to pass. What we think of may be enormous—the cosmic times and spaces, for example—whereas the inner state may be the most fugitive and paltry activity of mind. Yet the cosmic objects, so far as the experience yields them, are but ideal pictures of something whose existence we do not inwardly possess but only point at outwardly, while the inner state is our very experience itself; its reality and that of our experience are one. A conscious field *plus* its object as felt or thought of *plus* an attitude towards the object *plus* the sense of a self to whom the attitude belongs—such a concrete bit of personal experience may be a small bit, but it is a solid bit as long as it lasts; not hollow, not a mere abstract element of experience, such as the "object" is when taken all alone. It is a *full* fact, even though it be an insignificant fact; it is of the *kind* to which all realities whatsoever must belong; the motor currents of the world run through the like of it; it is on the line connecting real events with real events. That unsharable feeling which each one of us has of the pinch of his individual destiny as he privately feels it rolling out on fortune's wheel may be disparaged for its egotism, may be sneered at as unscientific, but it is the one thing that fills up the measure of our concrete actuality, and any would-be existent that should lack such a feeling, or its analogue, would be a piece of reality only half made up.[322]

If this be true, it is absurd for science to say that the egotistic elements of experience should be suppressed. The axis of reality runs solely through the egotistic places—they are strung upon it like so many beads. To describe the world with all the various feelings of the individual pinch of destiny, all the various spiritual attitudes, left out from the description—they being as describable as anything else—would be something like offering a printed bill of fare as the equivalent for a solid meal. Religion makes no such blunder. The individual's religion may be egotistic,

---

322 Compare Lotze's doctrine that the only meaning we can attach to the notion of a thing as it is "in itself" is by conceiving it as it is *for* itself; i. e., as a piece of full experience with a private sense of "pinch" or inner activity of some sort going with it.

and those private realities which it keeps in touch with may be narrow enough; but at any rate it always remains infinitely less hollow and abstract, as far as it goes, than a science which prides itself on taking no account of anything private at all.

A bill of fare with one real raisin on it instead of the word "raisin," with one real egg instead of the word "egg," might be an inadequate meal, but it would at least be a commencement of reality. The contention of the survival-theory that we ought to stick to non-personal elements exclusively seems like saying that we ought to be satisfied forever with reading the naked bill of fare. I think, therefore, that however particular questions connected with our individual destinies may be answered, it is only by acknowledging them as genuine questions, and living in the sphere of thought which they open up, that we become profound. But to live thus is to be religious; so I unhesitatingly repudiate the survival-theory of religion, as being founded on an egregious mistake. It does not follow, because our ancestors made so many errors of fact and mixed them with their religion, that we should therefore leave off being religious at all.[323] By being religious we establish ourselves in possession of ultimate reality at the only points at which reality is given us to guard. Our responsible concern is with our private destiny, after all.

You see now why I have been so individualistic throughout these lectures, and why I have seemed so bent on rehabilitating the element of feeling in religion and subordinating its intellectual part. Individuality is founded in feeling; and the recesses of feeling, the darker, blinder strata of character, are the only places in the world in which we catch real fact in the, making, and directly perceive how events

323 Even the errors of fact may possibly turn out not to be as wholesale as the scientist assumes. We saw in Lecture IV how the religious conception of the universe seems to many mind-curers "verified" from day to day by their experience of fact. "Experience of fact" is a field with so many things in it that the sectarian scientist, methodically declining, as he does, to recognize such "facts" as mind-curers and others like them experience, otherwise than by such rude heads of classification as "bosh," "rot," "folly," certainly leaves out a mass of raw fact which, save for the industrious interest of the religious in the more personal aspects of reality, would never have succeeded in getting itself recorded at all. We know this to be true already in certain cases; it may, therefore, be true in others as well. Miraculous healings have always been part of the supernaturalist stock in trade, and have always been dismissed by the scientist as figments of the imagination. But the scientist's tardy education in the facts of hypnotism has recently given him an apperceiving mass for phenomena of this order, and he consequently now allows that the healings may exist, provided you expressly call them effects of "suggestion." Even the stigmata of the cross on Saint Francis's hands and feet may on these terms not be a fable. Similarly, the time-honored phenomenon of diabolical possession is on the point of being admitted by the scientist as a fact, now that he has the name of "hysterodemonopathy" by which to apperceive it. No one can foresee just how far this legitimation of occultist phenomena under newly found scientist title may proceed—even "prophecy," even "levitation," might creep into the pale.

Thus the divorce between scientist facts and religious facts may not necessarily be as eternal as it at first sight seems, nor the personalism and romanticism of the world, as they appeared to primitive thinking, be matters so irrevocably outgrown. The final human opinion may, in short, in some manner now impossible to foresee, revert to the more personal style, just as any path of progress may follow a spiral rather than a straight line. If this were so, the rigorously impersonal view of science might one day appear as having been a temporarily useful eccentricity rather than the definitively triumphant position which the sectarian scientist at present so confidently announces it to be.

happen, and how work is actually done.[324] Compared with this world of living individualized feelings, the world of generalized objects which the intellect contemplates is without solidity or life. As in stereoscopic or kinetoscopic pictures seen outside the instrument, the third dimension, the movement, the vital element, are not there. We get a beautiful picture of an express train supposed to be moving, but where in the picture, as I have heard a friend say, is the energy or the fifty miles an hour?[325]

Let us agree, then, that Religion, occupying herself with personal destinies and keeping thus in contact with the only absolute realities which we know, must necessarily play an eternal part in human history. The next thing to decide is what she reveals about those destinies, or whether indeed she reveals anything distinct enough to be considered a general message to mankind. We have done as you see, with our preliminaries, and our final summing up can now begin.

I am well aware that after all the palpitating documents which I have quoted, and all the perspectives of emotion-inspiring institution and belief that my previous lectures have opened, the dry analysis to which I now advance may appear to many of you like an anti-climax, a tapering-off and flattening out of the subject,

---

324 Hume's criticism has banished causation from the world of physical objects, and "Science" is absolutely satisfied to define cause in terms of concomitant change—read Mach, Pearson, Ostwald. The "original" of the notion of causation is in our inner personal experience, and only there can causes in the old-fashioned sense be directly observed and described.

325 When I read in a religious paper words like these: "Perhaps the best thing we can say of God is that he is *the Inevitable Inference*," I recognize the tendency to let religion evaporate in intellectual terms. Would martyrs have sung in the flames for a mere inference, however inevitable it might be? Original religious men, like Saint Francis, Luther, Behmen, have usually been enemies of the intellect's pretension to meddle with religious things. Yet the intellect, everywhere invasive, shows everywhere its shallowing effect. See how the ancient spirit of Methodism evaporates under those wonderfully able rationalistic booklets (which every one should read) of a philosopher like Professor Bowne (The Christian Revelation, The Christian Life, The Atonement: Cincinnati and New York, 1898, 1899, 1900). See the positively expulsive purpose of philosophy properly so called:—

"Religion," writes M. Vacherot (La Religion, Paris, 1869, pp. 313, 436, et passim), "answers to a transient state or condition, not to a permanent determination of human nature, being merely an expression of that stage of the human mind which is dominated by the imagination.... Christianity has but a single possible final heir to its estate, and that is scientific philosophy."

In a still more radical vein, Professor Ribot (Psychologie des Sentiments, p. 310) describes the evaporation of religion. He sums it up in a single formula—the ever-growing predominance of the rational intellectual element, with the gradual fading out of the emotional element, this latter tending to enter into the group of purely intellectual sentiments. "Of religious sentiment properly so called, nothing survives at last save a vague respect for the unknowable *x* which is a last relic of the fear, and a certain attraction towards the ideal, which is a relic of the love, that characterized the earlier periods of religious growth. To state this more simply, *religion tends to turn into religious philosophy.*—These are psychologically entirely different things, the one being a theoretic construction of ratiocination, whereas the other is the living work of a group of persons, or of a great inspired leader, calling into play the entire thinking and feeling organism of man."

I find the same failure to recognize that the stronghold of religion lies in individuality in attempts like those of Professor Baldwin (Mental Development, Social and Ethical Interpretations, ch. x) and Mr. H. R. Marshall (Instinct and Reason, chaps. viii. to xii.) to make it a purely "conservative social force."

instead of a crescendo of interest and result. I said awhile ago that the religious attitude of Protestants appears poverty-stricken to the Catholic imagination. Still more poverty-stricken, I fear, may my final summing up of the subject appear at first to some of you. On which account I pray you now to bear this point in mind, that in the present part of it I am expressly trying to reduce religion to its lowest admissible terms, to that minimum, free from individualistic excrescences, which all religions contain as their nucleus, and on which it may be hoped that all religious persons may agree. That established, we should have a result which might be small, but would at least be solid; and on it and round it the ruddier additional beliefs on which the different individuals make their venture might be grafted, and flourish as richly as you please. I shall add my own over-belief (which will be, I confess, of a somewhat pallid kind, as befits a critical philosopher), and you will, I hope, also add your over-beliefs, and we shall soon be in the varied world of concrete religious constructions once more. For the moment, let me dryly pursue the analytic part of the task.

Both thought and feeling are determinants of conduct, and the same conduct may be determined either by feeling or by thought. When we survey the whole field of religion, we find a great variety in the thoughts that have prevailed there; but the feelings on the one hand and the conduct on the other are almost always the same, for Stoic, Christian, and Buddhist saints are practically indistinguishable in their lives. The theories which Religion generates, being thus variable, are secondary; and if you wish to grasp her essence, you must look to the feelings and the conduct as being the more constant elements. It is between these two elements that the short circuit exists on which she carries on her principal business, while the ideas and symbols and other institutions form loop-lines which may be perfections and improvements, and may even some day all be united into one harmonious system, but which are not to be regarded as organs with an indispensable function, necessary at all times for religious life to go on. This seems to me the first conclusion which we are entitled to draw from the phenomena we have passed in review.

The next step is to characterize the feelings. To what psychological order do they belong?

The resultant outcome of them is in any case what Kant calls a "sthenic" affection, an excitement of the cheerful, expansive, "dynamogenic" order which, like any tonic, freshens our vital powers. In almost every lecture, but especially in the lectures on Conversion and on Saintliness, we have seen how this emotion overcomes temperamental melancholy and imparts endurance to the Subject, or a zest, or a meaning, or an enchantment and glory to the common objects of life. The name of "faith-state," by which Professor Leuba designates it, is a good one.[326] It is a biological as well as a psychological condition, and Tolstoy is absolutely accurate

326 American Journal of Psychology, vii. 345.

in classing faith among the forces *by which men live.* The total absence of it, anhedonia, means collapse.

The faith-state may hold a very minimum of intellectual content. We saw examples of this in those sudden raptures of the divine presence, or in such mystical seizures as Dr. Bucke described. It may be a mere vague enthusiasm, half spiritual, half vital, a courage, and a feeling that great and wondrous things are in the air.[327]

When, however, a positive intellectual content is associated with a faith-state, it gets invincibly stamped in upon belief,[328] and this explains the passionate loyalty of religious persons everywhere to the minutest details of their so widely differing creeds. Taking creeds and faith-state together, as forming "religions," and treating these as purely subjective phenomena, without regard to the question of their "truth," we are obliged, on account of their extraordinary influence upon action and endurance, to class them amongst the most important biological functions of mankind. Their stimulant and anæsthetic effect is so great that Professor Leuba, in a recent article,[329] goes so far as to say that so long as men can *use* their God, they care very little who he is, or even whether he is at all. "The truth of the matter can be put," says Leuba, "in this way: *God is not known, he is not understood; he is used*—some times as meat-purveyor, sometimes as moral support, sometimes as friend, sometimes as an object of love. If he proves himself useful, the religious consciousness asks for no more than that. Does God really exist? How does he exist? What is he? are so many irrelevant questions. Not God, but life, more life, a larger, richer, more satisfying life, is, in the last analysis, the end of religion. The love of life, at any and every level of development, is the religious impulse."[330]

---

327 Example: Henri Perreyve writes to Gratry: "I do not know how to deal with the happiness which you aroused in me this morning. It overwhelms me; I want to *do* something, yet I can do nothing and am fit for nothing. . . . I would fain do *great things.*" Again, after an inspiring interview, he writes: "I went homewards, intoxicated with joy, hope, and strength. I wanted to feed upon my happiness in solitude, far from all men. It was late; but, unheeding that, I took a mountain path and went on like a madman, looking at the heavens, regardless of earth. Suddenly an instinct made me draw hastily back—I was on the very edge of a precipice, one step more and I must have fallen. I took fright and gave up my nocturnal promenade." A. Gratry: Henri Perreyve, London, 1872, pp. 92, 89.

This primacy, in the faith-state, of vague expansive impulse over direction is well expressed in Walt Whitman's lines (Leaves of Grass, 1872, p. 190):—

"O to confront night, storms, hunger, ridicule, accidents, rebuffs, as the trees and animals do. . . .

Dear Camerado! I confess I have urged you onward with me, and still urge you, without the least idea what is our destination,

Or whether we shall be victorious, or utterly quell'd and defeated."

This readiness for great things, and this sense that the world by its importance, wonderfulness, etc., is apt for their production, would seem to be the undifferentiated germ of all the higher faiths. Trust in our own dreams of ambition, or in our country's expansive destinies, and faith in the providence of God, all have their source in that onrush of our sanguine impulses, and in that sense of the exceedingness of the possible over the real.

328 Compare Leuba: Loc. cit., pp. 346–349.

329 The Contents of Religious Consciousness, in The Monist, xi. 536, July 1901.

330 Loc. cit., pp. 571, 572, abridged. See, also, this writer's extraordinarily true criticism of the notion

At this purely subjective rating, therefore, Religion must be considered vindicated in a certain way from the attacks of her critics. It would seem that she cannot be a mere anachronism and survival, but must exert a permanent function, whether she be with or without intellectual content, and whether, if she have any, it be true or false.

We must next pass beyond the point of view of merely subjective utility, and make inquiry into the intellectual content itself.

First, is there, under all the discrepancies of the creeds, a common nucleus to which they bear their testimony unanimously?

And second, ought we to consider the testimony true?

I will take up the first question first, and answer it immediately in the affirmative. The warring gods and formulas of the various religions do indeed cancel each other, but there is a certain uniform deliverance in which religions all appear to meet. It consists of two parts:—

1. An uneasiness; and
2. Its solution.

1. The uneasiness, reduced to its simplest terms, is a sense that there is *something wrong about us* as we naturally stand.
2. The solution is a sense that *we are saved from the wrongness* by making proper connection with the higher powers.

In those more developed minds which alone we are studying, the wrongness takes a moral character, and the salvation takes a mystical tinge. I think we shall keep well within the limits of what is common to all such minds if we formulate the essence of their religious experience in terms like these:—

The individual, so far as he suffers from his wrongness and criticises it, is to that extent consciously beyond it, and in at least possible touch with something higher, if anything higher exist. Along with the wrong part there is thus a better part of him, even though it may be but a most helpless germ. With which part he should identify his real being is by no means obvious at this stage; but when stage 2 (the stage of solution or salvation) arrives,[331] the man identifies his real being with the germinal

that religion primarily seeks to solve the intellectual mystery of the world. Compare what W. Bender says (in his Wesen der Religion, Bonn, 1888, pp. 85, 38): "Not the question about God, and not the inquiry into the origin and purpose of the world is religion, but the question about Man. All religious views of life are anthropocentric." "Religion is that activity of the human impulse towards self-preservation by means of which Man seeks to carry his essential vital purposes through against the adverse pressure of the world by raising himself freely towards the world's ordering and governing powers when the limits of his own strength are reached." The whole book is little more than a development of these words.

331 Remember that for some men it arrives suddenly, for others gradually, whilst others again practically enjoy it all their life.

higher part of himself; and does so in the following way. *He becomes conscious that this higher part is conterminous and continuous with a* more *of the same quality, which is operative in the universe outside of him, and which he can keep in working touch with, and in a fashion get on board of and save himself when all his lower being has gone to pieces in the wreck.*

It seems to me that all the phenomena are accurately describable in these very simple general terms.[332] They allow for the divided self and the struggle; they involve the change of personal centre and the surrender of the lower self; they express the appearance of exteriority of the helping power and yet account for our sense of union with it;[333] and they fully justify our feelings of security and joy. There is probably no autobiographic document, among all those which I have quoted, to which the description will not well apply. One need only add such specific details as will adapt it to various theologies and various personal temperaments, and one will then have the various experiences reconstructed in their individual forms.

So far, however, as this analysis goes, the experiences are only psychological phenomena. They possess, it is true, enormous biological worth. Spiritual strength really increases in the subject when he has them, a new life opens for him, and they seem to him a place of conflux where the forces of two universes meet; and yet this may be nothing but his subjective way of feeling things, a mood of his own fancy, in spite of the effects produced. I now turn to my second question: What is the objective "truth" of their content?[334]

The part of the content concerning which the question of truth most pertinently arises is that "more of the same quality" with which our own higher self appears in the experience to come into harmonious working relation. Is such a "more" merely our own notion, or does it really exist? If so, in what shape does it exist? Does it act, as well as exist? And in what form should we conceive of that "union" with it of which religious geniuses are so convinced?

It is in answering these questions that the various theologies perform their theoretic work, and that their divergencies most come to light. They all agree that the "more" really exists; though some of them hold it to exist in the shape of a personal god or gods, while others are satisfied to conceive it as a stream of ideal tendency embedded in the eternal structure of the world. They all agree, moreover, that it acts as well as exists, and that something really is effected for the better when you throw your life into its hands. It is when they treat of the experience of "union" with it that their speculative differences appear most clearly. Over this point pantheism

332 The practical difficulties are: 1, to "realize the reality" of one's higher part; 2, to identify one's self with it exclusively; and 3, to identify it with all the rest of ideal being.

333 "When mystical activity is at its height, we find consciousness possessed by the sense of a being at once *excessive* and *identical* with the self: great enough to be God;, interior enough to be *me*. The "objectivity" of it ought in that case to be called *excessivity*, rather, or exceedingness." Récéjac: Essai sur les fondements de la conscience mystique, 1897, p. 46.

334 The word "truth" is here taken to mean something additional to bare value for life, although the natural propensity of man is to believe that whatever has great value for life is thereby certified as true.

and theism, nature and second birth, works and grace and karma, immortality and reincarnation, rationalism and mysticism, carry on inveterate disputes.

At the end of my lecture on Philosophy I held out the notion that an impartial science of religions might sift out from the midst of their discrepancies a common body of doctrine which she might also formulate in terms to which physical science need not object. This, I said, she might adopt as her own reconciling hypothesis, and recommend it for general belief. I also said that in my last lecture I should have to try my own hand at framing such an hypothesis.

The time has now come for this attempt. Who says "hypothesis" renounces the ambition to be coercive in his arguments. The most I can do is, accordingly, to offer something that may fit the facts so easily that your scientific logic will find no plausible pretext for vetoing your impulse to welcome it as true.

The "more," as we called it, and the meaning of our "union" with it, form the nucleus of our inquiry. Into what definite description can these words be translated, and for what definite facts do they stand? It would never do for us to place ourselves offhand at the position of a particular theology, the Christian theology, for example, and proceed immediately to define the "more" as Jehovah, and the "union" as his imputation to us of the righteousness of Christ. That would be unfair to other religions, and, from our present standpoint at least, would be an over-belief.

We must begin by using less particularized terms; and, since one of the duties of the science of religions is to keep religion in connection with the rest of science, we shall do well to seek first of all a way of describing the "more," which psychologists may also recognize as real. The *subconscious self* is nowadays a well-accredited psychological entity; and I believe that in it we have exactly the mediating term required. Apart from all religious considerations, there is actually and literally more life in our total soul than we are at any time aware of. The exploration of the transmarginal field has hardly yet been seriously undertaken, but what Mr. Myers said in 1892 in his essay on the Subliminal Consciousness[335] is as true as when it was first written: "Each of us is in reality an abiding psychical entity far more extensive than he knows—an individuality which can never express itself completely through any corporeal manifestation. The Self manifests through the organism; but there is always some part of the Self unmanifested; and always, as it seems, some power of organic expression in abeyance or reserve." Much of the content of this larger back-

335 Proceedings of the Society for Psychical Research, vol. vii. p. 305. For a full statement of Mr. Myers's views, I may refer to his posthumous work, "Human Personality in the Light of Recent Research," which is already announced by Messrs. Longmans, Green & Co. as being in press. Mr. Myers for the first time proposed as a general psychological problem the exploration of the subliminal region of consciousness throughout its whole extent, and made the first methodical steps in its topography by treating as a natural series a mass of subliminal facts hitherto considered only as curious isolated facts, and subjecting them to a systematized nomenclature. How important this exploration will prove, future work upon the path which Myers has opened can alone show. Compare my paper: "Frederic Myers's Services to Psychology," in the said Proceedings, part xlii., May, 1901.

ground against which our conscious being stands out in relief is insignificant. Imperfect memories, silly jingles, inhibitive timidities, "dissolutive" phenomena of various sorts, as Myers calls them, enters into it for a large part. But in it many of the performances of genius seem also to have their origin; and in our study of conversion, of mystical experiences, and of prayer, we have seen how striking a part invasions from this region play in the religious life.

Let me then propose, as an hypothesis, that whatever it may be on its *farther* side, the "more" with which in religious experience we feel ourselves connected is on its *hither* side the subconscious continuation of our conscious life. Starting thus with a recognized psychological fact as our basis, we seem to preserve a contact with "science" which the ordinary theologian lacks. At the same time the theologian's contention that the religious man is moved by an external power is vindicated, for it is one of the peculiarities of invasions from the subconscious region to take on objective appearances, and to suggest to the Subject an external control. In the religious life the control is felt as "higher"; but since on our hypothesis it is primarily the higher faculties of our own hidden mind which are controlling, the sense of union with the power beyond us is a sense of something, not merely apparently, but literally true.

This doorway into the subject seems to me the best one for a science of religions, for it mediates between a number of different points of view. Yet it is only a doorway, and difficulties present themselves as soon as we step through it, and ask how far our transmarginal consciousness carries us if we follow it on its remoter side. Here the over-beliefs begin: here mysticism and the conversion-rapture and Vedantism and transcendental idealism bring in their monistic interpretations and tell us that the finite self rejoins the absolute self, for it was always one with God and identical with the soul of the world.[336] Here the prophets of all the different religions come

336 One more expression of this belief, to increase the reader's familiarity with the notion of it:—

"If this room is full of darkness for thousands of years, and you come in and begin to weep and wail, 'Oh, the darkness,' will the darkness vanish? Bring the light in, strike a match, and light comes in a moment. So what good will it do you to think all your lives, 'Oh, I have done evil, I have made many mistakes'? It requires no ghost to tell us that. Bring in the light, and the evil goes in a moment. Strengthen the real nature, build up yourselves, the effulgent, the resplendent, the ever pure, call that up in every one whom you see. I wish that every one of us had come to such a state that even when we see the vilest of human beings we can see the God within, and instead of condemning, say, 'Rise, thou effulgent One, rise thou who art always pure, rise thou birthless and deathless, rise almighty, and manifest your nature.' . . . This is the highest prayer that the Advaita teaches. This is the one prayer: remembering our nature." . . . "Why does man go out to look for a God? . . . It is your own heart beating, and you did not know, you were mistaking it for something external. He, nearest of the near, my own self, the reality of my own life, my body and my soul.—I am Thee and Thou art Me. That is your own nature. Assert it, manifest it. Not to become pure, you are pure already. You are not to be perfect, you are that already. Every good thought which you think or act upon is simply tearing the veil, as it were, and the purity, the Infinity, the God behind, manifests itself—the eternal Subject of everything, the eternal Witness in this universe, your own Self. Knowledge is, as it were, a lower step, a degradation. We are It already; how to know It?" Swami Vivekananda: Addresses, No. XII., Practical Vedanta, part iv. pp. 172, 174, London, 1897; and Lectures, The Real and the Apparent Man, p. 24, abridged.

with their visions, voices, raptures, and other openings, supposed by each to authenticate his own peculiar faith.

Those of us who are not personally favored with such specific revelations must stand outside of them altogether and, for the present at least, decide that, since they corroborate incompatible theological doctrines, they neutralize one another and leave no fixed results. If we follow any one of them, or if we follow philosophical theory and embrace monistic pantheism on non-mystical grounds, we do so in the exercise of our individual freedom, and build out our religion in the way most congruous with our personal susceptibilities. Among these susceptibilities intellectual ones play a decisive part. Although the religious question is primarily a question of life, of living or not living in the higher union which opens itself to us as a gift, yet the spiritual excitement in which the gift appears a real one will often fail to be aroused in an individual until certain particular intellectual beliefs or ideas which, as we say, come home to him, are touched.[337] These ideas will thus be essential to that individual's religion;—which is as much as to say that over-beliefs in various directions are absolutely indispensable, and that we should treat them with tenderness and tolerance so long as they are not intolerant themselves. As I have elsewhere written, the most interesting and valuable things about a man are usually his over-beliefs.

Disregarding the over-beliefs, and confining ourselves to what is common and generic, we have in the *fact that the conscious person is continuous with a wider self through which saving experiences come,*[338] a positive content of religious experience which, it seems to me, is literally and objectively true as far as it goes. If I now proceed to state my own hypothesis about the farther limits of this extension of our personality, I shall be offering my own over-belief—though I know it will appear a sorry under-belief to some of you—for which I can only bespeak the same indulgence which in a converse case I should accord to yours.

The further limits of our being plunge, it seems to me, into an altogether other dimension of existence from the sensible and merely "understandable" world. Name it the mystical region, or the supernatural region, whichever you choose. So far as

337 For instance, here is a case where a person exposed from her birth to Christian ideas had to wait till they came to her clad in spiritistic formulas before the saving experience set in:—

"For myself I can say that spiritualism has saved me. It was revealed to me at a critical moment of my life, and without it I don't know what I should have done. It has taught me to detach myself from worldly things and to place my hope in things to come. Through it I have learned to see in all men, even in those most criminal, even in those from whom I have most suffered, undeveloped brothers to whom I owed assistance, love, and forgiveness. I have learned that I must lose my temper over nothing, despise no one, and pray for all. Most of all I have learned to pray! And although I have still much to learn in this domain, prayer ever brings me more strength, consolation, and comfort. I feel more than ever that I have only made a few steps on the long road of progress; but I look at its length without dismay, for I have confidence that the day will come when all my efforts shall be rewarded. So Spiritualism has a great place in my life, indeed it holds the first place there." Flournoy Collection.

338 "The influence of the Holy Spirit, exquisitely called the Comforter, is a matter of actual experience, as solid a reality as that of electro-magnetism." W. C. Brownell, Scribner's Magazine, vol. xxx. p. 112.

our ideal impulses originate in this region (and most of them do originate in it, for we find them possessing us in a way for which we cannot articulately account), we belong to it in a more intimate sense than that in which we belong to the visible world, for we belong in the most intimate sense wherever our ideals belong. Yet the unseen region in question is not merely ideal, for it produces effects in this world. When we commune with it, work is actually done upon our finite personality, for we are turned into new men, and consequences in the way of conduct follow in the natural world upon our regenerative change.[339] But that which produces effects within another reality must be termed a reality itself, so I feel as if we had no philosophic excuse for calling the unseen or mystical world unreal.

God is the natural appellation, for us Christians at least, for the supreme reality, so I will call this higher part of the universe by the name of God.[340] We and God have business with each other; and in opening ourselves to his influence our deepest destiny is fulfilled. The universe, at those parts of it which our personal being constitutes, takes a turn genuinely for the worse or for the better in proportion as each one of us fulfills or evades God's demands. As far as this goes I probably have you with me, for I only translate into schematic language what I may call the instinctive belief of mankind: God is real since he produces real effects.

The real effects in question, so far as I have as yet admitted them, are exerted on the personal centres of energy of the various subjects, but the spontaneous faith of most of the subjects is that they embrace a wider sphere than this. Most religious men believe (or "know," if they be mystical) that not only they themselves, but the whole universe of beings to whom the God is present, are secure in his parental hands. There is a sense, a dimension, they are sure, in which we are *all* saved, in spite of the gates of hell and all adverse terrestrial appearances. God's existence is the guarantee of an ideal order that shall be permanently preserved. This world may indeed, as science assures us, some day burn up or freeze; but if it is part of his order, the old ideals are sure to be brought elsewhere to fruition, so that where God is,

---

339 That the transaction of opening ourselves, otherwise called prayer, is a perfectly definite one for certain persons, appears abundantly in the preceding lectures. I append another concrete example to reinforce the impression on the reader's mind:—

"Man can learn to transcend these limitations [of finite thought] and draw power and wisdom at will. . . . The divine presence is known through experience. The turning to a higher plane is a distinct act of consciousness. It is not a vague, twilight or semi-conscious experience. It is not an ecstasy; it is not a trance. It is not super-consciousness in the Vedantic sense. It is not due to self-hypnotization. It is a perfectly calm, sane, sound, rational, common-sense shifting of consciousness from the phenomena of sense-perception to the phenomena of seership, from the thought of self to a distinctively higher realm. . . . For example, if the lower self be nervous, anxious, tense, one can in a few moments compel it to be calm. This is not done by a word simply. Again I say, it is not hypnotism. It is by the exercise of power. One feels the spirit of peace as definitely as heat is perceived on a hot summer day. The power can be as surely used as the sun's rays can be focused and made to do work, to set fire to wood." The Higher Law, vol. iv. pp. 4, 6, Boston, August, 1901.

340 Transcendentalists are fond of the term "Over-soul," but as a rule they use it in an intellectualist sense, as meaning only a medium of communion. "God" is a causal agent as well as a medium of communion, and that is the aspect which I wish to emphasize.

tragedy is only provisional and partial, and shipwreck and dissolution are not the absolutely final things. Only when this farther step of faith concerning God is taken, and remote objective consequences are predicted, does religion, as it seems to me, get wholly free from the first immediate subjective experience, and bring a *real hypothesis* into play. A good hypothesis in science must have other properties than those of the phenomenon it is immediately invoked to explain, otherwise it is not prolific enough. God, meaning only what enters into the religious man's experience of union, falls short of being an hypothesis of this more useful order. He needs to enter into wider cosmic relations in order to justify the subject's absolute confidence and peace.

That the God with whom, starting from the hither side of our own extra-marginal self, we come at its remoter margin into commerce should be the absolute world-ruler, is of course a very considerable over-belief. Over-belief as it is, though, it is an article of almost every one's religion. Most of us pretend in some way to prop it upon our philosophy, but the philosophy itself is really propped upon this faith. What is this but to say that Religion, in her fullest exercise of function, is not a mere illumination of facts already elsewhere given, not a mere passion, like love, which views things in a rosier light. It is indeed that, as we have seen abundantly. But it is something more, namely, a postulator of new *facts* as well. The world interpreted religiously is not the materialistic world over again, with an altered expression; it must have, over and above the altered expression, *a natural constitution* different at some point from that which a materialistic world would have. It must be such that different events can be expected in it, different conduct must be required.

This thoroughly "pragmatic" view of religion has usually been taken as a matter of course by common men. They have interpolated divine miracles into the field of nature, they have built a heaven out beyond the grave. It is only transcendentalist metaphysicians who think that, without adding any concrete details to Nature, or subtracting any, but by simply calling it the expression of absolute spirit, you make it more divine just as it stands. I believe the pragmatic way of taking religion to be the deeper way. It gives it body as well as soul, it makes it claim, as everything real must claim, some characteristic realm of fact as its very own. What the more characteristically divine facts are, apart from the actual inflow of energy in the faith-state and the prayer-state, I know not. But the over-belief on which I am ready to make my personal venture is that they exist. The whole drift of my education goes to persuade me that the world of our present consciousness is only one out of many worlds of consciousness that exist, and that those other worlds must contain experiences which have a meaning for our life also; and that although in the main their experiences and those of this world keep discrete, yet the two become continuous at certain points, and higher energies filter in. By being faithful in my poor measure to this over-belief, I seem to myself to keep more sane and true. I *can*, of course, put myself into the sectarian scientist's attitude, and imagine vividly that the world of sensations and of scientific laws and objects may be all. But whenever I do this, I hear that inward monitor of which W. K. Clifford once wrote, whispering the word "bosh!" Humbug is humbug, even though it bear the scientific name, and the total expression of human experience, as I view it objectively, invincibly urges me beyond the narrow "scientific" bounds. Assuredly, the real world is of a different temperament—more intricately built than physical science allows. So my objective and my subjective conscience both hold me to the over-belief which I express. Who knows whether the faithfulness of individuals here below to their own poor over-beliefs may not actually help God in turn to be more effectively faithful to his own greater tasks?

# Postscript

In writing my concluding lecture I had to aim so much at simplification that I fear that my general philosophic position received so scant a statement as hardly to be intelligible to some of my readers. I therefore add this epilogue, which must also be so brief as possibly to remedy but little the defect. In a later work I may be enabled to state my position more amply and consequently more clearly.

Originality cannot be expected in a field like this, where all the attitudes and tempers that are possible have been exhibited in literature long ago, and where any new writer can immediately be classed under a familiar head. If one should make a division of all thinkers into naturalists and supernaturalists, I should undoubtedly have to go, along with most philosophers, into the supernaturalist branch. But there is a crasser and a more refined supernaturalism, and it is to the refined division that most philosophers at the present day belong. If not regular transcendental idealists, they at least obey the Kantian direction enough to bar out ideal entities from interfering causally in the course of phenomenal events. Refined supernaturalism is universalistic supernaturalism; for the "crasser" variety "piecemeal" supernaturalism would perhaps be the better name. It went with that older theology which to-day is supposed to reign only among uneducated people, or to be found among the few belated professors of the dualisms which Kant is thought to have displaced. It admits miracles and providential leadings, and finds no intellectual difficulty in mixing the ideal and the real worlds together by interpolating influences from the ideal region among the forces that causally determine the real world's details. In this the refined supernaturalists think that it muddles disparate dimensions of existence. For them the world of the ideal has no efficient causality, and never bursts into the world of phenomena at particular points. The ideal world, for them, is not a world of facts, but only of the meaning of facts; it is a point of view for judging facts. It appertains to a different "-ology," and inhabits a different dimension of being altogether from that in which existential propositions obtain. It cannot get down upon the flat level of experience and interpolate itself piecemeal between distinct portions of nature, as those who believe, for example, in divine aid coming in response to prayer, are bound to think it must.

Notwithstanding my own inability to accept either popular Christianity or scholastic theism, I suppose that my belief that in communion with the Ideal new force comes into the world, and new departures are made here below, subjects me to being classed among the supernaturalists of the piecemeal or crasser type. Universalistic supernaturalism surrenders, it seems to me, too easily to naturalism. It takes the facts of physical science at their face-value, and leaves the laws of life just as naturalism finds them, with no hope of remedy, in case their fruits are bad. It confines itself to sentiments about life as a whole, sentiments which may be admiring and adoring, but which need not be so, as the existence of systematic pessimism proves. In this universalistic way of taking the ideal world, the essence of practical religion seems to me to evaporate. Both instinctively and for logical reasons, I find it hard to believe that principles can exist which make no difference in facts.[341] But all facts are particular facts, and the whole interest of the question of God's existence seems to me to lie in the consequences for particulars which that existence may be expected to entail. That no concrete particular of experience should alter its complexion in consequence of a God being there seems to me an incredible proposition, and yet it is the thesis to which (implicitly at any rate) refined supernaturalism seems to cling. It is only with experience *en bloc*, it says, that the Absolute maintains relations. It condescends to no transactions of detail.

I am ignorant of Buddhism and speak under correction, and merely in order the better to describe my general point of view; but as I apprehend the Buddhistic doctrine of Karma, I agree in principle with that. All supernaturalists admit that facts are under the judgment of higher law; but for Buddhism as I interpret it, and for religion generally so far as it remains unweakened by transcendentalistic metaphysics, the word "judgment" here means no such bare academic verdict or platonic appreciation as it means in Vedantic or modern absolutist systems; it carries, on the contrary, *execution* with it, is *in rebus* as well as *post rem*, and operates "causally" as partial factor in the total fact. The universe becomes a gnosticism[342] pure and simple on any other terms. But this view that judgment and execution go together is that of the crasser supernaturalist way of thinking, so the present volume must on the whole be classed with the other expressions of that creed.

I state the matter thus bluntly, because the current of thought in academic circles runs against me, and I feel like a man who must set his back against an open door

341 Transcendental idealism, of course, insists that its ideal world makes *this* difference, that facts *exist*. We owe it to the Absolute that we have a world of fact at all. "A world" of fact!—that exactly is the trouble. An entire world is the smallest unit with which the Absolute can work, whereas to our finite minds work for the better ought to be done within this world, setting in at single points. Our difficulties and our ideals are all piecemeal affairs, but the Absolute can do no piecework for us; so that all the interests which our poor souls compass raise their heads too late. We should have spoken earlier, prayed for another world absolutely, before this world was born. It is strange, I have heard a friend say, to see this blind corner into which Christian thought has worked itself at last, with its God who can raise no particular weight whatever, who can help us with no private burden, and who is on the side of our enemies as much as he is on our own. Odd evolution from the God of David's psalms!

342 See my Will to Believe and other Essays in popular Philosophy. 1897, p. 165.

quickly if he does not wish to see it closed and locked. In spite of its being so shocking to the reigning intellectual tastes, I believe that a candid consideration of piecemeal supernaturalism and a complete discussion of all its metaphysical bearings will show it to be the hypothesis by which the largest number of legitimate requirements are met. That of course would be a program for other books than this; what I now say sufficiently indicates to the philosophic reader the place where I belong.

If asked just where the differences in fact which are due to God's existence come in, I should have to say that in general I have no hypothesis to offer beyond what the phenomenon of "prayerful communion," especially when certain kinds of incursion from the subconscious region take part in it, immediately suggests. The appearance is that in this phenomenon something ideal, which in one sense is part of ourselves and in another sense is not ourselves, actually exerts an influence, raises our centre of personal energy, and produces regenerative effects unattainable in other ways. If, then, there be a wider world of being than that of our every-day consciousness, if in it there be forces whose effects on us are intermittent, if one facilitating condition of the effects be the openness of the "subliminal" door, we have the elements of a theory to which the phenomena of religious life lend plausibility. I am so impressed by the importance of these phenomena that I adopt the hypothesis which they so naturally suggest. At these places at least, I say, it would seem as though transmundane energies, God, if you will, produced immediate effects within the natural world to which the rest of our experience belongs.

The difference in natural "fact" which most of us would assign as the first difference which the existence of a God ought to make would, I imagine, be personal immortality. Religion, in fact, for the great majority of our own race *means* immortality, and nothing else. God is the producer of immortality; and whoever has doubts of immortality is written down as an atheist without farther trial. I have said nothing in my lectures about immortality or the belief therein, for to me it seems a secondary point. If our ideals are only cared for in "eternity," I do not see why we might not be willing to resign their care to other hands than ours. Yet I sympathize with the urgent impulse to be present ourselves, and in the conflict of impulses, both of them so vague yet both of them noble, I know not how to decide. It seems to me that it is eminently a case for facts to testify. Facts, I think, are yet lacking to prove "spirit-return," though I have the highest respect for the patient labors of Messrs. Myers, Hodgson, and Hyslop, and am somewhat impressed by their favorable conclusions. I consequently leave the matter open, with this brief word to save the reader from a possible perplexity as to why immortality got no mention in the body of this book.

The ideal power with which we feel ourselves in connection, the "God" of ordinary men, is, both by ordinary men and by philosophers, endowed with certain of those metaphysical attributes which in the lecture on philosophy I treated with such disrespect. He is assumed as a matter of course to be "one and only" and to be "infinite"; and the notion of many finite gods is one which hardly any one thinks it worth while to consider, and still less to uphold. Nevertheless, in the interests of intellectual clearness, I feel bound to say that religious experience, as we have studied it, cannot be cited as unequivocally supporting the infinitist belief. The only thing that it unequivocally testifies to is that we can experience union with *something* larger than ourselves and in that union find our greatest peace. Philosophy, with its passion for unity, and mysticism with its monoideistic bent, both "pass to the limit" and identify the something with a unique God who is the all-inclusive soul of the world. Popular opinion, respectful to their authority, follows the example which they set.

Meanwhile the practical needs and experiences of religion seem to me sufficiently met by the belief that beyond each man and in a fashion continuous with him there exists a larger power which is friendly to him and to his ideals. All that the facts require is that the power should be both other and larger than our conscious selves. Anything larger will do, if only it be large enough to trust for the next step. It need not be infinite, it need not be solitary. It might conceivably even be only a larger and more godlike self, of which the present self would then be but the mutilated expression, and the universe might conceivably be a collection of such selves, of different degrees of inclusiveness, with no absolute unity realized in it at all.[343] Thus would a sort of polytheism return upon us—a polytheism which I do not on this occasion defend, for my only aim at present is to keep the testimony of religious experience clearly within its proper bounds. [Compare p. 130 above.]

Upholders of the monistic view will say to such a polytheism (which, by the way, has always been the real religion of common people, and is so still today) that unless there be one all-inclusive God, our guarantee of security is left imperfect. In the Absolute, and in the Absolute only, *all* is saved. If there be different gods, each caring for his part, some portion of some of us might not be covered with divine protection, and our religious consolation would thus fail to be complete. It goes back to what was said about the possibility of there being portions of the universe that may irretrievably be lost. Common sense is less sweeping in its demands than philosophy or mysticism have been wont to be, and can suffer the notion of this world being partly saved and partly lost. The ordinary moralistic state of mind makes the salvation of the world conditional upon the success with which each unit does its part. Partial and conditional salvation is in fact a most familiar notion when taken in the abstract, the only difficulty being to determine the details. Some men are even disinterested enough to be willing to be in the unsaved remnant as far as their persons go, if only they can be persuaded that their cause will prevail—all of us are willing, whenever our activity-excitement rises sufficiently high. I think, in fact, that a final philosophy of religion will have to consider the pluralistic hypothesis more seriously than it has hitherto been willing to consider it. For practical life at any rate, the *chance* of salvation is enough. No fact in human nature is more characteristic than

343 Such a notion is suggested in my Ingersoll Lecture On Human Immortality, Boston and London, 1899.

its willingness to live on a chance. The existence of the chance makes the difference, as Edmund Gurney says, between a life of which the keynote is resignation and a life of which the keynote is hope.[344] But all these statements are unsatisfactory from their brevity, and I can only say that I hope to return to the same questions in another book.

344 Tertium Quid, 1887, p. 99. See also pp. 148, 149.

# About the Authors

The chief author of *Alcoholics Anonymous* was **Bill Wilson**, or "Bill W." Born in 1895 in East Dorset, Vermont, Wilson battled alcoholism throughout his life, until a 1934 spiritual conversion experience left him sober and convinced of the role a higher power could play in helping alcoholics achieve sobriety. Wilson joined the Oxford Group, and with fellow recovered alcoholic Dr. Bob Smith, began working with a fellowship of alcoholics, teaching the spiritual principles that had changed their own lives. In 1938, Wilson was selected to be the principal author behind the group's text; he is also the author of the group's "Twelve Traditions." He died in 1971.

Born in 1851, **Henry Drummond** grew up as one of five children in Stirling, Scotland. After attending Edinburgh University, Drummond studied divinity at New College, Edinburgh. While at New College, Drummond became involved in evangelical work in 1873. Upon graduation, Drummond spent a year assisting at the Barclay Church in Edinburgh, where he first delivered some of the addresses contained in *The Greatest Thing in the World*. In 1877, Drummond went on to become a lecturer, and then a professor, in Natural Science at the Free Church College of Glasgow. While there, he wrote his first book, *Natural Law in the Spiritual World* (1883), which postulated a scientific theory of continuity between the physical and spiritual worlds, and which became popular among both religious and scientific communities. He died in 1897.

An influential figure in the early New Thought movement, **Ralph Waldo Trine** was born in 1866, in Mount-Morris, Illinois. The author of over a dozen books, he started off as a correspondent for the *Boston Daily Evening Transcript* before writing his widely popular *In Tune with the Infinite*. Informed by the ideas of thinkers as varied as Ralph Waldo Emerson, Johann Gottlieb Fichte, and Henry Drummond, *In Tune with the Infinite* went on to sell over 2 million copies. Trine died in 1958, in Claremont, California.

Born in 1886 in Ireland, **Emmet Fox** was trained as an electrical engineer but instead pursued a life as a spiritual teacher and lecturer in the United States. In 1931, he became the minister of the Church of the Healing Christ in New York City. An acclaimed and influential philosopher, spiritual teacher, and writer whose works, such as *The Sermon on the Mount*, were an early inspiration for Alcoholics Anonymous, he died in France in 1951.

**James Allen** was born in Leicester, England, in 1864. He took his first job at fifteen to support his family, after his father was murdered while looking for work in America in 1879. Allen worked as a factory knitter and later as a private secretary. In 1901, he published his first book, *From Poverty to Power.* He soon left secretarial work to devote himself full-time to writing and in 1903 completed his third, and best-known, work: *As a Man Thinketh.* Allen completed nineteen books during his career, several of which were published posthumously. While not widely known during his lifetime, Allen came to be seen as pioneering voice of contemporary inspirational literature. He died at age 47 in 1912.

Episcopal minister **Sam Shoemaker** was one of the earliest writers and philosophers behind Alcoholics Anonymous, working alongside Bill Wilson to develop the ideas the group is known for today. Shoemaker was born in Baltimore in 1893, and, after attending Princeton, spent several years in China, where he first encountered Frank Buchanan. Shoemaker became an ordained Episcopal priest in 1921, and became a key early member of Buchanan's Oxford Group religious movement. Bill Wilson said of Shoemaker, "It was from Sam Shoemaker that we absorbed most of the Twelve Steps of Alcoholics Anonymous, steps that express the heart of AA's way of life . . . he passed on the spiritual keys by which we were liberated." Shoemaker published over 30 books, and maintained a ministry at New York's Calvary Church for 26 years. He died in 1963.

**William James** was the father of American psychology, pioneering concepts related to free will, spirituality, and pragmatism. Born to the famous James clan (brother Henry was an acclaimed novelist, sister Alice a noted diarist) in New York City in 1842, he received his medical degree from Harvard in 1869, and spent almost his entire professional career teaching psychology and philosophy there. James published numerous influential books over the course of his career, including some of the earliest American textbooks on psychology, *The Will to Believe*, and *The Varieties of Religious Experience*, which was considered a classic almost immediately after its 1902 publication. James died in 1910.